Retracing Footsteps

Lakeside Cemetery,
Bay Village, Cuyahoga County, Ohio

*A Genealogical Study of Those Buried in
or Associated With Lakeside Cemetery
and Their Families.*

**Written and Compiled by
Catherine Burke Flament
for the
Bay Village Historical Society**

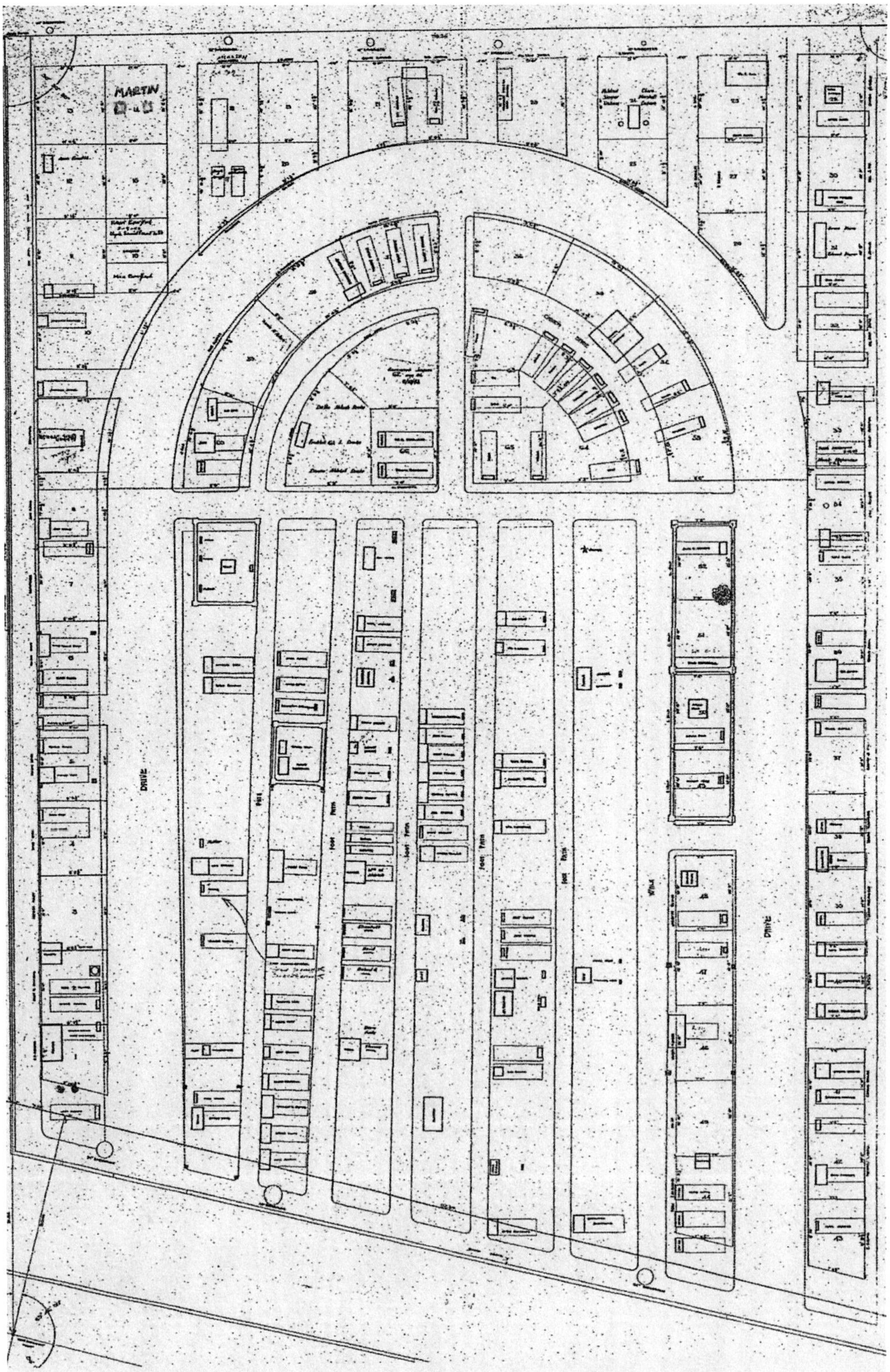

Plot map of Lakeside Cemetery as of 2025

Pedigrees
Ancestors
Relatives

Retracing Footsteps

Lakeside Cemetery, Bay Village, Cuyahoga County, Ohio

By Catherine Burke Flament
for the Bay Village Historical Society

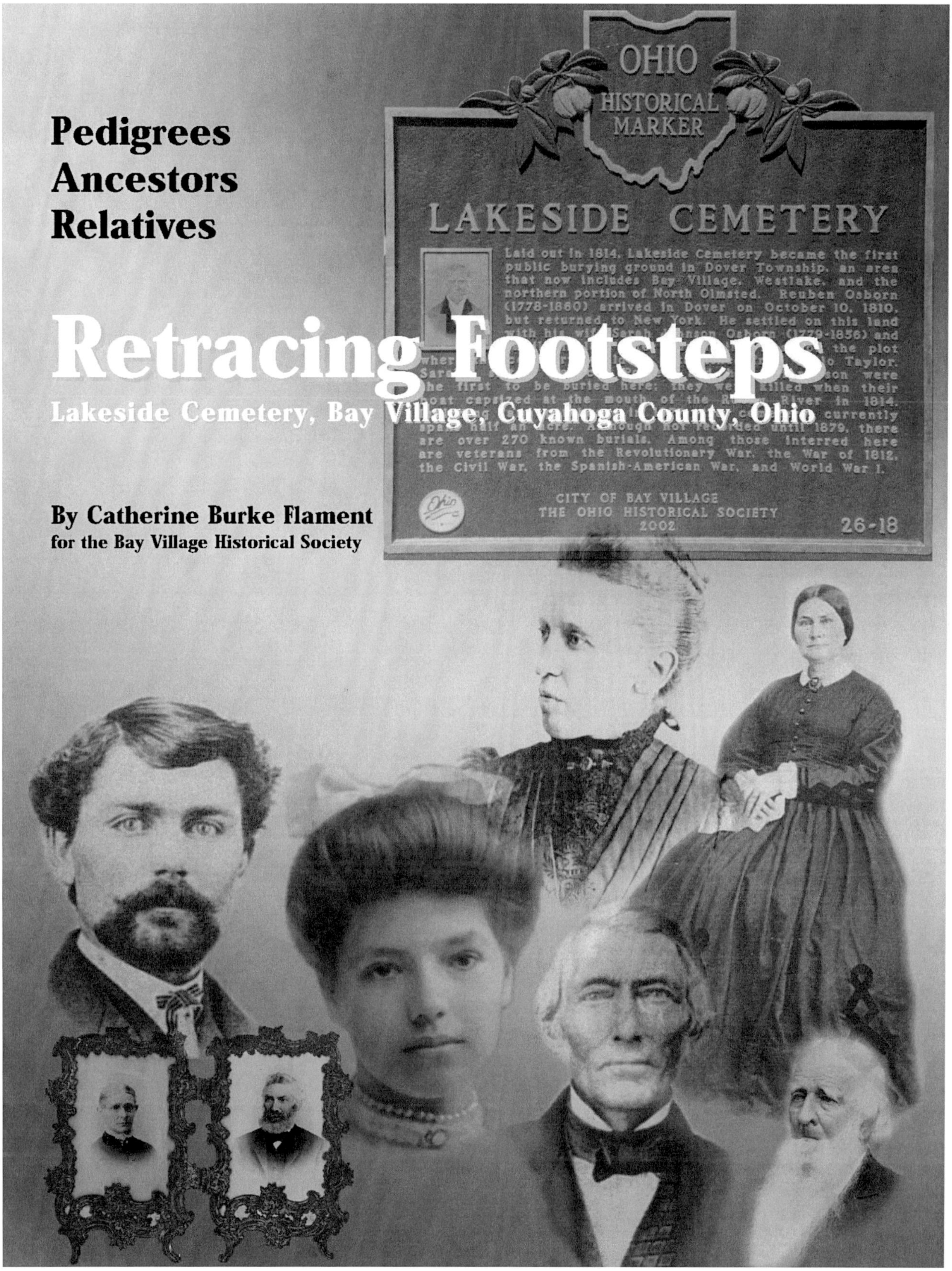

4th printing 2025
Cover designs by Gene Zvara, 2006.

Information on our webstie regarding Lakeside Cemetery:
website: https://www.bayhistorical.com/lakeside-cemetery-tour/

Published by and may be ordered from:
Bay Village Historical Society
P.O. Box 40187
Bay Village, OH 44140-0187
www.bayhistorical.com

There is a history in all men's lives."

Shakespeare, King Henry IV, Pt. III, i.80.

Dedication

To my husband and daughters
with love and appreciation.

Table of Contents

Dover - Her past, present and future.
Proof positive that her pioneers did not
'Take hold of the plow and look back.'"

A.P. Johnson, Jamestown, N.Y.
A Pioneer Celebration, 1875

Acknowledgements

Special thanks to those who helped in so many ways: Louella Meyer, an amazing woman who has become a special friend, who faithfully proofread the manuscript numerous times in addition to checking the index. Doris Gorgas, entered more than 14,000 names into the main index, a grueling job to say the least. Gene Zvara scanned and worked his magic on the photographs for the book. Joyce Dougherty painstakingly proofread the bibliography for errors. Eric Eakin, whose professional writing skills always amaze me, assisted with the final proofreading, photographs and some special touches.

Martin Chomoa, engineering technician for the City of Bay Village from 1961 to 1982, organized the extensive plotting of the cemetery and supervised transcribing the gravestones for the City of Bay Village during his tenure. The groundwork available saved me numerous hours when getting the project underway.

B.J. Schwartz has been an incredible inspiration who never faltered with her encouragement as I worked on the manuscript. Her knowledge of the general history of Lakeside Cemetery and tireless work to improve the cemetery itself are an inspiration. The effort she and her husband Ed have put forth over the years to beautify and protect it are unmatched and continue as this book is published.

Jeanne Parks, a special friend and neighbor, for her suggestions and clues when I would encounter stumbling blocks while researching. Ingrid Abrams and Keith Sheldon for listening to me as I attempted to sort out the maze of families and for assisting with general research as the book began.

Judith Cetina, director of the Cuyahoga County Archives, and her staff, especially Carolyn Svetz, for assistance when viewing the original records of Cuyahoga County. Genealogist Christy Wiggins of the Fairview Public Library Branch of the Cuyahoga County Library and her staff, graciously assisted me as I researched families. The late Richard E. Ross, local veterans' advocate; David Maier, commissioner, and Laurene Rutkowski, Memorial Affairs Officer, with the Cuyahoga County Veterans Service Commission, Cleveland, Ohio, for their assistance in procuring grave markers for the Unknown Soldier and Harry E. Rehling. (Laurene also researched military records.)

Paul Beaudry, researched sources at the Rhode Island Historical Society Library, Providence, R.I., providing access to some sources that would not have been available otherwise. Deanna Cooper of St. Paul Lutheran Church, Westlake, Ohio, assisted when viewing the church records and data cards. Helen A. Shaw, Chicago, Ill., researched the original naturalization papers that are now housed at the National Archives, Great Lakes Region, in Chicago. Joe Zaccagnini, recorders manager and archivist, Cuyahoga County Recorders Office, assisted with the research of the original cemetery deeds.

Bay Village Mayor Deborah Sutherland, along with the Bay Village City Council and Cahoon Memorial Park Trustees, supported the placement of an Ohio Historical Marker at the cemetery and allowed improvements to be made. James Sears, service director for The City of Bay Village, assisted with the cemetery improvements. (Jim has consistently gone out of his way to provide knowledgeable suggestions and to incorporate improvements in a timely and professional manner.) James M.

Wasniak, city planner for The City of Bay Village, and Corinne Wood, Bay Village Service Department, assisted with records.

Nancy Cleary graciously lent a hand with her camera and shared her artistic skills by assisting with photos of the grave markers that needed to be retaken.

Judi Ballard and Lynn Sebring, German teachers at North Olmsted High School, translated the headstone inscribed in German. The West Side Hungarian Reformed Church, Puritas Road in Cleveland, procured a translation of the Hungarian marker. Eleanor Gnandt, Penfield Township, Ohio, clerk personally checked marker inscriptions and records for Penfield Cemetery.

It is with deep regret that during the last year, four of those who had taken a special interest in the book, and were very special individuals have passed away. Gay Rothaermel Menning, an extremely knowledgeable resource of local history, was always willing to lend her expertise. Gay was the compiler of the original publication for the historical society, Bay Village: A Way of Life. Dick Ross, an individual who was always willing to get involved and never wavered in his tireless dedication to Bay Village. His smile, laugh and positive outlook remain an inspiration. George Serb, a lifelong Bay Village resident, was known and loved by everyone who met him. George gave tirelessly to the community for his entire life. Sarah Dodd Wymer, a truly remarkable woman whose memory my family will always treasure. Sarah would drive over two hours to come to visit us in her oversized van. Watching this tiny woman climb down when she was over 90 always amazed us. Her recall and stories about Bay Village in the early days were fascinating and a joy to hear. All of these individuals assisted in various ways throughout the research and will be deeply missed by many.

I can never truly express my gratitude to the descendants of the individuals buried here for their tremendous support. The family stories and photographs that have been carefully handed down from generation to generation have made this book come alive. The friendships I have made across the miles have been incredible and I will treasure each of them. I came to know so many of these families and was invited to become part of their lives. Through the years I hope these friendships will continue.

Specific family acknowledgments are located in the back of the book.

You can kiss your family and friends good-bye
And put miles between you,
But at the same time you carry them with you
In your heart, your mind, your stomach,
Because you do not just live in a world
But a world lives in you.
Frederick Buechner

Introduction

This book had its genesis about 1996 when local teacher, mother and Girl Scout leader Catherine Burke Flament decided to create a scouting patch to encourage scouts to delve into the history of the community. The patch that was designed included an option to explore Lakeside Cemetery in Bay Village, Ohio. Little did Flament realize that her initial probing into the history of the little-known cemetery would, years later, lead to the publishing of the most complete and historically accurate accounting of the lives, and deaths, of those interred there.

Early settlers arrived from New England, and later Europe, leaving behind their families and friends. The sacrifices to which they were subjected when relocating to the unknown took courage and perseverance. Who were they and what did their lives entail? The pages that follow not only provide insight into their everyday lives but expand to include how their ancestors and descendents contributed to the communities in which they settled. You don't need to have a family member buried in Lakeside Cemetery to enjoy the intriguing stories of those who came before us.

Now, imagine what it must have been like for these individuals, 100 or even 200 years ago, who made the decision to leave their homes and move on. What were their expectations? How much did they know about the places to which they would be moving? Did they know exactly where they would settle and call home, or would they come to a brook or level plot and decide this was what they sought? It wasn't like today when you are able to go on the internet and peruse the area to see what the homes look like, chose the amenities you would like, check out the school district, local surroundings and take a virtual tour. These pioneers left on a leap of faith, courageous heart and sense of adventure.

Arriving at their destination wasn't an easy adjustment. The land must be cleared, food sources evaluated and a shelter built. Through this book it is hoped that you will experience the challenges and adjustments faced by families such as the Cahoons or Osborns. What was going through Lydia Cahoon's mind as she ran through the woods assuming Indians were close behind? Experience the recollections of those on horseback, in a wagon, sleigh, or inter-urban train and discover how these things impacted their lives.

Sit back, relax and read about the varied and colorful individuals who rest at Lakeside Cemetery. Olaf Aslaksen left Norway at a young age to sail the world, only to meet his wife to be at the tip of South America. Gypsy families such as the Yankos routinely passed through, staying for a short time on their travels; this family, however, would leave behind a son. The Wischmeyer family brought their German traditions with them, running a hotel and winery on Lake Road. Read a letter from Ichabod Briggs to Sarah Case as their love affair blossomed. Sterling Rumbaugh died in the flu epidemic of 1918 after joining the Navy. Frances Willard Jaycox's mother was an ardent prohibitionist, very dedicated to the cause. An unknown soldier would unwittingly find these shores his final resting place; how far had he traveled? Jacob Wagner, only 19 years old, washed ashore. What brought him to this place, far from his home in Cincinnati?

Autobiographies from two time periods are included to allow the reader to compare the times. Margaret Dickson Van Allen Cahoon recalls the burning of Washington during the early years of our nation and continues her recollections through her life in early Dover Township. She knew first hand those we only read about in history books. You will discover the recollections of Florence Eppink Musil, a Krumwiede descendent, as she talks about the trials and joys of the time with memories of Cleveland and Dover some 100 years later.

Ever thought of using Virginia Snake Root in a recipe? Become intrigued with the fascinating remedies of Selden Osborn who rode horseback, assisting those who were ill. Recipes of different kinds are included for a variety of tasty treats. You may find them a bit vague, but nonetheless interesting.

Crossing your neighbor always has its drawbacks. Philo Taylor launched a curse against the mouth of the Rocky River a few years before the death of Rebecca Porter. How did William Comstock's daughter Sylvia really die? Is the family legend true?

Then there are those whose lives are intertwined with these families. John Ketchum lived with the Wolf family for years. He ran away to join the Civil War only to be caught as a spy; he escaped in a daring move.

Explosions, train accidents, slipping away in their sleep; these are all ways those interred came to rest here. Some at a "ripe old age" while others in the prime of their life. Some before they had a chance to experience life.

It is hoped that through reading this book you will have a better understanding of the fabric of the lives of those buried in Lakeside Cemetery and other cemeteries in the area. A part of history is portrayed by those who may or may not be historically significant, but who helped mold the Northeastern Ohio community into what it is today. In gratitude to those who preserved their history through written and oral testaments, this book has been able to expand to not only include raw statistics but personal accounts that make the times come alive.

Perhaps Flament had a calling from beyond to bring those buried there into the present, into the light, into your hands, into your consciousness, so they could live again, if only for a short time, through your interest.

Do not think, dear reader, that cemeteries are dead places. Quite the contrary. They are like libraries; from the outside they may be unimposing, but inside they are filled with drama, pathos, discovery, dishonor, pain and love. All you need to do is to look inside.

I hear the tread of pioneers
Of nations yet to be;
The first low wash of waves, where soon
Shall roll a human sea.
Each rude and jostling fragment soon
Its fitting place shall find,
The raw material of a State,
Its muscle and its mind!
John Greenleaf Whittier.

History of the Area

Bay Village, Ohio, formerly Dover Township, and surrounding areas were home to wandering tribes of Erie Indians when the first white men explored the area, about 1600 A.D. The lands were fertile hunting and fishing grounds. An important Indian trail in Ohio is now Lake Road, beside which Lakeside Cemetery sits.

In 1778, the State of Virginia made this part of the country its Northwest Territory during the Revolutionary War. New York, Pennsylvania, Massachusetts and Connecticut, however, also laid claim to the lands. Finally, in 1780 and 1781, because of the confusion and the need for the 13 new United States to come to an agreement, all the states except Connecticut gave up claims to the area. Connecticut refused to give up what it called its Western Reserve, the land extending 120 miles west of the Pennsylvania border on the northern shore of what is now Ohio.

The Connecticut Land Company was formed after Connecticut sold most of the land of the Western Reserve on September 2, 1795, to a group of private investors. One of the members of the company was a surveyor named General Moses Cleaveland. He and 51 others, including two women, made the trip on horseback from Connecticut in 68 days to the new land that the investors had purchased. They arrived on the banks of the Cuyahoga River with their Indian guides in July 1796. The party explored, surveyed and marked off land into townships five miles square, rather than following the pattern set by Congress of six-mile-square grids. The exceptions to this were the uneven areas along the lake shore. The ranges would be numbered progressively, starting at the border of Pennsylvania, and townships were numbered, beginning at the 41st parallel, from the south to the north.

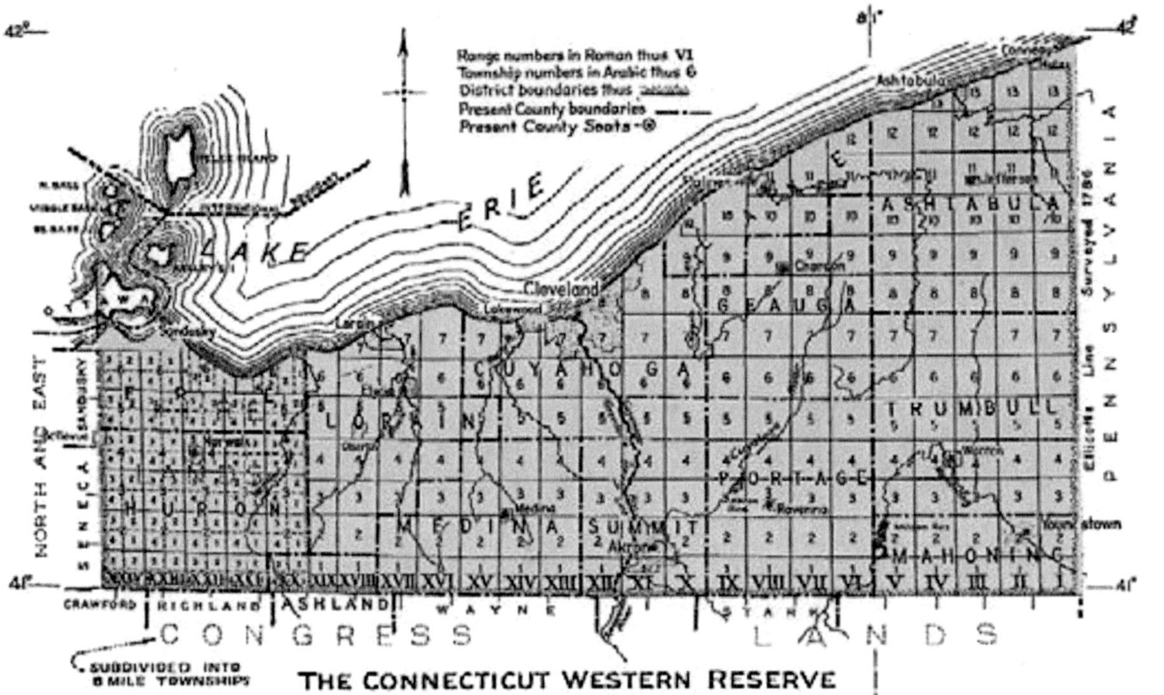

THE CONNECTICUT WESTERN RESERVE
Subdivided into 5 mile Townships

In addition to selling land in the Reserve to the Connecticut Land Company, Connecticut gave 500,000 acres to Connecticut citizens who had lost their homes and farms during the Revolutionary War due to raids by the British, who often burned the homes of those supporting the revolution. Unfortunately it would be years before titles would transfer to those (or their heirs) who had experienced the loss. These smaller sections of land on the western end of the Reserve became known as the "Firelands" or the "Sufferers' Lands."

Relinquishing the Western Reserve to the Connecticut Land Company created numerous problems for the more than 1,000 individuals who were living in the area at the turn of the century regarding who had jurisdiction over the area. Following a number of proposals, governmental control was passed to Governor Arthur St. Clair of the Northwest Territory in April 1800. Trumbull County was promptly formed on July 10, 1800, encompassing all of the Western Reserve with the county seat as Warren. Title to the land west of the Cuyahoga River would not be completely cleared from Indian claims until the Treaty of Fort Industry in 1805 after which it was quickly surveyed. Settlers did not settle on the land to the west of the Cuyahoga River until this time due to Indian claims.

President Thomas Jefferson signed the bill creating the state of Ohio on February 19, 1803. The new legislature met for the first time on March 1, 1803, which became Ohio's official date of birth. As chance would have it, a joint resolution was never signed admitting Ohio to the Union until 1953. President Dwight D. Eisenhower signed the document making the resolution retroactive to 1803.

Ohio, the 17th state, was the first state carved from the Northwest Territory. The Northwest Territory included the states we now know as Ohio, Illinois, Indiana, Michigan, Wisconsin and part of Minnesota. Chillicothe became the first capital until repeated political disputes moved it to Zanesville, then back to Chillicothe. A compromise was reached when it was decided to locate the capital within 40 miles of the center of the state. An area was chosen and named after the discoverer Columbus.

The township lines between the Cuyahoga River and the lands to the west were surveyed and laid out in 1806. The Western Reserve had been carefully evaluated to equalize each share. Purchasers invested $26,087 to be assigned a township in this region, many combining funds with others to afford the land. Drawings were previously conducted in 1796 and 1802 for other areas of the Reserve with the last two being held in 1807 and 1809. Two men from Connecticut bought Township Number 7, Range 15, as part of the third draft. Bordered by Lake Erie on the north, the township of Olmsted on the south, Rockport on the east and Avon on the west, this would be the 29th lot to be picked that day. They invested $31,087 for the 25 square miles, and an additional 3,000 acres.

The owners, Nehemiah Hubbard Jr. (1752-1837) and Joshua Stow(e), named it Dover Township. It is unclear as to how the name was chosen. Dover was a popular name in Ohio with five listings in 1850 causing frequent problems with mail and deliveries. Perhaps the name was used because the cliffs along the lake looked like the high, white cliffs of Dover, England.

JOSHUA STOW.

Stow and Hubbard were both from Middletown, Conn., and never settled in the Reserve although relatives of both men did. Joshua Stow was part of the surveying party of General Cleaveland, acting as a commissary manager in charge of food and drink, and would help to develop the settlement of Summit County. He purchased all of Stow Township and is said to have made 13 trips from Connecticut to that area over the years, taking a vested interest in its development. Travel at the time was by horseback, taking up to one month each way. Over the years Joshua was appointed postmaster, tax collector and associate judge of the court in Middletown. He wrote Article 7 of the Connecticut Constitution following his deep belief that individuals should be able to join the church of their choice, the Congregational Church being the "official" church of Connecticut up to this time. Joshua and his wife, Ruth Coe, are both buried in Middletown.

Hubbard also purchased Range 1, Township 3, now Hubbard Township in Trumbull County, Ohio. He had Samuel Tylee, who would settle in Hubbard, act as his agent since he never traveled to the area. Hubbard also sent his brother Isaac's sons to act as land agents on his behalf. His nephew, William, arrived with his family in 1834. William would become active in Ashtabula County's Anti-Slavery Society shortly after arriving, as had his brothers. His restored home is now open to the public as the Hubbard House Underground Railroad Museum in Ashtabula. Large numbers of slaves were aided by the Hubbard family on their way to the Canadian border. Nehemiah Hubbard was a merchant after serving a short time in the Revolutionary War, president of two banks and religious professor.

Hubbard and Stow engaged Philo Taylor, Mr. White and Datus Kelly as their sales agents to sell the lots to new settlers in Dover Township. Philo Taylor had arrived in the Cleveland area in 1806, settling with his family in Rockport in 1808. Taylor had agreed to find land that was suitable and then pay for it later. Philo felled trees and built a log cabin for he and his family on the east side of the mouth of the Rocky River in the Clifton Park lagoon area. Upon proceeding to pay for the land, he was informed that his land was to be used to plan a new town, Granger City, and was asked to settle elsewhere. Taylor put a curse on the land, which may have worked since the area met numerous problems preventing its development. While living in Dover Township, he opened a saw mill and the first tavern, in addition to being a ship owner. Taylor built the "Prudence" in 1821 and sailed vessels between Port Huron and Buffalo. Being involved in a variety of adventures, he is said to have moved to Newburgh where he helped to found Cleveland's first bank and was active with political affairs. Datus Kelly, a surveyor from New York, the nephew of Joshua Stow, arrived in 1811 with his wife Mary Dean. Later, in 1834, he and his brother, Ira, would purchase Kelley's Island where he would move in 1836.

County borders for the present Bay Village changed over the next few years. Geauga County was formed in 1805 from Trumbull County, extending 15 miles east of Black River Township. A subsequent reduction in area quickly followed with the formation in 1808 of Cuyahoga County being carved from Geauga. Official records would not begin until 1810 for Cuyahoga County when it was organized. The name derived from the Indian word meaning "crooked," or "winding stream" was originally used for the Cuyahoga River which divides the city of Cleveland in half. Cleveland became the county seat, as it remains today. County borders originally extended to the Black River.

In 1811 Dover Township became the second township organized in Cuyahoga County, the first being Cleveland. The county commissioner included the areas of Township 7 in Ranges 15, 16, 17 and the area in Range 18 east of the Black River. Dover Township expanded on March 6, 1812, to include the area west of the town of Dover and Township 6 in Range 16; east of the east line of the Firelands, and north of Township 5, Ranges 17, 18 and 19.

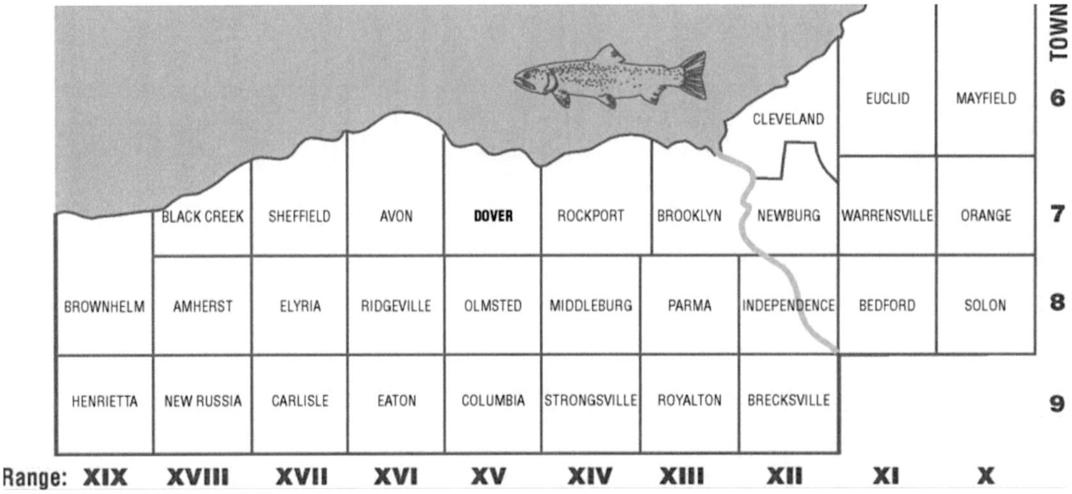

The first election of officers for the township was held in the home of Philo Taylor on April 6, 1812. The 18 individuals who would vote that day included Azariah Beebe, John Brittle, Joseph Cahoon, Noah Davis, Moses Eldred, John Jordan, Andrew Kelso, George Kelso, Ralph Lyon, Daniel Perry, Asahel Porter, Joseph Quigley, Lyman Root, Joseph Root, Jonathan Seeley, David Smith, Philo Taylor and Timothy Wallace. Daniel Perry, Joseph Quigley and Asahel Porter would become trustees; Asahel Porter, clerk and Philo Taylor, treasurer.

In 1822, Lorain County evolved from parts of Cuyahoga, Huron and Medina Counties with its northeastern border that of Dover Township. Lorain, named after the province Lorraine, France, was not organized until 1824 when records would officially start. Dover thus became the northwestern border of Cuyahoga County as it remains today. Avon Township, directly to the west of Dover Township, would eventually be divided into Avon Township to the south and Avon Lake Township to the north in 1915. Both have achieved city status since then.

Rockport, the township to the east of Dover, would become established in 1814, subsequently being divided into Rocky River, Lakewood, Fairview Park and the West Park area of Cleveland.

Kingston, to the south of Dover Township, was settled in 1814. It was renamed Lenox in 1822 only to be renamed Olmsted. Officially established in 1827, Olmsted Township is now recognized as North Olmsted (with the addition of the northern portion that was originally part of Dover), Olmsted Falls and Olmsted Township. The name Olmsted derived from Aaron Olmstead, one of the first land owners who never settled in Ohio. His son, Charles Olmstead, who inherited the land, requested the name of Lenox be changed to Olmstead. This was contingent on his father's library, comprised of 500 books, being donated as a circulating collection for the area. Traveling by oxcart from Connecticut, the books made possible the first lending library in the Western Reserve. The 153 remaining volumes are currently housed at the present North Olmsted Public Library. Through the years the name was misspelled, resulting in the variation of Olmsted which is used by the communities today.

"The settlers were elegant and educated gentlemen and ladies
Who had never known hard work.
Their history of privation and suffering had been repeated again and again
By the pioneer fathers and mothers,
Who opened up the now great and rich country
Lying between the Hudson and the prairies –
The greatest work ever done by any generation of mortal men."
Excerpt from the obituary of Margaret A. Van Allen Cahoon, wife of Joel B. Cahoon, 1894

Settlement of Dover

As early as 1799 a man named Joseph Cahoon visited Ohio. He had lived in Salisbury, Herkimer County, N.Y., until 1799 when he moved to Newark, N.J., where he operated a tide mill. In 1803 he returned to Salisbury. In 1807, realizing the beauty and potential of the area, he bought Lot 95 on the Lake Erie shore at the mouth of a creek. About 1808 he was living in Vergennes, Vermont, where he ran a mill on Otter Creek. Two years later, at age 48, with his wife, five sons and three daughters including the recent husband of daughter Mary, George Sexton, and all their belongings packed into a covered wagon, they set out for the six-week trip to their new home.

The Cahoon family stopped their wagon on the morning of October 10, 1810, near a bubbling little creek. Cahoon, a miller by trade, had picked the land knowing he would need water power to turn his mill.

With winter approaching, Cahoon and his sons, with nothing more than axes and muscle, built a log cabin in four days. Animal skins covered the windows; the door was the bottom of the wagon.

The afternoon of the Cahoon's arrival, after righting a wagon spilled at the Rocky River, Asahel and Rebecca Johnson Porter, their two daughters, together with her 17-year-old brother, Leverett Johnson, and her brother-in-law, Reuben Osborn, arrived from New York. The Porters claimed Lot 94 to the west of the Cahoons and Leverette immediately began clearing Lot 58 to the south in what is now Westlake.

Reuben, unlike the others in his party, returned to Camden, N.Y., until May of 1811 when he resettled with his family in Dover. It is assumed that he immediately settled on Lot 93, located just to the west of the Porter's, also on Lake Erie. He began building in 1814 the house currently found in Cahoon Memorial Park near Rose Hill Museum. It is the oldest frame structure between Cleveland and Lorain. Reuben donated the land that would become Lakeside Cemetery.

By 1818, Joseph Cahoon had built a four-bedroom frame house on a grassy hillside above the creek in Dover Township. He called it "the most beautiful spot in America." The house stands today as the Rose Hill Museum, filled with Cahoon and other early settlers' memorabilia.

Cahoon and his family would be some of the first settlers in what is now northwest Cuyahoga County. George Peake, a mulatto, considered the first permanent black settler in Cleveland, was perhaps the first permanent settler in the area. Philo Taylor had arrived in April of 1808, but was forced to move. George had been a soldier serving with the British during the French and Indian War. He settled in Rockport, Township 7, Range 14, after purchasing a 103-acre lot that lay southwest of Hayes School in Lakewood. Rockport, directly east of Dover Township, would eventually be divided into Rocky River, Lakewood, Fairview Park and the West Park area of Cleveland. Arriving in April of 1809 at the age of 87 with his wife and two sons, George Jr. and Joseph, they were the first to travel what is now known as Detroit Road. The road extended from Cleveland to the Huron River, eventually continuing to Detroit, Mich., hence its name. The road, which was the first state highway, had been cut making it wide enough for a wagon to travel following an Indian path to Rockport.

Two more of Peake's sons, James and Henry, would join him shortly after his arrival. George's invention of a hand gristmill proved to be a drastic improvement over the "stump mortar and spring-pole pestle" method used at the time. The stones used were 18 to 20 inches across and made a valuable contribution to the quality of meal produced. George was said to have been a "highly respected" citizen of the area, helping many settlers who followed. He died at the age of 105 in September, 1827.

Noah Davis settled in Township 7, Range 16 of Dover Township. He arrived in what is now Avon Lake in 1812 but rather than settle permanently in the area, moved on within a year. Wilbur Cahoon, step-brother of Joseph, would lead a group from Montgomery County, N.Y., in the summer of 1814 to become the first permanent settlers of Range 16. Not all in the caravan chose to continue the trek to Dover, as some remained in Ashtabula until 1815. Wilbur Cahoon's home was in the southern portion of the township in the area that is now Avon. Township number 7, Range 16's name would evolve from Dover to Xeuma in 1818, renamed Troy and finally Avon in December 1824.

Wischmeyer Hotel

Settlers came fast between 1811 and 1818. They hacked out homesteads about a half-mile apart on the lakeside dirt road. They were farmers, millers, shoemakers, blacksmiths, teachers and more.

The Bassett family came in 1811, then the Halls and Crockers. The Saddlers and Footes came in 1815, the Aldriches in 1816, the Winsors in 1817, and the Wolfs in 1818. Almost all of those families left a permanent impression on the community. By 1840 Dover Township's population was 960.

German immigrants began to arrive in the middle of the century. The vineyards of Dover Township established the area as America's second-largest grape-producing region in the late 19th Century.

After the Civil War, the lakeshore of Dover Township attracted affluent Clevelanders as an ideal location for summer homes. In 1901, residents in the northern part of the township voted to form Bay Village, also referred to as North Dover, an area occupying about 4.5 square miles. It was incorporated as the Village of Bay on May 1, 1903, and achieved city status in 1950. During the first half of the 20th Century, Dover Village remained essentially rural, and farms, truck gardens, and flower gardens continued to flourish. The population grew from 450 in 1910 to 3,700 in 1940 to 17,846 in 1980 and 16,087 according to the 2000 Federal Census. Bay Village is primarily a residential community today with a minimal number of businesses and virtually no available land.

The first election for officers of the Hamlet of Bay was held on February 18, 1903, at the office of the Oviatt Manufacturing Co., pursuant to a proclamation issued by Reuben Osborn and William O. Mathews, authorized agents of the petitioners for the Hamlet of Bay. On April 15, the following officers were sworn into office for the Village of Bay: Reuben Osborn, mayor; William W. Aldrich, clerk; J. Currier, treasurer; Frank C. Sites, marshall; Council members for two years: H.P. Foote, Julius Wischmeyer and Calvin Osborn; Council members for one year: Frank Meilander, Burrett Sadler and William O. Mathers. Perry Powell was elected assessor.

The central portion of Dover Township, comprised of 15.9 square miles, became incorporated into Dover Village in 1911. This area would be renamed Westlake in 1940 due to the continued confusion of multiple areas of the state being referred to as Dover.

Dover Township's southern region combined with portions of Olmsted to the south to form North Olmsted in the fall of 1908. Upon reaching a population of 5,000 the area reached the status of becoming the city of North Olmsted in 1951.

Here through winter's piercing blast
And summer's cooling breeze they dwelt,
A happy family,
Giving one and then another of their cherished ones
Into the keeping of those who loved them long and well,
Till all had made for themselves homes
And by their own firesides told the tales of pioneer life.
When the bidding came for our pioneers to leave the home
They so loved on Erie's pebbly shore
They quietly removed to that "a beautiful land,
The far away home of the soul."
The Cahoon Pioneer Celebration, 1874

History of Lakeside Cemetery

When comes life, so comes death.

Life in the early years of Dover Township, Ohio, was difficult. Death among children and loved ones was a frequent occurrence. When disease found its way to the area, there was little one could do but try not to associate with others until the threat passed. Times were hard but families were harder. Their closeness and sense of community became vitally important, almost a matter of life and death.

The half-acre Lakeside Cemetery was founded in 1814 out of necessity when Asahel Porter's wife, Rebecca, their infant son, Dennis, and a man named George Smith were killed. They were returning along with Noah Crocker from Cleveland when their boat capsized at the mouth of the Rocky River during a sudden storm. Reuben Osborn, one of the area's first settlers, donated the land for the burials

Osborn first visited Dover in October 1810 with other family members. He returned to Camden, N.Y., until the following spring when he returned with his family. Reuben officially purchased the 81 acres of the eastern portion of Lot 93 on which he had settled from Philo Taylor on November 7, 1815. The deed was not officially recorded until April 30, 1816. (Delays were frequent in the documentation of records.).

The cemetery at this time was comprised of what is now known as the center section, also known as the "Original Part." A tombstone is found in Row 6 of the old section for Rebecca, her husband Asahel, and their infant son, Dennis. Two small, older stones, assumed to be the originals, are present with initials "A.P." and "R.P."

Rebecca Porter was not the first recorded death in Dover Township. Rebecca Smith, wife of Abner Smith, died September 27, 1811, in her 52nd year. It has been said that she was "buried upon the family farm and afterwards removed to the cemetery on the lake," which would be Lakeside. Rebecca was consequently moved again and is currently buried along with her husband at Evergreen Cemetery on Columbia Road in North Olmsted, Ohio. Evergreen, also located in Dover Township, opened in 1820 and is close to the Smith's home on Center Ridge Road. Considering the method of burial at the time, it seems unlikely that Rebecca Smith would have been moved twice. Records are not available for this time period so it may never be known exactly how many times Rebecca was exhumed. Since there is an early reference to her burial at Lakeside, she is included in this book.

Cemetery Records and Expansion

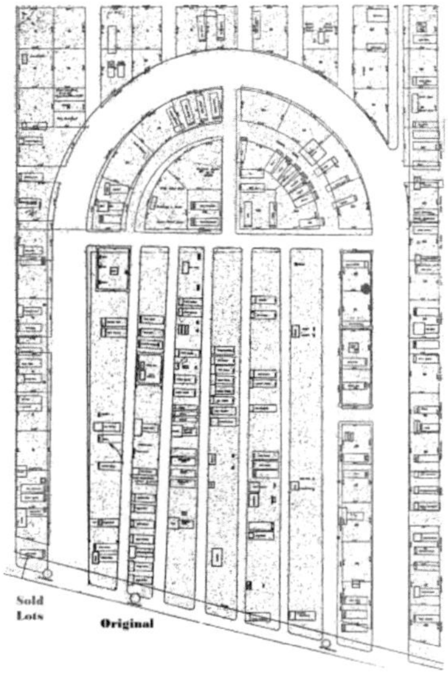

The year 1877 brought the addition of land surrounding the "original part" of the cemetery. The Trustees of Dover purchased more of Lot 93 to the north, east and west of the existing cemetery from David Deforest Osborn, Reuben's grandson, for $94.40. David also signed a quit claim deed to the trustees for the cemetery itself, receiving $1.00 consideration.

A strip 28 feet wide was purchased for $140 to the east of Lot 93 from Charles and Babette Hassler. The Hasslers owned the former Porter property that is part of Lot 94. Additions created a horseshoe layout to bring the cemetery to its present size of approximately half an acre. The original part is now located in the interior of the drive with the eastern row and northern half circle comprised of the newly acquired land. The outer areas of the horseshoe drive were all acquisitions from 1877 purchases. Lots were numbered and sold from this new area primarily from 1879 to the early twentieth century. Prices for the individual lots, most in the $5.00 range, are documented throughout the book.

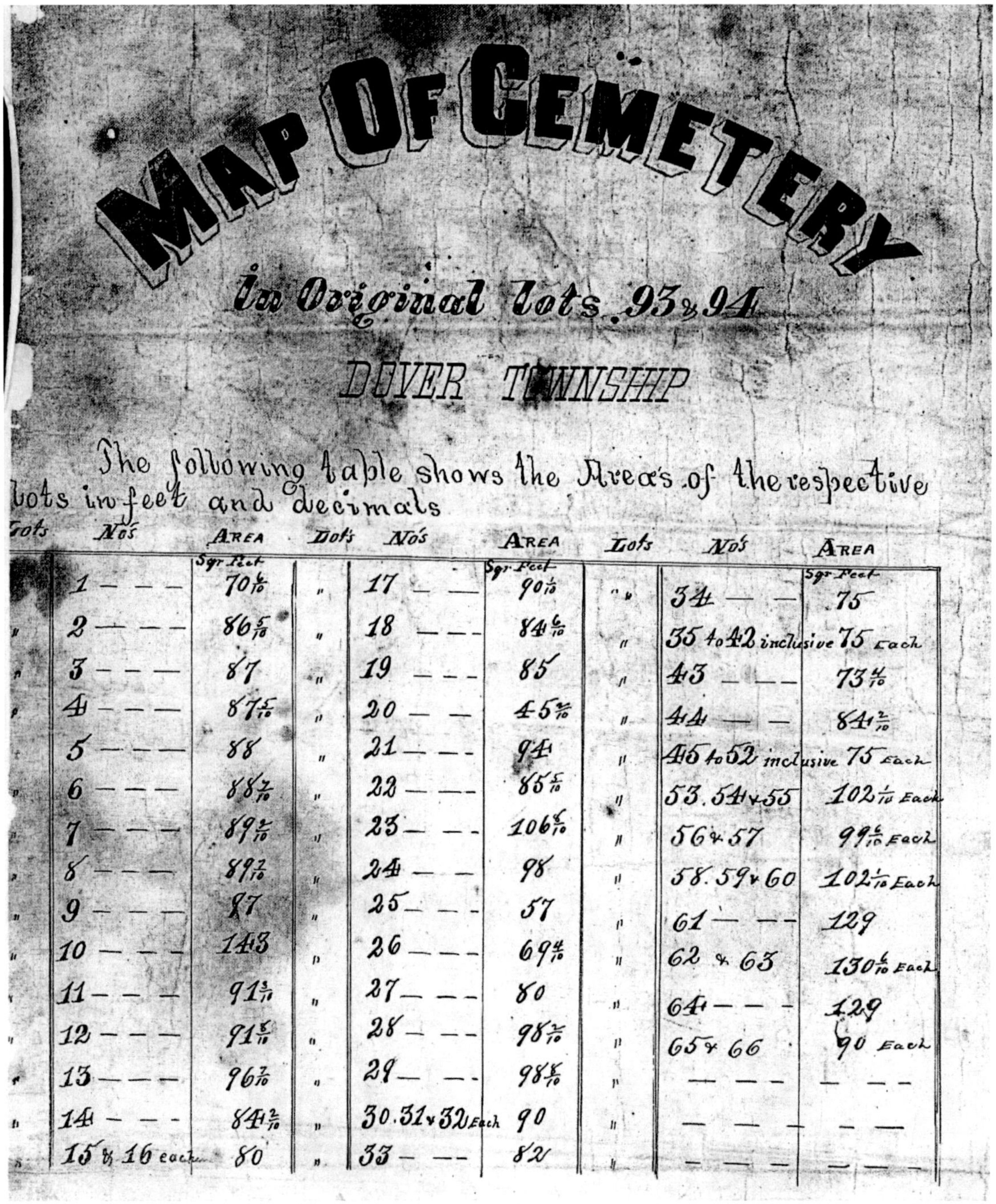

MAP OF CEMETERY

In Original Lots 93 & 94

DOVER TOWNSHIP

The following table shows the Area's of the respective lots in feet and decimals

Lots	No's	Area Sqr. Feet	Lots	No's	Area Sqr. Feet	Lots	No's	Area Sqr. Feet
	1 — — —	70 6/10	"	17 — —	90 1/10	"	34 — —	75
"	2 — — —	86 5/10	"	18 — — —	84 6/10	"	35 to 42 inclusive	75 Each
"	3 — — —	87	"	19 — — —	85	"	43 — — —	73 4/10
"	4 — — —	87 5/10	"	20 — —	45 2/10	"	44 — —	84 2/10
"	5 — — —	88	"	21 — — —	94	"	45 to 52 inclusive	75 Each
"	6 — — —	88 7/10	"	22 — — —	85 5/10	"	53. 54 & 55	102 1/10 Each
"	7 — — —	89 2/10	"	23 — — —	106 6/10	"	56 & 57	99 6/10 Each
"	8 — — —	89 7/10	"	24 — —	98	"	58. 59 & 60	102 1/10 Each
"	9 — — —	87	"	25 — — —	57	"	61 — — —	129
"	10 — — —	143	"	26 — — —	69 4/10	"	62 & 63	130 6/10 Each
"	11 — — —	91 3/10	"	27 — — —	80	"	64 — — —	129
"	12 — — —	91 8/10	"	28 — — —	98 2/10	"	65 & 66	90 Each
"	13 — — —	96 7/10	"	29 — — —	98 8/10	"	— — —	— — —
"	14 — — —	84 2/10	"	30. 31 & 32 Each	90	"	— — —	— — —
"	15 & 16 each	80	"	33 — — —	82	"	— — —	— — —

Original table showing the areas of respective lots in feet and decimals.

The recording of internments at Lakeside Cemetery began in 1879 after the expansion of the cemetery. Records are not complete, nor consistently entered in the book, throughout the period of notations from 1879-1919. At times dates were not recorded chronologically which may indicate a delay in inclusion leading to inaccuracy and omissions. There are approximately 270 known burials at Lakeside who were either recorded in the Book of Interments or who may be identified with headstones. There may be many burials in the original part lacking documentation, but we will never know how many. When looking at the layout of the cemetery there are areas where gaps exist, especially in the sixth row which seems to be the oldest.

Burials do include two Revolutionary War soldiers; five soldiers from the War of 1812; nine Civil War soldiers, including one "Unknown Soldier," one soldier from the Spanish American War, two from World War I, one during World War II, and one from the Korean War.

The Cahoon Will

The Last Will and Testament of Ida Maria Cahoon, granddaughter of the first family in Bay Village, specified that the cemetery be forever maintained. Ida had an interest in the cemetery because her grandparents, the first settlers of Bay Village, and her entire immediate family, consisting of her parents and all of her siblings, were interred there.

A portion of "Item 21" in the will of Ida Cahoon reads: "The Lakeside Cemetery situated west of said land on Lot Numbers Ninety three (93) and Ninety-four (94) in the Village of Bay, in which lie buried many early settlers, is to be sacredly cared for and if need be, protected upon the North by stone wall, but never to be removed from its present location.

"If any of the conditions be violated or said Mayor or Village Council refuse to accept said trust, then and in that event, I give, devise and bequeath the land and Real Estate, in this item named and described to the Board of Trustees of the School Teachers Pension Fund of Cleveland, Ohio, and their successors in office forever as a home for the use of the retired Teachers of the Public Schools of the City of Cleveland, Ohio."

A number of flat tombstones were damaged by vandals around 1969 and the stones were laid flat to preserve them. During the early 1970s the cemetery seemed to fall into disrepair. Unfortunately, one night, after repeated rains, about 40 feet of land was lost on the north, or lake, side of the cemetery. At least one casket was said to have been partially exposed in the washout. A rebuilding process was begun. The City of Bay Village and the Army Corp of Engineers installed gabions, or steel wire mesh baskets filled with stones, and added land to the north.

Recent Improvements

To draw attention to the significance of Lakeside Cemetery, Catherine Burke Flament in 2001 proposed to the Cahoon Memorial Park Trustees that an Ohio Historical Marker be erected at the site. The trustees, under the leadership of Mayor Deborah Sutherland, endorsed the proposal and the process was begun.

The Ohio Historical Marker Program, sponsored by the Ohio Historical Society, originally began in 1929 with the placing of wooden road sign markers to identify major routes of marches in military campaigns through Ohio. The current program recognizes people, places and events of local, state and/or national historical significance. In 1957, cast aluminum signs in the shape of Ohio replaced the original wooden markers.

Lakeside Cemetery was approved as a significantly historical site and a marker was dedicated during the Memorial Day festivities on May 27, 2002. This was also the 70th anniversary of the American Legion's participation in the parade. Osborn descendants who were present for the unveiling included Kathy O'Connor Johnson, George Morgan, Sally O'Connor, Delbert and Betty Osborn, and Glenn and Ruth Osborn. The marker was included under the umbrella of the Ohio Bicentennial initiative which was celebrated in 2003.

The marker with a photograph of Reuben Osborn states:

Lakeside Cemetery

Laid out in 1814, Lakeside Cemetery became the first public burying ground in Dover Township, an area that now includes Bay Village, Westlake, and the northern portion of North Olmsted. Reuben Osborn (1778-1860) arrived in Dover on October 10, 1810 but returned to New York. He settled on this land with his wife Sarah Johnson Osborn (1779-1856) and family in 1811, later purchasing most of the plot where the cemetery would be established from Philo Taylor. Sarah's sister, Rebecca Porter, and her infant son were the first to be buried here; they were killed when their boat capsized at the mouth of the Rocky River in 1814. Including land purchased in 1877, the cemetery currently spans half an acre. Although not recorded until 1879, there are over 270 known burials. Among those interned here are veterans from the Revolutionary War, War of 1812, Civil War, Spanish-American War, World War I, World War II and the Korean War.

Small metal grave markers had been placed on the graves of veterans over the years but many were in a state of disrepair and few remained. To clearly identify all veterans buried at Lakeside Cemetery, the members of Bay Village Post 135 of the American Legion took it upon themselves to identify all of the graves of veterans and honor them with engagement-appropriate cast bronze markers. The project was completed with the metal markers set in concrete before the Memorial Day Parade of 2004.

In 2003 a committee was formed to raise money to replace a combination of fence styles, including rotting wooden and chain link fences, that surrounded the cemetery. The effort was led by Billie Jo "B.J." Schwartz, who at the time lived across the street from the cemetery and who, with husband Edward, owned the slivers of land that surround the cemetery on the west, north and east sides.

Questers Dover on Erie Chapter 821 spearheaded the project with the assistance of the Bay Village Historical Society. Following fundraising efforts and the generosity of private donors, sufficient funds were raised to erect a black metal fence around the cemetery. A new black and bronze sign was affixed to the fence along Lake Road and three other bronze plaques were placed on the fence to honor significant donors after the fence installation during the spring of 2005. The largest donation coming from the family of Michael Joseph Maloney has been honored with an individual plaque. Michael is buried elsewhere.

Benches were created from the top ledge and sandstone sides of the Wolf Road bridge that was rebuilt in 2005. Two benches were installed by the City of Bay Village at the north end of the cemetery to provide a resting place for those visiting the cemetery. Gary and Katy Dix Brahler generously donated a weeping cherry tree in the spring of 2004 that is planted near one of the benches.

Plans were underway to beautify the cemetery with additional plantings which started in the spring of 2006.

In 2025, after repeated damage to the fences, the city installed bollard posts at each enterance to create a walking path through the cemetery.

In Summary

The cemetery has undergone some major transformations in the last few years. Over the years it had been neglected at times but after the efforts of a concerned group of citizens, the cemetery has been revitalized which hopefully will be continued.

When this publication was originally printed, it was determined that there were no available lots. However, in 1980, the city estimated that there were 77 empty graves. These available graves had been previously purchased from the city, but not all of the plots in each lot had been used by the owners. In some areas of the Old Section, a lack of headstones may indicate that the graves are occupied but currently unmarked.

In 2010, the City of Bay Village repurposed lots 13 and 14 in Potters Field as cremation plots. At that time, Dick Martin, who had served on city council for 32 years, and his wife Betsy were approved to purchase their final resting place in lot 14. Lot 13 has a large black walnut tree covering 2/3's of the area.

Using This Book as a Reference

This book was written as an aid when researching families who are associated with Lakeside Cemetery and to offer insight into the lives of those buried there. After years of researching, I found it frustrating to uncover information from a source and then be unsure of where it originated in order to verify its authenticity. This publication is designed to help eliminate this problem as well as to sort out discrepancies found when researching. For those who are intrigued by local history or have a curiosity about those who walked these shores, this book will reveal fascinating and sometimes touching accounts of the daily lives of these individuals, and sometimes the overwhelming challenges they faced and triumphs they celebrated.

The burials are organized by lot or row numbers followed by the number of markers in that particular row. The lot numbering begins on the west side of the cemetery going from the south (Lake Road) to the north (Lake Erie). There are multiple numbers used at the north end along the lake in the corner sections. The numbers proceed from west to east along the north (lake) end and proceed from north to south following the east fence line. The numbering continues passing to the west side of the car path and retraces from the south to the north. Multiple lots are located in the half circle formed at the northern end. The eastern half circle is where the Joel Butler Cahoon family is buried and is retained as a unit in the book in spite of the fact that the numbers are not chronological and skip to the western half circle and back. The central area is primarily considered the "Original Part" with the exception of the eastern row.

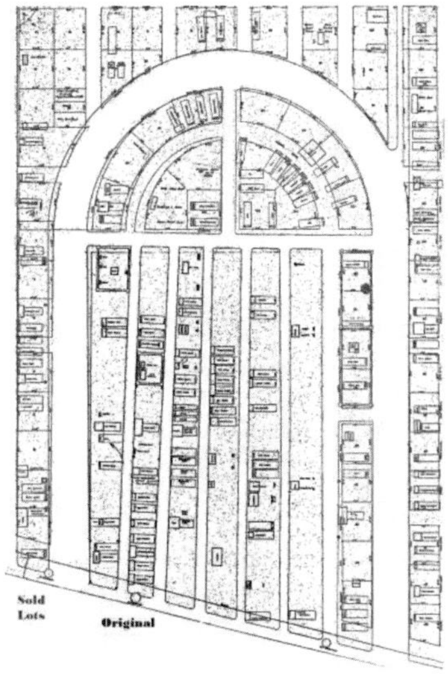

When an exact location of a burial has not been listed, but a spouse, parents, etc. is buried in a specific lot, the individual is listed with them with an asterisk (*) before the name. Italics have been used when the person has been moved to another cemetery or may never have been buried at Lakeside Cemetery.

Records were kept in a special book which lists the cemetery as "Lake Side." This may very well have been a printing error as other references have the name listed using one word. The cemetery was referred to in a number of ways through the years in obituaries, etc. as "Osborn Cemetery," "Lake Road Cemetery" and "Bay Village Cemetery."

The "Lake Side Cemetery List of Interments" included the following categories: Name of Person, Age, Residence, Nativity, When Interred, No. of Lot and Remarks. Most categories were usually completed. When reference is made to cemetery records in the book, the nativity is not listed if it states "American."

John Ware, 1879, was the first entry on the list. Internments previous to this had been identified only by tombstones placed on the grave. Theoretically, dozens of burials took place in Lakeside Cemetery that cannot be documented due to lack of concrete evidence. When examining the spacing in the original section of the cemetery one finds numerous spaces, especially in the row of the earliest burials. The impermanence of early grave markers may very well account for the lack of later burials in this area.

When reading the list of interments, after Oct. 2, 1890, the next listing is 1894, but there were burials between these years. Between 1900 and 1905 the records were very haphazard. Dates were mixed up; it was as if individuals were trying to remember who was buried and wrote the information down at a later date. The records in the book cease in December 1919. Burial permits recorded information starting in 1910. Obviously the records are directly correlated to the care that was taken by the recorder to document burials that took place.

Later burials include: Eleanor L. Burko in 1992 and Eleanor's husband, Walter W. Burko, in 1994. Both of these burials were in Lot 9. Since this time, there have been four additional burials that are included in the addendum of this book.

Sources were extracted precisely as found in each document. Incorrect spellings were retained for the reader to evaluate. It is common to uncover inconsistencies in genealogical research and is a clue as to how precise the compiler was when recording the information. Remember these sources may shed light on additional information that is not able to be uncovered elsewhere. When conflicts are uncovered they should be taken into account. Consider the date the reference was written. How close was it to the actual event? Do you feel the individual was estimating statistical and accompanying information they provided or were they truly knowledgeable? Was the informer a relative or acquaintance? Multiple sources are quoted where possible to allow the reader to evaluate the accuracy of the resource material. Keep in mind that incorrect data should not be totally discounted, it may be a clue to an adjacent family member.

Headings listing the person or monument associated with the specific lot are in bold for the individual buried in the lot. Italic has been used if an individual has been moved to another cemetery, may not be buried at the site but is listed in the official records or has multiple headstones. Direct descendants or ancestors are listed in bold italic letters with others in italic the first time they are mentioned in a citation.

Inscriptions were transcribed in the same manner. A few mistakes were found with names or dates on the tombstones themselves. When this occurred multiple references are cited to establish the correct information. When it was difficult to decipher writing on a marker, the questionable word or phrase is accompanied by a question mark (?).

Information on Federal census records was not always repeated if it duplicated a previous census. In some, information was listed under another branch of the family. The information is generally listed under the individual or spouse's plot, rather than their child's if both were buried at Lakeside Cemetery.

Ancestors are included from the time the family immigrated to the United States if possible. Descendants are included to provide information as to where branches of the family settled. The majority of those buried at Lakeside Cemetery were related to others buried there. Relationships were established through original documents as much as possible.

When young children were buried in Lakeside Cemetery, an attempt was made to elaborate on their parents, and, if possible, siblings, to give a glimpse of their lives and the families of which they were part.

Since the former Avon Township (Avon and Avon Lake), Dover Township (Bay Village, Westlake and the northern portion of North Olmsted) and Rockport Township (Rocky River, Fairview Park, most of Lakewood and the West Park area of Cleveland) are all in Ohio, the state may not be listed when they are mentioned.

Access to resources changed as the book progressed and has continued to broaden. Now the internet has become a valuable resource. One precaution should be mentioned: As others are expanding their knowledge of genealogy, you should be wary of those who are more interested in the amount of information they are able to accumulate, rather than the accuracy. The interaction between family descendents and fellow researchers for this publication proved to be significant and invaluable.

This book is meant to compliment a previous Bay Village Historical Society publication, Bay Village: A Way of Life. Additional information about Bay Village families, their homes and early life in the area are included in this publication. Readers are encouraged to use both when delving into information about the early years of Dover Township to get a full picture of its families and lifestyles. You may find some overlap between this book and the "Way of Life" book so many anecdotes were not duplicated here to avoid repetition. There were also a significant number of individuals buried in the cemetery who settled in surrounding areas, other than Dover/Bay Village. Therefore, this publication expands its reach to other communities whereas the "Way of Life" publication concentrates on the Bay Village community.

Abbreviations :

abt. - about
ae. - age
al. - alien, not a U.S. citizen
b. - born
bef. - before
BRP - Burial or Removal Permit, Bureau of Vital Statistics (Bay Village City Hall)
BTP - Burial Transit Permit, (Bay Village City Hall)
bur. - buried
BV - Bay Village, OH (previously called Dover)
BVCH - Bay Village City Hall (Papers in cemetery file)
BVWL - Bay Village: A Way of Life
c - circa (around/approximately)
certif. - certificate
CB - Certificate of Birth, Division of Vital Statistics, Year, File No. (Ohio Department of Health, Columbus)
Ch'n - children
CD - Certificate of Death, Division of Vital Statistics, Year: File No. (Ohio Historical Soc. Pre 1945, Ohio Dept. of Health: 1945-; Columbus)
CL - Cemetery list of interments, not included in chronological listing in ledger.
CLD - cemetery lot deed
Co. - county
Cong. - Congregational
CYBV - census reference for Bay Village, Cuyahoga County, Ohio
CYDO - census reference for Dover, Cuyahoga County, Ohio
CYRP - census reference for Rockport, Cuyahoga County, Ohio
Cuy Co. - Cuyahoga County, Ohio (Cleveland area)
d. - died

ds. - days
dau. - daughter
ECF - Estate Case File (wills)
FC - Federal Population Census
fr. - father
IEC - Independent Evangelical Church abstracts
inter - interment
LI - "List of Interments," Lake Side Cemetery record book (Bay Village City Hall)
LOAV - census reference for Avon, Lorain County, Ohio
LCMR - Lorain County Marriage Records
min. - minutes
mo. - mother
mos. or ms. - months
MR - Marriage Records, Cuyahoga County, OH- Cleveland Archives (volume, page)
Na. - naturalized citizen
no. - number
occup. - occupation
PBL - Probate Court Birth Records, Lorain Co., Ohio (volume: page, line number)
PD - Probate Court Death Records, Dover, Cuyahoga Co., Ohio (volume: page or reference number)
PDL - Probate Court Death Records, Lorain Co., Ohio, volume: page, line number.
PFH - Pease Funeral Home Records (Western Reserve Historical Society)
rel. - religion
res. - residence
SL - "Sale of Lots," Lake Side Cemetery book (Bay Village City Hall)
unm. - unmarried
yrs. - years
VR – Vital Record
WRHS - Western Reserve Historical Society
WWR - Memorial to the Pioneer Women of the Western Reserve.

Photo Credits

History of the Area:

Knepper, George W. The Official Ohio Lands Book. The Auditor, State of Ohio. "Connecticut Western Reserve – Firelands Map." Permission granted to reproduce from the Auditor of State of Ohio.............xv

"Moses Cleaveland." A History of the City of Cleveland by James Harrison Kennedy, 1896. Frontispiece. Permission granted to reproduce by The Western Reserve Historical Society, Cleveland, OH….................xv

"The Connecticut Western Reserve." Permission granted to reproduce from The Ohio Historical Society…..xvi

"Joshua Stow." A History of the City of Cleveland by James Harrison Kennedy, 1896. p. 29. Permission granted to reproduce by The Western Reserve Historical Society, Cleveland, OH……………………........xvii

"Lorain and Cuyahoga County Townships." Catherine Burke Flament and Gene Zvara……………………..xviii

Settlement of Dover:

"Reuben Osborn House." Eric Eakin. 2005………………………………………………………...….…...xix

"Rose Hill Museum." Eric Eakin. 2005………………………………………………….…..…………....xx

"Wischmeyer Hotel." Bay Village Historical Society. Wischmeyer Family File. Rose Hill Museum, Bay Village, OH. Undetermined date…………………………………………………………..……..…….. xx

History of Lakeside Cemetery:

"Reuben Osborn." Sally O'Connor. Family Photograph. Undetermined date………………......…………...xxii

"Map of Cemetery." Permission granted to reproduce from City of Bay Village. Lakeside Cemetery File..xxiv

"Ida Maria Cahoon." Bay Village Historical Society. Cahoon Family File. Rose Hill Museum, Bay Village, OH. Undetermined date……………………………………………………..……………….....xxv

"Cahoon Memorial." Bay Village Historical Society. Cahoon Family File. Rose Hill Museum, Bay Village, OH. Undetermined date……………………………………..………..xxv

Sylized cemetery map showing plots. Gene Zvara. 2006. ……………………………………………….xxxiv

Lakeside Cemetery Maps and Photographs:

Cemetery plot maps. Permission granted to reproduce from the City of Bay Village and Cahoon Trustees, Bay Village, OH.

General cemetery photographs. Eric Eakin and Catherine Burke Flament. 2005-2006, 2025.

Cemetery tombstones. Catherine Burke Flament, Bay Village, OH. 1998-2006. Additions by Nancy Cleary, Westlake, OH. 2005.

Individual portraits provided by family members and the Bay Village Historical Society.

"Walter W. and Eleanor L. Burko." Olan Mills Portrait Studios. Permission granted to reproduce by Olan Mills Portrait Studios. p. 21.

Catherine Burke Flament. Ohio School Pictures. Permission granted to reproduce by Ohio School Pictures. Back cover.

Unofficial Rendering of the Cemetery Showing Lots and Most Burials.

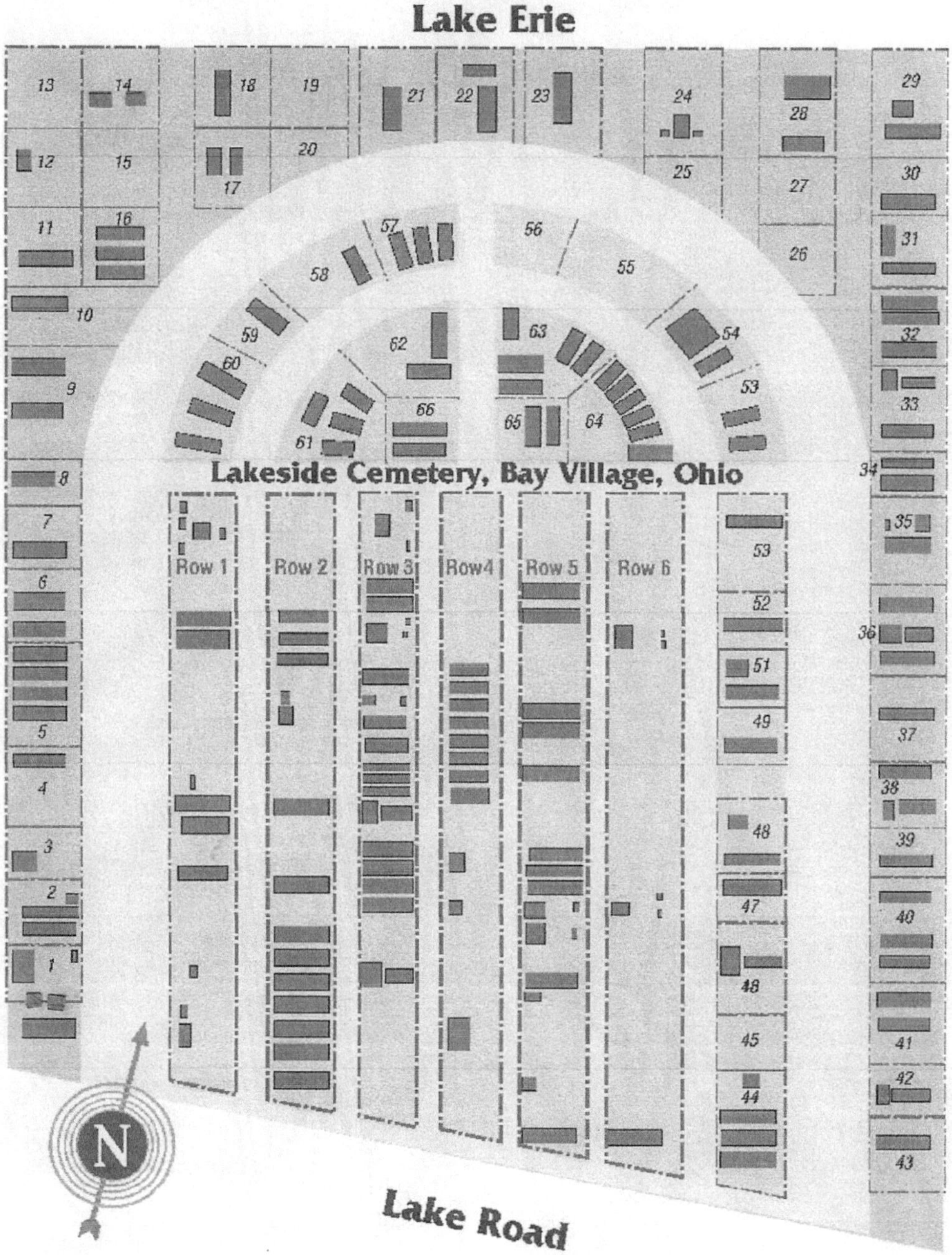

Original drawing by Gene Zvara.

Cemetery Internments by Lot

Those buried in the same lot are listed together. Immediate families that are included in adjoining lots are listed as a unit using both lot numbers together. The page numbers indicate where the information for the specific individual begins. Surnames of women are in parenthesis, but do not include a first marriage if they had been previously married unless the first husband is also buried at Lakeside. Names in italics are those who are associated with a lot but have been moved to another cemetery, or the burial was included with the cemetery records but probably did not occur. Some individuals were not identified in a specific lot; it is assumed they are buried with other family members and have been marked with a * if a relationship was established with another burial.

Numbers in the Original Section such as Row 1-1/3 indicate multiple markers for an individual or individuals in the family. Markers labeled "mother" or "father" or individual stones with one person's name, were included along with the primary marker. The Cahoon family, who have an entire section, have been organized in the book as listed on the cemetery monument, rather than the lot numbers as the lot numbers are not consecutive. The Cahoon plot is shown in the photograph to the right.

Purchased Lots

Original Part

Original Part Unidentified Plot

Those Interred in an Unidentified Area

Those Who Have Been Moved to Another Cemetery or Are Included in the Cemetery Records But May Never Have Been Buried Here.

Addendum

Alphabetical Cemetery Internments

Lot	*Name*	*Birth*	*Death*
Row 4-1	Aldrich, Aaron III	1795	1856
Row 4-1	Aldrich, Aaron Winsor IV	1815	1890
Row 4-1	Aldrich, Elizabeth	1794	1869
Row 3-7	Aldrich, Harriet Emma	1847	1851
Row 4-1	Aldrich, Henry Winsor	1822	1892
Row 3-5	Aldrich, Ida	1856	1910
Row 4-1	Aldrich, Mabel L.	1865	1881
Row 3-6	Aldrich, Martha	1818	1875
Row 3-8	Aldrich, Martha Bassett	1842	1848
Lot 16	Aldrich, Mary Ann	1851	1921
Row 4-1	Aldrich, Mary Ann	1822	1910
Row 4-1	Aldrich, Sarah Elizabeth	1853	1858
Row 3-5	Aldrich, William W.	1817	1903
Lot 18	Aslaksen, Bernice	1916	1916
Lot 18	Aslaksen, Herbert Barth	1917	1917
Lot 18-1	Aslaksen, John	1901	1921
Lot 18-1	Aslaksen, Louisa Malvina	1877	1948
Lot 18-1	Aslaksen, Olaf	1867	1954
Lot 34-6	Axam, Maria	1825	1895
Lot 23	Bambam, Frederick	1841	1901
Lot 23	Bambam, Lena	1837	1911
Row 3-10	Bassett, Martha Hall	1790	1835
Row 3-11	Bassett, Nancy	1823	1867
Row 3-9	Bassett, Nathan	1785	1842
Lot 6-13	Beard, Arthur H.	1882	1880
Lot 6-14	Beard, Emma Valara	1855	1927
Lot 6-13	Beard, Nelson	1887	1887
Lot 6-14	Beard, Nelson	1851	1907
Lot 5-10	Beard, Rolen	1890	1890
Lot 32	Beard, Willie	1888	1882
Lot 29	Bender, Elizabeth	1851	1929
Lot 33	Body, Mary	1854	1920
Unspec.	Brais, Jenny Mary	1883	1909
Row 1-8	Braman, Betsey	1807	1848
Row 2-9	Braman, Horace	1831	1891
Row 1-8	Braman, James	1837?	1838
Row 1-8	Braman, Louisa	1829	1831?
Row 2-10	Braman, Lydia	c1837	1864
Row 1-8	Braman, Otis	1805	1852(7)
Row 2-8	Braman, Sarah	1840	1933
Lot 9-18	Burko, Eleanor Louise	1916	1992
Lot 9-18	Burko, Walter William	1915	1994
Unspec.	Burlingame		1882
Lot 44-4	Burlingame, Gilbert	1844	1900
Lot 44-4	Burlingame, Hiram	1809	1891
Lot 44-4	Burlingame, Rebecca	1813	1902
Lot 57-3	Burrell, Vernon	1863	1907
Lot 63-5	Cahoon, Charles Oscar	1839	1853
Lot 63-9	Cahoon, Daniel Kenyon	1838	1890
Lot 53-1	Cahoon, Elizabeth	1830	1914
Lot 63-6	Cahoon, Ida Marie	1852	1917
Row 4-8	Cahoon, Joel	1831	1838
Lot 63-10	Cahoon, Joel Butler	1793	1882
Lot 63-8	Cahoon, John Joseph	1834	1894
Lot 64-13	Cahoon, John Marshall	1847	1899
Row 4-3	Cahoon, Joseph	1762	1839
Lot 65-15	Cahoon, Laura Ellen	1841	1917
Lot 64-12	Cahoon, Leverett Judson	1845	1886
Row 4-3	Cahoon, Lydia	1768	1834
Lot 63-7	Cahoon, Lydia Elizabeth	1835	1917
Lot 64-11	Cahoon, Margaret	1810	1894
Lot 65-16	Cahoon, Martha W.	1844	1903
Lot 64-14	Cahoon, Mary Emma	1849	1857
Lot 54-2	Cahoon, Thomas H.	1832	1907
Row 4-14	Campbell, Eliza	1814	1854
Row 6-2	Case, Charlotte	1790	1826
Row 6-2	Case, Moses	1781	1868
Lot 8-16	Close, John	1875	1904
Lot 35	Comstock, Mary Jane	c1834	1882
Row 5-11	Comstock, William	1826	1855
Lot 52-17	Conkey, Silas E.	1834	1880(3)
Lot 27	Conklin, Carrie G.	1881	1890
Lot 27	Conklin, James Monroe	1838	1900
Lot 27	Conklin, Susan	c1839	1919
Row 2-15	Coppin, Eliza Ann	1820	1861
Row 2-17	Coppin, James	1818	1874
Row 2-16	Coppin, Willie	1846	1863
Lot 59	Cowley, Elizabeth	1837	1916
Lot 59	Cowley, John	1858	1892
Lot 5-9	Crist, Margarett F.	c1853	1886
Lot 5-9	Crist, Mary Ann	1886	1887
Lot 28	Darby, Emma J.	1877	1957
Lot 40	David, Henry	c1839	1890
Lot 24	Davider, Henry	1835	1898
Unspec.	Deutsel, Ludwig	1865	1910
Row 4-15	Dodd, Annie	1836	1924
Row 4-15	Dodd, Charles	1835	1887
Row 4-16	Dodd, Charles	1870	1871
Lot 61-9	Drake, Della Myrtilla	1863	1895
Lot 61-9	Drake, Emma Irene	1860	1933
Lot 61-9	Drake, Frederick Lincoln	1862	1941
Lot 9	Dranse, Erdine Elizabeth	1870	1950
Row 2-6	Eddy, Caleb	1791	1869
Row 2-5	Eddy, Charles F.	1853	1854
Row 2-5	Eddy, Hiram J.	1851	1854
Row 1-11	Eddy, Margaret Griswold	1802	1869
Row 2-7	Eddy, Rebecca	1788	1849
Lot 43	Edson, Calvin Riley	1832	1880
Lot 54-3	Ellis, Effie H.	1863	1888
Lot 45-6	Elmer, Helen V.	1846	1930
Lot 45	Elmer, Lewie	1865	1918
Lot 45-5	Elmer, Washington	1837	1925

Lot	Name	Birth	Death
Orig. Part	Eppink, Infant	1890	1890
Row 4-2	Eugene C. Oviatt	1864	1864
Lot 16	Everard, Mary Ann	1851	1921
Lot 16	Everard, Mary Ann	1892	1936
Lot 16	Everard, Robert	1854	1921
Unspec.	Fichle, Infant	1925	1925
Row 2-12	Foote, Betsy H.	1826	1828
Row 2-12	Foote, Catherine	1806	1886
Row 2-12	Foote, Catherine P.	1838	1923
Row 3-1	Foote, Dama	1794	1866
Row 3-3	Foote, David	1760	1851
Row 3-4	Foote, Elizabeth	1764	1844
Row 2-12	Foote, Henry P.	1844	1919
Row 2-11	Foote, Ransom	1803	1846
Row 3-2	Foote, Richard L.	1854	1856
Row 2-12	Foote, Statira J.	1842	1845
Row 3-1	Foote, Thomas	1788	1856
Lot 33	Gerbick, Maude	1881	1944
Row 5-3	Geuder, Lina	1858	1858
Lot 35	Gibbs, Henry	c1830	1898
Lot 35	Gibbs, Mary Jane	c1834	1882
Row 5-2	Goodrich, James	1846	1848
Row 5-15	Grant, Alonson Atwell	1835	1863
Row 2-4	Griswold, Etmer L.	1865	1866
Row 1-10	Griswold, Luman	1799	1845
Row 2-4	Griswold, Luman Loami	1838	1867
Lot 33	Gunziger, Carl	1886	1886
Lot 29	Haag, Infant	1914	1914
Lot 39	Hahn, Frederick	1879	1884
Lot 18-1	Hardy, Louisa Malvina	1877	1948
Lot 42-18	Hassler, Anna	1858	1942
Lot 41-17	Hassler, Babette	1832	1879
Lot 41-17	Hassler, Carl F.	1820	1906
Lot 42-18	Hassler, Edna M.	1885	1964
Lot 43-20	Hassler, Fritz	1840	1892
Lot 42-18	Hassler, Getrude M.	1888	1966
Lot 42-18	Hassler, Laura M.	1884	1988
Lot 41-17	Hassler, Mathilda L.	1865	1947
Lot 42-18	Hassler, Robert C.	1890	1983
Lot 30	Hayes, Fannie J.	1868	1914
Row 3-15	Hayes, Joseph	1829	1905
Row 3-16	Hayes, Mary Jane	1832	1922
Lot 33	Heckerman, Bertha C.	1873	1907
Lot 33	Heckerman, Frank	1868	1954
Lot 33	Heckerman, Maude	1881	1944
Lot 10	Heron, Caroline	1889	1890
Row 1-6	Hilliard, William Silas	1813	1854
Lot 28	Hinz, Augusta	1850	1945
Lot 28	Hinz, Fred	1852	1911
Lot 57-2	Jaycox, Burrell Anson	1893	1904
Lot 62	Jaycox, Francis Willard	c1890	1894
Lot 62-10	Jaycox, Genevieve C.	1859	1946
Lot 62-10	Jaycox, George Anson	1857	1926
Lot 57-1	Jaycox, George Ernest	1881	1895
Unspec.	Johnson, William J.	1875	1934
Lot 19-2	Knaggs, Frank John	1863	1931
Row 5-1	Krumwiede, Heinrich Wm	1816	1899
Lot 9	Krumwiede, Infant	c1904	c1904
Orig. Part	Krumwiede, Infant	1909	1909
Lot 9	Krumwiede, Infant	c1903	c1903
Lot 9-17	Krumwiede, Katherine M	1870	1904
Orig. Part	Krumwiede, Leslie	1903	1905
Lot 9-19	Krumwiede, Lillian Sophie	1890	1974
Row 5-1	Krumwiede, Sophia	1822	1874
Lot 31-3	Kupfer, Edward W.	1860	1926
Lot 31-3	Kupfer, Emma	1859	1951
Lot 42-19	Lieberich, Theodore	1848	1910
Row 5-14	Loomis, William Henry	1841	1842
Lot 6-14	Lucas, Emma Valara	1855	1927
Lot 5-9	Lucas, Margarett F.	1850	1886
Lot 33	Lukacs, Mary	1854	1920
Lot 14C	Martin, Elizabeth Ross	1930	2016
Lot 14C	Martin, Treagh Richard	1930	2011
Lot 3	Mawby, John	1886	1886
Lot 42-18	Mayer, Anna	1858	1942
Lot 42-18	Mayer, J. Robert	1858	1942
Row 6-1	McMahon, Charlotte	1836	1862
Orig. Part	Miller, David	1841	1879
Lot 29	Miller, remains of		1897
Lot 1	Morgan, Mary Ann	1918	1918
Lot 28	Neubaum, Augusta	1850	1945
Lot 7	Oliver, Antonia	1824	1911
Lot 48-10	Osborn, Angenette E	1835	1880
Lot 43-21	Osborn, Bessie	1873	1897
Lot 2-5	Osborn, Betsey	1839	1912
Lot 1-3	Osborn, Chester Arthur	1889	1890
Lot 24	Osborn, Clare Marshall	1874	1952
Lot 43-21	Osborn, Clayton Selden	1873	1911
Lot 1-1	Osborn, David Deforest	1853	1902
Lot 46-7	Osborn, Eunice	1846	1940
Lot 43	Osborn, Gladys	1896	1896
Lot 43-21	Osborn, John Eldin	1897	1962
Row 5-8	Osborn, John Ruple	1844	1856
Row 4-13	Osborn, Julia	1813	1833
Lot 46-7	Osborn, Lucy M.	1886	1955
Row 5-6	Osborn, Mary Elizabeth	1851	1922
Row 5-8	Osborn, Mary R.	1843	1844
Lot 24	Osborn, Mildred	1870	1952
Row 5-8	Osborn, Nancy	1813	1890
Row 5-6/7	Osborn, Nettie Pearl	1878	1882
Row 4-11	Osborn, Polly	1804	1870
Lot 46-7	Osborn, Reuben	1847	1919
Row 4-9	Osborn, Reuben	1778	1860
Row 5-6	Osborn, Samuel Foster	1842	1897
Row 4-10	Osborn, Sarah	1779	1858
Row 5-8	Osborn, Selden	1809	1867
Lot 48-10	Osborn, Sherman	1834	1886
Orig. Part	Peake, Horace Leroy	1897	1899
Orig Part	Peake, Robbie D.	1896	1899
Lot 34	Pellett, Elizabeth Ann	1854	1919
Lot 34-6	Pellett, John	1825	1902

Lot	*Name*	*Birth*	*Death*
Lot 34-6	Pellett, Maria A.	1825	1895
Lot 59-5	Peters, Annie M.	1865	1893
Unspec.	Peters, Cuvier	1883	1919
Lot 21	Pickering, George	1858	1914
Unspec.	Pickering, Martha Jane	c1859	1930
Row 6-3	Porter, Asahel	1782	1820
Row 6-3	Porter, Dennis	1814	1814
Row 6-3	Porter, Rebecca	1777	1814
Lot 9-17	Quell, Katherine Marie	1870	1904
Lot 1-2	Read, Mabel P. Meddick	1922	2016
Lot 1-1	Read, True Ellis	1919	2003
Lot 62-12	Rehling, Harry Ernest	1896	1989
Lot 62-11	Rehling, Lucille G.	1888	1957
Row 2-13	Rentschler, Regina	1806	1871
Lot 38-11	Rentschler, Regina K.	1834	1918
Lot 43-21	Repp, Bessie	1873	1897
Row 5-13	Rowell, Isaac	1774	1845
Row 5-12	Rowell, Jerusha	1781	1867
Lot 58-4	Rumbaugh, Sterling L.	1894	1918
Row 3-14	Sadler, Christopher	1756	1839
Row 3-12	Sadler, Elizabeth	1793	1872
Row 3-13	Sadler, Sophia	c1760	1851
Row 3-12	Sadler, William	1791	1875
Lot 22-8	Sarles, Elizabeth	1871	1932
Lot 22-8	Sarles, George F.	1867	1905
Lot 22-6	Sarles, Ray D.	1898	1908
Lot 29	Scheible, Elizabeth	1851	1929
	Scheible, Elizabeth	c1852	1929
Lot 29-1	Scheible, George	1855	1947
Lot 29-1	Scheible, Rosie	1862	1892
Lot 33	Schneeberger, Bertha C.	1873	1907
Lot 36-9	Scholl, Anna	1838	1904
Lot 31-3	Scholl, Emma	1859	1951
Lot 36-7	Scholl, Rudolph	1827	1904
Lot 36-8	Scholl, William	1865	1882
Lot 10-20	Schulz, Johannes F.	1819	1886
Lot 31-4	Scoll, Otto	1857	1902
Lot 9-18	Seitz, Eleanor Louise	1916	1992
Lot 9	Seitz, Erdine Elizabeth	1870	1950
Lot 9-19	Seitz, Jay Henry William	1885	1950
Lot 9-19	Seitz, Lillian Sophie	1890	1974
Orig. Part	Seitz, Wilbur Lawrence	1913	1915
Lot 24	Sleeper, Mildred	1870	1952
Unspec.	Smith, Rebecca	c1751	1811
Lot 29-1	Solomon, Rosie	1862	1892
Row 2-1	Stevens, Benjamin	1795	1871
Row 2-3	Stevens, Chauncey B.	1833	1913
Row 2-2	Stevens, Lovica	1796	1862
Lot 60-7	Sunk, Friedrieka	1833	1888
Lot 60-6	Sunk, Louis	1831	1904
Lot 10-21	Szabo, Elizabeth	1862	1908
Lot 30	Thorsen, Fannie J.	1868	1914
Lot 7	Tomanek, Antonia	1824	1911
Lot 7	Tomanek, John M.	1818	1887
Lot 12-23	Trestik, Anna	1863	1927
Lot 40	Tuttle, Dexter	1807	1879
Lot 49-12	undetermined, Louisa		
Row 6-6	Unknown Soldier		
Unspec.	Wagner, Jacob	c1861	1880
Lot 4-7	Ware, John	1826	1879
Lot 4-8	Ware, Lydia	1833	1882
Lot 10-21	Warga, Elizabeth	1862	1908
Lot 27	White, Susan	c1839	1919
Lot 19-2	Wilkshire, Walter	1871	1924
Lot 2-4	Williams, Barney	c1852	1895
Lot 2-5	Williams, Betsey	1839	1912
Row 1-3	Willis, Alfred H.	1846	1927
Row 1-4	Willis, Carl	1878	1878
Row 1-3	Willis, Fannie M.	1839	1908
Row 4-6	Winsor, Henry	1835	1855
Row 4-6	Winsor, Henry	1813	1896
Row 4-6	Winsor, Martha	1815	1882
Row 4-6/7	Winsor, Nancy Maria	1839	1849
Lot 40-16	Wischmeyer, Amelia L.	1878	1911
Row 1-5	Wischmeyer, Fredrick	1863	1864
Lot 39-13	Wischmeyer, Henry	1832	1901
Lot 51-16	Wischmeyer, Henry	1872	1959
Lot 40-15	Wischmeyer, Julius	1875	1909
Lot 11-22	Wischmeyer, K.	1826	1902
Lot 40-14	Wischmeyer, Louis A.	1865	1899
Lot 51-15	Wischmeyer, Olga W.	1869	1948
Lot 38-11	Wischmeyer, Regina K .	1834	1918
Lot 51-14	Wischmeyer, Matilda	1866	1922
Row 2-14	Wolf, Alfred Charles	1865	1867
Lot 49-11	Wolf, Alfred Marion	1828	1896
Row 1-13	Wolf, Anna	1808	1894
Lot 50-13	Wolf, Arthur H. J.	1874	1900
Lot 50-14	Wolf, Caroline	1846	1930
Row 1-16	Wolf, John	1790	1859
Row 1-12	Wolf, Michael	1829	1862
Row 1-14	Wolf, Philapena	1760	1851
Lot 66-14	Wuestenberg, Charles	1832	1891
Lot 66	Wuestenberg, Ida May	1866	1884
Lot 66	Wuestenberg, Melville	1881	1886
Lot 66-13	Wuestenberg, Rebecca	1836	1918
Potters F.	Yanko, Infant	1927	1927

Purchased Cemetery Lots

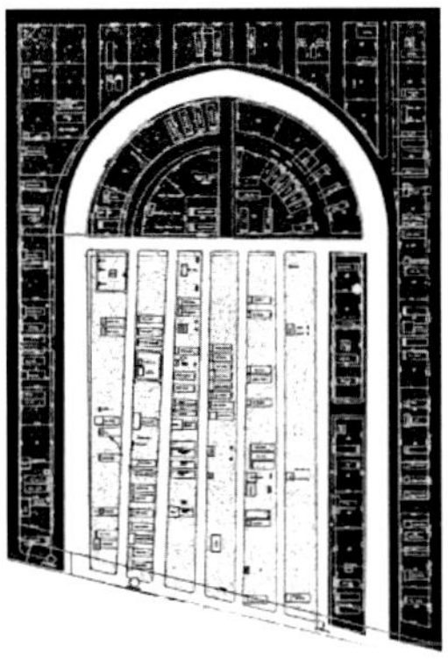

Purchased lots darkened.

"A chip from the old block," -
Children of the Dover pioneers.
The second growth like the parent stock,
May they prove straight in the grain
And free to branch.

Toast by A.P. Johnson
Cahoon Sixty-third Anniversary Celebration of the Settlement of Dover, August 28th, 1873.

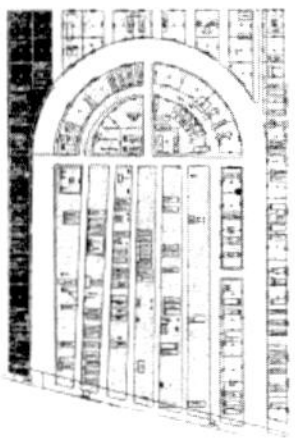

Sold lots begin with Lot 1 at Lake Road at the southern end and proceed toward Lake Erie on the western side of the cemetery.

Lot 1 *Owner: D. D. Osborn of Dover purchased March 1877 for $4.24* SL **See Addendum for current burials.*

Lot 1-1 David Deforest Osborn

FATHER

DAVID DEFOREST OSBORN
BORN FEB 21, 1853
DIED FEB 8, 1902
THE ANGEL OF THE LORD ENCAMPETH
ROUND ABOUT THEM THAT FEAR HIM
AND DELIVERETH THEM

David was the youngest son of Selden Osborn and Nancy Ruple (Row 5:7) and husband of Rose Mitchell.

The State of Ohio, Cuyahoga County, ss. I Certify that on the 15th day of January 1879 ***Mr. David D. OSBORN*** and ***Rose MITCHELL*** were legally joined in marriage. H.M. Walker Marriage Record, Cuyahoga County, OH, vol. 22, p. 143.

OSBORN, David, 27, farmer; ***Rose,*** 21, wife; ***Julia***, 4/12 yrs. *(4 months old)*, b. Jan, daughter; ***Nancy***, 65, mother; *WOERHMANN, Frederick*, 16, Servant, Laborer. 1880 FC OH CYDO, p. 99, lines 5-9, house no. 311.

OSBORN, David. Owned land; Acres: Improved - Tilled, including fallow and grass: 41, Permanent meadow: 3, Unimproved - Woodland: 12. Farm Values: Land and buildings - $5,000, Machinery - $175, Live Stock - $250, Cost of building and repairing in 1879 - $75. Labor: Paid for wages in 1879 - $125, weeks hired labor in 1879 - 28. Estimated value of all farm production: $500. Grass lands: acreage: 3 mown, 20 not mown, 4 tons hay. 2 horses, 3 milch cows, 1 other, 3 calves dropped, 3 cattle sold living. 300 pounds of butter made on the farm. Sheep: on hand June 1, 1880 - 25, 18 lambs dropped, 1 purchased, 18 sold living, 18 fleeces, weight - 94 lbs. 11 swine. 35 barnyard poultry on farm. Eggs produced in 1879: 200 dozen. Indian corn: 7 acres, 400 bushels; oats: 6 acres, 120 bushels; wheat: 4 acres, 100 bushels; potatoes: 1 acre, 65 bushels. Orchards - apple: 2 acres, 100 bearing trees, 100 bushels. Total value of orchard products: $50. Vineyards: 1 acre. Amount of wood cut: 25 cords. Value of forest products - $550. "Schedule 2. Production of Agriculture in Dover Township, Cuyahoga County, OH," enumerated June, 1880, p. 33.

OSBORN, David D., 47, b. Feb 1853, b. Ohio, fr. b. Mass, mo. b. Ohio, farmer, married 21 yrs.; ***Rose G.***, wife, 40, b. Aug 1859, b. England, parents b. England, 5 children born, 4 living; ***Julia E.***, dau., 20, b. Jan 1880, student; ***Effie R.***, dau., 16, b. Aug 1883, student; ***Leslie D.***, son, 14, b. May 1886, at school; ***Mabel I.***, dau., 9, b. May 1891; all children born in Ohio. 1900 FC OH CYDO, p. 21B, lines 69-75.

The children of ***Selden OSBORN*** *(Row5:8)* were given parcels of land. They raised berries, fruit and many grapes. In a small way raised oats, corn and wheat, only to supply their needs. Life was hard, requiring many extra hours in summer to prepare the fruit for the market, which was sold for the most part in the stalls on Broadway in Cleveland. The person selling the fruit must rise at one A.M. and drive some fourteen miles to market as it was in full swing at five in the morning. Then too, he must get the pickers and take them back as far as Rocky River during the time when the harvest was at its best. Prices received did not bring much profit.

I recall many happy memories, as I think back over the years. Father gave us all the pleasures and conveniences, all the strength that his means could give. He bought us an organ, although he could not sing a note or carry a tune, but he loved music. We had a gas well, which I greatly appreciated for it saved me the hated chore of washing lamp chimneys and filling the lamps. He later built a water tank and put water in the house. We children were justly proud of the "Surrey with the Fringe on Top." We thought it gave us a certain prestige noted by the young fry of the Dover Congregational Church.

Going to church in summer was a delight with the horse and surrey, but winter made up for it. As there were no paved roads and only dirt and mud, it often took one hour to reach it, when the mud was deep and the horses could only walk. In the severest weather, there was a problem of keeping warm. We would heat bricks and with straw on the floor of the spring wagon and with the help of Buffalo robes, we managed to keep fairly warm. After we reached the church we put the bricks on the long stove to be heated for the return journey. Julia Osborn Scott *(daughter of David)*, "Osborn Family History," p. 7.

David OSBORN, 49; res. Bay Village; interred Feb 10, 1902; Lot 1. "List of Interments," Lakeside Cemetery, Bay Village, OH.

The personal estate of ***David Deforest OSBORN*** lists the following upon his death: Two Horses ($37.50 ea.), Three Cows ($33 1/3 ea.), One Buggy ($40), One Buggy ($25), 15 Bush Rye ($7.50), 1 Lot of Hay and Straw ($10), 1 Set of Double Harness ($15), 1 Single Harness ($2), 1 Market Wagon ($5), 1 Market Wagon ($60), 1 Light Double Wagon ($10), 2 Plows ($10), 1 Lot of Corn ($5). 1 Harrow ($8), 60 Chickens .30 cents ($18). 1 Lot of Farm Tools ($20); $125 in the bank and 36 acres of farm land in Dover. Estate of David D. Osborn, Probate Court, Cuyahoga County, OH, #27739, Book 26, p. 310.

The Osborn family decided to have ***David OSBORN'S*** body moved to Evergreen Cemetery because the possibility of widening Lake Road was being discussed. David's place of burial was the first plot to the north of Lake Road and would have had to be moved. A family plot was purchased in Evergreen Cemetery so that this would not be a problem in the future. Jeanne Osborn Sanford

Request made on Dec 5, 1944, by ***David L. OSBORN***, ***Mabel O. MEDDICK*** *and* ***Julia O. SCOTT***, three of his five children, to remove the remains of ***David Deforest OSBORN*** to Evergreen Cemetery, Westlake, OH. Letter in city cemetery file, Bay Village City Hall, Bay Village, OH.

David D. OSBORN was interred at Evergreen Cemetery on Nov 20, 1945, in a wood box. He is in lot 135, grave 4, section E-2. Others in plot: ***Rose OSBORN***, bur. 1/25/1943; ***David Leslie OSBORN***, 81, d. 5/12/1968, Avon, OH, Congestive Heart Failure, res. 29127 Lake Road, Bay Village; ***Katherine C. OSBORN***, 87, d. 6/2/1976, Ashland, OH, res. 485 North Columbia, Columbus, OH, Medullary Failure, undertaker: Jenkins. Evergreen Cemetery, Westlake, OH.

Wife of David Deforest Osborn, Rose Mitchell:

Parents of Rose Mitchell: ***Tho. MITCHALL***, 40, farmer, value of real estate $1200, personal property $200; ***Eliza***, 40; ***Thomas***, 11; ***Mark***, 9; ***Mathew***, 8; ***Michael***, 5; ***John***, 3; ***Rose***, 2; all born in England; ***Willie***, 4 months old., b. Ohio. 1860 FC OH CYDO, p. 56, lines 24-32, house no. 428.

MITCHEL, Thomas, 45, farmer, value of real estate $3500, personal estate $445; ***Eliza***, 48, keeping house; ***Thomas***, 21, Laborer; ***Michael***, 15; ***John***, 13; ***Rose***, 11; all b. England; ***Yankey***, 10, b. Ohio; ***Warreen***, 7, b. Ohio. 1870 FC OH CYDO, p. 26, lines 7-14, house no. 218.

Rose's older brother, Thomas MITCHELL (1849-1927), married David's older sister, Julia OSBORN (1849-1912), see (OP 5: 7).

The following reminiscence was part of a paper shared with the Bay Village Reading Club by Mrs. Rose Osborn:

The Nickel Plate railroad was built 45 years ago and the Lake Shore Electric 31 years ago. Cleveland seemed far away before these roads were opened. When I first came to what is now Bay Village in 1879, a bride of 20 years, there were only 11 houses between Wischmeyers and Bradley road. Now, on land that originally belonged to the Osborns, there are 19 houses facing Lake road. We used kerosene lamps and made tallow candles. We made soft soap, saving all the grease and mixing it with lye from wood ashes. We cooked the soap outdoors in big iron kettles and it took all day.

On grapes after paying for baskets and shipping we made four or five cents on a 9-pound basket. We used to get 15 cents a pound for butter, and 8 to 10 cents for a dozen eggs. Three and four pound chickens sold for 35 cents apiece. Our taxes were around $30 a year while now the same land is paying $3,345.

We had little time for visiting in the summer but we made up for it in the winter - those wonderful sleigh rides. It seems as if we had sleighing all winter. How many remember the dry summer weather when dust was six inches deep and we couldn't leave our doors or windows open? Those were the good old days - but I don't think I care to go back to pioneering. Suburban News and Herald, undetermined date, p. 8, col. 1.

OSBORN, Rose, head, 51, widow, 5 children born, 4 living, b. England, parents b. England, year of immigration 1860, Manager, General Farm, owns farm; ***Leslie***, son, 23, b. Ohio, fr. b. Ohio, trade: laborer working on own farm; ***Mabel I.***, dau., 18, b. Ohio, profession none; ***SCOTT, Julia E.***, dau., 30, married 5 yrs., 1 child born and living, ***SCOTT, David O.***, grandson, 4, b. Ohio. 1910 FC OH CYDO, p. 3A, lines 10-15, house no. 54. *Rose was living in* *the Selden Osborn house, across and just west of the cemetery.*

I am happy to pay tribute to the memory of a dear, departed friend, ***Mrs. Rose OSBORN***, a Christian pioneer mother.

One might think that the countless home tasks with few conveniences, which we now accept as necessary aides, was sufficient in attending to her home and family. She was excellent in that capacity; but always civic-minded, she served many years on the School Board on the little Red School House on Lake Road -- now so much missed as it was a landmark along with the Osborn's fine homesteads on Lake Road.

As I recall her, (coming as I did a bride 39 years in August) worshipping at the Congregational Dover (now Westlake) Church with my husband's parents, I noticed her across the aisle on the very first Sunday as an attractive widow, wearing the long, black veil customary then and sitting with a seat full of her children.

Her husband passed on a few months before I came to Bay. With few conveniences or modern equipment then, she managed the farm, her son being too young for full responsibility. With her family and a 14 room house you'd say "a full job." It was at that time that some city friends urged her for summer board. She enlarged the dining room to accommodate them. It was nothing for her in those days to say (when we talked on the church steps), "I must hurry home, we have 20 or 25 boarders to get dinner for." Most of the preparation she had done before church. The baking was accomplished mainly with her own capable hands. Her children were able assistants and she was helped by a maid - no, a hired girl, some of the time.

Crops also had to be marketed, and her son accomplished this long journey to the city with a team of horses, making frequent stops on the poor road to rest the horses enroute. It was a big role the pioneer mother played. She exemplified the type of Christian Hospitality that endeared her to her friends and guests alike. I can vouch for it, for I was privileged to enjoy it on many occasions. She stood for the best in life.

The Old Pioneer would fight if necessary for his or her creed, whatever the kind, be it Hard Shelled Baptist or Loud Amen Methodist or may be the Holy Roller type. The years have softened and moderated denominations until we have blended, and today we hear little concerning creed, but instead all Christians of different kinds - as this Methodist Church - working for the same end, salvation for all. Some of the Osborns united with this church, as it began to seem unnecessary to go out of Bay to church. We knew how eager and active and faithful Rose was in this church for many years until her strength failed. Her chief source of discontent in later years was that she was unable to do for the church or to attend services as she had always loved to. However, she kept her interest and longed for the uplifting things pertaining to the Kingdom.

She will be happy to join her friends and loved ones in heavenly pursuits. We loved her, who knew her, but age made it easy to let her slip away a while to rest. From the family files of Sally O'Connor.

OSBORN: Rose (nee ***MITCHELL***), wife of the late ***David***, mother of ***Mrs. Julia SCOTT, Mrs. Effie MORGAN*** (deceased), ***David Leslie OSBORN*** and ***Mrs. Mabel MEDDICK***, grandmother and great-grandmother. Friends may call at the Clifford Pease Funeral Home, 2914 Dover Center rd., Westlake, O., where services will be held Monday, Jan 25, at 2:30 p.m. Undetermined newspaper article, Osborn File, Rose Hill Museum, Bay Village, OH.

Rose MITCHELL OSBORN, d. Jan 22, 1943, 10:45 p.m. at 29059 West Lake Rd., Bay, Cuyahoga Co., Ohio, of myocarditis; widow of ***David***; b. Aug 25, 1858, Surrey Co., England; fr. ***Thomas MITCHELL***, b. Surrey Co., mo. ***Eliza LETTS***, b. Surrey Co.; 84 yrs. 4 mos. 27 days; Informant *Julia O. SCOTT*, 27715 Lake Road, Bay Village; bur. Evergreen, Westlake, undertaker Clifford Pease Fun. Home. Ohio Certificate of Death, Division of Vital Statistics, 1943, certif. 876.

Children of David Deforest Osborn and Rose Mitchell:

Julia Elizabeth OSBORN, b. 31 Jan 1880, Dover, Cuyahoga Co., Ohio; d. 26 July1962, Amherst, Lorain Co., Ohio; m. 20 Dec 1904 *to Louis Stewart SCOTT* (b. 17 Aug 1882, d. 1 Oct 1950). ***Rose Effie OSBORN***, b. 22 Aug 1882, Dover; d. 4 June 1941, Bay Village, OH; m. *George Edward MORGAN*, 28 Oct 1903. ***David Leslie OSBORN***, b. 25 May 1887, Dover; d. May 1968; m. 20 Mar 1914 to *Katharine CLEMENTS* (b. 20 May 1889; d. 2 June 1976). ***Chester Arthur OSBORN***, b. 6 May 1889, Dover; d. 1 July1890, Dover. ***Mabel Irene OSBORN***, b. 11 May 1891, Dover; d. 11 Mar 1969, Bay Village; m. 15 Apr 1914 to *Warren Andrew MEDDICK* (d. Dec 1968). "Osborn Family History" by Julia E. Osborn, original documents, cemetery inscriptions and Susy O'Connor Thielen.

Julia O. SCOTT was the chairman of the Early Settlers Committee which sponsored the One Hundred and Twenty-Fifth Anniversary of the founding of Dover Township, October 11-12th, 1935. The headquarters was the library of Dover-by-the-Lake (formerly the Cahoon homestead), Lake Road, Bay Village. *Dr. Jesse L. SADDLER* was the General Chairman, *Harry E. GLASSER*, Secretary and *William M. SUTCLIFFE*, Treasurer. Activities included dedication of the football field, Cahoon Memorial Service at Lakeside Cemetery by the Com. Perry Chapter-Daughters of 1812, Covered Wagon Parade - Library Grounds, Spinning Demonstration by *Mrs. Eunice OSBORN*, Square Dance - High School Students, Clog Dance - *Mr. Hugh LARSON* with *Mr. Yank Mitchell*, Fiddler, Old Fashioned Turkey Shoot at Dover-Bay Gun Club, Fire Drill - Village of Bay Volunteer Fire Dept. Pageant with the Old Time Quartet, Reading by *Myra OSBORN*, Mayor listed as Dr. Jessee L. Saddler. Program of the "125th Anniversary Settlement of Bay Village," Cahoon Collection, Rose Hill Museum, Bay Village, OH.

Julia OSBORN SCOTT was a librarian and would often show us around the library, now Rose Hill, showing us books that she thought we might enjoy. Probably because of her extensive reading in a variety of subjects, she could hold our attention with a large repertoire of stories. Julia had one son, ***David Osborn SCOTT*** (b. 20 Feb 1906, m. *Phyllis McLAUGHLIN*). Sally O'Connor, Kathy O'Connor Johnson and Susy O'Connor Thielen.

Librarian of Bay Village Remembers Early Days

When ***Mrs. Julia OSBORN SCOTT*** goes to New Mexico next week, Bay Village will lose not only its favorite librarian but one of the community's oldest residents...

Looking out of the window at the home where she was born, 20959 Lake Rd., she recalled today the days when that highway was a narrow lane where horse-drawn carriages raised "too much dust."

Just across the street is her grandfather's home, built in 1813, the oldest house between Cleveland and Lorain. In the nearby cemetery are the graves of settlers her mother used to tell her about, including a family drowned fording Rocky River.

After attending Oberlin Academy, Mrs. Scott studied library work at Baldwin University in Berea, which later merged with Wallace College. In those days she knew everyone in Westlake, Olmsted Falls, Berea and Rocky River.

She left teaching for marriage in 1904, when she was 24. But in 1922 she returned to community life as librarian in a library of 800 volumes. In 24 years she had done all the work there except the cataloguing and now there are 12,000 books.

She knows who has read each book, and can tell just by talking with a new resident which he will want. Sometimes children come in and ask for books for their parents, and Mrs. Scott always knows what to send home.

Mrs. Scott retired September 1 and will leave for New Mexico next week to live with her son. All the reading she is doing now is southwestern history, but the country will not be new to her. She has been west nine times, and has hiked the hills and fished the streams there.

Still busy at 66, she doesn't think she'll go into library work there although she has talked about it. If she does anything it may be to write a fourth grade reader about her childhood experiences.

A reception will be given in her honor Sunday afternoon from 4 to 6 at the Community House. The public is invited to the program which was arranged by a committee of representatives of all the adult and young people's groups in the city. She expects it will "just be the neighbors," but there are few of the 5,000 residents she doesn't know as well as she did the 1,800 who lived there in 1900. Undetermined source, newspaper article provided by David O. Scott, Jr.

Mrs. Julia OSBORN SCOTT, teacher and librarian for the Bay Village Public Library the last 24 years, died yesterday in Amherst, O., at the age of 81.

Mrs. Scott's residence was at 29059 Lake Road, Bay Village, where she was born and spent nearly all her life.

She attended Oberlin and Baldwin-Wallace Colleges.

She was a charter member of the Bay Village Women's Club, the Bay Village Reading Club, the Bay Village Golden Agers, and the Bay Village Historical Society, and was a member of Lincoln Chapter of the Order of the Eastern Star.

She is survived by a son, ***David O.*** of Missoula, Mont.; a brother, ***David L.***, and a sister, ***Mrs. Mabel O. MEDDICK***, both of Bay Village.

Services will be at 1:30 p.m. Monday in the Jenkins funeral home, 2914 Dover Center Road, Westlake. Undetermined source, newspaper article provided by Sally O'Connor. *Roseffie Morgan, sister, was deceased at this time.*

Julia SCOTT was the Bay Village librarian at Rose Hill for 24 years from 1922 until 1946. Osborn Family File, Rose Hill Museum, Bay Village, OH.

Julia O. SCOTT, d. 14 Sept 1962 of Arterio sclerosis generalized at Amherst Nursing Manor for 7 weeks, Amherst, Lorain Co., Ohio; b. 1/31/1881, Bay Village; Librarian, City of Bay Village; usual residence 29059 Lake Rd; Divorced; Informant *Mabel MEDDICK*, Bay Village; Jenkins Funeral Chapel, bur. Evergreen Cemetery. Ohio Certificate of Death, Division of Vital Statistics, 1962, certif. 67549.

SCOTT. ***Julia O. SCOTT*** (nee *OSBORN*), late residence, 29059 Lake Rd., Bay Village, mother of ***David O.*** of Missoula, Mont., grandmother of three, great-grandmother of two, sister of ***David L. OSBORN, Mrs. Mabel O. MEDDICK*** and the late ***Rose Effie MORGAN***. The family will receive friends From 2-4 And 7-9 P. M., Sunday at the Jenkins Funeral Chapel, 2914 Dover Center Rd., Westlake, where services will be held Monday, Sept 17, at 1:30 p. m. Sept 16 1962. The Plain Dealer.

Husband of Julia Osborn Scott, Louis S. Scott:

Louis S. SCOTT, d. 2 Oct 1950, Rickly Memorial, Springfield Twp., Clark Co., OH, length of stay 7 mo., 14 days, usual residence Ohio Masonic Home, Springfield, 70 yrs. 1 mo. 15 ds.; b. 12 Aug 1880, Pittsburgh, son of *Holland SCOTT* and *Delia DENNIS*; Hotel Clerk; Divorced; bur. Ohio Masonic Home Cem., Springfield, OH. Ohio Certificate of Death, Division of Vital Statistics, 1950, certif. 59654.

Son of Julia Elizabeth Osborn and Louis Scott:

David O. SCOTT, was born February 20, 1906 at home in Bay Village. He went to high school in Rocky River and was an all-star center. His major in Forestry at the University of Michigan led him into a 33 year career with the U.S. Forest Service in the New Mexico and Arizona areas. He retired as a forest entomologist in Missoula, Montana.

He married ***Phyllis McLAUGHLIN*** in Silver City, New Mexico on October 28, 1933. Phyllis passed away in 1964. The Scott's had three children: ***David Osborn SCOTT, Jr.***, b. 3 Oct 1934; ***Julia Ann SCOTT McVAY***, b. 15 Oct 1938 and ***Phyllis Jean SCOTT ANDERSON***, b. 24 Sept 1948.

In 1969 he married ***Maurine THOMSON***, they resided in Ephraim, Utah. He enjoyed a twenty years affiliation with the Lions Club, had a great sense of humor and liked everyone. He loved the outdoors - animals, plants, bugs and birds. David passed away

January 28, 1998 in Orem, Utah, a month from his 92nd birthday. David O. Scott, Jr. and undetermined newspaper article.

Roseffie OSBORN MORGAN*, see burial of her daughter, Mary Ann (Lot 1:2), below.*

David Leslie OSBORN always had an extensive, well maintained garden full of vegetables in addition to apple trees. He frequently admonished- "Never buy a pig in a poke." Uncle Les's house was built from lumber from an old ship. David and Catherine had two daughters, Nancy and Jean. Sally O'Connor, Susy O'Connor Thielen and Kathy O'Connor Johnson.

David L. OSBORN, 27; res. N. Dover, O.; b. do. *(same)*; occup. Farmer; fr. *David,* mo. *Rose MITCHELL.* Married ***Katherine CLEMENTS***, 24; res. East Cleve'd, O; b. Cleveland, O.; occup. none; fr. *Robert J.*, mo. *Katie C. MCGREW*; neither previously married. State of Ohio, Cuyahoga County, ss. I Certify That on the 26th day of March 1914 Mr. David L. Osborn and Miss Katherine Clements were by me legally joined in marriage. Rev. Edward E. Leeper, Lakewood O. Marriage Record, Cuyahoga County, OH, vol. 88, p. 411.

OSBORN, Leslie D., 42, owns home and radio, value of home $15,000, married, age at marriage 26, b. Ohio, fr. b. Ohio, mo. b. England, occup. agent for Oil Co.; ***Katharine,*** wife, 40, age at marriage 24, b. Ohio, parents b. Ohio; ***Jean K.***, dau. 12, b. Ohio; ***Nancy***, dau. 13, b. Ohio. 1930 FC OH CYBV, ED 18-534, 29127 Lake Road, p. 16A, lines 28-31.

David Leslie OSBORN, beloved husband of ***Katharine*** *(nee* ***CLEMENT****),* father of ***Mrs. Nancy O. SEBASTIAN*** of Columbus and ***Mrs. Jean O. SANFORD*** of Ashland, O. grandfather, and brother of ***Mrs. Warren MEDICK*** *(sp.)* and the late ***Julia SCOTT*** and ***Rose Effie MORGAN***. Funeral services Tuesday, May 14 at 1:00 p.m. at the Jenkins Funeral Chapel, Dover Center, Westlake, O. May 14, 1968. The Plain Dealer.

Chester Arthur OSBORN *is buried in Lot 1:3.*

Mabel OSBORN MEDDICK was an extremely fine hostess, which was important as her husband, *Warren MEDDICK*, was named President and then Chairman of the Board of Elwell-Parker Electric Co. in Cleveland after he had been with the company 22 years. He had previously held the position of vice president and sales manager since 1939. He always drove Chryslers and ordered the newest innovation of the time. Always very professional, always the businessman. They had two children, ***Jack MEDDICK*** (d. 2002) and ***Pat MEDDICK READ***.

Every year the whole family would come together for a huge family picnic in Meddick's back yard after the Memorial Day services. We could all park there, join the parade and walk back. Extended family was always welcome. She baked great cookies. We were allowed to go down to the beach if we checked in first with "Aunt Mabel" and then had to check in when we finished swimming. This was the best part as there was usually a good conversation and cookies were offered. Sally O'Connor, Kathy O'Connor Johnson and Susy O'Connor Thielen.

Mabel OSBORN started the Reading Club in Bay Village which was comprised of about twelve couples, including singles and widows. The group met in peoples' livingrooms over a period of seventy-five years, finally disbanding in the 1980's. Mabel was known to keep a diary and lived in the Selden Osborn house at 29059 Lake Road, almost directly across the street from the cemetery, near the road. Billie Jo Schwartz

Mabel I. OSBORN, 22; res. Bay, O.; b. N. Dover, O.; occup. none; fr. *David,* mo. *Rose MITCHELL.* Married ***Warren A. MEDDICK***, 25; res. 7500 Rutledge Ave.; b. La Mar, Mo., occup. Salesman; fr. *Chas. V.*, mo. *Cora KNIGHT;* neither previously married. Marriage to be solemnized by Rev. E. A. Leper, Lakewood, O. The State of Ohio, Cuyahoga County, ss. I Certify That on the 15th day of April 1914 Mr. Warren A. Meddick and Miss Mabel I. Osborn were by me legally joined in marriage. Rev. John R. Stalker. Marriage Record, Cuyahoga County, OH, vol. 88, p. 482.

MEDDICK, Warren A., 40, value of real estate $10,000, owned a radio, age when married 23, b. Missouri, parents b. Michigan, Sales Manager, Manuf. Road Equip.; ***Mabel I.***, wife, 38, age at marriage 22, b. Ohio, fr. b. Ohio, mo. b. England; ***Jack W.***, son, 13, b. Ohio; ***Mabel P.***, dau., 7, b. Ohio; ***OSBORN, Rose***, mother-in-law, 71, widow, b. England, parents b. England, immigrated 1859, Naturalized citizen. 1930 FC OH CYBV, ED 18-534, 29059 Lake Road, p. 16A, lines 48-50 and p. 16B, lines 1-2.

MEDDICK. ***Mabel MEDDICK*** (nee ***OSBORN***), beloved wife of the late ***Warren A.***, dear mother of *John W. (Jack)* and *Mrs. Patricia READ*, grandmother of six, sister of the late ***Julia SCOTT, Rose Effie MORGAN***, and ***David Leslie OSBORN***. Funeral services Thursday, Mar 13, at 1:30 P. M. at Jenkins Funeral Chapel, 2914 Dover Center Rd., Westlake, where friends may call 2-4, 7-9 P. M. Wednesday. Cleveland Necrology File, Cleveland Press, Mar 12 1969.

Husband of Mabel Osborn Meddick, Warren A. Meddick:

MEDDICK. ***Warren A. MEDDICK***, beloved husband of ***Mabel*** (nee *OSBORN*), father of ***John W. (Jack)*** and ***Mrs. Patricia READ***, grandfather of six. Funeral services Monday, Dec 16 at 1:30 p.m. at The Jenkins Funeral Chapel, 2914 Dover Center Rd., Westlake, where friends may call From 2-4 And 7-9 P.M. Sunday. The family suggests contributions may be made to the Shrine Crippled Children's Hospital. Dec 15 1968. The Plain Dealer.

Lot 1-2 Osborn Monument

OSBORN

Lot 1-3 **Mary Ann Morgan** no marker

David DeForest OSBORN and ***Rose MITCHELL'S*** daughter ***Rose Effie***, born in 1882, married ***George Edward MORGAN*** and lived at 29039 Lake Road directly across from the cemetery. Mr. Morgan served as mayor of Bay Village in 1922, serving from Jan 1-Dec 31. Bay Village Historical Society, Bay Village: A Way of Life, pp. 17, 127.

The Morgan's daughter, Mary Ann, is buried in this plot. She originally was buried next to her grandfather, although his body was moved in 1945 to Evergreen Cemetery in Westlake.

Mary Ann MORGAN; res. Bay Village; interred Aug 9th, 1918; Lot 1. "List of Interments," Lakeside Cemetery, Bay Village, OH

Mary Ann MORGAN, Bay, Cuyahoga Co.; d. Aug 8, 1918, 1:30 a.m., Hydrocephalis-5 mos. 21ds., Contributory: Spina bifida (sacral); b. Feb 19, Bay Village, fr. ***George MORGAN***, b. Elyria, O., mo. ***Effie OSBORN***, b. Bay Village; 5 mos. 20 ds. old; informant Mrs. Geo. Morgan, Bay Village; bur. Bay Village, Aug 9, 1918, undertaker C. Pease, Dover Center, O. Ohio Certificate of Death, Division of Vital Statistics, 1918, certif. 46808.

Parents of Mary Ann Morgan:

George E. MORGAN, 27; res. Chicago, Ills.; b. Elyria, O.; occup. Erecting Engineer; fr. *Geo. E. MORGAN*, mo. *Sarah E. CLARK.* Married ***Rose E. OSBORN***, 21; res. Bay Vill., O.; b. same; occup. none; fr. *D. D. OSBORN*, mo. *Rose MITCHELL*, neither previously married. Marriage to be solemnized by Rev. Leper, N. Dover, O. The State of Ohio, Cuyahoga County, ss. I Certify that on the 28th day of Oct 1903 Mr. George E. Morgan and Miss Rose E. Osborn were by me legally joined in marriage. Rev. Edward A. Leper. Marriage Record, Cuyahoga County, OH, vol. 58, p. 30.

MORGAN, Geo. E., 43, b. Ohio, fr. b. Ohio, mo. b. Ohio; ***Rose Effie***, wife, 37; ***Helen***, b. 15? *Difficult to read, taped over;* ***Serra***, 13; ***Ruth***, 5. 1920 FC OH CYBV, pp. 1B-2A.

MORGAN, George E., 53, owns home, no radio, value $35,000, 27 at time of marriage, b. Ohio, fr. b. Ohio, mo. b. New York, occup. Com'l traveler, industry Boilers and Radiators, veteran Sp.; ***Rose Effie***, wife, 47, age at marriage 21, b. Ohio, fr. b. Ohio, mo. b. England; ***Sarah L.***, dau. 23, b. Illinois, Librarian, Public Library; ***Ruth E.***, dau., 15, b. Ohio; ***George E.***, son, 13, b. Ohio. 1930 FC OH CYBV, ED 18-534, 29039 Lake Road, p. 16A, lines 23-27.

The first 4th of July celebration in Bay Village took place at the Morgan House, 29039 Lake Road, directly across from Lakeside Cemetery while George was mayor. The Salvation Army played and a light platform was set up on the roof so they could play at night. There were also fireworks shot off.

An awful accident happened that night in front of the cemetery. The bloody victims were hauled into the house, getting blood over everything.

George worked for Standard Plumbing. He was a self-made engineer, having studied on his own. He put the entire hot water heating system in the house on Lake Road.

During the depression, he worked for the WPA in the winter in Cleveland.

He had an office in Cleveland at 18th & Euclid Avenue above the old Vernor's Ginger Ale Building. Our mother ***(Ruth O'CONNOR)*** and friends, used to stop by after shopping and they'd go downstairs for a gingerale with cream - delicious!

He loved to go down to the beach during storms to watch the storms come in much to our grandmother's chagrin.

He was a veteran of the Spanish American War. George was a mechanical engineer at NACA, now NASA, when he died. Sally O'Connor, Kathy O'Connor Johnson and Susy O'Connor Thielen.

George E. Morgan, Ex-Mayor of Bay Village, is Dead at 72

George E. MORGAN, former mayor and councilman of Bay Village, died yesterday in his home, 594 Fordham Parkway, Bay Village, at the age of 72.

Mr. Morgan was mayor of Bay in 1922 and 1923. Also, for three terms in the 1920's, he was a member of the Village Council.

For many years Mr. Morgan was a sales engineer specializing in heating, ventilating and air-conditioning equipment. Since 1944 he has been connected with the National Advisory Committee on Aeronautics here.

The ex-mayor was a veteran of the Spanish-American War and was commander of Lakewood Camp, United Spanish War Veterans for 1946-7. He was one of the founders of the Men's Community Club of Bay Village and a member of Dover Masonic Lodge.

Surviving him is a son, ***George E., jr.***; three daughters, ***Miss Sarah, Mrs. Helen INGLIS*** of Piqua, O., and ***Mrs. Ruth O'CONNOR*** of Bay Village, and seven grandchildren.

Lakewood Camp, United Spanish War Veterans, will hold memorial services at 8 tonight in the Daniel's funeral home, 15800 Detroit Avenue, Lakewood. At 1:30 p.m. tomorrow Dover Lodge will conduct Masonic services in the funeral home. Burial will be in Lake View Cemetery. Dec 21, 1948, p. 17, cols. 1-3. The Plain Dealer.

George Edward MORGAN, d. 20 Dec 1948 at 594 Fordham Parkway, Bay Village, Ohio (res.); cause Coronary Thrombosis; lived in community 30 yrs., veteran of the Spanish War; divorced, occup. Mechanical Engineer, business NACA; wife ***Roseffie MORGAN;*** age 72, b. May 14th, 1876, Elyria, Ohio, fr. ***George E. MORGAN***, mo. --; Informant *George E. MORGAN, Jr.,* 1257 Virginia Ave., Lakewood; bur. Lakeview Cemetery *(Cleveland)*; Wm. Daniel, Funeral Director, 15800 Detroit Ave. Ohio Certificate of Death, Division of Vital Statistics, 1940, certif. 74398.

This was a favorite story we always told at family gatherings about ***Roseffie OSBORN MORGAN***, as we found it so funny.

Trying to avoid a salesman at the front door, Roseffie crawled through the house on her hands and knees to the kitchen where she could go about her business, as she started to stand up, there he was at the back door looking in at her.

She took in boarders for a while to help support her family. Sally O'Connor, Kathy O'Connor Johnson and Susy O'Connor Thielen.

Recipes of Roseffie Morgan:

Hermits.

(Mrs. G. E. Morgan)

One-half cup sugar, one cup lard and butter creamed, two eggs. Add to this one-half cup raisins, one-half cup currants, one-half cup sour milk, four cups sifted flour, cinnamon and nutmeg, one teaspoon soda.

The Village Cook Book, p. 35. (c1911-1915).

CHICKEN LOAF

1 chicken	1/3 c. cold water
2 T. gran. gelatine	seasoning

Boil the chicken in sufficient water to cover, when meat is ready to fall from the bone, cool. Strain the liquor and continue to cook until it is reduced to 3 cups.

Remove all skin and bones and lay the light and dark meat alternately in a mold. Season the liquor, add the gelatine which has been soaked 1/2 hr. in the cold water. When thoroughly dissolved pour the liquor over the meat and set away to harden.

Mrs. Geo. E. Morgan
The Dover Cook Book, p. 7.

Mrs. Rose E. MORGAN Services for Mrs. Rose Effie Morgan, 58, a member of a pioneer Bay Village family, will be tomorrow at 2 p.m. at the Clifford Pease funeral home, 2914 Dover Center Road, Westlake. Mrs. Morgan died yesterday at her home 242 Bradley road, Bay Village.

Osborn Road in the village is named after Mrs. Morgan's great-grandfather, ***Reuben OSBORN***, who settled there in 1811. She was a charter member of the Bay Village Reading Club and active in village affairs.

Surviving Mrs. Morgan are her mother, ***Mrs. Rose OSBORN***; three daughters, ***Mrs. Helen INGLIS, Mrs. Ruth O'CONNOR*** and ***Miss Sarah MORGAN***; a son ***George***; two sisters, ***Mrs. Julia SCOTT*** and ***Mrs. Warren MEDDICK***, and a brother ***D. Leslie OSBORN***. June 5, 1941, p. 21, col. 4. The Plain Dealer.

Roseffie MORGAN, d. June 4, 1941, 12:30 p.m. at 242 Bradley Rd., Bay Village, Cuyahoga Co., Ohio of acute lymphatic leukemia and anemia about 4 mos.; divorced from ***George***; housewife; 58 yrs. 9 mos. 12 ds.; b. Aug 22, 1882, Bay Village to ***David Deforest OSBORN***, b. Bay Village and ***Rose MITCHELL***, b. England; informant *George E. MORGAN,* 242 Bradley Rd.; Clifford Pease Funeral Home, Westlake; burial Evergreen Cemetery, Westlake. Ohio Certificate of Death, Division of Vital Statistics, 1941, certif. 35050.

Siblings of Mary Ann Morgan:

Helen Elizabeth MORGAN, b. 11 Aug 1904; d. 12 Jan 1990; m. 12 Sep 1928, Bay Methodist Church, Bay Village, OH to *John Cockins INGLIS* (b. 14 June 1957); *Issue: John Cockins INGLIS, William Darling INGLIS, George Morgan INGLIS and Robert Scott INGLIS.* ***Sara Louise MORGAN***, b. 25 Dec 1906; d. 18 Sep 1992, Bay Village. ***Ruth Eleanor MORGAN***, b. 23 Nov 1914, Bay Village; d. 8 Mar 1995, Bay Village; m. 26 Nov 1938, Bay Methodist Church to *Robert Joseph O'CONNOR* (b. 30 Oct 1915, Wellsville, NY; d. 13 Apr 2001, Marion, Ohio). ***George Edward MORGAN, Jr.***, b. 16 Jan 1917; d. 13 July 1996, Duluth, St. Louis Co., MN; m. 17 Mar 1945 to *Louise LaClair TAYLOR*; *issue: George Taylor MORGAN, Jean MORGAN and Robert MORGAN.* With few exceptions, the Osborns were tall, especially for the times. *Julia OSBORN SCOTT* and Ruth Morgan O'Connor were exceptions. Tall meaning 5'8" to 6'+. Susy O'Connor Thielen

Helen E. MORGAN, 24; res. Bay Village, O; b. Chicago, Ill., occup. Librarian; fr. *Geo. E. MORGAN*, mo. *Rose E. OSBORN.* Married ***John C. INGLIS***, 24, res. Columbus, O.; b. do *(same)*; occup. student; fr. *Wm. D. INGLIS*, mo. *Alice M. COCKINS*; neither previously married. The State of Ohio, Cuyahoga County, I certify, that on the 12th day of September 1928, Mr. John C. Inglis and Miss Helen E. Morgan were by me legally joined in marriage. Rev. L.A. Ensley Marriage Record, Cuyahoga County, OH, vol. 154, p. 348.

Helen MORGAN INGLIS liked to entertain, with a husband who was a minister and four sons, it was a good thing. They lived in different areas when he was serving the Presbyterian church, St. Charles, Mo., and Piqua, OH, for a lengthy stay. Helen also was a librarian for a short time and member of the Martha Devotion Huntington Chapter of the DAR. Sally O'Connor, Kathy O'Connor Johnson and Susy O'Connor Thielen.

Sara L. MORGAN was a children's librarian. She served in Cleveland libraries and on their bookmobile, Bay High School for a few years in the 50's, also at the Ashland Public Library. She loved animals, especially her dogs. She always brought us the greatest books and read to us especially when we were little. She lived nearby, so we enjoyed her company often. Sally O'Connor, Kathy O'Connor Johnson and Susy O'Connor Thielen.

Ruth MORGAN, 23, res. Bay Village, O; b. do *(Bay Village)*; occup. nurse; fr. *George*, mo. *Rose OSBORN.* Married ***Robert J. O'CONNOR***, 23, res. 27950 Osborn Rd., Bay, O; b. Wellsville, N.Y.; occup. Steelworker; fr. *James P.*, mo. *Helen SLEEPER*; neither previously married. The State of Ohio, Cuyahoga County, I Certify that on the 26th day of November, 1938, Mr. Robert J. O'Connor and Miss Ruth Morgan were by me legally joined in marriage. Rev. Ralph Taylor Alton, Bay, O. Marriage Record, Cuyahoga County, OH, vol. 185, p. 418.

Ruth MORGAN O'CONNOR'S family fondly nicknamed her "Boots" since she always played with her booties as an infant. Growing up in Bay, a special childhood memory for Ruth was the day that "Susy," the family lamb, followed her to Church.

Ruth was a registered nurse graduating from Fairview Park Hospital School of Nursing and junior college in St. Charles, Missouri, while living with her sister, ***Helen INGLIS,*** and her husband, ***John***. She was employed by Fairview Hospital in Cleveland, Bradley Road Nursing Home and finally Good Samaritan Nursing Home in Avon where she retired. The last home she shared with her husband, ***Robert***, before she died was on Bradley Road. Robert relocated to the Marion, Ohio area to be near his daughters, Sally and Kathy.

Ruth was a member of the Martha Devotion Huntington Chapter of the DAR. Kathy Johnson and Billie Jo Schwartz.

Children of Ruth and Robert O'Connor:

Sally Ann O'CONNOR, b. 13 June 1940, Lorain, Lorain Co., OH. ***Susan Ruth O'CONNOR***, b. 20 Jan 1944, Lorain; m. 25 June 1966, Bay Methodist Church, Bay Village, OH to *Bruce Edward THIELEN* (b. 21 June 1944, Cincinnati, Hamilton Co., OH). *Issue: Andrew Bruce THIELEN*, b. 5 Oct 1968, Jacksonville, Duval, FL; *Scott Joseph THIELEN*, b. 20 Dec 1969, Seoul, Korea; *Alexander Robert THIELEN*, b. 29 Mar 1971, Meridian, Lauderdale Co., MS; *Kathy Xuan THIELEN*, b. 20 Feb 1974, Saigon, Viet Nam.

Kathryn Helen O'CONNOR, b. 21 Aug 1946, Cleveland, Cuyahoga Co., OH, m. 2 May 1970, Bay Methodist Church to *Randall Boyd JOHNSON* (b. 9 Mar 1944, Southgate, Los Angeles Co., CA). *Issue: Jennifer Wren JOHNSON*, b. 12 Jan 1972, Columbus, Franklin Co., OH; *Tracy Ann JOHNSON*, b. 9 July 1976, Marion, Marion Co., OH; m. 28 July 2001, Galena, Delaware, OH to *Christopher Scott JOHNSON* (b. 24 July1974, Kettering, Montgomery, OH). Susy O'Connor Thielen

Ruth M. O'CONNOR, d. 8 March 1995 11:10 a.m., b. 23 Nov 1914, Bay Village, OH, 16 yrs. of schooling. Ohio Certificate of Death, Division of Vital Statistics, 1995, certif. 27197.

Husband of Ruth Morgan O'Connor, Robert O'Connor:

Robert J. O'CONNOR, age 85 of Prospect. Formerly of Bay Village, died Friday April 13, 2001 in Marion. Memorial services will be held Saturday April 28, 2001 at 11 a.m. at The Prospect United Methodist Church, Prospect, and on Sunday April 29, 2001 at 2 p.m. at the Bay United Methodist Church, Bay Village. The Rev. David Hoffman will be officiating both services. The family will receive friends one hour prior to each service. Jenkins Funeral Chapel, Westlake and Stofcheck Funeral Home, Richwood are handling arrangements. April 26, 2002. The Plain Dealer. All rights reserved. Reprinted with permission.

Robert J. O'CONNOR, b. October 30, 1915; d. April 13, 2001, Marion, OH. Memorial Card for Robert J. O'Connor.

Parents of Robert O'Connor:

O'CONNOR, James P., 40, owns home valued at $10,000, owns radio, b. Ohio, parents b. United States, age at marriage 23, Com't Traveler Mfg. Battery; ***Helen S.***, wife, 40, age at marriage 23, b. Pennsylvania, parents b. Pennsylvania; ***Kenneth***, son, 15, b. New York, occup. newsboy street; ***Robert J.***, son, 14, b. New York, occup. newsboy street. 1930 FC OH CYBV ED 18-534, p, 21A, 27950 Osborn Rd., lines 25-28.

George MORGAN served in WWII and always marched with the American Legion during the Memorial Day parade in Bay Village. He worked most of his life with Pittsburgh Steamship Company, a Great Lakes ore shipping company, in a management position with Human Resources. He and ***Jack MEDDICK*** built boats and rafts that they sailed or paddled on Lake Erie. Sally O'Connor, Kathy O'Connor Johnson and Susy O'Connor Thielen.

When the Osborn's got together and started telling stories, they would laugh so hard they would have tears running down their cheeks. Susy felt in today's society our close knit family would be a rarity. We knew all of our cousins and most second and third cousins across the branches of the family tree. The family was very open and welcomed all new additions to the family with open arms. We were constantly bathed in family history.

When our mother died, it was the first time that there was not an Osborn living in Bay Village. When my dad moved down to Prospect, it pretty much ended visits to Bay of Osborn descendants. Sally O'Connor, Kathy O'Connor Johnson and Susy O'Connor Thielen.

Lot 1-4 Chester Osborn

CHESTER

CHESTER ARTHUR
SON OF
DAVID AND ROSE
OSBORN
BORN MAY 6, 1889
DIED JULY 1, 1890

Chester was the fourth child of David Deforest Osborn (Lot 1: 1) and Rose Mitchell.

Chester OSBORN, 13 mo.; res. Dover; interred July 1, 1890; Original part. "List of Interments," Lakeside Cemetery, Bay Village, OH.

Lot 2 *Owner: Betsey R. Williams of Dover purchased Sept 26, 1895 for $6.06* SL

Lot 2-4 Barney Williams

BARNEY

Thomas M. (Barney) WILLIAMS, b. 1852, d. 21 Sept 1895, Cuyahoga Co., m. 22 July1873, Cuyahoga Co. to ***Betsy OSBORN***. Marianne Ruple Gardner, The Descendants of Balthazar (Baltus) Ruple Pennsylvania, New Jersey, Ohio, p. 25. *Barney's name as Thomas was unable to be substantiated in any other documents and the original source for this citation was undetermined.*

WILLIAMS, Barney, 28, married, farmer, b. Ohio, fr. b. England, mo. b. Ireland; ***Betsy R.***, 40, wife, Keeping House, b. Ohio, fr. b. New York, mo. b. Ohio. 1880 FC CYDO, p.99, house 313, lines 22-3.

WILLIAMS, Barny *(sp.)*. Owned land; Acres: Improved - Tilled, including fallow and grass: 16, Permanent meadow: 4. Farm Values: Land and buildings - $3500, Machinery - $100, Live Stock - $100. Cost of building a repair in 1879: $10. Labor: Paid for wages in 1879 - $50, weeks hired labor in 1879: 8. Estimated value of all farm production: $300. Grass lands: acreage: 5 mown, 2 not mown, 5 tons hay. 1 horse, 1 milch cow, 1 calf dropped and 1 purchased, 2 cattle sold living. 100 pounds of butter made on the farm. 2 swine. 20 barnyard poultry on farm, 100 dozen eggs produced in 1879. Indian corn: 3 acres, 200 bushels; oats: 4 acres, 130 bushels; wheat: 1 acre, 35 bushels; potatoes: 1 acre, 50 bushels. Orchards - apple: 2 acres; peaches: 2 acres, 50 bearing trees, 3 bushels. Total value of orchard products: $4. "Schedule 2. Production of Agriculture in Dover Township, Cuyahoga County, OH," enumerated June, 1880, p. 33.

Barney WILLIAMS; res. Dover; interred Sept 23, 1895; Lot 2. "List of Interments," Lakeside Cemetery, Bay Village, OH.

Barney WILLIAMS, 9-21-1895, age 43, Lakeside Cemetery, Bay Village, cem. rec. Cleveland Necrology File, roll 86.

Lot 2-5 Betsey R. Osborn Williams

BETSEY

Betsey was the daughter of Selden Osborn and Nancy Ruple (OP 5:7) and sister of David Deforest Osborn (Lot 1:1).

WILLIAMS, Betsey, 51, head, widow, b. Oct 1839, married 3? years *(crossed out)*, 0 children born and living, b. Ohio, fr. b. New York, mo. b. Ohio; *Marton, May*, 27, female, boarder, b. Ohio, parents b. Ohio, single, b. May 1873. 1900 FC OH CYDO, p. 21B, lines 86-7.

WILLIAMS, Betsy R., 70, widow, 1 child born *(assumed error)*, 0 living, b. Ohio, fr. b. Conn.; ***MARTIN, Mary A.***, niece, 32, single, b. Ohio, fr. b. England, seamstress; *SEHNERT, Henry B.* boarder, 37, single. 1910 FC OH CYDO, p. 2B.

Mrs. Betsey WILLIAMS, d. Mch. 14, 1912 at 9 a.m., County of Cuyahoga, Village of Bay, cause of death: Senile Gangrene, for 365 days Contributory: Atheromatic Arteries, several years; b. Oct 22, 1838, Bay Village, fr. ***Seldon*** *(sp.)* ***OSBORN***, b. New York State, mo. ***Nancy RUFLE*** *(Ruple)* b. Ohio State; 73 yrs., 4 mos., 22 days; Widowed; occup. housewife. I attended deceased from Sept 1st 1911 to March 14, 1912, Geo. Lathrop, M.D.; bur. Bay Village Cem., Undertaker Jas. A. Pease and Son, Dover, Ohio. Ohio Certificate of Death, Division of Vital Statistics, 1912, certif. 13439.

Mrs. Betsy R. WILLIAMS, beloved wife of the late ***Barney WILLIAMS***, entered into rest March 14, 1912, at her home, Bay Village, O., aged 73 years. Funeral at her late residence, Monday, March 18, 1912, at 2 p.m. standard time. Cleveland Necrology File, March 15, 1912.

Betsy R. WILLIAMS, 72; res. Bay Village; interred Mar 18th, 1912; Lot 2. "List of Interments," Lakeside Cemetery, Bay Village, OH

Betsy WILLIAMS, cause of death Senile Gangrene, permit issued Mar 18, 1912 by I.C. Powell. Burial Permit.

Lot 2-6 Williams Monument

BARNEY WILLIAMS
DIED SEPT 21, 1895
AGED 43 YRS.
BETSEY HIS WIFE
DIED MAR 14, 1912
AGED 72 YRS.
AT REST

WILLIAMS

Lot 3 *Owner: Matthias Mawby of Avon purchased July 22, 1886, for $6.09* SL

Lot 3 John Mawby no marker

MAWBY, John; b. 1886, July 5; Ohio, Lorain Co., Avon; male; fr. ***Mathias B. MAWBY***, mo. ***Mary Ann BRITCHFORD***. Probate Court Birth Records, Lorain County, Ohio, vol. 2, p. 122.

John MAWBY; male; d. 1886, July 22, Avon; 17 days old; b. Avon; Hem. of brain. Probate Court Death Records, Lorain County, Ohio, vol. 2, p. 66, line 2785.

Baby MAUBY, 3 weeks; res. Avon; English; interred July 23, 1886; Lot 3. "List of Interments," Lakeside Cemetery, Bay Village, OH.

MAUBY, M.B.; Lot 3, Aug 19, 1886; vol. 1, p. 294. Bay Village City Hall Cemetery Records, assumed to be a payment record.

Presumed grandparents of John Mawby:

MAWBY, SIMON, 63, Farmer, Paralysis, b. England, parents b. England; ***Mary***, 68, wife, keeping house, b. England, parents b. England; ***Matthias***, 26, son, Farmer, b. England; ***Ramos***, 17, grandson, working farm. 1880 FC OH LRAV p. 336B, lines 27-30. *The Mawby family is living next to Adam and Maggie Lucas Crist. Maggie, Lot 5:9, died within two weeks of John.*

Parents of John Mawby:

MAWBY, Matthias B. (Mary A.), Beach Park, farmer, fruit grower, Lake Shore. ***MAWBY, Matthias, Jr***...Beach Park, fruit grower, Lake Shore Rd. ***MAWBY, Lucy M.***, Beach Park, Lake Shore Rd. *Fred'k (Florence)*...Beach Park; *Ivan, Stanley,* Lake Shore Rd. 1910 Lorain County Rural Directory, Avon.

MAWBY-Mary Ann, beloved wife ***Matthias B.***, mother of ***Lucy B.*** and ***Matthias B., jr.***, died at her home, Avon Lake, Friday, March 28. Funeral Monday at 2 p. m., at church, Stop 56 Lake road. Cleveland Necrology File, Mar 30, 1924.

Mary Ann MAWBY, d. Mar 28, 1924, Avon Lake, Lorain Co., Ohio of Carcinoma of Stomach; 67 yrs. 3 mos. 14 ds.; b. Dec 14, 1856, Willoughby, Ohio to ***Samuel BIRCHFORD***, b. England and ***Mary Ann PAIGE***, b. England; married to ***Mathias MAWBY***; informant *Lucy MAWBY*, Avon Lake; undertaker Geo. Batikey?, Lorain; burial Avon Lake Cemetery. Ohio Certificate of Death, Division of Vital Statistics, 1924, certif. 16616.

MAWBY: Mathias B., aged 84, at his home in Avon Lake, O., Monday evening, Feb 8, 1932, beloved father of ***Mathias, jr.*** and ***Lucy MAWBY***. Services from Avon Lake Church, Thursday at 2 o'clock. Friends invited. Cleveland Necrology File, Feb 10, 1932.

Matthias B. MAWBY, bur. Feb 11, 1932; Lake Shore Cemetery, Avon Lake, OH. Lot 34 purchased by M. B. Mawby, June 20, 1914. Lake Shore Cemetery Records, Avon Lake, OH.

MAWBY. Father ***Matthias B.*** 1847-1932, Mother ***Mary Ann*** 1856-1924, Son ***Matthias B.*** 1890-1974, Daughter ***Lucy*** 1884-1965, *Henry W. WALKER* 1856-1942. Lake Shore Cemetery (Avon Lake Cemetery), Avon Lake, OH. Recorded by Catherine Burke Flament.

A relationship between the Mawby family and Henry Walker was not established. He is listed as living next-door to Simon Mawby in the 1880 census.

Henry W. WALKER, d. May 16, 1942, Avon Lake, Lorain Co., Ohio of Cerebral Hemorrhage 1 day, Arterio Sclerosis and Prostatic Hypertrophy 10 yrs.; single; retired; b. Oct 26, 1856, Avon Lake, Ohio, to *John WALKER*, b. England and *Emma*, b. England; 85 yrs. 6 mos. 20 ds.; informant *Miss. L. MAWBY*, Avon Lake; funeral firm Reichlin Cooley, 2920 Bdwy. *(Broadway)*, Lorain, Ohio; burial Avon Cemetery. Ohio Certificate of Death, Division of Vital Statistics, 1942, certif. 31028.

Siblings of John Mawby:

Matthias B. MAWBY, 28, res. Avon Lake, O., b. Avon, O., occup. Grape grower, fr. *Matthias*, mo. *Mary BRIDGEFORD*. Married ***Dayse CONABEE***, 28, res. 1475 Crawford Rd., b. Lorain, Ohio, occup. Music teacher, fr. *William H.*, mo. *Frances PADLEY*, neither previously married. The State of Ohio, Cuyahoga County-ss. I Certify, That on the 19th day of Sept 1916 Mr. Matthias B. Mawby Jr. and Miss Dayse Conabee were by me legally joined in marriage. Rev. E.L.Waldorf Marriage Record, Cuyahoga County, OH, vol. 100, p. 246.

Matthias MAWBY, b. 27 Apr 1890, d. Apr 1974, Edmonds, Snohomish, WA 98020. Social Security Index.

Matthais Mawby

Matthais** (sp.) **B. MAWBY, 84, of 1152 2nd Ave., S., Edmonds, died April 28 in Edmonds.

He was born April 27, 1890, in Avon Lake, Ohio, and had been a resident of Edmonds for the past nine years.

Mr. Mawby leaves a daughter, ***Mildred BALL*** of Edmonds; a grandson, ***Louis Ball Jr.*** and one great-grandson.

Mr. Mawby was sent to Avon Lake, Ohio, for services and interment, with local arrangements by Beck's Funeral Home, Edmonds. Edmonds Tribune-Review, Edmonds, Washington; May 8, 1974, p. 2, col. 4.

Wife of Matthias: ***MAWBY, Mrs. Dayse***, late residence Oregon City, Ore., former residence Avon Lake; passed away Feb 6; beloved mother of ***Mildred BALL***; grandmother of ***Louis A.***, sister of *Earl CONABEE*, and nieces and nephews. Funeral services and interment, Wednesday, Feb 11, in Oregon City, Ore. Cleveland Press, Feb 9, 1953.

Lucy M. MAWBY, d. Mar 23, 1965, St. Joseph's Hospital, Lorain, OH; b. Jan 15, 1884, Ohio; res. 32531 Lake Rd., Avon Lake; homemaker, never married. Ohio Certificate of Death, Division of Vital Statistics, 1965, certif. 021484.

Lot 4 *Owner: Lydia Ware of Avon purchased on Jan 20, 1879, for $5.25* SL

Lot 4-7 John Ware

FATHER
JOHN WARE
1826-1879

The State of Ohio, Cuyahoga County, ss. I certify that on the 3 day of Dec 1864, ***Mr. John WARE*** and ***Miss Lydia BRAYMAN*** were by me legally joined in Marriage. Allen Durrow, Pastor Marriage Record, Cuyahoga County, OH, vol. 12, p. 22.

AVON.
(Too late for last issue)
February 4th

Two cases of insanity, four deaths, two church donations, several spelling schools, negative decisions on the question of county supervision of schools, several oyster suppers, one case of trouble in a school just over the Avon line in Dover, much anxiety among the saloonists, lull in taking up the married relation, and occasional musical soirees make up the Avon news for the last three weeks.

The cases of insanity….The deaths are ***John WARE*** and *Mrs. Geo. T. DEEG*, heart disease; *Mrs. Alice PRESLEY* and *Horace BARROWS*.

The Baptists give their pastor a donation at the parsonage on Feb 12.

Supt. Wean, of the Wellington schools, promises us a lecture of county supervision at some future date. Many would like to hear him on this question which but few understand.

About forty witnesses were summoned before the grand jury from this town, to testify against the saloon interest. TREBLIG. The Elyria Constitution, Elyria, Ohio, Thursday, Feb 13, 1879, p. 2, col. 5.

WARE, John; d. 1879, Jan, 19, Avon; married; 53 yrs., 5 mos., 3 days; b. Philadelphia; cause: heart disease; res. Avon. Probate Court Death Records, Lorain County, Ohio, vol. 2, p. 7, line 308.

John WARE; res. Avon; interred Jan 21, 1879; Lot 4. "List of Interments," Lakeside Cemetery, Bay Village, OH.

Lot 4-8 Lydia Braman Ware

MOTHER
LYDIA WARE
1833-1882

Probably the daughter of Otis Braman and Betsy Riley (OP1:8) and sister of Horace Braman (OP 2:9).

DIED.

Ware.-In Elyria, July 23, at 9 p.m., at the residence of her sister, *Mrs. A. B. BRAMAN,* ***Mrs. Lydia WARE,*** in the 48th year of her age.

The bereaved friends of the late Mrs. Lydia Ware, desire to tender their heartfelt thanks to the choir who furnished the music for the funeral service; to the friends who furnished the flowers for the occasion, the friends who by their various offices of love, gave touching and appropriate expressions of sympathy in their great sorrow. Elyria Weekly Republican, Elyria, OH, Thursday, Aug 8, 1882, p. 5, col. 5. *Lydia probably died at the residence of her sister Miss Adelia Braman.*

Lydia WARE; res. Elyria; interred July 25, 1882; Lot 4. "List of Interments," Lakeside Cemetery, Bay Village, OH.

Lots 5/6 *Owner: Nelson Baird of Avon purchased on October 2, 1882, for $5.28* SL

Lot 5-9 Margarett Lucas Crist

MAGGIE CRIST
DAU. OF
V. & E. LUCAS
DIED AUG 5, 1886
AGED 36 YRS.

Maggie is the sister of Emma Lucas Beard in Lot 6, next to this one, and daughter of Valentine Lucas and Elizabeth Stumpf.

The State of Ohio, Cuyahoga County, ss. I certify that on the 20 day of February 1872, ***Mr. Adam CRIST*** and ***Miss Maggie LUCAS*** were, by me, legally joined in Marriage. W.H. Goodrich Marriage Record, Cuyahoga County, OH, vol. 16, p. 373.

CHRIST, Adam, 29, Farmer, b. Ohio; ***Margarett***, 28, wife, keeping house, b. Ohio, parents b. Hess D.; ***Harry***, 6, son, b. Ohio; ***Cora***, 4, daughter, b. Ohio; ***Baby***, 1/12 yr., b. Ohio. 1880 FC OH LRAV p. 336B, lines 22-26. Census recorded June 21, 1880. *The "Baby" would be named Arthur, see 1900 census below. The Crist's were living next to Simon Mawby in this census. Maggie died within two weeks of John Mawby; see Lot 3.*

CRIST-Maggie, wife of ***Adam H***,. and beloved daughter of ***Valentine*** and ***Elizabeth LUCAS*** of Cleveland, O., Saturday evening, Aug 7, aged 37 years. Funeral Tuesday, Aug 10, at 1 p.m. from Avon Lake, O. Cleveland Necrology File, August 10, 1886, roll 17.

There are numerous age and year discrepancies within the following entries.

CRIST, Margarett F.; d. 1887, Aug 7, Avon; 34 yrs.; b. Cleveland; Housewife; Dropsy & Inf. of brain, res. Avon. Probate Court Death Records, Lorain County, Ohio, vol. 2, p. 66, line 2775. *Year of death conflicts, 1886-1887 records were combined and date may have been recorded incorrectly.*

Maggie CRIST, 37; res. Avon; German; Aug 10/16, 1886. "List of Interments," Lakeside Cemetery, Bay Village, OH.

Parents of Maggie Lucas Crist:

The State of Ohio, Cuyahoga County, ss. I hereby certify, that on the 27th day of October A.D. 1849, I duly solemnized the Marriage Contract between the said ***Valentine LUCAS*** and ***Elizabeth STUMPF***. Marriage Record, Cuyahoga County, OH, vol. 5, p. 28.

LUCAS, Valentine, 28, Grocer, b. Germany; ***Elizabeth***, 23, b. Germany. 1850 FC OH CY Ward 2, p. 214.

LUCAS, Valentine, 49, brick mason, b. Hesse Darmstaudt; ***Eliza***, 44, b. same; ***Amelia***, 15 attending school; ***William***, 11; ***George***, 10; ***Frank***, 7; ***Henry***, 5; all children b. Ohio. 1870 FC OH CY Cleveland, 7th Ward, p. 207, lines 3-9.

LUCAS, Valentine, 58, Works in Rolling Mill, 2 mos. unemployed, b. Hessen D., fr. b. Hessen D., mo. b. Hessen D.; ***Elizabeth***, 54, Keeping House, b. Hessen D., fr. b. Hessen D., mo. b. Hessen D.; ***LUCAS, George, P.***, 19, son, Printer, b. Ohio; ***Frank***, 17, son, Prentice Machinist, b. Ohio; ***Henry***, 15, son, Clerk in Notion Store, attended school, b. Ohio; ***Elizabeth***, 26, daughter, Home, b. Ohio. 1880 FC OH CY Cleveland, Ward 7, house 386, p. 238B, lines 49-50, p. 239C, lines 1-4.

Valentine LUKAS, b. Germany, date of arrival August 1855, date of naturalization Oct 18, 1880, witness C. Beck. Court of Common Pleas, Cleveland, Cuyahoga County, Ohio. Certificate Journal 77, p. 427. U.S. Dept of Labor, Immigration and Naturalization Service, Record at Cuyahoga County Archives.

Lucas, Valentine; 1822 - 9-11-1893. Age 71. Woodland Cemetery Cleveland, Ohio. Woodland Cemetery Records and Cleveland Necrology File, reel 051.

Valentine LUCAS, 71 yrs., of dropsy, bur. 11 Sept 1893, res. 74 Lymon; ***Elizabeth LUCAS***, 70, bur. 2 May 1897, res. 20 Spencer St. Sect. 31, Lot 15-16-17, sub sect. 4, 1st grave, NE corner. Woodland Cemetery Records, Cleveland, OH. *Valentine was found living at the same address in the 1877-78 Cleveland City Directory.*

Maggie's husband remarried in 1887. According to the census below, he is buried elsewhere. The following record is included to show Maggie probably had a son, Arthur.

CHRIST, Adam, 48, head, b. Aug 1851, Germany, parents b. Germany, immig 1852, Na., married 13 yrs.; *Margaret*, 49, wife, b. May 1851, Ireland, parents b. Ireland, immig 1854, 4 children born, 4 living; ***Arthur***, 20, son, b. May 1880, Ohio, fr. b. Germany, mo. b. Ohio, farm laborer; following children b. Ohio, fr. b. Germany, mo. b. Ireland; *Anna*, dau., 11, b. Oct 1888; *Valentine*, son, 10, b. Jan 1890; *Vincent*, son, 6, b. Jan 1894; *Isador*, son, 4, b. May 1896. 1900 FC OH LOAV, p. 17A, lines 18-24.

Margaret Crist, the second wife of Adam, is found in the 1910 Avon Census as being the head of household and a widow. Adam evidently passed away between 1900 and 1910, p. 4A. Adam is not listed in the Cemetery Inscriptions of Lorain County; it is presumed he is in an unmarked grave.

*CHRIST, Margaret (wid. of Adam)...*Beach Park, *Isadore, Vincent,* Walker Rd.

*Christ, Valentine...*Beach Park, farmer, Walker Rd.

1910 Lorain County Rural Directory, Avon, p. 48.

There are two "B" markers, one at the southeast corner of the headstone and one at the southwest foot of the grave by the drive. One is assumed to be for Mary Ann Crist, infant daughter of Adam Crist and Maggie Lucas.

Lot 5 Mary Ann Crist no marker

Infant daughter of Adam Crist and Maggie Lucas who died two weeks after her mother, Maggie.

CRIST, Mary Ann, b. 1886, July 15, Ohio, Lorain Co., Avon; fr. ***Adam CRIST***, mo. ***Margarett LUCAS*** of Avon. Probate Court Birth Records, Lorain County, Ohio, vol. 2, p. 122.

CRIST, Mary Ann; d. 1887, Aug 21, Avon; 1 yr. 7 days; b. Avon; no cause of death listed. Probate Court Death Records, Lorain County, Ohio, vol. 2, p. 66, line 2776. *(Mary Ann is not listed at Lakeside but may be one of the infant markers.)*

There are a number of misspellings included with the Beard family. The grave markings on the plat map and the actual markers do not coincide. i.e., Arthur - mother and " blank grave" with two names listed on the marker, etc.

The Beard family that follows are listed as a unit with the monument.

Lots 5/6-10 Rolen Beard

ROLEN

Lots 5/6-11 Emma Valera Lucas Beard

(Officially listed as the grave of Arthur H. Beard, assumed for Emma Beard, Lot 6, below.)

MOTHER

Lots 5/6-12 Nelson Beard

FATHER

Lots 5/6-13 Arthur H. Beard
Nelson Beard

<u>ARTHUR</u>
NELSON

Lots 5/6-14 Beard Monument

BEARD
EMMA V. HIS WIFE NELSON A. BEARD
1855-1927 1851-1907
ARTHUR 1880-1882
NELSON 1887-1887
ROLEN 1890-1890

(There are two "B" markers, one at the n/w corner of the tombstone and one to the n/e corner of the plot)

Lots 5/6-14 Nelson Beard

Nelson BEARD successfully farmed a large farm which he owned on the east side of Jaycox Road in Avon, now Avon Lake, OH, growing strawberries, vegetables, potatoes and some grain. His success was so well known that he was many times referred to as the "Strawberry King." He also owned two smaller farms, one on Jaycox Road near Lake Road and the other a 15 acre farm on Lake Road near Bay Village. He donated 2-3 acres of the Jaycox Road smaller farm when the Interurban Line was to pass through Avon Lake and because of this, Stop 49 was erected for his family's convenience. He also donated land on his Lake Road farm and was given Stop 42 as a permanent stop for the Interurban Electric cars. Nelson passed away at age 55.

Emma, his wife, continued running the farm after Nelson's death, hiring help, but found it was too much for her to keep up. She built a home on the Lake Road side of the property as there were 13 acres of land on the south side of the road with fruit trees. She, her daughter, ***Flossie BEARD WALKER***, and granddaughter, ***Hazel WALKER***, moved into the new home when the farm was sold. The family members swam in Lake Erie, getting access to the lake by climbing down a ladder to the water. It was later changed to wood steps.

Emma was a strict but kind woman who was always willing to lend a hand with the work. There are fond memories of her standing on the back porch as her granddaughter would leave to catch the Interurban to take music lessons in Bay Village.

When Emma suddenly became ill, her granddaughter, Hazel Walker, was instructed to run to the next farm of *Annie HAAG (mother of infant in Lot 29)* to call the doctor. Emma passed away at the age of 72 before Hazel had time to return. Hazel W. McCutcheon

The State of Ohio, Cuyahoga County, ss. I Certify that on the 12 day of November 1878 ***Mr. Nelson A. BEARD*** and ***Miss Valara E. LUCKAS*** were by me legally joined in marriage. Charles S. Pomeroy Marriage Record, Cuyahoga County, OH, vol. 22, p. 67.

BEARD, Nelson, head, 49, b. Mar 1851, b. Ohio, fr. b. Penn, mo. b. Ohio, married 21 yrs., farmer; ***Emma***, wife, 45, b. Feb, 1855, b. Ohio, parents-Germany, 6 children born, 3 living; ***Clarence***, son, 15, b. Jan 1885, at school; ***Flossie***, dau., 8, b. Sept 1891, at school; owned farm free. 1900 FC OH LOAV p. 14B, lines 75-78.

BEARD, Nelson; d. 1907, Mar 17, Avon, Pneumonia; 55 yrs., 11 mo., 17 days; b. Avon, farmer. Probate Court Death Records, Lorain County, Ohio, vol. 5, p. 6.

Nelson BAIRD, Lot 5. "List of Interments," Lakeside Cemetery, Bay Village, OH.

Grandparents of Nelson Beard:

Philip BEARD, 67, b. Maryland; ***Catherine***, 60, b. Penn.; *Mary*, 21, b. Penn.; *Rufus LOCKWOOD*, 9, b. Ohio. 1850 FC OH LRAV p. 469, house 1199, family 1233, lines 9-12. *Nextdoor to **Abraham BEARD**, 26, Farmer, b. Penn.; Almira C.*, 20, b. Ohio; *John*, 1, b. Ohio. Lines 6-8, family 1232 who is next to ***Philip BEARD***, 28, farmer below. *See census listed under "parents" for Philip.*

BEARD, Catherine**, wife of **Philip**,* 1790-1868. *Son: **Abraham 1823-1880; ***Emily***, his wife, 1822-1894. *Graves are not next to each other.* East Pittsfield Cemetery, Pittsfield Twp., Lorain Co., OH.

Parents of Nelson Beard:

The State of Ohio, Cuyahoga County, ss. I Certify that on the 30th day of January 1847 ***Mr. Phillip BEARD*** and ***Miss Tarissa MITCHELL*** were by me legally joined in marriage. Marriage Record, Cuyahoga County, vol. 4, p. 383.

BEARD, Philip, Pvt., Co. G, 107th Ohio Inf., enlisted 22 Aug 1862, Avon Lake, Ohio and was discharged 15 July 1865, Charleston, SC due to the close of the War. He had served 2 years 10 mos. 22 days. Philip was admitted to the Ohio Veterans Home from Avon Lake, OH on 12 Nov 1903 to RB Cottage and then admitted to the Home hospital on 9 Dec 1903. He expired on 2 Sept 1904 at 11:30 p.m. He is buried in their cemetery in Section G, Row 3, Marker 30. His date of birth is listed as 31 Mar 1821. His disability for admission to the hospital was given as old age. He received a $12 pension per month under certificate 531628. He owned no property and gave his previous occupation as farming. He was supported by his pension. He had five sons, no names given although his next of kin was listed as ***Elmer BEARD***, Avon Lake, OH. "1890 Eleventh Census of the United States Special Schedule, Surviving Soldiers, Sailors and Marines, and Widows, Etc.," Dover Township, 2, #22.

Enlisted as a Private... at the age of 41; Enlisted in Company G, 107th Infantry Regiment Ohio, 9 September 1862; Mustered out... in Charleston, OH. "Official Roster of the Soldiers of the State of Ohio," 1886.

Philip BEARD Jr., 28, Farmer, value of real estate $625, b. Penn.; ***Theressa***, 18, b. NY; ***Elmas A.***, 1, male, b. Ohio. 1850 FC OH LRAV p. 469, house 1199, family 1231, lines 3-5. *See information listed previously on his parents, who were two farms away.*

Phillip BARD, 39, Value of real estate $1500, personal property $600; b. Pa.; ***Theresa***, 29, b, Pa.; ***Elmer***, 11, b. Ohio; ***Nelson***, 9, b. Ohio; ***Charles***, 7, b. Ohio; ***Albert***, 5, b. Ohio; *Rosella VAN KNAPP*, 18, b, NY. 1860 FC OH LRAV.

BAIRD, Phillip, 49, farmer, value of real estate $2600, personal estate $800, b. Penn; ***Theresa***, 39, b. New York; ***Elmos***, 21, farm laborer; ***Nelson***, 19, sailor; ***Charles***, 14; ***Albert***, 10; ***Newton***, 3; all children born in Ohio. 1870 FC OH LRAV p. 348, lines 16-22.

BEARD, Elmas, 51, b. Mar 1849, Ohio, fr. b. Penn, mo. b. Ohio, farmer; ***Elizabeth***, wife, 43...; ***Philip***, father, b. Mar 1821, 79, wd., b. Penn, parent's b. Maryland... 1900 FC OH LRAV p. 20B, lines 39-43. *Elmas's three closest neighbors are also buried at Lakeside: William Frederick HINZ, George SCHEIBLE and Antonia TOMANEK.*

Philip BEARD had a large home on the north side of Walker Road in Avon Lake. He fought in the Civil War for almost three years, leaving his wife and children. He would later live with his sons, moving from one to another every year. Philip received $9.00/month pension after serving in the Civil War. The *TOMANEK* family helped Philip get settled in the Soldier Home in Sandusky, OH where he lived during his final days and was buried in the cemetery there. Hazel Walker McCutcheon

Siblings of Nelson Beard:

BEARD, Elmas A., (Elizabeth),...fruit grower, Lake Shore Rd. Lorain County Rural Directory, 1910, p. 55.

Elmas Arthur BEARD, d. April 13, 1924, 11:30 a.m., Avon Lake Village, Cuyahoga Co., Ohio of Dilatation of Heart and Aorta with Arterio-sclerosis and High Blood Pressure; 75 yrs. 27 ds.; Married; Fruit Grower; b. Mch. 16, 1824, Avon to ***Philip BEARD***, b. Penn. and ***Theresa MITCHELL***, b. Penn.; informant Mrs. Geo. Andrews, 1444 W. 74th St., Cleveland; undertaker C. Pease; burial Avon Lake, O. Ohio Certificate of Death, Division of Vital Statistics, 1924, certif. 20601.

Elizabeth BEARD, d. Feb 13, 1941, 10:15 a.m. of Post Influenza Pneumonia with Myocarditis 12 ds., 1444 W. 74th St., Cleveland, Cuyahoga Co., Ohio; 84 yrs. 3 mos. 12 ds.; Widow of ***Elmas BEARD***; b. Dec 1, 1856, Avon Lake, Ohio to *Joseph OSTERMAN*, b. Germany and *EMMA ___*, b. Germany; informant Gladys E. Andrews, 17200 Clifton Blvd., Lakewood, Ohio; undertaker Clifford Pease, Westlake, Ohio; bur. Avon Lake Cemetery. Ohio Certificate of Death, Division of Vital Statistics, 1941, certif. 9214.

BEARD, Chas. I., (Malinda), Beach Park, P.O., farmer, *Hattie*, Glen. 1910 Lorain County Rural Directory, Avon, p. 55.

BEARD Elmas A. 1848-1923; ***Elizabeth*** 1856-1941; ***BEARD Charles I.*** 1853-1933; ***Malinda C.*** 1857-1945. Lake Shore Cemetery (Avon Lake Cemetery), Avon Lake, OH. Read by Catherine Burke Flament.

Lots 5/6-14 Emma Valara Lucas Beard

Emma is the daughter of Valentine Lucas and Elizabeth Stumpf, and the younger sister of Maggie Lucas Crist (Lot 5).

BEARD, Emma, 64, Owns farm, Widow, b. Ohio, parents b. Germany, occup. none; ***WALKER, Flossie***, dau., 28, Widow, b. Ohio, parents b. Ohio, occup. Clerk, Retail Drygoods; ***WALKER, Hazel***, Grand-daughter, 6, b. Ohio, parents b. Ohio; ***JAYCOX, Grace***, Grand-daughter, 15, attending school, b. Ohio, fr. b. Wisconsin, mo. b. Ohio. 1920 FC OH LOAV, p. 4A, lines, 11-14.

MRS. EMMA BEARD

Funeral services for ***Mrs. Emma BEARD***, 72, who died at her home in Avon Lake Saturday following an attack of heart trouble, will be held in Bay Village church, Stop 32, Lake rd., at 2 o'clock Tuesday afternoon. The

Rev. Endly will officiate. Interment will be in the family plot in Bay Village cemetery.

Mrs. Beard was a pioneer resident of Avon Lake, having resided there for more than 50 years. She was a member of the Presbyterian church of Cleveland.

She leaves one son, ***Clarence BEARD*** of Lakewood and two daughters, ***Mrs. Lulu JAYCOX*** of Wisconsin and ***Mrs. Flossie WALKER*** of Avon Lake. Five grandchildren, one great grandchild and two brothers, ***Frank LUCAS***, Columbus and ***William LUCAS***, California, also survive. Lorain Times-Herald, Lorain, OH, Monday, April 25, 1927, p. two, col. 5. *A similar obituary was found in the Lorain Journal, Mon., April 25, 1927, p. 2, col. 6, "Pioneer Avon Lake Resident is Dead. Mrs. Emma Beard, 72, Succumbs After Heart Attack."*

Emma V. BEARD, heart, d. 4/22/1927. Pease Funeral Home Records, Mss. 4809, Register of Funerals, 1927, Western Reserve Historical Society.

Emma Valara BEARD, 72, Avon Lake, Acute Indigest Pectoris, issued April 24, 1927. Bureau of Vital Statistics, Burial or Removal Permit, Bay Village, OH.

Children of Nelson Beard and Emma Lucas other than those buried with them:

Clarence BEARD, son of ***Nelson,*** was a very reserved and intelligent man, graduating from high school in Lorain and Dyke College in Cleveland. He was employed as Head Bookkeeper for the Acorn Refinery. He was married twice and there were no children from either marriage. He and his second wife lived on Wyandotte in Lakewood, OH. Hazel McCutcheon

Clarence W. BEARD, 36; res. 1592 Wyandotte Ave.; b. Avon Lake, O; occup. Clerk; fr. *Nelson*, mo. *Emma LUCAS;* no. of times previously married once; Div. 1917 C.P.Ct. Married ***Florence M. BLACKBURN***; 28; res. 1457 Woodward Ave.; b. Cleveland, O; occup. none; fr. *William H*., mo. *Hancy S. HUDSON*; never previously married. State of Ohio, Cuyahoga County, I Certify that on the 8th day of October 1921, ...were by me legally joined in marriage. Rev. W.S. Cook, Lakewood, O. Marriage Record, Cuyahoga County, OH, vol. 124, p 161.

Clarence W. BEARD, beloved husband of the late ***Florence M___ BLACKBURN***...former residence, 10109 Lake Ave.,...Klanke Funeral Parlor, 12629 Detroit Ave., Lakewood. Cleveland Necrology File, Oct 29, 1966.

BEARD, Florence M. (nee ***BLACKBURN***), beloved wife of ***Clarence W***., sister of *Harriett BLACKBURN*, aunt of *Robert W. MAST*, and *Mrs. Florence G. CALL*, residence. 10109 Lake Ave. The family will receive friends From 2 To 5 And 7 To 10 P. M. at Klanke Funeral Parlors. 12629 Detroit ave., Lakewood, where services will be held Monday, Apr 8th, at 1:30 p. m. Cleveland Press, Apr 6 1957.

Clarence and ***Florence BEARD*** are buried at Lakewood Park Cemetery, Rocky River, OH. Clarence died at the Oakridge Rest Home in Westlake on Oct 25, 1966, after a six month stay. He had been the Vice-Pres. of a paint manufacturing company. Ohio Certificate of Death, Division of Vital Statistics, 1966, certif. 075530.

Lulu BEARD JAYCOX, daughter of ***Nelson***, was born on Jaycox Road and married ***Lewis JAYCOX***. They had three children including a son, ***Flynn*** and a daughter, ***Grace***. They lived in the state of Oregon. Hazel Walker McCutcheon

Flossie and Hazel, her daughter, were living with her parent's in the 1920 census.

Flossie BEARD WALKER, daughter of ***Nelson,*** is remembered by her daughter as a hard-working , loving mother. She helped her mother on the farms and was employed part time with the Bailey Company. When her mother passed away, Flossie found she was unable to continue working due to family obligations. Tourists became her source of employment from this point on. Flossie had a sign in front of her home on Lake Avenue, that she would light every night, listing it as a "Tourist Home." Three rooms and bath were available upstairs, while she stayed on the first floor, with the price being $1.50-2.00 a night. The sign seemed to be enough and advertising was never needed, turning away those she was unsure of. Flossie continued to take in boarders until in her eighties, she died at 97 years of age *(conflicts with death certificate)*. Hazel Walker McCutcheon

Flossie BEARD WALKER, b. 28 Sept 1891, Avon Lake, Lorain Co., OH; divorced; 94 yrs. old, d. 20 Sept 1986, Lorain Community Hospital, Lorain, OH, of Cardiac Arrest; res. 31856 Lake Rd., Avon Lake, OH; informant Hazel McCutcheon; Burmeister Funeral Home, Avon Lake; bur. Elmhurst Park Cemetery, Avon, OH. Ohio Certificate of Death, Division of Vital Statistics, 1986, certif. 069521.

Lots 5/6-14 Arthur H. Beard

Arthur was the oldest son of Nelson Beard and Emma Lucas.

BEARD, Arthur; 1882, Jan 28th, Avon; 1 year, 4 mo.; b. Avon; cause of death Croup. Probate Court Death Records, Lorain County, Ohio, vol. 2, p. 28, line 1193.

Lots 5/6-14 Nelson Beard, II

Nelson was the fourth of six children of Nelson Beard and Emma Lucas.

Baby BAIRD, 5 wks.; res. Avon; interred Nov 2, 1887 in Lot 6. "List of Interments," Lakeside Cemetery, Bay Village, OH.

(Probably Nelson listed above. Refer to family tombstone that follows.)

Lots 5/6-14 Rolen Beard

Rolen was the fifth child of Nelson Beard and Emma Lucas.

Rollon BEARD, 6 mos.; res. Avon; interred July 20, 1890; Lot 6. "List of Interments," Lakeside Cemetery, Bay Village, OH.

Lot 7 *Owner: A. H. Tomanek of Avon purchased Dec 17, 1887, for $5.32* SL

Lots 7-15 John M. Tomanek

HUSBAND

A.H. TOMANEK, 69; res. Avon; German; interred Dec 18, 1887; Lot 7. "List of Interments," Lakeside Cemetery, Bay Village, OH.

The individual identified in the previous record is incorrect. According to the family, John Tomanek would be the individual buried here. A.H. Tomanek, as listed above, purchased the lot on Dec 17th for his father. A. H. is buried in Lake Shore Cemetery, Avon Lake, OH.

Johann M. and ***Antonie OLIVER THOMANEK*** (original spelling) (Antonie 1824-1911), arrived in Baltimore aboard the Leocadia with their four children on 26 June 1865. Their last residence was listed as Neurcisch, Bohemia. The children who traveled with them were: ***Johann***, 14, (b. Oct 1850, m. *Mary*, lived in Warren, living in Minnesota in 1914); ***Anna***, 13, (1852-1917, bur. Woodland Cem., Cleve., m. *John JIRILE* (b.1845, d. 1909)); ***Franz***, 7 (1859-1896) and ***Anton Henry*** ("A.H."), 5 (b. 17 May 1860, m. *Clara FREY*, d. Jan 1926). John and his son John were both coachmakers. The family settled in Cleveland, living at 186 Croton St., Cleveland, and moved to Avon Lake around 1876. John became a naturalized citizen on April 14, 1873. He and his son John, also living on Croton, worked for *Jacob LOWMAN and Son*, in the carriage trade.

After John's death in December of 1887, A.H. inherited the family farm of forty acres with all the stock and implements on Lake Road, Stop 45, Avon Lake, provided he care for his mother, Antonie, for the remainder of her life and was to pay his brothers and sister $750 compensation. She did live with him until her death in 1911. A.H. became a builder and developed 45 allotments in Avon Lake. The main street was to be called Tomanek but was recorded as Tomahawk, which is how it is referred to today. Nancy Veits and Donna DeChant.

In 1876 ***John TOMANEK*** bought 32 acres of what is now called Lake Road from *Albert* and *Abbie ALLYN*. Mary Jean Dunker, Letter to the Editor, undetermined newspaper, October 1991, Rose Hill Museum, Bay Village, OH.

I, ***John TOMANEK,*** hereby make my Last Will and Testament; living after me my son *John* shall receive $250.00. My daughter *Anna* shall receive $350.00. My son *Frank* shall receive $150.00 providing he returns home within three years....For my wife shall be secured $500.00 but should she live with our son *Anton* until her death, the said $500.00 shall then belong to him in consideration of which he shall provide for her until then. In case she cannot get along with him, he shall pay her the said $500.00 as she directs and she may dispose of the same as she chooses. Should Antone die sooner than his mother his successors shall pay her the said $500.00 on demand. She may also take everything that she has had possession of while there and go wherever she likes...The farm of forty acres with all the stock and implements shall belong to my son Anton after the lawful opening and reading of this my last Will. In consideration of which he shall pay his brothers and sister $750...Will dated Sept 27, 1887 *(witnessed by George SCHEIBLE, Lot 29)...* Application to Probate Will...John Tomanek, Avon who died 12 December 1887...Those listed: ***John TOMANEK***, son, Akron, Ohio; ***Anna JIRELE***, daughter, 21 Burwell St...Cleveland, Ohio; ***Anton TOMANEK***, son, Avon Lake; ***Frank TOMANEK***, son, address unknown. Will of John Tomanek, Late of Avon, Probate Court, Lorain Co., Ohio, Docket #4, page 104 and Record of Wills, vol. 9, p. 252.

Children of John Tomanek and Antonie Oliver:

In 1874, son ***Frank*** is mentioned as living on Trumbull and working as a laborer. He worked as a trimmer at Lowman's and lived on Croton St. with his father in 1875. By 1876 Frank is listed in the City Directory as being a cigar maker for *Alois PALDA* and then *F.E. KELSEY*. Cleveland City Directories, provided by Nancy Veits.

JIRELE, John, 30, Carriage & Wagon Manufacturing, b. Bohemia, fr. b. Bohemia, mo. b. Bohemia; ***Anna***, 28, wife, Keeping House, b. Moravia, fr. b. Moravia, mo. b. Moravia; ***Belena***, 4, daughter, b. Ohio; ***Victor***, 3, b. Ohio. 1880 FC OH CY Cleveland Ward 6, Croton Street, p. 182C, house 46, lines 28-31. *Possible family of John: John JIRELE*, 55, Widowed, Blacksmith, b. Bohemia; *Vincene*, 19, son, Moulder, b. Bohemia; *Anna*, 17, dau. b. Bohemia; *Otto*, 14, son, blacksmithing, b. Ohio; *Theodore*, 12, son, at school, b. Ohio living also on Croton St. 1880 FC OH CY Cleveland Ward 6, p. 184C, house 74.

JIRILE Family Plot: #1, ***John*** (father) 1848-1909; #2 ***Anna THOMANEK*** (mother) 1852-1917; #3, ***Belena*** (daughter) 1875-1895; #4 ***Victor*** (son)1876-1962 and *Aline GOUVY* (wife) 1862-1940. Woodland Cemetery, Cleveland, OH, as read by Nancy Veits.

Anton TOMANEK inherited the farm from John that was approximately 33 acres. The acreage was well cared for with a vineyard, apple and peach orchards in addition to berry patches of all varieties. Anton, a farmer, was called the "50 center" because he would sit on the front porch and give wine and 50 cents to passers by. He served as the postman and delivered mail once a week, a bugle would be sounded if there was mail for a family. Nancy Veits

TOMANEK-Anton H., beloved husband of ***Clara***, father of ***Robert, Frank, William, Carl*** and ***Mrs. Marie SCHULTZ***, Jan 18, age 64. Funeral from the late residence, Stop 44, Lake Road, Avon Lake Village, Thursday, Jan 21, 2 p.m. Cleveland Necrology File, Jan 21, 1926.

Carl J. TOMANEK was the second village fire marshall (1930's) and the first "motorcycle policeman." Mary Jean Dunker, October 1991, Letter to the Editor, Pamphlet file, Avon Lake Library.

Lake Shore Cemetery, Avon Lake, OH:
TOMANEK Anton H. 1860-1926; ***Clara*** 1862-1955; ***Frank*** 1889-1919.
William TOMANEK, Ohio, CPL Co. F. 112 Engineers, World War I, June 30 1891- Jan 14 1959.
Carl J. TOMANEK, Ohio, Pvt. 1 Cl. 112 Engrs. 37 Div., April 20 1898-April 5 1941.
Elizabeth C. TOMANEK, June 29, 1899-May 26, 1991. ***Valborg F. TOMANEK***, 1895-1993.
Robert Anton TOMANEK, Ohio, Pvt. U.S. Marine Corps, Oct 12, 1887-May 2, 1945. Cemetery inscriptions as read by Catherine Burke Flament. *Elizabeth and Valborg are daughters of Olaf and Louisa Malvena Aslaksen, Lot 18-1.*

Lot 7 Antonia Oliver Tomanek

no marker

Antonia, wife of John Tomanek, was living with her son Anton H. Tomanek in the following census.
TOMANEK, Antone, 40, b. May 1860, Moravia, parents b. Moravia; immig. 1865, No. yrs. in U.S. 35; married 14 years; ***Clare***, wife, 37, b. Oct 1862, Ohio, parents b. Germany, 5 children born, 5 living; ***Robert***, 12, son, b. Oct 1887; ***Frank***, 11, son, b. Jan 1889; ***William***, 8, son, b. Jan 1891; ***Mary***, 6, dau., b. Sept 1893; ***Karl***, 2, son, b. Apr 1898; all children b. in Ohio; ***Antoinette***, 73, mother, b. Dec 1826, Moravia, parents b. Moravia, immig. 1865, 5 children born, 3 living; *KOVAC, John*, 26, servant, b. May 1874, Bohemia, parents b. Bohemia, immig 1893, Al. 1900 FC OH LOAV pp 20A/B, lines 47-55.
TOMANEK, Antoinette *(wid. Jno.)*, Beach Park, Lake Shore Rd. ***TOMANEK, Antone H. (Clara)***, Beach Park, farmer, Lake Shore Rd. ***TOMANEK, Frank***, Beach Park, farmer. ***TOMANEK, Robt.***, Beach Park, farmer. 1910 Lorain County Rural Directory, Avon.
Antonia TOMANEK, d. Nov 6, 1911, Avon, Lorain Co. of Endocarditis and Bronchial Pneumonia after 4 days. Contributory: Chronic Rheumatism-Arthritis Deform__, Osteomelitis- long bones for years. b. Dec 25, 1824, foreign born; 86 yrs., 10 mo., 11 days, widowed, farmer's wife; fr. ***Frank OLIVA***, foreign born, mo. not known, foreign born.

Informant Mrs. Tomanek, Beach Park, Ohio. Bur. Dover, Bay Village, Nov 8, 1911; undertaker George J. Wagner, Avon, Ohio. Ohio Certificate of Death, Division of Vital Statistics, 1911, certif. 60066.
Antonia TOMENAK *(sp.)*; res. Avon; Bohemia; interred Nov 8, 1911; Lot 7. "List of Interments," Lakeside Cemetery, Bay Village, OH.
Antonia TOMANEK, 86, female, white, Endocarditis Bronchial Pneumonia, bur. Dover, Bay Village, removal via wagon, issued Nov 8, 1911, undertaker Geo. J. Wagner, Avon, O. Bureau of Vital Statistics, Burial or Removal Permit, Bay Village, OH.

Lot 8 *Owner: John Close of Dover purchased for $5.38*

SL

Lot 8-16 John Close

JOHN CLOSE
1875-1904
CLOSE

The State of Ohio, Cuyahoga County, ss. ***John CLOSE, Jr.***, 24, Dover, O., b. Berea, O., Merchant, fr. *John CLOSE*, mo. *Kate SCHMIDT*, prev. married none, applicant Frank Sites. Married ***Josephine SUNK***, 23, Dover, O., b. Dover, O., occup none, fr. *Louis SUNK*, mo. *Freda NIGHT*, prev. married none. Marriage solemnized by Rev. Vernon W. Wager, Dover, O. I Certify, That on the 22nd day of Feby, 1900 John Close and Josephine Sunk were by me legally joined in marriage. Marriage Record, Cuyahoga County, vol. 50, p. 103.
CLOSE, John, 23, head, b. June 1876, Ohio, parents b. Germany, clerk, years married 0; ***Josephine***, 23, wife, b. June 1876, Ohio, parents b. Germany, no children. 1900 FD CYDO, p. 9A, line 43-44. *John and Josephine were living nextdoor to her father.*
John CLOSE; res. Dover; German; interred Feb 10, 1904; Lot 8. "List of Interments," Lakeside Cemetery, Bay Village, OH.

Wife of John Close, Josephine Sunk Close Braise:
John was the son-in-law of Louis Sunk and Friedrieka Frank/Night/ (Lot 60). After his death, Josephine, his wife, married Arthur Brais, widower of Jenny Mary Vogt (buried at Lakeside in an undetermined lot) on 10 Nov 1909 (MR). Arthur died July 19, 1923, in Bay Village (Cleveland NF), there were no children listed in the 1920 census. It is also interesting to note that Josephine's husband and father both died in the same year, 1904.
BRAIS: Josephine M., residence, 528 Dover rd., Bay Village, wife of the late ***Arthur***, sister of ***Mrs. John MOORMANN, John SUNK, Mrs. Emil VAN DORN*** and ***Mrs. Charles BAILEY***. Now at Clifford Pease Funeral Home, 2914 Dover Center rd., Westlake, Ohio, where services will be held Monday, Dec. 1, at 3 p. m. Cleveland Necrology File, Nov 30 1941, reel 009.
Mrs. Josephine M. BRAIS, 528 Dover Center Rd., Bay, Ohio; 65 yrs. 5 mos. 14 days., widowed, husband:

Arthur; b. 14 June 1876, Dover, O.; fr. ***Ludwig SUNK***, b. Germany, mo. Do not know; d. Nov 28, 1941, of an acute hemorrhage and bronchopneumonia while living at 528 Dover Center. Funeral firm Clifford Pease, bur. Evergreen Cemetery, Westlake, OH, Section O, Lot 27, grave 3, Lot owner: *John SUNK*. Ohio Certificate of Death, Division of Vital Statistics, 1941, certif. 65394 and Evergreen Cemetery, Westlake, OH.

Lot 9 *Owner: Krumwiede purchased for $5.82* SL

Lot 9-17 Katherine Quell Krumwiede

KATE KRUMWIEDE
1870-1904

Katherine (Kate) Marie QUELL KRUMWIEDE, was the oldest child of ***Henry*** and ***Anne QUELL***. In the 1870 census they were living in Cleveland, Ward 11 (p. 39, roll 1192). Her siblings included: Twins: ***Jewel,*** never m. and ***Lydia*** m. *Paul WAGNER*; ***Hulda*** m. *William HAAG* and ***Henry***, d. Westlake, res. Rocky River, 88 yrs., m. *Louise HABER*. She married ***Louie KRUMWIEDE*** (b. 24 May 1867, Dover, Cuyahoga Co., OH), son of *William KRUMWIEDE* and *Sophia SCHARNHARST (OP 5:1)* in Cleveland, Ohio. Kate died during the summer of 1904 of a ruptured appendix at Huron Rd. Hospital, leaving five children; ***Lillian "Sophie"*** *(Lot 9:19)*, ***Will, Arthur, Louise*** and ***Leslie*** *(Lot 9:19)*. Leslie and Lillian are both buried in this lot. Just before Kate died, she pointed up and said, " There's ***Herbie***," this was the name of her son who had died before her. When Kate died, the children went to live with Kate's mother in Cleveland at W. 67th and Hope. This was the same home where Leslie, another child of Kate's, had died.

Her husband, Louie, later married ***Nellie BRUGGERS***, who was ten years older than their daughter Sophie. Nellie was the widow of *George BRUGGERS* (b. 16 Dec 1874, Deaconess Hosp., Cleveland, OH; m. 4 June 1902, probably, Cuyahoga County; d. 25 May 1906, Deaconess Hosp., bur. Monroe Street Cemetery, Cleveland, OH) and they had a daughter, *Dorothy Helen BRUGGERS* (b. 20 June 1905, Dover; d. 5 Oct 1993; m. *James HINKEL*). Louie died October 1, 1945 in Wakeman, Huron County, Ohio. He is buried in the family plot at Birmingham Cemetery, Birmingham (Wakeman area), OH, along with Nellie, ***Kenneth KRUMWIEDE***, their son and Kenneth's wife, *Hazel. Another child of Louie and Nellie is buried in the Original Part, see "Undetermined Lots."* Esther Seitz Matousek

The State of Ohio, Cuyahoga County, ss. I Certify that on the 16th day of July 1889 ***Mr. Louie KRUMWIEDE*** and ***Miss Katie QUELL*** were by me legally joined in marriage. A.W. Koprittke Marriage Record, Cuyahoga County, vol. 33, p. 245.

KRUMWIEDE, Lewis, 33, head, b. May 1867, Ohio, parents b. Germany; farmer, married 11 yrs., owned farm with mortgage; ***Katie***, 28, wife, b. Nov 1871, Ohio, parents b. Germany, 4 children born, 3 living; ***Sopha (sp.)***, 8, dau., b. Nov 1891, Ohio; ***William***, 7, son, b. Jan 1893, Ohio; ***Arthur***, 5, son, b. Apr 1895, Ohio. 1900 FC OH CYDO, p. A22, lines 32-36.

KRUMWEIDE, Katie, 33, white, female, mother; b. Cleveland; res. Dover, Ohio, d. Huron St. Hos., duration 3 ds., cause appendicitis, fr. b. Ger., mo. b. Ger.; Dover Cemetery, Ohio; phys. J.C. Wood; undertaker Geo. C. Lang. June 29, 1904. CRD, film 1977439.

KRUMWIEDE-Katherine M. QUELL, beloved wife of ***Louie KRUMWIEDE***, at Huron Street hospital, aged 33 years. Funeral Friday at 1:30 p.m. sun time, from Second U.B. church, Elton and Dudley streets. July 1, 1904. The Plain Dealer.

Parents of Kate Quell Krumwiede:

QUELL, Henry, 30, Worker-lumberyard, b. Hanover, parents foreign born; ***Anna***, 21, Keeping house, b. Hanover, parents foreign born; *FINK, Margaretta*, 17, b. Ohio, parents foreign born. 1870 FC OH CY Cleveland, Ward 11, p. 39.

QUELL, Henry, 1840-1916, Age 76, West Park Cemetery, Cleveland, Ohio. cem. rec. Cleveland Necrology File.

QUELL: Anna M., age 88 years, widow of the late ***Henry***, mother of ***Henry, Julia, Mrs. Lydia E. WAGNER*** and

Mrs. Hulda M. HAAG. Friends may call at the home of the daughter Mrs. Wagner, at 2067 Arthur ave., Lakewood, O. after Sunday noon. Funeral services at the First United Brethren Church, W. 42 and Orchard st., Monday, Nov 29, at 2:30 p.m. Cleveland Necrology File, Nov 29 1937.

Siblings of Kate Quell Krumwiede:

Henry QUELL, Jr., 26, res. 14 Hope St., b. Cleveland, occup. patternmaker, fr. *Henry QUELL*, mo. *Anna VIETS*. Married ***Louise HABER***, 23, res. Dover, O., b. same, fr. *Philip HABER;* mo. *Lizzie KRUMWIDDE (sp.)*, 29 Nov 1905. The State of Ohio, Cuyahoga County, ss. I Certify, That on the 29 day of Nov 1905 Henry Quell and Lizzie Krumwidde were by me legally joined in marriage. Marriage Record, Cuyahoga County, vol. 62, p. 203. *Lizzie is the daughter of William and Sophia Krumwiede, OP 5:1.*

Henry QUELL, b. 21 Dec 1878, fr. ***Henry QUELL***, mo. ***Anna VEITS***; res. 1331 Linda St., Rocky River; occup. Wood pattern maker (Ret.) at Wellman Engineering; d. 24 Sept 1967 at the Oakridge Nursing Home, Westlake, OH; Funeral Director, Roger Baker, 206 Front St., Berea, bur. Westpark Cemetery, Cleveland. Informant *Wesley QUELL*, 19218 Davinwood, Cleveland 35, Ohio. Ohio Certificate of Death, Division of Vital Statistics, 1967, certif. 067258.

Julia E. QUELL, d. 12/4/60, Otterbein Home Hospital, Lebanon, Warren Co., OH, length of stay 3 1/2 mo. of Cerebral thrombosis, heart disease; 76 yrs. old; usual res. farm, outside city limits, Berea, OH; never married; b. 2/17/84, Cleveland, Ohio; fr. ***Henry QUELL***, mo. ***Anna VIETS***; nurse; funeral home: Johnsons, 115 N. Broadway, Lebanon; bur. 12/6/60, Otterbein Cemetery, Lebanon, R #1. Ohio Certificate of Death, Division of Vital Statistics, 1960, certif. 092492.

Lydia Elizabeth QUELL, 23, res. 6712 Hope Ave., S.W.; b. Cleveland, fr. *Henry QUELL*, mo. *Anna VIETZ*. Married ***John Paul SCHINSKY***, 26, res. Cincinnati, O., b. Henrietta., O., occup. Asst. Supt., fr. *John SCHINSKY*, mo. *Catherine BECKER*; neither previously married. Lydia Elizabeth Quell and John Paul Schinsky were legally married on 26 June 1907, Cuyahoga County, O. Marriage Record, Cuyahoga County, OH, vol. 66, p. 427.

Lydia E. WAGNER, d. Sept 22, 1969, 1:30 p.m., East Haven Nursing Home, Elyria, Lorain Co., 85 yrs., cause: Acute Coronal Occlusion, Heart Disease; m. ***J. Paul WAGNER***; b. Feb 17-84, Cleveland, O.; fr. ***Henry QUELL***, mo. ***Anna VEITS***; res. 405 20th Ave., N.E., St. Petersburg, Florida; Daniel's Funeral Home, Lakewood, Ohio; bur. Lakewood Park Cemetery, Rocky River, Ohio; informant Mr. J. Paul Wagner, 405 20th Ave., N.E., St. Petersburg, Florida. Ohio Certificate of Death, Division of Vital Statistics, 1969, certif. 069646.

Hulda QUELL, 20, 6712 Hope Ave., b. Cleveland, fr. *Henry QUELL*, mo. *Anna VIETZ*. Married ***William C. HAAG***, 26, res. 2217 West 33rd St., b. Middleburg, Ohio, clerk, fr. *Andrus*, mo. *Barbara BECKER*; neither previously married. The State of Ohio, Cuyahoga County, ss. I Certify, That on the 22nd day of June 1910 Hulda Quell and William C. Haag were by me legally joined in marriage. Marriage Record, Cuyahoga County, OH, vol. 75, p. 328. *William Haag is the brother of Leonard C. Haag, son-in-law of George Scheible and Rosie Solomon (Lot 29), father of the infant buried with them.*

Hulda HAAG, d. 3-29-69, Lorain Community Hospital, Lorain, Lorain Co., OH; cause: Medullary depression, toxemia, uremia; 79 yrs., b. Jan 20, 1890, OH.; fr. ***Henry QUELL***, mo. ***Anna VEITS***; widowed; Baker Funeral Home, 206 Front Street, Berea; bur. Apr 1, 1969, Woodvale Cemetery, Middleburg Heights, Ohio. Ohio Certificate of Death, Division of Vital Statistics, 1969, certif. 020711.

Children of Kate Quell and Louis Krumwiede:

Lillian Sophia KRUMWIEDE, b. 19 Nov 1890, Dover; d. 19 Oct 1974; m. 30 Jan 1913, Cuyahoga Co. to *"Jay" Henry William SEITZ (buried this lot)*. ***William H. KRUMWIEDE***, b. [8] Jan 1893, Dover; d. 20 Dec 1975, Bradenton, FL; m. *Amie HUNT [presumed same individual* b. 23 Nov 1893, d. Jan 1982, res. Bradenton, FL] . ***Arthur E. KRUMWIEDE***, b. [3]Apr 1895, Dover; d. 29 Nov 1975, Avon Lake, OH, bur. Avon, OH; m.1 27 Apr 1916, Cuyahoga Co. to *Phoebe THOMPSON* (b. 28 July 1895, Dover Twp., d. 22 Apr 1969, Nursing home in Avon, res. Olmsted Falls, OH, bur. Avon); m.2 1970 to *Helen NAZEL*. ***Margaret Louise KRUMWIEDE***, b. 3 Oct 1900, Dover; d. 10 Oct 1991, Lorain Co.; m.1 30 Oct 1920, Bay Village, *Glenn Irving BEARD* (b. 5 Oct 1898, d. 16 Feb 1962, Lorain Co., OH); m.2 9 Nov 1967, *William ARCHIBALD* (d. 12 Mar 1974). ***Stillborn girl KRUMWIEDE***. ***Leslie KRUMWIEDE***, b. cSept 1903, d. 7 Feb 1905. ***Herbert KRUMWIEDE****, died before his mother in 1904.* Esther Seitz Matousek, Carol P. Reed and [Social Security Records].

Following in the footsteps of their grandfather, ***William H.*** and ***Arthur E. KRUMWIEDE*** became carpenters and builders. There are fine Krumwiede-built homes all over the west side of Cleveland and Bay Village today, Nantucket Row and Winston Drive being two fine examples. Bay Village Historical Society, Bay Village: A Way of Life, p. 53.

William H. KRUMWIEDE, age 82, passed away Saturday, December 20 at Bradenton, Fla. Formerly of Lakewood. Beloved husband of ***Amie*** (nee *HUNT*). Father of ***Katherine PASCOE*** of Sarasota, Fla., and the late ***Martha BLASE***. Grandfather of five, great-grandfather of two. Brother of ***Louise ARCHIBALD, Dorothy HINKEL, Kenneth*** and the late ***Sophia SEITZ*** and ***Arthur***. The family suggests contributions may be made to The American Cancer Society. Funeral services Tuesday, December 23 at 1:30 p.m. at the Jenkins Funeral C hapel, 2914 Dover Center Rd., Westlake, where friends may call from noon until service time Tuesday. Dec 22, 1975. The Plain Dealer.

Arthur E. KRUMWIEDE, 21, Bay Village, b. same, Carpenter, fr. *Louie,* mo. *Kate QUELL*. Married ***Phoebe B. THOMPSON***, 21, res. Bay Village, b. Dover, occup. none, fr. *Henry A.*, mo. *Nellie BAKER*, neither previously married. The State of Ohio, Cuyahoga County, ss. I Certify, That on the 27th day of April 1916 Arthur E. Krumwiede and Phoebe B. Thompson were by me legally joined in marriage. D.W. Knight Marriage Record, Cuyahoga County, OH, vol. 96, p. 255.

KRUMWIEDE, Arthur E., 35, renting home for $30/month, owns radio, age at marriage 21, b. Ohio, parents b. Ohio, Builder home construction; ***Phoebe***, wife, 39, age at marriage 21, b. Ohio, fr. b. Dublin, Ireland, mo. b. Pennsylvania; ***Robert***, son, 11, b. Ohio; ***Lawrence T.***, 7, b. Ohio. 1930 FC OH CYBV ED 18-534, 29724 Lake Road, p. 19A, lines 1-4.

Arthur E. KRUMWIEDE of 33089 Lake Rd., Avon Lake, husband of ***Helen***, father of ***Robert*** and ***Lawrence***, brother of ***William, Kenneth, Louise ARCHIBALD, Dorothy HINKEL***, grandfather of 11, great-grandfather of 12. Funeral services Tuesday, Dec 2 at 2:30 p. m. Friends may call at The Burmeister County Line Funeral Home, 32000 Detroit Rd. (Rt. 254). Avon, O. Dec 2, 1975. The Plain Dealer.

Phoebe B. KRUMWIEDE, 7601 River Rd., Olmsted Falls, wife of ***Arthur E.***, mother of ***Robert A., Lawrence***, sister of *Clara C. FOULDS*, grandmother of 13, great-grandmother of nine. Funeral service 11 a.m. Wednesday, Apr 23. Friends may call at The Burmeister County Line Funeral Home, 32000 Detroit Rd. (Rt. 254), Avon, O., 2-4 And 7-9 P. M. Tuesday. Cleveland Press, Apr 22 1969.

Glenn I. BEARD, 24, res. Avon Lake, b. same, farmer, fr. *Charles*, mo. *Malinda TITUS*. Married ***Margaret L. KRUMWIEDE***, 20, res. Bay Village, b. same, occup. none, fr. *Louis*, mo. *Catherine QUELL*, neither previously married. I Certify, That on the 30th day of October 1920 Glenn I. Beard and Margaret L. Krumwiede were by me legally joined in marriage. Rev. Virgil E. Turner Marriage Record, Cuyahoga County, vol. 120, p. 107.

BEARD, Charles I 1853-1933, ***Malinda C.*** 1857-1945. Lake Shore Cemetery, Avon Lake, Ohio, as read by Catherine Burke Flament.

Lot 9 Leslie Krumwiede no marker

Leslie KRUMWEIDE is the son of ***Louis KRUMWEIDE*** and ***Kate QUELL***. Esther Seitz Matousek

KRUMWEIEDE, Leslie, 17 mos., male, single, b. Ohio, cause of death convulsions, res. 14 Hope, Ward 2, place of death res., duration of illness 2 ds., fr. b. Ohio, mo. b. Ohio, cemetery Dover Lake, phys. Dr. Summers, undertaker Geo. C. Lang. February 7, 1905. CRD: film 1977439.

Leslie KRUMWEIDE, 17 mo.; res. Bay Village; German; interred Feb 9th, 1905; Lot 9; Original Part. "List of Interments," Lakeside Cemetery, Bay Village, OH. *Lot 9 is not in the Original Part. It is assumed that Leslie is here.*

Lot 9 Infant Krumwiede no marker

____ ***KRUMWEIDE***, res. Bay Village, German, listed after 1903, interred Lot 9. "List of Interments," Lakeside Cemetery, Bay Village, OH.

Lot 9 Infant Krumwiede no marker

____ ***KRUMWEIDE***, res. Bay Village, German, listed after 1904, interred, Lot 9. "List of Interments," Lakeside Cemetery, Bay Village, OH.

Both of the infants listed previously are presumed children of ***Louis KRUMWIEDE*** and ***Kate QUELL***. One of them is probably ***Herbie KRUMWIEDE***, who died before his mother Kate. The other is the twin sister of ***Leslie*** or ***Herbie***. The baby was stillborn. Two infants' graves are located below the Burkos'. Esther Seitz Matousek.

No birth records were found for a Krumwiede from 1895-5 in Cleveland.

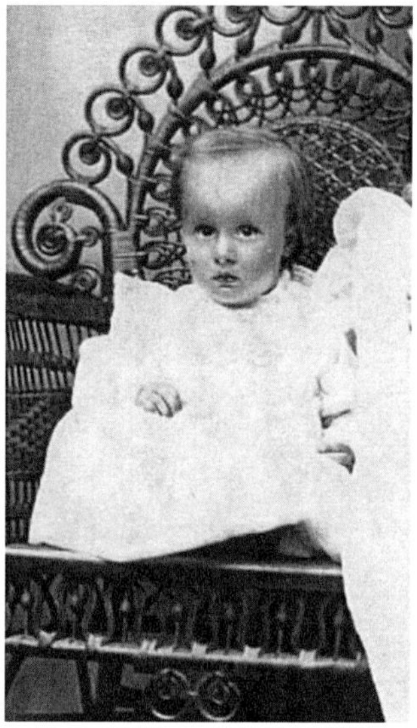

Photo of Herbert (Herbie) Krumwiede.

Lot 9-18 Burko Marker

BURKO
FATHER MOTHER
WALTER W. ELEANOR L.
1915-1994 1916-1992
IN LOVING MEMORY

Lot 9-18 Walter William Burko

Walter (Bill) William BURKO was born March 3, 1915, son of ***John BURKO*** and ***Domicela ZABOLOTNY*** (b. 14 Au 1873, Poland) in Holyoke, Mass. He was raised in Cleveland. He married ***Eleanor SEITZ*** and moved to Rock Creek, Ohio to raise their children. In later years they lived in Westlake on Marview Dr. He was a member of the Masonic Lodge and Eastern Star. Esther Seitz Matousek

BURKO, ***Walter W. BURKO, Sr.***, beloved husband of the late ***Eleanor*** (nee ***SEITZ***), dear father of ***Robert*** (wife *Jenne*), ***Edythe MAYABB (Mrs. John), Patricia MCCASKEY (Mrs. Coleman), Walter William Jr.*** (wife *Lyn*), ***Dee LOCKRIDGE, Richard,*** and ***Peggy HEIDECKER (Mrs. Tom)***, brother of ***Anne KOTULA (Mrs. Mike)***, and ***Helen KORYNOSKI (Mrs. Nick)***, grandfather and great-grandfather. Memorial services Saturday, Feb 26 at 3 p.m. at Jenkins Funeral Chapel, 2914 Dover Center Rd., Westlake. Feb 24, 1994, Section C, p. 7. The Plain Dealer.

Walter W. BURKO, Sr. buried May 5, 1994, Lot 9. Cemetery Listing, not in ledger.

Photograph reprinted with permission by Olan Mills Portrait Studio.

Lot 9-18 Eleanor Louise Seitz Burko

Eleanor Louise BURKO was the daughter of ***Jay Henry William SEITZ*** and ***Lillian Sophia KRUMWIEDE*** *(this lot).* She was born July 17, 1916, in Cleveland. When she was a year old the family moved to Bay Village. She was named valedictorian as a graduating senior and would go on to college. Eleanor graduated from Western Reserve, Flora Stone Mather in Cleveland. She married Bill and after raising her children returned to the work force. She was an active member of Eastern Star in Rock Creek and Westlake. Esther Seitz Matousek

BURKO, ***Eleanor Louise BURKO*** (nee ***SEITZ***), age 76, beloved wife of ***Walter William BURKO, Sr.***, dear mother of ...*(see Walter above)*, dear sister of ***Esther MATOUSEK*** and the late ***Raymond*** and ***Wilbur SEITZ***. Funeral services to be held Saturday, July 25 at 11 a.m. at Jenkins Funeral Chapel, 2914 Dover Center Rd., Westlake where friends may call 2-4 and 7-9, Friday. 23 July 1992, section C, p. 3, col. 2. The Plain Dealer.

Eleanor Louise BURKO died 7-21-92 in Westlake, OH of cardiopulmonary arrest. Ohio Department of Health, Burial Transit Permit, Bay Village, OH.

Lot 9-19 Seitz Marker

SEITZ

FATHER	MOTHER
JAY H.W.	LILLIAN S.
1885-1950	1890-1974

THE LORD IS MY SHEPHERD

Lot 9-19 Jay Henry William Seitz

Jay Henry William SEITZ was born July 18, 1885, the son of ***Henry August SEITZ*** (b. Nov 24, 1843, Germany; m. 16 Dec 1869, Cleveland; d. April 29, 1925, Bay Village) and ***Susanne Catherine BARTCHY*** (b. March 5, 1847, OH; d. Oct 29, 1937, Bay Village). ***Lillian*** became his bride in 1913 and they moved to Dover in 1917. Jay had two sisters, ***Anna***, who married *John RUMBAUGH, (see Lot 58-4)* and ***Erdine***, who married *Hugo DRANSE (info Lot 9).*

Jay and his wife ***Sophie*** were great baseball fans and loved to go to the Cleveland Indians' games. They originally attended games at League Park and continued when the original stadium was built downtown along the lake. He died suddenly April 7, 1950, as he was returning to work following a visit to the Old Stone Church in Cleveland on his lunch hour.

Jay and Lillian had four children:

Wilbur Lawrence, b. Oct 1913, bur. April 1915 *(buried OP)*. ***Eleanor Louise*** *(bur. this lot).* ***Raymond Warren***, b. 16 May 1920, Bay Village; m. *Victoria Patricia BAJOREK* (dau. of *Andrew BAJOREK* and *Josephine*

MIGALA; b. 21 Aug 1915, Cleveland; d. 6 Jan 1992, Cleveland; bur. Holy Cross Cemetery) 11 Nov 1950, Cleveland; d. 8 Dec 1952, Cleveland, bur. Holy Cross Cemetery, Brook Park, OH and ***Esther Ruth*** (living).

Their son worked at Bay Sweet Shop as the "soda jerk" when he was young.

Their home was on Foote Road near Bassett. Esther Seitz Matousek

Jay H. W. SEITZ, 27, res. 10717 Hathaway Ave., b. Cleveland, O., occup. clerk, fr. *Henry A.*, mo. *Susan C. BARTCHY.* Married ***Sophia KRUMWIEDE***, 22, res. Bay Village, Ohio, b. Bay Village, occup. none, fr. *Louis*, mo. *Katherine QUELL*, neither previously married. The State of Ohio, Cuyahoga Co., ss., I Certify, That on the 30th day of January 1913 Jay H.W. Seitz and Sophia Krumwiede were by me legally joined in marriage. Rev. J. Grant Walter Marriage Record, Cuyahoga County, OH, vol. 83, p. 375.

SEITES** (sp.)**, Jay, Foote Ave. (at Bassett Rd.) 35, b. Ohio, fr. b. Germany, mo. b. Ohio, bookkeeper at bank; ***Sophie***, wife, 29, b. Ohio, parents b. Ohio; ***Elenor** (sp.)*, dau., 3 5/12, b. Ohio. 1920 FC OH CYBV p. 6A.

SEITZ, Jay H., 44, owns home valued at $10,000, owns radio, age at marriage 27, b. Ohio, parents b. Germany, teller Bank Co.; ***Sophia***, wife, 39, age at marriage 22, b. Ohio, parents b. Ohio....1930 FC OH CYBV, ED 18-534, 29617 Foote Road, p. 19A, lines 5-9.

SEITZ, Jay H.W. of 3039 W. 51 St., beloved husband of ***Sophia***, father of ***Raymond SEITZ, Mrs. Eleanor BURKO, Mrs. Esther SULTER***, and grandfather, brother of the late ***Erdina*** and ***Ann***; suddenly Friday afternoon. Friends may call at the Geo. C. Lang Funeral Home, W. 95th at Lorain Ave. where services will be held Monday, April 10 at 1 p.m. Cleveland Necrology File, April 10, 1950.

Lot 9-19 Lillian Sophia Krumwiede Seitz

Sophie (***Lillian***) is the daughter of ***Louis KRUMWIEDE*** and ***Katherine Marie (Kate) QUELL*** *(this lot)*. Sophie was a homemaker who enjoyed baking and would sell bakery: kuchen, pecan rolls and bread to others. *Florence DIETZ*, the principal of Forestview School in Bay, tasted her bread after coming for dinner one night and asked to buy it. Bread was going for 9 cents a loaf at the time, she offered to pay 25 cents and would come from Lakewood to buy two loaves every two weeks. Sophie died of breast cancer. Esther Seitz Matousek

SEITZ - Lillian (Sophie) SEITZ** (nee **KRUMWIEDE**)*, beloved wife of the late ***Jay, dear mother of ***Eleanor BURKO (Mrs. W. William), Esther BITSKO***, and the late ***Raymond*** and ***Wilbur***. Grandmother and great-grandmother, sister of ***Will, Arthur, Louise ARCHIBALD, Dorothy HINKEL***, and ***Kenneth***. Funeral services Tuesday, Oct 22, at 2 P.M. at Jenkins Funeral Chapel, 2914 Dover Center Rd., Westlake, where friends may call from 2-4 and 7-9 P.M. Monday. Oct 21, 1974. The Plain Dealer.

Lillian S. SEITZ, d. Oct 19, 1974 at Parma General Hospital, Cuyahoga Co., Ohio, age 83, funeral director Charles J. Lokar, 2914 Dover Center Rd., Westlake, O. Bureau of Vital Statistics, Burial or Removal Permit, Bay Village, OH.

Lot 9 *Wilbur Lawrence Seitz no marker

***Wilbur Lawrence SITES** (sp.)*, 19 mo.; res. Bay Village; German; interred Apr 15, 1915. "List of Interments," Lakeside Cemetery, Bay Village, OH. *Wilbur is not listed as being buried in a specific lot in cemetery records, it is assumed he is buried here with his parents, Jay H. W. SEITZ and Lillian "Sophie" Krumwiede.*

The Seitz family lived at 10717 Hathaway, Cleveland, OH. ***Wilbur***, born in October of 1913, was their first-born child. Just before his death, Wilbur had gone with his mother, ***Sophie***, to her parents' home on Walker Road so that she could help look after them. He had a cold when they left which became worse. Just before Wilbur died in his mother's arms, he pointed up. Esther Seitz Matousek

Lot 9 *Erdine Seitz Dranse* no marker

Buried Lakeview Cemetery, Cleveland, OH.

Erdine DRANSE is listed on the cemetery plot map. There may have been preliminary plans for Erdine to be buried at Lakeside. *Her brother, Jay H.W. Seitz (this lot) and nephew, Sterling Rumbaugh, (lot 58-4) are buried here.* Plot map, Lakeside Cemetery, Bay Village, OH.

Erdine SEITZ DRANSE is buried at Lakeview Cemetery, Cleveland, Ohio, with her husband, ***Hugo***, and parents, ***Henry August SEITZ***, and ***Susanne Catherine BARTCHY*** *(see Lot 9:19)*. She was never interred here. She was the sister of ***Jay H.W. SEITZ*** *(buried this lot)*. Erdine Elizabeth was born on Sept 15, 1870, in Alliance, OH. She married ***Hugo H. DRANSE*** (b. 5 Oct 1870, Cleveland) who died of small pox on March 30, 1904, in Cleveland. He was a private in the 5th Regiment of the Ohio National Guard. They had a daughter, ***Hazel Ramona DRANSE*** (b. 14 Nov 1898, Cleveland; d. 19 Nov 1970, Cleveland), who married ***Martin Heinrich Wilhelm ALBERS***, 25 June 1921 in Bay Village. Erdine died March 21, 1950 at home on Foote Rd. in Bay Village, of heart failure. Evelyn Albers Badt

The State of Ohio, Cuyahoga County, ss. I Certify that one the 20th day of Oct 1897 ***Hugo H. DRANSE*** and ***Erdine E. SEITZ*** were legally joined in marriage. Rev. Wilson

R. Stearly. Marriage Record, Cuyahoga County, OH, vol. 45, p. 448.

SITES** (sp. Seitz), **Henry A., 77, married, immigrated 1859, Naturalized citizen 1869, b. Beveria *(Bavaria)*, mother tongue German; parents both b. Beveria, fruit farmer; ***Susan C***., 63, b. Ohio, parents b. Switzerland; ***Erdine DRANSE***, 49, widow, occup. none; *Hazel,* niece, 21, single, b. Ohio, parents b. Ohio, stenographer at Furnace Co.; *DUNCAN, Elizabeth*, sister-in-law, 70, Widow, b. Ohio, occup. none, Bassett Rd. 1920 FC OH CYBV, p. 6B.

DRANSE ***Erdine E. DRANSE*** (nee ***SEITZ***), age 79 years, beloved wife of the late ***Hugo***; mother of ***Mrs. Hazel ALBERS***, and grandmother; sister of ***Anna RUMBAUGH*** (deceased), and ***Jay SEITZ***. Friends may call at the Clifford Pease Funeral Home, 2914 Dover Center Rd., Westlake. Services at Bay Methodist Church (Lake Rd., Bay Village) Thursday, March 23, at 1:30 p.m. Burial at Lake View Cemetery. Cleveland Necrology File, March 22, 1950.

Erdine Elizabeth SEITZ DRANSE was born Sept 15, 1870, Alliance, Ohio; d. March 21, 1950, Bay Village, OH. Cause of death: heart failure. Ohio Certificate of Death, Division of Vital Statistics, 1950, certif. 14828.

Single grave between Lots 9 and 10.

Lot 9/10-20 Johannes Frederick Schulz

HIER RUHET IN
ERFIEDEN
JOHANNES F.
SCHULZ
GEST
DEN 9 FEB 1886
ALTER
66 JAHRE 2
MONATE

SCHULZ

Translation from German
HERE RESTS IN
PEACE
JOHN F. SCHULZ
DIED
9 FEB 1886
AGE
66 YEARS 2
MONTHS

John is not listed on the "List of Interments." Honored as a Civil War veteran, no pension or disability records were found. The following may be his service record:

Thirty-Seventh Infantry, Company H. ***John SCHULTZ***, enlisted Oct 16, 1861. Mustered out with the Reg. History of Cuyahoga County, p. 105.

SCHULZ, Frank, 44, farmer; Value of Real Estate $2,000, Value of Personal Estate $300; b. Germany, both parents foreign born; ***Merio** (sp.),* 42, keeping house; b. Germany; __ *(line for last name)* ***Marie***, 13; ***Mary***, 11; ***Anna***, 9; ***Cathrine***, 6; all children b. Ohio. 1870 FC OH CYDO, p. 256, lines 39-40 and p. 257, lines 1-4. *Living next to Rudolph Scholl.*

SCHULTZ, Frederick, 59, farmer, b. Prussia, parents b. Prussia; ***Mary***, 53, wife, b. Hanover, parents b. Hanover; ***Kate***, 16, daughter, at home, b. Ohio, fr. b. Prussia, mo. b. Hanover. 1880 FC OH CYDO p. 100A, lines 47-49, house 335.

SCHULTZ, Frederick. Owned land; Acres: Improved - 21 tilled, including fallow and grass, 9 permanent meadows, Unimproved - 2 woodland. Farm Values: Land - $2500, Machinery - $100, Live Stock - $100. Estimated value of all farm production: $300. Grass lands: acreage: 5 mown, 6 not mown, 5 tons hay. 1 horse, 2 milch cows, 1 other, 2 calves dropped, 1 cattle sold living. 200 pounds of butter made on the farm. 1 swine. 25 barnyard poultry on farm, 110 dozen eggs produced in 1879. Indian corn: 4 acres, 100 bushels; Oats: 2 acres, 60 bushels; rye: 1 acre, 20 bushels; wheat: 2 acres, 30 bushels; potatoes: 1 acres, 100 bushels. Orchards - apple: 6 acres. Amount of wood cut: 20 cords, Value of forest products - $15. "Schedule 2. Production of Agriculture in Dover Township, Cuyahoga County, OH," enumerated June, 1880, p. 36.

John F. SCHULZ married ***Maria Clara POTTING UHLMANSIEK SCHMIDT***, 18 February 1869 in Dover Township, Ohio at St. Paul Lutheran Church, it was her third marriage. John died 9 Feb 1886. She was from Barkhausen, Germany. The Schulz's never had children of their own. Mary Clara Potting's first husband was *Ernst UHLMANSIEK* of Wehringsdorf, Germany. They married at Zion Lutheran Church on 6 Sept 1855 and would have four daughters: ***Clara Marie UHLMANSIEK***, b. 14 Jan 1857, m. *Ernst Henry KOENIG* 6 July 1876, Trinity Lutheran Church; ***Maria Eleoner UHLMANSIEK***, b. 19 Sept 1859, m. *John Frederick HEIL* at Trinity Lutheran Church; ***Anna Eleonore UHLMANSIEK***, b. 14 Aug 1861, m. *William FANGMEIER* at Trinity Lutheran; ***Katherina Maria UHLMANSIEK***, b. 29 Nov 1863, m. *Frederick Johann ALBERS,* 10 Feb 1887, St. Paul's Lutheran Church, Dover Township, OH. Ernst died 7 Sept 1863 and is buried at Erie Street Cemetery. Her second husband was *Henry William SCHMIDT*, they were married at St. Paul's Lutheran Church, Dover Township, Ohio on 31 March 1864. Henry died in December 1867. The Schulz's lived on Bassett Rd. at the Railroad tracks. Mary Clara died 15 June 1888 and was buried at Monroe Street Cemetery and later transferred to the Heil plot at St. Paul Lutheran Cemetery. Carl Siek

John SCHULZ, 9/2/1886. "St. Paul Lutheran Church Comp. Index of Deaths 1867-1890," vol. .3, p. 155.

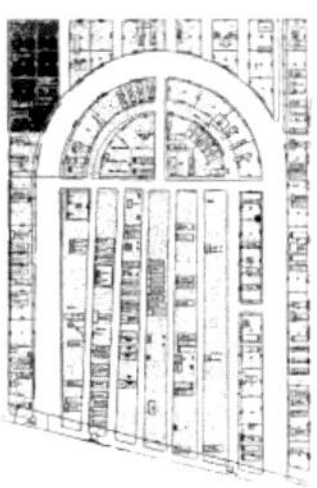

Potter's Field

Lots 10-16: *Originally designated as "Potter's Field" on plat map, "not to be sold."* SL

Lot 10 Caroline Heron no marker

Caroline HERON, 8 ms., Dover, German, July 12, 1890, Potter's Field. "List of Interments," Lakeside Cemetery, Bay Village, OH.

A birth or death record other than that of the cemetery's could not be found. The Heron name does occur in the Cahoon family but Caroline does not seem to tie in. There was also a marriage record uncovered for Arthur W. HERRON to Lillian SCHNEEBERGER (Marriage Record, Cuyahoga County, OH, vol. 60, p. 189) and another for Chas. F. HERRON to Carrie GIBBS (Marriage Record, Cuyahoga County, OH, vol. 26, p. 401). It is unclear if either of these couples ties in with those at the cemetery and is related to Caroline.

Deeds were found showing that some of the "Potter's Field" lots were sold in the 1920's.

Lot 10-21 Elizabeth Warga Szabo

ITT NMUGSZIK
SZABONE
WARGA ERZSEBET
SZUL 1862 AUG 23
MEG HALT
1908 JAN 17
ALDAS ES BEKE
LENGJEN
DRAGA HAMOAI
FELETT
ERZSEBET

REST IN PEACE

Translation from Hungarian

HERE RESTING IN PEACE
WIFE OF SZABO *(married surname)*
WARGA *(maiden name)*
ELIZABETH
BORN 1862 AUG 23
DIED
1908 JAN 17
BLESSINGS AND PEACE
BE WITH THE DEAR ASHES OF
FELETT *(name of who wrote saying)*

ELIZABETH

Elizabeth is labeled on the official city cemetery map as Margaret Erzsebet. According to the marker this name is incorrect.

The Hungarian name of Szabo translated into English is Taylor, as in a tailor. "ne" at the end of a woman's name means "Mrs." West Side Hungarian Reformed Church, Puritas, Cleve.

BODY IS HELD HIGH IN WIRES

Her body stretched across the telegraph wires, high in the air, where she alighted when hurled from the Nickel Plate track by a fast train at North Dover, ***Mrs. Elizabeth SABO***, forty five, died last night before she could be rescued.

The accident occurred at the Nickel Plate crossing of the Dover Center road. Mrs. Sabo had been visiting friends near the scene of the accident. About 8 o'clock, with a shawl pulled around her head and a basket on her arm, she started for home, a mile west of the village.

Taking the tracks for a short cut, she had gone about 200 yards when the approach of a freight train from the west caused her to step over on the other track. The noise of the freight prevented her hearing the approach of the westbound express as it bore down upon her.

The wild whistling of the express engine attracted the attention of people standing on the station platform. As they looked the form of the woman shot high in the air. Still clutching her basket Mrs. Sabo fell across the wires. Depot Master *W.N. KIDD* and *Marshal BEARDESLEY* secured a ladder and climbed the pole. The body lay about 10 feet from the pole, entangled in a mesh of wires. Reaching the top of the poles the men pulled the body toward them with a pole. As they did so the woman gave a gasp and died. Elyria Republican, Elyria, OH, Thursday, Jan 23, 1908, p. 2, col. 2.

Dover Lake

Mrs. SEBO of North Dover, aged 50 was killed by a Nickel Plate train last Friday evening. She had been calling on a neighbor and had crossed the track safely in front of an approaching train and failed to see another train on the other track rapidly coming near and too late to heed the warning. Notice of funeral later. Elyria Republican, Elyria, OH, Thursday, Jan 23, 1908, p. 7 col. 3.

There is a possibility that Mrs. Sabo's husband is related to *Michael SABO* who lived in the Cleveland area. Mike Jones

Lot 10-22 Kasper Wischmeyer

K. WISCHMEYER
1826-1902

Kasper WISCHMEYER, 77; res. Dover; German; interred Nov 20, 1904; Lot 10. *Note date discrepancy.* "List of Interments," Lakeside Cemetery, Bay Village, OH.

Casper WISCHMEYER Nov 17th, 1904 *(Wischmeyer family handwritten note at Rose Hill Museum, Bay Village, OH. The note lists the parents at the top and all children below. Casper is included in the list.)*

The following census record was found, which may be the person listed above. The date of birth is incorrect. It has not been determined how Kasper is related to the Wischmeyer family.

Wishmeyer, Casper, 61, widowed/divorced, carpenter, b. Hanover, parents b. Hanover; ***Mary***, 23, dau., single, b. Ohio; ***Lizzie***, 21, dau., b. Ohio; ***Fredericka***, 17, dau., single, b. Ohio; all children's parents b. Hanover. 1880 FC CY Cleve, Ward 6, p. 103B.

Lot 11 *North 1/3 of Lot 11 was sold to Frank Trestik for $8.33 on March 31, 1927.* CLD

(The marker for Anna Trestik is in the northern end of Lot 12 according to the plat map.)

Lot 11-23 Anna Trestik

ANNA
TRESTIK
1863-1927

TRESTIK, Frank, 48, renting house, occup. molder-foundry, b. B&M Austria; fr. b. Austria, mo. unknown (Au); ***Annie***, wife, 56, b. Austria, parents b. Austria; renting Lake Rd., both immig. 1903, Na. 1909. 1920 FC OH CYBV, p.1, lines 64-5. 1910 census: 2 child. b and living, m. 15 yrs. 1910 FC OH CY 22 WD Cleve, p. 63. lines 98-99.

Naturalization: ***TRESTIK, Frank***, 2311 W. 37 St., Cleveland, Ohio; b. Austria Sept. 13, 1871; Port: April 9, 1903, Baltimore; Nat.: 1 Mar 1909; Witnesses: Carl P. Assmus, 2318 St. Clair Ave. Edward Pokrandt, 2115 St. Clair Ave. Court of Common Pleas, Cuyahoga County, Cleveland, Ohio, 91271, vol. 3, p. 170.

Mrs. Anna TRESTIK, d. Mar 6, 1927, County of Cuyahoga, City of Cleveland, Charity Hospital, 2nd Ward; res. Osborn Rd., Bay Village, Ohio; married ***Frank TRESTIK***; b. June 11, 1861 Czecho-Slovakia; 65 yrs., 8 mos. 25 days; Hwf. *(Housewife)*; fr. Do not know, mo. *Francis NOVAK*, b. Do not know.. I hereby certify I attended the deceased from Feb 12, 1927 to March 6, 1927 and that death occurred, on the date stated above at 9:35 a.m. Cause: Chronic Myocarditis with myocardial failure, duration 2 yrs.; no operation or autopsy, Robert N. Wright, M.D., Charity Hospital; bur. Bay Village, March 9, 1927, Undertaker C. Pease, 2835A-Dover Center, O. Informant Frank Trestik, Bay Village, Ohio RFD. Ohio Certificate of Death, Division of Vital Statistics, 1927, certif. 14224.

Lot 12 *sold with Lot 16 to Robert Everard, resident of Bay, July 21, 1921, for a combined cost of $50.00.* CLD

Lots 13 and 15 *No burials listed.* 14 has new burials.

Lot 16 *sold with Lot 12 to Robert Everard, resident of Bay, July 21, 1921, for a combined cost of $50.00.* CLD

Lot 16 Robert Everard no marker

The State of Ohio, Cuyahoga County, ss. I Certify that on the 24th day of October 1888 ***Mr. Robert EVERARD*** and ***Mary Ann ALDRICH*** were by me legally joined in marriage. Rev. Geo. M. Heard Marriage Record, Cuyahoga County, OH, vol. 32, p. 269.

EVERHARD, Robert, 46, head, b. May 1854, England, parents b. England, immig. 1874, 26 years in the U.S., Naturalized citizen, married 11 yrs., farmer; ***Mary***, 49, wife, b. May 1851, Ohio, fr. b. New York, mo. b. Mass, 1 child born, 1 living; ***Mary A.***, 8, b. Apr 1892, dau., b. Ohio, fr. b. England, mo. b. Ohio. 1900 FC OH LOAV, p. 17B, lines 98-100.

EVERARD, Robt., (Mary A.)...Beach Park, farmer, ***Mae,*** Walker Rd. 1910 Lorain County Rural Directory, Avon, p. 50.

EVERHARD, Robert, 65, married, immig. 1873, Na. 1880, general farmer; ***Mary***, wife, 68; ***Mary Ann***, dau., 27, single, librarian-public library; *Margaret HASKEL*, boarder, 22, single, "American citizen, b. in Macedonia," fr. b. Bulgaria, mo. b. Iowa, high school teacher. 1920 FC OH CYBV, p. 1A.

EVERHARD, Robert, 75, value of real estate $30,000, no radio, b. England, parents b. England, immigrated 1874, Naturalized citizen; ***Mary A. E.***, daughter, 38, single, b. Ohio, fr. b. England, mo. b. Ohio, no occupation. 1930 FC OH CYBV, ED18-534, p. 22B, 30606 Lake Road, lines 70-71. *Living next door to Fred L. Drake (Lot 61-9).*

ROBERT EVERARD

Robert EVERARD, 90, 418 Second street, died at Elyria Memorial hospital at 12:15 p.m., Thursday, after a brief illness. Born in Thornby, Northamptonshire, England, May 7, 1854, Mr. Everary *(sp.)* came to this country when 19 years of age and resided in Lorain county most of his life.

On October 24, 1888 he was united in marriage to ***Mary Ann ALDRICH*** of Bay Village. She died July 2, 1921. An only daughter ***Mary A.E. EVERARD***, with whom he lived for many years preceded her father in death October 1, 1936.

Mr. Everard was a member of the Avon Baptist church for many years, transferring his membership to the First Baptist church of this city when he established his residence here eight years ago. For the past four years he had resided at the home of *Mr.* and *Mrs. Fred SEEKINS* on Second street.

The body is at the Taylor Funeral Home where friends may call and where funeral services will be held Sunday at 2:30 p.m. The Rev. J. Irving Reese will officiate and burial will be made in the cemetery at Bay Village. Chronicle Telegram, Elyria, Ohio, March 1945, p. 2, col. 3.

Robert EVERHARD, 3-4-45, Elyria Burial Permit no. 83. Cemetery Plot Map, Bay Village City Hall.

Robert EVERARD, male, white, widowed, wife: ***Mary A. EVERARD***; b. 5/17/1854, Thornby, Northamptonshire, Eng.; age 90 yrs. 9 mos. 24 days; retired; fr. ***Vincent EVERARD***, b. England; mo. ***Elizabeth EVERARD***, b. England.; d. Mar 1, 1945, 1:15 p.m., Elyria Memorial Hospital, Elyria, Lorain Co., cause Cerebral. Length of stay at hospital 4 days. Lived in this community 8 yrs. Usual Residence 418 2nd Street, Elyria, Lorain Co., OH. In the US 71 yrs. Informant *John EVERARD*, 250 9th St., Elyria, OH. Bur. 3/4/45, Lakeside Cemetery, Bay Village, OH. Embalmer R.W. Schmittgen, Funeral Director C__. L. Taylor, Elyria. Ohio Certificate of Death, Division of Vital Statistics, 1945, certif. 16354.

John C. EVERARD, the informant listed above was born 11 Sept 1888 in Ohio, and died 12 Feb 1966 at Elyria Memorial Hospital. His parent's were *John G. EVERARD* and *Annie BIGGS*. He was a teacher with the Cleveland Public School System and is buried at Ridgelawn Cemetery, Elyria. It is not known how or if he is related to Robert, above. Ohio Certificate of Death, Division of Vital Statistics, 1966, certif. 012658.

Parents of Robert Everard:

EVERARD Vincent, England Dec 11, 1813 - July 19, 1874; ***Elizabeth,*** Mar 20, 1818 - Mar 24, 1879. Lot A, row 6, 13-14th plot from Detroit Rd., Garfield Cemetery, Sheffield, OH, as read by Catherine Burke Flament. *Difficult to read.*

Vincent EVERARD, England Dec 11, 1817. Garfield Cemetery, Sheffield, OH. Sheffield City Hall, Sheffield, OH (next to cemetery), read by Catherine Burke Flament and Genealogical Workshops of the Lorain County Historical Society, Cemetery Inscriptions of Lorain County, Ohio 1980, Garfield Cemetery, p. 431.

EVERARD - On March 24th 1879, at Avon Lake, Lorain county, Ohio, ***Mrs. EVERARD,*** widow of the late ***Mr. Vincent EVERARD***, formerly of Naseby, Northamptonshire, England. Elyria Weekly Republican, Elyria, OH, Thursday, March 27, 1879, p. 5, col. 4.

Northamptonshire, (or Northampton), south-midland, county of England; area, 629,912 acres, population 272,555. Although the surface appearance of the county is generally hilly there are no elevations of considerable altitude. In some localities, particularly the W. and SW., the scenery is especially attractive; while here and there throughout the county rich woods and well-watered vales afford pleasing aspects. Throughout the whole county, farming is successfully prosecuted, all kinds of cereal and green crops being raised; while upon the splendid pastures large numbers of cattle are reared, principally for the London market. Northampton is celebrated for its ash trees, old oaks, and elm avenues. . . Iron is largely found, and although worked as early as the time of the Roman occupation, its modern manufacture dates only from 1850. . . Apart from ironworking, the great industry of the county is centred in the manufacture of boots and shoes in the town of Northampton and the towns of the middle of the county. Bartholomew's Gazetteer of the British Isles, 1887.

Lot 16 Mary Ann Aldrich Everard

no marker

Mary Ann ALDRICH EVERARD, taught school in Dover in a wooden schoolhouse on Lake Road. She married ***Robert EVERARD***, a native of England. The lived in Sheffield and the Dover area, at one time living in part of the Aldrich house. Gertrude Aldrich Barker Rose, "Genealogy of the Aldrich Family," p. 16.

Mary Ann ALDRICH, dau. of ***Henry Winsor ALDRICH*** and ***Mary Ann STEVENS***, b. 27 May 1851, d. 2 July 1921, m. 24 Oct 1888, ***Robert EVERARD*** (b. 7 May 1854, England, d. Mar 1945, Bay Village, O), child: ***Mary Ann Elizabeth*** *(Mae)* b. 9 April 1892, unmarried, d.-. George H. Drake, "Aldrich Generation Chart," p. 10, Rose Hill Museum, Bay Village, OH.

Mary Ann ALDRICH, b. at Dover..., m. to ***Robert EVERARD,*** of Sheffield, Ohio (b...at Thornby, Northamptonshire, England), she d. at the Aldrich home, ...res. Avon Lake and Bay Village, Ohio. Abram W. Foote, Foote Family Comprising the Genealogy and History of Nathaniel Foote, vol. II, p. 704.

Mary Ann EVERARD inherited land from her father, ***Henry W. ALDRICH***, upon his death. One plot was 280 feet from Bradley Road on the north side of Lake Road. It was 70 feet wide at Lake Road extending north in a pie shape to 136+ feet at Lake Erie. The second lot was to the east of that lot and was 302.96 feet wide, extending from Lake Erie to the south side of Lake Road. "The Estate of Henry W. Aldrich," Drake Family Papers, Rose Hill Museum, Bay Village, OH.

From a separate note paper found in ledger of interments:

Mary Ann EVERHARD, age unknown, interred July 5, 1921, Lot 15.

Mary Ann EVERARD, d. 3 July 1921, Bay, Cuy. Co., OH; res. Lake Rd.; married to ***Robt. EVERARD***; b. 27 May 1851, Bay Village, O.; 70 yrs., 1 month, 5 days; fr. ***Henry W. ALDRICH***, b. Watertown, NY; mo. ***Mary Ann STEVENS***, b. Lee, Mass. Cause of death Myocarditis, 5 years. Geo. Lathrop, M.D., Dover Center, O.; Informant *Mrs. Chas. DRAKE*, Avon Lake, O., R.F.D; bur. Bay Village, July 5, 1921; undertaker C. Pease, Dover Center, O. Ohio Certificate of Death, Division of Vital Statistics, 1921, certif. 37412 and added information re date of death.

Mary Ann EVERARD, BV, 70, Mitral Stenosis and incompetency, Lakeside Cemetery, undertaker Clifford Pease, Dover, Ohio, July 5, 1921. Burial Removal Permit.

Lot 16 Mary Ann Eliz. Everard no marker

Mary Ann Elizabeth EVERARD, b. Avon, Ohio, Apr 9, 1892; res. Bay Village, Ohio; unmarried. Daughter of ***Mary Ann ALDRICH*** and ***Robert EVERARD.*** Abram W. Foote, Foote Family Comprising the Genealogy and History of Nathaniel Foote, vol. II, p. 704.

Miss Mary EVERARD was a member of the Library and Museum Committee for the City of Bay Village in 1920. Min., Ordinances & Resolutions, Bay Village, OH, 1918-1921.

MISS MAE EVERARD

Miss Mae EVERARD, daughter of ***Robert*** and the late ***Mary Ann EVERARD,*** passed away at her home in Bay Village Thursday morning, October first.

Funeral services will be held at the Clifford Pease Funeral Home, 2914 Dover road, Dover Center, Saturday, October 3rd at 2:30. Chronicle Telegram, Elyria, Ohio, Oct 2, 1936, p. 2, col. 3.

Mary Ann EVERARD, d. 1 Oct, 1936, 4 a.m.; Bay, Cuyahoga Co., OH. res. 30663 Lake Rd.; Single, Librarian; b. April 9, 1892, Avon, Ohio; 44 yrs. 5 months 22 days. Fr. ***Robert EVERARD,*** b. Northamptonshire, England; mo. ***Mary Ann ALDRICH***, b. Bay Village, Ohio. I hereby certify, that I attended deceased from Sept 26, 1936 to Sept 30, 1936, I last saw her alive on Sept 30, 1936. Cause of death Cerebral embolism 9/26/36. C.W. Stoll, M.D., Dover Center. Informant *Robert EVERARD*, 30663 Lake Road, Bay Village. Bur. Lake Cem., Bay Village, Oct 3, 1936. Funeral Director Marion E. Pease, Dover Center, O., embalmed. Ohio Certificate of Death, Division of Vital Statistics, 1936, certif. 64421.

These families, and many others, are rooted deep, like fine old trees: enriching the land which nourished them.

Mrs. L.F. Ferster

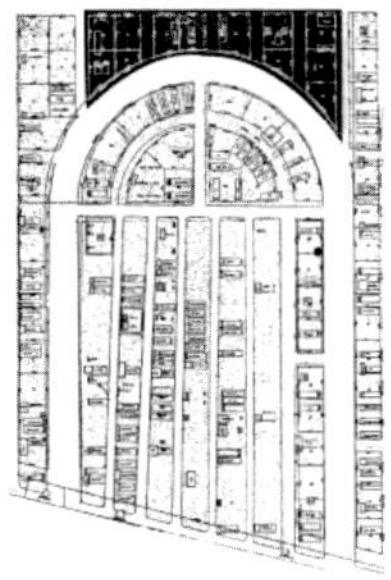

Sold lots located along the north (lake) side of the cemetery.

Lot 17/18 *Owner: Aslaksen purchased Lot 17 for $5.41, Lot 18 for $5.08* SL

Lots 17/18-1 Aslaksen Marker

	ASLAKSEN	
SON	MOTHER	FATHER
JOHN	MALVENA	OLAF
1901-1921	1877-1948	1869-1954

Lots 17/18-1 Olaf Aslaksen

Olaf *(Olav)* was born 29 Aug 1867 near Oslo in Norway, the oldest son of ***Yens ASLACHSEN*** of Tvedestrand and ***Halvordine (Dina) Pebsea SIMONSON*** originally from Holmestrand, Norway who married c1865. Yens was a boat builder. The family home in Holmestrand was named Aslaksborg, located only a few yards from the Lutheran church they attended and where Yens, Dina and their son, *Johnny* and Dina's parents are buried. Their children were: ***Olav***, b. 1867; ***Valborg***, b. 1872; ***David***, b. 1884 in Holmstrand and ***Johnnes*** b. 1885, d. 1889.

Olaf left Norway in 1883, at the age of sixteen, and decided to go out on his own sailing as a cabin boy. His adventures took him to the Falkland Islands off the southern coast of Argentina, Punta Arenas and up the west coast of South America. Mention of him is made in the book Uttermost Part of the Earth by *E. Lucas BRIDGES* telling of adventures he had with the author. While in the Falkland Islands he met and married ***Louisa Malvina***

HARDY. They would have thirteen children, most born in South America, specifically Chili and Argentina.

Life on the seas became a career as Captain Aslaksen sailed on ocean vessels and later on freighters traveling the Great Lakes.

Olaf and Louisa Malvina came to America from the Falkland Islands through Norway in 1904 and settled in Cleveland near the zoo. Olaf's brother David immigrated with them and their parents would follow. Yens and Dina, their parents, choose not to stay in the United States and returned to Norway, it was their wish to die in their native country. In 1915, the Aslaksen's moved to Cove Road in Avon Lake where they would raise their children. Nancy Veits and Donna DeChant.

Olaf ASLAKSEN was born in Norway in a small town called Lillefjord, near Oslo and his parents were inn-keepers He was a ship's captain and owned his own ship, carrying consignments around the Cape, up the western coast of South America to Panama. On one trip, he made a stop in the Falkland Islands, which was a British Crown Colony also known as the Malvinas. There he saw a girl who caught his interest. He completed his journey and finished his deliveries and turned back for the return trip. He hadn't forgotten the girl in the Falklands so he stopped there and found her. Her name was ***Malvena Louisa HARDY*** (named after the Malvinas) and her father was the colonial governor of the Falklands. Olaf married Malvena and took her back to his home in Norway.

Olaf and Malvena became the parents of sixteen children, thirteen of whom survived. In 1905, they came from Norway to Cleveland and then to Avon Lake to be in the country. They had a small family farm on Cove, where Westwinds development is now. They kept a few animals for their own use and raised enough crops to provide feed for the animals. Malvena did most of the farm work with help from the children as Olaf was now sailing the Great Lakes.

During WWI Olaf was a high seas merchant mariner. He finally retired from sailing after WWII and he died in 1954. Olaf died in a state hospital in Toledo. May Aslaksen Palmer, granddaughter; personal interview by Jeanne Parks; United Church of Christ, Avon Lake, OH; 9 Oct 2002.

Old Avon Lake Sea Dog Awaits Cook's Release

When the gates of Leavenworth penitentiary, out in Kansas, swing open to release *Dr. Frederick A. COOK*, former polar explorer, as they are expected to do soon, he will have a loyal friend in Lorain Co. waiting for him...

Himself a grizzled old sea dog of a long line of Viking ancestors, ***Capt. ASLAKSEN*** still remembers Doc Cook fondly from the days they first met nearly 30 years ago...

Only a few days ago, the former sea captain sent a letter to Doc Cook wishing him health and success, and inviting the doctor to visit him.

Captain Aslaksen is 60 and has been a navigator since his youth. His friendship for the former explorer began nearly three decades ago when Cook's vessel of the Nordenschold Antarctic expedition sailed into the harbor at Ushuaia, Tierra del Fuego, on the rim of southern civilization.

The sea captain met Cook there during the month or more that his vessel laid up for supplies. The captain recalls that an epidemic of measles broke out among the natives and that young Doc Cook worked ceaselessly administering to the stricken natives. Capt. Aslaksen was one of the few white men in the southern port.

Many years after, when the sea captain had retired, he met Cook in Cleveland. They have continued the friendship thruout the years.

Captain Aslaksen still remains faithful to the former explorer whose name was a national byword 20 years ago and whose expeditions caused international controversy. The captain still remained faithful when Cook was sentenced to federal prison on charges of fraud.

'I don't believe it,' the captain says when he hears reports of Cook's alleged fraud. He remembers Doc Cook for the many pleasant hours they spent together and for his humanitarian efforts fighting disease in Tierra del Fuego. Newspaper article provided by Nancy Veits, "Old Avon Lake Sea Dog Awaits Cook's Release," undetermined source.

Olaf ASLAKSEN, d. 9-1-1954, Toledo State Hospital, Lucas County, Toledo, Ohio; Length of stay 15 yrs.; usual residence Ohio, Lorain Co., Avon Lake, 210 Cove Ave.; widowed; b. Aug 29, 1867, Norway; fr. ***Olaf ASLAKSEN***, mother unknown; 87 yrs. old; occup. Seaman, Retired; citizen U.S.A., never in the U.S. Armed Forces, informant J.J. Mehlman M.D., Toledo State Hospital. I attended patient from 8/15/1939 to 9/1/1954, and that death occurred at 7:05 a.m., medical condition arteriosclerosis - 15 yrs., bur. 9-8-54 Bay Village Cemetery, Bay Village, Ohio, funeral director F.L. Burmeister. Ohio Certificate of Death, Division of Vital Statistics, 1954, certif. 57979.

Ethel, Louise, Betty, Ruth, Valborg, Agnes, Dena; Malvena and Olaf; Arthur and Irene Aslaksen; Avon Lake, 1934.

ASLAKSEN, CAPT. OLAF SR., residence 210 Cove Ave., Avon Lake, beloved husband of the late ***Malvina***, father of ***Volberg TOMANEK, Dena COFFEEJOHN, Elizabeth TOMANEK, Ethel NELSON, Olav Jr., Agnes ARNOLD, Ruth NELSON, Louise WELLNER, Irene MCCOWAN*** and ***Arthur***, brother of ***Volberg NOLL*** and ***David***, grandfather and great-grandfather. Friends may call at the Burmeister Funeral Home, 163 Avon-Belden Rd., Avon Lake, where services will be held Wednesday,

Sept 8 at 2 p.m. Cleveland Necrology File, Cleveland Press, September 7, 1954, roll 3.

Lots 17/18-1 Louisa Malvena Hardy Aslaksen

Louisa Malvina HARDY, b. 7th May 1877, female, fr. ***Frederick HARDY***, mo. ***Eliza HARDY*** formerly ***CONGDON***, fr. mason, signed by F. Hardy, father, res. Stanley on 14th May 1877. Registrar Arthur Bailey. Falkland Islands Registry of Birth.

Louisa Malvina (Vinny) HARDY was born 7th May 1877 in the Falkland Islands, one of thirteen children born to ***Frederick HARDY*** and ***Eliza Ann CONGDON***. The children were: ***Frederick James HARDY***, b. 1863; ***Louisa Ann HARDY***, b.1864; ***William Michael HARDY***, b.1865; ***Mary Margaret HARDY***, b. 1867; ***Albertina HARDY***, b. 1869; ***Arthur HARDY***, b. 1871; ***Frank HARDY***, b. 1872; ***George HARDY***, b. 1874; ***Walter HARDY***, b. 1875; ***Louisa Malvina HARDY***, b. 1877; ***Albert Percy HARDY***, b. 1878; ***Herbert HARDY***, b. 1882 and one child who lived only days, ***Unnamed HARDY***.

Eliza Congdon Hardy, was probably born in Cornwall, England. First written knowledge of her is when she went to the East Stonehouse Registration District to register the birth of a son, Frederick James, born 20 Feb 1863. She signed with an "X" and the address recorded is 10 St. Mary Street, East Stonehouse where the Royal Barracks are located. There is a tradition of sewing in the family and Eliza is said to have been a handmaiden to the Queen. Eliza died "while dishing up lunch" when Vinny was only 10 yrs. old in Port Stanley. The youngest child was five at the time.

Vinny's father was from Puddletown, Dorset, England, stationed with the British in the Falkland Islands as a private in the 31st Co. of Royal Marines. Frederick returned to England, married Eliza and then settled in Port Stanley, Falkland Islands, earning his living as a stone mason and bricklayer. She registered the birth of their son, Frederick James, who was born 20 Feb 1863 with an "X" as her mark, at the East Stonehouse Registration District. The Hardy's were living at 10 St. Mary Street in East Stonehouse where the Royal Marine Barracks were located. In later years Frederick traveled to Punta Arenas, Chile and lived with George or Herbert. He died there in 1917. Nancy Veits

RITES SET FOR MRS. ASLAKSEN

AVON LAKE-Funeral services will be held tomorrow for ***Mrs. Louise Malvena ASLAKSEN***, 73, who died Saturday morning at St. Joseph's hospital, Lorain, O.

Mrs. Aslaksen had been in ill health for about 15 years, but became gravely ill during the week.

Born in the Falkland Islands, (at the tip of South America), of English parents, she married ***Olav ASLAKSEN*** from Norway 54 years ago.

Aslaksen was a captain on the oceans and later on the Great Lakes, and they visited many countries, their 13 children being born in different parts of the world.

Surviving besides her husband are ***Mrs. Valborg TOMANEK, Mrs. Elizabeth TOMANEK, Olav, jr., Mrs. Agnes ARNOLD, Mrs. Ruth NELSON, Mrs. Irene MCCOWAN***, and ***Arthur*** of Avon Lake; ***Mrs. Dena COFOJOHN***, Belleville, Ky.; ***Mrs. Ethel NELSON***, Cleveland; ***Mrs. Louise FARAGHER*** of Lorain.

Preceding her in death were her children ***John, Bernice*** and ***Herbert***.

Services will be at 2 p.m. at the Burmeister funeral home, with Rev. Paul J. Folino of the Avon Lake Congregational church officiating. Burial will be in Bay Village cemetery. Newspaper article provided by Nancy Veits, undetermined source.

Louisa Malvena ASLAKSEN, d. Lorain Co., Lorain, Ohio, St. Joseph Hospital, length of stay 1 day; usual residence Ohio, Lorain, Avon Lake Village, Cove Ave.; b. May 7, 1877; Falkland Islands S.A.; fr. ***Frederick HARDY***, b. England, mo. ***Louisa CONGDON***, b. England; 71 yrs. 2 mo. 10 days; housewife - own home, Married to ***Olav Sr.*** who is 80 yrs. old; informant *Agnes ARNOLD*, 151 Lear Road, Avon Lake, O. bur. 7-20-48, Bay Village Cem., Bay Village, Ohio, Fred L. Burmeister, The Burmeister Funeral Home, 163 Avon-Belden Rd., Avon Lake, Ohio. D. July 17, 1948, 7:45. I attended the deceased from July 1, 1938 to July 17, 1948 and that I last saw her alive on July 17, 1948. Cause Coronary thrombosis - 24 hrs. due to Arterio-sclerosis - 10 yrs. Ohio Certificate of Death, Division of Vital Statistics, 1948, certif. 44415.

ASLAKSEN, LOUISA M. (nee ***HARDY***); late residence, Avon Lake, O.; beloved wife of ***Olav***; mother of...; grandmother and great-grandmother; Saturday. Friends may call at the Burmeister Funeral Home, 163 Avon-Belden Rd., Avon Lake, where services will be held Tuesday, July 20 at 2 p.m. Interment Bay Village Cemetery. July 19, 1948. The Plain Dealer.

There is a bracket in the List of Interments section of the Cemetery book connecting the next two entries. The burial permit seems to somewhat combine the two. According to the death certificates, which should be correct, the information has not been recorded correctly for the two infants.

Lots 17/18 Bernice Aslaksen no marker

Bernice Aslaksen was the daughter of Olaf Aslaksen and Malvena Hardy, buried this lot.

Baby Bernice ASLACHAN (sp.), Lake Rd., Avon Lake, May 2, 1916. Pease Funeral Home Records, Mss. 4809, Ledger Jan 1916-Aug 20, 1922, p. 20, Western Reserve Historical Society.

Bernice ASLACHSEN (sp.), d. April 29, 1916, Avon Lake, Lorain Co., Ohio, Acute Cerebral Meningitis, Acute Endocarditis (Luetic); b. March 4, 1916, Avon Lake; fr. ***Olan ASLACHSEN***, b. Norway, mo. ***Malvine HARDY***, b. Ireland; 2 mos. 25 days *(should be one month if DOB is* *correct)*, bur. May 1, Bay Village, Dover, O., undertaker J.A. Pease; informant Olan Aslachsen, Avon Lake, O. Ohio Certificate of Death, Division of Vital Statistics, 1916, certif. 35233.

Infant ASCALASKN *(sp.)*, 29 days; res. Bay Village; Polish; interred May 3d, 1917-18; Lot 17. List of Interments, Lakeside Cemetery, Bay Village, OH. *(listed after Herbert Barth Aslaksen, year may be off)*

Lots 17/18 Herbert Barth Aslaksen no marker

Herbert Barth Aslaksen was the son of Olaf Aslaksen and Louisa Malvena Hardy, buried this lot.

Herbert Bartle ASLAKSEN, d. Oct 30, 1917, 3 a.m., Avon Lake, Lorain Co., Ohio, cause *(difficult to read)* S__ mouth like Illio Polities *(sp.)*, duration 29 days; b. Oct 1, 1917, Avon Lake, Ohio, 29 days old; fr. ***Olaf ASLAKSEN***, b. Norway, mo. ***Melvena HARDY***, b. Falkland Island; bur. Oct 31, 1917, Bay Village, O., undertaker C. Pease, Dover Center, O.; informant Olaf Aslaksen, Avon Lake, O., R.F.D. Ohio Certificate of Death, Division of Vital Statistics, 1917, certif. 65931.

Herbert Barth ASLAKSEN, Avon Lake, male, 29 days, Liver Mouth Babe?, undertaker - C. Pease, Dover Center, Oct 30, 1917. Bureau of Vital Statistics, Burial or Removal Permit, Bay Village, OH.

Herbert Barth ASCALASKEN *(sp.)*, 7 weeks; res. Bay Village; Polish; interred Oct 30, 1917; Lot 17. "List of Interments," Lakeside Cemetery, Bay Village, OH.

Lots 17/18-1 John Aslaksen

John ASLAKSEN was the fourth child of ***Olaf*** and ***Malvena ASLAKSEN***. He was killed by an Interurban train on the tracks in front of his home at Cove in August of 1921. The weather was stormy that day and he was driving a 1917-1918 Ford when he died. He is remembered as a very handsome young man. May Aslaksen Palmer and Nancy Veits

CAR VICTIM IS HERO OF DARING RESCUE AT SEA

John ASLAKSEN, 20, Stop 40, Lake Shore Electric, near Dover, who was instantly killed yesterday morning when an interurban street car crashed into a Ford auto in which he was seated and which had stopped on the tracks almost directly in front of his home, was a joint hero with his father, ***Captain Olaf ASLAKSEN***, of one of the epic sea rescues of the Atlantic coast, two years ago.

Captain Aslaksen, two-years-ago, was master of an ocean freighter, on which his son was his chief aid. On one stormy winter-night their wireless picked up a distress call off the Newfoundland banks.

Against the judgment of most of the ship officers, the captain urged by his son, started toward the sinking ship, and in a twenty-four hour battle with the storm succeeded in reaching the craft, a tanker, saving a crew of a score and towing the tanker into the nearest port. The feat at the time was said to be one of the most daring in the history of the North. Lorain Times-Herald, Lorain, OH, Wed., August 3, 1921, p. 2, col. 1.

The Interurban, Lake Shore Electric, started traveling through Dover in 1897 and had its last run on May 15th, 1938 out of Public Square in Cleveland at 12:41 a.m. The Lake Shore territory extended 116 miles from Cleveland to Toledo, dividing near Huron and rejoining at Fremont. The trolley was used by salesmen, brought people to the city, provided transportation for city dwellers to go to the beaches and was a cheap way to ship milk, produce, hardware and newspapers.

In 1908 alone there were 4,761,000 paid fares. An hourly service was provided from Cleveland to Elyria via Beach Park and South Lorain with the trip taking 90 minutes. The Interurban trip could be extended to Detroit and Chicago and traveled at approximately 60 miles an hour. Harry Christiansen, New Lake Shore Electric, Trolley Trails, vol. 4, pp. 524, 534, 662 and Bay Village Historical Society, Bay Village: A Way of Life, p. 69.

The Lake Shore Electric stops in the Bay Village area were: #13 Clague Road, #19 Columbia Road, #23 Dover Center, # 24 Cahoon, #27 Ellenwood and Huntington, #29 Osborns, #32 Bassett and #35 Bradley Road. There were a few other stops but not all numbers were used. The trolley would only stop if necessary and the stops ranged from a small platform to a small building. The Dover substation is now Baycrafters shop in Huntington Metro Parks on Lake Road. Sarah Dodd Wymer

John ASLAKSEN, res. No. Four Ohio Stop 40 (Dover Centre *(sp.)*) for 10 years; d. Avon Lake, Lorain Co., Aug 2, 1921, Automobile Accident hit by Lake shore elec. Car at stop 40. Fracture skull___ and ribs right side, contributory___ hemorrhage brain, at crossing, coroner report; single; Electrician, employer: Auto; b. Dec 10, 1900, Punta Arenas (Chile), South America; fr. ***Olaf ASLAKSEN***, b. Norway, mo. ***Louise Malvina***, b. Falkland Isl., South America; 20 yrs. old; bur. Aug 5, 1921, Bay Village, Ohio, undertaker Mastick and Daniels, 14622 Detroit; informant Olaf Aslaksen, Stop 40, Avon, Ohio. Ohio Certificate of Death, Division of Vital Statistics, 1921, certif. 45885.

ASLAKSEN-John, beloved son of ***Olaf*** and ***Louise***, suddenly Tuesday, August 2. Funeral services from the residence of his parents, Stop 40, Lake Shore Electric, Avon, Ohio, Friday, Aug 5, at 2 p.m. Cleveland Necrology File, August 2, 1921, roll 3.

John ASLAKSEN, Norwegian, b. South America, d. Avon, Ohio, St Car Accident Lake Shore, Aug 2, 1921, single, religion P, fr. ***Olaf***, b. Norway, mo. ***Louise Malvina***, b. South America. Cost: Casket $195, Outside Box $15, Embalming $20, Hearse $10, Carriages to Cemetery $10, Death Notices in 2 newspapers $3, Flowers $6, Opening of Grave $8, Lining of Grave, Flowers $15. Total $259. Record of Funeral Mastick and Daniels, Lakewood.

Lot 19/20 *Owner: R.D. Scott (on plat map) purchased Lot 19 in June 1920 for $5.10, Lot 20 for $2.71* SL *Deeded on June 8, 1920 to R.D. Scott for $50.00, sold to Belle Wilkshire on July 30, 1924 for $50.00.* CLD

Lots 19/20-2 Frank John Knaggs

FRANK J. KNAGGS
1866-1931

Frank J. Knaggs is the brother-in-law of Walter Wilkshire who is buried in the same plot.
The date of birth recorded on the stone is incorrect and should read 1863.

Frank KNAGGS, 38, res. 19 Mueller Ave., b. Canada, machinist, fr. *James KNAGGS*, mo. *Hannah MARSHALL*. Married ***Jane TRAYTE***, 35, res. 237 Meldren Ave., b. England, fr. *Wm. TRAYTE*, mo. *Jane STEPHENS*, neither previously married. The State of Ohio, Cuyahoga County, ss., I Certify that on the 23rd day of Sept 1903 Frank Knaggs and Jane Trayte were by me legally joined in marriage. Rev. John H.W. Fortescue Cove. Marriage Record, Cuyahoga County, OH, vol. 56, p. 414.

KNAGGS, Frank, 45, married 8 years, b. Canada, fr. b. Canada, mo. b. England, immigrated 1892, alien, Superintendent, Hardwood ___ Co., renting home; ***Jane***, 44, 0 children born; immigrated 1883, occup. none. Four family dwelling, 116th Street near Detroit Ave., Cleveland. 1910 FC OH CY Cleveland Ward 1, ED 54, p. 2A, lines 22-23.

KNAGGS, Frank, renting, 49, not a citizen, b. Canada, fr. b. Canada, mo. b. England, Machinist, Dry Dock; ***Jane***, wife, 52, b. England, parents b. England; ***TRAYTE, Jane***, mother, 87, b. England, parents b. England. Wooster Rd. 1920 FC OH CYRR, ED 54, p. 4A, lines 45-47.

Frank KNAGGS, 19220 Telbir, Rocky River, O.; d. Jan 6. 1931, 4:30 a.m., Rocky River, Cause Naso pharougial milignousn, Cancer, contributory: Mitrol Insufficiency, attended by doctor March 2, 1930-Jan 6, 1931; married ***Jane KNAGGS***; Wood Carver; b. July 22, 1863, Meaford, Ontario, Canada, fr. ***James KNAGGS***, b. Toronto, Canada, mo. ***Anna MARSHALL***, b. Toronto, Canada; 66 yrs. 5 mos. 14 ds.; bur. Bay Village, O., Jan 8, 1931, undertaker Clifford Pease, Dover Center, O., body embalmed; informant *Belle WILKSHIRE*, 19220 Telbir Ave., Rocky River, O. Ohio Certificate of Death, Division of Vital Statistics, 1931, certif. 914.

KNAGGS: Frank, beloved husband of ***Jane*** (nee ***TRAYTE***), Jan 6, 1931. Services at residence 19220 Telbir Avenue, Rocky River, O. Thursday, Jan 8, at 2 p.m. Cem. Rec. 1866-1931, age 65, Lakeside Cem., Bay Village, Ohio. Cleveland Necrology File, Jan 8, 1931, roll 45.

Frank and ***Jane KNAGGS*** never had children. Sarah Dodd Wymer, former Bay Village resident.

Ancestors of Frank Knaggs:

I. ***William KNAGGS***, b. 1 Apr 1784, Bransdale, Yorkshire, England; d. unknown, possibly Ontario, Canada; m. ***Sarah PEACOCK***, b. unknown, Bransdale; d. unknown, ?Ontario. Information from the Marshall family bible, 1794-1930's, provided by Suzanne Evanson-Myers with additional research by her.

II. ***James KNAGGS***, b. 13 Nov 1830, Etobicoke, Ontario, Canada; d. 9 Oct 1925, bur. Lakeview Cemetery, Meaford, Ontario; m. ***Hannah (Anna) MARSHALL*** (dau. of *Andrew MARSHALL* (b. Nov 1777, Pickering, Yorkshire, England; d. 20 Aug 1852, Pickering) and *Jane LAWNSBOROUGH* (b. March 1805, Yorkshire; d. 13 Nov 1869, Pickering); b. 7 Mar 1830, christened in the Church of England 9 Mar, Pickering, Yorkshire, England; d. 6 Nov 1898, Meaford; bur. Lakeview Cemetery); moved to Meaford/St. Vincent, Grey Co., Ontario by 1871. A marriage record exists in the Bishop's Transcripts for *Andrew MARSHALL* and *Jane LAWNSBOROUGH*, 14 Feb 1823, Whitby, Yorkshire. It has not been substantiated that these are Hanna's parents. Frank's father, James, was a farmer and musician; most of the family were accomplished musician and singers. They were active in the local Anglican church, fireman's picnics and concert halls.

Issue of James Knaggs and Hanna Marshall: ***Pricilla Jane*** (*Lilly* or *Lillian*) ***KNAGGS,*** b. 18 May 1856; d. 16 Nov 1930, Meaford, Ont., bur. Lakeview Cemetery; never married. ***James P. KNAGGS***, b. 11 Apr 1857; musician and carpenter, m. *Cecelia ALBERY* (dau. of *Robert ALBERY*; b. c1853, NY); immig. to US 1884, Na. 1901, lived Buffalo, NY; woodworker 1922, Airplane Mechanic 1926-30; d. c1935 Buffalo, NY; burial place unknown. ***William (Billy) John KNAGGS***, b. 18 Nov 1859; farmer and musician with the Meaford Band, m. *Martha Jane CRAWFORD*; d. 1946, Lakeview Cemetery, Meaford, Ont. ***Sarah KNAGGS***, b. 10 July 1861; accomplished singer/vocalist for the church and in the community; d. 2 Feb 1884 of inflammatory rheumatism, Meaford; bur. Lakeview Cemetery, Meaford, Ont. ***Francis John (Frank) KNAGGS***, 26 July 1863 in the area of Etobicoke (Toronto), Ontario, Canada. ***Thomas Edward KNAGGS***, b. 5 Sept 1866; m. *Anna May MURRAY* (b. 6 July 1882, d. Oct/Nov 1959, Fort Erie, Ont.); resided in Bridgeburg (Fort Erie), Ont.; volunteer fireman and multi-business who lost most of his wealth in Fort Erie, Canada during the Great Depression; d. 1950, St. Paul's Anglican Church Cemetery, Fort Erie Ont., CA. ***David Marhall KNAGGS***, b. 29 July 1869, whereabouts unknown. Information from the Marshall family bible, 1794-1930's, provided by Suzanne Evanson-Myers with additional research by her.

William John KNAGGS (b. 18 Nov 1859) and ***Sarah KNAGGS*** (b. 10 July 1861) were baptized 6 Aug 1875. ***James, Frank*** and ***Thomas*** (age 18) ***KNAGGS*** were confirmed on Sept 23, 1884. ***James KNAGGS*** (age 94) bur. Oct 12, 1925 Meaford (Lakeview) Cem.; ***Mrs. Anna KNAGGS***, wife of James Knaggs, (age 68), Nov 28, 1897, Meaford Cem.; ***Sarah KNAGGS***, Feb 14, 1884, age 22, bur. Meaford Cem.; ***Lillie KNAGGS*** *(Priscilla)*, age 75, Nov 16, 1930, Lakeview Cem.; ***Martha Jane KNAGGS***, age 70, Dec 27, 1938. Christ Church Anglican Records, Meaford, Ontario, Canada.

KNAGGS, James, male, 39, b. Ontario, rel. Church of England, Anglican, origin English, occup. farmer, district Grey North (037), sub-div. St. Vincent (H), Division 2, Page 6. 1871 Census Index of Ontario, National Archives of Canada.

Wife of Frank Knaggs, Jane Trayte:
KNAGGS: Mrs. Jane, wife of the late ***Frank J.***, sister of *Oscar W. TRAYTE* of Painesville and ***Mrs. Belle WILKSHIRE*** and *Roland M. TRAYTE.* Residence 2744 Mayfield Road, Cleveland Heights. Services at De Vand Funeral Home, 11130 Euclid. Thursday at 3 p.m. Cleveland Necrology File, October 27, 1932, roll 45.

Lots 19/20-3 Walter S. Wilkshire

WALTER WILKSHIRE
1871-1924

(Original small metal marker placed in front of the grave.)
Spanish-American Veteran
Philippine Islands Porto *(sp.)* Rico
1898-1902
Army United Navy

Walter WILKSHIRE served in the military during the Spanish-American War. Walter was married to ***Belle TRAYTE*** who had emigrated to the U.S. from England when she was 12. Unfortunately the couple would separate for many years. He moved to California and lived with his sister. Belle may have lived with her sister, ***Jane KNAGGS***, on Superior Ave. in Cleveland during this period. Belle worked in a millinery factory on W. 9th Street in Cleveland with *Elvie POWELL DODD*. She was a tall woman (5'7") who was a little hefty. The Wilkshire's never had children. They reunited in the 1920's and he started a shop where he made lamps; he was known as a good craftsman. They had *Wirt DODD (see OP 4:16)* build the house for them on Foote Rd. behind the *RUMBAUGH* home *(see Lot 58-4)* which is where Walter passed away. The lot was narrow so the Dutch Colonial was situated so the side was to the street. Sarah Dodd Wymer, former Bay Village resident.

The State of Ohio, Cuyahoga County, ss. I Certify that on the 25th day of December 1890 ***Mr. Walter WILKSHIRE*** and ***Miss Belle TRAYTE*** were by me legally joined in marriage. Henry D. Aves Marriage Record, Cuyahoga County, OH, vol. 35, p. 226.

Walter was married to ***Clara Isabelle TRAYTE*** (b.16 Aug 1866, d. 30 Nov 1946), dau. of ***William TRAYTE*** (Aug 24, 1840-July 18, 1918) and ***Jane STEVENS*** (Oct 6, 1833-Dec 22, 1923), Jane disinterred from Rocky River, OH; Sec. 22, lot 875. Belle is buried in Lakeview Cemetery, Cleveland with her sister, ***Jane TRAYTE KNAGGS***, wife of ***Frank*** - above. Sec. 5, Lot 966. Lakeview Cemetery, Cleve./Certif. of Death.

Walter S. WILKSHIRE served during the Spanish American War with the L5 Ohio Inf. (S), Sgt. Maj. + B 46 US. vol. Inf. He received a military pension (application 1391 646 Certif. 1285452) and applied as an invalid while living in California. Belle received a widow's pension after his death (application 1222 346 Certif. 972 274 XC2718-143). Veteran Pension Record, microfilm, National Archives. Records held with Veterans Administration.

Walter S. WILKSHIRE, Fifth Regiment, Ohio Volunteer, Company L, private, res. Fernandina, FL, 27 yrs. Ohio Soldiers in the War with Spain 1898-99, p. 387.

Walter S. WILKSHIRE; Foot *(sp.)* Rd., Bay Village, married; wife ***Belle WILKSHIRE***; d. July 22, 1924, Bay, Cuyahoga Co., died sudden at house in bed no medical aid or cau. Probably chron. myocarditis arteri-sclerosis, contributory: chron. nephritis; 53 yrs. 6 mos., b. Jan 22, 1871, Cleveland, Ohio; fr. ***Wm. WILKSHIRE***, b. England; mo. ***Nellie SUNDERLAND***, b. England; occup. mnfg. Elec. Taxs; bur. Bay Village, undertaker C. Pease, 2835 A. Dover Center, O., bur. July 24, 1924. Informant *Mrs. Belle WILKSHIRE.* Ohio Certificate of Death, Division of Vital Statistics, 1924, certif. 38261.

WILKSHIRE - Walter S., beloved husband of ***Belle WILKSHIRE*** (nee *PRAYTE (Trayte)*), suddenly, July 22, age 53 years. Funeral from late residence, Foot*(sp.)* avenue, Bay Village, O., Stop 32, Thursday, July 24, at 2:30 p.m. Cleveland Necrology File, July 23, 1924.

Parents of Walter Wilkshire:
The State of Ohio, Cuyahoga County, ss. I Certify, That on 20th day of Jany 1868 ***Mr. William WILKSHIRE*** and ***Miss Ellen SUNDERLAND*** are by me legally joined in Marriage. A.J. Washburn, Rector. Marriage Record, Cuyahoga County, OH, vol. 14, p. 151

WILKSHIRE, William, 36, Gas filler, value real estate $3,000, value of personal estate $600, b. England, parents foreign born, Citizen of U.S.; ***Ellen***, 23, b. Ohio, father foreign born; ***William***, 13, b. Mass.; ***Henry***, 10, b. Mass.; ***Della***, 8/12 yr. *(8 months old)*, b. Oct in Ohio. 1870 FC OH CY Cleveland, 6th Ward, p. 105, lines 7-11.

WILKSHIRE, William, 50, Plummer *(sp.)*, b. England, parents b. England; ***Ellen***, 32, wife, keeping house, b. New York, fr. b. England, mo. b. Scotland; ***Della M.***, 10, dau., b. Ohio; ***Walter S.***, 9, son, b. Ohio; ***Libbie H.***, 5, dau., b. Ohio. 1880 FC OH CY Cleveland Ward 2, p. 101C, lines 39-43.

Brother of Walter: ***William WILKSHIRE***, d. Apr 27, 1914, 4:00 p.m. at Cooley Farms, Warrensville, Cuyahoga Co., Ohio of Chronic nephritis; 59 yrs. 10 mos. 2 ds.; Married; Tinner; b. June 25, 1854, Mass. to ***Wm. WILKSHIRE***, b. England and (mother) not obtainable, b. England; informant H. H. Ward, Cooley Farms; undertaker S.W. Mather, 3227 West 25th, Cleveland; burial Brooklyn Heights Cem. Ohio Certificate of Death, Division of Vital Statistics, 1914, certif. 21208.

Wife of Walter Wilkshire, Clara Isabelle Trayte:

Clara Isabelle WILKSHIRE, d. Nov 30, 1946, 2:45 p.m. at Cleveland State Hospital, Cleveland, Ohio. 76 yrs. 3 mo. 12 days; usual residence 2193 Bellfield, Cleveland Hts., O.; cause Cerebral Thrombosis for 48 hrs., due to cerebral-arteriosclerosis…; b. 18 Aug 1870, London, England, occup. housework; fr. ***Wm. TRAYTE***, b. England, mo. ***Jane STEVENS***, b. England; Informant *Roland M. TRAYTE*, 2193 Bellfield Rd., bur. Lake View, 12-2-46. Ohio Certificate of Death, Division of Vital Statistics, and Maher Melbourne Funeral Home, South Euclid, OH.

WILKSHIRE: C. Belle, wife of the late ***Walter***; sister of *Roland M. TRAYTE*, the late *William, Ernest, Oscar, Herbert* and *Mrs. Willa DRYER*, ***Mrs. Jane KNAGGS***; Saturday, Nov 30, 1946. Friends may call at Charles Melbourne & Sons Colonial Home, 12777 Euclid Ave., where services will be held Monday, Dec 2, at 3 p.m. Newspaper death notice provided by Maher Melbourne Funeral Home, South Euclid, OH.

Frank KNAGGS and ***Walter WILKSHIRE*** *(this lot)*, both married into the Trayte family. The following is a sketch of their wives' genealogy:

William TRAYTE, b. 24 Aug 1835, Walworth, Surrey, England; d. 18 July1918, Cleveland, Cuyahoga Co., OH; m.1 30 June 1854, St. Barnabas, Middlesex, England to ***Jane EDMONDS*** (b. 1836, d. 1854); m.2 7 Jan 1856, St. John's Church, Paddington, England to ***Jane STEVENS*** (b. 6 Oct 1833, Strowbridge, Witshire, England; d. 22 Dec 1923, Cleveland, OH).

Issue: ***William Thomas TRAYTE***, b. 30 Nov 1856, Kentish Town, London, Eng.; d. 31 May 1858, London; bur. Highgate Cemetery, London. ***Wilhelmina Mary TRAYTE***, b. 18 Sept 1858, Kentish Town; d. 28 June 1916, Cleveland; m. 5 Jan 1893, Cleveland to *John H. DRY(ER)* (b. 1856, m.; d. 3 Apr 1933, Cleveland). ***William Atkins TRAYTE***, b. 19 July1860, Kentish Town; d. 20 June 1892, Cleveland. ***Jane TRAYTE***, b. 25 Sept 1862, Kentish Town; d. 24 Oct 1932, Cleveland; m. *Francis John (Frank) KNAGGS* (b. 26 July1863, Etobicoke/Toronto, Ontario, Canada; d. 6 Jan 1931, Rocky River, Cuyahoga Co., OH). ***Ernest Stevens TRAYTE***, b. 25 Sept 1864, Kentish Town; d. 7 Mar 1931, Cleveland; m. 28 Dec 1892 to *Alice Mary OTT* (b. Dec 1892; d. 30 Jan 1930, Cleveland). ***Clara Isabelle (Belle) TRAYTE***, b. 18 Aug 1866, St. Paul's Road, Highbury Islington, London, Eng.; d. 30 Nov 1946, Cleveland; m. 25 Dec 1890, Cleveland to *Walter S. WILKSHIRE* (b. 1871; d. 22 July1924, Bay Village, Cuyahoga Co., OH). ***Oscar William TRAYTE***, b. 10 Apr 1869, Broadstairs, Kent, Eng.; m. *Daisey Beverly* (b. 1868, Michigan). ***Herbert Horace TRAYTE***, b. 10 June 1871, Broadstairs; d. 21 June 1919, Cleveland; m. 29 Nov 1899, Cleveland to *Elizabeth Jane (Bessie) GALLOWAY*. ***Horacio Roland Melrose TRAYTE***, b. 4 Apr 1874, Swanage, Dorset, Eng.; d. 15 Mar 1959, Euclid, Cuyahoga Co., OH; m. 24 June 1915 *Cora GUISE* (b. 19 Dec 1890; d. 19 May 1970, Novelty, OH). Except for William Thomas, who died as an infant, the family came to the U.S. in August 1881, on the S.S. California of the "Anchor Line." They were salon passengers on this U.S. Mail Steamer from London to New York. Herbert J. Trayte

Jane TRAYTE KNAGGS, is buried in Lakeview Cemetery, Cleveland, with her sister, ***Belle WILKSHIRE***, wife of ***Walter*** *(below)*. Her parents, *William* and *Jane TRAYTE* are also at Lakeview (Sect. 22, Lot 875). Lakeview Cemetery, Cleveland death notice.

William TRAYTE, Practical Carpenter and Builder, res. 74 Allen, business 85 Allen and 19 Hickox. 1883 Cleveland City Directory.

TRAYTE-William, beloved husband of *Jane* and father of *Ernest S., Oscar W., Herbert H., Roland M.,* ***Mrs. F. KNAGGS*** and ***Mrs. W. S. WILKSHIRE***. Funeral from residence of son, Ernest S., 1158 E. 102d st…1835-1918. Lakeview Cem. Prospect List. Cemetery record. Cleveland Necrology File, July 20, 1918.

William TRAYTE, d. July 18, 1918, 11233 Superior Ave., 25th Ward, Cleveland, Cuyahoga Co., Ohio of Arterio-sclerosis; 78 yrs. 11 mos. 25 ds.; Married; Carpenter Contractor, General Contractor; b. Aug 24, 1840, England to *William TRAYTE*, b. England and *Nancy* (unclear), b. England; informant *Mrs. Clara WILKSHIRE*, 11233 Superior; undertaker Charles Melbourne, 1315 E. 77th; burial Lake View. Ohio Certificate of Death, Division of Vital Statistics, 1918, certif. 41928.

TRAYTE-Jane, widow of ***William***, mother of …at residence of daughter, 1850 Wooster road, on Saturday, December 22, age 90. Services at parlors of Charles Melbourne & Sons, 12737 Euclid avenue, Monday, December 24, at 2 p. m. Cleveland Necrology File, Dec 22, 1923.

It is assumed the following headstones are for George and Martha Jane Pickering below. Neither Frank Knaggs nor Walter Wilkshire had children. The map may be inaccurate.

Lot 20-4 *(assumed Lot 21)* George Pickering

FATHER

Lot 20-5 *(assumed Lot 21)*Martha Jane Pickering

MOTHER 

Lot 21 *Owner: Robert Pickering of Bay Village purchased May 4, 1914, for $6.79* SL

Lot 21 George Pickering

FIND MAN IN LAKE, FOUL PLAY FEARED

Bay Village Residents Discover Body and Coroner Byrne Will Investigate.

Marks on Head Lead to Suspicion of Death by Violence.

After a preliminary investigation of the drowning of ***George PICKERON*** *(sp.)*, 55, Dover, whose body was found in the lake off Gleason's pier in Bay Village early yesterday morning, Coroner P.J. Byrne last night said he would conduct *(a)* thorough inquiry today.

Pickeron's body was found at daybreak on the sands at the foot of the pier by *Thomas GLEASON* and *James SEASOL*, both of Bay Village. They found Pickeron's coat floating on the water and after a search saw the body.

Coroner Byrne was told Pickeron had been fishing off the pier with friends Saturday night. He remained after the others of the party went home, Coroner Byrne was told.

Marks about the head caused the coroner to believe Pickeron may have met with violence.

Fish Pole Found.

Pickeron's lantern and a basket of fish were found upset on the dock where he had been fishing. His fishing pole was nearby. His friends were inclined to believe he stumbled and fell into the water just after he gathered up his fishing outfit to depart. They believe the marks on his head were made as the body struck a pile of the dock.

The body was taken to the morgue of Pease & Co., Bay Village. Monday, May 4, 1914, p. 1, col. 3. The Plain Dealer.

George PICKERING, d. May 2, 1914, Bay Village, Lake Erie, Cuy Co., Ohio, Found on Lake Shore - small wound in back of head. Looks like Accidental Drowning. Looks Peculiar. P. J. Byrne, coroner. Married; farmer; b. Oct 1, 1858, England, fr. ***Robert PICKERING***, b. England, mo. ***Anna FOSTER***, b. England; 55 yrs. 7 mos. 2 ds.; bur. Bay Village, May 4, 1914, undertaker Jas. Pease & Son, Dover, O. Informant *Robt. PICKERING*, No. Dover, O. R.F.D. Ohio Certificate of Death, Division of Vital Statistics, 1914, certif. 26736.

George PICKERING; res. Bay Village; English; interred May 5th, 1914 ; Lot 21. "List of Interments," Lakeside Cemetery, Bay Village, OH.

Lot 21 *Martha Jane Pickering

Martha, wife of George Pickering, was not identified officially in a specific lot. It is assumed that she is buried with her husband in the family plot beneath the stone "Mother." Martha passed away on April 14, 1930, but is listed with her son in the 1930 census that was recorded on April 26, 1930.

Cabbage Salad
(Mrs. George Pickering)

One-half cup vinegar (stirred into two well beaten eggs), cook until it thickens. When cool, add two tablespoons rich, sweet cream with salt, pepper, mustard and sugar to taste. Pour this over one-half cabbage that has been sliced very thin. The Village Cook Book, p. 23. (c1911-1915)

Thin Cookies
(Mrs. George Pickering)

One cup butter, one cup sugar, three eggs, all beaten together to a cream, use just enough flour to mix and roll thin. The Village Cook Book, p. 36. (c1911-1915)

PICKERING, Rob, head, own farm, Bassett Rd., 31 yrs., single, immig. 1889, b. Canada, fr. b. England, mo. b. Canada, occup. Express Mgr., R.R.Co.; ***Martha***, mother, 61 yrs., widow, immig. 1889, Naturalized or Alien: Pa, b. Canada, fr. b. England, mo. b. Scotland. 1920 FC OH CYBV p.6A, lines 43-4.

PICKERING, Robert F., 41, single, owns home valued at $10,000, no radio, b. Canada, fr. b. England, mo. b. Canada, English, immigrated 1889, Naturalized citizen, Fruit farmer; ***Martha J.***, mother, 71, widow, b. Canada, fr. b. England, mo. b. No. Ireland, immigrated 1889, Alien. 1930 FC OH CYBV, Ed 18-534, p. 21A, 29428 Osborn Rd., lines 2-3.

PICKERING: Martha J., wife of the late ***George*** and mother of ***Robert PICKERING***, at residence, 29428 Osborn Road, Bay Village, Ohio. Funeral from Bay Village M. E. Church, Stop 32, Wednesday, April 16, at 2:30 p.m. Wed., April 16, 1930, p. 27, col. 5. The Plain Dealer.

Mrs. Martha Jane PICKERING, 29428 Osborn Rd; d. April 14, 1930, 1 p.m., Bay Village, Cuyahoga Co., O., Hypostatic pneumonia, 2 ds., contributory: Epithelioma of nose; widow of ***George PICKERING***; b. Aug 16, 1858, Guelph, Ontario, Canada, *parents not listed*; 71 yrs. 7 mos. 28 ds.; bur Bay Village, April 16, 1930, undertaker C. Pease, Dover Center, embalmed; informant ***Robert PICKERING***, 29428 Osborn Rd., Bay Village. Ohio Certificate of Death, Division of Vital Statistics, 1930, certif.

21299 and Bureau of Vital Statistics, Burial or Removal Permit, Bay Village, OH.

Son of George and Martha Pickering:

Robert PICKERING was a bachelor who lived with his mother. Sarah Dodd Wymer, former Bay Village resident.

There was another Pickering family in Avon Lake with a number of similarities. John, b. Nov 1834, England, m. 42 yrs., immigrated 1849. John and Ellen had a son named George, b. in Ohio, Mar 1867. Next door to them was Robert Pickering, b. 1875, Ohio, with both parents b. England. There may have been a relationship which might be the reason George settled in the area . 1900 FC OH LRAV, p. 4A, lines, 39-47. John is also in the 1870 FC OH LRAV, p. 359, lines 1-8 and 1880 FC OH LRAV, p. 325D, lines 20-3.

PICKERING Frank, 1873-; *Grace*, 1876-1951; *Robert*, 1875-1937; *Mabel*, 1879-1938. *PICKERING George*, 1867-1930; *Miriam*, 1879-1972. Genealogical Workshops of the Lorain County Historical Society, Cemetery Inscriptions of Lorain County, Avon Center (Mounds) Cemetery, Avon, OH, p. 81. Read by Catherine Burke Flament.

Lot 22 *Owner: Mrs. Sarles purchased July 30, 1908, for $5.98* SL

Lot 22-6 Ray D. Sarles

(new marker; north end)
RAY D. SARLES
1898-1907

Lot 22-7

D.
SARLES
1898-1907

(original marker; foot of grave)

The date of death on the stones is incorrect, it should read 1898-1908. See information following parents.

Lot 22-8 Sarles Marker

SARLES

FATHER	MOTHER
GEORGE F.	ELIZABETH
1867-1905	1871-1932

Lot 22-8 and 9 George F. Sarles

The State of Ohio, Cuyahoga County, ss. I Certify that on the 7th day of January 1888 ***Mr. George F. SARLES*** and ***Miss Lizzie KEYSE*** were by me legally joined in marriage. E. Hitchens J.P. Marriage Record, Cuyahoga County, OH, vol. 31, p. 274.

SARLES, George, 31, head, b. Sep 1868, Ohio, parents b. Ohio, married 12 yrs., fisherman; ***Lizzie***, 29, wife, b. Apr 1871, Ohio, parents b. Ohio, 5 children born, 3 living; ***Ben***, 8, b. July 1891, Ohio; ***Harry***, 5, son, b. May 1895, Ohio; ***Ray***, 1, son, b. Aug 1899, Ohio. 1900 FC OH CYDO, p. 21 A/B, lines 49-53. *Living one house east of Henry Wischmeyer.*

George SARLES was born Oct 27, 1867, in Norwalk, OH, the son of ***William Henry SARLES (SEARLES)*** (b. Westchester, Co., NY Aug 18 or 19, 1820; m. 20 May 1844, Milan, Erie Co., OH; d. Aug 14, 1893; fought in the Civil War, Co. M I, Reg't Ohio Volunteers Heavy Artillery from Milan, OH) and ***Lydia Ann KNAPP*** (d. June 14, 1901). William and Lydia were divorced and remarried five times. George married ***Elizabeth KEYSE*** and was employed as a street car conductor.

Children of George Sarles and Elizabeth Keyse: ***Benjamin Franklin SARLES,*** b. 9 July1890, Huron, OH; m. 20 Oct 1915, Cleveland, Cuyahoga, OH to *Grace HAUGHTON* (b. 28 Jan 1891, d. 19 Apr 1969, Oakland, CA); res. Painesville, Lake Co., OH, occup. employed by the City of Euclid, OH; d. 14 July1964, Painesville. ***Harry William SARLES,*** b. 6 May 1895, Rocky River, Cuyahoga, OH; m. 18 Mar 1918, Wickliffe, OH to *Ferol May BONES* (b. 18 Mar 1896, d. 2 Jan 1950); res. Painesville, occup. during W.W.I worked in shipyards in Rocky River, later a carpenter; d. 3 Sep 1983, West Palm Beach, Palm Beach, FL. ***Ray D. SARLES***, b. 1898 *(see above).* ***Lloyd James SARLES***, b. 6 July1901, Bay Village, OH; m. 28 Mar 1925 to *Caroline Mary JOHNSON* (b. 7 Sept 1903 Mt. Vernon, West Chester, NY; d. 11 Nov 1961, West Palm Beach); res. Juno Beach, FL; occup. painter; d. 26 May 1964, West Palm Beach. George died in Lakewood, Ohio in a street car accident on July 30, 1905. Raymond Sarles family genealogy collection.

HURT IN CRASH, MAN DIES BY LIVE WIRE

Lake Shore Electric Express Jumps Curve and Motorman is Killed.

CONDUCTOR IS INJURED.

Heavy Car Loaded With Newspapers Smashes Into Trolley Pole - Sand on Tracks.

While running at full speed early yesterday morning the Lake Shore Electric express jumped the curve at Clifton boulevard and slid along the roadway on its side. Motorman ***George SEARLES*** *(sp.)*, of North Dover, was crushed under the wreckage and then killed by coming in contact with live wires. Conductor *Ernest PORTER*, also of North Dover, was badly injured, but he was able to crawl from the wreck and summon assistance.

Sand on Track.

The heavy rain during the night washed considerable sand down on the curve. It is thought that the motorman did not notice this, nor that he was so near the curve. When the car swung into it, Searles and Porter, the only men on the car, were thrown to the floor. Searles jumped to his feet, shut off the power and applied the airbrakes. The car lurched on to the straight track and the front trucks left the rails, throwing the car over on its side. It slid for thirty feet along the ground, and was stopped by an iron pole supporting the trolley wires. The blow shook the trolley wires from their fastenings and they fell to the ground. The car was torn free of the rear trucks, which shot on up the track for several hundred feet.

Motorman is Killed.

Searles' left leg was torn from his body when the crash came and he was pitched headfirst through the vestibule. His skull was fractured. He fell on the sputtering trolley wires and was instantly killed.

Porter, who was inside the car, sustained a crushed ankle and received many cuts and bruises. He crawled out of the wreckage and to the home of County Surveyor *William H. EVERS*, near by, from where he called Mastick's ambulance. Among the people who quickly gathered about the wreck was a man on a bicycle. Porter borrowed it and rode to Rocky River, where he notified the car dispatcher and also the wife of Searles. He then went to his home. Searles' body was taken to his home. He leaves a widow and four children. He had been in the employ of the road for three years.

The express car carried a heavy load of newspapers for Western Ohio towns. It left the Public Square at 4:30 o'clock, a half-hour late. Cleveland Leader, Monday, July 31, 1905, p. 12, col. 2.

George SEARLES, 39, res. Dover, cause of death accidental, July 30, 1905, certifying phys. coroner Sieghstine?, burial Osborn Cemetery, funeral at house. Funeral Expenses: Casket $50, Outside box $4, Shroud $6, 6 prs. of gloves $1, washing of remains $2, Keeping in Ice, in Freezer, or Embalming $8, 2 carriages to cemetery $12, Hearse $8. Daniel's Funeral Home Record.

Geo. SARLES, 38; res. Bay Village; interred Aug 1, 1905; Lot 22. "List of Interments," Lakeside Cemetery, Bay Village, OH.

Children of George Sarles and Elizabeth Keyse:

Benjamin F. SARLES, 25, res. Rocky River, b. Lorain, O., occup. Salesman. Married ***Grace E. HOUGHTON***, 24, res. 46 Allendale, E.C., b. Cleveland, O, fr. *Frank,* mo. *Mary FURNAL*, neither prev. married. The State of Ohio, Cuyahoga County, ss. I Certify that on 20 Oct 1915 the marriage of Benjamin F. Sarles and Grace E. Houghton was solemnized by Dr. Thomas A. King, Mars Ave., Lakewood, O. Marriage Record, Cuyahoga County, OH, vol. 94, p. 321.

Lloyd J. SARLES, 23, res. Rocky River, b. Dover, O., Clerk, fr. *George,* mo. *Elizabeth KEYES.* Married ***Caroline M. JOHNSON***, 21, res. 2084 Olive Ave., b. New York City, fr. *Thomas,* mo. *Caroline VAN FELT;* neither previously married. The State of Ohio, Cuyahoga County, ss. I Certify that on the 28th day of March *1925 Mr. Lloyd J. Sarles* and Miss Caroline M. Johnson were by me legally joined in marriage. Rev. D.L.B. Goodwin. Marriage Record, Cuyahoga County, vol. 139, p. 410.

Lot 22-9 George Sarles

FATHER

GEORGE F. SARLES 1867-1905

(original marker)

Lot 22-8 and 10 Elizabeth Keyse Sarles

Elizabeth KEYSE was born in 1871 in Rockport Twp., Ohio, the daughter of ***Henry*** (d. Feb 1882) and ***Katherine KEYSE*** (d. Nov 1898). Raymond Sarles family genealogy papers

Elizabeth SARLES, d. at residence Dec 13, 1932, 1732 Lakeview, Rocky River, Cuyahoga Co., Influenza 12/8/32 and Pneumonia 12/12/32; widow of ***George SARLES***; 61yrs. 7 mos. 23 ds.; b. Apr 21, 1871, Rocky River; fr. ***Henry KEYSE***, b. England, mo. ***Catherine ODON***, b. Cleveland, O; Informant *Lloyd SARLES,* 6137 Wareham Rd., Parma, bur. Cahoon, Dec 14, undertaker Wm. Daniels, 15800 Detroit Ave., Lakewood, O. Ohio Certificate of Death, Division of Vital Statistics, 1932, certif. 69491.

SARLES, Elizabeth, beloved mother of ***Benjamin F., Harry W.*** and ***Lloyd J.***, sister of ***Fannie KRUEGER, Nellie WILKINS*** and ***Frank KEYSE***. Services at residence,

1732 Lakeview Rd., Rocky River, Saturday, December 17th, at 2:30 p.m. Cleveland Necrology File, December 17, 1932, roll 71.

Family of Elizabeth Keyse Sarles:

Lot C-74 ***Henry KEYSE,*** 02/?/1882; ***William KEYSE,*** *07/?/1881;* both moved from Lot C-63 on 4/4/1931. Lot C-72, ***Katherine KEYSE,*** 11/07/1898. Other Keyse at Cemetery: Lot B-6 ***Cora Mary*** 1868-05/07/1962, 96 yrs.; ***Kittie Irene***, 1889-1900 (dau. of Wm.), 11 yrs.; ***Wm. J.*** 1861-1892, 31. Lot C-21 ***Everett***, 12/12/1902-3/23/1903, 1 yr.; ***James***, 12/06/1822-12/20/1897, 75 yrs. Lot 43, ***Frankey C.***, 3/15/1863-9/15/1864, 1 yr.; ***Martha J.***, 5/08/1843-11/12/1872, 29 yrs. Barbara Musselman, Fairview Park Cemetery (Rockport Cemetery), Cuyahoga County, OH. Records at Fairview Park City Hall and Fairview Park Branch of the Cuyahoga County Library.

Siblings of Elizabeth Keyse Sarles:

The State of Ohio, Cuyahoga County, ss. I Certify that on the 20th day of March 1884, ***Mr. Charles KRUEGER*** and ***Miss Fannie KEYSE*** were united in marriage. J. E. Canfield, J.P. Marriage Record, Cuyahoga County, OH, vol. 27, p. 247.

KRUEGER, Fannie A., age 67, mother of ***Arthur, Russell*** and ***Hazel,*** sister of ***Frank*** and ***Nellie,*** at her late residence, 1018 E. 141st St., Aug 8. Now at the parlors of the Millard Son & Raper Co., Carnegie at E. 105th St., where services will be held Friday at 2:30 p.m. Aug 10, 1933, p. 17., col. 3. The Plain Dealer.

KRUEGER, Fannie Alice, d. Aug 8, 1933, 11 a.m., 1018 E. 141 St., Cleveland, Cuyahoga Co., Ohio of Myocarditis for 2 yrs.; widow of ***Charles KRUEGER***; b. Aug 13, 1866, Rocky River, Ohio, fr. *Henry KEYES,* b. Unknown, mo. unknown; 67 y. 11 mos. 25 days; occup. at home; informant *Russel E. KRUEGER* (son), 1133 E. 144 St.; undertaker The Millard Son & Raper Co., 2092 E. 105th St., burial Lakeview, *(Cleveland, OH).* Ohio Certificate of Death, Division of Vital Statistics, 1933, certif. 44258.

Nellie KEYSE, 20, res. Rocky River, b. Rockport, fr. *Henry KEYSE*, mo. *Catherine ODON*, neither previously married. Married ***Edward J. WILKINS***, 22, res. 628 St. Clair St., City *(Cleveland),* b. Clio, Mich., occup cook, fr. *Geo. J. WILKINS*, mo. *Kate ERCLESTIN (sp.?)*; 11 Dec 1899, Cuyahoga County, OH. Marriage Record, Cuyahoga County, OH, vol. 49, p. 463. *Film dark and difficult to read.*

Lot 22-10 Elizabeth Keyse Sarles

MOTHER
(original marker for Elizabeth Sarles)

Lot 22 Ray D. Sarles

Son of George Sarles and Elizabeth Keyse.

Ray D. SEARLS *(sp.)*, 9; res. Rocky River; interred Feb 26, 1908. "List of Interments," Lakeside Cemetery, Bay Village, OH.

Ray D. SARLES, 9, Rocky River; d. Feb 26, 1908, Lakewood Hospital, chief cause of death Meningitis, contributing Measles, duration of illness two weeks; b. July 18, 1898, Lakewood, OH, fr. b. Norwalk, OH, mo. b. Rocky River; occup scholar; burial Dover Osborn Cemetery, undertaker Mastick, Physician A.H. Marvin. Board of Health of Lakewood Village, Burial Removal Permit.

SARLES-Ray D., Wednesday, February 26, age, 9 years, son of ***Elizabeth*** and the late ***George SARLES***, Rocky River. Funeral at M.E. church, North Ridge rd., Saturday at 1 p.m. Burial at Osborn cemetery, Dover. Cleveland Necrology File, February 29, 1908, reel 71.

Lot 23 *Owner: Mrs. Lena Bambam of Dover purchased Jan 1901, for $7.48* SL

Lot 23 Frederick Bambam no marker

Frederick and Lena were living with their son in this1900 census record.

BAMBAM, Fred T., 43, b. Dec 1856, Germany, parents b. Germany, Immig. 1872, Na., married 19 yrs., farmer; ***Lizzie R.***, 39, wife, b. Mar 1861, Germany, parents b. Germany, Immig. 1872, 6 children born, 6 living; ***William***, 18, b. May 1882, day laborer; ***Anna G.***, 16, b. Feb 1884; ***Fred J.***, 13, b. June 1886; ***Ferdnand,*** 11, b. Aug 1888; ***Augusta A.***, 9, b. May 1891; ***Elsa,*** 5, Dec 1894. All children b. in Ohio. ***Fred Sr.***, 59, father, b. Feb 1841, Germany, parents b. Germany, Immig 1872, married 33 yrs., unable to read/write; ***Lena***, 63, mother, b. Oct 1836, Germany, parents b. Germany, immig 1872, 1 child born, 1 living, unable to read/write. 1900 FC OH CYDO p. 2A, lines 37-46.

Frederick BAMBAM, 60; res. Dover; German; interred Jan 15, c1901; Lot 23. "List of Interments," Lakeside Cemetery, Bay Village, OH.

Friedrich BAMBAM, 59 years, 17 Jan 1901, p. 334. "Independent Evangelical Church," p. 3.

Children of Frederick Ludwig Theodor Bambam (son of Frederick and Lena Bambam) and Louise Raeder:

Wilhelm Friedr. August, confirmed 26 Maerz *(March)*1896.

Auguste Sophia Catharina, 5th child, b. 8 April 1891, bap. 10 Mai *(May)*1891.

Else Anna, 6th child, b. 14 Mai 1894, bap. 27 Mai. St. Paul Lutheran Church, Westlake, OH.

BAMBAM, William F., age 71, father of *Alvira HARDING, Laverne BUESCH, Beatrice CARLEY* of Flint, Mich., *Arthur, Eleanor* and *Richard*; brother of ***Anna ROCKY, Gussie HANES*** and the late ***Ferd,*** grandfather and great-grandfather, late residence, 3353

W. 59 Pl. Friends may call at Sauer's Funeral Home, 5303 Storer Ave., where services will be held Friday, Sept. 18, at 3 p. m., Rev. Walter K. Klein officiating. Interment Sunset Memorial Park. Cleveland Press, Sep 17 1953.

Anna BAMBAM, 30, res. 2171 East 18th St., b. Cleveland, O., fr. *Fred*, mo. *Louise RADER*. Married ***Thomas J. ROCKEY***, 25, res. 1871 East 18th St., b. Los Angeles, Cal., waiter, fr. *Thomas T.*, mo. *Ella LANG*. State of Ohio, Cuyahoga County, I Certify that on the 7th day of March 1914 Anna Bambam and Thomas J. Rockey were legally joined in marriage. Marriage Record, Cuyahoga County, OH, vol. 88, p. 349.

ROCKY, Thomas J. of Willoughby, O., beloved husband of *Anna*. Friends may call at Davis Funeral Home, 4154 Clark Ave July 28, 1963. The Plain Dealer.

Ferdinand BAMBAM, 32, 3818 Carnegie Ave., b. Cleveland, Carpenter, fr. *Fred*, mo. *Louise RAEDER*. Married ***Alice O. BOUSKA***, 23, 3802 Prospect, b. Austria, fr. *Joseph G.*, mo. *Veronica TRISKA*. Neither previously married. State of Ohio, Cuyahoga County, I Certify that on the 27th day of February 1918 Ferdinand Bambam and Alice O. Bouska were legally married by me. M.J. Penty, J.P. Marriage Record, Cuyahoga County, OH, vol. 108, p. 225.

BAMBAM, Ferdinand L., age 62, of Detroit Rd., R.D. 1, Elyria, O., passed away suddenly... Member of K. of P. Lakewood Lodge 729...husband of ***Alice A. BAMBAM***, brother of ***William, Mrs. Anne ROCKEY*** and ***Mrs. Augusta HANES***...Sudro-Curtis Funeral Home, Elyria. Cleveland Necrology File, June 1 1951.

Lot 23 ***Lena Bambam*** no marker

Lena is listed on the cemetery plot map in the same plot as Frederick, but Lena may be buried at Brooklyn Heights Cemetery with her son.

Lot 514 BAMBAM, no headstones:

Lena BAMBAM, bur. 5/5/1911, 514 Linwood; ***Fred BAMBAM***, bur. 2/12/1917, d. 2/8/1917, 58 years; ***Louise BAMBAM***, bur. 4/18/1908, 46 years; ***Elsie***, bur. 6/12/1907, 13 years *(daughter of Frederick L)*. Interment Records, Brooklyn Hts. Cemetery, Cleveland, OH.

BAMBAM, Lina geb SASS - MECKL SCHW, 73 years, 2 May 1911, p. 360; ***Frederick BAMBAM***, *(b.)* 27 Dec 1858, Mkl. Schwerien, 8 Feb 1917, p. 380; ***Louise BAMBAM***, geb Raden in Striethof, Pom., 46 years, 11 April 1908, p. 352. "Independent Evangelical Church," p. 3.

Mrs. Lena BAMBAM, d. May 2, 1911, 9 p.m. at 3232 W. 48th St., Cleveland, Cuyahoga County, OH. b. Oct 16, 1837, Germany; 73 yrs.; retired; father ***Frederick BAMBAM***, *(Assumed mistake, that this is the name of her husband due to the last name.)* b. Germany; mother Don't Know, b. Germany; informant *Frederick L. BAMBAM*, 3232 West 48 St. Cause of death Myocarditis - 1 year and Senility. R.H. Sunkle, M.D., 2107 Clark; burial Brooklyn Hgts., OH; bur 5/5/1911; undertaker S.W. Mather, 3227 W. 25th St. Ohio Certificate of Death, Division of Vital Statistics, 1911, certif. 25804.

I, ***Lena BAMBAM*** of the City of Cleveland...being seventy five years of age...Second: Bequeath to ***William BAMBAM*** an adopted child the sum of five Dollars...Third: All the rest of my property and effects...to my son ***Frederick SASSE*** also known as ***Frederick BAMBAM*** and his heirs. Signed with her mark (X) on 30 April 1910. Probate Will, Cuyaghoga County, OH, 1911 56216, vol. 86, p. 441.

Fred L. BAMBAM, d. Dec 12, 1917, 8 p.m., 4129 Train Ave., Ward 4, Cleveland, Cuyahoga Co., Ohio, cause Acute Myocarditis; married; b. Dec 27, 1859, Germany; fr. ***Fred BAMBAM***, b. Germany, mo. don't know, b. Germany; occup. Time Keeper; Informant *Mary (HAGEN) BAMBAM, (wife)* (same address); bur. B. Hgts Cemetery, undertaker S.W. Mather, 3227 W. 25th St. Ohio Certificate of Death, Division of Vital Statistics, 1917, certif. 9004; Cleveland Necrology File, Feb. 10, 1917, roll 3 and Marriage Record, Cuyahoga County, OH, vol. 76, p. 42 .

Elsie Anna BAMBAM, 13 years, 10 June 1907, p. 350. "Independent Evangelical Church," p. 3.

BAMBAM, Elsie Anna, 13, female, b. Ohio, Endocarditis, res. 4129 Train, d. at res., ill 4 ms., b. Germany. Died June 10, 1907. Probate Court Death Records, Cuyahoga County, Ohio,

BAMBAM, Elsie Anna, 13, F., res. 4129 Train... City Deaths, Cleveland, OH.

The family below is thought to be related due to the proximity of the graves, the exact relationship is unclear.

Lot 512, BAMBAM:

Carl BAMBAM, bur. 7/5/1924, age 76; ***Lena BAMBAM***, bur. 2/13/1919, age 67, Linwood *(wife)*; ***Fred BAMBAM***, bur. 11/25/1910, age 29, *(son)*; ***Rudolph***, bur. 11/11/1933, age 49 *(son)*; ***John KOLAR***, bur. 11/3/1943, age 65. Interment Records, Brooklyn Heights Cemetery, Cleveland, OH.

Bambam, Charles, 63, married 39 yrs., b. Germany, immigrated 1871, laborer, lumberyard; ***Lena***, 60, wife, # children b. 7, living 3, b. Germany, immig. 1871; ***Fred***, 28, b. Ohio, musician, Dancer; ***Rudolph***, 26, b. Ohio, works tinner, pan factory... 1910 FC OH 2-WD Cleveland Twp., Roll 1166, p. 196, lines 1-6.

Carl BAMBAM, d. July 2, 1924, res. 3203 W. 44th St., Ward 3, Cleveland, Cuyahoga Co., Ohio., cause Heart Endocarditis and Dropsy; widowed, wife ***Lena BAMBAM***; b. March 30, 1848, Meklenburg, Germany; fr. ***John BAMBAM***, b. Meklenburg, mo. ***Sophia BEAUTZ***, b. Meklenburg, Germany; Laborer-Lumberyard; 76 yrs 3 months 2 days; In U.S. and this city 51 years. Informant *William BAMBAM* (son, same address), bur. Brooklyn Hgts. Cem.; undertaker S.W. Mather Co. Ohio Certificate of Death, Division of Vital Statistics, 1924, file 38302.

Lena BAMBAM, d. Feb 13, 1919, 11:30 a.m., 3203 W. 44th St., Ward 5, Cleveland, Cuyahoga, Ohio; cause Carcinoma of Liver, Dropsy General; married; b. May 28, 1851, Germany; fr. ***John BOLL***, b. Germany, mo. don't know, b. Germany; Housewife; 67 yrs. 8 mo. 15 days; bur. Brooklyn Heights, undertaker Henry Dress (ink splotch). Ohio Certificate of Death, Division of Vital Statistics, 1919, file 9522.

Lena BAMBAM, geb 28 May 1851 Sternberg Mklschw., 13 Feb 1919, p. 388; ***Friedrich BAMBAM***, 29 yrs., 23 Nov 1910, p. 359. "Independent Evangelical Church," p. 3.

Lots 24/25 *Owned by: Mrs. H. Daveter of Dover purchased Aug 20, 1898, for $10.85, who resold to R. Osborn in December 1918, who resold/bequeathed to Clare M. Osborn.* SL

Lot 24 *Henry Davider*

no marker, moved

Heinrich DAVIDER was moved from Lakeside to St. Paul Lutheran Church Cemetery, Westlake, OH, in December of 1910 to section B, Lot S 1/2 3. He was married on 10 Nov 1859 to ***Eleanora Maria MEYER*** (b. 25 Sept 1836, Hanover, Germany, dau. of *August Meyer* and *Elizabeth Gerkeworkruian*?, d. 30 Mar 1927, bur. St. Paul Cemetery). St. Paul Lutheran Church, Westlake, OH. *Heinrich's monument is the tallest in the church cemetery, located in the middle section to the west of the driveway.*

Henry FOOTE sold a strip of the western end of his farm in 1898, forming the Eagle Cliff subdivision along the lake. The Daviders lived just south of it on Bradley Road. Bay Village Historical Society, Bay Village: A Way of Life, pp. 54, 89

Henry DAVIDER, Lot 97, which is located at the north west corner of what is now Bay Village, bordering Avon Lake. His lot was north of *Henry MEILANDER*, south of *Henry P. FOOTE* and west of *Henry W. ALDRICH*. 1880 Map of Dover Twp.

DAVIDER, Henry, 45, farmer, b. Prus(s)ia, parents b. Prusia; ***Ellen***, 42, wife, b. Hanover, parents b. Hanover; ***Mary***, 19; ***Herman***, 16; ***William***, 12; ***Henry***, 10; ***August***, 8; ***Mattie***, 5. All children b. Ohio. 1880 FC OH CYDO, p. 99, lines 4-11.

DAVIDER, Henry. Owned land; Acres: Improved - Tilled, including fallow and grass: 29, Permanent meadow: 7, Unimproved - Woodland: 4. Farm Values: Land and buildings - $4,000, Machinery - $100, Live Stock - $200. Estimated value of all farm production: $400. Grass lands: acreage: 8 mown, 5 not mown, 10 tons hay. 1 horse, 3 milch cows, 3 other, 1 calf dropped, 1 cattle sold living, 1 slaughtered. 300 pounds of butter made on the farm. 5 swine. 30 barnyard poultry on farm, 175 dozen eggs produced in 1879. Indian corn: 6 acres, 250 bushels; oats: 4 acres, 170 bushels ; rye: 1 acre, 20 bushels; wheat: 2 acres, 50 bushels; potatoes: 3 acres , 300 bushels. Orchards - apple: 1 acre, 30 bearing trees, 20 bushels. Total value of orchard products: $10. "Schedule 2. Production of Agriculture in Dover Township, Cuyahoga County, OH," enumerated June 1880, p. 34.

Henry DAVETER, 63; res. Eagle Cliff; German; interred Aug 20, 1898; Lot 24. "List of Interments," Lakeside Cemetery, Bay Village, OH.

Wife of Henry Davider, Eleanora Meyer:

DAVIDER, Ellen, 65, b. Sept 1837, yrs. married ?3, 7 children born, 6 living; unable to write, own farm free; ***Will F.***, 32, b. Apr 1868, farm laborer, single; ***Henry C.***, 30, b. Nov 1870, farm laborer, single; ***August F.***, 26, b. Nov 1873, merchant, single; ***Martha M.***, 25, b. Apr 1875, clerk, single. 1900 FC OH CYDO, p. 7A, lines 33-37.

The following census record of Henry's son's family is included to show Henry's place of birth, number of children and where Elenora was living in 1910.

DAVIDER, Henry C., 39, married 5 yrs., b. Ohio, parents b. Germany, married 5 yrs., farmer, general farm; ***Lydia A.***, wife, 37, 2 children born, 2 living, b. Ohio, parents b. Germany; ***Flora A.***, 4; ***Erwin W.***, 2; ***William F.***, brother, 41, single, b. Ohio...farm laborer; ***Elnore M.***, mother, 73, wd., 7 children born, 6 living, b. Germany, parents b. Germany, immig. 1870 *(incorrect due to children's DOB)*, able to read and write. 1910 FC OH CYDO p. 1A, lines 30-35.

DAVIDER-Eleanora, widow of the late ***Henry***, mother of ***Mrs. Mary SCHUZE, Mrs. Martha HOLMES, William, Henry, August*** and the late ***Herman H.***, March 30, aged 90 years. Services from late residence, Bradley road, Bay Village, April 2, at 2 p. m., and St. Paul's Lutheran church, Detroit road, Dover, at 3 p. m. Cleveland Necrology File, Mar 31, 1927.

Ellenora Marie DAVIDER, d. 30 March 1927, Bradley Rd., Bay Village, Cuyahoga County, OH of a Paralytic Stroke; spouse ***Henry DAVIDER***; b. Sept 25, 1837, Germany, fr. ***MIER***, b. Germany, mo. Do not know; 90 yrs. 7 mos.; housewife; Informant *Henry DAVIDER*, West Dover; bur. St. Paul's Lutheran, Dover Village; undertaker C. Pease, Dover Center. Ohio Certificate of Death, Division of Vital Statistics, 1927, file 14023.

Children of Henry Davider and Eleanora Meyer:

Maria DAVIDER; Herman DAVIDER; William Friedrich DAVIDER, b.17 April 1868 Cleveland, m. 23 Oct 1919, *Eleanora WUEBKER*, d. 8 May 1949; ***Johann Heinrich Christian (Henry) DAVIDER***, b. 5 Sept 1870, Dover, m. 10 Nov 1904 to *Lydia STOCKHAUS*, St. Paul Church, Dover, [*Lydia Anna DAVIDER*, res. 29402 Foote Rd.; b. 17 Sept 1872, Cleveland, Ohio, fr. *John STOCKHAUS*, b. Germany; d. Feb 24, 1944, at res. of Coronary Embolism, rel. Ev. Lutheran, St. Paul's Lutheran Cemetery] d. 22 Feb 1956, Arteriosclerotic Heart Disease; ***Franz Heinrich August DAVIDER***, b. 1872; ***August DAVIDER*** and ***Martha DAVIDER***. St. Paul Lutheran Church, Westlake, OH, [Pease Funeral Home Records; Mss. 4809; Western Reserve Historical Society, Cleveland, OH, Record of Funeral, p. 203].

Mary DAVIDER, b. OH; m. *SCHULZE*. ***Herman H. DAVIDER***, b. 1863, OH; m. *Cecelia GIREMAN* (b. 1867, d. 1934) - 2 children; d. 29 Aug 1926, Lakewood, OH, bur. with wife at Lakewood Park Cem., Rocky River, OH. ***William F. DAVIDER***, b. Apr 1868, OH; m. *Elnora "Ella" WUEBKER*, dau. of *Casper WUEBKER* and *Louise A. BAXTER* (d. 1954); 1 child. ***Henry C. DAVIDER***, b. Nov 1870, OH. ***August F. DAVIDER***, b. Nov 1873. ***Martha M. DAVIDER***, b. Apr 1874, Dover Twp., OH; m. *Charles J. HOLMES* (b. NY). Keith M. Sheldon, Descendents of Early Bay Village Families, pp. 339-343.

The State of Ohio, Cuyahoga County, ss. I Certify that on the 24th day of May 1885 ***Mr. Emil SCHULZE*** and ***Mary DAVIDER*** were by me legally joined in marriage. J. Rupprecht, Pastor. Marriage Record, Cuyahoga County, OH, vol. 28, p. 494.

SCHULZE: Mary, widow of ***Emil***, mother of *Selma McCARRAN*, sister of ***Martha HOLMES, William*** and ***Henry DAVIDER***, at Lutheran Home for Aged. Friends received at Erving Dress Funeral Home, 8624 Lorain ave., until 12 noon Sunday. Services at St. Paul's Lutheran Church, Westlake (Dover, O.), Sunday, Jan 12, at 2 p. m. Cleveland Necrology File, Jan 11, 1941.

SCHULZE-Emil, husband of ***Mary SCHULZE*** (nee ***DAVIDER)*** and father of ***Selma***, at residence, Bradley road, Bay Village, stop 35, Sept 21, age 62 yrs. Funeral from late residence at 2 p. m. from Lutheran church, Dover, Ohio, Wed., Sept 24, at 3 p.m. Cleveland Necrology File, Sept 24, 1919.

The State of Ohio, Cuyahoga County, ss. I Certify that on the 14th day of April 1891 ***Mr. Herman DAVIDER*** and ***Cacelia*** *(sp.)* ***GEIERMAN*** were by me legally joined in marriage. J. Rupprecht, Pastor. Marriage Record, Cuyahoga County, OH, vol. 28, p. 494.

DAVIDER, Herman H., beloved husband of ***Celia*** and father of ***Walter H.*** and ***Robert H.***, Sunday at 3 p. m. Services at late residence, 17457 Shaw avenue, Lakewood, Tuesday, Aug 31, at 2:30 p. m. 1863 - 1926. Lakewood Park Cemetery Rocky River, Ohio. Cleveland Necrology File, Cemetery record, Aug 31, 1926.

Herman H. DAVIDER, d. 8-29-1926, 17457 Shaw Ave., Lakewood, Cuyahoga, OH, of Bright's Disease; married, wife ***Cecelia DAVIDER***; Builder; b. Nov 7, 1863, Cleveland, O.; fr. ***Henry DAVIDER***, b. Germany, mo. ***Eleanor*** ____, b. Germany; bur. Lakewood Cemetery, undertaker Wm. Daniel, 15800 Detroit. Ohio Certificate of Death, Division of Vital Statistics, 1926, file 49537.

DAVIDER: Celia, beloved wife of the late ***Herman H.***, mother of ***Robert H.*** and ***Walter H.***, sister of *George* and *Ollie GIERMAN*, at 16802 Delaware Ave. Now at Klanke-Parr Funeral Home, 15407 Detroit Ave., Lakewood. Funeral service will be held at St. James' Church, corner Granger and Detroit, Monday, Jan 8, at 9 a.m. Cleveland Necrology File, Jan 7 1934.

Celia DAVIDER, d. Jan 5, 1934, 7:30 a.m., 16802 Delaware Ave, Lakewood, Cuyahoga Co., Ohio of Chronic Myocarditis and Mitral Insufficiency with Chronic Hypertension starting in Jan 1928; widow of ***Herman H.***; b. May 31, 1866, Delphos, Ohio to *Herman GIERMAN*, b. unknown, mother unknown; informant *Robert DAVIDER*, 16802 Delaware Ave.; undertaker Klanke-Parr Inc., 15407 Detroit Ave., Lakewood; burial Lakewood Park *(Rocky River, Ohio)*. Ohio Certificate of Death, Division of Vital Statistics, 1934, file 1891.

The State of Ohio, Cuyahoga County-ss. I Certify, That on the 23rd day of October 1919 ***Mr. William DAVIDER*** and ***Eleanora WRIEBKER*** *("ie" underlined, correct name Wuebker)* were by me legally joined in marriage, after due publication of bans as provided by law. Rev. F. Reinking. Marriage Record, Cuyahoga County, OH, vol. 103, p. 375.

Parents of Eleanora Wuebker Davider:

WUEBKER, Casper, owns farm, owns radio, 64, age at marriage 21 years, b. Germany, parents b. Germany, immigrated 1884, Naturalized citizen, farmer; ***Louisa B.,*** wife, 65, age at marriage 21, b. Ohio, parents. b. Germany; ***Alma***, daughter, 22, b. Ohio; ***Erma***, daughter, 22, b. Ohio. 1930 FC OH CY Dover Twp., ED 18-534, Bradley Road, p. 24A, lines 6-9.

William DAVIDER was appointed Street Commissioner Aug 31, 1920 and resigned March 15, 1921. Minutes, Ordinances & Resolutions, Bay Village, OH, 1918-1921. *This particular job seemed to be an appointed one and reappointed frequently according to the city minutes. He may have held this job for a longer period of time.*

DAVIDER, William H., 62, owns home with value of $48,500, owns radio, age at first marriage 52, b. Ohio, parents b. Hanover, Germany, Proprietor of fruit farm; ***Eleanor M.***, wife, 41, age at first marriage 31, b. Ohio, fr. b. Germany, mo. b. Ohio; ***Harold***, son, 7, b. Ohio. 1930 FC OH CYBV ED18-534, p. 22A, 206 Bassett Rd., lines 1-3.

William H. DAVIDER, res. 382 Bassett Rd., Bay Village, husband of ***Ella*** (nee ***WUEBKER***); retired gardener…rel. Lutheran, Rev. Wm. Single, d. May 8, 1949, res., cause Chr. Myocarditis with Decompensation-2 wks., Chr. Bronchitis-3 wks.; St. Paul's Lutheran Cemetery. Pease Funeral Home Records, Mss. 4809, Western Reserve Historical Society, Cleveland, OH, Record of Funeral, p. 269.

DAVIDER, William, husband of ***Ella*** (nee ***WUEBKER***); father of ***Harold***; brother of ***Henry***. Friends may call at the Clifford Pease Funeral Home, 2914 Dover Center Rd., Westlake, where services will be held Tuesday, May 10, at 2 p. m. Cleveland Necrology File, May 9, 1949.

DAVIDER: Ella DAVIDER (nee ***WUEBKER***), wife of the late ***William***, mother of ***Harold***, and grandmother, sister of *Fred WUEBKER, Edward WUEBKER, Edna OSTER, Herbert WUEBKER, Alvina KOCH, Rose WOEHRMANN, Alma MEYER* and the late *Irma THOMSEN*. Visitations at time of service only. Funeral services Monday, May 25, at 1 p. m. at The Jenkins Funeral Chapel, 2914 Dover Center Rd., Westlake. May 24, 1964. The Plain Dealer.

The State of Ohio, Cuyahoga County-ss. I Certify, That on the 10th day of November 1904 ***Mr. Heinrich DAVIDER*** and ***Miss Lydia STOCKHAUS*** were by me legally joined in marriage, after due publication of banns as provided by law. Rev. J. Rupprecht Marriage Record, Cuyahoga County, OH, vol. 57, p. 312.

Henry DAVIDER, 49, fruit farm; ***Lydia***, wife, 47; ***Flora***, dau., 14; ***Erwin***, son, 11; ***Elenor***, mother, 83, widow, yr. of immig. 1858, naturalized citizen 1860, b. Germany. 1920 FC OH CYBV, p. 7A, lines 4-8. *Next door* ***DAVIDER, William***, 50, General Farmer; ***Elenor***, wife, 38?, b. Ohio, parents b. Germany. 1920 FC OH CYBV, p. 7A, lines 9-10.

DAVIDER, Henry C., value of real estate $20,000, owns radio, 34, b. Ohio, parents b. Hanover, Germany; Proprietor of fruit farm; ***Lydia K.***, wife, 57, b. Ohio, parents b. Hanover, Germany; ***Flora M.***, daughter, 24, b. Ohio, Stenographer, Mfg. Paper ?; ***Erwin W.***, son, 22, b. Ohio, Truck driver, Laundry. 1930 FC OH CYBV ED18-534, p. 22A, 196 Bassett Rd., lines 4-7.

DAVIDER, Henry C., beloved husband of the late ***Lydia*** (nee ***STOCKHAUS***), father of ***Mrs. Flora HISER*** *(Frank H.)* and ***Ervin***, residence, 29402 Foote Rd., Bay Village. The family will receive friends from 2 to 4 and 7 to 9 P.M. Friday at the Pease-Jenkins Funeral Home, 2914 Dover Center Rd., Westlake, where services will be held

Saturday, Feb 25, at 1:30 p. m. Cleveland Press, Feb 24, 1956.

DAVIDER: Lydia, (nee ***STOCKHAUS***), wife of ***Henry***, mother of ***Flora*** and ***Corp. Erwin*** in Hawaii, sister of *Mrs. John WOEHRMANN, Sr., Mrs. Henry BRAUER, Mrs. Fred ARING* and *Theodore STOCKHAUS*. Now at Clifford Pease Funeral Home, 2914 Dover Center rd., Westlake, O. Services at St. Paul's Lutheran Church, Detroit rd., Westlake, Monday, Feb 28 at 2:30 p.m. Cleveland Necrology File, February 26, 1944.

Lydia Anna DAVIDER, d. Feb 24, 1944, 11 a.m. at 29402 Foote Road, Bay Village, Cuyahoga Co., Ohio, of Coronary Embolism due to Cardio and vascular disease and Hypertension for 5 yrs.; 71 yrs. 5 mos. 7 ds.; married to Henry, 72 yrs. old; b. Sept 17, 1872, Cleveland, Ohio, fr. ***John STOCKHAUS***, b. Germany, mo. b. Germany; informant *Flora M. DAVIDER*, 29402 Foote Rd.; undertaker Clifford Pease; burial St. Paul's Lutheran, Westlake, Ohio. Ohio Certificate of Death, Division of Vital Statistics, 1914, file 10075.

August F. DAVIDER, 48, res. 5511 Euclid Ave.; b. Bay, O.; occup. plumber; fr. ***Henry***, mo. ***Eleanor MYERS***. Married ***Florence BOND***, 48; res. Bay, O.; b. Beloit, Wis.; occup. none; fr. *Theophilus*, mo. *Loraine ROGERS*; previously married once. The State of Ohio, Cuyahoga County, ss. I Certify, That on the 11th day of December 1920 August F. Davider and Florence Bond were by me legally joined in marriage. Rev. William W. Bustard Marriage Record, Cuyahoga County, OH, vol. 120, p. 42.

DAVIDER: August, husband of ***Florence***, brother of ***William, Henry, Mrs. Mary SCHULTZE*** and ***Mrs. Martha HOLMES*** of Canada. Friends may call at Charles Melbourne & Sons' State Home, 12737 Euclid Ave. Services on Thursday, April 20, at 1 p.m. Cleveland Necrology File, Apr 20, 1933.

August DAVIDER, d. April 18, 1933, Cleveland State Hosp., Cleveland, Cuyahoga Co., Ohio of Hemorrhagic Pupura and Secondary Anemia…; 60 yrs. 4 mos. 19 ds.; married to ***Florence E. DAVIDER***; Plumber; b. Nov 30, 1872, Bay Village, Ohio, to ***Henry DAVIDER***, b. Germany and ***Eleanor MEYER***, b. Germany; informant *Mrs. Florence DAVIDER*, 1897 E. 89th St.; undertaker Charles Melbourne, 12737 Euclid Ave., Cleveland, Ohio; burial Thompson, Ohio. Ohio Certificate of Death, Division of Vital Statistics, 1933, certif. 20933.

Charles J. HOLMES, 40; res. 15 Eaton St.; b. Erie Co., N.Y.; occup. Engineer; fr. *Cyress HOLMES*, mo. *Louisa J. MEADE;* previously married once. Married ***Martha M. DAVIDER***, 26; res. Eagle Cliff, Ohio; b. do; occup. none; fr. ***Henry DAVIDER***, mo. ***Eleanor MEYERS***, never previously married. The State of Ohio, Cuyahoga County, ss. I Certify, That on the 15th day of April 1902 Charles J. Holmes and Martha M. Davider were by me legally joined in marriage. Rev. T.C. Lawrence Marriage Record, Cuyahoga County, OH, vol. 53, p. 434.

Lot 24/25-11 Osborn Marker

CLARE
MARSHALL
OSBORN
MARCH 5, 1874
DECEMBER 12,
1952

MILDRED
SLEEPER
OSBORN
JANUARY 27,
1870
NOVEMBER 9,
1952

Lots 24/25 Clare Marshall Osborn

Clare Marshall Osborn is the third of five children of Reuben Osborn and Eunice Chadwick, who are buried in Lot 46.

Clare Marshall OSBORN was born in Dover, the son of ***Reuben*** and ***Eunice CHADWICK OSBORN***. He graduated as a civil engineer from Case University. Most of his career was spent as a city manager in Lorain, OH; Kenosha, WI; Wilmette and Kenilworth, IL.

He and his wife ***Mildred*** had two children, ***Hazel*** (b. 12 Feb 1905, d. Dec 1979, New York City, NY), who never married, and ***James Marshall*** (b. 22 Apr 1906, d. 10 Oct 1976) who married *Marie-Louise MONTGOMERY* (b. 27 Sept 1905, Minneapolis, MN; d. 23 Dec 1968, New Haven, CT, dau. of *John Flournoy* and *Hedwig Wildi MONTGOMERY* of New York City) on 7 November 1929, New York City, NY. Hazel, James and Marie-Louise left their bodies to science, so there were no burials or tombstones.

Clare suffered his first stroke in the late 1940's. After the death of his wife, he moved to be near his daughter in Pittsburgh, PA where he died within a short period of time. J. Marshall Osborn

OSBORN, Rubin, 52, b. Aug 1847… ***Eunice***, 54, wife, b. Jan 1846…***George***, 30, son, b. Jan 1870… ***Clare***, 26, b. Mar 1874, son; ***Lucy***, 14, dau., b. Jan 1886…*See Reuben (Lot 46) for full citation.* 1900 FC OH CYDO, p. 21B, lines 80-85, house 462.

Clare M. OSBORN, 36, b. Ohio; ***Mildred S.***, 36, b. Illinois; ***Hazel M.***, 5, b. Ohio; ***James M.***, 3, b. Ohio. 1910 Miracode Index, Ohio, district 89.

CLARE MARSHALL OSBORN

My grandfather, ***Clare Marshall OSBORN***, was born in Bay Village, Ohio, in the old Osborn homestead on Lake Erie. He graduated as a civil engineer from Case. After graduation, he traveled to Chicago to help lay out the railroad which was being built out of Chicago to the West (I think that it was the Aurora and Elgin Railroad). He lived in a rooming house in Wheaton while he was working on laying out the railroad. In the same rooming house was a school teacher named ***Mildred SLEEPER***, and the two of them soon became engaged. He brought her back to Bay Village to meet his parents. On Sunday when he took her to church, there was a young woman who was very interested in my grandfather, and who fainted when she saw him with his fiancée. (*Hazel* told me that as a child she could not believe that anyone would faint over her father.)

My grandfather lived in Bay Village while both ***Hazel*** and my father *(James Marshall)* were born, and soon after that moved to East Cleveland. My grandfather became a city manager by profession, that is, he would be hired by a city to run the city, acting as a mayor would, but running things apolitically. I am not sure what his position was in East Cleveland. My father told me that his chief memory of living in East Cleveland is that his father would sit on the back porch in the evening, and if he heard an owl, he would start making sounds back to the owl, and pretty soon the owl would start moving closer until it was in a nearby tree talking to my grandfather.

My father also told me that as a young child he admired the way that my grandfather could cut with his axe, and he hoped that after his father's death he would be able to inherit his axe. Then they moved to Lorain, Ohio, where my grandfather was city manager. My father told me that at this time his parents like everyone else in town believed that it was absolutely forbidden to work on Sunday. Sunday was devoted to going to church and sitting home and reading the Bible. However, unlike most of the others, my grandparents believed that it was all right to go for a ride in the car on Sunday as long as it was for pleasure. Because of this heresy, some of the children that lived on the same block were forbidden to play with my father.

When my father was high school age, my grandfather became city manager of Kenosha, Wisconsin. After a few years, the politicians in Kenosha became unhappy that my grandfather was not doing what they wanted done, and they forced him out (probably about 1925). He then became city manager of Wilmette, Illinois, a suburb on the north side of Chicago. Probably about 1936 he became city manager of Kenilworth, Illinois. Since Kenilworth had only a few hundred people, this was a semi-retirement position. They built a house in Kenilworth in about 1937, where they lived the rest of their lives.

My grandfather made a comfortable income over the years, but he was not fortunate in his investments. At the beginning of the Depression, he lost all of his savings because the bank that he had it in went bankrupt. When he got to the point where he had more money to save, he bought some stocks that did poorly. I remember my father telling me that his father had bought some railroad stocks that proceeded to go down significantly in the years after he bought them.

My earliest memory of my grandfather was when my grandparents visited us in England, probably in 1936. During that visit, my grandfather built a kite for ***Tom*** and me, and then he built us a puppet theater. I next saw him when we returned to the USA in 1938, and we all flew out to Chicago to see them. And then we would visit periodically over the years as I grew up. My grandfather always took me down to the Museum of Science and Industry on the south side of Chicago. He could explain how anything worked, and seemed to be able to construct or repair anything. He was always kind and patient and ready to help.

About 1949 my grandfather had a stroke, but recovered pretty well from it and went back to work, although at a reduced pace. A couple of years later he had a second stroke, which hit him much harder. In the fall of 1952, when I went out to graduate school in Chicago, I went to see my grandparents. He got up with effort to greet me and for a minute or so he listened attentively to me, but could not speak. But then he just could not keep up the mental effort of listening, and he sat down in front of the television set again. When my grandmother died in November of 1952, we were not sure if he fully understood what had happened and why we were all there. But a few days later it seemed to hit him. Hazel moved him to Pittsburgh where she was then living, and put him in an apartment next to hers. But he did not last more than a couple of months.

My grandfather had more integrity than anyone that I have known, and he was known for this quality by others. He seemed completely at peace with himself, and ready to accept others as they were. He was always even tempered and helpful. With his ability to understand and figure out anything mechanical and electrical, he would have been able to move into the age of computers and the Internet with no problem. He was also interested in genealogy. He is the one who traced back the Osborn family to *Thomas OSBORN* in New Haven, and who gave me the information that I have about my Osborn ancestors before him. J. Marshall Osborn

CLARE MARSHALL OSBORN

Clare Marshall OSBORN, village manager of Wilmette from 1930 through 1934 and, more recently, village manager of Kenilworth, died in Pittsburgh, Pa., last Friday, December 12, at the age of 79.

In ill health since suffering a heart attack three years ago, Mr. Osborn died only 10 days after his arrival in Pittsburgh to make his home with a daughter, ***Miss Hazel M. OSBORN***. Grief for his wife, ***Mrs. Mildred SLEEPER OSBORN***, 82, who died at their Kenilworth home November 11, only a month previously, was thought to have been a contributing factor in his death.

Funeral services were held Monday afternoon in Westlake, Cuyahoga County, Ohio, where he was born and received his early education.

A graduate of Oberlin Academy in Lorain County, Ohio, he held a degree in civil engineering from Case School of Applied Science in Cleveland. After seven year in private engineering work, including building electric railway, docks, shipyards, and similar projects, he was appointed city engineer of Lorain, Ohio, then a city of 40,000 population, in 1908. Ten years later he was named first city manager for

East Cleveland, Ohio, where he organized the manager system.

From 1922 to 1928 he served as city manager in Kenosha, Wis., and from there went to Shorewood, Wis., a suburb of Milwaukee, to serve in a similar capacity. He became Wilmette's first village manager in July of 1930 when *Earl E. ORNER* was village president. He resigned from this position four years later during the presidency of *Carbon P. DUBBS*, succeeding *Felix L. STREED* four years later as village manager of Kenilworth where he served from 1936 until he resigned in 1948 due to ill health.

Headed Rotary Club

Other titles he held during his long career included president of the Wilmette Rotary Club (1943-44), president of the National City Managers Association (1921-22), and state engineer for the public works administration (1934-36), and he also was a member at one time of the Wisconsin City and Regional Planning Association.

Surviving besides his daughter, an instructor at the University of Pittsburgh, are a son, ***James M.***, an instructor *(Correction by J. Marshall Osborn, James was an associate professor working on research exclusively, not teaching.)* at Yale University, New Haven, Conn.; a sister, ***Miss Lucy OSBORN*** of Bay Village, Ohio; and two grandchildren, ***Marshall***, a graduate student at the University of Chicago, and ***Thomas*** a freshman at Princeton University. 12/15/52 Newspaper article provided by Kenilworth Historical Society, Kenilworth, IL

OSBORN, CLARE M., late residence, 645 Melrose Ave., Kenilworth, Ill. (first city manager of East Cleveland); husband of the late ***Mildred***; father of ***Hazel*** and ***James***, and grandfather, brother of ***Lucy***; memorial funeral services will be held at the Clifford Pease Funeral Home, 2914 Dover Center Rd., Westlake, Monday, Dec 15, at 2 p.m. Please omit flowers. Cleveland Necrology File, Dec 15, 1952.

Son of Clare Osborn and Mildred Sleeper:

JAMES OSBORN, 70, A LITERARY SCHOLAR
Specialist in 17th-and 18th-Century English Literature, Was at Yale

By Werner Bamberger

James M. OSBORN, a Yale University English scholar and literary detective, died Sunday at Yale-New Haven Hospital. He was 70 years old and a resident of New Haven.

Mr. Osborn, a literary historian at Yale University from 1938 to 1972, was a specialist in 17th- and 18th-century English literature. His title at Yale was research associate in English and curator of the James Marshall and ***Marie-Louise OSBORN*** Collection, one of the leading private collections of literature of that period. It is in the school's Beinecke Rare Book and Manuscript Library.

A graduate of Wesleyan University, Mr. Osborne first turned to investment banking and then decided to go into literature, taking a master's degree at Columbia University.

Detective Work on Ballad

Among his feats as a literary detective was the discovery in 1964 of a hitherto unknown manuscript "Select Meditations," by *Thomas TRAHERNE*, a 17th- century mystic.

He also established that a ballad quoted by *SHAKESPEARE* in "Much Ado About Nothing" had not been written by Shakespeare but predated the playwright by about 100 years. It was Benedick's song, and Mr. Osborn managed to discover a manuscript of the song.

And in 1956, at a rare book sale in London, he picked up a manuscript that turned out to be the earliest known autobiography in English, a work written in 1576 by an English composer, *Thomas WHYTHORNE*.

Mr. Osborn's interests were not confined to English literature, a subject on which he wrote several books, including "Young Philip Sidney," "Dryden, Facts and Problems," and "The Beginnings of Autobiography in England."

In 1949, on his Whirlwind Hill Farm in Wallingford, Conn., he started breeding Holstein cattle and 20,000 of his Holstein cows are in herds throughout the country.

Received Many Awards

He also served on the executive committee of the National Municipal League, which, in 1962, honored him with its distinguished citation award.

After he retired from Yale in 1972 he remained active as curator of the collections named after him and his wife, who died in 1968.

His work earned him three honorary degrees, from Kenyon College, McGill University and St. John's University, and a doctor of letters from Oxford University. He was the first American to earn this degree in English literature from Oxford, which is conferred after a rigorous assignment of a candidate's published contributions to scholarship.

He is survived by two sons, ***James M. Jr.***, a professor of mathematics at the University of Wisconsin, and ***Thomas M.***, and a sister, ***Hazel OSBORN***.

A memorial service at Yale is to be held some time next month. Tuesday, October 19, 1976. Copyright © 1976 by The New York Times Co. Reprinted with permission.

James M. Osborn Dies; Noted for Yale Collection

James Marshall OSBORN, whose English manuscripts and letters comprise the heralded Osborn Collection at Yale's Beinecke Rare Book and Manuscript Library, died Sunday, Oct 17, 1976, Yale-New Haven Hospital. He was *(blank after)*

Osborn began searching for rare English literary pieces 42 years ago in London. Today the collection encompasses a variety of English literature and history from the reign of *Mary TUDOR* to the mid-twentieth century. The earliest manuscript in the collection is the fragment of a Palm Sunday sermon dated before 1025 A.D.

Among the notable documents in the collection are the works of playwright *Richard Brinsley SHERIDAN*, music historian *Dr. Charles BURNEY* and *Edmund BURKE*.

Mr. Osborn was the author of nine books, several based on his research with unpublished documents in his collection.

He was awarded a Doctor of Letters degree from Oxford University for the high quality of his books and his contribution to scholarship in 1968.

He was a research assistant in English literature at Yale University and at one time the owner of a 250 acre farm in Wallingford where he bred prized Holstein-Friesian calves.

He was born April 22, 1906, in Cleveland, Ohio, son of the late ***Clare Marshall*** and ***Mildred OSBORN***.

He is survived by two sons, ***Dr. James OSBORN Jr.***, a mathematics professor at the University of Wisconsin, and ***Thomas M. OSBORN*** of Los Angeles; and a sister, ***Hazel OSBORN*** of New York. He was predeceased by his wife, ***Marie Louise OSBORN***.

He lived at 123 York St. and formerly on Edgehill Rd.

Private funeral services will be held. A memorial service will be conducted at Yale. New Haven Register; New Haven, CN, October 19, 1976.

Lots 24/25-11 Mildred Sleeper Osborn

Mildred SLEEPER OSBORN was the daughter of ***James Taylor SLEEPER*** (b. 6 July1829, d. 24 Dec 1887) and ***Delia Wilson BELLOWS*** (b. 1837, d. 2 Mar 1872) who m. 1854. J. Marshall Osborn

MILDRED SLEEPER OSBORN

My grandmother was born on January 27, 1870 in Palatine, IL. She was teaching school and living in a boarding house in Wheaton when she met my grandfather. She was four years older than my grandfather, which she tried to hide for many years. Since my grandfather was in his early twenties when they were married, I think that she felt very self-conscious about being that much older, and may not have wanted his parents to know. When my father ***(James)*** and ***Hazel*** were in their late teens, they became bothered by the fact that some of the dates and ages associated with their mother's family were not consistent with each other, and they confronted their mother about it, and she admitted to being older than she had been claiming.

My grandmother told me that her father had fought in the Civil War, and she once showed me her father's sword which she kept in her closet. She had some relatives somewhere in Michigan, and Hazel told me that when my grandparents were living in Kenosha, she would take her children on the ferry from Milwaukee across Lake Michigan to visit these relatives. Hazel told me that once the crossing was so rough that she (Hazel) fell on the ferry and broke her arm.

My grandmother tended to worry a lot about everything. When her children were away at college she insisted that they write her at least once a week so that she would know that they were all right. (I believe that I have a lot of those letters.) When I knew her, she always seemed to have a very concerned look on her face. She seemed too concerned to really talk with us or to do anything with us.

After my grandfather had his strokes, she worried a lot about him. And I think that this worrying contributed to the fact that she died first, in November of 1952. J. Marshall Osborn

Lot 26 *Owner: G.L. Osborn of Bay Village purchased June 12, 1920, for $4.86* SL

Lot 27 *Owner: J.M. Conklin of Avon purchased Feb 1, 1890, for $5.25* SL

Lot 27 James Monroe Conklin

no marker

According to the death certificate of his son, James was born in Olean, New York.

CONKLIN, James, 41, laborer, b. NY, parents b. NY; ***Susan***, 41, wife, keeping house, b. Ohio, fr. b. NY, mo. b. Penn.; ***Minnie M.***, 9, b. Mich.; ***Albert M.***, 7, b. Mich. 1880 FC OH CYDO, p. 97, lines 40-43, house 288.

CONKLIN, James M., 62, b. Jan 1838, married 32 yrs.; ***Susan***, 61, b. Dec 1838, Ohio, parents b. New York, 4 children born, 2 living; ***Minnie***, 29, b. Aug 1870, Michigan, single; renting house. 1900 FC OH LOAV, p. 20A, lines 8-10, house 410.

James is recognized as a Civil War veteran on Memorial Day.

There are eight James Conklins indexed in the1870 Michigan census; none of them appeared to be the individual named here.

J.M. CONKLIN, 60; res. Avon; interred Jan 26, 1900; Lot 27. "List of Interments," Lakeside Cemetery, Bay Village, OH.

Son of James Monroe Conklin and Susan White:

The State of Ohio, Lorain County, ss. I do hereby certify, that ***Mr. Albert M. CONKLIN*** and ***Miss Ada B. PAYNE*** were joined in Marriage by me on the 29 day of Feby A.D. 1896. Rev. Frank Dann. E.H. Hinman, Probate Judge. "Lorain County Marriages," Film 168, p. 214.

CONKLIN, Albert M. (Ada B.)...Motorman, Glen. 1910 Lorain County Rural Directory, Avon.

Albert CONKLIN, 37, b. Ohio; ***Ada***, wife, 33, b. Ohio; ***George***, son, 7, b. Ohio; *Louise PAYNE (Laura Mitchel Payne, b. Avon Lake from death certificate)*, mother-in-law, 65, b. Ohio. "1910 Census Miracode Index, Lorain, OH," district 84, visit 118.

Albert M. CONKLIN, d. July 1, 1941, Steve Moore Rd., Avon Lake, Lorain Co., Ohio of Coronary Thrombosis 2 min. and Coronary Sclerosis; 68 yr. 7 mos. 16 ds.; b. Nov 16, 1872, Middleton, Ohio to ***Monroe CONKLIN***, b. Olean, New York and ***Susan WHITE***, b. Middleton; married to ***Ada (CONKLIN)***; Retired Electric Rail Motorman; informant Glen A. Conklin; undertaker Sidney B. Royce Co. Ohio Certificate of Death, Division of Vital Statistics, 1941, certif. 52057.

Lake Shore Cemetery, Avon Lake, OH: ***Albert M. CONKLIN***, bur. 7-3-1941 also ***Ada Bell CONKLIN***, bur. 5-16-1948. Lots 5 and 6 purchased June 2, 1922 by A.M. Conklin. Lake Shore Cemetery Records, Avon Lake, OH.

Lake Shore Cemetery, Avon Lake, OH: ***CONKLIN. Albert M.*** 1872-1941. ***Ada B.*** 1876-1947. ***Leonard CONKLIN*** 1899-1905 Inscriptions as recorded by Catherine Burke Flament

Lot 27 Susan White Conklin

no marker

According to the death certificate of her son, Susan's maiden name was White and she was born in Middleton, Ohio.

Susan CONKLIN, 80; res. Avon; interred Dec 27, 1919; Lot 27. "List of Interments," Lakeside Cemetery, Bay Village, OH.

Death certificate not found in Lorain or Cuyahoga County.

Lot 27 Carrie G. Conklin no marker

Daughter of James Monroe Conklin and Susan White.

CONKLIN, Carrie G.; d. 1890, Feby 2, Avon, Inf. Rheumatism; single; 9 yrs., 10 days; b. Dover, O. Probate Court Death Records, Lorain County, Ohio, vol. 3, p. 91.

Carrie G. CONKLIN, 9; res. Avon; interred Feb 2, 1890; Lot 27. "List of Interments," Lakeside Cemetery, Bay Village, OH.

Lot 28 *Owner: F. Hinz purchased Mar 21, 1911, for $6.87*

SL

Lot 28-12 Hinz Monument

HINZ

(back)

FRED HINZ
JULY 7, 1852 MARC 20 1911
AUGUSTA HINZ
FEB 22, 1850 MAY 16, 1945

Lot 28-12 William Frederick Hinz

The family home in Avon Lake is just over the Bay border on the north side of Lake Rd. at the bend. The Hinz family had a sizeable farm consisting of an orchard, berries and grapes. Art Aslaksen.

Fred HINZ emigrated from Germany in 1873 and then sent for ***Augusta*** to join him. They married in Cleveland in 1877 and moved to Huntington farm in 1879 where Mr. Hinz worked for *John HUNTINGTON* as farm manager. The Huntington farm in Bay Village is today the Huntington Metropolitan Park. In 1895, the Hinz family settled in Avon Lake. Fred and Augusta would have three sons;

Arthur George HINZ, b. 13 Feb 1878, m. *Marie Elise LAISY*, d. in the '50's. They had a son, *William Frederick HINZ*, (b. 10 Nov 1912, d. 3 Aug 1980) who had one daughter, *Leslie HINZ d'ACUNZO*. ***William R. (Bill) HINZ***, m. *Ruth*, d. at home in Bay Village, no children. ***Johann Harry (Jack) HINZ***, m. *Katherine*, res. Lake Rd., Bay Village, they had two daughters, *Sally Kay HINZ* and *Jacqueline HINZ*. Leslie Hinz d'Acunzo

Mr. and ***Mrs. HINZ*** owned a farm at 1618 East 38th Street, Cleveland, Ohio. My grandfather, *John BUEHNER*, who was born in Waldberg, Germany, met them when he came to this country. He actually worked for them on 38th Street. Mr. and Mrs. Hinz purchased property in Avon Lake, Ohio. They had asked my grandfather to work and help manage the farm. However, he was desirous to live more in the city. Therefore, when he married *Margaret ZEIER*, he and she rented the property on 38th Street from the Hinz family. Every month they took the train out to the Hinz farm at Stop 37 to pay their rent. My parents, upon their marriage, moved into the East 38th Street property and every month they would help my grandfather pay the rent and travel to Stop 37.

Mr. and Mrs. Hinz were very close to my family and were wonderful, gentle and giving people. Over the years my family bought grapes from them to make home made wine and often was given other farm products. In fact, when the Hinz family finally sold the 38th Street property, they sold it to *Joseph BUEHNER*, my cousin.

My sister recalls that Mrs. Hinz was only upset once about her farm area. This was because a new road was extended out through Avon. It cut across her farm property separating her house on one side of the road and part of her farm on the other side of the road. Hon. Ann Dyke, letter July 20, 2004, Rose Hill Museum, Hinz Family File.

On the 30th day of March 1877 ***Augusta NEUBAUM*** was married to ***W. Frederick HINZ***. Signed April 2, 1877, Cleveland, Cuyahoga County, Ohio. Original marriage certificate in the possession of Leslie Hinz d'Acunzo.

William Frederick HINZ Naturalized Citizen Feb 27, 1893; Declared his intention to become a citizen 3 Febry 1891; b. July 7, 1852, Strasburg, Germany; immig. Sept 1873; farmer, Dover. Cuy Co. Pleas Court, Cuy Co., Cleveland, Ohio. Naturalization Papers, Cuy Co. Archives.

HINES (sp.), ***William F.***, 28, farmer, b. Loaban, parents b. Loaban; ***Augusta***, 22, wife, b. Loaban, parents b. Loaban; ***Arthur G.***, 2, b. Ohio; ***NEUBAUM, August***, 48, father-in-law, b. Loaban, laborer; ***Minnie***, 47, mother-in-law, b. Loaban; *GRAFF, Frederick*, 17, servant, laborer, b. Wirtenburg, parents b. Wirtenburg. 1880 FC OH CYDO, p.99, lines 31-36, house 309.

HEINZ (sp.), ***William***, 47, b. July 1852, married 23 yrs.; ***Agusta*** *(sp.)*, 44, b. Feb 1856, immig 1873, 3 children born, 3 living; ***Arthur***, *22*, b. Apr 1878, salesman H. Q___?; ***William***, *16*, b. Aug 1883, at school; ***John***, 14, b. Feb 1886, at school; *BRUNING, August*, 27, b. Mar 1873, Germany, parents b. Germany, immig. 1896, Al; ***DARBY, Emma***, 21, b. Aug 1878, Ohio, parents b. Ohio, servant. 1900 FC OH LOAV, p. 20A, lines 32-38, house 414. *Neighbors in this order Elmas (Philip) Beard, George Scheible and Anton Tomanek's.*

DOVER LAKE

Fred W. HINTZ *(sp.)* died at his home Monday, March 20, at the age of 60 years. He had been ailing for a year past, but the end came quietly. The funeral occurred from the home at Eagle Cliff, on Thursday, at 2 p.m., and services were conducted by their minister from Cleveland. A male quartet from Cleveland, sang. He leaves a wife and three sons. Burial was made in Lakeside cemetery, Bay Village. Evening Telegram, Elyria, OH, Wednesday, Mar 29, 1911, p. 6, col. 5.

Wm. Frederick HINZ, d. March 20, 1911, 3 p.m., Avon *(Lorain Co.),* Ohio, Inflammation of m__ge of brain-25 ds. and Digestion disturbance-30 ds.; married; farmer; b. July 7, 1852, Germany; fr. ***Michael HINZ***, b. Germany, *mo. not listed*; 58 yrs. 8 mo. 13 ds.; bur. Bay Village, May 23, 1911, undertaker Jas. A. Pease & Son, Dover, O.; informant *Arthur HINZ*, 793_ Lorain Ave., Clev., O. Ohio Certificate of Death, Division of Vital Statistics, 1911, certif. 16259.

Wm. F. HINZ, 58; res. Avon; German; interred Mar 20, 1911; Lot 28. "List of Interments," Lakeside Cemetery, Bay Village, OH.

Wm. Frederick HINZ, Inflammation of Meurugh of Brain, issued March 22, 1911 by Lawrence Heckel. Bureau of Vital Statistics, Burial or Removal Permit, Bay Village, OH.

Lot 28-12 Augusta Neubaum Hinz

Raised Doughnuts

(Mrs. Fred Hinz)

One quart scalded milk, when cool set sponge with one yeast cake, one teaspoon of butter and lard, one heaping tablespoon sugar, two eggs, a little nutmeg, one teaspoon salt. Add all to sponge and add enough flour to stir sponge with spoon. When light put on moulding board. Roll. Cut and let rise. Fry in deep fat. The Village Cook Book, p. 35. (c1911-1915).

Maid Marks 50th Year With Same Family Mistress Will Serve Her Tomorrow on Anniversary

By Marie Daerr

Tomorrow 93-year-old ***Mrs. Augusta HINZ*** is planning to play maid for a day.

She will turn the tables on 67-year-old ***Miss Emma DARBY*** and together the two women will celebrate an anniversary that undoubtedly will make thousands of Cleveland matrons turn green with envy - 50 years as mistress and maid.

Today Mrs. Hinz and Miss Darby, who naturally is more "part of the family" than maid, sat in the Hinz living room at 31620 Lake road, Bay Village, and chuckled frequently as they let their minds run over the years from the day 17-year-old Emma, dressed in a black skirt "down to my ankles" and a white shirtwaist came from Berlin Heights, near Norwalk, to start working for Mrs. Hinz.

Emma came to replace one of two maids who helped Mrs. Hinz keep house - a job that included cooking for hired men. At that time the family lived on Huntington Park, which ***Fred HINZ***, who has been dead for 30 years, managed.

"***Jack*** was only 8 then, ***Will*** was 10 and ***Art*** was 15," reminisced Mrs. Hinz, naming her sons.

"Emma just about raised those boys. Even today, when they come to see us, they ask Emma where to find things."

* * *

How do a mistress and maid remain on good terms all 50 years?

"Do you know the secret?" asked Mrs. Hinz, a twinkle in her eye.

"I've always liked to talk - Emma liked to listen."

Emma chuckled.

"It's a good combination."

"When I got cross - and I know I did sometimes, Emma would bear with me," continued Mrs. Hinz.

"We always co-operated, too. You could call our relationship a partnership, I guess. Even today we bake together. When we make kuchen, Emma does the stirring and I do the trimming."

Fifty years ago, reminisced Mrs. Hinz and Emma, bread was home-baked, on a coal range. Water came from the pump and carpets were swept with a broom, wet paper and muscle.

"Things are easy today," commented Emma.

* * *

Probably one of the secrets of Mrs. Hinz and Emma's partnership is their youthful outlook on life. At 93, Mrs. Hinz plays cards, goes to parties and reads without glasses. She regrets she stopped playing the piano seven or eight years ago. Today she is dressed in a printed voile and had a blue bow in her coiffure. Emma wore a gay print too - and a gardenia in her hair that has not even begun to turn gray.

The Hinz home is a gathering place for the family, Mrs. Hinz and Emma admitted. The three sons live in the immediate neighborhood and every morning they drop in for a cup of coffee.

"Will comes in at 7:30 and the others follow soon after," said Mrs. Hinz.

When Mrs. Hinz had a birthday last Feb 22, the whole neighborhood congregated to honor "Mother Hinz." Seven birthday cakes were among the gifts. Mrs. Hinz was born in Germany, coming here when she was 16. Her first home was on Kinsman road, near E. 55th street.

There are three grandchildren in the Hinz family: ***Fritz***, 30; ***Sally*** 20, and ***Jacqueline***, 18. Cleveland Press, August 31, 1944, p. 1.

Mrs. Augusta Hinz, Pioneer Here, Dies
Came to U.S. in 1863 on Sailing Ship

By Charles J. Patterson

Mrs. Augusta HINZ, a pioneer settler of western Cuyahoga County, died yesterday at the age of 94 in her home, at Stop 38, Lake road, Avon Lake Village.

Born in Baden, Germany, she came to the United States in a sailing ship when a child of 12.

Her husband, ***W.F. HINZ***, had emigrated to Cleveland from the same town before her. After their marriage some years later he built their first home in E. 38th street.

In 1879 the couple moved to a home near the present Huntington Park, Bay Village, where Mr. Hinz was associated with the late *John H. HUNTINGTON* of the Standard Oil Co. in farming and fishing. In 1895 the family moved just over the line into Lorain County where Mrs. Hinz lived until her death. Mr. Hinz died almost 35 years ago.

Last September, Mrs. Hinz received national notice when she celebrated the 51st year of association with her maid, ***Miss Emma DARBY,*** who through long years of service and association had become part of the Hinz family.

When Mrs. Hinz reversed their roles and played maid for the day, the story became unique in these days of servant problems.

Mrs. Hinz was a member of the Avon Lake Union, an old settlers' organization, the Altenheim Home for the Aged, the Avon Lake Garden Club and the Avon Lake 500 Club.

She is survived by her sons, ***Arthur G.*** of Avon Lake, ***William R.*** and ***John H.***, both of Bay Village; her grandchildren, ***W. Fred HINZ, Sally Kay HINZ*** and ***Jacqueline HINZ*** and a great-grandson *(daughter)*, ***Leslie Dustin HINZ.***

Services will be conducted at 2:30 Saturday afternoon at the Pease Funeral Home, Dover Center road, Westlake. Cleveland Press, May 17, 1945, p. 22.

Augusta HINZ, d. May 16, 1945, 4:30 a.m., at her residence 31620 West Lake Rd., Avon Lake, Lorain Co., of Coronary thrombosis - 3 days due to Artereo sclerosis, also Secondary Anemia 3 mos., 93 yrs. 2 mos. 24 days old; lived in community 66 yrs., widow of ***Wm. Frederick***; b. Feb 22, 1852, Baden, Germany, in U.S.A. 81 yrs., fr. ***August NEUBAUM,*** b. Germany, mo. ***Minnie,*** b. Germany; occup. housewife; informant *W.R. HINZ*, Bay Village, Ohio; bur. Lakeside, Bay Village, Funeral Director Marion E. Pease, Westlake, Ohio. Ohio Certificate of Death, Division of Vital Statistics, 1945, certif. 29598.

Sons of Fred Hinz and Augusta Neubaum:

Otto George HEINZ, fr. *Friedrich Wilhelm HEINZ*, b. 13 February 1878, confirmed 10 April 1892. p. 204.

Wilhelm Robert HINZ, fr. *Friedr. Wilh. HINZ*, b. 22 August 1883, Dover, confirmed 3 April 1898. p. 209.

Johann Harry HINZ, fr. *HINZ*, b. 8 February 1886, conf. 8 April 1900. p. 211. St. Paul Lutheran Church, Confirmation Records.

Married 50 Years

Couple to Observe Golden Anniversary

By Frieda Meyer

AVON LAKE - Golden Wedding anniversary of ***Mr.*** and ***Mrs. Arthur G. HINZ***, 31734 Lake Rd., will be observed Sunday at the home of their son and daughter-in-law, ***Mr.*** and ***Mrs. William F. HINZ***, 1182 Elbur Lakewood, with open house from 1 to 4 p.m.

The couple was married Oct 20, 1904 in Cleveland by *Rev. August KIMMEL* of German Reformed Church, Cleveland, who also married Hinz's parents and christened him.

Miss Martha SEITZ, Lakewood, was bridesmaid at the wedding, and ***William R. HINZ***, a brother of the bridegroom was best man. Both are expected to be at the anniversary celebration.

Recall Trip

Mrs. Hinz, in telling of the wedding, recalled their honeymoon trip by train to Washington, D.C. and Niagara Falls.

Both Mr. and Mrs. Hinz, the former ***Marie LAISY***, were born in Cleveland. Their parents early settlers in

Cleveland's west side, had stands in the farmers' market on Lorain St., in what was then the outskirts of Cleveland, now W. 73rd, and the families became well acquainted.

In later years, the west portion of the Laisy farm on Lake Road near the county line in Avon Lake, was purchased by the senior Hinz, and the families became neighbors.

Lake Resident

A.G. Hinz, said in reminiscing, he has lived along the lake for 63 years. He also recalled the many years his father was supervisor of the Huntington farm in Bay Village, which today is the Huntington Metropolitan Park.

Mrs. Hinz has been an active member of the board of directors of the Altenheim home for the aged, Cleveland for 35 years, is a member of Lake Shore Union society and Avon-on-the-Lake garden club. She is a West high school graduate.

Hinz, too, graduated from West high school, Cleveland, and for 32 years was in the wholesale hardware business with the Leutkemeyer Co., Cleveland. He took active part in the organizing of the Ohio Fruit Growers Co-operative Ass'n., Inc., and is its president. He is also president of the Ohio Grape Growers Institute. He is a member of the Masonic and Elk Lodge.

The couple has one son, ***William Fred HINZ***, and one grand-daughter, ***Leslie Dustin (Dusty) HINZ***.

A family dinner at the Westwood Country club will follow the open house celebration. Lorain Journal, Lorain, OH, Oct 18, 1954.

William HINZ, b. 22 Aug 1883, d. Mar 1974, res. Avon Lake, Lorain, OH, issuing state Ohio. Social Security Index.

HINZ William R. 1883-1974, ***Ruth D***. 1883-1972. Lake Shore Cemetery, Avon Lake, OH. Read by Catherine Burke Flament.

John H. HINZ, 90, d. July 17, 1976, 12:05 p.m. at 31686 Lake Road, Bay Village, Cuyahoga Co. (residence) of ASHD c CHF for 8 weeks; b. 8 Feb 1886 to ***William F. HINZ*** and ***Augusta MIBAUM***; President, Chemical Distributor; Veteran of WW I; buried Lakewood Park Cemetery, Rocky River, Ohio, Saxton-Klanke Funeral Home, 13215 Detroit Ave., Lakewood; informant W.F. Hinz, 22220 Hilliard Rd, Rocky River. Ohio Certificate of Death, Division of Vital Statistics, 1976.

Lot 28 Emma J. Darby

EMMA DARBY
1877-1957
(behind Hinz Memorial)

Emma worked with the Hinz family (above) for over 50 years (see article above regarding Augusta Hinz and Emma).

Sponge Cake
(Miss Emma Darby)

Five eggs (white and yokes beaten separately). Add gradually one-half teaspoon cream of tartar. Beat until stiff. Beat into these gradually (with an egg beater) one cup granulated sugar sifted. Then the well beaten yolks. Then add one teaspoon lemon extract, one cup of sifted flour, (add a little at a time). Bake in a slow oven until it nearly rises to the top of the pan. Then a quick fire until done. Requires about forty minutes.

The Village Cook Book, p. 48. (c1911-1915).

Emma DARBY, d. May 2, 1957, Altenheim, 7719 Detroit Ave., Cleveland, Cuy. Co. of Artereo Sclerotic Heart Disease due to chr. Sinusitis (severe) chr. Bronchitis with Prelatic bronchiectasis; married *(this is believed to be incorrect and was listed next to "never married")*; b. Aug 12, 1877, Berlin Hts., O., fr. ***Sylvester DARBY***, mo. ***Elzina BEACH***; 79 yrs. old, occup.; Housekeeper; informant Johanna Szucs, bur. 5-4-57, Bay Village Cemetery, embalmed, funeral home Leimkuehler's, 6722 Franklin, Cleveland. Ohio Certificate of Death, Division of Vital Statistics, 1957, certif. 036929.

DARBY, Emma, late residence, the Altenheim. Friends received at the Leimkuehler Funeral Home, 6722 Franklin Blvd., where services will be held Saturday, May 4, at 2 p.m. Cleveland Necrology File; Cleveland Press, May 3, 1957, roll 103.

The Altenheim is a nursing home that was opened in 1890 by the West Side German Women's Society. It was founded to provide care for individuals of German descent over 65 years old. It remained at 7719 Detroit Rd., Cleveland until 1980 when it was relocated in Strongsville. In 1923 the restrictions were dropped in regard to nationality and ancestry. David D. Van Tassel and John J. Grabowski, The Encyclopedia of Cleveland History, p. 20.

Ancestors of Emma Darby:

I. ***Martin A. DARBY*** (b. 1790, NH, d. 16 Aug 1848) and ***Betsey HUMISTON***, (b. 1796, CT). *Issue*: ***Sylvester DARBY***; ***Chester DARBY***, b. 1833, NY; ***Lowry DARBY***, b. 1836, NY; ***Almiry DARBY***, b. 1841, Henrietta Twp., Lorain Co., OH. Sue Heys, Descendant Report (not all research documented).

II. ***Sylvester DARBY***, b. 1825, NY; d. 1882, Berlin Heights, Erie Co., OH; m. 1854, Florence Twp., Erie Co., OH to ***Wealthy A. BEACH*** (b. 1839, OH; d. 1879 Berlin Heights).

Issue: ***Ida DARBY***, b. 1858, Berlin Heights. ***Nellie A. DARBY***, b. Sept 1859; d. 1910, OH; bur. Riverside Cemetery, Berlin Hts., OH; m. 15 Nov 1876, Berlin Heights to *Alfred HEYS* (b. 14 Nov 1849, Bury, England, son of *Richard HEYS* (b. England) and *Liza Ann SCOWLES* (b. England); d. 21 July 1920, OH; bur. Riverside Cemetery, Berlin Heights, OH); 6 children. ***Ephraim J. DARBY***, b. 29 Apr 1862, Berlin Twp.; m. 13 Jan 1885, Erie Co. to *Belle F. CARTER* (b. 1858, IA); owned apple orchards; d. 1950; bur. Birmingham Cemetery, Birmingham, OH. ***Thomas Jesse DARBY***, b. 1867, Berlin Hts.; m. 2 Apr 1890, Berlin Heights to *Margaret HORNBERGER*. ***Emma J. DARBY***. Sue Heys, Descendant Report (not all research documented).

S. DARBY, 28, Laborer, b. Ohio; ***A. DARBY***, 21, b. Ohio; ***Ida DARBY***, 2, b. Ohio; ***A. DARBY***, 11/12 *(11 months old)*; *F. LUCAS*, 30, b. Ohio, laborer. 1860 FC OH Erie Co., Township, p. 339, lines.

Sylvester is living with his daughter in the census below.

Alfred HAYES, 31, Laborer, b. England, parents b. England; ***Nellie A.***, 21, wife, Keeping House, b. Ohio, fr. b. NY; ***Richard***, 1, son, b. Ohio, fr. b. England, mo. b. Ohio; ***DARBY, Sylvester***, 54, father-in-law, b. NY, fr. b. NY, mo. b. NY.; ***DARBY, Jessie***, 13, brother-in-law, at school, b. Ohio, fr. b. NY, mo. b. NY. 1880 FC OH Erie Co., Berlin Hts., p. 14C, lines 47-50 and p. 14D, line 1.

Siblings of Emma Darby:

Nettie Anna HEYS, d. June 13th, 1910, Berlin Township, Erie Co., Ohio of Cerebral softening for 3 months; 50 years 5 mos. 19 ds.; married; b. Dec 25, 1860, Berlin Hts., Ohio to ***S. DARBY***, b. New York and ***Elzina BEACH***, b. unknown; housewife; informant *Alfred HEYS*; undertaker C.?H. Judson, Berlin Hts., O.; bur. Riverside Cem. Ohio Certificate of Death, Division of Vital Statistics, 1910, certif. 31545.

Alfred HEYS, d. 21 July 1920, Berlin Township, Erie Co., Ohio of Broncho pneumonia for 1 month, contributory Gastritis (chronic) for 2 years; widowed, wife ***Nettie A. HEYS***; he was b. 14 Nov 1849, Bary, England; fr. *Richard HEYS*, b. England, mo. *Liza Ann SCOWLES*, b. England; informant *C.A. HEYS*, bur. Berlin Hights *(Heights)*, Ohio, 23 July 1920, undertaker N.L Pease, Wakeman. Ohio Certificate of Death, Division of Vital Statistics, 1920, certif. 47546.

The life given us by nature
is short,
But the memory of
a well-spent life is eternal
Cicero

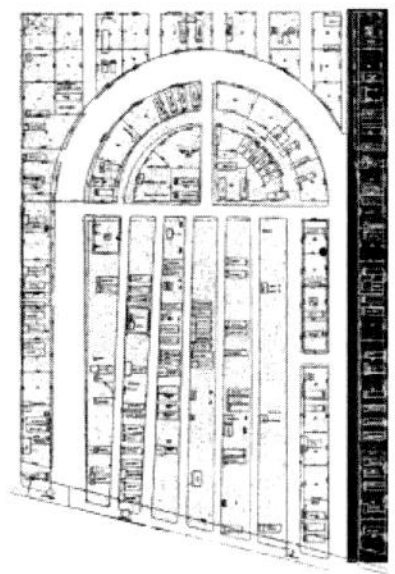

Lot 29 begins at the northern portion, toward Lake Erie, of the eastern side of the cemetery, and proceeds to Lake Road on the south.

N.E. Corner Remains of Miller no marker

Remains of Miller, "children" written above it; residence West Dover; April 2, 1897; N.E. Corner. "List of Interments," Lakeside Cemetery, Bay Village, OH.

There were numerous Miller's found in the Avon area specifically. A death record or other reference was not uncovered to identify this individual.

Lot 29 *Owner: George Scheible of Avon purchased July 21, 1892, for $6.92* SL

Lot 29-1 Scheible Monument

ROSIE SCHEIBLE
OCT 22, 1862
JULY 21, 1892
GEORGE
1855-1947

SCHEIBLE

Lot 29-1 Rosa Solomon Scheible

George immigrated from Germany c1879 and was married twice, Rosie being his first wife.

Rosie's daughter's marriage certificate, see below under Infant Haag, also lists her maiden name as Solomon.

SCHEIBLE, George m. ***SOLOMON, Rosa*** on 27 Nov 1883 by J. Brown Jr., JP. Edith Johnson Minderman; Marriages From the Probate Court, Ottawa County, Ohio, 1840-1890; p. 131.

Lot 29-1 George Scheible

George is thought to have resided at Put-in-Bay for an unspecified period of time. His brother, ***Simon,*** migrated from Germany after George and spoke little English. George's daughter, ***Anna,*** and her husband, took over the family farm and cared for the brother's until they passed away. Richard Haag, phone conversation, 26 March 2006

The State of Ohio, Cuyahoga County, ss. ***George SCHEIBLE*** having made application for a Marriage License for himself and ***Lizzie BENDER*** of said County...I certify that on the 1st day of June 1893...were legally joined in marriage. Rev. M. Ratsch. Marriage Record, Cuyahoga County, OH, vol. 39, p. 336.

SCHEIBLE, George, 45, b. Feb 1855, Germany, parents b. Germany, immig. 1874, Na., farmer, married 7 yrs.; ***Elizabeth***, 48, wife, b. Dec 1851, Ohio, parents b. Germany, no children born or living; ***Anna***, 15, daughter, b. Apr 1885, Ohio, parents b. Germany. 1900 FC OH LOAV, p. 20A, lines 44-6, house 416. *Anna was a daughter of Rosie above, Elizabeth apparently never had children.*

SCHEIBLE, George, 67?, immigrated 1879, Naturalized citizen 188-, b. B--er *(Bavaria seems to be crossed out for all with this listing)*, language German, parent same, fruit farmer; ***Elizabeth***, wife, 65, b. Ohio, parents b. B--er; ***Simon***, brother, immigrated 1910?, Alien. 1920 FC OH LOAV, p. 4A, lines 6-8. *Their daughter Anna and her husband, Leonard Haag, were living next door.*

GEORGE SCHEIBLE DIES IN AVON LAKE

AVON LAKE - ***George SCHEIBLE***, 92, believed to be Avon Lake's oldest resident, died yesterday at the home of his daughter, ***Mrs. Leonard HAAG***, 31902 Lake rd.

Scheible had been a farmer in this vicinity until his retirement 10 years ago. He was born in Germany. Prior to moving here he resided in Port Clinton, O.

Surviving besides his daughter, with whom he resided, are a brother ***Simon***, also of the same address; two grandchildren and two great-grandchildren.

The body is at the Burmeister funeral home where funeral services will be at 2 p.m. Friday with *Rev. Vernon O. GRABEL*, pastor of the Lutheran church, officiating. Burial will be in Bay Village cemetery. Lorain Journal, Lorain, OH, Aug 20, 1947, p. 9, col. 4.

SCHEIBLE, George, residence, 31902 Lake Rd., Avon Lake; beloved father of ***Anna HAAG***; brother of ***Simon*** of Avon Lake and ***Mary MESSMER*** of Germany; grandfather and great-grandfather; Tuesday. Friends may call at the Burmeister Funeral Home, 163 Avon-Belden Rd., Avon Lake, where services will be held Friday, Aug 22, at 2 p.m. Aug 20, 1947. The Plain Dealer.

George SCHEIBLE, d. Aug 19, 1947, 10:15, Avon Lake Village, Lorain Co. of senile myocarditis with failure, 1 month due to senility; usual residence 31902 Lake Rd., Avon Lake, in community 61 yrs., in U.S.A. 68 yrs.; widowed, wife ***Elizabeth***; b. Feb 7, 1855 in Bremgarten, Germany, 92 yrs. 6 mos. 12 days; fr. ***Andrew SCHEIBLE***, b. Germany, mo. ***Anna HESS***, b. Germany; occup. Farmer, retired; informant Anna Haag, 31902 Lake Rd.; buried Bay Village Cemetery, funeral home Burmeister Funeral Home, 163 Avon-Belden Rd, Avon Lake, Ohio. Ohio Certificate of Death, Division of Vital Statistics, 1947, certif. 51710.

Brother of George Scheible:

Simon SCHEIBLE, b. 1862; bur. 27 Apr 1953; Lake Shore Cemetery, Avon Lake, OH. Lake Shore Cemetery Records and inscription at Lake Shore Cemetery, Avon Lake, OH. Read by Catherine Burke Flament.

Lot 29 *Elizabeth Bender Scheible

no marker

Elizabeth Bender Scheible, George Scheible's second wife, may be buried here with her husband. No lot number was provided with the interment records, and there is no marker inscribed with her name.

Elizabeth SCHEIBLE, Avon Lake, Lorain Co.; d. 10/30, 1929, Acute cardiac dilatation, due to myocarditis senilis-suddenly, Contributory Bronchitis acute-7ds.; married ***George SCHEIBLE***; b. 12/22-1851, Parma, Ohio, fr. ***Henry BENDER***, b. Germany, mo. ***Julia*** -, b. Germany; 77 yrs. 10 mo. 8 ds.; informant *Anna HAAG*, Avon Lake, Ohio; bur. Bay Village, O., Nov 1, 1929, undertaker E.C. Haag, Berea, Ohio, embalmed. Ohio Certificate of Death, Division of Vital Statistics, 1929, certif. 65650.

SCHEIBLE, Elizabeth (nee ***BENDER***), beloved wife of ***George***, mother of ***Mrs. Anna HAAG***, sister of ***Mrs. Kate TRAPP*** of Berea, ***Dena*** and ***Henry BENDER*** of Cleveland at her home, stop 42 Lake Road, Avon Lake, Ohio, age 78. Funeral from her late residence Friday, Nov 1, at 2 p.m. Burial in Bay Village Cemetery. Oct 31, 1929, p. 29, col. 5. The Plain Dealer.

Siblings of Elizabeth Bender Scheible:

The State of Ohio, Cuyahoga County, ss. I Certify that on the 22 day of Nov 1883 ***Mr. Jacob TRAPP*** and ***Kate BENDER*** were by me legally joined in marriage. Marriage Record, Cuyahoga County, OH, vol. 27, p. 95.

Kate TRAPP, d. 19 July, 1932, Middleburg Heights, Cuyahoga Co., Ohio of Carcinoma of Signoid Colon for 9 mos.; 76 yrs. 7 mos. 29 ds.; res. East Bagley Road; married to ***Jacob TRAPP***; she was b. Nov 20, 1855, Parma, OH; housewife; fr. ***Henry BENDER***, b. Germany, mo. ***Katherinea FLICK***, b. Germany; informant *Jacob TRAPP*, Berea Home; undertaker E.C. Haley, Berea*?*, burial at Woodvale . Ohio Certificate of Death, Division of Vital Statistics, 1932, certif. 40649.

TRAPP: Kate (nee ***BENDER***), beloved wife of ***Jacob***, mother of ***Louise*** and ***Mrs. Julia WEINLE***, sister of *Christina BENDER*, at her home on East Bagley Rd., Berea, O., Tuesday, July 19, 1932, age 76 years. Funeral from her late residence, Thursday, July 21, at 2:30 p. m. Burial Woodvale Cemetery. Cleveland Necrology File, July 21, 1932.

Jacob TRAPP, d. Oct 9, 1938, Middleburg Hgts., Cuyahoga Co., Ohio of Cerebral apoplexy and Arterio Sclerosis; widower of ***Kate TRAPP***; b. Mar 22, 1860,

Brooklyn, Ohio, fr. *Frank TRAPP*, b. Germany, mo. *Augusta SCHMIDT*, b. Germany; 78 yrs. 6 mos. 17 days; informant *Mrs. Julia WEINLE,* Berea, Ohio; undertaker Emil C. Haag Co., Berea, burial at Woodvale, Berea. Ohio Certificate of Death, Division of Vital Statistics, 1938, certif. 56154.

TRAPP, Jacob, beloved husband of the late ***Kate*** (nee ***BENDER***) father of ***Louise*** and ***Mrs. Julia WEINLE***, brother of *John,* at his home on E. Bagley rd., Berea, O., age 78 years, Funeral services at his late residence, Tuesday, Oct 11, at 2:30 p. m. 1860-1938. Woodvale Cem. Berea, O. Cleveland Necrology File, Oct 1938.

BENDER-Henry, brother of ***Christina BENDER*** and ***Mrs. Kate TRAPP***, passed away suddenly Tuesday, Feb 25, 1930, at the residence, 5306 Wetzel Avenue. Age 72 years. Remains at the G.H. Busch & Son Funeral Home, 4334 Pearl Road, where services will be held Friday, Feb 28, at 2 p. m. 1930. age 71. Brookmere Cemetery, Cleveland, Ohio. Cleveland Necrology File, Feb 27, 1930.

Henry BENDER, d. Feb 25, 1930, 5306 Wetzell *(sp.)* ave., Cleveland, Cuyahoga Co., Ohio of Cerebral Apoplexy on Feb 25th and Artereo sclerosis; 71 yrs. 10 mos. 9 ds.; b. March 16, 1858, Parma Village, Ohio to ***Henry BENDER***, b. Germany and ***Catherine FLICK***, b. Germany; Retired Farmer, last worked 1920; Single; informant *Christina BENDER*, 5306 Wetzell *(sp.)* ave.; undertaker G. H. Busch and Son, 4334 Pearl rd.; bur. Brookmere. Ohio Certificate of Death, Division of Vital Statistics, 1930, certif. 8398.

Lot 29 Infant Haag no marker

Infant HAAG; res. Avon; interred Mar 14, 1914; Lot 29. "List of Interments," Lakeside Cemetery, Bay Village, OH.
The child buried here was the daughter of ***Anna*** and ***Leonard HAAG***. Richard Haag, phone conversation, 26 March 2006.

Parents of Infant Haag:
George and Rosie Scheible's daughter Anna's marriage certificate shows Rosie's maiden name.

Leonard C. HAAG, 25, res. and b. Middleburgh, O., machinist, fr. *Andrew HAAG*, mo. *Barbara BECKER*, prev. married none. Married ***Anna SCHEIBLE***, 21, res. 7905 Guthrie Ave., b. Avon, occup. none, fr. *George SCHEIBLE*, mo. maiden name *Rose SOLOMON*, prev. married none. Marriage to be solemnized by Rev. Royce, Parma, O. The State of Ohio, Cuyahoga County, ss. I Certify That on the 6 day of June 1906 Leonard C. Haag and Anna Scheible were by me legally joined in marriage. Rev. Reinhold Reuss Marriage Record, Cuyahoga County, OH, vol. 63, p. 238.

Leonard HAGG *was the brother of* ***William C. HAAG***, *husband of* ***Hulda QUELL*** *(see Lot 9-17) and brother-in-law of* ***Kate Quell KRUMWIEDE***, *Lot 9.*

HAAG, Leonard C., 38, b. Ohio, fr. b. Bavaria, mother tongue German, Fruit Farmer; ***Anna,*** wife, 34, b. Ohio, fr. b. Bavaria, spoke German, mo. b. Austria, spoke German; ***George I.***, 12, b. Ohio; ***Carl W.***, 10, b. Ohio. 1920 FC OH LOAV, p. 4A, lines 2-5.

HAAG, Leonard C., residence 31902 Lake Rd, Avon Lake; beloved husband of ***Anna***; father of ***George L.***, and ***Carl W.***, brother of ***Dan, William, Rose VANDEN MOTTER, Carl*** and ***Estelle*** and grandfather. Friends may call at the Burmeister Funeral Home, 163 Avon-Belden Rd., Avon Lake, where services will be held Monday, April 5 at 3 p.m. Cleveland Necrology File, Apr 4, 1954.

Leonard Christ HAAG, b. Oct 30, 1881, Middleburg Twp., OH son of ***Andrew HAAG*** and ***Barbara BECKER***; farmer; d. April 2, 1954, Bayview Hospital, Bay Village; res. 31902 Lake Rd., Avon Lake, OH Avon Lake Cemetery, F. L. Burmeister, embalmer. Ohio Certificate of Death, Division of Vital Statistics, 1954, certif. 22854.

Leonard C. HAAG, bur. Apr 5, 1954, Lake Shore Cemetery, Avon Lake, OH. Lot purchased by L.C. Haag Apr 12, 1926. Lake Shore Cemetery Records, Avon Lake, OH.

HAAG ***Anna Haag*** (nee ***SCHEIBLE***), residence 31902 Lake Road, Avon Lake, beloved wife of the late ***Leonard C.***, mother of ***George L, Sr.***, and the late ***Carl (Walter)*** and ***Celia Louise***, grandmother of four, great-grandmother of eight...Burmeister Funeral Home...Family suggests contributions to the American Cancer Society. Cleveland Press, Oct 3, 1968.

Lake Shore Cemetery, Avon Lake, OH: ***HAAG Thomas A.*** 1968, ***Anna*** 1885-1968, ***Leonard C.*** 1881-1954, ***Todd L.*** 1968, ***Simon SCHEIBLE*** 1862-1953. Read by Catherine Burke Flament.

Brothers of Infant Haag:

HAAG, Carl W. Services for Carl W. Haag, chief of the Avon Lake fire department since 1946, will be at Burmeister funeral home, 163 Avon-Belden Road, Avon Lake, at 2 p.m. today. Mr. Haag, who was 55, died Monday in St. Joseph Hospital, Lorain.

Mr. Haag was a volunteer fireman and later a deputy volunteer fireman from 1934 until he was made chief in 1946.

Surviving are his wife, ***Mary;*** two sons, ***Carl W. Jr.*** and ***Richard L.***; a daughter, ***Rosemary A.***; his mother ***Mrs. Anna HAAG***, and a brother, ***George L.*** He lived at 31900 Lake Road, Avon Lake. Cleveland Necrology File, Apr 28, 1965 *Carl is buried at Holy Cross Cemetery, Cleveland, OH.*

Carl Walter HAAG, d. April 26, 1965 at St. John Hospital, Lorain , Lorain Co., OH after a stay of three weeks of Cancer of the lung with Metastases to Spinal Cord for four months; residence 31900 Lake Rd., Avon Lake, Ohio; Fire Chief, Avon Lake Fire Dept.; b. Avon Lake, July 18, 1909 to ***Leonard C. HAAG*** and ***Anna SCHEIBLE***; 55 yrs. old; informant *Mrs. Mary HAAG*, 31900 Lake Rd., funeral dir. Burmeister Funeral Home, 163 Avon-Belden Rd., Avon Lake; bur. Holy Cross Cemetery, Cleveland, Cuyahoga Co., Ohio. Ohio Certificate of Death, Division of Vital Statistics, 1965, certif. 038228.

George HAAG, b. 4 May 1907, d. April 1981, Port Charlotte, Charlotte, FL. Social Security Index.

Lot 30 *Owner: Mrs. J. Hay of Cleveland purchased Mar 10, 1914, for $6.30* SL

Lot 30-2 Fannie J. Hayes Thorson

FANNIE
HAYES
THORSEN
1868-1914

Fannie Hayes Thorsen is the daughter of Joseph Hayes and Mary Campbell (OP 3:15-17).

Fanny J. THORSEN; res. Los Angles, Cal.; English; Mar 12, 1914; lot 30. "List of Interments," Lakeside Cemetery, Bay Village, OH. *The last name is believed to be misspelled and should be Thorson.*

Fannie J. THORSON, Los Angeles, Cal., died March 5, 1914, Pernicious Anemia, age 45, b. Ohio, physician Wm. E. Hall, to Cleveland, Ohio. Bureau of Vital Statistics, Burial or Removal Permit, Bay Village, OH.

THORSON-Fanny HAYES, March 6, at Los Angeles, beloved daughter of ***Mrs. J. HAYES***, 8024 Cedar ave., Cleveland, and sister of ***David HAYES, Dr. W (William). C. HAYES, J.(Joseph)B. HAYES, jr., Mrs. R. (Rene) MALLE*** and ***Miss Bessie M. HAYES***. Funeral to be held Thursday, Mar 12, at 3 p.m. from the residence, 8024 Cedar ave. Cleveland Necrology File, Mar 12, 1914, roll 80.

Possible child of Fannie Hayes Thorson:

Earl R. THORSON, b. 12/13/1894, Ohio; mother's maiden name ***HAYES***, male, d. Los Angeles, CA 6/26/1961, 66 years old. "California Death Index 1940-1997," California Home Page, Vital Search.

Lot 31 *Owner: O. Scholle, listed: "O. Scholle ?," purchased for $6.30* SL

Lot 31-3 Kupfer marker

KUPFER

EMMA	EDWARD W.
JAN 1, 1859	MAR 9, 1860
JUNE 16, 1951	SEPT 20, 1926

Lot 31-3 Emma Scholl Kupfer

Emma (Amelia) is the daughter of Rudolph and Anna Scholl (Lot 36), and sister of Otto Scholl (below) and Willie (Lot 36). Edward and her surname was signed as Kuepfer in her father's will.

"***Auntie Em***" as she was affectionately known to others was unable to read or write. Her home was always welcome to others and there was always something special to eat. She was extremely friendly and a close friend of ***Elvie POWELL DODD***. She and Edward never had children and lived across from the creek on Cahoon. While the middle school was being built she took in boarders of laborers working on the building. She worked as a cook for wealthy families on the east side of town and in Cleveland, but during the depression she wasn't employed. During this time to make ends meet, she would sell tablecloths and other items that wealthy families would give her that had "worn out." She also had a room off to the side of her house where she wove rugs. ***Edward***, a Swiss immigrant, was known to be from a wealthy family but didn't have a trade. He was not as friendly and inviting a figure as his wife. Sarah Dodd Wymer

Recipe shared by Emma:

Doughnuts
(Mrs. E. Kupfer)

Two-thirds cup of sugar, two eggs beaten, beat lightly together; two tablespoons melted butter, one-half cup sweet milk, one teaspoon salt, two heaping teaspoons baking powder, one pinch grated nutmeg. Add flour enough to roll and cut. Cook in hot fat.

The Village Cook Book, p. 34. (c1911-1915).

KUPFER, Emma, head, 71, own home, no radio, value of house $7,000, widow, b. Ohio, fr. b. Baden, Germany, mo. b. Wurtenberg, Germany, no occup. 1930 FC OH CYBV, ED 18-534, 467 Cahoon Road, p. 15A, line 6.

KUPFER, EMMA, wife of the late ***Edward***; sister of ***Mrs. Alice MARTIN*** and ***Charles*** and ***Albert SCHOLL***. Friends may call at the Clifford Pease Funeral Home, 2914 Dover Center Rd., Westlake, where services will be held Monday, June 18 at 2 p.m. Cleveland Necrology File, June 18, 1951, roll 127.

Emma KUPFER, female, white, d. June 16, 1951, 9:30 a.m. at 467 Cahoon, Bay Village (usual residence) of Generalized Arteriosclerosis (for years) and Old Age; widow; b. Jan 1, 1859 in Westlake (Dover), Cuy. Co., Ohio to ***Rudolf SCHOLL*** and ***Maria Anna GLASER***; 92 yrs.; Housewife; Informant *Lillian B. OSBORN. (Lillian is the daughter of John GLASSER and Mary BEELER, see Lot 48).* Physician attended deceased from June 1950 to June 16, 1951, W.R. Kutzenmeyer, MD, 589 Dover Rd.; Funeral Director Marion E. Pease; burial 6/18/51, Lakeside Cemetery, Bay Village. Ohio Certificate of Death, Division of Vital Statistics,1951, certif. 36684 and Bureau of Vital Statistics, Burial or Removal Permit, Bay Village, OH. 51-37.

Lot 31-3 Edward William Kupfer

CUPFER** (sp.)*, ***Edward, 40, b. May 1860, married 12 yrs., book agent; ***Emma***, 37, b. Oct 1862, no children born or living. 1900 FC OH CYDO, p. 21B, lines 62-3, house 458.

KUPFER, Edward W., 50, married 21 yrs., Swiss-German, bookkeeper-Cigar Mfg.; ***Emma S.***, 51, b. Ohio, parents b. Germany, immig 1881, Al. 1910 FC OH CYBV p. 2B, lines 87-8.

KUPFER, Edward, 59, rented house Lake Rd. near Bassett, immigrated 1881, naturalized 1915, b. Bern, Switzerland, parents b. Switz., merchant-furniture polish; ***Ema*** *(sp.)*, 61, b. Ohio, fr. b. Baden, Ger., mo. b. Wertenberg, Ger. 1920 FC OH CYBV, Lake Road, p. 2A, lines 4-5.

Edward William KUPFER, Cahoon Rd., Bay; d. Sept 20, 1926, 4:40 a.m.; married ***Emma S. KUPFER***; b. Mar 9, 1860, Switzerland, fr. ***Rudolph KUPFER***, b. Switzerland, mo. ***Ferona LEINBERGER***, b. Switzerland; occup. book__?; 66 yrs. 6 mos. 11 ds.; informant Emma Kupfer; bur. Bay Village, Sept 22., 1926, undertaker C. Pease. Ohio Certificate of Death, Division of Vital Statistics, 1927, certif. 78707.

KUPFER-Edward William, husband of ***Emma*** (nee ***SCHOLL***), at residence Kahoon *(sp.)* road, Stop 24, Bay Village, Ohio, Sept 20; age 66. Funeral at his residence, Wednesday, Sept 22, at 3 p.m. Cleveland Necrology File, Sept 22, 1926, roll 127.

Lot 31-4 Otto Scholl

OTTO

This is assumed to be ***Otto SCHOLL***, son of ***Rudolph*** and ***Anna SCHOLL*** *(Lot 36)*, brother of ***Emma KUPFER***, above and ***William SCHOLL***, *(Lot 36)*.

Otto SCHOOL, res. Bay Village, German, interred between 1900-04, Lot 31. "List of Interments," Lakeside Cemetery, Bay Village, OH.

SHOLL, Rudolph…Anna…Otto, 43, son, single, b. Jan 1857, Ohio, parents b. Germany, (no occupation listed). 1900 FC OH CYDO, p. 9A/B, lines 50-52, house 190.

SCHOLL, Otto, 45 years, 7 Sept 1902. "Independent Evangelical Church Abstracts," p. 61.

SCHOLL, Otto, Sunday morning at 2 o'clock, in his 45th year. Funeral Tuesday, Sept 9, 2 p.m. sun time. From Wischmeyers, Dover, O. Cleveland Necrology File, Sept 9, 1902.

Lot 32 *Owner: Mrs. Mary Beard purchased June 1, (no year listed) for, $6.30* SL

Lot 32 Willie Beard no marker

Willie BEARD, 6; res. Dover; interred Mar 29, 1888, Potter's field, removed to Lot 32. "List of Interments," Lakeside Cemetery, Bay Village, OH.

Lot 33 *Owner: Charles Gunziger of Dover. O. purchased Sept 11, 1886 for, $5.74* SL

Lot 33 Mary Lukacs Body no marker

Mary BODY, res. Cahoon St., d. Nov 24, 1920, Dover, Cuyahoga Co., Ohio, cause Acute appendicitis for 3 ds. contributory Large umbilical hernia for several years; *slash through marital status and no husband listed*; occup hwf.; b. Sept 11, 1854, Hungary, fr. ***John LUKACS***, b. Hungary, mo. ***Julia KIHAN***, b. Hungary; 66 yrs. 2 mos. 13 ds; bur. Bay Village, Nov 27, 1920, undertaker C. Pease, Dover Center, O., informant *Albert B. BODY*, Bay Village, O. Ohio Certificate of Death, Division of Vital Statistics, 1920, certif. 68103.

Albert, who was the informant for Mary's death certificate, may be her son but is not listed in the obituary. The following provides information about his parent's. Mary died after the census was taken but was not listed.

BODY, Adalbert, male, 42 yrs., immig. 1904, Na., b. Szatmar, Hungary, mother tongue Magyar Hungarian, parents. b. Szatmar, Hungary, draftsman; ***Ida***, wife, 28, immig 1906, Na., b. Szatmar, Hungary; ***Adalbert Jr.***, son, 10, b. Ohio; *BEN_, Mary*, boarder, 48, widow, immig. 1907, b. Gonor, Hungary, parents same, house at Dover Center Rd. 1920 (Jan 2-3), FC OH CYBV, p. 4B, lines 73-6.

Mary BODY, aged ___, Hungarian, interred 1921, sublot 33. Note in Cemetery file, Bay Village City Hall, Bay Village, OH.

Mary BODY, Dover, 66, Acute Appendicitis, undertaker - C. Pease, Dover Center, O., Nov 27, 1920. Bureau of Vital Statistics, Burial or Removal Permit, Bay Village, OH.

BODY-Maria, widow of ***John BODY***, beloved mother of ***Bela BODY***, died Wednesday noon at her residence, Stop 24, Dover, Ohio. Funeral from her Dover home, 2 p.m. Saturday, Nov 27. Friends invited. Cleveland Necrology File, Nov 25, 1920, roll 8.

Lot 33-5 Heckerman Marker

HECKERMAN
FRANK MAUDE
1868- 1881-1944

Lot 33-5 Frank H. Heckerman

Franz Heinrich Herrmann HECKERMANN...geb 9 Dec, bap. 12 Dec 1868. St. Paul Lutheran Church, Baptismal Records, p. 17.

Frank H. HECKERMAN, 38, Dover, O., b. Dover, O., carpenter, fr. *C.H.*, mo. *Mary PETERS*. Married ***Maude M. GIRBECH***, 27, res. 1302 W. 25th St., b. Austria, fr. *Milos*, mo. *Maude NEWARK*; neither previously married. I Certify that on 11 Nov 1908 Frank H. Heckerman and Maude M. Girbech were legally married by me in Dover, Cuyahoga County, O. D.T. Miller, J.P. Marriage Application filed and issued Nov 11, 1908. Marriage Record, Cuyahoga County, OH, vol. 71, p. 217.

Frank HECKERMAN and ***Maude GERBICK*** worked for a family that owned a mansion later becoming the Sheppard's house. He was the gardener and she was the maid. There were two sisters and a brother who owned the mansion and had two beautiful Russian Wolf Hounds.

Maude and Frank were hard working and determined to better themselves. They had a berry patch and apple orchard near the south tracks (Electric Rd.). The Interurban Electric cars ran just north of their property. Later when our family lived there for a short time, we rode the cars to school (now Bay Village Middle School). My Aunt and Uncle owned several homes on Foote Rd. off Bassett. During "haying" time, someone threw a pitchfork yelling, "Watch out below," just as Uncle Frank looked up. He lost an eye and wore a glass one after that.

Aunt Maude was the only daughter in the family, having three brothers: ***Sam***, ***Mike*** and ***John***. They sailed from Hamburg, Germany on the S.S.Europa, leaving Yugoslavia around 1900. They possibly left six brothers or so in Europe. John did return to Europe, while Sam and Mike had a business together on the west side of the Cuyahoga River near the Flats.

The Heckerman's had two sons, ***Amos*** and ***Daniel***. Amos was very interested in planes, building and flying them during the 1920's. He owned a car and of course a motorcycle. While driving the motorcycle on Lake Road *(not sure of location)*, he attempted to pass a car and ran head-on into an oncoming vehicle, resulting in his death.

Dan joined the Navy/Air Force and ferried the wounded back to the states in World War II, in addition to flying bombs over Guam for the fighters. He worked at the Pentagon for awhile and gave several speeches here at the Old Hollenden Hotel. He died in San Jose, California in 1978 and was buried with the title of Commander in the Presidio Navy Cemetery in San Diego. Mildred G. Offutt

The Sheppard house that is referred to above was the Lawrence Mansion. *Washington LAWRENCE,* up to the time of his death in 1900, was president of the National Carbon Company. He also developed for his family and friends in 1890 one of the oldest golf courses in the United States, the Dover-Bay Country Club in Bay Village.

Washington married *Harriett COLLISTER* in 1863 and reared seven daughters. In 1883 the Lawrences owned a summer home in Dover-Bay and eventually purchased land east of Clague Road to the township line between Lake Erie and the railroad tracks. This farmland was owned by *Joseph BROWN, A.C. PHINNEY, Joseph BROWN, Jr.* and *Mary GANT*. The Lawrence family was occupying the Phinney farmhouse in 1897, which was directly across from the mansion being built. By April of 1899 the family had started occupying the mansion which is now part of Cashelmara Condominiums. The home was still not completed when Washington died in 1900 of an illness after surviving a fall from the second floor of his new house as he was inspecting construction.

The daughters lived in the mansion or in the surrounding lakeside summer homes situated around their parents' home as they married. *Maude, Cora BROWN* a widow, and *Ella* with her husband *William MATTHEWS* lived in the mansion with Mrs. Lawrence.

The new mansion when finished contained eight bedrooms on the second floor alone. The third floor contained a ballroom, two bedrooms, an enormous linen closet, and the servants' quarters. There were seven servants, including gardener and handyman.

The last members of the Lawrence family living in the mansion were Ella and Will Matthews, and Maude, who enjoyed holding welfare meetings in the front parlor. When Maude died in 1948, Ella and Will Matthews sold the property, which then became the Bay View Osteopathic General Hospital. Monies were advanced by the Sheppard family, and the father and three sons were resident doctors. Bay Village Historical Society, Bay Village: A Way of Life, pp. 74-76.

Frank HECKERMAN helped to plow the sidewalks in the winter with a one-horse plow. Those traveling down Lake Road were also able to purchase items grown on his nearby farm. Kay Laughlin and George Serb.

HECKERMAN, Frank, 40, b. Ohio, parents b. Ohio, laborer, coal yard, owns home free; ***Maude***, 30, 1 child born and living; ***Emil***, 1/12, b. Ohio; ***Henry***, nephew, 20, b. Ohio, parents b. Ohio, teamster, road work, own farm. 1910 FC OH CYDO, lines 37-40.

HECKERMAN, Frank, 50, b. Ohio, parents b. Germany, basket maker at Basket factory; ***Maude***, wife, 39, yr. of immigration 1894?, naturalized by marriage, b. Demesha, Australia *(sp.)*, parents b. Australia; ***Amiel***, son, 10, b. Ohio; ***Dan***, son, b. Ohio; ***GERBIC, Irene***, boarder, 13, b. Ohio. 1920 FC OH CYBV p. 5A, lines, 9-13, Dover Center Rd. *Irene was the daughter of Maude's brother.*

HECKERMAN, Frank, 62, owns house valued at $7,500, no radio, age at marriage 40, b. Ohio, parents b. Ohio, Laborer farm; ***Maud***, 48, wife, age at marriage 26, b. Czechoslovakia, parents b. Czechoslovakia, language spoken at home before coming to the U.S. Bohemian, immigrated 1899, Naturalized citizen; ***Daniel***, 18, son, single, b. Ohio, Window trimmer Dept. Store. 1930 FC OH CYBV ED 18-534, 29412 Foote Road, p. 19A, lines 44-46.

Frank HECKERMAN, d. May 15, 1954, Bay View Hospital, Bay Village, OH. Usual residence 29414 Foote Rd., Bay Village. Widower, b. Dec 9, 1867, West Dover, Cuy. Co., Ohio, 86 yrs. old. Occup. Farmer, kind: Fruit Farm; fr. ***Henry HECKERMAN***, mo. ***Elizabeth PETERS***. Was deceased ever in the armed forces? No; Informant *Dan HECKERMAN.* Burial, 5/18/54, Lakeside Cemetery, Bay Village. Funeral Director Marion E. Pease. Ohio Certificate of Death, Division of Vital Statistics, 1954, certif. 29379.

Medical Certification Deferred, Supplementary Certification: Probable Bronchopneumonia, Cerebral Hemorrhage. Coroner S.R. Gerber. Ohio Certificate of Death, Division of Vital Statistics, certif. 348W.

Frank HECKERMAN: 5-18-54 Notation on plot map, Lakeside Cemetery File.

Parents of Frank Heckerman:

ECKERMAN** (sp.), **Henry, 43, farmer, b. Hanover, parents b. Hanover; ***Anna M.***, 41, wife, b. Hanover, parents b. Hanover; ***August***, 20, laborer; ***Louie***, 17; ***Louisa***, 15; ***Frank***, 11; ***Henry***, 9; ***Bertha***, 7. All children b. in Ohio. 1880 FC OH CYDO, p. 95 A, lines 43-50.

ECKERMAN** (sp.), **Henry. Owned land; Acres: Improved - Tilled, including fallow and grass: 24, Permanent meadow: 6. Farm Values: Land and buildings - $2,000, Machinery - $175, Live Stock - $200. Estimated value of all farm production: $300. Grass lands acreage: 10 mown, 3 not mown, 8 tons hay. 4 horses, 2 milch cows, 1 other, 2 calves dropped, 2 slaughtered. 200 pounds of butter made on the farm. 5 swine. 25 barnyard poultry on farm, 100 dozen eggs produced in 1879. Indian corn: 3 acres, 100 bushels; wheat: 5 acres, 60 bushels; potatoes: 3 acres, 250 bushels. Orchards - apple: 1 acre, 30 bearing trees. "Schedule 2. Production of Agriculture in Dover Township, Cuyahoga County, OH," enumerated June, 1880, p. 25.

Siblings of Frank Heckerman:

HECKERMAN, August, 70, value of home $5000, no radio, age at marriage 24, b. Ohio, fr./mo. b. Germany; ***Louise***, wife, 66, age at marriage 21, b. Ohio, fr./mo. b. Germany; ***Wilbert J.***, son, 27, single, truck driver. 1930 FC OH CY Dover Village, ED 18-534, p. 24A, Bradley Road, lines 32-34.

August Frank HECKERMAN, d. 8 Aug 1932, Fairview Park Hospital, Cleveland, Cuyahoga Co., Ohio; res. 1047 Bradley Rd., Dover Village of Hypertrophied Prostate and Broncho-Pneumonia; 72 yrs. 7 mos. 8 ds.; Fruit Grower; Married to ***Louisa HECKERMAN***; informant *Wilbert HECKERMAN*, 1047 Bradley; undertaker Clifford Pease, Dover Center, O.; burial St. Paul Lutheran Cemetery *(Westlake, OH)*. Ohio Certificate of Death, Division of Vital Statistics, 1932, certif. 46759 and St. Paul Lutheran Church, Death Records, p. 361.

HECKERMAN, August, head, 70, own house, no radio, value of house $5,000, age at marriage 24 yrs., b. Ohio, parents b. Germany; ***Louise***, wife, 66, age at marriage 21 yrs., b. Ohio, parents b. Germany; ***Wilbert J.***, son, 27, single, b. Ohio, Truck Driver. 1930 FC OH Dover Twp., ED18-584, Bradley Road, p. 24A, lines 32-34.

HECKERMAN: August F., husband of ***Louise*** (nee ***BAISCH***), father of ***Mrs. Florence FISCHER, Mrs. Fred BEHRING, Irving*** and ***Wilbert***, at 1047 Bradley Rd. Services at St. Paul's Lutheran Church, Detroit Rd., Dover Village, Thursday, Aug 11, at 3 p. m. 1860 - 1932. St. Paul's Cemetery Cleveland, Ohio. Cemetery record; Cleveland Necrology File, Aug 11 1932, reel 036.

Wilbert HECKERMAN, 27; res. W. Dover, O.; b. W. Dover; occup. Driver; fr. *August*, mo. *Louise BAISCH.* Married ***Bertha REED***, 21; res. N. Olmsted, O.; b. New York City, fr. *George*, mo. *Ruth PARKINSON*; neither previously married. Marriage solemnized by Wm. Single, W. Dover, O. The State of Ohio, Cuyahoga County, ss. I Certify, That on the 19th day of August 1930, Wilbert Heckerman and Miss Bertha Reed were by me legally joined in marriage. Marriage Record, Cuyahoga County, OH, vol. 162, p. 386.

HECKERMAN. ***Wilbert J. HECKERMAN***, late residence, 5675 Cornell Rd., North Ridgeville beloved husband of ***Bertha A.***, father of ***Donald*** and ***Mrs. Mildred LOWTHER***, grandfather of four, brother of *Mrs. Florence FISHER* and *Mrs. Nettie BEHRING*. The family will receive friends 2-4 And 7-9 P. M. Sunday at the Jenkins Funeral Chapel, 2914 Dover Center Rd., Westlake, where services will be held Monday. Oct 14 1962. The Plain Dealer.

The State of Ohio, Cuyahoga County, ss. I Certify that on the 13 day of Nov 1888 ***Mr. Fred H. HECKERMAN*** and ***Miss Clara GUELKER*** were by me legally joined in marriage. *(He was under 21 and needed consent.)* William Fuller. Marriage Record, Cuyahoga County, OH, vol. 32, p. 304.

HECKERMAN, Louis, age 85 years; husband of the late ***Carrie*** (nee ***GUELKER***); father of ***Mrs. Bertha WUEBKER, Alfred, Carl, Mrs. Edith HUNGER***, grandfather and great-grandfather; brother of ***Frank***, ***Henry*** and ***Mrs. Lydia KIDNEY***. Friends may call at the late residence, 741 Bassett Rd., Westlake. Services at St. Paul's Evangelical Lutheran Church, Detroit Rd., Westlake, Monday, Dec 15, at 3 p. m. Dec 13 1947. The Plain Dealer.

Louis HECKERMAN; d. 12 Dec 1947, 7:20 p.m. at his residence 741 Bassett Rd., Westlake of Coronary Thrombosis 4 hrs., Generalized Arteriosclerosis 10 yrs. and Asthmatic Bronchitis 15 yrs.; 85 yrs. 2 mos. 29 ds.; widower of ***Clara***; Farmer; Lutheran; b. 13 Sept 1862 to ***Henry HECKERMAN***, b. Germany and ***Elizabeth PETERS***, b. Germany; bur. Evergreen Cemetery; charge to *Mrs. Wm. WUEBKER*, Litchfield, Ohio; order given by *Al HECKERMAN*, 773 Bassett. Funeral costs $531.67, which included casket for $330, funeral car $12, 2 Plain Dealer notices $8.45, 1 Press 3.95, 1 News $2.25. Pease Funeral Home Records, Mss. 4809, Western Reserve Historical Society, Cleveland, OH, Record of Funeral, p. 162.

Louis and ***Clara HECKERMAN*** had six children; ***Bertha*** who moved to Litchfield; ***Henry*** who died of small pox, married *Grace* having one child, *Melvin*; ***Richard*** who died of small pox; ***Alfred*** (b. 20 Nov 1899, Dover) m. *Eleanor DREGER*, they had three daughters; ***Carl*** and ***Edith***. Betty Clifford

HECKERMAN: Clara (nee ***GUELKER***), wife of ***Louis***; mother of ***Mrs. Bertha WUEBKER, Alfred, Carl, Mrs. Edith HUNGER*** and the late ***Henry*** and ***Richard***; grandmother and great-grandmother; sister of *Mrs. Anna WESTERFELD* and *Mrs. Regina*

BOEHNKER. Friends may call at the late residence, 741 Bassett Rd., Westlake, Services at St. Paul's Evangelical Lutheran Church, Detroit Rd., Westlake, Saturday, June 22, at 3 p. m. June 21 1946. The Plain Dealer. Reprinted with permission, Cleveland Necrology File.

Clara Marie HECKERMAN, d. 19 June 1946 at residence 741 Bassett, Westlake, OH, of Coronary Embolism and Coronary Sclerosis and Generalized Arterio-sclerosis; b. 18 March 1870, Dover Twp.; fr. ***Friedrick W. GUELKER***, b. Germany, mo. ***Marie ENGEL***, b. Germany; order given by *Edith HUNGER*, 674 Bradley; cemetery Evergreen. Pease Funeral Home Records, Mss. 4809, Western Reserve Historical Society, Cleveland, OH, Record of Funeral, p. 162. *There are members of the Engel family buried in Lake Shore Cemetery, Avon Lake; it was not determined if this was the same family.*

Henry HECKERMAN, 30; res. Litchfield, O.; b. Dover, O.; Farmer; fr. *Louis*, mo. *Carrie GUELKER.* Married ***Grace E. KIDNEY***, 27; res. Dover; b. Dover; occup. none; fr. *William*, mo. *Anna ORING*; neither previously married. Marriage solemnized by W.J. Zoul, J. P., Shaker Hts., O. The State of Ohio, Cuyahoga County, ss. I Certify, That on the 15th day of December 1919, Henry Heckerman and Grace E. Kidney were by me legally joined in marriage. M. Penty, J.P. Marriage Record, Cuyahoga County, OH, vol. 114, p. 493.

HECKERMAN-Henry L., husband of ***Grace*** (nee ***KIDNEY***), Thursday, July 30, age 35 years. Funeral from home of his parents, ***Mr.*** and ***Mrs. Louis HECKERMAN***, Bassett road, Dover Village, O., Sunday, Aug 2, at 3 p. m. 1889 - 1925. Evergreen Cemetery Cleveland, Ohio. Cemetery record, Cleveland Necrology File, reel 036. Date of Interment 20 Apr 1925, Sect I, Lot 20, grave 1. Evergreen Cemetery.

HECKERMAN-Richard, son of ***Louis*** and ***Clara***, at German hospital, April 15, age 23 years. Funeral from residence, Bassett rd., Dover, Ohio, April 18, at 2 p. m. Auto funeral. 1893 - 1917. Evergreen Hills Cemetery, Chagrin Falls, Ohio. April 18, 1917 Cemetery record; Cleveland Necrology File, reel 036. Spinal Meningitis, Jas. Pease Undertaker, bur. Sect. I, Lot 20, grave 3. Evergreen Cemetery Records.

The State of Ohio, Cuyahoga County, ss. I Certify, That on the 20th day of July 1927, ***Alfred Louis HECKERMAN*** and ***Eleanora Bertha DREGER*** were by me legally joined in marriage, after due publication of bans as provided by law. Filed September 28, 1927, Rev. Wm. J. Single Marriage Record, Cuyahoga County, OH, vol. 136, p. 301.

Louisa Marie HECKERMAN GUNZIGER ZEECK, b. 18 Oct 1864, Dover; m.1 ***Charles GUNZIGER***; m.2 ***Otto ZEECK*** (b. c1870); d. 24 May 1945, St. Joseph Hospital, Lorain, Lorain Co., OH, bur. Evergreen Cemetery, Westlake, OH. *Information under son, Infant Gunziger, this lot.*

Frank HECKERMAN, b. 9 Dec 1868, d. May 1954, bur. Lakeside Cemetery. *See Lot 33.*

Heinrich Wilhelm Carl HECKERMAN, b. 1874. St. Paul Lutheran Church records.

Henry HECKERMAN, b. 28 Jan 1871; fr. ***Henry HECKERMAN***, mo. ***Elizabeth PETERS***; m. ***Blanche***; Ret'd basket maker, d. 26 Oct 1948 of acute myocarditis, one week; bur. Evergreen Cemetery, Westlake, OH. Pease Funeral Home Records, Mss. 4809, Western Reserve Historical Society, Cleveland, OH, Record of Funeral, p. 223.

Henry HECKERMAN, 77, d. Westlake, internment 29 Oct 1948, Section I, Lot 33, grave 2, Evergreen Cemetery, lot owner *Louisa GUNZIGER*. ***Carl HECKERMAN***, 66, Westlake, Ohio, undertaker Clifford Pease, internment 28 Apr 1941, grave 3. Evergreen Cemetery, Westlake, OH.

***Bertha HECKERMAN SCHNEEBERGER**, this lot.*

Sons of Frank Heckerman and Maude Gerbick:

Amos HECKERMAN died in a motorcycle accident. Their son ***Dan***, was a Commander in the Air Force who flew wounded back during World War II. He was a pioneer in flying World War I planes with double wings. He was a very good looking and charming man. He may have had two sons. Dan passed away in California of cancer in 1978. Mildred Gerbick Offutt

HECKERMAN - Amos E., son of ***Frank*** and ***Maude*** (nee ***GERBICK***), brother of ***Dan***, suddenly, Sept 23, age 20 years. Funeral from residence of parents, 29412 Foote Road, Bay Village, Thursday, Sept 26, 1929, at 2:30 p.m. Sept 25, 1929, p. 25, col. 2. The Plain Dealer. Reprinted with permission.

Amos Emil HECKERMAN, d. Sept 24, 1929 in Road at Stop 14 and Lake Road, Bay, Cuyahoga Co., Ohio of Fracture of Skull - Acc. Auto, Stop 15 Lake Road, contributory Hemorrhage and Shock; res. 29412 Foote Rd., Bay Village, Ohio; 20 yrs. 2 ds.; Excavator Engineer; b. Sept 22, 1909, Bay Village to ***Frank HECKERMAN***, b. Dover, Ohio and ***Maud GERBICK***, b. Jugo-Slavia, Austria; informant Frank Heckerman, 29412 Foote Rd.; undertaker C. Pease, Dover Center; Cremation. Ohio Certificate of Death, Division of Vital Statistics, 1929, certif. 56941.

Dan HECKERMAN, 22; res. 1347 St. Charles, Lwd. *(Lakewood)*; b. N. Dover, O.; occup. Trimmer; fr. *Frank HECKERMAN, mo. Maud GERBICK.* Married ***Hester HERMAN***, 21; 3810 Silsby Rd.; b. Dayton, O.; occup. Saleslady; fr. *Harry HERMAN*, mo. *Edith HUGHES*; neither previously married. The State of Ohio, Cuyahoga County, ss. I Certify, That on the 11th day of February 1931 Dan Heckerman and Hester Herman were by me legally joined in marriage. Rev. William P. Thomas. Marriage Record, Cuyahoga County, OH, vol. 164, p. 70.

Dan HECKERMAN, b. 29 April 1911, d. 31 Jan 1978, Last benefit San Jose, Santa Clara, CA Social Security Index and California Death Index.

No obituaries, death notices or funeral notices were found in the San Jose Mercury from February 1-10, 1978. San Jose Public Library, San Jose, California.

Burial was not able to be verified at Presidio Naval Cemetery, San Francisco for Dan Heckerman.

Lot 33-5 Maude Gerbick Heckerman

Maude was a very businesslike person and worked as a maid. She had two brothers who were also born in Yugoslavia and lived in the area, ***Mike*** and ***Sam***. Mildred G. Offutt

Maude HECKERMAN; d. 29424 Foote Rd., Bay Village, Ohio (usual residence), Aug 12, 1944, 9:20 a.m., Cancer of stomach with metastesis-1 yr., arteriosclerosis-5yrs.; married; husband ***Frank***, 74 yrs. old.; b. 9 Sept 1881, Jugo-Slavia; 62 yrs. 11 mos. 3 days; fr. ***Mike GERBICK***, b. Jugo-Slavia, mo. do not know, b. Jugo-Slavia; bur. 15 Aug 1944, Lakeside Cem., Bay Village, undertaker Marion E. Pease, Westlake; informant W. Gunziger, E. Oviatt, Bay V. Ohio Certificate of Death, Division of Vital Statistics, 1944, certif. 53465.

HECKERMAN, MAUDE, residence 29424 Foote rd., Bay Village, wife of ***Frank***, mother of ***Lieut. Dan***, U.S.N.R., and grandmother, sister of ***Sam GERBICK***. Friends may call at the Clifford Pease Funeral Home, 2914 Dover Center rd., Westlake, until Tuesday noon. Services at Bay Village Methodist Church, Tuesday, Aug 15 at 2 p.m. Cleveland Press, August 14, 1944, p. 18.

Siblings of Maude Gerbick Heckerman:

Sam GERBICK, b. Feb 2, 1875, in Austria-Hungary, Yugoslavia; m. ***Bertha KASSAY*** (b. Budapest, Hungary; d. 1976 Costa Mesa, CA); d. Feb 7, 1953, at his home 36130 Detroit Rd., Avon, Lorain County, OH. He was a retired Steel Worker. Sam is buried at Lakewood Park Cemetery, Rocky River, OH. Mildred Gerbick Offutt and Ohio Certificate of Death, Division of Vital Statistics, 1953, certif. 11418.

GERBICK, Samuel, residence, 36130 Detroit Rd., Avon, O.; beloved husband of ***Bertha***; father of ***Ella DANNEMILLER, Theodore, John, Mildred OFFUTT, Charles*** and ***Dorothy KNIGHT***, and grandfather. Friends may call at the Burmeister Funeral Home, 163 Avon Belden Rd., Avon Lake, where services will be held Tuesday, Feb 10, at 2 p. m. Cleveland Necrology File.

Mike and ***Sam GERBICK*** had a business together in Cleveland on the west side of the Cuyahoga River, near the Flats. Mildred Gerbick Offutt

GERBICK: Michael, beloved father of ***Mrs. Edith MIDDLETON***, and grandfather, brother of ***Mrs. Maude HECKERMAN*** and ***Sam GERBICK***. Friends may call at the Branch-Kauffman Funeral Home, 16605 Detroit ave., where services will be held Wednesday, Feb 16, at 2 p. m. Cleveland Necrology File, Feb 15 1938.

Michael GERBICK, d. Feb 14, 1938, 7:15 a.m. at Cleveland City Hospital, Cleveland, Cuyahoga Co., Ohio of Cerebral Hemorrhage (right) on Feb 10, Cardiac Hypertrophy and Dilatation, Passive Hyperemia of Liver, Kidneys and Spleen; 65 yrs. 2 mos. 10 ds.; b. Dec 4, 1872, Jermaja, Yugoslavia; res. 1212 Main St.; Divorced from ***Theresa FISHER***; Merchant Coal and Lumber, spent 30 years in this occupation, last worked Feb 1938; informant Edith Middleton; undertaker Branch Kauffman, 16605 Detroit Ave.; burial West Park Cem. Ohio Certificate of Death, Division of Vital Statistics, 1938, certif. 8279.

Lot 33 Bertha Heckerman Schneeberger

no marker

Bertha Schneeberger was the daughter of Henry C. Heckerman and Marie Peters, sister of Frank, this lot, and aunt of Carl Gunziger (infant) below.

Bertha Christiana Maria HECKERMAN, b. 3 June 1873. St. Paul Lutheran Church Baptismal Record.

The State of Ohio, Cuyahoga County, ss. I Certify that on the 18th day of Feby 1892 ***Mr. George SCHNEEBERGER*** and ***Miss Bertha HECKERMAN*** were by me legally joined in marriage. Chas. L. Selzer, Mayor of the Village of Brooklyn Marriage Record, Cuyahoga County, OH, vol. 36, p. 463.

George SCHNEEBERGER, b. Apr 1869, 31 yrs., parents b. Switz.; ***Bertha***, b. Jan 1873, parents b. Ohio, 27 yrs., married 8 yrs., 2 children b/living; ***Florence***, b. Sept. 1898, 1 yr.; ***Elmer***, b. Mch 1900, 2/12 yrs. All b. Ohio. 1900 FC OH, Ashtabula Co., Conneaut Twp., p. 200, lines 3-6.

Bertha SCHNEUBERGER; res. Buffalo, NY; German; interred Dec 20, 1907, Lot 33. "List of Interments," Lakeside Cemetery, Bay Village, OH.

Bertha SCHNEEBERGER, 35, d. Dec 18, 1907 at 12:30 p.m., Pneumonia, Buffalo, NY. Bureau of Vital Statistics, Burial or Removal Permit, Bay Village, OH.

Obituary/death notices for Bertha were not included in the Buffalo newspapers. Buffalo and Erie County Public Library.

Husband of Bertha Heckerman Schneeberger, George Schneeberger:

Father of George: The State of Ohio, Cuyahoga County, SS. I certify, That on the 2d day of January 1866, ***Mr. Jacob SCHNEEBERGER*** and ***Miss Mary KALLICKEN*** were by me legally joined in Marriage. D. Stephan, J.P. Marriage Record, Cuyahoga County, OH, vol. 12, p. 264.

Remarriage: ***George SCHNEEBERGER***, 51, res. N. Dover, O; b. Cleveland. occup. Basket maker, fr. *Jacob*, mo. *Mary KOELLIKE.* Married *(Mrs.)* ***Clara M. MAJO***, 34, res. 2049 W. 85th St., b. Cleveland, O., occup. Circular work, fr. *William COLLIER*, mo. *Carrie MACKENZIE*; both individuals married once before, spouse deceased, married name of Clara: Majo. I certify that George Schneeberger and Clara M. Majo were legally married on 23 August 1924, Cuyahoga County, O. W.J. Zoul, J.P. Marriage Record, Cuyahoga County, OH, vol. 137, p. 240.

Daughter of Bertha Heckerman and George Schneeberger:

Edward F. DOROW, 23; res. Bay Village; b. Dover, O.; occup. Farmer; fr. *C.H.*, mo. *Augusta DRYER*. Married ***Florence B. SCHNEEBERGER***; 20; res. Bay Village, O.; b. Conneaut, O.; occup. none; fr. *George*, mo. *Bertha HECKERMAN*; neither previously married. State of Ohio, Cuyahoga County, I Certify that on 31st day of Jan 1919 that Edward F. Dorow and Florence B. Schneeberger were by me legally joined in marriage. M.J. Penty, J.P. Marriage Record, Cuyahoga County, OH, vol. 111, p. 216.

DORROW, Edward F., 60; res. 6620 Franklin Ave., Cleveland, Ohio; d. Cleveland of corenous of esophagus, undertaker Glen Jenkins; bur. Evergreen, 6 Sept 1955, Sect. 1, Lot 41, grave 5. Evergreen Cemetery, Westlake, Ohio.

Parents of Edward F. Dorow:

DOROW, Carl H., husband of the late ***Augusta***, father of ***Henry, Albert, Edward,...***, Pease Funeral Home, Aug 24, 1943 *(death notice).* Cleveland Necrology File.

DOROW, Augusta, wife of ***Charles***...St. Paul's Lutheran Church, June 25, 1927. Cleveland Necrology File.

Baby DOROW *(not named),* female, d/b. April 27, 1920, 7:00 A.M., Dover, Ohio, 1 hour old., cause Atelectasis, congenital; res. No. Ridge Rd., Dover, Cuyahoga Co., fr. ***Edwin F. DOROW***, b. Dover, mo. ***Florence SCHNEEBERGER***, b. Buffalo, NY; Informant Edwin F. Dorow, Pease Funeral Home, bur. Evergreen Cemetery. Ohio Certificate of Death, Division of Vital Statistics, 1920, certif. 27946.

Lot 41, Section I, Lot owner Edwin Dorow: Undetermined grave - ***Baby DOROW;*** Grave 5 - ***Edward F. DOROW***, res. 6620 Franklin, Cleveland, 60 yrs., undertaker Glen Jenkins, interment 9/6/1955; ***Albert R. DOROW,*** res. Bay Village, 58 yrs., d. Bay Village, undertaker Burmeister/Avon, OH, interment 4/7/1951, ashes. Evergreen Cemetery, Westlake.

Lot 33 Carl Gunziger

no marker

Carl Gunziger is the nephew of Frank Heckerman and Bertha Schneeberger, in this lot, his mother being their sister.

Baby GUNZIGER, 10 ds.; Dover; German; Sept 11, 1886; Lot 33. "List of Interments," Lakeside Cemetery, Bay Village, OH.

Carl GUNSICKER *(sp.)*, d. Aug 9, 1886, Dover, 11 days, b. Dover, parents ***Charles*** and ***Louisa***, disease Lung Fever. Probate Court Death Records, Cuyahoga County, Ohio, vol. 3, p. 146, line 16.

Parents of Carl Gunziger:

Charles GUNZIGER, 16, was listed as a servant of Joel Cahoon in the 1880 Dover Census, p. 98A.

The State of Ohio, Cuyahoga County, SS. I Certify that on the 13th day of Oct 1883 ***Mr. Charles GUNZIGER*** and ***Miss Louisa HECKERMANN*** were by me legally joined in marriage. *(He was under 21 and needed consent.)* William Fuller Marriage Record, Cuyahoga County, OH, vol. 27, p. 28.

GUNZIGER, Charles, b. Oct 1865, 34 yrs. married 17 yrs., b. Ohio, fr. b. Germany, mo. b. Germany, occup. sawmill___; ***Louisa***, wife, b. Nov 1865 Ohio, 34 yrs., 2 children born and living, fr. b. Ohio, mo. b. Ohio; ***Josephine***, dau., b. Feb 1885, Ohio, 15 yrs., at home; ***Walter***, b. Jan 1888, Ohio, 12 yrs. 1900 FC OH CYDO, p. 4A. *Note: Carl is not listed as a child in the above census under "number of children born."*

GUNZIGER, Charles Sep. 13, 1865 - Apr 21, 1920 (d. Dover, res. Dover); ***Josephine E. POWER*** 1885-1920; ***Elizabeth R***. Sept 7, 1834 - July 1, 1921 (d. and res. West Dover, cause Old Age, C. Pease undertaker); ***MOORMAN, Oscar*** 1893-1915. Sect. I, Lot 54 Evergreen Cemetery Inscriptions and Records, Westlake, OH.

Oscar MOORMAN, d. Sept 26, 1915, Cleveland, Cuyahoga Co., Ohio of Bullet in abdomen...homicide; Single, Clerk; b. Sept 16, 1893, Dover, Ohio; fr. ***John MOORMAN***, b. Germany, mo. ***Minnie SUNK***, b. Germany; res. 2173 W. 63rd St.; Informant John Moorman, Bay Village; bur. Lutheran Cem., Dover, Ohio; undertaker J.A. Pease, Dover, O. Ohio Certificate of Death, Division of Vital Statistics, 1915, certif. 48433.

Charles GUNZIGER, d. Apr 21, 1920, First Ave., Dover, Cuy; b. Sept 13, 1864, Switzerland; 55 yrs. 7 mos. 8 days; Machinist; fr. ***Jacob GUNZIGER***, b. Switzerland, mo. ***Elizabeth FLORA***, b. Switzerland; cause acute pericarditis, myocarditis and endocarditis with rupture of left ventricle; informant *Mrs. Chas. GUNZIGER*, Bay Village, O.; bur. Evergreen, undertaker C. Pease, Dover Center, O. Ohio Certificate of Death, Division of Vital Statistics, 1920, certif. 27945.

Louisa remarried after the death of Charles Gunziger:

Otto ZEECK, 56, res. Dover, O.; b. Germany; occup. Labor; fr. *John ZEECK*, mo. *Bertha SCHUTT;* previously married once, div. Mar 15-27 C.P.Ct. Married ***Louise****(sp.)* ***GUNZIGER***, 62, res. Dover; b. do; fr. *Henry HECKERMAN,* mo. *Mary PETERS;* previously married Once, married name Gunziger, Dec Marriage to be solemnized by Rev. A.B. Meldrum, Old Stone Church. The State of Ohio, Cuyahoga County, I Certify, That on the 15th day of March 1927 Otto Zeeck and Louise Gunziger were...legally joined in marriage. Marriage Record, Cuyahoga County, OH, vol. 148, p. 206.

Louisa Marie ZEECK, b. 18 Oct 1864, Dover, Cuy. Co., OH, 80 yrs.; parents ***Henry C. HECKERMAN*** and ***Marie PETERS***; d. 24 May 1945, St. Joseph's Hospital, Lorain Co., OH; res. 26971 First St., Westlake, OH; bur. Evergreen Cem., Westlake. Buried with ***Otto ZEECK***, d. Westlake, 77 yrs., Coronary; undertaker Marion Pease, internment 5/19/1948. Section E-2, Lot 64, lot owner Anna Zeeck. Evergreen Cemetery Records and Ohio Certificate of Death, Division of Vital Statistics, 1964.

Paternal grandmother of Carl Gunziger:

GUNSIGER *(sp.)*, ***Elizabeth,*** head, 76, Widow, no. of children born 14, no. living 8; b. Germany, parents b. Germany; immigrated 1866; own farm with mortgage. ___***ter***, son, 30, single, b. Ohio; parents b. Germany; Fruit Farmer. 1910 FC OH CYDO, p. 14B, lines 98-9.

Elizabeth R. GUNZIGER, d. July 1, 1921, 11:15 p.m., West Dover Rd., Dover, Cuy Co., Ohio; Widowed, housewife; 87 yrs. 9 mos. 6 days; b. Sept 7, 1833, Switzerland, fr. ___ ***FLORA,*** b. Switzerland, mo. Do not know; Informant *Geo. GUNZIGER*, Collinwood, Ohio; bur. Evergreen, undertaker C. Pease, Dover Center, O. Ohio Certificate of Death, Division of Vital Statistics, 1921, certif. 37414.

Son of Elizabeth and Jacob Gunziger:
George C. GUNZIGER, 25, res. West Dover, O., b. Olmsted Falls, O., Watchman, fr. *Jacob GUNZIGER*, mo. *Elizabeth FLURY.* Married ***Lillian GUELKER***, 16, res. West Dover, O., b. Cincinnati, Ohio, fr. *Ernest GUELKER*, mo. maiden name unknown; neither previously married. The State of Ohio, Cuyahoga Co., ss. I Certify, That on the 23rd day of Mar, 1903 Mr. George C. Gunziger and Miss Lillian Guelker were by me legally joined in marriage. Rev. Herman H. Rippe. Marriage Record, Cuyahoga County, OH, vol. 55, p. 367.

Siblings of Carl Gunziger:
Horace H. POWER, 33, res. Dover, O., b. Conneautville, Pa., Decorator, fr. *Wm. E.*, mo. *Fanny BILLINGS*, previously married once. Married ***Josephine E. GUNSIGER*** *(sp.), 24*, res. Dover, b. Dover, occup. none, fr. *Chas.*, mo. *Florence HECKERMAN*, never previously married. The State of Ohio, Cuyahoga County, ss. I Certify that on the 7th day of Nov 1908 Mr. Horace H. Power and Miss Josephine E. Gunsiger were by me legally joined in marriage. William Brown J.P. (E. Clev'd., O.) Marriage Record, Cuyahoga County, OH, vol. 71, p. 202.
Josephine Elizabeth POWER, d. Oct 12, 1920, 11:10 p.m., Dover Center, Cuyahoga Co., Ohio, of Brain Abscess contracted from fertilizer accidentally inhaled; married, Hwf.; b. Feb 8, 1885, Dover, O., fr. ***Chas. GUNZIGER***, Switzerland, mo. ***Alma HECKERMAN***, Dover, Ohio; Informant *Mrs. Chas. GUNZIGER*; bur. Evergreen, undertaker C. Pease, Dover Center, O. Ohio Certificate of Death, Division of Vital Statistics, 1920, certif. 62514.
Walter E. GUNZIGER, 22; res. North Dover, Ohio; b. North Dover; Steam Fitter; fr. *Chas. GUNZIGER*, mo. *Louisa HECKERMAN.* Married ***Hattie F. KOON***, 22 ; res. North Dover, Ohio; b. Wollottville, Ind.; occup. none; fr. *Frank*, mo. *Hattie ROY*; neither previously married. The State of Ohio, Cuyahoga County, ss., I Certify, That on the 6th day of June 1910 Walter E. Gunziger and Hattie F. Koon were by me legally joined in marriage. William Brown, J.P. Marriage Record, Cuyahoga County, OH, vol. 75, p. 231.
Walter Edward GUNZIGER, 32, res. Dover, O.; b. do.*(same)*; occup. Steam Fitter; fr. *Chas. GUNZIGER*, mo. *Louisa HECKERMAN*; previously married once. Div. June 6, 1915 Fort Wayne, Ind. Married ***Marguerite VAN ALSTINE***, 29, res. So. Euclid, O.; b. Diamondale, Mich.; occup. Telephone Operator; fr. *Miles VAN ALSTINE*, mo. *Esther SHOOTS*, never previously married. The State of Ohio, Cuyahoga County, ss. I Certify, That on the 20th day of October 1920 Walter E. Gunziger and Marguerite Van Alstine were by me legally joined in marriage. William Brown, J.P. Marriage Record, Cuyahoga County, OH, vol. 120, p. 66.
Walter GUNZIGER, b. 16 Jan 1888, d. May 1966, residence Bay Village, Cuyahoga Co., OH. Social Security Index.

Lot 34 *Owner: John Pellett of Dover. O., purchased Dec 1895, for $5.25* SL

Lot 34 Elizabeth Ann Pellett no marker

Elizabeth Ann PELLETT, d. Dec 5, 1919, 4:45 a.m., Ward 3, Cleveland, Cuyahoga Cty.; Single, Occup. none; b. Sept 28, 1854, Dover, Ohio; 65 yrs., 2 mos., 7 ds. old; fr. ***John PELLETT***, b. England; mo. ***Maria AXUM***, b. England. Informant *Miss Eva PELLETT*, 16300 S. Park, Cleveland. I attended deceased from Nov 10, 1919 to Dec 5, 1919. d. Carcinoma of the liver. J.C. Simon, 6617 Lorain Ave.; bur. Bay Village, Dec 7, 1919; undertaker C. Pease, Dover Center, O. Ohio Certificate of Death, Division of Vital Statistics, 1919, certif. 67620 and Bureau of Vital Statistics, Burial or Removal Permit, Bay Village, OH.
Elizabeth PELLETT, res. Bay Village; English; interred Dec 6, 1919; Lot 34. "List of Interments," Lakeside Cemetery, Bay Village, OH.
Elizabeth A. PELLETT, 7506 Lorain Ave., Cleveland, Ohio; cancer, d. Dec 5, 1919, funeral requested by *Mrs. Eva PELLETT*, 16300 So. Park Blvd., Shaker Heights, Cleve., Ohio. Pease Funeral Home Records, Mss. 4809, Register Of Funerals, 1919-22, p. 174, Western Reserve Historical Society.

Lot 34-6 Pellett Marker

JOHN
PELLETT
1825-1902
MARIA A.
PELLETT
1825-1895

Christ died for us.

Lot 34-6 John Pellett

PELLET*(sp.)*, ***John***, 34, farmer, b. England, real estate value $300, personal property $150.; ***Maria***, 34, b. England; ***Helina***, 13, female, b. England; ***Christopher***, 9, male, b. England; ***Elizabeth***, 5, female, b. Ohio; ***Evangaline***, 1, female, b. Ohio. 1860 FC OH CYDO pp. 46-7, lines 39-42.
PELLATT*(sp.)*, ***John***, 45, farmer, b. England; ***Maria***, 45, occup. KH, b. England; ***Elizabeth***, 15, b. Ohio; ***Evangeline***, 11, b. Ohio; ***Reuben***, 5, b. Ohio; ***Electa***, 3, b. Ohio; *DODD, John*, 60, Blacksmith, b. England. 1870 FC OH CYDO, p. 255, lines 6-12.
PELLETT, John, 55, machinist, parents b. England; ***Maria***, 55, parents b. England; ***Elisabeth***, 22, dau., at home, b. Ohio; ***Reuben***, 15, son, laborer, b. Ohio; ***Electa***, 13, dau., b. Ohio. 1880 FC OH CYDO p. 97, lines 1-5, house 29. *Eva, their daughter, was working as a domestic servant for Sherman Osborn (Lot 48-10) in 1880. This was just after Sherman's wife died.*
PELLETT, John, Owned land; Acres: Improved - Tilled, including fallow and grass: 16, Permanent meadow: 13, Unimproved - Woodland: 30. Farm Values: Land and buildings - $5500, Machinery - $150, Live Stock - $50. Labor: Paid for wages in 1879 - $75. Estimated value of all farm production: $800. Grass lands: acreage: 4 mown, 10 not mown, 6 tons hay. 2 horses, 1 milch cow, 1 other, 1 calf dropped, 2 cattle sold living. 100 pounds of butter

made on the farm. Oats: 1 acre, 50 bushels; potatoes: 1 acre, 60 bushels. Orchards - apple: 1 acre, 100 bearing trees, 60 bushels. Total value of orchard products: $30. Vineyards: 7 acres, grapes sold in 1879 - 16,000, 45 gals. of wine made in 1879. Amount of wood cut: 10 cords, Value of forest products - $8. "Schedule 2. Production of Agriculture in Dover Township, Cuyahoga County, OH," enumerated June, 1880, p. 22.

PELLETT, John, 75, b. May 1825, England, immig 1853, Na., married 56? yrs.; ***Lizzie***, 39, dau., b. June 1860, Ohio, single. 1900 FC OH CYDO, p. 21A, lines 89-90, house 445.

John PELLETT property east of *Henry WISCHMEYER'S, (Lot 39-13)* Lake rd. south to the railroad tracks, Lot 96, 33 acres, house near Canterbury. 1880 Map of Dover Twp.

John PELLATT *(sp.)*, res. Bay Village, English, Lot 34. "List of Interments," Lakeside Cemetery, Bay Village, OH.

John PELLETT late of the township of Dover...died on or about July 1, 1902, leaving no widow and the following named persons his next of kin ***Reuben PELLETT***, son, Dover, O.; ***Elizabeth PELLETT***, dau., Dover, O.; ***Eva PELLETT***, dau., Nottingham *(near East Cleveland)*, O.; ***Electa MITCHELL***, dau., Lorain. He left household goods worth $50.00 and 58 Acres of Land in Dover, Ohio, the probable value of which will not exceed $1500. I Give, Devise and Bequeath to my daughter Electa Mitchell the west one half acre, from the lot I now own in Lot 87.; to my daughters Eva and Elizabeth Pellett, one half acre of land and house where I now reside, north of Lake road,...; to my daughter Elizabeth in addition, one fourth of the balance of all the oral estate of which I may divide? Except 1/2 acre below divided...my son Reuben, the east one half acre from the acre I now own in Lot No. 87. Also the remaining three fourths of all lands not otherwise devised, together with all the farming tools on said lands. Cuyahoga County, OH, Probate Court Estate Case File, 28857.

Lot 34-6 Maria Axam Pellett

Mrs. John PELLETT; res. Dover; English; interred Nov 8, 1895; Lot 34. "List of Interments," Lakeside Cemetery, Bay Village, OH.

Children of John Pellett and Maria Axam:

Eleanor M. PELLETT, d. Feb. 16, 1884, Dover, Cuyahoga County, Ohio of typhoid fever; age 36 yrs. 7 mos., b. London, England; Clerk; fr. ***John PELLETT***, mo. ***Maria AXAM***. Record of Death, Cuyahoga County, Ohio, vol. 2, p. 246.

Elizabeth Anna PELLETT, see above.

Eva Pellett worked and lived with the following:

MURFEY, Charles P. (?), head, 59, b. Ohio, married 23 years, Vice President Bank; *Florence S.*, wife, 47, b. Ohio, two children born and living; *Spencer L.*, 22, b. Ohio; *Clerence A.*, 20, b. Ohio; ***PELLETT, Eva***, 45, b. Ohio, parents b. England, servant, private family; *BROCK, Elvina O.*, 27, servant, b. Ohio, parents b. Germany; *SNYDER, Joseph*, 27, servant, b. Ohio. 1910 FC OH CY Cleveland Hts., ED 435, p. 31, Bluestone Road, lines 33-39.

MURFEY, Charles L., head, 67, b. Ohio, parents b. Vermont, President of Bank; *Florence,* wife, 48, b. Ohio, parents b. New York; *Spencer*, son, 32, b. Ohio, parents b. Ohio, no occupation; ***Eva C. PELLETT***, Companion, 47, b. Ohio, working for private family; *CLEMENTS, Sam*, Butler, 34, b. Kentucky, parents b. Kentucky; *Blanche*, wife, 24, b. Illinois, fr. b. Missouri. 1920 FC OH CY Shaker Heights, p. 14A, lines 10-16.

PELLETT: Eva C., daughter of the late ***Mr.*** and ***Mrs. John PELLETT*** of Bay Village, sister of ***Mrs. Electa MITCHELL***. Funeral Wednesday at 3:30 p.m. from the residence of *C. L. MURFEY*, 16300 South Park Blvd. Cleveland Necrology File, Dec 19, 1934.

Eva Claire PELLETT, d. Dec 17, 1934, 8 a.m., 16300 So. Park Blvd., Shaker Heights, Cuyahoga Co., Ohio of Senile Degeneration of Heart and Aorta; 77 yrs. 1 day; single; b. Dec 16, 1857, Bay Village, Ohio, to ***John PELLETT***, b. London, England and ***Myria AXAM***, b. London, England; length of stay in Shaker Hts. 19 years, 9 months; informant *C.A. Murfey*, 16300 So. Park Blvd.; undertaker J.H. Brown & Son, Inc., 18128 Carnegie Ave.; bur. Lakeview Cemetery. Ohio Certificate of Death, Division of Vital Statistics, 1934, certif. 71176. *Eva is listed as being a servant with the Murfey family in the 1910 census so was with the family longer than 19 years.*

Charles L. Murfey died Aug. 13, 1936, and Florence Murfey on August 3, 1955. Their son Clarence is buried at Lake View Cemetery. Cleveland Necrology File.

PELLETT: Reuben S., father of ***Mrs. Eleanor JONES***, ***Mrs. Ruby MANNING***, ***Earl***, ***Arthur***, and brother of ***Eva PELLETT***, ***Mrs. Electa MITCHELL*** and the late ***Elizabeth*** of Lake Road, Bay Village, O. April 19, 1930. Now at Clifford Pease Funeral Home, Dover Center Road, Dover Center, O., where services will be held Monday, April 21, at 2:30 p.m. Burial will be at.... cem. rec. 1875-1930, Lakewood Park Cemetery, Rocky River, Ohio. Cleveland Necrology File, 1930.

Reuben Selden PELLETT, d. April 19, 1930, 3:02 a.m., Lutheran Hospital, Cleveland, Cuyahoga Co., Ohio of Mitral Insufficiency about 3 yrs., asthma and chronic...Nephritis; res. 26504 Lake Rd., Cuyahoga, Ohio; divorced; b. Sept 14, 1864, Bay Village, Ohio, fr. ***John R. PELLETT***, England, mo. ***Maria AXAM***, b. England; 65 yrs. 7 mos. 5 days; retired; Informant *Earl PELLETT*, 3285 West 98th Street; bur. Lakewood Cem., undertaker C. Pease, Dover Center. Ohio Certificate of Death, Division of Vital Statistics, 1930, certif. 3559.

Reubin *(sp.)* ***S. PELLETT***, res. Stop 21 Lake Road, Bay Village, 65 yrs., b. Dover, d. Lutheran Hosp., cause Mitral Insufficiency, d. April 19, 1930, Lot 417, Section 3, Grave 2. Buried next to ***Arthur M. PELLETT***, 60, res. 3128 W. 136th St., Cleve, husband of ***Jeanette*** (nee ***McDERMOTT***), son of ***Jennie Pellett REEDER*** and the late ***Ruben*** *(sp.)*, d. Jan 22, 1958, Grave 3; and ***Arthur PELLETT***, died when a child about 40 years ago, ashes in cremation vault, interment Aug 13, 1982, Grave 3. Lakewood Park Cemetery, Rocky River, OH.

Children of Reuben Pellett and Jennie Payne:

Arthur E. JONES, 35, res. 1513 Lincoln Ave., Cleveland, O., occup. Pressman, fr. *Grosvenor*, mo. *Margaret CONLEY*, previously married once, Divorced 2/14/20, C. T. *(P.?)* Ct. Married ***Eleanor PELLETT***, 27, 7323 Madison Ave., b. N. Dover, O., occup. Operator, fr. *Reuben*, mo. *Jamie PAYNE*, never previously married.

The State of Ohio, Cuyahoga County, ss. I Certify, That on the 3rd day of June 1918 John Reeder and Jennie Pellett were by me legally joined in marriage. W. J. Zoul, J.P., Shaker Hts., O. Marriage Record, Cuyahoga County, OH, vol. 117, p. 311.

William EUCKER, 20, res. 5017 Bridge Ave., b. Cleve'd., O., occup. Driver, fr. *Geo.*, mo. *Effie HEISE.* Married ***Ruby PELLETT***, 18, res. 5017 Bridge Ave., b. Avon, O., fr. *Reuben*, mo. *Jennie PAYNE*, neither previously married. Marriage to be solemnized by Wm. Brown, J.P., E. Cleve'd., O. Consent of Gdn. *(guardian)*. The State of Ohio, Cuyahoga County, ss. I Certify, That on the 6th day of December 1913 William Eucker and Ruby Pellett were by me legally joined in marriage. Marriage Record, Cuyahoga County, OH, vol. 86, p. 441.

Edward F. MANNING, Jr., 21 (8-25-15), res. 1836 W. 28th St., b. Cleveland, Ohio, occup. Surveyor, fr. *E. F.*, mo. *Mary F. ROSE.* Married ***Ruby M. PELLETT***, 20, res. 5907 Ellen Ave., b. Avon, O., occup. none, fr. *Reuben*, mo. *Jennie PAYNE*, neither previously married. Marriage to be solemnized by W.J. Zoul, J.P., Orange, O. The State of Ohio, Cuyahoga County, ss. I Certify, That on the 30th day of October 1915 Edward F. Manning, Jr. and Ruby M. Pellett were by me legally joined in marriage. Marriage Record, Cuyahoga County, OH, vol. 94, p. 138.

Earl C. PELLETT, 26, res. 14960 Lakewood Hts. Bld., b. Dover, O., occup. Printer, fr. *Reuben*, mo. *Jennie PAYNE*, never previously married. Married ***Annamae SCHULTZ***, 20, res. 14960 Lakewood Hts. Bld., b. Youngstown, O., occup. none, fr. *William SCHULZ*, mo. *Jennie SENIA*, previously married once, married name *GRAHAM*, Div. 12-21-28, C. P. Ct. Marriage to be solemnized by M.J. Penty, J.P., Warrensville, O. Consent of mother. The State of Ohio, Cuyahoga County, ss. I Certify, That on the 26th day of February 1929 Earl C. Pellett and Annamae Schultz were by me legally joined in marriage. Marriage Record, Cuyahoga County, OH, vol. 156, p. 66.

Earl PELLETT, 31, res. 2130 Alger Rd., L.O., b. Bay Village, O., occup. Printer, fr. *Reuben PELLETT*, mo. *Jennie PAYNE*, previously married once, Dec'd. *(dece ased)*. Married ***Pauline COLDREN***, 24, res. 2130 Alger Rd., L.O., b. Chillicothe, O., occup. Waitress, fr. *Otis COLDREN*, mo. *Sarah MEYERS*, never previously married. Marriage to be solemnized by Rev. W.K. Klein, Bridge Ave. The State of Ohio, Cuyahoga County, ss. I Certify, That on the 7th day of July 1933 Earl Pellett and Pauline Coldren were by me legally joined in marriage. Marriage Record, Cuyahoga County, OH, vol. 169, p. A10959.

Arthur PELLETT, 18, 5907 Ellen Ave., b. N. Dover, O., occup. Driver, fr. *Reuben*, mo. *Jennie PAYNE.* Married ***Mildred LEONARD***, 18, res. 6607 Wakefield Ave., b. New York City, occup. none, fr. *Joseph*, mo. *Mary POOLEY.* Marriage to be solemnized by W.J. Zoul, J.P., Orange, O. Consent of mother. The State of Ohio, Cuyahoga County, ss. I Certify, That on the 24th day of May 1916 Arthur Pellett and Mildred Leonard were by me legally joined in marriage. Marriage Record, Cuyahoga County, OH, vol. 96, p. 417.

Arthur PELLETT, 41, res. 13501 Lakewood Hts. Blvd., b. Bay, O., fr. *Reuben*, mo. *Jennie REEDER*, previously married once, Div'd. *(divorced)* 1928. Married ***Jeanette C. McDERMOTT***, 38, res. 2232 W. 89th St., b. Cleveland, O., clerk, fr. *John*, mo. *Katherine LOVELL*, never married. The State of Ohio, Cuyahoga County, ss. I Certify, That on the 14th day of November 1938 Arthur Pellett and Jeanette McDermott were by me legally joined in marriage. Rev. Walter K. Klein, Bridge Ave. Marriage Record, Cuyahoga County, OH, vol. 185, p. 472.

Arthur M. PELLETT, d. 11 Jan 1958 at Fairview Park Hospital, Cleveland, Cuyahoga Co., Ohio of coronary artery occlusion; res. 3128 W. 136th St., Cleveland; occup. clerk at State Liquor Store; married; b. 19 June 1897 to ***Ruben** (sp.)* ***PELLETT*** and ***Jennie PAYNE***; bur. Lakewood Park Cemetery, Rocky River, OH; funeral home The McGorray Bros. Co., 3040 Lorain Ave., Cleveland. Ohio Certificate of Death, Division of Vital Statistics, 1958, certif. 001588.

Reuben's wife remarried after the divorce:

John REEDER, 39, res. 4302 Bailey Ave., b. Cleveland, O.; occup. Hard Wood Finisher; fr. *John*, mo. *Marie LANGE*; never previously married. Married ***Jennie PELLETT***, 46, res. 5907 Ellen Av.; b. Avon, O.; occup. none; fr. *Selden PAYNE*, mo. *Laura MITCHEL*; previously married once. The State of Ohio, Cuyahoga County, ss. I Certify, That on the 3rd day of June 1918 John Reeder and Jennie Pellett were by me legally joined in marriage. M.J. Penty, J.P. Marriage Record, Cuyahoga County, OH, vol. 109, p. 132.

Electa MITCHELL of 3356 W. 94th St., wife of the late ***Charles***; mother of the late ***Olive UNKE***; grandmother of ***Mrs. Audrey QUAYLE***; Thursday afternoon. Friends may call at the Geo. C. Lang Co. Funeral Home, W. 95th St. and Lorain Ave., where services will be held Saturday, March 15, at 3 p.m. Mar 15, 1947, p. 16, col. 2. The Plain Dealer.

Electa E. MITCHELL, d. 13 Mar 1947, 4 p.m. of Coronary thrombosis for one hour at her residence 3356 W. 94th, Cleveland, OH; b. 8 April 1868, Bay Village to ***John PELLETT***, b. St. Mary's, England and ***Marie AXUM***, b. England; in community 50 years; 78 years 11 months 5 days; buried Lutheran Cem., informant *Mrs. Audrey QUAYLE*, 3356 W. 94th. Ohio Certificate of Death, Division of Vital Statistics, 1947, certif. 14725.

Daughter of Electa Pellett Mitchell:

William UNKE, 25, res. 2915 Coburn Ave., b. Cleveland, O., occup. Paper Ruler, father: *Wm.*, mother: *Minnie GLUTH.* Married ***Olive M. MITCHELL***, 20, res. 7506 Lorain Ave., b. Cleveland, O., occup. none, father: *Charles*, mother: *Electa PELLETT.* Neither previously married. Cuyahoga County, OH. Marriage Record, Cuyahoga County, OH, vol. 96, p. 220.

UNKE-Olive M., beloved wife of ***W.R. UNKE*** and daughter of ***Mr.*** and ***Mrs. Charles MITCHELL*** Friday at 9:45 a.m., age 23 yrs. Funeral from late residence, 3806 Denison ave, Monday, at 2 p.m. Cleveland Necrology File, October 27, 1918.

Olive M. UNKE, d. Oct 25, 1918, 3806 Dennison Ave., Cleveland, Cuyahoga Co., Ohio of Lobar Pneumonia for 5 ds. and Chronic Myocarditis for one year; 23 yrs.

8 ds.; married; b. Oct 16, __, City to ***Charles MITCHELL***, b. U.S.A. and ***Electa PELLETT***, b. U.S.A.; undertaker Wm. Wischmeier, 2560 W. 25th St.; buried Lutheran Cem., informant *William R. UNKE*, 3806 Denison Ave. Ohio Certificate of Death, Division of Vital Statistics, 1918, certif. 60969.

Lot 35 *Owner: Harry Gibbs of Dover, O., purchased for $5.25* SL

Lot 35 Henry Gibbs no marker

Previously recorded stone that is currently missing.

HENRY GIBBS
DIED AUG 2, 1898
AGE 68
JANE

(Stone set down into ground)
Cuyahoga County Cemetery Inscriptions, p. 140.

An attempt was made to determine if a stone had sunk, but none was detected.

The State of Ohio, Cuyahoga County, SS. I certify that on the first day of January 1863 ***Mr. Henry GIBBS*** and ***Miss Mary J. COMSTOCK*** were by me legally joined in Matrimony. Wm. Green J.P. Marriage Record, Cuyahoga County, OH, vol. 11, p. 46.

GIBBS, Henry, 47, farmer, b. England, parents b. England; ***Jane***, 46, wife, b. England, parents b. England. 1880 FC OH CYDO, p. 97, lines 44-45, house 289.

GIBBS, Henry. Rents for fixed money rental. Acres: Improved - 4 Tilled, including fallow and grass, 12 permanent meadow, Unimproved - 18 woodland. Farm Values: Land and buildings - $2500, Live Stock - $15. Estimated value of all farm production: $100. Grass lands: acreage: 1 mown, 1 ton hay. 1 horse. Indian corn: 1 acre, 15 bushels; oats: 1 acre, 30 bushels; potatoes: 1 acre, 30 bushels. Vineyards: 6 acres, 1500 lbs. grapes sold in 1879. "Schedule 2. Production of Agriculture in Dover Township, Cuyahoga County, OH," enumerated June, 1880, p. 29.

Henry GIBBS, 68; res. Centere Village, P.A.; English; interred Aug 2, 1898. "List of Interments," Lakeside Cemetery, Bay Village, OH.

Lot 35 Mary Jane Comstock Gibbs no marker

____*GIBBS (presumed Jane)*; res. Avon; English; interred August 20, 1882; Lot 35. "List of Interments," Lakeside Cemetery, Bay Village, OH.

Note in cemetery file from 1980 lists "Jane died Aug 20, 1882" next to Henry Gibbs' tombstone inscription.

Lots 36/37 *Owned by: Rudolph Scholl of Dover, purchased Feb 26, 1882 for $5.25 each* SL

Lot 36-7 Rudolph Scholl

FATHER

Rudolph SCHOLL, Naturalization Country Baden, Date of arrival June 1854, Date of naturalization Oct 3, 1861, Common Pleas Court, Cuyahoga Co., Cleveland, Ohio. Journal E, p. 227, Cuy Co. Archives.

SCHOLL, Rodolph, 44, farmer, b. Germany; ***Annie***, 32, wife, b. Germany; ***Otto***, 13, male; ***Amelia*** *(sp.)*, 9, male; ***Alice***, 7, female; ***Wm***., male, 5; ***Louie***, 2, male; children b. Ohio. 1870 FC OH CYDO p. 256, lines 32-38, house 262.

SCHOLL, Rodolph, 53, farmer, b. Baden, parents b. Baden; ***Anna***, 42, wife, b. Witenburg, parents b.Witenburg; ***Emma***, 21, dau., at home; ***Alice***, 17, dau., at home; ***William***, 14, son, laborer; ***Louie***, 11, son, at school; ***Leonard***, 8, son; ***Rodolph***, 3, son; ***Albertus***, 9/12 yrs., born in Sept, son; all children b. Ohio. 1880 FC OH CYDO, p. 97, lines 16-24, house 292.

SCHOLL, Rudolf*(sp.)*. Owns land. Acres: Improved - 2 tilled, including fallow and grass, 2 permanent meadows, Unimproved - 6 woodland. Farm Values: Land and buildings- $400, Live Stock - $25. Estimated value of all farm production: $100. Grass lands: acreage: 1 mown, 1 ton hay. 1 milch cow, 1 calf dropped, 1 cattle sold living. 100 pounds of butter made on the farm. Potatoes: 1 acre, 70 bushels. "Schedule 2. Production of Agriculture in Dover Township, Cuyahoga County, OH," enumerated June, 1880, p. 30.

SHOLL, Rudulph *(sp.)*, 73, b. Apr 1827…; ***Anna***, 62, b. Apr 1838, 9 children born, 8 living, married 44 yrs., can't read; ***Otto***, 43, single, son, b. Jan 1857; own farm. 1900 FC OH CYDO, p. 9A/B, lines 50-52, house 190.

Rudolph SCHOOL *(sp.)*, 77; res. Bay Village; German; interred May 1, 1904; Lot 37 *(Possibly Lot 36?)*. "List of Interments," Lakeside Cemetery, Bay Village, OH.

SCHOOL *(sp.)*, res. Bay Village, German, Lot 36 *(Directly below listing for Rudolph, Lot 37)*. "List of Interments," Lakeside Cemetery, Bay Village, OH.

I, ***Rudolph SCHOLL***, of the township of Dover…Give and Bequeath to my beloved wife ***Anna SCHOLL*** in lieu of her dower the use of my property during her natural life and after her death to my children as follows: to my sons ***Otto SCHOLL*** *(Lot 31)* and ***Charles SCHOLL*** (Chicago, Illinois) the sum of One Dollar ($1.00) each. The balance to be divided equally share and share alike among the rest of my children vis.: my two Daughters ***Emma KUEPFER*** *(Lot 31)* (790 Prospect St., Cleveland, O) and ***Alice MARTIN*** (5 Little St., Cleveland, Ohio) and my sons ***Amiel SCHOLL*** (Emmile, Willoughby, Lake Co, Ohio), ***Louis SCHOLL*** (North Dover,Ohio), ***Rule SCHOLL***

(Lexington St., Cleveland) and ***Albert SCHOLL*** (North Dover, Ohio)...(Application for probate information, April 29, 1904, signed by Edward W. Kuepfer, resides at No. 576 Kinsman Street). Cuyahoga County, OH, Probate Court Estate Case File, 33927.

Children of Rudolph Scholl and Anna Glasser:

The State of Ohio, Cuyahoga County, ss. I Certify that on the 21st day of March 1883 ***Mr. William MARTIN*** and ***Miss Alice SHUCK (SCHOLL)*** were by me legally joined in marriage. N. Wiers, Pastor. Marriage Record, Cuyahoga County, OH, vol. 26, p. 202.

Louis SCHOLL resigned as Road Commissioner in 1917 and is listed again in this position in 1918 and 1920. Louis may have served in this capacity for a number of years. Minutes, Ordinances & Resolutions, Bay Village, OH, 1918-1921.

SCHOLL: Louis, residence 396 Dover rd., Bay Village, husband of ***Nellie*** (nee ***McCABE***), father of ***Louis***, and grandfather. Now at Clifford Pease Funeral Home, 2914 Dover rd., Dover Center, where services will be held Monday, Dec 23, at 2:30 p. m. 1935, age 67. Evergreen Cem., Dover, O. Dec 23, 1935, p. 21, col. 3. The Plain Dealer.

Louis SCHOLL, d. Dec 20, 1935, Bay, Cuyahoga Co., Ohio of Arterio Sclerosis with Chronic Arthritis; res. 396 Dover Rd., married to ***Ellen Mary SCHOLL***; Farmer; b. Sept 13, 1868, Dover Village, Ohio to ***Rudolph SCHOLL***, b. Germany and ***Anna GLASSER***, b. Germany; *informant Louis SCHOLL*, 502 Cahoon Rd., Bay; undertaker Clifford Pease, Dover Center, O.; burial Evergreen Cemetery. Ohio Certificate of Death, Division of Vital Statistics, 1935, certif. 77052.

Ruly SCHOLL, 24, 62 Bolivar St., b. Dover, O., Cigar Dealer, fr. *Rudolph SCHOLL*, mo. *Mary Ann GLASSER.* Married ***Effie M. HOLCOMB***, 18, res. 62 Bolivar St., b. Cleveland, fr. *F. W. HOLCOMB*, mo. *Margaret ROBINSON;* neither previously married. The State of Ohio, Cuyahoga County, ss. I Certify, That on the 23rd day of Jany. 1901 Mr. Ruly Scholl and Miss Effie M. Holcomb were by me legally married. Rev. M.J. Grable Marriage Record, Cuyahoga County, OH, vol. 51, p. 373.

SCHOLL: Ruly E., dearly beloved husband of ***Effie*** (nee ***HOLCOMB***), father of ***Mabel***, grandfather of ***Joan Kay;*** residence, 17400 Clifton blvd. Friends may call at William R. & Roy A. Daniels Funeral Home, 15800 Detroit, where services will be held Wednesday, Aug 23, at 3 p. m. Cleveland Necrology File, Aug 23, 1939.

Ruly E. SCHOLL, d. Aug 20, 1939 at his residence 17400 Clifton Blvd., Lakewood, Cuyahoga Co., Ohio of Coronary Thrombosis; 62 yrs. 10 mos. 23 ds. Married to ***Effie SCHOLL***; Retired Broker; b. Sept 27, 1876, Dover Center, Ohio to ***Rudolph SCHOLL***, b. Germany and ***Anna GLASER***, b. Germany; informant Effie Scholl, undertaker Wm. R. Ray Daniels, 15800 Detroit Rd.; burial Lakewood Cemetery. Ohio Certificate of Death, Division of Vital Statistics, 1939, certif. 47795.

The State of Ohio, Cuyahoga County, ss. I Certify that on the 16th day of February 1916 ***Mr. Albert SCHOLL*** and ***Miss Emma KARNOWSKI*** were by me legally joined in marriage. J. Wefel Marriage Record, Cuyahoga County, OH, vol. 98, p. 173.

SCHOLL. ***Albert SCHOLL***, age 88, beloved husband of the late ***Emma*** (nee ***CARNIS***), father of ***Mrs. Leona HAWKINS***, grandfather of ***Susan*** and ***Bill***. Funeral services Friday, May 9, at 2:30 p.m. at Jenkins Funeral Chapel, 2914 Dover Center Rd., Westlake, where friends may call from 2-4 and 7-9 P.M. Thursday. Cleveland Press, May 8, 1969.

SCHOLL: Emma (nee ***KARNISS***), beloved wife of ***Albert***, mother of ***Leona*** May, Oct 22. Services at the residence, 1443 Wayne Ave., Lakewood, Saturday, Oct 24, at 2:30 p.m. Cleveland Necrology File, Oct 23, 1931.

Mrs. Emma SCHOLL, d. Oct 22, 1931, 3:05 p.m. at 1443 Wayne Ave., Lakewood, Cuyahoga Co., Ohio of Cerebral Hemorrhage and Blood pressure 260/150; 46 yrs. 6 ms. 10 ds.; Married to ***Albert SCHOLL***; Hwf.; b. April 12, 1885, Cleveland to ***Chas. KARNISS***, b. Germany and ***Wilhelma WURZOK***, b. Germany; informant Albert Scholl; undertaker Clifford Pease; burial Lakewood Park, Rocky River, Ohio. Ohio Certificate of Death, Division of Vital Statistics, 1931, certif. 59115.

Lot 36-8 William Scholl

WILLIAM
SON OF
R. & A. SCHOLL
BORN DEC 10, 1865
DIED MAR 19 1882
We miss thee Willie

SCHOLL

SCHOLL, Willie, d. March 19, 1882, Dover, 16 yrs. 3 m. 9 d., b. Dover, parent ***Rudolph SCHOLL***, disease scarlet fever. Probate Court Death Records, Cuyahoga County, Ohio, vol. 2, p. 131.

Between Lots 36 and 37-9

Anna Glasser Scholl

MOTHER

Assumed marker for Anna Glasser, wife of Rudolph Scholl (above), b. c1838, Germany. Anna died one month after her husband, Rudolph.

SCHOLL-Anna, widow of ***Rudolph SCHOLL***, in her sixty-sixth year. Funeral Friday, June 10, at 2 p.m., sun time, from the old homestead, Stop 23, North Dover, O. Cleveland Necrology File, June 10, 1904.

SCHOLL, Anna, 66 years, 7 June 1904, 342. "Independent Evangelical Church Abstracts," p. 61.

Lot 37-10 William Scholl

WILLIE

Two markers for the same person? See Lot 36-8.

William SCHOLL; res. Dover; German; interred March 19,1882; Lot 37. "List of Interments," Lakeside Cemetery, Bay Village, OH.

Lots 38/39 *Owned by: Regina Wischmeyer of Dover, purchased Feb 27, 1880 for, $5.25 each* SL

Lot 38-11 Regina Rentschler Wischmeyer

MOTHER
1834-1918

Regina was the wife of Henry Wischmeyer, also of Germany.

Her mother, Regina Rentschler (OP 2:13), probably father and sister, Caroline Rentschler Wolf (Lot 50-14), are also buried here.

Regina WISCHMEYER; d. July 6, 1918, Bay, Cuy Co., Ohio; b. April 15, 1834, Wurtenberg, Germany; 84 yrs., 2 mos., 21 ds.; cause Stroke of Paralysis; fr. ***Frederick RENCHLER*** *(sp.)*, b. Germany; mo. __ ***LAPP***, b. France; bur. Bay Village, July 9, 1918; undertaker C. Pease, Dover Center, O., Informant *Olga Wischmeyer*, Bay Village, O. Ohio Certificate of Death, Division of Vital Statistics, 1918, certif. 45854.

Wisch(meyer), Regina geb ***Rentschler*** 25 April 1834 Wurt. died 6 July 1918. "Independent Evangelical Church Abstracts."

Wischmeyer-Mrs. Henry, mother of ***Henry, Olga, Mathilda*** and ***Mrs. George MILLER***, Sat., July 6, age 84. Funeral services Tuesday, July 9, 2 p.m. at the late residence, Lake rd., Bay Village, Ohio. Cleveland Necrology File, July 9, 1918

Regina WEISHMYER *(sp.)*, res. Bay Village, German, Lot 39. "List of Interments," Lakeside Cemetery, Bay Village, OH.

Parents of Regina Rentschler Wischmeyer:

Regina Katharine RENTSCHLER was born in Diefenbach, Wurtenburg, Germany on 15 Apr 1834, the daughter of ***Jacob Friedrich RENTSCHLER*** and ***Regina Katherina LAPP*** *(OP 2:13)*. Her family immigrated to America in 1850. Records from Church of Zavelstein, Wurtenburg, Germany, provided by Norma Garber.

The ***RENTSCHLER*** family settled on the west side of Cleveland. Nov 29, 1907, p. 10, col. 6. The Plain Dealer.

Lot 38-12 Wischmeyer Monument

WISCHMEYER

There is a reference on the new plot map that Louisa Wischmeyer is buried in this lot. There is no evidence to substantiate this and it is believed that a mistake was made when reading the List of Interments. Louis A. is listed in Lot 39. There were no references to anyone by the name of Louisa in the Wischmeyer family records.

Lot 39-13 Henry Wischmeyer

FATHER
1832-1901

Henry WISCHMEYER came out from Cleveland in 1874, and began to raise grapes upon a tract of fifty acres...In 1874 he built upon his land a wine cellar with a capacity of ten thousand gallons, and manufactures considerable wine every year. Crisfield Johnson, History of Cuyahoga County, p. 442.

The Wischmeyer family arrived in Dover in 1872. Wischmeyer Family Papers, Rose Hill Museum, Bay Village, OH.

A resort hotel was built above the Wischmeyer wine cellar in 1874 which could accommodate seventy guests. His hotel became a regular stopping place for business men traveling from Sandusky to Cleveland, who could not return home the same day after making their wine purchases. The hotel became a popular resort for affluent Clevelanders and guest arrived who traveled not only on the interurban but also from out of state via the railroad. Bay Village Historical Society, Bay Village: A Way of Life, p. 50. *The hotel was located on the north side of Lake Road at Glen Park Drive and torn down in 1962 due to a new ordinance stating businesses were not allowed on Lake Road in Bay Village. The family home still stands on the south side of Lake Road, near Glen Park Drive at 26565 Lake Road.*

Henry Wischmeyer, father, born July 23, 1832 - died April 30, 1902. Paper listing Henry Wischmeyer family dates of birth and death, Wischmeyer Family Papers, Rose Hill Museum.

United States of America, The State of Ohio, Cuyahoga County, ss: To all who shall see these presents - Greeting: Know Ye, That on the 2 day of Nov Anno Domini 1860 at a Probate Court, held at the Probate Office of the City of Cleveland, in and for the County of Cuyahoga and State of Ohio, personally came ***Henry WISCHMEYER***, a native of Hanover who produced a Certificate of his intention to be Naturalized, and become a Citizen of the United States....Absolutely and entirely Renounce and Abjure all allegiance and fidelity to every Foreign Prince, Potentate, State or Sovereignty, whatsoever, and particularly to George V King of Hanover whose subject he was.

This is, Therefore, to Certify, that the said Henry Wischmeyer is admitted a Citizen of the United States. 2 Nov 1860, Dan R. Tilden, Probate Judge. Original Naturalization Certificate, Wischmeyer Family Papers, Rose Hill Museum.

To all People to whom these Presents shall come---Greeting: Know Ye, That *Mr. Kinsley SHERMAN* and *Sarah I. SHERMAN*, husband and wife of Cleveland, Ohio for the consideration of One Thousand Dollars received to and full satisfaction, of ***Henry WISCHMEYER*** the following tract or lot of land, situated in the township of Dover being in the county of Cuyahoga and in the State of Ohio, and is known as a tract of Fifty Acres of land off from the east side of a tract of Eighty seven acres of land in lot no. ninety six (96)...commencing at the North West corner of lot no. 96, thence easterly along the Lake shore Eighty five acres more or less to the North West corner of land once owned by *Abner SMITH* ... and 50 acres of land herein described. Received and transferred April 8th 1862 in Cuyahoga County, vol. 115, pages 135 & 136. Original Warranty Deed, Rose Hill Museum, Wischmeyer Family Papers.

Know all Men by these Presents, That *William P. GARDNER* and *Ruth GARDNER* (husband and wife), the Grantors for the consideration of Four thousand dollars received to our full satisfaction of ***Henry WISCHMEYER***...situated in the Township of Dover...being a part of original Township Lot No. 96...bounded on the west by Dover Center Road: On the North by Lake Erie: On the East by lands formerly owned by *Geo. R. SMITH* (now by Henry Wischmeyer): On the South by Lot No. 86 and is so much of the west part of said Lot No. 96 as contains thirty seven acres of land. Excepting there from six acres sold off the same and deeded by said Smith to *Joel B. CAHOON* in the North West corner of said Lot 96 which said six acres is bounded north by Lake Erie & South by the Lake Shore Road. The land herein conveyed contains thirty one (31) acres. Thirty one acres was purchased on December 23, 1884, sealed in the State of Louisiana, Parrish of St. Landry, La. Where the Gardeners appeared. Original Warranty Deed, Rose Hill Museum, Wischmeyer Family Papers.

WESCHMIER *(sp.)*, ***Henry***, 47, farmer; b. Hanover, parents b. Hanover; ***Ragina***, 46, wife, b. Wirtenburg, parents b. Wirtenburg; ***Ardelaid*** *(sp.)*, 21, at home; ***Louis***, 15, laborer; ***Matilda***, 13; ***Olga***, 11; ***Henry***, 7; ***Julius***, 5; all children b. in Ohio; *LYSIN, Louis*, 36, servant, laborer, b. Bierland, parents b. Bierland; *KOCHERBROAD, John*, 23, servant, laborer, b. Leuxemburg *(sp.)*, parents b. Leuxemburg. 1880 FC OH CYDO p. 97, lines 6-15.

WISCHMEYER, Henry. Owned land (rented for fixed amount of money); Acres: Improved - 20 tilled, including fallow and grass, 25 (25) permanent meadow, Unimproved - 5 (5) woodland. Farm Values: Land and buildings- $6000 (3,000), Machinery - $150, Live Stock - $250 (45). Labor: Paid for wages in 1879 - $400. Weeks of hired labor: 110. Estimated value of all farm production: $1500 (300). Grass lands: acreage: 2 mown, 10 not mown, 2 tons hay. 3 horses, 2 (1) milch cows, 1 other, 2 (1) calves dropped, 2 (1) cattle sold living, 1 died, strayed stolen and not recovered. 200 (100) pounds of butter made on the farm. 4 (2) swine. 80 (100) barnyard poultry on farm. 300 (30) dozen eggs produced in 1879. Oats: 5 acres, 250 bushels; rye: 2 acres, 65 bushels; potatoes: 8? (1) acres, 100 (70) bushels. Orchards - apple: 3 (10) acres, 120 (1000) bearing trees, 300 (100) bushels; peaches: 1 acre, 40 bearing trees. Total value of orchard products: $150 (50). Vineyards: 5 (15) acres, 16000 (2000) lbs. grapes sold in 1879, 200 (400) gallons wine made in 1879. "Schedule 2. Production of Agriculture in Dover Township, Cuyahoga County, OH," enumerated June, 1880, p. 30.

WISCHMEYER, Henry, 67, head, b. July 1832, Germany, in US 1854, 46 yrs. Na., married 46 yrs.; ***Regina***, 66, wife, b. May 1834, Germany, 8 children born, 5 living; ***Henry***, 26, b. Oct 1873, farm laborer; ***Julus***, 24, b. May 1876; ***Amela***, 36, b. June 1863 *(incorrect)*; ***Olga***, 30, b. May 1869; all children b. Ohio; *BANGER, Eugin*, 23, b. Oct 1876, Ohio, parents b. Germany, day laborer, in US 1899. 1900 FC OH CYDO p. 21A.

Henry WISCHMEYER, Lake Erie to approximately Wolf Road, Glen Park to the Cahoon property, lot 96, 44 61/100 acres. 1880 Map of Dover Twp.

Mr. WISCHMYER, 69; res. Bay Village; German; interred May 3, 1902; Lot 39. "List of Interments," Lakeside Cemetery, Bay Village, OH.

Children of Henry Wischmeyer and Regina Rentschler:

Adelheid Karolina Regina WISCHMEYER, b. 24 Feb 1859; d. 28 Oct 1922, Pease Funeral Home, bur. Evergreen Cem. (Ohio Certificate of Death, Division of Vital Statistics,1922, certif.51741); m. Nov 18, 1884 to *George R. MILLER* (son of *Peter*; d. 7 Sept 1942 [Pease Funeral Home Records, Mss. 4809, Western Reserve Historical Society, Cleveland, OH, Record of Funeral, p. 77]) (St. Paul Lutheran Church Records, pp. 67, 89, 354 and Marriage Record, Cuyahoga County, OH, vol. 28, p. 102); they would have one son, *Richard MILLER*, res. 591 Dover Center Rd. ***Frederick WISCHMEYER*** *(possible)* 1863-1864 *(OP:1)*. ***Louis A. WISCHMEYER*** 1865-1899 *(Lot 40)*. ***Matilda WISCHMEYER*** 1866-1922 *(Lot 51)*. ***Olga WISCHMEYER*** 20 Feb 1869-1948 *(Lot 51)*. ***Henry WISCHMEYER*** 1872-1959 *(Lot 51)*. ***Julius John WISCHMEYER*** 1875-1909, m. *Amelia WEGEWARDT* (1878-1911) *(Lot 40)*. *Accumulated from Wischmeyer references used in this book.*

Adelheid Karolina Regina WISCHMEIER, b. 24 Feb 1859. Confirmation record, 1873, p. 67; St. Paul Lutheran Church, Westlake, OH.

The State of Ohio, Cuyahoga Co., ss. I Certify that on the 18th day of November 1884 ***Mr. George MILLER*** and ***Miss Addie WISCHMEYER*** were by my legally joined in marriage. J. Rupprecht, C.P. Marriage Record, Cuyahoga County, OH, vol. 28, p. 102.

Georg** (sp.) **MUELLER & Adelheid WISCHMEIER m. 18 November 1854, St. Paul Lutheran Church, Westlake, OH. St. Paul Lutheran Church Marriage Records, p. 89.

Adelaide MILLER, Dover Center, Bay, Cuyahoga County, OH; d. Oct 28, 1922, Right sided hemoplegia 17 ds., arterio sclerosis, 63 yrs. 8 mos. 4 ds.; Married to ***George MILLER***; b. Feb 24, 1859, Cleveland, Ohio, fr. ***Henry WISCHMEYER***, b. Germany, mo. ***Regina RENSLER***, b. Germany; Evergreen Cemetery, Westlake, undertaker C. Pease. Ohio Certificate of Death, Division of Vital Statistics, 1922, certif. 51741.

MILLER: GEORGE R., residence 591 Dover Center rd., Bay Village; husband of the late ***Adelaide*** (nee ***WISCHMEYER***), father of ***Richard***, grandfather of ***Richard J.*** and ***Charline***. Friends may call at Clifford Pease Funeral Home, 2914 Dover Center rd., Westlake, O., where services will be held Saturday, Sept 19, at 2:30 p.m. Sept 19, 1942, p. 17, col. 2. The Plain Dealer.

Child of Adelaide Wischmeyer and George Miller:

MILLER, Richard E., 32, res. Bay Village; b. Do.; occup. Engineer; fr. *George*, mo. *Adelaide WISCHMEYER*. Married ***Anne C. McCAMANT***, 27, res. 1298 Brockley Ave.; b. W. Lafayette, Ohio; occup. none; fr. *Geo. E.*, mo. *Jane TURNEY*; neither previously married. The State of Ohio, Cuyahoga County, ss. I Certify, That on the 5th day of August 1918 Richard E. Miller and Anne C. McCamant were by me legally joined in marriage. Marriage Record, Cuyahoga County, OH, vol. 109, p. 442.

MILLER, Richard M., head, 44 yrs., own home and radio, value of home $13,500, age at marriage 31, b. Ohio, fr. b. Wirtenberg, Germany, mo. b. Ohio, Consult. Make Engines, Industry Lake Boat; ***Anne C.***, wife, 39, 27 at time of marriage, b. Ohio, parents b. Ohio; ***Richard I.***, son. 3, b. Ohio; ***Charline M.***, dau., 1 4/12 yrs., b. Ohio. 1930 FC OH CYBV, ED18-534, 26816 Lake Road, p. 12A., lines 16-19.

MILLER. ***Richard E. Miller***, beloved husband of ***Charline Ann*** (nee ***McCAMANT***), father of ***Richard I.***, and the late ***Charline Mary***, grandfather of two. Funeral Services Tuesday, Aug, 6, at a time to be announced at the Jenkins Funeral Chapel, 2914 Dover Center Rd., Westlake, where friends may call from 2-4 and 7-9 p.m. Sunday and 3-5 and 7-9 p.m. Monday. Cleveland Press, Aug 3, 1968.

MILLER, Anne, residence, 26816 Lake Rd., Bay Village, wife of ***Richard E.***, mother of ***Richard I.*** and ***Charline***; daughter of *George* and the late *Emma Janet McCAMANT*; sister of *Mrs. Florence SMITH* and *Edgar P. McCAMANT*...Clifford Pease Funeral Home...March 6 at 2 p.m. Cleveland Necrology File, Mar 5, 1949.

Children of Richard Miller and Anna McCamant:

Richard MILLER was influential in starting the Bay Boat Club that is located on what was Cahoon land just west of Dover Center off Lake Road. He lived on Lake Road and passed away of cancer. ***Charline*** died shortly after high school. Norma Wolf Garber

MILLER, Charline Mary, dau. of ***Richard E.*** and the late ***Anna***; sister of ***Richard L.***, residence, 26816 Lake Rd., Bay Village...Daniel's Funeral Home. Cleveland Press, Aug 8, 1955.

Henry and ***Regina WISCHMEYER*** had a foster child, ***Mabel BLAIR*** who lived with them. Mabel married a ***WHELPLEY*** and moved away from Dover, near Milan, OH. She outlived all of the Wischmeyer children and was the last one to live in the family home on Lake Rd. until it was sold by ***Dick MILLER***. She then moved across the street living with neighbors until she passed away. Norma Wolf Garber

Arthur W. WHELPLEY, 31, res. 3806 Cedar Ave., b. Kirtland, O., occup. Salesman, fr. *Wm. P? WHELPLEY*, mo. *Margaret WELLS*. Married ***Mable G. BLAIR***, 23, res. N. Dover, O., b. Charlotte, Mich., occup. Stenographer, fr. *Chas. E. BLAIR*, mo. *Nellie L. LOVESS*; neither previously married. The State of Ohio, Cuyahoga County-ss. I Certify, That on the 29th day of November 1906 Mr. Arthur W. Whelpley and Miss Mable G. Blair were by me legally joined in marriage. Rev. Paul P.F. Sutphen Marriage Record, Cuyahoga County, OH, vol. 65, p. 185.

Arthur WHELPLEY, 33, b. Ohio; ***Mabel***, 26, b. Michigan; *Virginia*, mother, 72, b. Ohio. 1910 FC OH CY Cleve., ED 323, visit 70.

WHELPLEY, Arthur W., 44, married, b. Ohio, fr. b. Ohio, mo. b. New York, Grocery salesman; ***Mable** (sp.)*, wife, 36, b. Michigan, fr. b. Pennsylvania, mo. b. Michigan, no occupation. 1920 FC OH Lake County, Willoughby Twp., Willoughby Village, ED 99, Union Street, p. 14B, lines 77-78.

WHELPLEY. ***Mabel G. Whelpley*** (nee ***BLAIR***), beloved wife of the late ***Arthur***, dear friend of *Emeline A. ROLIE, Mary BOGNOR*, both of Bay Village and *Helen STANLK* of Avon. Funeral services Thursday, Mar 25, at 1 P.M. at Jenkins Funeral Chapel, 2914 Dover Center Rd., Westlake, where friends may call From 2-4 and 7-9 P.M. Wednesday. Burial In Mentor, O. Cleveland Press, Mar 24, 1971.

Mabel WHELPLEY, d. 21 March 1971, Fairview General Hosp., Cleveland, OH, intestinal obstruction; res. 26565 Lake Road, Bay Village; b. 5 Aug 1883, Indiana, fr. -- ***BLAIR***, mo. not known; widowed; occup. storekeeper, Grocery Store Owner; bur. Mentor Cemetery, Mentor, Lake County, Ohio; informant Emeline A. Rolfe; Jenkins Funeral Chapel, Inc., Westlake, Ohio. Ohio Certificate of Death, Division of Vital Statistics, 1971, certif. 016711.

WHELPLEY, Arthur W. of Collins, O., passed away Aug 27, 1947; beloved husband of ***Mabel BLAIR***; brother of *Mrs. E.R. BARNES* of St. Louis, Mo. Funeral services Saturday, Aug 30, at 11 a. m. from the L.D. Gerber Funeral Home, Wakeman, O. Interment Mentor, O. Aug 29 1947. The Plain Dealer.

Lot 39 ***Frederick Hahn***

unmarked, moved

Frederick Hahn is the grandson of Regina Lapp Rentschler (OP 2:13), nephew of Caroline Rentschler Wolf (Lot 50-14) and Regina Rentschler Wischmeyer (Lot 38-11).

Frederic R. HAHN, 3; res. Dover; German; interred July 26, 1884; Lot 38. Body removed to Cleveland, August 28th, 1884. "List of Interments," Lakeside Cemetery, Bay Village, OH.

Frederick HAHN, buried at Highland Cemetery, 1888, from Dover, died 1884. Removed to Lake View Cemetery. City of Cleveland Cemeteries.

Frederick HAHN, b. 2 July 1879; d. Aug 28, 1884; bur. 14 Feb 1908, Lake View Cemetery, Sect. 1, Lot 14 B, lot in name of *J.L. HAHN*. Lake View Cemetery Assoc., Cleveland. *Frederick was moved to Lake View Cemetery following his mother's death in November.*

Frederick *is buried with his parents,* ***Joseph L. HAHN*** *and* ***Adelheide RENTSCHLER.*** Adelheide, mother of Frederick, is the sister of ***Regina WISCHMEYER*** *(Lot 38-11).* Other family members buried in the family plot are; *Vernon BURKE, Mrs. Bertha M. BURKE, Sigismund J. F. HAHN, Joseph O. HAHN, Mrs. Helen B. HAHN, Vernon H. BURKE, Matilda H. BURKE* and *Elmer Ellsworth MCINTYRE* at Lake View Cemetery, Cleveland, OH. Frederick's stone at Lake View reads: "Freddie 1879-1884." Cemetery marker read by Ingrid Abram. Lakeview Cemetery Association, Cleveland, OH.

Parents of Frederick Hahn:

The State of Ohio, Cuyahoga County, ss. I Certify that on the 17th day of December 1863, ***Mr. Joseph L. HAHN*** and ***Miss Ada RENTHLER*** *(sp.)* were by me legally joined in Matrimony. Fredk. A. Brand, Justice of Peace. Marriage Record, Cuyahoga County, OH, vol. 11, p. 242.

Mrs. Adelheide HAHN, born Aug 19, 1843, d. Nov 28, 1907. Lake View Cemetery Records

Adelheide HAHN-64 yrs.- wife of J.J. Hahn, at her residence, Nov 28, 1907. Burial private. Cleveland Necrology File, roll 33.

Joseph L. HAHN b. Jan 18, 1832, in Germany; d. Sept 21, 1909, 2064 E. 81st, Cleveland. Lake View Cemetery Records and Ohio Certificate of Death, Division of Vital Statistics, 1909, certif. 45273.

Joseph L. HAHN, d. 2064 E. 81st St., Cleveland, Ward 21, Cuyahoga County, Ohio.; b. 1832, 77 yrs., widowed, b. Germany, fr. *Joseph HAHN*, b. Germany, mo. *Adelaide HAHN*, b. Germany; d. Sept. 21, 1909 of Brights Disease for one year. Bur. Lakeview Cemetery, Sept 23, undertaker: J. and W. Koebler, 2340 E. 55th. Information provided by *S.J. HAHN*, Conneaut, O. Ohio Certificate of Death, Division of Vital Statistics, 1909, certif. 45273.

MRS. ADELAIDE HAHN DIES
Daughter of Pioneer Resident of
West Side and Mother of
Mrs. Vernon Burke.

Mrs. Adelaide HAHN, wife of ***Joseph L. HAHN*** and daughter of ***Frederick REUTSCHER***, *(sp.)* one of the pioneer residents of the West Side, died yesterday morning after a long illness. She returned from Europe while ill in September, after a prolonged stay abroad and had been in poor health since.

Mrs. Hahn was the mother of ***Mrs. Vernon H. BURKE***, ***Joseph HAHN*** of this city and ***S.J. HAHN*** of Conneaut. She is also survived by her husband. She was sixty-four years old.

The funeral will take place tomorrow morning from the residence of her daughter, Mrs. Burke, 2064 E. 81st. The burial will be private. Friday, Nov 29, 1907, p. 10, col. 6. The Plain Dealer.

Siblings of Frederick Hahn:

Tillie B. HAHN m. ***Vernon H. BURKE***, Cuyahoga County, Ohio. Marriage Record, Cuyahoga County, OH, vol. 40, p. 237.

Matilda H. BURKE age 97 years, wife of the late ***Vernon H. BURKE Sr.***, mother of ***Vernon H. BURKE Jr.***, on Tuesday, July 13. Residence, Forest Park Towers. The family will receive friends From 7-9 P. M. at the East Cleveland Home of Rinear and Son, 13136 Euclid Ave. High Mass will be conducted by Rev. Fr. Peterson and Rev. Fr. Cook at St. James Episcopal Church, 55th and Whittler Ave., July 15 at 11:30 a.m. Interment in the family plot in Lake View Cemetery following church services. June 15 ? Cleveland Necrology File, roll 97.

Vernon H. BURKE, d. Charity Hospital, Ward 11, Cleveland, Cuyahoga County, Ohio; b. December 21, 1866, 51 years, 20 days; attorney-at-law; fr. *John F. BURKE*, b. Ireland, mo. *Helen STEWART*, b. Scotland; d. January 10, 1918, Intestinal obstruction, general peritonitis 7 ds. and appendicitis; res. 2064 East 81st Street; bur. Lake View Cemetery, Jan 12,

1918. Ohio Certificate of Death, Division of Vital Statistics, 1918, certif. 1210.

Joseph O. HAHN, 28, res. 2058 E. 81st St., b. Dover, O., Salesman, fr. *J.L.*, mo. *Adelaide RANTSCHLER (sp.)*, never previously married. Married ***Helen J. BASSETT***, 27, res. 2103 E. 90th St., b. Warren, O., no occup., fr. *Horace P.*, mo. *Hortener JUSTINE*, never previously married. Marriage to be solemnized by Rev. J.H. Goldner, E. 100 St. Filed Mar. 6, 1909. The State of Ohio, Cuyahoga County. I Certify, That on the 6th day of March 1909 Mr. Joseph O. Hahn and Miss Helen J. Bassett were legally joined in marriage. Marriage Record, Cuyahoga County, OH, vol. 72, p. 67.

HAHN: Joseph O., beloved husband of ***Helen B. HAHN*** (nee ***BASSETT***), brother of ***Mrs. Vernon H. BURKE*** and ***Sig J.F. HAHN*** of Painesville, O., at his residence, Feb. 9, 70 Euclid ave., Willoughby, Ohio. Services at residence, Tuesday, Feb. 11, at 2 p.m. Burial Lake View Cemetery, Cleveland, Ohio. Cleveland Necrology File., Feb. 11, 1936.

Helen B. HAHN, wife of ***Joseph O. HAHN***, 1881-1963. Headstone, Lake View Cemetery, Cleveland.

HAHN, Joseph Oscar, b. May 17, 1884; d. Feb 9, 1936; from Willoughby; Sect. 1, Lot 14-B. The Lake View Cemetery, Cleveland, O.

HAHN, Sigismund, J.F., of Painesville, O.; brother of ***Mrs. Vernon H. BURKE, Sr.***, and the late ***Joseph HAHN***; uncle of ***Vernon H. BURKE, jr***. Services, and interment private Tuesday, afternoon. July 5, 1954. Cleveland Necrology File, Roll 115.

Lot 40 *Owner: B. Tuttle of Dover (later reference: Benjamin Tuttle), purchased on Feb 25, 1879, for $5.25* SL

This lot was transferred to the Wischmeyer family. The Dexter Tuttle family is buried at Evergreen Cemetery, Westlake, OH.

Lot 40-14 Louis Alfred Wischmeyer

LOUIS
1865-1899

Louis Alfred was the second child of Henry Wischmeyer (Lot 38:11) and Regina Rentschler (Lot 39:13).

WISCHMEIER: father ***Heinrich***; mother ***Regina***; b. 10 April, bap. 2 July, ***Louis Alfred***; godparents *Louis KRUGER* and *Alfred WOLF (Lot 50-15)*. Baptismal Record, St. Paul Lutheran Church, 1865, Book 1, p.11.

Louis WISCHMEIER, age 34, died 26 May 1899, RR accident. Coroner's Files 1833-1900.

Louis WISCHMEYER was killed by a train of the Lakeshore Electric Interurban line at Bradley Road. Norma Wolf Garber

Louis WISCHMEYER died May 26. Wischmeyer Family File, Handwritten note, Rose Hill Museum, Bay Village, OH.

Louis A. WISCHMEYER, 34; res. Dover; German; interred May 29, 1899, Lot 39 *(plot map shows Lot 40)*. "List of Interments," Lakeside Cemetery, Bay Village, OH.

Lot 40-15 Julius John Wischmeyer

JULIUS
1875-1909

Julius was the youngest child of Henry Wischmeyer (Lot 38:11) and Regina Rentschler (Lot 39:13).

The State of Ohio, Cuyahoga County, ss. I certify that on the 5th day of Dec 1904, ***Mr. Julius WISCHMEIER*** *(sp.)* and ***Miss Emilie WEGEWARTH*** were by me legally joined in marriage, after due publication of banns as provided by law. Rev. J. Rupprecht Marriage Record, Cuyahoga County, OH, vol. 57, p. 337.

Johann Julius WISCHMEIER *(sp.)*, Bay Village, 29 yrs. 5 m. 6 d. to ***Emilie Louise WEGEWARTH***, Dover, Ohio, 26 y. 8 mo. 23 d. were married 15 Dec 1904, 7 p.m. St. Paul Lutheran Church, Marriage Record, p. 307.

Julias WEISHMEYR *(sp.)*, 34; res. Bay Village; German; interred May 19, 1909. "List of Interments," Lakeside Cemetery, Bay Village, OH.

Julius John WISCHMEYER, Bay Village, Cuyahoga; d. May 17, 1909, 11:40 p.m.; Asthma one day; b. July 10, 1875, N. Dover, Ohio, fr. ***Henry WISCHMEYER***, b. Germany, mo. ***Regenia RENSHLER*** *(sp.)*, b. Germany; 34 yrs. 10 mos. 7 ds.; Married; Farmer; Informant *Mrs. Geo. MILLER*, North Dover, Ohio; bur. N. Dover, O., Lake Rd., May 20, 1909, undertaker Jas. A. Pease & Son, Dover, Ohio. Ohio Certificate of Death, Division of Vital Statistics, 1909, certif. 23565.

WISCHMEYER-Julius, Monday, May 17, 11 p.m., at his residence, Bay Village, O., aged 33 years 10 months. Funeral Thursday, May 20, 1909, 2 p.m., standard. Take Lake Shore Electric R.R., Stop 22. Columbus papers please copy. Cem. rec. 1875-1909, age 34, Lakeside Cemetery, Cleveland, Ohio. Cleveland Necrology File, May 19, 1909, roll 86.

Lot 40-16 Amelia Wegewardt Wischmeyer

AMELIA
1878-1911

Amelia, wife of Julius Wischmeyer, was the daughter-in-law of Henry Wischmeyer (Lot 39) and Regina Rentschler (Lot 38).

Mrs. Emilie Louise WISCHMEIER, geb. *(maiden name)* ***WEGEWARDT***, geb. *(born)* 22 March 1878, Koressow, Tom.?; d. 13 April 7 p.m., bur. 17 April, 2:30 p.m., 33 yrs. 22 days, 1911. St. Paul Lutheran Church Records, p. 347.

DOVER LAKE

Mrs. Julius WEISHMYER *(sp.)* died very suddenly Thursday evening at the home of her mother in Dover. She had walked from Bay Village at noon and was in usual health. Heart failure is supposed to have been the immediate cause of death. Her husband died two years ago and they had no children. The funeral will occur at the Lutheran church Monday at 2:00 p.m. Burial at Lakeside cemetery, Bay Village. Evening Telegram, Elyria, OH, Wednesday, April 19, 1911, p. 4, col. 6.

Mrs. Amilia Louisa WISCHMEYER, d. April 13, 1911, Cuyahoga County, Township of Dover; b. March 22, --78, Germany; 33 years, 21 days; widowed, Housewife; fr. ***Christian WENGERWART***, b. Germany, mo. ***Louisa HERTGEL***, b. Germany; Cause of death Valvular Heart Disease, Sudden Death, Contributory Influenza Bronchial, signed Calvin O. Clemens, M.D.; Informant *Anna Wengerwart*, N. Dover, O.; burial Bay Village, April 17, 1911, Undertaker Jas. Pease Sons, Dover, O. Ohio Certificate of Death, Division of Vital Statistics, 1911, certif. 20528.

Amelia L. WISCHMEYER, 33; res. Dover; German; interred April 17, 1911; Lot 40. "List of Interments," Lakeside Cemetery, Bay Village, OH.

Mrs. Amelia L. WISCHMEYER, Valvular Heart Disease, issued April 17, 1911 by C. Pease. Bureau of Vital Statistics, Burial or Removal Permit, Bay Village, OH.

Wischmeyer-Mrs. Amelia (nee ***WEGEWARDT***), age 33 years at North Dover, suddenly at 6:30 p.m., Thursday, April 13. Funeral at 2:30 p.m. Monday, April 17. Friends invited. Conveyances furnished. Stop 23, Lake Shore Electric. Cleveland Necrology File, April 17, 1911, roll 86.

Parents of Amelia Wegewardt Wischmeyer:

WEGEWARDT, Christian, 1839-1905. St. Paul's Cemetery Dover, Ohio. Cleveland Necrology File, reel 084.

Assumed mother: ***WEGEWARDT, Louise***, d. 21 May, 1915, Cuyahoga County, OH. Ohio Certificate Of Death, Division Of Vital Statistics, Index, 1915, certif. 27537.

Louise WEGEWARDT, 64, b. Ger.; ***Anna***, 26, b. Ger.; ***Ester***, 11, b. Ohio. 1910 FC OH CY East Cleveland, ED11, 168.

Lot 40 *Dexter Tuttle* unmarked, moved

Dexter TUTTLE, 71; res. Dover Lake Shore; interred Feb 26, 1879; Lot 40 *(note year)*. "List of Interments," Lakeside Cemetery, Bay Village, OH.

Dexter TUTTLE, born Sept 10th, 1807 in Rowe, Berkshire Co., Mass. came with his family (***Chester*** born 1792, ***Lucy*** born 1796, ***Ezra*** born 1798 and ***Benjamin*** born 1804) via Connecticut with single ox-bow cart, in 1823 when he was 16 years old. They forded Cuyahoga River and Rocky River at Silverthorn Hotel (Westlake Hotel). They lived in present Rocky River and helped build the first plank bridge. Property was where the Beachcliff Theatre and A&P were built. Benjamin moved on to Albion (half-way between Medina and Cleveland) and became the father of ***Lyman TUTTLE*** who was professor of music and composer at Baldwin College, Berea.

Dexter married ***Amelia WEIDNER*** (b. 3 Dec 1811, d. 30 Aug 1896) about 1828 and settled in Dover Twp. in 1836. They cleared woods at Stop 19 Lake Rd (old Hall Rd) for log cabin placed on west side of Tuttle Creek north of Old Wagon Rd. (Lake Rd.). Their family consisted of seven boys and one girl who died young…Dexter Tuttle lived in log cabin until he and Ezra built the present house at 25547 Lake Rd. (*HARTER* residence) about 1840-50 where they raised chickens and sheep and sold them to the Silverthorn Hotel. Amelia used wool from sheep to make clothing for her family after carding, spinning and weaving it. They also had a saw mill and logs taken to Cleveland and Sandusky. Dexter acquired property from lake to Nickel Plate R.R. (100 acres) and at the age of 71 years died (1878). Amelia lived 18 years longer and was 85 years old in 1896. She was blind the last seven years and was taken care of by ***Marius*** who never married. Flora Tuttle Renfrew, "Tuttle Family Story." *Flora, b. 1881, was the daughter of Frederick J. TUTTLE. Her maternal grandparents were Henry and Mary BATES who purchased the (John) WOLF (OP 1:12) house on Detroit Rd. in Westlake.*

Dexter TUTTLE married ***Permelia*** *(sp.)* ***WIDENER***, May 1, 1833, Cuyahoga County, OH. Marriage Record, Cuyahoga County, OH, vol. 1, p. 479.

The Evergreen Cemetery Interment Record has very little information. It is unclear when Dexter was moved to Evergreen or if a lot was purchased by the family and Dexter was originally buried in Evergreen Cemetery.

Evergreen Cemetery, Lot 31, section A, lot owner ***Ezra*** and ***Marius TUTTLE***: ***Dexter TUTTLE***, interment in 1878; *Amelia TUTTLE*, Dover, OH, b. Rochester, NY, date of interment 9/18/1896. Evergreen Cemetery Records, Westlake, OH.

Dexter TUTTLE, Sep. 1807-Feb 1878. ***Amelia WEIDNER***, his wife, Dec 3, 1811-Aug 30, 1896… *Children and their family members with them are* ***Ezra*** 1837-1921; m. *Victoria E. CLAGUE* 1839-1930 (Ezra's son, ***Edward A.***, m. *Henrietta LIEHR* 1874-1926). ***Benjamin F.***, b. June 10, 1835; d. Nov 27, 1889. ***Marius***, b. June 21, 1839; d. May 10, 1906. ***Frederick J.***, b. April 20, 1845; d. July 20, 1928; m. *Mary*. ***Jane***, b. Apr 26, 1852; d. Nov 26, 1932. ***Wallace W.***, b. March 26, 1849; d. Feb 21, 1906; m. *Mary ZIMMERMAN*, 1858-1930. Evergreen Cemetery, tombstone inscription, Westlake, OH. Section A, Lots 30-31, 34-35. *The Tuttle family has a large monument with small stones surrounding it listing the above information.*

Petition for letters of Administration, 15th of May 1912. ***Dexter TUTTLE*** died on or about 22nd day of February, 1878, leaving his widow (She died Aug 30, 1896) and the following persons as his next of kin: ***Mary TUTTLE,*** dau.-in-law; ***Elizabeth*** and ***Ida TUTTLE***, grand-daughters and sons ***Fred*** and ***Ezra TUTTLE***; all of the Village of Bay, Dover Township; ***Angelo***, son, of Kansas and ***Samuel J.***, son, of Lincoln, Nebraska. Cuyahoga County, OH, Probate Court Estate Case File, 60979.

Children of Dexter Tuttle and Amelia Weidner:

Benjamin TUTTLE, b. 10 June 1835; d. 27 Nov 1889, Dover Twp., Cuy. Co., OH; never married. ***Ezra W. TUTTLE***, b. 1837; m. 31 May 1873, Cuy. Co. to *Victoria CLAGUE*; d. 1921. ***Marius TUTTLE***, b. 21 June 1839; d. 10 May 1906. ***Angelo Michael TUTTLE***, b. 15 Jan 1841; m. 19 Apr 1866, Cuy. Co. to *Jennifer A. BEARD* (b. 28 June 1849, Cuy Co.; d. 25 Oct 1920; bur. Colfax Church Cem., Wilson Co., KS); d. 22 Sep 1918 KS, bur. Colfax Church Cem. ***Samuel J. TUTTLE***, b. 2 Aug 1844; m. 1 June 1870 to *Bianca F. KIES* (b. 1851, MI); d. 14 Feb 1927, Lincoln, Lancaster Co., NE; bur. Wyuka Cem., Lincoln, NE. ***Frederick J. TUTTLE***, b. 30 Apr 1845, Dover Twp., Cuy. Co.; m. *Mary Jane WARWICK* (b. 26 Apr 1852 England; d. 26 Nov 1932, Cleveland, Cuy Co, OH); d. 29 July 1928, Cuy. Co. ***Wallace W. TUTTLE***, b. 26 Mar 1849; m. 4 Dec 1877, Cuy. Co. to *Mary ZIMMERMAN* (b. 1858, OH; d. 1930); d. 21 Feb 1906. ***Daughter TUTTLE***, b. unknown, d. young. All children born Dover Twp., Cuy. Co. Keith M. Sheldon, Descendants of Early Bay Village, pp. 623-28.

Ezra W. TUTTLE, d. July 23, 1921, 6:30 p.m., Bay, Cuyahoga, Co., Ohio of Broncho-pneumonia, 3 days; m. ***Victoria***; Farmer; b. Feb 12, 1837, Bay, Ohio; fr. ***Dexter TUTTLE***, b. Connecticut, mo. ***Amelia WEIDNER***, b. Penna.; Informant *E. A. TUTTLE*; bur. Evergreen Cemetery, Dover, Ohio; undertaker C. Pease, Dover, Ohio. Ohio Certificate of Death, Division of Vital Statistics, 1921, certif. 37413. *Ezra married Victoria CLAGUE whose homestead is now the Clague House Museum in Westlake, OH.* Ohio Certificate of Death, Division of Vital Statistics,1931, certif. 37413.

Marius TUTTLE had a great sadness in his young life. The beautiful young school teacher whom he loved very dearly and possibly would have married, was taken very ill and passed on. I do not remember her name. Each time he would get out this Family Album he would speak particularly about her with great reverence. He never loved again. He was short in stature, good looking and a good man. Notes by Flora Tuttle Renfrew, Rose Hill Museum.

TUTTLE, Angelo, 30 farmer; ***Mary***, 25, Keeping House; ***Frank***, 4; ***Lillie***?, *1*. 1870 FC OH Lorain Co., Elyria, p. 363, lines 20-23.

The daughter of ***Dexter*** and ***Amelia TUTTLE*** lived approximately two years. She is not listed in the family bible. Notes by Flora Tuttle Renfrew, Rose Hill Museum.

Lot 40 Henry David unmarked

Henry DAVID, 51; res. Dover; German; interred Feb 18, 1890; Lot 40. "List of Interments," Lakeside Cemetery, Bay Village, OH.

Additional information was not found on Henry David.

Lot 41 *Owner: Charles Hassler of Cleveland purchased Aug 15, 1879, for $5.25* SL

Lot 41-17 Hassler Marker

HASSLER

BABETTE	MATHILDA	CARL
1832-1879	1865-1947	1820-1906

Lot 41-17 Babette Lieberich Hassler

Babetta HASSLER, 47; res. Cleveland; German; interred Aug 16, 1879; Lot 41. "List of Interments," Lakeside Cemetery, Bay Village, OH.

Babette migrated to Dover in 1854 with her husband ***Carl HASSLER***. She died in August, 1879 at their home, 28838 Lake Road. Carl temporarily left Dover moving to Cleveland that same year, and proceeded to live on a number of farms. ***Mathilda*** was the daughter of Babette and Carl (Charles) Hassler. Bay Village Historical Society, Bay Village: A Way of Life, pp. 40-41.

Lot 41-17 Mathilda L. Hassler

Mathilda L. HASSLER, d. 379 Bassett Rd., BV on Mar 27, 1947; Terminal broncho pneumonia, cerebral hemorrhage; 81; undertaker - E.H. Saxton, 13215 Detroit Ave., Lkwd. Bureau of Vital Statistics, Burial or Removal Permit, Bay Village, OH.

HASSLER, Mathilda L., sister of the late ***Robert***, aunt of ***Laura M., Edna M., Gertrude, Robert C.***, and ***Helen HASSLER*** of Bay Village, O., passed away Mar 27. Friends may call at the Saxton Funeral Home, 13215 Detroit Ave., where PRIVATE services will be held Sat. afternoon. Please omit flowers. Cleveland Necrology File, Cleveland Press, Mar 27, 1947, roll 35.

Lot 41-17 Charles F. Hassler

HASS** (sp.)**, Chas, 50, farmer, Value of real estate $8000, Personal Property $830, b. Germany; ***Barbary***, 37, Keeping House, b. Germany; ***Robert***, 11, b. Ohio; ***Gustavus***, 8, b. Ohio; ***Matilda***, 4, b. Ohio. 1870 FC OH CYDO, p. 30, dwelling 257, lines 36-40.

Charles HASSLER, 28838 Lake Rd. House purchased from *Mr. BAKER* in 1854/5, not sure who built or when, probably built 1830. Known as Castle Garden. "Old Houses in Bay Village," West Life, Oct 3, 1960.

Charles HASSLER, 60, ret. Farmer, b. Bavaria, fr. b. Bavaria, mo. b. Bavaria; ***Robert***, 21, son, single, Bookkeeper, b. Ohio, fr. b. Bavaria, mo. b. Germany; ***Augustus***, 18, son, clerk seed store, b. Ohio; ***Matilda***, 14, dau. b. Ohio; *BOYLAN, ____*, 17, servant. 1880 FC OH CY Cleve Ed 2, p. 39, house 63, dwelling 297, lines 7-11.

Chas. F. ***HASSLER***, 86, d. 8/14, 1906, b. 1820, Germany, single, place of death residence 9924 So. Boulevard, cause of death old age, bur. Lake View Cemetery, parents b. Germany, undertaker Fred Beilstein. Removed to Dover, Ohio Sept 1906. Burial Permit, City of Cleveland, roll 1977542.

HASSLER-Charles F., Tuesday, August 14, aged 80 years, at residence of his son, ***Robert HASSLER,*** 9024 S. Boulevard N.E. Funeral services at residence Friday, Aug 17, 2 p.m., standard time. Burial private. Please omit flowers. Cleveland Necrology File August 17, 1906, roll 35 *(incorrect age listed).*

Second card: ***HASSLER, Carl***, 1820-1906, age 86, Lakeside Cemetery, Cleveland, cem. rec. Cleveland Necrology File, roll 35

Charles HASSLER, 86; res. Cleveland; German; interred Aug 14, 1906; Lot 41. "List of Interments," Lakeside Cemetery, Bay Village, OH.

Lot 41/42-18 Hassler Marker

The family of
ANNA MAYER
1858-1942
&
J. ROBERT
1858-1942
HASSLER
EDNA M.
1885-1964
GERTRUDE
1888-1966
ROBERT C.
1890-1983
LAURA M.
1884-1988

Lot 41/42-18 Anna Mayer Hassler

Robert and ***Anna HASSLER*** were very involved in the German community, belonging to a German Lutheran Church in Cleveland and active in the Verein Social Club. Helen Hassler Bircher

In 1981 the Hassler Center for Family Medicine opened in a building directly across the street from the main hospital. This center, home of the hospital's residency in family practice, was named in memory of ***John Robert HASSLER*** and his wife ***Anna***, who were among the original supporters of the Society for the Christian Care of the Sick and Needy when it was founded in 1892. Their support was continued through two of their children, ***Laura*** and ***Robert HASSLER***.

At its dedication on November 8, 1981, the center was described by *Dr. Germaine R. HAHNEL*, who chaired the department of family practice and directed the hospital's residency program in family medicine, as a facility that "represents Fairview's serious and growing commitment to preparing physicians for the specialty of family medicine."

Ever looking to serve its patients better, in 1992 Fairview continued a major renovation of its Birthing Center and started renovations and expansions of the Hassler Center for Family Medicine and the emergency and admitting departments. The Centennial History of Fairview General Hospital, pp. 67, 79. *Unfortunately, neither Robert or Laura was able to attend the dedication ceremony. The Center has since been renamed the Center for Family Medicine.* Dr. Germaine Hahnel

HASSLER, Anna, wife of the late ***Robert***, mother of ***Laura, Edna, Gertrude, Robert C.***, and grandmother of ***Helen***, sister of ***Mrs. John N. KIPP***, sister-in-law of ***Matilda L.***, at her residence, 379 Bassett rd., Bay Village, Friday, Dec 4. Friends may call Saturday at the Clifford Pease Funeral Home, 2914 Dover Center rd., Westlake. Funeral services will be private. Kindly omit flowers. Cleveland Necrology File, Dec 6, 1942, roll 35.

Mrs. Anna HASSLER, d. Dec 4, 1942, 4:40 a.m., Bay Village, Cuy. Co., Arterio-sclerosis with Hypertension-20 yrs., Chron. Myocard. Degen.-10 yrs., Carcinoma of Vagina-6 mos.; res. 379 Bassett Rd., widowed, husband ***Robert***; b. Dec 27, 1859, Cleveland, Ohio, fr. ***Matthew MAYER***, b. Germany, mo. ***Mary RUHL***, b. Germany; 82 yrs. 11 mos. 24 ds., Hwf., informant *Edna M. HASSLER*, 379 Bassett Rd., cremated J.D. Deutsch Crematory, funeral firm Clifford Pease, Westlake. Ohio Certificate of Death, Division of Vital Statistics, 1942, certif. 74450.

Sister of Anna Mayer Hassler:

John N. KIPP, 57, res. 7212 Superior Ave., b. Cleveland, O., occup. Decorator, fr. *Martin*, mo. *GLENZER*, married once before, spouse dec'd. Married ***Mary M. MAYER***, 53, 10929 Soull Ave., b. Cleveland, O., occup. none, fr. *Mathew*, mo. *Mary RUHL*, never married. The State of Ohio, Cuyahoga County-ss. I Certify, That on the 17th day of May 1916 Mr. John N. Kipp and Miss Mary M. Mayer were by me legally joined in marriage. Rev. J.S. Huebschmann Marriage Record, Cuyahoga County, OH, vol. 96, p. 371.

KIPP, Lena *(nee* ***MAYER****)*, age 95 years, 3 months, widow of the late ***John N.***, mother of *Lottie HOLIZBERGER, Elizabeth RYAN, Edward, Carl, Celia SCHIKOWSKI, Hilda SAXTON* and *Albert*, aunt of ***Laura, Edna, Gertrude, Robert HASSLER***, grandmother, great-grandmother, July 7, at her residence, 8551 Woodbridge Rd., Cleveland Heights. Family will receive friends From 2-5 And 7-10 P. M. Wednesday at the Brickman & Sons Funeral Home, 7204 Superior Ave., where services will be held Thursday, July 10, at 11 a. m. Please omit flowers. Cleveland Press, July 9, 1958.

KIPP: John, beloved husband of ***Lena*** (nee ***MAYER***), father of *Lottie, Lill, Edward, Carl, Cecelia, Hilda, Albert*. March 10. Friends may call at Brickman's Funeral Home, 7204 Superior until noon. Wednesday, March 13 Services at First Evangelical Church, Thornhill and Arlington, Wednesday, at 2 p.m. Cleveland Necrology File, Mar 12, 1940.

Lot 41/42-18 John Robert Hassler

J. Robert is the son of ***Charles HASSLER*** *(Lot 41-17).* Bay Village Historical Society, Bay Village: A Way of Life, p. 40.

The State of Ohio, Cuyahoga County, ss. I Certify that on the 9th day of May 1883 ***Mr. Robert HASSLER*** and ***Miss Anna MAYER*** were by me legally joined in marriage. Ferdinand Bueller Marriage Record, Cuyahoga County, OH, vol. 26, p. 272.

HASSLER, Robert J., agt., *D.W. LOUD*, r. 39 *William also residing with him:* ***Chas. F.***, retired. The Cleveland City Directory, 1890.

DOVER LAKE

Mr. HASLAR'S *(sp.)* family, of Cleveland, has moved to the summer home on Bassett road, formerly owned by their uncle, ***Theodore LIEBRICH***. Evening Telegram, Elyria, OH, Wednesday, June 14, 1911, p. 4, col. 5.

HASSLER, Robert, head, 71, owns house valued at $40,000, no radio, age at marriage 25, b. Ohio, parents b. Bavaria, Germany, no occup.; ***Anna***, wife, 71, age at marriage 25, b. Ohio, parents b. Baden, Germany; ***Laura M.***, dau., 46, single, b. Ohio, teacher Public School; ***Edna M.***, dau., 45, single, b. Ohio, occup. none; ***Gertrude***, 42, dau., single, b. Ohio, Social Worker in Education; ***Robert C.***, son, 39, widower, President Lumber Co.; ***Helen Y.***, granddaughter, 1 9/12 yrs., b. Ohio, parents b. Ohio. 1930 FC OH CYBV, ED 18-534, 379 Bassett Road, p. 18B, lines 59-65.

Robert HASSLER, d. Mar 13, 1942, 9:40 p.m., Bay, Cuyahoga Co., Cerebral Thrombosis and Arterio sclerosis; res. 379 Bassett Rd., Married to ***Anna***; b. July 25, 1858, Bay Village, Retired, 83 yrs. 7 mos. 18 ds.; fr. ***Charles HASSLER***, b. Germany, mo. ***Babette LIEBRICH***, b. Germany; informant *Laura M. HASSLER*, 379 Bassett Rd. Bur. Bay Village, O., March 16, 1942, funeral firm Clifford Pease. Ohio Certificate of Death, Division of Vital Statistics, 1942, certif. 14763.

Robert and ***Anna HASSLER*** at one time lived at East 30th and Central in Cleveland. They were two of the first people to contribute to what is now Fairview General Hospital. W. Wilson Caldwell

HASSLER: Robert, husband of ***Anna***, father of ***Laura, Edna, Gertrude*** and ***Robert C.***, brother of ***Matilda L.***, grandfather of *Helen*, at his residence, 379 Bassett rd., Bay Village. Friday, March 13. Private services at Clifford Pease Funeral Home, 2914 Dover rd., Westlake. Kindly omit flowers. Cleveland Necrology File, Mar 16, 1942.

Lot 41/42-18 Edna M. Hassler

Edna HASSLER, daughter of ***Robert*** and ***Anna***, was single and was not employed outside the home. Martha Bangert

Edna M. HASSLER, d. at her residence 379 Bassett Rd., Bay Village, Ohio, 1-31-1964, 11:45 p.m.; length of stay in Bay Village 49 yrs.; b. 8/24/1885, Cleveland, Ohio; 78 yrs. old; Homemaker; fr. ***Robert HASSLER***, mo. ***Anna MAYER***; informant *Robert HASSLER*, Bay Village, Ohio; Cause of death Chronic endocarditis - 3 mos., Chronic heart failure, Arterio sclerosis - 10 years., no autopsy. I attended the deceased from Jan 2, 1950 to Jan 31, 1964 and last saw her alive on, Jan 31, 1964. Russell M. Arnold, M.D., Avon Lake, Ohio; cremation, 2/1/1964, Cleveland Cremation Co., Cleveland, Ohio; Jenkins Funeral Chapel, Inc., 2914 Dover Center Rd., Westlake, Ohio. Ohio Certificate of Death, Division of Vital Statistics, 1964, certif. 010151.

Edna M. HASSLER, 1885-1964, buried Feb 3, 1964. "List of Interments," Lakeside Cemetery, Bay Village, OH. *Not in chronological ledger.*

HASSLER, ***Edna M. HASSLER***, late residence 379 Bassett Rd., Bay Village, sister of ***Laura, Gertrude*** and ***Robert***, aunt of ***Helen*** and ***Jack BIRCHER***. *(Jack was the husband of Helen).* At her request PRIVATE services will be held. Feb 3, 1964. The Plain Dealer.

Lot 41/42-18 Gertrude Magdalen Hassler

Gertrude Magdalen HASSLER, female, b. Feb 4, 1888; fr. ***Robert HASSLER***, 29 yrs., b. North Dover, Traveling Salesman; mo. ***Anna MAYER***, 29 yrs., b. Cleveland, Housewife; 3 children born alive to this mother, 3 children living; res. 39 William St., Cleveland. Updated/corrected birth certif. March 26, 1926, signed by mother, Anna Mayer Hassler, Bassett Rd., Bay Village. Certificate of Birth for Cleveland, Cuy Co. Archives. *Birth recorded in index but not on Microfilm of Birth Records. The extract above is from the original at the Archives.*

Gertrude HASSLER, d. Dec 9, 1966, 7:20 a.m., 379 Bassett Rd., Bay Village, Cuyahoga County (her residence), length of stay in Bay Village 52 yrs.; 78 yrs. old; b. 2/4/1888, Cleveland, Ohio; never married; school teacher, Cleveland School Board; fr. ***Robert HASSLER***, mo. ***Anna MAYER***; Informant *Robert HASSLER*, Bay Village, Ohio; Death caused by Cancer of the Breast, 4 yrs.; I attended the deceased from Sept 1940 to Dec 9, 1966 and last saw her alive on Dec 8, 1966, Russell M. Arnold, M.D., Avon Lake, Ohio; cremation 12/10/1966, Cleveland Cremation Co., Cleveland, OH; Jenkins Funeral Chapel, 2914 Dover Center Rd., Westlake, OH. Ohio Certificate of Death, Division of Vital Statistics, 1966, certif. 091944.

HASSLER ***Gertrude HASSLER***, late residence, 379 Bassett Rd., Bay Village, sister of ***Laura, Robert*** and the late ***Edna***, aunt of ***Helen*** and ***Jack BIRCHER*** at her request private services were held, Monday, Dec 12. Cleveland Necrology File, Dec 14, 1966, roll 35.

Lot 41/42-18 Robert C. Hassler

Male infant, b. November 27, 1890; mo. ***Anna HASSLER***, German, 31 yrs.; fr. ***Robert HASSLER***, German, 32 yrs. old; b. 39 Williams Street; Medical Attendant J. Laisy, MD. *Return of Birth*, City of Cleveland, Cuy Co. Archives. *Birth recorded in index but not on Microfilm of Birth Records. The extract above is from the original at the Archives, assumed to be Robert C. Hassler.*

Robert HASSLER married ***Helen YENSEN*** of Cleveland, who he had met at Ohio State University. She had a brother *Howard* who moved to Columbus, their father had died earlier. The Hassler's had one daughter, ***Helen Y.*** Helen Yensen Hassler died while giving birth to her daughter and is buried by herself at Lakeview Cemetery. Helen Hassler Bircher and Martha Bangert. *Helen BIRCHER passed away 19 July 2000, while living in Willoughby, OH.*

Robert C. HASSLER*,* 36, res. Bay Village, O., b. Cleveland, O., occup. Lumberman, fr. *Robert,* mo. *Anna MAYER.* Married ***Helen YENSEN****,* 30, res. 1836 Knowles St., b. Cleveland, O., occup. none, fr. *Peter*, mo. *Clara MAGRUDER*; neither previously married. The State of Ohio, Cuyahoga County-ss. I Certify, That on the 7th day of May 1927 Mr. Robert C. Hassler and Miss Helen Yensen were by me legally joined in marriage. Rev. Louis F. Ruf. Marriage Record, Cuyahoga County, OH, vol. 148, p. 432.

Robert HASSLER and ***Helen YENSEN*** met at Ohio State University and later married. She died on 22 July 1928 after the birth of their daughter, ***Helen***, on July 19th. He then chose to move back to Bay Village with his daughter so that his three single sisters would be able to help raise her. It proved to be a strict upbringing for Helen.

Wirt DODD built the Hassler home on Bassett which had a small orchard in the back where they grew apples which were sold. W. Wilson Caldwell

Robert HASSLER was a member of the Bay Village City Council in 1920 and was part of the Library and Museum Committee. Minutes, Ordinances & Resolutions, Bay Village, OH, 1918-1921.

The Hassler's owned land on Bassett Road with an apple or peach orchard on the land that is presently the Bay Village High School Stadium. A man, presumably ***Robert*** (or "Bob"), would spray the apple trees with a yellow substance that smelled like sulfur using a pumping machine drawn by a horse. Whenever he would start, people would run to close their windows as quickly as possible because of the smell. He was always nice to the neighborhood children and was never upset if someone would run through the orchard, although children stayed in their own yards as a general rule. Esther Seitz Matousek

Robert HASSLER, and his sister ***Laura***, established The Hassler Scholarship Fund to encourage college attendance and school and living experience in other countries outside of the United States of qualified and worthy Bay High School students and graduates. Twenty-five thousand dollars was entrusted to the Bay Village Board of Education as a principal sum to establish the fund. The Board accepted the donation at the December 21, 1976, board meeting. The income earned from the fund was divided with eighty-five percent of the fund used to provide one or more scholarships. Fifteen percent is used to provide assistance to those in the American Abroad program of the American Field Service International Scholarship or its successor. The first award from the income earned was awarded in 1978. The award committee is selected by The Bay Village Women's Club Foundation. The Club has been generous through the years by supplementing the interest earned from the fund to create scholarships.

In 2001, upon the death of Robert's only child, ***Helen BIRCHER***, a larger amount was given to the School Board in the name of the Laura and Robert Hassler Charitable Trust Fund for the same purpose. The interest from these two funds, at the decision of the School Board, is to be included as part of The Bay Village Women's Club Foundation annual scholarships which are chosen and awarded by the Foundation's Scholarship Committee. Louella Parsons Meyer, The Bay Village Women's Club.

Robert C. HASSLER, d. February 23, 1983, 7:05 a.m., Fairview General Hospital, Cleveland, OH, inpatient; 92 yrs.; b. Nov 27, 1890, Ohio, never in the armed forces, widowed; occup Lumber; res. 379 Bassett Rd., Bay Village, OH; fr. ***J. Robert HASSLER***, mo. ***Anna MAYER***; informant *Laura C. HASSLER*, same address; cause of death Cardiac failure due to UTT prob. Septic Shock, COPP; no autopsy; Robert C. Landes, 18200 Lorain Ave., Cleveland, Ohio; Cremation Feb 23, 1983, Sunset Memorial Park, North Olmsted; Jenkins Funeral Chapel, Inc., 2914 Dover Center Rd., Westlake, Ohio. Ohio Certificate of Death, Division of Vital Statistics, 1983, certif. 008236.

Wife of Robert C. Hassler:

HASSLER -Helen YENSEN, wife of ***Robert*** passed away Sunday morning, July 22. Funeral Wednesday at 2:30 p.m. from the late residence, 3247 Dellwood Road, Cleveland Heights. Burial private. Please omit flowers. Cleveland Necrology File, July 23, 1928.

Helen HASSLER, d. July 22, 1928, 11:25 a.m., Maternity Hospital, 5 Ward, Cleveland, Cuyahoga, Ohio of Cardiac failure (30 min.), Caesarian Section (30 min.); res. 3247 Dellwood Rd., Cleveland Hts. Married to ***Robert HASSLER***; b. February 18, 1897, Cleveland; fr. ***Peter YENSEN***, b. U.S., mo. ***Clara MAGRUDER***, b. U.S.; 31 yrs. 5 months 4 days, housewife at home; Informant *Robert C. HASSLER*, 3247 Dellwood, C. H.; bur. Lake View Cemetery, July 25, 1928. Ohio Certificate of Death, Division of Vital Statistics, 1928, certif. 42178.

Helen YENSEN HASSLER, b. 18 Feb 1907 *(incorrect year)*; d. 22 July 1928, bur. Lakeview Cemetery, Cleveland, OH: Sect. 5, Lot 8-16 (only burial in lot). Lakeview Cemetery records.

Father of Helen Yensen Hassler:

Peter YENSEN, beloved husband of ***Clara E.***, father of ***Howard M.*** and the late ***Mrs. Helen HASSLER***, brother of *Mrs. Tina BEBER*, *Christ* of Sandusky, O., and *Richard* of Port Clinton, O., entered into rest Saturday, Oct 31. Funeral service from Sharer-Parrish Chapel, 2436 Prospect Ave., Monday, Nov 2 at 2:30 p.m. Interment at Port Clinton, O. Cleveland Necrology File, Nov 2, 1931.

Christian F. YENSEN (brother) d. 24 Dec 1932, Sandusky, Erie Co., OH; husband of *Rosamond*; b. 12 Oct 1846, Germany; Christian Scientist - no doctor, cause of death unknown; bur. Port Clinton. Ohio Certificate of Death, Div. of Vital Statistics, 1932, certif. 70701.

Peter YENSEN, d. Oct 31, 1931, 1:30 a.m., 1836 Knowles St., East Cleveland, Cuyahoga, Ohio of Chr. Intestinal nephritis - 5 yrs., acute cardiac dilatation and/or edema of lungs-4yrs.; married to ***Clara E.***; b. Jan 9, 1858, Port Clinton, Ohio; 73 yrs. 9 months 22 days; retired for 13 yrs.; fr. ***Peter YENSEN***, b. Germany, mo. ***Sophia RICHARDSON***, b. Germany; informant *H.W. YENSEN*, 4408 Eastway, Toledo; bur. Port Clinton, O., undertaker Sharer-Parrish, Inc. Ohio Certificate of Death, Division of Vital Statistics, 1931, certif. 63229.

Brother of Helen Yensen Hassler:

Howard Magruder "Pete" YENSEN, b. 28 June 1902, Cleveland, OH; d. 22 Jan 1980, Williamsburg, VA, after a short illness. A native of Cleveland, Ohio, Mr. Yensen was a resident of Williamsburg for seven years. He retired after 40 years as an executive with Ohio Bell Telephone Co. wife *Hilda R.*; son *Peter R. YENSEN* of Boston, Mass.; a daughter *Susan YENSEN SCHUPP* of Rochester, NY. Cremation and memorial services Port Clinton, OH. The Virginia Gazette, Williamsburg, VA, Jan 23, 1980, vol. 51, No. 4, p. 24, col. 5 and Soc. Sec. Index.

Lot 41/42-18 Laura M. Hassler

Laura HASSLER taught German at both Lincoln and Rhodes High Schools for the Cleveland Board of Education. W. Wilson Caldwell

Laura M. HASSLER, d. Feb 23, 1988, 11 p.m., 379 Bassett Rd., Bay Village, Cuyahoga County (her residence); 103 yrs.; b. March 1, 1884, Ohio; never married; school teacher, Cleveland School System; fr. ***Robert HASSLER***, mo. ***Anna MAYER***; Informant W. Wilson Caldwell, 28849 Bassett Rd., Westlake, Ohio 44145; Death caused by Respiratory Arrest due to Bilateral Pneumonia (Organism Unspecified); Cremation Feb 27, 1988, Westshore Cremation, Westlake, OH; not embalmed; Jenkins Funeral Chapel, Westlake, OH. Certificate of Cremation and Ohio Certificate of Death, Division of Vital Statistics, 1988, certif. 017249.

HASSLER Laura M. Hassler, beloved aunt of ***Helen BIRCHER***. Private services. Contributions to the American Cancer Society. Arrangements By Jenkins Funeral Chapel. A trust 100 funeral home. Feb 28, 1988, p. 15, sec. D. The Plain Dealer. All rights reserved. Reprinted with permission.

Original beneficiary in ***Laura HASSLER'S*** will was ***Miss Luise LIEBERICH*** whose address in Oct 1964 was Damenheim, Ansbach, Bavaria, Germany. This will was later revoked. Helen Bircher

Lot 42 *Owner: Theodore Leibrich of Dover purchased Oct 13, 1880, for $5.25* SL

Lot 42-19 Theodore Lieberich

THEODORE
LIEBERICH
1848-1910

Theodore was ***Charles HASSLER'S*** brother-in law and owned twenty-five acres of land where the house at 379 Bassett was built. Bay Village Historical Society, Bay Village: A Way of Life, p. 41.

Theodore's last name is spelled inconsistently throughout documents, as illustrated below.

LEIBRICH, Frederick T. Owned land; Acres: Improved - 22 tilled, including fallow and grass, 3 permanent meadow. Farm Values: Land - $2,000, Machinery - $100, Live Stock - $75, Cost of building or repairing in 1879: $50. Estimated value of all farm production: $200. Grass lands: acreage: 10 mown, 5 not mown, 10 tons hay. 1 horse, 2 other. 5 swine. Indian corn: 5 acres, 250 bushels; oats: 2 acres, 85 bushels. Apple orchard: 3 acres, 180 bearing trees. "Schedule 2. Production of Agriculture in Dover Township, Cuyahoga County, OH," enumerated June, 1880, p. 33.

Theo. LEIBRICH, 25 acres, Lot 93. 1880 Map of Dover Twp.

LEIBRICH, Frederick, 32, single, farmer, b. Bavaria, parents b. Bavaria. 1880 FC OH CYDO, p. 99, line 30, house 316. *Living between Sherman Osborn (Lot 48:10) and Calvin Riley Edson (moved from Lakeside Cemetery).*

Application of ***Theodore LIEBERISH*** for Admission to Citizenship of the United States of America. Now comes Theodore Lieberish and respectfully represents to the court, that he is an alien, and a subject of Bavaria; that he was born, on or about 3rd day of April 1848, at the village of Ausbach in Bavaria; that he first arrived in the United States on or about the 15th day of December 1868; that on the 20th day of August 1869, he duly declared his intention to become a citizen of the United States of America, the certificate of such declaration being now here produced in court... that he is by occupation a Farmer, and now resides at Dover, Cuyahoga county, Ohio., signed Theodor (*no "e")* Lieberick. AFFIDAVIT - ***Robert HASSLER*** (39 Wilson St.) of lawful age, being duly sworn according to law....That he is by occupation a Salesman and resides in the city of Cleveland...that for more than the last five years he has been personally acquainted with the above named applicant Theodore Lieberisch who now resides in the Town of Dover..... He became a naturalized citizen of the United States on 1 Nov 1890. United States District Court, Naturalization Papers for Theodore Lieberich, No. 8634, Chicago, IL.

LIEBRICH, Frederick, 52, single, b. Bavaria, parents b. Bavaria, farmer. 1900 FC OH CYDO, p. 99, line 30, house 316.

LIBERHRECH, Theodore *(sp.)*, 62, single, immig 1868, Na., own income, own house free, Bassett Rd. 1910 FC OH CYBV, p. 2B, line 56, house 39.

Edward Frederick Theador LEIBRICH, d. May 16, 1910, 8 p.m., Village of Bay, Cuyahoga County, Ohio; b. April, 1848, Barvaria *(Bavaria)*, 63 yrs., 1 month, 12 days; Single, occup. Farmer; fr. ***John LEIBRICH***, b. Barvaria; mo. ***Margaret HEINLEIN***, b. Barvaria; informant *Miss Matilda HASSLER*. I hereby certify, that I attended deceased from Jan 1st 1908 to May 15th, 1910 that I last say him alive on May 14th, 1910. Cause of death Organic Disease of heart with enlargement of ? and dropsy. Duration 2 yrs.; Geo. C. Lathrop, Dover, O.; burial Bay Village, May 16, 1910; Undertaker Jas. A. Pease & Son., Dover, Ohio. Ohio Certificate of Death, Division of Vital Statistics, 1910, certif. 2516 7 and Bureau of Vital Statistics, Burial or Removal Permit, Bay Village, OH.

LIEBERICH-Theodore, Sunday, May 15. Funeral Tuesday, May 17, from North Dover M.E. church at 2 p.m. Take 1 p.m. car to stop 32. Cem. rec. 4/3/1848-5/15/10, age 62, Lakeside Cem., Bay Village, Ohio. Cleveland Necrology File, May 17, 1910.

Theodore LEBERICK *(sp.)*; res. Bay Village; German; interred May 15, 1910; Lot 42. "List of Interments," Lakeside Cemetery, Bay Village, OH.

Theodore LIEBERICH late of the twp. of Dover…died on or about May 15th 1910 leaving no widow and the following persons named as next of kin - Sisters in Germany: ***Laura HETZEL*** and ***Amalia HOEFLICH***; ***Robert HASSLER***, nephew and ***Matilda HASSLER***, niece of 9924 So. Boulevard; Nephews and nieces and children of ***Ernst LIEBERICH*** deceased brother of descendent in Germany: ***Hans LIEBERICH, Laura L. KOPPEL, Frieda L. SCHNITZLEIN, Lena L. DORN, Matilda L. WAGLEIN, Oscar LIEBERICH*** all of Germany; Nephews and nieces and children of ***Fred LIEBERICH*** deceased brother of decedent in Germany: ***Rodolph, Ludwig*** and ***Louisa LIEBERICH*** and ***Matilda LIEBERICH KOBERLIN***; nephews and niece and children of ***Matilda HETZEL*** deceased sister of decedent in Germany: ***Augusta H. VOLKHARDT*** and ***Karl HETZEL***. Signed May 21, 1910, Cleveland. He left approximately Forty seven Hundred dollars in money, bank note and mortgage and 15 ½ acres of land in Bay Village valued at Forty five Hundred dollars. Robert Hassler and Matilda Hassler were to receive One Hundred Dollars ($100.00) each in addition to the second provision providing for the above mentioned assets to be split. Signed 1 March 1902. Cuyahoga County, OH, Probate Court Estate Case File, 53036.

Lot 43 *Owner: C. Osborn*

Mrs. Lovisa Edson purchased this lot on Sept 5, 1880 for $5.25 and resold to Clayton Osborn. SL *Calvin Riley Edson was originally buried here and then moved to another cemetery. Refer to section providing information on those who were moved.*

Lot 43-20 Fritz Hassler

FRITZ HASSLER
1840-1892

HASSLER, Fred, d. Oct 24, 1892, Cleveland, single, 32 yrs. *(age discrepancy)*, male, occup. Baker, rel. Prot., b. Germany, fr. ***Geo. HASSLER***, mo. ***Justina***, disease cancer, res. 175 Alabarna?, Cleveland, Cuy. Co., O., undertaker F. Beilstein, bur. Lot 42, Lake Side, rec. June 19, 1893. Probate Court Death Records, Cuyahoga County, Ohio, vol. 7, p. 12905.

HASSLER, Fritz, 1840-1892, age 52, Lakeside Cemetery, Cleveland, Ohio, cem. rec. Cleveland Necrology File, Roll 35.

Lot 43-21 Osborn Marker

OSBORN
BESSIE R. CLAYTON
1873-1897 1873-1911
JOHN E.
1897-1962

Lot 43-21 Bessie Repp Osborn

Bessie died in April, shortly after the birth of their son, John, in March of 1897. Clayton, her husband, would die of heart failure when John was only fourteen years old. Gladys, who died at the age of six months, may have been their first child,.

Bessie OSBORN, 23; res. West Dover; interred April 22, 1897; Lot 43. "List of Interments," Lakeside Cemetery, Bay Village, OH.

The State of Ohio, Cuyahoga County, ss. I Certify that on the 9th day of July 1895 ***Mr. Clayton S. OSBORN*** and ***Miss Bessie K. REPP*** were by me legally joined in marriage. Rev. Livingston Taylor. ***S.F. OSBORN*** having made application for a Marriage License for Clayton S. Osborn and Bessie K. Repp of said County. S.F. Osborn. Marriage Record, Cuyahoga County, OH, vol. 42, p. 322.

Lot 43-21 Clayton Selden Osborn

Clayton was the son of Samuel Osborn and Mary Crocker (OP 5:6).

The remains of ***Clayton OSBORN***, who died of heart failure, aged 38, at St. John's hospital, Cleveland, were brought to Bay Village, Saturday afternoon and interred in Lakeside cemetery by the side of his wife and infant daughter. Evening Telegram, Elyria, OH, Wednesday, June 28, 1911, p. 6, col. 1.

Clayton Selden OSBORN, d. June 23, 1911, St. John Hosp., Cleveland, Cuy. Co. of Mitral regurgitation and Acute dilatation of heart for 11 mos.; b. June 9, 18*(blank)*, Dover, Ohio, 38 yrs., 13 days; widowed, occup. Machinist; fr. ***Samuel OSBORN***, b. Dover, mo. ***Mary CROCKER***, b. Dover; burial Bay Village, June 24, 1911, undertaker James A. Pease, Dover, O. Ohio Certificate of Death, Division of Vital Statistics, 1911, certif. 31717.

OSBORN-Clayton Seldon, at St. John's Hospital, Thursday, June 22. Interment at Bay Village. Services private. Cleveland Necrology File, June 23, 1911, roll 62. *Date contradicts death certificate.*

Clayton OSBORN, 38; res. Cleveland; interred June 24, 1911; Lot 43. "List of Interments," Lakeside Cemetery, Bay Village, OH.

Clayton S. OSBORN, Mit. Regurg., issued June 23, 1911, by C.E. Ford, M.D. Bureau of Vital Statistics, Burial or Removal Permit, Bay Village, OH.

Lot 43-21 Gladys Osborn

The obituary of Clayton Selden Osborn states that his infant daughter is buried next to her mother, Bessie.

Gladys OSBORN, 6 mo.; res. Dover; October 31, 1896 *(written after 1897 date, directly below Bessie)*; Lot 43. "List of Interments," Lakeside Cemetery, Bay Village, OH.

Lot 43-21 John Eldin Osborn

Son of Clayton Osborn and Bessie Repp:

John Eldon OSBORN, b. 1897, d. 1962, m. ***Fern*** ___; *Issue:* ***Jack***, deceased; ***Rex***, res. Cuyahoga Falls, O. Fern may have married someone in the Carter Lumber family. Ronal d G. Osborn

Possible: ***John OSBORN***, 24, Roomer, b. Ohio, fr. b. Ohio, mo. b. Ohio; laborer at U.S. Express Co. 1920 FC OH Franklin Co., City of Columbus, Precinct A, West 4th Avenue, dwelling 53, family 60, ED 259, p. 3A. Enumerated Jan 8, 1920. *John's age would have been 23 at the time, there were no other John Osborn's or Osborne's close in age in the 1920 census.*

John Eldin OSBORN, d. 12 May 1962, between 12 M & 6:00 A, 503 West Fourth St., Dayton, Montgomery County, Ohio. Residence 503 W. Fourth St., divorced, b. 3-9-97, Dover, Ohio, 65 yrs. old.; fr. ***Clayton OSBORN***, mo. ***Bessie REPP***. Occup. Retired, Kind of business or industry Gentile Air Depot. Was deceased in U.S. Armed Forces? Yes, War #1. Informant Marion E. Pease, 2940 Dover Rd., Westlake, O. Cause of death Cerebral anoxia, natural death. Burial cremation 5/18/62, Sunset Crematory, Columbus, Ohio. Funeral Firm R.L. Ullmer & Son, 3701 W. 3rd St., Dayton, Ohio. Ohio Certificate of Death, Division of Vital Statistics, 1962, certif. 38909.

John was employed at the Gentile Air Force Depot according to his death certificate:

The former Johnson flying school site in Wilmington was taken over by the United States military in 1944. Opened as an Army Signal Corps storage facility, the field was renamed Gentile Air Force Depot in 1951 in honor of *Major Don (Dominic) S. GENTILE*, a World War II flying ace from Piqua, Ohio. Today the facility is commonly identified as DESC, which stands for the Defense Electronic Supply Center, its last main tenant. In 1993 DESC was placed on a list of military bases to be closed. The city of Kettering, is spearheading redevelopment of the vacated 135 acre property. Mary Ann Johnson, A Field Guide to Flight: On the Aviation Trail in Dayton, Ohio, p. 130.

On the death certificate for John Eldin Osborn it is stated that he served in World War I. It is believed that this information is incorrect. It was not necessary for those employed at the Air Force Base to be in the armed service. The following records were checked by the Veterans' Memorial Affairs Office in Cleveland, Ohio which failed to produce evidence of his service: VSC records, VA Administration, Recorder's Office, and the Governor's Office in Columbus, Ohio. Laurene Rutkowski, Veteran's Memorial Affairs, Cleveland, OH.

OSBORN, John E., 64, of 503 West Fourth Street, Saturday (Ullmer & Son). Dayton Journal Herald, May 15, 1962, p. 30, col. 2.

"The Cradle - The ballot box of our pioneer mothers: They voted 'early and often,' and always carried the election."

Toast by L. H. Johnson at the eleventh Cahoon Celebration 1870.

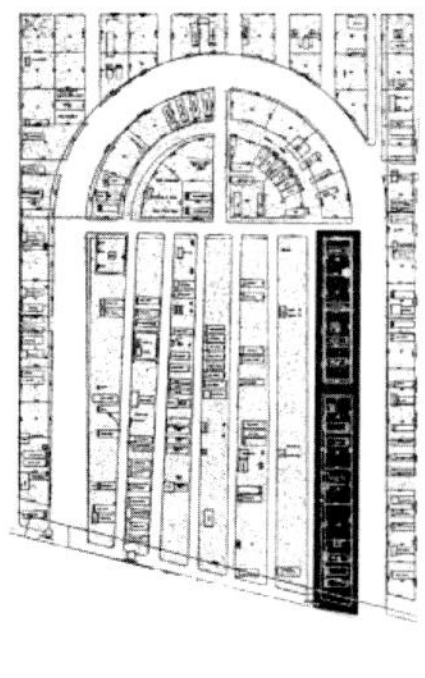

The following lots are in the central section of the cemetery surrounded on three sides by a car path in a horseshoe ring. Lot 44 is directly west of Lot 43 on the other side of the path. These lots start at the southern end and proceed north toward Lake Erie.

Lot 44 *Owner: Hiram Burlingame of Rockport purchased Oct 1, 1879, for $5.89* SL

Lot 44-1

Assumed marker for Gilbert Burlingame.

BROTHER

Lot 44-2

Assumed marker for Hiram Burlingame.

FATHER

Lot 44-3

Assumed marker for Rebecca Burlingame.

MOTHER

Lot 44-4 Burlingame Monument south

(Top appears to be missing.)

HIRAM BURLINGAME
BORN 1809
DIED JULY 18, 1891
AGED 82 YRS.
REBECCA,
1813-1902
GILBERT,
1844-1900
BURLINGAME

WASHINGTON
1837-1925
HELEN V.
1846-1930
LEWIE
1865-1918
ELMER

Lot 44-4 Hiram Burlingame

The State of Ohio, Cuyahoga County, ss. This certifies that I have this day united in marriage ***Hiram BURLINGAME*** and ***Rebecca GANT*** by virtue of a license from the Clerk of the Court of Common pleas. Feby 18th 1836, Genye? Hoadley, Justice of the Peace. Marriage Record, Cuyahoga County, OH, vol. 3, p. 201.

The State of Ohio, Cuyahoga County ss. before me *Aaron ALDRICH* one of the town Justices of the peace for said County personally came *George GOIT* who being duly sworn according to Law deposeth and Faith that on the first day of June 1835 in the County of Cuyahoga ***Hiram BURLINGAME*** did meet him in the highway of Dover between the dwelling of *Adin LINTY* and *Anania BROWNS*, and did there violently lay hands on, and strike him and this *(deposition)* says that Hiram Burlingame is guilty of the fact charged and further this *(deponent)* saith not sworn to and *(subsen.)* before me at the County *(aforsaid)* this first day of June 1835. George G. Gout. *(words difficult to decipher)* Aaron Aldrich Papers Collection, File 3-36, Rose Hill Museum, Bay Village, OH.

BURLINGAME, Hiram, 41, sailor, b. Vermont; ***Rebecca***, 37, b. Vermont; ***Charlotte***, 10 *(incorrect age)*; ***Gilbert***, 6; ***Jasper***, 12; ***Ira***, 10; ***Helen***, 5; all children b. O.; *Jesse GANT*, 60, occup Mason, b. Mass; ***Ira***, 26, sailor, b. Ohio. 1850 FC OH CYDO, p. 214B, lines 34-42, house 3711.

Hiram BURLINGAME, 51, Sailor, b. Vt.; ***Rebecca***, 49, b. Vt.; ***Charlotte***, 23; ***Casper***, 21; ***Ira***, 19, ***Gilbert***, 14, ***Hellen***, 13; all children, b. Ohio. 1860 FC OH CY Rockport, p. 9, lines 33-39, house 67.

BURLINGAME, Hiram, 71, farmer, b. Vermont, parents b. Vermont; ***Rebbecca*** *(sp.)*, 68, b. Vermont, parents b. Vermont. 1880 CY Rockport 319B, lines 11-12, house 153.

BURLINGHAM, Hiram, d. July 18, 1891, Rockport, 82 yrs. 24d., male, white, occup sailor, rel P., b. Ruthland *(Rutland)*, Vermont, fr. ***Rufas***, mo. ***Emma***, disease old age, clergy Barth, Lake Side Cemetery. Probate Court Death Records, Cuyahoga County, Ohio, vol. 5, p. 5735.

Ancestors of Hiram Burlingame:

I. Our first American Ancestor, ***Roger BURLINGHAM***, son of ***Thomas and Elizabeth (HOWARD) BURLINGHAM***, was born in Kent Co., Eng. Jan 24, 1620, died Mashantatack (Cranston), RI on Sept 1, 1718. At the age of 16 he enlisted in the British Army… he held the rank of Captain. About 1646 he married ***Jacolyn HUNTINGDON*** and to them was born a son, born in 1648. …He was ordered to America and he landed with his troops at Boston, Mass., May 10, 1650. Soon after reaching America, he resigned… and went up to the Connecticut Colony for the purpose of purchasing a farm, with the intention of bringing his wife and son to America, only to learn that his wife had died in the meantime… The name Burlingame is a corruption of the English Burlingham… He and *Thomas GRIFFIAN* purchased 100 acres of land, Feb 16, 1656 at Pequot (now New London), Conn… Roger Burlingame and his family were of the Quaker faith… Roger married secondly, Warwick, R.I. Oct 3, 1663 ***Mrs. Mary (LIPPITT) BARLINGSTONE***, (b. Providence Plantations, Mar 3, 1643, d. Mashantatack, R.I. July 5, 1718, dau. of ***John*** and ***Martha LIPPITT***). Mary's first husband had drowned while fishing six weeks after they married. Mary's father was involved in the original organization for the state of Rhode Island. Roger and Mary would have children. Burlingame Manuscript, Rhode Island Historical Society Library, Providence, RI, vol. 1, pp. 2, 7.

II. ***John BURLINGAME***, son of Roger Burlingame and Mary Lippitt Barlingstone, was b. Warwick, R.I. Aug 1, 1664; d. Warwick, June 24, 1719; m. his first cousin at Warwick, Nov 19, 1688, ***Mary Knowles LIPPITT***, (b. Warwick c1666, d. Cranston, R.I. Jan 13, 1708, dau. of ***Moses LIPPITT*** and ***Mary KNOWLES***). They had nine children, the third oldest was John. Burlingame Manuscript, vol. 1, p. 8, #2 .

III. ***John BURLINGAME***, son of John Burlingame and Mary Lipid; b. Cranston, R.I., 1690; died in Cranston, Feb 12, 1755; m. c1710 to ***Sarah BRIGGS*** (b. 1688, d. Cranston June 4, 1763, dau. of ***Daniel*** and ***Lydia BRIGGS***). John and Lydia had seven children, the oldest was John. Burlingame Manuscript, vol. 1, p. 17, #14.

IV. ***John BURLINGAME***, son of John Burlingame and Sarah Briggs; b. Cranston, R.I. June 6, 1712; d. Cumberland, R.I. July 5, 1786; m. at Providence, R.I. Apr 28, 1738 to ***Elizabeth (Betsy) PLIMPTON***, dau. of ***Jeremiah PLIMPTON*** of Attleboro, Mass. They had at least nine children, the youngest being John. Burlingame Manuscript, vol. 1, p. 36, #77.

V. ***John BURLINGAME***, son of John Burlingame and Elizabeth Plimpton; b. Cumberland, R.I., 1760; d. Ira, Vt. 1822; m. ***Esther HARMON*** (b. Suffield, Conn. 1762, dau. of ***Nehemiah HARMON*** and ***Abigail NORTON***). They had at least seven children, the second being Rufus. Burlingame Manuscript, vol. 1, p. 79, #312.

VI. ***Rufus BURLINGAME***, son of John Burlingame and Esther Harmon; b. Ira, Rutland Co., Vt., c1786; d. Defiance, Co., O., Nov 4, 1855; m. ***Eunice***__, (b. c1786, d. Defiance., O. Jan 12, 1863). Resided Vermont, Mass., Penns. and Ohio and is said to have had a large family. Known issue: ***William***, d. Geneva, O. 1892; ***Hiram***, b. 1809, d. Rocky River, O.; ***Henry H.***, b. May 16, 1818, d. Nov 26, 1886; ***Edwin Rufus***, b. Aug 8, 1823, d. Nov 19. 1899. Burlingame Manuscript, vol. 2, p. 174, #856.

Rufus J. BURLINGAME, b. 1786 in VT; bap. Ira (VT) Baptist Church, 25 Dec 1808; d. 4 Nov 1855, Ira, VT (family bible); m. to ***Eunice***, (bap. Ira (VT) Baptist Church 18 Dec 1808; d. 12 Jan 1863 (family bible)). *Issue:* ***Henry H.*** b. 16 May 1818 (tombstone and family bible); d. 27 Nov 1886, Sheridan Twp., Calhoun, Michigan; bur. Marengo, Calhoun, Michigan. (County Records 2:61); m. 31 Jan 1846 to *Cornelia Melvina HUTCHINS* (b. 20 Oct 1825, New York; d. 1 Dec 1891, Sheridan; bur. Marengo). ***Hiram***, b. 1809. ***Edwin Rufus***, b. 1823. ***William***. Carlene DeMaso

VII. ***Hiram BURLINGAME***, son of Rufus and Eunice Burlingame, born Ira, Vt. 1809, died Rocky River, O. Married ***Rebecca***, born in Vt. 1813, died. 1850 resided Newberry Town, Cuyahoga Co., O. and gave his occupation as sailor. Known issue: ***Washington; Esther; L***__*.;* ***Jasper*** b. 1838; ***Charlotte*** b. 1840, m. *MCMAHON*; ***Ira*** b. 1840; ***Gilbert*** b. 1844, d. He was on deed list in 1873 for Avon Township, Lorain Co., O. ***Helen*** b. 1847. Burlingame Manuscript, vol. 3, p. 317A-B, #2129.

The above reference lists Hiram and Rebecca as having eight children. The census record for 1850 lists only five and the 1900 census reports Rebecca gave birth to five. Hiram and Rebecca married in 1836 according to the record that follows and the first date of birth recorded above is for Jasper in 1838. The names of the oldest children have no dates for birth or death. Washington ELMER was the name of Helen's husband, Lewis (L) was her son's name and Esther was the name of Gilbert's wife. Therefore it is thought that there was a mistake made by the compiler of this manuscript for Hiram's descendants, including their children's spouses and child as their own children.

Brother of Hiram Burlingame:

William BURLINGAME, b. Mass.; d. 1892, Geneva, Ashtabula Co., OH; arrived Lorain Co. 1836, moved Ashtabula Co. 1870; m. ***Melissa BAKER***, b. abt 1818, Penn.; d. 5 May 1865, Sheffield Twp., Lorain Co., OH, age 47 yrs., 17 d.; bur. 1865 Garfield Cem. *Issue:* ***Thomas Corwin BURLINGAME***, b. 22 Dec 1846, Sheffield Twp.; d. 1912; bur Ridgelawn Cem., crypt 55 east; m. 28 Nov 1871, Sheffield to *Eva M. BEMIS* (dau. of *Uriel Moore BEMIS* and *Mary STANDEN*; b. 22 Dec. 1853; bur. Ridgelawn Cem., crypt 56, east). ***Sarah BURLINGAME,*** m. *William SMITH.* ***Henry C. BURLINGAME***, d. 5 yrs.; bur. 1868 Elmwood (interment from Garfield Cem.), Sect. B, Lot 20, #0111. ***Eunice BURLINGAME*** m. *Daniel BALL.* ***Maria BURLINGAME*** m. *Harry PACKHAM.* ***Lucy BURLINGAME*** m. *B. SHAW.* ***William BURLINGAME.*** ***Martha BURLINGAME*** m. *BRAINARD.* ***Mina BURLINGAME***, m. *BRAINARD*; bur. 1886, Sect. B., Lot 20, Gr. 3, Elmwood Cem., age 14. Cheryl A. Bakker and Garfield Cemetery, Sheffield, Ohio as read by Catherine Burke Flament.

Children of Hiram Burlingame and Rebecca Gant:

The State of Ohio, Cuyahoga County, ss. I Certify that on the 27th day of Dec, 1866 ***Mr. Jasper M. BURLINGAME*** and ***Miss Sarah M. JACKSON*** were by me legally joined in marriage. Lewis Burton Marriage Record, Cuyahoga County, OH, vol. 13, p. 125.

BURLINGAME, Jasper M. 10/31/1858 *(Winnagle states1838)* - 8/20/1908. ***BURLINGAME, Sarah M***, d. 7/23/1921 (same plot). Oakwood Cemetery, Warren, Trumbull Co., OH. The area was formerly Howland Twp. Mrs. Roscoe Winnagle recorded Cemetery inscriptions in the 1920's. Trumbull County Cemetery Inscriptions, 1800-1930, p. 127.

The State of Ohio, Cuyahoga County, ss. I Certify that on the 13th day of May, 1878 ***Mr. Ira BURLINGAME*** and ***Miss Mary A. GREEN*** were by me legally joined in marriage. A.M. Wagar, J.P. Marriage Record, Cuyahoga County, OH, vol. 1, p. 428.

Lot 44-4 Rebecca Gant Burlingame

BURLINGAME, Rabecka, 86, head, b. July 1813, widow…5 children born, 4 living, owns house free of mortgage; ***Ira***, son, b. Dec 1840, widower, Ohio, mail carrier; owned house. 1900 FC OH CYRR 13A, lines 24-25, dwelling 263.

Rebecca BURLINGAME, 88; res. Rocky River; interred Feb 1, 1902; Lot 44. "List of Interments," Lakeside Cemetery, Bay Village, OH.

Rebecca BURLINGAME'S will, executor ***Washington ELMER***, Lake Rd, Rocky River Hamlet, Ohio. The following bill was included:

J.A.Mastick, Furniture and Undertaking

1 Casket	$50.00
Outside box	2.00
Three carriages	17.00
Notice in paper	1.00
Rushing and Chiffon	1.25
Hearse	6.00
Sickle of flowers	3.75
Burial of Rebecca Burlingame	$81.00

Family members listed in the will are: ***Jasper BURLINGAME***, son, Mineral Ridge, O.; ***Helen V. ELMER***, daughter; ***Ira BURLINGAME***, son; grandsons: ***Frank BURLINGAME***; ***Harry BURLINGAME***, minor over 14; ***Burt BURLINGAME***, minor under 14; ***Mace BURLINGAME***, minor under 14; granddaughters: ***Mabel BURLINGAME***; ***Minnie BURLINGAME***; ***Florence BURLINGAME***, minor over 14; ***Lattie DRAKE***, East Saginaw, Mich. All of the above were listed as living in Rocky River, Ohio, unless stated otherwise. Cuyahoga County, OH, Probate Court Estate Case File, 27327.

Lot 44-4 Gilbert H. Burlingame

The State of Ohio, Cuyahoga County, ss. I Certify, That on the 18th day of November, 1869 ***Mr. Gilbert H. BURLINGAME*** and ***Miss Etty GREEN*** were by me, legally joined in Marriage. D. Dean, J.P. Marriage Record, Cuyahoga County, OH, vol. 15, p. 324.

BURLINGAME, Gilbert H., 55, b. Sept 1844, Ohio, parents b. Vermont, fisherman, married 31 yrs.; ***Esther J.***, 50, wife, b. Feb 1850, Ohio, fr. b. New York, mo. b. Germany, 9 children born, 7 living; ***Mable C.***, 22, b. Aug 1877, laundress; ***Harry D.***, 16, b. Sept 1883, section hand; ***Florence A.***, 12, b. May 1888; ***Mace J.***, 10, b. Aug 1889; ***Gilbert H.***, 8, Jan 1892, ***Winnefred***, 2, b. May 1898, all children born in Ohio; *KEMPHER, William*, 33, b. May 1867, Ohio, parents b. Germany, single, boarder, section hand; *SOUDEGOAD, Fred*, 19, b. June 1880, Denmark, parents b. Denmark, single, boarder, plower hand; renting house. 1900 FC OH CYRR, p. A11, lines 37-47, house 223.

Gilbert BURLINGAME, 56; res. Rocky River; interred Dec 10, 1899 *(year discrepancy)*; Lot 44. "List of Interments," Lakeside Cemetery, Bay Village, OH.

Gilbert H. BURLINGAME, late, of the Village of Rocky River, died on the 7th of Dec 1900 leaving; ***Esther J.***, widow…; ***Minnie E.A. LAMBERSON***, daughter, 22; … Cuyahoga County, OH, Probate Court Estate Case File, 23965.

Wife of Gilbert Burlingame, Esther Green:

Esther J. BURLINGAME, April 15, 1926, 6 p.m., 19228 Detroit Rd., Rocky River, Cuyahoga Co., Ohio of Chronic Myocarditis; widowed, husband ***Gilbert BURLINGAME***; b. Feb 25, 1870, Cleveland, Ohio; fr. ***Daniel GREEN***, b. Ohio, mo. ***Caroline DEGG***, b. Germany; 56 yrs. 1 mo. 21 days; housewife; Informant *Mable HAYES*, Detroit, Michigan; bur. Fairview Village, undertaker Leimkuehler, 6722 Franklin Ave. Ohio Certificate of Death, Division of Vital Statistics, 1926, certif. 22009.

Children of Gilbert Burlingame and Esther Green:

Gilbert H. BURLINGAME, 22, res. Lakewood, O., b. same, occup. Iceman, fr. *G.H.*, mo. *Esther J. GREEN*. Married ***Fern MAC LEAN***, 19, res. Lakewood, O., b. Detroit, Mich., occup. none, fr. *William*, mo. *Mary HYSLOP*; neither previously married. Marriage to be solemnized by Rev. Morreshead, Lkwd., the State of Ohio, Cuyahoga County, ss. I Certify, That on the 27th day of July 1915 Mr. Gilbert H. Burlingame and Miss Fern MacLean were by me legally joined in marriage. Rev. Joseph Mottershead *(The name is spelled differently than earlier in the record)*. Marriage Record, Cuyahoga County, OH, vol. 93, p. 341.

Mabel C. BURLINGAME, 29, res. Rocky River, O., b. do *(same)*, occup. none, fr. *Wm.? BURLINGAME*, mo. *Hester* (c.u.u.), previously married none. Married to ***Herbert R. Hays***, 40, res. 384 Prospect St., b. Galion, O., occup. bartender, fr. *Wm. HAYS*, mo. *Susan SEAGER*, married previously once. The State of Ohio, Cuyahoga County, ss. I Certify that on the 30th day of Sept 1905 Herbert R. Hays and Mabel C. Burlingame were legally married by Rev. Charles Bayard Mitchell. Marriage Record, Cuyahoga County, OH, vol. 62, p. 1.

Mace BURLINGAME, 34, res. 2935 Woodland Ave., b. Rocky River, occup. Chauffeur, fr. *Gilbert*, m. *Esther GREEN*, previously married Once, Div. 3-30-23 C. P. Ct. Married ***Mayme STIER***, 35, res. 3397 E. 130th St., b. Cleveland, O., occup. Clerk, fr. *Mathew WINTRICH*, mo. *Anna BASTGEN*, Previously married once, married name *STIER*, dec'd. The State of Ohio, Cuyahoga County, ss. I Certify, That one the 16th day of June 1923 Mace Burlingame and Mayme Stier were by me legally joined in marriage. W.J.Soul, J.P. Marriage Record, Cuyahoga County, OH, vol. 130, p. 465.

Lot 45 *Owner: Hellen of Rockport* (Helen V. Elmer?) *purchased Oct 1, 1879, for $5.25* SL

Lot 45-5 Washington Elmer

WASHINGTON

Declaration for Pension 23rd day of Feby. 1907/23rd day of June 1921…***Washington ELMER***, of Rocky River… enrolled at Sackets Harbor, Jefferson County, New York State *(with Capt. Lt. J. S. Evans - 1925 paper)*…on the 19th day of August 1862 as a Private in Company I, 10th Regiment, N.Y. Heavy Artillery…in the Civil War and was HONORABLY DISCHARGED at Washington, D.C. on the 2d of June 1865. Personal description at enlistment: Height 5 feet 10 inches; complexion dark, color of eyes grey; color of hair dark, that his occupation was farming, born Jan 27th, 1837 at Jefferson Co., NY. He lived in Jefferson Co., NY after leaving the service til 1866 and since that time in Rocky River, Ohio...Received a pension of $12.00 in 1907. Disability in 1921: Bad eye sight, crippled, and old age. Signature: X (his mark) *(Another paper states family records concerning his birth have been destroyed and there are no church records).* Civil War Pension File, National Archives, Certificate 474 468 No. 607 610.

General Affidavit for Pension. By *Frederick J. TUTTLE*, 44, Rocky River, 9th April 1889. ***Washington ELMER***...is a farmer and laborer by occupation, and from that year (1867) to the present has resided in his immediate neighborhood. When he first saw claimant in 1867 he was suffering from disease of kidneys and bladder...was weak and emaciated, had pains in his back...and he has continued to so suffer up to the present time. That in consequence of said disabilities... claimant has been unable to any time since 1867, to perform more than one-fourth as much labor as a sound able-bodied man. Civil War Pension File, National Archives, Certificate 474 468 No. 607 610.

The State of Ohio, Cuyahoga County, SS. I certify that on the 12 day of August 1869 ***Mr. Washington ELMER*** and ***Miss Hellen BURLINGAME*** were, by me, legally joined in Marriage. I.A. Thome, Min Marriage Record, Cuyahoga County, OH, vol. 15, p. 219.

Neither ***Washington*** or ***Helen*** were previously married. Helen Elmer

When and where were you married? ...Cleveland, O. by J.A. Thoms, Pastor of First Congreg. Church. Washington Elmer July 9, 1915, Civil War Pension File, National Archives, Certificate 474 468 No. 607 610.

ELMER, Washington, 40, laborer, b. New York, parents b. New York; ***Hellen***, 34, wife, b. Ohio, parents b. Vermont; ***Louis***, 15, son, at home, b. Ohio. 1880 FC OH CYRP, p. 319D, lines 13-15, house 154.

Washington ELMER, 19217 Lake Rd., Rocky River, Cuyahoga Co., Oct 16, 1925, 7 p.m., Broncho-Pneumonia for 3ds., Contributory Myocarditis; married ***Helen V. ELMER***; Retired; b. Jan 27/37, New York State, fr. ***Jonathan ELMER***, b. Vermont, mo. b. Vermont; 88 yrs. 8 mos. 20 ds.; informant *Helen V. ELMER*; bur. Cahoon Cemetery, Oct 19, 1925, undertaker William Daniel's, 15800 Detroit. Ohio Certificate of Death, Division of Vital Statistics, 1925, certif. 55698.

ELMER-Washington, beloved husband of ***Helen V.,*** age 88 years, Friday, Oct 16. Services at late residence, 19217 Lake road, Rocky River, Monday, Oct 19, at 2 p.m. Burial private. Cleveland Necrology File, Oct 18, 1925, roll 23.

Washington ELMER...retired, rel. Christian, b. Jan 27, 1837, fr. ***John ELMER***, b. Vermont, mo. unknown, interment Cahoon Cemetery, Grey Hearse. Record of Funeral, Busch-Saxton-Parker-Daniels.

Parents of Washington Elmer:

Jonathan ELMER came to Jefferson County about 1819 or '20 at that time being 16 or 17 years of age. He worked out among the farmers until his marriage with ***Cynthia CARPENTER***, when he located at Sackets Harbor, a few years later removing to Pillar Point, in the town of Brownville, where he engaged in boat building and carpentering. He subsequently engaged in farming, and died in this town in January, 1855. His wife died in 1887.

They had 13 children, viz.; ***Silas M., Minerva, William M., Melissa, Washington R., Wellington H., Roxanne, Adelaide, Arvilla, Elvira, Ruth, Alice***, and ***Edward B***. (Twelve of these attained maturity.) Geographical Gazetteer of Jefferson County, NY 1684-1890, Town of Brownville, 1890, page 295.

John ELMER, 78, b. VT, Farmer, fr. b, VT, mo. b. VT; ***Syntha ELMER***, b. NY, 66, wife, fr. b. NY, mo. b. NY. 1880 FC NY Jefferson, Brownville., p. 161C.

Lot 45-6 Helen Burlingame Elmer

HELEN V.

Daughter of Hiram Burlingame and Rebecca Gant (Lot 44-4).

Helen Viola BURLINGAME was born February 26, 1846 at Cleveland, Ohio. Helen Elmer, Civil War Pension File, National Archives, Certificate 474 468 No. 607 610.

Helen V. ELMER, d. Aug 18, 1930, 1:30 a.m., Rocky River, Cuy Co., Myocarditis from 1/11/1930; res. 19127 Lake Rd., widow of ***Washington ELMER***; b. Feb 26, 1856 *(this year appears to be incorrect)*, Vermont, 84 yrs. 6 ms. 8 ds., housewife; fr. ***Hiram BUILINGAR*** *(sp.)*, b. Vermont, mo. ***Rebeca GOTT***, b. Vermont; informant Frank Stone, Lakewood, O., bur. Osborn *(Cemetery)* 8/20, 1930, undertaker Wm. Daniel's, 15800 Detroit, body embalmed. Ohio Certificate of Death, Division of Vital Statistics, 1930, certif. 46683.

Helen ELMER, died Aug 18, 1930, at home, 19127 Lake Rd., rel. Christian Church, b. Feb 26, 1---, fr. ***Hiram BURLINGAME***, b. Vermont, mo. ***Rebecca GOTT***, b. Vermont, bur. Osborn Cemetery. Record of Funeral, Wm. Daniels.

Helen V. ELMER, Rocky River, 84, Myocarditis, place of bur. Osborn *(Cemetery)*, undertaker Wm. Daniels, 15800 Detroit Ave., Lakewood, issued Aug 20, 1930. Bureau of Vital Statistics, Burial or Removal Permit, Bay Village, OH.

ELMER: Helen V., wife of the late ***Washington***, mother of the late ***Louie***, aunt of *Helen VOUBLER*, Monday morning. Services at residence, 19127 Lake Road, Rocky River, Wednesday, Aug 20, 1930, at 2 p.m. Cleveland Necrology File, August 20, 1930, roll 23.

Lot 44/45 Lewis Elmer

Lewis is listed on the official plot map being buried in Lot 44.

Dept. of the Interior, Bureau of Pensions, Ques. No. 5 Have you any children living? Yes, ***Lewis MCKENNA*** a child of my wife's *(Helen Burlingame)* born about Aug, 1864. Washington Elmer, Feby 9, 1898.
State name/birth of children: ***Lewie ELMER,*** born June 5, 1865. Adopted child now an invalid. Washington Elmer, July 9, 1915. Washington Elmer's Civil War Pension File, National Archives, Certificate 474 468 No. 607 610.

Lewie ELMER, Rocky River, Cuyahoga Co.; d. March 28, 1918, 8:30 p.m., Broncho-Pneumonia-2 ds., Contributory Epilepsy; b. Sept 5, 1865, Rocky River, fr. ***Washington ELMER***, b. New York, mo. ***Helen BURLINGAME***, b. Cleveland, Ohio; single; occup. none; 53 yrs. 6 mos. 13 ds.; bur. Cleveland Cremation, March 30, 1918; undertaker W.R. Daniels, 15800 Detroit Ave. Ohio Certificate of Death, Division of Vital Statistics, 1918, certif. 14883.

ELMER-Lewie, beloved son of ***Washington ELMER***, Thurs., March 28, at 8:30 p.m., aged 53 yrs. Funeral services from the late residence, Lake rd., Rocky River, Sat. March 30, at 1 p.m. Funeral private. Kindly omit flowers. Cem. rec. - 1918, age 53. Cleveland Crematory, Cleveland, Ohio. Cleveland Necrology File, March 30, 1918, roll 23.

Ashes of ***Lewis ELMER***, res. Rocky River, interred 1918, Lot 44. "List of Interments," Lakeside Cemetery, Bay Village, OH.

Lot 46 *Owner: Reuben Osborn purchased Nov 2, 1887, for $5.25* SL

Lot 46-7 Osborn Monument

OSBORN

REUBEN
OSBORN
1847-1919
EUNICE
CHADWICK
OSBORN
1846-1940
DAUGHTER
LUCY M.
OSBORN
1886-1955

Lot 46-7 Reuben Osborn

Reuben is the son of ***Selden OSBORN*** and ***Nancy RUPLE*** *(OP 5:8)*. He married ***Eunice CHADWICK*** in 1870 and lived at 29202 Lake Rd. Reuben was the first mayor of Bay Village after it seceded from Dover. Reuben was the inventor of the "Flying Harness," used by firemen and hung from the ceiling to facilitate fast harnessing of horses for the fire wagon. Their children were ***George, Irving, Clare, Luella (Mrs. A. K. GLENDENNING)*** and ***Lucy***. Bay Village Historical Society, Bay Village: A Way of Life, pp. 16-17.

The State of Ohio, Cuyahoga County, ss. I Certify, That on the 21 day of April 1869 ***Mr. Ruben OSBORN*** and ***Miss Eunice CHADWICK*** were, by me legally joined in Marriage. H.B. Hall. Marriage Record, Cuyahoga County, OH, vol. 15, p. 164.

OSBORN, Reuben, 32, Farmer, b. Ohio, fr. b. NY, mo. b. Ohio; ***Eunice***, 34, wife, b. Ohio, fr. b. Mass.; mo. b. Ohio; ***George***, 10, son, at school, b. Ohio; ***Luella***, 8, dau., b. Ohio; ***Clare M.***, 6, dau. *(son)*, b. Ohio; ***Irwin***, 2, son, b. Ohio; *UGAMEYER, Henry*, 16, servant; ***DODD, Bessie***, 16, servant, single, Domestic Servant *(dau. of Charles and Annie Dodd, OP 4:16)*. 1880 FC OH CYDO, p. 99A.

OSBORN, Reuben. Owned land; Acres: Improved - 35 tilled, including fallow and grass, 9 permanent meadow, Unimproved - 15 woodland. Farm Values: Land - $5000, Machinery - $150, Live Stock - $250. Cost of building and repairing in 1879: $100. Labor: Paid for wages in 1879 - $150. Weeks hired labor in 1879: 40. Estimated value of all farm production: $800. Grass lands: acreage: 4 mown, 14 not mown, 8 tons hay. 2 horses, 3 milch cows, 3 calves dropped, 1 purchased, 4 cattle sold living. 300 pounds of butter made on the farm. 32 sheep on hand June 1, 1880, 18 lambs dropped, 5 purchased, 15 sold living, 17 fleeces, weight: 90 lbs. 7 swine. 45 barnyard poultry on farm, 250 dozen eggs produced in 1879. Indian corn: 10 acres, 450 bushels; Oats: 3 acres, 150 bushels; wheat: 2 acres, 36 bushels; potatoes: 2 acres, 300 bushels. Orchards - apple: 2 acres, 125 bearing trees, 300 bushels; peaches: 1 acre, 40 bearing trees, 25 bushels. Total value of orchard products: $200. Vineyards: 1 acre. Amount of wood cut: 50 cords, Value of forest products - $550. "Schedule 2. Production of Agriculture in Dover Township, Cuyahoga County, OH," enumerated June, 1880, p. 33.

OSBORN, Rubin *(sp.)*, 52, b. Aug 1847, Ohio, occup. farmer, married 30 yrs.; ***Eunice***, 54, wife, b. Jan 1846, Ohio, fr. b. Mass, mo. b. Ohio, 5 children born and living; ***George***, 30, son, b. Jan 1870, occup. farm laborer; ***Clare***, 26, son, b. Mar 1874; ***Lucy***, 14, dau., b. Jan 1886, at school; all children born in Ohio; *HAGEDORN, Gus*, 22, farm laborer, b. Oct 1877, Ohio, parents b. Germany; own home free. 1900 FC OH CYDO, p. 21B, lines 80-85, house 462.

The first election for officers of the Hamlet of Bay was held on February 18th, 1903, at the office of the Oviatt Mfg. Co., pursuant to Proclamation issued by ***Reuben OSBORN*** and *Wm. O. MATHEWS*, authorized agents of the petitioners for the Hamlet of Bay. April 15th, Reuben Osborn was elected Mayor for the Village of Bay. Hamlet minutes, Record Book, Bay Village City Hall.

Reuben OSBORN was chosen first mayor and he held this office seven years. In an old scrap book I read that out of 110 voters 40 were candidates for office. Ferster, Louis F.,

"Tells of Pioneer Days in Dover, Bay Village," Suburban News and Herald, p. 8, col. 1, paper by Mrs. Rose Osborn.

The Osborn's were orchardists and marketed apples...The Osborns also did a lot of fishing as did most of the settlers. Osborn Collection, Rose Hill Museum, p. 5.

OSBORNE, Reuben, head, 63, married 40 yrs., b. Ohio; ***Eunice***, wife, 64, 5 children born and living; ***Lucy***, dau., 29, single, b. Ohio. 1910 FC OH CYDO, p. 3A, lines 7-9.

"Let us visit vintage homes"

The following is an excerpt from this article.

Available records tell little of ***Reuben OSBORN*** except that he ... developed a suspended harness for fire horses that was used for many years. *(Article written about Reuben OSBORN, his grandfather.)*

Meg Algren MARINO, the Press expert in residence on suspended harnesses, describes that contraption thusly:

"One of the major problems of early-day fire-fighting was getting to the fire before the fire burned out. It wasn't so much the time it took the horses to get there once they were harnessed as it was the harnessing itself. Sometimes this would take five to seven minutes.

"A suspended harness was developed that would be dropped down onto the horses standing in position in front of the fire engine. The horses were tied with breakaway halters and so well trained that they would leave their stalls when the bell rang, take their positions in front of the engine and wait for the harness to be lowered."

Whether it was Osborn's harness, or some variation of it, that came to be a fixture in American firefighting companies is not known. It is known that English fire crews were so impressed with the device that they sent experts over to study the Yankee technique. Julian Krawcheck, "Let us visit vintage homes," Cleveland Press, Press Magazine, first in the series, "Cleveland Historical Houses," Aug 24, 1976, p. A8.

DOVER LAKE

The one hundredth anniversary of the settling of the grandfather of the Osborns, at Dover lake, was celebrated at the home of ***Reuben OSBORN***, Wednesday, May 17th of the sixty-one remaining descendants forty-five were present. Evening Telegram, Elyria, OH, Thursday, May 25, 1911, p. 6, col. 2.

Reuben OSBORN, 72; res. Bay Village; interred June 16 *(date of death)*, 1919, Lot 46. "List of Interments." Lakeside Cemetery, Bay Village, OH.

Reuben OSBORN, Pernicious Anemia, issued June 19, 1919. Bureau of Vital Statistics, Burial or Removal Permit, Bay Village, OH.

OSBORN-Reubin, aged 73, husband of ***Eunice Frederick*** *(should read CHADWICK)*, passed away Monday, June 16. Funeral at residence, Lake road, Bay Village, O., at 2 p.m. Thursday. Cleveland Necrology File, June 18, 1919, roll 62.

Lot 46-7 Eunice Chadwick Osborn

OSBORN, Eunice, 73, widow, b. Ohio, fr. b. Massachusetts, mo. b. Ohio; ***Lucy***, daughter, 33, b. Ohio, parents b. Ohio; ***MEDDICK, Warren A.***, head, 31, b. Missouri, fr. b. Missouri, mo. b. Michigan, salesman for Engineering and Manufacturing; ***Mable*** *(sp.)*, 28, b. Ohio, fr. b. England, mo. b. Ohio; ***John W.***, 3 5/12 yrs., b. Ohio; ***Rose OSBORN***, mother-in-law, 61, widow, immigrated 1859?, Nat. by marriage, b. England, parents b. England. 1920 FC OH CYBV ED 509, p. 1B, Lake Road, lines 92-98.

Bay Women's Club

By Mrs. L.F. Ferster

A stage setting of antiques greeted the members of the Bay Village Women's Club at their last meeting, Thursday, November 14...The program was presented by the Literature group...*Mrs. F.W. DUTTON*, was dressed in a quaint old mustard color silk poplin, trimmed with brown taffeta - the wedding gown of ***Mrs. Eunice OSBORN***, and loaned by her for the occasion...

When ***Reuben OSBORN*** married Eunice Chadwick, sixty-one years ago next April, he brought his bride to the home of his grandfather, the lovely old white clapboard farm house, with green blinds, on the north side of Lake road, at Stop 30, where Mrs. Eunice Osborn still lives. Reuben's grandfather, also a ***Reuben OSBORN***, came west in a covered wagon, drawn by oxen, from Connecticut *(to Camden, NY in 1803 and Ohio in 1811)* - bringing his family with him, over the trackless forests, finally settling on the shores of Lake Erie, and building in 1811, a log cabin, which was replaced by the present home in 1814. Another grandson, ***David (DeForest)***, lived across the street, in a home which has grown large and rambling, after the fashion of old houses, comfortably adding a room or a wing, as the need of the family demanded - and his widow, ***Mrs. Rose OSBORN***, still lives in this other fine old home. Reuben Osborn *(grandson)*, was the first mayor of Bay Village, he and his brother David led the fight which separated the village from the township of Dover, and they helped form the government under which the village has prospered for twenty-five years.

...The Women's Club is proud to boast that Mrs. Eunice Osborn and her sister-in-law, Mrs. Rose *(Mitchell)* Osborn, are two of its staunchest supporters. So, Mrs. Dutton, in Mrs. Osborn's slim white wedding dress, with the jaunty brown taffeta trimmed basque, and stiffly full skirt, gave us an inspiring glimpse of the significance of the lives of all such sturdy families all over our country. Undetermined source, newspaper article provided by David O. Scott, Jr. c1928.

OSBORN, Eunice C., 84, own home valued at $25,000, no radio, widow, b. Ohio, fr. b. Mass., mo. b. Ohio; ***Lucy***, 44, daughter, single, b. Ohio, parents b. Ohio, no occup.; *DIMICK, Mildred*, 21, lodger, single, b. Ohio, parents b.

Ohio, occup. Stenographer Village Hall. 1930 FC OH CYBV, ED 18-534, 29202 Lake Road, p. 16B, lines 60-62.

Recipes shared by EuniceChadwick Osborn:

Best Johnny Cake

(Mrs. Reuben Osborn)

Three cups of sour milk, three tablespoons melted butter or fat, one-half cup of sugar, one egg, one teaspoon salt, three even teaspoons soda, one and one-half cups flour, one and one-half cups cornmeal, one even teaspoon baking powder in flour. Dissolve soda in a little water and add the last thing before it goes in the oven. The Village Cook Book, p. 19. (c1911-1915).

Salmon Loaf

1 can salmon	salt and pepper to taste
2 eggs	Milk
1 c. crackers	1/2 c. thin cream

Remove bones and fat from salmon. Save out one egg yolk. Crush crackers and mix well with the eggs and salmon, add enough milk to form a loaf. Bake 1/2 hr. When serving the loaf pour over it a sauce made from the liquor in the can, one egg yolk and cream, heat and thicken. Garnish with lemon and parsley.
Mrs. Reuben Osborn The Dover Cook Book, p. 10.

Widow of First Mayor of Bay Village Dies at 94

Death yesterday cut a link between Bay Village and the pioneer days of old when it took ***Mrs. Eunice Chadwick OSBORN*** in her 95th year. She was the oldest resident of the village.

Ill for 10 weeks, Mrs. Osborn died in the old family home at 29202 Lake road, which she had first entered as a bride 70 years ago and which had been built in 1814.

The oldest house between Cleveland and Lorain, it is a symbol of Mrs. Osborn's early life and the struggle of the country's early settlers. Bark still clings to the logs of the old rafters in the basement which is built on uncemented lake stones. The basement stairway is of black walnut.

Known as "Aunt Eunice" to almost every resident of Bay Village, Mrs. Osborn was active until her last illness. During the hard weather of the past winter she had walked every Sunday to services at the Bay Village Methodist Church.

Her mind retained its full powers through the years and she frequently recalled many of the early events in the village.

Among these were the great log jam when pine logs stretched out into Lake Erie as far as the eye could see when they jammed on their way down from Michigan to the mills in Cleveland. Expert lumbermen had to be called down from Saginaw, Mich., to break the million-foot jam.

She recalled the political fight when the village seceded from Dover on the issue of "taxation without representation." Her husband then became the first Bay Village mayor.

Those were in the days when she was known as a cook. The days when the family whose turn it was to provide the periodic church dinner did just that without any help. In those days she baked 40 pies and helped prepare other food for groups that numbered up to 125 persons.

Surviving the aged lady are her sons, ***George*** of Bay Village and ***Clare*** of Chicago; her daughters, ***Mrs. A. K. GLENDENNING*** and ***Lucy***, both of Bay Village; her sister, ***Mrs. Ada GADD*** of Ann Arbor, Mich.; seven grandchildren and seven great-grandchildren. Her late husband, ***Reuben***, served as mayor of Bay Village for seven years.

Services at 3 p.m. tomorrow will be at the Bay Village Methodist Church. Cleveland Press, August 23, 1940, undetermined page, cols. 2-3.

"AUNT EUNICE" OSBORN

(obituary)

...And she looked back with nostalgia to "harder times than we face now," to when all persons seemed to be kind, and the children with little enjoyed life to the deepest. She was a lifelong church worker. Until her death she would visit community centers to sew for the needy and until the end she baked home-made bread.

Of such stuff were our ancestors. And in these days when we feel we may have grown too soft as a people, it is good to review the conquering virtues of our pioneers. Undetermined newspaper article, Osborn Family File, Rose Hill Museum, Bay Village, OH.

MRS. EUNICE CHADWICK OSBORN

......Born on Cleveland's West Side *(Middleburg Hts. According to George's obituary)*, ***Mrs. OSBORN*** spent all her life in Greater Cleveland where she was active in Methodist Episcopal Church circles..... Aug 23, 1940, p. 12, col. 5. The Plain Dealer. All rights reserved. Reprinted with permission.

Eunice CHADWICK OSBORN, d. Aug 22, 1940, 9:30 a.m., Bay, Cuyahoga Co.; Chronic Myocarditis-1930, Myocardial failure-Aug 19, 1940, Gen. Arteriosclerosis-1920; res. 29202 Lake Road; widowed, husband ***Reuben***; b. Jan 5, 1846, Ohio, fr. ***Marshall CHADWICK***, b. Lee, Mass., mo. ***Jane STOCKING***, b. Dover Twp., Ohio; 94 yrs. 7 mos. 17 days, Hwf., informant *Lucy OSBORN*, Bay Village, Ohio RFD; bur. Bay Village, funeral firm Clifford Pease, Dover Center, Ohio. Ohio Certificate of Death, Division of Vital Statistics, 1940, certif. 48498.

Eunice Chadwick OSBORN, 94, died Aug 22, 1940 of Chronic Myocarditis, myocardial failure at 29202 Lake Rd, BV, undertaker Clifford Pease. Bureau of Vital Statistics, Burial or Removal Permit, Bay Village, OH.

OSBORN: Eunice CHADWICK, residence, 29202 Lake rd., Bay Village, wife of the late ***Reuben***, mother of ***George, Mrs. A. K. GLENDENNING, Clare, Irwin*** (deceased) and ***Lucy***, grandmother and great-grandmother. Services at Bay M.E. Church, Bassett and Lake rd., Saturday, Aug 24 at 3 p.m. Cleveland Necrology File, Aug 24, 1940, roll 62.

Maternal Grandparents of Eunice Chadwick Osborn:
Before "Grandma Osborn" married ***Reuben***, the second, she was ***Miss Eunice CHADWICK***, whose own grandmother and grandfather, ***Joseph*** and ***Jane STOCKING***, were among the early settlers of the village. Helen Allyn, "Home Weathers Storms of 118 Years," Cleveland Press, Oct 6, 1932, first page of the section, col. 5.

I. ***George STOCKING***, b. Suffolk, England about 1582, emigrated to America in 1633 and settled in Cambridge, Mass.; d. 25 May 1683, Hartford, Conn. at the age of 101; m.1 in England to ***Anna*** ____; m.2 ***Agnes SHOTWELL WEBSTER***, widow of *John WEBSTER*. George and Anna had four children, the oldest and only son being Samuel. George Stocking, The Stocking Ancestry, Comprising the Descendants of George Stocking Founder of the American Family, pp. 2, 3.

II. ***Deacon Samuel STOCKING***, b. England; emigrated with his father in 1633 and in 1650 removed from Hartford to Middletown, Conn. where he became one of its founders; d. 3 Dec 1683; m. 27 May 1652, ***Bethia HOPKINS*** (dau. of ***John*** and ***Jane HOPKINS*** and granddau. of ***Samuel HOPKINS***. one of the signers of the Mayflower Compact, in 1620). The sixth of their nine children was George. Stocking, pp. 3, 4.

III. ***George STOCKING***, b. 20 Feb 1664; d. 17 Feb 1714, buried in the old cemetery in Portland (originally East Middletown, later called Chatham), Conn.; m. ***Elizabeth*** ____(d. 16 Nov 1787, East Middletown, Conn.; m.2 *Deacon Samuel HALL*, of East Middletown) The oldest of their six children was Steven. Stocking, pp. 4, 6, 7.

IV. ***Steven STOCKING,*** b. 20 Aug 1694, d. 1789; m.1 1 July 1722 to ***Elizabeth HALL*** (from Portland, Conn.); m.2 24 Feb 1757 to widow ***Sarah ANDREWS*** (d. 29 July 1790). Steven resided in Chatham, Conn.; was commissioned ensign in militia in 1732. The oldest of the seven children of Steven and Elizabeth was Joseph. Stocking, pp. 6, 7.

V. ***Captain Joseph STOCKING,*** b. 28 June 1723; m. 1 Nov 1753 to ***Sarah SHEPHERD CORNWALL*** (b. 1727, d. 1820, dau. of ***John SHEPHERD*** and ***Sarah CLARK*** of East Middletown, widow of *William CORNWALL*). Joseph moved from East Middletown (now Portland), Conn. to Ashfield, Mass. before the Revolution where he owned a farm. He was a sergeant of the Sixth Col, Second Conn. Regt. The oldest of their seven children was Abraham. Stocking, pp. 7, 12.

VI. ***Abraham STOCKING***, b. 26 Sept 1754, Ashfield, Mass.; d. after 1832, York, Livingston Co., NY; m. ***Abigail (Nabby) SMITH***; private in the Rev. War 22 Sept to 18 Oct 1777. The oldest of his five children being Joseph. Stocking, pp. 12, 25.

VII.***Joseph STOCKING*** , b. 1782; m. ***Jane FISHER***. Issue*:* ***Sophronia STOCKING***, d. young. ***Justus STOCKING***, d. No child. ***Jonathan Smith STOCKING***, m. *Sabrina LILLY*; issue: *Constant* and *Darwin*; res. Brighton, O. ***Sophrina STOCKING,*** b. 1812, m. *Stephen SCRANTON.* ***Richard Weldon STOCKING***, d. unm. ***Abner STOCKING***, m. *Gracia PORTER*; issue: *William* and *Delia*; res. Bennett Station, Neb. ***Abigail STOCKING***, m.1 *ROBINSON*; m.2 *FINNEY*. Res. Vineland, NJ. ***Herod STOCKING***, b. 5 July1819; m. 3 Nov 1841 to *Adaline FITCH;* issue: *Charles F. STOCKING* (1842-1898, m. 1875 *Sarah E. WICKHAM*), *Roselle STOCKING* (1845 - d. young), *Joseph STOCKING* (1848 - d. young), *Joseph Chester STOCKING* (b. 1852, m. 1876 to *Lydia A. BRADBROOK*) and *Willis Marshall STOCKING* (b. 1861, m. 1886 *Emma ROCHTY*); carpenter; res. Grand Rapids, O. ***Jane STOCKING***, m. *Marshall CHADWICK.* ***Martha STOCKING***, d. at Dover, O. unm. ***Joseph STOCKING***, unm; res. Dover Center, O. Stocking, pp. 46, 47, 90.

Joseph STOCKING came with his uncle, *Jonathan SMITH*, in 1811, and purchased land from the latter, in Dover. He returned to Massachusetts for his family, but postponed their trip on account of the war of 1812. In 1815 Joseph and ***Jane FISHER STOCKING***, with five children, along with others came from Lee, Mass., settling upon what is known as the Stocking farm, near Dover Center. Their early housekeeping was somewhat primitive and amusing. The dining table was the family chest, around which pumpkins were placed for chairs. Mrs. Stocking was "Aunt Jenny" to all her friends. Her quiet life, full of devotion to her family, ended when eighty-three years were completed. Her daughter, *Mrs. Sophronia SCRANTON*, lives upon the old place...*Mrs. ROBINSON, Mrs. Marshall CHADWICK*, and *Miss Martha STOCKING* were Mrs. Scranton's sisters. Memorial to the Pioneer Women of the Western Reserve, p. 60, and Crisfield Johnson, History of Cuyahoga County, p. 437.

Joseph STOCKING...was born in Ashfield, Franklin Co., Mass., November 1, 1781, and in 1815 came to Dover township, Cuyahoga Co., Ohio, with his family, including *Jonathan S. (STOCKING).* They traveled with an ox-team, the journey occupying six weeks, other immigrants coming at the same time. Mr. Stocking had visited the locality twice before bringing his family - once in 1811 or '12, and again in 1814. He built a log house on the site where he last resided. When he first came to Dover township there was but one frame building in Cleveland, that place, in fact, being a mere point, a nucleus around which a village afterward grew up from which was evolved the great city of Cleveland. Mr. Stocking was prominent and active in the township, and was equally active in its religious and educational interests. His first Presidential vote was cast for Jefferson, and it is said he voted at every Presidential election afterward, his last vote being cast for Hayes. He died February 23, 1877, aged ninety-five years, three months, twenty-two days, having been a resident of Dover township, Cuyahoga county, over sixty years. He lived to see the wilderness transformed into fruitful fields, and towns and cities rise up out of the dense forest; he lived to hear the rush and roar of the railroad train where once could be heard naught but the howling of wolves, the angry growling of no less ferocious bears, and the war-whoop of the Indian. But to essay to mention what was consummated in those three score years would be to attempt a history of all the Northwest, with its most wonderful growth and marvelous development.

In Dover township, Cuyahoga county, in November, 1836, Jonathan S. Stocking married ***Sabrina LILLY***, born in Ashfield, Mass., daughter of ***Austin LILLY***, who came from New England in pioneer times. Jonathan S. Stocking lived in Cuyahoga county till 1836, in which year he moved to Brighton township, Lorain county, and in company with *Harry HAWES* bought 222 acres of heavily-timbered land, and they felled the first tree that ever felt the axe on that farm. This land cost them six dollars per acre, but it proved a valuable property. Jonathan Stocking died here in 1890, aged eighty years, two months, seventeen days, his wife in 1887, aged seventy-two years, four months, five days and they are interred at Brighton Center. He was very successful, not only in general farming but also in stock raising, and was a hard-working man up to within two years of his death. In politics he was first a Whig, and, after the formation of the party, a staunch Republican. Mrs. Stocking, in Church relationship, was an Episcopalian. They were parents of children as follows: ***C. D.***, subject; ***Byron***, deceased in infancy; ***Elmus B.***, who enlisted in Company K, One Hundred and Seventy-eighth O. V. I.*(Civil War, Ohio Volunteer Infantry)*, was detailed to hospital work at Wilmington, S. C., and while handling corpses in the dead house became poisoned (he died at home at the age of twenty-two years); ***Abigail***, who died in 1865 when sixteen years old; ***Ralph G.***, deceased in infancy; and ***Darwin***, a farmer of Brighton township.. "C. D. Stocking," Commemorative Biographical Record of The Counties of Huron and Lorain, p. 1092.

Joseph STOCKING, 66, farmer, b. Mass.; ***Jane***, 69, b. Mass.; ***Joseph***, 24, farmer; ***Martha***, 26; ***Abigail ROBINSON***, 33, b. Ohio; ***Richard STOCKING***, 37, occup. none, b. Mass., idiotic; ***Elizabeth I. ROBINSON***, 8, b. Ohio. 1850 FC OH CYDO, p. 213B, lines 15-21, dwelling 3692. ***Abigail STOCKING*** married ***William ROBINSON***, Cuyahoga County, 16th day of September, 1838. Marriage Record, Cuyahoga County, OH, vol. 4, p.19

Living next door: ***Abner STOCKING***, 36, farmer, b. Mass.; ***Gracia***, 32; three children listed. Dwelling 3691.

S. Porter SMITH, 40; wife, *Ruth*, 30, b. Ohio, two children. Dwelling 3693.

Chester STOCKING, 43, farmer, b. Mass.; ***Eliza***, ink blotch over age, three others. Dwelling 3694.

Joseph STOCKING, 78, farmer, b. Mass.; ***Jane***, 78, b. Ohio; ***Meldin***, 49, farmer, b. Ohio; ***Martha***, 36, b. Ohio; ***Joseph***, 34, b. Ohio, farmer. 1860 FC CYDO, p. 63, lines 32-36.

Mrs. Joseph STOCKING, Maiden Name ***Jane FISHER***; Arrived Dover 1815; Where From or Where Born Lee, Mass.; Last Residence Dover, O.

Mrs. Abner STOCKING, Maiden Name ***Gracia PORTER***; Arrived Dover 1815; Where From or Where Born Dover; Last Residence Firth, Neb. Women of the Western Reserve Prior to 1840, p. 18.

STOCKING, Abner, ?-1854, age 38; ***Eliza***, bur. 26 Apr 1889, 74, b. Mass., Lot 8E, Old Cemetery; ***Joseph Sr.***, 1781-1877; ***Joseph***, ?-1908, age 82, b. Dover, d., Dover, Lot 8E, Old Cemetery; ***Welden R.***, bur. 30 Mar 1888, age 75, b. and d. Dover. Evergreen Cemetery Records, Westlake, Ohio and Cleveland Necrology File.

Parents of Eunice Chadwick Osborn:

Vital Record information of Lee, Mass., for the Chadwick family is available on line at www.rootsweb.com/~maberksh/towns/lee.lee-vr.html.

The State of Ohio, Cuyahoga County, ss. I hereby certify, that on the 3rd day of March A.D. 1845, I duly solemnized the Marriage Contract between the said ***Marshall CHADWICK*** and ***Jane STOCKING***. John Keys, Pres. Min. Dover Marriage Record, Cuyahoga County, OH, vol. 4, p. 267.

Marshall CHADWICK (1810-1858) and ***Jane STOCKING*** (1821-1916) had six children, five were: ***Eunice CHADWICK***, b. 1846, d. 1940, m. *Reuben OSBORNE* (b. 1847, d. 1919). ***Martha Ann CHADWICK***, b. 1849, d. 1922. ***Bricena CHADWICK***, b. 1851, d. 1939. ***Jane CHADWICK***, b. 1853, d. 1874. ***Adah CHADWICK***, b. 1857, d. 1942. Osborn File, Rose Hill Museum, Bay Village, OH.

CHADWICK, Marshall, 1858, age 48, Evergreen Cemetery, Dover, Ohio. Cleveland Necrology File

Mrs. Marshall CHADWICK, maiden name ***Jane STOCKING***, Came to Dover 1819, last residence Tecumseh, Mich. Women of the Western Reserve Prior to 1840, p. 18.

Children of Reuben Osborn and Eunice Chadwick:

George L., b. Jan 1870; d. 4 Oct 1943; m. *Blanche* (d. 15 Mar 1944). ***Louella B.***, b. 1872; d. 30 Dec 1946, Cuy. Co., OH; bur. Evergreen Cem., Westlake, OH; m. *Amos GLENDENNING* (b. 1872, d. 1 Apr 1939, Lakewood, Cuy Co., OH, bur. Evergreen Cemetery; third child of *Walter GLENDENNING* (b. 9 Feb 1841 Canada, d. 22 Aug 1916, North Olmsted, Cuy. Co.) and *Susannah A. CHUTE* (b. 1842, d. 8 Feb 1917, North Olmsted, both bur. Evergreen)). ***Clare Marshall***, b. 1878, d. Dec 12, 1952 *(bur. Lot 24-11)*, wife *Mildred SLEEPER*. ***Irwin***, b. 1878; m. 9 Apr 1907 to *Amy REED* (b. c1882, Iowa; d. 2 Nov 1946); res. 1910, Columbus, OH; for many years 2862 Croyden Rd, Shaker Hts., OH; d. 2 Nov 1935, bur. Oberlin, OH. 1child, d. pre 1910 and 2 dau.. ***Lucy M.***, b. 28 Jan 1886, d. 26 May 1955 *(bur. this lot)*, never married. All children b. OH. Rose Hill Museum, Osborn File; Evergreen Cem., Westlake; 1880 FC OH CYDO, p. 23, 1910 FC OH Franklin, 12W Columbus, p. 85, lines 99-100.

George L. OSBORN, 30, b. Dover, O., Carpenter, fr. *Reuben OSBORN*, mo. *Eunice CHADWICK*. Married ***Blanch****(e)* ***A. NEFF***, 29, res. 31 Alexander St., b. Cleveland, O., fr. *Malchoir NEFF*, mo. *Josephine BICHMAN;* neither previously married. The State of Ohio, Cuyahoga County, ss. I Certify that on the 26th day of Nov 1900 George L. Osborn and Blanch A. Neff were by me legally joined in marriage. John P. Brennan Marriage Record, Cuyahoga County, OH, vol. 51, p. 224.

OSBORN, George L., 60, own home valued at $7,000, owns radio, age at marriage 31, b. Ohio, parents b. Ohio, Carpenter, house construction; ***Blanch****(e)* ***H.***, 59, wife, age at marriage 29, b. Ohio, fr. b. Baden Germany, mo. b. Holland, no occup. 1930 FC OH CYBV, ED 18-534, p. 16B, 29337 Lake Road, lines 67-68.

Mr. George OSBORN, d. Oct 4, 1943, Fairview Hosp., Cleveland, Cuyahoga Co., Ohio; cause Myocardial degeneration and chronic asthma; res. 29337 West Lake Rd., Bay Village; married to ***Blanche*** (73 yrs.); Carpenter; 73 yrs. 8 mos. 22 days; b. 12 January 1870, Bay Village, Ohio; fr. ***Reuben OSBORN***, b. Bay Village, mo. ***Eunice CHADWICK***, b. Middleburg Hts., Ohio. Informant *M. M.*

OSBORN, Watertown, NY; bur. Evergreen Cem., Westlake, undertaker Clifford Pease, Westlake. Ohio Certificate of Death, Division of Vital Statistics, 1943, certif. 60587.

George OSBORN, rel. Protestant. Pease Funeral Home Records, Mss. 4809, Western Reserve Historical Society, Cleveland, OH, Record of Funeral, p. 208.

Blanche A. OSBORN, d. Mar 15, 1944, 1:30 A.M. at home 29337 Lake Rd., Bay Village, Cuyahoga Co., Ohio of Uremia, Myocarditis; in this community 44 yrs.; widow of ***George***; 73 yrs. 6 mos. 14 ds.; b. Sept 1, 1870, Cleveland, O. to ***Melchoir NEFF***, b. Baaden Baaden, Germany, mo. ***Josephine BECKMAN***, b. Holland; informant *Merle OSBORN*, 169 Bowers Ave., Watertown, NY; funeral director Clifford Pease, Westlake, Ohio; Evergreen Cemetery. Ohio Certificate of Death, Division of Vital Statistics, 1944, certif. 21901.

Blanche A. OSBORN, religion Catholic. Pease Funeral Home Records, Mss. 4809, Western Reserve Historical Society, Cleveland, OH, Record of Funeral, p. 208.

OSBORN, George, internment 7 October 1943, Grave 1, Lot No. 137, Section E-2, lot owner Blanche Osborn; ***Blanche OSBORN***, grave 2. Owned by Merle Osborn. Evergreen Cemetery Records, Westlake, OH.

The State of Ohio, Cuyahoga County, ss. I Certify that on the Fourth day of November 1896 ***Mr. Amos K. GLENDENNING*** and ***Miss Luella H. OSBORN*** were by me legally joined in marriage. Rev. William J. Frost, D.B. Marriage Record, Cuyahoga County, OH, vol. 44, p. 260. *The spelling of Luella changes with the records.*

GLENDENNING, Amos K.,48, b. Ohio, b. Ohio, parents b. Canada, Plumber in a plumbing shop; ***Louella***, wife, 47; ***Donnald*** *(sp.)*, son, 21, Plumber in a plumbing shop; ***Robert***, son, 12, attended school. 1920 FC OH CYBV ED509, p. 1B, lines 76-79.

GLENDENNING, Amos K., 58, value of house $20,000, owns radio, age at marriage 24, b. Ohio, parents b. Canada, Proprietor Hardware; ***Luella***, wife, 57, age at marriage 22, b. Ohio, parents b. Ohio; ***Robert A***, son, 23, b. Ohio, Store Manager, Plumbing and Hardware. 1930 FC OH CYBV, ED 18-534, 29219 Lake Road, p. 16B, lines 57-59.

Luella OSBORN GLENDENNING, widow of ***Amos***, mother of ***Donald*** and ***Robert***; res. 603 Bassett Rd., Bay Village, occup. housewife, d. Dec 29, 1946 at 6:25 a.m. of cause Carcinoma of vulva with metastasis due to neglect (C.S.) and Senility at residence, 74 yrs. 6 mos. 3 days; rel. Christian Scientist, clergyman Fred Fisher, C. S; Pease Funeral Home, Funeral 31 Dec 1946, Tues., Cemetery Evergreen, Sect. N, Lot 1 Grave 3. Pease Funeral Home Records, Mss. 4809, Western Reserve Historical Society, Cleveland, OH, Record of Funeral, p. 89; Cleveland Necrology File; Ohio Certificate of Death, Division of Vital Statistics, 1946, certif. 72643 and Evergreen Cemetery, Westlake.

Husband of Luella Osborn Glendenning:

Amos Kindell GLENDENNING, d. April 1, 1939 at 1311 Edanola Ave., Lakewood, Cuyahoga Co., Ohio of Chronic Myocarditis starting in Feb 1939; b. April 21, 1871, Dover, Ohio, son of ***Walter GLENDENNING***, b. Ontario, Canada and ***Susan CHUTE***, b. Ontario, Canada; married to ***Luella GLENDENNING***; Merchant and Plummer *(sp.)*; informant *D. O. GLENDENNING*, Lake Rd., Bay Village; undertaker Clifford Pease Funeral Home; bur. Evergreen Cemetery, Sect. N, Lot 1, Grave 2, lot owner: *Mary E. Osborn (Westlake, Ohio)*, 4/3/1939. Ohio Certificate of Death, Division of Vital Statistics, 1939, certif. 23575 and Evergreen Cemetery, Westlake.

Parents of Amos Glendenning:

Walter GLENDENNING, a blacksmith and farmer, b. 9 Feb 1841, Canada; d. 22 Aug 1916, North Olmsted, Cuy Co., OH; and ***Susannah A. CHUTE***, b. 1842, Canada; d. 8 Feb 1917, North Olmsted, OH. Both buried Evergreen Cemetery, Westlake, OH. 1880 FC OH CYDO, p. 23, and Ohio Certificate of Death, Division of Vital Statistics, 1916, certif. 78725.

Susan Amelia GLENDENNING, d. 8 Feb 1917, North Olmsted, Cuyahoga Co., Ohio of Pleura Pneumonia for four days; widowed; b. Sept 26, 1841, Aeton, *(Ontario?)*, Canada to ***George CHUTE***, b. Nova Scotia and ***Cynthia HERSHEY***, b. Nova Scotia *(Canada)*; 75 yrs. 4 mos. 12 ds.; informant *Wm. GLENDENNING*, No. Olmsted, O.; undertaker J.A. Pease & Son, Dover, O.; bur. Evergreen. Ohio Certificate of Death, Division of Vital Statistics, 1917, certif. 81896.

OSBORN, Irwin Selden, husband of ***Amy*** (nee ***REED***), res. 2862 Croyden Rd. *(Shaker Hts.)*, father of ***Dorothy Anne*** and ***Amy Ruth***, son of ***Mrs. Reuben OSBORNE***, of Bay Village. Now at Clifford Pease Funeral Home…where services will be held Tuesday, Nov 5, at 1:30 p.m. Burial at Oberlin, O. Cleveland Necrology File, Nov 4, 1935.

Irwin OSBORN, d. Nov 2, 1935, 6:45 a.m., Hanna House *(part of University Hospital)*, Cleveland, Cuyahoga Co., Ohio of Myocarditis…Broncho Pneumonia; res. 2862 Croyden Rd., Cleveland Hts., Ohio; 57 yrs. 9 mos. 8 ds.; wife ***Amy***; Consulting Engineer; b. Jan 24, 1878, Bay Village, Ohio to ***Reuben OSBORN***, b. Bay Village and ***Eunice STOCKING*** *(Chadwick)*, b. Berea, Ohio; informant *Mrs. Irwin Seldon OSBORN*; funeral director Clifford Pease, burial Oberlin. Ohio Certificate of Death, Division of Vital Statistics, 1935, certif. 64831.

OSBORN: Amy REED, age 65, mother of ***Mrs. Robert S. SHUNK*** and ***Mrs. Paul HORST***; sister of *Arthur F., Ralph A.* and *Nellie REED*; passed away suddenly. Wednesday, Oct 16, Oberlin, O. Services will be held Friday, Oct 18, at Fairchild Chapel, Oberlin. Friends may call at Sedgeman's Funeral Home, Oberlin, O. Oct 18 1946. The Plain Dealer.

Lot 46-7 Lucy M. Osborn

DOVER LAKE

Lucy OSBORN is taking vocal lessons in Cleveland. Evening Telegram, Elyria, OH, Wednesday, April 12, 1911, p. 7, col. 1.

Recipes shared by Lucy Osborn:

BAKED PEAS

1 can peas	1 ½ c. milk
2 T. butter	1/2 t. salt
1 T. flour	1/4 t. pepper

Make a white sauce of the butter, flour, milk and seasoning then pour over the peas and bake until brown.

POTATOES AU GRATIN

1 pt. diced cooked potato	1 c. grated cheese
2 T. butter	1 pt. milk
2 T. flour	Seasoning

Blend flour and butter over a slow fire, add milk gradually, season with salt and pepper. When thick remove from fire, add cheese and potatoes, pour into a baking dish, grate cheese on top and bake 1/2 hr.

PINK LUNCHEON MENU

Salmon Loaf Stewed Potatoes
Creamed Cauliflower
Whole Tomato Salad
Oatmeal Bread and Butter
Radishes Stuffed Olives
Strawberry Gelatine Pink Frosted Cakes
Candy Nuts
Coffee

Miss Lucy Osborn
The Dover Cook Book, pp. 14, 16, 89.

MISS LUCY OSBORN

Born on a farm on Lake Road in Bay Village, ***Miss Lucy OSBORN*** was a member of one of the first families to settle there.

Miss Osborn, 69, the daughter of ***Reuben*** and ***Eunice OSBORN***, died yesterday at Lakewood Hospital. She had lived in Bay Village all her life and at the time of her death was living at 31616 Westlake Rd. She was a charter member of the Reading Club of Bay Village and The Bay Village Women's Club. She also was a member of Bay Village Congregational Church.

There are no members of her family surviving her.

Services will be at 3 p.m. tomorrow at the Burmeister Funeral Home, 163 Avon-Belden Road, Avon Lake. Burial will be in Bay Village Cemetery. Undetermined newspaper article, Osborn Family File and similar article in May 28, 1955, p. 22, col. 1. The Plain Dealer.

Lucy M. OSBORN, buried May 28, 1955. "List of Interments," not included in chronological listing in ledger.

Lot 47 *One-half purchased by Reuben Osborn and one-half by Sherman Osborn, on Nov 2, 1887 for $2.63.* SL *(assumed this was the price each paid). Presently listed under: Sherman Osborn.*

The plat map lists the next two headstones in reverse order. It is assumed that Selden's grave was also confused. He has been listed here therefore under the "Father" headstone.

Lot 47-8

MOTHER

Lot 48 *Sherman Osborn of Dover purchased on April 28, 1881, for $5.25.* SL

Lot 48-9 (*Selden Osborn*)

"Selden Osborn" is handwritten on the plat map and it is assumed that this is a mistake. Selden is found in fifth row of the Original Part. This is probably Sherman.

FATHER

Lot 48-10 Osborn Monument

SHERMAN OSBORN
DIED
NOV 3, 1886
AGED
52 Yrs. 7 Mo. 2 D.
OSBORN

ANGENETTE E.
WIFE OF
SHERMAN OSBORN
DIED
Apr 27, 1880
AGED
44 YRS. 9 M. 27 D.

Lot 48-10 Sherman Osborn

Sherman Osborn is the oldest child of Selden Osborn and Nancy Ruple (OP 5:8).

Marriage of Sherman and Angenette not indexed in Cuyahoga County.

OSBORN, Sherman, 36, b. Ohio; ***Angenette***, 35, b. Ohio; ***Albert***, 10, b. Ohio; ***Calvin***, 4, b. Ohio; *STARK, John*, b. Germany. 1870 FC OH CYDO, p. 33, dwelling 279.

OSBORN, Sherman, 45, farmer, b. Ohio, fr. b. NY, mo. b. Ohio; ***Albert***, 20, son, farm laborer; ***Calvin***, 14, son, at school; ***Emily***, 8, dau.; all children b. in Ohio; ***Julia***, 31, sister, House Keeper; ***PELLETT, Eva***, 21, domestic servant *(daughter of John Pellett and Maria Axam, Lot 43-6)*. 1880 FC OH CYDO, p. 99, lines 24-29, house 315.

OSBORN, Sherman. Owned land; Acres: Improved - 17 tilled, including fallow and grass, 12 permanent meadow, Unimproved - 8 woodland. Farm Values: Land and buildings - $3500, Machinery - $250, Live Stock - $350. Cost of building and repairing in 1879: $20. Labor: Paid for wages in 1879 - $100, hired labor 25 weeks in 1879. Estimated value of all farm production: $350. Grass lands: acreage: 4 mown, 5 not mown, 8 tons hay. 5 horses, 4 milch cows, 4 calves dropped, 4 cattle sold living. 300 pounds of butter made on the farm. 25 swine. 70 barnyard poultry on farm, 300 dozen eggs produced in 1879. Indian corn: 4 acres, 350 bushels; Oats: 3 acres, 150 bushels; wheat: 1 acre, 47 bushels. Orchards - apple: 2 acres, 100 bearing trees, 150 bushels. Total value of orchard products: $75. Amount of wood cut: 30 cords, Value of forest products: $25. "Schedule 2. Production of Agriculture in Dover Township, Cuyahoga County, OH," enumerated June, 1880, p. 33.

The State of Ohio, Cuyahoga County, ss. I Certify that on the 12th day of Feby 1884 ***Mr. Sherman OSBORN*** and ***Mrs. Myra L. YODER*** were by me legally joined in marriage. S. Z. Kauffman, Rockport, O. E. B. Evans having made application for a Marriage License… Marriage Record, Cuyahoga County, OH, vol. 27, p. 203.

OSBORN, Sherman, d. Nov 5, 1886, Dover; married; 52 y. 1 m. 2 d.; b. Dover, farmer; parents ***Sheldon*** and ***Nancy***; disease Typhoid fever, residence Dover. Probate Court Death Records, Cuyahoga County, Ohio, vol. 3, p. 146.

Sherman OSBORN, 52; res. Dover; interred Nov 8, 1886; Lot 48. "List of Interments," Lakeside Cemetery, Bay Village, OH.

Second wife of Sherman Osborn, Myra Yoder:

Myra OSBORN, 56, b. New York; ***Harvey A. YODER***, son, 30, single, b. Ohio. 1910 FC Index OH Cuyahoga Co., Cleveland.

Creole Beef Loaf

(Mrs. Myra L. Osborn)

Grind together twenty cents worth of round steak and five cents worth of fresh pork, with one small onion, a little celery, salt and pepper to taste. Mix this with one cup milk, one cup toasted bread crumbs, one beaten egg, one heaping teaspoon butter; form into beef loaf. Put into hot oven for ten minutes; then cover with good half can of tomatoes. Bake one and one-half hours. Basting often. Keep the tomatoes heaped on top. Serve with gravy of tomatoes. The Village Cook Book, p. 9. (c1911-1915).

Myra OSBORN, 66, Widow, b. NY, parents b. NY; ***Harvie A. YODER***, son, 40, b. Ohio, fr. b. NY, mo. b. Ohio *(Parental birth information appears to be reversed)*, Foreman, Amer. Sh__. 1920 FC OH CYBV, Bassett Road, p. 5B.

Son of Myra Yoder Osborn:

Myra OSBORN and ***Harvey YODER***, her son, lived at 343 Bassett. Harvey was appointed the first full-time Marshal of Bay Village on June 12, 1923. Marshal Yoder cut a dashing figure riding about on his motorcycle. Unfortunately he was killed when struck by a Lake Shore Electric Railway car while he was driving a new Ford out of the police station down Dover Center Road on July 25 *(should read 20)*, 1925. Bay Village Historical Society, Bay Village: A Way of Life, pp. 92, 127.

YODER-Harvey A., beloved son of ***Mrs. Myra L. OSBORN***, Bay Village, O., suddenly, July 20, age 45 years. Funeral from M. E. Church, Bassett and Lake Roads, Bay Village, Stop 32, Lake Shore Electric, Wednesday, July 22, at 2 p. m. 1870-1925. Evergreen Cemetery Cleveland, Ohio. Cleveland Necrology File, July 22, 1925, reel 087.

Harvey YODER, Bay Village, 46, male, bur. 22 July1925, Grave 1; ***Myra L. OSBORN***, 92 of Elyria; d. of myocarditis, internment 9 April 1946; undertaker Carl Taylor, Elyria, OH. Grave 2; Lot owner Myra L. Osborn, Section M, Lot 19. Evergreen Cemetery, Westlake, OH.

Lot 48-10 Angenette Phinney Osborn

OSBORN-Nettie At her home, in Dover, April 27, of lingering consumption, Nettie, wife of ***Sherman OSBORN***. A patient sufferer gone to rest. Leader, Apr 29, 1880, Cleveland Necrology File, roll 62.

OSBORN, Agnett, d. April 27, 1880, Dover, married, 45 yrs., b. Dover, farmer's wife, parents ***Calvin*** and ***Alma PHINNEY***, disease consumption. Probate Court Death Records, Cuyahoga County, Ohio, vol. 2, p. 82.

Nettie OSBORN, 45; res. Dover; interred April 29, 1880; Lot 48. "List of Interments," Lakeside Cemetery, Bay Village, OH.

Grandfather of Angenette Phinney Osborn:

Sylvanus PHINNEY, 71, Farmer; b. Mass.; ***Catherine***, 56, b. NY. 1850 FC OH CYDO p. 216A, lines 2-3, dwelling 3725. Next door to *Edwin PHINNEY*, 34, merchant, b. Ohio; *Phoebe*, 34, b. Vermont; 4 children. p. 215B, lines 38-42, p. 216A, line 1.

PHINNEY, Sylvanus, -1852, age 73, Evergreen Cemetery, Westlake, OH. Evergreen Cemetery, Westlake.

Parents of Angenette Phinney Osborn:

I Certify that on the 19th day of Augt. 1834, I solemnized the marriage contract between ***Calvin PHINNEY*** and ***Emaline MARTIN***, both of Dover, Cuyahoga County. John Hing Stated supply in the Church at Dover. Rec'd Oct 21, 1834. Recorded Feb 7, 1835. Marriage Record, Cuyahoga County, OH, vol. 3, p. 116.

Calvin PHINNEY, 39, Merchant, b. Mass.; ***Emeline***, 29, b. Vermont.; ***Anngennette***, 16, b. Ohio; ***Sylvanus***, 12, b. Ohio; ***Sylvester***, 10, b. Ohio; ***Sanford***, 4, b. Ohio; *Charlotte SAWYER*, 27, no occup. listed, b. NY; ***Emma PHINNEY***, 8/12, b. Ohio; *Nancy STOUP*, 17, b. Germany; *Charles FISHER*?, 20, Shoemaker, b. Germany; *John GARCH*, 35, Shoemaker, b. Germany. 1850 FC OH CYDO, p. 216A, lines 36-42 and p. 216B, lines 1-4, dwelling, 3731.

Calvin PHINNEY followed *Eli CLEMENS* as postmaster of Dover. Bay Village Historical Society, Bay Village: A Way of Life, p. 64.

Phinney, Calvin; -1870, age 61. Evergreen Cemetery, Westlake.

Siblings of Angenette Phinney Osborn:

State of Ohio, Cuyahoga County, I Certify That on the 16th day of April 1863 ***Mr. Sylvester A. PHINNEY*** and ***Miss Lucy ROSE*** were by me joined in marriage. Tracy L. Waite, Minister. Marriage Record, Cuyahoga County, OH, vol. 11, p. 113.

First wife of Sylvester Phinney:

PHINNEY Lucy R. wife of ***S. A. PHINNEY*** Died Aug 5, 1869 Aged 27 yrs. 11 m. 2d.; ***Merton***...Infant Son Died Sept 9, 1869, Aged 1 mo. 16 ds. Maple Ridge Cemetery inscriptions, Westlake, OH. Read by Catherine Burke Flament.

State of Ohio, Cuyahoga County, I Certify That on the 15th day of May 1873 ***Mr. Sylvester A. PHINNEY*** and ***Miss Kate L. ROSE*** were by me joined in marriage. Tracy L. Waite, Minister. Marriage Record, Cuyahoga County, OH, vol. 17, p. 182.

PHINNEY-Sylvester A., Sept 25, age 75. Funeral from late residence, Butternut Ridge Rd., North Olmsted, Stop 43, Elyria Line, Sept 28 at 2 p.m. eastern time. Cem record 1840-1916, Evergreen Cemetery, Cleveland, Ohio. Cleveland Necrology File, Sept 28, 1913.

Second wife of Sylvester Phinney:

Kate L. PHINNEY, sister of ***F. J. ROSE***, Seville, O., ***Mrs. Arthur BURDETTE***, Sheffield, O., ***Mrs. Eliza WILLIAMS***, Elyria, O. Services at late residence, 211 Wooster street, Elyria, O., Sunday, Oct 16, at 2 p.m. Burial at Evergreen cemetery, Dover Village. Cleveland Necrology File, Oct 16, 1927.

Children of Sherman Osborn and Angenette Phinney:

Albert D. OSBORN, 70, head of household, owns home valued at $10,000, owns radio, single, b. Ohio, farmer; ***Calvin E.***, 64, brother, age at marriage 26, b. Ohio, farmer; ***Lillie B.***, 58, sister-in-law, age at marriage 21, b. Ohio, parents b. Hoeniger, Germany; ***Emily P.***, 57, sister, single, b. Ohio, no occup. 1930 FC OH CYBV, ED 18-534, 29560 Lake Road, p. 17A, lines 11-14.

Albert Deverde OSBORN, d. Sept 29, 1950, 3:00 p.m. at his residence 29560 Lake Rd., Bay Village, Cuyahoga Co. of a Cerebral Hemorrhage for one week, Generalized Arterio Sclerosis for 20 yrs., Arthritis D. 15 yrs. at 90 yrs. 7 mos. 16ds.; b. 13 Feb 1860, Dover Twp. to ***Sherman OSBORN*** and ***Angenette PHINNEY***; Single, Retired Boat Steward on the Great Lakes; bur. Evergreen Cemetery, Westlake, Ohio; Marion E. Pease funeral director. Ohio Certificate of Death, Division of Vital Statistics, 1950, certif. 10384.

OSBORN, Albert D., son of the late ***Sherman*** and ***Angenette*** (nee ***PHINNEY***); brother of ***Emily*** and ***Calvin*** (deceased)...Clifford Pease Funeral Home...Westlake, OH. Cleveland Necrology File, Sept 30, 1950.

Neither ***Albert*** nor ***Emily*** married. Albert d. 29 Sept 1950, Emily d. 5 Dec 1955. Mrs. True (M. Patricia) Read, Letter 22 Oct 1999, Rose Hill Museum.

The State of Ohio, Lorain County, ss. I do hereby certify that ***Mr. Calvin E. OSBORN*** and ***Miss Lillie B. GLASSER*** were joined in marriage by me on the 2nd day of April A.D. 1893. *(Application made on April 15th, filed and recorded on April 26th)* Frank H. Young. Lorain County Marriage Records, Administration Bldg., Lorain, OH.

OSBORN, Cal, b. June 1865, married 7 yrs., b. Ohio, parents b. Ohio; ***Jennie***, wife, b. Aug 1870, no children born, b. Ohio, parents b. Ohio; ***Emily***, sister, b. Oct 1871, b. Ohio. 1900 FC OH CYDO ED 213, lines 91-3, dwelling 465, p. 21, house 465. *There is a discrepancy with Cal's wife. A marriage certificate was found showing he married Lillian in 1893 although her date of birth is different. It is believed that this is a mistake.*

OSBORN, Calvin E., Ohio, 35 *(incorrect age)*, m. 15 yrs., Farmer, General Farm; ***Lily***, wife, b. Ohio, parents b. Germany, 38, children b./living 0; ***Emily***, sister, 38, single, b. Ohio; ***Albert***, brother, 50, single, Sailor on Lakes. 1910 FC OH CY Village of Bay, p. 2B, lines 79-82, dwelling 45.

OSBORN, Calvin D., 54, b. Ohio, parents b. Ohio, General Farmer; ***Lillian***, wife, 47, b. Ohio, fr. b. Wertenberg, Germany, mo. b. Himiega, Germany; ***Emily***, sister, 47, single, b. Ohio, no occup.; ***Albert D.***, brother, 59, single, b. Ohio, General Farmer. 1920 FC OH CYBV ED 509, p. 1B, lines 52-55.

Calvin Eugene OSBORN, d. 13 Jan 1948, 8 p.m. at his residence 29560 Lake Road, Bay Village, Ohio of hypostatic pneumonia for 2 days due to congestive heart failure; Married to ***Lillian*** age 75; farmer, b. 19 June 1866, Dover Twp. to ***Sherman OSBORN***, b. Dover Twp., Cuy Co. and ***Angenette PHINNEY***, b. Dover Twp.; Informant *Lillian B. OSBORN*, bur. Evergreen Cemetery, Westlake. Ohio Certificate of Death, Division of Vital Statistics, 1948, certif. 8276.

OSBORN.- Calvin A., will be buried in the old family plot in Evergreen, after services...at Clifford Pease Funeral Home....Mr. Osborn was born 80 years ago at 29560

Lake Rd...and lived there all his life, died yesterday after a long illness. From the time he was a youth until a year ago he had farmed the lands around his home. A hunting enthusiast, he was one of the founders and active in the Dover Bay Gun Club. He attended the Bay Methodist Church. He and his wife, ***Mrs. Lillian GLASSER OSBORN***, were married in Lorain, O., 55 years ago. Surviving are his wife; a brother, ***Albert,*** and a sister, ***Miss Emily OSBORN.*** Undetermined newspaper article, Pease Funeral Home Records, Mss. 4809, Western Reserve Historical Society, Cleveland, OH.

Calvin Eugene OSBORN, res. 29560 Lake Rd., husband of ***Lillian*** (nee ***GLASSER***) (age 75); d. Jan 13, 1948, and 8 P.M. at res., 81 yrs. 6 mos., 24 days, cause Hypostatic Pneumonia (2 days), Congestive Heart Failure and Aortic Insufficiency Arteriosclerosis; b. June 19, 1866, Dover Twp., occup. Farmer; Pease Funeral Home, Evergreen Cemetery. Pease Funeral Home Records, Mss. 4809, Western Reserve Historical Society, Cleveland, OH, Record of Funeral, p. 173.

Wife of Calvin Osborn:

OSBORN, Lillian B., residence 2463 Breezewood Dr., Westlake, O. formerly 29560 Lake Rd., wife of the late ***Calvin***. Burmeister Funeral Home, 163 Avon Belden Rd., Avon Lake, O. Cleveland Press, June 27, 1958.

Mrs. Calvin Osborn, 86, Long a Bayite, Dies

The oldest living member of Bay Methodist Church, ***Mrs. Calvin OSBORN***, 86, died Thursday. Mrs. Osborn, who was a member of the Sunshine Circle at the church, passed away at her home, 2463 Beechwood Dr., Westlake.

Mrs. Osborn was born in Cleveland and had moved to Bay Village following her marriage more than 60 years ago. Her husband was a real estate dealer and active participant in the Bay Gun Club prior to his death some years ago. The couple has resided at 29560 Lake Rd, Bay Village, before Mr. Osborn's death. No near relatives survive.

Funeral services were held Saturday afternoon at the Burmeister funeral home, Avon Lake. Burial was in Evergreen Cemetery, Westlake. Newspaper article provided by Sally O'Connor, undetermined source.

Lillian Barbara OSBORN, d. 26 June 1958 at her residence 2463 Beechwood Dr., Westlake, Ohio of Broncho-pneumonia and Cerebra-Vascular Accidents (3-4), Arteriosclerosis b. 30 March 1872, dau. of ***John GLASSER*** and ***Mary BEELER***., informant *Mrs. Loretta A. THOMAS*, Pease Funeral Home, bur. Evergreen Cemetery. Ohio Certificate of Death, Division of Vital Statistics, 1958, certif. 40922.

Emily Phinney OSBORN, d. 5 Dec 1955, 8:50 p.m. at Cedarcrest Sanitarium, 29560 Lake Rd. for 3 mos. of Cerebral Thrombosis; b. 5 June 1872, Dover, OH to ***Sherman OSBORN*** and ***Angenette PHINNEY***, Never Married, Seamstress.; informant *Mabel MEDDICK*, bur. Evergreen Cemetery, Westlake, funeral director Marion E. Pease. Ohio Certificate of Death, Division of Vital Statistics, 1955, certif. 332.

OSBORN, Emily, residence 29560 Lake Rd., Bay Village; sister of the late ***Albert*** and ***Calvin***; sister-in-law of ***Mrs. Lillian OSBORN***...at Burmeister Funeral Home, 163 Avon-Belden Rd., Avon Lake...services...Dec 8 at 1:30 p.m. Cleveland Necrology File, Dec 7, 1955.

Evergreen Cemetery, Section M, Lot 17 ***OSBORN, Emily P.***, 83, d. Westlake, Cerebral Thrombosis. Lot 18, Grave 1. ***OSBORN, Albert D.***, res. 29560 Lake Rd., Bay Village, 90, d. Bay Village, Cerebral Hemorrhage. Grave 2 ***Lillian B.***, res. 2463 Beachwood, Westlake, 86, d. Westlake, Pneumonia/Cerebral Accident. Grave 3 ***Calvin E.***, Lake Rd., Bay Village, 81, pneumonia. Undertaker Marion Pease *(conflicts with newspaper)*, Grave 3. Evergreen Cemetery Records, Westlake, OH.

OSBORN - Lillian B., 1872-1958; ***Calvin E.***, 1866-1948; ***Emily P.***, 1872-1955; ***Albert D.***, 1860-1950. ***Myra L. OSBORN***, 1853-1946. Evergreen Cemetery, Westlake, OH, as read by Catherine Burke Flament.

Lots 49-52 have a stone enclosure around them. There is a partition between 50 and 52.

Lots 49/50 *Owner: A. Wolf of Dover purchased on May 17, purchased in 1879 for $5.25 each* SL

Lot 49-11

FATHER

Lot 49-12 Louisa ____

LOUISA

It has not been determined who Louisa is. She was not identified with the Wolf family but may be in the Pomfrett family described below. Reference to James Pomfrett follows,

for what may be a payment for her grave. There is a possibility this may be a granddaughter of James. The records for the time period are disorganized and not complete.

POMFRETT, James; Lot 49, Sect. 3; April 3, 1897, vol. 1 p. 94. *Typed page with cemetery information at Bay Village City Hall.*

POMFRETT. (West) ***Jas. POMFRETT*** born Jan 18, 1834, died Jan 3, 1905. *(North)* ***Susan****, wife of Jas. POMFRETT,* born Nov 5, 1828 died Nov 1, 1894. ***Sarah SAMMONS*** 1856-1924 *(Daughter of James and Susan). (South)* ***G.T. POMFRETT*** 1866-1921. *(Son of James and Susan).* ***James****,* son of *G & E POMFRETT* 1891-1914; Flat individual stones: *George, Sarah, James, Father, Mother.* Maple Ridge Cemetery inscriptions, Westlake, OH and read by Catherine Burke Flament.

Children of James Pomfrett and Susan Honewell:

James POMFRETT and ***Susan HONEWELL*** were the parents of three known children: ***Sarah POMFRETT***, b. Feb. 1856, Eng., d. 25 Nov. 1924, m. *William SAMMONS*; ***Elizabeth POMFRETT***, b. June 1860, m. *James JENKINS*; ***George Thomas POMFRETT***, b. 3 Apr. 1866, m. ***Eliza GIBSON***. Workman, Jeanne B., Maple Ridge Cemetery, Westlake, Cuyahoga County, Ohio, p. 72.

The State of Ohio, Cuyahoga Count, ss. I certify that on the 16th day of March 1876 ***Mr. William SAMMONS*** and ***Sarah PAMFERT*** *(sp.)* were by me legally joined in Marriage. Rev. Jacob Winslow, Pastor Marriage Record, Cuyahoga County, OH, vol. 20, p. 50.

SAMMONS-Sarah (nee ***POMFRETT***), sister of ***Mrs. James JENKINS***, Nov. 25, age 68 years. Funeral from residence of her sister, *Mrs. James JENKINS*, Hall road, North Olmsted, Stop 24, Elyria line, Friday, Nov. 28, at 2 p. m. Cleveland Necrology File, November 25, 1924, reel 071.

Elizabeth POMFRETT married ***James JENKINS***, 19 Feb 1879, Cuyahoga County, Ohio. Marriage Record, Cuyahoga County, OH, vol. 22, p. 113.

The State of Ohio, Cuyahoga County, ss. I Certify that on the twenty-fifth day of December 1890 ***Mr. George POMFRETT*** and ***Miss Eliza GIBSON*** were by me legally joined in marriage. Frank D. Stevick, Min. Marriage Record, Cuyahoga County, OH, vol. 35, p. 224.

POMFRETT George T., own farm, 53, b. Ohio, parents b. England, occup. farming; ***Eliza***, 56, immigrated 1878, naturalized citizen, b. England, parents b. England; ***Walter H.***, son, 13, b. Ohio; *SAMMON, Sarah*, sister, 62, immigrated *(year unclear)*, naturalized citizen, b. England, parents b. England. 1920 FC OH CY North Olmsted, ED 69, p. 4B, lines 58-61.

POMFRETT George Thomas, husband of ***Eliza POMFRETT***, and father of ***Mrs. William SCHULTZ***, ***Walter***, and brother of ***Mrs. Sarah SAMONDS*** and ***James JENKINS***, June 4, age 65. Funeral from late residence, Hall road, North Olmsted, Tuesday, June 7, at 2:30 p.m. Cleveland Necrology File, June 4, 1921.

George Thomas POMFRETT, d. June 4, 1921, 5:15 p.m., No. Olmsted, Cuyahoga Co, Ohio of Carcinoma of stomach, Gastric Ulcer; res. Hall Rd.; 55 yrs. 2 mos. 1 day; Farmer; husband of ***Eliza POMFRETT***; he was b. April 3, 1866, Lakewood, Ohio; fr. ***James POMFRETT***, b. England; mo. ***Susan HANWELL***, b. England; informant *Mrs. Sarah SAMONNS*, Bay Village, O; undertaker C. Pease, Dover Center, O., burial Maple Ridge. Ohio Certificate of Death, Division of Vital Statistics, 1921, certif. 53485.

Children of George Pomfrett and Eliza Gibson:

POMFRETT-James W., of Dover, O., beloved son of ***George*** and ***Eliza POMFRETT***, Friday, Feb 6, 1914, aged 22. Funeral at the residence of his parents Monday, Feb 9, 1914, at 1 p.m. standard time. February 8, 1914 Cem. rec. 1891-1914 Maple Ridge Cemetery Dover, Ohio. Cleveland Necrology File.

Mr. James W. POMFRETT, d. Feb 6, 1914, 3:40 a.m., German Hospital, Ward 8, Cleveland, Ohio of General Peritonitis 2 ds., contributory Perforating Gastric Ulcer; Single; b. Sept 11, Olmsted, O., 22 yrs., 9 mos., 11 ds.; fr. ***George POMFRETT***, b. Rockport, O., mo. ***Eliza GIBSON***, b. England; where was disease contracted if not at place of death: North Olmsted, O.; undertaker Jas. Pease & Son, Dover, O.; buried Maple Ridge Cem, Feb 9. Ohio Certificate of Death, Division of Vital Statistics, 1914, certif. 7389.

Lot 50-13 Arthur H. J. Wolf

ARTHUR

See Wolf Monument that follows.

Lot 50-14 Wolf Monument

(Parts of monument worn and difficult to read)

ARTHUR H. J. WOLF
June 28, 1874
June 8, 1900

Peaceful be thy silent slumber, Husband.

ALFRED M. WOLF
Born Oct 19, 1828
Died Jan 4, 1896

CAROLINA
His Wife
Born May 26, 1846
DIED June 3, 1930
In hope of eternal life.

WOLF

Lot 50-14 Arthur H. J. Wolf

Arthur H. J. WOLF was the son of ***Alfred WOLF*** and ***Caroline RENTSCHLER***. He was born at 3 a.m. on Friday, August 28, 1874 in Dover. Arthur never married but was dating *Mabel BLAIR WHELPLEY*, foster child of *Henry* and *Regina RENTSCHLER WISCHMEYER* when he died of too much patent medicine on June 8, 1900 in Dover. Wolf Family Bible in the possession of Norma Wolf Garber and interview with Norma Garber.

Arthur WOLF, 26, res. Bay Village, interred 1900, Lot 51. "List of Interments," Lakeside Cemetery, Bay Village, OH.

Lot 50-14 Alfred Marion Wolf

Alfred Marion WOLF, born in Dover, was the son of ***John WOLF*** *(OP 1:13)* and ***Ann ANDERSON*** *(OP 1:15)*. He married ***Caroline RENTCHLER***, who was 17 years younger than he, on March 9, 1865 in West Dover. They would have four sons, all born in Dover: ***Alfred Charles WOLF***, b. 24 Dec 1865, d. 15 Nov 1867*(OP 2:14)*. ***George Saul WOLF***, b. 24 Jan 1868, d. 19 April 1958 in Milan, OH where he is buried with his wife, m. 31 Jan 1894 in Allegan, MI to *Ida SHARP* (dau. of *Adelbert SHARP* and *Mary PORTER*, b. 24 Jan 1876 in Chicora, MI; d. 20 July 1942, Milan, OH). ***Albert Horace WOLF***, who became the second mayor of Bay Village; b. 29 Feb 1872; d. 28 Dec 1931; m. 1 May 1897 *Florence Margarite MALLE* (b. c1877, Balogna, France; d. c10 Nov 1964, Bay Village, OH) dau. of *Gerard Joseph MALLE* (b. 14 March 1836, France; d. 10 March 1912 Ohio Certificate of Death, Division of Vital Statistics, 1912, certif. 14242) and *Celina CARTIGNY* (b. 2 Feb 1841, France, d. 15 Dec 1925, Bay Village. Ohio Certificate of Death, Division of Vital Statistics, 1925, certif. 67795), all bur. in Evergreen Cem. ***Arthur H.J. WOLF***, b. 28 Aug 1874; d. 8 June 1900 *(buried this lot)*.

Alfred served during the Civil War as one of the "100 day" soldiers that Lincoln had requested. He served on garrison duty in forts surrounding Washington as a line of fortification around the capitol.

The smoke house on Alfred's property served as the local jail when needed. When vagrants were released in the morning they frequently smelled like smoke!

Alfred died mysteriously 4 Jan 1896 while on his way home. His body was found below the trestle of the interurban line in Rocky River near where the sewage plant is today. It is thought he may have had an accident while walking home or he had money on him and was murdered. Norma Wolf Garber and Susan Wolf.

The State of Ohio, Cuyahoga County, SS. I certify, That on the 9th day of March 1865, ***Mr. Alfred WOLF*** and ***Miss Caroline RENTSCHLER*** were by me legally joined in Marriage. Lorenso Warner M. G. Marriage Record, Cuyahoga County, OH, vol. 12, p. 101.

WOLF Alfred M. - Private, Company I, Regiment 150 O.N.G., Inf., enlisted 5 May 1864, discharged Aug 23, 1864, length of service 3 Mos. 18 Days. Special Schedule Surviving Soldiers, Civil War, S.D. 6; E.D. 157, line 25 Dover, Ohio.

Alfred WOLF, Rank, private, Company I, 150 Reg't. Ohio Inf. (applied for pension) ...Acquired rheumatism during the service - Has had weak eyes and shortness of breath about 7 years - during this period he has been unable to do any work. Height 5 feet 9 inches; weight 140 pounds, 63 years. vision r. eye 6/20, left eye 1 ½ / 20 March 16, 1892. Civil War Pension File application 1084772, certif. 799 326, National Archives.

150th Regiment served for 100 days. The regiment was raised in Cleveland, Co. I from Dover, Olmsted and Rockport. The Regiment was mustered in May 5th, 1864, sent to Washington, divided and companies were assigned to different forts about Washington. Some of those serving in the 150th were *Joseph STOCKING, Jr., Frederich TUTTLE,* ***Alfred WOLF****, Albert WHICHT, Reuben HALL, Zibia HALL, Erastus LILLEY, Jerome OSBORN, James C. PORTER, Hiram SMITH, Jr., Orpheus SMITH* and *Amos SPERRY.* Reuben Hall, "Reminiscences of Dover Pioneer Life, 1810-1910," p. 16.

Be it remembered that on the 5th day of January A.D. 1896...the dead body of a man...was found at a point 2 miles west from Rocky River, Rockport, Cuyahoga county; I visited the house of deceased at West Dover and there found the dead body...January 6, I summoned the following persons, to-wit: *Fred HINZ, H. WISCHMEYER, Charles HAHN, C. C. DEAN, M--? FARR, Wm. GUTHER* and *Dr. G. C. LATHROP* to appear before me at the late residence...to inquire how...the said person came to his death. The said ***Alfred WOLF*** was married, about 68 years of age, a resident of Dover, and a native of Ohio, had grey eyes, grey hair, and beard and mustache, Dark complexion, and was about 5 feet 9 ¾ inches in height...and was a farmer by occupation, with the following marks and wounds upon his body: a slight wound on the top of the head, being the only visible mark on any part of the body. ...Alfred Wolf came to his death on the 4th day of January 1896, at about 8 o'clock P.M. at or near the Dean trestle so called of the Nickel Plate RR about 2 miles west of Rocky River station in Rockport Twp, by accidentally falling from the top of said trestle to the ice below, a distance of 28 feet, death being caused entirely by said fall and then freezing. J. M. Hurst, Acting Coroner. Civil War Pension File application 1084772, certif. 799 326, National Archives, Washington, D.C.

WOLF, Alfred. Owned land; Acres: Improved - 43 tilled, including fallow and grass, 3 permanent meadow, Unimproved - 26 woodland. Farm Values: Land and buildings- $6000, Machinery - $250, Live Stock - $200. Labor: Paid for wages in 1879 - $300. Weeks of hired labor: 102. Estimated value of all farm production: $600. Grass lands: acreage: 8 mown, 8 not mown, 12 tons hay. 4 horses, 1 milch cows, 1 other, 2 calves dropped, 1 purchased, 8 cattle sold living, 1 slaughtered. 100 pounds of butter made on the farm. Sheep: 8 on hand June 1, 1880, 6 lambs dropped, 1 purchased, 14 sold living, 4 fleeces, 24 lbs. weight. 10 swine. Poultry on farm: 40 poultry, 18 other. 200 dozen eggs produced in 1879. Indian corn: 12 acres, 600 bushels; oats: 4 acres, 280 bushels; wheat: 10 acres, 250 bushels; potatoes: 1 acre, 150 bushels. Orchards - apple: 1 acre, 40 bearing trees, 10 bushels. Total value of orchard products: $5. Amount of wood cut: 100 cords, Value of forest products - $75. "Schedule 2. Production of Agriculture in Dover Township, Cuyahoga County, OH," enumerated June, 1880, p. 26.

Alfred and ***Caroline WOLF'S*** home stood where the Bay Lodge now stands at Bradley and Wolf Rds. Norma Wolf Garber

Alfred WOLF; res. West Dover; interred Jan 9, 1896; Lot 49. "List of Interments," Lakeside Cemetery, Bay Village, OH.

Children of Alfred Wolf and Caroline Rentschler:

My brother ...***George*** lives at 232 Hamilton St. in Cleveland, O. Albert H. Wolf, Deposition B extracted from Civil War Pension File application 1084772, certif. 799 326, National Archives.

WOLF, George S., 62, owns farm valued at $31,000, age at marriage 26, b. Ohio, fr. b. Ohio, mo. b. Germany, Fruit farmer; ***Ida I.***, wife, 54, age at marriage 18, b. Michigan, fr. b. New York, mo. b. Vermont; ***Hiram E.***, son, 20, b. Ohio, machinist manufacturing machines. 1930 FC OH CYBV, ED 18-534, 563 Bradley Road, p. 20A, lines 22-24.

The State of Ohio, Cuyahoga County, SS. I Certify, That on the 4th day of May 1897, ***Mr. Albert H. WOLF*** and ***Miss Florence M. MALLE*** were by me legally joined in Marriage. Rev. W. J. Frost Marriage Record, Cuyahoga County, OH, vol. 45, p. 24.

Parents of Florence Malle Wolf:

MALLE-Gerard Joseph, suddenly Sunday, March 10, at his residence, Center Ridge rd., Dover, O., age 76 years. Funeral from his late residence, Thursday, March 14, at 1:30 p. m., standard. Carriages will meet the Lake Shore Electric car at stop 23, leaving Cleveland at 9 and 10. 1836-1912. Evergreen Cem. Dover Ohio. Cleveland Necrology File, March 13, 1912.

MALLE-Celina, widow of the late ***Gerard MALLE***, mother of ***John, Rene, Matilda, Mrs. B. F. REED*** and ***Mrs. Horace WOLFE***, Dec 15, age 85 years. Funeral from home of her daughter, Mrs. Horace Wolfe, Bradley road, Bay Village, Friday, Dec 18, at 2:30 p. m. Cleveland Necrology File, Dec 17, 1925, reel 054.

A. Horace WOLF, who became the second mayor of Bay Village from 1910 to 1915, remained on the homestead property left him by his father, ***Alfred***, at 492 Bradley Road. Horace had two sons, ***Joseph*** and ***Salem***. Salem built a farm south of his father at 496 Bradley Road. Horace had an airport in the 1920's located on all the land behind St. Barnabas Church. The large homestead was purchased by the City of Bay Village for the Senior Citizens. The house was 101 years old in 1973 when it was torn down to make way for the new Jaycee Community House. Bay Village Historical Society, Bay Village: A Way of Life, pp. 29-30.

WOLF, A. Horace, 58, owns house valued at $35,000, age at marriage 25, b. Ohio, General Farmer; ***Florence A.***, 52, wife, age at marriage 20, b. Ohio, parents b. France; ***Caroline***, 83, widow, mother, b. Ohio, parents b. Wuertenburg, Germany; *KETCHUM, John*, lodger, 84, widowed, b. Ohio, parents b. Ohio. 1930 FC OH CYBV, ED 18-534, 492 Bradley Road, p. 20A, lines 25-28.

John Ketchum was living with George JAYCOX (Lot 62-10) in the 1870 census and later lived with the Wolf family for years. While living with the Wolf family in his later years, John was almost blind and would spend time rocking on the porch. He liked to go down in the basement to get some "spirits" and Horace could never figure out how he would never spill a drop. One day he was in the basement without John knowing when he observed him go up to the spiket with his cup and place his finger in the cup to check the height of the drink going in. Norma Wolf Garber

Spy in Civil War.

Funeral services will be held this afternoon in Bay Village for ***John KETCHUM***, 87-year-old Civil War veteran who served with the Union forces as a spy at 15 and who was believed at the time of his death to have been the youngest Civil War veteran alive. He died Sunday.

Mr. Ketchum was born in Bay Village and lived there until he joined the army in Cleveland when he was 14. Soon after his mother learned of his enlistment she took him home, but he ran away a short time later and re-enlisted under an assumed name, joining Company G of the 107th Ohio Infantry. He became a spy in Charleston, S.C.

He was captured by the Confederates and sentenced to be shot at sunrise of the day following. During the night, as his guard slept, he escaped. He spent many hours hiding in a river, and the long period in the water permanently crippled him.

Mr. Ketchum came back to Cleveland in 1865 and was employed about ten years later by ***Horace WOLF*** to help with light duties around Wolf's farm in Bay Village. He remained at the Wolf farm until his death. In 1906 a fall from a ladder on the farm resulted in partial paralysis, and he had been an invalid since that time. Oct. 26, 1932, p. 1, col. 2. The Plain Dealer.

KETCHUM, John, 88; res. and d. Bay Village, Ohio; cause of death carcinoma; undertaker Clifford Pease, bur. 26 Oct 1932, Evergreen Cemetery, Sect. C2, Lot 88. Evergreen Cemetery, Westlake, Ohio.

Presumed parents of John KETCHUM:

Charles KETCHUM, 27, Farmer and Laborer, value of land $375, b. NY; ***Catherine***, 27, b. Ireland; ***Stephen***, 6, b. O.; ***John***, 4, b. O.; ***Franklin***, 2, b. O. 1850 FC OH LOAV p. 469, lines 33-37.

Albert Horace WOLF, d. Dec 28, 1931, Bay Village, Cuyahoga Co., Ohio of Cardiosclerosis (Angina) Pectoris and Arterio-sclerosis; 59 yrs. 9 mos. 29 ds. Married to ***Florence M. WOLF***; res. Bradley Rd.; b. Feb 29, 1872, Bay Village, Ohio to ***Alfred M. WOLF***, b. Germany and ***Caroline RENTSCHLER***, b. Germany; informant *Joseph A. WOLF*; undertaker Clifford Pease, Dover Center, O.; burial Evergreen, Dover, O., Dec 31, 1931. Buried Grave 3, Lot 19, Section R with Florence. Ohio Certificate of Death, Division of Vital Statistics, 1931, certif. 70153 and Evergreen Cem.

Joseph WOLF, son of ***Horace***, has managed the farm since his father's death a few years ago. Oct, 26, 1932, p. 1. The Plain Dealer. All rights reserved. Reprinted with permission.

Lot 50-14 Caroline Rentschler Wolf

Caroline is the daughter of Regina Lapp Rentschler (OP 2:13), sister of Regina Rentschler Wischmeyer (Lot 38) and aunt of Frederick Hahn (Lot 39), he being the son of Adelheide Rentschler Hahn. A third sister, Sophia Wilhelmina married Charles Hahn.

Caroline, wife of ***Alfred***, was the daughter of ***Jacob Friedrich RENTCHLER*** and ***Regina LAPP*** *(OP 2:13)*. She was born in Wurtenburg, Germany and moved with her family to the U.S. when she was two. She loved to travel and was in San Francisco when the great earthquake struck, promptly returning home. There is a picture that the family has when she attended the Chicago World's Fair as she stood in front of the tallest building that stood 11 stories high! She was an accomplished quilter and cook, always churning her own butter. Norma Wolf Garber

The World Fair of 1893 was officially called the World's Columbian Exhibition, to celebrate the landing of Christopher Columbus in America. The fair is thought to have shaped modern America as it headed into the twentieth century. Twenty seven million visitors viewed the exhibition during the six months it was open.

I am 71 years of age, having been born May 26, 1846, at Kingdom of Wertenberg, Germany. West Dover, O. 2/7, 1917, signed ***Caroline WOLF***.

I am the widow of ***Alfred WOLF***...neither of us had been previously married and I have not married since his death...my parents are both dead and left me no property....My husband left a will under which I was to have the life use of our place on which I have lived ever since his death and after my death the property was to be divided between our two sons ***Horace*** and ***Arthur***. At the time my husband died we had three children. ***George***, then married, and Horace and Arthur then unmarried. George was practically unprovided for under my husbands will-as all that was left him was a vacant lot on Carton St. in Cleveland, O. near Newberg rolling mills as George had married contrary to his fathers wishes...Horace and Arthur made their home with me until Horace got married May 4, 1897-and since then he has lived on next place to me-He is now 28 years of age....Arthur continued to live with me until his death, at 26 years of age, June 8, 1900-he was never married...This farm contains about 112 acres-82 acres my husband inherited from his parents and ever since my husbands death I have rented it to my two sons Horace and Arthur-no one else-and each one of us took one third of what the place produced. Caroline Wolf, Nov 26 1900 Deposition A.

A few years before claimant's husband died their house burned down and he then built their present large house-but expended all the money he had in the house and was never able to furnish it and so it stands vacant with only three rooms scantily and poorly furnished. E. B. Olmsted, Special Examiner.

All of the above are extracted from Civil War Pension File application 1084772, certif. 799 326, National Archives.

Caroline WOLF, d. June 3, 1930, 6:30 p.m.; 492 Bradley, Bay Village, Cuyahoga County, Ohio; b. 26 May 1856, Germany; 84 yrs. 7 days; Widow of ***Alfred M. WOLF***; occup. Hwf; fr. ___***RENSELLER***, b. Germany; mo. ___ ***SCHNAUFER***, b. Germany; informant *A. H. WOLF*, 492 Bradley. I hereby certify, that I attended deceased from Dec 25, 1929 to June 3, 1930. I last saw her alive on June 3, 1930. Cause of death myocarditis serilis (Acute cardiac dilatation), Suddenly; contributory Arterio-sclerosis (General). Burial Bay Village, June 7, 1930; Undertaker Clifford Pease, body embalmed. Ohio Certificate of Death, Division of Vital Statistics, 1930, certif. 34732.

Caroline WOLF, 84, died June 3, 1930, suddenly (do not know), Acute Cardiac Dilation at 492 Bradley Rd., BV, undertaker Clifford Pease, Dover Center. Bureau of Vital Statistics, Burial or Removal Permit, Bay Village, OH. and burial booklet.

WOLF, Caroline, wife of the late ***Alfred M. Wolf***, mother of ***George*** and ***Horace***, June 3, 1930, age 84 years. Funeral from home of her son, Horace Wolf, 492 Bradley Road, Bay Village, Ohio, Saturday, June 7, at 2 p.m. June 7, 1930. The Plain Dealer. All rights reserved. Reprinted with permission.

Lots 51/52 *Owner: C. Wolf of Dover purchased on May 17, 1879 for $5.25 each* SL

The following Wischmeyer descendants are three of the children of Henry (Lot 39) and Regina Rentschler (Lot 38) Wishcmeyer, none of them married. A stone enclosure surrounds their plots including that of Silas Conkey.

Lot 51-14 Sophia Matilda Wischmeyer

1866
MATILDA
WISCHMEYER
1922

Sophia Mathilda was probably named after her aunt, sister of her mother, Wilhelmina Sophia Rentschler Hahn. She went by the name Sophia. Sophia Hahn's son, Frederick, was buried in the cemetery for a short time (Lot 39).

Sophia Mathilde WISCHMEIER, geb. *(born)* 29 Sept 1866, confirmation April 1881. St. Paul Lutheran Church, Confirmation records, p. 71

Matilda WISCHMEYER was an artist and studied in Europe. Some of her work exists today. Norma Wolf Garber

Cream Cookies

(Miss Tillie Wischmeyer)

Two cups granulated sugar, one cup butter, one cup sour cream, three eggs, one-half teaspoon grated nutmeg. The Village Cook Book, p. 35. (c1911-1915).

The Wischmeyer daughters, ***Matilda*** and ***Olga***, never married, were very quiet and cooked at the Wischmeyer Hotel. Kay Laughlin

Matilda WISCHMEYER, Bay, 56, Papillo-cystoma of ovary, undertaker C. Pease, Dover Center, Ohio, Dec 9, 1922. Bureau of Vital Statistics, Burial or Removal Permit, Bay Village, OH.

Matilda WISCHMEYER, Lake Road, Bay Village, d. Dec 7, 1922; single; b. Sept 29, 1866, Bay Village; 56 yrs. 2 mos. 8 ds; cause pappilo cystoma of ovary, attended by doctor Sept 1920-Dec 7, 1922, operation preceded death 1921-2; fr. ***Henry WISCHMEYER***, b. Germany; mo. ***Regina Cathrine RENTSCHLER***, b. Germany; Informant *Henry WISCHMEYER*, Bay Village. Ohio Certificate of Death, Division of Vital Statistics, 1922, certif. 62608.

WISCHMEYER-Matilda, sister of ***Henry*** and ***Olga WISCHMEYER***, December 7. Funeral from late residence, Stop 22, Lake road, Bay Village, O., Saturday, December 9, at 2:30 p.m. Cleveland Necrology File, December 7, 1922, roll 86.

Wischmeyer sisters. Exact identity undetermined, thought to be Matilda and Olga.

Lot 51-15 Olga Wilhelmine Wischmeyer

OLGA
WISCHMEYER
FEB 19, 1869 MAR 27, 1948

Olga Wilhelmine WISCHMEIER born 20 February 1869, confirmed 18 March 1883. St. Paul Lutheran Church, Confirmation Record, p. 72.

Olga WISCHMEYER was a member of the Library and Museum Committee for the City of Bay Village. Minutes, Ordinances & Resolutions, Bay Village, OH, 1918-1921.

Jelly Roll

(Olga Wischmeyer)

One cup sugar, five eggs (the yolk and sugar together and the white beaten separately), one cup of flour, one teaspoon baking powder. A little flavoring, lemon or vanilla. The Village Cook Book, p. 48. (c1911-1915).

WISCHMEYER, Olga. Residence 26565 Lake Rd., Bay Village, sister of ***Henry***. Friends may call at the Clifford Pease Memorial Home, 2914 Dover Center Rd., Westlake, where services will be held Tues., Mar 30, at 3 p.m. Cleveland Necrology File, roll 86.

Olga Wilhelmina WISCHMEYER, res. 26565 Lake Rd., Bay Village, O. occup. housewife; d. 3/27/48, 7:30 P.M. at residence; Coronary Embolism, contrib. Arteriosclerotic Heart Disease 10 yrs., Hypertension 15 yrs., age 76 yrs. 1 mo. 8 days; b. Feb 19, 1872, Dover Twp., Cuy. Co., Ohio; religion Christian Scientist; Pease Funeral Home...Funeral expenses: Casket $530, vault $100, dress Blue Crepe $25, funeral car $12, tent rental $5, opening of grave $20, 6 line death notice in 3 papers $4.70, Sales tax $19.65. Total $756.35. Pease Funeral Home Records, Mss. 4809, Western Reserve Historical Society, Cleveland, OH, Record of Funeral, p. 194.

Olga WISCHMEYER, died in Cuyahoga on March 27, 1948, Coronary Embolism, 76, undertaker Marion E. Pease, Westlake. Bureau of Vital Statistics, Burial or Removal Permit, Bay Village, OH.

Children of Henry and Regina Wishcmeyer.

Lot 51-16 Henry C. Wischmeyer

HENRY
WISCHMEYER
SEPT 27, 1872 JULY 4, 1959

Henry WISCHMEYER worked with his father, ***Henry***, raising grapes. He became very skilled making model and full size boats. Building boats may have provided income for him during the winter months. Many of his models are on display at Rose Hill Museum, Bay Village. Norma Wolf Garber

Great Lakes Historical Museum in Vermilion, Ohio, also has a collection of Henry's model boats.

WISCHMEYER, Henry C., head, own home valued at $12,000, owns radio, 57 yrs., single, b. Ohio, fr. b. Hamburg, Germany, mo. b. Wirtenberg, Germany, farmer; ***Olga W.***, 60, b. Ohio, no occup.; *McMAHON, Mike*, servant, 62, widow, b. Ohio, parents b. Irish Free State, laborer, Fruit Farm. 1930 FC OH CYBV, ED 18-534, 26565 Lake Road, p. 12A, lines 2-4.

Henry C. WISCHMEYER, d. Cuyahoga Co., Cleveland, Ohio, Fairview Hospital. Length of stay 3 days. Usual residence 26565 Lake Rd., Bay Village, OH, farm. Date of death July 4, 1959; 10:50 a.m. Born 9/27/1873, Bay Village, Ohio; age 86; farmer; fr. ***Henry WISCHMEYER***; mo. ***Regina RENTCHLER***. Never in armed forces. Informant *R.E. MILLER*. Cause of death Subarochnoid Hemorrhage, due to Pulmonary edema, due to Early broncho pneumonia. Autopsy performed. Burial 7/7/1959, Lake Side Cemetery, Bay Village, Ohio. Embalmer Glen A. Jenkins, Pease Jenkins Funeral Home, Inc. 2914 Dover Center Rd., Westlake, Ohio. Ohio Certificate of Death, Division of Vital Statistics, 1959, certif. 046693.

WISCHMEYER, HENRY C., residence 26565 Lake Road, Bay Village, foster brother of ***Mable BLAIR WHELPLEY***, uncle of ***Richard E. MILLER***. Family may receive friends from 2-4, 7-9 P.M. MONDAY at the Pease-Jenkins Funeral Home, 2914 Dover Center Rd., Westlake, where services will be held Tuesday, July 7, at 1:30 p.m. Cleveland Necrology File, roll 86.

Henry WISCHMEYER; interred July 7, 1959. "List of Interments," Lakeside Cemetery, Bay Village, OH.

Lot 52-17 Silas E. Conkey

SILAS E. CONKEY
BORN JUNE 1, 1834
DIED AUG 28,
1880(3)
(Year unclear)

Verification of Silas Conkey's identity has not been found, this may be the individual buried at Lakeside but it could not be substantiated further.

Silas E. CONKEY, State Served NY, Enlisted Date 21 December 1863, Enlist Rank Private, Enlist Age 29, Enlist Place Grand Island, NY, Army Union. Company K, Unit 2NY Mounted Rifles, Rank -Induction: Sergeant, Rank -Discharge: Private. American Civil War Records, Box 000551, Extraction 0027, Record 00002616.

Grand Island was located just north of Buffalo, NY, in Erie County.

The Departed,
we reverence their names,
and would emulate their virtues.

A toast by Mrs. J.B. Cahoon, Cahoon Fifty-third Anniversary Celebration of the Settlement of Dover, Oct 10, 1863.

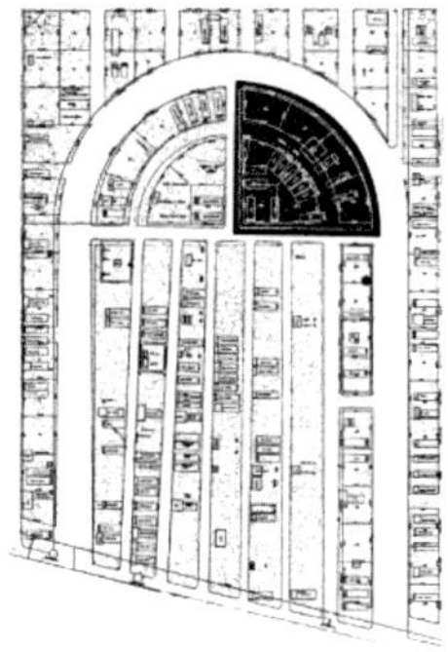

Lots 53-56 and 63-65 comprise the Joel B. Cahoon plot and are included as a unit. The plot is located in the north eastern portion of the cemetery in a quarter circle formation.

Lot 54/55 Cahoon Memorial

Lots 53-56: (Monument centered between Lots 54-55, Thomas Cahoon and family located in 53-54, Lot 56 is empty.) Estate of Dover. Cuyahoga Co., O.

Lots 53, 54 and 55 were $7.14 each, purchased May 30, 1888

Lots 63-65: (Burials) Heirs of Joel B., Cahoon Estate of Dover. Cuyahoga Co., O.

Lot 63 was $9.14, Lot 64 was $9.03 and Lot 65 was $6.30 SL

The Cahoon Monument having four sides, lists the parents, Joel Butler and Margaret Van Allen Cahoon, on the south west side. Thomas Havenner Cahoon, the oldest child and only one who married, is listed on the north east side with his wife and their only child who married and died at the age of twenty-four. The northwest side lists the first five children who died and continues on the south east side with the remaining five.

The burials were organized with Thomas and his family being placed in the southern portion of the outer circle next to each other. Joel and Margaret, the parents, are located in the middle flanked with two male children on each side, forming an arch. Oscar and Emma who died as children are in the outermost corners of this arch. The four remaining daughters are located in the inner portion of the circle. Information on each individual is organized by the inscriptions on the monument, not by lot number.

JOEL B. CAHOON
BORN IN SALISBURY, NY
AUG 27, 1793
DIED SEPT 28, 1882
MARGARET A. VAN ALLEN
WIFE OF
JOEL B. CAHOON
BORN IN WASHINGTON, D.C.
FEB 8, 1810 - JUNE 21, 1894
"I SHALL BE SATISFIED WHEN I AWAKE, WITH THY LIKENESS."

THOMAS HAVENNER CAHOON
JULY 7, 1832 - APRIL 16, 1907
HIS WIFE
ELIZABETH HUGHES CAHOON
NOV 19, 1830 - OCT 4, 1914
EFFIE H. CAHOON ELLIS
AUG 1, 1863 - APR 18, 1888
CAHOON

CHARLES OSCAR CAHOON
OCT 12, 1839 - JUNE 7, 1853
MARY EMMA CAHOON
AUG 20, 1849 - APRIL 17, 1857
LEVERETT JUDSON CAHOON
NOV 14, 1845 - AUG 16, 1886
DANIEL KENYON CAHOON
JAN 25, 1838 - FEB 15, 1890
JOHN JOSEPH CAHOON
JAN 9, 1834 - MARCH 4, 1894

JOHN MARSHALL CAHOON
JULY 20, 1847 - AUG 8, 1899
MARTHA WASHINGTON CAHOON
FEB 22, 1844 - MAY 19, 1903
LYDIA ELIZABETH CAHOON
AUG 16, 1835 - MAR 29, 1917
LAURA ELLEN CAHOON
DEC 12, 1841 - JUNE 2, 1917
IDA MARIA CAHOON
MAR 17, 1852 - NOV 28, 1917

Individual stones surround the monument.

(Lot 63/64) **Joel Butler Cahoon**

JOEL B. CAHOON

Joel Butler CAHOON was the third son of the first settlers of Bay Village, ***Joseph*** and ***Lydia CAHOON***. He was seventeen when his family settled in the area. He married ***Margaret A. VAN ALLEN*** July 14, 1831. He and his family moved back to Dover in 1842 and moved into the vacant family home, Rose Hill, 27715 Lake Road. His children would occupy the home until 1917 when ***Ida Maria***, the last of Joel and Margaret's descendants, passed away. *The last three daughters died within an eight month period.* The home and surrounding land were generously donated to the city by the Cahoon family. Rose Hill became a library from 1919 until 1960. The will stipulated that if the home ceased to be a library it should become a museum. Rose Hill is owned by the City of Bay Village with a museum operated by the Bay Village Historical Society. The museum has room displays in the basement, main and second floor which include a small local history and genealogy library in addition to a shop. The museum always has an impressive display featuring a collection or local history that is changed a few times a year. Bay Village Historical Society, Bay Village: A Way of Life and Rose Hill Museum.

July 14 1831, ***CAHOON, Joel B.*** to ***VAN ALLEN, Margaret***. Margaret E. Myers, Marriage Licenses of Frederick County, 1811-1840, p. 35.

Joel Butler CAHOON and ***Margaret DICKSON VAN ALLEN*** would have eleven children of which only *Thomas*, the eldest, would marry. All are buried in the family plot along with *Elizabeth HUGHES*, the wife of Thomas, and their only child, *Effie CAHOON ELLIS*. The children of Joel and Margaret were: ***Thomas Havenner*** 1832-1907, ***John Joseph*** 1834-1894, ***Lydia Elizabeth*** 1835-1917, ***Daniel Kenyon*** 1838-1890, ***Charles Oscar*** 1839-1853, ***Laura Ellen*** 1841-1917, ***Martha Washington*** 1844-1903, ***Leverett Judson*** 1845-1886, ***John Marshall*** 1847-1899, ***Mary Emma*** 1849-1857, ***Ida Maria*** 1852-1917. Cahoon Collection, Rose Hill Museum.

The Cahoon estate, which is the scene of the celebration of this interesting family each year, is one of the largest and most beautiful in the country. The estate consists of nearly 400 acres of which 110 acres are vineyards. Part of the estate overlooks Lake Erie from a cliff 60 feet high, while in other places the land slopes down to the water's edge. It is at one of these places that one of the best bathing beaches is located. Loose article in Cahoon Reunion Notebook, Rose Hill Museum, Bay Village, OH.

Story told by Joel: He arrived in Dover at the age of 17, 51 year ago. The next Saturday started for Newburgh mill for meal and venison hams. In the vicinity of the mill found Indian wigwams. Old squaw was very friendly, (Voice-"young squaw" - uproarious laughter which quite embarrassed the patriarch) -- but he continued - squaw gave me piece of raw meat, nipped away at it, no salt on it, could not eat, - squaw then gave me dried venison, eat, and bought 120 pounds of saddle venison for one dollar - came home with hams and meal, and the family enjoyed a feast of 'hasty pudding' and venison. Usually went to mill on horseback - horses ran in woods and lived on rushes in winter. On one occasion went down to Rocky river for meal on foot. Shelled three pecks of corn, and helped "*black Pete*" grind it in a hand mill. Forded river next morning with grist on back, got home and had a nice johnny-cake for dinner. ***Mr. Cahoon*** related his pioneer experiences with a freshness and gusto greatly enjoyed by the old and young folks. "Dover Pioneer Pic-Nic," Cahoon Family Reunion Notebook, Newspaper article: 1861.

In the spring of 1813, a certain *Col. WADSWORTH* recruited *Leverett TERRELL* and ***Joel B. CAHOON*** (then living temporarily in Ridgeville Twp.) to join *General W.H. HARRISON* at Fort Meigs. Joel enlisted in Mar 1813 in Capt. D. Mills' company of Ohio militia, serving in the War of 1812 under *Major (or Col.) CROGHAN*. From Fort Meigs (on the Maumee River near Toledo), Joel's company marched with General Harrison to Detroit; and in battle with the British and Indians at Fort Malden, Leverett Terrell was shot and seriously wounded. Joel carried him off the field and dressed his wound, saving his life. In early 1814, serving under Major Croghan, he went north to Fort Michilimackinac (or Mackinaw; at the straits of Mackinac) in an expedition against the British. Joel B. Cahoon eventually was mustered out of service in 1814 at Warren, Ohio.

After leaving the army (and until 1822), Joel carried the public mail by horseback from Cleveland to Maumee City (near Toledo), and then returned to his birthplace, Salisbury, N.Y. (whereupon he spent 3 years in the salt harvesting business and operating a canal boat, near Salt Point, N.Y.). During 1825-26, Joel and his brother, ***Daniel CAHOON***, started and operated a canal store at Boston in Summit Co., Ohio. For the next 16 years (1826-42), Joel and Daniel worked on various "public works" projects as contractors, building canals, aqueducts, viaducts and railroads in Penn., Maryland, Indiana, and southern Ohio. Joel and ***Margaret*** lived first in Maryland, then Cincinnati, returning in 1842 (by horsedrawn carriage) to his father's estate in Dover Twp., Cuyahoga Co.; and they had 11 children. Joel was a farmer and inventor, applying for patents for a shingle making machine and a method of constructing plank roads. Jeff Sigsworth, The Cahoon Family of Scotland (Who Came to Cuyahoga County), p. 19.

Returning home after the War of 1812, he ***(Joel CAHOON)*** was the western mail carrier between Cleveland and Maumee City. On horseback he followed the winding corduroy road through the great swamps, sleeping at night near a smoldering log underneath which he had built a fire. In 1822 he visited Herkimer, N.Y., where he worked in a mill and saved enough money to start business as a contractor. Returning to this state he formed a partnership with his brother ***Daniel***, and they soon had contracts for turnpikes and later for work on the canal, with an office at Boston, O. On the completion of the northern sections of the canal, the firm followed this up with several years of profitable engineering work in the vicinity of Pittsburgh and in the state of Maryland.

...Contracting in the east becoming scarce, the Cahoon brothers removed west in 1842 to complete some project of public works near Cincinnati, the Joel Cahoon family making their home in North Bend. Daniel, the brother, died and Joel closed up his affairs and returned to his farm at Dover.

As Farmer

Here he took up the work laid down by his father a decade before. The grist mill was again set in motion, the saw mill repaired and Joel resumed the life of a farmer until a severe illness incapacitated him from active work.

...July 14, 1881, ***Mr. and Mrs. Cahoon*** celebrated their golden wedding. For two years he had been a paralytic and recently unable to walk and about a year later, on Sept 28, 1882 he died. Mrs. Cahoon died in 1894 at the age of 84; both had been steadfast members of the Early Settlers Association since it was organized. S. J. Kelly, "Cahoon Pioneer Association," undetermined newspaper source, Cahoon Collection, Rose Hill Museum, Bay Village, OH.

The venerable host was eighty-six years of age on Wednesday of this week. He has lived a busy, strong and industrious life. He came with his father to this nook in 1810; was building a grist-mill on the day of *Commodore (Oliver H.) Perry's* victory, and heard the guns of the contending fleets; he went out in the world to business; was one of the contractors of the second railroad built in America; lived a long life among men, and has come back to this quiet nook to spend in quiet and peace the remainder of his days. Last winter he received a slight shock of paralysis, and is suffering from it more or less. He had a word of greeting for all, and no one entered more heartily into the spirit of the occasion. "Old and Young," Cahoon Family Reunion Notebook, Newspaper article, 1879.

Joel Butler CAHOON, the third son of ***Joseph*** and ***Lydia K. CAHOON***, was his father's assistant in clearing the farm, erecting and operating the mills, and fitting the place for a home until 1822.

When the call for men to defend their country came in 1812, he marched away with Col. Croghan to the defense of Mackinac; being mustered out of service at Warren, O., in 1814. He rode horseback through the wilds and marshes, carrying the mail from Cleveland to Maumee City at a later day.

For twenty years he was actively engaged as a contractor, in building canals, aqueducts, viaducts and railroads in Pennsylvania, Maryland, Indiana and southern Ohio. Ida M. Cahoon, History of the Cahoon Family, p. 30.

Joel B. Cahoon, *Private*, Capt. Delanne Mills' Company (Probably from Portage Co.) Roster of Ohio Soldiers in the War of 1812, Adjutant General of Ohio. Transcription, 1916, vol. 2, p. 309.

CAHOON, John B., 76, farmer, value of real estate $20,000, personal estate $800, b. N.Y.; ***Margaret***, 60, KH *(keeping house)*, b. Meriland *(Maryland)*; ***D.K.***, 32, occup. at home, b. same; ***L.E.***, 34, at home, b. same; ***Laura***, 29, at home, b. Ohio; ***Marthy W.***, 25, Teaches school, b. Ohio; ***Leveret J.***, farmer, personal estate $120, b. Ohio; ***J. Marshal***, 22, farmer, b. Ohio; ***Ida M.***, 18, at home, b. Ohio. 1870 FC OH CYDO, p. 30, lines 20-28.

CAHOON, Joel B. Owned land. Acres: Improved - 63 tilled, including fallow and grass, 51 permanent meadow, Unimproved - 20 woodland. Farm Values: Land and buildings- $12,000, Machinery - $400, Live Stock - $600. Cost of fertilizer purchased in 1879: $40. Labor: Paid for wages in 1879 - $300, weeks labor hired: 80. Estimated value of all farm production: $4000. Grass lands: acreage: 10 mown, 20 not mown, 10 tons hay. 4 horses, 2 milch cows, 2 calves dropped, 1 calf purchased, 2 sold living. 200 pounds of butter made on the farm. 3 swine. 100 barnyard poultry on farm, 400 dozen eggs produced in 1879. Oats: 10 acres, 400 bushels; rye: 5 acres, 35 bushels, potatoes: 3 acres, 300 bushels. Orchards - apple: 6 acres, 200 bearing trees, 600 bushels; peaches: 3 acres, 350 bearing trees, 200 bushels. Total value of orchard products: $400. Vineyards: 40 acres, 120,000 lbs. of grapes sold in 1879, 2,000 gallons of wine made in 1879. Amount of wood cut: 50 cords, Value of forest products - $1,000. "Schedule 2. Production of Agriculture in Dover Township, Cuyahoga County, OH," enumerated June, 1880, p. 31.

Mr. Joel B. CAHOON, a son of ***Joseph***, still survives, having wintered the storms of 87 years....Almost three months ago he was prostrated by a third stroke, which has confined him ever since to his bed. "Dover's Settlement," Cahoon Family Reunion Notebook, Newspaper article 1880.

OBITUARY.
JOEL B. CAHOON.

Joel B CAHOON, third son of ***Joseph*** and ***Lydia KENYON CAHOON***, was born in Salisbury, Herkimer county, N.Y., August 27th, 1793. The story of his life, stretching over a space so vast, is full of interest. His father's family removed when he was a small child to Vergennes, Vt., but, this locality not suiting them as a permanent home, in 1799 Mr. Cahoon visited Ohio with a view to settling in this now famous State. Visits to different parts of the State were made, and in 1810 it was decided to locate upon the shore of Lake Erie, twelve miles west of Cleveland. To the New Englander this seemed a dangerous undertaking, and upon the morning of their departure from Vergennes the people assembled upon the village green to bid them farewell after the "man of God" had offered prayer and given them his final blessing. For six weeks the travelers, in their covered wagon drawn by four horses and saddle-horses behind, bore steadily on their way through forests, streams yet unbridged, and over hills, steep and rugged, till the bright sun of October 10th lit the valley and hillside with golden, mellow light, the wagon halted at their first home and the first settlement of Dover was made. For several years the subject of this sketch remained with his father, aiding in the various duties or clearing the forest and farming as well as building the first grist-mill west of the Cuyahoga River, upon Cahoon Creek, the raising of which was in progress at the time of the Battle of Lake Erie. The farm-life was soon after this changed to soldier's, he remaining in service till the War of 1812 was declared at the end.

In 1822 he started out into the busy world, soon acquiring a small capital with which to start a business in company with his brother ***Daniel***.

They took contracts for building locks on the Pennsylvania Canal, being very successful, using the profits thus acquired enabling them to go into stone work, and three or four years were passed in this manner. In 1880 the second railroad of the many which now make the United States prosperous was commenced. In company with *Hon. James K. MOREHEAD*, for many years M.C. from Pennsylvania, three sections of the celebrated B & O. R.R. near Frederick were constructed. The following year he took the contract for building the Lateral Branch of the road from Frederick, Md., to Point of Rocks, an excavation upon it still being known as "Cahoon's deep cut." While in Frederick, he formed the acquaintance of ***Mrs. M. A. VAN ALLEN***, of

Washington, D.C., a lady many years his junior, to whom on July 19th, 1831, he was married. No other proof of the wisdom of his choice is necessary than that more than fifty years have been passed in happy companionship. The good fortune which attended him this far was not always to last, for in 1836 he sustained such heavy losses as to nearly exhaust his heretofore abundant treasury. In view of more prosperous business he moved to Kentucky, then to Indiana, but four years after, when engaged upon a heavy contract, the State of Indiana suspended payment, again depriving him of his gains. The last of his engagements upon public works was in 1842 in North Bend, near Cincinnati, at which time occurred the death of a brother so closely associated with him. This bereavement following his losses in business caused him to think of returning to the home and friends of his youth, and in the autumn he removed to the farm in Dover, engaging in farming and milling till age prevented active life. When the labor was laid aside he sat in comfort by his pleasant hearth enjoying the companionship of life long friends. Three years ago he received a shock of paralysis, and a year later another, which completely prostrated him, but after a time his health was restored, though without the use of his limbs. The same energy which characterized his earlier life was apparent this time, as he patiently and cheerfully waited, expecting to regain the use of his disabled members, never being discouraged or unhappy, but always recognizing some beauty and comfort in his surroundings. He was a member of the Baptist Church in Dover many years, and his latter days were filled with peace and confidence in the blessed promises. His character was never stained. Strictly honest, upright and manly, he was respected by the entire community around him.

He was a man with very few advantages of education except home culture and self improvement, still well informed and intelligent as well as active in business, who battled with the world and was above it, living a strictly temperate, virtuous life. Belonging in part to the last century he witnessed the grand improvements of the age, each as in travel and transportation, the telegraph machinery, etc.; Cleveland, with its four or five houses, grow to a city of 200,000 inhabitants; the Cuyahoga, spanned by its grand viaduct, in place of the ferry of seventy years ago, and the whistle of the locomotive, as it passed the home of the pioneer, railroad contract tracks of a much more rapid transit than ...wagon of 1810.

More than this he outlived his generation. The early pioneers have long since passed from earth given then brothers and sisters who gathered around the home hearth not one remains. He sat in the doorway at Rose Hill watching with unimpaired interest the everlasting, ever beautiful waters, he may *(have)* caught a glimpse of the other country, he whose gateway he was patiently, calmly waited till the hinges would turn and permit an entrance to "an eternal day" with those he loved.

About two months since he was taken ill, and most of the time was in great pain. Thursday evening the end of this beautiful life was reached, and in the same room in which his mother died over forty years ago he breathed his last, bequeathing to his children a priceless legacy in his good name. Newspaper article, undetermined source, Cahoon Collection, Rose Hill Museum, Bay Village, OH.

An Old Pioneer Gone

To the Editor of the Leader:

Little do those who enjoy the luxuries of life as it is to-day realize the labor and time necessary to prepare the unbroken forests of the home of man. Only occasionally do they think of a time when things were not as they are now. Yesterday the past was brought forcibly to the minds of many as the last loving duties were performed for one of the oldest of Cuyahoga's pioneers.

The sun never shone brighter at Rose Hill, the birds never warbled softer notes, and the waves never caressed the shore more gently than upon the funeral day when loving hands bore away from the dear home ***Joel B. CAHOON***, who seventy years ago made the first settlement in Dover. He was closely identified with early days, and all their little incidents. It was upon Cahoon creek that the first grist-mill west of Cleveland was built. It was himself who carried the mail from Cleveland to Maumee City on horseback seventy years ago, and marched away a soldier in 1813. Then, when the farm seemed too narrow for him, he moved out into the busy world, engaging in active life for twenty years before returning to the farm. While away in Maryland, Pennsylvania, Kentucky and Indiana, he was engaged in the construction of some of our first railroads and canals doing a very extensive business. But when age deprived him of his strength he walked in and out among his loved ones with cheerful countenance, and pleasant words. For more than twenty years he was the host at the Cahoon Pioneer Celebration, which is annually held upon his grounds, and it was a sad sight to see the venerable men with bowed heads stand by the side of his form as it lay beneath the tree he planted sixty-eight years ago upon his lawn.

From all surrounding towns came those who respected and loved him, to meet him for the last time at Rose Hill. A double quartette sang, "He's Gone," which was followed by the reading of Scripture. *Rev. John R. JEWETT*, a friend of many years, offered prayer in a feeling and affectionate manner after which was sung the 1000th hymn. *Rev. F. TOLHURST*, of Cleveland, who had visited Mr. Cahoon frequently during five years past and held religious conversation with him, made a few remarks upon the 6th and 7th verses of the 12th chapter of Ecclesiastes. He spoke of the long, useful, busy and excellent life now ended. He spoke of the gentleness, and patience, and reliance upon God in his latter days, and the assurance he had given his dear ones of the home beyond.

"Asleep in Jesus" was sung, after which the five sons bore the casket from the room he so dearly loved. Upon the sixth handle was a black ribbon which told of the other son, whose chair had long been vacant. How fitting that the same hands which ministered to his wants with so much tenderness, during his helplessness, should be the last to carry him.

At the Harris vault, in Erie Street Cemetery, gathered a number of friends to meet the sad procession, and *Mrs. J.C. FITZPATRICK* sang very beautifully, "Abide With Me," before the burial service was read. Then the last look was taken of that calm, beautiful face, which eighty-nine years had failed to impair, and we left him sweetly sleeping in his quiet home, while his soul had reached the beautiful city with "an eternal day." Cleveland, September 30. Newspaper clipping, Joel B. Cahoon Family Papers, Rose Hill.

Joel was originally buried in the vault of his dear friend, *J.A. Harris*. He is remembered here at the annual Cahoon reunion. *J.A. HARRIS*...pioneer, Mayor of Cleveland, editor of the Cleveland <u>Herald</u> and latterly as a vineyardist, where he enjoyed a few years in the vine rows. Newspaper article 1875.

Wm. O. CAHOON of Elyria: "To the memory of my old friend of some fifty years: We lament to-day the absence of our worthy friend and long-tried acquaintance, *J.A.HARRIS*...an acquaintance of many years of his social, literary and political life. He expressed sorrow at his removal from our midst and referred to his valuable service in our annual meetings, where for so many years he performed the duties of Secretary. "The Cahoon Pioneer Celebration," Reunion notebook, Rose Hill Museum, Newspaper article 1876.

The President referred to Mr. Harris as a pioneer, as Mayor of Cleveland, as editor of the Cleveland <u>Herald</u> and latterly as a vineyardist, where he enjoyed a few years in the vine rows.

In all offices of trust he acquitted himself well. His present illness was very severe, but he had the love and friendship of hosts of friends. "A Pioneer Celebration," Sixty-Fifth Anniversary Cahoon Reunion. 1875. Undetermined newspaper article, Cahoon Collection, Rose Hill Museum, Bay Village, OH.

CAHOON, Joel B., b. Herkimer, NY, m. ***Mrs. Margaret VAN ALLEN***, nee ***DICKSON***, widow of ***John D. VAN ALLEN***, dau. of ***John Calhoun DICKSON.*** Frederick City, Maryland, 7/14/1831. <u>Memorial Record of the County of Cuyahoga and City of Cleveland</u>, p. 400.

CAHOON, Joel B, d. Sept 28, 1882, Dover, 89y. 1m. 1d., b. New York, parents: ***Joseph*** and ***Lydia CAHOON***, disease paralysis, residence Dover. PD 2:185.

Joel B. CAHOON was moved from Erie Street Cemetery on Oct 7, 1882, to his final resting place at Lakeside Cemetery. Erie Street Cemetery, Cleveland, Ohio.

(Lot 64) Margaret Dickson Cahoon

MARGARET A.
CAHOON

Margaret DICKSON was the daughter of ***John Calhoun DICKSON*** and ***Elizabeth REASER***. Margaret, their only child was born in Washington on Feb 8, 1810. John and Elizabeth spent their married lives in Washington City, D.C. where they are buried.

Margaret's first marriage was to ***John Douglas VAN ALLEN*** of New York City on Aug 14, 1827. He died in Philadelphia, Pa., March 4, 1829 leaving her a widow and orphan. She moved back to Washington to live with family friends and met ***Joel CAHOON*** in November, 1830 while on a trip to Frederick. Margaret subsequently married him and had eleven children. Margaret Dickson Van Allen Cahoon, "Autobiography of Margaret Dickson Van Allen Cahoon."

The Autobiography of Margaret Dickson Van Allan Cahoon

My father, ***John Calhoun DICKSON***, was a native of Gulbuoy, Ireland. He came to the United States under the care of an uncle and resided in Philadelphia until he was eighteen, when he went to St. Mary's County, Md., where he remained a short time, then removed to Washington, D.C. ***Elizabeth,*** daughter of ***Jacob*** and ***Margaret HARDMAN REASER,*** was born in Frederick Town, Md., Nov. 13, 1770, and was married to my father in that city May 1, 1800. They went to Washington City where they spent the remainder of their lives. I was their only child and was born February 8, 1810. My father died Oct. 2, being 59 years and three days old, and my mother's life ended March 29, 1828. They are buried in the Congressional Cemetery in Washington, a space for a grave between theirs being reserved, by my father's request for their only child. When only three days old I was baptized by *Rev. Mr. MCCORMICK*, pastor of Christ Protestant Episcopal, at the Navy Yard. I was sent to school very early, before I was four years old. My first teacher was an elderly lady who taught in a building which had been used for a stonecutters shop, when the first Capitol was being built. I remember her as a very kind lady, whom I called *Grandma ELFERD*. I was taken to school by riding on horseback before my father or the man servant. I do not know that I acquired much knowledge in this school but remember distinctly the little pallet made for me when sleep overtook me.

Mrs. HALEY was my second teacher. This was after the war of 1812, as the first school building was destroyed by the British. The way to this school was through the Capitol Grounds, being a small enclosure, you would think so to compare the present with the past. She rewarded us with nuts and candy. My next teacher was *Mrs. NOY*, a very lovely lady, sister of the Washington Postmaster. In *Mr. TIPPET'S*, the next school I attended where the monitor system was observed, one day his assistant whipped every scholar, why we never knew.

While a pupil in *Miss WHITE'S* school the Pawnee tribe of Indians came to Washington on business with "The Great Father." The pupils of Miss White's Seminary, having heard of the magnanimous deed of one of the chief's of that tribe in rescuing a white woman from the funeral fire, resolved to show in a measure their appreciation of his valor on that occasion, had a large gold medal made to present to him. On one side of the medal was a representation of the event - the fire, the woman bound to the stake, the chief with two horses ready to rescue her. On the reverse side was inscribed, "Presented by the young ladies of Miss White's Seminary, Washington City, D.C."

I would like to narrate the proceedings as I remember them. Each pupil contributed two dollars, which was placed in Miss White's hands to order the medal and make the purchases. We were to have a gay dress for the squaw and beads for the papoose. On the appointed day the teacher and pupils assembled in the schoolroom which was in the old Washington Bank. The scholars were in the cloakroom. The Indians came and seated themselves on the floor. Then Miss White led her pupils in the schoolroom. On our entrance the Indians smoked the pipe of peace and it was handed to each of us. *Miss Mary RAPINE*, the oldest scholar, presented the medal and made an admirable speech. The Chief's reply was quite eloquent, being translated by their interpreter, and the gifts to the squaw and papoose, appeared to delight him as much as the medal. He became very demonstrative when the beads were placed on the baby's neck. Mary Rapine wore a crimson crape dress, and broad white satin scarf, which seemed to please the Indians very much. All were happy – we in giving and they in receiving.

We had two May parties while I was attending the school. The pupils voted for the queen, and she selected her maids of honor, crown bearer, and floras. We had a throne decorated with flowers and evergreen. The floras, carrying little baskets filled with flowers, preceded the queen who was guarded by four maids of honor, followed by the pupils and last by the crown bearer and her assistant. The line of pupils divided and the crown bearer and her assistant passed up to the stage and placed the crown on the head of the queen. The assistant put a garland of flowers around her shoulders. They then conducted her to and seated her on the throne. The crown bearer made a short speech to which the queen replied. After this reply the six little floras each repeated a verse and handed her their baskets to select a flower from. The rest were cast at her feet. The Queen was congratulated by the teacher and pupils. The rest of the day was spent in play. These May parties were held in the woods about two miles out of the city, and we enjoyed them very much.

Miss White was a native of Salem, Mass., and I think was the only Congregationalist in the city at that time. She rewarded us for good conduct and being at the head of our classes by allowing us gold medals. We were permitted to wear the medals a week and were very much pleased to have them over Sunday. I often received the medal for being at the head of the class, sometimes had three at once, but on account of whispering never received one for good conduct.

I next attended *Thomas WHEAT and Son's* Hamiltonian school at the Navy Yard. Mr. Wheat was an intimate friend of my father's and a prominent member of the Ebenezer Church. After some time I was placed under the instruction of *Mr. Noah BRASHEARS*, where I was taught to understand Grammar more fully than every before. He was the author of "Brashears' Grammatical Tables." Mr. Brashears also paid particular attention to Orthography and Reading. It was while in this school I received a copy of *THOMSON'S* "Seasons" as a prize awarded by the votes of the audience for reading *COWPER'S (William)* poem, "Cruelty to Brutes Censured."

I was sent to *Don* and *Madame TASTUS* who were Spaniard's. Here I received my first lessons in painting. I was only a short time under their tuition. The Madame ate our dinners. *Mrs. STONE*, an English lady who was considered a superior teacher for young ladies, was the principal of the last school I attended. I liked all of my teachers, but think Miss White and Mr. Brashears were remarkably fine. The instruction received from them has remained in memory through all my life, and for which I am very grateful.

I have written a long chapter on education as I consider it of great importance.

Among the earliest recollections of the war of 1812, I remember distinctly my father coming into the house on the morning of August 24, 1814, and telling my mother that the British were coming up the Eastern Branch of the Potomac and would be in the city in a short time, requesting her to use all possible haste to be ready, as he had engaged a hack to take *Mother*, *sister* and me to Frederick City about forty miles distant where Mother's sister lived. I also recollect our journey, stopping at a spring to eat our lunch, and that it was a very warm day. The news was carried from Washington daily to Frederick by a man on horseback called the Express, who called out as he rode through the streets: "The British in the City"; "The Capitol in Flames"; "*General ROSS* Horse Shot From Under Him"; "The British have taken possession of the President's House." I used to sit on my aunt's portico every evening to hear the news, not that I really understood the meaning of it all, yet I knew there was something dreadful about the war, and was anxious to hear from my *father* who remained in Washington and whom I loved dearly.

While we were in Frederick father was a prisoner for one day and compelled to walk to the President's House, about two miles, a greater distance than he had walked for many years. When the soldiers entered the house to search for firearms and take father prisoner, he was reading for morning devotion in the family Bible, which I have given to *Marshall*. A few days before the British came our money, silver and other valuables were put in boxes and buried in the garden. We spent about a week in Frederick and returned to Washington where we found things much changed. Father took me to the Capitol and there we saw the walls of the House of Representatives and Senate Chambers all blackened with smoke, the eagle over the Speaker's chair blackened and broken, and the names of *(Adm. Sir George) COCKBURN* and *(John) ARMSTRONG* written on the walls and columns. Armstrong was the Secretary of War in 1812. It was said by some he was bribed. The Capitol buildings were so mutilated the citizens of Washington feared Congress would be removed to some other city.

A number of citizens formed an association to erect a building, which was called "The Brick Capitol," to be ready for occupancy at the opening of the next session of Congress and it was accomplished. This building was only a few rods from our home and father owned stock in it. It was used afterward by Commissioners of Ghent, also as a prison in the war of the Rebellion. It was with some of the interest of this stock that we bought the scholarships in the Ohio Wesleyan University. We sold the stock to a *Mr. ADAMS* of Washington and used the avails in purchasing the six acres from *Mr. SMITH*. After peace was declared, the city was illuminated with candles, put in tin sockets and potatoes cut flat to hold the lights, they were placed at the little panes of glass, some to form designs and mottoes. I remember my father's taking one to a thickly populated part of the City to see the "Beautiful Sight." Quite different from the Electric lights now used. Remember when you read this it took place seventy-five years ago, and I am glad that I can and do rejoice with you in the wonderful improvements.

President (James) MADISON resided for a short time until his former residence was repaired at the Octagon House, in the corner house of a row called the Six Buildings. I have seen *Mrs. Dolly MADISON* many times talking to her pet parrot. She was a very commanding looking lady and wore elegant looking turbans. It was a source of great pleasure to me when a child to look upon her lovely face. I was present at the inauguration of *President MONROE* which took place at the Brick Capitol March 4, 1817, a temporary platform having been erected for that occasion. I became acquainted with *Virginia GOUVERNEUR*, a granddaughter of the President's while on a visit to *Major ADLUM'S* who was a relative of my mother's and who is said to be the father of grape culture in the United States.

When a child, my father took me to every session to visit the judges of the Supreme Court. They appeared to be interested in my education, asking me how I progressed in my studies, having me read, and pronouncing words for me to spell. At one time *Justice LIVINGSTON* gave me colander to spell, saying, "If you spell it correctly, Margaret, you shall have the nicest hat in the city and you may have two trials, for the Chief Justice could not spell it." He thought I would spell it right but I lost the hat. The impression made on my young mind caused me ever to remember those great men with much veneration.

Those I remember distinctly are *Chief Justice MARSHALL* of Virginia, who was a very plain, mild gentleman, remarkably polite; *Justice STORY* of Connecticut, bright and cheerful in his appearance; *Justice Brockholst LIVINGSTON* of New York, who was a very dignified person; *Justice Bushrod WASHINGTON*, a nephew of *General WASHINGTON*; *Justice JOHNSON* of New York; and *Justice DUVAL* of Maryland. The judges all boarded at the same house. On my way to Miss White's school I passed through the Capitol grounds, and often stopped on my return when Congress was in session to hear the debates. It was then I heard *Henry CLAY, John RANDOLPH, John C. CALHOUN, Edward EVERETT, Daniel WEBSTER*, and many other notable men. Mr. Randolph boarded opposite the Capitol and could be seen almost any morning – especially if he was to speak on an important subject-riding on a gallop followed by his servant John and a number of hounds. Whenever it was known that Mr. Randolph was to speak the galleries of the House of Representatives were crowded. This he did not always appreciate as an instance will prove. On one occasion, on looking up and seeing the galleries mostly filled by ladies he said, "I think those ladies would be much better employed at home darning their husband's stockings."

Messrs. Everett and Webster were very intimate friends. They boarded near each other and the same carriage served both families. *Mr. O'BRIEN* was the member from Maine when in 1820 it was admitted as a State into the Union. He frequently came and requested the privilege to hoe in our garden for exercise. *Hon. Elias KEYES* visited Father often and wrote him a letter saying he wished to rent rooms, "One for a family room, another for a bed chamber" also that "he would furnish his own provender," and directed the letter to "*John C. DICKSON* the grate gardener, Washington City." I believe he was Governor of Vermont at one time. *Hon. James BUCHANAN*, then Senator from Pennsylvania, visited us twice every session always bringing us a letter from Mother's aunt who lived in Lancaster and taking our answer when he returned. He was a fine looking gentleman, very polished and prepossessing in his manners. When *Commodore (Stephen) DECATUR* was killed in the duel at Bladensburg, I saw the party on their way to the fatal field.

Commodore Decatur was a brave naval officer and was accused of cowardice by *Commodore (James) BARRON*, who was the challenger. He was buried at Kalorama in a vault belonging to *Col. TAYLOR* (name crossed out). "He was followed to his grave by the President of the United States, and the most illustrious men of our times. The same cannon which so often announced the splendid achievements of Decatur, now marked the periods of bearing him to the tomb. Their reverberating thunder mournfully echoed through the metropolis, and also vibrated through a heart tortured to agony." He tried to avert the duel, saying to Commodore Barron, "I have not challenged you, nor do I intend to challenge you; your life depends upon yourself." I have written a long account of this brave officer for the reason that my father held him in great esteem, and I remember how often and sorrowful I used to look at a fine oil portrait we had of him. I attended the funeral and recollect how sad the people appeared.

When *General (Marquis de) LAFAYETTE* visited Washington in 1824 a procession of girls from *Mr. MCLEOD'S* school, dressed to represent the States of the Union, met him at the East gate of the Capitol grounds and repeated the lines which were sung to *General WASHINGTON* as he crossed the bridge at Princeton.

Welcome, mighty chief once more!
Welcome to this grateful shore!
Now no mercenary foe
Aims again the fatal blow,
Aims at thee the fatal blows.

Virgins fair and matrons grave,
Those thy conquering arm did save,
Build for thee triumphal bowers.
Strew ye fair, his way with flowers.
Strew your hero's way with flowers.

During the singing of the last two lines, the ground in front of LaFayette was strewn with flowers by the young ladies. The scene was truly beautiful, LaFayette showing considerable emotion! They then joined the procession at the East portico of the Capitol. Here he received the citizens and I am pleased to say I had the honor of shaking hands with such an illustrious and venerable general.

In my childhood there was no Sabbath Schools except for colored people. I attended classes in Catechism every Saturday afternoon at Ebenezer M. E. Church taught by the minister in charge. My father united with the church about

1812 under the ministry of *Rev. Andrew HEMPHILL*, "He was a Good man, full of the Holy Ghost and of faith." Mother united with the church soon after, *Rev. Mr. MONTGOMERY* being the pastor. My father's house was always a home for the Methodist preachers and I will mention the names of a few who visited us frequently: *Rev* Hemphill, *WATT*, Montgomery, *MONROE, WAUGH, PEYTON, SLICER, WILSON*, and *KEPPLER*. Father was one of the charter members of the Ebenezer Station, which was the only M. E. Church in Washington at the time. I always enjoyed the visits of our ministers, and judging from the notice I received from them I must have been quite a favorite. Grandpa Watts gave me the first religious book I ever owned, having for its title, "The Life of Jesus a Token for Little Children," which I prized very much. Father was a subscriber for the Methodist Magazine when it was first published and continued taking it until it was superceded by The Christian Advocate and Journal.

I was taught to remember the Sabbath day and keep it holy, which had a good effect on me in after life. I have heard many of the celebrities of our church preach, namely, *Bishops SOULE, Vaughn EMORY, BAKER, SIMPSON, THOMSON, FOSTER, MERRILL, PECK, ANDREWS, FOWLER, JOYCE, and FOSS. Also Revs. SUMMERFIELD, Lorenso DOUR, MOFFIT, BASCOM, Peyton HAMMET, Stephen ROZZEL, Adam POE, Louis R. FECHTIG, French J. EVANS, and John P. DURBIN*. I heard Dr. Durbin preach the most eloquent sermon to which I ever listened in the House of Representatives from Philippians 2 and from the fifth to the eleventh verses inclusive. He concluded his sermon by quoting the last stanza from *THOMSON'S* "Hymn to the Seasons," beginning with "Should fate command me the farthest verge." I never heard anything so fine. It still rings in my ears, and the angelic countenance of the speaker til....to my vision. I also was permitted to hear *Miss Harriet LIVERMORE*, sister to *Senator LIVERMORE*, many times. The sermon that I will speak of in particular was in the House of Representatives during *President John Quincy ADAMS* administration from Samuel, 23 Chapter, 3, 4 verses.

I united with the Ebenezer M. E. Church in Washington City when I was eleven years old, Rev. Yelverton Peyton being pastor. I suppose my name is on the records yet. In consequence of my many removals and the care of my children for sometime, I rarely attended church but I followed my early teachings reading the Bible, and having my children commit portions of it to memory, and reading religious books, and never lost my love for the church of my youth. I was and am a firm believer in her doctrines and polity. I again united with the M. E. Church in Dover in 1851, *Mr. PLUMMER* receiving me into the church. Since that time I have endeavored to be a humble follower of my Lord and Master. During my residence in Dover I have heard Bishop Simpson preach some very impressive sermons. The last time I heard the saintly Simpson was at the dedication of the Brooklyn M. E. Church.

I was married to ***John Douglas VAN ALLEN*** August 16, 1827, the *Rev. William RYLAND* officiating. I remained with my mother until March 1828, when I went with Mr. Van Allen to New York city, his native place. We boarded with his oldest sister, ***Susan VAN GUIESON***, who was very kind and loving to me. Mr. Van Allen had three other sisters; ***Margaret FRANK, Maria CARROL, Caroline HAGERMAN*** and a brother ***Peter***, all living in New York. April 3, I received a letter from *Miss Ellen HICKEY* who was one of our most intimate friends bringing the sad intelligence that my dear mother was very ill. We started as soon as possible for Washington and on our arrival found that mother's death occurred one week previous. She had passed away about two hours after Miss Hickey's letter was written, being sick but one day. The friends who were with her and so kindly cared for her assured me that everything that human skill could do was done, but of no avail. *Dr. Frederick MAY*, our family physician spent the entire day with her. Mr. Havenner, her dearest friend, was kneeling by her bedside praying with her, holding her hand in his when death loosed the clasp. The *Rev. Norval WILSON* officiated at the funeral, and she was laid away in the Congressional Cemetery. This was the second sorrow in my life.

I returned to New York and remained there until May, when we went to Philadelphia. Mr. Van Allen, going to work for *Mr. SHUTHERS*, I remained in Philadelphia until November, when I went to Harrisburg, and on our journey homeward we visited mother's aunts and cousins in Lancaster - were very cordially received and kindly treated. We arrived in Philadelphia Dec. 3 and Mr. Van Allen was never out of the house after. He did not seem to suffer much pain, but gradually grew weaker, and on the fourth of March 1829 he was taken from me, leaving me an orphan and a widow. Another deep sorrow added to the death of my dear mother, but God who had watched over me in years past, provided a friend in Mr. Havenner, who had been my guardian, and for whom I have always had the tenderest love. He wrote to me immediately, to come to Washington, saying that as long as he had a home I should share it with his children. I always found it just as he said, I feel grateful to him not only for the house, but the kind counsel and fatherly love bestowed upon me.

While a widow, I spent my time at my ***Aunt Proctor's*** *(sp.?)* in Fredricksburg, Va. ***Aunt Micheal*** in Frederick, Md., and at Mr. Havenner's the latter place being my home. While I was in Fredricksburg the remains of "Mary the mother of Washington" were removed from the former burial place, the old farm of the Washington family to the site where in May the corner stone was laid by *President JACKSON*. At the present time, Jan 18, 1890, there is a lawsuit between The Ladies Association and a real estate firm who pretend to claim the site which was bought from a gentleman with whom I was well acquainted.

I visited my Aunt in Frederick early in November 1830 and it was when there that I was introduced to your Pa. He paid particular attention to me and said he was pleased with me the first time he saw me. An attachment was formed which resulted in our marriage. The ceremony was performed at the residence of my Aunt Micheals, *Rev. MCSCHAEFFER* officiating; ***Cousin Ellen*** *(BINNEY)*was brides maid and *Mr. George RICE*, groomsmen. I was dressed in a light gray Gros di Naples silk, made surplice waist, a thread lace inside handkerchiefs, the shirt full with three large sized tucks, White silk stockings and white satin slippers. My hair was dressed high wearing a high comb, two puffs each side, and long curls at the back. A head dress made of white satin braids so as to form a coronet, I carried a very fine linen cambric handkerchief made of a square of the material and beautifully marked with indelible ink. It was large enough to make a half dozen pocket handkerchiefs today.

Mr. Cahoon wore a suit of crape dressed black cloth, white vest, white cravat, white silk socks and morocco pumps. Your uncle ***Daniel***, Aunt and family, *Mr. and Mrs. HAVENNER* their sons, *John Fletcher*, and *Charles Wesley*, *Captains PARRISH* and *Weems, Mr. and Mrs. SIMMONS* and *Mrs. EVETT* were the wedding guests. In the fifty-nine years that have passed since that memorable day to me, great changes have taken place. Of all the guests assembled on that day, *cousin* ***Ellen BINNEY*** is the only one that has not crossed the "River of Death." She, aunt's colored servant, *Susan (VAN GUIESON)* and myself are the persons that are living who were present at the time of our marriage.

Your Pa and Uncle had a heavy rock contract on the Baltimore and Ohio Rail Road known as the Cahoon deep cut. They had planned they would have some very heavy blasts on the next day, your Pa and I accompanied by the most of the wedding guests drove to the section about a mile distant and your uncle had the fuses in readiness so that when we arrived about fifty blasts went off making a tremendous noise, and throwing out the largest blocks of limestone I ever saw. After remaining at the section about two hours, we returned to Aunt's and partook of a delicious dinner. Rather a novel way to entertain a bride, you think but it pleased me, because it delighted your Pa and Uncle.

Here let me acknowledge my love, gratitude and respect for my dear aunt, who after my mother's death filled her place more than any other person. She was tender and careful of me all the time I was near her and very indulgent of *Thomas* and *Joseph* when children. As long as life lasts I hope to remember her gratefully. We remained at aunt's a few days and then went to New Market, Frederick County, Md., where your Pa had section seven on the B. & O.R.R. to build. We boarded at *Mr. OWING'S* Hotel which was a very pleasant home and where we formed many pleasant acquaintances. When this contract was completed we returned to Frederick and boarded with *aunt*. On the 28th of November, the first passenger cars drawn by horses, came to Frederick, having on board *Mr. THOMAS* the president of the board of directors, the engineers and superintendents of the Baltimore and Ohio Railroad. In honor of the occasion the citizens of Frederick gave a banquet to which your Pa and Uncle were invited. It was a gala day for Frederick, as much so then as the viaduct was to Cleveland, the cars had never run any further than *ELLICOTTS Mills*, twelve miles from Baltimore. The next day we went to Hancock, Md. and boarded with *Mrs. OLIVER* who was very kind and motherly to me. Your Pa had a contract with the B. & O. R.R. to supply them with ties. He had to be away from home as his business was chiefly with the lumbermen in the mountains. It was while we were at this place *Mrs. CHARLTON* sent a horse with mother's side saddle for me to visit her. Your Pa, Mrs. Oliver and I accepted the invitation and had a very pleasant visit at her home in Pa. *A page of the manuscript appears to be missing*

...to *Mr. CROMWELL'S* to board, Your Pa had several miles of McAdamsed road to build. Here I saw the great shower of meteors on October 13. It appeared as though it were raining stars. We returned to Frederick and on the ninth of January, our son ***John Joseph***, who has the name of his two grandfathers, was born. We went to Williamsport, Md., where your Pa had another contract with the Chesapeake and Ohio Canal Co. We remained here about one year, boarding at Brown's Hotel. Your Pa, *Thomas*, *Joseph* and I left Frederick May 1, 1835, for a visit to Dover, Ohio, by stage; arrived in Cleveland the fifth. We put up at the Franklin House, kept by *Mr. SCOVILLE.* In the morning your Pa asked Mr. Scoville where he could get a hack to take him to ***Leverett JOHNSON'S*** in Dover. He pointed him to the stable back of a crockery store on the opposite side of the street, saying it was the only hack in Cleveland. We reached Dover about noon, your ***Aunt Abby*** *(Abigail CAHOON JOHNSON)* was the first one to meet us, she seemed pleased to see me. I thought she appeared shy and embarrassed. Soon your uncle Leverett came in and I felt more at ease. They sent your ***Cousin Asahel*** to the lake to inform your ***Grandpa*** *(Joseph Cahoon)* of our arrival. The next morning very early we heard some one talking in the sitting room. Pa recognized his voice and immediately went out to see him. I followed very soon and received a warm and loving reception as did the two boys. I already loved him not only as the father of my husband, but for the many loving letters I had received from him since my marriage, one in particular, the first one we received after our marriage. I will give you a sentence or two, and you will be able to form your own opinions. He commenced the letter in saying,

"Dear,

What shall I say, I have been saying child, I now say Dear Children, Every new connection lays me under renewed obligations to strive for their happiness, this my feelings would prompt me to do by wishing you all the happiness that an accommodating world, and a well regulated life can afford you, the reason for this desideratum I must leave for you to pursue, and bring to your view a happiness far superior to any worldly happiness."

Two years later your uncle visited Ohio, making the journey on horseback, to visit his venerable and aged father. He spent about three weeks with the different members of the family and his visit delighted Father that he was quite overcome. As he expressed himself "he thought he would pass off the stage of life." This proved to be true, for the day that *Daniel*, your uncle, intended starting on his return your grandpa was taken sick and became so ill that Daniel remained, and the next day the family was shocked by his sudden death. The most of his children were with him at the time he passed away. It was always a great consolation to your uncle that he could be with your Grandpa in his last moments.

Before this I ought to have mentioned ***Mother*** *(Lydia)* ***Cahoon's*** death, but will speak of it now in connection with that of your Grandpa, Your Grandma was taken suddenly ill while alone, Father having been detained at your uncle *Leverett's* on account of a violent thunderstorm. The granddaughter, ***Selisia*** *(possibly Silicia HEATH WRIGHT)*, was at Newburg to visit her mother. When Father returned very early in the morning he found her very ill, scarcely able to speak, and after inquiring from her relative to her sickness went to ***Brother Amos*** *(CAHOON)* for assistance. Nothing could relieve her and in a few hours, she who was so loved and lovely was removed from them by death. The old neighbors who have frequently told me how much they missed her, also spoke of her many deeds of kindness, and amiable qualities. Your Uncle Daniel selected the following to be inscribed to their memories.

"The terrors of Death had not power to alarm him,
He felt not its sting, he feared not the tomb;
For the smiles of his Savior in mercy had met him,
Oh, Death thou art anguished! Oh, Grave where's thy gloom?
Then calm be the spot where her form now reposeth,
May the friends who so loved her visit the grave,
And find, though the cold sod her ashes encloseth,
She lives in the presence of Him who can save."

The next Monday, your ***Aunt Mary*** *(GRIFFITH)*, uncle ***William*** *(Ovington Cahoon)* and *Mr.(Ebezener) Griffith* came to see us, and we accompanied them to Elyria, making your uncle's (Wm.) house our home. Your Grandpa invited all his children home to dine with him. He requested me to have a Maryland dinner, I made potato pies. When we were seated at the table he said, "Daughter you forgot the tea" and when I told him we never had tea for dinner in Maryland, he replied, "We will not have tea, we want a Maryland dinner." He enjoyed the gathering very much.

After spending four weeks very pleasantly with our relatives we left Ohio and turned our faces homeward. We bought a pair of horses, that we named Montezuma and Pizarro, also a Jersey wagon with two seats. We had the seats so arranged that the children could sleep there when we were driving, also had a stationary umbrella to protect them from the sun. We made our journey from Ohio to Maryland in ten days, having had a delightful journey. I kept an account of our expenses and found the cost of our return trip was twenty-seven dollars, a journey of four persons, two horses and a toll! We arrived in Frederick June 13 and went to board with an old friend *Mrs. EVITT* who had a beautiful residence called "Bears Folly" just in the suburbs of the city. On the 16 of August to our delight our daughter ***Lydia Elizabeth*** was born. September 17 we went to Clear Spring, thirty-six miles from Frederick and boarded at *BOYD'S* Hotel, until April when we commenced keeping house for the first time. Your Pa and uncle had two very large contracts on the Chesapeake and Ohio Canal. Your uncle had the management of the Round Top work, which was twenty miles west, and your Pa had the work that was two miles distant. It was at Clear Spring *Thomas* was sent to school to *Mrs. MILLER*. *Joseph* also attended a short time. The birth of ***D. Kenyon*** Jan 25 in Clear Spring Md. added another son to our family, August 21, 1838. I've started to seek a home in the South. We chartered a stage, *Pa., uncle Thomas, Joseph, Lydia, Kenyon* and I were the passengers. We had a very pleasant journey to Wheeling, where we had expected to take a steamboat to Cincinnati, but on our arrival we found the Ohio river so low we were detained several days, and accepted the hospitality of *Wm. NEWMAN* and wife, old Maryland friends, who heard of our coming, and came to the hotel and insisted on removing our baggage, and having us remain with them until we decided upon our mode of traveling to Cincinnati. We were so cordially entertained that I quote a line from *(Robert) BURNS* which I wish to impress on your minds.

"When thou meetest thy mother's friend
Remember him for me!"

We hired a private conveyance to Cincinnati. From there we took passage on the little Steamer Return and even to the Louisville House for a few days, obtained board in a private boarding with *Mrs. INGHAM*, Main street, remained there until late in November. We then went to Hamburg, Indiana, eight miles from Louisville. This place was inhabited principally by men who followed running flat boats for an occupation and were the most ignorant and degraded people I ever met, although I had not any personal acquaintance with them. *Mr. SMITH*, the gentleman with whom we boarded, kept the stage house and was a large landholder. His wife was very kind to me and remarkably so to the children, proving to me that often beneath a rough exterior, we find a kind heart. *Thomas* and *Joseph* attended school here, kept by *Miss DOUR (sp.?)*, a great niece of the eccentric *Lorenzo DOUR*. She was an excellent teacher, and she was the first teacher I ever knew to teach orthography by sound. We remained here nearly two years, your Pa having a contract on the Crawfordsville and Salem Road with the State of Indiana. The State suspended payment and of course the work had to stop. Our next home was at New Albany where we boarded with *Mrs. ELDERKIN*.

On October 12 we had a nice little black-eyed boy whom we called ***Charles Oscar.*** In November we returned to Louisville and remained until May, when we went to Cleves, O. Here we boarded a few weeks until the log cabin was ready for occupancy. The cabin was built on *Mr. Richard HUGHES'* farm. Log cabins were very much in vogue at that time, the campaign of 1840. It was built of green Buckeye logs, had a sitting and dining room combined, two bedrooms, and kitchen. We had a latch string hanging out, also a barrel of cider near the door. Several companies of delegates from Indiana passed by the door on their way to pay their respects to *General HARRISON* at North Bend. They would "about face and salute with three hearty cheers for Tippecanoe and Tyler too," which always was returned heartily and an invitation to drink a glass of cider. On July 7, 1841, your Pa, *Thomas*, and *Joseph* attended the burial of *President HARRISON* on high hill at North Bend from which you can look upon the three States of Ohio, Kentucky and Indiana.

It was while living here that "Death came unbidden on to the household band "and took from us our dearly beloved brother *Daniel* who died in Cincinnati with congestive chills October 7, 1841. He and your Pa had been in business twenty-one years and your Pa said they never had an angry word. We laid him away in the Gano Cemetery.

December 12 we had another daughter who we named ***Laura Ellen*** and we all thought she was a very sweet little sister. While living here we formed warm and lasting friendships. I forgot to say Pa and Uncle were engaged in building locks and aqueducts on the Cincinnati and White Water canal.

After the death of your uncle your Pa decided he would quit public works and go to his old farm in Dover, to which I acquiesced and the children were delighted with the plan. We left the Log Cabin August 19, spending two days in Cincinnati. Here we bought the carriage in which all the family traveled to Dover. It was the only carriage in the town for several years. On our journey we visited Brother ***Franklin*** and family at Norwalk. We arrived at Elyria the 27th, were the guests of Sister ***Mary GRIFFITH***, who was then at the Mansion House. After visiting the relatives, we went to Rockport, rented a house until we could get possession of our home at Rose Hill. The place had been badly neglected, having been rented for a long time. Your Pa went up every day and made such repairs as he could that it might be comfortable. *Mr. OVIATT* who was occupying a part of the house was not willing to move until June. 29 November we moved to the home at Dover; which has been my home for forty-seven years. A home I love. There is so much associated with and about it which makes it very dear indeed, almost sacred to me. It has been the birthplace of five of my children. Here, too, I have days of pleasure, also of sorrow. Here I have been called to drink deep of the cup of sorrow in the removal of my dear husband and three dearly loved children.

"Things are around us that have ceased to be,
And starry hopes, extinguished long ago,
Still link us to the past."

As this home has been in possession of the family for three generations, I hope it will continue for many years; and if it should be there is no longer one of the name to inherit it, I hope it may have founded upon it a benevolent institution bearing the name of Cahoon.

In the fall of 1842 your Pa commenced repairing the grist and sawmills. He sawed considerable ship plank, which he sold for fifteen dollars a thousand, thought to be a great price then. We succeeded pretty well in business matters owing to your Pa's good management and industry. February 22 another baby was added to our household, in the person of a daughter whom we named ***Martha Washington***. When I came here many of the relatives thought I would not remain long as it was so lonely, but I thought it was for our interest and as I had through my married life, tried to suit myself to our circumstances – I was contented with my situation. Your cousin ***Ruth*** visited me frequently and cheered me very much by her happy face and agreeable conversation. It is a pleasure to me now to think of her cheerful company. November 14 our son ***Leverett Judson*** came to us, and was named after his Uncle *Leverett JOHNSON*, who came to Dover the same day as your Pa did, and was nearly the same age, also married your Pa's youngest sister. A warm friendship was formed that lasted until death loosed the cord that bound them. The name of Judson was for the noted Baptist Missionary sent to India 1812.

About this time the Outward Bound was built on our beach. I then formed the acquaintance of *Mrs. Lyman CROWL* and *Mrs. Susan SNOW*, both of whom were cherished friends. They were the first acquaintances in Cleveland. Nothing of much interest occurred for some time except the birth of my three youngest children, ***John Marshall*** August 20, 1847. ***Mary Emma*** August 20, 1849. ***Ida Maria*** March 17, 1852. They were all lovingly welcomed, making the number eleven.

"Each time I thought how near, how dear,
The little children God has sent us;
How full they made our house of cheer,
And how their presence did content us.
Hard if but one were laid away,
This year or next as might or may be.
Our hearts would ache, would burn or break,
And now - another baby.
"Ah, so I thought, and so I said,
In ecstasy of peace and pleasure,
As bending down I kissed the head
Of any last weest, sweetest treasure;
O dear child of my life and love,
Whatever you are, whatever you may be,
I take you from the Christ above,
And thank Him for - another baby."

In September we were called to mourn the death of Sister *Mary GRIFFITH*, a favorite sister. *Dr. PIERCE* preached her funeral sermon, taking for his text, at her request, "Prepare to meet thy God!"

We had for many years desired much to visit Washington, but our limited means, and family cares prevented, until March 1853. Your Pa, *Marshall* and *Ida* and I made the long anticipated visit, arriving at Washington March 3. The morning of the 4th your Pa went to the Capitol to witness the inauguration of *Franklin PIERCE*, the fourteenth President of the United States. I saw the procession from Pennsylvania Avenue. This was the first journey on a railroad. We were very cordially received by our friends and had a delightful visit to my old home, also visiting many places of note that I had been familiar with in my girlhood days which was very pleasing to me. After spending two weeks in Washington, we bade adieu to our loved friends, and went to Frederick City to visit ***Cousin Margaret RICE*** and my dearly beloved ***Aunt Micheal***, who were overjoyed to see us. Cousin Margaret and I were as dear to each other as sisters for many years, seeing each other every day. The memory of her and *Mr. RICE* are very dear to me. We remained with them some weeks. Mr. Rice, Mrs. Rice, your Pa and our little ones left on the Baltimore and Ohio Railroad for Baltimore to look on Cousin *Ellen BINNEY* for mother and sister. After spending a short time and enjoying ourselves, we left Baltimore on the B & O R. R. and had a delightful ride, enjoying the scenery very much, arrived at home, where we found all well and glad to welcome us home again after an absence of six weeks.

When I left home I promised the nicest present should be given to the one who behaved the best during my absence. It was voted by acclamation that *Oscar* should receive the gift. I think you were all pretty good children. I have visited Washington twice since. In the spring of 1872 in company with *Marshall*, and in 1885 accompanied by *Leverett* and *Ida*, I spent my seventy fifth birthday at ***Bettie HAVENNER MCEWENS***. The remaining members of Mr. Havenner's family with old friend *Daniel SMITH* and his son *Dr. Thomas SMITH* were invited to Bettie's to tea on that day. *Mr. William ROWE* asked the blessing. We all enjoyed the occasion and I presented all the guests with a souvenir. I think what made it very appropriate to have the birthday reception at the home of the granddaughter of *Mrs. HAVENNER* who was guest at my mother's at the time of my birth. I went to my old home which my father and mother had purchased eighty five years ago and showed *Leverett* and *Ida* the room in which I was born; we also visited the graves of my dear departed parents.

In about two months after this pleasant visit, the first great sorrow came to our family. We had had many disappointments and losses which were of a financial character.

"These portentous clouds which hang their pall
Athwart life's mountain tops may melt away
And leave no trace behind; the loss of wealth
Or outward things.
The sun breaks forth, and the familiar summits, as of old,
May gleam out again. Not so the nomic shroud
O'erspread by death! Death! It is like the rush
Of the remorseless avalanche."

Although we had been married twenty years, we had never known of being bereft of any of our children. The first link was broken in our family circle June 7, 1853, when "Death the insatiate archer," entered our home and removed from us our dear ***Oscar***. This was so unexpected, as we did not consider him ill until a few hours before his departure. We were so overcome with grief it seemed impossible to bear the separation, but He who said, "I will never leave thee nor forsake thee," sustained and comforted us in this great loss, of a remarkably obedient, loving and thoughtful son. His last words to us as he kissed us were, "Goodbye, meet me in heaven." May God grant that we may all so live that Oscar's dying request will be fulfilled.

"Angels in the home of beauty, where ye dwell,
Guard what we have loved so well!
Crowned with light above,
Where no tender ties are breaking;
In the land of love,
Seraphs are his welcome waking."

1854 *Lydia* visited Washington, Frederick and Baltimore, remaining eighteen months. *Cousin Margaret RICE'S* death occurred while she was in Frederick. In April 1857 another great sorrow came to us in the death of our dear little ***Mary Emma***. She was sick six weeks, being first attacked with Rheumatism, which terminated in the disease of the heart. She was very patient during her illness and talked to me about several pieces of poetry she had learned, would ask me the meaning of many of them, and when I would explain them, she answered "Oh yes, I know now." She was lovely in life and beautiful in death.

"Peace! She sleeps at last,
The fitful dream of life is ended,
Death is with the past.--
Brightly hath her soul ascended.
Dark the waves, but winged angels waft her o'er,
Vainly we deplore; time will ne'er restore.
Softly now her white feet press the shining shore,
Blessed now forever more."

Thomas' marriage to ***Elizabeth HUGHES*** of Cleves, this took place March 27, 1860, being the only important event in the few following years, it being the first and only marriage in our family.

One cause of anxiety during the war was our failure to hear from *Joseph*, whose home had been in Memphis and who remained in the South through the dark days of the Rebellion. In April 1865, after an absence of seven years, he returned to us, making us a visit full of pleasure. That same Spring your Pa was very ill, and being advanced in years, never fully recovered his former great strength and endurance. Then *Leverett* and *Marshall* took charge of the business and farm.

On October 10, 1860, we celebrated the fiftieth anniversary of the settlement of Dover, by *Father CAHOON* and his family by having a family reunion at Rose Hill. This was so delightful to all participating it was decided to have it a yearly occurrence. This plan was carried out for nineteen years, at which time all of the original excepting your Pa, had passed beyond earthly bidding, and his strength would not permit of the excitement attending the meeting. In 1885 we held our last reunion, the second generation taking up the duties laid aside by their fathers and honored the memory of the energy, fortitude and will of those who made it possible to enjoy the homes, founded for their posterity. These meetings were interesting to many friends outside of the family, among whom were *Drs. KIRTLAND* and *GARLICK, Messers. HARRIS, ROOT,* and *DAY*, who took particular pleasure in them, and added to the interest by the prominent and pleasing part they contributed to the exercises. Dr. Kirtland acted as President and Mr. Harris, Secretary, when they were present. Dr. Kirtland said these reunions were an oasis in the desert to him. Our first reunion was held on the site where the first house was built. The rubbish was removed that had gathered over the old hearth stone, a fire made and water boiled in the same tea kettle which was used by your *Grama (Lydia Kenyon Cahoon)* fifty years previous in preparing the first supper in D.

On the 14 July 1881, we celebrated our golden wedding at Rose Hill, receiving our friends from 4 to 9 P.M. The day was beautiful, all that we could have desired. There were 150 guests present. It was a day never to be forgotten. I often seem to live the day over again. In the morning we exchanged rings, again plighting our love. The rings were engraved with our initials and the date of the anniversary.

"O chain of love! O ring of gold!
O marriage true and tried!
That binds with tenderness untold
The old man and his bride!"

The many letters of congratulations we received from absent friends afforded us much pleasure, and it is still a delight to peruse them, they bring to memory recollections of many loved ones who have gone to that "Bourne from whence no traveler returns."

Our hearts were more deeply moved than at any other time during the day, when you nine children, kissed us and offered us your loving congratulations; missing the two loved ones who were not with us, but wait to greet us in that better land. The events of this memorable day are so indelibly impressed on your minds, that I do not think it necessary to write more particularly,

We felt some anxiety fearing the excitement of the day might be too fatiguing for your Pa. Though he seemed much exhausted that evening, he rested well, and in a few days appeared as well as usual. The happiness that day brought to him was a buoy that renewed his strength. I think it was one of the happiest days of his life. *Mr. CAHOON* continued to get a little stronger gradually, keeping the same cheerful spirit, always seeing the bright side of everything.

He had for so many years prophesized contrary to the opinion of nearly everyone that there would be a railroad where the Nickle Plate now is, often saying, "I may not live to see it but there will be a railroad pass through Dover," and when his prediction came to pass, *Leverett* and *Marshall*, carried him in their arms and placed him carefully in the carriage, then drove up to the track, so he might see what he had so often looked for. This pleased him so much. We had planned to have him visit you in Cleveland as soon as the passenger cars were put on the road, and he was very happy in anticipation of the trip and the visit. But alas for our hopes, in a short time he was taken sick and grew weaker. We did not apprehend any danger, the doctor encouraging us in our belief. I was his constant companion. He often said he was so glad I could be with him all the time, frequently he would say he was afraid he did not appreciate the children's tenderness and gifts to him. He often told me he was willing to depart whenever his Master would say, "Come up higher". Yet he was not tired of life, this world was very beautiful to him. Once he appeared very drowsy, I said to him you appear to be so sleepy, he replied, "I think sometimes I will go to sleep, and wake to an eternal day." He continued to grow weaker until half past nine of the evening of September 28, the end came, and while loved ones were kneeling by his bedside, supplicating the Father of all mercies to smooth the way and to walk with my dear husband through the valley and shadow of death, he was taken from me, after having spent fifty-one years of happy wedded life.

"Ah! Tho' broken be the golden bowl today,
Hence, with tears away, dim not the beauteous day!
Tho' on earth the silver cord be loosed for aye,
The spirit wakes in endless day.
"All his grief is stilled.
The weary watch, the faint endeavor,
All his hopes fulfilled.
Perfect joy is won forever."

It is impossible for me to express to you how desolate I felt. I had relied on your Pa for advice in almost every step of my life, ever finding him affectionate and considerate of my happiness. Fifty one years we had spent in happy wedded life and it seemed as though my heart was rent asunder. The grief at this separation had a great tendency to impair my health, which before this time had been remarkably good. After the death of my dearly loved husband, I received every attention and loving kindness from you dear children, which in a great measure assuaged my grief and loneliness, and for which I hope the Lord will reward and bless you. Margaret Dickson Van Allen Cahoon, "Autobiography of Margaret Dickson Van Allen Cahoon." Ministers names verified for correct spellings by the Baltimore-Washington Conference, Commission on Archives and History, United Methodist Church, Lovely Lane Museum, Baltimore, MD.

Joel B. and ***Margaret Ann CAHOON*** *(note Margaret's middle name)* - May many years of peace, happiness and prosperity be added to their lives. Sentiment by President Kirtland (Cahoon Assoc.), Cahoon Pioneer Celebration, 28 Aug 1871, newspaper clipping, Cahoon Collection, Rose Hill Museum.

In 1818 ***Joseph CAHOON*** built a frame house upon the hill west of his log cabin, which, remodeled, still stands. To this home, in 1842, his son, ***Joel P. CAHOON***, brought his wife, ***Margaret DICKSON VAN ALLEN***, and their six children. The journey from Cincinnati was made with a two-seated top carriage, the first in Dover. Mrs. Cahoon was a native of Washington, D.C., being four years old when the British invaded that city, burned the Capitol, and took her father prisoner. She had seen *Dolly MADISON* as mistress of the White House and clasped the hand of *LAFAYETTE* when he was the nation's guest, in 1824. She conformed herself to the mode of life so different from all she had enjoyed, giving all her energy to improve in education and culture her new home. Patriotism, devotion to religion, hospitality, and cheerfulness were a part of her life. She originated the Cahoon pioneer celebration, which commemorates the anniversary days since Dover passed its fiftieth milestone, The gentle ***Lydia***, to whose place she succeeded, was fondly cherished, and when her eighty-four beautiful years had passed she left as mistress of the sacred home the first daughter born to her within its walls. Cahoon, Ida M., Memorial to the Pioneer Women of the Western Reserve, Part 1, p. 62.

2nd Annual Fair of the Dover Agricultural and Mechanical Society, Sept 3, 1858. Domestic Manufacturing: ***Mrs. J.B. CAHOON***; 2nd Place - counterpane, 1st Place - Patch Quilt, 1st Place - Grape Preserves. Westlake, Looking Back to Dover, A Collection of Writings.

The eightieth anniversary of the settlement of the village of Dover was fittingly celebrated there yesterday at the home of ***J.M. CAHOON***, a grandson of ***Joseph CAHOON***, the first settler...The dinner was served in the big red barn connected with the old homestead. It was a glorious feast of all the fruits of the productive acres of the Cahoon family. The fact that ***Margaret CAHOON***, the oldest of the family, a daughter-in-law of Joseph Cahoon, took her part in preparing the feast, was generally commented upon. She is eighty years old, and it is said that she baked eight of the apple pies which helped to make up the sumptuous dinner...

The house of J.M. Cahoon was beautifully decorated with flags and bunting yesterday. Family relics were seen on every hand. In front of the house was an old kettle brought by the family from Vermont. A majestic tree stands before the old homestead which was started from a sprout that one of the sons had used for a whip, and which he afterwards thrust into the ground after a long jaunt through the woods, little thinking when he did it that it would grow into a great tree...

"It is a beautiful thing to think of that day when old Joseph Cahoon and his wife sat upon this romantic spot to think over their future and to reflect upon the burden of their journey just over. Compare them as they sat down to their first repast eighty years ago upon this very spot with us who have just been seated at a sumptuous feast. They looked forward to their future with just as much hope as we look forward to our future to-day. The next eighty years will be to us just what we make it. A happy, faithful, and Christian life will make a true and noble nature. My acquaintance with the Cahoon family

HAS BEEN VERY PLEASANT.

I only knew the younger members of the family. When I see sons and daughters so faithful in cherishing the memories of father and mother I believe those sons and daughters are worthy of being loved and cared for themselves. These frequent gatherings, I believe, are most beneficial. As the young grow up, they will learn the beauties of a life of faithfulness and devotion to truth. They will be taught lessons which they can never forget. They will grow in manhood and learn to forget and despise the evil things of life." *Hon. D. J. NYE*, Elyria "The First Settler," newspaper article, 1890, Cahoon Collection, Rose Hill Museum.

EIGHTY YEARS OLD.
Mrs. Margaret A. Cahoon Celebrates Her Birthday at the Home of Her Daughters -A Sketch of Her Long Life-Her Recollections of Early Historical Events in America.

Mrs. Margaret A. CAHOON, of Rare *(Rose)* Hill Farm, Dover, celebrated her eightieth birthday yesterday afternoon and evening at the residence of her daughters, No. 1916 Broadway. The frost of four score winters set lightly on Mother Cahoon. Her hair is as white as snow, but her mind is as clear and active as it was half a century ago. Mrs. Cahoon was born in Washington, D.C., on February 8, 1810. Her early life was spent in that city, and she received the best education that the private schools of the Capital then afforded. She is rich in reminiscences of the early days in Washington city. Just before the invasion of the city by the British, during the war of 1812, she, with the remainder of the family, was sent to a place of safety, while her father and the servants remained behind. While holding prayer with his servants one morning her father was taken prisoner by the British, but was released a few days later. Although but four years of age at the time, Mrs. Cahoon remembers of returning to the city, and seeing the blackened walls of the Capitol, which had been burned by the invaders. She resided in Washington when the early statesmen were in their prime, and her personal acquaintance with *Edward EVERETT, John RANDOLPH, James BUCHANAN*, and many others, is among her pleasantest memories. She has always taken a great interest in the political affairs of the country, and even now she reads every line of Congressional news that is published in the daily papers. Mrs. Cahoon was married in 1831, at Frederick, Md., to ***Joel B. CAHOON***. Mr. Cahoon was one of the pioneer railroad contractors of the country, and was then engaged in constructing a section of the Baltimore & Ohio Railway. For eleven years Mr. and Mrs. Cahoon resided in Maryland, Kentucky, Indiana, and Southern Ohio, and in 1842 they removed to Dover. Mrs. Cahoon has lived on the same farm ever since, and she is greatly attached to her charming home. Her husband died on the farm in September, 1882, one year after the celebration of the fiftieth anniversary of their wedding. He was known as a man of strong character, and was a pioneer of note. Mr. and Mrs. Cahoon had eleven children, eight of whom are living. They are ***Thomas***, of Franklin avenue; ***Joseph*** of Memphis, Tenn.; ***J. Marshall***, of Dover; and ***Misses Lydia, Laura, Martha***, and ***Ida*** of No. 1916 Broadway. The daughters are teachers in the public schools. A favorite son, ***Leverett J.,*** died in August, 1886, and since that time Mrs. Cahoon has left some of her cheerfulness, and has failed more rapidly than for some years previous. Mrs. Cahoon is an ardent member of the Methodist Episcopal Church, her father being one of the first Methodists in Washington.

The reception lasted from 3 o'clock in the afternoon until 9 o'clock in the evening, and more than two hundred people called to pay their respects to the venerable lady. Many were present from abroad. Many beautiful and costly mementos of the occasion were presented, and the display of flowers was imposing. In serving the refreshments a tray was used which did service when Mrs. Cahoon was christened. She was assisted in receiving by the venerable *Mrs. J. A. MARSHALL. Mrs. J. T. BOWMAN*, who is almost eighty years of age, was expected to assist in the honors, but she was prevented from being present on account of illness.

Mrs. Cahoon has been engaged from some time in writing a history of the interesting events of her life. She expected to have it finished by her eightieth birthday, but she met with an accident last fall, and the completion of the valuable paper has been delayed.

Joseph CAHOON, the father of Mrs. Cahoon husband, settled on Rose Hill farm in Dover in 1810, and it has remained in the family during all these years. He was one of the noted pioneers of the Western Reserve. Newspaper article, Cahoon Collection, Rose Hill Museum.

MRS. JOEL B. CAHOON
An Early Settler of Cuyahoga County is Laid to Rest in Dover - A Tribute to the Memory of a Gifted Christian Woman.

She had been reared in the atmosphere of luxury and refined society, such as existed in Old Virginia and Maryland a hundred years ago. In her father's house and elsewhere she met *Chief Justice MARSHALL, Justice Jay RANDOLPH, WEBSTER, CLAY* and other great men. She lived in Washington when it was burned by the British in 1814, and shook hands with Lafayette in 1824. From surroundings and society of this kind she was suddenly transferred to the wilds of Cuyahoga county, and entered upon the battle of subduing the great forest; raising in the meantime a family of ten or twelve children who were thoroughly educated and in every way well equipped for life. Of a remarkably happy and cheerful temperament, she successfully met and overcame all the dangers and deprivations of the times and conditions of pioneer life in Northern Ohio. The daughters adopted the profession of teachers, and have successfully followed that calling; the sons becoming enterprising and successful business men of this community.

The old homestead of several hundred acres, called Rose Hill, after the Virginia and Maryland style, situated on the bank of the lake, in the township of Dover, is one of the most picturesque, beautiful, and highly cultivated farms in Northern Ohio-a vast vineyard covering a large part of the farm. It is now in charge of ***Mr. Marshall CAHOON***, an enterprising man of energetic character. From a commanding promontory jetting into the lake his grandfather looked out toward the scene and heard the guns of *COMMODORE PERRY'S* victory in 1814.

At the lifelong home of this good woman the old neighbors and friends gathered in large numbers last

Saturday, and laid tenderly by the side of her companion in life, who died ten or twelve years ago, all that remains to earth of ***Mrs. CAHOON***. The spot where she rests is a most beautiful one on the bank of the lake, strewn and surrounded with roses and other flowers in great profusion. The most sacred love and friendship watered those flowers with tears, and she was where

"The storms that wreck in wintry sky,
No more disturbed her deep repose
Than summer's latest sigh
That shuts the rose."

(James Russell) LOWELL asks: "What is so rare as a day in June! Days then, if ever, come perfect." I will answer, a life and character that of this noble pioneer Christian woman is more rare than even a day in June. Her life seemed as perfect as any day in June. Two predominant sentiments or passion stood out boldly in her life and conversation: love of country and love of church. She knew and associated with the fathers of the Republic and of the Methodist Church. Her admiration for Washington was only equaled by that for John Wesley. She was deeply read in the literature of the nation and of the church. Her reading to the very last was the highest and best, and her religious character the deepest and most sincere. Her sweet and precious memory will long be cherished, and her gentle life an inspiration to all who knew her.

"Life's race well run,
Life's work well done,
Life's crown well won,
Now comes rest."

Cleveland Leader, June 26, 1894.

OBITUARY
Mrs. Margaret A. Cahoon

Mrs. Margaret A. CAHOON, who passed from earth to immortality at the residence of her daughter in this city last Thursday, was so rare, so worthy a character that more than the usual mention should be made when life is ended.

She was the only child of ***John Calhoun DICKSON*** of Washington, D.C. She was born in that city when this wonderful century was but ten years old.

Her girlhood was passed most favorably in the best schools, associated with many choice spirits, who ever remained dear to her...In 1827 she married ***John Douglass VAN ALLEN***, a marble cutter, engaged in the building of the capitol, but soon removed to New York, afterward to Philadelphia, from whence she returned at nineteen a widow and an orphan.

July 14, 1831, she married ***Joel P.*** *(should be B.)* ***CAHOON*** at Frederick, Md., living in that vicinity for a few years while her husband carried on his contracts for constructing several sections of the B. & O. railroad.

Kentucky, Indiana and North Bend, O., in turn furnished a residence till in 1842 the family came to the farm in Dover settled by Mr. Cahoon's father *(Joseph Cahoon)* in 1810, which for more than fifty years has been her loved home, where she has dispensed free-hearted hospitality and cheered every heart her influence reached.

Her intellectual attainments were a delight to all. Her love of books and her excellent memory gave her great power to entertain, while the patriotism which filled her inspired others.

With her father and mother she joined the first church of the Methodist Episcopal denomination in Washington....

Sorrows had accumulated fast in recent years, each one leaving its impress upon her brave heart and healthy frame, till she had less strength than courage. Her devoted husband and three manly sons were laid away, still she could say:

"My hope I cannot measure,
My Savior has my treasure
And he will walk with me."

She came to the city to make an address in one of our public schools Memorial day, being most successful in her effort, and spent the following week very pleasantly, after which the fatal illness occurred. From beautiful Rose Hill on Saturday afternoon, June 23, were held the last services according to her wish. *Mr. Walter E. WRIGHT* sang "In Heavenly Love Abiding." *Rev. Dr. F. S. HOYT* read Psalm 103 and St. John 14, verses 1 to 28, and followed with a tender tribute to one whose Christian character, womanly, exalted life had for years inspired him.

Rev. Levi GILBERT, D.D., very feelingly spoke of her later years and those last beautiful days, when he found her waiting at the gate ready to enter into the city of God. *Rev. Dr. Russel B. POPE* offered a prayer of thanksgiving that this life had been so beautiful, so helpful, so patriotic, ideal and complete.

Mrs. HOLLIDAY and Mr. Wright sang "Spirit, Leave Thy House of Clay," and the loved form was borne by her two sons and four nephews to be laid with her husband and five children in Lake Side cemetery. In connection with the burial service Dr. Pope read at the open grave the hymn beginning

"Shall man, O God of light and life,
Forever molder in the grave?"
As she lay there surrounded by
her own roses we could but think,
Fold back thy mantle, fringed with green,
Broidered with leaf and blossom,
And take her tenderly to rest,
Dear earth, upon thy bosom."

In the June sunshine, honored by a large acquaintance, loved by hosts of friends, with the glory of immortality upon her quiet face, with gratitude to God Who gave and to God Who took, under tears and lilies, she sleeps till the glad resurrection morn. Newspaper article, Margaret Cahoon Family Papers, Rose Hill Museum, Bay Village, OH.

CAHOON-Mrs. M.A. Cahoon, aged 84 years, died at the residence of her daughters, 1916 Broadway at 9 o'clock a.m., June 21. Funeral from her late residence, Rose Hill, Dover, at 2 o'clock standard time, Saturday, 23d. N.B. Nickle Plate trains leaving Pearl st. station at 11:19 a.m. will stop at Dover for those wishing to attend the funeral. Cleveland Necrology File, June 23, 1894.

CAHOON, M.A., Mrs. 84, white, female, widow, 1916 Broadway, Ward 25, d. city, b. Virginia, cause of death paralysis, Phys. Dr. Jewitt, cemetery Denver, O., undertaker Hogan T. Harris. June 21, 1894. CRD, roll 1977437.

Mrs. Joel CAHOON, 84; res. Dover; interred June 21, 1894; Lot 65. "List of Interments," Lakeside Cemetery, Bay Village, OH.

(Lot 54) Thomas Havenner Cahoon

THOMAS

Thomas Havenner CAHOON, oldest child of ***Joel*** and ***Margaret CAHOON***; b. 7 July1832, Fredericktown, Frederick Co., MD; d. 16 Apr 1907, Cleveland, Cuyahoga Co., OH; m. 27 Mar 1860 Cincinnati, Hamilton Co., OH to ***Elizabeth HUGHES***. Cahoon Family Charts and Gen. Data, Rose Hill.

Thomas was named after a close friend of his mother, Thomas Havenner, and was the only child in the family to marry.

T. H. CAHOON, 374 Franklin street, Cleveland, Ohio, has for many years been a well-known citizen of this place and since 1887 has been retired from active business, enjoying the fruits earned by a life of honest industry.

Mr. Cahoon was born in Fredericktown, Maryland, July 7, 1832, son of ***Joel*** and ***Margaret CAHOON***, the former a native of Vermont and the latter of Washington, District of Columbia. The mother is still living at the old homestead in Dover township, this county, she having attained her eighty-fourth year...

T. H. CAHOON spent his early life in working on his father's farm and in attending the district school. In 1851 he came to Cleveland and began learning the trade of ship carpenter. This business he followed for fifteen years. Then he ran a plaining mill, and in 1876 engaged in the lumber business in this city, being a member of the firm of Cahoon & Hutchinson. In this business he continued until 1887, when he retired, as above stated.

Mr. Cahoon was a member of the City Council of Cleveland in 1882, and it was largely owing to his vote and influence that the ordinance was passed which granted the Johnson line franchise over Scoville avenue, thereby making an opening for a single fare from Brooklyn through the city.

Mr. Cahoon was married, March 27, 1860, on the Miami river, near Cincinnati, Ohio, to ***Miss Elizabeth HUGHES***...

Both Mr. and Mrs. Cahoon are members of the Presbyterian Church, and he is a member of the I.O.O.F. and the A.O.U.W., both of which organizations he has passed all chairs. He has represented Ohio in the National Council of the A.O.U.W. Politically, he has always been a Republican. Memorial Record of the County of Cuyahoga and City of Cleveland, pp. 369-70.

THOMAS H. CAHOON DEAD

...former member of the city council from the old Tenth ward...had been ill for several months...was associated with the firm of Moore, Cahoon & Co., manufacturers, and Cahoon and Hutchinson. He retired from active business life some years ago...He was a member of the Erie Lodge...and North Wing Encampment, and was long a member of the Old Stone Church. News clipping in Thos. H. Cahoon Family Papers, Undetermined newspaper, Rose Hill Museum, Bay Village, OH.

CAHOON-Thomas Havenner, at his residence, Tuesday evening, April 16, 1907. Funeral services Friday, April 19, at 2 p.m. standard, from his late residence, 5217 Franklin ave. N.W. Burial at Lake Side cemetery, Bay Village, O., at 3:30 p.m. Kindly omit flowers.

Members of North Wing, Encampment, No., 88, and Erie Lodge, no. 27, are requested to meet at Phoenix Hall, No. 950 Lorain st., near Harbor, Friday, April 19, at 1 o'clock, standard, to attend the funeral of our late brother, Thomas Cahoon.

A. H. GLOVER
Chief Patriarch,
GEORGE H. FLETCHER,
Noble Grand

Newspaper article, undetermined source, Cahoon Collection, Rose Hill Museum, Bay Village, OH and Cleveland Necrology File, April 19, 1907, roll 12.

Thomas H. CAHOON, 74; res. Cleveland; interred Apr 18, 1907; Lot 64. "List of Interments," Lakeside Cemetery, Bay Village, OH.

Thomas H. CAHOON, 74 yrs. 9 mts. 9 days, d. April 16, 1907, Cleveland, O., six o'clock, diabetes, duration 54 days, retired, b. Fredrick, Md., fr. ***Joel B. CAHOON***, b. Salisbury, NY, maiden name of mo. ***DICKSON***, b. Washington, D.C. Burial Removal Permit and Cleveland Record of Deaths, film 1977542.

(Lot 53) Elizabeth Hughes Cahoon

ELIZABETH

Elizabeth Hughes Cahoon was the wife of Thomas Havenner Cahoon, oldest son of Joel Butler and Margaret Cahoon. Ancestors of Elizabeth Hughes Cahoon.

I. ***Ezekiel HUGHES***, b. 22 Aug 1767, North Wales, Great Britain; d. 2 Sept 1849, Watership Township, Hamilton Co., OH; m.1 1803 to ***Margaret BEBB***, of North Wales (d. within less than a year of her marriage), m.2 ***Mary EWING*** (b. 4 June 1785, Northumberland co., Pa.; dau. of *Thomas* and *Ann EWING*, Presbyterians from the North of Ireland, her father was a soldier in the Revolutionary Army). Ezekiel emigrated to the United States in April, 1795, stopping in Philadelphia for about one year, moving west in 1796. In 1803 he purchased from the U.S. Govt. Sections 15 and 16 T. 1, R. 1 East, Watership township, on which he settled until his death. *Issue*: ***Anna HUGHES***, b. 6 Mar 1806; ***Richard HUGHES***, b. 8 Feb 1808; ***Jane HUGHES***, b. Dec 1810, m. 9 Dec c1852 to *William WAKEFIELD*, of New Haven, Hamilton co., O. (d. c1855); ***Thomas HUGHES***, b. 1812, m. *Jane Augusta BOND*; ***Wm. HUGHES***, b. 1814, d. 1845, m. *Amarilla ROBINSON*; ***John HUGHES***, b. 1816, m. *Mary B. CLARK*; ***Martha HUGHES***, b. 25 Dec 1818, d. 24 May 1882; ***Edward HUGHES***, b. 1830 *(crossed out and 1820 written by hand)*, m. 1850 to *Mary DAVIS*; ***James HUGHES***, b. 1823, d. 1840; ***Rebecca HUGHES***, b. 28 May 1826, m. July1842 to *Rev. B. W. CHIDLAW*. "Haire Genealogy," pages 1-23 removed from an early book, p. 10, author, publisher and date unknown. Rose Hill Museum, Bay Village, OH.

II. ***Richard HUGHES***, b. 8 Feb 1808; m. 30 Jan 1830 ***Elizabeth ELDER*** (b. 13 Nov 1807, dau. of *John* and *Mary ELDER*, came from Pennsylvania and settled in Whitewater township in 1819). There were born to them two sons and six daughters. Issue: ***Elizabeth HUGHES***, b. 19 Nov 1830, m. 27 March 1860 to *Thomas H. CAHOON*; ***John Milton HUGHES***, b. 1832, d. age of two; ***Mary Jane HUGHES***, b. 28 Oct 1834, m. 27 Sept 1854 to *Joseph CILLEY*, one dau. *Ellen Florence CILLEY*, b. 11 Oct 1855; ***Frances Scott HUGHES***, b. 24 June 1838, m. 14 July1887 to *George W. HAIRE*; ***Martha Elder HUGHES***, b. 5 Aug 1840, m. 5 Oct 1872 to *Edward M. GRISWOLD*, one dau. *Stella GRISWOLD*; ***Ezekiel HUGHES***, b. 28 Dec 1845, m. 30 May 1879; ***Rebecca HUGHES***, b. 2 Feb 1848. *Only five daughters are listed in the book although "six" are mentioned. Handwritten in book is:* ***Margaret HUGHES*** *was born Sept 12 1845. This date would conflict with the birth of Ezekiel in Dec of 1845, if in fact this is the sixth daughter.* "Haire Genealogy," pages 1-23 removed from an early book, p. 10, author, publisher and date unknown. Rose Hill Museum, Bay Village, OH.

Mr. (Thomas Havenner CAHOON) was married, March 27, 1860, on the Miami river, near Cincinnati, Ohio, to ***Miss Elizabeth HUGHES***, daughter of ***Richard*** and ***Elizabeth HUGHES***. Her grandfather Hughes came with *Governor BEBB* from Wales to this country, and it is recorded of him that he bought the first tract of land west of the Miami river. Richard Hughes was born in 1808, was married January 21, 1830, and died August 25, 1850. His wife was born in Pennsylvania in 1807, emigrated to Ohio with her parents, ***John ELDER*** and wife, in 1815, and died September 6, 1870. She was a most estimable woman and a devoted Christian. Mr. and Mrs. Hughes had a family of eight children. Memorial Record of the County of Cuyahoga and City of Cleveland, p. 370.

Elizabeth HUGHES was from Cleves, Ohio, *(located on the Ohio River in the south west corner of Ohio)* when she married ***Thomas CAHOON***. This was the first and only marriage of Joel Cahoon's children. Margaret Dickson Van Allen Cahoon, "Autobiography of Margaret Dickson Van Allen Cahoon."

Elizabeth H. CAHOON, 79, Head, Widow, 0 children born/living, fr. b. Ohio, mo. b. Ohio, b. Penns., Own Income, Owns house; *BORZA, Nicholas*, Lodger, 22, single, fr./mo. b. R ? Roumanian, b. R ? Roumanian, Clerk at bank; *CRAY, Blanche*, 37, Head, widow, 1 child b. and living, fr./mo. b. O., b. O., Dressmaker at Shop, Renting house; *CRAY, Nellie*, dau., 15, fr. b. O., mo. b. O., b. O. 1910 FC OH CY Cleveland, Ward 3, Enum. Dist. 88, Franklin Ave., Dwelling 247, Family 305-6, lines 77-80.

BAY VILLAGE

Wednesday, Oct 7, at 3:30 p.m., ***Mrs. Elizabeth HUGHES CAHOON***, wife of the late ***Thomas H. CAHOON***, long prominently identified with business interests in Cleveland, was laid to rest in Lakeside cemetery beside her husband and daughter, in the Cahoon family lot. For fifty years she had been a member of Old Stone church. Her pastor, *Rev. A.B. MELDRUM*, officiated, assisted by *Rev. MICKEY*, of Bethany Presbyterian church. The choir sang three selections at the residence, 5217 Franklin avenue, and *Edwin H. DOUGLASS*, a long-time friend, sang most impressively at the burial, "Beautiful Isle of Somewhere." A large number of friends went from here to the final service in the quiet little "God's acre" beside the lake to testify their appreciation of a cherished friend. Many beautiful floral tributes of baskets and sprays of roses, dahlias, lilies, heliotrope and asters told of the esteem in which she was held.

Mrs. Aaron BULLOCK and *Miss BULLOCK* came from Elyria to Mrs. Cahoon's funeral.

Some additional news included in the article:

On Sunday, October 11, a temperance program will be presented at the church services.

Mrs. Anna SUNK HORNING died at her home on Dover Center road October 8. Her funeral was held from the Lutheran church October 11.

Grape harvest is about completed. The crop has been abundant and of excellent quality.

Miss ZIPP, of Cleveland, with *John ZIPP, Jr.*, and *Franklin FISHER*, spent the week-end with *Mr. Louis ZIPP*, celebrating Mr. Zipp's birthday.

Mrs. A.R. MILLER returned to her home this week, bringing with her a fine baby boy, *Robert Abram MIL. (assumed Miller)*

A political meeting is to be held here October 19. Newspaper clipping, marked: Friday, Oct 16, 1914, undetermined source, Cahoon Collection, Rose Hill Museum, Bay Village, OH.

CHURCH RECEIVES $3,000 BY CLEVELANDER'S WILL

The Bethany Presbyterian Church, Clinton avenue and W. 65th street, was bequeathed property valued at about $3,000 by the will of ***Mrs. Elizabeth CAHOON***, who died October 3. The local W.C.T.U. *(Women's Christian Temperance Union)* and the Presbyterian Board of Relief for Disabled Ministers were also beneficiaries of her estate, valued at $8,000.

The Bethany church was given the Cahoon property at 1872 W. 47th street. Mrs. Cahoon ordered the proceeds of the sale of her homestead at 5217 Franklin avenue to be given to the Presbyterian home. She also gave $1,000 to relatives and $100 to the W.C.T.U. Newspaper article, undetermined source, marked Oct 13th 1914, Tuesday, Cahoon Collection, Rose Hill Museum, Bay Village, OH.

Elizabeth HUGHES CAHOON, d. Oct 4, 1914, 8 p.m., 5217 Franklin St., Ward 3, Cleveland, Cuy. Co. of chronic intestinal nephrites, 84 yrs., 11 mos., 21ds.; widowed, b. Ohio, fr. ***Richard HUGHES***, mo. ***Elizabeth ELDER***, physician *C.D. ELLIS*, 12214 Detroit, bur. Lakeside Cemetery, undertaker S.W. Mather, 3227 W. 25th Ohio Certificate of Death, Division of Vital Statistics, 1914, certif. 54120.

CAHOON-Elizabeth HUGHES, wife of the late ***Thomas H. CAHOON***, at 5217 Franklin ave. N.W., Sunday, Oct 4, at 8 p.m. Funeral services at late residence, 5217 Franklin ave., Wednesday, Oct 7, at 2 p.m. Interment at Lakeside cemetery, Bay Village, 3:30 p.m. Cincinnati papers please copy. Cleveland Necrology File, October 7, 1914.

Elizabeth H. CAHOON; res. Cleveland; interred Oct 6, 1914; Lot 64. "List of Interments," Lakeside Cemetery, Bay Village, OH.

(Lot 54) Effie Cahoon Ellis

EFFIE

Thomas H. CAHOON, son of *Joel Butler* and *Margaret Van Allen CAHOON*, m. ***Elizabeth HUGHES***, they had one daughter, ***Effie H.***, b. Cleveland, Ohio. Effie married ***Dr. C. N. ELLIS***. Orval O. Calhoun, Our Calhoun Family, vol. 2, p. 156.

The State of Ohio, Cuyahoga County, SS. I Certify that on the 24th day of October 1883 ***Mr. Clifton D. ELLIS*** and ***Miss Effie H. CAHOON*** were by me legally joined in marriage. J.W. Simpson Marriage Record, Cuyahoga County, OH, vol. 27, p. 48.

Effie CAHOON ELLIS, 25, res. Cleveland, interred 1888, Lot 64 (found in Lot 54). Removed from River Side Cemetery in 1907. "List of Interments," Lakeside Cemetery, Bay Village, OH.

Effie ELLIS, 24, died 18 April 1888 of consumption (TB), married, res. 374 Franklin Ave., Cleveland, OH. Buried April 20, Sect. 24, Lot 98, Grave 1. Removed from Riverside Cemetery, Cleveland 5 March 1907. The lot she was originally buried in has the graves of *Laura, Charlotte, Christian* and *George AUER*; *Carrie* and *Robert MCDOWELL*; *Arthur E. KREWSON* and an *infant*. The lot may have been sold to this family after Effie was removed to Lakeside. Riverside Cemetery, Cleveland, OH.

Effie Cahoon's husband, Clifton Ellis:

C.D. ELLIS, M.D., a physician and surgeon at No. 433 Pearl street, Cleveland, was born in Christian county, Kentucky, August 6, 1860, a son of ***William*** and ***Anna (HARRISON) ELLIS***, natives respectively of Maryland and Kentucky. In early life the father was engaged at the tailor's trade, later, at the breaking out of the late war, opened a general supply store at Hopkinsville, Kentucky, which he continued until 1878, and in that year became owner and manager of the Hopkinsville Flouring Mills. The latter was destroyed by fire in the fall of 1882. Mr. Ellis then became the first manufacturer of artificial ice in that part of the State, which business is still conducted by his son, *F.L. ELLIS*. During the late war, he was a staunch Union man. He has served as Councilman of Hopkinsville eight terms, and in every way a most worthy and highly esteemed citizen. He is now eighty-three years of age. Mrs. Ellis died in 1885, at the age of sixty-four years.

C.D. Ellis, M.D., the youngest in a family of four children, all now living, attended the public schools of Hopkinsville, completed the studies in the Hopkinsville high school, and graduated in the class of 1883. After spending eighteen months in the practice of medicine at Emporia, Kansas, Dr. Ellis came to Cleveland in 1885. In addition to his general practice, he is a professor of Osteology and Minor Surgery in the Cleveland University of Medicine and Surgery, also Visiting Physician and Secretary of the Advisory Board in the Homeopathic Hospital, a lecturer in the Training School for Nurses, and President of the Hahnemann Society. Surgical clinic is held by the Doctor every Friday afternoon at the college throughout the year.

He was married in 1883, to ***Miss Effie CAHOON***, a daughter of ***Thomas*** and ***Lizzie CAHOON***, who reside at 374 Franklin avenue, Cleveland. His *(Her)* father has been Councilman of this city. Mrs. Ellis died in 1888, at the age of twenty-seven years, having been a consistent member of the Presbyterian Church. In 1890 the Doctor was united in marriage with *Miss May B.*, a daughter of *Capt. George* and *Mary WARNER*, of this city. Mrs. Ellis is a member of the St. John's Episcopal Church. In his social relations, the Doctor is a member of the Royal Arcanum, the Golden Chain, the Homeopathic Round Table Club, and was formerly Treasurer of the State Homeopathic Medical Society, of which he is now a member. In political matters, he is identified with the Republican Party. Memorial Record of the County of Cuyahoga and City of Cleveland, p. 182.

Clifton D. ELLIS, graduated from Cleveland Homeopathic Medical College, Cleveland, Ohio as a physician in 1883. Physicians' and Dentists' Directory of the State of Ohio, 1905.

The State of Ohio, Cuyahoga County, ss ...I Certify that on the 8th day of Oct 1890 ***Mr. Clifton D. ELLIS*** and ***Miss May Bell WARNER*** were by me legally joined in marriage. Henry D. Aves. Marriage Record, Cuyahoga County, OH, vol. 35, p. 68.

DR. C.D. ELLIS' FUNERAL TODAY
Lakewood Physician Practiced 35 Years.

Funeral services for ***Dr. Clifton D. ELLIS***, pioneer Lakewood physician, will be held at 1 p.m. today at his residence, 12214 Detroit avenue, Lakewood. Burial will be in Lake View Cemetery.

Dr. Ellis died Saturday. He practiced for nearly thirty-five years. For years he had offices on W. 25th street near Franklin avenue. N.W.

He was born in Hopkinsville, Ky., and received his medical training at Western Reserve university. He was a member of the Westwood Country Club and the Clifton Club.

Three years ago Dr. Ellis' health began to fail. He continued his practice until about a year ago. Last winter he went to Arizona to recuperate. Four weeks ago he was brought home, slightly worse.

Dr. G.G. FROST, Dr. W.L. HOBART, Dr. W.H. PERRY, Dr. C.L. GRABER, Dr. W.E. WELLS, Dr. N.W. SHETTER and *Dr. G.R. WILKINS* will act as pall bearers. Monday, June 28, 1926, p. 4, col. 4. The Plain Dealer.

June 28, 1926 ***ELLIS-Dr. Clifton D.***, beloved husband of ***May*** (nee ***WARNER***), Saturday morning, June 26. Funeral services from his late residence, 12214 Detroit avenue, Lakewood, Monday, June 28, at 1 p.m. Cleveland Necrology File, June 28, 1926.

(Lot 63) Charles Oscar Cahoon

OSCAR

Charles Oscar CAHOON, fifth child of ***Joel*** and ***Margaret CAHOON***; b. 12 Oct 1839, New Albany, IN; d. 7 June 1853, Dover, OH. Cahoon Family Charts and Gen. Data, Rose Hill.

CAHOON- In Dover, June 7th, ***Charles Oscar*** son of ***J. B.*** and ***A. M. CAHOON*** aged 13 years and 7 months. Cleveland Necrology File, June 9, 1853.

(Lot 64) Mary Emma Cahoon

MARY

Mary Emma CAHOON, tenth child of ***Joel*** and ***Margaret CAHOON***; b. 20 Aug, 1849, Dover, OH; d. 17 Aug 1857, Dover. Cahoon Family Charts and Gen. Data, Rose Hill.

In April 1857 another great sorrow came to us in the death of our dear little ***Mary Emma***. She was sick six weeks, being first attacked with Rheumatism, which terminated in the disease of the heart. She was very patient during her illness and talked to me about several pieces of poetry she had learned, would ask me the meaning of many of them, and when I would explain them, she answered "Oh yes, I know now." She was lovely in life and beautiful in death. Margaret Dickson Van Allen Cahoon, "Autobiography of Margaret Dickson Van Allen Cahoon."

(Lot 64) Leverett Judson Cahoon

LEVERETT

Leverett Judson CAHOON, eighth child of ***Joel*** and ***Margaret CAHOON***; b. 14 Nov 1845, Dover, OH; d. 16 Aug 1886, Dover; never married. Cahoon Family Charts and Gen. Data, Rose Hill.

CAHOON, L.J. & J.M. Owned land; Acres: Improved - Tilled, including fallow and grass: 5, Permanent meadow: 10, Unimproved - Woodland: 44. Farm Values: Land and buildings- $2500, Machinery - $102, Live Stock - $400. Cost of building and repairing in 1879 - $200. Labor: Paid for wages in 1879 - $500, weeks hired labor in 1879 - 100. Estimated value of all farm production: $200. Horses: 3, Milch Cows: 1, Calves dropped: 1, Cattle sold living: 1. Pounds of butter made on the farm: 100. Indian corn: acres - 3, bushels - 100; potatoes: acres - 2, bushels - 250. Orchards - apple: acres - 2. Vineyard: acres - 4. "Schedule 2. Production of Agriculture in Dover Township, Cuyahoga County, OH," enumerated June, 1880, p. 31.

The company was called to order and ***L.J. CAHOON*** chosen president of the day, and *L.H. JOHNSON,* secretary. The president tendered thanks for the honor conferred, and expressed his surprise that they should select the "baby" of the family. This created some merriment, considering that he occupies a space six feet two perpendicularly, and tilts the scale at 235. "Rose Hill Pioneers," Reunion Notebook, Newspaper article 1885.

Leverett Judson CAHOON, helped his Dad with the farm work until ***Joel*** became too ill to work in 1861. As a lad, in his teens, he and his brother, ***Patrick*** *(John Marshall)*, became proprietors of the Cahoon Store around 1860. The family owned a strip of land on the east side of Dover Center Road where they had an orchard. Here they built a brick building and opened a hardware store. They sold rope, nails, chain, baskets, axes, hoes and seed. The New York Central approached them about building the Nickel Plate Railroad tracks along the south side of their property. They requested a lease of the property for the tracks. The family decided that they would lease them the property if a train station was erected on the site. The Dover train station was built on the property. Leverett worked in the store until the death at Rose Hill. "The Joel Butler Cahoon Family," (Bay Village Historical Society).

The Cahoon store referred to above was on Dover Center Road just north of the railroad tracks. It was torn down in 2000, after being occupied by Reehorst Cleaners since the 1960's, to make way for a new CVS Pharmacy. Robert E. Reehorst

Card in the Rose Hill Cahoon Collection:

LEVERETT J. CAHOON J. MARSHALL CAHOON

L. J. & J. M. CAHOON
GROWERS AND SHIPPPERS OF
FRUIT
NORTH DOVER, OHIO.
ON NICKEL PLATE R. R.

Leverett J. Cahoon

To the Editor of the Leader:

Leverett Judson CAHOON*,* fifth son of the late ***Joel B.*** and ***Margaret A. CAHOON****,* was born at Dover, O., November 14, 1845. Here, on Rose Hill farm, he lived the length of his useful life, and here, when unable to battle with disease, he rendered up that life. As a youth, he was very promising, possessing rare mental ability, and improving his time at study at the district and select schools of his native place. When seventeen years of age and preparing to enter college, the severe illness of his father compelled him to resign all thought of a higher education, to take charge of the farm and his father's business. With the unselfishness and cheerfulness which ever characterized him, he entered upon the duties pressed upon him. How nobly he performed them with the assistance and advice of his younger brother, ***Marshall***, his friends well know. Lying upon the bank of the lake and possessing the proper qualities of soil for the culture of grapes, the farm gradually was devoted to that branch of fruit growing until eighty acres of beautiful vineyard attest to the work he did in that line. The location also was propitious for fisheries, and with energy of purpose, he entered into that industry, never faltering in any branch of business which previously occupied his attention. He spent several winters in the schoolroom, where he was the object of the admiration of his pupils, the trusted teacher of many who now live in this vicinity. He seemed to feel that a great trust was given into his keeping when his honored father felt the hand of time resting heavily upon his snowy head, and with tenderness almost exceptional the strong son cheered the declining years of his life and helped to lay him to his final rest. Then he accepted as his most sacred duty the care of his grieving mother, who has always shared his home. For her and the four sisters who gathered around him for counsel, he had nothing but affection and support. All these years of his manhood he had been unconsciously working himself into prominence by his excellent habits, his great mental strength and public spirit, as well as his utter thoughtlessness of self when someone else or his town would receive benefits. He planned much for the future, more even than the past can show, but it was not to be. In the fall of 1884 he dislocated his knee while stepping from a train, and before he could again use his limb, contracted a severe cold, causing pleuro-pneumonia. From his illness, which was long and serious, he never fully recovered.

Still he could not rest, but was ever busy with both head and hands planning improvements, and executing plans already formed. Not till Saturday, August 7, did he place himself in the hands of his physician, so anxious was he to be at his business and reluctant to accept the situation. Disease had taken a firm hold, and after one week of suffering from the dread typhoid fever, he was taken from us. At 8 o'clock, Monday, August 16, a thrush came and sang at the open door of the sick chamber a sweet song of morning praise. At the same time the feeble breathing ceased, leaving the home full of grief at the sudden loss of a noble son and brother. Three days later, at 11 o'clock, hundreds had gathered from near and far, some from other States, and many from distant parts of Ohio, to perform the last rites of a true friend. Within the quiet sitting-room, so dear to him, surrounded by *(damaged section)*....beautiful flowers, lavishly laid by loving hands near him, lay the form of him ...He lay in a rich black casket, showing the full figure, in dress suit of black with nobleness of his character depicted upon his face. *Mrs. J.C. FITZPATRICK* began the service by sweetly singing, "Come, Ye Disconsolate," and was followed by *Rev. R.B. POPE* in fervent prayer. The Arion Quartet then sang impressively, "Lead Kindly Light." Many beautiful, consoling selections from the Scripture were then read, after which Dr. Pope, simply, eloquently, and with comfort in his words, spoke of his cheer, his hospitality, his generous nature, his great business ability, his progressive thought, and his manliness. He referred to his strength in health, the fine robust figure, calling him a giant in form as well as in mind. He spoke of Leverett as taking the work from the hand of his worthy father, who had continued that of his good father, the settler of this town, who founded the home at beautiful Rose Hill. Now life's labor o'er, they form a grand trio, ***Joseph, Joel***, and Leverett, three generations of noble men.

"Thy Will be Done" was sweetly sung by the "Arions," which was the last exercise before leaving the cemetery. At the vault the Dover Lodge of F. & A. Masons conducted the services. *Mr. Josiah N. HURST*, with feeling, read the beautiful service, the order responding with reverence. The quartet three times lent the charm of their beautiful voices to the services, which made them complete. The eight trusted friends bore him within the structure which is to shelter him. There, with the perfume of blossoms which covered him and the tears of those who mourn fresh upon his narrow home, we left him, carrying in our sad hearts the memory of a life, short but well lived, loving, true, and kind.

"Speak no more of his renown;
Lay all earthly fancies down;
God accept him, Christ receive him."

Newspaper article, The Leader, Cahoon Collection, Rose Hill Museum, Bay Village, OH.

L. J. CAHOON, d. August 16, 1886, Dover, single, 40y. 9m. 2d., b. Dover, farmer, parents ***J. B.*** and ***Margaret***, disease Typhoid fever. PD 3:146.

CAHOON, Leverett J.- At his residence, Rose Hill, North Dover, O., Monday morning, August 16, 1886, Leverett J. Cahoon, son of the late ***Joel B. CAHOON***. Funeral from his late residence, Thursday, Aug 19, at 11 a.m. Friends invited. Morning Leader, Cleveland, August 18, 1886, p. 5, col. 5. Similar notice in Aug 17, p. 3, col. 4. The Plain Dealer.

Leverett CAHOON, 40, res. Dover; interred Oct 9, 1886, Lot 64. "List of Interments," Lakeside Cemetery, Bay Village, OH. *Date assumed incorrect.*

(Lot 63) Daniel Kenyon Cahoon

KENYON

Daniel Kenyon CAHOON, fourth child of ***Joel*** and ***Margaret CAHOON***; b. 25 Jan 1838, Clear Springs, MD; d. 15 Feb 1890, Cleveland, OH, never married. Cahoon Family Charts and Gen. Data, Rose Hill.

Daniel Kenyon CAHOON, was called Kenyon. We do not know what he did for a living. He never married. He was a Mason. "The Joel Butler Cahoon Family," (Bay Village Historical Society).

CAHOON, D. Kenyon - Saturday, February 15th, 1890, at the residence of his sisters, 1916 Broadway, D. Kenyon Cahoon, aged 52 years. Funeral from residence of his sisters, Tuesday, Feb 18th, at 10:30 a.m. Cleveland Necrology File, February 17, 1890.

D. Kenyon CAHOON, 52; res. Dover; interred Feb 15, 1890; Lot 63. "List of Interments," Lakeside Cemetery, Bay Village, OH.

CAHOON, D.K., d. Feb 15, 1890, 1916 Broadway, single, 52 y, b. M.S., disease pneumonia. PD 4:179.

(Lot 63) John Joseph Cahoon

JOSEPH

John Joseph CAHOON, second child of ***Joel*** and ***Margaret CAHOON***; b. 9 Jan 1834, Fredericktown, Frederick Co., MD; d. 4 Mar 1894, Dover, OH; never married. Cahoon Family Charts and Gen. Data, Rose Hill.

John Joseph CAHOON was named after his two grandfathers. "The Joel Butler Cahoon Family," (Bay Village Historical Society).

DEATH OF J. J. CAHOUN.

A Well-Known Mechanical Engineer of Memphis, Tenn., Passes From Life at Dover - A Resident of the South Since 1859.

Mr. J. Joseph CAHOUN *(assumed misspelling)* died on Sunday afternoon at 2:30 o'clock at his mother's home in Dover. Mr. Cahoun was born in Frederick, Md., but when a lad his parents made their home near Cleveland and here his boyhood years were passed. In 1857 he visited several Southern cities, settling upon Memphis, Tenn., as his place of residence and that city continued to be his home. From earliest childhood he evinced a mechanical genius, which developed with his years. His inventions were specially profitable to the cotton industry of the South, and attracted the

attention of many Eastern and foreign capitalists. He possessed many characteristics of a true genius, being thoughtful, philosophical, and decided in his opinions, though possessing much quiet humor. He was a true friend. As a son and brother his love was ardent and beautiful. When his robust frame began suddenly to fail he immediately placed himself in the care of his loved ones, and bravely and patiently endured till the end came. He was the second son of the late ***Joel B. CAHOUN***, so long prominently identified with every interest in this vicinity. ***Messrs. Thomas H. CAHOUN***, of this city, and

J. Marshall CAHOUN are his brothers. Mr. Cahoun was unmarried, and had just passed his sixtieth birthday. Newspaper clipping from the Cahoon Family Papers, Rose Hill Museum.

John Joseph CAHOON invented the cotton compress, receiving a patent on June 29, 1875. Cahoon Family Papers, Rose Hill Museum.

CAHOON-J. Joseph Sunday, March 4, 1894, at Rose Hill, Dover, O., of consumption, J. Joseph Cahoon of Memphis, Tenn., second son of the late ***Joel B. CAHOON***. Funeral services will be held at the family residence in Dover Wednesday, March 7, at 11 a.m. St. Louis (Mo.) and Memphis (Tenn.) papers please copy. Cleveland Necrology File, March 7, 1894.

(Lot 64) John Marshall Cahoon

MARSHALL

John Marshall CAHOON, called Pat, was the ninth child of ***Joel*** and ***Margaret CAHOON***; b. 20 July1847, Dover, OH; d. 8 Aug 1899, Dover; never married. Cahoon Family Charts and Gen. Data, Rose Hill.

See Agricultural Production Schedule for J. M. with Leverett above.

Post Office Department,

OFFICE OF THE FOURTH ASSISTANT POSTMASTER GENERAL,

Washington, D.C., May 7, 1892.

John Marshall Cahoon, Esq.

Sir: The Postmaster General has appointed you Postmaster at North Dover, County of Cuyahoga, State of Ohio, in which capacity you will be authorized to act...

Very Respectfully, E.G. Rathbone
Fourth Assistant Postmaster General.

Card in the Rose Hill Cahoon Collection:

J. M. CAHOON
GENERAL INSURANCE AGENCY.
REPRESENTING
(Companies listed)
Total Assets Represented, $25,000,000
NORTH DOVER, O.

VIOLENT DEATH.
John M. Cahoon Fatally Injured in A Runaway Accident last Evening.

John Marshall CAHOON, one of the best known residents of North Dover, died at his home, "Rose Hill," at 11 o'clock last evening from injuries received by being thrown from his buggy.

Mr. Cahoon was the youngest son of the late ***Joel B.*** and ***Margaret A. CAHOON***, who were the first settlers of Dover township, making their home there in 1810. *Reference is to the grandparents of John Marshall, Joseph and Lydia.* The family is well known in the vicinity. Mr. Cahoon owned large vineyards and a store.

Last evening about 5 o'clock Mr. Cahoon left the house on the way to the store which is about half a mile distant. He went by a short cut instead of going by the road and on the way is a steep ravine. It is thought that while descending into this ravine the buggy made a short turn and capsized, frightening the horse, which ran away. Mr. Cahoon was dragged some distance by the frightened animal and it is thought struck against a tree or stump. The members of the family at the house heard the noise of the runaway and hastened to the scene. Mr. Cahoon was picked up unconscious and taken to the house in a buggy. *Dr. E.H. JEWETT* of this city, an old friend of the family was at the house at the time, spending a vacation. ***Dr. C.D. ELLIS*** of Detroit road and *Dr. C.W. STAHL* of Dover Center were also called. The efforts of the physicians, however, proved to no avail. Several ribs had been broken and penetrated the lungs, causing internal hemorrhages, from which he died at 11 o'clock without regaining consciousness.

Mr. Cahoon was a single man and lived at "Rose Hill" with his sister, ***Martha***. Three other sisters, the ***Misses Ida, Lydia*** and ***Laura CAHOON***, are school teachers in this city. ***Mr. Thomas CAHOON*** of Franklin avenue is the brother of the deceased. Article in the Cahoon Family Papers, Rose Hill Museum. *The accident occurred on a path near where the Interurban tracks were by the swimming pool.*

DEEPLY DEPLORED
Is the Death of J. Marshall Cahoon -A Tribute to His Memory

To the Editor of the Leader.

It seems but justice to the memory of ***J. Marshall CAHOON***, whose life so suddenly ended last Tuesday evening, that a few words of appreciation be spoken.

Born in the home of his ancestors-the family home for eighty-nine years-he passed his life beneath its roof, emulating the characteristics of his father and grandfather.

When but a mere lad it became the duty of his brother, ***Leverett***, and himself to take charge of the farm, with its extensive vineyards. Both became men of plans and purposes, broadening out into business incident to their surroundings and having taste for the beautiful, they added to the natural attractiveness of Rose Hill. Thirteen years ago a sudden illness deprived him of his brother's counsels and companionship. Bravely he took up life's duties, caring with a beautiful tenderness for his aged mother, and devoting himself to his four sisters.

His public spirit aided Dover in ever improving enterprise while he looked hopefully into the future for greater things. His Christian life began when a boy, continuing through the years in the interest of the Dover Lake Shore Methodist Episcopal Church particularly, but in the earnest helpfulness to all of his fellow men. He daily lived a cheerful, earnest Christian life. In the church and Sunday school he was a willing worker, esteemed because of his pure life. His large circle of friends grieve to-day that in the midst of this great usefulness, while vigorous and enterprising, his life should have so tragic an ending.

"Only the actions of the just
Smell sweet and blossom in the dust."

The large and beautiful grounds at Rose Hill were crowded by friends and sympathizing neighbors on the Saturday afternoon, on the funeral occasion. *Elder KIMBLE*, his pastor, and others spoke warmly and eloquently of this active life and labors, public and private, in the neighborhood where he had always lived. His extensive vineyard and orchards and farm are monument to his enterprise and industry, keeping up the reputation of a family which has occupied the homestead for a hundred years. Newspaper clipping in the Cahoon Family Papers, Rose Hill Museum.

HIS CARRIAGE OVERTURNED.

FATAL ACCIDENT TO JOHN M. CAHOON, OF NORTH DOVER.

He was a Prominent Business Man And Fruit Grower-Found Lying by the Wayside.

John M. CAHOON, a prominent business man and fruit grower of North Dover, O., was killed by an unfortunate accident while driving yesterday.

Mr. Cahoon lived on his farm called "Rose Hill." Several miles from his home is a store that he owned. Every day he drove from his home to the store. The road that he used is not frequented by many teams. It leads through a dark and steep ravine. In some manner the carriage became overturned, throwing Mr. Cahoon to the ground. The horse ran several feet and then stopped with the overturned carriage still attached to him. The crash of the carriage as it went over attracted some small boys who immediately gave the alarm.

Mr. Cahoon was taken to his home in a semi-conscious state. Several ribs were broken and one punctured the lungs. The accident occurred at 5 o'clock in the afternoon. Mr. Cahoon died at 11 o'clock from the internal hemorrhage. *Dr. HEWITT* and ***Dr. C.D. ELLIS*** of Cleveland, who happened to be staying in Dover, attended Mr. Cahoon.

Mr. Cahoon leaves four sisters and one brother. Three of the sisters teach in the Cleveland schools. They are the ***Misses Lydia CAHOON, Laura CAHOON*** and ***Ida CAHOON***. The other sister, ***Miss Martha CAHOON***, lives at Dover. Mr. Cahoon's brother, ***Thomas CAHOON***, lives on Franklin avenue in this city. Newspaper clipping in the Cahoon Family Papers, Rose Hill Museum.

UNDER THE BLUE SKY.

THE FUNERAL SERVICES OF MARSHALL CAHOON WERE HELD.

Many Friends Gather Upon the Beautiful Lawn to Hear the Last Tribute to a Dover Citizen.

The funeral services over the remains of ***J. Marshall CAHOON***, of Dover, were held yesterday afternoon at Rose Hill, his late home. The services were attended by several hundred friends, among them many Cleveland men. The beautiful lawn overlooking the lake was arranged with seats and the services were held in the open air.

The Arion Quartet, of this city, opened the impressive services by singing the Twenty-third Psalm. *Rev. Z. WAGER*, pastor of the Dover Methodist Episcopal Church, read from the Scriptures and made remarks eulogistic of the career of Mr. Cahoon. The quartet sang "One Sweetly Solemn Thought," and *Rev. D.P. JULMER*, a former pastor of the Dover church, spoke feelingly of his acquaintance with Mr. Cahoon.

Gilbert ELLIOTT spoke of Mr. Cahoon as a citizen, praising his integrity, patriotism, and enterprise. *Horatius BONAR* recited an original poem appropriate for the occasion, and Rev. Dr. Kemble, presiding elder of the Cleveland district, offered prayer. The remains were taken to Lakeside Cemetery. The pall-bearers were *Roy L. GLEASON*, *Reuben OSBORN*, *A.J. MICHAEL*, ***Dr. C. D. ELLIS***, *H.P. FOOTE* and *H.C. BOWMAN*. Newspaper clipping in the Cahoon Family Papers, Rose Hill Museum.

CAHOON-John Marshall Cahoon, youngest son of the late ***Joel B***. and ***Margaret A. CAHOON***, Tuesday evening, August 8, 1899, at his home, Rose Hill, North Dover, O. Funeral services will be held from his late residence at 2 p.m. standard time, Saturday, Aug 12. Lorain and Cleveland electric cars stop at Cahoon rd. Cleveland Necrology File, Aug 11, 1899.

J.M. CAHOON, 52; res. Dover; interred Aug 11, 1899; Lot 64. "List of Interments," Lakeside Cemetery, Bay Village, OH.

In Memoriam

Whereas:

Since the last meeting of the Directors of The Commercial Adding Machine Co. it becomes our sad duty to record the death of ***Mr. J.M. CAHOON*** who has been a director of this company since its organization.

Therefore be it Resolved:

That this board, in appreciation of his services in the organization of this Company, direct that this resolution of respect be spread upon the minutes of this meeting and that a memorial page be set aside for that purpose and an engrossed copy be sent to his immediate relatives, to whom we extend our heartfelt condolence.

Directors:

Wm. F. SAYLE, Geo. L. RATSTON, Wm. M. WRIGHT, J.C. McLELAND, E.W. SCHLEGEL. A.E. MERKEL. Cleveland, Ohio, Oct. 20th, 1899. Cahoon Family Papers, Rose Hill Museum.

(Lot 65) **Martha Washington Cahoon**

MARTHA

Martha Washington CAHOON, seventh child of ***Joel*** and ***Margaret CAHOON***, b. 22 Feb 1844, Dover, OH; d. 19 May 1903, Dover; never married. Cahoon Family Charts and Gen. Data, Rose Hill.

Martha Washington CAHOON was born on George Washington's birthday, thus the middle name. She was a school teacher. One of her first teaching jobs was in Toledo, OH. She journeyed to Toledo and boarded in a rooming house for the year. At the end of the year, she returned home to Dover. She became a teacher in the Cleveland School System. She was a member of the Commodore Perry Chapter of the Daughters of 1812. She was an artist, and many of her paintings hang in Rose Hill. When she became ill, she retired to Rose Hill where she was nursed by her sisters for seven months until her death. She never married. She died of sclerosis. "The Joel Butler Cahoon Family," (Bay Village Historical Society).

CAHOON-Martha Washington Tuesday evening, May 19, 1903, Martha Washington, third daughter of the late ***Joel B.*** and ***Margaret A. Cahoon***. Services at Rose Hill, Dover, O., Friday, May 22, at 2 p.m. May 22, 1903 and May 21, 1903, p. 8, col. 5. The Plain Dealer. All rights reserved. Reprinted with permission.

Martha CAHOON, 59, single, b. Ohio, Cause of death sclerosis, res. 1916 Broadway, Ward 17, d. res., duration of illness 7 mos., fr. b. NY, mo. b. DC, cemetery Lakeside and Dover, phys. E.H. Jewitt, undertaker B.S. Harris. May 19, 1903. CRD: film 1977439.

Martha W. CAHOON, 59; res. Dover; interred May 19, 1903; Lot 65. "List of Interments," Lakeside Cemetery, Bay Village, OH.

(Lot 63/65) **Lydia Elizabeth Cahoon**

LYDIA

Lydia Elizabeth CAHOON, third child of ***Joel*** and ***Margaret CAHOON***; b. 16 Aug 1835, Frederick, MD; d. 29 Mar 1917, Bay Village, OH; never married. Cahoon Family Charts and Gen. Data, Rose Hill.

South School will not be remembered by many. It was a two-room frame building, once located on the site which now is occupied by Barkwill School. But, undoubtedly, members of the class...can talk profusely on South School and its importance years ago. *Students pictured with "**Miss KUHOON** (teacher)."* "These Studied at Old South School," Cleveland Press, undetermined date, Lydia Cahoon Family Papers, Rose Hill Museum.

WAR DAUGHTERS SEE PATRIOTISM WANE

Photograph of Misses Lydia, Laura and Ida Cahoon.

The roar of cannon drifted across the waters of Lake Erie. It was a hundred years ago, on a hot August day.

A young man who was hewing timbers for his mill on the banks of Dover creek stopped and listened anxiously to the sound, trying to tell from the rising and falling of the rumble which way the fight was going.

For he, young ***Joel CAHOON***, knew the meaning of that battle when *Commodore PERRY* was fighting with the British. He knew what terrors defeat would bring to the people of Ohio, and he was thrilled when he thought of what happiness a victory would bring.

"How many of us realize, as he did," asks Miss Lydia Cahoon, his daughter, "the importance of the battle to the progress of which my father listened so anxiously?"

Parents in War

The ***Misses Laura, Lydia*** and ***Ida CAHOON*** of North Dover are among the few living persons whose parents went through the war of 1812. They are members of the United States Society of Daughters of 1812.

Their father, fired with enthusiasm after hearing the cannon of Perry's ships, enlisted in the army and served during the campaigns of Colonel George Crogan, the hero of Fort Stephen.

Their mother was among those who fled from Washington before the invading began.

In their home at North Dover, built by their father more than a century ago, they are treasuring silver and keepsakes buried in the yard of the Washington house while the British occupied the town.

Thus surrounded all their lives by relics and traditions of the war time in whose shadow they were brought up, they feel a love for the flag and a patriotism which they fear is wanting in too many American homes today.

Lydia Elizabeth CAHOON was a little, tiny lady. She loved to cook and was often in the kitchen. "The Joel Butler Cahoon Family," (Bay Village Historical Society).

Will Ride in Parade

"We hope the Perry centennial will bring back to people the importance of the stirring war history in whose making my father took a part," said Miss Lydia Cahoon Thursday as she accepted the invitation of the women's committee to ride in the grand final parade, planned for September 17.

"For years we taught in Cleveland's public schools and did our part to fill the minds of hundreds of future citizens with the reverence for our country's history which we always have felt.

"We hope the people of Cleveland will celebrate in the same reverence.

"Yet, looking at it from the point of view of money alone, it was Perry's victory which made possible the present commercial prosperity of Cleveland. I hope that people won't forget this, at least, amid the gaiety of parades and fireworks." Cleveland News, Sept 4, 1913.

PIONEER RESIDENT OF BAY VILLAGE, IS DEAD

MISS LYDIA CAHOON, WAS WELL KNOWN IN NORTHERN PART OF THIS COUNTY

Miss Lydia CAHOON, daughter of the late ***Joel CAHOON***, one of the pioneer residents of Bay Village, died at her home in that place yesterday afternoon at four o'clock, aged 84 years.

The funeral services will be held Monday afternoon from her late home, at two o'clock; Eastern time. Newspaper clipping, Lydia Cahoon Family Papers, Rose Hill Museum, Bay Village, OH.

On Monday, April 2nd, 1917, at two o'clock, the funeral services of ***Lydia Elizabeth CAHOON*** were held in her late residence, Dover Village, *Dr. F.W. LUCE* presiding…"This bible from which I am reading this sacred lesson," said Dr. Luce, "is an heirloom in the family. The ancestors of Miss Cahoon were not only devout Christians, but were devoted to the cause of their Country. The maternal Grand-father was reading from these pages in 1814 when taken prisoner by the British as they invaded Washington D.C."…Dr. Luce spoke as follows: "It is utterly useless for me with mere words to undertake to add luster to the character of this good woman whom we mourn today. Any words of mine would be like a feeble and unworthy attempt to add luster to the new light or to give delicacy and beauty to the colorings and shading of these flowers.

"True goodness is true greatness, and service is the medium of character. In this light we are today remembering and paying tribute to a truly great and truly good character. Gentleness is greatness; kindness is service, and these words define in their truest sense, some of the elements of the character of this good woman. - Gentle as a June Zephyr, - kind as the hand of Charity and Love itself, - modest in her activities, - always faithful to any duty; she will be remembered while memory lasts, by those who knew her. - - Sweet in her home life; -loved by all who knew her, - I think it would be impossible to conceive of her as having an enemy...those who knew this dear one most closely, recognize most her delicate and kindly courtesy, her beauty and Christlike sincerity of character." Memorial Service for Lydia E. Cahoon, Lydia Cahoon Family Papers, Rose Hill Museum.

BAY VILLAGE

The community lost this last week one of its most useful and loved members. ***Miss Lydia E. CAHOON*** passed peacefully on to eternal life, on Thursday, March 29, at 4:05 p.m., after an illness of three months…Her mother, ***Margaret A. CAHOON*** was a woman of unusual intellectual ability and charming ways, many of which were prominent in her eldest daughter, Lydia.

Miss Cahoon was educated at *Mrs. GREEN'S* Select School in Dover, and at *Miss Linda T. GUILFORD'S* Seminary in Cleveland. She will be remembered by many as their teacher for she taught in Cuyahoga County schools, in Toledo, and in the Cleveland public schools.

In Cleveland she had a foreign element, often not one English speaking student. To them she taught the love of country and the flag under which they lived, as one of the essentials of citizenship. She retired from teaching fourteen years ago, returning to the Rose Hill home of her family. She interested herself in the religious and social life of her home village, contributing largely to building the new M.E. church and parsonage. Each year she with her sisters, entertained at a June festival at Rose Hill that was attended by hundreds of her friends. She was a charter member of Saturday Club and also of Commodore Perry Chapter, Daughters of 1812, of which she was chaplain ever since its organization.

On Monday, April 2, a large number of friends assembled at Rose Hill to attend the last services for Miss Cahoon. She lay in a bower of beautiful flowers, the room being garlanded with roses, lilies, carnations, jonquils, violets and dainty ferns.

Rev. Dr. F.W. LUCE, district superintendent of Cleveland district, paid a beautiful tribute to her gentleness, kindness, courtesy and real goodness. *Dr. W.C. ENDLEY*, a former pastor, and *Rev. D.W. KNIGHT* assisted in the service.

Miss Margaret WRIGHT, of Cleveland, sang in a sweet clear voice, "One Sweetly Solemn Thought," and "O Paradise." *W.E. WRIGHT* sang a favorite hymn, "In Heavenly Love Abiding." *Mrs. C.B. TOZIER*, founder of Commodore Perry Chapter, U.S.D. of 1812, spoke feelingly of her friend, giving her data in the Chapter, she being a real daughter, and the chaplain who prepared the beautiful ritual that would be used for her today. At the close of their service each member of the chapter placed a white carnation upon the loved sister.

Six friends, *C.G. BARKWELL, W.O. MATHEWS, Dr. A.S. COOLEY, Edward COWLEY, Geo. H. BROWN* and *R.S. HOOVER*, bore her from the loved and sacred home and she was tenderly laid to rest by her dear ones in Lakeside Cemetery.

Her memory is as fragrant as the valley lilies that lay upon her breast.

Dr. and *Mrs. W.C. ENDLEY, Judge* and *Mrs. D. J. NYE, Mrs. Aaron BULLOCK* and *Miss BULLOCK* and *Mrs. W.E. CAHOON* from Elyria; *Mrs. Joseph JAMESON* and *Mr.* and *Mrs. Leverett J. CAHOON* of Avon; and *Mr.* and *Mrs. Henry DOUGHERTY*, of Wellington, attended the funeral of Miss Cahoon, last Monday.

Special services have been given at the church this past week.

The Ladies' Aid society postponed its meeting for two weeks because of the death of its founder. *Miss May HOLLENBACH*, of Cleveland, spent some time at Rose Hill, the past week.

Little *Edward COWLEY* is very much better.

The grading at Cahoon hill goes steadily on.

Newspaper clipping, Lydia Cahoon Family Papers, Rose Hill Museum, Bay Village, OH.

CAHOON-Lydia Elizabeth, eldest daughter of the late ***Margaret A.*** and ***Joel B. CAHOON***, and dearly beloved sister of ***Laura E. CAHOON*** and ***Ida M. CAHOON***, at her residence, Rose Hill, Bay Village, O., Thursday, Mar 29, 1917. Funeral services at late residence West Lake, cor. Cahoon rd., Stop 24, Lake Shore Electric, Monday, April 2, at 2 p.m. Cleveland Necrology File, April 1, 1917.

Lydia Elizabeth CAHOON, d. Mar 19, 1917, 4:05 p.m., West Lake Road, Bay Village, Cuyahoga County, Ohio; b. Aug 16, 1835, Maryland; Single, Retired; fr. ***Joel B. CAHOON***, b. New York; mo. ***Margaret DICKSON***, b. Washington D.C. Informant *Ida M. CAHOON*, Bay Village, O. I hereby certify, that I attended deceased from Jany. 7, 1917 to Mar 29, 1917, that I last saw her alive on Mar 29, 1917, *C.D. ELLIS, M.D.*, 1730 W. 25th St. Cause of death Pneumonia, contributory age. Burial Lakeside Cemetery, Apr 2, 1917, Undertaker Geo Sharer and Son, 2436 Prospect Ave. Ohio Certificate of Death, Division of Vital Statistics, 1917, certif. 16180.

Lydia E. CAHOON, 82; res. Bay Village; interred April 1, 1917. "List of Interments," Lakeside Cemetery, Bay Village, OH.

Lydia Elizabeth CAHOON, Pneumonia, issued April 2, 1917 by A.L. Miller. Burial Removal Permit.

(Lot 65) **Laura Ellen Cahoon**

LAURA

Laura Ellen CAHOON, sixth child of ***Joel*** and ***Margaret CAHOON***; b. 12 Dec 1841, Cleves, Hamilton County, OH; d. 2 June 1917, Bay Village, OH; never married. She had a bright, pleasant personality and a happy face.

Cahoon Family Charts, Gen. Data, Rose Hill and "The Joel Butler Cahoon Family," (Bay Village Historical Society).

TEACHER DEAD AFTER 45 YEARS IN SCHOOLS

Photo of Miss Laura E. Cahoon

THOUSANDS OF PUPILS MOURN AGED TEACHER

"Now, before we work today,
We will not forget to pray
To God, who kept us thru the night,
And waked us with the morning light."

Thousands of Cleveland men and women thought of this verse Monday when they read that ***Miss Laura Ellen CAHOON*** is dead.

When they were in the first grade at school, they used to say the verse daily with their teacher. The teacher was Miss Cahoon.

Funeral services for Miss Cahoon will be held at the family home in Bay Village at 2:30 p.m. Wednesday. She died Saturday in St. John's hospital.

Miss Cahoon began teaching in Cleveland schools about forty-seven years ago. She taught in Charter Oak, Union, Barkwill and Detroit schools for 36 years, and in schools in Dover, Avon and Sheffield for eight years before she came to Cleveland.

When Miss Cahoon resigned as teacher in Detroit School two years ago she said:

"I'll miss the voices of the children. I always taught the first grade except for one year when I took the second."

Miss Cahoon kept a flag always above the door of her schoolroom. Every morning the children saluted it and gave the pledge of allegiance.

"A child's earliest lesson should be in patriotism," she said.

Miss Cahoon once gave this advice to young teachers:

"Never go into the work of preparing a child for life simply as a means of making a living. Unless you love children and love to work with children, your place isn't with them. A little girl or boy is the most precious thing in the world."

Miss Cahoon was a member of the Daughters of 1812. She had been historian of the Commodore Perry Chapter and was recently elected chaplain of the chapter. She was the granddaughter of ***Joseph CAHOON***, founder of Dover-tp. Newspaper clipping, Undetermined source, Cahoon Collection, Rose Hill Museum, Bay Village, OH.

BAY VILLAGE

A very impressive memorial service was held at the church at the regular meeting of the Ladies' Aid Society for the late secretary, ***Miss Laura E. CAHOON***, whose very sudden passing away was a shock to her many friends. *Miss LIGGETT* and *Miss Lucy OSBORN* sang appropriate hymns, "One Sweetly Solemn Thought," and "In Heaven Love Abiding," *Miss Julia OSBORN SCOTT* read Psalm 41, and *Mrs. Jesse L. SADDLER* gave an account of the beautiful funeral service for Miss Cahoon. *Dr. Duston KEMBLE, Rev. D.W. KNIGHT, Rev. Joseph CALLISTER* and *Dr. W.C. ENDLY*, each bore a part in the service. Mrs. Saddler read the tribute paid Miss Cahoon as a teacher by *Miss Augusta C. THOMPSON*, principal of Detroit school, where Miss Cahoon taught for eight years. *Mrs. BAILEY* read a poem written by Miss Cahoon for the church anniversary in 1907. *Mrs. Russell POPE*, who presided, added items of interest regarding Miss Cahoon and read a letter from *Mrs. ELLINWOOD*, whose absence in Asheville, N. C., prevented her attendance. The room was beautifully decorated and Miss Cahoon's picture was draped with flowers and the flag she loved.

Mrs. Emma S. BENHAM called on her brother, *F.C. SITES*, Friday, on her way to spend two weeks with friends in Avon.

Miss HINE of Youngstown spent the week end with Miss Cahoon.

Miss Cahoon and Mrs. Bailey called upon Dr. Endly and family on Lake avenue, Elyria, last Thursday.

Mrs. John HUNTINGTON is living on her beautiful farm this month.

Miss HOLLENBACH and *Miss MOORE* of Cleveland visited Rose Hill on Saturday. Newspaper clipping, Undetermined source, Cahoon Collection, Rose Hill Museum, Bay Village, OH.

BAY VILLAGE

The announcement of the death of ***Miss Laura E. CAHOON***, June 2, 1917, brought sorrow to many homes in our midst. Miss Cahoon had been ill just one week, and few knew of her serious illness.

But two months previous, her older sister, ***Miss Lydia E. CAHOON***, had been laid to rest in the family lot in Lakeside cemetery. The sorrow of this bereavement bore heavily upon Miss Laura, she being unable to rise above the burden and life held no charms for her.

When illness came, she said she would not recover and that she would like to go.

Wednesday at 2:30 o'clock a host of friends gathered to pay their tribute of affection to the dear one gone.

Dr. Duston KEMBLE of Lisbon, an old time friend, had charge of the services. *Miss Margaret C.F. WRIGHT*, of Cleveland, opened the service with a sweet rendering of "My Jesus as Thou Wilt," and was followed by prayer of Dr. Kemble and Scripture reading by *Rev. J.Q. CALLISTER* of Polk, O. *Miss Maude WILLIAMS,* of Cleveland, a former pupil sang "Safe in the Arms of Jesus," with variations. *Dr. Wm. C. ENDLY*, of Elyria, a former pastor and a friend of more than thirty years, delivered the address; speaking of his coming to this home on his first appointment and receiving inspiration from the Christian mother who was to him, also, a mother. He spoke of Laura's love of nature, of the beautiful, of her poetic trend, of her great work as a teacher, and of her faith, submission and longing for the other world since, two months ago, her dear sister was taken.

Mrs. Augusta C. THOMPSON, who was principal of Detroit school during the years Miss Cahoon taught in that building, told of how she was loved and honored among her associates, how she amplified the humble little people who came under her care.

She told of the daily morning prayer, the daily salute to the flag, of the lessons of patriotism, of her original ideas in training and of her free generosity at all times.

Mrs. C.B. TOZIER, founder of Commodore Perry Chapter U.S.D. of 1812, having recently read in the autobiography of Miss Cahoon's mother, attributed much of Miss Laura's patriotism and love of the best in life to the influence of the unusually gifted mother. She spoke of her as historian of the chapter for two years, and as recently elected chaplain to succeed her late sister, Miss Lydia E. Cahoon, both being Real Daughters.

Miss Wright sang "My Faith Looks Up to Thee," and then the Commodore Perry Chapter U. S. D. of 1812, whose silken flag stood at her head, rendered their beautiful ritual and laid their white carnations upon the loved form. At Lakeside cemetery the committal service was read, by Dr. Kemble, Miss Williams rendered "Abide With Me," and surrounded by a wealth of summer's bloom sent by loving friends, having beautiful memories of her long and useful life, she lies near many dear ones who precede her to the Heavenly Land.

Miss Anna C. HAVENNOR of Santa Barbara, California, was present at Miss Cahoon's funeral as also was *Mrs. Dr. E.P. HAWLEY* of Clement, Cal.

Mrs. C.E. FRENCH of Toledo, O., is spending a week at Rose Hill.

Many Elyria friends and relatives attended Miss Cahoon's funeral Wednesday. Newspaper clipping, Undetermined source, Cahoon Collection, Rose Hill Museum, Bay Village, OH.

Laura Ellen CAHOON, West Lake Road, Bay, Cuy. Co.; d. June 2, 1917, 10 p.m. Femme Hernia Strangulated, Hernia-15 yrs., *C.D. ELLIS, M.D.* 1730 W. 25th; b. Dec 12, 1841, Ohio…; 75 yrs. 5 mos. 21 ds; single; Informant/undertaker Geo. Sharer and Son, 2436 Prospect; bur. Lakeside Cem., June 6, 1917. Ohio Certificate of Death, Division of Vital Statistics, 1917, certif. 38096.

CAHOON-Laura Ellen, second daughter of the late ***Margaret A.*** and ***Joel B. CAHOON*** and dearly beloved sister of ***Ida M. CAHOON***, Saturday, June 2, 1917. Services at late residence, Rose Hill, Bay Village, O., cor. West Lake and Cahoon rds., Stop 24, Lake Shore Electric, Wednesday, June 6, at 2:30 o'clock, eastern time. Cleveland Necrology File, June 6, 1917.

Laura CAHOON; res. Bay Village; interred June 2d, 1917. "List of Interments," Lakeside Cemetery, Bay Village, OH.

(Lot 63) **Ida Maria Cahoon**

IDA

Ida Maria CAHOON, youngest child of ***Joel*** and ***Margaret***; b. 17 Mar 1852, Dover, OH; d. 28 Nov 1917, Bay Village, OH; never married. Cahoon Family Charts and Gen. Data, Rose Hill.

Ida M. CAHOON received her "Teacher's Certificate" on April 15, 1871, in Cleveland and was "qualified to teach Reading, Writing, Orthography, Geography, Grammar and Arithmetic." Ida taught for the Cleveland School System. Teaching Certificate and notes, Rose Hill Museum, The Bay Village Historical Society.

The Cahoon Family Centennial at Dover

…Monday, October 10th, 1910 marked the century line of the eve…so interesting to the Cahoon family. Beautiful souvenir invitations were sent from Vermont to California, inviting the descendants of ***Joseph*** and ***Lydia CAHOON*** to gather at Rose Hill and have a feast of good things and a feast of reason to follow.

Rose Hill had been polished for the occasion. Flags floated everywhere. Providence sent a glorious sunshine to light the scene and give it the touch an October day must have to be perfect. A large number came, not in covered wagons over unbridged streams, but the trolly car stopped on the edge of the grounds, and many automobiles were there.

The officers were ***Miss Ida M. CAHOON***, Rose Hill, president; ***Miss Lydia E. CAHOON***, Rose Hill, first vice president; *Mr. Everett CAHOON*, Akron, second vice president; *Mr. Walter E. WRIGHT*, Cleveland, third vice president; *Capt. Frank B. HOLLENBACH*, Cleveland, secretary; *Mr. H.R. DAUGHERTY*, Wellington, treasurer.

The beautiful dinner was served upon beautifully arranged tables, decorated with autumn blossoms and sprigs of barberry, and placed under a huge tent on the lawn. Bag-pipe music enlivened the occasion. The venerable *Dr. F.S. HOYT*, of Lorain, asked a blessing upon all, before the roast pig, fried chicken; vegetables, apple pies, cakes, luscious fruits and ice cream were enjoyed. The committee having this feature of the function in charge deserve the highest praise. They brought their best in bountiful quantity and knew just how it must be carried out. Surely our grandmothers must have been clever, or how would this generation be so capable?…

Among those present were, *Mr. Levi CAHOON, Mr. Wilbur CAHOON, Mr. Paul CAHOON* and *Mrs. Huldah C. NESBITT*, of Barabor, Wis.; *Mrs. Mary W. McCroden*, of Jersey City, N.J.; *Mr. and Mrs. Elbert CAHOON*, of Watertown, Ia.; *Mr. H.J. CAHOON, Misses Carrie* and *Maude CAHOON, Judge* and *Mrs. D.J. NYE, Mrs. John B. CAHOON, Mrs. Aaron BULLOCK* and *Miss BULLOCK*, of Elyria; *Mr.* and *Mrs. Alvah BULLOCK* of Toledo, *Mr.* and *Mrs. Jos. CAHOON* and family, *Mr.* and *Mrs. Jos. JAMESON, Mrs. C. SWEET* and *Mrs. Geo. HURST*, of Avon; the *ANDREWS family* of Lakewood; *Mrs. L.H. JOHNSON* and *Mr. Leverett C. ALDRICH,* of Ashtabula; and large numbers from Cleveland, Dover, Bay Village, Vermilion, Avery and Florence. *Rev. W.N. ROBERTSON*, of Port Clinton; *Rev* and *Mrs. COLLISTER*, of Monroeville and *Dr. G.A REEDER*, president of Baldwin University, Berea, were also present. I.M.C. *(Ida Maria Cahoon?)* Undetermined source, Newspaper article, Cahoon Collection, Rose Hill Museum, Bay Village, OH.

Parfait

(Miss Ida M. Cahoon)

One teacup maple syrup, yolks four eggs beaten lightly and put in with syrup and boil in double boiler until it thickens a little. Beat through and add whites of four eggs beaten lightly. Also one pint of whipped heavy cream. Mix it and beat well. Pack in a mold and set in a pail with salt and pounded ice for four hours.

Peach Pudding

(Miss Ida M. Cahoon)

Fill a buttered baking dish with sliced peaches, and pour over them a batter made as follows: One-half cup sugar, one egg, one cup flour, one tablespoon butter, one-half cup sweet milk, one teaspoon baking powder. Bake in a moderate oven until brown. Serve with cream and sugar.

The Village Cook Book, p. 41. (c1911-1915).

The June Festival

HELD ANNUALLY AT ROSE HILL ON THE THIRD WEDNESDAY OF JUNE IS THE GALA DAY FOR THE

Ladies Aid Society

- At that time the roses are most fragrant, the skies the bluest, and the bird songs the sweetest, and the work of the year is put upon sale.
- Light refreshments are served all afternoon and supper at 4:30 p.m.
- Fine automobile roads, and Lake Shore Electric cars to Stop 24, - form means of reaching Rose Hill, on West Lake Road corner Cahoon Road. Invite your friends and join in our next June Festival.

The Village Cook Book, p. 12.

By 1912, some church members from the eastern part of the village were growing tired of traveling the long distance to Bassett and Lake Roads. ***Miss Ida CAHOON***, a staunch Methodist and member of the school board, arranged for the red-brick school house at Lake and Columbia Roads to be used. Services were held by the *Rev. W.C. ENDLEY* and *Mr. John RUMBAUGH*, Sunday School Superintendent. The new group was offered the choice of a church service or Sunday School classes. The members opted for the Sunday School program so that the children could participate. Firmly established by 1917, our daughter church ran off and joined the Presbyterians. Carol K. Meermans, Bay United Methodist Church, 175th Anniversary booklet, 2002.

Mrs. McIntosh Heads Ohio Daughters of 1812.

Mrs. George McIntosh was elected president of the Ohio Society, United States Daughters of 1812, at the annual meeting Wednesday at the Woman's Club. Vice regents, *Mrs. W.D. CALDWELL*, Canton; *Mrs. Helen Wolcott DIMICK*, Toledo; secretary, *Mrs. Laura S. GOODHUE*; treasurer, *Mrs. A.E. SMITH*; registrar, *Mrs. A.M. HOLCOMB*; historian, ***Miss Ida CAHOON***; chaplain, *Mrs. A.B. COE*; surgeon, *Mrs. O.E. JONES*. The Ohio society will subscribe their quota for seven vases to be placed by the national society at the George Washington memorial at Valley Forge. Newspaper article, undetermined source, Cahoon Collection, Rose Hill Museum, Bay Village, OH.

MAY LOOSE LAND FATHERS HELD
Residents of Bay Village Have Queer Tangle With Homestead Property.
Lawyer in South Dakota Claims They Have No Right to It.

If the contention set up in common pleas court here by *Ernest C. JOHNSON*, an attorney of Black Hills, S. Dak., succeeds, he may come into an interest in valuable Bay Village land.

Misses Ida, Lydia and ***Laura CAHOON***, who for many years have believed themselves the owners of the land, attempted to sell it a few weeks ago for $12,000 and in order to give unclouded title, brought proceedings in court to clear up any possible claim against the property.

They claim that an ancestor, ***Joseph CAHOON***, the first settler in Dover township, deeded the land to their father, ***Joel CAHOON***, in 1837. The deed was lost, they declared, before being recorded.

Now comes *Ernest JOHNSON*, through his lawyers, Horr & Lewenthal, with a denial that they have good title to the property. The fact that the records display no deed to their father shows, he says, that no deed was ever made, and that although they have deemed themselves owners for many years, they have no rightful possession.
Newspaper article, Tuesday, Nov 12___, Cahoon Collection, Rose Hill Museum, Bay Village, OH.

BAY VILLAGE

The annual Guest Day of the Ladies' Aid society was a real success.

Dr. and *Mrs. F.W. LUCE*, of Cleveland, were the honored guests. Dr. Luce gave a very excellent address after the chicken dinner and *Miss EVANS* rendered a piano solo.

The church is making plans for special meetings after Christmas. Five students from Berea will spend a week in evangelism in this village.

On Wednesday evening the Men's club will hold a meeting at the church with supper at 7:00 p.m. and address from some one connected with the State Agricultural college on matters relating to insect pests.

The Committee on Village Hall is busy completing the interior arrangements and furnishings, preparatory to opening the new hall.

The mayor, clerk and road committee were guests of a Galion Ohio firm one day last week. Their trip will result in better equipment for good roads in Bay Village.

Mr. SCOTT, of Stop 35 is planning to erect a $7000 residence upon his new lake front acre purchased from *H.P. FOOTE*.

F.C. SITES returned from the Palace Poultry show in New York City where he was one of the judges. He has been asked to act in a like capacity at the same show next year.

The ***Misses CAHOON*** were hostesses to the Saturday club the 12th of this month. About twenty-five were present. *Miss RUGGER* formerly of the Oberlin Conservatory of Music was a guest, as also were *Miss Lucille BROWN* of Lakewood and *Miss Jennie E. JOHNSON* and *Miss Margaret JONES* of Cleveland.

Christmas greens, barberry bushes and bitter-sweet berries were used as decorations. The surprise program was a reading of one of *George Bernard SHAW'S* short dramas, which was greatly enjoyed. The refreshments bore Christmas decorations and were in accord with the holiday season.

Miss *Ada G. HINE* spent the weekend at Rose Hill.

The stewards meet with *Mr.* and *Mrs. J.D. RUMBAUGH* Monday evening the 14th.

Miss Olive P. BAILY will leave Tuesday to spend a month with *Mrs. MILES* of Springfield, Pa.

She was given a farewell tea at Rose Hill the night before leaving.

The Christian Endeavor solicit of the people of Dover and Bay Village any kind of clothing, fruit and vegetables....to pack and deliver to Cleveland charities.

Also magazines and any good reading. A call has come from Columbus State penitentiary. The freight will be paid.

A gentleman from Cleveland spoke at the Congregational church Sunday in the interest of the Anti-saloon league....

Edgar EVANS of Fields visited at the home of *Mrs. Myra OSBORN* Sunday.

The Men's club of Bay Village, will meet at the Methodist church Wednesday evening. A lecture will be given by *Mr. GOODMAN* of Wooster. A 25 cent supper will be served. Newspaper article, 9 Nov 1914, undetermined source, Cahoon Collection, Rose Hill Museum, Bay Village, OH.

Ida CAHOON was crippled with a club foot and you were able to hear her coming down the steps with the thumping of her crutch on the steps. Ida also had a "droopy" eye encouraging her to always turn her head when being photographed. Osborn Papers, Rose Hill Museum; Sally O'Connor and Kay Laughlin.

Ida M. CAHOON, Rose Hill, Lake Rd., Bay, Cuy Co. died on Nov 28, 1917, 8:00 p.m., Cerebral Hemorrhage and Apoplexis-12 days, Myocarditis-5yrs., *C.D. ELLIS, M.D.*; b. Mar 17, 1852, Dover, O...65 yrs. 8 mos. 11 ds.; Informant *Walter E. WRIGHT*, 4139 East 94 St., Cleveland, bur. Bay Vil., Lakeside Cem. on Dec 2, 1917, Undertaker Geo. Sharer & Son, 2436 Prospect Av. Ohio Certificate of Death, Division of Vital Statistics, 1917, certif. 69410.

CAHOUN-Miss Ida M., daughter of the late ***Joel B.*** and ***Margaret A. CAHOUN***, at the residence, Rose Hill, Village of Bay, early Wednesday night. Services at the First M.E. Church, Bay Village, Stop 32, Lake Shore Electric, Sunday, Dec 2, at 2 p.m. eastern time. Cleveland Necrology File, December 2, 1917.

Ida M. CAHOON, res. Bay Village, interred 1917. "List of Interments," Lakeside Cemetery, Bay Village, OH.

The early-day home of the Cahoons was willed by the last heir *(Ida)*, to become the Village library. The Cahoon barn was converted into a community hall. ***Ida Marie***, d. 1917, willed the land to become Cahoon Park. A condition of the gift banned boating, bathing, games and sports on Sunday. William Ganson Rose, Cleveland: The Making of a City, pp. 1066-1067.

Ida, the tallest of the sisters, was very involved with the Methodist Church in the village and gave much of her time to the church. The sisters allowed a Methodist Church Camp to convene yearly on the property south of the barn. Because Ida was the last to die, she is referred to when talking about the Cahoon Will which was drawn up by the family in 1882, the year before Joel's death. Some of the stipulations of the will were to keep the home, barn and grounds as a memorial park and museum, which was given to the citizens of Bay Village as a gift with a $25,000 trust fund. There was to be no swimming, boating, organized sports played on Sunday, and no liquor served on the property. If the land was not wanted or cared for, the land would become property of the Cleveland Teacher's Retirement System. Her book Looking Forward is in the Museum library. "The Joel Butler Cahoon Family," (Bay Village Historical Society).

The Cahoon home, Rose Hill, opened as Dover-by-the Lake Library in May of 1921 as stipulated in the will of ***Ida CAHOON***. The library would become part of Cuyahoga County Public Library in 1949. A new library was built in the late 1950's at the corner of Dover Center and Wolf Roads as the city grew. This building would be replaced by another facility on Cahoon Road in April of 1981. Rose Hill was later converted as a museum operated by the Bay Village Historical Society. Cuyahoga County Public Library and Rose Hill Museum.

And can it be
that in a world so full and busy,
the loss of one creature
makes a void in any heart,
so wide and deep that nothing
but the width and depth of eternity
can fill it up!

Charles Dickens

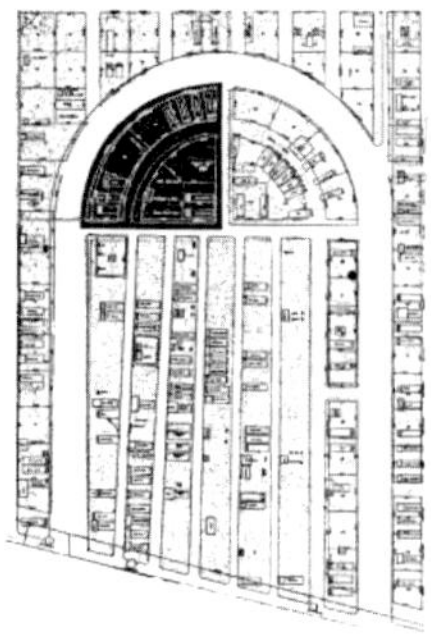

Quarter circle, adjacent and west of the Cahoon Memorial.

Lot 57 *Owner Anson Jaycox of Avon Lake purchased for $6.97* SL

Lot 57-1 George Ernest Jaycox

Name plate missing.

Metal plate is missing listing the name. Previously read as "***George L . JAYCOX.***" Cuyahoga County Cemetery Inscriptions, p. 138. *Assumed mistake recording middle initial.*

George Ernest Jaycox was the son of George Anson Jaycox and Genevieve Burrell (Lot 62-10).

JACOCK, George Ernest; b. 1881, Oct 17, Lorain; fr. ***Anson JACOCK***, mo. ***Jennie BURRELL***, Lorain. *George seemed to have used his middle name, Anson, when he was younger, probably to avoid confusion with his father, George.* PBL 2:52, line 2314. *(Note: owner of lot Anson Jaycox)*

George Anson JAYCOX and ***Genevieve JAYCOX*** had four children: (1) ***George Ernest JAYCOX***, b. 17 Oct 1881, d. 12 Sept 1895 ... *Complete citation under George A. Jaycox, Lot 62-10.* Porter Matteson, Mattesons in America, A5 and B5, no page numbers.

JAYCOX, George E., d. 1895, Sept 12, Avon; single; 13 yrs. 26 days; b. Avon; Struck by lightning. PDL 3:36.

George JAYCOX; res. Avon; interred Sep. 15, 1895; Lot 57. "List of Interments," Lakeside Cemetery, Bay Village, OH.

Lot 57-2 Burrell Anson Jaycox

Name plate missing.

Metal plate is missing listing the name. Previously recorded as "***Burrel JAYCOX.***" Cuyahoga County Cemetery Inscriptions, p. 138.

Burrell A. Jaycox was the son of George Anson Jaycox and Genevieve Burrell (Lot 62-10).

George Anson JAYCOX and ***Genevieve JAYCOX*** had four children: (4) ***Burrell Anson JAYCOX***, b. 26 August 1893, d. 13 June 1904. Porter Matteson, Mattesons in America, A5 and B5, no page numbers.

JAYCOX, George A., 44, head;... ***Genevieve***, 40, wife...; ...***Burrell***, 6, son, b. Aug 1893, Ohio. 1900 FC OH LOAV p. 14B, lines 63-67, house 300.

JAYCOX, Burrell A.; d. 1904, June 13, Avon, heart failure; 10 yrs., 9 mos., 18 days; b. Dover; res. Avon. PDL 5:38.

Burrel JACOX, res. Avon, died 1903-4, Lot 57. "List of Interments," Lakeside Cemetery, Bay Village, OH.

Lot 57-3 Vernon Burrell

VERNON _______

The top of the tombstone has a metal plate, half of it is broken and missing. Previously recorded as "***Vernon BURREL.***" Cuyahoga County Cemetery Inscriptions, p. 138.

Vernon was the brother of Genevieve Burrell Jaycox (Lot 62:10).

AVON

The funeral of ***Vernon BURRELL*** was held at the Avon Lake church January 2. He was the eldest son of ***George BURRELL*** and was born in Avon June 1863. His death which occurred in Kiefer, Okla., Dec 27 was caused by pneumonia. Elyria Republican, Elyria, OH, Thursday, Jan 9, 1907, p. 5, col. 4.

Vernon BERRELL *(sp.)*, 44; res. Kiefer, Okla.; interred Dec 27, 1907. "List of Interments," Lakeside Cemetery, Bay Village, OH.

Ancestors of Vernon Burrell:

BURRELL

Assumed great-grandfather of Vernon:

Arnold BURRELL, d. June 15, 1842, 76y.

Assumed grandparents of Vernon:

Catherine BURRELL, wife, Jan 30, 1800 - May 1, 1871; ***Ald BURRELL.***, Sept 30, 1795 - Feb 20, 1883.

Abraham, son A & C, d Jan 14, 1839, 16y. 2m. 19d.; *Caroline C.*, Jan 9, 1821 - Sept 29, 1890; *Alva James,* son Arnold & Cath., d. May 14, 1833, 8y. 8m.; *Alvah J.*, son A & C, d. Aug 18, 1824, 10m. Garfield Cemetery, Sheffield, OH, Lot B, Row 11. Sheffield City Hall, Sheffield, OH (next to cemetery); read by Catherine Burke Flament; and Genealogical Workshops of the Lorain County Historical Society, Cemetery Inscriptions of Lorain County, Ohio 1980, Garfield Cemetery, p. 434.

The eldest ***Arnold BURRELL*** (1766-1842) married twice, his first wife was ***Lois*** and they would have twelve children, with records of only seven. He arrived in Sheffield, Lorain Co., Ohio in 1833 and married his second wife, ***Mary***. They would have seven more children. Arnold was the brother of ***Captain Jabez BURRELL***, who surveyed the land of Sheffield in June, 1815 after leaving Sheffield, Berkshire Co., Mass. He would bring his family in 1816. Jabez's home later became the last station in Lorain County of the Underground Railroad. The home remained in the family until the last heir died in 2001. The Burrell homestead is currently owned by the Lorain County Metro Park System and will be open to the public.

Arnold and Lois had a son, ***Arnold***, who is believed to be the grandfather of ***Vernon BURRELL*** and lived in Elyria. Their family home still stands on Gulf Road. Thomas K. Hoerrle and <http://members.tripod.com/~Range17/>.

Grandfather: ***BURRELL, Arnold***, Males: 3, 5-10 yrs.; 1, 10-15 yrs.; 1, 20-30 yrs.; 1, 40-50 yrs. Females: 2, under 5; 1, 10-15 yrs., 1, 16-20 yrs.; 1, 40-50 yrs.

Next to assumed great-grandfather:

BURRELL, Arnold: 70-80 yrs. 1840 FC OH, Lorain Co., Elyria, p. 94.

Burrell, Arnold, 54, Joiner and Carpenter, value of real estate $2,000, b. NY; ***Catherine***, 50, b. NY; ***Caroline***, 29; ***Hiram***, 24, Farmer; ***Catherine***, 22; ***George***, 19, Farmer; ***Aurora***, male, 17, Farmer; ***Daniel***, 14; ***Sophia***, 12; ***Mary***, 10. All children b. Ohio, George and those younger attending school. 1850 FC OH Lorain Co., Elyria Township, p. 530, lines 19-28.

BURRELL, Arnold, 74, Farmer, value of real estate $4800, value of personal estate $2000, b. New York; ***Catharine***, 71, Keeping House, b. New York; *BLODGETT, Caroline,* 45, b. Ohio; ***Burrell, James***, 15, b. Ohio; *REEVE, Carrie*, 4, b. Ohio *(See burial reference below)*. Living next to *BURRELL, Alva J.*, 34, Farmer, *Sophia*, 33; *Emma*, 14; *Charles*, 5. 1870 FC OH Lorain Co., Elyria Township, p. 459, lines 6-14.

Captain Jabez Burrell wass the brother of the eldest Arnold Burrell. ***BURRELL, Jabez, Esq***., d. Sept 25, 1833, 66y.; ***Mary***, wife, d. Aug 26, 1831, 60y. Garfield Cemetery, Sheffield Twp, Lorain County OH. Sheffield City Hall, Sheffield, OH (next to cemetery), read by Catherine Burke Flament; and Genealogical Workshops of the Lorain County Historical Society, Cemetery Inscriptions of Lorain County, Ohio 1980, Garfield Cemetery, p. 431.

Parents of Vernon Burrell:

Vernon's mother, Eunice Pellett Burrell, died when he was approximately four years old. (Reference: sister's death certificate, Lot 62:10).

BURRELL - In Avon, on the 12th inst., of Consumption, ***Eunice D***., wife of ***George BURRELL***, aged 32 years.

Mrs. Burrell leaves a husband and two interesting children, besides a large circle of friends to mourn her early death. Her husband has lost a true and devoted wife, and her children a fond and indulgent mother. May our Heavenly Father guide and protect them in their journey through life. Elyria Independent Democrat, Elyria, OH, Wed. Aug 14, 1867, p. 2, col. 5.

BURRELL; Eunice D., wife of ***George A***.; Born July 20, 1835; Died Aug 12, 1867; *Eliza*, wife *A. A*., d Dec 1, 1835, 29y; *Rhoda*, dau. *AA & E*, d July 2, 1844, 3m 15d. 11-13th plots.
Next to this plot is:
REEVE, Mary L., wife *H*., d Aug 10, 1866, 27y.; *Frank*, son *ML & H*, d. May 8, 1864, 3y 16d.
The next plot is: Arnold, see grandparents above.
Garfield Cemetery, Sheffield, OH, Lot B, row 11. Sheffield City Hall, Sheffield, OH (next to cemetery), read by Catherine Burke Flament; and Genealogical Workshops of the Lorain County Historical Society, Cemetery Inscriptions of Lorain County, Ohio 1980, Garfield Cemetery, p. 434.

George Burrell, Vernon's father, married a second time to Ellen between 1867-1870. Marriage for George A. Burrell and Ellen not found in Lorain or Cuyahoga County.

BURRELL, George A., 40, sleigh manufacturer, b. Ohio; ***Ellen M***., 32, Keeping house, b. Ohio, mother of foreign birth; ***Jane***, 10, At School, b. Ohio; ***Vernon***, 7, At School, b. Ohio. 1870 FC OH Elyria Village, Elyria Township, Lorain County, p. 498, lines 1-4.

BURRELL, George, 45, Carpenter, b. Ohio, fr. b. NY, mo. b. NY; ***Ellen***, 40, wife, b. Ohio, fr. b. Mass., mo. b. Conn.; ***John***, 10, b. Ohio; ***Frank***, 6, b. Ohio; ***Jennie***, 20, school teacher, b. Ohio; ***Vernon***, son, 18, Machinist, b. Ohio. 1880 FC OH Lorain Co., Elyria Village, ED 171, p. 491C.

BURRELL, Geo. A., d. 1896, Aug 31, married, 66 yrs. 2 mos. 12 days, d. Elyria, b. Elyria, carpenter, Consumption, res. Elyria. Record of Death, Lorain County, 1896, pp. 86-7.

BURRELL, John 1870-1895; ***George A.*** 1830-1896; ***Ellen M.*** 1837-1924. Ridgelawn Cemetery, Elyria Township, Lorain County, OH. Genealogical Workshops of the Lorain County Historical Society, Cemetery Inscriptions of Lorain County, Ohio 1980, Ridgelawn Cemetery, p. 252.

G. A. BURRELL. Estate File: Died 30 August 1896, ***Ellen BURRELL***, widow.

BURRELL, Geo. A., *Henry RIMBACH*, Furniture Dealer and Undertaker, 74 West Broad Street. 1896, Sept 1 One Casket $50, Preserving body and services $5, Hearse & carriages $16.50, Singers $5.00. Total $76.50

Those listed in the estate: ***Jennie JAYCOX***, dau., Avon Lake. ***Vernon BURRELL***, son, Mantua, O. ***Frank BURRELL***, son, Elyria, O. ***Geo. BURRELL***, grandson, Avon, O. ***Joseph BURRELL***, grandson, Avon, O. Estate File 4299, Lorain County, Ohio.

Ellen Maria BURRELL, d. May 9, 1924, 3:25 a.m., 849 Bond, Elyria, Lorain Co., Ohio of Pneumonia - Hypostatic for 8 days and artereo sclerosis for 10 yrs.; widow of ***Mr. Geo. BURRELL***; b. August 28, 1837, Elyria, Ohio, fr. ***Francis RANSOM***, b. Mass., mo. ***Elizabeth KOEHLEY***, b. Isle of Man; 86 yrs. 8 mos. 11 ds.; undertaker Wm. C. Sudro, Elyria; bur. Ridgelawn Cem. Ohio Certificate of Death, Division of Vital Statistics, 1924, certif. 29387.

Lot 58 *Owner J.D. Rumbaugh of Bay Village purchased Dec 8, 1819 for $7.15 (The number 8 had been altered, it is assumed they fixed the wrong number and it should read 1918)* SL

Lot 58-4 Sterling L. Rumbaugh

STERLING

S. L.
RUMBAUGH
1894-1918
U. S. NAVY

Sterling Rumbaugh's mother, Anna A. Seitz, was the sister of Jay H. W. Seitz (Lot 9-19).

Sterling was the son of ***John RUMBAUGH*** (b. PA; m. 29 Dec 1892, Grace Reform Church, Cleveland) and ***Anna A. SEITZ***. He died of pneumonia at the Great Lakes Naval Training Center after recently joining the Navy. This may have been a result of the flu epidemic that was so widespread at the time.

Sterling had one sister, ***Gladys Dorothy***, b. 2 Feb 1899, Dover, d. 18 May 1961, Rocky River, OH, bur. Lakewood Park Cemetery, Rocky River, OH; m. 15 Sept 1921, Cleveland, *Floyd Quincy GRAHAM* (b. 21 April 1895, Volant, Lawrence Co., PA). Esther Seitz Matousek

Since its founding in 1911, the Training Center has prepared men and women for duty in Naval Service. Great Lakes, the home to the Navy's single Recruit Training Command, is home to 15 of the Navy's Technical service schools. It is located on the western shore of Lake Michigan midway between Chicago and Milwaukee.

President William H. TAFT dedicated the station on October 28, 1911. *Edward ARPEE*, who has written a history of the base, expresses his amazement that the new station was able to handle the huge influx of new sailors that poured through the gates at the outbreak of World War I. There were only about three dozen permanent buildings at that time, some of which are still in use around Ross Field and Camp Barry. Building Four became a barracks, where cots were set up under hammocks to double capacity. In Camp Paul Jones, brand new sailors slopped around in ankle deep mud and slept in small tents with three small cots per tent.

More than 100,000 men trained at Great Lakes during the First World War. They fought the enemy's undersea raiders and faced the mighty German battleships. They helped convoy more than a million soldiers to Europe and back. A few went into the interior of the European continent manning giant naval guns mounted on railroad flatcars. Many of these gunners were trained on gun mounts located on the present lakeshore recreational area. Great Lakes Naval Training Center, History of Great Lakes, <www.ntcgl.navy.mil/history.htm>, June 2002.

In the last months of the last year of the Great War, when the flower of European manhood was already lost in the trenches and battlefields, a fresh horror was visited upon the world: The Spanish Influenza.

By most accounts, the plague (and that's what it was, probably the most vicious in history) began at Camp Funston, Fort Riley, Kansas. In March of 1918, a single soldier, *Albert GITCHELL*, reported to sick call in the morning. By day's end, there were nearly a hundred soldiers ill.

Within months, it had swept the world in a whirlwind of destruction. They called it "The Spanish Influenza; La Grippe; and other names. Ironically, American soldiers and Sailors who were being sent to save democracy and lives probably spread it. Over the course of a year, three waves of the Flu hammered humanity. Upwards of 50 million people died; more than 700,000 in the United States alone.

I know it's almost unbelievable, and partly because most Americans today know little or nothing about the calamity. Three quarters of a million Americans died, but it doesn't stand out in the history books. Part of the reason is human nature. War is one thing. It involves warriors fighting against each other. No matter what weapons they use, the phenomenon is within our area of understanding.

Not so with plagues. Too small to see, too deadly to comprehend, too much for the heart and mind to accept, their memory is psychologically repressed by the survivors. It has happened before in history. After a plague goes away, people go on with their lives, and put the memory out of their minds. It is said that in the United States, after it was over, most people simply refused to talk, or even think about what happened. Such protective devices help us cope.

Great Lakes was affected by the pandemic (a worldwide epidemic), but not as badly as one would expect. We had nearly 50,000 Sailors here at the time, training for the Great War, brought together in relatively confined areas and spaces. That was the Flu's playground.

However, under the watchful care of *Admiral MOFFETT* and his staff, especially his medical staff, Great Lakes managed to keep our losses to a minimum. As I searched through our magazine of the time, *Great Lakes Recruit*, there is barely a mention of the Flu. *The Great Lakes Bulletin* of 1918 and 1919 keeps the story straight, but short....

21 September. "*Lieutenant Commander MINK* said that it is imperative for the men on the Station to wear warm clothing, and not to take any chances of contracting cold during the present cold wave."

23 September. Official statement by Commandant Moffett. "To dispel alarming and often exaggerated accounts that have been circulated, the total population of the Station is 45,000. There are about 4,500 cases of Spanish influenza. Precautionary measures [are] reducing the number of cases and the number of deaths. The situation in general is much improved."

29 October. "Good shoes guard against flu says doctor."

14 December. "Flu again halts several parties."

14 December. "Warning sounded against return of flu Dr. Mink urges precautions"

1 January 1919. "Sickness decrease 40 percent. Camp Barry first in health for last week."

15 January. "Slight increase in illness. Commander Mink issues a warning."

We may be fragile creatures, at the mercy of hostile men, and microbes. True enough. But Americans, and humanity itself, has the heart to endure, the soul to dream, and the will to go on.

A scholar, *Sir William HAMILTON*, once wrote, "My study of antiquities has kept me in constant thought of the perpetual fluctuation of everything. The whole art is, really, to live all the days of our life; and not, with anxious care, disturb the sweetest hour that life affords the present! Admire the Creator, all his works and do all the good you can upon the earth; and take the chance of eternity without dismay." "The Influenza Epidemic of 1918 and the Music of Life," History of Great Lakes, Great Lakes Naval Training Center, www.ntcgl.navy.mil/history.htm, 14 July 2004.

INFLUENZA HITS CAMPS

Washington, Dec 12 - A total of 338,257 cases of influenza were listed in the army camps and military centers with approximately 17,000 deaths during the epidemic, according to the War Department summary.

About 24,000 other deaths from causes acquired from influenza and pneumonia were also recorded in that period. Elyria Evening Telegram, Elyria, OH, Thursday, Dec 12, 1918, p. 5, cols. 4-6.

"Influenza 1918" is the story of the worst epidemic the United States has ever known. Before it was over, the flu would kill more than 600,000 Americans--more than all the combat deaths of this century combined.

American troops were bringing the flu back home. First hundreds, then thousands, of soldiers were lining up outside infirmaries and hospitals at army bases across the country, falling ill with a swiftness that defied belief.

It was a flu unlike any other. People could be healthy in the morning and dead by nightfall. Others died more slowly, suffocating from the buildup of liquid in their lungs.

October saw the epidemic's full horror: more than 195,000 people died in America alone. There was a nationwide shortage of caskets. In Philadelphia, the dead were left in gutters and stacked in caskets on the front porches. Trucks drove the city streets, picking up the caskets and corpses. People hid indoors, afraid to interact with their friends and neighbors. http://www.pbs.org/wgbh/amex/influenza/filmmore/description.html.

In 1918 America was caught up in the last horrific year of World War I. Yet the war had nothing to do with the extreme measures being taken. Deadly influenza, the so-called "Spanish-flu," was sweeping the country, spreading terror everywhere.

Once started, the disease moved west in lethal waves that appeared to follow the lines of the railroads. The speed with which it killed was appalling, the loss of life unimaginable. By the time it had run its course in America, the epidemic took more than 600,000 lives.

It was said every family lost someone. Certainly it seemed that way. http://www.pbs.org/wgbh/amex/influenza/filmmore/transcript/index.html

RUMBAUGH, John D., 41, head, b. Ohio, fr. b. Penns., mo. b. Ohio, General farmer, married 17 yrs.; ***Anna A.***, wife, 38, b. Ohio, fr. b. Germany, mo. b. Ohio, 2 children born and living; ***Sterling L.***, 16, son, b. Ohio; ***Gladys D.***, dau., 11, b. Ohio; Bassett Road, own farm, free. 1910 FC OH CY Bay Township, p. 2A, lines 29-32.

RUMBAUGH-Sterling, passed away Sunday at 10 a.m. at Great Lakes Training Station. Funeral services from First M.E. Church of Bay Village, O., Thursday, Dec 12, at 2 p.m. Take Lake Shore Electric car to stop 32. Cleveland Necrology File, Dec 11, 1918, roll 70.

Sterling RUMBAUGH, 24; res. Bay Village; German; interred Dec 11, 1918; Lot 58. "List of Interments," Lakeside Cemetery, Bay Village, OH.

Parents of Sterling Rumbaugh:

State of Ohio, Cuyahoga County ss., I Certify that on the 29th day of Dec 1892 ***Mr. John D. RUMBAUGH*** and ***Miss Anna SEITZ*** were by me legally joined in marriage. Rev. Wilson R. Stearly Marriage Record, Cuyahoga County, OH, vol. 39, p. 83.

Father: ***John Daniel RUMBAUGH*** b. 25 June 1868, Penn. (son of ***George*** and ***Amanda***); d. 12 July 1950, Orlando, FL, residence Winter Park, FL. Florida Certificate of Death, Division of Vital Statistics, Orange Co., file 15, certificate 11379056.

Mother: ***Anna A. RUMBAUGH***, b. 16 March 1872, Alliance, OH; dau. of ***Henry A. SEITZ***, b. Germany and ***Suzzanne*** *(sp.)* ***BARTCHY***, b. Ohio; d. 21 Mar 1946, Florida Sanitarium and Hosp., Orlando, FL. Florida Certificate of Death, Division of Vital Statistics, Orange Co., 1946, certificate 11379461.

RUMBAUGH, John, 62, renting $40/month, no radio, age at marriage 24, b. Ohio, fr. b. Pennsylvania, mo. b. Ohio, Broker in Real Estate; ***Anna A.***, wife, 58, age at marriage 21, b. Ohio, fr. b. Germany, mo. b. Ohio. 1930 FC OH CYBV, ED 18-534, 387 Hall Rd., p. 6B, lines 77-78.

Sister of Sterling Rumbaugh:

Floyd Q. GRAHAM, 26, res. 4217 W. 24th St., b. Volant, Pa., occup. Real Estate, fr. *William*, mo. *Elizabeth MCCONNELL*. Married ***Gladys D. RUMBAUGH***, 22, res. Bay Village, b. Cleveland, occup. none, fr. *John D.*, mo. *Anna SEITZ*, neither previously married. The State of Ohio, Cuyahoga Co., ss. I Certify that on the 15th day of September 1921, *Mr. Floyd Quincy Graham* and *Miss Gladys Dorothy Rumbaugh* were by me legally joined in marriage. Rev. D.W. Knight, Shaker Heights. Marriage Record, Cuyahoga County, OH, vol. 124, p. 25.

GRAHAM, Gladys R. Wife of ***Floyd Q.***; mother of ***Joyce MITCHELL*** of Cincinnati, O., and grandmother; residence, Westlake Hotel, Rocky River. The family will receive friends at the Zeis Funeral Home, 16105 Detroit Ave. Services will be held at the Rocky River Methodist Church, Saturday, May 20, at 1:30 p. m. In lieu of flowers contributions may be made to the Heart Fund. Cleveland Necrology File, Cleveland Press, May 20 1961, reel 113.

Floyd GRAHAM to *Ruth BELL*, Cuyahoga County, Ohio. Marriage Record, Cuyahoga County, OH, vol. 627, p. 307.

GRAHAM. ***Floyd Q. GRAHAM***, age 77, of Centerburg, O., former resident of 2825 S. Mareland Blvd., Tuesday, Columbus, husband of *Ruth* (nee *BELL*), father of ***Mrs. William (Joyce) MITCHELL***, grandfather of ***Graham E.*** and ***William Allen MITCHELL Jr.*** Friends may call 3-5 And 7-9 P.M. Friday at the Snyder-Melick Funeral Home, Centerburg, O., where funeral services will be held Saturday at 2 P.M. Burial Eastview Cemetery, Centerburg, O. Please omit flowers. Contributions may be made to The Heart Fund. Cleveland Necrology File, Cleveland Press, May 18 1972, reel 113.

Lot 59 *Owner Edw. Cowley of Bay Village purchased for $7.15* SL

Lot 59-5 Anna Schmit Peters

Mother

ANNIE M. PETERS
1865 - 1893
REST IN PEACE

Annie PETERS, nee ***SCHMIT***, was the wife of ***John Henry PETERS***. She died at the age of twenty-eight leaving four sons and a daughter, ***Alvina***. John Henry married a widow with children of her own after Annie's death. Bay Village Historical Society, Bay Village: A Way of Life, pp. 53-54.

Anna M. SCHMIT, b. 18 Jun 1865; d. 29 Feb 1893, Dover Twp., OH; m. *John Henry PETERS* (b. 31 Aug 1856 at sea, son of *Henry Wilhelm TONSING* and *Marie Elizabeth PETERS* of Brockhausen, Germany; d. 19 Jan 1921, Rocky River, OH; bur. Lkwd. Park Cem.; gardener; m.2 *Emma M._*. (CD 1921 998)). Issue: ***Harvey PETERS***, [b. 24 Jan 1882, OH]; m. *Pauline C. SEEMEL*, d. 3 May 1971, [Cuy. Co., OH]. ***Harry PETERS***, 1884, d. 25 Mar 1976. ***Alvina Caroline PETERS***, b. 30 Jun 1886, Dover; d. 2 Jul 1953, Bay Village, bur. Evergreen Cem., Westlake, OH; m. *Ernest August WUEBKER*, (b. 25 Feb 1884, NY, NY, son of *Friedrich WUEBKER*, b. 1855; d. 9 Dec 1887, Comet, OH and *Ernestine FRANKE*, b. 1858, Hanoi, Silesia, Germany; d. 28 Jul 1927, Lkwd. Hosp., Lakewood, OH, bur. Evergreen Cem., d. 29 Jan 1979, Bay Village, bur. Evergreen Cem.). ***Paul PETERS***, res. Minneapolis, MN, dau. Leona and two sons?. ***Carl PETERS,*** res. Minneapolis, MN, train engineer with route to Chicago. Fanta and Soc. Sec. Index

Maternal ancestor of Annie M. Schmit Peters:

Die 13 Feb 1836 ego matrimonio e conju ***Georgius SCHIRGER*** et ***Margaretham RAPP*** tostes suerunt *Michael BALMER* et *Joanes TUCIAN*. St. Mary's Catholic Church, Tiffin, OH 1831-2002, frame 400.

George SCHURGER m. to ***Margaret RABB***. Issue: ***Elizabeth SCHURGER***, ***Catherine SCHURGER*** *(Sr. Mary Kostha)*, b. 28 Aug 1848, Tiffin, OH; d. 29 Feb 1940. ***Mary SCHURGER*** *(Sr. Mary de Pazzi)*, b. 1 Mar 1850, d. 26 Mar 1893. The later two sisters were nuns, entering the convent on 6 Sept 1872 and 15 May 1873 respectively. Both taught at St. Mary's of the Woods, South Bend, IN. It is thought there were other children. Wayne I. Fanta.

Georgius SHURGER, die 1853 obit. St. Andrew Catholic Church, Liberty, Seneca, OH 1850-2001, p. 117.

Elizabeth SCHURGER, b. c1843; died young; m. ***John N. SCHMIT*** (Smith in some sources, he did not remarry.). Issue ***Catherine (Kate) SCHMIT***, b. 1861, WI; d. Apr 1940, bur. Calvary Cem., Lorain Co., OH; m. *Christian ZIMMER*. ***John G. SCHMIT*** (called Jack), b. 22 Mar 1863, Waupaca Co. WI. ***Anna M. SCHMIT***. ***Nicholas SCHMIT***. ***Mary SCHMIT***, m. *John WEBBER*. ***Christian SCHMIT***. ***Mathilda SCHMIT***. The Schmit's were pioneers in Wisconsin, and it is believed they backtracked to Ohio. Fanta

Spouse of Annie Schmit, John Henry Peters:
John Henry Peters, son of William.

William PETERS, 56, farmer, b. Hanover; ***Mary***, 50, b. Hanover; ***John***, 14, b. Hanover; ***Mary***, 9, b. Hanover; ***John H.***, 4, b. Ohio; ***Frederick W.***, 1, b. Ohio. 1860 FC OH CYDO p. 51, lines 29-34. *House located between Henry Wischmeyer and Thomas Powell.*

PETER, Wm., 65, farmer, b. Germany; ***Mary***, 48, KH, b. Germany; ***Henry***, 24, carpenter, b. Ohio; ***John Henry***, 14, b. Ohio; ***Fredrick***, 12, b. Ohio; ***Louisa***, 5, b. Ohio. 1870 FC OH CYDO p. 35, lines 12-17. *He is also living with his parents in the 1880 census for Dover. John Henry's brother, "Henry, 24," is the father of Cuvier H. Peters who was buried at Lakeside and moved to Evergreen.*

Second marriage of John:

PETERS, John, b. Aug 1857, married 19 yrs., b. Ohio, parents b. Germany, Farmer, owns farm; ***Mary L.***, wife, b. Mar 1862, No. children 8, living 7, b. Germany, parents b. Germany; All children fr. b. Ohio, mo. b. Germany. ***Emma R.***, b. Aug 1883, 16 yrs., b. Minnesota; ***Alvina***, b. June 1886, 13 yrs., b. Ohio; ***Richard***, b. Aug 1887, 12 yrs., b. Illinois; ***Paul W., Carl W., Arthur L.***, all 9 yrs., b. June 1890, Ohio; ***Walter E.***, b. Aug 1896, 3, b. Ohio; ***Flora***, b, June 1898, 1, b. Ohio; ***Olga F.***, b. Feb 1899, 1; ***Elizabeth Mary***, mother, b. Feb 1820, 80, widow, No. children 6, No. living 4, b. Germany, parents b. Germany. 1900 FC OH CYDO, p. 7B, lines 84-95, house 154. *Wife's name probably incorrect, blending of children from previous marriages.*

Children of John Henry Peters and Annie Schmit:

Baptismal Records for those listed as the children of ***Johann PETERS*** and ***Anna*** (nee ***SCHMITT)*** St. Paul Lutheran Church, Westlake, OH, Baptismal Records.

Heinrich Wilhelm Harvy PETERS, baptized 24 February? 1882, b. 19th. p. 49.

Alvina Caroline PETERS, b. 30 June, baptized 25 July 1886. p. 61.

Paul Walter PETERS, 4th child, b. 13 June 1889, bap. 23 June 1889. Taut Register, p. 3.

Carl Wilhelm PETERS, 5th child, b. 13 June 1889, bap. 23 June 1889. Taut Register, p. 3.

Ernest A. WUEBKER, 22, N. Dover, b. New York City, Mail Carrier, fr. *Fred WUEBKER*, mo. *Ernestina FRANKE* married ***Alvina C. PETERS***, 20, res. and b. W. Dover, O., fr. *Jno. PETERS*, *mo. Anna SMITH*. State of Ohio, Cuyahoga Co., I Certify That on the 16th day of Aug 1906 Ernest…and Alvina…were by me legally joined in marriage. Rev. J. Rupprecht, N. Dover, O. Marriage Record, Cuyahoga County, OH, vol. 64, p. 38.

WUEBKER, Ernest A., 46, value of real estate $20,000, no radio, age at marriage 23, b. NY, parents b. Germany, Mail carrier Rural Delivery; ***Alvina C.***, 43, wife, age at marriage 20, b. Ohio, fr. b. United States, mo. b. at sea, Fruit farmer; ***Vera A.***, 20, Stenographer Banking; ***Carl E.***, 19; ***Elaine M***, 15. All children b. Ohio. 1930 FC OH CYBV, ED 18-534, 584 Bradley Road, p. 20A, lines 7-11.

Lot 59 John Cowley unmarked

John was born in Jurby, Isle of Man. The Isle of Man is 220 square acres and is situated in the Irish Sea between Ireland and England. Jurby is eight square miles, located in the northwestern part of the island, surrounded by water on two sides. The area was primarily an agricultural area of flat lowlands. The names of Cowley and Kewley were both common on the island.

The State of Ohio, Cuyahoga County, ss. I Certify that on the 25th of September 1874, ***Mr. John COWLEY*** and ***Miss Elizabeth MOORE*** were, by me, legally joined in Marriage. Newburgh, O. G.R. Bowman, Mins. Marriage Record, Cuyahoga County, OH, vol. 18, p. 159.

COWLEY, John, June 3, 1892, Dover, married, 34 y. 5 d., fisherman, Rel. Prot., b. Jurby, Isle of Man, fr. *John COWLEY*, mo. *Kittie KEWLEY*, heart disease, residence Dover, Cuy., O., clergy Rev. M. Stowe, undertaker James Pease, buried in Lot 59, Lake Side Cemetery, date of record June 10, 1893. PD 7:12238.

John COWLEY, Manx, interred 6-6-1892, Lot 59. *(Notation made in records in 1916 directly above **Elizabeth**).* "List of Interments," Lakeside Cemetery, Bay Village, OH. *Year discrepancy*

Parent's of John Cowley:

COWLEY, John, 42, farmer; ***Cathrine***, 38, K.H., ***Cathrine***, 18, works in vineyard; ***Christiana***, 15, works in vineyard; ***John E.***, 13; ***Thomas Henry***, 6; ***Wm.***, 4; all b. Isle of Man; ***Fredrick***, 2/12, b. Apr, b. Ohio. 1870 FC OH CYDO, p. 254, lines 8-15.

COWLEY, John, Country of Allegiance: Great Britain, Date of arrival August 1864, Date of Naturalization Aug 4, 1874. Renounces allegiance and fidelity to Victoria Queen of Great Britain and Ireland. Naturalization Records, Common Pleas Court, Cleveland, Cuy. Co., Ohio; Journal No. 51, p. 336.

Catherine A. COWLEY, Aged 73 yrs.; ***John S. COWLEY***, Aged 78 yrs. *(with **Thomas H.**, etc. as listed below)* Maple Ridge Cemetery inscriptions, Westlake, OH, as read by Catherine Burke Flament.

Siblings of John Cowley:

COWLEY Thomas H. Father 1864-1937; ***Charlotte S.*** Mother 1870-1954; ***Wm. H. COWLEY*** 1868-1908. Maple Ridge Cemetery inscriptions, Westlake, OH, as read by Catherine Burke Flament

COWLEY: Thomas H., residence 6209 Barton rd., husband of ***Charlotte***, father of ***Ray*** and ***Howard***, brother of ***Dennis***, Services at the Congregational Church, Barton and Lorain rds., North Olmsted, Thursday, Dec. 9, at 1 p.m.

Child of John Cowley and Elizabeth Moore:

Edward COWLEY, 25; res. 2049 Cannon St.; b. Dover, Ohio; occup. Engineer; fr. *John COWLEY*, mo. *Elizabeth MOORE.* Married ***Lillian Gertrude THORNTON***, 25; res. 1711 Harvard St.; b. Youngstown, Ohio; fr. *Wm. THORNTON*, mo. *Harriet PARKER*; neither previously married. The State of Ohio, Cuyahoga County, ss. I Certify, That on the 24 day of Dec 1901…were by me legally joined in marriage. Rev. W.J. Cadman Marriage Record, Cuyahoga County, OH, vol. 53, p. 195.

COWLEY: Edward, residence, 26823 Russell rd., Bay Village; husband of ***Lillian***, father of ***Mrs. Hazel ZAHN***, ***Edward*** and ***Blanche***. Friend may call at Clifford Pease Funeral Home, Dover rd., Dover Center, where services will be held Thursday, April 13, at 2:30 p. m. 4/10/1939. age 62. Lakewood Park Cemetery Rocky River, Ohio. Cleveland Necrology File, Apr 13, 1939, reel 17

Edward COWLEY, res. 26823 Russell Rd., Bay, Cuyahoga County, OH; Married to ***Lillian***; Retired Assistant Supt. of Mails, 62 yrs. 1 mos. 8 days, b. March 2, 1877, Bay Village, OH, fr. *John COWLEY*, b. Isle of Man, mo. *Elizabeth MOORE*, b. Isle of Man; deceased attended from 9/2/36 to 4/10/39, I last saw him alive on 4/10/39 at 10:45 a.m., cause of death Cerebral Hemorrhage, Hypertension - 20 yrs., Adenoma of thyroid (non-malignant) - 20 yrs.; Informant *Hazel ZAHN*, 609 Glenwood Ave., Youngstown, OH; bur. Lakewood Park Cemetery, Funeral Firm Clifford Pease. Ohio Certificate of Death, Division of Vital Statistics, 1939, certif. 22685.

Children of Edward Cowley and Lillian Thornton:

Blanche Gertrude COWLEY, d. April 20, 1939, res. 26823 Russell Rd., Bay Village, Cuyahoga Co., OH; b. Nov 3, 1908, Cleveland, Ohio, fr. *Edward COWLEY*, b. Bay Village, mo. *Lillian THORNTON*, b. Youngstown, Ohio; 30 yrs. 5 mos. 17 ds; bookkeeper; cause of death Mytrol stenosis and Chronic Pancreotitis since 1936; informant *Hazel COWLEY ZAHN*; bur. Lakewood Park Cemetery, Funeral Firm Clifford Pease. Ohio Certificate of Death, Division of Vital Statistics, 1939, certif. 22686.

ZAHN: Hazel COWLEY, 125 Eastern Heights blvd. Elyria, wife of ***Albert A.***, mother of ***Janet***, daughter of ***Edward*** (deceased) and ***Lillian COWLEY*** sister of ***Edward***; Now at the Clifford Pease Funeral Home, 2914 Dover Center rd., Westlake where services will be held Wednesday, Feb. 16 at 2 p.m. Cleveland Necrology File, Feb. 14, 1944, reel 88.

Mrs. Hazel COWLEY ZAHN, res. 125 Eastern Hgts., Elyria, Lorain, Ohio; d. Feb 13, 1944, 41 yrs., rel. Protestant, Rev. Ray Utterback; fr. *Edward COWLEY*, b. Bay Village, mo. *Lillian THORNTON*, b. Youngstown, Ohio. Pease Funeral Home Records, Mss. 4809, Western Reserve Historical Society, Cleveland, OH.

Lot 59 Elizabeth Moore Cowley unmarked

Elizabeth COWLEY, 79; res. Bay Village; Manx; interred May 20, 1916; Lot 59. "List of Interments," Lakeside Cemetery, Bay Village, OH.

Elizabeth COWLEY, d. May 18, 1916, Bay, Cuyahoga County, Myocarditis followed by Si__ dropsy-1yr., doctor attended from Sep. 1st, 1915 to May 18, 1916; b. July 7, 1837, Isle of Man, fr. ***Edward MOORE***, mo. *(left blank)*, b. Isle of Man; widow; 78 yrs. 10 mos. 11 ds.; Informant *Edward COWLEY*, Bay Village, O.; bur. Bay Village, May 21, 1916. Ohio Certificate of Death, Division of Vital Statistics, 1916, certif. 29981.

Lot 60 *Owner S. Sunk of Dover, Cuy Co., O. purchased Feb 9, 1888 for $7.15* SL

Lot 60-6 Louis Sunk

LOUIS SUNK
1831-1904

SUNK, Louie, 47, farmer, b. Prusia *(sp.)*, parents b. Prusia; ***Loretta*** *(?)*, 46, wife, keeping house, b. Prusia, parents b. Prusia; ***Anna***, 16, dau.; ***John***, son, 12, laborer; ***Frederick***, 9, son; ***Emma***, 7, dau.; ***Josie***, 5, dau.; children b. Ohio. 1880 FC OH CYDO, p. 98A, lines 32-38.

SUNK, Louie. Owned land; Acres: Improved - 2 tilled, including fallow and grass, 13 permanent meadow, Unimproved - 2 woodland. Farm Values: Land and buildings- $1000, Machinery - $25, Live Stock - $45. Estimated value of all farm production: $200. Grass lands: acreage: 1 mown, 1 ton hay. 1 horse, 1 milch cow, 1 calf dropped, 1 calf sold living. 100 pounds of butter made on the farm. 2 swine. 13 barnyard poultry on farm. 30 dozen eggs produced in 1879. Potatoes: 1 acre, 60 bushels. Vineyards: 5 acres, 2000 lbs. grapes sold in 1879. "Schedule 2. Production of Agriculture in Dover Township, Cuyahoga County, OH," enumerated June, 1880, p. 31.

SUNK, Lewis, b. May 1833, 67 yrs., Wd., married 49 yrs. *(X'd out)*, b. Germany, parents b. Germany, immig. 1870 *(this is in conflict with John Carl's death certificate stating he was b. in NY in 1868)*, 30 yrs., Na., farmer; ***DAVIS, Freda***, dau., b. Feb 1872, 28 yrs., married, 8 yrs., 2 children born and living, b. Ohio, parents b. Germany; ----- ***Wally***, son, b. Sep. 1894, 5 yrs., b. Ohio, parents b. Ohio; ----- ***Rutha***, dau., b. Aug 1897, 3 yrs., b. Ohio. 1900 FC OH CYDO p. 9A, lines 39-42.

The 1874 ***Louis SUNK*** family farmhouse was at 527 Cahoon. Bay Village Historical Society, Bay Village: A Way of Life, p. 95.

Louis SUNK, property between Lake and the Railroad tracks to the west of Dover. Part of Lot 85, 17.61 acres. 1880 Map of Dover Twp.

Luis SUNK, 77; res. Dover; German; interred 1904, Lot 60. "List of Interments," Lakeside Cemetery, Bay Village, OH.

Children of Louis Sunk and Friedrieka Frank :

MOORMAN, Minnie (nee ***SUNK***), age 95 years, wife of the late ***John***, mother of ***Mrs. Nettie Warnke***, ***Frank***, ***Mrs. Celia Scherler***, ***Mrs. Mae Dieterich***, ***Robert***, and the late ***Albert***, ***Mrs. Edith MURTON***, ***Arnold***. ***Oscar*** and ***Mrs. Eunice BOBLAND***, grandmother, great-grandmother and great-great-grandmother. Friends may call at the Clifford Pease Funeral Home, 2914 Dover Center Rd., Westlake, where services will be held Monday, June 7, at 1:30 p.m. Cleveland Necrology File, June 5 1954, reel 136.

MOORMAN, John, 1926, age 71. Evergreen Cemetery Dover, O. Cemetery record and Cleveland Necrology File, reel 058.

The State of Ohio, Cuyahoga County, ss. I Certify that on the 13th day of January 1886, ***Mr. Philip HORNING*** and ***Anna SUNK*** were by me legally joined in marriage. Marriage Record, Cuyahoga County, OH, vol. 29, p. 183.

Philip HORNING, 52, married 24 yrs., b. Ohio, parents b. Germany, General Farmer, Owns farm with mortgage; ***Anna***, wife, 45, 6 children born and living, b. Germany, parents b. Germany, immigrated 1864?; ***Fred***, son, 22, b. Ohio, Fisherman on Lakes; ***Orey***, son, 17, b. Ohio, Apprentice in Machine Shop; ***Esther***, daughter, 10, b. Ohio; ***Meta***, daughter, 5, b. Ohio. Dover Center Rd. 1910 FC CY Bay Township, p. 3B, lines 95-100.

HORNING-Mrs. Anna, Oct. 8, age 70 years, beloved wife of ***Philip HORNING***, at her residence, Dover Center rd., Bay Village. Funeral from the German Lutheran church Sunday, Oct. 11, at 2:30 p. m. sun time. Cleveland Necrology File, Oct 10, 1914, reel 039.

HORNING: Philip, at residence, 492 Dover Rd., Bay Village, father of ***Fred***, ***Arthur***, ***Ora*** and ***Mrs. Meta OLSEN***. Now at Clifford Pease Funeral Home, 2914 Dover Rd., Dover Center, O., where services will be held Sunday, Dec. 16, at 2:30 p. m. 1934. age 75. Evergreen Cemetery Dover, Ohio. Dec 15 1934, Evergreen Cemetery record and Cleveland Necrology File, reel 039.

Philip HORNING, res. and d. Bay Village, OH, 75, cerebral hemorrhage, under Clifford Pease, inter 12/16/1934. Sect. F-2, Lot 33. Lot owner Ora Horning. Evergreen Cemetery Records, Westlake, OH.

The State of Ohio, Cuyahoga County, ss. I Certify that on the 25th day of August 1892 ***John C. SUNK*** was married to ***Annie H. WARNKE*** (17 yrs. old). Marriage Record, Cuyahoga County, OH, vol. 38, p. 295.

John SUNK, 51, b. New York, parents b. Germany, Fruit Farmer; ***Anna***, wife, 45, b. Ohio, parents b. Germany. 1920 FC OH CYBV, p. 2A, lines, 2-3, Jan. 24, 1920.

SUNK, John, husband of ***Anne*** (nee ***WARNKE***), brother of ***Mrs. Minnie MOORMAN***. Friends may call at the Clifford Pease Funeral Home, 2914 Dover Center rd., Westlake. Services at St. Paul's Evangelical Lutheran Church, Detroit rd., Westlake, Sat., March 16, at 3 p. m. Cleveland Necrology File, Mar 1946, reel 079.

John Carl SUNK, husband of ***Anna*** (nee ***WAHRNKE)***, res. 27336 Second St., d. 3/13/46 at res., cause Myorcarditis senilis with Cholecystitis, Bronchial Asthma, 77 yrs. 6 mos. 24 days; Ret'd Bridge-building, employer Railroad Co.; b. 8/19/1868, Albany, NY, fr. ***Louis SUNK***, b. Germany, mo. ***Fredericka FRANK***, b. Germany; rel. Lutheran, services at St. Paul's Ev. Luth. Church, Evergreen Cemetery. Pease Funeral Home Records, Mss. 4809, Western Reserve Historical Society, Cleveland, OH, Record of Funeral, p. 47.

SUNK, John C. 1868-1946 ***Anna H***. 1875-1952. Evergreen Cemetery Inscriptions, Westlake, OH; as read by Catherine Burke Flament.

Anna, who was from Cleveland, was young when she married ***John SUNK***, her mother had died in childbirth. The Sunk's would never have children and they lived on Dover Center across the street from the red brick school house (now painted). Lois Beheim

SUNK, Anna H. (nee ***WARNKE***), of 3117 W. 99 St., wife of the late ***John***, sister of *Mrs. Caroline KUHRT, Mrs.*

Ada MOORMAN, and *Albert WARNKE.* Saturday morning. Friends may call at the George C. Lang Co. Funeral Home, W. 95 at Lorain Ave. Services Tuesday, Oct. 21, at St. Paul's Evangelical Lutheran Church, 27971 Detroit Rd., at 2 p. m. Oct 20 1952 Cleveland Necrology File, reel 160.

The State of Ohio, Cuyahoga County ss., I Certify that on the 13th day of October 1892 ***Lawrence DAVID*** and ***Frieda SUNK*** were by me legally joined in marriage. Rev. W.C. Endy. Marriage Record, Cuyahoga County, OH, vol. 38, p. 397.

Frieda is listed as living with her father in the 1900 census; her husband may have died and she remarried according to the death record listed below.

Freda Louise VAN DORNE, wife of ***Emiel*** (69 yrs. old); res. 505 North Abbe Rd., Elyria; bur. 10/19/1945, cause Cerebral Hemorrhage, 73 yrs. 7 mos. 25 days; (cemetery records 63 yrs.), b. Feb 21, 1872, Dover, fr. ***Louis SUNK***, b. Germany, mo. b. Germany; bur. Evergreen Cemetery. Buried with *Emil C. VAN DORNE*, North Ridgeville, OH, internment 10/23/1947 and her son, ***Walter C. DAVIS***, 50, res. and d. Broadview Heights, OH, undertaker S.W. Mather, Cleveland, inter 10/11/1943. Lot 31 L. Pease Funeral Home Records, Mss. 4809, Western Reserve Historical Society, Cleveland, OH, Record of Funeral, p. 23.

VAN DORNE, Frieda, residence No. Abbe rd., Elyria, O., wife of ***Emiel***, mother of ***Mrs. Ruth DIETERICH, Mrs. Beatrice LESCHER***, grandmother and great-grandmother, sister of ***Mrs. Minnie MOORMAN*** and ***John SUNK***. Friends may call at Clifford Pease's Funeral Home, 2914 Dover Center rd., Westlake, where services will be held Fri., Oct. 19, at 3:30 p. m. Cleveland Necrology File, Oct 17 1945, reel 082.

VAN DORNE, Emiel, residence 505 N. Abbe Rd., Elyria, O. husband of the late ***Frieda*** (nee ***SUNK***), father of ***Mrs. Beatrice LESCHER*** and ***Mrs. Ruth DIETERICH***, and grandfather. Friends may call at the Clifford Pease Funeral Home, 2914 Dover Center Rd., Westlake, where services will be held Thurs., Oct. 23, at 2:30 p. m. Cleveland Necrology File, Oct 22 1947, reel 082

Charles BAILEY to ***Emily SUNK***, 12 Nov 1896, by the Mayor of Glenville, Cuyahoga County, O. Marriage Record, Cuyahoga County, OH, vol. 44, p. 231.

BAILEY, Emma A.--Beloved wife of ***Charles***, mother of ***Earl, Frenchie, Mrs. Helen MIKITA***. Now at Clifford Pease Funeral Home, 2914 Dover Center rd., Westlake, O., where services will be held Tuesday, March 24, at 2:30 p. m. Cleveland Necrology File, Mar 23 1942, reel 004.

Emma Anna BAILEY, d. March 22, 1942, 12:30 a.m. of Cerebral Hemorrhage March 20 and myocarditis for 5 yrs. at Cedar Crest Sanitarium, Westlake, Ohio; res. 26704 East Oviatt Rd., Bay Village; married to ***Charles***; Hwf.; 68 yrs. 1 day; b. March 1874, Bay Village to ***Louis SUNK***, b. Germany, mo. Do not know, b. Germany; informant Frenchie L. Bailey, Bay Village; funeral firm Clifford Pease; bur. Evergreen Cemetery, Westlake. Ohio Certificate of Death, Division of Vital Statistics, 1942, certif. 14766.

Emma Ann BAILEY, wife, *(no spouse listed)*, charge to: Estate of Aid for the Aged; occup. Hwf.; d. March 22, 1942, Cedar Crest Sanitarium; b. March 21, 1874, Bay Village, Ohio, rel. Protestant, Cong., Rev. Ray Utterback; Evergreen Cemetery. Pease Funeral Home Records, Mss. 4809, Western Reserve Historical Society, Cleveland, OH, Record of Funeral, p. 39.

Josephine SUNK, m.1 ***John CLOSE*** *(Lot 8-16)* and m.2 ***Arthur BRAISE*** *(see Jenny Mary BRAISE, "Not In Specified Lot").*

Lot 60-7 Friedrieka Frank Sunk

FRIEDRIEKA FRANK
WIFE OF
LOUIS SUNK
DIED FEB 11?, 1888
AGED 54 YS. 4 M.

(saying illegible)
SUNK

"Sunk," grave outlined. Inscription worn and difficult to read.

Mrs. SUNK, 52, res. Dover, German, interred Feb 1888, Lot 60. "List of Interments," Lakeside Cemetery, Bay Village, OH.

Frances SUNK, d. Feb 11, 1888, Dover, married, 44 y. 4 m., b. Germany, parent ***Joseph FRANK***, disease spinal complaint. PD 3:218. *Age and name discrepancies.*

ZUNK, Loier; Lot 60, July 7, 1890; vol. 1 Pg. 378. *Record found on typewritten page with cemetery statistics at City Hall. Could this have been misread from Louis Sunk? From other dates on the page it may not have been a burial, but the date of a payment for a lot.*

Lot 60-8 Friedrieka Frank Sunk

Assumed marker for Friedrieka Sunk, above.

MOTHER

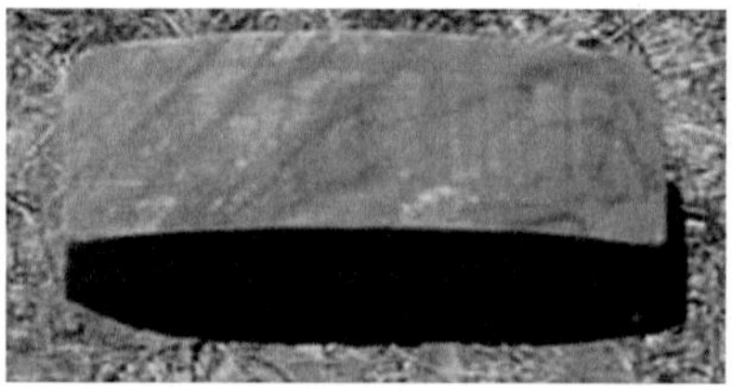

Lot 61 *Owner: F. Drake purchased March 11, 1895 for $9.03* SL

Lot 61-9 Drake Marker

DRAKE
DELLA ALDRICH 1863-1895
FREDERICK L. 1862-1941
EMMA ALDRICH 1860-1933

Lot 61-9 Della Aldrich Drake

Fred DRAKE married ***Della Myrtle ALDRICH*** (b. 14 July 1863), dau. of ***Henry Winsor ALDRICH*** *(OP 4: 1)* and ***Mary Ann STEVENS*** *(OP 4:1)*, in 1884. While living in West Cleveland, Della died of scarlet fever. Fred then brought his two children, ***Florence*** and ***George***, with him to live with his mother-in-law ***Mary Ann ALDRICH***. Fred built a house on the twenty acres his wife had received at the death of her father. In 1896, Fred married Della's older sister, ***Emma ALDRICH*** and moved into the new home he had built in Dover. He and Emma would have a daughter, ***Marjorie***, and then twins, ***Marion*** and ***Herbert***. Herbert lived only twenty days. "Genealogy of the Aldrich Family," p. 17; and Bay Village Historical Society, Bay Village: A Way Of Life, p. 81.

Della Myrtilla ALDRICH, dau. of ***Henry Winsor ALDRICH*** *(OP 4: 1)* and ***Mary Ann STEVENS*** *(OP 4:1)*, b. 6 July 1863, Dover, d. 11 Mar 1895, m. 4 Dec 1884, ***Frederick Lincoln DRAKE*** (b. 11 June 1862 Oskaloosa, Iowa, d. 19 Oct 1941, Grafton, Ohio). *Issue:* ***Florence Mabel DRAKE***, b. 20 June 1886, DeSmet, Kingsbury Co., SD; d. 6 Jan 1973, Florence, Freemont Co., CO; m.1 1918+ *Glen ROBINS*, m.2 *Chas. DAVIS*. ***George Henry DRAKE***, b. 21 Oct 1891, Cleve; m. 24 June 1914, *Susan Marguerite GUTHERY*, La Rue, O (b. 24 Oct 1891). George H. Drake, "Aldrich Generation Chart," p. 11.

DRAKE, Della, 32, white, female, mother, res. Silk *(Silk St. Cleveland)*, Ward 41, d. at residence, born US, cause of death scarlet fever, phys. Fred Klim, cemetery North Dover, undertaker E. H. Saxton. March 11, 1895. CRD, roll 1977437.

Deceased: *Della DRAKE,* d. Mar. 11, Scarlet Fever, age 32, physician Fred Kline. Paid for by: ***F.L. DRAKE***, Silk St., W End: Casket, $50.00. Box, $4.00. Wagon to Dover, $12.00. (Carriage by M.M. $8.00), Preserving Body and Attendance, $8.00. Total $74.00 Saxton Funeral Home Records, Lakewood, OH.

Mrs. F. DRAKE; res. Dover; interred March 11, 1895; Lot 61. "List of Interments," Lakeside Cemetery, Bay Village, OH.

Lot 61-9 Fredrick Lincoln Drake

Frederick Lincoln DRAKE, b. June, 1862 , son of ***Rev. George Wolf*** and ***Laura (EASTMAN) DRAKE*** of Oskaloosa, Ia.; mason and contractor, res. Bay Village, Ohio. Abram W. Foote, Foote Family Comprising the Genealogy and History of Nathaniel Foote, vol. II, p. 704.

The State of Ohio, Cuyahoga County, SS. I Certify that on the 4th day of December 1884 ***Mr. Fred L. DRAKE*** and ***Miss Della ALDRICH*** were by me legally joined in marriage. G.W. Nead, Minister Marriage Record, Cuyahoga County, OH, vol. 28, p. 134.

The State of Ohio, Cuyahoga County, ss. I Certify that on the 5th day of November 1896 ***Mr. Fred L. DRAKE*** and ***Miss Emma I. ALDRICH*** were by me legally joined in marriage. Rev. W.K. Dennis Marriage Record, Cuyahoga County, OH, vol. 44, p. 214.

DRAKE, Fred L., 39, b. Aug 1860, Iowa, fr. b. Mass, mo. b. Iowa, mason, married 4 yrs.; ***Emma J.***, wife, b. Oct 1860, Ohio, parents b. Mass, 2 children born and living; ***Marjorie A.***, 1, b. Aug 1898, Ohio; ***George H.***, 8, b. Oct 1891, Ohio; ***Mary A.***, 6/12, b. Nov 1899, Ohio; ***Florence M.***, 13, dau., Oct 1886, Ohio; *ABEN, Joseph A.*, 68, widower, b. Dec 1831, Switzerland, parents b. Switz., laborer; own farm free. 1900 FC OH CYDO p. 7A, lines 44-50, house 145.

Fred L. DRAKE, own home, free of mortgage, 57, b. Iowa, parents b. Ohio, general farmer, res. on Bradley Rd.; ***Emma***, wife, 60; ***Marjorie***, dau., 21, attending school; ***Marion***, 20, attending school. 1920 FC OH CYBV, p. 7A.

DRAKE, Fred L., 67, value of home $12,700, owns radio, age at first marriage 24, b. Iowa, occup. Mason, brick contractor; ***Emma***, wife, 69, age at first marriage 34, b. Ohio, fr. b. Rd. Island, mo. b. Massachusetts. 1930 FC OH CYBV ED18-534, p. 22B, 30724 Lake Rd., lines 72-73.

DRAKE Fred L., husband of the late ***Emma***, father of ***Mrs. Florence DAVIS, George, Mrs. Marjorie COLLETT, Mrs. Marion HITCHCOCK***, now at Clifford Pease Funeral Home, 2914 Dover Center rd., Westlake, where services will be held Tuesday, Oct 21, at 2:30 p.m. Cleveland Necrology File, Oct 21, 1941, roll 21.

Fred Lincoln DRAKE, d. Oct 19, 1941, 12:30 p.m., Grafton, Lorain Co., Ohio, Cerebral Hemorrhage 10/11/41, contributory Hypertension, Arteriosclerosis, Chronic Prostate; res. State Route 57; widowed, wife ***Emma***; b. Aug 12, 1862, Iowa, fr. ***George W. DRAKE***, b. Mich., mo. ***Laura EASTMAN***, b. New York; 79 yrs. 2 mos. 7 ds., Mason Contractor, informant *Nelson G. Hitchcock*, Grafton, Ohio, Funeral Firm Clifford Pease, Westlake. Ohio Certificate of Death, Division of Vital Statistics, 1941, certif. 61882.

Parents of Fredrick Lincoln Drake:

George W. DRAKE to ***Laura A. EASTMAN***, Married Sept 8, 1846, Lorain County. Marriages Lorain County 1824-1865, p. 33.

Laura Eastman and Rev. George W. Drake, Lakeside, MI on their 50th Wedding Anniversary, 1896.

Rev. George Wolfe DRAKE was a graduate of Oberlin College in 1834 and received an M.D. degree at Western Reserve. He planned to be a medical missionary and went to Oskaloosa, Iowa where his father, ***Fred DRAKE***, was born. He married ***Laura EASTMAN*** on 8 Sept. 1846. She died 22 March 1916, Lakeside, MI. He may have founded a college out west. He had a hotel located at or in Blue Island, Chicago and later moved to Lakeside Michigan where his daughter, ***Mary DRAKE MURPHY***, ran a summer resort. George died 16 March 1909, Lakeside, MI and is thought to be buried there. There is a monument for Geo. W. Drake at Oberlin Cemetery. Fred Drake, back of family photograph of Laura and George Drake, Rose Hill Museum, Bay Village, OH.

Children of Frederick L. Drake and Della Myrtle Aldrich:

Florence DRAKE, b. 20 June 1886, m. *Charles DAVIS*, res. 917 W. 2nd St., Florence, Co. ***George H. DRAKE,*** b. 13 Oct 1891; m. *Susan Marguerite GUTHERY*; res. 30663 Lake Rd., Bay Village, O. Family Chart, Foote Family Papers, Rose Hill Museum.

Florence Mabel DRAKE, b. ...DeSmet, S.D.; graduated Cleveland School of Art 1908; m. July 2, 1919 to ***Glenn ROBBINS***, b. Aug 27, 1874, at Bannack, Mont., son of *E. Leonard* and *Emma (BRUCE) ROBBINS*; miner and stock ranchman; served through the war in 10th U.S. Secret Service; res. Denver, Colo. Abram W. Foote, Foote Family Comprising the Genealogy and History of Nathaniel Foote, vol. II, pp. 705-6.

DAVIS. Florence M. Davis *(nee* ***DRAKE****)*, age 86, formerly of Bay Village, O., wife of the late ***Charles D. DAVIS*** of Florence, Colo., sister of ***George H. DRAKE*** of Bay Village, ***Mrs. Nelson G. HITCHCOCK*** of Avon Lake and ***Mrs. J.R. MCGUIRE*** of Apache Jct., Ariz., passed away Saturday, Jan 6. Services will be held at The Florence Funeral Parlors, Florence, Colo. on Wednesday, Jan 10 at 1 p.m. Jan 9, 1973. The Plain Dealer.

George Henry DRAKE, b. Cleveland, Ohio, Oct 23, 1891; graduated Ohio State University, 1914; m. June 24, 1914 to ***Susan Marguerite GUTHERY***, dau. of *John H.* and *Lavina (BROCKELSBY)* of Larue, Ohio, b. Oct 24, 1891; attended Ohio Wesleyan University, Delaware, Ohio, and Western College, Oxford, Ohio; he is an estimating engineer for the N.Y. Central R.R. Co., Cleveland; res. Lakewood and Bay Village, Ohio. Foote, vol. II, p. 706.

DRAKE, George H., 38, value of house $18,000, owns radio, age at first marriage 22, b. Ohio, fr. b. Iowa, mo. b. Ohio, occup. Civil Engineer Railroad Transportation; ***Marguerite J.***, wife, 38, age at marriage 22, b. Ohio, parents b. Ohio; ***Virginia G.***, daughter, 14, b. Ohio; ***Guthery W.***, son, 13, b. Ohio. 1930 FC OH CYBV ED18-534, p. 22A, 30470 Lake Rd., lines 38-41.

Oldest Bayite recalls Bay's early history

...One special man who remembers a much simpler life in the early 1900's is ***Mr. George Henry DRAKE***, 83.

...In 1904, there were exactly three students in his graduating class from the brick schoolhouse. These were the students who chose the colors blue and white to represent the school.

What we know today as Bay Village didn't look the same 80 years ago. Coal-oil lamps and candle lanterns were used instead of electricity. Families made their own soap from fat and lye.

Classrooms were segregated with the boys on one side and the girls on the opposite side of the room. There were no paved roads or other modern conveniences, according to Mr. Drake.

He recalled one of his favorite sports, which was riding horse-drawn sleds or wagons. Leaning back in his chair, the octogenarian told of a memorable Christmas when he received a tricycle, but usually, as he explained, the children would "dream of Santa Claus and when we woke up, if we found an orange in our stocking, we were happy."

George Drake has always been a very religious Methodist, and as a boy, he had *Ida CAHOON* as a Sunday School teacher. She gave him a Bible, which he still owns, for coming to school every Sunday for a year.

George's father, ***Fred DRAKE***, was a musician...

Mr. Drake entered Ohio State University and studied engineering. In his sophomore year, he met ***Marguerite GUTHERY*** and "fell in love with her right then." In fact, the student was so distracted by her he had to take five years of college instead of four since he flunked calculus. Marguerite Guthery became Mrs. George H. Drake a week after graduation in 1914.

When George's Grandmother Aldrich *(Mary Ann STEVENS ALDRICH, OP 4:1)* died, George received some lakefront property on which he built a house in 1920 and four cottages along the beach. He acquired the Aldrich homestead at 30663 Lake Road in 1945 and he and Marguerite have remained in that home since....

It is so obvious that this couple still enjoys each other's company. Speaking with sincerity, Mr. Drake analyzed, "I've made many mistakes in my life, you know, but the best thing I ever did was marry you," he told his wife...

Both of the Drakes are warm, open people who love their village and the memories of its past. Marguerite Drake is a charming, outgoing lady who specializes in making her visitors feel at home. Next month, Mr. Drake will be 84. The 5-ft. 5-in. engineer has much to be proud of in his lifetime. He loved to make and cut jewelry from stones he would buy or find such as turquoise, jade and tiger eye. He also made pottery, panned for gold in Colorado, and enjoyed taking pictures. Knowing about his ancestors fascinated him and in their home he and Marguerite treasure many antiques given to them by family and friends. Laura Mogyordy, undetermined newspaper article, c September 1975, Drake Family Papers, Rose Hill Museum, Bay Village, OH.

George Henry DRAKE, age 87 years, was born in Cleveland, Ohio, October 21, 1891, and died August 21 (1979) at 2:10 a.m. He was graduated from West High School in Cleveland and also received a degree in mechanical engineering at Ohio State University, where he played clarinet in the marching band.

One week after graduation, he was married to ***Marguerite GUTHERY*** of LaRue, Ohio, who came to Cleveland to reside for five years prior to moving to Bay Village to continue living on his great-grandfather Aldrich's land, purchased from The Connecticut Land Company in the early 1800's.

He continued to work in Cleveland for many years--first as a structural draftsman for The City of Cleveland, later for the New York Central and Wheeling and Lake Erie Railroads. He was assistant engineer for several years with the Federal Public Housing Administration of Cleveland. His last 17 years were spent in the engineering department of the municipality of Bay. He was a life-long member of the Bay United Methodist Church, active in The Bay Village Historical Society, and designed plaques for 12 Landmark homes in Bay Village. He also belonged to the Reading Club founded in our church in 1912. After retirement, 12 trips were made to Chile to visit daughter ***Virginia***, residing there. His son, ***Guthery***, remained near his side. Four grandchildren and eight great-grandchildren brought much joy and happiness to him. "Unto whom much is given, great things are expected." He was indeed an extraordinary man. Drake File, Rose Hill Museum, Bay Village, OH.

A PERSONAL TESTIMONY

For sixty-five years I shared ***George's*** life. It was so wonderful to grow old beside him...he did it so gracefully. Through good times and bad, he was consistently patient, forgiving, gentle, generous, and extremely sensitive. We had many marvelous times together, and I am deeply grateful for the life and love he gave me; but I am also in pain and grief over the things we shall never again do together. "A live *(life)* well-loved makes every yesterday a dream of happiness and every tomorrow a vision of hope."...***Marguerite Drake*** Funeral Booklet for George Henry Drake 1891-1979, copy at Rose Hill Museum, Bay Village, OH.

Marguerite DRAKE began painting in 1955, exhibiting her artwork that was inspired by the landscape and sights of Chile, at Bay Village Public Library. ***George*** and Marguerite's daughter, ***Virginia***, met a Chilean businessman who had been visiting Cleveland and became ***Mrs. MUJICA***. She is now living on a 1,200 acre estate beside the Andes at Hacienda Esmeralda, 65 miles from Santiago, Chile. A recent trip to visit their daughter was the inspiration for the art that was displayed at the library, although Mrs. Drake enjoys landscapes in general.

The five feet two Mrs. Drake, studied art at Western College for Women and Ohio Wesleyan before her marriage. George, an engineer, is now assisting the community's engineer, *William S. SADLER*. George and Marguerite live at 30663 Lake Road. Their son, ***Guthery W.***, lives only 600 feet away, at 30506 Lake Road. "Her Paint Brush Links Chile and Bay Village," undetermined newspaper article, Drake Family File, Feb. 19, 1961.

Children of Frederick L. Drake and Emma Irene Aldrich:

Marjorie Lucille DRAKE, b. 3 (31) Oct 1897, Dover Twp., OH; m.1 Dec 1927 (8) to *Robt. COLLETT* (b. 14 June 1876, d. 15 July1956); m.2 3 June 1962 to *John MCGUIRE* (b. 8 Oct 1892, d. 6 May 1977); res. 2921 W. Palm Lane, Phoenix, Ariz. ***Marion Elizabeth DRAKE*** (twin), b. 1 Nov 1899, Dover Twp.; m. 20 Oct 1922 to *Nelson HITCHCOCK* (b. 5 Mar 1898, d. 17 Nov 1964); res. Grafton, O. ***Howard Paul DRAKE***, (twin), b. 1 Nov 1899; d. 21 Nov 1899. Stevens Family Chart, Foote Family Papers, Rose Hill Museum and George H. Drake, "Aldrich Generation Chart," p. 10.

Marjorie Lucile DRAKE, b. Bay Village...attended Oberlin Conservatory; graduated Colorado Springs College: School of Music, 1922; violinist; res. Colorado Springs, Colo. Abram W. Foote, Foote Family Comprising the Genealogy and History of Nathaniel Foote, vol. II, pp. 705-6.

Marion Elizabeth DRAKE, b. Bay Village...; attended Oberlin Conservatory and Colorado College; m. ... (b. Mar 5, 1898, son of *Willis N.* and *Mary (BENZING) HITCHCOCK*, of Grafton, Ohio); graduated Ohio State University, 1920; dairy farming; res. Grafton, Ohio. Abram W. Foote, vol. II, pp. 705-6.

Nelson G. HITCHCOCK, 24, b. and living in Grafton, O., occup. farmer, fr. *Willis N.*, mo. *Mary BENZING*. Married ***Marion E. DRAKE***, 22, b. and living in Bay Village, fr. *Frederick L.*, mo. *Emma I. ALDRICH*. Neither previously married. The State of Ohio, Cuyahoga County, I Certify that on the 20th day of October 1922 Nelson G. Hitchcock and Marion E. Drake were by me legally married. Rev. Virgil E. Turner Marriage Record, Cuyahoga County, OH, vol. 128, p. 198.

HITCHCOCK. ***G. Nelson Hitchcock***, age 66 of Grafton, O., beloved husband of ***Marion***, father of ***Marion LISLE*** of Avon Lake, ***Jane HARRIS*** of Denver, Colo., ***Ruth BESHIRE*** of Medina and grandfather, brother of *Eleanor SHELDON* of Grafton, passed away Nov 17. Funeral service and Memorial F. and A.M. service will be held Thursday 2 p. m. at the Grafton Methodist Church. Burial Nesbett Cemetery, Grafton. Friends received at the Russell D. Fulton Funeral Home, 1028 Main St., Grafton, Wednesday 2-4 and 7-9 P. M. Nov 18, 1964. The Plain Dealer.

HITCHCOCK Nelson G., 1898-1964; ***Marion D.***, 1899- ***HITCHCOCK Mary BENZING***, 1874-1938; ***Willis Nelson***, 1870-1949. Nesbett Cemetery, Grafton, OH. Genealogical Workshops of the Lorain County Historical Society, Cemetery Inscriptions of Lorain County, Ohio, Nesbett Cemetery, p. 289.

Marion D. HITCHCOCK, d. 27 May 1994, 10:30 a.m., Nursing Home, Avon Lake, OH; b. 1 Nov 1899, Bay Village, OH; 14 yrs. of school; fr. ***DRAKE***, mo. ***ALDRICH***. Ohio Certificate of Death, Division of Vital Statistics, 1994, certif. 39132.

Lot 61-9 Emma Aldrich Drake

Emma, daughter of Henry Winsor ALDRICH and Mary Ann STEVENS (OP 4:1), became the second wife of Fred Drake after her sister's death.

Emma Irene ALDRICH, dau. of ***Henry ALDRICH*** and ***Mary Ann STEVENS***, b. 6 Oct 1859; m. 15 Nov 1896 to ***Frederick Lincoln Drake***, widower of her sister. George H. Drake, "Aldrich Generation Chart," p. 10.

DRAKE, Emma Aldrich, beloved wife of ***Frederick L.***, mother of ***Mrs. Marjorie D. COLLETT*** and ***Mrs. Marion D. HITCHCOCK***, April 2. Now at Clifford Pease's Funeral Home, 2914 Dover Center Rd., where services will be held, Tuesday, April 4, 2 p.m. Cleveland Necrology File, April 4, 1933, roll 21.

Emma Aldrich DRAKE, Grafton, 73y 5m 26d, Cerebral Hemorrhage, undertaker Clifford Pease, Dover Center, O., issued April 3, 1933. Burial Removal Permit.

Lot 62 *Owner: James Jaycox of Avon purchased for $9.14, and resold to Anson Jaycox.* SL

Lot 62 *Frances Willard Jaycox*

moved, no marker

Frances was moved to Elmwood Cemetery, her father's brother, George Anson Jaycox, is buried here (Lot 62-10) along with her mother's uncle, William Silas Hilliard, (OP 1:6) and great-grandparents, Luman and Margaret Marilla Griswold (OP 1: 10-11).

Francis W. JAYCOX, res. Avon, 1894, Lot 62. Removed to Lorain, Ohio. "List of Interments," Lakeside Cemetery, Bay Village, OH.

Frances Willard JAYCOX was the four year old daughter of ***James JAYCOX*** (son of *George JAYCOX* and *Mary MATTESON*) and ***Ida Lorinda HILLIARD*** (dau. of *Joseph Warren HILLIARD* 1819-1867 and *Lorinda GRISWOLD* 1829-1895 (*see OP 1:10)*). Her mother, Ida, attended Oberlin College for training to become a teacher. Ida was an ardent prohibitionist and founded the Women's Christian Temperance Union in Lorain which is named after her. Frances was named after *Frances WILLARD* of Evanston, IL, a famous national leader in the movement. Ida was also active in the Daughters of the American Revolution, the original Methodist Church in both Avon and Lorain, and a woman's group called Sorosis that recently celebrated their 100th anniversary. The family lived in Avon where James sold grapes and bought and sold land until about 1898. During the 1890's James attended the Oberlin Business College and the family at some time moved to 1026 4th St., Lorain where he continued to deal in real estate. Ida purchased a large family plot in Elmwood Cemetery in Lorain and had Frances moved there. She and James, along with their two other daughters and their husbands are also buried in the family plot. Karen Boas

Funeral Card for Frances Jaycox:

In Loving Remembrance of
Frances Jaycox,
Died May 1_ *(date illegible)* 1894
A precious one from us has gone,
A voice we loved is stilled;
A place is vacant in our home,
Which never can be filled.
God in His wisdom has recalled
The boon His love has given;
And though the body slumbers now,
The soul is safe in Heaven.

Card in the possession of Karen Boas

Parents of Frances Willard Jaycox:

Frances's father, James M. Jaycox, was the brother of George Anson Jaycox, below.

The State of Ohio, Lorain County. I Hereby Certify, that on the 18th day of August A.D. 1879, I duly solemnized the Marriage Contract between ***Mr. James M. JACOX*** *(sp.)* and ***Miss Ida L. HILLIARD***. I.H. McConnell, MG. LCMR: 1872-1885, p. 1004.

James M. Jaycox

James M. JAYCOX, a well-known fruit grower of Avon township, is a native of same, born in 1849, son of ***George*** and ***Mary (MADISON) JAYCOX***, both of whom were born in New York State...

James M. Jaycox was brought up on the home farm in Avon township, in the common schools of which place he received his education, and later engaged in mercantile business in Lorain. He now gives his attention to the culture of, as well as the buying and selling of grapes and since embarking in this business has handled over 400,000 baskets of fruit. Since 1880 he has resided on his present farm in Avon township, where he has eight acres devoted to grapes, and also raises other fruit; he is the owner of forty-one acres of land in Avon township. In 1879 Mr. Jaycox was married, in Elyria to ***Miss Ida L. HILLIARD***, a native of Wisconsin, daughter of ***Joseph W. HILLIARD***, who was a blacksmith, and an early settler of Avon township, whence he subsequently removed to Wisconsin, where he died. To Mr. and Mrs. Jaycox have been born three children, namely; ***Ethel***, ***Lora*** and ***Francis***. Politically our subject is a staunch member of the Republican party, and held the position of postmaster of Avon Lake for seven years. Socially he is a member of Avon Tent No. 1 K.O.T.M., French Creek. He is secretary and treasurer of the Lorain County Grape Growers Shipping Association, which organization has a membership of 125,

and in 1893 shipped 150 carloads of grapes from Avon station. Our subject and wife are both active workers in all religious movements; Mrs. Jaycox is an ardent worker in the temperance cause, and is president of W.C.T.U. of Avon Lake. They are both members of the M. E. Church, in which Mr. Jaycox holds offices of steward and trustee, and he has served as superintendent of the Sabbath school for many years. "James M. Jaycox," Commemorative Biographical Record of The Counties of Huron and Lorain, pp. 983-4.

PNEUMONIA IS FATAL TO J. M. JAYCOX

James M. JAYCOX recently appointed city sealer of weights and measures, died early this morning at his home, 1026 4th st., after an illness of about three weeks. He was taken ill the last day of December, just before he was to have taken office and had never been able to assume his new duties.

The illness not thought serious at first was a light case of grippe. He was in bed when *Mayor L.M. MOORE* gave him his commission. A few days later his sickness developed into pneumonia, and about a week ago his strength began to fail. His death had been expected for several days.

Mr. Jaycox was 66 years old. He was born on his father's farm near Avon where he lived a number of years. He was married to ***Ida HILLIARD*** in August, 1879. He continued at his occupation of farming until 1899, when he was elected county commissioner at which time he moved to Lorain. He served the county two terms in that position.

Since coming to Lorain Mr. Jaycox has occupied a large part of his time in real estate and as an insurance agent. During 1914 and 1915 he was tax assessor. Mr. Jaycox spent his entire life in Lorain county, either in Lorain or at Avon. He was a charter member of the Maccabees at the latter place

Mr. Jaycox is survived by his widow and two daughters, ***Mrs. Herman KOEPKE***, of Lorain, and ***Mrs. R.E. BICKEL*** of South Bend, Ind., and an adopted daughter, ***Miss Dorothy***, who lives at the Jaycox home. He is also survived by several sisters and brothers: ***Mrs. John BURE***, of Avon, ***Mrs. Stephen KETCHUM***, of Lorain, ***Mrs. H .G. BRAUN***, of Lorain, ***G.A. JAYCOX*** and ***William JAYCOX***, of Avon.

Mrs. Ketchum was called from her home yesterday morning, where her husband, *Captain KETCHUM*, had died only a few hours earlier, to the deathbed of her brother.

Funeral services will be held at the First Methodist church, of which Mr. Jaycox was a member, at 1:30 p.m. Saturday. The body will be taken to the church at 12:30 to lie in state until the time of the funeral. Rev. J. R. Jacob will preach the funeral sermon. Burial will be made in Elmwood cemetery.

The pallbearers will be *Frank COLEMAN, L. M. MOORE, James EDMUNDS, Thomas BOWEN, P. C. DODGE, Jerry GREENWOOD*. Lorain Times-Herald, undetermined date.

James Monroe JAYCOX, b. 1849; d. 1916, Avon Lake, OH (son of ***George JAYCOX*** and ***Mary MATTISON***); m. ***Ida Lorinda HILLIARD*** (b. 9 Sep 1855 in Avon Lake, OH; d. Avon Lake, OH). Ida graduated from Oberlin College in Lorain Co., OH and immediately taught in the Avon school. Her father-in-law was the superintendent of the schools and donated the school and church to the town. She was nationally involved in the temperance and women's suffrage movements as well as the Methodist church. She was a member of the Daughters of the American Revolution (DAR 163619). *Issue:* ***Ethel Annabelle JAYCOX***, b. 17 Apr 1881, Avon, OH; d. June 1969, Lorain, OH; m. *Reuben Edward BICKEL* in 1912, Lorain, OH. ***Lora Mae JAYCOX***, b. 1886, Avon, OH; d. 5 Feb 1966, Lorain, OH; m. *Herman F. KOEPKE*. ***Frances JAYCOX,*** b.1890, Avon; d. 1894, Avon. ***Dorothy HARPER*** (an adopted cousin). Victor Grant Hilliard, Jr. Dorothy Harper was the granddaughter of one of James's siblings who's mother died in childbirth. She married *Harry HOUFF,* lived most of her life in Indianapolis and passed away in 1997. Victor Grant Hillard, Jr. and Karen Boas.

Mrs. Jaycox, Lorain Dry Leader, Taken by Death

Former W.C.T.U. Head and Active Temperance Worker for 60 Years Dies in Home Here

Mrs. Ida L. JAYCOX, 77, friend of Frances E. Willard and other temperance leaders and president of the Lorain branch of the W.C.T.U. for 33 years, died this morning at her home at 1026 4th st.

The end which came following an illness of 13 months, was peaceful, according to members of the family. Mrs. Jaycox lapsed into a coma, and passed away quietly.

Her death brings to a close a 60-year career devoted to the call of temperance. From the time she was 16 years of age, Jaycox put her best effort into her work of fighting what she considered the "evils of drink."

Attended Oberlin

Mrs. Jaycox was born in what is now Sheffield Lake Village in 1855. Her father was a blacksmith, and the year after she was born he took this family and his smithing into a pair of two-horse wagons and started for Wisconsin to start up a new shop.

They settled near LaCrosse, Wisconsin where her father died. In 1873 her mother moved into LaCrosse to send her children to school. They lived there for __ years then came to Lorain. *(Mother was Lorinda Hilliard Aldrich, see Wm. Aldrich OP 3:5)*

Mrs. Jaycox and her sister ***(Anna Serelda HILLIARD)*** entered Oberlin college to take teacher training courses, and after her work there she taught school at Avon and at Sheffield Central. Lorain Times-Herald, undetermined date. (Karen Boas)

MRS. IDA L. JAYCOX

Yesterday, a Lorain woman died who had given 60 yrs. of her life to the temperance cause.

There were many who may have disagreed with the views of ***Mrs. Ida JAYCOX***, but none who doubted her sincerity, her belief that in prohibition society was to find new growth and spirit.

Born in Lorain before the Civil War, she not only observed the development of the community, but played an active part in that development.

She was present when the first sparks of the prohibition movement came to life in this country...sparks that were destined to kindle a force that swept the nation and became a factor thruout the civilized world.

The early leaders of that movement were her friends – *Mrs. Francis WILLARD (believed to be Miss Frances), Anna GORDON, "Mother STEWART," Mrs. Frank FARNSWORTH* (*Margaret Marilla GRISWOLD FARNSWORTH*, dau. of *Luman GRISWOLD* and *Margaret Marilla SMITH, OP 1: 10-11*). For 35 years she served as president of the W.C.T.U. organization in Lorain.

The life of Mrs. Jaycox closely parallels the history of the cause she served so faithfully.

Loyal to that cause, she worked long and hard in its behalf. And in so doing, she won the esteem of not only those who believed as she did, but of those who did not. Lorain Times-Herald, undetermined date, (additions by Karen Boas).

Ida L. JAYCOX, d. City of Lorain, Lorain Co., OH, res. 1026 4th Street; Oct 17, 1932, Carcinoma small intestines, secondary in liver 27 mos., carcinoma left breast operated 6 yrs. ago, senility. Widow of ***James M. JAYCOX***; b. 9/9/1855; age 77 yrs. 1 mo. 8 days.; b. Sheffield Lake, Lorain Co., OH; fr. ***Joseph HILLIARD***, mo. ***Matilda GRISWOLD***. Informant *Mrs. R. BICKEL*, 1026 4th St., Lorain. Burial Elmwood 10/20, 1932; undertaker The Wickens Memorial, Lorain, Ohio. Ohio Certificate of Death, Division of Vital Statistics, 1932.

Lot 62-10 Jaycox Marker

JAYCOX

GENEVIEVE C. GEORGE A.
1859-1946 1857-1926

Lot 62-10 George Anson Jaycox

(steel vault)

George may have used his middle name to avoid confusion when he was younger, since his father's name was also George.

JAKOX (sp.), George, 59, farmer, value of real estate $7000, personal property $1500, b. New York; ***Mary***, 49, Keeping house, b. New York; ***Eliza***, 23, no occupation, b. Ohio; ***James***, 21, Farm Laborer, b. Ohio; ***Alice***, 16, b. Ohio; ***Anson***, 13, b. Ohio; ***Henry***, 11, b. Ohio; ***Minnie***, 6, b. Ohio; ***William***, 2, b. Ohio; *KETCHUM, Emily*, 18, no occupation, b. Ohio; *KETCHUM, John*, 24, Sailor, value of real estate $750, b. Ohio; *JACOX, Seir(sp.)*, 26, b. Ohio. 1870 FC OH LOAV, p. 1, lines 27-34.

The State of Ohio, Lorain County, I Hereby Certify, that on the 25th day of November A.D. 1880, I duly solemnized the Marriage Contract between ***Mr. Anson JAYCOX*** and ***Miss Jennie BURRELL***. C.C. West. LCMR: 1872-1875, p. 1079.

George Anson JAYCOX married ***Genevieve BURRELL*** on 25 Nov 1880, and died May 22, 1926 in Lorain. ***Issue***: ***George Ernest JAYCOX***, b. 17 Oct 1881, d. 12 Sept 1895 *(buried Lot 57)*. ***Lucile JAYCOX***, b. 14 August 1888, m. 20 Nov 1920 to *Harry E. REHLING*; res. 718 Lakeside, Lorain, Ohio *(bur. this lot)*. ***Vern Burrell JAYCOX***, b. 10 July 1891, m. 15 Sept 1913 to *Daisy MARTIN*, 4 children: *Burrell Frederick JAYCOX*, b. 2 June 1914. *Wm. Earl JAYCOX*, b. 21 July 1915. *Myrtle Ellen JAYCOX*, b. 15 Jan 1915. *Walter JAYCOX*, b. 25 May 1921. ***Burrell Anson JAYCOX***, b. 26 August 1893, d. 13 June 1904. Porter Matteson, Mattesons in America, A5 and B5.

JAYCOX, George A., 44, head, b. Feb 1856, Ohio, parents b. New York, farmer, married 19 yrs.; ***Genevieve***, 40, wife, b. Oct 1859, Ohio, parents b. Ohio, 4 children born, 3 living; ***Lucile***, 11, dau., b. Aug 1888, Ohio; ***Vernon***, 8, son, b. July 1891, Ohio; ***Burrell***, 6, son, b. Aug 1893, Ohio. 1900 FC OH LOAV p. 14B, lines 63-7, house 300.

JAYCOX, Geo. A., (Genevieve),...Beach Park, farmer; ***Vernon***, Jaycox Rd. 1910 Lorain County Rural Directory, Avon, p. 55.

GEORGE A. JAYCOX

Funeral services for ***George A. JAYCOX***, who died Saturday at his home, 718 A-st., were held Tuesday afternoon. *The Rev. G. A. HOUCK* officiated with interment in Bay Village cemetery in charge of Funeral Director Sidney B. Royce. Lorain Time-Herald, May 25, 1926, p. 8, col. 5.

George A. JAYCOX; 718 A St., Lorain; married, wife ***Elizabeth JAYCOX***; b. Feb 1, 1857, Avon, O.; 69 yrs., 3 mo., 21 d.; retired farmer; fr. ***George JAYCOX***, b. New York, mo. ***Mary MATTISON***, b. New York; d. 5 a.m., May 22, 1926 of Hypostatic Pneumonia (4 days), contributory Arterio Sclerosis - 10 yrs.; bur. Bay Village, undertaker Sidney B. Royce, Lorain; informant *Mrs. Geo. A. JAYCOX*. Ohio Certificate of Death, Division of Vital Statistics, 1926, certif. 33134.

Ancestors of George Anson Jaycox:

I. ***Samuel Benedict JAYCOX*** of NY and ***Sarah MORRISON*** of CT who arrived c1820 in Avon. Karen Boas

Saml. L. JACOX, 27, Farmer, value of real estate $400, b. NY; ***Malinda***, 23, b. NY; ***Sarah A.***, 3, b. NY; ***Sarah***, 63, b. Conn.; ***Saml .B. JACOX***, 68, Farmer, value of real estate $400, b. NY. 1850 FC OH Lorain Co., Avon Twp., p. 468, lines 34-38. *Next to George JACOX.*

Headstone Inscriptions, Lake Shore Cemetery, Avon Lake, OH:

Samuel B. JACOX, Died Jan 27 1855, Aged 72 y. *Stone resting against a tree, rest of marker missing.*

Sarah, wife of S.B. JACOX, Died Jan 29 1833, Aged 67 yrs. 3 mos.?. Death caused by suffocation by a kettle of coals in their sleeping room. Read by Catherine Burke Flament

II. ***George JAYCOX*** m. ***Mary MATTESON*** (dau. of *Estys MATTESON* and *Lydia PHILLIPS*). George donated the land for the first public church and school in Avon. The original family home is on Lake Rd, just east of where Jaycox meets Lake Rd. facing west. Karen Boas

III. ***George Anson JAYCOX*** was born Feb 1, 1857 in Avon Lake, OH. His nickname was "Tone." Karen Boas

Parents of George Anson Jaycox:

George JAYCOX, father of our subject, was reared in his native state *(New York)* up to the age of 15 years, and in 1828 migrated west with his parents, ***Samuel*** and ***Sarah JAYCOX***, who were also natives of New York. They settled in an early day in Avon Township, Lorain Co., Ohio, where they passed the remainder of their lives. George Jaycox also took up a farm in the woods of Avon township, where he became a prominent citizen. He was a lifelong Republican, an active member of the party, and held various township offices. He died in 1873, his wife surviving him three or four years. They were the parents of ten children: ***Charles JAYCOX***, who died at the age of seven years; ***Jane JAYCOX*** wife of *J. BURE(BUER)*, of Avon township, who was a soldier in the Civil War; ***Eliza JAYCOX***, wife of *O. MOORE*, of Avon township, who also served in the Civil War; ***James M. JAYCOX*** *(see Francis in lot above)*; ***Emily JAYCOX***, wife of *J. KETCHAM*, residing in Lorain; ***Alice JAYCOX***, wife of *H. G. BROWN (BRAUN)* of Lorain; ***Anson JAYCOX***, married who makes his home in Dover township, Cuyahoga county; ***Henry JAYCOX*** a resident of Lorain; ***Minnie JAYCOX***, wife of *J. BROWN* of Lorain; and ***William JAYCOX***, living in Avon township. Full citation on James M. Jaycox, History of Lorain County, Ohio, pp. 983-4.

George JAYCOX (b. 1811, d. 1874) and ***Mary MATTESON JAYCOX*** (b. 13 Apr 1820, d. 15 Oct 1881, dau. of *Rev. Estys MATTESON*) m. 11 Aug 1841. *Issue:* ***Charley JAYCOX***, b. 1842, d. 1852. ***Jane JAYCOX***, b. 13 Dec 1846, d. 20 Sep 1921, m. *John BUER* (d. 1924). ***Elide JAYCOX***, b. 1847, d. 1911, m. *Orlo A. MOORE*. ***James JAYCOX***, b. 1849, d. 1916, m. *Ida HILLIARD* (b. 1855, d. 1932) *(dau. originally buried this lot, see above)*. ***Emma JAYCOX***, b. 1851, d. 1927, m. *Johnson KETCHAM*. ***Alice JAYCOX***, b. 1854, d. (29 Apr, Lorain, OH; death cert. 23576) 1925, m. *Henry BRAUN* (b. 1853, d. 1938). ***George JAYCOX***, b. 1 Feb 1857, Avon Lake, Ohio; d. 22 May 1926, Lorain, Ohio; m. 25 Nov 1880 *Genevieve BURRELL* (b. 1859, d. 8 Aug 1946). ***Henry A. JAYCOX***, b. 1861, d. 1913, m.1 *Louise BOUSE* (b. 1867, d. 1904), m.2 *Mary LAPP*. ***Minnie JAYCOX***, b. 1864, d. 1904, m. *Johnson BRAUN* (b. 1857, d. 1946). ***William JAYCOX***, b, 1867, d. 195_, m. 20 July 1903 *Maryette KENELLY*. Porter Matteson, Mattesons in America, pages not numbered. The Porter manuscript is

George JAYCOX, Sr., b. 1813, Albany, NY. Marilyn Ross

George JAYCOX, 39, value of real estate $1200, b. NY; ***Mary***, 26, b. NY; ***Jane***, 5, b. NY; ***Lovisa***, 4, b. NY; ***James***, 2, b. Ohio; *Betsey LOCKWOOD*, 25, b. Penn. 1850 FC OH Lorain Co., Avon, p. 935, lines 39-42, p. 936, lines 1-2.

Lake Shore Cemetery, Avon Lake, OH.

George JAYCOX, Feb 9 1811, Feb 6? 187_. *Very difficult to read.* Read by Marilyn Ross as Feb 14, 1871.

Mary JAYCOX, died Oct 15, 1881.

Charles, son of ***George M. JACOX***, died Jan 22, 1850, aged 7 years 2 mos. and 19ds. Aye mourners cease to languish on the grave of him so loved far removed from pain and anguish. He's a chanting hymns above.

MOORE: Elide JAYCOX 1847-1911, ***Winnie M.*** 1881-1882, ***Maud*** 1883-1885, ***Earl O.*** 1885-1887, ***Almyra*** 1887-1888.

KETCHAM: *There are numerous graves on the east side of the cemetery where the inscriptions are very difficult to read.* Read by Catherine Burke Flament.

Maternal Ancestors of George Anson Jaycox:

I. ***David MATTESON*** of Montville. Porter Matteson, Mattesons in America, A 1-5.

II. ***William MATTESON***, b. 24 Jan 1762, d. 6 Apr 1850, Harmony near Panama, Chautauqua Co., NY; ***Mehitable MATTESON***, dau. of *Zarababel MATTESON*. Served sporadically with the Conn. Militia from 1780-81. The third of thirteen children was Estys. Porter Matteson, A 1-5.

III. ***Estys MATTESON***, b. 12 Feb 1791; d. 9 Nov 1857, Avon, Ohio; m. 1810 ***Lydia PHILLIPS*** (d. Avon); was in the War of 1812. The second of seven children was Mary. Porter Matteson, A 1-5.

IV. ***Mary MATTESON*** *(mother of George).* Porter Matteson, A 1-5.

Estys MATTESON, 59, Farmer, b. Vermont; ***Lydia***, 56, b. Vermont; ***Munroe***, 16, b. NY; ***William***, 31, b. NY; ***Lydia***, 24, b. NY; ***Archibald***, 3, b. O.; ***Alsina***, female, 11/12, b. O. 1850 FC OH Lorain Co., Avon, pp. 468-9.

Lake Shore Cemetery, Avon Lake, OH.:

Estys MATTESON, Died Nov 9 1857, Aged 66 yrs. 9 mos.

Lydia P. MATTESON, Died Jan 18 1858, Aged 64? Yrs. 5m. 12 d.

Their son: ***Victor***, d. Aug 22, 1850, 16 yrs. "Being himself amiable and lovely was loved by all."

The estate of ***Estys MATTESON*** mainly consisted of personal property. List of persons purchasing property: *Orrin MOORE, George JACOX* (also spelled Jaycox in document), *Smith JACOX, A.L.MATTESON, Wm. MATTESON, Elijah JACOX* and wife *(Anna).* Estate File 13730, Lorain County as read by Sherry Spenzer.

Children of George Jaycox and Genevieve Burrell:

George Ernest and Burrell Anson Jaycox, the children of Genevieve and George A., are both buried in Lot 57 along with Vernon Burrell, Genevieve's brother. The lots are located next to each other.

JAYCOX, Vernon B., res. 1250 W. Erie St., Lorain, O; Enlistment Division: National Army; Enlistment Location: Lorain, O.; Date 30 Mar 1918; b. Avon Lake, O.; Age 26 8/12 Years; Assigns Comment 16 Co 4 Training Battalion 158 Depot Brigade to 20 Apr 1918; Co E 330 Infantry to 1 Aug 1918; Co E 16 Infantry to Discharge Private St. Mihiel; Meuse-Argonne; Defensive Sector. Wounded in Action slightly 4 Oct 1918. American Expeditionary Forces 12 June 1918 to 13 March 1919. Honorable discharge 27 March 1919. Ohio Military Men, 1917-18, Volume 9.

JAYCOX, Vernon B., b. 10 July 1891; d. Dec 1964, Denver, Adams, CO 80221; Issued OH (Before 1951). Social Security Index.

Lot 62-10 Genevieve Burrell Jaycox

Genevieve is the sister of Vernon Burrell, this lot.

According to the 1880 census, listed with Vernon, Genevieve was a teacher by profession.

Genevieve C. JAYCOX, female, widowed, d. Lorain Co., Lorain, St. Joseph Hosp., length of stay 4 hrs.; d. August 9th, 1946, 1:50 p.m. Cause of death Cerebral Hemorrhage, Other conditions Genrl. Arteriosclerosis. D?.A. LaFleur, M.D. In this community 76 yrs. Usual res. Ohio, Lorain Co., Lorain, 718 Lakeside Ave; b. Oct 17, 1859, Avon Lake, Ohio; age 86 yrs. 9 mos., 22 days.; occup. at home; fr. ***George BURRELL***, b. Elyria Township, OH, mo. ***Eunice PELLETT***, b. Avon, Ohio. Informant *Mrs. Harry REHLING*, 718 Lakeside Ave. Burial, cremation or other Aug 10-46, Bay Village, Ohio, Embalmer/Funeral Director J. Ford Thompson, Lorain, O. Ohio Certificate of Death, Division of Vital Statistics, 1946, certif. 49415.

Genevieve JAYCOX, age 86, 8/10/46. Plot map

Lot 62-11 Lucille Jaycox Rehling

LUCILLE
GENEVIEVE
REHLING
1888-1957

Lucille is the daughter of George Anson Jaycox and Genevieve Burrell (this lot), b. 14 August 1888. She married Harry E. Rehling Nov 20, 1920. Around 1950 the couple resided at 718 Lakeside, Lorain, OH.

Mrs. Lucille Rehling

Mrs. Lucille JAYCOX REHLING, 68, died this morning at her home, 718 Lakeside Ave., after a six-month illness.

A native of Lorain, she was graduated from Lorain High School in 1906. She studied teaching at Western Reserve University and taught in the Lorain elementary schools for 12 years. She was a member of the Delaware Ave. Methodist Church and the Women's Society of Christian Service.

Surviving are her widower, ***Harry E.*** and several cousins.

Friends may call this evening at the Reichlin-Cooley Funeral Home, 2920 Broadway, where services will be held Monday at 1:30 p.m. with *Rev. Joseph LONG* officiating. Burial will be in Bay Village Cemetery, Bay Village.

The family requests expressions of sympathy take the form of contributions to the Cancer Society. Lorain (Ohio) Journal, Sat., June 15, 1957, p. 10, col. 4.

Lucille REHLING, buried June 17, 1957. CL

Lucille G. REHLING, d. June 15, 1957, 12:15 A.M., 718 Lakeside Ave., Lorain, Lorain Co., Ohio, Metastatic Carcinoma site undetermined - 4 months, lived 68 yrs. in Lorain; married, res. 718 Lakeside Ave., not a farm; b. 8/14/1888, Lorain, O., 68 yrs. old, housekeeper; fr. ***Anthony JAYCOX***; mo. ***G. BURRELL***, informant *Harry E. REHLING*, J. S. Hawthorne, M.D., Lorain, O. attended deceased from Dec 1956 to 6-15-57, last seeing her alive on 6-1-57; buried 6/17/1957 Bay Village Cemetery; embalmer Donald R. Zilch, funeral firm Reichlin Cooley, 2920 Broadway, Lorain, Ohio. Ohio Certificate of Death, Division of Vital Statistics, 1957, certif. 040316. *George JAYCOX, father of Lucille, used "Tone" as his nickname which may be why Harry provided Anthony as her father's first name.*

Lot 62-12 Harry Ernest Rehling

HARRY ERNEST
REHLING
US ARMY
WORLD WAR I
JUL 22 1896
MAR 13 1989
BENEVOLENT
HUSBAND
AND FATHER

Harry did not have a stone when research for this book was initiated. Records were uncovered that he served in the military during World War I. A military marker was placed on the grave in March 2001 through the Veterans' Service Commission. The marker was blessed and dedicated at the Memorial Day Parade and Cemetery Commemoration May 28th of that year by Fr. Timothy Gareau of St. Raphael Church, Bay Village.

Notation made in cemetery file for Jaycox/Rehling plot shows "Harry" and "mail to Mrs. Harry Rehling." Letter also found acknowledging the burial of Harry E. Rehling on April 13, 1989, at Lakeside Cemetery.

Harry REHLING was born in Richmond, Indiana, to ***William REHLING*** and ***Anna HOLTGRIEVE***. He had at least one brother, ***George***, who is believed to have worked for Bethlehem Steel in Dayton, OH; and a sister, ***Nellie*** who would visit the family in the summer. Harry served in the U.S. Army with the Cavalry during World War I until July 17, 1917. His first marriage was to ***Lucille JAYCOX** (this lot)*, daughter of ***Anthony*** and ***G. JAYCOX***. Following Lucille's death in 1957, Harry married ***Helen (Nell) Catherine GRAMBLEY*** on February 22, 1963. Nell (b. 22 Feb 1923, Columbus, OH; d. 20 Dec 1983; bur. Lorain County, OH) was the daughter of *William GRAMBLEY* and *Nellie SMITH*, and the mother of five children. His step-children remember Harry as a caring individual who provided a loving home for his new family. Harry and Nell had one child, ***Harry Ernest Jr***., who was stillborn on 11 Feb 1966 at St. Joseph's Hospital in Lorain, OH. "Little Hank" as he was lovingly referred to by family members is buried at Calvary Cemetery. Nell passed away in 1983. Harry lived on his own for a short time and then moved in with his step-daughter, ***Karen SZABO***. His eye sight had been declining for years, and after his 80th birthday he had become blind, but able to function with assistance. A cigar smoker, he was diagnosed with colon cancer after a short illness. Karen Szabo

REHLING, Harry E., 659872, white, res. 2887 Romana Place, Cincinnati, O. NA *(National Army)* LB 1 Norwood, O. Oct 15/18 Br. *(born)* Richmond, Ind., July 10/96. Det *(detachment)* 1 ASP *(Air Service, Aircraft Production)* Washington DC to Mch 3/19; 4 Co. Cp. *(Camp)* Meigs DC to disch. Sgt. Nov 10/18; Sgt. 1 cl Jan 22/19 hon disch Mch 5/19. Prior serv. NG *(National Guard)* June 26/16. Dayton O.; NG Disch Nov 23/17 SCD. *(Surgeons Certificate of Disability)*. Official Roster of Ohio Soldiers, Sailors and Marines, World War 1917-18, vol. 14 POK-ROS, p. 14052.

Harry Rehling

ASHTABULA - ***Harry E. REHLING***, 92, of Ashtabula, Ohio, died Tuesday at Ashtabula County Medical Center.

A former resident of the Lorain area of 66 years, he was also a former resident of Beach Park Towers, Avon Lake. Rehling was a retired store keeper at the American Ship Building Company, retiring in 1961 with 25 years of service.

He was a former member of the American Legion Post No. 30, Lorain. He was also a U.S. Army veteran, serving during World War I.

Survivors include daughters ***Mary Lou, Virginia*** and ***Karen Sue SZABO***; sons ***Christopher*** and ***Paul***; and 11 grand-children. He was preceded in death by a son, ***Harry Jr***.

A memorial service will be Saturday at 4 p.m. at St. Joseph's Church, 3330 Lake Ave., Ashtabula.

The family suggests memorial contributions may be made to St. Joseph's Church or to the Society for the Blind.

Arrangements were handled by the Burmeister Funeral Home. "Journal," Lorain, OH, March 16. 1989, p. 23, cols. 1-2.

Harry Ernest REHLING, male, d. Mar 14, 1989, Ashtabula County Medical Center, Ashtabula, Ashtabula Co., Multiple Organ Failure - 3 days, Gangrenous Cecum - 7 days, Carcinoma of the Splenic Flexure - years, 92 yrs. old; b. July 22, 1896, Richmond, Indiana; widowed, occup. Construction Engineer - Ship Building; res. 1316 West 40th Street, Ashtabula, 44004, educ. unknown; fr. ***William Frederick REHLING,*** mo. ***Anna HOLTGREIVE***; informant *Mrs. Karen SZABO*, 1316 West 40th St.; Brookside Crematory, Parma, Burmeister Funeral Service, 163 Avon Belden Road, Avon Lake, OH 44012. Ohio Certificate of Death, Division of Vital Statistics, 1989, certif. 024734.

Brother of Harry Ernest Rehling:

REHLING, George H., age 78, of 3700 Ridgeway Rd., Kettering, died Saturday at Kettering Memorial Hospital. He was a Vice President of Wyckoff Steel Co., retiring in 1961 after more than 40 years with the Company. He was an honorary member of the Dayton City Club, and a member of the Oakwood Kiwanis Club and Dayton Country Club. Survived by his wife, ***Mary Edna***; 2 daughters, ***Mrs. Marianna REHLING-GOODMAN*** of New York City and ***Mrs. Dorothy Jeanne WILLIS*** of St. Clair, MI, a brother, ***Harry E***. of Lorain, O.; a sister, ***Mrs. Nellie THOMAS*** of Crowley, TX; 6 grandchildren and 3 great grandchildren. Services 1:30 p.m. Tuesday from the Routsong Funeral Home, Brown St. at Irving Ave., Rev. Lester McMannis officiating. Burial Woodland Cemetery. There are no visiting hours. If desired, friends may make memorial contributions to the charity of their choice. Dayton Daily News, Mon. Feb 5, 1973, p. 39, col. 2. *Woodland Cemetery is directly opposite the University of Dayton.*

George Herman REHLING, d. Feb 3, 1973, Kettering Medical Center, Kettering, Montgomery Co., Ohio, 78 yr., cause Cerebral vascular accident; b. Feb 8, 1894, Indiana, fr. ***William REHLING***, mo. ***Anna HOLTGREIVE*** (?); married, spouse ***Mary Edna CLAPPER***; res. 3700 Ridgeway Rd., Kettering; Routsong Funeral Home, 6 Oakwood Ave., Dayton; bur. Woodland Cemetery, Dayton, Ohio. .Ohio Certificate of Death, Division of Vital Statistics, 1973, certif. 01444.

George H. REHLING - born 2/8/1894, died 2/3/1973, buried 2/6/1973; ***Mary Edna REHLING*** - born 4/7/1897, died 2/3/1979, buried 2/6/1979; ***Marianne REHLING GOODMAN*** (cremation interment) - buried 7/1/1996 (no other information) Buried at Woodland in Section 101, Lot 3730. Woodland Cemetery & Arboretum, Dayton, OH.

Son of Harry Ernest Rehling:

Harry REHLING, Jr., bur. 11 Feb 1966, Sect. 8B, Infant grave 450. Calvary Cemetery, Lorain, OH.

Lot 66 *Owner: C. L. Wuestenberg of Dover purchased March 28, 1884 for $6.30 SL*

Lot 66-13 Rebecca Mueller Wuestenberg

MOTHER
REBECCA M. WUESTENBERG
1836-1918

Rebecca MUELLER (MILLER), wife of ***Charles L. WUESTENBERG***, was born in July of 1834 or 1836 in Pennsylvania. Her father's name was originally *MELLINGER*. She died August 15, 1918. Robert W. Hoff, Wuestenberg Family Group Sheets.

WESTENBERG-Rebecca, widow of the late ***Dr. C. L. WESTENBERG***, died Aug 15, at the home of her daughter, Waycross, Ga., aged 82 yrs. Funeral Monday, Aug 19, at 2 p. m., from the residence of her daughter, 1292 W. 111th st. Burial at Bay View cemetery. Cleveland Necrology File, August 18, 1918, roll 085.

Rebecka WUESTENBERG, 82; res. Cleveland; German; interred Aug 19, 1918; Lot 66. "List of Interments," Lakeside Cemetery, Bay Village, OH.

Lot 66-14 Charles Louis Wuestenberg

FATHER
CHARLES L. WUESTENBERG
1832-1891

Charles L. WUESTENBERG was born in Prussia in 1832. He married ***Rebecca MUELLER*** on 7 Sept 1853 in E. Liberty, Allegheny Co., PA. They lived in Pittsburgh before moving to Cleveland. He practiced Dentistry and had a tobacco shop. Charles died 24 July 1891 from an inflammation of the liver. Charles and Rebecca had fourteen children: ***Emma Rebecca WUESTENBERG***, b. 20 June 1854, Pittsburgh, Allegheny Co., PA; m. 11 July 1877, in Berea, Cuyahoga Co., OH to *Ira Weston DISBRO*; d. 30 June 1938, Cleve, OH, bur. Lakeview Cem. ***Mary A. WUESTENBERG***, b. 7 May 1856, Pittsburgh; m. *W. L. LIPPERT,* four children. ***Lillie Ricks WUESTENBERG***, b. 30 Mar 1858, Pittsburgh; m. 1 Nov 1877, Cuy. Co., OH to *Charles M. BIRDSALL;* missionary. ***Charles Albert WUESTENBERG***, b. 28/29 Nov 1860, Pittsburgh; m. *Jessie D.;* d. 17 Mar 1927, Berkeley, Alameda Co., CA; bur. Sunset View Cem. ***John Clarence WUESTENBERG,*** b. 28 Jan 1862, Rochester, Beaver Co., PA; m. *Anna Lillian FISTLER*; d. 20 Jan 1926, bur. Cypress Lawn, CA. ***Alice M. WUESTENBERG***, b. 28 Aug 1864; m. 12 Nov 1884 to *Loren R. WRIGHT.* ***Ida May WUESTENBERG***, b. 28 Jan 1866; d. 1884, bur. Lakeside Cem., Bay Village. ***Annie Rebecca WUESTENBERG***, b. 12 Oct 1867, PA; m. *Ben WELLER.* ***Robert C. WUESTENBERG***, b. 20 Oct 1869, Middleburg, OH; m. *Lee DANTA.* ***Laura K. WUESTENBERG***, b. 15 Aug 1871, Middleburg; m. *J.D. JONES,* "Chaplain-Bethel;" res. 1565 E. 84th, Cleve. O. ***Carl Louis WUESTENBERG***, b. 18 May 1873, OH; m. twice. ***Eva WUESTENBERG***, b. 9 Mar 1875; waitress; res. 9208 St. Clair; m. 1914, *Jack MCCALLUM.* ***Mabel WUESTENBERG***, b. 26 Apr 1877; never married; res. So. Cal. ***Melville G. WUESTENBERG***, b. 9 Aug, 1881; adopted?; d. 1886, bur. Lakeside.

Early in the 20th century, most of the family dropped the "u" and adopted the name Westenberg. Robert W. Hoff, Wuestenberg Family Group Sheets.

Children of Charles L. Wuestenberg and Rebecca Mueller:

DISBRO, Ira W., 28, Physician, b. Ohio; ***Emma R.***, 25, wife, b. Pennsylvania; ***Ira Reginald,*** 10/12, b. Aug, son, b. Ohio; *TOBEBEN, Paglina*, 14, Servant, b. Ohio; *BEAUCHAMP, Thos*., 38, Boarder, Machinist, b. England. 1880 FC OH CYW7, p. 229C.

DISBRO: Emma R., widow of the late ***Dr. Ira W. DISBRO***, mother of *Mrs. GNY (should be **Guy A** and **Ira**),* ***Roger*** and ***Earl*** in her 85th year. Services at Wade Chapel, Lake View Cemetery, Saturday, 1 p. m. Burial private. Please do not send flowers. Cleveland Necrology File, July 2 1938, reel 020; Guy A. Disbro, Sr., Aug 27, 1966, reel 104.

DISBRO-Dr. Ira W., aged 54, Wednesday, November 7th, 10:15 a. m. Funeral from late residence, 7905 Superior ave., at 2 p. m., Friday Nov 9th. Burial private. Cleveland Necrology File, Nov 9, 1906, reel 020.

Emma Rebecca DISBRO, b. June 20, 1854; d. June 30, 1938; bur. Sect. 25, Lot 1105. Lakeview Cemetery, Cleveland, OH.

LIPPERT-Mary A., beloved wife of ***William L.***, mother of ***Alice M. COLE, Theodore M., C. Louis*** and ***Harry W. LIPPERT***, suddenly at 8:30 p. m. Monday. Funeral services from her late residence, 1671 Chesterland avenue, Lakewood, 2:30 p. m., Wednesday, March 24. Burial Lakewood Park Cemetery. Cleveland Necrology File, Mar 23, 1926 reel 050.

East Rockport Central School, 1879, was the first combination grade and high school as a brick building on Warren Road in Lakewood. S.H. Herriman was appointed as the first superintendent and teacher of the higher department at a salary of $75 per month. There were three teachers. During this administration and that of ***William L. LIPPERT***, who succeeded him from September 1882 until August 1888, more emphasis was placed on the curriculum and educational improvements.

Lippert served as principal of Lakewood High School served from 1881-1888. Charles P. Lynch, "Lakewood Public Schools," Story of Lakewood, OH by Lindstrom, E. George; Margaret Manor Butler, The Lakewood Story; Lakewood Board of Education, "A Compilation of Histories, The Lakewood Public Schools," [Lakewood Public Schools].

William L. LIPPERT William L. Lippert, a former principal of Lakewood High School and a member of the Cleveland Public Library staff for forty-three years, died today at the Elyria Oma Home for the Aged. He was 88 years old. It was through Mr. Lippert's efforts that the first high school was built in Lakewood, a Cleveland suburb, and he later served as a teacher and principal at the school. While working at the library he urged board members to establish a newspaper and magazine room. The idea was vetoed, but later was adopted. He was born at Warrensville, Ohio, in 1855, and was one of the oldest living graduates of Baldwin-Wallace College. A daughter, ***Mrs. Alice M. COLE***, survives. Cleveland Necrology File, Apr 10 1943, reel 050 and Copyright © 1943 by The New York Times Co. Reprinted with permission.

Possible additional marriages from the information provided above. The State of Ohio, Cuyahoga County, ss. I Certify that on the 28 day of January 1885 ***Mr. John C. WESTENBERG*** and ***Miss Mattie DAVIS*** were by me legally joined in marriage. Chester L. Foote. Marriage Record, Cuyahoga County, OH, vol. 28, p. 199.

The State of Ohio, Cuyahoga County, ss. I Certify that on the 23rd day of September 1891 ***Mr. J. Clarence WESTENBERG*** and ***Miss Cynthia E. WINTERS*** were by me legally joined in marriage. Rev. Burt Eshtes Howard. Marriage Record, Cuyahoga County, OH, vol. 36, p. 202.

WRIGHT: Alice M., 1565 E. 84th St., Tuesday, Remains at Frank J. Patterson's Parlors, 10913 Superior Ave., where services will be held Friday, Nov 23, at 2 p. m. Cleveland Necrology File, Nov 22, 1934, reel 087.

Laura W. JONES, d. January 8, 1932 at 5:40 p.m. of Cancer of Cecum; res. 1565 E. 84th St., Ward 1, *(Cleveland)*, housewife, widow; 60 yrs. 4 mos. 23 ds.; b. 8/15/1871, Berea, O. daughter of ***Chas. Louis WATENBERG***, b. Germany and ***Rebecca MILLER***, b. Butler, Pa.; informant *Alice M. WRIGHT*, 1565 E. 84th St.; burial Lakewood Park Cemetery, undertaker Frank Patterson, 10913 Superior Ave. Ohio Certificate of Death, Division of Vital Statistics, 1932, certif. 277.

JONES: Laura W., widow of the late ***J.D.***, at residence, 1565 E. 84th St., Friday. Funeral services at Euclid Avenue Baptist Church, Euclid Ave. E. 18th St., Monday at 2 p. m. Cleveland Necrology File, Jan 10, 1932, reel 042.

Laura W. JONES, d. Jan 8, 1932, Section 1, Lot 490, Grave 5, buried with ***Alice M. WRIGHT***, d. Nov 20, 1934, age 72, Grave 6. Lakewood Park Cemetery, Rocky River.

John David JOMES *(should read JONES)*, d. April 5, 1926 at 11:00 p.m. of General paralysis of insa__; res. 1565 E. 84th St., Ward 1 *(Cleveland)*; Minister married to ***Laura W. JAMES*** *(JONES)*; 80 yrs. 11 mos. 5 ds.; b. *(blank)*, Cleveland, Ohio, fr. ***David JONES***, b. Newark, NJ, mo. ***Mary J. McMILLAN***, b. Scotland; informant *Mrs. Laura W. James*, 1565 E. 84th St., burial Riverside Cemetery, undertaker The Hogan Co., 1345 Superior., T. _.Patterson. Ohio Certificate of Death, Division of Vital Statistics, 1926, certif. 3691.

JONES-Chaplain J.D., beloved husband of ***Laura W***., and father of ***Loren P. JONES*** and ***Mrs. Ella J. SCHROCK***, and grandfather of *Lawrence, Arthur, Homer, Ella* and *Lydia SCHROCK*, at his residence, 1565 E. 84th street, Monday, April 5, at 11 p. m. Funeral services at Euclid Avenue Baptist Church, Euclid avenue and E. 18th street, Thursday, April 8, at 2:30 p. m. Cleveland Necrology File, Apr 8, 1926, reel 042.

Chaplain Jones was married previously to Lydia Pepperday who is buried with him at Riverside Cemetery. A marriage certificate for Laura and John was not found in Cuyahoga County.

The State of Ohio, Cuyahoga Co., ss., I Certify that on the 18th day of May 1869, ***Mr. John D. JONES*** and ***Miss Lydia J. PEPPERDAY*** were by me legally joined in marriage. Peter Bellwood Marriage Record, Cuyahoga County, OH, vol. 15, p. 168.

JONES-Lydia PEPPERDAY, wife of ***Chaplain J.D. JONES*** of the Floating Bethel, passed away at 11:30 p. m., April 30. Funeral service May 2, at 2:30 sun time, from residence, Library ave., cor. of Pearl st. Cleveland Necrology File, May 2, 1901, reel 042.

Riverside Cemetery, Cleveland, Ohio. Section 10, Lot 335; owner John D. Jones:

Grave 1 ***Lydia J. JONES***, 56, married; b. England; d. 1 May 1901, Cleveland of cancer, undertaker B.E. Harris, bur. 2 May; res. 3 Library Ave., Cleveland. Stone: Mother, 1846-1901.

Grave 2 ***John D. JONES, Jr***., 28, single; b. Cleveland; d. Cleveland of tuberculosis; undertaker B.E. Harris; res. 3 Library Ave., Cleveland. Stone inscription: John D. Jr., 1875-1903

Grave 3 ***Lida JONES***, 23, single; b. US; d. 15 Aug 1904 of tuberculosis, bur. 17 Aug; Hogan undertaker; res. 225 Vannese Ave., Cleveland. Stone inscription: Lida Jane, 1881-1904

Grave 4 ***John D. JONES***, 80, married; b. Cleveland; d. 5 Apr 1926 in Cleveland of Paresis, bur. 8 Apr; res. 1565 East 84th, Cleveland. Stone inscription: Husband, Chaplain J.D. Jones, 1845-1926.

Grave 5 ***Lawrence E. SCHROCK***, 41, married; b. Ohio; d. 14 June 1947, Cleveland of Mesenterie thrombosis; undertaker Nosek, 3282 E. 55th St.; res. 4304 Denison Ave., Cleveland. Stone: Lawrence E. Schrock, 1905-1947.

SCHROCK, Lawrence E., residence, 4303 Denison Ave., beloved husband of ***Dorothy*** (nee ***KESSLER***), father of *Lois Neuman*, son of ***Ella*** and the late ***John***, brother of *Arthur, Homer, Ella* and *Lydia SCHULER*. Passed away Sat. Services at A. Nosek & Sons Funeral Home, 3282 E. 55, Tues., June 17, at 2 p. m. June 14 1947. Cleveland Necrology File, reel 072.

Grave 6 ***Ella J. SCHROCK***, 86, widow; d. 22 Dec 1969, Cleveland, cause of death deferred, bur. 24 Dec, Brown-Forward Funeral Home, 17022

Chagrin Blvd.; res. 3246 E. Overlook Rd. Stone inscription: Ella Jones Schrock, 1883-1969.

SCHROCK. Ella Schrock (nee ***JONES***), beloved wife of ***John George*** (deceased), mother of ***Arthur*** *V.*, of New Providence, N. J., ***Homer P., Ella A., Lydia SCHUELER (Mrs. Robert T.)*** and ***Lawrence*** *E.* (deceased), grandmother of four, great-grandmother of one, late residence, 3246 East Overlook Rd. Those who wish may send contributions to the Heights United Presbyterian Church, 3217 Washington Blvd., Cleveland Hts., O., or to the Homecrafters Shop, 13017 Larchmere Rd., Shaker Heights, O. Services will be held at 11 a.m. on Wednesday at Brown-Forward, 17022 Chagrin Blvd. Dec 24 1969, The Plain Dealer.

SCHROCK: John G., age 56, beloved husband of ***Ella*** (nee ***JONES***), father of ***Lawrence, Arthur, Homer, Ella*** and ***Lydia***, brother of *Herman* of Jefferson, O., *Joseph* of Euclid, O., *Jacob* and *Amelia* of Trumbull, O., passed away Sunday afternoon at his home in Strongsville, O. Now at the Behm Funeral Parlors, Madison, O. Services Wednesday, Jan 6, 1932, at 2 p. m. Jan 5 1932. Cleveland Necrology File, reel 072.

The Floating Bethel Mission and its founder, the ***Reverend John Davis JONES***, have received little attention from Cleveland's historians. The Floating Bethel Mission was one of numerous religious based charitable works undertaken by Clevelanders to save the souls of their fellow citizens, to keep them from sin, and to help them in sickness and in need. The mission's special task was to serve sailors in the lake shipping trade, and in 1887 it boasted "the largest Sailor Congregation" and "the best located and patronized" reading room on the lakes.

Although this "independent unsectarian work" was under the direction of a board of trustees, with a president, a secretary, and a treasurer, the main force behind its work was the Rev. John Davis Jones. Indeed, it is the longevity and dedication of "the one-armed Missionary" that provides the Floating Bethel Mission with much of its distinctiveness. For more than five decades, the Rev. Jones enjoyed the financial and moral support of some of the city's leading citizens for his work along the docks and among the poor.

The Rev. John Davis Jones (April 30, 1845-April 5, 1926) became a well-known figure on the streets of Cleveland as he ministered to the sick and needy along the lakefront and in the flats. The founder of the Floating Bethel Mission and "a pastor-at-large to the poor of the city," the Rev. Jones was a native Clevelander, one of eight children born to *David JONES*, one of the founders of the area's first rolling mill. According to his obituary, Jones first went to sea as a cabin boy, later advancing to mate, before enlisting in the Union army in 1861. He served in the Seventh Ohio Volunteer Infantry during the Civil War until he was discharged with a disability; then he re-enlisted in the navy. While serving on the gunboat *Yantic,* he was rendered partly deaf by a cannon explosion during a battle. Following the war, Jones worked on the lakes during the summers and with the railroads during the winter season. His work on the railroads led to further disability: an accident "cost him an arm and part of a foot."

Jones' religious work reportedly began following his own conversion in 1867 "at a noonday service conducted by the Young Men's Christian Association." Jones began distributing religious tracts along the docks, but soon extended his work into hospitals and local prisons. By the early 1870's, he was preaching in a Methodist church; in 1876 he was ordained a sailor evangelist; and on December 12, 1877, he was ordained minister of the Woodland Avenue Presbyterian Church, where he served until failing health forced him to retire in 1924. When and how the Rev. Jones came to establish the Floating Bethel Mission is unclear, but the name he chose for his mission clearly proclaimed its original intent: he used a boat to take the word of God to men who made their living on the open waters of Lake Erie. By the late 1870's, Jones had, according to *William Ganson ROSE*, "fitted an old scow in grand style" to attract sailors to his ministry; by the mid 1880's, the Sailors Floating Bethel and City Mission Chapel was in operation on land at 165 River Street, with Jones as chaplain and superintendent. A powerful speaker, Jones reportedly combined material service with his religious services, giving tickets to his Sunday prayer meetings that permitted their collectors to redeem a certain number for shoes or clothing. In addition to his own work on behalf of the sick and needy, the Rev. Jones was active in the founding of the Jones' Home for Friendless Children. He claimed to have influenced his uncle and aunt, *Carlos L.* and *Mary B. JONES*, to donate their land and home for the orphanage.

Throughout its history, the Floating Bethel Mission had trustees and officers in addition to the Rev. Jones, but it remained largely a one-man operation. The Rev. Jones not only held the services and ministered to those in need, but was also the Mission's fundraiser. Among those he solicited for aid was an old acquaintance, *John D. ROCKEFELLER*. According to Jones, he and Rockefeller were classmates together at both the Brownell School and "the Baptist Church Sunday School" at the corner of Ohio and Erie streets.

"His big heart keeps him poor and his nose on the grindstone all the time," wrote *L.M. BOWERS* of the Rev. Jones in 1902 to Rockefeller. "He cannot keep a dime when he sees suffering and his pocket is of course empty most of the time." One of Rockefeller's closest advisors, *Starr J. MURPHY*, gave his approval to the Rev. Jones' work in both 1905 and 1906. Murphy argued that while "the work is not of a kind which makes a general appeal to modern ideas of philanthropy...the work seems to be one which carries a ministry of love and comfort to many people." "I should think it worth maintaining," Murphy reported, "at least during the lifetime of Chaplain Jones.... [who is] a man of advanced years, and of lovable personality."

Not everyone was so favorably impressed by the Rev. Jones or the Floating Bethel Mission. The Cleveland Chamber of Commerce established a Committee on Benevolent Associations to assess the work of each charitable organization and to endorse those it believed were doing worthy work. Such endorsement was denied to the Floating Bethel Mission on two grounds. The Benevolent Associations found that the Floating Bethel Mission "absolutely refused to cooperate in its relief-giving work with the other relief organizations of the city." The Floating Bethel "seems rather to consider these organizations as its rivals and to vie with them for support." Both of these tendencies ran counter to the committee's belief "that cooperation is a fundamental principle of all charities." The committee also determined that the Floating Bethel's "administration of charity...is not always of the wisest and most effective character, tending occasionally to pauperize rather than to uplift." The charge that its actions tended to pauperize rather than uplift the poor was perhaps the most damning charge that could be leveled against a charitable organization according to the tenets of modern charitable work at the turn of the century.

The Rev. Jones understood the poor and needy as dignified individuals deserving of help, with few questions asked. The one-armed missionary, a veteran charity worker with a clear religious point of view, and with ties to some of the oldest families and wealthiest individuals in Cleveland, was certainly a formidable opponent for younger scientific charity workers. His failing health in 1924 and death two years later were the only thing that drove him from the field. In the spring of 1925, the Floating Bethel's board of trustees notified donors that Jones's "increasing physical disability" had prompted them to sell the property at 1322 West 11th Street and "give up the Charter of the Institution." Jones, the trustees argued, was "in no condition mentally or physically to carry on any work": poor eyesight due to cataracts on both eyes, a failing memory, and fainting spells made it "dangerous for him to be on the streets." Yet he continued to try to raise funds and minister to the needy, and the trustees felt compelled to urge his former supporters to refuse his appeals: "Former subscribers sympathetically inclined will be doing the Chaplain a great kindness if they hereafter refuse his appeal of funds." Proceeds from the sale of the Floating Bethel property had been used to pay the debts Jones had incurred on the institution's behalf, and the remainder was used to establish a trust fund for Jones and his wife. Jones died in 1926. Adapted with permission from "John D. Rockefeller's Philanthropy and Problems in Fundraising at Cleveland's Floating Bethel Mission and the Home for Aged Colored People," by Kenneth W. Rose, Ohio History, vol. 108, pp. 146-152 and 156-157. Paul Hillmer, "John D. Rockefeller and Civic Affairs in Cleveland," pp. 3-6.

The Jones Homes for Children, once home to "friendless boys," is now a service center for children and is the focus of the Jones Home Subdivisions National Register District and is an example of the many social services available in the neighborhood. Neighborhood Link. Welcome to Clark-Fulton, "Neighborhood Tour." Cleveland: Cleveland State University. 12 July 2004 http://www.nhlink.net/neighborhoodtour/clark-fulton/.

JONES-J.D. JONES, Jr., aged 28, son of ***Chaplain J.D. JONES***, at his residence, 3 Library ave., after a sickness of nearly ten years. Funeral Saturday at 2:30 p. m. sun time. Take Scovill and Pearl or Jennings and Brooklyn car to Library ave. Cleveland Necrology File, June 6, 1903, reel 042. *J. D. was a son from Chaplain Jones' first marriage, but died after the Chaplain married Laura.*

Wife of Carl Louis: ***WESTENBERG: Harriet***, beloved wife of ***Carl L.***, sister of Mrs. Robert Weissenstein, passed away suddenly Sunday, Jan 16. Now at Merle Owen Funeral Home, 15848 Euclid, where services will be held Tuesday, Jan 18, 2:30 p. m. Cleveland Necrology File, Jan 18 1938, reel 085.

Husband of Eva: ***John H. McCALLUM***, d. May 4th, 1944, 9:30 a.m., Lakewood Hospital, Lakewood, Cuyahoga Co., Ohio, Probable fracture of the skull, hemorrhage of the brain, internal injuries…, at hospital two days; 66 yrs. 8 mos. 3 ds.; b. Sept 1, 1878, Glencoe, Ontario, Canada, fr. ***Hugh McCALLUM***, b. Glencoe, mo. ***Annie FERGUSON***, b. Mosaic Township, Canada; Purchasing Agent for Cleveland-Buffalo Transit; married to *Eva M.*, age 66 years; res. 1292 W. 111th St., Cleveland, Cuyahoga Co.; in this community and U.S.A. 50 years; informant A. H. McCallum, 11821 Detroit Ave.; funeral director Daniels, 15800 Detroit Ave.; burial Lakewood. Ohio Certificate of Death, Division of Vital Statistics, 1944, certif. 30998.

Lot 66 Ida May Wuestenberg

no marker

Ida May WUESTENBERG was born Jan 28, 1866, the daughter of ***Charles L.*** and ***Rebecca WUESTENBERG***. Robert W. Hoff, Wuestenberg Family Group Sheets.

Ida M. WUESTENBERG, 18; res. Dover; German; interred March 28, 1884; Lot 66. "List of Interments," Lakeside Cemetery, Bay Village, OH.

Lot 66 Melville G. Wuestenberg

no marker

Melville WUESTENBERG, 5; res. Dover; German; interred Dec 22, 1886; Lot 66. "List of Interments," Lakeside Cemetery, Bay Village, OH.

WUESTENBURG, Melvin, d. Dec 22, 1886, 5 yrs. 4 m. 6 d., b. Rockport, parents ***Charles*** and ***Rebecca***, disease diphtheria. PD 3:146.

Melville G. WUESTENBERG, ***Charles*** and ***Rebecca's*** youngest child, was born August 9, 1881. It is thought by some family members that he may have been adopted. Robert. W. Hoff, Wuestenberg Family Group Sheets.

Original Part

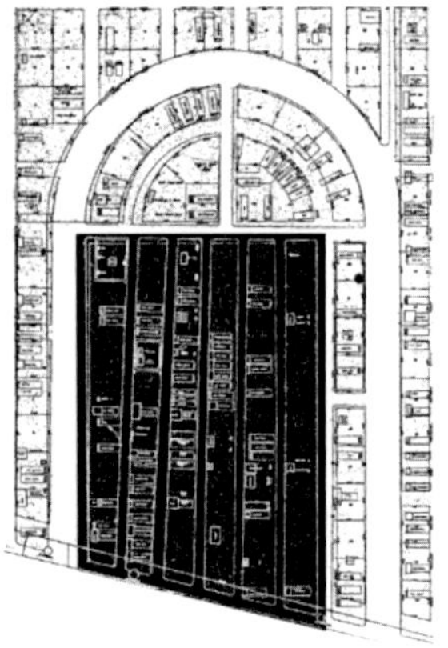

Original portion darkened.

Our Forefathers -
May we ever cherish their memories
and strive to imitate their virtues.

Toast made by request of Mr. H.M. Addison, Jeffersonville, Indiana
Cahoon Fifty-Sixth Anniversary Celebration of the Settlement of Dover,
Oct 10, 1866.

The original portion of the cemetery dates back to 1814. It is in the central area surrounded by the drive, excluding the row next to the drive on the east, and the half circle section to the north. All of the graves are probably not marked because of the age of the burials where markers may have been lost or no longer exist because of their composition or impermanence.

"The cradle, the ballot box of our pioneer mothers: 'They voted 'early and often,' and often carried the election".

Toast by L.H. Johnson at the eleventh Cahoon Celebration
1870.

First row to the east of the west drive starting from the road and proceeding north toward the lake.

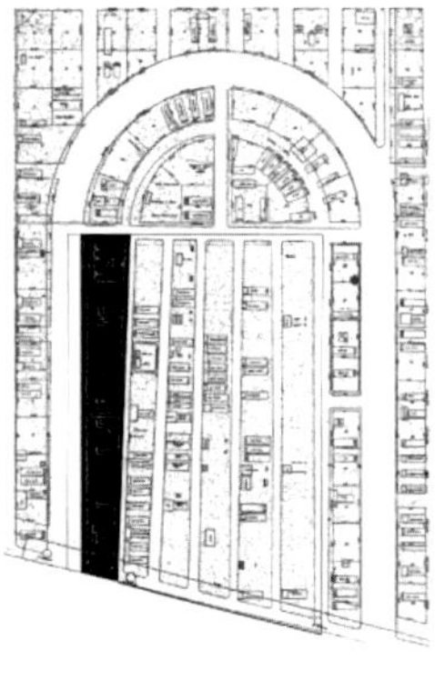

Graves identified as OP (Original Part), followed by - Row: Number of marker in row

OP 1:1 Alfred H. Willis

Assumed to be for Alfred H. Willis

FATHER

OP 1:2 Fannie Carter Grant Willis

Assumed to be for Fannie Willis

MOTHER

OP 1:3 Willis Monument

WILLIS

ALFRED H.
1846-1927
FANNIE M.
HIS WIFE
1839-1908

OP 1:3 Alfred H. Willis

The State of Ohio, Lorain County, I Hereby Certify, that on the 24th day of September A.D. 1874, I duly solemnized the Marriage Contract between ***Mr. Alfred WILLIS*** and ***Miss Fanny GRANT***. H.M. Walker. Lorain County Marriages : 1872-1885, p. 779 (110). *Fannie is assumed to be Fannie Carter Grant, widow of Alonson Grant OP 5:16. Besides the name, the year of birth also coincides.*

WILLIS, Alfred H., carpenter, 416 Washington St.; ***Fannie M., Mrs***. and ***Vernon E.***, jeweler. 1906 Lorain County Directory, Vol.1, pp. 288-9.

ALFRED H. WILLIS

Alfred H. WILLIS, 322 Eighth-st., died Tuesday evening following an illness extending over a period of many years.

Mr. Willis has been a resident of Lorain over 35 years, coming here from Avon Lake where he was born 81 years ago. He is survived by a sister, ***Miss Harriet WILLIS***, Eighth st., and one son ***Vernon E. WILLIS*** of West Erie av.

Services will be conducted from Thompson's Mortuary Friday at 1:30 p.m. with burial in the family lot at Dover Bay. The Lorain Times-Herald, Dec 15, 1927.

Alfred H. WILLIS, 322 8th St., Lorain, Lorain Co.; d. 12-13, 1927, 9:45 p.m., Dilatation of Heart 1 da., Contributory: Senility with old hemorrhage of brain; Widower of ***Fannie M. WILLIS***; b. May 2, 1846, Avon, O., fr. ***Wm. W. WILLIS***, b. England, mo. ***Lucy HALFRED***, b. England; Retired Merchant; 81 yrs. 7 mos. 11 ds.; informant *V. E. WILLIS*, 1439 W. Erie Ave., Lorain; bur. Bay Village, 12/14/27, undertaker J. Ford Thompson, Lorain. Ohio Certificate of Death, Division of Vital Statistics, 1927, certif. 70666.

Parents of Alfred H. Willis:

William WILLIS, b. 5 February 1802, England and ***Lucy HALFRED***, b. 26 Feb 1804, England; m. 24 February 1825. *Issue:* ***Mary WILLIS***, b. 1829, Blaby, Leices Tuchrise, England; m. 1858, Plainfield, Illinois to *Peter SCHOTT*; d. 1886. ***Ann E. WILLIS***, b. 1 Mar 1833, Blaby, England; m. c1855 *Lorenzo Croyden BEMENT* (b. 25 Oct 1823, Suffield, CT; d. 11 Feb 1911 of myocarditis, bur. Evergreen Cem.); d. 6 Oct 1905, Dover Township, OH; bur. Evergreen Cemetery, Westlake, OH. ***Hariette WILLIS***, d. after Feb 9, 1930 *(from photo)*. Phyllis J. Gaddy

William WILLIS, 49?, farmer, value of real estate $1260; ***Lucy***, 44; ***Mary***, 19; ***Ann***, 1_?; ***James***, 14?; ***Phebe***, 12; ***Joseph***, 9; ***Alfred***, 4; ***Harriet***, 1; all b. England. 1850 FC OH LRAV p. 937, lines 9-17. *Difficult to decipher.*

WILLIS, William, 68, farmer, value of real estate $6300, personal property $1000, b. England; ***Lucy***, 65, b. England; ***Alfred***, 24, farm hand, b. Ohio; ***Harriet***, female, 22, farm hand, b. Ohio; ***Phoebe***, 31, at home, b. England. 1870 FC OH LRAV p. 361, lines 21-25.

WILLIS - William, d Feb 5, 1894, 92y; ***Lucy***, wife, d Oct 6, 1889, 84y 7m 10d; ***James***, May 20, 1836-Apr 13, 1872 GAR; ***Harriet***, 1848-1941. Avon Mounds (Center) Cemetery, Avon, OH.

Sibling of Alfred H. Willis:

The State of Ohio, Cuyahoga County, ss. I hereby certify, that on the 29th day of August A.D. 1854, I duly solemnized the Marriage Contract between the said ***Lorenzo C. BENNETT*** and ***Ann WILLIS***. I.R. Henry, M.G. Marriage Record, Cuyahoga County, OH, vol. 5, p. 531.

Ann BEMENT, res. Dover, OH, 72, b. England, interment 10/5/1905, Sec. G, Lot 6, owner Ann Bement. ***Lorenzo BEMENT***, res. Dover, OH, 87, b. Dover, cause of death Myocarditis, undertaker Jas. Pease, interment 2/11/1911, Sec. G, Lot 5, Grave 1. ***Frances K. BEMENT***, res. Oberlin, OH, 85, d. Oberlin, OH, cause infirmity of age, undertaker Glen Jenkins, interment 11/24/1956, Sec. G, Lot 6, Grave 1. ***Lucy Permilia BEMENT***, res. Westlake, 72, d. Kansas City, Missouri, cause cerebral arteriosclerosis, undertaker Clifford Pease, interment 11/1/1940, Sec. H, Lot: 6, Grave 3. Evergreen Cemetery, Westlake, OH.

OP 1:3 Fannie Carter Grant Willis

Fannie's first husband, Alonson Grant, (OP 5:16) died during the Civil War. She then lived with her sister Amanda's family before marrying Alfred Willis.

BATES, Alfred, 41, Farmer, value of real estate $12,700, personal property $1200, b. New York; ***Amanda***, 38, Keeping House, b. Ohio; ***Alise***, 16; ***Everett***, 14; ***Daniel***,

12; ***Charles***, 10; ***Elsie***, 3; ***EDMOND, James***, 20, b. Ohio; ***GRANT, Fanny***, 30, No Occupation, Value of Personal Estate $800, b. Ohio; ***GRANT, Sarah***, 10, at home, b. Ohio, attended school. 1870 FC OH LRAV p. 362, lines, 6-15. *The Grant Family History lists a son, Maurice Alonson. He was not found in the census recorded above. There was one farm between Alfred Willis's family and the Bates family at the time.*

Fannie M.C. WILLIS, 69, d. Dec 14, 1908, 6 a.m., Lorain, Lorain Co., Ohio, cause of death Apoplexy, duration Im. *(immediate),* Housewife, married. Permission is granted to remove for burial at Dover Lake, Cuyahoga Co., Ohio on the 15th day of December. George Uickeun *(sp.),* shipping undertaker. Ohio State Board of Health, Transportation of Corpse Permit.

Fannie WILLIS, res. Lorain, Ohio; interred Dec 15, 1908; Original Part. "List of Interments," Lakeside Cemetery, Bay Village, OH.

Lorain, O, Apoplexy, housewife, married, b. Ohio. Burial Removal Permit, City of Bay Village, OH.

Family of Fannie Carter Willis:

It is thought that ***Fannie CARTER WILLIS'S*** parents may have died pre-1850, her father c1846 . Terrill Bates Black. *She is found in the 1850 census living with the Edmonds family. Nancy Edmond may have been her sister; this has not been proven. Note that in the 1870 census when she is living with the Bates family, James Edmond, an infant in the following census, has also been enumerated with the family. The 1850 census is very light and difficult to read.*

Alexander EDMUND, 39; ***Nancy***, 25; ***James***, 3/12; ***Fanny CARTER***, 10; ***Sylvia Ed….***, 1?; a male is listed, 20, farmer. 1850 FC OH LRAV p. 936, lines 15-20.

The Bates family owns a photograph of the 60th wedding anniversary of ***Amanda CARTER*** and ***Alfred BATES*** who lived in Elyria, Ohio, at the time. On the back it identifies ***Alfred WILLIS*** and states he is the brother-in-law of Amanda Carter Bates. Terrill Bates Black

Amanda BATES, b. 5 Nov 1830, Ohio; fr. ***John CARTER***, b. unknown; mother unknown; residence 108 Spruce St., Elyria; d. 2 Oct 1913, bur. Elyria Cemetery. Ohio Certificate of Death, Division of Vital Statistics, 1913, certif. 59142.

Amanda's obituary provided family information:

Mrs. Alfred BATES…Her maiden name was ***Amanda CARTER***. She was born in Trumball County, Ohio, November 5th 1830. When but a few years of age, she came with her parents to Rochester, Lorain County, where she lived until the age of 16. She came to Avon where she was married to ***Alfred BATES*** on May 15th 1853. They have lived in Elyria since 1879. She was the mother of six children, four boys and two girls. Two of these have passed away… Elyria Telegram, Elyria, OH, October 3, 1913.

OP 1:4 **Carl Willis**

Son of Alfred H. Willis and Fannie M. Carter.

CARL *(top)*

Inscription worn and difficult to read.

Infant son
of
A.H. & F.M.
WILLIS
Died
Mar 18, 1878
Aged 19 Dy.

OP 1:5 **Fredrick Wischmeyer**

FREDRICK

WISCHMEYER
BORN
MAR 24, 1863
DIED
AUG 10, 1864

This may be a child of Henry Wischmeyer Sr. (Lot 39), and Regina Rentschler (Lot 38), but this has not been documented. Regina in the 1900 census states she had 8 children, of whom only 5 were living.

OP 1:6 **William Silas Hilliard**

Marker cracked and set in concrete.

In Memory
WILLIAM S.
HILYAR
Who imparted this life
March 25, 1854
Aged 41 Years
22 days

(in corner)
Millerd Shribe
Cleveland W.S.

*William S. HILYAR is presumed to be **William Silas HILLIARD**. Research uncovered a William Silas Hilliard with the dates of birth and death exactly the same as William S. Hilyar in this grave.* The Hilliard name has been found in records to be spelled numerous ways, the general progression of Hilliard was Hilyar, Hilyard, Hilliard. William's brother, ***Joseph***, married ***Lorinda GRISWOLD***. Lorinda's second husband was ***William W. ALDRICH** (OP 3:5).* Karen Boas *Lorinda's parents are buried within three plots of William (OP 1: 10-11).*

William Silas HILLIARD was born on 3 Mar 1813 in Hebron, Tolland Co., CT. He died on 25 Mar 1854 in Avon Lake, Lorain Co., OH. He was married. William had a daughter who lived in Wisconsin. Victor Grant Hillard, Jr.

Ancestors of William Silas Hilliard:

I. ***William HILLARD***, b. abt. 1614 in England. He arrived in Boston in the spring of 1653 on the ship "Elizabeth and Ann" out of London. He was a carpenter at the age of 21 and purchased land at Plymouth Colony for the first time in 1637. He was married to ***Esther*** in Duxbury of the Plymouth Colony in Oct. 1640 and they had three children, the oldest and only son being William. Victor Grant Hillard, Jr.

II. ***William HILLARD***, b. abt. 1641, probably Duxbury, Plymouth Co., MA; d. 24 Jan 1713/14, Little Compton, Bristol Co., MA; bur. Old Commons Cemetery, Little Compton, Newport Co., RI; m. 12 June 1671, Hingham, Plymouth Co., MA to ***Deborah WARREN*** (dau. of *John WARREN* and *Deborah WILSON*; b. 1652/3, Exeter, Rockingham Co., NH; d. 15 Feb 1717/18, Little Compton, Bristol Co., MA; bur. Old Commons Cemetery). The youngest of twelve children was Jonathan. Hilliard

III. ***Jonathan HILLARD***, b. 8 Nov 1696, Little Compton, Bristol Co., MA; d. 5 Oct 1741 in Stonington, New London Co., CT; m. 13 May 1716, Little Compton, Bristol Co., MA to ***Abigail WILBOR*** (dau. of *William WILBOR* and *Sarah TALLMAN,* b. 1 Apr 1697; d. 5 Oct 1741 Stonington, New London Co., CT); bur. Hillard Cemetery, North Stonington. The fifth of seven children was Isaac. Hilliard

IV. ***Isaac HILLARD***, b. 2 Oct 1726 in Stonington, New London Co., CT; m. 5 Apr 1751, Westerly, Washington Co., RI to ***Victoria COATES*** (dau. of *Robert COATES* and *Mary*; b. 17 Oct 1723 in Stonington). Their second child was Jonathan. Hilliard

V. ***Jonathan HILLARD***, b. 27 Feb 1754, Stonington, New London Co., CT; d. 1803, probably Groton, New London Co., CT; m. bef. 1771 to ***Mary WILLIAMS*** (b. 1750, d. 1809, probably in Groton). He served as a private in Capt. Ezra Cary's Company, Connecticut Militia. Their eighth and youngest child was William. Hilliard

VI. ***William HILLIARD** (note spelling change of last name),* b. 30 Dec 1784, Groton, New London, CT; d. 9 Feb 1872, Springfield, Walworth, WI; m. 2 Sep 1803, Groton to ***Elizabeth LEWIS*** (b. 2 Feb 1783, Stonington, New London, CT; dau. of *Henry LEWIS* (b. 1757 Westerly, RI; d. c1836 LaGrange, Lorain Co., Ohio) and *Betsy (Polly) JACKSON* (b. c1762, d. c1807); d. 12 Mar 1859, Richmondville, Schoharie Co., NY). He served in the Navy during the War of 1812.

Issue: ***Diana HILLIARD***, b. 24 Nov 1804, Groton, New London, CT; d. 6 Apr 1895, Lincoln, Kewaunee Co., WI; m. 1842, Champlaine, Clinton Co., NY to *John PLUGH* (b. Clinton Co.). ***Eliza HILLIARD***, b. 17 June 1810, Berne, Albany, NY; d. 21 Oct 1853, Newark Valley, Tioga Co., NY; m. *McCULLOGH*. ***William Silas HILLIARD***, b. 3 Mar 1813, Hebron, Tolland, CT; d. 25 March 1854, Avon Lake, OH. ***Henry Lewis HILLIARD***, b. 3 Feb 1815, Hebron; d. 22 Oct 1853, Alto, Fond du Lac, WI; m. bef. 1838 in NY to *Malvina M. MILLER* (b. 1 Jan 1816, Duanesburg, Schenectady Co., NY; d. Oct 1889 in Waupun, Fond du Lac Co., WI); five children. ***Phebe Angeline HILLIARD***, b. 24 May 1817, Marlboro, Ulster, NY; d. btwn 1870-79, La Crosse, WI; m. Marlboro, Ulster Co., NY to *John SADDLEMIRE*. ***Joseph Warren HILLIARD***, b. 7 Aug 1819, Berne, NY; d. 22 Mar 1867, La Crosse, La Crosse, WI; m. 1 Dec 1847 to *Lorinda GRISWOLD (dau. of Luman and Margaret Marilla Griswold OP 1: 10-11, second wife of William Aldrich OP 3:5).* ***Valentine HILLIARD***, b. 9 Dec 1821, Berne, NY; d. 26 Dec 1864, Springfield, WI. ***Marion HILLIARD***, b. 28 Oct 1823, Berne, NY; d. possibly Davenport, NY; m. 1843, Davenport, Delaware Co., NY to *Edward FEAK*. ***Samantha Ann HILLIARD***, b. 15 Jan 1828, Berne, NY; m. *George W. ROBINSON* (b. c1820, England). Hillard and Daughters of the American Revolution, vol. 164, p. 200.

Father of William Silas Hilliard:

Town of Holland...The following is a list of the officers from 1866 to date:

1874...***Wm. HILLYARD***, *Ole W. JOHNSON*, *Isaac CLARK*, Constables.

1879...*P. VAN LOON*, ***William HILLIARD***, *Ole HALTER*, Constables.

History of La Crosse County, Wis., Chicago, Western Historical Society, 1881, p. 708. *(notice spelling of Hilliard in 1874)*

Sibling of William Silas Hilliard:

The State of Ohio, Cuyahoga County, ss. I hereby certify, that on the 1st day of December A. D. 1847, I duly solemnized the Marriage Contract between the said ***Joseph W. HILLYARD*** and ***Lorinda GRISWOLD***. N. S. Worden, Minister Gospel Marriage Record, Cuyahoga County, OH, vol. 4, p. 445. *(Their granddaughter is Frances Willard Jaycox, who is buried in Lot 62.)*

OP 1:7

Marker presumed for Otis Braman.

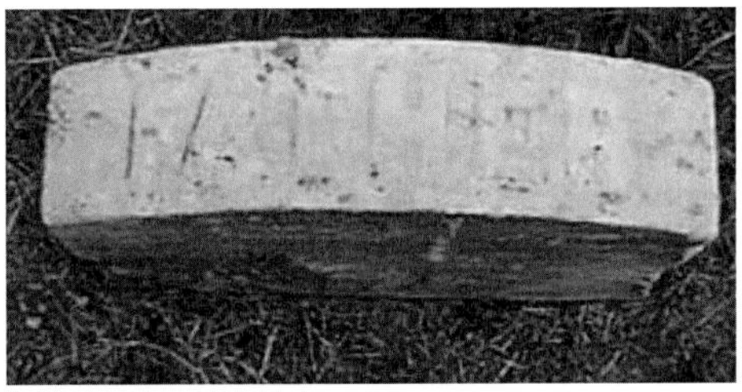

FATHER

OP 1:8 Braman Monument

OTIS BRAMAN
BORN
Oct 12., 1805
Died Oct 3, 1852(7)
BETSEY BRAMAN
Wife of
OTIS BRAMAN
Born Mar 14, 1807
Died July 4, 1848
BRAMAN

LOUISA
BORN
NOV 5, 1829
Died Aug 6, 1831(?)
JAMES
Born Apr 16, 1837 *(?)*
Died Feb 3, 1838
Children of
O&B BRAMAN

OP 1:8 **Otis Braman**

Otis Braman and Betsey Riley are the parents of Horace Braman (OP 2:9) and Lydia Braman Ware (Lot 4).

Otis BRAMAN, 44, farmer, b. NY, value of land $2250, ***David R.***, 21, farmer, ***Morris***, 18, farmer, ***Lydia***, 16, ***Elvira***, 14, ***H. A-ag***, 10 male, ***Adelia***, 5. All children b. Ohio. 1850 FC OH AVLR, p. 935, lines 6-12.

Otis BRAMAN bought land from the Conn. Land Company. Abram W. Foote, Foote Family Comprising the Genealogy and History of Nathaniel Foote, vol. II, p. 706.

Ancestors of Otis Braman:

I. ***Thomas BRAMAN***, b.1614 England; d. 1657/9, Taunton, Bristol, MA, m. before 1650 to ***Jane KINGSLEY*** (c1630/1633 in England); at least three sons, the youngest was Thomas. Linda Laird

II. ***Thomas BRAMAN***, b. 1649; d. 1709; m. 20 Jan 1685, Taunton to ***Hannah FISHER*** (b. 1 Feb 1666, Tauton, MA; d. 1714); ten children. Thomas came to Mass. with two or three brothers in 1652. Their second child was a son, Daniel. Laird

III. ***Daniel BRAMAN***, b. 13 Oct 1688; d. 1753-56, Taunton; m. 25 Nov 1714, Norton, Bristol, MA to ***Rachall CAMPBELL*** (b. 31 Jan 1692, Norton, dau. of *Sylvanus CAMPBELL* and *Mary LEONARD*); five children. They had a son, Daniel. Laird

IV. ***Daniel BRAMAN***, b. 13 Feb 1718, Norton; d. Nov 1, 1758, Norton; m. 22 Sep 1750, Norton to ***Bethiah WASHBURN*** (b. 24 May 1729, Kingston, Plymouth, MA; d. 22 Sep 1750, Norton, dau. of *Ichabod WASHBURN* and *Bethiah PHILLIPS*); four children. They had a son, Daniel. Laird

V. ***Daniel BRAMAN***, b. 17 Feb/Mar 1752, Norton; d. 18 Apr 1816; m. 28 Nov 1774, Norton to ***Silence CLAPP*** (b. 5 May 1755, Walpole, MA; d. Oct 8, 1822, dau. of *Seth CLAPP* and *Mary BULLARD*); fifteen children. The third child was Otis. Laird

VI. ***Otis BRAMAN***, b. Aug, 10, 1779 in Norton, Bristol, Mass.; farmer; d. Sept 17, 1844 in Carlisle, Franklin Co., OH; m. Jan 1, 1805 in Westport, Essex Co., NY to ***Lydia FELT*** (dau. of *Aaron FELT* (b. 1 Sept 1742, Lynn, Mass., d. July 1801, Temple, NH) and his first wife *Tabitha UPTON*, (b. 20 Mar 1745; d. 1789, Temple, NH) who married in Reading, Mass, 21 May 1766). Lydia was b. 21 Sept 1784, Temple Twp., Hillsboro, NH. Otis served in the War of 1812. Laird

Issue: ***Otis BRAMAN***, b. 20 Oct 1805 in Wadham's Mills, Essex, NY; d. Oct 2, 1857, Avon, Ohio; m. Oct 28, 1826 in Alexandria, NY to ***Betsey RILEY***, (d. 4 July 1849, Avon, OH). ***Silence BRAMAN***, b. Apr 5, 1807, Wadham's Mills, NY; d. Oct 4, 1853, Elyria, Ohio; m. Apr 5, 1831, Carlisle, Ohio to *Hiram HARRIS*, (b. 17 Oct 1796, Washington Co., NY; d. 11 June 1868, LaGrange, OH). ***Daniel BRAMAN***, b. Jan 31, 1809, Genesee, NY; d. Dec 8, 1882, Garden Valley, Wis.; m. May 6, 1834, Carlisle, Ohio to *Belinda FALKNER*, (b. 15 Aug 1814, Medina, OH, dau. of *Henry FALKNER* and *Frances THROCKMORTON* of Medina). ***Anson BRAMAN***, b. May 30, 1811, Bethany, Genesee, NY; d. Jan 14, 1886, Saluda, NC; m. Dec 24, 1835, Ohio to *Emeline VINCENT* (b. 10 Oct 1818, Berkshire Co., Mass.; dau. of *John T. VINCENT* and *Sally MARTIN*); nurseryman and fruit-grower; 5 children. ***Samantha BRAMAN***, b. Feb 26, 1813, NY; d. Oct 26, 1855, Ohio; m. as 2nd wife Dec 26, 1833, Ohio to *Henry Sedolphus ROCKWOOD* (b. June 30, 1809, Champion, Jefferson Co., NY, son of *David ROCKWOOD* and *Susanna GRIFFITH* of Boston, Mass.; druggist; m.3 *Cynthia BRAMAN*, sister of Samantha). ***Elvira BRAMAN***, b. Feb 24, 1815, Bethany, NY; d. Mar 1823, Genesee Co., NY. ***Jason Jarvis BRAMAN***, b. Jan 12, 1817, Bethany, NY; m.1 Jan 29, 1837, Bethany to *Phoebe SUTTON* (d. Feb 3, 1845 in Detroit, Mich.); m.2 Sept 17, 1857, Oregon to *C.E. DELAMATER* (b. Mar 14, 1837, Ohio, dau. of *John DELAMATER* and *Ellen FORSYTH*). He was a surgeon during the Civil War. ***Azubah BRAMAN***, b. Feb 3, 1819, Bethany, NY; m. April 16, 1850, Elyria, Ohio to *Edson Sheldon FRARY* (b. Dec 26, 1820, Dorset, VT; d. May 9, 1862 Jackson, Mich.; builder; son of *Sheldon FRARY* and *Maria UNDERHILL* of Olmsted, Ohio). ***Cynthia BRAMAN***, b. Apr 13, 1821; m. Mar. 1857 in Detroit, Mich. to *ROCKWOOD*, deceased sister's husband. ***Emeline BRAMAN***, b. Feb 26, 1825, NY/Avon, Ohio; m. Oct 27, 1868, Coldwater, Mich. to *Reuben Clinton AMES* (b. Nov 6, 1819, Potsdam, NY, son of *Willard AMES* and *Amy FERRIS* of Potsdam, farmer); resided Litchfield, Mich. ***Charles BRAMAN***, b. Aug 10, 1827, NY/Ohio; d. May 21, 1847, Cassville, Wis. John E. Morris, The Felt Genealogy, 1893 and Laird.

VII. *Otis BRAMAN*, b. 20 Oct 1805, (Wadham's Mills, Essex Co.), NY; m. *Betsy RILEY*; d. 1857. Laird and (Mary Jane Turner)

Parents of Otis Braman:

BRAMAN Otis, d Sept 17, 1844 (2), 65 y; *Lydia*, wife, d. Sept 14, 1844, age 60 y. Tombstone inscription, LaPorte Cemetery, Carlisle Twp., OH.

Otis BRAMAN: Males: 2 under 10, 2: 10 yrs-15, 1: 16-18 yrs., 2: 18-26, 1: 26-45 yrs., 1: 45 and older, Females: 3 under 6 yrs., 1: 10-15 yrs., 1: 16-26 yrs. 3 involved in agriculture. 1820 FC NY Genesee County, Leicester Twp., p. 51.

Lydia FELT BRAMAN, mother of ***Otis BRAMAN***, descends from ***George FELT*** who was found in Charlestown, Massachusetts in 1633. He was born in 1601, and the tradition relates that he came to America with *ENDICOTT* who arrived in September, 1628. There is testimony of George Felt himself that the year of his advent in this town was that already named, for in 1681 he describes himself as about 80 years of age, and testifies "that the town of Charlestown gave him an house plott of two acres of land lying in the common on the left hand as you go to Cambridge betwixt the ground that was *Rice MORRISSES* and *GOBLE'S*, which is now in the hands of *Thomas WELCH Senr.*, which plott was given him about forty-eight years since."

The wife of George Felt was ***Elizabeth***, daughter of widow ***Prudence WILKINSON***, whose home was in Charlestown. John E. Morris, The Felt Genealogy, 1893, p. 9. *The Felt Genealogy is extremely well documented.*

Sibling of Otis Braman:

BRAMAN, Anson, 59, nurseryman, value of real estate $10000, person estate $3500, b. New York; ***Emeline***, 50, b. Mass.; ***Jeanette***, 25, at home, b. Ohio; ***Emily***, 22, at home, b. Ohio. 1870 FC Lorain Co., Elyria Village, Elyria Township, family 254, p. 485, lines. 4-7.

Son of Anson:

William A. BRAMAN. Few men exercised a stronger and wider influence in the affairs of Lorain County than the late William A. Braman, who was in his sixty-ninth year when he died at Elyria April 12, 1905. In early life hard work and self-reliance were his portion, but in later years he was a vigorous force in the republican party of Lorain County, was both broad minded and practical in promoting everything good in his home city, and was highly successful in business, being president of Elyria Savings and Banking Company at the time of his death.

He was born in Carlisle Township of Lorain County, October 24, 1836. His Scotch ancestors came to America about 1700, locating in Boston, and several of them were revolutionary soldiers and the family was represented in the War of 1812. One characteristic which has persisted through a number of generations is splendid physical development. Mr. Braman himself stood six feet three inches in height, and it is said that his grandfather ***(Otis BRAMAN)*** and two brothers and two sisters were each six feet or more in height. Grandfather Braman was one of the pioneer settlers in Lorain County, coming from Genesee County, New York, to Avon Township in 1822. William A. Braman was the son of ***Anson*** *(brother of Otis, this lot)* and ***Emeline (VINCENT) BRAMAN***. His father was born in Genesee County, New York, May 30, 1811, grew up partly in Avon Township, and for many years was a farmer and nurseryman in Carlisle Township. He was in the nursery business at Elyria from 1855 to 1872, and then removed to Michigan. *Emeline VINCENT* was born in Massachusetts October 8, 1818, and had come with her parents in 1834 to Carlisle Township, where she was married the following year.

...Apparently everything he undertook proved successful...He taught country school in order to pursue advanced studies in higher institutions. In 1864 he began dealing in live stock, and in 1870, associated with *Mr. BOYNTON*, he took up the cheese business. In the spring of 1874 he was one of the organizers of the firm of Braman, Horr & Warner, manufacturers and general dealers in butter and cheese. This business became one of the most extensive of its kind in Northern Ohio.... In 1890 a stock company was organized by leading republicans in Elyria and Lorain County to purchase the Elyria Republican, which it was determined should become a temperance republican paper, true to the best interests of the party and in favor of temperance and moral interest. The directors of this company insisted upon Mr. Braman taking the position of editor, though he was without practical experience in that profession. He took the position at first only temporarily, but was unable to relinquish it for eight years, and made of it a journal notable for its high ground and standards as a republican paper and an exponent of temperance and every other reform. He was not only an able editor but made the Republican self-supporting financially.

In later years Mr. Braman was best known as a banker. For twenty years or more he was a director in The Savings Deposit Bank Company, for several years was vice president, and also president of The First National Bank of Lorain, and was a director of The Penfield Avenue Savings Bank at Lorain from its organization in 1895. Subsequently his banking interests were concentrated in the Elyria Savings & Banking Company, of which he was president.

The ideals of useful citizenship were seldom better exemplified than in the career of William A. Braman. Always with credit he filled various positions of responsibility and honor. Personally he was dignified in his demeanor, possessed an impressive personality, and in everything was thoroughly American and patriotic. It was truthfully said of him that he was a better American than he was a partisan.

In politics his father had been an old line democrat, but in spite of that affiliation Mr. Braman had gone with the new republican party in 1856 and voted for *John C. FREMONT*. William A. Braman came to manhood about the time the republican party was organized and about the time the great national crisis was evolved between the North and the South. Like many others he was influenced by an early reading of Uncle Tom's Cabin, and he was an ardent boy partisan of Fremont in 1856. In 1860 he cast his first vote for *Abraham LINCOLN*, and thereafter for more than forty years was a champion of the best in the grand old party *(GOP)*. While living in his home Township of Carlisle he filled most of the township offices, trustee, clerk, treasurer, and at the age of thirty-one was appointed county commissioner for one year. In 1877 he was elected county treasurer by a majority of 2,800, the largest given to anyone on the ticket. He filled that place with fidelity and efficiency for two terms of two years each, receiving a nomination without opposition. In 1887 he was nominated and elected to the State Legislature, in which he served two terms. He was a member of the Finance Committee in both sessions of the Legislature, and among other things established the provision that each state institution should be regularly visited and inspected by a legislative committee. While in the Legislature he also showed himself an effective force in behalf of temperance reform. It was largely due to his efforts that the township local option law was passed and also the Sunday law, prohibiting sale of liquor on Sunday. Mr. Braman was one of the strongest supporters of *Major MCKINLEY* in his first nomination for governor of Ohio, and did some effective work in consolidating the party on that candidate. For many years Mr. Braman was president of the Lorain County Humane Society, and though an intensely practical and busy man, the influences of humanitarianism were always guiding factors with him. For many years he was a member of the city council at Elyria, and was a trustee of the local schools for nineteen years. He was president seven years of the Lorain County Agricultural Society and for three years was president for the Farmers Institute.

April 27, 1865, he was married to ***Miss Sophia E. PATTERSON***, daughter of *Hiram PATTERSON*. Mrs. Braman is still living in Elyria. To their marriage were born three children, ***Theodore W.***, who was born in 1867, and is now deceased; ***Charles M.***, born in 1869; and ***Belle Louise***. Standard History of Lorain Co., Ohio, vol. II, pp. 643-644.

OP 1:8 Betsey Riley Braman

Children of Otis and Betsey Braman:

The State of Ohio, Cuyahoga County, ss. I Certify that on the 10th day of Sept 1860 ***Mr. David R. BRAMAN*** and ***Miss Elizabeth W. ALDRICH*** were by me legally joined in Marriage. S.W. Adams Clergyman Marriage Record, Cuyahoga County, OH, vol. 10, p. 91.

David BRAMAN, [d. 4 Oct 1909]; {res. Kansas}]; m. 10 Sept 1860 to ***Elizabeth Winsor ALDRICH***, (dau. of *Aaron ALDRICH III* and *Elizabeth WINSOR (OP 4:1);* b. 12 Sept 1832, Dover; [d. 4 Oct 1909]). George H. Drake, "Aldrich Family - Thirteen Generation Chart," p. 1, 9, 10, 12; [Gertrude Aldrich Barker Rose, "Genealogy of the Aldrich Family," pp. 8, 9]; {Women of the Western Reserve Prior to 1840} and Ima Aldrich Slaby.

BRAMAN, D.R., 41, farmer, value of real estate $16,800, personal property $1600, b. Ohio; ***Elisabeth***, 36, K.H. *(Keeping House)*, b. Ohio; ***NESBITT, W.J.***, 14, b. Ohio; ***NESBITT, Gerome***, 12, b. Ohio; ***NESBITT, Annie E.***, 5, b. Ohio. 1870 FC OH CYDO p. 257, dwelling 280, lines 25-29.

JOHNSTON, Charles, 45? Lawyer.....***BRAMAN, Alvira***, 35, Domestic, value of personal property $200, b. Ohio; ***BRAMAN, Adelia***, 25, Dress Maker, value of personal property $200, b. Ohio... 1870 FC OH Lorain, Elyria, p. 486, dwelling 245, lines 32-39.

NEVINS, Fred, 38, Laborer, b. Ohio?, fr. b. NY, mo. b. NY; ***Almira***, 43, Keeping House, b. Ohio, fr. b. NY, mo. b. NY; ***BRAMAN, Adelia***, 33, single, Dressmaker, b. Ohio, fr. b. NY, mo. b. NY. 1880 FC OH Lorain Co., Elyria, p. 454C, lines 5-7, house 267.

Adelia BRAMAN, 65, head, single, b. Ohio, parents b. NY, nurse, employer: general. East Avenue. 1910 FC OH Lorain Co., Elyria, ED. 111, p. 4, house 49.

Adelia B. BRAMAN, 1844-1916; ***Alvira BRAMAN NEVINS***, 1835-1910; ***Frederick B. NEVINS***, 1841-1911. Also buried in this cemetery: *NEVINS William J.*, 1835-1908; *Thirza F.*, 1839-1909. Ridgelawn Cemetery, Elyria, Lorain Co., OH.

OP 1:8 Louisa Braman

Louisa BRAMAN, daughter of ***Otis*** and ***Betsey BRAMAN***; b. Nov. 5, 1829; d. Aug 6, 1831 *(year of death unclear)*. Cemetery marker.

OP 1:8 James Braman

James BRAMAN, son of ***Otis*** and ***Betsey BRAMAN***; b. Apr 16, 1837 *(year unclear)*; d. Feb 3, 1838. Cemetery marker

OP 1:9

Marker presumed for Betsey Braman.

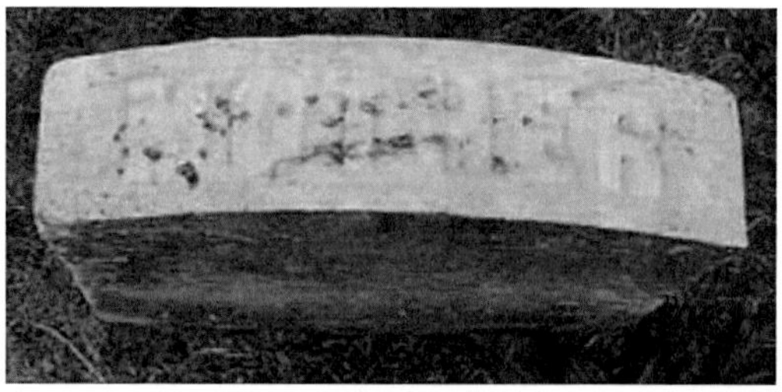

MOTHER

OP 1:10 **Luman Griswold**

LUMON GRISWOLD
DIED
JUNE 8, 1845
Aged 45 y. 10 d.

Luman Griswold is the former husband of Margaret Smith Griswold Eddy, in the next plot. Their son, Luman Loami Griswold is buried with his son in OP 2:4.

The spelling of Luman is inconsistent throughout the records, frequently being spelled Lumon. It is thought that Luman is correct.

Luman GRISWOLD; b. 28 May 1799, the son of ***David GRISWOLD,*** (b. 1 Oct 1765, Sharon Lithchfield, CT; d. prob. 1840-50, Orange Twp., Cuyahoga County, OH) and ***Polly***. Luman m. ***Margaret Marilla SMITH***, *(OP 1:11)* 22 Nov 1826, Geauga County, OH; d. 8 June 1845 in Lorain County, OH. Karen Boas

Will of Luman Griswold:

To all people whom it may concern. Know ye that I, ***Luman GRISWOLD*** of Avon township Linn County State of Ohio, being weak in body but of sound mind & memory by the grace of God do hereby make & publish this my last will & testament as follows (?) after any just & honest debts are all paid I do hereby give & bequest all that remains of my estate both real & personal of every (name) and nature whatsoever or wherever it may be found unto *William SADLER (OP 3: 13)* and *Kaleb EDDY (Caleb Eddy, OP 2: 6)* of Dover township Cuyahoga County State aforesaid in trust with them for the use & benefit of my beloved wife & children to be by them appropriated for the purchase of land at their discretion to make a home for my family & to be the property of my wife as long as she remains my widow in case of marriage or at her decease to be equally divided among my surviving children. And further more I the testator do hereby constitute and appoint the said William Sadler and Kaleb Eddy the sole & only executors of this my last will & Testament. In testimony whereof I have hereunto set my hand and seal this thirty first day of May A.D. one thousand eight hundred & forty five. Luman Griswold. Will provided by Carrie A. Stave.

Ancestors of Luman Griswold:

I. ***Thomas GRESWOLD,*** b. about 1562, Solihull, Warwick, England; m. 1587, ***Elizabeth SHUCKBURGH*** (b. about 1565; d. after 1602 Tanworth-in-Arde, Warwick, England). *This line is traced back to c1041 in Kennilworth, Warwick, England.* Robert L. French and Esther G. French, The Greswolde Family: 12 Generations in England.

II. ***Edward GRESWOLD,*** chr. 5 Aug 1594, Tanworth, Warwick, England; d. 20 Aug 1633, Cubbington, Warwick, England; m. 20 May 1618 Draytron, Oxford, England to ***Margaret BLENCOE*** (b. about 1590, Merston, Northants, England; d. 16 June 1633, Cubbington). French and French.

III. ***Michael GRISWOLD,*** b. about 1620, Cubbington; d. 26 Sept 1684, Wethersfield, Hartford Co., CT; m. 1645 in Wethersfield to ***Anne***. Esther Griswold French and Robert Lewis French, The Griswold Family, The First Five Generations in America.

The Griswold Family Association owns and maintains an historic house in Wethersfield, Connecticut. The original house was owned by ***Michael GRISWOLD***; most of the house as it exists today was constructed in 1730 by his son, ***Michael***. Griswold Family Association, Home Page, <http://www.griswoldfamily.org/>, (cited 12 July 2004).

IV. ***Jacob GRISWOLD,*** b. 15 Apr 1660, Wethersfield; d. 22 July1737, Wethersfield; m. 10 Dec 1685, Wethersfield to ***Mary Frances WRIGHT*** (b. 15 Apr 1665, Wethersfield; d. 25 Apr 1735, Wethersfield). French and French, The Griswold Family, The First Five Generations in America.

V. ***Ephraim GRISWOLD,*** b. 23 Sept 1704, Wethersfield; d. Spencertown, Columbia, NY; m. 19 Dec 1726, East Haddam, CT to ***Mehitable RILEY*** (b. 6 Mar 1702/03), divorced 18 Aug 1746. French and French, The Griswold Family, The First Five Generations in America.

VI. ***Azariah GRISWOLD***, b. 10 Sept 1727, East Haddam, CT; d. after 1820, Cuy. Co., OH; m. 18 Feb 1753, Sharon, Litchfield, CT to ***Olive BROWN***. French and French, The Griswold Family, The First Five Generations in America.

VII. ***David GRISWOLD***, b. 1 Oct 1765, Sharon, Lithchfield, CT; d. after 1820 (source: Griswold Family Association), prob. 1840-50 (source: Karen Boas), Orange Twp., Cuyahoga County, OH); m. ***Polly PARKER*** *(BAKER)* (b. 24 May 1769, CT; dau. of ***Matthew PARKER*** (b. 1712, d. 1800) and ***Edith HANES*** (b. 1723, d. 1796); d. after 1849, OH). French and French, The Griswold Family, The First Five Generations in America.

David GRISWOLD, Male: 0-10 yrs.: 1, 10-16 yrs.: 1, 45+ yrs.: 1, Females: 10-16 yrs.: 1, 16-26 yrs.: 1. 1820 FC OH Cuyahoga Co., Orange Twp.

The following was written about Luman's mother, Polly Griswold, which relates information about his childhood.

Mrs. David GRISWOLD (Polly BAKER) was married in 1787 and emigrated from the state of Vermont, settling in Orange in 1816, on what is now the *James BELL* farm near Chagrin river. She is believed to have been *Mrs. (Serenus) BURNETT'S* first white neighbor.

Having built their log house, she, with her husband, proceeded to prepare a place for the planting of their first crop. Having felled the trees and cleared off the brush they, with an ax, made holes in the ground, into which they dropped kernels of corn, pressing it to place with the foot. Tradition says that this primitive method of preparing a seed bed proved eminently successful, and the virgin soil returned an abundant harvest.

Time never hung heavily on the hands of this pioneer wife and mother. The responsibility of clothing the family rested upon her. She carded, spun, wove and colored the wool and flax grown upon their own farm, using the bark, berries and leaves of certain trees and shrubs for dye-stuffs, supplemented by the indispensable blue dye-tub. Butternut and walnut barks made a durable if not handsome color for men and boys wear; white oak, chestnut and the berries of sumac made lighter shades for dresses and aprons for mother and the girls.

After spinning and weaving came the cutting and making, and each housemother was her own dressmaker and tailoress. Mrs. Griswold often sewed late into the night by the light of the hickory bark fire, while the wolves kept noisy vigil just outside. Three sons and three daughters grew under her loving care and guidance, and went out from that lowly house to do their appointed work in the world's great battlefield. Memorial to the Pioneer Women of the Western Reserve, Orange Township, *(Cuyahoga County, Ohio),*1897, pp. 596-597.

Siblings of Luman Griswold:

David GRISWOLD, b. July 3, 1794; d. Mar 28, 1860; bur. Garfield Cemetery, Sheffield Twp. Lorain, Co., OH; m. 30 Dec 1829 to ***Betsy D. HUTCHINS*** (dau. of *Moses* and *Sarah HUTCHINS* and half sister of *Margaret Marilla SMITH*). ***Henry GRISWOLD*** m. *Diena*. ***James GRISWOLD. Edith GRISWOLD*** m. *HULBERT*. ***Betsy GRISWOLD*** m. *McFARLAND*. ***Mary GRISWOLD*** m. *SMITH*. Karen Boas

David GRISWOLD, b. July3, 1791(4); d. Mar 28, 1860. Lot A, row 2. Cemetery records for David B. Griswold. Garfield Cemetery, Sheffield Twp., Lorain County, OH. Sheffield City Hall, Sheffield, OH (next to cemetery), read by Catherine Burke Flament and Genealogical Workshops of the Lorain County Historical Society, Cemetery Inscriptions of Lorain County, Ohio 1980, Garfield Cemetery, p. 432.

Children of Luman Griswold and Margaret Marilla Smith:

Lorinda GRISWOLD, b. 5 June 1829; d. 17 Jan 1895, bur. Holman, Wisconsin with her first husband and children; m. 1 Dec 1847, Cuyahoga Co. O. [MR 4 445] to *Joseph Warren HILLIARD* (son of *William HILLIARD* and *Elizabeth LEWIS*, brother of *William S. HILLIARD OP 1: 6*; b. 7 Aug 1819, Berne, Albany Co., NY; d. 22 March 1867, LaCrosse Co., WI); m.2 21 Jan 1878 to *William ALDRICH (OP 3:5)*. ***Lucy GRISWOLD*** m. *Asa SADLER (son of William SADLER and Elizabeth TRYON, OP 3:12)*. ***Rosina GRISWOLD*** m. *Caleb Reynolds EDDY (son of Caleb EDDY who would become Margaret's second husband after Luman's death OP 2:6-7, their children bur. 2:5, see lot information)*. ***Rosetta GRISWOLD*** m. *Ed DAILY*. ***Orilla GRISWOLD*** m. *Oliver CARTER*. ***Malinda GRISWOLD*** m. *Isaac CASE (son of Moses CASE OP 6:2)*. ***Luman Loami GRISWOLD*** *(OP 2:4)*. ***Margaret Marilla GRISWOLD*** m. *Frank FARNSWORTH*. All children b. Orange Twp., Cuyahoga County, OH. Karen Boas, Victor Grant Hillard, Jr. and Marriage Certificate.

Children of Lorinda Griswold and Joseph Warren Hilliard:

William Luman HILLIARD, b. 19 Sept 1848, Sheffield {Avon Lake}, Lorain Co., OH; d. 5 Sept 1937, Fosston, Polk Co., MN; m. 22 Feb 1868, La Crosse, La Crosse, WI to *Mary Ophelia LOCKMAN* (b. 2 July1850, La Crosse; d. 4 Feb 1930, Lengby, Polk Co., MN). ***Henry Cephas*** *(called Cephas)* ***HILLIARD***, b. 25 Nov 1849, Sheffield; d. 27 Mar 1872, LaCrosse Co., WI; unmarried. ***Charles*** *(Charlie or Charley)* ***Edward HILLIARD***, b. 28 Nov 1850, Sheffield; d. 10 Feb 1941, Lengby, Polk Co., MN; m. 13 June 1869, LaCrosse, LaCrosse Co., WI to *Matilda M. HEATH* (b. 9 Apr 1854, Marengo, McHenry Co., IL; d. 9 Apr 1854, Marengo). ***Joseph Chipman HILLIARD***, b. 5 Jan 1852, Sheffield; death unknown, possibly Arizona. ***Margaret Elizabeth*** *(Lizzie)* ***HILLIARD***, b. Aug 1854 Sheffield, m. *William E. BENNETT* (b. Feb 1850, WI). ***Ida Lorinda HILLIARD***, b. 9 Sept 1855 Sheffield; m. *James JAYCOX (see Lot 62)*. ***George Washington HILLIARD***, b. 22 Feb 1858, LaCrosse; d. 22 July 1870, LaCrosse Co., [struck by lightning]. ***John Wesley*** *(Wesley)* ***HILLIARD***, b. July1859, LaCrosse; d. 1948, Brainerd, Crow Wing Co., MN; m. before 1890, MN to *Lillie May HUSTIS* (b. 21 Nov 1869, MN). ***Anna*** *(Annie)* ***Serelda HILLIARD***, b. 21 Mar 1861, LaCrosse; d. c. 1965, possibly [CA] or {Butte, Jefferson, MT}; m. 12 July1887 to *Howard E. GILL*. He deserted the family when the children were young. ***Herbert Warren HILLIARD***, b. 17 June 1862, LaCrosse; d. Aug 1862 LaCrosse. [Karen Boas] and {Victor Grant Hilliard, Jr.}, *information agreed unless indicated.*

The State of Ohio, Cuyahoga County, ss. I Certify that on the 14th day of September 1845 ***Mr. Asa SADDLER*** and ***Miss Lucy GRISWOLD*** were by me legally joined in marriage. Marriage Record, Cuyahoga County, OH, vol. 4, p. 308.

Oliver CARTER, 27, Cabinet Maker, b. New York; ***Orilla***, 17, b. New York. 1850 FC OH LRAV p. 456, lines 24-25, house 1010.

Melinda GRISWOLD *was the third wife of* ***Isaac CASE***, *son of* ***Moses*** *(OP 6:4)*.

Melinda CASE, 44, Keeping house, b. Ohio, fr. b. Vt., mo. Canada; ***Lilly***, 21, daughter, Teaching school, b. Ohio; ***Hurley***, 19, son, Farming, b. Ohio; ***Edna***, 7, daughter, b. Ohio; ***Newton***, 33, son, Sailor, b. Ohio. 1880 FC OH Lorain Co., Sheffield, p. 6A, lines 46-50.

Melinda CASE, d. Feb 15, 1917, 206 Woodland, Oberlin, Lorain Co., Ohio, of Pneumonia; widowed; b. March 10, 1836, Solon, Ohio to ***Luman GRISWOLD***, b. U.S. and ***Margaret SMITH***, b. U.S.; 80 yrs. 11 mos. 5 ds.; undertaker Allen & Hayden, Oberlin, bur. Sheffield T.P., Lorain Co.; informant Mrs. L.C. Cuyler, 206 Woodland Ave. Ohio Certificate of Death, Division of Vital Statistics, 1917, certif. 11948.

CASE Isaac L., Jan 25, 1819 - May 7, 1876. ***Malinda C. GRISWOLD*** wife of ***Isaac CASE*** 1836 - 1917; ***Nina Lorett***, dau. IL&MC, d May 7, 1868, 6y 18d; ***Edna***, 1873 - 1901. Lot owned by ***David GRISWOLD***. Lot A, row 2, Garfield Cemetery, Sheffield Twp., Lorain County, OH. Sheffield City Hall, Sheffield, OH; inscriptions read by Catherine

Burke Flament and Genealogical Workshops of the Lorain County Historical Society, Cemetery Inscriptions of Lorain County, Ohio 1980, Garfield Cemetery, p. 432.

Melinda Case, d. pneumonia, Oberlin, funeral director Allen & Hayden, Oberlin, Permit No. 8, primary district 755, interment 2-17-1917. Garfield Cemetery, Sheffield Twp., Lorain County, OH. Sheffield City Hall, Sheffield, OH. *Isaac Case is the son of Moses Case, see OP 6:4 for additional information.*

The State of Ohio, Cuyahoga County, ss. I certify that on the 24th day of December 1861 ***Mr. Charles H. FARNSWORTH*** and ***Miss Marilla M. GRISWOLD*** were by me legally joined in marriage. L. Smith, Clergyman. Marriage Record, Cuyahoga County, OH, vol. 10, p. 256.

A JUST REWARD

Awaited the Coming of Hicksville's Lady, Mrs. M.M. Farnsworth - Death was Sudden but She was Ready

Photograph of Mrs. Farnsworth that was not clear enough to reproduce.

"I have fought a good fight" are Biblical words so appropriate to the parting of ***Mrs. M.M. FARNSWORTH*** from her friends last Thursday morning as "Welcome thou good and faithful servant," greeted her on yonder side of Jordan.

Death, although it came quickly found this highly respected lady ready. She had finished her course, she had kept the faith, hence it follows that there awaited her coming a just reward.

Words fail in paying tribute to her. The large representative audience at the M. E. church Sunday afternoon was the best tribute to her. Young and old gathered to take a parting look at the form of Mother Farnsworth. Already the impress of her life had been stamped on theirs and because of that unseen tie that binds hundreds braved the elements to pay silent homage to her.

Rev. D.G. Hall, her pastor, conducted the service and eulogized her in a brief but appropriate address. *Attorney L.E. GRIFFIN* read the obituary prepared by himself and so full of good things, and true, too, that it is reproduced here herewith in its entirety out of respect for the honored dead and as an incentive to those on this side of the silent waters.

Mention of the music must be made. The choir sang very sweetly but the ladies quartet comprised of *Misses Nina PHILLIPS* and *Mary PETTIT* and *Mesdames G.D. SIMMONS* and *J.W. WRIGHT* touched the hearts of those who mourn in their beautiful selection so well rendered.

Present also was a male quartette from Milford township, young men who are sons of former pupils of the deceased, whose songs in the past had found lodging in the soul of the departed and by request they sang two numbers. They were *Messrs. Clarence WEISS, Daniel SCHOTT, Arthur KRILL* and *George KRILL.*

Many were present from Milford, the former home of Mother Farnsworth.

The following account of the life of the deceased carefully edited by Mr. Griffin is fraught with interesting facts and words of commendation. Read it.

Margaret Marilla Farnsworth was born in Lorain county, Ohio, June 5, 1843, and died at her home in Hicksville, early Thursday morning, February 12, 1914, after an illness of but a few hours, aged 70 years, 8 months and 7 days.

She is survived by the aged husband, ***Francis O. FARNSWORTH***, three sons and their families and one sister. The sons are ***William F.***, residing in Allegan county, Michigan, ***Luman O.***, residing at Paulding, Ohio and ***Arthur G.***, residing at Auburn, Indiana. The grandchildren of the three families of her sons number ten and the sons and their families are all present.

Mrs. Farnsworth, lovingly known as "Mother" Farnsworth by so many, was the youngest of a family of eight children of ***Luman*** and ***Margaret GRISWOLD***. She never knew the tender care of a father, for he died when she was but two years old and the burden of the large family was bravely assumed by the mother.

Speaking of her own early life, Mrs. Farnsworth once wrote, "I early learned to suffer and be strong, to labor hard and be cheerful, to be tired and keep sweet.

"When seven years of age, at a time when most little ones are keeping house, with their dolls, I had begun the practical duties of life and at that tender age was earning my board, and in all my after life my feet have trod the rugged road of the toiler."

Her education was obtained in the public schools of Lorain county where she made such progress that after a two year teacher's course at Berea college, at the age of 15 years, she came to Defiance county and began her work as a teacher in the public schools.

She was married to ***Charles FARNSWORTH*** of Milford township, this county, in 1860, and a year later he hearkened to the call of his country for troops to suppress the rebellion of the South, and enlisted in Co. F, 111th O. V. I. and went to the fields of battle with the gallant boys of that company, most of whom were from the western townships of this county.

He never returned to his young bride for death claimed him as a result of exposure and sickness, near Murfreesboro, Tenn.; in the year 1862. In after years the surviving members of Co., F., 11th O. V. I., in sympathy with her bereavement and in honor of the dead, elected her an honorary member of their ranks.

Thus, at the very threshold of her young life, a girl of but 18 years, she was bereft of the husband of her first love.

After a widowhood of more than four years, and after the close of the war, on New Years day 1867, she married Francis O. Farnsworth, brother of her deceased husband, and to this union was born the three sons that survive.

She united with the M.E. church when but ten years old and lived a devoted Christian life during all of the years that followed, being an active worker in her younger days in the missionary society and the other women's organizations of the church. In the home the family altar was maintained and at the meal time the blessing was asked, and a Godly example was not only set to her own household but before all with whom she was associated.

The activities of her life work were in the home, in the public schools, in the church and its societies, in the G.A.R. and W.R.C., on the public platform and elsewhere as an advocate of temperance reforms and measures, and along all those other avenues of endeavor that engage the attention of good women.

She was not only a teacher in the public schools of this county before her marriage but she continued to teach during her widowhood and after her second marriage, teaching in all, in the public schools of this county, sixty-one terms of school.

Six years of teaching was in the village schools of Hicksville and with the exception of two terms taught at Sherwood, all her school work was done in the townships of Farmer, Milford and Hicksville.

She was known as one of the best loved and most successful teachers of her time, and in the schools which she taught nearly 2000 different pupils were under her influence and tuition. It was during her teaching in the public schools of Hicksville that a medal was given to her and to the pupils of her room, by the judges of school work exhibited at the Ohio Centennial celebration, held in Columbus.

She was one of the pioneer temperance workers and advocates, not only of this vicinity, but of Ohio, and enlisted in that cause at a time when all who were enlisted in it were not only deemed to be fanatics, but were branded as such.

Her enlistment in the cause of temperance and the abolition not only of the open saloon, but as well of the whisky jug from the harvest field, a half century ago, was at a time when the movement was not only unpopular but its success was looked upon as only the stream of idealists and little notice was taken of it as it was thought to be doomed to failure and defeat.

Her advocacy of temperance and temperance reforms and measures was not confined to the lecture platform at home and abroad, but was carried on through the public press and through periodicals devoted to that reforms, and to this work she devoted much time and energy.

Her stand upon this great moral question brought her into association with many of the great leaders of the movement in the state and nation and brought her many calls from far and near for addresses and lectures and it is a matter of common knowledge that *Mother (Eliza Daniel) STEWART*, one of the great world leaders and factors in the temperance cause, spent the last five years of her life in the home of Mrs. Farnsworth and was assisted by her in the completion of Mother Stuart's "Memoirs of the Crusade."

For nearly a score of years she was president of the Defiance County W.C.T.U. and was also president for a number of years of its local organization. For a time she was district organizer for that society, and while such, organized many local unions, held many meetings and conventions and devoted much time to the temperance cause.

It was a great source of pride and satisfaction to her life to witness the partial triumph of the cause of temperance for which she and her associates had so long striven and prayed and to realize that the heart and intelligence and conscience of the whole nation has been so educated and uplifted that the handwriting is already appearing upon the walls of the banquet chamber of King Alcohol, announcing that the days of the open saloon are numbered.

And it is to her efforts and the efforts of such as she and to their prayers and their tears and struggles, that the present attitude of this nation upon this question is attributable.

She was the prime mover in the organization of the Old 'Settlers' Society of the Maumee Valley, of which she was the honored president at the time of her death. She formulated and wrote its constitution and bylaws and from the date of its organization spent much time in the compilation of its records, the enrollment of members, supervising and arranging for its annual gatherings and doing all things so necessary to be done for its success and welfare. At its last annual meeting, held last August at the fair ground in this city, it was a matter of very keen regret and disappointment not only to her but to all its membership, that she was not able to attend, and although she was absent in body, the worth and esteem in which she was held by her old time friends, was evidenced by the fact that she was unanimously re-elected president for another year.

She was not only a public speaker upon the subject of temperance and kindred subjects, but her ability and merit were recognized by the state of Ohio, in her selection and employment by its Agriculture Department, as one of its lecturers before the Farmers' Institute of the state during the year of 1910. As a writer it may be said of her that she was the author of many poems upon differing and varying subjects, and of merit and poetic beauty.

For more than a half century, this woman has resided in the township of Hicksville and Milford and during that whole time, she has been a positive, inspiring, courageous and honored factor and leader of all those forces and movements and organizations and influences that have to do with the betterment of mankind and the moral and spiritual uplift of her fellowman.

I think that I do no injustice to any when I say that taking it all in all, for more than a half century the blessed influence of her life has touched more lives with the radiance of its blessing than the life of any other woman who has lived in our midst during that period.

The impress of her noble character has been left upon hundreds and hundreds of young lives that came under her influence and teaching and which have since budded into manhood and womanhood, uplifted by the inspiration of her teachings and example, and who, in turn, have imparted the good influences and teachings to their children and thus a progressive series of noble impulses, lofty ambitions and pure and Christian characters has been projected, the Godly influence of which only eternity can tell.

This is the influence and power of a good and pure life and this is doubly the influence and power of her life.

I have marveled at the scope of the accomplishments and work of this woman. The mother of three children, who have all been born, cared for and nurtured by herself during these years of her life's activity, and who have all testified to me that no hired nurse ever put them to bed or took their good-night kiss or heard their evening prayers, has yet been found time aside from her domestic ties and cares and duties, to accomplish the wonderful things that she did accomplish.

Her death, like her life, was without complaint. Not a word of fear, not a tremor. She was prepared. Undetermined newspaper, Hicksville, Ohio, Thursday, February 19, 1914. Provided by the Defiance Public Library from an obituary booklet.

FARNSWORTH, Charles F., Private, 22 yrs., entered service Aug. 13, 1862, period of service 3 yrs., d. March 27, 1863, at Murfreesboro, Tenn. Official Roster of the Soldiers in the War of the Rebellion (Civil War), Co. F., 111th Regiment Ohio Volunteer Infantry, p. 61.

OP 1:11 Margaret Smith Griswold Eddy

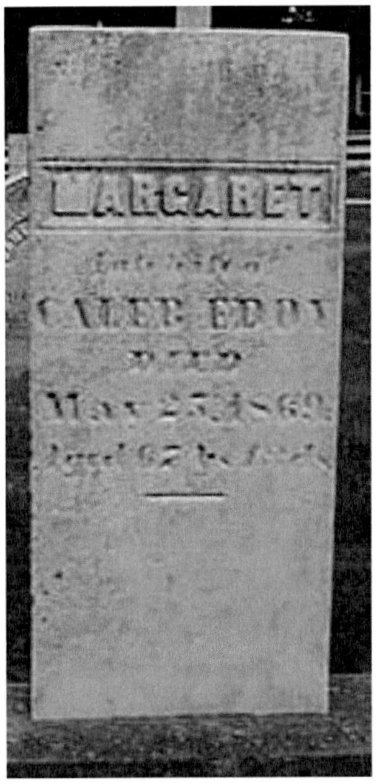

MARGARET
late wife of
CALEB EDDY
DIED
May 25, 1869
Aged 67 ys. 13d.

Margaret was first married to Luman Griswold above. Their son, Luman Loami Griswold is buried with his son in OP 2:4.

Margaret Marilla SMITH, b. 12 May 1802 in Quebec, Canada, previously called Eastern or Lower Canada; dau. of ___***SMITH*** and ***Sarah*** (Sarah m.2 *Moses HUTCHINS*, fought in the Revolutionary War, d. mid 1830's, Geauga Co., OH), d. mid 1830 in Geauga, Co., OH; m.1 ***Luman GRISWOLD***, (*OP 1:10*) 22 Nov 1826 in Geauga County, OH. They had eight children, seven daughters and one son. Margaret m.2 ***Caleb EDDY*** *(OP 2:6);* she d. 25 May 1869 in North Dover, OH. Caleb Eddy's son, ***Caleb Reynolds EDDY***, was married to Margaret's daughter ***Rosina***.

Her house was moved to 29506 Osborn Road. Karen Boas

References to some of Margaret's children from her first marriage to Luman GRISWOLD: ***Malinda C. GRISWOLD***, b. c1838, m. __*CASE*. ***Luman L. GRISWOLD***, b. May 1839, Cleve, d. 1 May 1867, Sheffield, O (*OP 2:4*); m. 27 June 1863, Elyria, O. to *Melinda E. SMITH*. ***Margaret M. GRISWOLD***, b. c1843; m. *FARNSWORTH*. *Civil War Pension File, National Archives, Certificate 837.212 No. 193.021 for Luman L. Griswold. See complete reference under Luman Griswold (OP 1:10)*

Margaret was enumerated twice in 1850. She completed the census in Avon and shortly thereafter married Caleb Eddy, thus moving to Dover and was included again for Dover.

Margaret GRISWOLD, 47, b. Canada; ***Rosetta J.***, 19; ***Malinda***, 14; ***Lumon L.***, 12; ***Margaret***, 6. All children b. Ohio. 1850 FC OH LRAV, p. 467, lines 15-19.

About this time in our history settlers increased in number quite rapidly. A family named Hutchins settled on lot twenty-one, with his wife, and two daughters by a former husband, ***Jane*** and ***Margaretta SMITH***, and the following children by ***HUTCHINS***: *Nancy, Sarah, Diana, Jacob*, and *Caleb*. They came from York State. Mrs. Hutchins' family was from Canada. Mr. Hutchins came in 1816, remained about fourteen years, sold his improvements to *William B. Gray*, and went to Burton, where the old people soon died. Pioneer and General History of Geauga County, p. 725.

122. ***Moses HUTCHINS***, 3, (***Thomas*** 1, ***Edward*** 2) was born in Charlton, Worcester County, Mass. in 1760...He served in the army...After leaving the army he returned to Athol, Mass. and on the 9th of September 1779 he married ***Susannah THAYER*** of Richmond, New Hampshire...In 1790 he was living...in Queensbury, Washington County, New York. He was head of a family of four males under sixteen years of age, one male over sixteen and three females. In 1812 he appeared in Burton Township, Geauga County, Ohio and in 1814 he crossed over the Cuyahoga River to Middlefield Township, Geauga County. In 1816 he purchased Lot 21 in Middlefield Township...When Moses arrived in Middlefield Township he was married to a ***Mrs. Sarah SMITH***, whom he must have married about 1807 as Sarah had two daughters, by her first marriage, who were born about 1802 and 1804. In addition Sarah had two sons and three daughters after her marriage to Moses. The oldest of these children was born about 1808. Sarah Smith was noted as being from a Canadian family. The histories record that Moses came to Middlefield from York state. No information is available on Moses' first wife, Susannah Thayer, nor on any children from this marriage. Moses Hutchins died in Burton Township, Geauga County, Ohio on June 22, 1834. Jack Randolph Hutchins, Genealogy of Thomas Hutchins of Salem, Massachusettes, pp. 99-100.

Margaretta "Margaret" SMITH HUTCHINS was born about 1804, the daughter of ***Sarah SMITH*** and her first husband. On the 22nd of November, 1826 She married ***Luman GRISWOLD***... In 1834 Luman and Margaret moved from Burton Township to Chagrin Falls. Margaret later lived in Akron *(should be Avon)*, Ohio. Jack Randolph Hutchins, p. 106.

Sister of Margaret Griswold Eddy: ***Jane SMITH HUTCHINS*** *(Jane probably did not take on the Hutchins name)* was born in Canada East (Quebec) about 1800.

She moved to Ohio with ***Moses HUTCHINS***, her step-father, and her mother in 1812. On September 21, 1827 Jane married ***Mathew FLEMING***, as his second wife. He died in Burton, Ohio on December 10, 1831. Jane was living in 1880. Jack Randolph Hutchins, Genealogy of Thomas Hutchins of Salem, Massachusettes, p. 106.

Margaret's second marriage was to ***Caleb EDDY***. They died within four days of each other from a fever. Bay Village Historical Society, Bay Village: A Way of Life, p. 36. *Caleb is buried in OP 2:6. According to his obituary, both Caleb and Margaret died of heart attacks.*

Stone enclosure surrounding the Wolf family plot:
The primary Wolf family monument is made from sandstone. Unfortunately the marker is almost entirely illegible. Norma Wolf Garber was able to provide some of the information that could not be read.

OP 1:15 *(OP 1:12-16)* Wolf Monument

Most of the inscriptions are illegible on the Wolf plot. The legible portions have been recorded and if somewhat clear have been verified with Mrs. Norma Garber. The portions that were illegible have been left with blanks. The markers have been organized below as they are listed on the monument.

JOHN WOLF
BORN _____?
DIED _____?

Inscription illegible
Previously read as:
John Wolf
Born Oct 28, 1790
Died Aug 17, 1859

Philapena
MOTHER OF
Born on

Previously read as:
Philapena,
Mother of John Wolf,
Born 1760,
Died June 30, 1851

ANN
ANDERSON
WIFE OF
JOHN WOLF
BORN MAR 14, 1808
DIED JUNE 23, 1894

THY...EDE...
MICHAEL WOLF
SON OF
JOHN AND ANNA WOLF
BORN DEC 20, 182*?*
DIED...1862

Inscription illegible.
Previously read as:
Michael,
Son of John and Anna Wolf,
Born Dec 20, 1820
Died Feb 3 or 8, 1862

The year of birth is thought to be an error due to the census records, etc., it may well have been 1829.

Previous readings compiled in Cuyahoga County Cemetery Inscriptions, 1934.

Wolf area showing monument and individual markers surrounding. The family is included below as listed on the marker

OP 1:16 **John Wolf**

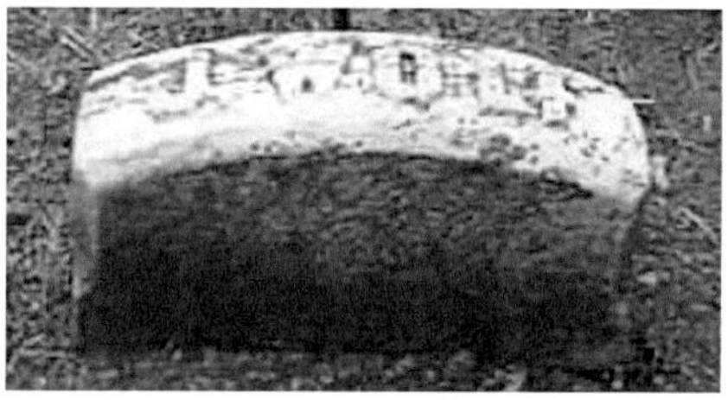

J. WOLF

John WOLF was the son of ***Michael*** and ***Philapena*** *(Philippina)* ***WOLF***. Michael died in Elizabethtown (now Hagarstown), Washington County, Maryland in July 1799 at about the age of 65. He was buried at St.Thomas Parish on July 21, 1799. Michael may have been previously married to ***Salome***, having a son ***Joh. Jacob***, b. Febr. 2, 1783, bap. Mar. 7, 1783 at the First Reformed Church of Baltimore, Maryland. Susan Wolf

John WOLF was born Oct 28, 1790. He fought as a private during the War of 1812 with the 2nd Co. commanded by *Captain John Foos* with the 3rd Regiment, Strongs Ohio

Militia, it is assumed he lived in the Columbus area when he was mustered in at Franklinton, OH. Twenty-eight-year-old, John Wolf arrived in Dover in 1818 after living in Rockport for five to six years. He settled on land which appears to be near Detroit and Clague Road. On March 1, 1826 he invested in land in Dover, presently the Bradley Road area. ***Anna ANDERSON***, of Blaine, PA, became his bride on Dec 19, 1827, he may have gone back to Pennsylvania to marry her. They had two sons, ***Alfred Marion WOLF*** *(Lot 49)*, b. 19 Oct 1828, d. 4 Jan 1896; ***Michael WOLF*** *(this lot)*, b. 20 Dec 1829, d. Feb 1862; and a daughter ***Mary Jane WOLF***, b. 29 Oct 1831 in Dover, d. 29 Oct 1854 in Grand Rapids, MI, m. 1 Nov 1849 to *William MILLER* (b. 4 July 1827, Dover). John died August 17, 1859, in Dover. Norma Wolf Garber

Wolf, John, Private; Roll of *Capt. John FOOS'* Company. (Probably from Delaware County) Roster of Ohio Soldiers in the War of 1812, vol. I, p. 46.

WOLF, John, Males - 26 to 45 yrs.: 1; Females - to 10 yrs.: 3, 26-45 yrs.: 1. 1820 FC OH CYDO, p. 53A.

WOLF, John, Males - under 5 yrs.: 2, 30-40: 1; Females - 10-15 yrs.: 1, 20-30 yrs.: 1, 30-40 yrs.: 1. 1830 FC OH CY Dover, p. 120, line 2.

WOLF, John, Males - 10 under 15: 2, 40 under 50: 1; Female - 5 under 10, 30 under 40: 1. Employed in Agriculture. 1840 FC OH CY Dover, p. 163.

WOLF, John, 61, farmer, b. Penn.; ***Ann***, 41, b. Penn.; ***Michael***, 21, farmer, b. Penn.; ***Henry MILLER***, 23, farmer, b. Penn.; ***Ann MILLER***, 20, b. Penn; value of real estate: $1300. 1850 FC OH CYDO, p.435, lines 5-9, house 3752. *Could Henry and Ann be John's daughter and son-in-law, William H. and Mary Jane Miller? Dates of birth are close.*

23319 Detroit Road in Westlake, OH was built by one ***John WOLF*** whose residence in Dover Township (Westlake) has been established by U.S. Census records during 1830, 1840 and 1850. Mr. Wolf is alleged to have owned a brick yard on the north side of North Ridge Road (Detroit Road) extending along Clague Road and encompassing the lands now utilized by the Crown water filtration plant. This was later known as the Asplin brick plant which may have been purchased from John. It is interesting that the brick yard area is the easterly terminus of Wolf Road leading to Bay Village. The brick yard property also contained a popular ice skating pond, of which photos exist in the "History and Civics of Dover Township." This area was later owned by the City Ice and Fuel Co.

It is interesting to note that the Pomeroy House in Strongsville, OH which was built in 1849 is identical to the Wolf house. The possibility exists that the Pomeroy house may have had brick supplied by John Wolf's brick yard and he became so enamored with it, purchased or bartered for the plans and built his home the following year. Alas, even if he did do the above, it was thought that there was a sudden death in the family during the construction of the Dover residence. Mr. Wolf never occupied his dream house. Therein lie the aforementioned "detail" differences between the Wolf house and the Pomeroy house. Due to the nature of the construction of these homes the roof was the last structural portion to be built, unlike today's frame houses. And that is where the detail differences lie. While both roofs are identical in geometry and pitch, the Pomeroy house contains a Frieze board, about 20" in height, just below the eave and similar to the Clague house (Westlake). The Dover home does not. It is assumed that upon the passing of his loved one, Mr. Wolf lost interest and directed that the detail be abandoned and simply add the roof to protect the structure. He never finished the interior of the house and it is said the house sat vacant until 1857 or 1858 when it was purchased by *Henry B. BATES*.

The architectural style of a home is always a difficult question as the classical architectural styles of homes are basically classified by the detail features and most houses are modifications, transitions or combinations of styles... We have determined that the house was Greek Revival with porch architecture influenced by the emerging Italianate style. Helen and Robert Porter III, "History of the Whispering Pines," present owners of the property, 2003.

There is no evidence of a death in the family when the house was built. There is a possibility that John may have built the house for his only daughter, Mary Jane, who married in 1849. She and her husband, William, moved to Michigan where she died in 1854. If the house was a gift to his daughter, John may have been upset that she was moving away and abandoned the home before it was completed. There is no proof of this theory; it is purely conjecture.

Child of John Wolf and Anna Anderson.

The State of Ohio, Cuyahoga County, ss. I hereby certify that on the 18th day of November 1849, I duly solemnized the Marriage Contract between the said. *William H. MILLER* and ***Mary Jane WOLF***. Dover. Rev. William M. Hitchcock. Marriage Record, Cuyahoga County, OH, vol. 5, p. 22.

Child of William Miller and Mary Jane Wolf:

Tabitha A. MILLER, b. 29 Aug 1850, Dover Twp., Cuy., Co.; m. 15 Feb 1870, ***Harvey W. LAMB***. Norma Wolf Garber

OP 1:14 **Philapena Wolf**

P. WOLF

Michael WOLF and wife ***Philippina***, baptismal sponsors for *Georg SCHNEIDER*, 3 Nov 1797, son of *Cooper* and his wife, *Eliz.*. Baptismal Records, Evangelical Lutheran Church of Elizabethtown (Hagarstown), Maryland.

Philapena WOLF moved to Dover sometime after her son, ***John*** *(below)*, and his wife ***Anna***, from Virginia. She was born in 1760 and died in 1851. Norma Wolf Garber

It is noted that Philapena is not listed in the 1850 census with John.

OP 1:13 Anna Anderson Wolf

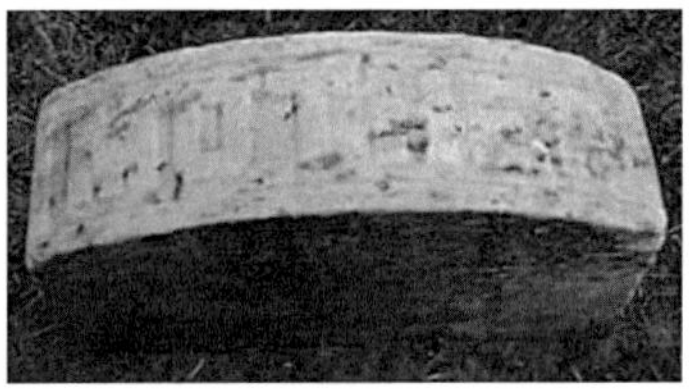

MOTHER

John WOLF'S wife was ***Anna ANDERSON***, she married John on Dec 19, 1827; there is a possibility that this was his second wife. Norma Wolf Garber

"Dear Althea,

Some time ago you asked me about what I knew about Our Family. Well dear not so very much, but will tell you what I know.

Grandmother WOLF (Anna ANDERSON) *was born in Blaine, Perry Co., Pa. the youngest of 18 children, 9 Boys & 9 Girls, she being the youngest, their Mother died while going through the Change. Grandma was Bound out to a family until she was 18 years old and was not treated very Kindly, then she met Grandpa and was Married. Came to Ohio and lived on the North Ridge now Rockport for a good many years. 3 children was born to them* ***Alfred*** *(your Grandpa)* ***Uncle Michael*** *and my Mother* ***Mary Jane****. Grandpa had been married before. A daughter 4 years younger than Grandma and a Son Older, so she had 2 Children to bigin (begin) with, but She Said they were very nice to her. Grandpa was about 30 years older than she was. Grandpa was born in Va., I don't know what part. I never heard of but two others,* ***Aunt Maltie*** *and* ***Johnathon****. Grandpas name was* ***John****...Oh yes, they sold their farm in Rockport and bought where Uncle lived, there was a house across the Road, they rented that until they could build. My Mother was Married there, and I was born there. When I was 2 years old Father & Mother went to Grandrapids, and was there about 2 years when Mother died with T.B. father took me back to Dover and I was there until Grandma was married to a Baptist Minister. Dec 21st 1931* Written by Tabitha Miller, daughter of Mary Jane Wolf Miller. Letter in the private collection of Norma Wolf Garber.

WOLF, Mrs. John, maiden name ***Ann ANDERSON***; last res. Dover. ***MILLER, Mrs.__***, maiden name ***WOLF, Mary Jane***. Women in the Western Reserve before 1840, p. 23.

In ***John WOLF'S*** will, dated 17 November 1857, " I give and devise to my Beloved Wife ***Ann WOLF*** the use of my property Both Real and personal during the time She remains my widow and when she ceases to be such or at her Decease... I give and devise to My Son ***Alfred WOLF***". Cuyahoga County, OH, Probate Court Estate Case File, B 1504. *Ann did remarry and the land reverted to Alfred.*

The State of Ohio, Cuyahoga County, SS. I Certify, That on the 12th day of Feby 1867 ***Mr. Joseph G. FENTON*** and ***Miss (Mrs.)Ann WOLF*** were by me legally joined in Marriage. Allen Darrow, Pastor. Marriage Record, Cuyahoga County, OH, vol. 13, p. 169. *Second marriage*

Anna FENTON is found living with her son ***Alfred*** in the 1870 census. According to her tombstone, ***Anna ANDERSON*** was born 14 Mar 1808, making her 62 at the time. She is not living with him in the 1880 census. ***Alfred WOLF***, 41, farmer, Ohio; ***Carolin***, 24, b. Germany; ***George***, 2, b. Ohio; ***FENTON, Anna***, 62, b. Penn. 1880 FC OH CYDO p. 35

"I give and devise to my Mother, ***Ann CLARK*** if she should survive me, the sum of one Thousand Dollars for her support..." Will of ***Alfred WOLF***, dated 21st of May 1892. Cuyahoga County, OH, Probate Court Estate Case File. *This would show a possible third marriage for Anna although a marriage certificate was never found.*

Mrs. WOLF; res. Dover; interred June 22, 1894; Original Part. "List of Interments," Lakeside Cemetery, Bay Village.

LAMB, Harvey, b. Nov 1845, 54, married 30 yrs., b. Ohio, fr. b. NY, mo. b. Ohio, Proprietor Meat Cutter, own home with mortgage; ***Tobiatha A.***, wife, b. May 1850, 50, one child born and living, b. Ohio, fr. b. NY, mo. b. Ohio; ***George A.***, son, b. May 1875, 25, Meat Cutter. 1900 FC OH CY Glenville Village, ED 216, p. 17A, lines 26-28.

OP 1:12 Michael Wolf

M. WOLF

Michael WOLF was born Dec 20, 1829 in Dover, son of ***John WOLF*** and ***Anna ANDERSON***. He married ***Annis LAFLER*** and had a daughter, ***Mary Jane*** (b. 24 Nov 1852). Michael was sent home with extensive chest injuries after fighting in the Civil War and died in Dover shortly thereafter on 3 Feb 1862. Norma Wolf Garber

Michael WOLF died a week after he had been sent home with a bullet in his chest while fighting in the Civil War in 1862. Bay Village Historical Society, Bay Village: A Way of Life, p. 28.

The State of Ohio, Cuyahoga County, ss. I hereby certify, that on the 23 day of Nov A.D. 1851, I duly solemnized the Marriage Contract between the said ***Michael WOLF*** and ***Ann GRAFFLER***. J.K. Jewitt, Dover. Marriage Record, Cuyahoga County, OH, vol. 5, p. 183.

Annis LAFLER, the seventh of eleven children of ***Mary GRANT*** and ***David LAFLER***, b. Warrensville, O., Feb 10, 1835; d.s.p. *(without children)* Rockport, O., July 27, 1859; m. Oct 1852, ***Michael WOLF,*** of Dover, O. Arthur Hastings Grant, The Grant Family, A Genealogical History of the Descendents of Matthew Grant of Windsor, CT, 1601-1898, pp. 192-193 and Marriage Record, Cuyahoga County, OH, vol. 5, p. 183. *See Alonson A. Grant*, OP 5:16.

"Here through winter's piercing blast
and summer's cooling breeze
they dwelt, a happy family,
giving one and then another
of their cherished ones
into the keeping of those
who loved them long and well,
till all had made for themselves homes
and by their own firesides
told the tales of pioneer life.
When the bidding came for our pioneers
to leave the home they so loved
on Erie's pebbly shore
they quietly removed
to that "a beautiful land,
the far away home of the soul."

The Cahoon Pioneer Celebration, 1874

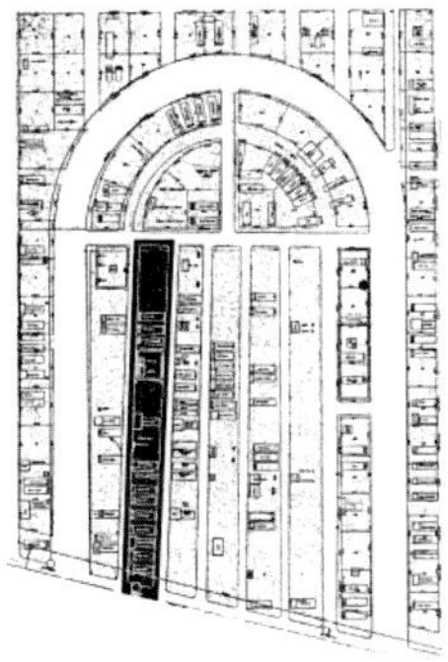

Second row east of the west drive starting from the road and proceeding north.

OP 2:1 **Benjamin Stevens**

BENJAMIN STEVENS
BORN
in Lee, Berkshire Co., Mass. May 19, 1795
DIED
FEB 5, 1871 AGED 75 YRS.

Lay *(Say)* if that we but live that Jesus died and rose again from out _____ also which sleep in Jesus with God living with him.

Benj. STEVENS, Males - under 5 yrs.: 1, 10-15 yrs.:1, 16-20 yrs.:1, 20-30: 2, 40-50 yrs.:1; Females - under 5 yrs.: 1, 10-15 yrs.:1, 16-20 yrs.:1, 40-50 yrs.:1. 1840 FC OH LOAV, p. 155.

Benjamin STEPHANS, 55, farmer, $2000 real estate value, b. Mass; ***Lovisa***, 53, b. Mass; ***Delia T.***, 25, b. Mass; ***Chauncey***, 16, farmer, b. Ohio, attended school; ***Sarah***, 10, b. Ohio, attended school. 1850 FC OH LRAV, p. 939, lines 31-35.

Benjamin STEPHENS, 63, farmer, value real estate $3,000, personal property $700; ***Visa***, 62, b. Mass.; ***Chauncy***, 25, b. Ohio, farmer; ***Sarah***, 18, b. Ohio; *Andrew HORREN?*. 1860 FC OH LRAV, p. 26, lines 20-24.

Ancestors of Benjamin Stevens:

I. ***Thomas STEVENS***, d. 1658, Stamford, Conn., (in that part of the town that is now called Darien). He was granted a house and lot in 1678 by the town of Stamford for services "against the common enemy." He had five sons, the third being *Benjamin* "The Ancestry of the Stevens Family," Rose Hill Museum, Bay Village, OH with extracts from the Vital Statistics of Lee, Mass. and Geraldine A. Hardway.

II. ***Benjamin STEVENS***, removed in 1680 to Bedford, Westchester Co., NY, which was then part of Stamford, Conn. About 1700-1710 he moved with his four sons to Danbury, Conn. "The Ancestry of the Stevens Family" and Hardway.

III. ***Nathaniel STEVENS***, m. ***Abigail BARNUM***, dau. of ***Thomas BARNUM***, said to be the first white female child born in the town of Danbury. They had six sons and two daughters. He made his will Feb 1, 1743 recorded at Fairfield, Conn. "The Ancestry of the Stevens Family" and Hardway.

IV. ***John STEVENS***, d. 1788, Lee, Mass.; m. ***Lydia BRAMAN***, a daughter of ***Benjamin BRAMAN*** (granddaughter of ***Richard BRAMAN***, son of ***Thomas BRAMAN***, one of the eight original settlers of Danbury in 1684). "The Ancestry of the Stevens Family" and Hardway.

V. ***Benjamin STEVENS*** and ***Sarah BIGELOW;*** b. 1760; Capt. Benjamin Stevens died of decay (old age) 11 June 1832 at age 72. He was one of the prominent men of the town (Lee, Mass.). He was repeatedly fence viewer, tithing man and surveyor of highways. According to plan of the old meeting house his pew was No. 34, half way up the broad aisle, which in New England was significant of aristocracy. He also had other pews, one of which was in the gallery for his servants. *Issue:* ***Susanna STEVENS***, b. 29 Aug 1785, Lee, Mass. ***Marcy STEVENS***, b. 29 Aug 1787, Lee, Mass.; m. *GOODSPEED*. ***Lucy STEVENS***, b. 20 Feb 1789, Lee, Mass.; m. 4 Apr 1835 to *John STRONG*. ***Sarah*** (*Sally*) ***STEVENS***, b. 8 Mar 1791, Lee, Mass. ***Chauncey Bigelow STEVENS***, b. 27 Jan 1793, Lee, Mass.; d. Mar 1883, Augusta, Miss.; educated at Lee and Lynn, Mass. studying medicine which, in those days of little surgery except bleeding of patients for all aliments, was little more than applied botany. He located in Ohio and m. *Elizabeth JACKSON*, who died shortly after the birth of a son named *Edward*. Edward was left with his mother's family and Chauncey went to Biloxi. He taught school for the family of *Bryant FERRILL* and his neighbor, among his pupils was *Lucy FERRILL*,

(d. c1882, Augusta, Miss.) who he later married. Opposition being offered to the marriage, they eloped and after being married went to Tangipahoe, Louisiana, later moving to Mobile, Alabama and then Augusta, Miss. ***Benjamin STEVENS,*** b. 19 May 1795 (17 May 1793), Lee, Berkshire Co., MA; d. 5 Feb 1871. "The Ancestry of the Stevens Family" and Hardway.

VI. ***Benjamin STEVENS*** m. Aug, 22, 1815 to ***Lovica FOOTE***, dau. of *David FOOTE* and *Betsy HAMBLIN (bur. OP 3:3-4). Issue:* ***John STEVENS,*** b. Lee, Mass., Dec 23, 1816; d. 2 June 1895; m. 28 Oct 1847 to *Betsey STRONG* [b. 3 Sept 1820, d. 10 Nov 1899], three children. ***Ransom Foote STEVENS***, b. Lee, Mass., May 20, 1820; m. Apr 8, 1846 to *Finetta M. RUPLE*, of Euclid, Ohio; d. Sept 8, 1890, at Byron, Mich.; three children. ***Mary Ann STEVENS*** *(OP 4:1),* b. Apr 9, 1822. ***Delia Taylor STEVENS***, b. Lee, Mass., Nov 30, 1824 [Nov 3, 1824]; m. Dec 22, 1859 to *William JAMESON…*; d. Avon, Ohio Dec 25, 1887, they had a son *Dr. George Chauncey JAMESON*. ***Benjamin Franklin STEVENS,*** b. Lee, Mass., June 5, 1827 [6 May 1827]. ***Chauncey Barnum STEVENS*** *(OP 2:3)* b. Sept 20, 1833, Avon, O. ***Sarah Bigelow STEVENS*** *(OP 2:8)* b. Mar 17, 1840, Avon. Abram W. Foote, Foote Family Comprising the Genealogy and History of Nathaniel Foote, vol. I, pp. 111-112 and vol. II, p. 706, [Handwritten paper, Stevens Family Papers, Rose Hill Museum].

Vital Record information for the *STEVENS* family is available on line for Lee, Mass. at: <http://www.rootsweb.com/~maberksh/vr.html>, 2005.

Children of Benjamin Stevens and Lovica Foote:

The State of Ohio, Cuyahoga County, ss. I hereby certify, that on the 8th day of April A. D. 1846, I duly solemnized the Marriage Contract between the said ***Ransom S. STEVENS*** and ***Finetta RUPLE***. John Barr, Justice Marriage Record, Cuyahoga County, OH, vol. 4, p. 348.

Finetta RUPLE, b. c1829, Cuyahoga, OH; d. 24 Mar 1898, Grandville, Michigan; dau. of *Cyrus RUPLE* (b. 7 Mar 1806, Collinwood, Cuyahoga Co., OH; d. 10 Mar 1875, Collinwood; bur. East Cleveland Cemetery, East Cleveland, OH) and *Tryphena BEERS*, his first wife (b. 1809, d. 3 Dec 1831, Collinwood; bur. East Cleveland Cemetery). *Issue:* ***Mary Ann STEVENS***, b. 22 Feb 1847, Brighton, Clark Co., OH; m. *ROBERTS.* ***Cyrus STEVENS***, b. 9 Jan 1850, Avon, Lorain Co, OH. ***Elihu Burritt STEVENS***, b. 29 Apr 1854, Avon. Marianne Ruple Gardner, The Descendants of Balthazar (Baltus) Ruple Pennsylvania, New Jersey, Ohio, pp. 18, 20, 49. *Cyrus was the brother of Nancy Ruple Osborn (OP 5:8).*

Ransom F. STEPHENS, 30, Farmer, value of real estate $1,000, b. Mass.; ***Finetta***, 21, b. O.; ***Mary***, 3, b. O.; ***Cyrus***, 5/12, b. O. 1850 FC OH LOAV, p. 470, lines 28-32.

Randsom STEPHENS, 39, Farmer, value real estate: $1,500, personal property $600, b. Mass.; ***Minerva,*** 32, b. Mass.; ***Mary,*** 14, b. Ohio; ***Cyrus***, 9, b. Ohio; ***Bird,*** 6, b. Ohio. 1860 FC OH LRAV, p. 26, lines 15-19. *Living next to Benjamin Stevens.*

William JAMESON, a native born farmer citizen of Avon township, is a son of *Joseph B.* and *Avis (SMITH) JAMESON,* the father a native of New Hampshire, the mother of Massachusetts, where they were married. In 1824 they came to Lorain county, Ohio settling in the woods of Avon township, where they opened up a farm and made a permanent home. Mrs. Jameson died in 1834, and Mr. Jameson subsequently married *Miss Mary HORR,* who died in Avon township in 1893; to that union were born four children, of whom *M.B.*, the only survivor, resides in Avon township.

William Jameson…was born in 1824, in Avon township, where he was reared, and received his elementary education in the common schools, supplemented by one term at Norwalk. He taught school for seven winters in Lorain and Cuyahoga counties, since when he was chiefly engaged in farming. In 1849, he located on a farm in Sheffield township, which is now known as Randall's Grove, and first built a log cabin thereon, which was afterward supplanted by a frame house. On that place he resided for sixteen years, improving the land, and then in 1865, bought an improved farm of 102 1/2 acres in Avon township, to which he himself has made many new improvements, and where he has since been successfully engaged in general farming; at one time he worked on this farm for twelve dollars per month. In 1852 Mr. Jameson was married in Birmingham, Erie county, to *Miss Laura LAMORE*, who was a native of LaGrange township, Lorain county, and the adopted daughter of *Dr. BEAMAN,* an early settler of French Creek. *Mrs. Laura JAMESON* died in 1859, leaving one child, *Clyde Burton,* who is married and has two children: *Everett E.* and *Norris Morey*; he resides in Buffalo, N.Y. In 1859 our subject wedded, for his second wife, ***Miss Delia F. STEPHENS,*** who was born in Berkshire county, Mass., daughter of ***Benjamin*** and ***Lovica (FOOTE) STEPHENS***, both natives of Massachusetts and early settlers of Avon township, where they died. To this union was also born one child, ***George Chauncey***, who graduated from the Philadelphia Medical University, class of 1893, and is now located in Oberlin, Ohio. His mother died in 1887. In politics Mr. Jameson is a Republican, and has served as assessor of Sheffield township. In religious faith he is a member of the Baptist Church at French Creek. "William Jameson," Commemorative Record of the Counties of Huron and Lorain, vol. II, p. 1136.

JAMESON, William; 45, Farmer, value of real estate $10,000, value of personal property $2000, b. Ohio; ***Delia***, 45, Keeping House, b. Ohio; ***Burton***, 13, male, b. Ohio; ***George C.***, 5, b. Ohio; *HORVIS, Martha*, 14, Domestic, b. Wisconsin. 1870 FC OH LRAV, p. 360, dwelling 318, lines 30-34.

JAMESON: William, d. Nov 24, 1895, 71yr.; *Laura B. LAMORE*, wife Wm., d. Mar 14, 1859, 29yr.; ***Delia STEVENS***, wife Wm., d. Dec 25, 1887, 63yr; *Lucina HORR*, dau. JB&MH, d. Oct 17, 1866, 23yr. 9m.; *Daniel*, son JB&Mary, d. Nov 10, 1849, 10yr. 7m. 21d.; *Joseph B.*, Dunbarton NH-d. June 8, 1867, 79yr. 6m. *Avis*, wife, d. July 13, 1834, 37yr. 4m.; *Mary HORR*, Pomfret, VT Apr 28, 1801-Avon, OH May 5, 1893. Avon Center (Mounds) Cemetery, Avon Township, Lorain Co., OH.

OP 2:2 Lovisa Foote Stevens

LOVISA FOOT
WIFE OF
BENJAMIN
STEVENS
born in Lee,
Berkshire Co.,
Mass.
in 1796, moved to
Ohio in 1831,
DIED DEC 6, 1862
AGED 66 Y 5 D

But God will
redeem my Soul
from the
power of the grave.
Psalms 19:15

Lovisa is frequently found with the spelling Lovica.

Lovica FOOTE, b. Nov 29, 1796, in Lee, Mass., dau. of ***David FOOTE*** and ***Betsy HAMBLIN*** *(OP 3:3-4)*. Abram W. Foote, Foote Family Comprising the Genealogy and History of Nathaniel Foote, vol. I, p. 111.

OP 2:3 Chauncey Barnum Stevens

CHAUNCEY B.
STEVENS
1833-1913

Chauncey Barnum STEVENS, son of ***Lovica*** *(Lovisa, above)* ***FOOTE*** and ***Benjamin STEVENS***, b. Avon, Ohio, Sept 20, 1833; unm.; d. at Avon, Ohio, June 10, 1913, at the Stevens Homestead where he was b. and where he had spent his whole life. A very quiet unassuming man, his sterling character, sound judgment and kindliness made him the "first citizen" in the neighborhood where he spent his life. He accumulated a modest fortune which he used generously in furnishing an education to a number of his nephews and nieces and in assisting his neighbors. He was widely known as "Uncle Chauncey." He was bur. in Lakeside Cemetery, Bay Village, Ohio. Abram W. Foote, Foote Family Comprising the Genealogy and History of Nathaniel Foote, vol. II, p. 705.

STEVENS, Chauncy, b. Sept 1833, 66 yrs., single, b. Ohio, parents b. Mass., farmer; *WESTCOTT, Hattie*, niece, b. May 1852, 48 yrs., wd., 2 children born and living, b. Ohio, father b. Mass., mother b. New York; ***Otis BRAMAN***, servant, *(nephew of Chauncey)* b. July 1875, 24, single, b. Ohio, parents b. Ohio, farm laborer. 1900 FC OH LRAV, p. 18, lines 9-11.

An interesting house that is still occupied on this road *(Walker)* is the one built by ***Chauncey STEVENS***. The front four rooms of this house were built before 1860 and the kitchen, woodshed and cellar were added after the Civil War. Walker, Milburn, Avon Lake Story, Ohio, 1965, p. 32.

"War veteran 1861-1865"

A five pointed cast metal star flag holder with the above inscription lies in front of the marker. The upper corner has the letter "F", lower points have "C" and "L" with the cross points having crossed rifles on the left and an anchor on the right. These are from the Grand Army of the Republic membership badge. The letters stand for the motto of the GAR "Fraternity, Charity and Loyalty." The anchor and crossed rifles represent the naval and land forces of the Union. This is a generic Civil War marker for Union Veterans who did not belong to the GAR, it is thought that only half of the Civil War Veterans joined the GAR at one time or another. This star was damaged in 2002 and new stars were placed at each veteran's grave in May, 2004. Dick Ross and Richard Orr, Past Commander-in-Chief, Sons of Union Veterans of the Civil War.

C. STEVENS PIONEER OF AVON DIES

Chauncey STEVENS, 80, a life-long resident of Avon and one of the district's wealthiest farmers, died yesterday of valvular heart trouble. He had been in poor health for a number of years.

Mr. Stevens was interested in farming land throughout the country and was widely known. He was born on the farm on which he died, and remained unmarried throughout his life.

Two sisters, ***Mrs. ALDRICH***, of Dover, O., aged 90, and ***Mrs. Harvey BRAMAN***, formerly of Lorain, now of Lakewood, aged 70 survive. There are a number of nieces and nephews.

Funeral services will be held at 1:30 p.m. Friday at the late home on Walker rd. Burial will be made in the Dover Methodist Episcopal cemetery. Lorain Times-Herald, June 12, 1913, p. 1, col. 4.

Chauncey Barnum STEVENS, d. June 10, 1913, 11:55 p.m., Avon, Lorain Co., Chronic Endocarditis for 400 days, Cystitis - 3 years, b. September 20, 1833, 79 yrs. 8 ms. 20 ds., single, b. Avon, O., Farmer; fr. ***Benjamin STEVENS***, b. Massachusetts, mo. ***Lovisa FOOTE***, b. Massachusetts; informant *Geo. C. JAMESON*, Oberlin, O., bur. Bay Village, June 13, 1913, undertaker Jas. A. Pease and Son, Dover, O. Ohio Certificate of Death, Division of Vital Statistics, 1913, certif. 72795.

AVON LAKE

The death of ***Chauncey B. STEVENS***, of Avon Lake, which occurred Tuesday, removed from this community, one of its best known residents. "Uncle Chauncey," as he was known to more than half of the people of Avon Lake, was 80 years of age. He was born and lived all his life on the same farm. He never married. A man of fine character, he was greatly beloved by all of his kin. The funeral services will be held Friday afternoon at 2 o'clock from his late home. Elyria Democrat, Elyria, Ohio, Thursday, June 12, 1913, p. 1, col. 6.

STEVENS-Chauncey B., Wednesday, June 11, aged 79 years. Funeral from his late residence, Walker rd., Avon, O., Friday, June 13, at 2 p.m. Friends invited. Cleveland Necrology File, June 13, 1913, roll 77.

Chauncy STEVENS, res. Avon; Original Part. "List of Interments," Lakeside Cemetery, Bay Village, OH.

OP 2:4 Luman Loami Griswold

LUMAN L.
GRISWOLD
Died May 1, 1867
Aged 28 Yrs. 11Mo. 23 Ds.
ETMER L.
son of
L.L. & M.E.
GRISWOLD
died Oct 5, 1866
Aged 1 year 3 ms. 7 Ds.

Luman Loami GRISWOLD, son of ***Luman GRISWOLD*** *(OP 1:10)* and ***Margaret Marilla SMITH GRISWOLD EDDY*** *(OP 1:11)* was born in Orange Twp., Cuyahoga County, OH.; m. ***Malinda E. SMITH***; d. 1 May 1867. Karen Boas and Carrie A. Stave.

Luman GRISWOLD's mother married Caleb EDDY (OP 2:6), a widower in 1850.

Lumon GRISWOLD, 22, b. Ohio; ***Margaret M.***, 19, b. Ohio, living with ***Caleb EDDY***, 69. 1860 FC OH CYDO, p. 48, lines 23-26.

The State of Ohio, Lorain County, SS I Hereby Certify, that on the 27th day of June A.D. 1863, I duly solemnized the Marriage Contract between the said ***Luman L. GRISWOLD*** and ***Malinda E. SMITH***. C.C. West, M.G. Marriage Record, Lorain County.

All references below are from the Civil War Pension File, National Archives, Certificate 837.212, No. 193.021 for Luman L. Griswold.

Luman L. GRISWOLD a Private of Captain A. H. Nickerson's Company of the 8th Regiment of the United States O.V.I. was enlisted by *H. WANEBURG* at Camp Chase, *(Cleveland)* Ohio on the 17th of August 1861 to serve three years; he was born in Cuyahoga County in the State of Ohio is Twenty Six (26) years of age, 5 feet 6 ½ inches high, Light complexion, Blue eyes, light hair, and by occupation when enlisted a Farmer. He was discharged at Columbus, Ohio August 22nd, 1864 because of his time having expired. The soldier desires to be addressed at North Dover, Cuyahoga Co., Ohio. Certificate of Disability for Discharge.

19th day of April 1894, 56 yrs. old, ***Melinda C. CASE*** residing in Oberlin, Lorain Co., Ohio, ***Luman L. GRISWOLD*** died at my house in Sheffield Township, Lorain Co., on or about May 1st 1867. The cause of his death was the effects of what the Doctors called Oxidized Rheumatism. Melinda C. Case, *sister of Luman. Scrofulous caries of the bones was also identified as a cause of death.*

10 Nov, 1896, Clay Center, Co. of Clay, Kansas, ***Laura SMITH***: I shall be 90 years of age next March. I have resided in Clay nine years...I made ***Lumon's*** *(sp.)* acquaintance when he was about twelve years of age at Avon, Lorraine Co., Ohio. He was there living with his mother ***Mrs. Margaret GRISWOLD*** who was a widow. He was smaller than most boys his age but had perfect health...His mother was a very healthy woman and *..had..* four children. By the time he was 18 years old he was as large and as stout as boys generally are. He lived some ten miles away from me, but worked about a mile from me sometime before the breaking out of the late war. It was about this time that he began to pay attention to my daughter the claimant, whom he afterwards married...He was never home on furlough and did not return until he came from the hospital. As I have understood it, he became sick during the marches before Richmond and on the James River...I think the soldiers first battle was at Romney and that the movements were in the Shenandoah Valley... His mother had moved to Dover some ten miles from Avon... He used to come to see my daughter and they were married *(in)* June...At the time of his marriage, his health was improving steadily, and his mother thought it would be better for him to be married and live with her in Dover. Laura Smith, *Mother-in-law of Luman.*

Third of March, 1897, at Hicksville, Co. of Defiance, Ohio. My age is 53 years, post office address is Hicksville, Ohio. I am a housekeeper for my family. My maiden name was ***Margaret M. GRISWOLD***; and ***Luman L. GRISWOLD***, ...was my brother. At the time my brother, Luman L. Griswold enlisted, his home was in Dover

Township, Cuyahoga Co., Ohio, where he was living with his mother now dead, and his stepfather ***Caleb EDDY***, also dead.

My home was there too...About the first of April 1861 I came to Farmer Township, Defiance Co., Ohio to teach school...He *(Luman)* had to use a crutch or cane for at least a year before his death. M.M. Farnsworth, *sister of Luman.*

General Affidavit. State of Kansas, County of Clay Centre, ss. In the matter of Pension Claim of ***Malinda RILEY***, Co. I 8 Reg. O.V.I., 5th day of Sept, 1890...*J.M. TITUS*, 61 yrs. That prior to the year 1867. In about that time I was a resident of Sheffield Lake, Lorain, Co., Ohio that I was well acquainted with ***Melinda SMITH*** who was my adopted daughter and that in the 27th day of June, 1863 said Melinda Smith was united in marriage to ***Luman GRISWOLD*** at Elyria, Lorain Co., Ohio the marriage being Solemnized by a *Rev. WEST*, a Methodist minister. That subsequent & immediately following their marriage, Mr. & Mrs. Griswold lived with me for one and one half years except so far as Luman Griswold was ? who for most of the time during said year and a half was in the army. That in the 1st day of May 1866 said Luman Griswold having returned from the Army died at Sheffield Lake, Lorain Ohio. That sometime in the year 1867 I removed to Linten Township. Allamakee Co., Iowa where I have since resided. Joseph M. Titus, *father-in-law of Luman.*

Deposition A., Case of ***Malinda E. RILEY*** (pension for ***Luman GRISWOLD***), No. 193021, 3rd, Feb, 1897, Sangatuck, Co. Of Allegan, Mich., *Lorenzo W. GRANT.* ...I knew him (Luman) intimately from boyhood up, and I was in his neighborhood about six months or a year after his discharge, (Aug 1864). Disease Luman had in service: He was sick, quite sick, when we were on the Peninsula. We were there July 1862. It seems to me that he was one who was affected badly with the bloody dysentery. I know many of us had that then...About August we were sent back to Fortress Monroe. We stayed there a short time and then went to Alexandria, Va. where we were in Convalescent Camp, about a week and then I was sent back to my regiment and left him there.

After my discharge we lived about ¼ mile apart a mile or a mile and one-half east of Sheffield Lake, Lorain Co., Ohio. I lived there until 1867, when I came here but he moved away from there about a year after discharge to the western part of the state...He died about one hundred miles away. It strikes me now that it was reported that he died of the sunstroke he had...I did hear that his bones became diseased in some way. Lorenzo W. Grant, *brother of Alonson Grant, grave OP 5:16.*

War Dept. Surgeon Generals Office: ***Lyman L. GRISWOLD***, Private, Co. I 8th Reg't was admitted to Camp Ohio, D.C., Dec 19th, 1862 for treatment for Chronic Diarrhea, and was transferred ... Harwood G.H., Washington, D.C., Mch 5, '63,...transferred G.H. Cleveland, O Apr. 6, '63,....returned to duty Augt. 10, 1864. Washington, D.C. Sept 25th, 1871.

Marriage Certificate, This is to Certify That by authority of a License under the Seal of the Probate Court of Lorain County ***Mr. Luman L. GRISWOLD*** and ***Miss Malinda E. SMITH*** were by me, on the 27th of June in the year of our Lord One Thousand Eight Hundred and Sixty Three legally united as Husband and Wife. Elyria June 27th 1863, C.C. Mott Marriage Certificate, Lorain County.

Certificate of Marriage. To the District Court of Allamakee County: This certifies, that on the 28 day of September A.D., 1868 at Rossveter in said County, according to Law, and by authority I duly JOINED IN MARRIAGE ***Mr. George RILEY*** and ***Malinda E. GRISWOLD*** ...my hand ...J.B.B. Baker. State of Iowa. *Malinda's remarriage after Luman's death.*

Case of ***Melinda E. RILEY***...***Laura E. JUDD***, 45 yrs. old, res. 553 South Sherman Street, Denver, Colorado, ***George RILEY*** died on Feb 21, 1883 at Hardin, Iowa and Melinda Riley has not remarried since. 27th Feb 1917. Residence 509 East 2, Avenue, Denver, Colorado. My mother, Melinda E. Riley...died at my home under date of July 5, 1927. Laura E. Judd, *daughter of Malinda Griswold Riley*

OP 2:4 Etmer L. Griswold

Etmer L. son of ***Lyman L.*** and ***Malinda E. GRISWOLD***; d. Oct 5, 1866; Aged 1 year 3 ms. 7 Ds. Cemetery Marker.

OP 2:5 Charles Franklin Eddy
Hiram James Eddy

Marker cracked and set flat in concrete.

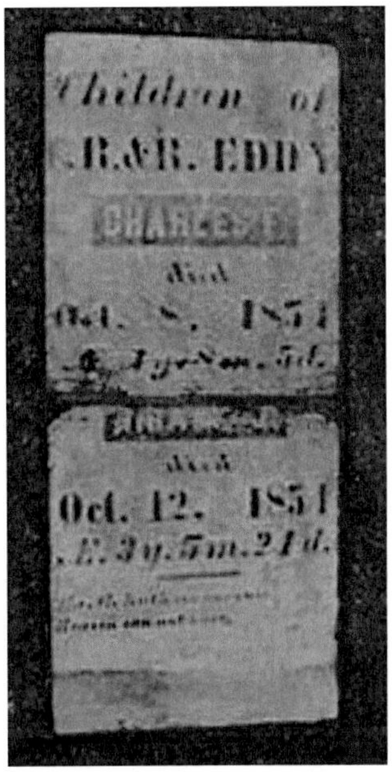

Children of
R. & R. EDDY
CHARLES F.
died
OCT 18, 1854
1 yr. 8 M. 5 d.
HIRAM J.
died
Oct 12, 1854
AE 3y. 5m. 24d.

Earth hath no sorrow Heaven can not cure.

The children buried here are the sons of Caleb Reynolds Eddy, Jr. and Rosina Griswold. Caleb Reynolds is the son of Caleb Eddy and Rebecca Reynolds in the next plot. Rosina Griswold Eddy, their mother, is the daughter of Luman Griswold

(OP 1:10) and Caleb Eddy, Sr.'s second wife, Margaret Smith Griswold Eddy (OP 1:11).

Parents of Charles F. and Hiram J. Eddy:

Caleb Reynolds EDDY, b. 18 Aug 1821, near Detroit, Michigan; d. 16 Dec 1899 at Belleville, Kans.; m. 19 Apr 1843 at Avon, O. to ***Rosina GRISWOLD*** (b. 19 Sept 1827 at Cuyahoga Co., O.; d. 27 Apr 1897 in Belleville, Kans., dau. of ***Luman*** and ***Margaret SMITH GRISWOLD*** *(OP 1: 10-11)*). He lived in Ohio until 1865 on his father's farm. Then he went to Iowa. They were very devout people, members of the Methodist Episcopal Church and great workers in the Church and in Sunday School. Mrs. Eddy used to tell her children that while she taught her Sunday School classes, she held her baby in her lap and had the next oldest seated by her side. This arrangement continued until the child was old enough to enter a class herself, when the place was taken by the next baby. Ruth Story Devereux Eddy, Eddy Family in America, p. 488, # 2869.

Caleb R. EDDY married ***Rosina GRISWOLD***, 19 April 1843. Marriages of Lorain County 1824-1865, p. 35.

Caleb R. EDDY, 29, b. Penn.; ***Rosina***, 23, b. Ohio; ***Caleb***, 6, b. Ohio; ***Henry***, 5, b. Ohio; ***Jane***, 2, b. Ohio; ***Loami GRISWOLD***, 42, b. Ohio. 1850 FC OH CYDO p. 216B, lines 21-24, dwelling 3735.

Caleb E. EDDY purchased one hundred and sixty acres of land in Linn Co., Iowa in August of 1869 for the sum of twenty four hundred dollars. Recorded in Cleveland, Cuyahoga Co., Ohio in August, 1869. Land was then purchased the following year in Adair Co., Iowa by Caleb and ***Rosina***. Land Deed provided by Carolyn Ames Raz

EDDY, Caleb R., 48, Value of real estate $550, b. Michigan; ***Rosanna***, 42, b. Ohio; ***Emma L.***, 12, b. Iowa; ***Amelia S.***, 8, b. Iowa; ***Ulysses S.***, 6, b. Iowa; ***Anna M.***, 4. 1870 FC Iowa, Linn Co., College Twp., p. 218, lines 14-19 for family, extends to line 28 for "R.R. Labor."

EDDY, Caleb R., 58, Farmer, b. Michigan; ***Rosina***, 52, wife, b. Ohio, keeping house; ***Emma L.***, 22, daughter, at home, b. Iowa; ***Serelda***, 18, daughter, at home, b. Iowa; ***Ulysses S.***, 16, son, at home, b. Iowa; ***Annie M.***, 13, daughter, at home, b. Iowa. 1880 FC Iowa, Adair County, Richland Township, p. 46C, lines 1-6.

C. R. EDDY was a charter member of the Pleasant Grove Church in Adair Co., Iowa which was organized in March 1881. Those in the family who were included in the 1881 records were: ***C. R. EDDY, R. EDDY, Emma EDDY, Serrelda EDDY, M. S. EDDY*** and ***Anna EDDY***. Adair County Historical Society, History of Adair County, Iowa, p. 557 and Elizabeth Jensen, Pleasant Grove United Church of Christ Records, Jan. 7, 1881.

Children of Caleb Reynolds Eddy and ***Rosina Griswold***:

Caleb Luman EDDY, b. 7 Apr 1844, N. Dover, Cuyahoga Co., OH; d. 4 Mar 1917, Fontanelle, Adair Co., IA; m. 19 Mar 1871, Solon, Johnson Co., IA to *Lucy Rachel KESSLER* (b. 10 Aug 1847, Taylorsville, O). Caleb served three years in Co. H of the 22nd Regt. of the Iowa Volunteers during the Civil War, later a stock raiser and farmer in Adair Co. ***Henry Reynolds EDDY***, b. 2 Nov 1845, N. Dover; d. 16 May 1925, Olathe, Johnson Co., KS; m. 11 Jan 1877 at A.A. Fay's, Stanley, Johnson Co., KS to *Ella M. FAY*. ***Rosina Jane (Jenny) EDDY***, b. 28 Sep 1848, N. Dover; d. 7 Apr 1924, Belleville, Republic Co., KS; m. 27 Nov 1867, Mt. Vernon, Linn Co., IA to *Abner Reed ARRASMITH*, (b. 15 Oct 1844, Solon; d. 7 April 1924, Belleville, KS; son of *Abner ARRASMITH* and *Elizabeth PEEKINPAUGH*). ***Hiram James EDDY***, b. 18 Apr 1850, Dover; d. 12 Oct 1853, at home in Dover *(buried. this lot)*. ***Charles Franklin EDDY***, b. 21 Feb 1852, Dover; d. 8 Oct 1853, at home in Dover, *(buried this lot)*. . ***Ella Malinda EDDY***, b. 16 Feb 1855, Dover; d. 2 Oct 1856. ***Emma Lorinda EDDY***, b. 1 Oct 1857, Brown Township, Linn Co., Iowa; m. 9 Mar 1881 at home in Richland Twp., Adair Co., IA. to *John Franklin EPHRAIMSON*. ***William Fredric EDDY***, b. 10 July1859, Greenfield Twp., Jones Co., IA; d. 11 July1859, at home in Greenfield Twp. ***Serrelda Amelia EDDY***, b. 29 Oct 1861, Fairview, Greenfield Twp., Jones Co., IA; d. 19 Nov 1950, Ottawa, Franklin Co., KS; bur. Highland Cem.; m. 27 Feb 1890, Munden, Republic, KS to *George Sidney WELLS* (b. 30 Mar 1864, Mt. Sterling, Crawford Co., WI; d. 12 Mar 1925, Ottawa, Franklin Co., KS; bur. Highland Cem.; son of *Nathaniel Wadsworth WELLS* and *Harriet Elizabeth MAYNARD*). Serrelda was a student in Holton, KS at Campbell University and became a teacher. ***Ulysses Sanford EDDY***, b. 5 Nov 1863, Putman Twp., Linn Co., IA; d. 6 July1893, Munden, Republic Co., KS; teacher. ***Annie Marilla EDDY***, b. 21 June 1866, Putman Twp.; m. 1 Dec 1885, Richland, Adair Co., IA to *Robert Ross HOPPER*, (d. 21 Oct 1920; son of *John HOPPER* and *Eliza Jane McGREGOR*). ***Mina Rebecka EDDY***, b. 6 May 1868, Dover; d. 31 Mar 1870 at home in Western, Linn Co., IA. ***Nellie EDDY***; b./d. 17 Dec 1870, at home in Western, Linn Co. Lucille Bennett Ames and Carolyn Ames Raz with records from the Caleb Reynolds Eddy Family Bible and Ruth Story Devereux Eddy, Eddy Family in America, p. 488, # 2869 and pp. 662-3, #5417-5423.

OP 2:6 **Caleb Eddy**

CALEB EDDY
DIED
May 21, 1869
AGED
77 yrs. 7 ms. 27 ds.

Women's Benefit Assoc. of the Maccabees metal marker at grave.

State of Ohio, Cuyahoga County on the 24th of this Instant was Joined in Marriage ***Caleb EDDY*** and ***Miss Rebecca REYNOLDS*** both of Euclid by me August 27th 1817, Enoch Munay, Justice of Peace. Marriage Record, Cuyahoga County, OH, vol. 2, p. 81.

Caleb EDDY had at least two brothers. ***David EDDY***, b. 7 Feb 1783, m. *Elizabeth*, lived first in PA but later went to Lorain Co., OH. *Issue*: ***Jesse EDDY***, b. 1814 Washington Co., PA, lived in Colombia Twp., Lorain Co. and in 1870 he was in Rochester Twp. ***Samuel EDDY***, b. 1799, d. 1880, went to Kenosha, WI. Karen Boas

Caleb EDDY, Males - 1: 5-10 yrs., 1: 30-40 yrs.; Females: 1: 10-15 yrs., 1: 30-40 yrs. 1830 FC OH CYDO, p. 119.

Caleb's second wife was ***Margaret Marilla SMITH GRISWOLD*** *(OP 1:11)*, widow of ***Lumon GRISWOLD*** *(OP 1:10)*. They married 3 Oct 1850. Her daughter, ***Rosina GRISWOLD***, married Caleb's son, ***Caleb Reynolds EDDY*** on 19 April 1843. Both marriages were in Lorain Co., OH. Karen Boas and Marriages Lorain County, 1824-1865, p. 35.

The State of Ohio, Lorain County, ss. I hereby Certify, that on the 3rd day of October A.D. 1850, I duly solemnized the Marriage Contract between the said ***Caleb EDDY*** and ***Margaret GRISWOLD***. J.R. Jewitt. MR, Lorain County.

Caleb EDDY, 59, farmer, b. Penn; ***Margaret***, 40, b. NY; ***Nancy***, 31, b. Ohio; ***Margaret GRISWOLD***, 7, b. Ohio. 1850 FC OH CYDO p. 216B, lines 21-24, dwelling 3735.

Caleb EDDY, 69, farmer; ***Margaret E.***, 58, b. Canada; ***Lumon GRISWOLD***, 22, b. Ohio; ***Margaret M. GRISWOLD***, 19, b. Ohio. 1860 FC OH CYDO p. 48, lines 23-26, dwelling 362.

Eddy - In Dover on the 21st, ultimately of heart disease, ***Mr. Caleb EDDY***, aged 78 years. Also, on the 25th, ultimately of the same disease, ***Margaret***, wife of Caleb Eddy, aged 67 years. Elyria Independent Democrat, Elyria, OH, June 2, 1869.

Ancestors of Caleb Eddy:

I. ***William EDDYE*** *(sp.)*, b. c1560, Bristol, Gloucestershire, England; d. 23 Nov 1616, Cranbrook, Kent, England; m.1 20 Nov 1587, Cranbrook, to ***Mary FOSTEN*** (dau. of *John FOSTEN* and *Ellen MUNN*); m.2 22 Feb 1613/14, Cranbrook, to ***Mrs. (Elizabeth) Sarah TAYLOR***, dau of *TAYLOR,* they would have one daughter. The ninth of eleven children of William and Mary was Samuel. Ruth Story Devereux Eddy, Eddy Family in America, p. 1.

II. ***Samuel EDDY***, b. c1608, Cranbrook; d. 12 Nov 1687, Swansea, Bristol Co., Massachusetts; m. 1630, England to ***Elizabeth SAVERY*** (dau. of *Thomas SAVERY* and *Margaret WOODRORKE*). Sailed to Plymouth in 1630 on the ship "Handmaid." The fourth of seven children was Obadiah. Eddy, pp. 1, 2.

III. ***Obadiah EDDY***, b. c1645 at Plymouth, Massachusetts; d. 1727, Plymouth; m. c1668 to ***Bennett ELLIS*** (dau. of *John ELLIS* and *Elizabeth FREEMAN*). The fourth of twelve children was Benjamin. Eddy, p. 4

IV. ***Benjamin EDDY***, b. c1676, Middleboro, Mass.; d. 24 Sept 1744, Halifax, Mass.; m. 8 Nov 1716 to ***Abigail PRATT*** or ***HATHAWAY***. The second of nine children was Caleb. Eddy

V. ***Caleb EDDY***, b. 21 Jan 1718/19, Middleboro, Mass; m. 11 July1745, ***Phoebe BABBIT*** (dau. of *Elkanah BABBIT* and *Mary HATHAWAY*). The fourth of five children was Caleb. Eddy

VI. ***Caleb EDDY***, b. 1754 (Family record of Mrs. Arrasmith); d. 21 Apr 1818; m.1 1779 to ***Esther***___ (b. 1756, d. 15 Oct 1786 (Morristown, NJ Book of Mortality, 11806)). *Issue*: ***Timothy EDDY***, b. 4 Mar 1781; ***David EDDY***, b. 7 Feb 1783; ***Elizabeth EDDY***, b. 9 Dec 1784, m. ___*EMMONS*. They had a dau., *Fanny* who m. ___*COLE*. m2 1778 ***Mrs. Nancy (MCELRAF) JONES***. *Issue:* ***Esther EDDY***, b. 9 Aug 1789; ***Caleb EDDY***, b. 25 Sept 1791; ***Sarah EDDY***, b. 4 Sept 1793; ***Phebe EDDY***, b. 12 Dec 1797; ***Samuel EDDY***, b. 24 Nov 1799; ***Isabel EDDY***, b. 2 Sept 1804. Eddy, children's records extracted from Eddy family bible in the possession of Mrs. Arrasmith, pp. 433-434.

VII. ***Caleb EDDY*** was b. 25 Sept 1791; d. May 21, 1869, at N. Dover, Cuyahoga Co., OH; m.1 1818 *(incorrect date, should be 1817)* to ***Rebecca REYNOLDS***. *Issue:* ***Nancy Rebecca EDDY***, b. 26 August 1819, North Dover, OH, m.1 *Solomon GILLETTE*, m.2 ___*MORSE* of Belair, Mich. ***Caleb Reynolds EDDY***, b. 18 Aug 1821, near Detroit, Michigan; d. 16 Dec 1899 at Belleville, Republic Co., Kans.; m. 19 Apr 1843 at Avon, O. to

Rosina GRISWOLD (b. 19 Sept 1827 at Cuyahoga Co., O.; d. 27 Apr 1897 in Belleville, Kans., dau. of *Luman* and *Margaret SMITH GRISWOLD (OP 1: 10-11)*). m.2 ***Margaret Marilla SMITH GRISWOLD***, the mother of his son's wife, who was almost twenty years younger than he. She d. 25 May 1869.

He was a soldier in the War of 1812 and received a land grant of 160 acres. About 1821 Caleb was living near Detroit, probably about 16 miles distant. Later he moved to a farm in Ohio about 15 miles west of Cleveland in Cuyahoga Co. This was a large farm of about 160 acres where he lived the rest of his days. Eddy, pp. 268, 433-4 (# 1283, 2869).

Daughter of Caleb Eddy and Rebecca Reynolds:
The State of Ohio, Cuyahoga County, ss. I hereby Certify, that on the 24th day of August A.D. 1853, I duly solemnized the Marriage Contract between the said ***Solomon K. GILLET*** and ***Nancy R. EDDY***. Aaron Aldrich, Justice Peace. Marriage Record, Cuyahoga County, OH, vol. 5, p. 396.

OP 2:7 Rebecca Reynolds Eddy

Marker intact but placed flat in concrete.

REBECCA
Wife of
CALEB EDDY
DIED
SEPT 20, 1849
AE 61*(?)* y. 1 M. 20 days

EDDY, Mrs. Caleb, Maiden Name _____ ***Rebecca***, Last Res. Dover. Women in the Western Reserve before 1840, p. 29.

Rebecca REYNOLDS was the first wife of ***Caleb EDDY***. Rebecca was the daughter of ___ ***REYNOLDS*** and ***Rebecca MORTON***. Family notes state that Rebecca was related to *John Morton,* who signed the Declaration of Independence, that her mother's ancestors were born in England and that her grandfather Reynolds was born in Ireland. Lucille Bennett Ames and Carolyn Ames Raz

"Two Braman children". *Notation on plot map.*

OP 2:8 Sarah Stevens Braman

SARAH S.
BRAMAN
1840-1933

Sarah Bigelow STEVENS, the youngest child of ***Benjamin STEVENS*** and ***Lovisa FOOTE*** *(OP 2:1-2)*, b. Avon, Ohio, Mar 17, 1840; m. May 4, 1871, in Lakewood, Ohio, to ***Horace BRAMAN*** of Avon; bur. Bay Village Cemetery; res. Lakewood, (*Elyria (vol. I, p. 112))* OH. *Issue:* ***Hattie Stevens BRAMAN***, b. Feb 25, 1873, at Avon, Ohio; teacher in Lakewood; res. Lakewood, Ohio, d. 16 Mar, 1965, bur. Lakewood Cem. *(Rocky River, OH).* ***Otis BRAMAN***, b. Avon, Ohio, June 27, 1875; farmer; res. on the farm his grandparents bought of the Conn. Land Company, unmarried. ***Frank BRAMAN***, b. Mar 27, 1880, Avon, Ohio; d. 1963; m. Apr 7, 1906 to *Ruth EDSON*, (b. Cleveland, Ohio, Mar 6, 1885, d. 1906); secretary of the Pittsburgh Oil Co., New York, NY; res. Sound Beach, Conn.; they had a son *Dandridge Arthur BRAMAN*, b. Lakewood, Ohio, Mar 22, 1916, living much of his life in Long Island Sound, NY and Old Greenwich, CT. Abram W. Foote, Foote Family Comprising the Genealogy and History of Nathaniel Foote, vol. II, pp. 702, 705-706; Stevens Family Chart; Foote Family Papers; Rose Hill Museum and Frank Braman.

BRAMAN, Sarah S., mother of ***Harriet, Otis*** and ***Frank***. Services at residence, 1433 Lincoln Ave., Saturday, Nov 25, at 2 p.m. Cleveland Necrology File, Nov 25, 1933, reel 9.

Sarah S. BRAMAN, 1433 Lincoln, Lakewood; d. Nov 23, 1933, 2 p.m., Lakewood, Cerebral Softening, onset Nov. 16, 1933, senility; 93 yrs. 8 ms. 6 days; b. Avon, March 17, 1840, fr. ***Benjamin STEVENS***, b. Lee, Mass., mo. ***Lovisa FOOTE***, b. Mass.; Informant *Harriett BRAMAN*, 1433 Lincoln; undertaker Wm. Daniels, 15800 Detroit, Lakewood, O., embalmed; bur. Bay Village, Nov 25, 1933. Ohio Certificate of Death, Division of Vital Statistics, 1933, certif. 64702.

Children of Sarah Stevens and Horace Braman:
BRAMAN. ***Harriett BRAMAN,*** sister of the late ***Frank*** and ***Otis***, residence, 1433 Lincoln Ave. Friends may call at the Daniel's Funeral Home, 15800 Detroit Ave., where services will be held Thursday evening, Mar 18, at 8:30 P. M. Interment Friday morning. Memorials are suggested to the Cleveland Society for the Blind. Cleveland Press, Mar 18, 1965. ***Harriett*** was blind. Frank Braman

BRAMAN, H. Otis., brother of ***Harriet S***. and ***Frank BRAMAN***, residence, 1433 Lincoln Ave. Friends may call at the Daniels Funeral Home, 15800 Detroit, where services will be held Wednesday, May 9, at 3 p.m. Cleveland Press, May 8, 1956.

Harriett BRAMAN, Grave 7; ***Otis BRAMAN,*** Grave 8; Section 1, Lot 192. Lakewood Park Cemetery, Rocky River, OH.

OP 2:9 Horace Braman

HORACE
BRAMAN
1831-1891

Horace was the son of Otis Braman and Betsey Riley (OP 1:8) and the brother of Lydia Ware (Lot 4). No evidence of children from this marriage was found.

The State of Ohio, Cuyahoga County, SS. I certify, That on the 24th day of Jany. 1864 ***Mr. Horace BRAMAN*** and ***Miss Lydia E. WINSOR*** were by me legally joined in Matrimony. John M____, Minister Marriage Record, Cuyahoga County, OH, vol. 11, p. 245.

After the death of his first wife, Lydia Winsor in 1864, Horace married Sarah Stevens in 1871.

Horace BRAMAN, b. Aug 6, 1832, at Avon, Ohio; m. ***Sarah Bigelow STEVENS***...; d. at Avon, Ohio, Apr 18, 1891. Abram W. Foote, Foote Family Comprising the Genealogy and History of Nathaniel Foote, vol. II, pp. 705-706.

BRAMAN, Horace; 1891, April 18, Avon, Dropsy; 58 yrs., 8 m., 12 days; b. Avon; farmer. PDL 3:3

BRAMAN, Horace, April 31, 1891, Avon, married, 58 y. 9m., religion Prot., b. Avon, fr. ***Otis BRAMAN***, Disease Abscess, last res. Avon, *(Lorain County)*, O., clergyman J. J. Gough, undertaker J. Pease, Lake Side Cemetery. PD 6:11502.

OP 2:10 Lydia Winsor Braman

LYDIDE
WIFE OF
HORACE BRAMAN
DIED
SEPT 24, 1864
AGED 27 YRS.

(Note spelling of first name. Inscription that follows illegible.)

Lydia E. Winsor Braman died exactly eight months after marrying Horace. She was the second oldest child of Henry Winsor and Martha Cahoon(OP 4:4).

BRAMAN, Mrs. Horace, Maiden Name ***Lydia WINSOR***; Year Came to Township or Born 1837; Where From or Where Born Dover, O.; Last Residence Berea, O. Women in the Western Reserve before 1840, p. 17.

Henry WINDSOR, 37, farmer, b. Ohio; ***Martha***, 36, b. Ohio; ***Lydia***, 12, b. Ohio... 1850 FC OH CYDO, page 217B, lines 37-42, dwelling 3750.

OP 2:11 Ransom Foote

Marker cracked and set in concrete.

RANSOM FOOT
DIED
Oct 11, 1846
crack through next number
AE 44? yrs.

Ranson FOOTE, the son of ***David FOOTE*** and ***Betsy HAMBLIN*** *(OP 3:3-4)* was b. Feb 15, 1803; m. Mar 28, 1824, ***Catharine PORTER***, d. Oct 11, 1846; res. Dover, OH. *Issue:* ***Lavias FOOTE***, b. Dover, May 16, 1825; m. Dover, June 14, 1849 to *Fayetta (Fuetta) LILLY* (b. Ashfield, Mass., Mar 4, 1828, dau. of *Austin LILLY*); d. July 14, 1882, Byron, Mich. ***Betsey Ham(b)line FOOTE*** *(OP 2:12)*, b. Oct 30, 1826; d. Aug 3, 1828. ***Ranson L. FOOTE***, b. Dover, July 23(2), 1828; m. Dover, Oct 1, 1853 to *Julia B. FARR* (b. Dover, June 23, 1833, dau. of *Algenon FARR* (b. c1805 re 1850 census) and *Sophrons SMITH* (b. c1807 re 1850 census); d. Mar 1907, bur. Royalton, Minn.); res. Long Beach, Cal. ***Angeline Porter FOOTE***, b. Apr 30, 1830; m. June 6, 1847, Cuyahoga Co., OH to *Joseph E. LAVAYEA* (b. Aug 8, 1819); d. Jan 7, 1890, Cleveland, O. ***Laura Alline FOOTE***, b. Dover, Jan 14, 1832; m. Berea, O., Sept 27, 1855 to *Alfred Goodwin BRIGHT* (b. New York State, July 7, 1832; d. Sept 9, 1875). ***Emeline P. FOOTE*** b. July 25, 1834; m. July 17, 1872 to *Thomas LIGGETT* of Cleveland (d. Feb 23, 1902). ***Asahel P. FOOTE***, b. May 25(2), 1836; m. 1880 to *Anna SUTHERLAND* (b. July 20, 1861, Bangor, Me., d. 1889, Minn.). ***Catherine P. FOOTE*** *(OP 2:12)*, b. Mar 16, 1838; d. Sept 5, 1923, Bay Village, OH; unm. ***Marietta Robinson FOOTE***, b. Mar 17, 1840; m. Dec 22, 1864 to *David F. MILLER* (b. Nov 6, 1841, Avon, O., *bur. OP, unidentified lot*); Res. Long Beach, Cal. ***Statira FOOTE*** *(OP 2:12)*, b. Mar 8, 1842; d. Mar 28, 1845. ***Henry P. FOOTE*** *(OP 2:12)*, b. Apr 21, 1844; d. Mar 13, 1919, Bay Village, OH; unm. ***Abigail S. FOOTE***, b. Oct 30, 1846; m. Aug 1, 1865 to *Thomas L. NILES* (b. Nov 23, 1832, Vt.; d. Jan 2, 1881). [All children b. Dover Twp., Cuyahoga Co., OH]. Abram W. Foote, Foote Family Comprising the Genealogy and History of Nathaniel Foote, vol. I, pp. 229-231, 362., (vol. II if discrepancy) [Keith M. Sheldon, Descendants of Early Bay Village Families, pp. 396-397].

Married March 28th 1824 in The State of Ohio, Cuyahoga County. I hereby certify that on the 28th day of March A.D. 1824 - in the presence & by the consent of the proper parents and Guardian, I joined together in marriage ***Ransom FOOT*** & ***Catharine PORTER*** according to law - Given under my hand & seal this 1st day of April A.D. 1824, Leverett Johnson, Justice of the Peace. Marriage Record, Cuyahoga County, OH, vol. 2, p. 44. *Leverett Johnson was the uncle of Catharine.*

Ransom and his family were living next to his parents in this census. ***Ransom FOOT***, males, 1: 5 yrs. under 10; 1: 10 and under 15; 1: 15 and under 20; 1: 30 and under 40; females, 2: under 5 yrs.; 1: 5 under 10; 2: 10 under 15; 1: 30 under 40. 1840 FC OH CYDO, p. 63.

Death was not a stranger to Ransom's family. He and Catharine had already lost their second born and between the 1840 and 1850 census they would not only lose another child, but Ransom himself died in 1846 leaving Catharine with ten children. Their son, Ransom, would become the head of household, marrying in 1853.

Ransom FOOT *(son of Ransom after Ransom's death)*, 22, Farmer, b. Ohio; ***Catherine***, 44, b. Conn.; ***Abigail***, 4; ***Laura***, 18; ***Emeline***, 16; ***Asahel***, 14; ***Catherine***, 12; ***Marietta***, 10; ***Henry***, 7; ***Servius***, 25, Farmer, b. Ohio; ***Fayette***, 22, b. Mass.; ***David***, 92, occup. none, b. Maine; *Joseph SCHELLING*, 22, Labour, b. Germany; *Olive HOUGH*, 5, b. Ohio. All children b. Ohio and had $300 real estate each except for Ransom who is listed as having $500. Catherine also had $300. 1850 FC OH CYDO p. 434, lines 23-36.

Children of Ransom Foote and Catharine Porter:
Future spouses of Ransom L. Foote and Laura Alline Foote:
Algernon FARR, 45, Farmer, b. Penn; *Sohpronia*, 43, b. Mass; ***Julia***, 17, b. Ohio; ***Walter***, 2, b. Ohio; ***Alfred BRIGHT***, 17, laborer, b. Ohio; *Julia SMITH*, 60, b. Ohio. 1850 FC OH CYDO, p. 214B, lines 20-25.

The State of Ohio, Cuyahoga County, ss. I hereby certify, that on the first day of October A. D. 1853, I duly solemnized the Marriage Contract between the said ***Ransom S. FOOT*** and ***Julia B. FARR*** A. Blakesly, V.D.M. Marriage Record, Cuyahoga County, OH, vol. 5, p. 412.

LIGGET-Emeline P. FOOT, wife of the late ***Thomas LIGGET***, mother of ***Mary E.***, Sunday, Nov 29, 9:30 p. m., age 91 years. Funeral services from the late residence, Stop 35, Lake Road, Bay Village, Wednesday, Dec 2, at 3:30 p. m. Burial at Lakewood Cemetery. Cleveland Necrology File, Dec 2, 1925, reel 050.

OP 2:12 Foote Monument

FOOTE

RANSOM 1803-1846
HIS WIFE
CATHERINE PORTER 1806-1886
BETSY H. 1826-1828
STATIRA J. 1842-1845
HENRY P. 1844-1919
CATHERINE P. FOOTE 1838-1923

OP 2:12 Ransom Foote

Information listed with individual marker OP 2:11.

OP 2:12 Catharine Porter Foote

Catharine was the daughter of ***Asahel PORTER*** and ***Rebecca JOHNSON*** *(OP 6:6-7).* She arrived in Dover with her parents, sister ***Emaline***, and uncles *Leverett JOHNSON* and *Reuben OSBORN* when she was four years old on the first day Dover was settled, October 10, 1810. Her mother and brother drowned in the Rocky River in April, 1814. Catharine and her two siblings were raised by her mother's sister, *Sarah Johnson OSBORN*. Bay Village Historical Society, Bay Village: A Way of Life, pp. 9, 13, 22.

Catharine PORTER, wife of ***Ranson*** *(sp.)* ***FOOTE*** was b. Nov 16, 1806 in Salem, Ct., d. Apr 6, 1886, res. Dover. Abram W. Foote, Foote Family Comprising the Genealogy and History of Nathaniel Foote, vol. I, p. 229.

FOOTE, Mrs. Ransom; Maiden Name ***Catherine PORTER***; Year Came to Township or Born 1810; Where From or Where Born Waterbury, Ct.; Last Residence Dover, O. Women in the Western Reserve before 1840, p. 17.

Mrs. Catherine FOOTE...spoke of the happy times when a young girl she used to visit Mrs. Hall in her hollow stump kitchen. (*Barnabas* and *Hannah HALL* arrived at what was then called Rushbank, now Dover, August 22d, 1811, after a weary journey by ox team of forty-one days from New England. For two weeks Mrs. Hall's kitchen was a large hollow sycamore stub...Sept 28, 1812, their log cabin with its contents, was burned by the Indians). She became well acquainted with the Indians, and had not learned to be afraid of them. She often played with Indian children, and tended the little ones. Her own young pioneer life had its hardships, but also its pleasures, and memory delighted to recur to the wilderness incidents. "The Pioneers, Eleventh Cahoon Celebration," Reunion Notebook, 1870.

Note: Chas. H. HALL, b. Nov 4, 1817; died Feb 6, 1895. *Barnabas HALL*, died May 29, 186?3, Aged 22 yrs. *Hannah* Died Sept 19, 19_8, Age 81 yrs., 8 mos. Maple Ridge Cemetery inscriptions, Westlake, OH as read by Catherine Burke Flament.

Mrs. Catherine FOOT said the going to mill narratives reminded her of the days when she had pounded corn with a pestle in a mortar burned out in the end of a log. It made good hasty puddings, samp, johnny cakes, &c. and she was taught to be thankful for such blessings. Mrs. F. is one of the "mothers of Israel," and came to Dover the same day with the Cahoon family. "Dover Pioneer Pic-nic," Cleveland Herald, Oct 10, 1861.

The little ***Catharine PORTER***, who as a maiden of three years came into Dover upon its natal day, married ***Ransom FOOTE***, lived a short distance west of her father's farm many useful years, devoted to her family and church, honored by a large acquaintance, and when full of years, her loved form was garlanded by the gentle hands of her great-grandchildren, and laid beside the husband taken from her in his prime. Her daughters are a living testimonial of her worth. Memorial to the Pioneer Women of the Western Reserve, p. 58.

Catharine FOOT, 79; res. Dover; interred April 6, 1886; Original Part. "List of Interments," Lakeside Cemetery, Bay Village, OH.

OP 2:12 Betsy Hamblin Foote

Betsey Hamline FOOTE, b. Oct 30, 1826; d. Aug 3, 1828. *Assumed to be Hamblin.* Abram W. Foote, Foote Family Comprising the Genealogy and History of Nathaniel Foote, vol. I, family information pp. 229-231, 362.

OP 2:12 Statira J. Foote

Statira FOOTE *(OP 2:12)*, b. Mar 8, 1842; d. Mar 28, 1845. Abram W. Foote, Foote Family Comprising the Genealogy and History of Nathaniel Foote, vol. I, family information pp. 229-231, 362.

OP 2:12 Henry P. Foote

Henry P. FOOTE, a farmer of Dover township, is a son of the late ***Ransom FOOTE***, who was born in Lee, Berkshire county, Massachusetts, February 15, 1803, and was brought by his father, ***David FOOTE***, in 1815, to Cuyahoga county, Ohio, who settled in the northwestern part of Dover township and lived there until his death. On arriving at the estate of manhood Mr. Ransom Foote married, March 28, 1824, ***Miss Catherine PORTER***, who was born in Waterbury, Connecticut , November 16, 1806, and whose father, ***Asahel PORTER***, emigrated to this State in 1810, settling also in Dover Township. Mr. Ransom Foote continued to reside on the old homestead of his father until his death, which occurred October 11, 1846. His wife died April 6, 1886. They had twelve children, namely: ***Lavias H.***, deceased; ***Betsey***, deceased; ***Ransom***; ***Angeline***, deceased; ***Laura***, the widow of *Alfred G. BRIGHT*; ***Emeline***, the wife of *Thomas LIGGETT*, of Cleveland; ***Asahel***;

Catherine; ***Maryette***, widow of *David MILLER*; ***Statira***, deceased; ***Henry P.***, our subject; ***Abigail***, the widow of *Thomas NILES*.

Mr. Foote, whose name heads this sketch, was born in Dover township April 21, 1844; was reared on his father's farm, and has all his life resided in his native township excepting the seven years he lived in Berea. He attended Baldwin University at Berea three years. Farming is his occupation, and he owns eighty-eight acres of the old homestead. He has been active in local offices, as well as in official relations in the Methodist Episcopal Church. Memorial Record of the County of Cuyahoga and City of Cleveland, p. 409.

Henry P. FOOTE, b. Apr 21, 1844, son of ***Ranson*** and ***Catharine PORTER FOOTE.*** He and (his sister) Catharine occupy the old home at N. Dover, O., on the shore of Lake Erie, unm. Abram W. Foote, Foote Family Comprising the Genealogy and History of Nathaniel Foote, vol. I, p. 231.

FOOT, Henry P., 36, farmer, b. Ohio, fr. b. Ohio, mo. b. Conn.; ***Catherine***, 73, mother, b. Conn., parents b. Conn.; ***Catherine P.***, 41, sister, keeping house, b. Ohio. 1880 FC OH CYDO p. 93, lines 8-10.

FOOT, Henry P.; owned land; Acres: Improved - 30 tilled, including fallow and grass, 10 permanent meadow, Unimproved - 40 woodland. Farm Values: Land and buildings- $8,000, Machinery - $125, Live Stock - $225. Labor: Paid for wages in 1879 - $300, Weeks hired labor - 25. Estimated value of all farm production: $700. Grass lands: acreage: 10 mown, 12 tons hay. 2 horses, 3 milch cows, 2 calves dropped, 3 cattle sold living, 1 slaughtered. 300 pounds of butter made on the farm. 60 barnyard poultry on farm, 300 dozen eggs produced in 1879. Barley: 4 acres, 157 bushels; Indian corn: 4 acres, 500 bushels; oats: 3 acres, 120 bushels; wheat: 6 acres, 150 bushels; potatoes: 2 acres, 200 bushels. Orchards - apple: 2 acres, 80 bearing trees, 200 bushels. Total value of orchard products: $100. Amount of wood cut: 100 cords, Value of forest products - $1,200. "Schedule 2. Production of Agriculture in Dover Township, Cuyahoga County, OH," enumerated June, 1880, p. 22.

FOOT, Henry P., 56, head, b. April 1844; ***Catherine P.***, 62, sister, b. Mar 1838; ***BRIGHT, Laura***, 68, sister, b. Jan 1832, widow, children born and living 6. 1900 FC OH CYDO p. A22, lines 7-9, house 475.

Henry P. FOOTE, d. March 12, 1919, 1 a.m., Bay, Cuyahoga Co., Angina pectoris & myocarditis (chronic), contributory Artereo-sclerosis for several years; Single, b. Apr 10, 1844, Dover, O., 75 yrs. old., Retired Farmer; fr. ***Ransom FOOTE***, b. U.S., mo. ***Catherine PORTER***, b. U.S., informant J.A. Gillette, Bay Village, bur. Bay Village, Mar 15, 1919, undertaker Saxton & Son, 13205 Detroit. Ohio Certificate of Death, Division of Vital Statistics, 1919, certif. 16513.

FOOTE-Henry P., age 75 years, March 13, at residence, Bay Village, O., Funeral Saturday 2 p.m., from M. E. church, Stop 32, Lake Road, Bay Village; take Lake Shore Electric cars; please omit flowers. Cem. Rec. 1844-1919, Lakeside Cemetery, Bay Village, Ohio. Cleveland Necrology File, Mar 15, 1919, reel 2.

Henry P. FOOTE; res. Bay Village; interred Mar 1919; Original Part. "List of Interments," Lakeside Cemetery, Bay Village, OH.

OP 2:12 Catherine P. Foote

Cathrine P. FOOTE, b. Mar 16, 1838; res. Dover, O. with ***Henry***; unm. Abram W. Foote, Foote Family Comprising the Genealogy and History of Nathaniel Foote, vol. I, p. 229.

Apple John

(Miss C. Foote)

One egg (two are better), one pint sweet milk, two tablespoons sugar, pinch of salt, one-third cup of flour. This is for a medium sized pie tin. Butter the tin and pour in the batter. Put in the apples which should be sliced, not too thin, and softened, in a steamer or the oven. Sift over a little cinnamon if you like and bake. Spread with butter and sugar. Serve warm.

The Village Cook Book, p. 19. (c1911-1915)

Catherine P. FOOTE, d. Sept 5, 1923, 9:30 a.m., Bay, Cuy. Co., Acute cardiac dilatation - 20 minutes, Contributory Arterio sclerosis & myocarditis - Several years 5 at least; Single, b. Mar 16, 1838, North Dover, Ohio, Retired; fr. ***Ransom FOOTE***, b. unknown (city), Mass., mo. ***Catherine PORTER***, b. Salem, Conn.; informant *Mary E. LIGGET*, West Lake Rd., bur. Bay Village, O., Sept 9, 1923, undertaker Saxton & Son, 13205 Detroit Ave. Ohio Certificate of Death, Division of Vital Statistics, 1923, certif. 53127.

FOOTE-Catherine P., sister of ***Mrs. E.P. LIGGETT*** of Bay Village, O., ***Mrs. M.P. MILLER*** of Long Beach, Calif. and the late ***H.P. FOOTE***, Wednesday, Sept 5, at 9:30 a.m., age 85 years. Services from her late residence, West Lake road, Bay Village, Friday, September 7 at 3 p.m. Cleveland Necrology File, Sept 7, 1923, roll 26.

Regina Rentschler and Alfred Wolf, her grandson in the next plot, are enclosed in a stone border.

OP 2:13 Regina Lapp Rentschler

Hier ruht in Gott
unsere liebe
MUTTER
Regina Katharina
Ehfrau von
Friedrick Rentschler
geb. Den 6 Feb 1806
gest. Den 15 Jan
1871

Wie wohl ist meinem
Leib
Nach ausgestandenen
Leiden
Wie wohl ist meiner
Seele
in jenen
Himmelsfreuden.

Translation by Judi Ballard.

Here lies with God
our dear Mother
Regina Katharina
Wife of
Friedrick Rentschler
born 6 Feb 1806
died 15 Jan 1871
How well is my Body
After enduring Pain (sorrow)
How well is my Soul
In those joys of Heaven.

Ancestors of Regina Lapp Rentschler :

I. ***Johann Ludwig LAPP***, b. 4 Feb 1741; d. 24 Aug 1806; m. 1765 to ***Anna Maria FREYIN*** (b. Freyh); carpenter from RoBwaag, Germany.

II. ***Phillip Jakob LAPP***, b. 3 Oct 1777; m. 30 Apr 1804 to ***Regina Barbara LAMMLE*** (b. 19 Nov 1776, d. 1842); immigrated to USA.

III. ***Regine Katherina LAPP***, b. 6 Feb 1806, Diefenbach, Germany; m. 11 Sept 1831, Diefenbach to ***Jakob Friedrich RENTSCHLER***, weaver, went to "Amerika." Records from Church of Zavelstein, Wurtenburg, Germany, and are "guaranteed to be right by the church of Zavelstein," provided by Norma Wolf Garber.

RENTSCHLER, Ragina, wid. ***Fred.***, laborer, h. 316 Taylor. 1868-9 Cleveland City Directory., p. 265.

Ancestors of Jacob Friedrich Rentschler, husband of Regina Lapp Rentschler:

I. ***Jakob RENTSCHLER***, m. 13 Nov 1694 to ***Katherina PFROMMER*** (dau. of *Bartholomai PFROMMER*).

II. ***Michael RENTSCHLER***, b. 17 Sept 1698; m. 30 Apr 1720 to ***Barbara***.

III. ***Johann Michael RENTSCHLER***, b. 8 Dec 1725; d. 2 Oct 1777; m. 2 Aug 1763 to ***Maria Barbara DITTUS*** (b. 2 July 1738; d. 17 Sept 1816; dau. of *Samuel DITTUS*, farmer).

IV. ***Samuel RENTSCHLER***, b. 16 Oct 1770; d. 1 Jan 1831; m. 16 Aug 1797 to ***Margarethe Barbara SPAR*** (b. 9 Mar 1768, d. 23 Mar 1839)

V. ***Jacob Friedrich RENTSCHLER***; b. 26 Sep 1799, Teinach, Diefenbach, Germany; m. on 11 Sept 1831 in Diefenbach to ***Regine Katharine LAPP***. *Kinder (Issue):* ***Jakobine Friederike RENTSCHLER***, b. 30.10.1828 *(date discrepancy or child from a previous marriage?)*, confirmed 1842; ***Regina Katharina RENTSCHLER***, b. 15.4.1834, conf. 16.4.1848; ***Sophie Wilhelmine RENTSCHLER***, b. 2.4.1836; conf. 1850; ***Jakob Friedrich RENTSCHLER***, b. 6.8.1838, d. 5 Mar 1841; ***Elisabetha Adelheid RENTSCHLER***, b. 18.12.1839, d. 23.6.1840; ***Anonymous RENTSCHLER***, b. 22.10.1841; ***Adelheid RENTSCHLER***, b. 19.8.1844; ***Caroline RENTSCHLER***, b. 26.5.1846. Family immigrated in 1850. Records from Church of Zavelstein, Wurtenburg, Germany, and are "guaranteed to be right by the church of Zavelstein," provided by Norma Wolf Garber.

Jacob Frederick RENTSCHLER, d. 24 March 1858 probably in Cleveland, OH. Norma Wolf Garber

It has not been determined where Frederick Rentschler, Regina's husband, is buried. The cemetery records start later and there is no tombstone for him at Lakeside, although he may very well be interred here.

RENSTATLER, Frederick, h. Taylor n. Lorain. 1856 Cleveland City Directory, p. 100.

A document believed to a Probate Court Record for ***Fredk RENTSCHLER***, dated March 1873, lists him as having owned sublots 18 and 19 of the part of the original lots 48 and 49 in the City of Cleveland. Those listed on the document are: ***Charles HAHN, Wilhelmina HAHN, Louis KRUGER, Fredericka KRUGER, H. WISCHMEYER, Regina WISCHMEYER, Alfred WOLF, Carolina WOLF, Joseph HAHN*** and ***Adelheid HAHN***. L. Kruger, atty. Provided by Norma Garber.

Children of Regina Lapp and Jacob Frederick Rentschler:

Regina Katharina RENTSCHLER *(Lot 38:11)*, b. 15 April 1834, dau. of ***Regina***, m. ***Henry WISCHMEYER*** *(Lot 38:13)*.

Carolina RENTSCHLER *(Lot 50:13)*, b. 26 May 1846 became the wife of ***Alfred Wolf*** *(Lot 50:13)*.

Sophia Wilhelmina (Mina) RENTSCHLER HAHN, inherited everything from her mother according to Regina's will. ECF: F1211 Mina Rentschler married ***Charles HAHN*** on the 26th of August 1855. MR 7 H004 She died in Rockport, December 30, 1900, leaving two children: ***Charles*** and ***Bertha Boylan HAHN***. ECF: 184307 Mrs. Sophia Hahn, widow of Charles Hahn, on the 30th inst., at the residence of her brother-in-law, *Henry WISCHMEYER*, at Dover, O. Funeral from Schifflin Christian church, cor. Dodge and Superior sts., Wednesday at p.m. standard, by funeral car. Cleveland Necrology File, Jan 2, 1901.

Adelheide RENTSCHLER HAHN. Ada Rentschler married ***Joseph L. (Louis) HAHN***, Dec 17, 1863, Cuy County. MR 11 242 Their son, ***Joseph O. HAHN***, lists his mother on his marriage certificate as Adelaide Rantschler. MR 72 67 She was born Aug 19, 1843, d. Nov 28, 1907. Her husband, Joseph L. was b. Jan 18, 1832, in Germany; d. Sept 21, 1909, 2064 E. 81st, Cleveland. Lake View Cemetery Records/. Ohio Certificate of Death, Division of Vital Statistics, 1909.

Fredericka RENTSCHLER KRUGER, Friederika geb Rentschler 30 Oct 18?? Diefenbach, D died 9 Feb 1908. Ingrid Abram, "Independent Evangelical Church Abstracts."

Fredericka KRUEGER, 79, b. Germany, cause Old Age; res. 1262 W. 116, Ward 26; d. res.; fr. b. Ger., mo. b. Ger.; Cemetery Woodland, Undertaker Black & Wright. PD of Cleveland, reel 1977543. *No marriage certificate was found in Cuyahoga County.*

OP 2:14 Alfred Charles Wolf

ALFRED CHARLES
ALFRED & CAROLINE
WOLF
BORN DEC 8, *Year illegible.*
DIED NOV 15, 1867
Inscription below illegible

Alfred Charles WOLF was the oldest child of ***Alfred Marion WOLF*** and ***Caroline RENTSCHLER*** *(Lot 50).* His nickname was thought to have been Freddie. He was born on Christmas eve, 1865. According to a notation in the family bible, he died Friday morning at 10:55 of scarlet fever. Norma Garber Wolf. *Freddie rests next to his grandmother, Regina.*

OP 2:15 Eliza Ann O'Brien Coppin

ELIZA ANN
O'BRIEN
wife of
JAMES COPPIN
DIED
JUNE 21, 1861
Aged 41 y. 1 mo.

Ann (Mrs. Aaron Winsor ALDRICH) *(daughter-in-law of Aaron ALDRICH and Elizabeth WINSOR OP 4:1),* maiden name ***O'BRIEN****;* ***Mary (Mrs. Sylvanus CROCKER)*** *(daughter was Mary Elizabeth CROCKER OSBORN OP 5:5),* maiden name ***O'BRIEN*** and ***Mrs. Thomas O'BRIEN*** (maiden name ***Elizabeth HALL***) are all listed as arriving in Dover in 1835, coming from Clarkson, NY. Women in the Western Reserve, Prior to1840, p. 18. *There is a possibility that Elizabeth is the mother of Eliza, Ann and Mary. This may be why the Coppin family is buried at Lakeside Cemetery, which was not near their home.*

The O'Brien family was not found in the 1820 or 1830 Federal Census for Clarkson, Monroe Co., New York.

There is a J. O'Brien in the 1840 census for Dover who may be Eliza's father. Mary married James one year prior to this census.
Males: 1 (under 5), 1 (10-15 yrs.), 1 (20-30 yrs.), 1 (40-50 yrs.). Females: 2 (5-10 yrs.), 1 (20-30 yrs.). 1840 FC OH CYDO p. 163.

OP 2 Willie Coppin

Stone previously read and currently missing:

Willie,
Son.
Died Nov. 13, 1863,
Age 17 years.

Willie COPPIN*, who is listed in the 1860 census that follows under his father, was probably the son of* ***James*** *and* ***Eliza Ann COPPIN****, born about 1847.*

OP 2:16 James Coppin

JAMES COPPIN
DIED
April 6, 1874
AE 56 yrs. 3 m.
& 19 DAYS

Possible: James COPPIN, b. 19 Dec 1817, Faversham, Kent, England; b. 30 Jan 1818. It should also be noted, as with most names, that there are many spellings to the name Coppin: Coppen and Copping included. Roy Copping *This is only a possibility and has not been documented further.*

James COPPIN and ***Eliza Ann O'BRIEN*** License is endorsed - Marriage Solemnized between these parties March 15, 1839 Before me. Wells Porter, Justice of the Peace. Marriage Record, Cuyahoga County, OH, vol. 3, p. 342.

James COPPIN, 32, farmer, value of real estate $300, b, England; ***Eliza***, 29, b. N. York; ***Sylvia***, 9, b. Ohio, attending school; ***William***, 4, b. Ohio; ***Phebe***, 2/12, b. Ohio. 1850 FC OH Lorain Co., Brownhelm, p. 435, lines 1-5.

James COPPIN, 43, farmer, b. England; ***Eliza***, 40, b. NY; ***Sylva***, 19, male, b. O.; ***William***, 13, male, b. O.; ***Ellen***, 10, female, b. O. 1860 FC OH LRAV p. 52, lines 26-30.

Possible marriages after the death of his first wife, Eliza.

James COPPINS to ***Caroline GRIGGS***, Marriage 22 Aug 1861. Marriages Lorain County, Ohio 1824-1865, p. 27.

COPPIN-RICHARDSON-By the same *(J.R. Faxon, Esq.)*, at Elyria, Feb 10th, 1868, ***Mr. JAMES COPPIN***, of Ridgeville, to ***Mrs. Elizabeth RICHARDSON.*** Lorain Constitutionalist, Elyria, OH, Wednesday, Feb 12, 1868, p. 2, col. 5.

COPPINS, James, 53, Farmer, value of real estate $1,800, Personal Estate $800, b. New York; ***Elizabeth***, 42, Keeping House, b. Ohio; ***Ellen***, 20, At Home, b. Ohio. 1870 FC OH Lorain Co., Elyria Township, p. 460, lines 22-24.

James COPPIN vs. *Joseph CAHOON.* Suit brought on acct for digging ditch and making bank. July 8th. Parties attended defendant confessed summons and joined issue and defendant plead on adjournment for more Evidence. Court adjourned to 15th ins. at 2 O'clock P.M. *Wm. HERST* and *Matthew GOODELL* acknd subpoena to appear on the 15th. Undetermined date. Aaron Aldrich Paper's Collection, File 3-36, Rose Hill Museum, Bay Village, OH.

SUDDEN DEATH.- ***Mr. James COPPIN***, while standing in the church in Ridgeville, where the election was being held, fell, and almost instantly expired on Monday afternoon. He left Elyria about noon, in his usual good health, and undoubtedly was stricken with heart disease.

A daughter of the deceased, ***Mrs. S. C. OWEN***, started from Cleveland the same day, for her future home in California, and was stopped at this place, while passing through on the evening train, when the sad news was broken to her. Elyria Independent Democrat, Elyria, Ohio, Wednesday, April 8, 1874, p. 3, col. 3.

Possible brother of James Coppin:
Charles COPPIN to ***Betsey O'BRINE***, Jan 18, 1848. Marriages Lorain County, Ohio 1824-1865, p. 27.

Daughter of James Coppin:
Charles E. OWENS to ***Sylvia C. COPPIN*** married 16 Nov 1873. Ohio, Lorain Co., Probate Court, Marriage Applications Rec. from 4/1872 through 4/1885, Lorain Co. Court 3, p. 730.

"The number of excellent women who once lived in Dover is so great that it is with reluctance we stay the pen... let it be remembered ...that the many unite to make the beautiful whole. My greeting to the living is one of cheer, of congratulation upon the rich inheritance which is ours, for 'We need not go abroad for stones to build our monumental glory.'"

Ida M. Cahoon, Chairman and Historian
Memorial to the Pioneer Women of the Western Reserve, 1896, p. 62.

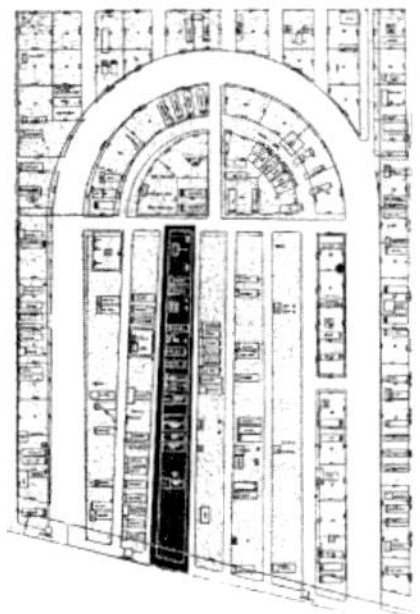

Third row east of the west drive starting from the road and proceeding north.

OP 3:1 Foote Monument

THOMAS FOOTE
SON OF
DAVID & ELIZABETH
FOOTE
BORN IN LEE,
BERKSHIRE C., MASS
MAY 21, 1788
MARRIED
MARCH 12, 1812
MOVED TO OHIO
1815
DIED
JULY 31, 1856
AGED 68 YRS.

DAMA
DAUGHTER OF
ABRAHM &
TEMPERANCE
PERRY
& WIFE OF THOMAS
FOOTE
WAS BORN IN LEE
BERKSHIRE C. MASS
DEC 9, 1794
DIED
JUNE 11, 1866
aged 71 yrs.

OP 3:1 **Thomas Foote**

Thomas FOOTE, son of ***David FOOTE*** and ***Betsey HAMBLIN*** *(OP 3:3-4)* b. May 21, 1788; m. Mar 12, 1812 to ***Dama PERRY***; d. July 31, 1856. *Issue:* ***Semantha FOOTE***, b. Sept 30, 1812; d. Oct 28, 1813. ***David FOOTE***, b. July 18(24), 1814(24) [Lee, MA]; m. Jan 1, 1844 to *Abigail CRANS* (b. Dec 4, 1824 [Proctorville,

OH]; d. Lorain, O., Apr 13, 1905); d. Jan 20 [30], 1887, Oscoda [Osceola], Iosco Co., Mich. ***Lyman Perry FOOTE***, b. Mar 22, 1817; m.1 Nov 24, 1842 to *Ruth Beng SMITH* of Dover (d. July 19, 1855); m.2 Oct 24, 1857 to *Rebecca Elsie TIEDEMAN*; d. Nov 23, 1889; res. Cleveland, O. ***Thomas FOOTE***, b. Mar 29(26), 1819; m.1 May, 1840 to *Candace E. PARK* (b. Sept 23, 1822, Dover, d. Feb 15, 1887); m.2 Sept 1878 to *Clara E. WILFORD* (b. Jan 6, 1854, Amherst, O.); d. Nov 1903; res. Lorain, O. ***Temperance R. FOOTE***, b. Dec 29, 1826; m. May 11, 1845 to *James M. GARDNER*, of Ramsey, Ill. (b. Watertown, NY, Dec 22, 1819, d. June 20, 1898); she was a school teacher at Dover. Abram W. Foote, Foote Family Comprising the Genealogy and History of Nathaniel Foote, vol. I, pp. 111, 229, 360-361, vol. II *If information conflicted, vol. II is in ( ). This does not apply to spouses DOB and DOD which are placed in ( ).* [Daphne Gawne]

OP 3:1 Dama Perry Foote

Wife of Thomas Foote:
Ancestors of Dama Perry Foote:

I. ***Edward PERRY***, b. 27 Jan 1598/99, England; m. ***Sarah*** (b. 1592, Devon, England; d. 1659, Sandwich, Barnstable, MA); d. England. Daphne Gawne

II. ***Ezra PERRY***, b. 1625, Devonshire, Eng.; d. 16 Oct 1689, Sandwich; bur. Old Sandwich Cemetery, Sandwich; m. ***Elizabeth BURGE*** (b. c1629, Eng.; d. 26 Sept 1717, Sandwich; bur. Old Sandwich Cemetery; dau. of *Thomas BURGE* (b. Sandwich) and *Dorothy WAYNES* (d. 1683)). Gawne

III. ***John PERRY***, b. 1 Jan 1655/56, Sandwich; d. 31 Oct 1732, Sandwich; m. ***Elizabeth CROWELL*** (d. 23 Apr 1727, Sandwich; dau. of *John CROWELL* (b. Yarmouth, MA; d. 1672) and *Elish.* Gawne

IV. ***John PERRY***, b. Apr 1684, Sandwich; d. 18 Apr 1739, Sandwich m. ***Abigail DAMON*** (b. Oct 1692, Scituate, MA; d. Apr 1764, Sandwich, MA; dau. of *Zachariah DAMON* (b. c1672, Scituate; d. 3 Sep 1730, Scituate) and *Martha WOODWORTH* (b. c1673, Scituate)). Gawne

V. ***Arthur PERRY***, b. 18 July1721, Sandwich; m. ***Catherine GIFFORD*** (b. 9 June 1732, Falmouth, MA; d. 5 Feb 1818, Lee, MA; dau. of *Justin* (b. 12 Oct 1691) and *Ruth GIFFORD* (b. 14 Feb 1698/99, Falmouth, MA)). Gawne

VI. ***Abraham PERRY***, b. 12 Mar 1766, Lee, MA; d. 17 Mar 1843; m. ***Temperance HATCH*** (b. 10 May 1768, Falmouth, MA; d. 28 Feb 1846; dau. of ***Lemuel HATCH***, b. 27 Feb 1733/34, Tolland, CT; d. c1827, Grand Isle, VT (son of *Joseph HATCH* (b. 3 Aug 1689; d. 1751, Falmouth, MA) and *Rebecca PARKER*) and ***Temperance HATCH***, b. 15 June 1736, Falmouth (dau. of *Edward HATCH* (b. 2 June 1703, Falmouth) and *Abia DAVIS* (b. 12 Oct 1707, Falmouth)). Gawne

VII. ***Dama PERRY***, b. 9 Dec 1793 *(varies from tombstone)*, Lee, Mass.; d. 14 June 1866, Dover, Ohio, m. ***Thomas FOOTE***. Gawne

Vital Record information for Lee, Mass. including the Perry family is available on line at: www.rootsweb.com/~maberksh/towns/lee.lee-vr.html

*Children of **Thomas Foote** and **Dama Perry**:*

*Children of **David FOOTE** and **Abigail CRANS**:* ***Isabel FOOTE***, b. Lorain, O., 27 Feb 1847; m. 10 Jan 1868 to *William PURCUPILL* of Lorain, O (d. 13 July1803 *(mistake in year)* at Lorain); 4 children. ***Ella A. FOOTE***, b. 10 Apr 1852, Lorain; m. 4 Oct 1870 to *Ira B. MANSFIELD* of Lorain (d. 16 Dec 1897, Chicago, Ill.). ***Ada E. FOOTE***, b. 15 Apr 1857, Vanar, Mich.; m. 25 Dec 1874 to *Eugene SANBORN* of Lorain; 8 children all b. Lorain. ***Herbert P. FOOTE***, b. 4 May 1860, Denmark, Mich.; m. *Mary SEINSATH*. Abram W. Foote, Foote Family Comprising the Genealogy and History of Nathaniel Foote, vol. I, p. 360.

*Children of **Lyman Perry FOOTE** and **Ruth Beng SMITH**:* ***Romelia M. FOOTE***, b. 17 Aug 1843; m. *William H. QUAYLE*, 4 children. ***Hiram S. FOOTE***, b. 8 June 1847, d. 30 July 1854. ***Florence R. FOOTE***, b. 9 July 1850, m. 11 Apr 1873 to *Henry E. LEUER*, 2 children. ***William FOOTE***, b. 15 May 1855, d. 1 Aug 1855.

Children of Lyman Perry FOOTE and Rebecca Elsie TIEDEMAN: ***Cora Elsie FOOTE***, b. 14 Feb 1860, m. 20 Aug 1881, *Christian NARTEN*, res. 1979 E. 82nd St., Cleveland, O., 5 children. ***Helen Peng FOOTE***, b. 23 May 1879, m. 24 July1901 to *William Elmer ROBERTS*, 2 children. Foote, vol. I, pp. 360-61.

*Children of **Thomas FOOTE** and **Candace E. PARK:*** ***Temperance FOOTE***, b. 1841, Dover; m.1 *Charles Augustus REED*, lawyer, of Ill. 1 child. He d.; m.2 *Milligan REED* (brother of August), 2 children. ***Corwin T. FOOTE***, b. 11 Apr 1847, m. *Clara M. COTTON*. ***Waldo Emerson FOOTE***, b. 22 Dec 1880, Amherst, O.; m. 10 June 1903 to *Olive C. PARSONS*, of So. Amherst, O., res. Amherst. Foote, vol. I, p. 361.

***FOOTE-Thomas** (died)*, at North Amherst, October 24, aged eighty-four years. Cleveland Necrology File, Nov 1, 1903.

The State of Ohio, Cuyahoga County, ss. I hereby certify, that on the 11th day of May A. D. 1845, I duly solemnized the Marriage Contract between the said ***James M. GARDNER*** and ***Temperance R. FOOTE***. Thomas Thompson, MG. Marriage Record, Cuyahoga County, OH, vol. 2, p. 296.

*Children of **Temperance R. FOOTE** and **James M. GARDNER**: Issue:* ***Mary A. GARDNER***, b. 16 Apr 1846, Dover; m. 21 Oct 1875 to *Isaac TRAIZER*, Georgetown, Ill.; ed. at Cleveland, O., music teacher; Methodist. ***George W. GARDNER***, b. 27 Jan 1848, Dover; res. Ramsey, Illinois.; m. 6 Mar 1895 to *Florence BALLARD* at Blenheim, Ontario, Canada; ed. Cleveland and Jamestown, NY; farmer; Methodist. ***Dewitt C. GARDNER***, b. 9 Dec 1851, d. Aug 1852. ***Emma T. GARDNER***, b. 22 July1853, Cleveland, O.; res. Ramsey, Ill.; m. 27 Aug 1868, Lexington, NY to *John C. MARTIN* (b. 17 July1826, Williamsport, Pa., d. 31 July1892); ed. Cleveland, and Jamestown, NY; 8 children. ***Cora E. GARDNER***, b. 8 Oct 1855, d. Aug 1856. ***Susie GARDNER***, b. 29 July1858, d. 16 June 1884. ***Minnie GARDNER***, b. 25 Jan 1860, d. 15 June 1878. ***Lena GARDNER***, b. 12 June 1864; res. Ramsey, Ill.; m. 14 Aug 1883, Vandalia, Ill. to *William HENNISON* (b. 11 Aug 1859, near Pittsburgh, Pa.); 4 children. Foote, vol. I, p. 229.

OP 3:2 **Richard L. Foote**

RICHARD L.
SON OF
R.L. & J.B. FOOT
Died
June 28, 1856
AE 1Yr. 8 M.

Richard FOOTE*,* b. Oct 22, 1854; d. in infancy; oldest child of ***Ransom L. FOOTE*** (b. July 22, 1828, Dover, son of *Ransom* and *Catharine PORTER FOOTE*; m. Oct 1, 1853) and ***Julia B. FARR*** (dau. of *Algenon FARR* and *Sophrons SMITH,* b. June 23, 1833 in Dover; d. Mar 1907, bur. Royalton, Morrison, Minn.).

Siblings of Richard: ***Harriett S. FOOTE***, b. May 3, 1856; m. Jan, 1881, *J.M. GOULD*; d. Mar 9, 1883. ***Ida B. FOOTE***, b. July 3, 1857; m. Aug 10, 1887, *J.M. BLACK* (he d. Feb 13, 1888) res. Royalton, Minn. ***Cora Dell FOOTE***, b. Feb 28, 1862; m. Dec 3, 1890 to *George Ames SAVORY* of Royalton, Minn. (b. May 9, 186_). ***Charles R. FOOTE***, b. St. Cloud, Stearns, Minn., Dec 22, 1863; m. Mar 19, 1896, Royalton, Minn. to *Mattie RICTOR*. ***Alphonso E. FOOTE***, b. Lasock, Minn., Nov 22, 1865; m. June 26, 1894, Wis. to *Ellen RICTOR*. ***Henry P. FOOTE***, b. Two Rivers, Minn., July 22, 1867; m. Mar 25, 1889, Little Falls, Morrison, Minn. to *Anna SHAMBROCK*. Abram W. Foote, Foote Family Comprising the Genealogy and History of Nathaniel Foote, vol. I, pp. 362-363, 478.

OP 3:3 **David Foote**

Marker cracked and set in concrete.

DAVID FOOT
DIED
Jan 31, 1851
AE 91 yrs.

Small marker
Revolutionary
War
Soldier

Martha Devotion
Huntington
and
Lakewood Chapter
NSDAR,
1977

David FOOTE, son of ***Jonathan FOOTE*** and ***Sarah FENNER***, b. Colchester, Ct., Sept 4, 1760; removed from Colchester, Ct., to Lee, 1775. Farmer, Lee; Whig; highway surveyor, 1794. In 1816, with his family he removed by way of Buffalo, N.Y., to Dover, Ohio, then a howling wilderness. The journey was made with horses and wagon, occupying three weeks: Presbys. Daphne Gawne

FOOT, David, Private, *Capt. Ezra Whittelsey's Co, Col. John Brown's* detachment of Berkshire Co. militia; enlisted Sept 11, 1777; discharged Sept 30, 1777; service, 20 days at the Northward; also *Samuel Goodrich's Co. Lieut. Col. Miles Powell's* Berkshire Co. regt.; enlisted July 18, 1779; discharged Aug 22, 1779; service, 1 mo. 10 days, travel included. at New Haven, Conn.; also, *Capt. Amos Porter's Co., Col. David Rocester's (Rosseter's)* regt.; enlisted Oct 14, 1780; discharged Oct 17, 1780; service, 3 days, on the alarm in Berkshire Oct 14, 1780; also same Co. and regt., enlisted Oct 18, 1780; discharged Oct 21, 1780; service, 4 days on the alarm in Berkshire of Oct 18, 1780. History of the Town of Lee, p. 128. "Massachusetts Soldiers and Sailors of the Revolutionary War," printed by the State in 17 Vols.

DIED.

In Dover, Cuyahoga Co., on the first inst. ***Mr. David FOOT***, in the 92d year of his age. The deceased emigrated from Berkshire Co., Mass., in the year 1815. He endured the privations and hardships, peculiar to a new country, with resolution and perseverance, and had the satisfaction of seeing the wilderness converted into fruitful and well cultivated farms. Through his long pilgrimage, he ever pursued a strict path of honesty and integrity, which won for him the confidence and esteem of all who knew him. It is not known that he ever had an enemy, and all seemed willing to acknowledge him to be one of the "noblest works of God," an honest man. He leaves a large family of children and grand-children who, while they acknowledge his loss, mourn not as those who have no hope.

His funeral was attended on the 2nd inst. by a large congregation of his relatives and friends, where they listened to a very interesting and thrilling discourse from the *Rev. John R. JEWETT* of the Methodist Episcopal Church.

"The winter of trouble is past,
The storms of affliction are o'er,
His struggle is ended at last,
And sorrow and death no more."

Com.

Lorain Argus, Elyria, OH, Feb 18, 1851, p. 3, col. 1.

Ancestors of David Foot:

I. Three brothers, ***Nathaniel, Pasco*** and ***John FOOTE*** came from Shalford, Colchester, England, in the brig "Ann." They landed at Plymouth in 1630. John died without issue, Pasco settled at Salem, Mass.

Nathaniel FOOTE, b. c1593; m. in England c1615, ***Elizabeth DEMING*** (b. c1595, d. 28 July 1683, she m.2

c1646 *Thomas WELLES.* He was one of the first settlers of Wethersfield, CT. He was magistrate, afterwards Governor of the Colony.); made a freeman 1633; d. c1644.

Mr. Foote married in England, about the year 1615, to Elizabeth Deming, sister of *Mr. John DEMING*, who was one of the first settlers of Wethersfield, and for many years one of the magistrates of the Colony of Connecticut, and one of the patentees named in its charter. His children were all born in England, except perhaps the youngest.

From all that we can learn, Mr. Foote came from Shalford, in Colchester, Eng., and settled in Watertown, Mass. The first mention I find of his name is in the Records of the Colony of Massachusetts Bay, in 1633, when he took the oath of freeman.

Nathaniel Foote, one of the first settlers of Wethersfield, Ct., belongs, not to that class of men who fill a large place in the world's history, because called by some great emergency into positions of power and influence, - but to that more meritorious class of pious and excellent person, who, born to the great inheritance of labor, walk meekly along the paths of common life, perform every duty, public or private, love and help their fellow men, and act always as if in their Great Task Master's eye. It is to such men that society owes at once its peace, stability and progress, and yet history takes no more such, and hence "The world knows nothing of its greatest men."

His business in life was that of agriculture, - necessarily the leading pursuit of New England in its early history.... And in every period of society the agriculture population has proved of the highest importance to the wealth, dignity and strength of a State. It is from this class of the population that the city and the village, that commerce and the arts, are ever drawing the bone and muscle of their laborers, and much of the energy of their directing force. In no other of the directing pursuits in society are there the same facilities for cultivating bodily energy, and the force and vigor of mind consequent upon a vigorous constitution.... Mr. Foote was an intelligent, pious and industrious farmer, and, like all of that class of farmers, he was from time to time summoned to the discharge of public trusts by his neighbors and townsmen.

Mr. Foote died in 1644, aged about 51 years, and was buried in the ancient burying ground in the rear of the Meeting House, where are gathered together the ashes of nine generations. He left behind him, surviving, a widow, two sons and five daughters. He left no will but the following is mentioned in his estate: The age of the five children living with their mother. ***Nath: FFOOTE***, 24years; ***Rob FFOOTE***, about 17 years; ***Frances*** about 15 year, ***Sarah*** about 12 years and ***Rebecka*** about 10 years. Abram W. Foote, Foote Family Comprising the Genealogy and History of Nathaniel Foote, vol. I, p. 17.

II. ***Nathaniel FOOTE***, b. c1620; m. 1646 to ***Elizabeth SMITH*** (dau. of *Lieut. Samuel SMITH*, Elizabeth m.2 *William GULL*); d. 1655. Foote, vol. I, p. 27.

III. ***Nathaniel FOOTE***, b. 10 Jan 1647, p. 27. (14 Jan 1648, p. 29) Wethersfield, Mass.; m. 2 May 1672, ***Margaret BLISS*** of Springfield, Mass. (dau. of *Nathaniel BLISS* of Springfield; d. 3 Apr 1745, Colchester); d. 12 Jan 1703, Wethersfield, CT; 9 children, 7th Josiah.

After residing in Hatfield two years, he removed to Springfield, like almost every householder, he was called into the service of his country against the Indians, and was actively engaged in the bloody and successful attack on their encampment at the falls in Connecticut river a few miles above Deerfield, since called Turner's Falls, in commemoration of the brave *Capt. Turner*, who commanded the expedition.

Although a carpenter by trade...he appears to have pursued the practice of law, his name frequently appearing on the records of the County Court as Attorney in cases before that court. Foote, vol. I, pp. 27, 29.

IV. ***Josiah FOOTE***, b. 27 Sept 1688; m. 7 Dec 1738 to ***Sarah WELLS*** (d. 3 Aug 1766); d. Dec 1778. Foote, vol. 1, pp. 35-36.

V. ***Jonathan FOOTE***, b. 23 Mar 1715; m. 25 May 1749 to ***Sarah FENNER*** (dau. of *John FENNER* of Saybrook, CT; d. 1791, ae. 61); d. 11 Nov 1803, Lee, Mass; res. Colchester, CT. and Lee, Mass. Foote, vol. I, p. 53.

Children of Jonathan FOOTE and *Sarah FENNER*: ***Freelove FOOTE***, b. 11 Mar 1749/50 (50), Colchester; d. 11 Nov 1803; m. 24 May 1769 to *Simon (Simeon) WRIGHT* (of Rutland, VT). ***Jonathan FOOTE***, b. 30 Mar 1752, Laybrook *(Old Saybrook?)*, Middlesex, CT; d. 26 May 1837, Lee, Berkshire, MA; m. *Deliverance GIBBS* (d. 28 Apr 1828, ae. 77), 23 Dec 1773, Colchester, New London, CT. ***Fenner FOOTE***, b. 5 Oct 1754, Colchester; d. 27 Apr 1847, Lee; m. 11 Mar 1779, Lee to *Sarah WILCOX* (d. 14 Jan 1840). ***Sarah FOOTE***, b. 12 Jan 1758, Laybrook; d. 1759-1852; m. c.1778, *Jesse CLARK* of Lee, Mass. ***David FOOTE***, b. Sept 4, 1760, Laybrook; d. aft. 1803; m. 12 Jan 1785, Lee to *Elizabeth HAMBLIN.* ***Asahel FOOTE***, b. 22 Apr 1763, Laybrook; d. 20 Mar 1841; m. 21 Aug 1793, Lee to *Anne ABBOTT.* ***Lovica FOOTE***, b. 1765; d. 1766-1859. ***Solomon FOOTE***, b. 1768, d. 26 Oct 1811. Stuart Cameron Freeman and Foote, vol. I, pp. 53-54.

VI. ***David FOOTE***, b. Sept 4, 1760; m. Jan 12, 1785 at Lee, Mass. to ***Betsy HAMBLIN***. Res. Lee, Mass. and Dover, Ohio.

Issue: ***Betsy FOOTE***, b. June 23, 1786; d. Nov 16, 1860; m. Nov 3, 1806 to *Noah CROCKER.* ***Thomas FOOTE*** *(OP 3:1)*, b. May 21, 1788, m. *Dama PERRY.* ***David FOOTE***, b. July 11, 1790; d. Oct 4, 1790, in Lee, Mass. ***Silas FOOTE***, b. Aug 18, 1791; d. July 14, 1828, Dover Twp., Cuy Co., OH; m. *Emeline SMITH* (d. 28 May 1882, Melrose, Todd Co., MN). ***Delia FOOTE***, b. May 3, 1794; d. Jan 6, 1852; m. Oct 7, 1818 to *Elisah TAYLOR*, of Lee, Mass. ***Lovica FOOTE*** *(OP 2:1)*, b. Nov 29, 1796, in Lee, Mass.; m. Aug 22, 1815 to *Benjamin STEVENS.* ***Temperance FOOTE***, b. Nov 7, 1800, Lee, Mass; d. Dec 1894, Amherst, Ohio; m. July 3, 1821 to *John Broughton ROBERTSON*, (b. at Ballston Spa., N.Y., Dec 26, 1797; d. Mar 7, 1875, Amherst, Ohio). ***Ranson FOOTE*** *(OP 2:11-12)*, b. Feb 15, 1803 [1802, *vital records of Lee, Berkshire, Mass.*]; m. *Cathrine PORTER.* ***Laura FOOTE***, b. Jan 6, 1807; m. Sept 3, 1824, *John D. TAYLOR*, of Lee, Mass. ***Caroline FOOTE***, b. Aug 5, 1809; m. Jan 14, 1830 to *Alexis*

MILLER of Lee, Mass. Foote, vol. I, pp. 53-54, 111-112 and Marriage Records.
Vital Record information for the FOOTE family is available on line for Lee, Mass. at: www.rootsweb.com/~maberksh/towns/lee.lee-vr.html

Children of David Foote and Elizabeth Hamblin:
Betsey** (FOOTE) **CROCKER, 64, value of real estate $600, b. Mass.; ***Sophia***, 41. 1850 FC OH CYDO p. 218A, lines 35-36.
The State of Ohio, Cuyahoga County, ss. I do hereby certify that on the fourth day of August 1822 I Joined in the State of Matrimony ***Silas FOOT*** and ***Emeline SMITH*** of Lawful age - given under my hand and Seal this 7th day of October in the year of Our Lord one thousand eight hundred and twenty two. Noah Crocker, Justice Peace Marriage Record, Cuyahoga County, OH, vol. 2, p. 3.
Sylvanus SMITH was the first settler in the part of the township which became known as Dover Center. He was a strong-charactered man, who advocated temperance vigorously in the settlement. But his sister married *Asa BLOOD,* who built and kept the first log tavern in that part of the township. Asa placed a post office in the tavern and *Mr. WOLVERTON* stopped his mail stage there three times a week. Smith's other two sisters married *Ansel RICE* and *Asher COOLEY.* A History of Westlake, Ohio 1811-1961, Book I, Chapters V and VI.
Delia FOOT m. ***Elisha TAYLOR*** of Newburgh 29 Oct 1812, Cuyahoga County, OH. Marriage Record, Cuyahoga County, OH, vol. 1, p. 100.
The State of Ohio, Cuyahoga County, I hereby certify that on the 27th day of June, I Joined in the State of Matrimony ***John B. ROBERTSON*** and ***Temperance FOOT*** at Dover. Given under my hand and seal ... in the year of our Lord 1821. Noah Crocker Justice Peace. Marriage Record, Cuyahoga County, OH, vol. 1, p. 167.
Mrs. Temperance FOOTE ROBERTSON was born in Lee, Mass., in 1800, and came to the Western Reserve in 1815, but returned to her native State to reside for a few years, after which, with her husband, ***John B. ROBERTSON***, she came to Amherst, where she lived until her death, at the age of ninety-three. She possessed fine intellectual ability, and, while keeping in memory those crucial tests of early settlement in the unbroken forest, later calmly contemplated the work of the brave women who so gladly gave up the comforts of civilization for the little environment of a few square miles in the wilderness, where life was essentially a struggle for competence. Pioneer Women of the Western Reserve, Amherst, p. 320.
Children of ***Temperance FOOTE*** *and* ***John Broughton ROBERTSON***: ***Sarah M. ROBERTSON****,* d. unm. ***Ebenezer ROBERTSON****,* d. ae. 10. ***Theodore ROBERTSON****,* m.1 *Laura JOHNSON*, m.2 *Harriet HOGEBOOM.* ***John B. ROBERTSON****,* b. Omaha, Neb.; d. Amherst, O.; m. 1850 to *Eliza BELDEN.* ***Franklin Nelson ROBERTSON***, b. Omaha, Neb.; m. *Louise CRELLIN.* ***Mary L. ROBERTSON****,* m. *Parks FOSTER* of Elyria, O. Abram W. Foote, Foote Family Comprising the Genealogy and History of Nathaniel Foote, vol. I, p. 112.
Daughter of Temperance Foote Robertson:
In October 1855, ***Parks FOSTER*** and ***Mary L. ROBERTSON***, a native of Lorain county, were united in marriage and had four children...***Sarah May*** is the wife of *S.L. KENT*, of New York City; ***Burton P.*** is a resident of Findlay, Ohio; ***Mary L.*** is the wife of *Arthur W. WALKER,* of Portsmouth, N. H.; and ***Miss Florence*** is a student of music at Boston, Mass. ***John B. ROBERTSON***, Mrs. Foster's father, was a native of Ballston, N. Y., and was well known in prominent Democratic circles. He was formerly a resident of Saratoga, N. Y., coming to Lorain county in 1830. He married ***Miss Temperance FOOT***, a native of Lee, Mass., and they had five children - three sons and two daughters - of whom two sons are living, in Lorain county and New York, respectively. Mr. Robertson died in 1875. His widow is now living in Amherst township, Lorain county, at the advanced age of ninety-three years.

Mrs. Foster passed her girlhood in Amherst township, where she was educated. It was after marriage, when her health began to fail, that she and her husband went South. She has ever been a hard worker in the interests of reform, a zealous Church woman, and was the one who took the initiative and most active part in the erecting of the present Baptist Church building. A member of several organizations, she acts as chairman of numerous committees. She is a live worker in the social interests of the Church, and raised the wherewithal to establish the Temperance Reading Room. In the Anti-Liquor League recently organized, she is one of the active workers, and a leader it its councils. She is a power in the family circle, and a counselor to her husband, at times aggressive when he may be mild or indifferent, but always on the side of right, to that end, in all things, fearless and unflinching. Commemorative Biographical Record of Huron and Lorain Counties, 1894, p. 548.
ROBERTSON John B., Dec 26, 1797-Mar 7, 1875; ***Theodore H.***, Mar 21, 1821-Dec 23, 1871; ***Temperance***, Nov 7, 1800-Dec 21, 1893; ***Sarah M.***, Apr 3, 1822-Dec 6, 1881; ***Ebenezer***, Apr 21, 1826-Dec 7, 1836. ***ROBERTSON John B.,*** Sept 19, 1828-July 7, 1896. Middle Ridge Cemetery, Amherst, OH. Genealogical Workshops of the Lorain County Historical Society, Cemetery Inscriptions of Lorain County, Ohio 1980, Middle Ridge Cemetery, pp. 33-34.
John D. TAYLOR to ***Laura FOOT*** Married 8th September 1824. I do hereby certify that John D. Taylor & Laura Foot were duly joined together in marriage, by me, on the 8th day of September A.D.1824. John McCrea, Pastor of the Church in Dover. Marriage Record, Cuyahoga County, OH, vol. 2, p. 57.
The reader will please excuse me for giving some of my own experiences and recollections of log cabin life, recollections both pleasing and sad, yet none of remorse for wrong done to others. When I was eighteen years old, I made the acquaintance of a Yankee girl of the genuine Plymouth rock stamp named ***Laura FOOT***, born in Berkshire county, Massachusetts, in 1806, her father having emigrated from the Berkshire Hills in 1816, and settled on the lake shore in Dover. Two years afterwards, we were married, after which I bought land for a farm in Rockport on the west side of Rocky river, on the road leading from Cleveland to Elyria, a dense wilderness of

heavy timber. In March, 1824, I built my log cabin on that land, and after cutting down all the trees that were liable to fall upon the house, I moved my wife with household goods into it. She was intelligent, pure-minded, with a great warm heart, and an expert in the art of house-keeping, and could spin and weave cloth, and commenced the business as soon as I could raise flax and buy some sheep for the wool.

After being settled in my cabin, I commenced in earnest clearing land for corn, potatoes, etc. My whole outfit being yoke of oxen, two cows, five hives for bees, and provisions enough to last through the Summer. I began to think that my wife was too good for me, and commenced to make myself better.

Our health was good, sleep sweet, and that cabin was a paradise to us. Three children were born to us in it. The first died in infancy. If it had lived till now it would be sixty-five years old. Dear old log cabin; scene of so much more joy than sorrow; so much more of sunshine than shadow.

Occasionally I visit it in my dreams, as also the better house, built before vacating the former one, where my wife died on September 8, 1858, the 36th anniversary of our wedding day. Extract by John D. Taylor, printed in the Cuyahoga West Tracer, vol. 19, #4, December 1995, p. 61.

Alexis MILLER to ***Caroline FOOT*** This Certifies that the Marriage Covenant was duly solemnized between Alexis Miller & Caroline Foot on the fourteenth day of January in the year of our Lord one thousand eight hundred and thirty by me John McCrea, Pastor of the Church in Dover, Recorded August 12th 1830. Marriage Record, Cuyahoga County, OH, vol. 2, p. 207.

MILLER, Alexis, 64, Farmer, value of real estate $2,500, personal estate $700, b. New Jersey; ***Caroline***, 61, b. Mass; ***Susan***, 20, b. Ohio; *Clyden FIELD*, 17, male; *Erviss FIELD*, 2; *Sariliam? FIELD*, 42, Farmer, value of real estate $1500. 1870 FC OH Lorain Co., Avon, p. 363, family 345, lines 11-16.

OP 3:4 Elizabeth Hamblin Foote

Marker cracked and set in concrete.

ELIZABETH
WIFE OF
DAVID FOOT
DIED
Jan 10, 1844
Aged 80 Years

Betsy HAMBLIN, sister of *Deliverance HAMBLIN*, b. Jan 1764, Lee, MA; dau. of ***Job HAMBLIN***, of Lee, Mass, formerly of Falmouth, Mass; she removed with her parents to Lee, 1772; m. June 1785, Lee, Mass. to ***David FOOTE***. Daphne Gawne

Falmouth, Barnstable County, Massachusetts. In 1602, sea *Captain Bartholomew GOSNOLD* sailed from England, landed on these shores, explored the region and gave Cape Cod its name. What is now known as Falmouth was first settled in 1660 and is located just north of Martha's Vineyard. The settlement received a charter in 1686 from Plymouth Colony to establish a town, which was originally called Suckanesset after the Indian name for the place. By the 1690s, the town became known as Falmouth, after the port in England from which Gosnold sailed. In the early years, Falmouth was primarily a farming community. From 1820 to the Civil War, Falmouth was a whaling port and throughout the 19th century produced many whalingmen who went on whaleships from Falmouth and other ports. Falmouth Historical Society, (cited July 2004). <http://www.falmouthhistoricalsociety.org/history.htlm>.

DIED-In Dover, Cuyahoga co., on the 10th inst. after a short illness, ***Mrs. Elizabeth***, wife of ***Mr. David FOOT***, formerly of Lee, Berkshire co., Mass., in the 80th year of her age.

She emigrated to this state in 1814, and settled in Dover while the town was yet a wilderness, and patiently endured all those privations and toils which were peculiar to the first settlers of this country. She has left an aged companion and several children, together with a large circle of grandchildren and other relatives to mourn her loss; but they mourn not as those who have no hope.

"Beneath a numerous train of ills
Our feeble flesh and heart may fail;
Yet shall our hope in thee, our God,
O'er every gloomy fear prevail."

Lorain Republican, Elyria, OH, Wednesday, Jan 17, 1844, p. 3, col. 3.

Ancestors of Elizabeth Hamblin Foote:

I. ***James HAMBLIN***, b. 1696, Barnstable, MA; d. after 1763; m. ***Mary CROCKER*** (b. 8 Apr 1700). Daphne Gawne

II. ***Job HAMBLIN***, b. c1744, Barnstable, MA; m. 18 Jan 1761, Sandwich, Barnstable Co., MA to ***Abigail GIFFORD*** (b. 28 Sept 1741, Sandwich, dau. of *Cornelius GIFFORD* (b. 9 Feb 1717/18) and *Elizabeth BARLOW* (b. Sandwich)). Gawne

III. ***Elizabeth HAMBLIN***, b. 1764, Cholchester, New London, CT. Gawne

Job HAMBLIN (1736-1815) served, 1780, as private in *Capt. Amos Porter's* company, *Col. David Rosseter's* regiment. He was born in Falmouth, Mass.; died in Lee, Mass. Job Hamblin and ***Abigail GIFFORD***, his wife, m. 1761. Daughter, ***Betsy HAMBLIN***, m. ***David FOOTE***. The National Society of the Daughters of the American Revolution, vol. 56, p. 133, DAR ID Number: 55283.

Possible father of Betsy Hamblin:
***Job HAMBLIN**,* Males: 10-16 yrs.: 1, 45+ yrs.: 1. Females: 45+: 1. 1800 FC Massachusetts, Berkshire Co., Lee, p. 261.
Vital Record information for the HAMBLIN family is available on line for Lee, Mass. at: www.rootsweb.com/~maberksh/towns/lee.lee-vr.html

OP 3:5 Aldrich Monument

Wm. W. ALDRICH
BORN
Oct 17, 1817
DIED
Nov 19, 1903

MARTHA
WIFE OF
Wm. W. ALDRICH
DIED
NOV 29. 1875
AGED
57 Yrs. 1 Ms. 22 Ds.
ALDRICH

HARRIET E.
ALDRICH
DIED
Nov 1, 1851
AGED
4 Yrs. 10 Ms. 2 Ds.
IDA
1856-1910

MARTHA H.B.
ALDRICH
DIED
Oct 23, 1848
AGED
6 Yrs. 4 Ms. 20 Ds.

OP 3:5 William Waterman Aldrich

William W. ALDRICH was the son of ***Aaron ALDRICH III*** and ***Elizabeth WINSOR** (OP 4:1)*, whose parents arrived in Dover from Rhode Island a year before his birth. The family left Dover in 1822 and moved to Hartwick, NY, then Watertown in 1828 before returning to Dover when William was twelve. Gertrude Aldrich Barker Rose, "Genealogy of the Aldrich Family," p. 10.

William Waterman ALDRICH, b. 17 Oct 1817, Dover; d. 19 Nov 1903, Lorain, Lorain Co., OH; m.1 5 Feb 1840, Dover to ***Martha BASSETT***; m.2 Jan 22, 1878 to ***Mrs. Lorinda (GRISWOLD) HILLIARD***. Ima Aldrich Slaby

William Waterman ALDRICH I was born in Dover, now Westlake. He married ***Martha BASSETT*** on 5 Feb 1840, Dover, O.

Issue: ***William Waterman ALDRICH II***, b. 1[7] Jan 1841; d. 2 June 1924, Bay Village, O., bur. Evergreen Cem. (Cleveland Necrology File); m. 12 June 1862,{Elyria, Lorain, O.} to *Laura Jeanette BATES* (dau. of *Daniel BATES* and *Rachel OMAN*, b. 6 Feb 1841, Avon, O.; d. 27 May 1931, BV, bur. Evergreen Cem.). ***Martha Hall Bassett ALDRICH***, b. 3 June 1842; d. 23 Oct 1848, Dover *(bur. this lot)*. ***Lucy Elizabeth ALDRICH***, b. 20[23] Apr 1844; d. 21 Aug 1895{[1894], Holland, Lucas, O.}; m. 23 May 1864 [5] to *Harrison Henry BATES* (son of *Daniel BATES* and *Rachel OMAN*, b. 5 Oct 1836, Avon, O.; d. 26 Nov 1902, Holland, O.).

Luther Melancthon ALDRICH, b. 6 June 1845; d. 6 Mar 19{32}, Traverse City, MI; m. 3 Oct 1872, {Elyria, Lorain Co., OH} to *Mary Elizabeth HURST* {dau. of *Frederick HURST* and *Ann BAKER*, b. 10 Jan 1855, Dover; d. 6 Mar 1921, Traverse City, MI}.

Hariette Emma ALDRICH, b. 3 Dec 1846; d (1) Nov 1851, Dover *(bur. this lot)*. ***Lucias {Lucius} Parker ALDRICH***, b. 10 July1850; d. 17 Jan 1940, Sandusky (Milan), Erie, O.; m. 4 Oct 1876[9] to *Minerva TAYLOR* (b. 22 Jan 1845, Reves, Saskatchewan, Canada; d. 20 Nov 1923, Milan, O. (1936)) *Death certificate not found in Ohio*. ***Evangeline St. Clair ALDRICH***, b. 1 Dec 1852; d. 22 Jan 1902, Elyria, O.; m. 1 Oct 1876 to *Thomas Jefferson BATES* (son of *Daniel Bates* and *Rachel OMAN*, b. 14 Sept 1848, Avon; d. 22 Dec 1915, Elyria, O.).

Celia Marthaetta ALDRICH, b. 10 Sept 1855; d. Dec 1932, Lorain, O.; m. 30 Sep 1879 to *Norton Buckley HURST* (b. 26 Feb 1851, Dover [Lorain], O.; d. 21 Oct 1930, Lorain, O.).

Ida Minerva (Margetta*) ALDRICH**, buried this lot,* b. 22 Oct/Nov 1856; d. 21(22*) Mar 1910, Gallipolis, Gallia Co.; Ohio, never married; ***Clara Emma ALDRICH, b. 19 Sep 1858; d. 5 Feb 1952, Pasadena, Los Angeles Co., Calif.; m. {27 Mar [Nov] 1881 (1887*)} to *Francis Asbury MILLIS* (b. 10 Nov 1859, Elyria, O.; d. 5 Oct 1938, Pasadena, Calif.). All of the Aldrich children were born in Dover. Rose, pp. 18-19.

Resources used if additions/contradictions: [George H. Drake, "Aldrich Generation Chart," pp. 1, 6-8] (Genealogy of William Bassett*), {Ima Aldrich Slaby}, Evergreen Cemetery Records.

William W. ALDRICH, son of ***Aaron ALDRICH***, received the advantages of a good common district school education until twelve years of age. Three years after that he attended school during the winter months. With this exception, he from choice, worked faithfully for his father until he was twenty-one years of age. These early years were spent in clearing up the forest, making roads, tearing down the old log dwelling, and replacing it with new structures. Often did he work until midnight to burn the log heap rolled together during the day. Homespun garments he wore, homespun tow and linen in summer, the fuller cloth in winter. Well does he remember the yoke of cattle and lumber wagon that, filled with father's family and neighbors, he so often drove to the old town house in Dover, where all denominations met under one roof to worship a common father.

At the age of twenty-one, Mr. Aldrich hired to his father for the term of one year, at eleven dollars per month; losing but a half day's time once in four weeks - this to attend covenant meetings.

February 5, 1840, Mr. Aldrich was married to ***Miss Martha BASSETT***, daughter of ***Nathan BASSETT***, of Dover. Renting his father's farm, he worked for one year, receiving one-third of its products to share. At this time, with twenty-five dollars as first payment, he commenced on a farm of his own. Five years, only, passed, when he was the owner of seventy-five acres of land. From this time, while he remained in Dover, he was ever active in business. His good wife, in every sense of the word a helpmate, by her wisdom and prudence, contributed to the success which followed.

Soon after the death of Mrs. Aldrich's father, who was killed by lightening, April 6, 1842, Mr. Aldrich took possession of the "old homestead," buying up the other heirs. To this valuable farm of one hundred and sixty-eight acres, he added many other acres.

Commencing, in 1844, in a small way, the slaughtering business, increasing trade led him to build a slaughter house, from which, for twenty-five years, he supplied Cleveland markets. At the same time, he was engaged on Lake Erie in a general coastwise trade. Wood and ship plank from Black River to Cleveland, limestone from Kelleys Island, and coal to Detroit, kept busy three scows - The "Mayflower," purchased from Livingstone & Phelps, of Black River; the scow "Consuello," of the same place; and finally, the scow "Wave," of Fairport, Ohio. All these ventures added to his capital, which he employed in general speculations; dealing largely in horses, cattle, sheep - in fact, in any thing that could be traded or sold.

In the spring of 1870, Mr. Aldrich removed to Elyria, where he purchased the *Charles ABBE* farm, paying for the same nine thousand dollars. Of Mr. Ashton he also bought a few thorough bred Hereford cattle, since which time he has made the breeding of that class a successful specialty, until the present day. Mr. Aldrich, when he first commenced the handling of Herefords, found it to be an "up-hill" business. At town, county, or State fairs, public opinion was against him; but his energy, skill, and business courtesy, soon set men everywhere thinking. And now, (as the old Grecians marked a happy day with a white stone,) Mr. Aldrich, in his travels through many States, finds very many white-faced Herefords that say to him, "Your toil and patience have made me worthy of notice." The issue of the first cow, "Florena," alone brought Mr. Aldrich two thousand, five hundred dollars. Competing at many of the State fairs, his success was unequalled, and to-day, Mr. W. W. Aldrich is recognized as the leading Hereford breeder of the United States, with only one exception, *Mr. T.L. MILLER*, of Illinois, who purchased his first stock of Mr. Aldrich.

Martha, the first wife of Mr. Aldrich, died November 29, 1875....On January 21, 1878, Mr. Aldrich took for his second wife ***Mrs. Lorinda (GRIWSOLD) HILLIARD***, of La Crosse, Wisconsin, with whom he is happily living. In her younger days, she was a resident of Avon, Lorain county, Ohio. For a time after her marriage with *Mr. (Joseph Warren) HILLIARD*, they resided in Avon and Dover, where they formed many strong friendships. After an absence of twenty years in Wisconsin, ten years as a widow, surrounded by a happy home, kind friends, and a large circle of acquaintances, all of them were reluctant to part with her, yet wishing her every joy and all happiness, they bade her farewell, as with her husband she returned to the friends of her youth. Mrs. Aldrich, in her fourteenth year, professed her faith in Christ, and united with the Methodist Episcopal church, and has ever since lived a consistent christian life.

Mr. W.W. Aldrich, on profession of his faith, was baptized by *Elder Moses WARE*, and united with the First Baptist church in Avon, Ohio, A. D. 1835, which membership he retained until January 27, 1836. At that time four brethren, viz: *A.A. Aldrich*, *Wm. W. Aldrich*, *Jesse ATWILL (Atwell)*, *Wm. NESBIT*, and *Sister ALEXANDER* met in conference, and resolved, with the advice of sister churches, to form a church in Dover. Said conference met February 24, 1836, and formed said church, Elder Ware giving the "right hand of fellowship."

On the 5th of March following, this little band met for church and covenant meeting, and voted Mr. W. W. Aldrich clerk of their body, which office he held for nine years. To this church did Mr. Aldrich belong until 1856, when on the death of his father and the removal of many of the members, the church was disbanded. Mr. Aldrich has never since united with a church, but has ever lived and maintained his first profession, by a well ordered life, and godly conversation.

Mr. Aldrich is yet hale and hearty, with a pleasant home, dear wife, kind children, and stands out as an example of what integrity, temperance, and economy may do for a man. History of Lorain County, Ohio, 1879, pp 141-143 and Traverse Region, 1884, p. 242.

In the spring of 1870 ***Mr. ALDRICH*** moved to Elyria where he purchased a large farm and was engaged in breeding Hereford cattle, which he continued till a short time since. Was one of the leading breeders of these cattle in Ohio. He moved to Northport, Mich., in the spring of 1881 and bought 300 acres of land. The first year he came he built a house, cleared twenty acres and built two miles of board fence. Traverse Region, 1884, p. 242.

Several years after ***Martha's*** death...***William (ALDRICH)*** moved to Northport, Mich. On Jan 21, 1878 he married ***Mrs. Lorinda HILLIARD*** of LaCrosse, Wis. She had been a former resident of Avon and Dover...she lived as a widow in Wisconsin ten years before marrying William Aldrich. They lived in Michigan eight years and then returned to Dover...In 1887, they removed to Lorain. His second wife died in 1896. After her death he remained in Lorain...He was a man of great physical strength and sustained until his last illness almost perfect health, with the exception of cataracts in both eyes, which were an affliction for eight years, being blind for two years. He spent the last years of his life with his daughter and family, ***Mrs. Norton HURST***, at whose home he died of Bright's disease on Nov 19, 1903. His funeral was held at the Hurst home, with *Rev. COOK*, the Baptist minister officiating. He is buried beside his first wife in the family plot at Lakeside Cemetery. Rose, p. 14.

Marriage Certificate of ***William W. ALDRICH***; occup. Herford Cattle Breeder; res. Elyria, Ohio; b. Ohio, fr. *Aaron ALDRICH*, mo. *Elizabeth ALDRICH*. He married ***Mrs. Lorrinda HILLIARD***, fr. *Luman GRISWOLD*, mo. *Margaret GRISWOLD*. The marriage was contracted at Lacrosse, Wisconsin on Jany 21, 1878. Methodist Episcopal ceremony, witnesses, *Joshua WINSLOW* and *Jeannette MONTAGUE*. Hereby Certify, that the foregoing marriage was consummated by me on the twenty-first day of Jany A.D.1878. J.E. Clouge, Minister. Marriage Certificate, Office of Register of Deeds of LaCrosse County, Wisconsin, vol. 4 of Marriage Records, p. 91.

Lorinda GRISWOLD HILLIARD, *William's* second wife, b. 5 June 1829, Cuyahoga Co., OH is the daughter of ***Luman GRISWOLD*** *(OP 1:10)* and ***Margaret Marilla SMITH GRISWOLD EDDY*** *(OP 1:11)*. She married her first husband, ***Joseph Warren HILLIARD*** (b. 7 Aug 1819, Berne, NY son of *William HILLIARD* and *Elizabeth LEWIS*, *brother of William S. HILLIARD (OP 1:6)*) on 1 Dec 1847 in Cuyahoga Co. and then moved to Sheffield Lake. They had several children before moving to Holman, Wisconsin where they completed their family of ten children. Three or four of the children died when they were young. Joseph was a farmer and blacksmith and the family lived next to an Indian reservation. He was kicked in the chest by a horse and died March 22, 1867 with all of the children under 18. The older boys ran the farm for awhile and then Lorinda moved into Lacrosse and ran a boarding house.

William Aldrich had one of the largest cattle raising businesses in the country and traveled extensively. He was actually the age of, and probably a friend of, Lorinda's parents. William and Lorinda married in Holman, but later returned to Ohio to live in Elyria. Lorinda always called William "Mr. Aldrich" or "Husband." William and Lorinda may have separated, with Lorinda returning to Wisconsin or possibly going to Minnesota. Lorinda died 17 Jan 1895. She is buried in Holman with Joseph, her first husband and the children who died young. Her gravestone is a new stone of granite, with the inscription "Mother, Lorinda Hilliard, 1830-1895" on it. One of the children of Joseph and Lorinda was *Ida HILLIARD JAYCOX*, the mother of *Frances JAYCOX*. Frances was buried and then removed from Lakeside *(Lot 62)*. Karen Boas

ALDRICH, William, 52, Farmer, value of real estate $9000; ***Martha***, 52, Keeping House, value of real estate $9600; ***Lucius***, 20, Farm laborer; ***Celia***, 15; ***Ida***, 12; ***Clara***, 11; *BRAMAN, Charles*, 15. All b. Ohio. All five children attending school. 1870 FC OH Lorain Co., Elyria, p. 462B, lines 27-33.

ALDRICH, William W. Owned land; Acres: Improved - 42 tilled, including fallow and grass, 3 permanent meadow, Unimproved - 4 woodland. Farm Values: Land - $5000, Machinery - $300, Live Stock - 300 $. Estimated value of all farm production: $900. Grass lands: acreage: 10 mown, 10 not mown, 12 tons hay. 3 horses, 2 milch cows, 1 other, 2 calves dropped, 2 cattle sold living. 200 pounds of butter made on the farm. 2 swine. 25 barnyard poultry on farm, 100 dozen eggs produced in 1879. Indian corn: 6 acres, 300 bushels; Oats: 4 acres, 150 bushels; wheat: 6 acres, 110 bushels; potatoes: 6 acres, 700 bushels. Orchards - apple: 2 acres, 100 bearing trees, 300 bushels. Total value of orchard products: $150. Amount of wood cut: 20 cords, Value of forest products - $15. "Schedule 2. Production of Agriculture in Dover Township, Cuyahoga County, OH," enumerated June, 1880, p. 36.

Newspaper excerpts, Northport, Michigan.

Thursday, 5 Aug 1880: The benefits of judicious advertising are apparent in the fact that *Mr. (Anson) Braman's* real estate in this township has all been disposed of since the insertion of his ad in our columns, for cash at a fair figure. ***Mr. W.W. ALDRICH*** of Ohio has just purchased the Washburn plane and village lots, which closes out the real estate in this township. He is a gentleman of means and culture and intends building on the village lots at once. He will prove a valuable acquisition to the town.

Thursday, 6 Sept 1880: ***Mr. W.W. ALDRICH*** of Elyria, Ohio, who has recently purchased a portion of the Braman property, contemplates spending the winter in town.

Thursday, 30 Dec 1880: ***Mr. W. ALDRICH*** of Elyria, Ohio, who purchased several village lots of A. Braman last summer, announces his intention, in a letter received by *Mr. CUTLER*, of removing to this place as soon as circumstances will permit, and of improving his property and buying more. Northport has lots of room for this kind of man.

Thursday, 6 Oct 1881: The I'lun property in this village, which was lately sold to ***W.W. ALDRICH***, has been converted into a handsome and convenient residence and is a credit to that part of the village in which it stands. A handsome portico and spacious additions give the exterior of the building a handsome and attractive appearance, while the interior plan of the house is convenient and tasty. The carpenters are now putting the finishing touches on the building preparing to its occupancy by Mr. Aldrich and family this winter.

Thursday, 9 Dec 1881: Our old friend and fellow citizen, ***W.W. ALDRICH*** and his estimable wife have arrived at Traverse City and will be here in a day or so. They will go into winter quarters in their newly prepared home in this village and are duly equipped for housekeeping. We understand that Mr. Aldrich has with him some choice blooded stock in the raising of which he has had much experience and has recalled great profit. We have not inspected the animals yet but when we do we shall have more to say regarding them.

Thursday, 26 Jan 1882: ***Mr. ALDRICH (Luther M.)*** and family of Ohio arrived in town last week. Mr. Aldrich is the son of ***W.W. ALDRICH*** and we believe will make this his permanent residence.

Thursday, 6 April 1882: HERFORD BULL I have a Thorough Bred Herford Bull, Pedigree perfect. He will be kept at Northport this season for the improvement of stock in Leelanau County. Price of services $2.00 to be paid at time of service. ***WM. W. ALDRICH***

Thursday, 13 April 1882: The clearing and improvements recently made by ***W. W. ALDRICH*** on the land opposite the farm of *R.A. DEGOLIN* in this township, have let the daylight in on the clearing south, and have converted what looked like a solid and impenetrable cedar swamp into pleasant farms.

Thursday, 22 June 1882: ***W.W. ALDRICH*** has built a neat picket fence around his lots on the corner of Mill and Third streets.

Thursday, 20 July 1882: "Practical Housekeeping" by *H.W. BEECHER*. ***Mrs. W.W. ALDRICH*** is agent for the excellent book.

Thursday, 12 July 1883: At a school meeting at Northport Monday evening, *William H. FRANKLIN* and *E.F. DAME* were re-elected trustees of school dis. No. 1 and *A. WRISLEY* and ***W. W. ALDRICH*** were elected in place of *Robert LEE* and *George N. SMITH* respectively.

Thursday, 1 Nov 1883: ***Mrs. W.W. ALDRICH,*** accompanied by her daughter, ***Miss Anna HILLIARD,*** were in town Saturday. The latter will teach the Omena school this winter.

Thursday, 13 Nov 1884: ***Mr.*** and ***Mrs. W.W. ALDRICH*** of Northport, will spend the winter outside, the former in Elyria, Ohio and the latter in Minnesota.

Thursday, 25 Dec 1884: ***W.W. ALDRICH*** started for the world's exposition at New Orleans last Monday evening. Leelanau Enterprise, Northport, Leelanau Co., MI as extracted by Ima Aldrich Slaby.

Record of Death - Probate Court. Mch 31, 1904, male, ***WM. ALDRICH***, d. 1903, Nov 19, Lorain. Condition Widowed, 86 yrs. 1 month, 2 days. b. Dover, occup Farmer, color White, Disease Bright's Disease, res. Lorain, informant Clayton Terrell. Record of Death, Probate Court, Lorain County.

William ALDRICH, Sr., 88; res. Lorain; interred 1903; Original Part. "List of Interments," Lakeside Cemetery, Bay Village, OH.

Children of William Aldrich and Martha Bassett:
Three of William and Martha Bassett's children married children of: ***Daniel Staples BATES***, b. 6 Feb 1804, Bennington, VT, (son of *Jacob BATES*, d. Bennington, VT) and ***Rachel OMAN*** (b. 18 Nov 1804, Proveland, Penn; d. 9 Feb 1894, Elyria, Ohio). The parents of Jacob Bates were massacred by Indians; he, as a child, was hidden and escaped with a younger sister.

Issue of Daniel and Rachel Bates: ***Alfred BATES***, b. 8 May 1829, Bennington, VT; d. 15 June 1914, Elyria; m. 1853, *Lucy (Amanda) CARTER*; served in the 19th Battery A *(Amanda Carter is the sister of Fannie CARTER WILLIS, OP 1:3)*. ***Amelia BATES***, m. *Steve GRISWOLD* (killed in the Battle of Atlanta, 186_). ***Alexander Hamilton BATES***, d. 1902, Rural Ohio; m. *Mary Ann GILBERT*. ***William Harrison (Harrison Henry) BATES***, d. 1902, m. *Lucy ALDRICH*, Co. E 42nd Inf. Shiloh, Red River campaign, Arkansas post at Vicksburg. ***Sarah BATES***, m. *William HOLT*. ***Laura Jeanette BATES***, m. *Wm. Waterman ALDRICH*. ***Thomas Jefferson BATES***, m. 11 Oct 1876, *Eva St. Claire ALDRICH*. Aldrich Family File, Rose Hill Museum, Bay Village, OH.

Harrison H. BATES, Private, Co. E., Forty-Second Regiment, Ohio Volunteer Infantry. Mustered into service Oct. 30, 1861; out Nov. 15, 1864. History of Lorain County , p. 94.

The first born child to ***William*** and ***Martha ALDRICH*** was a son, ***William Waterman II*** on Jan. 1, 1841. Since they were still living with his father, William was born in the old ***Aaron ALDRICH*** house. When William was a little over a year old, the family moved to Bassett Rd. where William I took over Martha's father's farm, following his death by being struck by lightning.

William II helped his father with farm work and in 1857, he bought seventy-six acres of land from *Christian SADDLER*, on Bassett Rd. He cleared the land, and farmed it. In 1852, he sold some of the property, probably to raise money to build a small house, consisting of two rooms, a kitchen and a bedroom. The outside walls were made of virgin poplar which he cut from his own woodland and took to the sawmill near Bradley Road to be milled.

On June 12, 1862, William II married ***Laura Jeanette BATES*** of Avon, Ohio. She was the sixth child of *Daniel* and *Rachel OMAN BATES.* She always used her middle name and several descendants have taken that name. William and Jeanette were both 21 years of age, since her date of birth was Feb. 6, 1841, when they were married at the Congregational parsonage in Elyria. While on their trip to be married in Elyria, they rode in a "spring" wagon. Jeanette was dressed in a blue silk dress, wearing a bonnet trimmed with orange blossoms. William had a broadcloth suit. While passing over a small plank bridge, one of the planks gave way and William was thrown into the water, and his wedding clothes were drenched, but they continued on their way to be married.

In 1864, William II was drafted to serve in the Civil War. Being in rather poor health at that time and having a wife and baby to support, he was permitted to hire a substitute to go in his place. For the sum of $500, *Charles MORTON* was drafted as a three year substitute. William had to borrow $300 at 20% interest to help pay for the substitute.

William and Jeanette lived out their entire lives in the same home they built with numerous additions through the years as their family grew. All seven girls were married in the parlor, and the funerals of William and Jeanette were held there. The house was surrounded by a spacious lawn and beautiful trees. They had a large flower garden, taken care of by Jeanette. The farm, generally, was given to the raising of vegetables, small berry variety of fruit, as well as the fruit orchard varieties. Only enough hay and grain were raised to feed the horses, and cow and a few chickens. The large family provided the farm help and William sold the produce on the Cleveland market.

They were members of the Congregational Church at Dover Center. Because of the distance, the family often attended services on Sunday afternoon or evening at the Methodist Church, at the corner of Bassett and Lake Roads. For many years Jeanette was a Dover news correspondent for the Elyria Newspaper.

Gradually, William sold off some of his land as it became harder to manage even with the aid of his son ***Clifton***. He died June 2, 1924 from complications of old age. He is buried in the Evergreen Cemetery in Westlake, Ohio.

Jeanette remained in the home, cared for by her daughter, ***Evalena***, and she was an invalid. While her body had deteriorated with diabetes and old age, she remained keen and alert, and had no use for glasses. She died on May 27, 1931, and she is buried beside her husband in the same cemetery. The house has been sold and remodeled slightly, but still retaining much of the outside appearance it is recorded in the National Register at 366 Bassett Road, Bay Village. Rose, pp. 19-21.

Children of Wm. Waterman ALDRICH and Laura Jeanette Bates: ***Imogene Rachel ALDRICH***, b. 6 May 1863; d. 24 Mar 1931, Westlake, Cuyahoga Co., OH; m. 10 Nov 1880, Dover to *George WILLIAMS* (b. 9 Apr 1859, Buffalo, NY; d. 25 Aug 1927, Westlake); both buried Evergreen Cemetery, Westlake, Cuyahoga Co., OH. ***Berthenia Capitola ALDRICH***, b. 2 May 1864; d. 26 Apr 1894, Carlisle Twp., OH with the birth of her sixth child; m. 24 June 1885, Dover to *Robert John SMITH* (13 Aug 1859, Carlisle Twp.; d. 22 July 1942, Carlisle Twp.); both buried Ridgelawn Cemetery, Elyria, Lorain Co., OH. ***Martha Bassett ALDRICH***, b. 25 Nov 1865; d. 12 Aug 1957, Chicago, IL; m. 27 Oct 1887, Dover to *Isaac BEAUCOCK* (b. 24 Feb 1861, Dover; d. 9 Dec 1935, Chicago). ***Evalena ALDRICH,*** b. 17 Mar 1867; d. 5 Mar 1956, Lorain, Lorain Co., OH; bur. Evergreen Cemetery; m.1 22 Mar 1892, Dover to *George LINDSE* or *LINDSLEY* (b. 18 May); m.2 22 Mar 1902, Chicago to *Heinrich LADE* (b. 8 Jan 1857, Esch, Germany; d. 19 Oct 1907, Chicago); m.3 18 July 1910, div. 18 June 1918, *John MEISTER* (b. Lorain); m.4 27 July 1919 to *Jack W. THOMSON* (b. 18 Aug 1864; d. 7 Sept 1929, 366 Bassett Rd., Bay Village, OH; Clifford Pease Funeral Home; father of *Mrs. Warren PAPE* and *Berahard LADE*). ***Howard Vincent ALDRICH,*** b. 22 Aug 1869; d. 6 Mar 1947, Cleveland, Cuyahoga Co., OH; m. 17 Nov 1889, Dover to *Alice McCARTEY* (b. 20 Feb 1873, Dover; d. 2 May 1964, Mentor, Lake Co., OH); ran store at Dover Center; both buried Evergreen Cemetery. ***Annabelle ALDRICH,*** b. 30 Oct 1873; d. 9 Oct 1950, Lakewood, Cuyahoga Co., OH; m.25 Feb 1896, Dover to *Clayton M. TERRY* (b. 19 Sept 1870, N. Eaton, Lorain Co., OH; d. 18 Oct 1948, Elyria, Lorain Co., OH); both buried Butternut Ridge Cemetery, N. Eaton, Lorain Co., OH. ***Edythe Amelia ALDRICH,*** b. 14 Aug 1876; d. 8 Jan 1961, Elyria; bur. Evergreen Cemetery; m. 5 Apr 1905, Dover to *Herbert M. BARKER* (b. 14 Aug 1871, Clarendon, NY; d. 23 Apr 1924, Elba, NY). ***Clifton Irving ALDRICH,*** b. 21 Nov 1878; d. 17 May 1970, Avon, Lorain Co., OH; m. 27 Aug 1903, Elba, NY to *Mary Adeline or Alzede BARKER* (b. 6 Aug 1882, Elba, NY, sister of *Herbert*; d. 10 Mar 1971, Bay Village; both buried Evergreen Cemetery, Westlake, OH. ***Gertrude Florence ALDRICH,*** b. 3 Apr 1880; d. 25 Dec 1949, Benton Harbor, Berrien Co., Michigan; m. 7 Mar 1907, Dover to *Frank L. SIMANTON,* professor at Michigan Univ. (b. 12 Sept 1875, Ashland, Ashland Co., OH; d. 18 Jan 1935, Benton Harbor); both buried Crystal Springs Cemetery, Benton Harbor. ***William Waterman ALDRICH III,*** b. 4 Sept 1882; d. 30 Sept 1946, Toledo, Lucas Co., OH; m.1 25 Dec 1906, Dover, to *Flossie MITCHELL*, div.?; m.2 *Ruby TEASDALE* (b. 12 Apr 1894, Meadville, PA; d. 25 Oct 1949, Elyria; both buried at Ridgehill Memorial Cemetery, Amherst, OH. All children b. Dover. Gertrude Aldrich Barker Rose, "Genealogy of the Aldrich Family," pp. 22-23; Aldrich File, Rose Hill Museum, Bay Village, OH and Cleveland Necrology File.

ALDRICH, Wm.; 29, Farmer, value of real estate $5000, personal property $500; ***Genett***, 29, Keeping House; ***Imogene***, 7; ***Berthenie***, 6; ***Martha***, 4; ***Everlina***, 3; ***Howard***, 9/12. All born in Ohio. 1870 FC OH CYDO, p. 257, dwelling 281, lines 30-36.

The youngest of William's children was born after the oldest two had married, ***Imogene*** in 1880 and ***Berthenia*** in 1881. Four of the girls taught school and all of them attended some college and educational training in Ada. They were all musical and four of the younger ones had a quartet which was popular locally.

Grandmother, ***Laura Jeanette BATES*** had three brothers go off to War, all joining with *Colonel GARFIELD*, a very popular nearby farmer. When he started to organize his battalion, they all enlisted, along with *Steve GRISWOLD*, Amelia's husband. He lost his life at the siege of Atlanta, being buried there.

In front of the barn was a fabulous flower garden, mostly white Easter lilies. They were all in bloom when Grandma Aldrich died and the florist gathered enough of them to make a blanket to cover her casket. When anyone married it was customary to send ten or twelve lily bulbs. Letter written by Grace Rollins Walz, Aldrich Family File, Rose Hill Museum, Bay Village, OH.

Article on Clifton Aldrich, son of Wm. Aldrich and Laura Jeanette Bates, Bay Village Park Superintendent, written as part of the sesquicentennial.

Park Superintendent Traces Family to First Settlement

The Aldriches must have been among the housewarming guests when *Joseph CAHOON* moved into Rose Hill in 1818.

So Cahoon would have been pleased that the job of readying the old house for the Bay Village sesquicentennial *(150 years)* fell to the great-grandson of his old neighbor.

Clifton ALDRICH has lived 82 years of Bay Village's history, and his father and grandfather before him were born on the farm in Dover Twp.

Now, as park superintendent, he has charge of 114 acre Cahoon Park, Rose Hill, and the old carriage house, now the Community House and fire station.

"I used to know every person in the village," he said. "But times change. Now I hardly know my next-door neighbor."

Settled Near Lake

The Aldriches arrived in Dover Twp. in 1814 or 1815, and settled along the lake at what is now Bradley Rd., a mile and a half west of Cahoon's mill. ***William ALDRICH*** was born in 1818, and his son ***William*** in 1841.

In 1878, when Clifton was born, William Jr. recorded he had spent $627 and taken in $626.

"He wrote in his diary that he had lost a dollar and gained a son," Aldrich said.

Civilization had proceeded so far that Clifton went to school in the red brick school house on the south side of Lake, instead of the log cabin across the street where his dad had studied.

"My mother used to tell how her mother would say, 'A nice venison stew wouldn't go bad for supper' and her father would walk out in the back yard and shoot a deer," he recalled.

Organized Village

In 1903, when the northern residents grew dissatisfied because trustees from the southern part of Dover spent all the township funds for southern roads, Aldrich was among the leaders who seceded and organized the Village of Bay. He was the first treasurer of the village, and organized its Fire Department.

Aldrich grew up on Bassett Road named after a grandfather of his, ***Nathaniel BASSETT***, who was a lieutenant colonel under *George WASHINGTON*. Until 20 years ago, he operated a 20-acre orchard on Osborn Road now the site of the Dodd-Aldrich allotment.

Moved to Park.

Bay officials coaxed him out of retirement to supervise the land left to the village by the last of the Cahoons. He and his wife ***Adeline***, moved into a 100-year-old house at 445 Cahoon Road, in the park itself. They celebrated their 57th anniversary this year.

Bay High School students and visitors to the park know him as "Gramps," and usually stop to chat a while.

Aldrich likes to leaf through the diaries, which recount, for instance, how his father had to borrow $300 at 20% interest to hire a substitute in the Civil War. But he's more interested in his children and grandchildren.

He has two sons and a daughter. None of them live in Bay Village.

"Times change," he shrugs "young people like to move around." Fred McGunagle, "Park Superintendent Traces Family to First Settlement," newspaper article provided by Sally O'Connor, undetermined date.

ALDRICH-William W., age 83 years 5 months, beloved husband of ***L. Jeanette*** (nee ***BATES***) and father of ***Mrs. G.A. WILLIAMS, Mrs. Isaac BEAUCOCK, Mrs. J.W. THOMSON, Howard V., Mrs. C.M. TERRY, Mrs. H.M. BARKER, Clifton I., Mrs. F.L. SIMANTON, William W., jr.***, and (deceased) ***Mrs. R.J. SMITH***, Monday, 8:45 p.m. Private service for relatives at the late residence, Bay Village, O., at 2 p.m., June 5. Public services at Dover Congregational church, Dover Village, at 3 p.m., June 5. Burial at Evergreen cemetery. Cleveland Necrology File, June 5, 1924, reel 001.

William Waterman ALDRICH, d. June 2, 1924, 8:45 p.m., Bay Village, Cuyahoga Co., Ohio of senile decay, contributory Inf. Peritonitis bladder caused by a puncture made 10 years ago…enlarged prostate; res. Bassett Rd. Married to ***Laura Jennette;*** Fruit Grower; b. Jan 1, 1841, Bay Village to ***Wm. Waterman ALDRICH***, b. Bay Village and ***Martha BASSETT***, b. Lee, Mass.; informant *Clifton I. ALDRICH;* undertaker C. Pease, Dover Center, O.; burial Evergreen. Ohio Certificate of Death, Division of Vital Statistics, 1924, certif.:32764.

ALDRICH: L. Jeannette (nee ***BATES***), wife of the late ***William***, mother of ***Mrs. Martha BEAUCOCK, Mrs. Evelyn THOMSON, Howard, Mrs. C.M. TERRY, Mrs. Edith BARKER, Clifton, Mrs. F.L. SIMINTON*** and ***William***, May 27, age 90 years. Services at residence, 366 Bassett Rd., Bay Village, Saturday, May 30, at 2:30 p. m. Cleveland Necrology File, May 30, 1931, reel 001.

Lucius Parker ALDRICH, d. Jan 17, 1940, Sandusky, Co., Ohio of Terminal Hypo static Pneumonia and Myocardial failure; widowed, wife ***Minerva ALDRICH***, he was b. July 10, 1850, Dover, Ohio; Farmer, 89 yrs., 5 months, 6 days, fr. ***William PARKER*** *(Waterman Aldrich)*, b. Con., Ohio, mother ***Mary BOSET*** *(Martha BASSETT)*, b. Con. Ohio; informant *Mr. Elmer ALDRICH*, funeral home Rawle Funeral Home, buried Milan, Ohio. Ohio Certificate of

Death, Division of Vital Statistics, 1940, certif. 2158. *(Parents' names incorrect.)*

Husband of Evangeline St. Clair ALDRICH: ***BATES, Thomas J.***, d. Dec 22, 1915, Elyria Mem. Hospital, 3rd Ward, Elyria, Lorain Co., OH of Chronic cystitis due to hypertrophy of prostate; 67 yrs. 3 mos. 8 ds.; b. Sept 14, 1848, Avon, OH to ***David BATES***, b. U.S. and ***Rachel OMAN***, b. U.S.; General Contractor; widowed; res. 105 Robson Ct., Elyria for 3 yrs. 3 ds.; undertaker Friday & Thomas, Elyria, bur. Elyria Cemetery, Dec 30th.; informant W. Bates, Elyria. Ohio Certificate of Death, Division of Vital Statistics, 1915, certif. 67662.

Norton B. HURST, husband of ***Celia***, was the owner of a large department store in Lorain, ruined by the tornado in the 20's or 30's. Aldrich File, Rose Hill Museum, Bay Village, OH.

HURST: Celia M., age 77 years, widow of the late ***N.B. HURST***, passed away at the home, 189 Lakeside Ave., Lorain, O., Saturday p.m.; mother of ***Ralph, Roy*** and ***Harvey***. Services Wednesday, 1:30, at First M. E. Church, 6th St., Lorain, O. Burial in Dover Cemetery. Cleveland Necrology File, Dec 13 1932.

Mrs. Celia HURST, d. Dec 10, 1932, Lorain, Lorain Co., Ohio of Lobar Pneumonia and Tuberculosis; 77 yrs. 3 mos.; widow of ***N.B. HURST***; Housewife; b. Sept 10, 1855, Dover, Ohio; dau. of ***Wm. ALDRICH***, Dover and ***Martha BASSETT***; informant *Roy HURST*, 189 Lakeside Ave., Lorain; undertaker Geo V. Schwartz, 1089 12th St., Lorain; burial Dover, Ohio. Ohio Certificate of Death, Division of Vital Statistics, 1932, certif.:72992

Husband of Celia Marthaetta Aldrich: ***HURST: Norton B.***, age 79, husband of ***Celia M.***, father of ***Ralph, Roy*** and ***Harvey***, brother of *J.D. HURST*, passed away Oct 21, 1930, at Lorain, Ohio. Funeral Friday, Oct 24, at 2 p. m. from First M. E. Church, Lorain, Ohio. Knights Templars services. Burial Dover Center, Ohio. 1851 - 1930. Evergreen Cemetery Dover, Ohio. Cleveland Necrology File, Oct 22 1930.

OP 3:6 Martha Bassett Aldrich

MOTHER

Martha BASSETT, daughter of ***Nathan BASSETT*** *(OP 3:9)* and ***Martha HALL*** *(OP 3:10)*, b. 7 July 1818, Dover, OH; d. 29 Nov 1875, Elyria, Lorain Co., Ohio, m. ***William ALDRICH***. Ima Aldrich Slaby

His (***William Aldrich's***) good wife, in every sense of the word a helpmate, by her wisdom and prudence, contributed largely to the success which followed. *(purchasing her father's farm)*...***Martha***, the first wife of Mr. Aldrich, died November 29, 1875, leaving eight children to mourn the loss of one, who, as wife, mother, and member of the Congregational church, filled well every function of the true woman. History of Lorain County, Ohio, pp. 142-143.

Martha BASSETT ALDRICH was a tiny person with a natural weight of less than 100 pounds. She was a fine wife, mother and member of the Dover Congregational Church. On November 29, 1875, she died from consumption at her farm home in Elyria, leaving a family of eight children to mourn her loss. ***Henry ALDRICH*** wrote home in May, 1875, that Martha had told him she had faith in her Savior, had talked to all her children, and had given them presents. She said her funeral should be conducted the same as funerals in the old days, and there was no need to make a fine show. She wanted a plain coffin and no costly carriage. She was buried from the Lakeshore Methodist Church. Gertrude Aldrich Barker Rose, "Genealogy of the Aldrich Family," p. 14 and Bay Village Historical Society, Bay Village: A Way of Life, p. 63.

ALDRICH.- In Elyria, on Monday the 29th of November, of Consumption, ***Mrs. Martha ALDRICH***, wife of ***Wm. W. ALDRICH***, aged 57 years and 4 months.

Funeral at the Methodist church in Dover, on Wednesday, at 1 o'clock p.m. Friends are invited to meet at her late residence, at 9 a.m. Elyria Independent Democrat, Elyria, Ohio, Wednesday, Dec 1, 1875, p. 2, col. 5.

OP 3:7 Harriet Emma Aldrich

HARIETTE

Harriet *(spelling varies)* ***Emma ALDRICH***, is the fifth child of ***William W. ALDRICH*** and ***Martha BASSETT***, b. 3 Dec 1846, d. 1 Nov 1851. Gertrude Aldrich Barker Rose, "Genealogy of the Aldrich Family," p. 18 and tombstone inscription.

OP 3:5 Ida Aldrich

Ida is indicated on the family marker above.

Ida Minerva (Margetta) Aldrich, is the ninth child of ***William W. ALDRICH*** and ***Martha BASSETT***, b. 22 Oct/Nov 1856. Dover; d. 21 Mar 1910, Gallipolis, Ohio; never married. Gertrude Aldrich Barker Rose, Genealogy of the Aldrich Family, p. 18.

According to Ida's death certificate, she had epilepsy and lived at the Ohio Hospital for Epileptics for over fifteen years.

The Ohio Hospital for Epileptics is now called Gallipolis Developmental Center where approximately 240 individuals with MR/DD reside today. "Testimony by Monty Blanton, President," OCSEA Assembly for Mental Health/ Mental Retardation/Ohio Veteran's Home, <http://www.ocsea.org/mrdd_testimony.html> and "The Holzer Heritage," Holzer Medical Center, <http://www.holzer.org/heritage2.html>, (cited July 31, 2004).

THE HOSPITAL FOR EPILEPTICS.

The Ohio Hospital for Epileptics at Gallipolis is the pioneer of its kind in the United States.

The problem of providing proper accommodations for epileptics has engrossed the attention of persons interested in nervous and mental diseases for many years. In Ohio, as far back as 1879, a bill for the establishment of a separate institution for their accommodation and treatment almost became a law, passing one branch of the legislature. Not, however, until 1890 was a law enacted providing for the establishment of a hospital for epileptics and epileptic insane. All epileptics resident in Ohio are eligible for admission to this institution, up to the measure of its capacity, each county being entitled to a number proportionate to its population. No discrimination is made on account of mental condition, age or sex.

The buildings, as originally planned, consisted of stone cottages having a capacity of fifty beds each, located symmetrically about a group of executive buildings and connected by tunnels with a central powerhouse, which was to furnish heat and light for all, and a central kitchen and bakery, flanked by two congregate dining-rooms, one for each sex. The whole group, with estimated accommodations for one thousand patients, was planned so compactly as to cover scarcely more than twenty-five acres, leaving the balance of one hundred acres of the original tract for ornamentation and gardens. The wisdom of this plan was seriously questioned, and subsequent experience and events have led to an entire modification of it, so far as practicable. Of the original thirty-six buildings, only thirteen have been built as designed. The location and design of six others, now nearly completed, have been materially changed. One hundred and twenty-five additional acres of land have been purchased and a cottage for the insane constructed at a distance of one-half mile from the original group. Other buildings, projected for the future, are to be much farther away, their precise location depending upon the possibilities in the selection and purchase of land, which may or may not adjoin the tract now owned by the state.

A tract of 110 acres of farm land has recently been purchased, on which a group of cottages will be erected, and in which the husbandmen among the male patients will be accommodated. This land adjoins the sewage-disposal beds of the Hospital, and it is intended to utilize the sewage for fertilizing the farm. It is purposed to expand the institution in the future by erecting small, homelike cottages for small and selected groups of patients, leaving the large central cottages with their common kitchen and congregate dining rooms for the accommodation of more advanced cases of epilepsy and for the infirmary class of inmates. A new style of architecture has been decided upon, by which it is believed the monotony of the present symmetrical groups of large stone cottages can be relieved.

A board of construction was appointed in 1890, which consisted of *James E. NEAL*, of Hamilton; *John E. VANCE*, of Gallipolis; *George H. BUNNELL*, of Sidney; *Lewis SLUSSER*, of Canton.

The hospital was opened for the reception of patients, November 30, 1893. Six more cottages have since been erected, and when the buildings now in course of construction are completed, which will be during the present year (1901), accommodations will have been made for 1,060 patients. The buildings will then consist of thirteen residence cottages with from fifty to seventy-six beds each; one laundry cottage for seventy-five patients; one cottage for the insane, with a capacity of 200; one schoolhouse; two industrial buildings, each containing eight large, well-lighted and well-ventilated rooms, accommodating twenty five patients each - in many of the manual industries commonly followed; one kitchen and bakery building; one ice machine and cold storage building, with a capacity of eighteen tons daily; two large congregate dining-rooms; one boiler, power, and electric light building; one waterworks building; one hospital building, accommodating sixty, and one administration building. The cost of the buildings up to the time when those under way shall have been completed, will be $565,000.

A pathological laboratory in which researches into the nature, cause, and prevention of epilepsy are carried forward, has been a feature of this institution for the past five years. Through the scientific studies pursued in this laboratory and published to the medical profession, the Ohio Hospital for Epileptics has achieved international fame. The medical profession of Ohio, and of the United States, is deeply interested in seeing this important work encouraged and properly supported, since it is realized that by this method alone can the mysteries as to the nature, cause, treatment and prevention of epilepsy be solved. The investigations already pursued by the scientific staff in this laboratory have already disclosed some very important facts relative to the cause and prevention of epilepsy.

Many of the patients came from almshouses, many from the lower walks of life, and were uncouth in their manners and dress, filthy in their habits, and rude in their conversation. The improvement most noticed by visitors has been the wonderful change in their deportment. The Biographical Annals of Ohio, A Handbook of the Government and Institutions of the State of Ohio, compiled under authority of the Act of May 12, 1902. Revised and enlarged edition of Ohio Statesmen and Hundred Year Book, by Col. W. A. Taylor, copyright 1892, pp. 878-879.

Gallipolis, OH had a population in the year 2000 of 4,180 people *(the population decreased by 1,000 since 1990)*. The city is located on the southern border of Ohio approximately half way across the state on the Ohio River and encompasses approximately 9 square miles. "Gallipolis, Ohio," Wikipedia, the On-line Encyclopedia, <http://en.wikipedia.org/wiki/Gallipolis,_Ohio>, (cited July 31, 2004).

Ida ALDRICH, interred March 21, 1910. "List of Interments," Lakeside Cemetery, Bay Village, OH.

Ida ALDRICH, d. Mch 21, 1910, 1:45 a.m., O.H.E. Gallipolis, Co. Gallia, Ohio, Double Labor Pneumonia – 3 days, Contributory Epilepsy; b. 1863, Ohio; 47 yrs. old; occup. none; How long at place of death 15 yrs. 6 mos. 8

ds.; Informant Mary L. Austin, M.D., Gallipolis, O.; bur. Lorain, Ohio, Mch 24, 1910, undertaker Hayward & Son; Former or usual res. Lorain, O. Ohio Certificate of Death, Division of Vital Statistics, 1910, certif. 14029. *Notice place of burial.*

OP 3:8 Martha Hall Bassett Aldrich

MARTHA

Martha Hall Bassett ALDRICH, is the second child of ***William W. ALDRICH*** and ***Martha BASSETT***, b. 3 June 1842, d. 23 Oct 1848. Gertrude Aldrich Barker Rose, "Genealogy of the Aldrich Family," p. 18 and tombstone inscription.

OP 3:9 Nathan Bassett

NATHAN
BASSETT
DIED March 30, 1842
Aged 55 yrs.
& 9 months
(saying - illegible)

Small upright stone in lane behind

marker, "N.B."

BASSETT, Nathan, ch. ***Cornelius*** and ***Remember***, June 29, 1785. Vital Records of Lee, Massachusetts, To the Year 1850, Births: Bassett. *In the Vital Records mentioning Nathan's mother, she is referred to as "Remember," a birth record was not found for her.*

BASSETT, Nathan 2d, ***Patty HALL***, June 14, 1810. Vital Records of Lee, Massachusetts, To the Year 1850, marriages: Bassett *(The original record indicates that this is Nathan's second marriage. A previous record states Nath[a]n and Azuba [Azubah, C.R.(church record)] Jones, Jan 12, 1797. This does not appear to be for this Nathan as he would have been 12 years old at the time.*

Nathan and ***Patty BASSETT*** came to Dover claiming the land her father had given her. At the corner of the present Lake and Bassett Roads (named for the family), the Indian trail turned south. They followed on until they reached a creek where they camped for a few days and planned to settle. This is near to and south of the present intersection of Wolf and Bassett Roads. Nathan built a log house on the bank of the creek and some rods back of that a log barn. He continued to clear the land and farm it. One source said he bought more acreage for 10 shillings an acre. Gertrude Aldrich Barker Rose, "Genealogy of William Bassett and Descendents 1620-1973," p. 29.

Nathan served much of the time from 1813 until 1839 as a town trustee. About 1840, there was a division on the subject of slavery, and a difference of opinion on church government. Until 1847 one group worshipped in the church building and the other in the town house. In 1847, the two bodies united and reorganized under the name of the Congregational Church of Dover with 41 members. Nathan Bassett and his family were members of the church, but Nathan died before this union.

Martha died July 10, 1835. Nathan continued to live on the same property until Mar 30, 1842, when he was struck by lightning and killed, while taking shelter in the barn during an early spring thunderstorm. Rose, p. 30.

Nathan arrived in Dover in 1811 with his wife ***Martha***. They resided on fifty acres given to them by Martha's father, ***Moses HALL***. "Nathan had a turning-lathe, and manufactured chairs, and was also known far and near as a great hunter and manager of bees." He served as a town trustee between 1813 and 1839. Crisfield Johnson, History of Cuyahoga County, pp. 437-438.

Ancestors of Nathan Bassett:

The first known ancestor of ***Nathan*** was ***William BASSETT***, who came from Bethnal Green, Middlesex County, England… A certain *John ROBINSON*, educator and teacher, with others known as the Scrooby group, broke away from the Church of England and later from a church in Amsterdam, and formed a peace-loving, God-fearing group in Leyden, Holland. A goodly number of exiles heard of Robinson and were drawn to Leyden because of him. Among them were *John CARVER, Samuel FULLER, John TILLEY, William BASSETT, Jonathan BREWSTER* and *Edward WINSLOW*. These men were to establish Plimoth Plantation and were to set the pattern for the New England community…

William and his third wife ***Elizabeth*** (probably ***TILDEN***), left Delft Haven in the Speedwell, July 22, 1620 and went to Southampton, England with other Pilgrims. There the Mayflower was awaiting them. The company was divided between the two vessels, the Mayflower and the Speedwell. They set sail Aug 5, 1620. The Bassett's were aboard the Speedwell. The ship leaked and both ships put in to Dartmouth, England for repairs, and set sail Aug 21. The Speedwell leaked again, and they put in to Plymouth, England for repairs. It was decided that the Mayflower should continue its journey, and those that could not get on the Mayflower (about 20 including William and Elizabeth) should return to England.

They sailed the following year 1621 aboard the Fortune, and William and Elizabeth landed at Plymouth in November of that year.

He is listed on the passenger list of the Fortune as an ironworker. He probably brought his blacksmith tools with him, as he was a blacksmith and a gunsmith. He brought with him eighteen books, including one by Robinson. This was considered a goodly collection at the time. Rose, pp. 2, 3.

I. ***William BASSETT***, b. England; d. 4 Apr 1667, Bridgewater, Mass.; m.1 ***Cecelia*** (Cecil in Dutch record) ***LIGHT***, m.2 13 Aug 1611 to ***Margaret OLDHAM***; m.3 c1621 ***Elizabeth (TILDEN*** ?) prior to their departure to America, (b. England, d. pre 1650, Bridgewater, Mass); m.4 the widow, ***Mary TILDEN LAMPHAM*** of Scituate, Mass, d. after 1667. Rose, pp. 1, 4.

II. ***William BASSETT***, their oldest child was b. 1624, Plymouth, Mass.; d. 29 May 1670, Sandwich, Mass; m. c1652 to ***Mary RAYNESFORD*** (b. 1 June 1632, Boston, Mass., d. 12 Apr 1694, Falmouth, Mass, dau. of *Deacon Edward RAYNESFORD* of Boston; m. 2 *James PERCIVAL* of Sandwich and Falmouth and had three children from this marriage). Rose, p. 4.

III. ***William BASSETT***, the second of their two children was b. 1656, Sandwich; d. 29 Sept 1721, Sandwich; m. 9 Oct 1675 ***Rachel WILLISON***. He spent some time in Boston and was one of the judges of the Inferior Court and later Registrate of Probate. Rose, p. 6.

IV. ***Nathan BASSETT***, the fifth of their six children was b. 1 May 1685, Sandwich; d. 24 Mar 1754, Barnstable, Mass; m. 22 Oct 1712 to ***Mary STETSON*** (b. 1 Mar 1691, Scituate; d. 1 Jan 1778, Barnstable; dau. of *Thomas STETSON* (b. 1643, Scituate) and *Sarah DODSON* (b. 26 Aug 1652)). Rose, p. 7.

V. ***(Deacon) Nathan BASSETT***, the oldest of their five children was b. 15 Aug 1715, Sandwich; d. 27 Dec 1791, Barnstable; m. 25 Oct 1739, ***Thankful FULLER*** (b. 19 Sept 1718, Barnstable; d. 18 Mar 1809 [1759], Lee, Mass. She was the dau. of *Lt. John FULLER* (b. Oct 1689, Barnstable; m. 16 June 1710; d. 20 July 1732, Barnstable) and *Thankful GORHAM* (b. 15 Feb 1690, Barnstable, [Scorton Neck, Sandwich, Mass]; d. 20 Jan 1759, Barnstable). Both of Thankful's parents were Mayflower descendants, her mother from *John* and *Elizabeth TILLEY* and father through *Edward* and *Ann FULLER*. Rose, pp. 7-12.

VI. ***Cornelius BASSETT***, the fourth of their seven children was b. 20 Jan, 1753, Barnstable; d. 21 Nov 1821, bur. Fairmount Cemetery in Lee; m. 1 Oct 1778 probably in Sandwich to ***Remembrance NYE*** (b. 15 Aug 1761, Lee; d. 19 Jan 1828, Lee; bur Fairmount Cemetery; dau. of *Benjamin NYE* (b. 16 Oct 1697, Sandwich, d. 13 June 1790) and *Rachel*), he was a blacksmith. Rose, pp. 21-23

Children of Cornelius and Remembrance: ***Elisha BASSETT***, b. 22 Jan 1782, Lee; d. 22 Dec 1822, Lee; m. 16 Nov 1805, Pittsfield, Mass. to *Elizabeth GOODRICH*. ***John BASSETT***, b. 3 Jan 1784, Lee; d. 27 June 1870, East Lee, Mass; m. 21 Nov 1811, Lee to *Salvina BAKER*. ***Nathan BASSETT***. ***Infant daughter BASSETT***, b. 13 July 1791, d. July 1791. ***Remembrance (Remember) BASSETT***, b. 6 May 1793, Lee; d. 30 May 1841, Lee; m. 3 Feb 1820, *David BAKER* II. ***Experience BASSETT***, b. 6 Mar 1796, Lee; d. 31 Aug 1869, Barrington, Mass; m.1 30 Dec 1818, *Horace LEWIS* (b. 1796, d. 27 Dec 1825), m.2 intention publ. 22 Apr 182?, *Stephen WALKER*. ***Rachel BASSETT***, b. 25 July1799, Lee; m. 2 Feb 1820, *John COFFEY*, N. Canaan, NY. p. 23.

VII. ***Nathan BASSETT***, the third of their seven children was b. 29 June 1785, Lee; d. 30 Mar 1842, Dover, Ohio; m. 14 June 1810 ***Martha (Patty) HALL*** (b. 20 Feb 1790, Lee; d. 10 July1835, Dover; dau. of *Moses HALL* and *Relief*). "Genealogy of William Bassett," p. 24, [Notes, Aldrich Family Papers], Rose Hill Museum, Bay Village, OH.

Nathan BASSETT can be traced back as a Mayflower descendent through ***Thankful GORHAM***, mother of ***Thankful FULLER BASSETT*** *(Mrs. Nathan)*. She was the daughter of ***Lieut. Col. John GORHAM*** (b. Feb 20, 1651 or 2, Marshfield, Mass.; d. Nov 11, 1716, Barnstable); m. Feb 24, 1674 or 5 to *Mary OTIS* (b. Jan 14, 1653 Hingham, Mass., d. Apr 1, 1733, Barnstable), son of ***Capt. John GORHAM*** (b. Benfield, Northamptonshire, Eng.; d. Feb 5, 1675 or 6 Swansea, Mass.); m. 1644 to *Desire HOWLAND* (b. Plymouth, Mass.; d. Oct 13, 1683, Barnstable), son of ***Elizabeth TILLY*** (b. 1607, England; d. Dec 31, 1687, Swansea) m. 1624 *John HOWLAND* (b. 1593, England; d. Feb 23, 1672 or 3, 80 yrs. old, Plymouth), daughter of ***John TILLY*** (b. England, d. Plymouth between Jan 11 and Apr 10, 1621) and *Elizabeth TILLY* (b. England, d. same). John Tilly 29th signer of Mayflower Compact. He, his wife and daughter, Elizabeth were aboard the Mayflower. John Tilly died that first winter as did his wife. John Howland was on board the Mayflower Nov 11, 1620; was an attendant to *Gov. CARVER*; was signer of Mayflower compact and later married Elizabeth Tilly. Rose and Bassett Family Papers, Rose Hill Museum.

Children of Nathan Bassett and Martha Hall:

Nathan BASSETT, b. 26 Mar 1811, Lee, Berkshire, MA; d. 31 Mar 1811, Lee. ***Vesta BASSETT***, b. 14 June 1812, Dover, OH; d. 22 June 1844; m.1 *Nathan SANFORD* (b. Sept 1805, d. 27 June 1839), m.2 ? *ROOT*. ***Lydia BASSETT***, b. 14 July 1814, Dover, OH; d. Dec 1887; m. *John PORTER*. ***Lucy BASSETT***, b. 27 Nov 1816, Dover, OH; d. 9 Jan 1845 of consumption; bur. Evergreen Cemetery, Westlake, OH; m. *Josiah HURST* (b. 1811, d. 9 Feb 1881). ***Martha BASSETT***, b. 7 July1818, Dover, OH; m. 5 Feb 1840, *William Waterman ALDRICH (both bur. OP 3:5)*. ***Harriet M. BASSETT***, b. 17 Oct 1820, Dover, OH; d. 17 Nov 1846, bur. Evergreen Cemetery, Westlake, OH; m. *Josiah HURST*. ***Nancy BASSETT***, b. 22 Aug 1823, Dover, OH; d. 1 Apr 1867 *(OP 3:12)*. "Genealogy of William Bassett and Descendents 1620-1973," pp. 23, 30 and Ima Aldrich Slaby.

Spouse: ***Josiah HURST***- February 9, at his residence in Elyria, in his 70th year, Josiah Hurst. Funeral services Friday, Feb 11, at 1:30 p. m. Friends of the family are invited. Burial at convenience of the family. 1881, Age 70. Evergreen Cemetery, Dover, O. Cleveland Necrology File, Feb 11, 1881.

Note: A marriage record was found in Cuyahoga

County for Josiah HURST and Martha G. PORTER, 11 Oct 1845. Marriage Record, Cuyahoga County, OH, vol. 4, p. 481.

OP 3:10 Martha (Patty) Hall Bassett

MARTHA
wife of
NATHAN
BASSETT
Died July 10, 1835
Aged 45 years
& 5 months

Small upright stone
in lane behind
marker, "*M.B.*"

Martha HALL BASSETT, b. 20 Feb 1790, Lenox, Berkshire, MA; dau. of ***Moses HALL*** (d. Ashtabula, Ohio) and ***Relief SWIFT*** (d. 28 Aug 1805, Lee, Berkshire, MA). Ima Aldrich Slaby

BASSETT, Mrs. Nathan; Maiden Name: ***HALL, Martha***; Year Came to Township or Born 1811; Where From or Where Born Lee, Mass.; Last Residence Dover, O. Women in the Western Reserve before 1840, p. 18.

Ancestors of Martha Hall Bassett:

Ichabod HALL immigrated to America from Wales and settled in Falmouth, Mass. He was on the muster roll of Capt. Shipley's Co. from June 26 to Dec 10, 1722. One of his sons, ***Ebenezer HALL***, was a commander of Mass. Volunteers for frontier defense and became distinguished as an Indian fighter, serving from June 1 to Nov 2, 1795 on the muster roll of *Capt. Joshua MOODERY'S* Co. at Stoughton, Mass.

Moses HALL, son of Ebenezer Hall, was a soldier in the Revolution, having enlisted in the Continental Army at the age of 18, near the close of the war. He was a drummer for *Capt. Enoch NOBLE'S* Co.; *Col. John ASHLEY'S* Reg. (Berkshire County). He enlisted Aug 1, 1777, and was discharged Aug 20, 1777, serving 20 days.

After the war was over, he was a cloth dresser and had a factory at Lee, Mass. Later on he removed to Lenox, which is in Berkshire Co., as is also Lee, and engaged in farming. While living in Lee, he was sworn into office as supervisor of highways.

Moses Hall was born about 1759 in Lee, Mass. and died in Ashtabula, Ohio. His first wife ***Relief----*** was born in 1769 and died Aug 28, 1805 in Lee, Mass. Moses and Relief Hall had a large family of children; some sources saying there are twelve...Relief must have died shortly after the birth of twins at the age of 36. She is buried in Falmouth Cemetery in Lee, Mass.

On Dec 5, 1805, Moses Hall married ***Lydia HINSDALE***. She must have been a very capable woman, assuming the responsibilities of such a family of children, several of them being very young. Then in 1811 she had the undertaking of a strenuous trip moving to Ohio with their accompanying families. Gertrude Aldrich Barker Rose, "Genealogy of William Bassett and descendents 1620-1973," p. 26.

Martha, called ***Patty***, was the second daughter of ***Moses HALL*** and ***Relief*** ___ of Lee, Massachusetts; b. 20 Feb 1790, Lee, Mass; m. 14 June 1810 to ***Nathan BASSETT***. In 1810 Moses Hall came and took up 2163 acres of land in Dover and he got his title from Hubbard and Stowe, agents of the Connecticut Land Co...for the consideration of $4,326.

Nathan Bassett and Martha (Patty) Hall...settled on Lot 82, Western Reserve No. 7, Range 15. Rose, pp. 27-28.

Moses HALL, after selecting his land in Dover, [sic] in 1810, returned to his home in Lee, Massachusetts, and in 1811 he moved west with his large family, of wife and twelve children, together with a few other families who came with their ox and horse teams and lumber wagons; and after a journey of five or six weeks, arrived at Ashtabula, Ohio, where he and the most of his family established a home, and where he continued to reside until his death, July 4, 1834.

Three of his children came on to Dover the same year (1811), namely, ***Martha HALL BASSETT***, ***Barnabas HALL***, and ***James HALL.***

Four of his other children came to Dover between 1820 and 1830, namely, ***Charles HALL***, ***Reuben C. HALL***, ***Edwin HALL*** and ***Nancy***, wife of *David INGERSOLL*.

Charles Hall, my father, came to Dover in 1821, and settled down as a pioneer in a log cabin which he had erected a little north of where *Mr. Thomas MITCHELL* now lives. He had married *Lucy SEYMOUR* of Plymouth, Ashtabula County, October 22, 1819, and in the fall of 1821, they gathered together their few household goods, and a stock of provisions for the winter, and loaded them into an ox cart, and with two yoke of oxen, and a boy to help drive them, they started for their new home in the wilderness of Dover. After getting here, father had fifty cents left, and twenty-five cents of this he gave to the boy to take him back to Ashtabula with one of the yoke of oxen, which left twenty-five cents for father and mother to commence pioneer life with in their new home. Surely, not an extravagant sum for a newly married couple to begin with.

Of the large tract of land which Moses Hall took up in Dover, he gave to his seven sons 100 acres each, and to his five daughters 50 acres each. Seven of his children settled in Dover, and five in Ashtabula.

After 1811 other families came from the eastern states and settled in Dover, and by 1825, the forest had become dotted with clearings, and log cabins erected to shelter the early settlers. The ring of the ax, and the crash of falling timber were familiar sounds. The land had to be cleared and the trees were cut down and piled into log heaps and burned before the pioneer could raise anything to live upon, and in this way very much valuable timber was destroyed. But what else could they do? There was no market for the lumber, and no mills to cut the trees into lumber. The cutting down of the trees and cutting them into logging lengths was generally done in the winter, and then in the spring or fall they were piled into log heaps ready to be burned. As it required three men and a yoke of oxen to do this work successfully, neighbors would change works, helping each other; one to drive the oxen and draw the logs together, and the other two with hand spikes to roll them together into heaps ready for burning.

When the field which had been chopped over was finished, the log heaps were fired; and it was a beautiful sight in the evening to see the glowing light which was cast on the surrounding forest.

The cleared fields were surrounded with a rail fence; the rails being made from trees near by, which were free to split. The Pioneer then had a hard task to get in the seed for the first two or three crops, as the land could not be ploughed on account of the stumps and roots, and he had to take his ox team and hitch them to a three-cornered drag and loosen the ground as well as he could to receive the seed for the first crop. But it is said that grit and perseverance will win, and in proof of this we can look at the beautiful fields which we have today. Reuben Hall, "Reminiscences of Dover Pioneer Life, 1810-1910," pp. 2-4.

HALL, Capt. Moses, and ***Lydia HINSDALE***, Dec 5, 1805. *Her father remarried and then moved to Ohio. The first marriage of Moses to Relief was not found in the records.* Marriages: Hall

HALL, with ***Capt. Moses***, Aug __, 1804, a. *(age)* 36. [Relief, Aug 28, 1805, G.R. *(gravestone record)*]. *This record indicates that Martha's mother died when Martha was only 14 or15 and the family was left with a number of young children, including twins.* Vital Records of Lee, Massachusetts, To the Year 1850, Deaths: Hall. http://www.rootsweb.com/~maberksh/towns/lee/lee-vr.html,.

Siblings of Martha Hall Bassett:

(Rev.) John HALL, b. 5 Nov 1788, Lennox, Mass.; m.1 Sept 1813 *Sarah BADGER* (d. 6 May 1828), m.2 1829 *Harriet WILSON* (d. early spring 1833), m.3 Sept 1837 *Pruder TRACEY* (d. 1853); d. 1869 (age 81), Ashtabula, Ohio; moved to Ohio before his parents. ***Martha (Patty) HALL****, see below.* ***Barnabus HALL***, b. 1791; m. 31 Dec 1810, *Hannah PHELPS* (b. 1792, d. 19 Sept 1873); d. 29 May 1863, Dover, Ohio; lived on Lot 62 in Dover. ***James HALL***, m. 1 Feb 1816, *Elizabeth INGERSOLL* of Dover; lived on Lot 57 in Dover until 1821 when he moved to Ashtabula, Ohio. ***Edwin HALL***, claimed land in Dover between 1820-30. ***Nansey HALL***, b. 3 Feb 1797; d. 19 Feb 1797, Lee, Mass. ***Charles HALL***, b. 12 Sept 1798, Lee, Mass; m. 22 Oct 1819, Plymouth, Ashtabula Co., Ohio, *Lucy SEYMOUR* (b. 1800, d. 1844); d. Apr 1878, Ashtabula; moved to Dover on Lot 48 in the fall of 1821. ***Nancy HALL***, b. 14 Apr 1800, Lee, Mass.; m. *David INGERSOLL* (b. 1796, d. Jan 1879); d. Apr 1879; lived on Lot 37 in Dover; they had seven children. ***Lucy HALL***, b. 29 May 1802, Lee, Mass. ***Relief HALL*** and ***Reuben HALL*** (twins), b. 9 Aug 1804. Gertrude Aldrich Barker Rose, "Genealogy of William Bassett and descendents 1620-1973," p. 27 and http://www.rootsweb.com/~maberksh/towns/lee/lee-vr.html, Births: Hall.

In 1811 ***James*** and ***Barnabas HALL***, with their wives, also ***Martha HALL***, wife of ***Nathan BASSETT***, came to occupy 2,100 acres of land purchased before leaving Lee, Mass. Mrs. Bassett's daughter, ***Vesta***, was the first white baby born in Dover. ***Lydia, Mrs. John PORTER***, was born in 1814, living all her life in Dover, where her daughter, *Mrs. GRIFFIN*, still resides. Mrs. Bassett's other daughters were ***Lucy, Harriet (HURST), Nancy***, and ***Martha***. The latter became ***Mrs. W.W. ALDRICH***, a careful attentive mother of a large family....

Of this family, at a later date, ***Nancy HALL***, wife of *David INGERSOLL*, a descendant of *Jonathan EDWARDS*, and worthy of the honor, came to brighten all associated with her...

Charles HALL married *Lucy SEYMOUR*, of Ashtabula, settling near his brothers in 1821. They both have passed away, leaving two sons, *Reuben* and *Ziba*, prominent residents of their native town. Pioneer Women of the Western Reserve, Dover, Cuyahoga County, 1897, pp. 58-9.

Sister of Martha Hall Bassett: ***David INGERSOLL,*** 55, farmer, value of land $5,400, b. Mass.; ***Nancy***, 50, b. Mass.; ***Chauncey***, 18, farmer, b. Ohio; ***Edward***, 12, b. Ohio; ***Jeanne*** *(last name had large mark over it)*, 16, b. Ohio. 1850 FC OH CYDO p. 223A, lines 31-36.

Nancy H. INGERSOLL, Born Apr 14, 1800, Died Apr 27?, 1879. *(west)* ***David INGERSOLL,*** Born Mar 3, 1795, Died Jan 21?, 1879; ***Edward S.*** Died Oct 23, 1859, Aged 21 yrs.; ***Chauncey H.*** Died Dec 11, 1854, Aged 22 yr. (north) ***Cornelia*** Died May 3, 182?9, age 4 mos.?; ***Lucy,*** Died Aug 26, 1833, Aged 5 mos.; ***William D. INGERSOLL*** Died Feb 2, 1849, Aged 27 yrs. *(east)* ***Elizabeth*** Died Feb 2, 1836, Aged 12 yrs.; ***Sarah P. INGERSOLL***, wife of *Rev. C.S. NOBTHBUP* Died June 24, 1849, Aged 29 yrs. Ingersoll Monument, Maple Ridge Cemetery, Westlake, OH.

OP 3:11 Nancy Bassett

NANCY
Daughter of
NATHAN & MARTHA BARRETT*
Died April 1, 1867
Aged 44 years.

**It is believed that the stone should read "daughter of Nathan and Martha Bassett".*

...of ***Martha*** and ***Nathan's*** children...a daughter ***Nancy***, born in 1823, died in 1867. Bay Village Historical Society, Bay Village: A Way of Life, p. 17.

Nancy BASSETT, daughter of ***Nathan BASSETT*** and ***Martha (Patty) HALL***, b. 22 Aug 1823, d. 1 Apr 1867. Gertrude Aldrich Barker Rose, "Genealogy of William Bassett and descendents 1620-1973," p. 30.

OP 3:12 Sadler Monument

WM. SADLER
Died
Mar 23, 1875
Aged 83 yrs. 6 m.

ELIZABETH
wife of
Wm. Sadler
Died
April 29, 1872
Aged 79 Yrs. 3 M. 17 D.

SADLER

OP 3:12 **William Sadler**

William was the son of ***Christopher SADDLER*** and ***Sophia ORTIZ***. During the War of 1812 he was a corporal under *Captain HARRIS* and participated in the Battle of Lake Erie as a sharpshooter. William Saddler I married ***Elizabeth TRYON*** of Clarence Station, in 1813. He then traveled with his father, Christopher, to settle in Dover in 1814 or 1815. In March of 1815, he traveled back to New York to bring his wife and infant daughter ***Sophia*** to Dover Township. Seven more children were born after arriving in Dover. William spoke German, English and Indian fluently and for many years was an interpreter for the Indians as well as Germans. Bay Village Historical Society, Bay Village: A Way of Life, pp. 18-19.

William SADLER was born Sept 23, 1791. ***Elzabah Betsy SADER*** *(sp.)* was born, Jan 12, 1792. Handwritten family papers provided by Carol Sadler Lenard.

William SADLER donated the land for the Bay Village Methodist Church at Bassett and Lake Roads. Carol Sadler Lenard

SADDLE, Wm. *(sp.)*, 59, farmer, value of real estate $1200, b. Penn.; ***Elizabeth***, 37*(incorrect age)*, b. NY; ***Wm.***, 18, b. Ohio; ***Lydia***, 14, b. Ohio. 1850 FC OH CYDO p. 217B, lines 6-9, dwelling 3745.

SADDLER, William, 69, value of real estate $7,000, personal property $600; ***Betsy***, 68; ***Lidia***, 22; ***Asa***, 14, b. Ohio, ***William Sadler***, 29, farmer, ***Ann E. Sadler***, 22, b. Mass. 1860 FC OH CYDO, p. 50, lines 32-37.

SADLER, Wm., 78, farmer, real estate $8,000, personal property $200, b. Penn; ***Betsy***, 76, K. H. *(keeping house)*, b. NY. 1870 FC OH CYDO, p. 34, lines 4-5.

Mr. William SADLER was born at Laurel Hill, Pennsylvania, September 23rd, 1791 and was eighty four years and six months old at the time of his decease, having lived over the time allotted to man. He removed from Laurel Hill to Clarence, New York and from thence to Dover, where he resided until his decease. He has left seven children to mourn his loss. Mr. Sadler was one of the pioneers of Dover having come here March 1818. He gained the love of the people for his cheerful and happy disposition, also for his kindness in time of trouble and affliction, and for his benevolence and hospitality. His house for many years was a home for the early itinerant Methodist ministers where they always received a cordial welcome. Let us cherish the memory of our departed friend. Friend after friend departs. Who has not lost a friend! There is no union here of hearts that has not here an end. An old friend. A paper in the possession of Carol Lenard, perhaps written for William's funeral.

I, ***William SADDLER***, of Dover Township, Cuyahoga County & State of Ohio.

Item 1st I give and devise to my son, ***Henry SADDLER*** and his heirs at my death, the Land Known as the Wilson Farm, Situated in the Township of Avon, Lorain County and State of Ohio. Being the east part of Lot. No. Thirty, and is bounded as the following...along the Lake Shore...

Item 2nd I devise and bequeath to my daughters ***Sophia POWELL, Mary A. WEED, Betsey CROCKER,***

Eunice CHRISTIE, Lydia SADDLER or heirs, at my death, all my Personal property to be divided in Equal amount.

Item 3. I do hereby nominate & appoint ***William SADDLER*** and ***John CHRISTIE*** Executors of this my last will and testament...

Signed Wm. Saddler, witnessed by *C.H. HALL* and *Samantha HALL*

Last Will of William Saddler, 13th day of December 1860.

Executor's Bond: John Christie and William Saddler are listed as principal and executors of the will of the late William Saddler and *Sherman OSBORN* and *Henry P. FOOTE* as sureties ...in the penal sum of Three Thousand Dollars... Signed John Christy, Wm. Sadler Jr., Sherman Osborn and Henry P. Foote. *Notice spelling differences.* EFC 1175.

Children of William Sadler and Elizabeth Tryon:
Sophia SADLER was born. Nov, 15. 1814. ***Henry SADLER*** was born. July, 4. 1817. ***Asa SADLER*** was born Oct 16. 1819. died Oct 28. 1896. ***Mary SADLER*** was born, May 10. 1822. ***Betsy SADLER*** was born. Apr 1. 1826. ***Eunice SADLER*** was born. Sept 24. 1830. ***William SADLER*** was born. June. 25. 1833. ***Lydia SADLER*** was born. Feb ll. 1837. ***Asa Wm. SADLER*** was born. Aug 7. 1846. Handwritten family papers provided by Carol Sadler Lenard.

Issue: ***Sophia SADDLER***, b. 1814, [Clarence, NY; d. 13 Apr 1880, Dover Twp.]; m. *Thomas B. POWELL*, [b. 1803, Olean, Cattaraugus Co., NY]. ***Henry SADDLER***, Methodist Minister, b. 1817, Byron Center; m. *Julia ROOT* of Clarence, N; d. 1899. ***Elizabeth SADDLER***, b. 1818, m. *Lewis CROCKER*. ***Asa SADDLER***, b. 16 Oct 1819; m. ***Lucy GRISWOLD*** *(dau. of Luman Griswold and Margaret Smith Griswold Eddy, OP 1:10-11)*; d. 1896, bur. Lakeside Cem., Cleve, *(not recorded at Lakeside)* Jan 1900. ***Mary Ann SADDLER***, b. 1822, m. *Joshua WEED*. ***Eunice SADLER***, b. 1826, m. *John CHRISTY*. ***William E. SADLER***, b. 25 June 1833 at Dover, Ohio; d. 5 Feb 1900 at Dover, bur. Evergreen Cem.; m. to *Ann Eliza LILLY* (b. 11 Sept 1838 at Ashfield, Mass.; d. 6 March 1915, Bay Village, OH, bur. Evergreen Cem.). ***Lydia C. SADDLER***, b. 1837; m1. *Cyrus GOODSPEED,* m2. *George N. GOODSPEED*, m3. *Charlie CHASE*. United States Daughters of 1812 application of Carol Lenard, 1981 and family group sheets. [Keith M. Sheldon, Descendants of Early Bay Village Families, p. 576].

I hereby certify that on the 4th day of Jany 1832, by virtue of a License from the Clerks of the Courts of Common pleas of Cuyahoga County, ***Thomas B. POWELL*** and ***Sophia SADLER*** were legally joined in marriage by me a Justice of the Peace. Marriage Record, Cuyahoga County, OH, vol. 2, p. 290.

Thomas POWELL, b. 1 Dec 1803, Olean, NY; resided in Dover, Ohio; d. 1844 at Dover; m. ***Sophia SADLER*** (b. 15 Nov 1814 at Clarence, NY, d. 15 Apr 1880). Their son, ***Perry POWELL*** was born 29 April 1836 in Dover, m. *Sarah MILNER* (b. 13 April 1847 at Mayfield, OH; resided in Lyons, O. and Dover; d. 23 Sept 1898). Sarah Dodd Wymer *Their daughter, Elizabeth would marry Henry F. PETERS (whose son, Cuvier PETERS, was moved to Evergreen Cemetery from Lakeside).*

Thomas POWELL, 56, farmer, b. Ohio; ***Sophia***, 45, b. NY; ***Perry W.***, 24, farmer, b. do.; ***Adie M.***, 18, b. Ohio; ***Elizabeth***, 15, b. Ohio; ***West***, 6, b. Ohio; *Frank SHULER*, 37, farm laborer, b. Germany. 1860 FC OH CYDO, p. 51, lines 35-40; p. 52, line 1.

POWELL, Thomas B, 76, farmer, b. NY, fr. b. NY, mo. b. RI; ***West T.***, 27, laborer, b. NY, fr. b. NY, mo. b. NY; ***Arabell***, daughter-in-law, b. Ohio, fr. b. Ohio, mo. b. Ohio; ***Jer***___?, 2, granddaughter, b. Ohio. 1880 FC OH CYDO p. 95B.

Passed to Spirit-Life.

Sophia POWELL, was born in Clarence, Erie county, N.Y., November 15th, 1814. She moved with her parents in 1816 to Dover, Cuyahoga county, Ohio and passed to spirit-life April 15th 1880, at her home in Dover. She was born a Spiritualist, and early embraced the beautiful philosophy of Spiritualism, and her life has not been in vain, for by her many good qualities of mind and heart, she won and held the love of all who knew her, and they will refer with affectionate remembrance to her many excellent traits of character. She leaves many examples worthy of imitation and a vacancy in her home and social circle difficult to fill. She leaves five children and a husband to mourn for her departure.

"Gone Home"

How true, "Death loves a shining mark,"
And aims its arrow well,
Secures our dearest ones of earth,
And bids us say farewell.
Cold death has taken from our home
Our darling mother dear;
Who bade us smile through bitter grief,
And dry the loving tear.
Think when you gather around at eve,
Her spirit hovers near,
So bid away the smothered grief'
And dry the loving tear.
Look up and smile for mother's sake,
Her sufferings now are o'er,
She's gone to join the spirit band,
Where death is known no more.
She passed away like dew from early flowers,
In life's well spent morn,
Left memory fraught with sweetness pure,
Like hope from heaven's first dawn.
There mother waits to greet us,
With the bright and shining hand,
Hoping soon to meet us,
In that bright and happy land.

Newspaper article in the possession of Carol Sadler Lenard.

We the undersigned,----children, of the late, ***Mrs. Sophia POWELL***, of Dover Cuyahoga Co. Ohio, deceased, April 15th 1880, do hereby appoint our brother ***Mr. West T. POWELL***, administrator of her money that is in the savings bank at Cleveland and a note against *Mr. David*

SITES of Dover. ***Mrs. Ada PEPPER, Mrs. Fidelia LILLY, Mrs. Libbie PETERS*** *(mother of Cuvier PETERS, moved from Lakeside Cemetery)*, ***Perry POWELL***. Note with Application for Letters of Administration, Probate Court, Cuyahoga County, State of Ohio.

Thomas POWELL, date of internment 11/1/1884; ***Sophia POWELL***, date of internment 4/18/1880, Lot 30, Section B, Evergreen Cemetery, Westlake, OH Lot 30B. Evergreen Cemetery Records.

Children of Thomas Powell and Sophia Sadler:

Perry POWELL, d. July 16, 1915, Bay, Cuyahoga Co., Ohio of Parenchymatous nephritis for 6 months and Valvular organic heart disease for many years; 79 yrs. 2 mos. 17 ds.; widowed, retired; b. Apr 29, 1836, Bay Village to ***Thos. B. POWELL***, b. Peugau?, NY and ***Sophia SADLER***, b. New York; informant I. C. Powell, West Dover, O.; undertaker Jas. A. Pease, Dover; bur. Evergreen Cem., Dover. Ohio Certificate of Death, Division of Vital Statistics, 1915, certif. 37328.

Mr. West T. POWELL, d. Jan 31, 1938, 11:30 p.m. at his res. 1919 E. 84th St., Cleveland, Cuyahoga Co., Ohio of Chronic Nephritis since April 1937 and Hypertension; Widowed; 84 yrs. old; b. Nov 19, 1853, Dover, Ohio to ***Thomas W. POWELL***, b. unknown and mo. unknown; informant *Mrs. Julie POWELL*, 7?982 E. 85th St., funeral director M. W. Mar___, 1802 Br____ford Rd., bur. Evergreen Cemetery, Dover Center. Ohio Certificate of Death, Division of Vital Statistics, 1938, certif. 6859.

Thomas and *Sophia's* granddaughter, daughter of *Perry*, would marry ***Wirt DODD***. Wirt's parents are buried in OP 4:13.

The State of Ohio, Cuyahoga County, ss. I Certify that on the 28th day of May, A.D. 1848, I duly solemnized the Marriage Contract between the said ***Henry SADLER*** and ***Julia Ann ROOT*** N.S. Worden, Minister Gospel. Marriage Record, Cuyahoga County, OH, vol. 4, p. 451.

Henry SADLER, 33, Farmer, Value of real estate $1,000, b. Ohio; ***Julia***, 35, b. NY; ***Althea***, 5/12, b. Ohio. 1850 FC OH CYDO, p. 216 B, lines 25-27.

DEATH OF AN OLD RESIDENT,
Henry F. Sadler of Byron Center Passed Away Monday Night.

Henry F. SADLER of Byron Center died Monday night, July 31, at his residence. He was born July 1817, at Dover, Ohio and was 82 years old a month ago. He came of both revolutionary and war of 1812 stock, both grandfathers having fought in the revolution, and his father in 1812. He was married May 28, 1848 to ***Julia A. ROOT*** of Clarence, NY, and in 1856 moved to Byron Center, where he had continually resided until his death. When he was 15 years old he became a member of the M.E. church, and was many years a local minister. It had been said of him that he preached more funeral sermons than any other minister in town, In politics he was a staunch republican until long after the civil war. In his old age he was often heard to remark that he stood by the republican party until the rebellion was put down, and now he was going to stand by the prohibitionist party until the whisky traffic was subdued.

His aged wife survives him and his two daughters, ***Mrs. Alice M. LOSEY*** of Byron, and ***Mrs. Alta M. STEWART*** of this city. His death was expected for several days. *"1899" written by hand.* Newspaper article in the possession of Carol Sadler Lenard.

The State of Ohio, Cuyahoga County, ss. I Certify that on the 15th day of November 1843 ***Mr. Noah CROCKER*** and ***Miss Betsy SADDLER*** were by me legally joined in marriage. Marriage Record, Cuyahoga County, OH, vol. 4, p. 236.

Noah CROCKER, 30, Farmer, value of real estate $700, b. O.; ***Betsey***, 24, b. O.; ***Alonson***, 4, b. O.; ***Nameless Babe***, 1/12, b. Ohio. 1850 FC OH AVLR p. 469, line 42 and p. 470, lines 1-3.

The State of Ohio, Cuyahoga County, ss. ***Asa SADDLER*** to ***Miss Lucy E. GRISWOLD*** I Certify that on the 14th day of Sept. A.D. 1845, I duly solemnized the Marriage Contract between the said Asa and Lucy E. Eluathan C. Gairt, Minister. Marriage Record, Cuyahoga County, OH, vol. 4, p. 236.

Son of Asa Sadler:

Louis Saddler

Louis, the only son of ***Mr.*** and ***Mrs. Asa SADDLER*** of Greenwood, died at the home of his parents of pneumonia, Tuesday evening, March 10. Louis Saddler was seventeen years of age, just budding into manhood, when the fatal malady cut the thread of the young life and brought sorrow to the household of the aged parents. The funeral services were held in the school house Thursday afternoon at 2 o'clock and the remains interred in the Greenwood cemetery. Newspaper article in the possession of Carol Sadler Lenard.

The State of Ohio, Cuyahoga County, ss., I Certify that on the 4th day of April 1850, I duly solemnized the Marriage Contract between the said ***Joshua WEED*** and ***Mary SADDLER***. Ohio City Adam Poe Marriage Record, Cuyahoga County, OH, vol. 5, p. 41.

Possible:

WEED, Joshua, 32, Carpenter, Value of Real Estate $300, b. Ohio; ***Mary A.***, 20, b. Ohio; ***William***, 63, b. N. H.; ***Abigail***, 21, b. Ohio. 1850 FC Michigan, Allegan Co., Newark, lines 14-17. *Unsure if correct family due to ages listed in 1860 census that follows.*

WEED, Joshua, 40, Carpenter and Joiner, value of real estate $2500, value of personal property $150, b. Ohio; ***Mary***, 37, b. Ohio; ***Perry***, 8, b. Ohio; ***George I.***, 3, b. Ohio; ***Lydia***, 1, b. Michigan. 1860 FC Michigan, Allegan Co., Newark, p. 103, house 678, lines 35-39.

The State of Ohio, Cuyahoga County, ss., I hereby certify, that on the 12th day of December A.D. 1849, I duly solemnized the Marriage Contract between the said ***John CHRISTY*** to ***Eunice SADDLER***. Avon. W.M. Hitchcock Marriage Record, Cuyahoga County, OH, vol. 5, p. 35.

CHRISTY, John, 26, Farmer, Real estate value $800, b. NY; ***Eunice***, 20, b. Ohio. 1850 FC OH Lorain Co., Penfield Twp., p. 505, lines 26-27.

CHRISTY, John, 38, Farmer, Value of real estate $3,000, personal value $800, b. England; ***Eunice***, 31, b. Ohio; ***Cecelia***, 9, b. Ohio; ***Rosilla***, 6, b. Ohio; ***Flora***, 4, b. Ohio; ***Ann***, 2, b. Ohio; ***Abejah***, male, 67, b. England. 1860 FC OH Lorain, Penfield Twp., p. 95, lines 23-27.

CHRISTIE, John, 48, Value of real estate $6,500, personal value $1365, b. England; ***Unis***, 41, Keeping House, b. Ohio; ***Celia***, 19; ***Rosetta***, 17; ***Flora***, 16, ***Annaza***, 14; ***Ida***, 12; ***John***, 6; ***Finta***?, 4; ***Arthur***, 1; ***Angelina***, 1; all children b. Ohio. 1870 FC OH Lorain, Penfield Twp., p. 564, lines 2-12.

CHRISTY, John, 58, Farmer, b. Isle of Man, fr. b. England, mo. Isle of Man; ***Eunice***, b. Ohio, fr. b. NY, mo. b. Penn.; ***Anna E.***, 23; ***Ida M.***,19; ***John E.***, 15, Work on farm; ***Elsie S.***, 13; ***Arthur B.***, 11; ***Angie B.***, 11; all children b. Ohio. 1880 FC OH Lorain Co., Penfield Twp., p. 541, lines 18-25.

Tombstone Inscription: ***CHRISTY - John***, Father; Dec 24, 1821 - Feb 19, 1899. ***Eunice***, Mother; Sept 24, 1830 - Aug 2, 1907. ***Elsie L.***, Daughter, Feb 27, 1867 - Sept 15, 1886. ***Angie B.***, wife of *A. B. STRONG;* May 6, 1869 - Jan 5, 1904. ***Arthur B.***; May 6, 1869 - April 8, 1935. ***John E.***; Jan 6, 1865 - Jan 19, 1941. ***Ida M.;*** Nov 7, 1860 - Jan 24, 1944. ***Abijah***, Grandfather; Apr 20, 1792 - May 12, 1869. Penfield Cemetery, Penfield, OH. Inscriptions read by Eleanor Gnandt, Penfield Twp. Clerk.

The State of Ohio, Cuyahoga County, ss., I Certify that on the 16th day of Sept 1858, ***Mr. William SADDLER*** and ***Miss Ann E. LILLY*** were by me legally joined in marriage. C.H. Hall. Marriage Record, Cuyahoga County, OH, vol. 9, p. 107.

William E. SADLER, b. 25 June 1833, Dover, Cuyahoga Co., Ohio married 16 Sept 1858 to ***Ann Eliza LILLY*** (b. 11 Sept 1858, Ashfield, Franklin Co., Mass. dau. of *Luther LILLY* and *Mary HOWES*; d. 6 Mar 1915, Bay Village, Cuyahoga Co., Ohio); fisherman, farmer; Methodist; d. 5 Feb 1900, Dover; both buried Evergreen Cemetery, Westlake, Cuyahoga Co. *Issue*: ***Frank SADLER***, b. 1861, Dover; m. 1891 to *Carrie MILLER*; d. 1929; bur. Evergreen Cemetery. ***Florence SADLER***, b. 6 June 1865, Dover; m. 30 Dec 1886 to *Silas STRIMPLE*; d. July 1938. ***Burrett Elihu SADLER***, b. 13 Aug 1869, Dover; m. 17 Nov 1909, Erie Co., New York to *Marie Caroline RAUSCH*; d. 2 Aug 1941, Bay Village; bur. Evergreen Cemetery. ***Jessie SADLER (SADDLER)***, b. 1874, Dover; d. 1947. ***Ralph Edward SADLER***, b. 1879, Dover; m. 1900 to *Ida BURT*; d. 1954; bur. Evergreen Cemetery. Carol Sadler Lenard

A PIONEER OF DOVER.

Brief Sketch of the Life of William Sadler, Who Died Last Monday.

With the death of ***Mr. William SADLER*** on the afternoon of Monday, Dover lost one of its old and prominent citizens.

Mr. Sadler's parents were among the earliest settlers of Dover, coming from Clarence, near Buffalo, N.Y., to Dover in 1815. His mother was the first Methodist in town and was instrumental in establishing a church of her denomination, giving the building site and much of the timber for the construction of the little church that now, after sixty years have passed, is a monument to her memory. With this church Mr. Sadler was identified. Mr. Sadler's father served his country in the war of 1812.

Of a large family of brothers and sister but one remains-***Mrs. Eunice SADLER CHRISTY***. Mr. Sadler's beautiful farm stretches out upon the bank of the lake, and in this quiet spot he had for many months felt that he must soon put aside earthly cares.

His wife, sons and daughter have the sympathy of a large circle of friends, who, in the sixty-six years that were given to him, have honored his integrity and felt his quiet, kindly interest in his fellow men. Newspaper article in the possession of Carol Sadler Lenard.

SADLER- At his home, Dover, Ohio, February 5, ***William SADLER***, aged 66 years. Funeral Thursday 9:30 a. m. Evergreen Cemetery Dover, Ohio. Cleveland Necrology File, February 7, 1900, reel 070.

SADLER-Ann Eliza, widow of ***William SADLER***, Mar 6, 1915, age 76 years. Funeral from late residence, Mar 9, 1915, at 1 p. m. eastern time. Cleveland Necrology File, March 8, 1915, reel 070.

Ann Eliza SADLER, d. March 6th, 1915 at 3 p.m., Bay, Cuyahoga Co., Ohio of Senile decay, Gradual decline for one year, 8 months…; 76 yrs. 5 mos. 22 ds.; Widowed, Housewife; b. September 11th, 1838, Ashfield Plains, Mass. to ***Luther LILLY***, b. Mass. and ***Mary HOWE***, b. Mass; Length of time at residence 38 yrs. 5 mos. 22 ds., In the state 73 yrs.; informant ***Jesse L. SADLER***, Bay Village; undertaker Clifton *(Clifford)* Pease; burial Evergreen Cemetery. Ohio Certificate of Death, Division of Vital Statistics, 1915, certif. 13420.

I hereby certify that on the 2nd day of Sept A.D. 1863, I duly solemnized the marriage contract between the said ***George W. GOODSPEED*** and ***Lydia C. SADDLER***. Cuyahoga Co. Marriage Record, Cuyahoga County, OH, vol. 1, before p. 1 and Marriage Record, Cuyahoga County, OH, vol. 12, p. 65.

OP 3:12 Elizabeth Tryon Sadler

Elizabeth TRYON, b. 12 Jan 1793, Clarence Station, NY; m. Dec 1813, Clarence Station, NY; d. 29 April 1872, Dover, OH. DAR application of Carol Sadler Lenard, Nat. 640373.

A worthy, faithful, energetic Christian woman of early days was ***Elizabeth TRYON***, who came from New York soon after her marriage to ***William SADLER***, a soldier in the war of 1812. When the Lake Shore Methodist Episcopal Church was organized in 1827 she contributed largely, giving the lot and much of the building material, being one of the five charter members. The others were *Rev. Eliphalet JOHNSON*, his gifted wife, *Margaret*, their daughter, *Rebecca*, and niece, *Catharine PORTER FOOTE*...The beloved Rev. Johnson preached here until he moved to Wisconsin in 1842.

All her life long Mrs. Sadler cherished the church she helped to build, the membership of which revere her memory. *Mrs. Ann Eliza LILLY SADLER*, her son's wife, is an enthusiastic worker in the same church. Pioneer Women of the Western Reserve, Dover, Cuyahoga County, pp. 60-1.

Dover Lakeshore Methodist Episcopal Church, our church's ancestor was established in 1827. Organized by ***Elizabeth SADDLER (Mrs. William)*** and led by the *Rev. Eliphalet JOHNSON*, brother of *Sarah OSBORN (Mrs. Reuben)*. The members of this new church held worship services in their homes or in the cabin built with walnut logs cut from the Saddler woods. In 1840 Elizabeth Saddler gave the land at Bassett and Lake Roads and much of the material for the construction of the church built by *Alvah MCKINLEY*. Seventeen members shared the cost. The little wooden church served until 1907, the congregation's eightieth Anniversary, when the membership outgrew it. That spring the decision was made to build a new brick church. Carol K. Meermans, Bay United Methodist Church, 175th Anniversary booklet, 2002.

CUYAHOGA. Monday evening, April 29th, ***Mrs. Betsy SADDLER***, one of the pioneers of Northern Ohio, passed away from earth. She was born in Clarence, N.Y., in 1792, and was married to ***Mr. Wm. SADDLER*** in 1813. They settled in Dover in 1815, sharing with the few inhabitants the privations incident to pioneer life. She had for sixty-two years been a member of the M. E. Church, being one of the seven who organized the first Methodist Church in the town. She was an exemplary Christian, ever evincing a deep interest in the good cause, and when death came was ready and waiting the happy change. C. Newspaper clipping in the possession of Carol Sadler Lenard.

SADLER, Elizabeth, d. May 30, 1872, Dover, married, 79y 4m. 26d., b. Dover, farmer, disease old age. PD 1:71 *(Place of birth as Dover, is incorrect, this would have been before the "first settler's" arrived.)*

Ancestors of Elizabeth Tryon Sadler:

Elizabeth TRYON, was the daughter of ***Ezra TRYON*** (b. 2 Aug 1760, d. May 1847) and ***Annah (Anner) BIDWELL*** (b. 6 July 1762, d. 23 Jan 1818, m. 14 Mar 1790). Ezra enlisted 1777 and fought as a private in the Revolutionary War from Connecticut in *Capt. Edward BULKLEY'S* Co., *Samuel B. WEBB'S* regiment and served until 1783. He was in the battles of Rhode Island, Springfield and Yorktown. In 1818 he applied and was approved for a pension in Wayne County, Ohio. DAR application of Carol Sadler Lenard, Nat. 640373.

Children of Ezra and Annah TRYON: ***David TRYON*** was born Feb 16, 1791 he has 11 children. ***Elizabeth TRYON SADLER*** was born Jan 12, 1793, she has 8 children. ***John TRYON*** was born March 8, 1794, he has 12 children. ***Abel TRYON*** was born Sept 23, 1795 died Sept 1, 1804. ***Mary TRYON SMITH*** was born Feb 23, 1797, 5 children. ***Oliver TRYON*** was born Jan 7, 1799 died Feb 27, 1814. ***Adah TRYON*** was born July 6, 1800 died 1856, 11 ch. ***Aneil TRYON*** was born March 25, 1806 died 1860, 4 ch. Handwritten paper in the possession of Carol Sadler Lenard.

E.
(Small stone at the foot of Sadler monument)

Wm.
(Small stone at the foot of Sadler monument)

OP 3:13 Sophia Ortiz Sadler

SOPHIA
WIFE OF
C. SADDLER

Sophia ORTIZ of Pennsylvania met ***Christopher*** during his travels with the army. When the war ended, he returned north to marry Sophia and together they journeyed to Clarence Station, New York. They would settle on farm land granted to him from his military service. The Saddler's had ten children most of whom stayed in New York. Bay Village Historical Society, Bay Village: A Way of Life, pp. 18-19.

Sophia ORTS *or* ***ORTZ***...was b. in Lancaster Co PA... sold*(ier)* d 23 Mar 1839 in Cuyahoga Co OH & his wife appl*(ied)* there 16 Oct 1848 aged 89. Wid*(ow)* d 6 Nov 1851. Virgil D. White, Genealogical Abstracts of Revolutionary War Pension Files, p. 2995. *(See complete text below with Christopher)*

Sophia ORTS (ORTZ) born 1759-1761 at Cocalico Township, Lancaster Co., Penna., died at Dover Township, Ohio on 11/6/1851, married 1781-1782 at Berks County, Penna. DAR application of Ruth E. Strimple Shook, Nat. 499277.

SADLER, Mrs. Christopher; Maiden Name: *ORTZ, Sophia*; Year Came to Township or Born 18--; Where From or Where Born Clarence, N.Y.; Last Residence Dover, O. Women in the Western Reserve before 1840, p. 24.

OP 3:14 **Christopher Sadler**

CHRISTOPHER
SADDLER
WAR OF 1776

Christopher SADLER was born in 1756 in Hesse Cassel, Germany. He was granted land after the war through the Connecticut Land Grant Company. That property extended from the lake to what is now identified as Wolf Rd. and from Saddler Rd. to Florence St. in Bay Village. The house built by ***William SADLER***, Christopher's son, at 29737 Lake, remained in the family until 1997. William had come with his father in a covered wagon, across the ice to the property. Carol Sadler Lenard

Christopher's son ***William***, convinced him to come to Dover with him after their home in Clarence Station, NY was burned out during an Indian uprising. The Sadlers traveled during the winter of 1814 or 1815. Two other sons arrived later, but chose not to stay. Bay Village Historical Society, Bay Village: A Way of Life, pp. 18-19. *(Further information on the family is provided in the book.)*

SADDLER, Christopher, Sophia *(wife)*, Cont Line (German), R9135, sol *(soldier)* was b in Germany (no date given) & he came to America in 1777 as a Pvt in the British Army & was taken prisoner & in the spring of 1778 he enl *(enlisted)* into the Rev Army, sol m. ***Sophia ORTS*** or ***ORTIZ*** in 1781 or 1782 near Reading in Berks Co PA & she was b. in Lancaster Co PA (no date given), sol. d. 23 Mar 1839 in Cuyahoga Co OH & his wife appl there 16 Oct 1848 aged 89, a son ***John SADDLER*** was aged 64 in 1848, a daughter (not named) m in 1818 to *Henry ONSTIEN* & he was a widower in 1848 aged 56, wid d 6 Nov 1851 & in 1852 ***Christian SADDLER, Wm. SADDLER*** & ***Christopher SADDLER*** of Cuyahoga Co OH claimed to be heirs of dec'd wid, Saddler family data given was: ***William*** b. 23 Sep 1791 (he was son of sol), ***Elizabeth*** b in Jan 1792, ***Sophia*** b 15 Nov 1814, ***Henry*** b in July yr. illegible, ***Asa*** b 16 Oct 1819 & ***Mary A***. b 7 May 1822. Virgil D. White, Genealogical Abstracts of Revolutionary War Pension Files, p. 2995.

Christopher SADLER (SADDLER)...assisted in establishing American Independence during the War of the Revolution, while acting in the capacity of Private (as a Dragoon) in independent corps under the command of General Count Pulaski. He rode horseback and carried a carbine and lance. He was in service over two years...Children of he and Sophie Orts (or Ortz)...: ***Henry SADLER*** , 1780, m. *Ester PETTON;* ***Chrisjohn SADLER***, b. 1783, d. 1866, m. *Eliza ROOT*; ***William SADLER*** #1, b/d. 1786; ***Betsy***, b/d. 1789; ***William SADLER*** #2, 9-23-1791, d. 1875 *(Lot 3:13),* m. 1813 to *Elizabeth TRYON*; ***Barbry S. (Barbara) SADLER***, b. 1792, d. 1862, m. *Benjamin REYNOLDS*; ***Catharine SADLER,*** b. 1796, d. 1870, m. *William STEVENS* [of Avon Lake, Lorain Co.]; ***Lydia SADLER***, b. 1799, d. 1880, m. *John TRYON*, (Child: *Rufus*); ***Susan SADLER***, b. 1801, d. 1838, m. *Henry ONSTINE*; ***Christopher SADLER,, Jr.***, b. 1803, d. 1868, m. *Mary Ann SNYDER*. DAR application of Ruth E. Strimple Shook, Nat. 499277, family group sheet of Carol Sadler Lenard and [Geraldine A. Hardway].

Christopher SADLER and ***Sophia ORTS*** was married 1778. ***Christopher SADLER*** was born near 1758. ***Sophia SADLER*** was born near 1767. ***Henry SADLER*** was born 1780. ***Christjohn SADLER*** was born Aug 1783. ***WM. SADLER*** was born 1786. ***Betsy SADLER*** was born 1789. ***Wm. SADLER*** was born Sept 23 1791. ***Barbry SADLER*** was born Feb 1792. ***Cathrine SADLER*** was born 1796. ***Lydia SADLER*** was born July 1799. ***Susan SADLER*** was born Feb 1801. ***Christopher SADLER*** was born Apr 1803. Handwritten paper provided by Carol Sadler Lenard.

Christopher SADDLER'S home, built about 1840, still stands today at 29737 Lake Road at the corner of Lake Road and Ruth Street. The home is one of the five oldest privately owned homes in Bay Village. The property remained in the Sadler family approximately 160 years. Within a short period of time after it was sold it was put up for auction to be offered at a Sheriff's sale, but removed at least twice until it was finally sold in the late spring of 2002 for $189,000. The charming white house with black shutters and a wrap around porch has its own gas well providing heat for the family. Rose Hill Museum Family Files and William R. Krause.

Children of Christopher Sadler and Sophia Ortiz:

I do hereby certify that on the 1st day of Jan 1818 that I joined ***William K. STEVENS*** and ***Catharine SADLER*** together in bonds of Marriage, said William and Catharine both of Dover and County of Cuyahoga, Dover. March 9th, 1818. Jedediah Crocker, Justice of the Peace. Marriage Record, Cuyahoga County, OH, vol. 1, p. 89.

William K. STEVENS and ***Catharine*** *(SADLER)* ***STEVENS***, were pioneer settlers in Huron county having moved there in 1819 from New York. Their children are - ***Harriet, John A., Catharine, Salina, Mary*** and ***Margaret***. Their son, John A. was born in Huron County in 1822 and married *Esther L.* (dau. of *Daniel* and *Permelia (Petty) HEATH* who had eight children). Wood Co., OH Atlas 1875-1912, p. 39.

William K. STEVENS of New York state and ***Catharine SADDLER*** had 7 children of which ***John*** is the oldest (b. 3 May 1822, Huron Co., in Bloom, now Erie Twp.). John began working at the age of seven and went West for a few years as a cowboy. He married 1849, Sherman Twp., Huron Co., OH to *Esther Linda HEATH* and moved to Wood Co. in 1853. They had the following children: *Daniel, John E., Amelia GILL, Zahm, Almina POTES, Prudence, Roxy Ann DOTS, Mary Elizabeth GILL* and *Emma Jane AMES*. "William K. Stevens," Commemorative Historical Biographical Record of Wood County, Ohio, p. 1362.

I do hereby Certify that ***John TRYON*** of Mohican in the County of Wayne and ***Lydia SADLER*** of Dover in the County of Cuyahoga were joined in the marriage state Jan 21, 1817. Marriage Record, Cuyahoga County, OH, vol. 1, p. 74.

OP 3:15

Marker is presumed to be for Joseph Hayes, see below.

FATHER

OP 3:16 Hayes Monument

HAYES

JOSEPH HAYES
BORN APRIL 14, 1829
DIED NOV 2, 1905
MARY J. HAYES
1832-1922

OP 3:16 Joseph Hayes

HAY, Joseph, 37, farmer, value of real estate $1,600, personal estate $500, b. England; ***Mary Jane***, 34, b. England; ***Florena***, 12, b. New York, attended school during the year; ***David***, 5, b. Ohio, attended school; ***Fannie Jane***, 3, b. Ohio. 1870 FC OH DO p. 25, lines 6-10.

HAY, Joseph, 46, farmer, b. England, parents b. England; ***Mary J.***, 43, wife, b. England, parents b. England; ***David***, 14, laborer; ***Fanny J.***, 12; ***Betty***, 9; ***William C.***, 6; ***Joseph B.***, 4; ***Bell M.***, Oct, 8/12; all children born in Ohio. 1880 FC OH CYDO, p. 93, lines 21-28.

HAYS, Joseph; owned land; Acres: Improved - 18 tilled, including fallow and grass, 5 permanent meadow, Unimproved - 5 woodland. Farm Values: Land and buildings- $2500, Machinery - $100, Live Stock - $225. Estimated value of all farm production: $300. Grass lands: acreage: 6 not mown. 3 horses, 2 milch cows, 1 other; 1 calves dropped, 2 cattle sold living. 230 pounds of butter made on the farm. 3 sheep on hand June 1, 1880; Spring 1880 - 3 fleeces, weight 15 lbs. 26 barnyard poultry on farm, 200 dozen eggs produced in 1879. Indian corn: 4 acres, 180 bushels; oats: 2 acres, 80 bushels; wheat: 3 acres, 40 bushels; potatoes: 2 acres, 100 bushels. Orchards - apple: 1 acre, 40 bearing trees. "Schedule 2. Production of Agriculture in Dover Township, Cuyahoga County, OH," enumerated June, 1880, p. 22.

HAY, Joseph, b. Apr 1832, 68, immig. 1857, 43 yrs., Na., married 47 yrs., farmer; ***Mary J.***, b. Feb 1835, 65, 10 children born, 7 living, immig. 1857, 43 yrs., Na., married 47 yrs. 1900 FC OH CYDO, p. 5A, line 30-31, house 95.

HAYES-Joseph, aged 76 years, at his residence, at North Dover, O. Funeral Sunday from residence at 2 o'clock standard. Toronto papers please copy. Cem. Rec. 1829-1905, Lakeside Cemetery, Bay Village, Ohio. Cleveland Necrology File, November 4, 1905, roll 35.

Joseph HAY, 80; res. Dover; nativity English; interred Novm 5th 1905; Original Part. "List of Interments," Lakeside Cemetery, Bay Village, OH.

An application to admit his will to probate was presented on Nov 16, 1905 to the State of Ohio by ***Floanna GUILD, David HAYES, Fannie THORSON, Bessie HAYES, William HAYES, Joseph HAYES*** and ***Belle MALLE***. Estate Case File, Cuyahoga County, 38005.

Children of Joseph Hayes and Mary Campbell:

David C. HAYES, 35, res. Lakewood, Ohio; b. Dover; occup. Machinist; fr. *Joseph HAYES*, mo. *Mary CAMPBELL*. Married ***Elsie DICKSON***, 34, res. Lakewood, b. Ridgeville, Ohio; occup. Seamstress; fr. *Henry DICKSON*, mo. *Minnie ROBINSON*; both previously married. The State of Ohio, Cuyahoga County, SS. I certify, That on the 23rd day of Nov 1901, Mr. David C. Hayes and Mrs. Elsie Dickson were by me legally joined in Marriage. G.W. Huddleston Marriage Record, Cuyahoga County, OH, vol. 53, p. 116. *Previous marriage not recorded in Cuyahoga County for Elsie.*

HAYES, David, 44, married 14 yrs., b. Ohio, fr. b. Ireland, mo. b. Ireland, occup. General Farmer, Renting; ***Elsie***, 44, no children, b. Ohio, parents b. Ohio. 1910 FC Lorain Co., Sheffield Twp., ED 126, p. 7B, lines 97-8, West Ridge Road.

The State of Ohio, Cuyahoga County, ss. I certify, That on the 28th day of Nov 1895, ***Mr. William C. HAYES*** and ***Miss Marie L. GRIFFIN*** were by me legally joined in Marriage. Rev. O__ Jenkins Marriage Record, Cuyahoga County, OH, vol. 43, p. 75.

HAYES, Dr. William C., 36, b. Ohio, No. of years married 14, occup. Physician; ***Marie***, 36, 1 child living, b. Ohio, fr. b. Ireland, mo. b. Ohio; ***Lois***, adopted daughter, 1 8/12 yrs., b. Ohio; *FISHEL, John*, 24, roomer, b. Penn., parents b. Germany, occup. clerk; *SUMMER, Ezra*, 24, b. Penn., parents b. Penn., occup. clerk. 1910 FC Lorain Co., Lorain City, Sheffield Township, Precinct D, ED 98, p. 5B, lines 1-3.

HAYES, Dr. William C., 46, widower, b. Ohio, parents b. England, Physician in Lorain; ***Lois***, dau., 11, b. Ohio, parents b. Ohio; *GRIFFEN, Harriet C.,* mother-in-law, 77, widow, b. Ohio, fr. b. Mass., mother b. Ohio, Housekeeper. 1920 FC OH Lorain, Lorain, 31st. Street, Sheffield Township, p. 1B, ED 25, lines 82-4.

William C. HAYES, 46, res. Lorain, O., b. Dover, O., occup. Phisician *(sp.)*, fr. *Joseph*, mo. *Mary CAMPBELL.* Married ***Nettie M. JARVIS***, 43, res. 12518 Detroit Ave., b. Cleve. O., occup. none, fr. *John MASON*, mo. *Naomi CROSS*; both previously married, spouses deceased. The State of Ohio, Cuyahoga County, ss. I certify, That on the 3rd day of August 1920, Mr. William C. Hayes and Miss *(should be Mrs.)* Nettie M. Jarvis were by me legally joined in Marriage. Rev. Chas. J. Pardee, West Park, O. *(also listed as Rev. H.W. Pardee)* Marriage Record, Cuyahoga County, OH, vol. 417, p. 463.

Previous marriages of Nettie:

The State of Ohio, Cuyahoga County, ss. I Certify, That on the 1st day of Nov 1894, ***Charles E. KANEEN*** and ***Henrietta MASON*** were by me legally joined in marriage. Rev. Francis M. Hall. Marriage Record, Cuyahoga County, OH, vol. 41, p. 233.

KANEEN, Charles E., 89; a resident of Cleveland, O., until 10 years ago; passed away Monday, Miami, Fla., clerk with General Motors Corp. for over 30 years. Charter Member Lakewood Masonic Lodge 602, F. and A. M. and the Knights of Pythius Hesperian Lodge, survived by daughter *Mrs. Gladys JARVIS*, one grandchild, two great-grandchildren. Funeral Wednesday, Miami, Arrangements by Pracey Funeral Home. Sep 22, 1959 The Plain Dealer.

John W. JARVIS, 43; res. 2572 West 41st St.; b. Canada; occup. Mover; fr. *John*, mo. *Mary*; number of times previously married Once (dec'd). Married ***Nettie May KANEEM***, 36, res. 3756 West 25th St., b. Cleve'd, O., occup. none, fr. *Jno. E. MASON*, mo. *Naomi CROSS*, number of times previously married Once, div. The State of Ohio, Cuyahoga Co., ss., I Certify that on the 1st day of Oct 1913, Mr. John W. Jarvis and Mrs. Nettie May Kanteen were by me legally joined in marriage. Wm. Brown, J.P. Marriage Record, Cuyahoga County, OH, vol. 86, p. 90. *Spelling of Kaneen inconsistent.*

HAYES-Dr. William C., beloved husband of ***Nettie N.*** (nee ***MASON***), father of ***Louis M. HAYES***, at residence, 1972 E. 31st street, Lorain, O., Tuesday, March 20. Funeral from late residence, Friday, March 23, at 2 o'clock. Cleveland Necrology File, March 20, 1923, reel 035.

W.C. HAYES, M.D.; husband of ***Nettie M. HAYES***, 1870-1923. Maple Ridge Cemetery, Westlake, OH.

Joseph B. HAYES, 23, Dover, O., b. Dover, Farmer, fr. *Joseph HAYES,* mo. *Mary CAMPBELL.* Married ***Annie F. MILEY***, 23, res. Dover, O., b. Cleveland, O., fr. *Patrick MILEY,* mo. *Mary LACEY*; neither previously married. The State of Ohio, Cuyahoga Co., ss. I Certify, That on the 10th day of May 1899 Mr. Joseph B. Hayes and Miss Annie F. Miley were by me legally joined in marriage. Rev. James O'Leary. Marriage Record, Cuyahoga County, OH, vol. 48, p. 442.

Rene MALLE, 26, Dover, Ohio, b. City, Farmer, fr. *Gerard MALLE*, mo. *Selina CARTIGNY.* Married ***Belle HAYES***, 20, Dover, b. Dover, occup. none, fr. *Joseph HAYES,* mo. maiden name *Mary CAMPBELL;* neither previously married. The State of Ohio, Cuyahoga County, SS. I certify, That on the 18th day of May 1899, Mr. Rene Malle and Miss Belle Hayes were by me legally joined in Marriage. William Brown, JP Marriage Record, Cuyahoga County, OH, vol. 48, p. 459.

Parents of Rene:

Gerard Joseph MALLE, d. March 10, 1912, 12:15 p.m., Dover, Cuyahoga Co., Ohio of Cerebral hemorrhage and Arterio sclerosis; 75 yrs. 11 mos. 26 ds.; b. March 14, 1836, France to ***Paul MALLE***, b. France, mother unknown; married; Mason and Plasterer; informant Harry Malle, Dover, O.; undertaker Jas. A. Pease & Son, Dover; burial Evergreen Cem., Dover. Ohio Certificate of Death, Division of Vital Statistics, 1912, certif. 14242.

Celina MALLE, d. Dec 15, 1925, Bradley Rd., Bay, Cuyahoga Co., Ohio of secondary infection of sub maxillary gland causing inability to take nourishment 2ds. and Bronchitis following___influenza, 16 ds.; 84 yrs. 10 mos. 13 ds.; b. Feb 2, 1841, France to *H. CARTIGNY,* b. France and *Myra A. HOURYZ*, b. France; widowed; informant *A. H. WOLF,* West Dover; undertaker C. Pease; burial Evergreen, Cem. Ohio Certificate of Death, Division of Vital Statistics, 1925, certif. 67795.

Rene's sister, Florence MALLE, married Albert Horace WOLF, son of Alfred Marian and Caroline WOLF (Lot 49). 1925 would bring a difficult year for Belle with the divorce and death of their son.

MALLE-Edward J., beloved son of ***Rene*** and ***Belle***, brother of ***Mrs. Pearl GOLLIN, Mrs. Grace TREVIS, Clarence, Ruth*** and ***Jean***, suddenly. Funeral at William Daniels' funeral home, 15800 Detroit avenue, Tuesday, June 9, at 2 p. m. Burial at Lakewood Cemetery. Cleveland Necrology File, June 9, 1925, reel 54.

Remarriage of ***Rene MALLE***, 53, res.18241 Sloane Ave., Cleveland, Conductor…previously married once, Div. Jan 1925 C.P.Ct. Married ***Lottie PETERMAN***, 56, res. 11720 Detroit Av., b. Farmington, O., fr. *Erwin BELDEN*, mo. *Amelia AMES*, previously married once, married name *PETERMAN*. June 27, 1925, Cuyahoga County, Ohio. Marriage Record, Cuyahoga County, OH, vol. 141, p. 7 Lottie passed away, Daniels Funeral Home Cleveland Necrology File, Roll #54

MALLE: Rene, beloved husband of *Sarah*; father of ***Mrs. John Gollin, Mrs. Grace WILLIAMSON, Mrs. Ruth GREENHAW, Jean*** and ***Clarence,*** *Mrs. Alice HALL, Mrs. William BARTH* and *Mrs. E. J. SMITH*; grandfather and great-grandfather; residence 1421 W. 84th St. Friends received at Klanke Funeral Parlors, 12629 Detroit Ave., Lakewood, where services will be held Tuesday, Dec 31, at 3 p. m. Dec 30 1946, The Plain Dealer. All rights reserved. Reprinted with permission.

Third wife of Rene:

MALLE, Sarah A. (nee ***BRENNAN***), beloved wife of the late *Rene*, mother of *P.C. JENKINS, Mrs. Gladys BARTH, Mrs. Dorothy SMITH* and the late *Mrs. Alice HALL* and *Irene JENKINS*, and foster mother of ***Mrs. Pearl GOLLIN*** and ***Clarence MALLE***, residence, 3617 Siam Ave. The family will receive friends From 3 To 5 And 7 To 10 P.M. at Klanke Funeral Parlors, 12629 Detroit Ave., Lakewood, where services will be held Monday, Apr 21, at 1:30 p. m. Cleveland Necrology File, Cleveland Press, Apr 1958, reel 133.

OP 3:16/17 **Mary Jane Campbell Hayes**

MOTHER

HAYES, Mary J., 80, widow, No. of children born 10, living 7, b. Ohio, parents b. Scot., occup. Own Income; ***Bessie***, 30, b. Ohio, father b. England, mo. b. Scot., occup. Stenographer Office, Rented Home. Carnegie Avenue South East. 1920 FC OH CY, Cleveland, ED 198, p. 4B, lines 79-80.

Mary J. HAYES, 2193 E. 89 St., Ward 18; d. Jan 1, 1922, 9 a.m., Chronic Valvular Disease-vibral incompetence; widowed; b. Feb 14, 1832, England, fr. ***Wm. CAMPBELL***, b. Scotland, mo. do not know; 89 yrs. 10 mos. 17 ds.; informant *Miss Bessie HAYES,* 2193 E. 89 St., Cleve.; bur. Bay Village, Jan 4, 1922, undertaker C. Pease, Dover Center. Ohio Certificate of Death, Division of Vital Statistics, 1922, certif. 908.

HAYES-Mary J., January 1 at 9 a.m., aged 90 years, at the residence of her daughter, ***Bessie M. HAYES***, 2193 E. 89th street. Funeral Wednesday, 1:30 p.m. at the residence. Burial at Bay Village. Funeral and burial private. Cleveland Necrology File, Jan 1, 1922, reel 35.

Mary HAYES, Cleveland, 89, Heart Disease, removal to Bay Village, undertaker C. Pease, Dover Center, O., interment Jan 4, 1922. Burial Removal Permit, City of Bay Village, OH.

Dr. Garlick asked to apply the wish of Don Quixote to Sancho Panza to the Cahoons:

When any of their descendants leave this wicked world may their eyes be closed by the soft fingers of great-grandchildren.

Cahoon Sixtieth Anniversary Celebration of the Settlement of Dover, August 27th, 1870

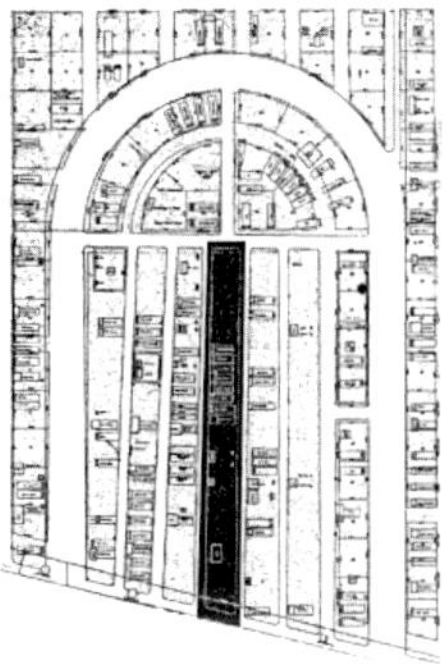

Fourth row east of the west drive starting from the road and proceeding north.

OP 4:1 Aldrich monument

AARON ALDRICH
BORN APR 27, 1795
DIED MAY 27, 1856
ELIZABETH
BORN DEC 22, 1794
DIED DEC 28, 1869

HENRY W. ALDRICH
BORN SEPT 12, 1822
DIED AUG 10, 1892
MARY ANN ALDRICH
BORN APRIL 9, 1822
DIED FEB 16, 1910

SARAH E.
BORN DEC 4, 1853
DIED AUG 28, 1858

MABEL L.
BORN
AUG 2, 1865
DIED
FEB 4, 1881

AARON W.
ALDRICH
BORN
OCT 5, 1815
DIED
APR 17, 1890

ALDRICH

OP 4:1 Aaron Aldrich

Aaron ALDRICH III, son of ***Aaron ALDRICH*** and ***Mary (Marcy) WATERMAN,*** b. 27 Apr 1795, Smithfield; d. 27 May 1856, Dover, O.; m. 11 Sept 1814, Smithfield to ***Elizabeth WINSOR*** (b. 22 Dec 1794, N. Smithfield, d. 28 Dec 1869, Dover, OH). Gertrude Aldrich Barker Rose, "Genealogy of the Aldrich Family," pp. 1, 2 and Aldrich File, Rose Hill Museum, Bay Village, OH.

Aaron and ***Elizabeth ALDRICH,*** after being married only two years, left Rhode Island with their one year old son ***Aaron IV*** and came to Dover, Ohio, arriving there in 1816. The journey to Ohio took six weeks of toilsome travel. Passing through Cleveland, only three dwellings were seen by them. They crossed the Cuyahoga River on a log ferry. At Rocky River, the Indians helped them float the wagon across. They continued their journey west following an old Indian trail. When they came to "Kelly's Hill," where the Bay View Hospital *(presently Cashelmara Condominiums)* of Bay Village now stands, one of the oxen slipped and fell while climbing the hill, breaking its leg. It had to be shot. It was skinned, using the hide to make shoes after it had been tanned and the meat was used as they continued their journey. With the help of a cow and the other ox, they went over the rough trail.

Their first home was a log cabin built in 1817 on the west side of Bradley Road, one half mile south of Bradley and Lake Roads in Bay Village. The house was on the north side of the creek where it crosses the road. There was no lumber or nails used in the building; hewed logs for the floor, split shakes for the roof, and a blanket for the door and window. Poles were used to keep the shakes in place. It had a stick chimney. The location is confirmed by a deed dated June 8, 1821 for 21 A and 60 rods of land on Lot 41, purchased from *Moses HALL*. Rose, pp. 9, 10.

Aaron ALDRICH III and his wife ***Elizabeth WINSOR ALDRICH (Betsy)***, arrived in 1816 from Rhode Island. The journey consumed six weeks of toilsome travel. Passing through Cleveland, Cuyahoga County, Ohio, only three dwellings greeted the eyes of Mr. A. and his companion, in the place of the so many fine mansions that make it now so beautiful. In the history of Mr. A. Aldrich, occurs one of the rare and single interpositions of divine providence, which it is pleasurable to record. Soon after his arrival amongst the woods of Dover, he became disabled from excessive labor. Having been reared in factory life, the labor of felling the forest was too much for him. What should he do? Disqualified as a woodsman; a growing family upon his hands, and in a country uncultivated, unexpected as the "manna" descended for the relief of the children of Israel, came a letter from a stranger, authorized by a company of strangers. This proposed a removal to Hartwick, Otsego county, N.Y., where he might take charge of a cotton factory, with a salary of eight hundred dollars per year, with house rent and firewood free. [In an agreement dated Aug 22, 1822, he was to manage all the manufacturing operations, except the weaving and go through the factory between nine and ten in the evening to see that everything was safe. For this he was paid the sum of one dollar and fifty cents per day or $469.50/year.] This proposal was accepted as a godsend. For several years he remained in this employ, each year increasing his compensation, until *Mr. Levi BEEBE*, of Watertown, N.Y. proposed higher wages, wishing Mr. Aldrich to put a cotton factory in operation at that place. Consenting, Mr. Aldrich remained at Watertown for nearly two years. [The family moved to Watertown, and on 4 May 1828, he began to work for Mr. Beebe, receiving $800 per year with house rent, firewood and garden free.] Finding himself provided with necessary means to found a home for himself and family, he again removed to Ohio. He re-settled in Dover in [October] 1829, [very close to where he had been the first time]. Habits of industry and economy secured for him a comfortable and beautiful home on the shore of Lake Erie, a few miles west of the romantic residence of *Ex-Governor WOOD*.

[He bought a farm of one hundred forty acres in Dover Twp., part of lots 92 and 98, which extend from the shore of Lake Erie south to what is now Wolf Road, west to Bradley Road, and east to land deeded to *Philo TAYLOR*, today the back lot lines of Saddler Road. The deed from *Nehemiah HUBBARD* and *Joshua STOW*, members of the Connecticut Land Co. says that Aaron and Betsy Aldrich paid $500 for 140 A. to *Eber LOOMIS*. The taxes on the farm in 1830 were $5.06.

[They built a log cabin on the north side of Lake Road where they lived until their frame house built across the road on the south side was completed. This home, 30663 Lake Road in Bay Village, is still standing, well preserved, and changed very little from its original design. It is a "Heritage House" in the National Register, very near to the southeastern part of the intersection of Bradley and Lake Roads. It is occupied at the present time by the wife of a great-grandson of Aaron and Betsy. *1980s.*

[He was very clever with tools. He made furniture and had a tannery across the road from the old house. Many of his tools are now in Rose Hill Museum, Bay Village. His sons helped with the farm work.]

Mr. A. Aldrich affords an example of industry, frugality, integrity, benevolence, piety and good will toward all men. Of a sound and discriminating mind, he was for many years selected as a magistrate in the township. In the discharge of his duties he was ever more anxious to adjust matters of difference by compromise than litigation, never an instigator of quarrels, but a peace maker. [He took an active part in offices in the township and was a member of the Whig Party.]

Mr. Aldrich and his wife were baptized and united with the First Baptist Church in Avon, Ohio, in 1832, elder Hans officiating. In 1836 Mr. Aldrich was one of the original five who met and formed the First Baptist Church of Dover, Ohio. For many years he maintained his Christian profession with uniform consistency, and the jeer of the infidel was put to silence by his godly life. [Meetings for the Dover Church were first held in the Lake Shore schoolhouse and in the town house. In 1845, a house of worship was built on *Justus STOCKING'S* land near North Dover and there the congregation continued until 1856, at which time, the church having by removals and death lost nearly all of its members, discontinued its services. Aaron was often referred to as Deacon Aaron Aldrich.]

Died, in Dover, on May 27, 1856, Deacon Aaron A. Aldrich, aged sixty-three years and one month. In his decease the Baptist church sustained an irreparable loss in member and office bearer; community mourned the loss of one who all joined in saying, 'He was truly a good man." To his family he was ever dear, and his memory is ever hallowed at the family altar which he so constantly visited, no matter what the pressure might be of worldly business. Six children are now grown to maturity and mostly settled in life. Two of these are companions of Baptist ministers in this State. History of Lorain County, OH, pp. 141-142 and [Rose, pp. 10, 11].

Letter from Mr. Beebe accepting Aaron Aldrich's decision to come to work for him: Addressed to Mr. Aaron Aldrich, Union Factory, near Cooperstown, N.Y.

Watertown 31, Jany. 1828

Mr. Aaron Aldrich
Cooperstown

Dear Sir,

We read yours of the 25th Inst. last evening and had begun to wonder at your silence where it would have been detained so long we cannot image! But, in perusing your letter, we are happy to find you so frank, - and hear you say, that you are at perfect liberty, to engage with us, and commence by the first of May next, that would answer our purpose - and we will depend upon you not making any engagement elsewhere - for we will give you fair, & full compensation for Yr. Services -

We have a first rate Master Weaver engaged and the offer, of a good, steady man, (of some experience, near by) to take charge of the Spinning, and over sight of the Carding, & C.- and if mutually satisfied we expect you to make a long pull with us - and, when we have an interview with you, will present some further inducements perhaps:- an opportunity for this chat, will be offered, when our L. Beebe comes to Otsego, say, in about two weeks - will then give you notice, where to meet him as it would not be advisable to have the interview at the Factory-

Our machines will be good, & the establishment pleasant and we entertain no fear of your capability- We repeat that you must not make any engagements that will disappoint us - as we have today, decided against one or two applications, which have been before us for sometime.-

You will therefore, make at your calculations to come here yourself, the first of May, even if the travelling should be such as to prevent the removal of your family at the time - mean time, if you choose to "talk of Ohio" it will not affect us-

Respectfully, Yours
Levi Beebe

Aldrich Family Boxes of Letters and Documents, 2-18, Rose Hill Museum, Bay Village, OH.

Ancestors of Aaron Aldrich:

I. ***William ALDRICH*** m. ***Mary***? (tabulated in Cheam Church: "daughter of Isabella of France and Edward II of England," Isabella was the daughter of Phillip IV of France and sister of Charles IV). Gertrude Aldrich Barker Rose, "Genealogy of the Aldrich Family," p. 1.

II. ***George ALDRICH*** of London, England, m.?. Rose, pp. 1, 2.

III. ***George ALDRICH***, b. 1605, Derbyshire, England; d. 1 Mar 1683, Mendon, Mass.; m. 9 Nov 1629, ***(C)Katherine SEALD*** (b. 1610, England, d. 11 Jan 1691, Mendon, Mass.).

First ancestors of Aaron's in America were George and Katherine Aldrich who arrived 6 November 1631, possibly on the Winthrop Fleet. He may have come over in the service of some wealthy man. George first settled in Dorchester, Mass. where he worked as a tailor, and their first three children were born. On Dec 7, 1636, he was made a freeman of the Massachusetts Bay Colony in Dorchester. Ten more children were born after they moved to Braintree, Mass. They then moved to Mendon, and he and six other men were the first pioneers of the town, and he was one of the first proprietors. Rose, pp. 1-3.

IV. ***Joseph ALDRICH***, b. 4 June 1635, Dorchester, Norfolk Co., Mass.; d. 27 Apr 1701, Smithfield, Providence Co., RI; m. 26 Feb 1662, Providence, Providence Co., RI, to ***Patience OSBORNE*** (b. Weymouth, Norfolk, Mass, d. 1705, Providence or Scituate, Providence Co, RI).

Joseph settled in Mendon in 1664, shortly after his father had founded the town. He was a member of the Society of Friends and tradition says that on this account at the time of King Philip's War, when the town was burned by the Indians, his house was left untouched. He left Mendon about the time that his father died and went to Providence, R. I., near Smithfield. He was a farmer as well as the first person in Providence to be chosen as "Scaler of Weights and Measures." Rose, p. 3.

V. ***John ALDRICH***, b. 21 Oct 1668, Braintree, Norfolk Co., Mass; d. 17 Mar 1735, Scituate; m. 20 Mar 1699, Providence, ***Martha EVANS*** (b. 19 Jan 1679, Rehoboth, RI.; d. 1735+, Scituate).

John was a miller by occupation who had considerable land holdings. He lived with his grandmother, Katherine Seald Aldrich, until her death, then moved to Rhode Island. He and his wife, Martha, lived in Scituate all their married life. Rose, pp.1, 3.

VI. ***Aaron ALDRICH I***, b. 1705, Scituate; d. 7 Nov 1769, Scituate; m. Scituate to ***Abiah BURGESS*** (b. Providence).

Aaron was a farmer, inheriting land from his father. He lived his entire life in Scituate. Rose, pp. 1, 3, 4.

VII. ***Aaron ALDRICH II***, b. 29 Sept 1743(5), Scituate; d. 1838 Edmeston, NY; m. ***Mary (Marcy) WATERMAN*** (b. 9 Oct 1769; d. Fall of 1832, Edmeston, NY).

Aaron was a private in the Rhode Island State Militia in the Revolutionary War, serving in *CRARY'S* Regiment in 1776. He was an "off and on" soldier. When the British threatened along the coast of Rhode Island, he dropped his farming and fought them. By 1849, Aaron and his wife had moved to Edmeston, Otsego Co., near Cooperstown. She died in 1832. He deeded his property to *Benjamin HOPKINS* and lived with Mr. Hopkins until his death in Edmeston in 1838. His son ***Olny*** went to see him two or three years before his death and he was blind. His children scattered from Smithfield, RI to Ohio and Wisconsin. Rose, pp.1, 4.

Children of Aaron Aldrich and Elizabeth Winsor:

Aaron Winsor ALDRICH IV, b. 15 [18] Oct 1815, Smithfield, RI *(this lot, date of birth disagrees with marker)*; d. 7 Apr 1890, Dover, Cuyahoga Co., O.; m. 4 Sept 1859 to *Ann O'BRIEN*, no children. ***William Waterman ALDRICH***, b. 17 Oct 1817, Dover; d. 19 Nov 1903, Lorain, Lorain Co., OH; m.1 5 Feb 1840, Dover to *Martha BASSETT*; m.2 Jan 22, 1878 to *Mrs. Lorinda (GRISWOLD) HILLIARD (OP 3:5)*. ***Julia Ann ALDRICH***, b. 10 Apr 1820, Dover; d. 22 Nov 1907; m. 11 June 1846, *James GOODRICH (see son's data, bur OP 5:2)* {res. White Pigeon, Mich.}. ***Henry Winsor ALDRICH***, b. 12 Sept 1822, [Hartwick, Otsego Co., NY]; d. 9 May 1892, *(tombstone says 10 Aug)* Dover; m. 4 May 1848, Avon, Lorain Co., Ohio to *Mary Ann STEVENS (this lot)*. ***Amy ALDRICH***, b. 4 Dec 1826, [Hartwick, NY]; d. 30 Dec 1896, Grafton, O.; bur. Nesbett Cem., Grafton; m. June 1846, *Rev. William. NESBETT* (b. 7 June 1799, d. 4 Dec 1865, Grafton, bur. Nesbett Cemetery). ***Elizabeth Winsor ALDRICH***, b. 12 Sept 1832, Dover; d. [4 Oct 1909]; m. 10 Sept 1860, *David BRAMAN* [d. 4 Oct 1909] {res. Kansas} *(son of Otis and Betsey Braman OP 1:8)*. George H. Drake, "Aldrich Family - Thirteen Generation Chart," pp. 1, 9, 10, 12; [Rose, pp. 1, 8, 9] {Women of the Western Reserve Prior to 1840} and Ima Aldrich Slaby.

The fifth child of ***Aaron*** and ***Betsy ALDRICH*** was ***Amy***, born in Hartwick, N.Y. on Dec 4, 1826. As a small child she moved with her family to Watertown, N.Y. and then back to Dover. She married ***Rev. William NESBETT***. They lived in Dover at first and they were among the original members of the First Baptist church of Dover. He was the man who built the windmill for his father-in-law, Aaron. They moved to Grafton, and both are buried in the Nesbett Cemetery of that town. Their oldest son, ***Robert***, lived in Grafton and he and his wife, ***Mary THORP***, had four children. One of their sons, ***Bert NESBETT***, was a well known dairy farmer in that town. Other children of Amy and William Nesbett were, ***John***, who lived in Cleveland; ***Daniel***, a well known Grafton farmer, who was killed by a railroad train; ***Jerome***, who lived in Grafton; ***Henry***, who lived in Cleveland; ***Amy***, who with her husband lived in Elyria, moving to California with her third husband; and ***William***, who was always an invalid. Rose, p. 17.

Letter from Amy Aldrich Nesbett around 1855 to "Aaron Aldrich, North Dover, Cuyahoga County, Ohio." Copied exactly from the original.

Dear Father Mother Brothers & Sisters

I am almost homesick to come down ther but the wether is so bad know I canont I looking for some of you to come every team I see the roads are HORIBLE muddy you must come to the conclusion to write directly there is as much travel here now as there used to be between Rocky River & Cleveland there is a great deal of fresh pork brought to the Station it is $6.50 since I was there I have spun enough for 20 yards of flannel and 7 yards of Satinett & dried apples enough for thirteen bushels. have got my of cloth made up my work well done up except for myself I have got two calico dresses I alpacca dress 1 flannel dress & have colored over my old yellow dress and have got to make it over I have colored that hard twisted yarn ame going to knit some socks to sell Mr Alden Thomsons Wife's daughter maried a Mr Sheldon who lives a few miles from here Mrs Sheldon went to help Mrs Lines killing hog day and took her boy 4 years old with her when they had done the hog work as mrs Sheldon told mrs lines she would mop her floor if she would heat the water when hot mrs Sheldon turned it in a pail and steped to get the mop when her own boy fell into the pail this occurred about sunset the boy lived until eleven the next day one man in this town became insane by Spirit Ruffings last winter was sent to the insane Hospital in

Columbus they pronounced him sane last summer and sent him home his idea was that all spirits were happy and he wanted to be a Su_ Spirit he hung himself two weeks ago ***Mr. Nesbett*** *preaches in Columbia every Sunday Mrs Watkins dried apples on shares so that I $5 to trade on and have got a due bill $13 50 Now to my dear Nepheyo* ***Wiliam Aldrich*** (II) *you seam very dear to me I hope you get a good education and make good use of it you can make yourself a likely man but no one else can make you so begin now to train you mind if you can write I shall go to the Post Office third Saturday in January for aletter little William don't you disappoint me write if not but three word Robert is sick with a cold and diareah I would fill this sheet full but must stop take care of Robert John is a great stout fellow he talks is as fat as his grandma this letter is to all my Frends Amy Nesbett*

Aldrich Family Boxes of Letters and Documents, 2-18, Rose Hill Museum, Bay Village, OH.

Some of Amy's children are living with her sister, Elizabeth BRAMAN, in the 1870 census after Amy's husband died in 1865. See David Braman with his parent's OP 1:8.

NESBETT, Jerome W., 21, farmer, b. Ohio, fr. b. Mass, mo. b. Ohio; *Amy A.*, 56, mother, Keeping House, b. Ohio, fr. b. Mass.; ***Elisabeth A.***, 17, sister, At Home, b. Ohio. 1880 FC OH Lorain Co., Grafton Twp., p. 493D, lines 11-13.

NESBET (NESBIT) Wm. I., Rev., d. Dec 4, 1865, 65y.; ***Amy A.***, wife, d. Dec 30, 1890 *(probably 1896, see above)*, 72y.; with ***Robert***, d. Sept 6, 1820, 66 y.; ***Mary***, wife, d. Aug 15, 1833, 77 y.; ***Catherine***, d. Oct 24, 1872, 84 y.; ***Elizabeth***, d. Jan 3, 1875, 81 y.; ***Nancy A.***, d. June 19, 1833, 43 y.; ***Sarah***, d. May 28, 1874, 78 y.; ***Mary***, d. Dec 11, 1872, 81 y. Nesbett Cemetery, Grafton Twp., Lorain County, OH. Genealogical Workshops of the Lorain County Historical Society, Cemetery Inscriptions of Lorain County, Ohio 1980, Nesbett Cemetery, p. 285.

The sixth and last child of ***Aaron*** and ***Betsy ALDRICH***, was ***Elizabeth*** born in Dover on Sept 12, 1832, probably the first child born in the old Aldrich homestead, since it was erected in 1829-30. She married ***David BRAMAN***. He was Capt. Braman and operated his brother-in-law, ***Henry ALDRICH'S***, scow, American Eagle, between Niagara Falls and Toledo as early as 1864. They had no children. Gertrude Aldrich Barker Rose, "Genealogy of the Aldrich Family," p. 18.

Statement Concerning the Personal Possessions of Mrs. E.W. Braman

Elizabeth W. ALDRICH married ***David R. BRAMAN*** and went to live in Kansas. She took with her a few books and keepsakes that were her father's and mother's and left a few articles of furniture at her old home, at this time belonging to her brother, ***H.W. ALDRICH***.

These were:
- 1 Old-fashioned high bookcase
- 1 Picture of Lincoln and his cabinet.
- 1 Chest of drawers.
- 1 Curly maple stand.
- 1 Rocking chair.

In 1905, a few years after her husband's death, at the age of 73 years, she returned to Ohio to make her home with ***Mary A. EVERARD***, one of her nieces At that time she wished to have the last three articles mentioned for her use. These, with an old-fashioned four poster bed, were placed in her room.

During her stay in Ohio, Aunt Elizabeth made several visits to other relatives, namely: The summer of 1908 she spent with her older sister, ***Julia Ann GOODRICH***, and niece, ***Julia GOODRICH GILLETTE***, in Somerville, a suburb of Boston, Mass. In the winter of 1908-09 she visited her cousin, ***Mrs. CLEMENS***, of Dover Center, Ohio, also a niece, ***Elizabeth NESBITT JEROME***, near Elyria.

In the summer of 1909 she returned, and was taken ill while at the old home with ***Mrs. H.W. ALDRICH***, and ***Mrs. Lucy PEEL***. *Dr. Celia O. CLEMENS* attended her. She died very suddenly after a short illness. ***Wm. W. ALDRICH***, a nephew, of Bay Village, assisted with the funeral arrangements. She left enough money to pay her funeral expenses, including railroad fare for her nephew, ***Daniel NESBITT***, and niece, ***Elizabeth NESBITT JEROME***, to accompany her body back to Alma, Kansas.

At the time of her death, her trunk containing clothing and a few keepsakes, including 2 brass candlesticks that were mother's, was at the old house. Aldrich file, Box 2, 18, Rose Hill Museum, Bay Village, OH.

OP 4:1 Elizabeth Winsor Aldrich

Elizabeth Winsor Aldrich was the wife of Aaron ALDRICH III, and aunt of Henry Winsor (OP 4:4).

Elizabeth WINSOR, b. 22 Dec 1794, Smithfield, Providence, RI, d. 28 Dec 1869, Dover Center, O.; dau. of ***Augustus WINSOR*** (b. 12 June 1764, Smithfield, m. 24 Aug 1783, d. 14 Nov 1837, Johnston, Providence, RI) and ***Nancy WATERMAN*** (b. 25 Sept 1765, Smithfield; d. 18 Nov 1804, Smithfield; dau. of *Andrew WATERMAN* (b. 1724, Smithfield; d. 6 Mar 1812, Smithfield; m. 1762) and *Margaret FOSTER* (b. 21 Mar 1737, N. Providence, Providence, RI, d. 28 Sept 1815, Providence)). Ima Aldrich Slaby

Mrs. Elizabeth ALDRICH died December 21, 1869. She was a faithful christian worker, was always kind to the poor and needy, and ever ready and willing to supply their needs. History of Lorain County, OH, p. 142.

Ancestors of Elizabeth WINSOR ALDRICH (and her sister, Lydia WINSOR WINSOR, mother of Henry WINSOR, OP 4:4).

I. ***Joshua WINSOR***, according to family tradition was the son of ***Samuel WINSOR*** of (Salisbury) England. He was born about 1617, possibly at Salisbury, Wiltshire Co., England. He died 1679, Providence and may have been buried on his home lot and later moved to North Burial Ground. He married ***Mary*** ___ (d. Feb 1654, Providence). James Windsor

In common with many other emigrants from England in those days, ***Joshua's (WINSOR)*** passage many had been advanced to him, and upon his arrival he became an indentured servant to *Governor John WINTHORP* in Boston. Apparently he was somewhat of a free thinker and ran into difficulties with the theocratic and fundamental views of the Boston colonist. *Roger WILLIAMS*, who had similar difficulties with the authorities in both Boston and Salem, somehow learned about Joshua Winsor, and being in the need of help in handling his property, wrote a letter to John Winthrop in the fall of 1638, from which I quote in part:

Sir, this is the occasion of this enclosed, I understand a servant of yours, Joshua - is some trouble to your selfe, as allso to others, & consequently can not (if he desire to feare the Lord) but himselfe be troubled & grieved in his condition, though otherwise I know not where under Heaven he could be better.

If it seem good in your eyes (wanting a servant) I shall desire him (not simply from you) but for your peace & his. I shall desire your best & full satisfaction in payment, & what summe you pitch on, to accept it wither from this bill, or if you better life from that debt of *Mr. LUDLOW*, for which he promised your worship to pay me 800 weight of tobacco but did not, & I presume your worship may with ease procure it; but I subscribe ex animo to your choice, & with respective salutacions & continued sighes to heaven for you & yours, rest desirous to (be)Your worships unfained though unworthy, Roger Williams

We know that Roger Williams succeeded in his plan, and Joshua Winsor came to Providence as the indentured servant of Roger Williams. Within two years he worked out his period of indenture, for in May 1640, he was one of twenty who signed the "Combination" of agreement as freeman.

It is not known for sure whether Joshua was married before he came to Providence, but possibly in 1643. He had four children: ***Samuel, Sarah, Susanna*** and ***Mary***. It is known that Joshua's wife died in 1654, for Roger Williams again in a letter dated 15 Dec 1654, this time writing to John Winthrop, Jr., Governor of Connecticut, said:

It had pleased God, sir, to take away (some few days since) the wife of our Joshua Winsor (once a servant to your deare father). She had a passionate wish that God should part them, & take away him or her. It pleased his Jealousie to heare her, & to take away a child in her wombe also, of which she could not be delivered.

From this comment, it would seem that Joshua and his wife had some difficulties, and from other records, it would seem that he was not an easy person to get along with, but according to *Olney Winsor*, "he appears to have been a person of some considerable talents and education, and of a serious and religious turn of mind; but no mention is made of his being a member of any particular church. John Osborne Austin, The Genealogical Dictionary of Rhode Island; Comprising Three Generations of Settlers Who Came Before 1690, p. 434; Dorothy Higson White and Mr. Kay Kirlin Moore, Descendents of Roger Williams, "Book 1, Waterman Line, Winsor Line," pp. 193-194; A Genealogical Dictionary of the Ancient Winsor Family in the United States, 1847 and James Windsor.

II. ***Samuel WINSOR***, b. 1644, at Providence, RI; d. 19 Sept 1705, Providence; m. 2 Jan 1677, Providence to ***Mrs. Mercy WILLIAMS WATERMAN*** (widow of *Resolved WATERMAN* and dau. of *Roger WILLIAMS* and *Mary BARNARD*, b. 15 July1640, Providence; d. after 1705, Providence).

28 Nov 1705, Administration of his estate to widow Mercy and eldest son, ***Samuel***. Inventory £250+. At his old dwelling house, 3 horses, 1/2 a mare and colt, 5 yearling cattle, 33 sheep and lambs, a swine, 18 loads of hay, apples, standing corn, and various tools in the shop, viz. vice, handsaw, joiner's tools, planes, saws, gouge, beetles, wedges, &c. Other articles at this old dwelling house were: tobacco, yarn, hops, books, spectacles, gun, 3 silver spoons, a silver dram cup, &c. At his farm in the woods were 3 pair of oxen, 8 cows, a bull, 4 heifers, a steer, a bible and other books, &c. Austin, p. 435 and Whte and Moore, p. 195.

Roger WILLIAMS, who settled in Narragansett Bay, called Providence by him, has been remembered on a 1936 stamp (Scott #777), commemorating the Rhode Island Tercentenary. The Winsor line is documented by the Roger Williams Family. Williams fourth child, ***Mercy WILLIAMS***, born at Providence, 15 July 1640, died circa 1705; married first in 1659 ***Resolved WATERMAN***, born July 1638, died August 1670; five children. Mercy married second ***Samuel WINSOR***, born 1644, died 19 September 1705; three children. Roger Williams Family Association website: www.rogerwilliams.org.

III. ***Joshua WINSOR***, b. 25 May 1682, Providence, RI; d. 10 Oct 1752, Providence, bur. ***Col. Abraham Winsor*** Lot Cemetery, Peach Blossom Lane, Smithfield; m.1 18 Oct 1706, Providence to ***Mary BARKER*** (dau. of *James BARKER* and *Sarah JEFFERAY*, b. 13 Mar 1678, Newport, RI; d. 30 Dec 1718, bur. same); m.2 3 Dec 1719, Providence to ***Deborah HARDING*** (dau. of *Abraham HARDING* and *Deborah GARDNER*; b. 6 Apr 1679, Providence; d. 24 July1756, Smithfield). Inventory of his moveable estate: "£3,559, 4 s, 10d, viz.: books new and old £18, 14 s 37 milled dollars £103, 12s, bonds, notes and book debts, pewter, 6 silver spoons £40, hour glass, 5 looms, double and twisted stocking yarn, linen, yarn, cooper's and carpenter's tools, old sword, fat cow, warming pan &c." Austin, p. 435, White and Moore, pp. 198-199.

IV. ***Abraham WINSOR***, b. 4 Oct 1720, Smithfield, RI; d. 20 Apr 1798, at Smithfield; m.1 2 Apr 1741 to ***Mary SMITH*** (dau. of *William SMITH* and *Mary SAYLES*, b. 1721, Smithfield; d. 4 Jan 1752, Smithfield in an epidemic, aged 30); m.2 24 Nov 1752 to *Sarah SMITH*, sister of Mary (b. 21 June 1725, Smithfield; d. 12 Nov 1802, Smithfield). Abraham and Mary had five children, he and Sarah had eight children the seventh being Augustus. White and Moore, pp. 216-217 and James Windsor.

V. ***Augustus WINSOR***, b. 12 June 1764, Smithfield, RI; d. 14 Nov 1837, Smithfield, age 74; m.1 ***Nancy WATERMAN***, (the dau. of *Captain Andrew WATERMAN (paternal ancestors of Andrew)* Resolved 4, 3, 2, Richard 1 and *Margaret FOSTER*. She was b. 25 Sept 1765 at Smithfield, RI; d. 18 Nov 1804 at Smithfield, age 40. She is bur. at Smithfield, her grave marked with a tombstone). m.2 ***Mrs. Martha STEERE EDDY*** (dau. of *Samuel STEERE* and *Martha COLWELL*, b. 25 Sept 1765, Smithfield; d. 18 Nov 1851, Smithfield).

Children of Augustus and Nancy WINSOR: ***Luciana WINSOR***, b. 1784; d. 12 Dec 1866 at Providence, RI, age 82; m. *Henry STONE*, 25 Apr 1813 at Smithfield, RI. ***Mary "Polly" WINSOR***, b. 1786; d. 1863; m. *Joseph BROWN*. ***Lydia WINSOR***, *(mother of Henry WINSOR OP 4: 4)* b. 1788; d. 1872; m. *Andrew WINSOR*. ***Abraham WINSOR***, b. 1790; d. 1883. ***Henry WINSOR***, b. 1793, d. 1828. ***Elizabeth "Betsy" WINSOR***, b. 1794; d. 1869; m. *Aaron ALDRICH*. ***Sarah Ann, "Sally Ann" WINSOR***, b. 1798; d. 1829; m. *Edward Scott RHODES*. ***Julia Ann WINSOR***, b. 1800; d. 1880; m. *John D. WELD* of Brimfield, Mass., on 31 Mar 1829, at Johnston, RI. ***Augustus WINSOR***, b. 19 June 1802; d. 11 June 1803. ***Nancy Waterman WINSOR***, twin; b. 6 Nov 1804, Springfield, Hampden, MA; d. 1864, Providence, Providence, RI, Rehoboth Cemetery; m. *Daniel J. [Ide] HUNT* (b. 24 June 1798, Rehoboth, Bristol, MA). ***Unnamed WINSOR***, twin, b. 6 Nov 1804, d. young. White and Moore, pp. 146-154, 286, 287 and James Windsor.

VII. ***Elizabeth WINSOR*** m. ***Aaron ALDRICH III*** *(see Aaron above).*

Sibling of Elizabeth Winsor Aldrich:

Mrs. Joseph BROWN (nee ***Mary WINSOR***), from Smithfield, R.I., was a descendant of *Lord Edward WINSOR*, also of *Roger WILLIAMS*. Her home was a charming location by the lake, where a long, useful life was passed. Her daughters who came with her were ***Lucina, Nancy, Mary, Rachel,*** and ***Elizabeth....Mrs. Aaron ALDRICH*** was a sister of Mrs. Brown, living where the beautiful Erie spread a fair scene before her. She was mother of a large family. ***Julia ALDRICH*** was a teacher in Dover, and married ***Rev. James GOODRICH***, of the Baptist Church. Memorial to the Pioneer Women of the Western Reserve, Part 1, p. 61.

Assumed letter from ***Julia Ann WINSOR WELD*** to her sister, ***Elizabeth ALDRICH*** in the early 1850's. Exact spelling and punctuation reproduced.

My Dear sister, I could not once have believed that so long a time could have elapsed without my seeing or writing to you, but seven years have quickly fled and with them many pleasures many pains and many hopes of dear delight, and knew ones have sprung up in their place. In addressing you my dear sister my thoughts unavoidably recur to by gone years. How short in retrospect appears the time back to my earliest recolection but short as it appears nearly half the time usualy allotted to man is past would that it were passed in a better manner. it is pleasing sometimes to retrace our steps to childhood's years when we were all sheltered beneath the paternal roof strangers to the cares and toils of tumultuous life when

The same fond Mother bent at night
Over each fair sleeping brow
She had each folded flower in sight
Where are those dreamers now

Scattered in different directions but though far distant we may still cherish those feelings of sisterly affection which is the life and delight of the family circle it is seldom that I see any of the family except ***Martha***. *I have lately made a visit to Seekonk found them all pretty smart.* ***Sister STONE*** *is not quite as well as she was in the winter but much better than I ever expected to see her she can use her hand a little about almost everything she and* ***Sarah*** *do the work a lone but they are both slender Sarah is an amiable girl.* ***Henry*** *is very much respected for his steady deportment and modesty of behaveiour* ***Semuel*** *begins to shave and feels considerable like a man and looks some like one* ***Waterman*** *is at work in the mill at present* ***Mr. STONE*** *is driving about as usual says he is going to Ohio in the fall.* ***Winsor*** *has got to be a stout looking boy I have now written about them all*

Henry of course can inform about his Fathers family better than I can sister. ***Lydia*** *mind is so engrossed with the great changes that are taking place that I seldom see or hear from her with out the most minute inquiry but it is not strange. Oh I was going to tell you about* ***Nancy*** *she was very well indeed when I was there a little more than a week ago and I have not heard from her since but am anxious to hear. there never was any body better suited to be sure and it is cause for thankfulness they have every thing comfortable convenient and as much style as is consistent with good judgment to say nothing of christianity. I need not say how much I want to see you and your family and your children are all so large that I suppose you and* ***Mr. Aldrich*** *enjoy your selves very much in going to meeting and visiting together have you a Preacher that suits you and is there much attention to religion generaly in* *that quarter and as it respects yourselves. I should be pleased to hear how you get along it is rather a low time. I believe in this neighbourhood.* ***Julia Ann's*** *health must be a great affliction to you as well as yourself (torn section missing) she is enabled to put her trust in God rmembering that he does not willingly afflict the children of men and in whatever he does he has gracious purposes to fulfill. I will send her* ***Mrs. ROWES*** *Devout exercises of heart and wish I had something more to send. give my love to all the family write about them all they must write tell* ***amey*** *uncle* ***Weld*** *talks some of coming their in the fall and she must try to get acquainted with him. I have no help but a little girl nine years old and don't expect any this summer it looks rather discourageing kiss little* ***Elizabeth*** *for me I have just been in to ask Father if he had any particular word to send he says no I don't as I have anything more than my love! our connexions generally are well I believe* ***James THUMBURS*** *wife died this winter cousin* ***hannah*** *you knew I suppose was moved to her uncle* ***Charles DYER*** *and is living in a very splendid maner Farther says tell* ***Betsey*** *I am in hopes to help her some before a great while. I must write to sister* ***Mary*** *and have so much to do that I cannot write more at present.*

Yours in love Farewell ***Julia A. Weld***

E. Aldrich

Note along the side of the paper: Our boys are very much unruly as you may see by the corner of this sheet. *Ink blotch near the corner.* Letter from Julia Winsor Weld to her sister Elizabeth Aldrich, c1850, Aldrich Papers, Rose Hill Museum.

OP 4:1 Henry Winsor Aldrich

Henry Winsor ALDRICH, fourth child of ***Aaron ALDRICH III*** and ***Elizabeth WINSOR***, b. 12 Sep 1822, [Hartwick, NY]; d. 9 May 1892, *(tombstone says 10 Aug)* Dover; m. 4 May 1848, Avon, Lorain Co., Ohio to ***Mary Ann STEVENS*** (b. 9 Apr 1822, d. 14 Feb 1916).

Issue: ***Lucy Stevens ALDRICH***, b. 1 April 1849; m. 23 Nov 1893 to *John PEEL*. ***Mary Ann ALDRICH***, *(Lot 16)* b. 27 May 1851, Dover; m. *Robert EVERHARD (Lot 16)*. ***Sarah Elizabeth ALDRICH***, b. 4 Dec 1853; d. 28 Aug 1858, Dover *(buried this lot)*. ***Metta Victoria ALDRICH***, b. 27 Aug 1856; m. 17 June 1885 to *Chas. George DRAKE* (b. 3 Dec 1863, d. 1923); d. 8 Feb 1944, Bay Village. ***Emma Irene ALDRICH***, b. 6 Oct 1859...; m... to *Frederick Lincoln DRAKE (Lot 61)*. ***Della Myrtilla ALDRICH***, b. 6 July1863,... m. *Frederick Lincoln DRAKE ...(Lot 61)*. ***Mabel. L. ALDRICH***, b. 1865, d. 1881, Dover *(buried this lot)*. Gertrude Aldrich Barker Rose, "Genealogy of the Aldrich Family," p. 17; George H. Drake, "Aldrich Family Generation Chart" pp. 10-11 and [Keith M. Sheldon, Descendents of Early Bay Families, p. 51].

After the death of his father, Aaron III, ***Henry ALDRICH*** bought out the heirs, on May 27, 1856, and had possession of the farm. Henry continued there as a farmer. He was drafted during the Civil War and hired *Duff BURRELL* for $250 on Oct. 9, 1862, to go in his place since he had five daughters and no sons to run his farm in his absence. He served in affairs of the community, being a trustee in Dover in 1864. He must have been in charge of road repairs for the township as he was to order out before July 1864, all persons in Road District, No. 1, to perform two days' labor on the highway improvement. Also, by 1864, he owned a scow, American Eagle, hauling raw material and merchandise between Niagara Falls and Toledo. His brother-in-law operated it. In 1869, a horse barn, 100 feet long was erected east of his house, and it was not torn down until 1979. In Nov. 1886, he had a windmill erected near the barn to pump water to the stock. It was built by his brother-in-law for ten dollars. Rose, p. 16.

ALDRICH, Henry, 48, Farmer, value of real estate $11,000, personal estate $1,650, b. NY; ***Mary***, 48, b. Mass.; ***Lucy***, 21, at home; ***Mary***, 19, at home; ***Mettie V.***, 12; ***Emma***, 10; ***Della***, 7; ***Mabell***, 5; all children b. Ohio; *JONES, Edward*, 21, Laborer, b. England. 1870 FC OH CYDO, p. 34, dwelling 285, lines 6-14.

ALDRICH, Henry W. Owned land; Acres: Improved - 63 tilled, including fallow and grass, 12 permanent meadow, Unimproved - 15 woodland. Farm Values: Land - $10,000, Machinery - $300, Live Stock - $225, Cost of building and repairing in 1879: $10. Estimated value of all farm production: $1,000. Grass lands: acreage: 15 mown, 20 not mown, 18 tons hay. 2 horses, 3 milch cows, 7 other, 3 calves dropped, 1 slaughtered. 300 pounds of butter made on the farm. 31 sheep on hand June 1, 1880, 9 lambs dropped, 3 sold living, 28 fleeces, 168 pounds. 7 swine. 40 barnyard poultry on farm, 200 dozen eggs produced in 1879. Indian corn: 15 acres, 620 bushels , Oats: 8 acres, 300 bushels; wheat: 4 acres, 40 bushels; potatoes: 1 acre, 80 bushels. Orchards - apple: 3 acres, 110 bearing trees, 300 bushels; peaches: 1 acre. Total value of orchard products: $150. Amount of wood cut: 30 cords, Value of forest products - $25. "Schedule 2. Production of Agriculture in Dover Township, Cuyahoga County, OH," enumerated June, 1880, p. 33.

ALDRICH, Henry W., Aug 10, 1892, Dover, married, 69 yrs. 10 m., male, farmer, b. New York, fr. ***Aaron ALDRICH***, mo. ***Elizabeth***, disease abscess, residence Cuy., O., physician, Dr. Lathrop, clergyman W.K. Dennis, Lake Side Cemetery, date of record June 24, 1893. PD 7:13482.

OP 4:1 Mary Ann Stevens Aldrich

Mary Ann Stevens Aldrich, was the daughter of Benjamin Stevens and Lovisa Foote(OP 2:1-2), wife of Henry Winsor Aldrich.

Mary Ann STEVENS ALDRICH was from an early Dover pioneer family, her grandfather ***David FOOTE*** coming here in 1815 a year before the Aldriches. She was born in Massachusetts in 1822 and came to Avon in 1832 with her parents at the age of ten. She lived in Avon thirteen years, when she married ***Henry***. Mary Ann died at the age of 94 years on Feb. 16, 1916, in their old home on Lake Road where she had lived for 65 years. At the time of her death she was the oldest living resident of Bay Village. She was looked after by her daughter, a widow, ***Mrs. Lucy PEEL***, and another daughter ***Mrs. Metta DRAKE,*** lived in the west half of the very large home. After her death, her grandson, ***George DRAKE***, as part heir, received lake front property on which he built a house in 1920, followed by four cottages along the lake. Gertrude Aldrich Barker Rose, "Genealogy of the Aldrich Family," p. 16.

George (DRAKE) and his five sisters followed a path through the woods behind their house to the old red brick schoolhouse on Lake Rd., but Mr. Drake preferred another route. "When I went to school," he confided, "I liked to stop at my grandmother's ***(Mary Ann ALDRICH)*** house, 'cause she would give me a piece of bread with butter and sometimes brown sugar on it!"

Henry DRAKE (should read ALDRICH), George's grandfather, owned approximately 145 acres of land extending from Lake Erie south to what is now Wolf Rd., east to today's Saddler Rd., and west to Bradley. Laura Mogyordy, "Oldest Bayite recalls Bay's early history," p. 3, undetermined newspaper article and Drake Family Papers, Rose Hill Museum.

Mary Ann STEVENS ALDRICH, daughter of ***Benjamin STEVENS*** and ***Lovica FOOTE(OP 2:1-2),*** b. Apr 9, 1822, at Lee, Berkshire, Mass.; m. Avon, Ohio, May 4, 1848 to ***Henry W. ALDRICH,*** of Dover, Cuyahoga County, Ohio…; d. Feb 16, 1916 at the Aldrich Homestead, Bay Village, which had been her home for sixty-five years; bur. at Lakeside Cemetery. She possessed the Christian virtues of thrift and conscientiousness, characteristic of the New England Puritans, "a meek and quiet spirit" and was distinguished for her patience. Her character is a beautiful and inspiring memory to her family. Abram W. Foote, Foote Family Comprising the Genealogy and History of Nathaniel Foote, vol. II, pp. 703-704.

Mrs. Mary Ann ALDRICH, d. February 16, 1916, 11:30 p.m., Bay Village, Cuy. Co., Ohio; b. April 9, 1822, Lee, Mass., 93 yrs. 10 mos. 7 days; Widowed, Housewife; fr. ***Benjamin STEVENS***, b. Mass., mo. ***FOOTE***, b. Mass.; Informant *Mary S. DRAKE*, Avon Lake, O. I hereby certify that I attended deceased from Oct 1st 1915 to February 1916, that I last saw her alive on February 16, 1916.; cause Old Age, contributory Indigestion and auto intoxication?, 4 ds.; Geo. Lathrop, M.D., Dover Center, O.; bur. Bay Village, Feb 19, 1916; Undertaker J.A. Pease and Son, Dover, O. Ohio Certificate of Death, Division of Vital Statistics, 1916, certif. 9404.

Mrs. Mary Ann ALDRICH, 94; res. Bay Village; interred Feb 19, 1916; Original Part. "List of Interments," Lakeside Cemetery, Bay Village, OH.

Children of Henry Winsor Aldrich and Mary Ann Stevens:

Lucy Stevens ALDRICH, b. 1 April 1849 at Dover; m. 23 Nov 1893 to ***John PEEL*** (farmer, of Pittsfield, O, b. 20 Dec 1829, in Leicestershire, England); she d. Bay Village, 27 Mar 1909 *(incorrect)*; res. Aldrich Homestead, Bay Village. Abram W. Foote, Foote Family Comprising the Genealogy and History of Nathaniel Foote, vol. II, p. 706.

Henry and ***Mary Ann ALDRICH*** had seven children. The eldest, ***Lucy***, married ***John PEEL***, and lived in Avon Lake. Mrs. Peel and another daughter, ***Mrs. Metta DRAKE***, cared for their mother in her later years, living in the west half of the very large family home. Gertrude Aldrich Barker Rose, "Genealogy of the Aldrich Family," p. 16.

PEEL-Lucy S. ALDRICH, widow of the late ***John PEEL***, sister of ***Mrs. Letta V. DRAKE*** and ***Mrs. Fred L. DRAKE***, April 21st, age 79, at residence, 30663 Lake Rd., Bay Village. Funeral from M. E. Church, Stop 32. Tuesday April 21, at 2 p. m. Cleveland Necrology File, Apr 22 1928, reel 063.

Lucy Stevens ALDRICH PEEL, d. April 21, 1928, at 1 p.m. at her res. 30663 Lake Rd., Bay Village, Cuy Co., OH of Apoplexy, 17 days.; widowed, 79 yrs. 20 days; housewife; b. Bay Village, April 1, 1849; fr. ***Henry W. ALDRICH***, b. Watertown, New York, mo. ***Mary Ann STEVENS***, b. Lee, Mass. Informant *Mary EVERARD*, Bay Village. Burial Avon Center, Ohio, April 24, 1928; undertaker C. Pease, Dover Center, O. Ohio Certificate of Death, Division of Vital Statistics, 1928, certif. 21294.

Possible family, Lucy not listed. ***PEEL John***, Dec 19, 1829-Mar 27, 1909; *Jane*, wife, Sept 12, 1836-June 10, 1891; *Joseph*, Dec 13, 1847-June 18, 1881, GAR; *William*, Dec 27, 1808-Sept 28, 1879; *Elizabeth*, Oct 10, 1808-Apr 23, 1892. Avon Center (Mounds) Cemetery, Avon, OH.

Metta Victoria ALDRICH, b. at Bay Village, Aug 27, 1856; graduate Oberlin College; m. 17 June 1885 to ***Chas. George DRAKE*** (son of *Rev. Andrew Jones* and *Sophia Butler COY DRAKE* of DeSmet, S.D.; b. 3 Dec 1856 at Peoria, Ill.; d. 1923 at Lakeside Hospital, Cleveland, O., bur. Evergreen Cem., Dover; he was a farmer at DeSmet and Bay Village). Abram W. Foote, Foote Family Comprising the Genealogy and History of Nathaniel Foote, vol. II, p. 705.

The fourth daughter of ***Henry*** and ***Mary Ann ALDRICH***, ***Metta Victoria***, married ***Charles DRAKE*** *(cousin of Frederick DRAKE who was married to her sisters, Della and Emma, Lot 61)*. They lived in the Avon Lake area and he was a farmer. They had two children, ***Charles*** and ***Mary Sophia, "Mamie".*** She never married and cared for her mother in the old Aldrich home. Metta died Feb. 8, 1944 at the age of 93, the last member of the Henry Aldrich family and oldest resident of Bay Village at the time of her death. Her daughter, Mamie, followed her in death a few months later. On April 25, 1945, ***George DRAKE***, son of her sister ***Della***, and grandson of Mary Ann, bought the homestead for $5400. As of 1981, this house had been occupied by some member of the Aldrich family since it was built in 1830. Rose, p. 17.

Metta Victoria ALDRICH DRAKE, d. February 8, 1944, 1 a.m., Bay Village, Cuyahoga Co. of Gradual exhaustion following cerebral hemorrhage …recent cerebral hemorrhage with paralysis of throat; res. 281 Bradley Rd., Bay Village, lived in the community 87 yrs.; widow of ***Charles G.***; 87 yrs. 5 mos. 11 dys., b. Aug 27, 1856 in Dover Twp. to ***Henry W. ALDRICH***, b. Rhode Island and ***Mary Ann STEVENS***, b. Lynn, Mass.; informant *C. H. DRAKE*, Bay Village; Clifford Pease Funeral Home, Westlake; bur. Evergreen Cemetery, Westlake. Ohio Certificate of Death, Division of Vital Statistics, 1944, certif. 10074.

Metta Victoria ALDRICH DRAKE, res. Bradley Rd, Bay Village; d. Feb 8, 1944 at res., cause Cerebral Hemorrhage, 87 yrs.; b. Aug 27, 1856, Dover Twp.; rel. Protestant; Evergreen Cemetery. Pease Funeral Home Records, Mss. 4809, Western Reserve Historical Society, Cleveland, OH, Record of Funeral, p. 198.

OP 4:1 Sarah Elizabeth Aldrich

Sarah Elizabeth ALDRICH, third child of ***Henry Winsor ALDRICH*** and ***Mary Ann STEVENS***, b. 4 Dec 1853, d. 28 Aug 1858. Gertrude Aldrich Barker Rose, "Genealogy of the Aldrich Family," p. 17 and George H. Drake, "Aldrich Family - Thirteen Generation Chart," pp. 10 -11.

OP 4:1 Mabel L. Aldrich

Mabel. L. ALDRICH was the youngest child of ***Henry Winsor ALDRICH*** and ***Mary Ann STEVENS***, b. 1865, d. 1881, Dover. Gertrude Aldrich Barker Rose, "Genealogy of the Aldrich Family," p. 17 and George H. Drake, "Aldrich Family - Thirteen Generation Chart," p. 11.

ALDRICH, Mabel L. - At her home in Dover, O., February 4, of bronchial pneumonia, Mabel L., youngest daughter of ***H.W.*** and ***M.A. ALDRICH***, aged 16 years and 2 days. Leader, Feb 22, 1881 and Cleveland Necrology File, reel 1.

ALDRICH, Mabel, d. Febry. 4, 1881, Dover, single; 16 yrs. 6 m. 2 d.; b. Dover, parents ***Henry ALDRICH*** and ***Mary A. ALDRICH***; disease measles. PD 2:82.

OP 4:1 Aaron Winsor Aldrich

Aaron W. ALDRICH, oldest child of ***Aaron ALDRICH III*** and ***Elizabeth WINSOR***, b. 15 Oct 1815, Smithville, RI; d. 7 Apr 1890, Dover, O.; m. 4 Sept 1859 to ***Ann O'BRIEN***, no children. George H. Drake, "Aldrich Family - Thirteen Generation Chart," p. 1.

Aaron Winsor ALDRICH married ***Ann O'BRIEN*** when he was almost 44 years old. They had no children. He spent most of his life working with his father on the old Aldrich homestead. Gertrude Aldrich Barker Rose, "Genealogy of the Aldrich Family," pp. 8, 11, 12.

Aaron is listed with ***Henry W. ALDRICH*** in the 1850 census as a farmer and in 1880 as a tanner who was widowed. 1850 FC OH CYDO, p. 217B, line 13 and 1880 FC OH CYDO, p. 99, line 45.

Ann (Mrs. Aaron W. ALDRICH), maiden name ***O'BRIEN; Mary (Mrs. Sylvanus CROCKER)*** (daughter was ***Mary Elizabeth CROCKER OSBORN*** *OP 5:5*), maiden name ***O'BRIEN*** and ***Mrs. Thomas O'BRIEN*** (maiden name ***Elizabeth HALL***) are all listed as arriving in Dover in 1835, coming from Clarkson, NY. Women in the Western Reserve Prior to 1840, p. 18. *There is a possibility that Elizabeth is the mother of Eliza Ann O'BRIEN COPPIN (OP 2:15) and Mary.*

It has not been determined when Ann O'Brien Aldrich died or where she is buried.

OP 4:2 Eugene C. Oviatt

EUGENE

EUGENE C. OVIATT
DIED
Nov 3, 1864
Aged
1 M. 10 DA.

Eugene, twin of Lillian Caroline, was the son of Dudley Luman Oviatt and Almira A. Phinney. There is a street named after the family in Bay Village but the Oviatt's moved to Rockport and later the Cleveland area.

Ancestors of Eugene Oviatt:

I. ***Thomas OVIATT***, d. 28 May 1691; m. ***Frances*** ___; appears in Milford about 1664/5 with his wife. He made frequent visits to England on business and mention is made of him carrying letters; town clerk in Milford 1689; business was that of Tallow Chandlery and soap maker. Of eight children the fifth was Samuel. Susan Woodruff Abbott, Families of Early Milford, Connecticut, p. 497.

II. ***Samuel OVIATT***, b. 24 Nov 1672; d. 1749/50; m. ***Mary*** (possibly *BALDWIN*); occup. soapboiler. Of six children the oldest was Samuel. Abbott, pp. 498-499.

III. ***Samuel OVIATT***, bap. 24 June 1711; d. c1767; m.1 16 Nov 1717 to ***Rebecca PRITCHARD*** (bap. 24 Oct 1697, dau. of *Benjamin PRITCHARD* and *Rebecca JONES*; probably d. bef. 11 Oct 1752); probably m.2 ***Rhoada*** ___. The second of nine children of Samuel was Samuel. Abbott, pp. 499-500.

IV. ***Samuel OVIATT***, b. 1 Apr 1722; d. 15 Jan 1805, Goshen, Conn.; m.1 ***Keziah PLUMB*** (b. 10 Mar 1724/5, dau. of *John PLUMB* and *Keziah ALLEN*; d. 23 Apr 1790, Goshen, Conn., ae. 66; bur. West Side Cemetery); m.2 ***Ruth SQUIRE***. In his will he leaves his wife the household furniture of hers she had when he married her. Samuel and Keziah had three children, the youngest being Benjamin. Abbott, pp. 500, 502-503.

V. ***Benjamin OVIATT***, b. 6 Sep 1755, Goshen, CT; d. 16 Sept 1832, Goshen, bur. Oviatt Cem., Goshen; m. 8 Dec 1774, Goshen to ***Elizabeth CARTER*** (b. 28 Aug 1754, Cornwall, Litchfield Co., CT; d. 1823, Goshen; her parents, *Nathaniel CARTER* (b. 27 Apr 1717, Killington, Middlesex, CT; d. Oct 1763 at Pau Pac, Pike, Penns.) and *Sarah BENNET* (b. 4 Mar 1709, Stonington, New London, CT; d. Oct 1763) were killed by Indians and she was held captive with her sister and brother through the winter. Their second child was Luman. Abbott, p. 508.

VI. ***Luman OVIATT***, b. 6 Sep [Oct]1777, Goshen, Litchfield Co., CT; d. 7 Dec 1838, Richfield, Summit Co., OH; m.1 10 May 1796, Goshen to ***Rhoda NORTON*** (dau. of *Miles NORTON* and *Ruth SQUIRE*, b. 29 (9) Aug 1777, [Litchfield]; d. 10 Jan 1821, Goshen in childbirth). *Issue:* 1. ***Birdsey (Birdseye) Norton OVIATT***, b. 1 Sept 1796, Goshen; d. 4 July 1825, New Orleans, LA of Yellow Fever; bur. Chapel Street Burying Ground; m. 28 May 1818, Portage, OH to *Abigail Laura HUDSON* (dau. of *David* and *Anna HUDSON*, founder of Hudson, OH; b. 30 June 1798; d. 24 Apr 1860); divorced; occup.: Clerk of Post Office in 1821 and stole $600, the scandal rocked the community. 2. ***Nelson G. OVIATT*** *(see below)*. 3. ***Keziah OVIATT***, b. 27 May 1800, Goshen; d. before 1871, Goshen; m. 14 Dec 1817-18 (27 Nov 1818, Frank C. Oviatt Collection, WRHS) to *Leonard B. CARR* (b. 1800, Goshen). 4. ***Rhoda OVIATT***, b. 21 Aug 1802, Goshen; d. 29 Mar 1880, Richfield, OH; m. 14 Dec 1820 to *Julius HUMPHREY* (b. 1800; d. January 1864, Louisville Hospital from disease contracted while there; he went South after *James SANBORN*, of the 64th O.V.I. who was sick in that hospital, but neither returned, James dying about two weeks after Mr. Humphrey.); removed to Richfield 1820. 5. ***Heman OVIATT***, b. 26 Aug 1804, Goshen; d. 31 Dec 1854, OH, bur. Copley Cemetery, Copley, Summit Co., OH, Western Section, Row 1; m. 10/25 February 1828 Goshen to *Eliza (Elizabeth) BALDWIN* (dau. of *Amos BALDWIN* and *Elizabeth BRYAN*, b. 10 Jan 1805 Norfolk, CT; d. 13 May 1883 at Pearl Street House, Copley; bur. Copley Cemetery); res. Copley. 6. ***Marcus OVIATT***, b. 15 Jan 1807, Goshen; d. 10 Oct 1854, CT; m. 12 Feb 1829, Goshen; two children b. Ohio in c1835 and c1838; 1850 census shows them in Watertown, CT (p. 395). 7. ***Infant OVIATT***, d. 1809. 8. ***Aaron OVIATT***, b. 4 (15) Aug 1810, Goshen where he was raised and educated; d. 1906 Copley; bur. Copley Cemetery, Western Section, Row 1; m.1 7 or 9 Jan 1833/35 to *Electa BROWN* (dau. of *Reuben BROWN* of Norfolk, CT; b. 30 Jan 1813, Norfolk, CT; d. 7 May 1846); Aaron removed to Akron, OH after Electa's death. m.2 11 Oct 1846 to *Marion B HOISINGTON* (dau. of *Salmon HOISINGTON* and *Mary B. HAWKINS*). Aaron then returned to Connecticut, resided there two years and removed to Copley, OH purchasing 123 acres which land he farmed about seven years, when he removed to Akron City. 9. ***Moses OVIATT***, b. 14 Mar 1813, Goshen; d. 11 Jan 1890, bur. Brookmere Cemetery, Cleveland, Cuy. Co., OH; m. 21 Aug 1840, Richfield to *Electa Almira SPAFFORD* (dau. of *Jacob SPAFFORD* and *Electa CHITTENDON*; b. 23 July 1818 Rutland, VT; d. 11 May 1878, Cleveland). Moses and Electa came to Parma Twp., OH by 1840. Moses owned over 150 acres (Lot 20 in the Blake Tract of Parma Twp.). 10. ***Harriett OVIATT***, b. 11 June 1815 Goshen; m. 21 Dec 1837 to *Washington B. BIGELOW* of Goshen (b. 1814 Broome, Schaharie Co., NY; d. 2 Apr 1853, Richfield. Washington later married 4 Oct 1842 to *Nancy HUNTLEY* (Richfield Historical Society Article). 11. ***Child OVIATT*** (daughter?), d. 27 Oct 1816, age 5 months. 12. ***Laura OVIATT***, b. 11 June 1818 Goshen; d. 2 June 1849; m. 6 Oct 1839, Goshen to *Jonathan SPAFFORD* (son of *Jacob SPAFFORD* and *Electa CHITTENDEN*, d. 2 June 1846). 13. ***Sarah Lucretia OVIATT***, b. 28 Nov 1822, Goshen; d. 9 Aug 1849, Goshen; m. 25 Sept 1839 to *James WADHAMS* (son of *Norman WADHAMS* and *Martha (Patty) NORTH*, b. 4 Feb 1815, Goshen; d. 17 Oct 1882 or Sept 1883). 14. *Lyman Benjamin* ***OVIATT***, b. 27 Sept 1826, Goshen; d. 12 Jan 1850, San Francisco, CA of typhoid fever; never married. 15. ***Samuel Platt OVIATT*** (Platt being Grandmother's maiden name), b. 14 July 1831 Goshen CT; d. 5 June 1895, bur. Goshen; m. 13 Oct 1858 to *Mary Jane CRANDALL.*

m.2 23 Dec 1821 to ***Alosia*** [***Aloria***] ***SANFORD*** (dau. of *Ephraim SANFORD* (b. 1779, CT; d. 1808; m. 1796) and *Sally PLATT* (b. 1779, Redding Co., CT); b. 1 July 1803, Johnstown, NY; d. 30 (19) Jan 1889, Goshen; m.2 19 Dec 1873 to *Hosea W. CRANDALL* (b. Goshen)). The second child of Luman and Rhoda was Nelson. Leah Krulik and [Abbott]

VII. ***Nelson G. OVIATT***, b. 9 Oct 1798, Goshen Twp., CT; d. 9 Jan 1870, Dover, Cuyahoga Co., OH; bur. Fairview Cemetery, Richfield, Summit Co., OH; m.1 8 Oct 1820, CT to ***Melinda HUMPHREY*** (possibly the dau. of *Dudley HUMPHREY* and *Polly M. SHERMAN*; b. 11 July 1798; d. 11 Aug 1851 (1854) of Erysipelas and internal fever, aged 56 yrs. 1 mo., newspaper notice: 25 Aug 1847). *Issue:* 1. ***Luther Melville OVIATT***, b. 14 July 1821, Goshen; d. 8 Aug 1889; bur. Woodland Cemetery, Cleveland; m. 17 July 1850, Cleveland to *Mary Elizabeth SMITH* MR 8 47 (b. 1831, Springfield, MA; d. 13 Aug 1889, bur. Woodland Cemetery; res. No. 3 Livingston St.). Luther came west with his family to Dover (Westlake), OH. He attended Western Reserve College at Hudson where he graduated in 1857 with honors and a knowledge of literature and classical languages of which he was always proud, and justifiably so. From college he went directly into the public school system of Cleveland, serving at various times as teacher, principal, and for two years as superintendent of instruction. Along the way two of his students were *John D. Rockefeller* and *Laura Spelman*, who in time would become *Mrs. Rockefeller*. Luther served as the First Librarian of Cleveland Public Library from 1869 to 1875. 2. ***Emily C. OVIATT***, b. 2 Aug 1822, Parma, OH; d. 5 Dec 1884, Richfield; m. 27 May 1841 to *Everett FARNHAM (FARNAM)* MR 4 101 (b. 18 Dec 1800, d. 15 Aug 1884). 3. ***Louisa Melinda OVIATT***, b. 10 Nov 1823, Parma, Cuyahoga Co., OH; d. 22 July 1880, Parma, bur. Lake View Cemetery, Cleveland, OH; m. 11 Sept 1853, Cuy. Co. MR 5 401 to *John H. BURRIDGE* (b. 1822; d. 17 Feb 1886, Cleveland of pneumonia). 4. ***Mary H. OVIATT***, b. 6 Apr 1825, Dover, Cuyahoga Co., OH; d. 23 May 1849, Richfield; m. 17 Apr 1841, Parma to *Stephen C. HODGMAN* MR 4 101. 5. ***Caroline Amelia OVIATT***, b. 6 Apr 1827, Dover, Cuyahoga Co.; d. 30 June 1848, Dover. 6. ***Dudley Luman OVIATT*** *(see below)*. 7. ***Laura M. OVIATT***, b. 25 Sept 1835, Dover, Cuyahoga Co., OH (1840 Parma: Women Who Came to the Western Reserve, p. 190); d. 19 July 1930, bur. Fairview Cem., Richfield; m. 28 Dec 1875, Summit Co. to *D. D. MORRELL*

m.2 of Nelson G., 2 Feb 1848, Cuyahoga Co., OH (MR 4 445) to ***Lucy M. WILCOX*** (b. 17 Oct 1800, Goshen; d. 5 May 1870, Richfield [bur. Fairview Cemetery]). The sixth child of Nelson and Melinda was Dudley Luman. Leah Krulik and [Keith M. Sheldon, Descendants of Early Bay Village, pp. 559-62].

VIII. ***Dudley Luman OVIATT***, b. 26 June 1832 Dover, Cuyahoga Co., OH; d. 9 Oct 1923 at his res. 13230 Detroit Rd., Lakewood, Cuyahoga Co., OH, bur. Riverside Cemetery, Cleveland, OH; m. ***Almira Abigail PHINNEY*** (b. 1834, Rockport, Cuyahoga Co., OH; d. 9 Nov 1917, services at late res. 13230 Detroit Ave., bur. Riverside Cemetery). *Issue:* ***Clarence Melville OVIATT***, b. 8 May 1857, Dover; d. 20 Dec 1938. [East Cleveland, Cuyahoga Co.]; bur. Riverside Cemetery; m.1 17 June 1885, Brooklyn, Cuyahoga Co., OH to *Georgia Electa GILBERT* (b. 11 Feb 1863, Cleveland; d. 11 Aug 1951, Cleveland, late residence 6801 Euclid Ave., Cleveland, OH; dau. of *George GILBERT* and *Martha A. OVIATT*); m.2 1924 *Johanna HINDEN* (b. 1874; d. 27 May 1925, Cleveland; bur. Riverside Cemetery). ***Lillian Caroline OVIATT***, twin of Eugene; b. 24 Sept 1864, Dover; d. 13 May 1922, at her residence La Verne, CA; bur. Riverside Cemetery; m. 16 June 1886, Lakewood to *Hoyt Verner BRIGHT* (b. 23 May 1863). ***Eugene OVIATT***, twin of Lillian; b. 24 Sept 1864, Dover; d. 3 Nov 1864, bur. Osborn Cemetery *(Lakeside Cemetery)*. ***Arthur Nelson OVIATT***, b. 22 Oct 1866; m. 14 May 1890, Cleveland to *Lydia Abbey GIBBS* (b. 20 June 1869, Cleveland; d. 22 July 1935, Bedford, Cuyahoga Co., OH CD 1935:41372). ***Rena Melinda OVIATT***, b. 29 Mar 1868, Dover; d. 1946, Pomona, CA; m. 1923 to *Hoyt Verner BRIGHT* (same husband as Lillian?). ***May Clara OVIATT***, b. 1875, Dover; d. Oct 1926, services at late residence 17825 Clifton Blvd., Lakewood; bur. Riverside Cemetery; m. 2 Jan 1913, Cleveland to *Thomas P. GRIMES* (b. 1879, Portsmouth, OH; d. 1953). Leah Krulik, Ohio Certificate of Death, Division of Vital Statistics, (CD year: certificate).

Each township in the Western Reserve had been divided into five square mile blocks. Hudson, Township 4, Range 10, comprised of 15,969 acres originally sold by lottery in January 1798. The Connecticut Land Company sold the township for $12,903.23 to fifteen individuals, one of whom was *David HUDSON*. ***Benjamin OVIATT***, *Stephen BALDWIN* and *Theodore PARMELE* jointly invested in one-eighth part of Hudson Township in 1800, one year after David Hudson had established the village.

Heman OVIATT, son of Benjamin settled in Hudson in 1801 on land a mile or so south of the village that was a gift from his father. The Oviatt land was near the old Indian trail referred to as the Stigmanish Trail. Indians frequently stopped at the Oviatt cabin and traded with them. Grace Goulder Izant, Hudson's Heritage, pp. 34-36, 60-61.

Grandparents of Eugene C. Oviatt:

The State of Ohio, Cuyahoga County, ss. I hereby certify, that on the 2nd day of February A. D. 1848, I duly solemnized the Marriage Contract between the said ***Nelson OVIATT*** and ***Lucy M. WILCOX***. Ohio City; Cyrus L. Burton, Minister Gospel. Marriage Record, Cuyahoga County, OH, vol. 4, p. 445.

Nelson OVIATT, 52, Farmer, b. Conn.; ***Lucy***, 50, b. Conn.; ***Dudley***, 18, Miller, b. Ohio; ***Laura***, 15, b. Ohio, attending school. 1850 FC OH CYDO, p. 215B, lines 28-31.

Parents of Eugene C. Oviatt:

The State of Ohio, Cuyahoga County, ss. I Certify, That on the 26th day of June 1856 ***Mr. Dudley L. OVIATT*** and ***Miss Almira A. PHINNEY*** were by me legally joined in Marriage. Veron D. Taylor Marriage Record, Cuyahoga County, OH, vol. 8, p. 44.

D.L. OVIATT, 28, Lumberman, b. Ohio; ***Almira***, 26, b. Ohio; ***Clarence***, 3, b. Ohio; *Fredrick STORK*, 24, Lumberman, b. Germany; *Sarah STORK*, 18, b. Ohio; *Elizabeth UPHINE*?, 18, Servant; b. Ohio. 1860 FC OH CYDO, p. 47, lines 13-18.

OVIATT, Dudly, 38, Lumber Man, Value of real estate $8,000, Personal: $2,500, b. Ohio; ***Almina***, 36, keeping house, b. Ohio; ***Clarence***, 13, b. Ohio; ***Arther***, 3, b. Ohio; A., 3/12 yr., b. March, b. Ohio; *CHADWICK, Martha*, 21, Domestic Servant, b. Indiana; *BROADY, Fred*, 23, Laborer, b. Ireland; *JOHNS, David*, 25, Laborer, b. England. The house next door of *Porter SMITH*, lists a child ***Lilian OVIATT***, 5, b. Ohio with no others with the same surname. 1870 FC OH CYDO, p. 37, lines 9-16.

OVIATT, Dudley. Owned land; Acres: Improved - 40 tilled, including fallow and grass, 5 permanent meadow, Unimproved - 35 woodland. Farm Values: Land and buildings - $6000, Machinery - $200, Live Stock - $500, Cost of building and repairing in 1879: $25, Cost of fertilizers purchased in 1879: $4. Labor: Paid for wages in 1879 - $300, Weeks hired labor in 1879: 80. Estimated value of all farm production: $300. Grass lands: acreage: 15 mown, 6 not mown, 15 tons hay. 5 horses, 6 working oxen, 2 milch cows, 2 calves dropped, 8 cattle purchased, 2 sold living, 1 died, strayed or stolen and not recovered.

100 pounds of butter made on the farm. 2 swine. 30 barnyard poultry on farm, 100 dozen eggs produced in 1879. Oats: 12 acres, 240 bushels; wheat: 6 acres, 25 bushels; potatoes: 1 acre, 40 bushels. Orchards - apple: 2 acres, 20 bearing trees, 10 bushels. Total value of orchard products: $5. "Schedule 2. Production of Agriculture in Dover Township, Cuyahoga County, OH," enumerated June, 1880, p. 31.

Dudley L. OVIATT, d. Oct 7, 1923, 9 p.m. at his residence, 13230 Detroit Ave., Lakewood, Cuyahoga Co., Ohio of Chronic Prostatitis for 15 years and Chronic cystitis; 91 yrs. 3 mos. 12 ds.; widower of **Elmira OVIATT**; retired; b. June 26, 1832, Richfield, Ohio to ***Nelson OVIATT***, b. Conn., mother unknown, b. Conn.; informant *Mrs. May OVIATT GRIMES*, 13230 Detroit Ave.; undertaker Wm. Daniels, 15800 Detroit Ave.; bur. Riverside Cemetery, Oct 12. Ohio Certificate of Death, Division of Vital Statistics, 1923, certif. :59308.

Almira Abigale OVIATT, d. Nov 9, 1917, 13230 Detroit, Lakewood, Cuyahoga Co., Ohio of Chronic Myocarditis for several years; Married; b. May 18th, 1834, fr. ***Benjamin PHINNEY***, b. unknown, mo. unknown; R.M. Oviatt, 13230 Detroit; undertaker W.R. Daniels, 15800 Detroit Ave.; Burial Riverside. Ohio Certificate of Death, Division of Vital Statistics, 1917, certif.: 70205.

Family of Almira Phinney Oviatt:

Benjamin PHINNY m. ***Lucretta THOMPSON*** (dau. of ***Pvt. Stephen THOMPSON*** (b. 6 May 1764, Goshen, Litchfield, Conn.) and ***Abigail HUTCHINSON*** (b. c1777, Bennington, Bennington Co., VT)); b. 6 Feb 1804, Hudson, Portage Co., Ohio; d. 11 July 1837, Avon, Ohio. Millard Thompson and B.M. Stercula, "The Thompson Family Magazine," undetermined issue.

Benjamin PHINNY, 45, occup. Merchant, b. Mass; ***Susan***, 84, b. Ohio; ***Almira***, 16, b. Ohio; ***Benjamin***, 6, b. Ohio. 1850 FC OH CYDO, p. 211B, lines: 10-13, dwelling: 3662.

Benjamin PHINNEY, 53, farmer, value of real estate: $20,000, personal property, $2,000, b. *(writing difficult to read)*; ***Eliza ?***, 43, female, b. Mass.; ***Benjamin***, 15, b. Ohio, attending school; ***Atta?***, 9, female, b. Ohio, attending school; *Elizabeth ROBINSON*, 18, b. Ohio, attending school. 1860 FC OH CY Rockport, p. 13, lines 22-26.

PHINNEY, Benj., d. Oct 27, 1865, 60yr. 2m.; ***Lucretia***, wife, d. July 1837, 32yr.; ***Catherine***, wife, d. Mar 8, 1842, 36 yr. Avon Center (Mounds) Cemetery, Avon, Lorain Co., OH.

Riverside Cemetery Lot 143, Section 10, owned by Dudley L. Oviatt. The monument states "OVIATT" on the front with the individual inscriptions on the back.

Dudley L. OVIATT, 91, widower; d. 9 Oct 1923, at his res. 13230 Detroit Ave., Cleveland of Chr. Prostatitis, bur. 12 Oct, Wm. Daniels Funeral Home, grave 3. Stone inscription: Dudley L., 1832-1923.

Almira A. OVIATT, 83, married; d. Nov 1917, at her residence - 13230 Detroit Ave., Cleveland, bur. 12 Nov 1917, grave 1. Stone inscription: Almira A., his wife, 1834-1917.

Lillian O. BRIGHT, 57, married; d. May 1922 of diabetes at her residence, bur. 26 May 1922, W.R. Daniels Funeral Director, grave 2. Stone inscription: Lillian C., wife of H. V. Bright, 1864-1922.

Johanna H. OVIATT, 50, married, b. Michigan; d. 27 May 1925, Cleveland of apoplexy, bur. 1 June 1925, Wm. R. Daniels Funeral Parlor; res. 5107 Clark Ave., Cleveland, grave 4. Stone inscription: Johanna Hinden, wife of Clarence M., 1874-1925.

Clarence M. OVIATT, 81, widower, b. Cleveland; d. 20 Dec 1938, E. Cleveland, OH of fracture at base of skull, J.H. Brown & Son Funeral Parlor, 8128 Carnegie Ave., grave 5. *No inscription on marker*. Riverside Cemetery Records, Cleveland, OH.

Siblings of Eugene C. Oviatt:

The State of Ohio, Cuyahoga County-ss. I Certify, That on the 17th day of June 1885 ***Mr. Clarence M. OVIATT*** and ***Miss Georgia E. GILBERT*** were by me legally joined in marriage. O.D. Patch Marriage Record, Cuyahoga County, OH, vol. 28, p. 372.

Clarence M. OVIATT, 67; res. 13230 Detroit Ave.; b. Dover; occup. Investments; fr. *Dudley L.*, mo. *Almira PHINNEY;* previously married once, Div. 1913 C.P.Ct. Married ***Johanna HINDEN***, 49; res. 4617 Clark Ave.; b. Detroit, Mich.; occup. Milliner; fr. *Joseph*, mo. *Barbara WAGNER*; never married. The State of Ohio, Cuyahoga County-ss. I Certify, That on the 25th day of August 1924 ... were by me legally joined in marriage. A.B. Meldrum Marriage Record, Cuyahoga County, OH, vol. 137, p. 260.

Johanna HINDEN OVIATT, d. May 27, 1925 at her residence 5107 Clark Ave., Ward 7, Cleveland, Cuyahoga Co., Ohio of Apoplexy and Cerebral Hemorrhage; 49 yrs. 6 mos. 17 ds.; married to ***Clarence M. OVIATT***; Millner; b. Nov 10, 1875, Cleveland, fr. *Joseph HINDEN*, b. Germany, mo. *Barbara WAGNER*, b. Germany; informant Clarence M. Oviatt; undertaker Wm. Daniels; River Side Cemetery. Ohio Certificate of Death, Division of Vital Statistics, 1925, certif.: 28043.

C.M. Oviatt First '38 Auto Fatality in East Cleveland

In the first traffic fatality of the year in East Cleveland, ***Clarence M. OVIATT***, 81, of 14715 Terrace Road in the suburb, was fatally injured late yesterday when he walked into the street in front of 14733 Euclid Avenue and was struck by an automobile.

Oviatt, an uncle of ***Douglas G.***, mayor of South Euclid, died of his injuries, which included a skull fracture, in Huron Road Hospital at 9:40 last night, four hours after he was hit.

East Cleveland police said Oviatt walked in front of a parked automobile and another one that was double-parked waiting to pull into a space at the curb, and was struck by a car that was passing the others.

The victim, a brother of ***Arthur N.***, Cleveland architect, and ***Mrs. Rena OVIATT WRIGHT*** *(BRIGHT)* of LaVerne, Cal., was the operator of a lumber concern here until 1910, when he joined a Memphis company dealing in timber. He returned in 1916 and looked after his properties after that time. Dec 21, 1938, p. 1, col. 1. The Plain Dealer.

OVIATT: Clarence M., passed away Tuesday, Dec 20, 1938, at the A. M. McGregor Home. Funeral services Thursday, Dec 22, at 2:30 p. m., at the J. H. Brown & Son., Inc., Funeral Home, 8128 Carnegie. Burial Riverside Cemetery. Cleveland Necrology File, Dec 22 1938, reel 062.

Clarence M. OVIATT, d. Dec 20, 1938, 9:40 p.m. Huron Road Hospital, East Cleveland, Cuyahoga Co., Ohio of Fracture of base of skull, Laceration and Hemorrhage of Brain. (Auto Accident) 12.20.38, Pedestrian struck by auto on street; res. A.M. McGregor Home, 14715 Terrace Rd.; widower of ***Johanna HINDEN OVIATT***; Retired; b. May 8, 1857, Dover, Cuyahoga Co., fr. ***Dudley L. OVIATT***, b. Richfield, Summit Co., Ohio, mo. ***Almira A. PHINNEY***, b. Avon, Lorain Co., Ohio; informant W.L. Schock, Matron, 14715 Terrace Rd., E. Cleve.; Funeral Firm J.H. Brown & Son Inc.; Burial Riverside Cemetery, Dec 22. Ohio Certificate of Death, Division of Vital Statistics, 1938, certif. 69719.

The State of Ohio, Cuyahoga County-ss. I Certify, That on the 16th day of June 1886 ***Mr. Hoyt V. BRIGHT*** and ***Miss Lillian C. OVIATT*** were by me legally joined in marriage. James A. Bolles D.D. Marriage Record, Cuyahoga County, OH, vol. 29, p. 375.

Hoyt Verner BRIGHT, b. Dover, Ohio, May 23, 1863; m. June 16, 1886, ***Lillian OVIATT*** of Cleveland, O. He is the son of ***Laura Alline FOOTE*** (daughter of ***Ransom FOOTE*** and ***Catharine PORTER***, *OP 2:12*) and ***Alfred Goodwin BRIGHT***. Abram W. Foote, Foote Family Comprising the Genealogy and History of Nathaniel Foote of Wethersfield, Conn. and His Descendants, vol. 1, p. 230.

Hoyt V. BRIGHT, 55, b. Ohio, bus. Manufacturing?; ***Lillian C.***, wife, 57, b. Ohio; ***Rena OVIATT***, 48, single, b. Ohio; the names of the maid and cook living with them are difficult to read. 1920 FC California, Los Angeles, San Dimas Twp., ED 569, p. 6A, lines 80-84.

Hoyt Verner BRIGHT, b. 15 May 1864, Ohio, mo. ***FOOTE***, fr. ***BRIGHT***, d. 11 Aug 1942, Los Angeles, CA. California Death Index

The State of Ohio, Cuyahoga County-ss. I Certify, That on the 14th day of May 1890 ***Mr. Arthur N. OVIATT*** and ***Miss Lida A. GIBBS*** were by me legally joined in marriage. Rev. Brainard Marc Burridge Marriage Record, Cuyahoga County, OH, vol. 34, p. 293.

Rena married Hoyt V. Bright, Lillian's husband, after Lillian passed away.

Rena OVIATT BRIGHT, b. 1 Jan 1874, Ohio, mo. ***FINNEY***, fr. ***OVIATT***, d. 14 May 1946, Los Angeles, CA. California Death Index.

May C. OVIATT, 32; res. Lakewood, O.; b. Dover; occup. none; fr. *Dudley*, mo. *Almira PHINNEY;* never married. Married ***Thomas P. GRIMES***, 33; res. 7209 Linwood Ave; b. Portsmouth, O.; occup. manager; fr. *Wm.*, mo. *Wallie A. ROUSH*; previously married once (dec'd). The State of Ohio, Cuyahoga County-ss. I Certify, That on the 2nd day of January 1913, Mr. Thomas P. Grimes and Miss May C. Oviatt were by me legally joined in marriage. Saml. Kabatchnick J.P. Marriage Record, Cuyahoga County, OH, vol. 83, p. 264.

May OVIATT GRIMES, d. Oct 2, 1926, 11 a.m. at residence 17852 Clifton Blvd., Lakewood, Ohio of Cerebral hemorrhage 6 mos.; married to ***T.P. GRIMES***; 50 yrs. 4 mos. 5 ds.; b. May 27, 1876, Dover, Ohio, fr. ***Dudley OVIATT***, b. Richfield, Ohio, mo. ***PHINNEY***, b. Avon; undertaker William Daniels, 15800 Detroit Ave.; bur. Riverside Cemetery. Ohio Certificate of Death, Division of Vital Statistics, 1926, certif. 61013.

OP 4:3 Cahoon Monument

CAHOON

FIRST SETTLERS OF
DOVER TOWNSHIP
OCT 10, 1810
IN MEMORY OF
JOSEPH CAHOON
WHO DIED
MAR 16, 1839
AGE 75 YRS.
IN MEMORY OF
LYDIA KENYON
WIFE OF
JOSEPH CAHOON
WHO DIED
AUG 13, 1834
AGED 65 YEARS
10 MO. 13 DAYS

OP 4:3 **Joseph Cahoon**

Joseph, the pioneer of Dover,
may we one and all,
be so unspeakably happy
as to be admitted on board
King Emmanuel's wagon,
and be carried up,
not to the rich land of Goshen,
but to the better land.

Sentiment offered by W. O. Cahoon at the Cahoon Sixty-third Anniversary Celebration of the Settlement of Dover, August 28th, 1873.

Referring to Joseph Cahoon and Lydia Kenyon:
Most of their children came to them in Salisbury, Herkimer Co., N.Y.

The youngest, ***Joseph Franklin***, was the first white baby boy born in Dover, O.

From New York they removed to Newark, N.J., where they had a tide mill, thence to Vergennes, Vt., where the Otter Creek formed the water power for the mill.

In 1799 Grandfather visited Southern Ohio with a view of settling there, writing verses to his wife telling of his impressions in the new country he found in the West.

In August, 1810, a covered wagon, drawn by four horses, with a saddle horse behind, was driven up to the village green, at Vergennes, Vt., where a religious service was held prior to the departure of ***Joseph*** and ***Lydia KENYON CAHOON*** with their family to make their home in the unsettled wilds of Northern Ohio.

The long journey led through dense forests, over unbridged streams, before "good roads," were agitated in this country.

Blazed trees and Indian trails were to direct their way.

The saddle horse was to relieve the tedious journey for the ladies, for we have been told Grandmother was accomplished in horsemanship.

The cow was to furnish milk, while the cream, suspended in a receptacle from the wagon reach, was churned into butter.

The iron tea kettle supplied hot water at the wayside camp fire, where meals were served.

The prayer was said, the tearful adieu was spoken, and westward they took their way, Joseph and Lydia Cahoon, with ***Amos, Mary, Joel, Abigail, Rebecca, Daniel, Benjamin*** and little ***William***.

Mary was the bride of ***George SEXTON***, and they came to make their home near her parents, stopping for a while at *Judge KINGSBURY'S* place, east of Cleveland.

Amos stopped at *William WILLIAMS* in Newburgh, and July 3, 1813, married "***Polly***," the miller's pretty daughter.

On the morning of October 10, 1810, the wagon halted in the ravine for the location had been reached where the new home was to be founded in the unbroken wilderness.

The golden light of October fell in richest abundance upon the oaks, chestnuts, hickories and elms which stood in majesty on either side.

Soft ripples from the blue expanse of Erie broke upon the pebble beach. Nature was at her best and the hearts of the travelers rejoiced in the attractive scene.

"I pray you hear my song of a nest,
For it is not long."

The father and sons set about building a log house, north of the Lake Road, east of the creek, completing it in four days.

Those of us who heard the story from dear lips, now forever closed, wish to repeat the tradition that those who succeed us in these celebrations may keep it for the future.

Apple trees were planted upon a clearing north-east of the house in which we live. A peach orchard grew upon the east hillside where the grove now stands, and another peach orchard was planted in the ravine west of the creek.

Doubtless the seed for these trees came from New England, as we know pear trees were grown from seeds brought from Connecticut which were in bearing from over fifty years.

While *Commodore Oliver Hazard PERRY* was fighting his famous battle upon Lake Erie, Sept 10, 1813, a grist mill was being raised by Grandfather Cahoon and his neighbors upon Cahoon Creek, east of our house.

Prior to this time the nearest flour mill was at Newburgh, eighteen miles away. Miles seemed longer when no streams were bridged, no hill graded, and a horse or ox bore the burden of the grain to be ground, than they do today with modern means of transportation. The stones for grinding the grain were quarried from the creek by Joseph Cahoon and his son *Joel*. They are placed as stepping stones at the entrance to our lawn, preserved as a part of the history of the place.

In 1818 the frame house was built where it now stands, upon one of the most picturesque sites in the country, thanks to the artistic tendencies of our ancestors.

As nails had to be transported by wagon from Pittsburgh they were very costly, so wooden pins were substituted for nails whenever possible in the building, which was truly a work of the hands, so little machinery being at their command.

The laths were split timbers, champered and sprung into grooves.

A saw mill had been erected a few rods north of the grist mill, upon the brook, in which the giants of the forests were converted into lumber. Ida M. Cahoon, History of the Cahoon Family, pp. 24-27.

Agreeable to statue, the freeholders and inhabitants of the town of Salisbury convened at the house of *Aaron HACKLEY, Esq*., on Tuesday, the 4th day of April, 1797. *Cornelius HUMPHREY* and Aaron Hackley, Esqs., superintended the meeting. Polls opened and proceeded to put in the town officers, and the following were chosen, that is to say.....***Joseph CAHOON*** and Alexander Ayers pound masters. Be it remembered that on the 15th day of January, 1798, Joseph Cahoon and *Isaiah KENYON*, merchants of the town of Salisbury, county of Montgomery and State of New York, was this day convicted before me, Cornelius Humphrey, one of the justices of the peace of said county, for retailing, on the 9th day of this instant--January--and at several other times, at their store in the town aforesaid, gin and other spirituous liquors by small measure to be drank in their house; without having a license or such permit in their house, out-house, yard or garden, or without having entered into such recognizance as is mentioned in the act entitled 'an act to lay a duty of excise on strong liquors and for the better regulating of inns and taverns,' passed March 1st, 1788. Given under my hand and sealed the 15th day of January, 1798. Cornelius Humphrey, J. P. The Town of Salisbury and Early Settlers and Settlements.

Joseph CAHOON lived in Salisbury, Herkimer Co., NY until 1799; Newark, NJ from 1799-1803, where he operated a tide mill; Salisbury, 1803-07; Vergennes, VT 1807-10 where he ran a planing mill on Otter Creek; and from 10 Oct 1810, Dover Twp., Cuyahoga Co., Ohio. On 3 December 1812, *Joel, Oliver* and *Ichabod TERRELL*, and *David BEEBE, Sr.*, of nearby Ridgeville Twp., (later part of Lorain Co.), deeded to Joseph Cahoon 60 acres of land at the center of Ridgeville Twp., in exchange for his promise to build a grist mill there. This deed was the first real estate transfer in Ridgeville Twp. The 18 x 20 foot mill was finished in the Spring of 1813. *Wyllis TERRELL, Sr.*, bought the mill from Joseph Cahoon later that year, and operated it until 1827. Jeff Sigsworth, The Cahoon Family of Scotland (Who Came to Cuyahoga County), p. 7.

Joseph CAHOON; Males: 3 0-9yrs., 2 16-25 yrs., and 1 45 and up. Females: 2 10-15 yrs., 1 16-25 yrs., 1 26-44 yrs. 1810 FC VT, Franklin Co, Vergennes, p. 70. *Joseph and Lydia were listed twice in the Federal Census due to the dates they were recorded.*

Dover was settled in 1810 when ***Joseph CAHOON*** purchased land from *Nemiah HUBBARD* and *Josiah STOW* through their agent *Datus KELLEY.*

CAHOON, Joseph; Male: 1 0-9 yrs., 2 10-15 yrs., 1 16-25 yrs., and 1 45 yrs. and up; Female: 1 16-25 yrs., 1 45 yrs. and up. 1820 FC OH CYDO, p. 52A.

The Cahoon's are of Scottish origin. The first known of this cognomen on American soil was born in Rhode Island about 1669. One hundred years later his grandson, ***Reynolds CAHOON***, with his family moved from Rhode Island to Massachusetts, the eldest, ***Joseph CAHOON***, then being of age. Three years after this he married ***Miss Lydia KENYON***, and soon moved to Salisbury, New York, engaging in milling and manufacturing. This business occupied his attention for a dozen years or more, with a little change of locality, 'til 1808, when the family moved to Vergennes, Vermont, this being only a transient dwelling place. Westward the course of the empire takes its way, and visions of rich lands, broad and beautiful, were ever before our hero's eyes, and the desire strengthened to "go up and possess it." The spirit of adventure entered the home of our grandfather, Joseph Cahoon, years before he could make final arrangements to journey to the wilderness of Ohio. In the year 1799 he went to the Ohio River in search of a suitable home, and was so charged with the place that he sent his wife a poem descriptive of the country. In 1810 the plans for his removal were perfected and the leave-taking on that bright August morning which witnessed their departure has been described as being very impressive. The family of eight children came in a four horse covered wagon, and saddle horse behind, instead of the express train of to-day. We are told that the townspeople gathered themselves together and protested against this movement to the end of the world, as they deemed it, and held religious exercises upon the green, bidding a sad farewell. Six weeks sufficed to accomplish their trip, and just as the forest, with its many tinted foliage, was about to be stripped of nut and leaf, the little party put an end to their wearisome journey and settled on this romantic spot which we now cherish as their and our home. Besides the children of Joseph and Lydia Cahoon, came ***George SEXTON***, who, two weeks before their departure from Vermont, married their eldest daughter ***Mary***, and with his bride joined the party. They stopped at Newburgh on *Judge KINGSBURY'S* farm, while the remainder of the company went to a less settled locality, passing on their way the thriving city of Cleveland, with its one frame building, the office of *Judge WALWORTH* and four log dwellings. Their own log house was soon built, and in four years' time two grist mills were built by this famous pioneer, the second being raised on the day of Perry's victory on Lake Erie, the sound of the battle reaching the ears of the busy workmen. Prior to this time all the grain used by the inhabitants of Dover was ground at Newburgh, the journey of 36 miles being frequently made on foot. It is 68 years since the first settlement was made in Dover. These long years have witnessed many changes. The dense forest has been felled and houses erected upon rich farms. The little settlement of Cleveland has grown into a great city. We look around in wonder from the stories our fathers tell us of the long ago to the present with its marvelous improvements, and say of the heroes who made these comfortable habitations, where are they? Few respond to the query, but "the low, green tent, whose curtain never outward swings," veils the form of many a cherished one. "The Cahoon Pioneers," Reunion Notebook, Rose Hill Museum, Newspaper article, 1878.

CAHOON, JOSEPH (1762-1839) Cahoon was born in Rhode Island, where he was raised in a family of devout Baptists. After several moves, he settled in Vergennes, Vt., where he lived until emigrating to the Western Reserve. A practical man, throughout his life he demonstrated a high degree of self-sufficiency. He was primarily a miller, with an additional talent for inventions. These included a cotton compress, *(This should be improvements of a cotton compress. This was invented by **John Joseph CAHOON**, his grandson. Correction by David Rooke, Western Reserve Historical Society from the Cahoon Family Papers Collection, The Bay Village Historical Society.)* a tie buckle machine, a grape hoe (drawn by 1 horse), and a shingle making machine. In Vermont he had invented a nail-making machine but was unable to procure a patent because of "collusion and fraud" by a patent clerk.

With his family, Cahoon left Vergennes for the Western Reserve in 1810. To wish them well, a public meeting was held in the village square. Cahoon had visited Ohio in 1799 so as not to purchase land sight unseen. He chose land west of the Cuyahoga near the lakeshore, where the climate seemed more favorable for the fruit trees he wished to plant. The family took the land route to Western Reserve and in autumn arrived in Cleveland, where they were briefly guests of *Jas. KINGSBURY.* On 10 Oct 1810 they arrived in Dover Twp., and in 4 days they erected a log cabin on Lot 95 (north of Lake Rd., at the mouth of Cahoon Creek.)

Within the first year, Cahoon planted seeds for apple and peach trees. On 10 Sept 1813, the family erected the first gristmill in the Western Reserve west of the Cuyahoga. As they finished notching the beams together, they could hear the distant guns of *PERRY'S* fleet off Put-in-Bay. Cahoon later built a sawmill, which enabled him, with his son ***Joel***, to build a frame house in

1818. When the fruit trees matured, Cahoon, always practical, took into account the excess fruit and built a distillery for the manufacturing of peach brandy. Cahoon was married to ***Lydia KENYON***. The Cahoon family remained in the original frame house, Rose Hill, until 1917. At that time the house was deeded to the community and used as a library until 1960, when it became the Rose Hill Museum. It is maintained by the Bay Village Historical Society. David D. Van Tassel and John J. Grabowski, The Encyclopedia of Cleveland History, p. 150.

Joseph CAHOON located upon land purchased of *Datus KELLEY*, the agent for Hubbard & Stowe, the Connecticut owners of this portion of the Western Reserve...In four days Mr. Cahoon had completed a log house, the big wagon-box having meanwhile served as a place of nightly repose for the females of the family. In 1818 Joseph Cahoon built the house now occupied by his son ***Joel B.***, and where he died in 1829, at the age of seventy-five. Crisfield Johnson, History of Cuyahoga County, Ohio, p. 436.

Joseph CAHOON, his wife ***Lydia***, and their children...settled...at the mouth of the creek running through lot No. 95, then 20 or 25 rods from the Lake, but now not more than half that distance...

The prices that pioneers had to pay for the necessaries of life were extremely high, especially during the War of 1812. Flour sold for $20 per barrel; nails, 30 cents per pound, and most other things in proportion. An old account-book of *Asahel PORTER* shows that *Miss Abigail TAYLOR* paid for six yards of calico, six shillings per yard - $4.50; and for six yards of cotton shirting, four shillings per yard - $3.00.

The first child born in the township was ***Franklin***, son of Joseph and Lydia Cahoon. The first couple married in the township were ***LEVERETT JOHNSON*** and ***Abigail CAHOON*** *(daughter of Joseph and Lydia)*. Mr. Johnson, who for many years was a prominent man in the affairs of our County, died April 19th, 1856. His wife, who is the oldest resident in the township, is still living, enjoying good health, and occupied the head of our dinner table on the 10th. ***Lydia CAHOON*** died August 13, 1834. ***Joseph CAHOON*** died March 17, 1839. ***Daniel CAHOON***, October 7th, 1841. ***Mary GRIFFITH***, September 19th 1849. ***Franklin CAHOON***, May 18, 1858. ***Rebecca GRIFFITH***, June 6th, 1859...The descendants of Joseph and Lydia Cahoon now living, are, six children, forty-nine grand-children, and sixty four great-grand-children.

The population of Dover in 1810 was 15. The population in 1860 is 1,884. "Celebration of the Fiftieth Anniversary of the Settlement of Dover," Cleveland Herald, H. M. Addison, Newspaper article, Cleveland, Oct 15th, 1860, Reunion Notebook.

FIRST LAW SUIT.

The first law suit was between *Loman C. BEEBE*, plaintiff and ***Joseph CAHOON***, defendant. It was held at the house of *David BEEBE*, June 17, 1813, and before *Asahel OSBORN*, a justice of the peace of Columbia. It was an action for damages, the plaintiff claiming unfaithfulness, wastage and poor work, on the part of defendant in the grinding of a quantity of wheat for plaintiff, in May of the above year. The decision of the court, rendered June 18, 1813 was in the following words:

"It appears, from evidence before this court, that, from twenty-eight bushels of wheat, which said plaintiff carried to said defendant's mill, said defendant made one hundred and eleven pounds' weight less flour, and that not so good as *Capt. Calvin HOADLEY* generally makes out of similar wheat. From a mature consideration of the evidence and circumstances, it is the opinion of this court that the said plaintiff, Loman C. Beebe, is entitled to receive of the said defendant, Joseph Cahoon, the sum of six dollars damage, and five dollars and seventy-seven cents costs of suit, for which judgment is rendered in favor of the plaintiff against defendant by this court." History of Lorain County, Ohio, Ridgeville, p. 163.

Down on the shore of the lake, a dozen miles from Cleveland, there opens a little inlet into the land, between whose overhanging banks one catches a glimpse of the long level of blue or the swaying whirlwinds of foam, according to the mood that has for the time befallen the changeful waters. A little brook that has its life up in the stone ledges beyond, here goes puling over a bed of shingle, and gives its existence into the ready embrace of the greater waters. On either hand hang great groves of trees, whose tops almost interlace over the two or three masts that idly rock with the slight motion of the current. A winding road leads up from either end of the old wood bridge, and marks the dusty trail of man across the face of nature.

In this little spot a miracle was wrought just sixty-nine years ago. A strong and stalwart man, whose heart and arms were built for the work of a pioneer, came into the presence of nature and laid his hands upon her, and bound her captive to his use. He took a few score of her great trees, hewed them and staked them together, and made him a house in which to escape the storms of winter and the hunger of the wild beast. He threw across the brook a rude dam, and the willing waters ground for him the first grist that machinery furnished in that section of Cuyahoga. Here, year after year, labored and wrought ***Joseph CAHOON***, and to-day two score descendants are reaping the harvest he sowed in such labor, such patience, and in the solitude of the unbroken wilds. "Old and Young," Cahoon Reunion Notebook, Rose Hill Museum, Newspaper article, 1879.

Seventy-three years ago this summer my grandfather and an aunt, took me with them on a visit to ***"Uncle Joseph's"*** in a one-horse wagon - there were no buggies then and we crossed the Cuyahoga River at the foot of a then steep lane-now Superior street-on a scow, which was pulled across the river by a rope fastened on either side - the only way of getting across there. At Rocky River we crossed in the same manner, but had to blow a tin horn tied to a tree to get the boat with the ferryman from the west side. The route to what is now Dover was by the Detroit road, which was the old Indian trail, on which the trees had been cut down in a space wide enough for the passage of wagons; and in low places and over little streams, made passable in wet weather by corduroy-logs laid crosswise-and by log bridges where space for water under them was necessary. We passed several log cabins in small clearings, but along much of the distance there was *(were)* woods on one or both sides of the road. We arrived at Dover late in the afternoon, having gone at the average rate of about two and one-half mile per hour, or ten times as long as I was in going there Saturday. The two trips and condition of the intermediate territory prove this to be a decidedly progressive age. "Cahoon Family Reunion," H. M. Addison, Cleveland, Aug 29, 1897, Newspaper article, Cahoon Reunion Notebook.

The descendants of the first settlers of Dover celebrated the fiftieth anniversary of the occasion by inviting their relatives and a few close friends to join them on Oct 10, 1860 at the family home of Rose Hill. One hundred and twenty people gathered at the first celebration. The day was spent by having a "sumptuous" dinner on the spot where the first log cabin was built by ***Joseph CAHOON*** and his sons. Numerous toasts were made and the party then adjourned to the house where they spent the time "most agreeably in social conversation." The first gathering was such a success that it was agreed upon to continue the celebration as an annual event. In 1869 the event was changed to the 28th of August to commemorate the birthday of Joseph Cahoon to "better accommodate the old pioneers who have been accustomed to attend these meetings." This continued to be held annually until 1881 with two hundred attending until ***Joel B. CAHOON'S*** health began to fail. Joel passed away in 1882 and the reunion's were held every five years starting in 1885 until at least 1910, celebrating the 100th anniversary of the Cahoon's arrival. Three hundred persons are recorded to have attended the celebration in 1910. The last Cahoon to occupy Rose Hill, ***Ida CAHOON***, passed away in 1917. Cahoon Reunion Notebook, Rose Hill Museum.

CELEBRATE SETTLEMENT.

Dover Township Residents Recall Coming of Cahoon Family Over 100 Years Ago.

The celebration of the 100th anniversary of the founding of Dover township, began yesterday afternoon, when a large crowd assembled in the Methodist church at Bay View and listened to commemorative addresses. The celebration this year is in charge of the Cahoon family, which is particularly appropriate, as ***Joseph CAHOON*** was the first settler.

Rev. L.J. ALDRICH of Dover conducted the services, which opened with an address by ***Miss Ida M. CAHOON*** on reminiscences of the early women settlers and the struggle they were forced to make for bare existences. *Reuben HALL* of Dover read a paper on the early church work. *Rev. Dan F. BRADLEY* of Pilgrim Congregational church of Cleveland, delivered the principal address of the afternoon. He chose the subject, "One Hundred Years Ago," and spoke of the evolution that had taken place since the first settler erected his log cabin in a clearing.

The Cahoon family presented the township with a handsome American flag, *Horace WOLFE*, mayor of Bay View, making the acceptance speech.

This afternoon ***Lydia, Laura*** and ***Ida CAHOON***, granddaughters of Joseph Cahoon, will give a dinner at their home, at Stop 24, Lake Shore Electric, to which 300 invitations have been sent out. Addresses will be made during the afternoon. Newspaper article, 1910, Cahoon Collection, Rose Hill Museum, Bay Village, OH.

Bay Village: CAHOON (Family Cemetery) - Included in Lakeside Cemetery now. Maxine Hartmann Smith, Ohio Cemeteries, p. 71.

Additional documentation of burials on the Cahoon property were not found and are questioned.

DIED

Of the Pleurisy, on the morning of the 16th inst., at his residence in Dover, Cuyahoga County, ***JOSEPH CAHOON***, aged 75 years.- Mr. Cahoon was among the earliest pioneers on the Western Reserve, and was more especially known for his zeal in the cause of the Christian religion, of which he manifested up to the hour of his death the brightest example. - COMMUNICATED. Elyria Advertiser, March 16, 1839, p. 3, col. 3.

For Joseph Cahoon

The terrors of death
had not power to alarm him,
He felt not his darkness
and feared not his sting,
The thought of his Saviors
kind mercy could calm him,
And his Spirit went upward
s on faith's ardent wings

D.K. Cahoon

Handwritten note, Cahoon Collection, Rose Hill Museum, Bay Village, OH.

Paternal Ancestors of Joseph Cahoon:

The song called "Loch Lomond" is about the Colquhouns and their lands. When the Scots were helping to fight off the Normans & the Druids, several were captured and for every two that were captured, they had to decide between them which one would return home and which one would die. Hence the Lyrics:

Ye'll tak the high road
and I'll tak the low road,
but I'll be in Scotland afore ye,
For me and my true love
will never meet again,
On the bonnie,
bonnie banks
of Loch Lomond.

The one that took the high road was returning home and the one taking the low road was to die. The bonnie banks of Loch Lomond was Luss, the Colquhoun lands, where our castle Rossdhu House still stands. Home for the Chiefs of the Clan.

The lineages of the Clan Chiefs are found in the centre of the Rossdhu Book and may be followed back from father to first born son to ***Maldouen***, 1st Clan Chief of Luss from 1150 AD until 1220 AD, & ***Umfridus***, 1st Clan Chief of Kilpatrick & of Colquhoun from 1190 AD until 1260 AD. Orval O. Calhoun, Our Calhoun Family, vol. 2, pp. 123-127 and Owen Calhoun.

I. ***Sir John COLQUHOUN*** (Cahoon or Calhoun in America) was born in Dunbarton-Shire, Scotland in 1595. He was the sixteenth chief of the Clan Colquhoun, eighteenth Laird of the Land of Luss, whose lands lay on the west of Loch Lomond, in Dumbarton-Shire. He was the first Baronet of Nova Scotia, Canada in 1617, whose brothers *William* and *George* made their home in Sweden, 1647. Ida M. Cahoon, History of the Cahoon Family, p. 17.

Alternate source:

William CAHOON was the second of two children born to ***Alexander COLQUHOUN***, b. 1599 and ***Marion STERLING***. Alexander was the third of eleven children born to *Sir Alexander COLQUHOUN*, 15th Clan Chief of Colquhoun, seventeenth child of ***Luss COLQUHOUN*** and ***Margaret Helen BUCHANAN***. Orval O. Calhoun, p. 33.

II. ***William CAHOON***, b. 1635, was the youngest of three sons of ***Sir John COLQUHOUN***. William probably emigrated to America before 1651 and in 1669, signed the agreement, and became a citizen of Swansea, R.I. He learned the brick making trade from *James LEONARD*. In 1660, with sixteen others, he purchased Block Island, Rhode Island. He married c1663 at Block Island to ***Deliverance PECK*** (b. c1635), they had at least two children, ***Joseph*** born 1665, Block Island, and ***James*** born 15 February 1671, Swansea, R.I. In "Hubbard's Narrative of Indian Wars" we find this record: "On the 24th of June, 1675, the alarm was sounded in Plymouth Colony, when eight or nine of the English were slain in and about Swansea, they being the first to fall in King Philip's War." William Cahoon was one of these nine killed by the Indians and buried in Swansea. We now find the Americanized spelling of the name. Ida M. Cahoon, Handwritten notebook on the Cahoon Family Reunions, Rose Hill Museum, Bay Village, OH; and Jeff Sigsworth, The Cahoon Family of Scotland, pp. 1, 2, 4 and the New Eng. Register vol. 52.

William (Cahoon) was a soldier in the war between Scotland and England and was captured. He was made an indentured servant and sold to Bex & Company to work for his freedom in the iron mines of Block Island, MA. Orval O. Calhoun, vol. 2, p. 33.

Officially made Swansea's first town brickmaker, December 24, 1673. ***William "CAHOONE"*** finally met with "success" as a Freeman in Swansea, Mass., when he was officially appointed as the sole brickmaker for that town. There is still in existence, in the Swansea Town Offices, the original bound volume entitled: "Proprietors Book of Grants and Meetings, 1668-1769." It includes the following entry: At a Town Meeting of the townsmen, December 24, 1673, It was Agreed upon by and Between the townsmen In the behalf of the town and William Cohoone (Cohoune/Cohowne?) brickmaker that for and in Consideration of a Lot and other Accommodations or Grants And Given by him from the town unto him the said William Cohoun. It was therefore Agreed and Concluded upon by the Parties Above so that the said William Cohoon Shall Supply all the Inhabitants with the town with Bricks at a Price not Exceeding Twenty Shillings a Thousand in current Pay Putting between Man and Man." Willliam's name is spelled differently in each instance, possibly indicating that he was illiterate.

On June 24, 2000, William Cahoone's direct descendants donated a commemorative plaque to the Swansea Historical Society, it will be affixed to a rock and erected near the site of the Cahoone Brickworks, close to the location of the Myles Garrisoned House along the Palmer River in Swansea, Mass. It states:

Near this spot stood
The Cahoone Brickworks from 1673-1675
founded and operated by
William Cahoone (Colquhoun)
of Luss, Scotland and Swansea, Massachusettes.
+++++
Taken prisoner during Cromwellian Wars (1650)
Indentured servant at
Quincy, Massachusettes (1651)
Freeman at Block Island (1664)
One of founders of Swansea, Massachusettes (1669)
Killed by Indians Eve of King Philip's War
While attempting to secure doctor
For wounded of Swansea (June 24, 1675
+++++
Presented by the Descendants June 24, 2000

Cahoone Website: http://personal.tmlp.com/richard/wilsoc.html, Richard and Deborah Cahoon Didick, The William Cahoone (Colquhoun) Society.

III. ***Joseph CAHOON***, the third of seven children born to William Cahoon and Deliverance Peck; b. c1665 at Block Island, RI?; m.1 ***Hannah KENT*** (b. 2 July 1667, Charlestown, Mass; d. 1699, Bristol, RI; dau. of *John KENT* (b. 1645) and *Hannah GRISWOLD* (1644-1690)), they had four children. m.2 30 Apr 1700 ***Elizabeth SCRANTON?*** of Swansea, Bristol and E. Greenwich; they had at least five children, the third being Ebenezer. Orval O. Calhoun, vol. 2, p. 33.

IV. ***Lieut. Ebenezer CAHOON***, b. 8 Oct 1706 at East Greenwich R.I.; m. 1728 to ***Mary REYNOLDS*** (b. 5 Feb 1704 (6), Providence, RI, dau of *Francis REYNOLDS* (b. 1662) and *Elizabeth GREENE* (b. 1668 of Providence, RI)). Lived at East Greenwich, North Kingston & Exeter. He was a house carpenter by trade. He fought in the British colonial army under *Sir William JOHNSON* during the French and Indian War in 1755 and helped to erect *Fort William HENRY* at the head of Lake George. Many real estate transfers in his name are recorded in East Greenwich Land Record vols. 5, 6 and 9. They would have at least five sons. Ida M. Cahoon, Handwritten notebook on the Cahoon Family Reunions, Rose Hill Museum, Bay Village, OH and Sigsworth, pp. 1, 2, 4 and Orval O. Calhoun, vol. 2, pp. 123-127.

One son, ***Capt. William CAHOON***, b. 1733, Greenwich; d. 26 Oct 1813, Chatham, Mass; m. *Elizabeth VAUGHN*. They would have at least eleven children, one being ***William CAHOON***, b. 2 June 1765, West Greenwich, R.I.; d. 1 Oct 1828, near Kirtland, Lake Co., Ohio; m.1 5 July 1787 to *Mehitable HODGE(S)* (b. 21 Dec 1765, West Greenwich, R.I.; d. 28 Mar 1809, Kirtland); m.2 *Mrs. Mary SMITH.* William and Mehitable had eight children, one being ***Reynolds CAHOON***, b. 30 Apr 1790, Cambridge, NY; d. 29 Apr 1861, South Cottonwood, Utah; m.1 11 Dec 1810 to *Thirza STILES* (dau. of *Daniel Olds STILES* and *Abigail FARRINGTON*, b. 18 Oct 1789, d. 20 Nov 1867); m.2 and 3 *on the same day*, 16 Jan 1846, (Nauvoo, Ill.?) to *Mrs. Lucinda ROBERTS JOHNSON* (b. 5 Mar 1806, Lincoln, Addison Co., VT) and *Mary HILDRATH* (b. 21 Oct 1806). About 1825 Reynolds' family moved to Kirtland, Lake Co., Ohio where he became active in the Latter-Day Saints (Mormon) Church, eventually becoming a High Priest.

The founder of the Mormon Church, *Joseph SMITH*, in 1830 sent one of his brothers (*Samuel SMITH*) west as the first missionary of the new church. By the spring of 1831, Samuel was preaching between Kirtland and Amherst, Lorain Co., Ohio and from June to Aug 1831, Reynolds joined him -- eventually preaching as far west as Independence, Missouri. They were the first Mormon missionaries to enter the states of Kentucky and Indiana. In Oct 1839, when the "Zarahemia Stake (regional branch)" was created at Montrose, Lee Co., Iowa, *John SMITH* (uncle of Joseph) was chosen president of the stake and Reynolds was appointed counselor. The Zarahemia Stake was the second most important community until 1842. Sigsworth, pp. 5 and 30.

Another son of Ebenezer was Reynolds.

V. ***Reynolds CAHOON***, b. 1735, East Greenwich or North Kingston, RI; d. 1815 in East Cleveland (now Euclid), Ohio; bur. Euclid Cemetery; m.1 5 Nov 1761 to ***Rebecca RATHBUN*** (dau. of *Joseph RATHBUN (RATHBONE)* and *Abigail WILBUR*, b. 27 Dec 1736 Exeter, RI; d. pre1761). *Issue:* ***Joseph CAHOON*** (b. 28 Aug 1762, Rhode Island, d. Dover, Ohio). ***Rebecca CAHOON***, b. 1764, RI; lived in New York State; m. 1789, possibly in Salisbury, Herkimer Co, NY to *Asa STILES* (son of *John STILES* (b. 1738) and *Betsy OLDS* (1740-1800) of Woodbury, Litchfield Co., Conn.; b. 1766, Brandon, VT.); moved to Warrensville Twp., Cuyahoga Co., OH c1811; they had at least four daughters and three sons. ***Reynolds CAHOON***, m.2 12 Feb 1769 *Mary RATHBUN*, sister of Rebecca (b. 22 Nov 1738). *Issue:* ***Benjamin CAHOON*** b. c1770, RI?; m. *Mary "Polly" AUBURN*; lived in Salisbury, NY; had at least seven children. ***Wilbur CAHOON***, b. 27 Dec 1772, Hancock, Berkshire Co., Mass./RI; d. 25 (27) Sept 1826, Avon, Lorain Co., OH; bur. Avon Mounds (Center) Cemetery, Avon; m. 1795, Salisbury to *Priscilla SWEET* (b.1772/3, RI; d. 2 May 1855/7, Avon Twp.; dau. of *Jesse SWEET* and *Hulda WHITFORD*, of East Greenwich, RI); lived in the "Royal Grant," Herkimer Co., NY, then to Ohio; eight children. ***Reynolds CAHOON***, b. c1775, Hancock, Mass or RI; d. 1844, East Cleveland (now Euclid), Cuyahoga Co., OH; came to Ohio pre 1815 and settled in E. Cleveland; m. with at least two daughters and one son. ***Abigail CAHOON***, b. 30 Apr 1779, Hancock, Mass. or RI; d. 15 Oct 1857 or 67; lived at Toledo, OH; m. 3 Sep 1798, Harpersfield, Delaware Co., NY or Salisbury, NY to *Aaron STILES* (brother of *Asa STILES*; b. June 1773 or 19 May, Woodbury, Litchfield Co., Conn. or Brandon, Rutland Co., Vt.; d. 19 Jan 1843), at least seven children. ***Hannah CAHOON***, b. c 1781, Hancock, Berkshire Co., Mass or RI; m. c1803 Salisbury, NY to *Belcher JOHNSON* (son of *Capt. Hezekiah JOHNSON*, b. c1778); lived at Salisbury, NY; had at least one son.

Reynolds Cahoon was a house carpenter who died in East Cleveland, Ohio in 1815. He had gone west to live with his son, Reynolds. Ida M. Cahoon; Handwritten notebook on the Cahoon Family Reunions, Rose Hill Museum, Bay Village, OH; Jeff Sigsworth, pp. 1, 2, 4, 6, 25; Orval O. Calhoun, vol. 2, pp. 128, 147 and Cahoon Family File at Rose Hill Museum.

The present Euclid Cemetery originated in 1864. The Nickel Plate Railroad was slated to go through the Baptist Cemetery in Euclid which was established in the 1820's. Approximately 30% of the graves were able to be found and were moved to Euclid at this time. There are no records of ***Reynold CAHOON***. Due to the time of Reynolds death, 1815, it is thought that he was probably buried on his own land. John Williams, Euclid Historical Museum, Euclid, OH.

Reynolds CAHOON *(parents of Joseph, living with his brother Reynolds).* Males: 10-15 yrs.: 1, 15-20 yrs.: 1, 20-30 yrs.:1, 50-60 yrs. Female: 5-10 yrs.: 1, 10-15 yrs.: 1, 15-20 yrs.: 1, 40-50 yrs.: 1. 1830 FC OH CY Euclid, p. 97.

Reynolds CAHOON *(parents of Joseph, living with his brother Reynolds).* Males: 20-30 yrs.: 1, 60-70 yrs.: 1. Females: 15-20 yrs.: 1, 20-30 yrs.: 1, 50-60 yrs.: 1. 1840 FC OH CY Euclid, p. 115.

Ancestors of Rebecca Rathbun Cahoon, mother of Joseph Cahoon:

I. ***John RATHBUN***, New Shoreham, RI; d. 1702; m. ***Margaret*** the same year. He came to Block Island with the first settlers, being one of the sixteen purchasers of the Island, April 1661. His will, dated 12 Feb 1702, mentions wife Margaret, sons ***John, William, Joseph, Samuel*** and ***Thomas***: daughters ***Sarah, Margaret*** and ***Elizabeth***. John Osborne Austin, The Genealogical Dictionary of Rhode Island; Comprising Three Generations of Settlers Who Came Before 1690, p. 159.

II. ***Joseph RATHBUN***, lived in New Shoreham, Kingston and Exeter, RI. He m. 19th of May 1691, ***Mary MOSHER***, daughter of *Rev. Hugh MOSHER* (b. 1633, d. 1713, res. Newport and Portsmouth, RI and Dartsmouth, Ma., first Pastor of the First Baptist Church of Dartsmouth) and *Rebecca HARNDEL* (dau. of *John* and *Sarah HARNDEL* of Newport, RI), who d. in 1748. He died in 1749. His will mentions sons ***Joseph*** and ***Benjamin*** besides seven daughters. Austin, p. 159.

III. ***Joseph RATHBUN***, b. 4 Oct 1707, resided at North Kingston. He m. 4 Sept 1734, ***Abigail WILBUR***, daughter of *Joseph WILBUR* (d. 4 May 1729, son of *William WILBUR*) and *Ann BROWNELL* (d. 2 Apr 1747, dau. of *Thomas* and *Ann BROWNWELL)* of

Little Compton, RI. His will, dated 8 Mar 1759 and proved 11 Sept 1759, leaves his Estate to his wife Abigail and children ***Jeremiah*** (minor), ***George, Joseph, Rebecca, Mary*** and ***Ann***. Exeter Probate Records Book 2, p. 69 and Austin, pp. 228-229.

IV. ***Rebecca RATHBUN,*** b. 27 Dec 1736, m. 5 Nov 1761 to ***Reynolds CAHOON***. ***Mary RATHBUN***, b. 22 Nov 1738, m. 12 Feb 1769 to ***Reynolds CAHOON***. Rathbun selection prepared for S.A. Johnson, 13 Jan 1900 by Prof. James Allen Kibbe. Rose Hill Museum, Cahoon Collection.

VI. ***Joseph CAHOON***, the first of two children born to ***Reynolds CAHOON*** and ***Rebecca RATHBUN***; b. Aug 28, 1762; served in the Rhode Island Militia during the Revolution and married ***Lydia KENYON*** [c1786]. They lived in Rhode Island; Massachusetts; Newark, N.J.; Salisbury, N.Y.; Vergennes, Addison Co., Vt. and Dover, O. The first nine children were born in Salisbury, Herkimer Co., N.Y. The twins and *Joseph* were born in Dover. *Issue:* ***Samuel CAHOON***, b. 1787; d. 29 Mar 1863, Ridgeville Twp., Lorain Co., OH; bur. Ridgeville Center Cemetery; m. 27 Apr 1818, Cuyahoga Co., OH to *Lucinda BARNUM* of Rockport (b. 1786, d. Ridgeville, dau. of *John BARNUM* (1757-1819)); res. Ridgeville Twp., OH. ***Amos CAHOON***, b. 7 Sept 1789; d. 27 Nov 1860, WI; m. 3 July 1813, Newburgh, Cuyahoga Co., OH to *Mary Polly WILLIAMS* (b. 8 Nov 1797, Suffield, Hartford Co., CT; d. 17 Mar 1874, bur. Lyons, WI, dau. of *William Wheeler WILLIAMS*); res. Ridgeville Twp. (1813-1818), Dover Twp. (1819-1835), WI (from 1835). ***Mary CAHOON***, b. 24 Oct 1791; d. 17 Sept 1849, m.1 1810, Vergennes, Addison Co., VT to *George SEXTON* (b. 31 Jan 1787 Bennington Co., VT; d. 7 Nov 1829 Ridgeville Twp., Lorain Co., OH; son of *Aaron SEXTON* and *Jane JAMESON*); m.2 4 July 1836, *Ebenezer GRIFFITH* (b. 1813, d. 26 Dec 1886); res. Ridgeville, O. ***Joel Butler CAHOON,*** b. 29 Aug 1793; d. 28 Sept 1882, Dover, OH; m. 14 July 1831, Frederick, Frederick Co., MD to *Mrs. Margaret A. VAN ALLEN*, nee *DICKSON (Lots 63/64).* ***Abigail CAHOON***, b. 6 May 1796; d. 1869 Dover Twp., bur. Evergreen Cemetery, Westlake, OH; m. July 1814 to *Leverett JOHNSON* (b. 1793, {Conn.}; d. 1856, bur. Evergreen Cem, Westlake, Cuyahoga Co., OH). ***Rebecca CAHOON,*** b. 1798; d. 1859; m.1 *Jacob HEATH,* m.2 *Ebenezer GRIFFITH*; {res. Cleveland}. ***Daniel Kenyon CAHOON***, b. 1803; d. 1841, North Bend, Hamilton Co., OH, bur. Spring Grove Cem., Cincinnati, Hamilton Co., O; unm. ***Benjamin Reynolds CAHOON***, b. 14 July 1805; d. 24 Sept 1872, Elyria, Lorain Co., OH; m. *Emeline (Elizabeth "Emma") HACKETT* (b. 4 Dec 1808, d. 19 Mar 1876, [Elyria]), res. Elyria, O. ***William Ovington CAHOON***, b. 10 Jan 1808; d. {20 July} 1878, Elyria, Lorain Co.; {bur. Ridgelawn Cemetery}; m.1 25 Dec 1831 *Nancy Dewitt ELDRED* (b. 4 July 1809, d. 1 Sept 1838, dau. of *Judge Moses ELDRED* {d.1857} and *Martha DEWITT*), m.2 *Melissa (Margaret) ELDRED* (b. 13 Feb 1821, Ridgeville, Lorain Co., OH; d. {25 May} 1888, sister of *Nancy Dewitt ELDRED*), res. Elyria. ***Twins*** who died in infancy, no names, b./d. c1811, Dover, OH *also listed as Salisbury, NY which would not be accurate if the date is accurate*. ***Joseph Franklin (Franklin) CAHOON***, the first white male child born in Dover, b. 1813; d. 1858, Lorain, Lorain Co., OH, bur. Avon Cemetery, Avon, Lorain Co. OH; m. *Nancy E. RULE* of Norwalk, O. Ida M. Cahoon, pp. 23-34; Descendants of Bay Village Families, pp. 221-34; [Cahoon annual reunion, Newspaper article, 1876, Rose Hill Museum]; {"Lorain County Researcher," Winter 1996, p., 7}; Orval O. Calhoun, vol. 2, p. 147.

Siblings of Joseph Cahoon:

Husband of Rebecca Cahoon: ***Asa STILES***, Males: 0-10 yrs.: 3, 10-16 yrs.: 1, 16-26 yrs.: 1, 45+ yrs.:1. Females: 0-10 yrs.: 1, 16-26 yrs.: 1, 45+ yrs.: 1. 1810 FC NY Clinton Co., Chazy, p. 24.

Asa STILES, War of 1812, 36 Reg't (Miller's) New York Militia, Private, Roll 200, Esct. 602. War of 1812 Soldiers.

Warrensville. This township is situated southeast from Cleveland, and was designated in the survey of the Western Reserve as township seven in range eleven. ***Asa STILES*** came to the Warren neighborhood from New York about 1812. He had three sons named ***Amos, Hiram*** and ***Wilbur***. He is listed as a trustee of Warrensville in 1820 and 1827, then treasurer in 1828. The total tax collected in Warrensville for the year 1821 was $6.05. Asa Stiles was compensated $1.55 as trustee for the year. Crisfield Johnson, History of Cuyahoga County, Ohio, pp. 529-531.

Asa STILES is listed in the 1820 census for OH, Cuyahoga Co., Warrensville Twp., p. 61.

Asa STILES, Males: 10-15 yrs.: 2, 20-30 yrs.: 1, 30-40 yrs.: 2, 60-70: 1. Females: 20-30 yrs.: 1, 30-40 yrs.:1. 1830 FC OH CY Warrensville Twp., p. 141.

Asa STILES, Old Cemetery, Shaker Hts., OH. Abstract of Graves of Revolutionary Patriots, vol. 4, #11912.

Warrensville West Cemetery is the oldest landmark in Shaker Heights, having the first burial in 1811, and the second oldest in Cuyahoga County. It stands at the center of the first settlement in Warrensville Township.

In 1812, ***Asa STILES*** came from New England to settle on Lot 43 in Warrensville Township. Purchasing 160 acres, the lot was situated in the NE corner of the old surveyors' trail at (Lee Road) and Old Salt Springs Road (Kinsman) which included the graves of *Lovisa WARREN* and *Betsey PRENTISS*. 1 3/10 acres was transferred soon after his arrival to the township for a cemetery which included these two graves. Asa buried his wife, ***Rebecca CAHOON STILES***, in the cemetery in 1824. Her stone and those of four other Stiles stand here as a monument to the family. Stones were found for ***Cloe*** and possibly ***Mary*** or ***Martin***. Asa is recorded as being in Row 8, grave 16. Records for this cemetery have been lost. Asa is honored with a flag each Memorial Day for his participation in the War of 1812. City of Shaker Heights, Planning Dept., Shaker Hts., OH.

Asa STILES, son of *John STILES* (b. 21 Aug. 1738, Stratford, Fairfield Co., CT; m. 13 Aug 1760) and *Betsy OLDS* (b. 10 Nov 1740, Woodbury, Litchfield Co., CT); b. 1 Mar 1767, Brandon, Rutland, VT; d. 12 Mar 1834 at the age of 68; m. ***Rebecca CAHOON*** (b. Exeter, NY). *Issue:* ***Hanna STILES***, b. 1790, New York City, NY; m. 1817, Warrensville, Cuy. Co., OH to *Wm. ADDISON*, children *Hiram* and *Harvey*. ***Betsy STILES***, b. 1792, New York City; d. 8 Dec 1861. ***Amos STILES***, b. 1794,

New York City; d. 21 Oct 1854; m. 1848. ***Wilbur STILES***, b. 1796, New York City; d. 10 Nov 1846. ***Rhoda T. STILES***, b. 1800, New York City. ***Hiram STILES***, b. 1804; m. *Mandana DUTY*. ***Electa STILES***, b. 1816, Bloomfield, Otsego, NY; d. 23 Sept 1888 at 158 Congress St., Warrensville, Cuy. Co., Ohio; m. *Calvin FISH* (b. 1816, Ellesburg, Jefferson Co., NY); children *Charles E*, b. 1847, O and *James W*., b. Nov 1850, O. Mike Jones

Wilbur CAHOON, was born in Hancock Township, Berkshire county, Massachusetts, December 27, 1772, but for a number of years he and his wife, ***Priscilla***, lived in Saulsbury *(Salisbury)*Township of Herkimer County, New York in which locality all their children but one were born. It was in the year 1814 that these worthy people, participating in that great westward movement which began about the close of the second war with Great Britain, left New York State for the far West. Wilbur Cahoon traded his 100 acres of land in Herkimer County for a tract of 800 acres, all covered with heavy forests in what is now Avon Township of Lorain County. Arriving here with his family after the numberless difficulties of travel in such times and circumstances, he established such rude accommodations as conditions permitted for his first home. A few years later in 1825 he erected the first frame house that was built in Avon. The tract of land which thus early came into the possession of the Cahoon family was in 1814 so isolated that in order to reach it Wilbur had to cut a trail for eight miles through the woods. Not until some time afterwards was a single settlement planted between the Cahoon habitation and the little hamlet at Cleveland, Ohio. What is now a great city at that time had only thirty houses. Wilbur Cahoon's distinction in the early history of Avon does not rest entirely upon his being the advance guard of the first settlers. His character and activities would have made him influential in any country. He was one of the early members of the Whig party and was the first justice of the peace elected for the jurisdiction now divided among the townships of Avon, Sheffield and Dover, all of which was at that time one township, Dover being now in the county to the east of Lorain. There were only two justices of the peace, and the other was *Isaac BURRELL*. Wilbur Cahoon and wife were charter members of the first Baptist Church established in Avon, and until a proper church edifice would be built meetings were frequently held at their home. Though he thus played a large and influential part in the early life of Avon, Wilbur Cahoon had lived there only twelve years until his death on September 27, 1826. His wife, Priscilla (Sweet) Cahoon, was born in Rhode Island, and died in Avon May 2, 1855, both having been laid to rest side by side in the old township. They were the parents of eight children, all but one lived beyond middle age....The journey from Herkimer to Lorain County brought many interesting recollections...A trip around the world in modern times is fraught with not half the difficulties which attended a migration from one of the eastern to one of the states of the Ohio Valley a century ago. It required the Cahoon family a month of tedious travel. The first objective point in their migration was Dover in Cuyahoga County, where Wilbur Cahoon had a brother, ***Joseph***, who in the local history of Dover is likewise distinguished as the first settler, having located there in 1810. After a visit at Joseph's home the family came on to their chosen spot in the Northern Ohio wilderness in Avon. History of Lorain County, 1879, pp. 708-9.

In the summer of 1814, ***Wilber CAHOON*** and family; *Nicholas YOUNG* and son *William*; *Lewis AUSTIN* and family; *Ephraim KEYES* and family, and two brothers, *Spink* and *Reuben COOPER*, with their wives, took their departure from Montgomery county, New York, for Ohio, the objective point being township number seven, in the sixteenth range. The cavalcade consisted of five horses, four yoke of oxen and five cows. Arriving at Ashtabula, Keyes and the brothers Cooper decided to remain there for a time. The other three families came on, and early in the fall reached the end of the ridge road, at *Barney HALL'S*, in Dover township, Cuyahoga county. Here the families remained until a road had been cut along the summit of the ridge to section eleven, in which the greater portion of the lands selected by Mr. Cahoon were situated. Soon a log house was constructed on this section, the first built by a permanent settler, and into this the family of Mr. Cahoon soon removed. This stood on the site of the present homestead residence, which was built in the year 1826, and was the first house built in the township of Avon.

Mrs. Cahoon was formerly ***Miss Priscilla SWEET***, of Rhode Island. The children were, ***Susan***, who married *Harley MASON*, and now lives in Erie county, this State; ***Jessie S***., who married *Marcus MOORE*, (deceased); ***Wilber***, who married *Theresa MOORE*, (died in California); ***Ora B***., who married *Jane T. JAMESON*, in section eleven, and to him we wish to acknowledge our obligations for valuable aid in collecting data for the history of Avon. His family numbers seven, all living. ***Orra***, the next child, married *Henry TITUS*, (deceased); ***Huldah*** died in 1826; ***Melissa M***. married *John C. STEELE*, (deceased); and ***Leonard***, who married *Mary TITUS*, and lives in Elyria.

Wilber Cahoon purchased his lands in Avon, of *Orrin ENSIGN*, (who had surveyed the township, and received in payment certain tracts, lying in different sections of the township), paying therefor in eastern lands. He had in addition to the three hundred acres in section eleven, about two hundred acres in section six. The spring following his settlement in Avon, he planted an orchard of one hundred trees on section eleven. The trees were procured at Newburgh, Cuyahoga county. The greater part of this orchard is still standing.

The first saw mill was erected on section eleven, in the fall of 1815, by Mr. Cahoon. The waters of the French creek were utilized to propel the rude machinery of this mill, which was in operation a full fifty years; now there is scarcely a vestige of it remaining. The first wheat in Avon was sown by Wilbur Cahoon on section eleven, in the fall of 1815. The previous season a crop of corn was raised on the same ground.

A Baptist church was not formed until the summer of 1817. In June of that year *Elder HARTWELL*, from the east, making a missionary tour through this portion of the Reserve, held meetings at the house of Wilbur Cahoon a few times, and traveled westward.

In the summer of 1818, Mr. Cahoon built a grist mill near the saw mill mentioned above, the water, propelling which, being supplied from the same pond. There were two run of stone. This mill was finally abandoned in consequence of a scarcity of water.

June 22, 1819, *Jabez BURRELL* and Wilber Cahoon were elected justices of the peace.

Mr. Cahoon did not live to witness the completion of the first frame house in the township. Suddenly and swiftly came the pale messenger; while in full health he was stricken down with apoplexy, and in one brief hour was dead. This was in 1826. His wife and mother survived him many years; she *(Priscilla)* died in 1857. History of Lorain County, Avon, pp. 271-275.

Of their eight children (***Wilbur*** and ***Priscilla SWEET CAHOON***), *Leonard* was the only one to be born in Avon Township, and he was its first native white child. All the other children were born in Herkimer County, New York. A Standard History of Lorain County, 1916, ed. G. Frederick Wright, vol. I, p. 101.

Wilbur CAHOON'S first name was for his mother's maternal great-grandfather, ***Joseph WILBUR***. In 1814, Wilbur and his family arrived in the township that was eventually named Avon. Wilbur and ***Priscilla*** were Avon's first permanent settlers. Wilbur built the first saw and grist mills in the village. Their eighth child, ***Leonard***, was born on 1 December 1814. He was the first white child born in Avon.

That Wilbur had learned his carpentry skills from his father is proven by the fact that the home he built still stands today on the banks of French Creek in Avon. He built the home in 1825, and only lived one year after its completion. Wilbur, died in Avon, Ohio of a stroke on 27 September 1826.
http://www.centuryinter.net/tjs11/gen/cahoon.htm. Sources: Jean Fischer, "Genealogy of the Cahoon Family"; Ida M. Cahoon, History of the Cahoon Family, p. 21; Jeff Sigsworth, Elyria, Ohio.

CAHOON, Wilber Esq., d Sept 25, 1826, 53y 9m; ***Priscilla***, wife, d May 2, 1855, 82y; ***Huldah***, dau, d July 16, 1826, 16y 3m.; ***Leonard***, d. May 3, 1890, 75y; ***Mary TITUS***, wife, d Sept 26, 1906, 88y; ***Susan CAHOON JAMESON***, Dec 24, 1850-Aug 13, 1931; ***Chas.***, 1849-1850; ***Jesse S. Esq.***, d Feb 28, 1836, 17y 10m. Avon Mounds (Center) Cemetery, Avon, OH.

Children of Wilbur Cahoon and Priscilla Sweet:

Susan M. CAHOON, b. c1797, Salisbury, Herkimer Co., NY; d. 16 Dec 1880, Florence Twp., Erie Co., OH; m. 29 Dec 1819 (or 1 Jan 1820) to *Harley MASON* (b. 30 June 1795, d. 28 Feb 1851, Florence). ***Wilbur CAHOON***, b. c1799, Herkimer Co.; d. 9 Sept 1852, California (where he was prospecting during the Gold Rush); m. 6 Apr 1826, Avon Twp., Lorain Co., OH to *Thirza MOORE* (dau. of *Joseph MOORE* (b. 1764, d. 1864) and *Hannah MILLER* (b. 1864, d. 1842), b. c1795); farmer and lumber mill operator. ***Jesse Sweet CAHOON***, b. 1803, Salisbury; d. 28 Feb 1836, Avon Twp. of cholera; m. 30 Nov 1831 to *Masena MOORE* (dau. of *Joseph MOORE* and *Hannah MILLER*; b. 22 July 1810, Willsboro, Essex Co., NY; d. 20 May 1896, Reedsburg, Sauk Co., Wis.). ***Ora B. CAHOON***, b. 11 or 25 May 1804, Salisbury; d. 17 Mar 1881, Avon Twp.; m. 10 Dec 1834 (or 15 Dec 1833), Avon Twp. to *Jane T. JAMESON* (dau. of *Joseph B. JAMESON* and *Thankful SMITH*, b. 1814, d. 29 Aug 1890). ***Nancy Melissa (Melissa) CAHOON***, b. c1805, Salisbury; d. 27 Aug 1851, Amherst Twp., Lorain Co., Ohio; m. 23 Jan 1833 to *John C. STEEL* (son of *John STEEL* and *Polly ST. JOHN*, b. c1807, Delaware Co., NY; first settler on the French Creek in 1817). ***Orra CAHOON***, b. Aug 1807, Salisbury; d. 18 (8) Apr 1875; m. c1835 to *Henry TITUS* (son of *Anson TITUS* (b1785, d. 1865) and *Hannah MOORE* (b. 1788, d. 1867), b. 17 June 1812, d. 20 Dec 1894). ***Huldah CAHOON***, b. Apr 1810, Salisbury; d. 16 July 1826, Avon Twp. ***Leonard CAHOON***, b. 1 Dec 1814, Avon Twp.; d. 3 May 1890, Avon Twp.; m. c1847, *Mary TITUS* (dau. of *Anson TITUS* and *Hannah MOORE*, b. 1818, d. 26 Sep 1906, she was a teacher in Avon Twp.). Jeff Sigsworth, The Cahoon Family of Scotland (Who Came to Cuyahoga County), pp. 30-37 and Ida M. Cahoon, History of the Cahoon Family, pp. 22-23.

Henry TITUS, a truly progressive and well-to-do farmer and fruit grower of Avon township, is a native of Essex county, N.Y., born in 1811, a son of *Anson* and *Hannah (MOORE) TITUS*, natives, respectively, of Connecticut and Massachusetts.

The parents of our subject were married in New York State, and in 1829, with their family, came to Ohio and to Lorain county, making a settlement in the woods of Avon township, where they cleared a farm, erecting a sturdy and comfortable log house. Here the father died in 1865, the mother some time later. Five children were born to this honored pioneer couple, as follows: *Treat*, residing in Avon township; Henry, our subject; ***Mary***, widow of ***Leonard CAHOON***, of Avon township; *Sarah*, widow of *William CURTIS*, of Port Clinton, Ohio; and *Joseph*, married, who is a resident of Iowa.

Henry Titus, the subject of these lines, was reared and educated in Essex county, N.Y., until the age of eighteen, when he came with his parents to Avon township, where he assisted in clearing the home farm. In 1846 he was married in Avon township to ***Miss Orrie CAHOON***, also a native of New York State, daughter of ***Wilbur*** and ***Priscilla (SWEET) CAHOON***, of the same State, who in 1809 came to Ohio and to Avon township, Lorain county, where they cleared a farm and passed the rest of their busy lives. To Mr. and Mrs. Titus were born three children, namely: ***John***, residing on the farm, who is married, and has four children: *Arthur, Clarence, Marietta* and *Edith*; ***Ora***, married, who resides in Wisconsin; and ***Hannah***, wife of *Glover MILLER*, a sketch of whom appears above. Our subject is the owner of as fine a farm as can be found in the township, comprising 140 acres of highly productive land, twenty-eight of which are devoted to the growing of grapes, eighteen at the present writing being covered with fruit-bearing vines. "Henry Titus," Commemorative Biographical

Record of the Counties of Huron and Lorain County, Ohio, p. 1115.

THE CENTENNIAL CELEBRATION OF AVON

September 10, a day made memorable by *Commodore Oliver Hazard PERRY* a century and a year ago, when by his brilliant victory on Lake Erie a peace began between Great Britain and the United States which has continued ever since unbroken, was chosen by the descendants of ***Wilber CAHOON*** to commemorate his memory.

It was just 100 years since this first settler of Avon entered the dense forest with his family, the wagon drawn by an ox team, and founded the first home in Avon township.

The journey had been made from Salisbury, N.Y. As they passed through Buffalo the smoking ruins told the tale of the war of 1812.

Four days before *Francis Scott KEY* wrote the soul-inspiring "Star Spangled Banner," which has but recently been sung by the school children of our great nation. Wilbur Cahoon could sing "Praise God, from whom all blessings flow," as he halted in the wilderness which was to be his home ever after.

In December following there came to the log cabin home a baby boy, whom they named ***Leonard***, he being the first child of Avon. It was the happy thought of his daughter, *Mrs. Susan CAHOON JAMESON*, who lives on the original farm, to gather together the numerous descendants of her grandfather, her other relatives and many friends at Beach Park on Thursday, September 10, 1914, to greet each other, feast upon the good things brought in well filled baskets and hear the story of the beginnings of things in Avon.

About three hundred responded to the invitation. Four grandsons were present - *H.J. CAHOON*, of Elyria; *Levi CAHOON*, of Baraboo, Wis.; *Joseph CAHOON*, of Avon and *Elbert CAHOON*, of Waterville, Ia. Six granddaughters were present. They were *Mrs. Lodema MASON POYER,* of Berlin Heights, O.; *Mrs. Hulda CAHOON NESBET*, of Baraboo, Wis.; *Mrs. Priscilla STIEL SWARTWOOD*, of Vermilion, O.; *Mrs. Hannah TITUS MILLER*, of Avon Lake, O.; *Mrs. Susan Cahoon JAMESON*, of Avon and *Mrs. Hariett CAHOON GIBSON*, of Cleveland.

All of the grandsons and daughters brought their sons and daughters to the number of twenty-five, while longing hearts in California, Wisconsin and Iowa yearned for the pleasure denied them that day.

I have no record of the great-great-grandchildren, but several fond mothers carried those in their arms that day who may hear the story and in another fifty years will hold an anniversary party in honor of their ancestors.

The Cahoons for centuries have been Baptists, so it was eminently fitting that *Rev. Mr. DAN*, a former pastor of the Baptist church in Avon, should act as chaplain of the day. His fervent prayer opened the day's events.

The officers chosen were: Hostess, Mrs. Susan C. Jameson; chairman, *Miss Ida M. CAHOON*; secretary, *Mrs. Daniel TITUS*; treasurer, *Elbert CAHOON*.

The program was as follows:

Music - "The Star-Spangled Banner," *Mrs. Iva CAHOON WALKER* and *Miss Rena TITUS*.

History - *Horace J. CAHOON*

Regrets - Standing in silence in memory of the departed. Greetings to those absent and those who are ill.

Music - "Auld Lang Syne," duet and chorus.

Toast - "The Schoolmasters Who Trained Us for Life's Duties." Responses by *Judge David J. NYE* and *Charles METCALF*.

Music - "Annie Laurie," Miss Rena Titus.

Henry WEST, of Tremont, O. made a few remarks, representing the family of *Thompson WILDER* , an early settler of Avon and near neighbor of Wilber Cahoon.

Music - "Oh, That We Two Were a-Maying," Miss Rena Titus and *Edwin HANAN*.

Others were to give short talks, but the day was coming to a close, many were far from home, and with the tones of "God be with you till we meet again" sounding in our ears the good-byes were spoken.

Not long after Mr. Cahoon came to Avon, a boy of 16? *(unclear on copy)*, who had walked from New York to grow up with the west came to find shelter in the log cabin and remained several months. This boy became the most famous surgeon in Northern Ohio. As the years passed on *Dr. Theodatus GARLICK*, when very venerable, applied this wish to the Cahoon family who had made his boyhood comfortable and happy, and in closing we will make it ours:

"When any of their descendants leave this wicked world, may their eyes be closed by the soft fingers of their great-grandchildren." I.M.C. *(assumed Ida M. Cahoon)*
Newspaper article, undetermined source, Cahoon Collection, Rose Hill Museum, Bay Village, OH.

Children of Joseph Cahoon and Lydia Kenyon:

Samuel(CAHOON) and his brother ***Amos*** first settled in Ridgeville Twp., in 1813. Samuel and ***Lucinda***, his attractive and intelligent wife, had at least five children. The Cahoons lived on a fine farm in Ridgeville Twp., where they owned a brick Italianate home (built about the 1840's). Lucinda's father, *John BARNUM*, was a pioneer settler of Rockport Twp. (now Fairview Park), Cuyahoga Co., and a relative of showman *Phineas T. BARNUM*. "Lorain County Researcher," Winter 1996, p. 6 and Ida M. Cahoon, History of the Cahoon Family, p. 27.

Samuel CAHOON to ***Lucinda BARNUM***. I Do hereby certify that the bond of Marriage was solemnized between Samuel Cahoon and Lucinda Barnum both of Ridgeville Township on the 27th day of April last by me. Ichabod Terrill, Justice of the Peace, June 2nd A.D. 1818. Marriage Record, Cuyahoga County, OH, vol. 1, p. 95.

Samuel CAHOON, b. 1787, m. ***Lucinda BARNUM***. *Issue:*

1. ***John Barnum CAHOON***, b. 4 Oct 1820, Ridgeville Twp., Ohio; d. 10 June 1898, Ridgeville Twp.; m.1 *Betsy Ann LYNES (LINES)* (b. 21 (25) Sept 1821, Harpersfield, Delaware Co., NY; d. 27 Sept 1871; dau. of *Sturgis*

LYNES and *Betsy LINDSLEY* or *LINDSAY*, he being an early surveyor of the Connecticut Western Reserve sent by General Moses Cleveland); m.2 *Sarah RULES or KALES* (b. c1825). 2. ***Daniel K. CAHOON***, b. Oct 1822 (1831), Ridgeville Twp.; d. 1842. 3. ***Cornelia CAHOON***, b. 1825, Ridgeville Twp.; d. 1 Dec 1868; m. 18 July 1857 to *Frank Egbert SHELDON (went by Egbert)*. 4. ***James M. CAHOON***, b. 3 Mar 1826, Ridgeville Twp.; d. 10 June 1898 (1908), Wakeman, Ohio; bur. Wakeman Cemetery; m. *Cynthia PARISH* (b. Mar 1823 (26), New York; d. 1916, dau. of *John PARISH*); lived in Wisconsin, returned to Ridgeville Twp., Ohio (1857-63) then purchasing a 160 acre farm near Wakeman, Ohio. 5. ***Sidney H. CAHOON***, b. 1829/30; d. 16 Apr 1836 Ridgeville Twp., at the age of six. Jeff Sigsworth, The Cahoon Family of Scotland (Who Came to Cuyahoga County), pp. 8, 9; and Orval O. Calhoun, Our Calhoon Family, vol. II, p. 147.

Before coming to Ohio, ***Samuel CAHOON*** attended Yale University; he engaged in ship building in Cleveland for a short time before moving to the Lorain County area. Samuel and his brother ***Amos*** settled in Ridgeville Twp. in 1813. During the War of 1812, Samuel was a mail courier for *General William H. HARRISON'S* army; he also helped to organize the militia at the blockhouse in Columbia Twp., and was made a Captain. ***Lucinda*** was one of the first members of the First Presbyterian Church of Ridgeville Twp. (organized in Dec 1822); this church later became the First Congregational United Church of Christ.

Samuel and Lucinda owned a farm on the middle ridge (Center Ridge Rd.) at the western side of Ridgeville Township. Their brick Italianate-style home (built in about the late 1840's) was once awarded a blue ribbon at the Lorain County Fair. The home is still standing, housing a scaffolding business and served as the home of the North Ridgeville Historical Society from 1977-1986. On 19 Dec 1828, for a consideration of $10, Samuel donated the land on Center Ridge Rd. for Ridgeville Twp.'s District No. 3 ("West End") school. Sigsworth, p. 8.

Samuel CAHOON, Males 26-45 yrs.: 1, Female 0-10 yrs.: 1, 26-45 yrs.: 1. 1820 FC OH CY Ridgeville Twp., p. 55.

CAHOON, Samuel C., Males 0-5 yrs.: 2, 5-10 yrs.: 2, 40-50 yrs.: 1; Females 5-10 yrs.: 1, 40-50 yrs.: 1. 1830 FC OH Lorain Co., Ridgeville Twp., p. 2, last line.

Mr. Samuel CAHOON, one of the resident Pioneers of Ridgeville, died last Monday. Elyria Independent Democrat, Elyria, OH, April 1, 1863, p. 3, col. 1.

The following is a record for the past year...two deaths, ***Lucinda BARNUM***, wife of ***Samuel CAHOON***, and ***Eugene CAHOON***, son of ***William O. CAHOON***. "Eleventh Cahoon Celebration," Weekly Herald, Sept 3, 1870.

Samuel C. CAHOON, d. Mar 29, 1863, 75 y.; ***John B.***, son *Sam., & Lucinda,* Oct 4, 1820 - June 16, 1898; ***Betsey Ann***, wife, Sept 25, 1821 - Sept 27, 1871; ***Sidney H.***, d. Apr 16, 1836, 6 y.; ***Daniel K.***, d. Aug 27, 1842, 10 or 19 y. 10 m.; ***Ellen***, grddau. S & L. Ridgeville Center Cemetery, Ridgeville Twp., OH

Amos CAHOON, see *Martha CAHOON WINSOR (OP 4: 6)*.

Soon after the marriage of ***George SEXTON*** and ***Miss Mary CAHOON***, at Vergennes, Vt., in the year 1810, they moved into Ohio, stopping at *Judge KINGSBURY'S*, Newburgh, Cuyahoga county, Ohio, where they remained until March 12, 1812; then, with family, Mr. G. Sexton moved into the west part of Ridgeville, Lorain county, Ohio on Center Ridge, lot thirty-nine. The location is now occupied by *John CAHOON*. He remained there three years and then sold to *Samuel CAHOON*, and moved farther west on the same road. Mr. Sexton was originally from Bennington county, VT. He resided in Ridgeville until his decease, November 7, 1829, aged forty-two years, leaving a widow and seven children, five of whom are since dead. Mrs. Mary Cahoon *(Sexton)* died September 17, 1849.

The two children living are ***Amos C. SEXTON***, who is a farmer in Orange, Cuyahoga county, Ohio; the other, ***C. Lester SEXTON***, of whom this sketch is written, following the same calling as his brother, resides in Ridgeville, Lorain county, Ohio. He was born at Newburgh, as above, on April 20, 1810.

Mr. C. Lester Sexton and *Frances C. PORTER* were married at Ridgeville, 5 Dec 1833. Soon after they removed to Ashland, Ashland county, Ohio. Returning to Ridgeville on the 9th of March, 1838, they commenced in the unbroken woods to make for themselves and children a home.

In Ridgeville they have since lived, with the exception of three years in Elyria, where Mr. Sexton engaged in brick making. Mr. Sexton is the father of five children. Mr. Sexton has filled, and now holds the office of township trustee. Still vigorous, at a ripe old age, loved and respected by his neighbors, he remains one of the makers of Ridgeville.

Jonathan A. SEXTON, a brother of George, arrived in town in 1812, and married here and settled. His wife was *Betsey SHELLHOUSE*. He lived on lot thirty-nine for several years and then moved to Carlisle, and later to Wisconsin, where he died. Soon after, another brother, *James SEXTON*, came into the township with his family, and settled on the lot on which his brother George last lived. He sold out in 1834, and eventually moved to Wisconsin and died there. His widow, who was a daughter of *Martin SHELLHOUSE*, is now (January, 1879,) living in St. Joseph, Mo., at the age of eighty-seven.

Soon after the arrival at Elyria, of *Judge ELY'S* first wife, Mr. Sexton's mother, and another lady, started on foot through the woods, to make a friendly call on the new-comer. The visit being made, the ladies commenced their journey home. Losing their way, the night coming on, they were forced to spend the night under a partially fallen tree. The next morning brought them kind neighbors, who had passed the night in vain in search of them. Such was "calling" in Lorain county pioneer life. History of Lorain County, Ohio, Ridgeville, pp. 160, 167-168.

Mary and ***George SEXTON*** came to Ridgeville Twp., by way of Newburgh, Cuyahoga Co., in the spring of 1812, they had a farm on Center Ridge Road, and had at least eight children. After George's death, Mary married ***Ebenezer GRIFFITH*** of Elyria, as his second wife, his first wife had died recently. In 1830, Ebenezer and *Reuben NICHOLS* had built the "Mansion House" hotel in downtown Elyria, the finest such establishment in the area (until the *BEEBE House* was built in 1846). "Lorain County Researcher," Winter 1996, p. 6 and Jeff Sigsworth, The Cahoon Family of Scotland (Who Came to Cuyahoga County), p. 8.

Children of Mary Cahoon and George Sexton: 1. ***Cyrus Lester "Lester" SEXTON***, b. 20 Apr 1810, Newburgh Twp., Cuyahoga Co., OH; m. 5 Dec 1833, Ridgeville Twp. to *Frances C. PORTER* (b. 1811; d. 27 Nov 1880, Ridgeville Twp.; dau. of *Ebenezer PORTER* (1775-1867) of Mass. and Ridgeville Twp.). 2. ***Amos C. SEXTON***, b. 1812 (22); m. 1837 (47), Lorain Co. to *Maria(h) EARL (LORD)* (b. 1829/30); lived in Ridgeville Twp. and Orange Twp., Cuyahoga Co. 3. ***Aaron SEXTON***, b. 1814, Ridgeville Twp.; d. 6 Oct 1839; m. 8 Oct 1837, *Mariah REYNOLDS* (she remarried 18 Aug 1842, Elyria to *Samuel COMSTOCK*). 4. ***Lydia K. SEXTON***, b. c1816; d. 1 Apr 1831. 5. ***Mary SEXTON***, b. c1818; m. *William P. HERRON*. 6. ***George J. SEXTON***, b. 1821; d. possibly of cholera 26 Oct 1839 (29), aged 18 yrs. 7. ***Abigail "Abby" SEXTON***, b. c1823; m. 14 Feb 1848, Elyria, Lorain Co. to *George BEEBE*. 8. ***Nancy SEXTON***, b. c1825; d. young. Sigsworth, p. 18.

We have heard many very pleasant things of ***Aunt Mary*** from those who knew her. Ida M. Cahoon, History of the Cahoon Family, p. 28.

GRIFFITH Mary, wife ***Ebenezer***, d Sept 17, 1849, 57y 10m 24d. Ridgeville Center Cemetery, Ridgeville Township, Lorain County, OH. Genealogical Workshops of the Lorain County Historical Society, Cemetery Inscriptions of Lorain County, Ohio 1980, Ridgeville Center Cemetery, p. 388.

SEXTON E. Porter, Apr 15, 1841-May 3, 1897, CO E 42 OVI; ***George***, Jan 31, 1787-Nov 7, 1829, 41y; ***George***, son *Geo & Mary*, d Oct 26, 1839, 18y; ***Lydia K.***, dau Geo & Mary, d Apr 1, 1831, 14y. Ridgeville Center Cemetery, Ridgeville Township, Lorain County, OH. Genealogical Workshops of the Lorain County Historical Society, Cemetery Inscriptions of Lorain County, Ohio 1980, Ridgeville Center Cemetery, p. 388.

GRIFFITH: Ebenezer, d. Dec 26, 1886, 73y War 1812?; ***Lillis***, wife, d. Nov 20, 1837, 15y?; ***Jerome***, their son, d. Sept 31, 1838, 15y 10m 20d. Ridgelawn Cemetery, Elyria, Lorain Co., OH. Genealogical Workshops of the Lorain County Historical Society, Ridgelawn Cemetery, p. 262.

Joel Butler CAHOON, see Lot 63.

In July 1814, the first marriage occurred in the town. ***Leverett JOHNSON*** first saw the fair ***Abigail CAHOON*** as she gathered nuts, when he came into the "forest primeval." A mutual feeling of tenderest affection was experienced, which culminated in the happiest manner. The wedding gown was made from six yards of pink cambric. As no minister was near, *Justice REED*, from Black River, came to officiate *(first wedding in Dover)*. Her home ever after was a mile west of Dover Center, where free-hearted hospitality reigned. Her gentleness and kindness made her lovable. Memorial to the Pioneer Women of the Western Reserve, p. 60. *It is interesting to note that Abigail's brother, Amos, married one month earlier in Newburgh before bringing his bride to Dover.*

Mrs. (Abigail or Abbie) JOHNSON, of Dover, widow of the ***Hon. Leveritt JOHNSON*** *(sp.)*, formerly Representative in the Ohio Legislature from Cuyahoga county. Mr. Johnson died in 1856 - his widow, daughter of ***Joseph*** and ***Lydia CAHOON***, numbers nearly three score and ten years...Her narration of pioneer life, especially in the fact that when at the age of fourteen she met with young Johnson of sixteen, who had come the day after her own arrival *(he arrived in the afternoon of the same day with his sister's family)* to enliven the solitude of the wilderness as her father's neighbor and then thought "he was the boy for her." So it proved and the "love at first sight" made Hymen's torch brighter and brighter through a long and useful wedded life. "Sixth Cahoon Celebration," Reunion Notebook, Newspaper article, 1865.

Leverett JOHNSON...began clearing land...on lot 58...and lived with the Porters on the weekend...During the week he lived alone in the wilderness...Johnson admitted it was sometimes darned lonesome. The first season, his home was a bark roof set against an old log of great size. He was not disturbed by the Indians, who were friendly and sometimes helped him in his work, and he kept the wild beasts away by a fire at night...He was carving a home in the forest and battling for her as men have endured, not always in the same way, but for the love of a woman. In 1814 he married ***Abigail CAHOON*** and took her to the new log house which he built that year. Johnson became prominent in the new community. He was justice of the peace from 1827 to 1833 and served five terms in the Legislature of the State of Ohio. He died in 1856 in his sixty-second year. He was the first director of the Dover Academy. As a legislator he had a varied experience. He began December 4, 1837, when *Governor Joseph VANCE* was in office and *Peter HITCHCOCK* and *Reuben WOOD* were on the Supreme bench. At this session of the Legislature imprisonment for debt was abolished. The next session was held December 3, 1838. *Wilson SHANNON* was governor. Mr. Johnson served in 1840 when *Thomas CORWIN* was governor and *John BROUGH* was auditor of the state. The legislative records of this session recite the fact that in receiving notice of his election, Governor Corwin made a felicitous speech. In the forty-seventh General Assembly, which convened December 4, 1848, Mr. Johnson was an influential member of the House. *Seabury FORD* was governor. In the Senate there was turmoil over the canvass of the vote and there were stormy scenes in both houses. At this time the vote for state officers was canvassed by the two branches of the General Assembly. Two members of the Free Soil party were elected to the Legislature and the whigs and democrats were evenly divided on joint ballot and the election of the United States senator was coming up. The vote in the organization of the House and Senate was disturbed by a contention over the seating of two men from Hamilton County. The Senate after much discussion and many ballots were taken finally perfected an organization but the House organization was more difficult. Upon a call, forty-two members responded and thirty-two failed to respond, less than a constitutional quorum responding as present. These forty-two and thirty-two factions each attempted an organization, *Benjamin F. LEITER* presiding over the forty-two and *A. T. HOLCOMB* over the thirty-two. These two rival Houses did not come together until January 3, 1849. The vote for speaker at that time on the first and second ballots stood Leverett Johnson, thirty-four, *John G. BRESLIN*, thirty-four, scattering two. On the third ballot Mr. Breslin was elected, receiving thirty-seven to Mr. Johnson's thirty-three. The Dover man was not elected speaker but he had received a high compliment in a stormy period. Mr. Johnson again served in the fifty-second Assembly, when *Salmon P. CHASE* was governor, who was elected by a small majority over *Henry B. PAYNE* of Cleveland. This session began in 1856. Mr. Johnson died while serving on this, his fifth term in the House. William R. Coates, A History of Cuyahoga County and the City of Cleveland, Dover, vol. 1, pp. 142-143.

Leveritt JOHNSON to ***Abey CAHOON***. Married 15th day of August 1814. State of Ohio, Cuyahoga County. This is to certify that I solemnized the marriage between Leverit Johnson and Abey Cahoon, on the 15th Inst. according to Law on testimony there of I have... Set my hand and Seal to the 20th Day of August 1814. John S. Reede - Justice Peace. Marriage Record, Cuyahoga County, OH, vol. 1, p. 35.

Children of Abigail CAHOON and Leverett JOHNSON: 1. ***Leverett Hubbard "Hubbard" JOHNSON***, b. c1816, m. *Marietta REED* 2. ***Dennis P. JOHNSON***, b. c1818, m. *Caroline CLEMENS*. 3. ***Asahel JOHNSON***, b. c1820, m. *Marie GILLETT*. 4. ***Clayton JOHNSON***, b. c1822, m. *Jane DICKENSON*. 5. ***Mary JOHNSON***, b. 1824, m. *Mr. ROSENCRANS*. 6. ***Rebecca JOHNSON***, b. c1826, m. *James SANFORD*. 7. ***Nancy JOHNSON***, b. c1828, never married. 8. ***Abigail JOHNSON***, b. c1831, m. *Charles GOSS*. 9. ***Pauline JOHNSON***, b. 1834, never married. All children b. Dover Twp. Jeff Sigsworth, The Cahoon Family of Scotland (Who Came to Cuyahoga County), pp. 21-22.

The State of Ohio, Cuyahoga County, ss. I hereby certify that on the 14th day of Nov A.D. 1852 I duly solemnized the Marriage Contract between the said ***Leverett H. JOHNSON*** and ***Marietta REED***. S.H. Waldo Marriage Record, Cuyahoga County, OH, vol. 5, p. 265.

The State of Ohio, Cuyahoga County, ss. I hereby certify, that on the 28th day of April A.D. 1842, I duly solemnized the Marriage Contract between the said ***Denise P. JOHNSON*** and ***Caroline M. CLEMONS***. Solomon Stevens Marriage Record, Cuyahoga County, OH, vol. 4, p. 144.

The State of Ohio, Cuyahoga County, ss. I hereby certify that on the 1st day of January A.D. 1854 I duly solemnized the Marriage Contract between the said ***Clayton JOHNSON*** and ***Jane E. DICKINSON***. A. Blakly V.D.M. Marriage Record, Cuyahoga County, OH, vol. 5, p. 449.

J. ROSENKRANS to ***Mary JOHNSON***. The said parties within named were joined in marriage March 21 by Rev. Joseph H. Payne, Dover, Cuyahoga Co. Marriage Record, Cuyahoga County, OH, vol. 3, p. 281. *(Marriage recorded in 1837.)*

The State of Ohio, Cuyahoga County, ss. I hereby certify that on the 13th day of April A. D. 1841, I duly solemnized the Marriage Contract between the said ***James H. SANFORD*** and ***Rebecca JOHNSON***. H.L Parish V.D.M Marriage Record, Cuyahoga County, OH, vol. 4, p. 97.

The State of Ohio, Cuyahoga County, ss. I hereby certify, that on the 17th day of May A.D. 1849, I duly solemnized the contract between the said ***Charles P. GOSS*** and ***Abigail P. JOHNSON***. Dover. S. W. Waldo Min. Gospel Marriage Record, Cuyahoga County, OH, vol. 4, p. 548.

Leverett JOHNSON, 56, Farmer, b. Conn.; ***Abigail***, 54, b. New Jersey; ***Hubbard***, 22, Farmer, b. Ohio; ***Clayton***, 20, Farmer, b. Ohio; ***Palelina***, 18, b. Ohio, attending school. 1850 FC OH CYDO, p. 222B, lines, 33-37. Living next-door *Asel JOHNSON*, 28, Farmer, b. Ohio; *Elisabeth*, 22, b. Ohio; *Celia*, 2, b. Ohio; *Asa M.*, 9/12, b. Ohio. Lines 38-41.

Mrs. Leverett JOHNSON. - One of the family of the first settlers of Dover, whose life has been made checkered by the vicissitudes of time. May she live to meet her friends on many more occasions of this kind, and may her remaining days be as calm and peaceful as the summer's eve. Toast by *C. FRENCH, Esq.* at the 53rd Anniversary of the Cahoon Settlement of Dover, 1863. Undetermined newspaper article, Cahoon Collection, Rose Hill Museum.

Death of a Pioneer Woman.

Rapidly the first settlers of Northern Ohio are being removed by death, and soon the last of the fathers and the mothers who, more than half a century ago, broke up the dense wilderness of the lake coast, and amid almost incredible privations and hardships established pleasant homes for their children and children's children, will "rest from their labors." It is well to ever hold in remembrances their enterprise, endurance, fortitude, and lives of many virtues and great usefulness.

Mrs. Abigail CAHOON JOHNSON, died at her late residence in Dover, May 3, 1869, aged 73 years. She was born in Salisbury, Herkimer county, New York, and emigrated with her father, ***Joseph CAHOON***, to Ohio in October, 1810. She was married to the late ***Hon. Leverett JOHNSON***, of Dover, in July 1814, the first marriage in that township. The deceased was the oldest inhabitant of the place, having been a resident of Dover for nearly fifty-nine years. Her presence at the Cahoon festivals in commemoration of the first settlement of Dover, will no longer bring joy to numerous descendants, relatives, and friends.

Mrs. Johnson became a member of the Congregational Church thirty years ago, and was an exemplary and consistent christian. In all the endearing relations of life she exemplified the highest christian character, and her "adorning was that of a meek and quiet spirit." Newspaper article, undetermined source, Cahoon Collection, Rose Hill Museum, Bay Village, OH.

JOHNSON, Abigail, wife of Leverett Johnson, Died May 3, 1869 aged 73 years. ***Leverett JOHNSON***, Died April 19, 1856, aged 6_ *(Unable to decipher age)* yrs. 10 m.; ***Nancy***

J., daughter of L. & A. Johnson, Died Feb. 19, 1849, aged 30 years; ***Pauline JOHNSON*** 1832-1908. Evergreen Cemetery, Westlake, OH, read by Catherine Burke Flament.

Jacob HEATH to ***Rebecca CAHOON*** Married Nov 16, 1823, State of Ohio---Cuyahoga County. I hereby certify that on the sixteenth day of November I Joined in the holy state of matrimony Jacob Heath and Rebecca Cahoon of Lawful age given under my hand and seal, twenty first day of November 1823. *Amos CAHOON,* Justice Peace Marriage Record, Cuyahoga County, OH, vol. 2, p. 10.

Rebecca CAHOON was born in Salisbury, NY in 1798-1859. She was 12 years young when she came with her family to Dover Township. She married ***Jacob HEATH*** and had a daughter, ***Silicia*** and a son. Unfortunately, her marriage did not last, and she was divorced. After the death of her sister, ***Mary***, she married ***Ebenezer GRIFFITH*** and lived in Newburg, OH. Silicia, a great favorite of all who knew her, married *James WRIGHT* of Cleveland. Their son, ***Walter WRIGHT***, became the Cahoon lawyer and processed the Cahoon Will. "Those Who Came," Cahoon family brochure, Rose Hill Museum, 2003.

Children of Rebecca CAHOON and Jacob HEATH: 1. ***Silicia HEATH,*** b. c1825, Cleveland; d. pre Aug 1876; m. c1848 to *James WRIGHT* of Cleveland. They had at least seven children, *(the third child, Amos Frank WRIGHT, would marry Henrietta WINSOR, great-granddaughter of Joseph Cahoon and Lydia Kenyon, granddaughter of Amos Cahoon, see OP 4:4).* 2. ***Franklin HEATH,*** b. c1830, Cleveland. Jeff Sigsworth, The Cahoon Family of Scotland (Who Came to Cuyahoga County), p. 22 and Cahoon Reunion Celebration newspaper article, August, 1876.

The State of Ohio, Cuyahoga County, ss. I hereby certify that on the 4th day of November A.D. 1845, I duly solemnized the Marriage Contract between the said ***James WRIGHT*** and ***Silacia COOHOWN*** *(sp.)*. J.W. Walden Minister Marriage Record, Cuyahoga County, OH, vol. 4, p. 336.

The State of Ohio, Cuyahoga County, ss., I hereby certify, that on the 14th day of November A.D. 1850, I duly solemnized the Marriage Contract between the said ***Ebenezer GRIFFITH*** and ***Rebecca (CAHOON) HEATH***. S.W. Adams. Marriage Record, Cuyahoga County, OH, vol. 5, p. 109.

Daniel Kenyon CAHOON was just a lad when he came to Dover. When a young man (about 1820), he was a clerk in the store of *Nathan PERRY (Jr.)* in downtown Cleveland, Ohio, the largest one in the city. He later worked with his brother ***Joel***, engaging in contracting for public work. He was unmarried, so made his home with his brother Joel, who reciprocated his unusual affection. The letters passing between them make it evident that he was a delightful gentleman, acquainted with business life and alert to the general topics of the time. While on a business trip to Cincinnati he was taken suddenly ill, and passed away before his relatives could reach him, but attended by his Masonic brethren, was laid to rest in Spring Grove Cemetery, Cincinnati. Ida M. Cahoon, History of the Cahoon Family, p. 27 and "Lorain County Researcher," Winter 1996, p. 6.

Benjamin CAHOON was born in Montgomery county, New York, July 14, 1805 and came to Dover with his parents in 1810. In 1835 he married ***Emeline HACKET***, and settled in Elyria, where he remained until his death, September 29th, 1872. He had been in very feeble health for several years, which prevented him from participating in the pleasures of the family meeting. "Cahoon Pioneer Celebration," Reunion Notebook, Newspaper article, 1873.

I certify that by virtue of a license from the Clerk of the Court of Common laws for Cuyahoga County, ***Benjamin CAHOON*** & ***Emaline HACKETT*** were in the 1st of Dec 1835 by me legally joined in marriage. June 12, 1836. Wm. Burton, Just. Peace. Marriage Record, Cuyahoga County, OH, vol. 3, p. 193.

Benjamin Reynolds CAHOON and his wife, ***Emeline "Emma" HACKETT***, had at least eight children. They lived in Cincinnati and Elyria, Ohio, where Benjamin was a stone cutter. In Elyria, his work could be seen in many fine stone buildings in the downtown business area. "Lorain County Researcher," Winter 1996, p. 6.

Benjamin Reynolds (CAHOON), made a journey to New Orleans in 1831, returning to Cincinnati, where he worked at his trade as stone cutter, for a time, before settling in Elyria, O., his permanent home. He married ***Miss Emeline HACKETT***, a most excellent wife and model mother...Uncle Benjamin was very fond of flowers, fruits and all the beautiful objects he could have about him and was excellent company among his many friends. Ida M. Cahoon, History of the Cahoon Family, pp. 32-33.

Children of Benjamin Reynolds CAHOON and Emeline HACKETT: 1. ***Eliza J. CAHOON,*** b. c1834, Cincinnati; d. 1843. 2. ***Helen CAHOON,*** b. 24 Dec 1836; d. 19 July 1924; m.1 *W.M. CLARK*, m.2 *Aaron H. BULLOCK (BULLOCH)* (b. 19 Jan 1825; d. 23 Oct 1909, son of *Aaron* and *Rebecca BULLOCK*); lived in Elyria. 3. ***Leverett J. CAHOON,*** b. c 1838, d. 1843. 4. ***Minerva CAHOON,*** b. 1 Mar 1838; d. 1 Dec 1915, Cuyahoga Co.; m. 17 Sept 1863, Lorain Co. to *Reuben HOLLENBACH (HOLLENBECK);* lived in Cleveland. 5. ***Silicia W. CAHOON,*** b. c1841, Elyria; d. 1843. 6. ***Jeanette Rebecca CAHOON,*** b. 26 Jan 1842; d. 1902 (12), Elyria. 7. ***Everett Benjamin CAHOON,*** b. 9 July 1847, Elyria; d. 6 Sept 1909, Akron; m. *Alice STEWART;* lived in Akron, Ohio; inventor. 8. ***Abigail Frances CAHOON,*** b. 7 Aug 1852, Elyria; m. *Dr. Fred W. SCHEERER,* Union Soldier; lived in Norwalk, Huron Co. Jeff Sigsworth, The Cahoon Family of Scotland (Who Came to Cuyahoga County),

p. 23 and notes at Rose Hill Museum, Cahoon Collection.

CAHOON, Benjamin, 65, Stone Mason, value of real estate $2500, personal estate $500, b. Vermont; ***Emeline***, 62, b. New York; ***Annette***, 29, Sewing, b. Ohio; ***Everette***, 22, Candy Maker, b. Ohio; ***Abbie***, 18, no occupation, b. Ohio. 1870 FC OH Lorain Co., Elyria Village, p. 486A., lines 16-20.

Died.-- ***Mr. Benjamin CAHOON***, an old resident of Elyria, and for some years an invalid, died at his home on East Avenue, on the 24th, aged 68 years. Newspaper article, undetermined source, Cahoon Collection, Rose Hill Museum, Bay Village, OH.

William O. CAHOON, was born in the State of New York and was only two years of age when his parents settled in Dover Township at Cuyahoga County in 1810. He lived there until he was about seventeen year of age, then went to the southern part of the state for a year or so, and on returning to the North located at Elyria in 1835, and made his home in that city until his death. He passed away in Elyria in 1878. In politics he was a republican and a free soiler, and in religion a Methodist. His wife died in Elyria in 1888. There were six children who lived to grow up, five sons and one daughter. The only one now living is ***Charles A. CAHOON***, deputy sheriff of Lorain County and a resident of Elyria. The oldest son, ***E.A. CAHOON***, was a member of Battery E., First Ohio Artillery, and served two and a half years with that command until his honorable discharge.

William E. CAHOON, another son, was for many years actively identified with merchandising and with public affairs in Elyria, was a veteran of the Civil war, and the memory which he left behind him was that of a thoroughly capable citizen, honest and true and steadfast in any position to which duty called him, and the type of man who makes any community the better for his presence. History of Lorain County, 1879, p. 710.

William Ovington Cahoon and his first wife, ***Nancy D. ELDRED***, had at least three children. After her death he married her sister, ***Melissa ELDRED***, sometimes recorded as ***Margaret***, they lived in Elyria and had at least six children. Their father was *Judge Moses ELDRED*, a pioneer of Dover Twp. (1811) and Ridgeville Twp. (1813). William was a stone mason or cutter, working with his brother ***Benjamin R. Cahoon***; they operated a stone quarry on the east branch of the Black River, selling the stone used for sidewalks in Elyria. "Lorain County Researcher," Winter 1996, p. 6.

Parents of Nancy D. Eldred and Melissa Eldred:

Moses ELDRED came from Rome, New York to Cuyahoga county, Ohio, settling on a farm west of Rocky River. He served in the War of 1812, following which he settled on what was known as the Shore Road, but later, finding that this was not to be the main thoroughfare, moved to a location on the Center Ridge Road, 2 1/2 miles east of Elyria, in Lorain County. There he built a log tavern and later a frame house, which, substantially built of timbers, is still standing as a landmark of pioneer times. He continued to conduct the tavern until his death, at the age of eighty-three years, made his home successively with his several children. A Standard History of Lorain County, Ed. G. Frederick Wright, p. 816, article on Dewitt Eldred, his grandson.

Moses ELDRED came into the township in December, 1813. He was a native of Massachusetts, whence he removed to Dover, Cuyahoga county, in March, 1811. His location in Ridgeville was on center ridge, lot forty-six. At the time of his settlement there was not a house west of him nearer than Florence, Erie county. He lived in Ridgeville until 1836, and then again took up his residence in Cuyahoga county, in Bedford, and later in Carlisle, where he died in June, 1857. Mrs. Eldred died in 1832. They had a family of ten children, six of whom are living. *Clark, Noah* and ***Melissa (Mrs. Wm. O. CAHOON)*** live in Elyria township, and *Francis* in Ridgeville. *Aaron* lives in Medina county, Ohio and *Jarvis* in Michigan.

Mr. Eldred served in the War of 1812, and was wounded in a skirmish with the Indians on the peninsula, near Sandusky, in September, 1812. *Joshua R. GIDDINGS*, then a young man, was in the same engagement, and carried Mr. E. from the field of battle. He was the first postmaster of Ridgeville, and at a subsequent period was associate judge for Lorain county. History of Lorain County, Ohio, p. 161.

CAHOON, William O., 68, Stone Mason, b. New York; ***Melissa***, 49, b. Ohio; ***Avine Stacia***, 33, b. Ohio; ***Ervin W.***, 24, Tinner, b. Ohio; ***Burton L.***, 21, Stone Mason, b. Ohio; ***Wesley***, 18, b. Ohio; ***Charles***, 9, b. Ohio; ***Lucy***, 30, b. Ohio. 1870 FC OH Lorain Co., Elyria Twp., p. 484B, lines 31-38.

Children of William O. CAHOON and Nancy D. ELDRED:
1. ***William E. CAHOON***, b. c1832, Elyria; d. 1 Nov 1834, Elyria. 2. ***Nancy Anastasia CAHOON***, b. 1834, Elyria; d. 29 Oct 1905; never married; res. Elyria. 3. ***Marquis Lafayette CAHOON***, b. c1836, Elyria; d. young.

Children of William O. CAHOON and Melissa ELDRED:
4. ***Melissa A. CAHOON***, b. c1841, Elyria; died in infancy, Elyria. 5. ***Amos Eugene (Eugene) CAHOON***, b. c1843, Elyria; d. 8 Mar 1870, Elyria; m. 3 Oct 1864, Amherst Twp., Lorain Co. to *Lucia (Lucy) NYE;* Battery E., 1st Ohio Artillery Union Army; res. Elyria. 6. ***William Erwin (Erwin) CAHOON***, b. 15 May 1846, Elyria; d. 18 Mar 1904, Elyria; m. 30 July 1874, Brooklyn, Cuyahoga Co. to *Mrs. Maria BUSH TAYLOR* (b. 1848, Fremont, Ohio; d. 21 Dec 1923, Elyria; dau. of *Rev. Eurotus H. BUSH* and *Mary GOODSELL*, Rochester, NY and Cleveland, OH); res. Elyria; Co. K of the 135th O.V.I. Union Army; tinner, Lorain County Recorder, Elyria Twp. assessor and title abstractor. 7. ***Burton L. CAHOON***, b. 1850/01, Elyria; m. 1871 to *Elizabeth KLEIN (CLINE)* (b. c1852); res. Elyria; quarryman. 8. ***Wesley CAHOON***, b. c1853, Elyria; res. Dakota Territory (N. Dakota); inventor. 9. ***Charles A. CAHOON***, b. Nov 1862, Elyria; d. after 1916, Elyria; m. 29 June 1892, *Honora V. (Nora) MEYERS* (b. Jan 1862, NY); res. Elyria; Lorain County Sheriff's deputy. Jeff Sigsworth, The Cahoon Family of Scotland (Who Came to Cuyahoga County), pp. 24-25.

W.E. CAHOON, is a native of the city of Elyria, where he resides, and was born May 15, 1846, a son of ***William O.*** and ***Melissa (ELDRED) CAHOON***...W.E. at the age of seventeen enlisted in Company K, One Hundred and Thirty-fifth O.V.I., one hundred days of service, which regiment was sent to Virginia, Maryland, Harper's Ferry, Martinsburg and Maryland

Heights, participating in the fight at *John BROWN'S* Schoolhouse. On his return home Mr. Cahoon learned the trade of a tinner, which he followed about twelve years, but accidentally losing his right arm while firing off a cannon on Decoration Day, 1874, he closed up his business in 1878. In 1875 he was elected assessor of Elyria township, filling the office four consecutive years; in 1882 he was elected county recorder, serving till January 1, 1892, since when he has been abstracter of titles.

Mr. Cahoon was married, July 30, 1874, to ***Mrs. M. P. (BUSH) TYLER***, who was born in Fremont, Ohio, daughter of *Rev. Enrotus H.* and *Mary (GOODSELL) BUSH*, both of whom were born in Rochester, N.Y. Politically our subject is a staunch Republican, and socially he is a member of the G.A.R. and Royal Arcanum. "W.E. Cahoon," Commemorative Biographical Record of the Counties of Huron and Lorain County, Ohio, p. 1137.

Mr. WILLIAMS remarked that he was pleased that the duty was given him to speak of his loved friend, ***William O. Cahoon***, with whose daily life he had long been acquainted. He knew him as a neighbor, a friend, a citizen of worth to the town which he had called home for nearly a century, and as a Christian gentleman. His sudden death, falling, though an old man, it seemed in the glory of manhood, was a shock he was tardy to comprehend. Today, with many who cherished the departed one, he came to the home of his babyhood, realized its beauties and compared them with the character of the man, so gentle, so kind to all he chanced to meet, and so thoroughly upright! As he looked up he saw a towering hickory straight and strong, and he failed to find another species of tree about him, and wondered as he sat beneath their shade, "Are the Cahoons all hickories? Are they all hard wood, useful in every station of life in which you find them?" Such was the character of William O. Cahoon…Most of his active life was spent in Elyria, and many of the buildings of that town were built under his direction. His thorough honesty, uprightness, sociability and kindness of heart gained him the respect and sincere esteem of all. For nearly half a century he had been a faithful member of the Methodist church and evinced his Christian character in everyday life. "Cahoon Pioneer Celebration," Reunion Notebook, Rose Hill Museum, Cleveland Weekly Leader, 1878.

William Ovington CAHOON, was a genial gentleman, whose face was always smiling. A troop of children followed his footsteps, and when his life was ended the little ones came to drop a flower until his form was covered with their loving offerings. Ida M. Cahoon, History of the Cahoon Family, p. 33.

Death of an old Resident.

Another pioneer of the Western Reserve has received the Master's call. ***William O. CAHOON***, died at his home on East Avenue, in Elyria, Saturday evening, July 20th at 11 o'clock. He was born in Salisbury, Herkimer county, N. Y., January 10th 1808, and two years later, when his father's family came from Vergennes, Vt., to settle in Dover, O., his residence on the Western Reserve was commenced. December 25th, 1831, he married ***Miss Nancy DeWitt ELDRED***, and after her death again married in 1839, ***Miss Melissa ELDRED***, both daughters of *Judge ELDRED*, of Lorain county. Most of his life was spent in Elyria, where he was a prominent business man. For three years he had been in much impaired health, but the latter months of his life had shown great improvement. His death was very sudden, and caused a shock to the entire community. He spent Saturday, July 20th, sitting on the lawn in conversation with his family, and at 10 o'clock separated in usual health. A few moments after retiring he was seized with coughing, probably burst a blood vessel, causing intense suffering and in less than an hour from the first attack he passed away. His only remark was to reassure the loved ones of his household of the firm hope of eternal life. He had been a member of the Methodist Episcopal Church for more than forty years, being ever known as an earnest, benevolent, working Christian, foremost in the performance of all church duties. He leaves a wife, daughter, and four sons, who have the sympathy of a large circle of friends who will miss the presence of him who is no more.

The funeral was attended by his pastor, *Rev. Mr. MCCONNELL*, Monday afternoon, at 4 o'clock, *Messrs. NELSON, MORSE, JONES, ALLEN, FULLER*, and *STARR*, firm friends of the deceased, acting as pall bearers. The high esteem in which he was held was evidenced by the large number who came to offer the last tribute of respect.

The remains were deposited in a beautiful place in the Elyria cemetery. The integrity, Christianity, and truth of his character is a worthy example to all.

We copy the above from the Cleveland Herald. The deceased was well known to all of our old citizens. He did the stone cutting work on our present Court House, the Jail and the old Presbyterian church in 1837. The notice of his life and social qualities are not overdrawn in the least. He was truly a good, conscientious, and honest man. Newspaper article, undetermined source, Cahoon Collection, Rose Hill Museum, Bay Village, OH.

Death of Mrs. Cahoon.

Another honored pioneer of Lorain county has gone to her rest. ***Mrs. Melissa ELDRED CAHOON***, widow of the late ***William O. CAHOON***, died at her residence in this city, on Tuesday evening. She was born in Ridgeville, sixty-seven years ago, and has spent all her mature years in Elyria, where she was honored for her many virtues by a wide circle of friends. The day of the funeral will be announced hereafter. Newspaper article, undetermined source, Cahoon Collection, Rose Hill Museum, Bay Village, OH.

Children of Joseph Franklin CAHOON and Nancy Eliza RULE:

Only one survived childhood, all b. Dover Twp. 1. ***Lydia E. CAHOON***, b. c1837. 2. ***William H. CAHOON***, b. c1839. 3. ***Martha S. CAHOON***, b. c1841. 4. ***James Franklin (Frank) CAHOON***, b. c1844; never married; served under *General SHERMAN* in the Civil War; d. Sandusky Soldiers' Home. Jeff Sigsworth, The Cahoon Family of Scotland (Who Came to Cuyahoga County), p. 25.

OP 4:3 **Lydia Kenyon Cahoon**

Joseph CAHOON married ***Lydia KENYON***, a very gentle, lovable daughter of an established Rhode Island family. Ida M. Cahoon, History of the Cahoon Family, p. 23.

Research was done on the Kenyon line in New England, but as Lydia was not found to be documented in any of the published lines, it is unclear from which line she descends.

Apparently, ***Joseph CAHOON*** lived in Ridgeville Twp. during the first half of 1813 while building the grist mill there ...After *General HULL'S* surrender of Detroit to the British and Indians in 1812, the families in the Western Reserve settlements lived in terror of "the tomahawk and the scalping knife of the red man." One day probably in the early summer of 1813, a man ran up to Joseph Cahoon's temporary cabin in Ridgeville Twp., shouting "The Indians are upon us!" ***Lydia CAHOON*** fled in terror with her baby (***Joseph F. CAHOON***, born earlier that year in Dover Twp.) along the trail (Center Ridge Road) toward Cleveland; she was five miles away before her husband overtook her, and satisfied Lydia that the report was just a false alarm. Jeff Sigsworth, The Cahoon Family of Scotland (Who Came to Cuyahoga County), pp. 7-8.

The first departure for the Better Land was ***Lydia KENYON***, wife of the pioneer ***Joseph CAHOON***, August 13, 1834, leaving behind her in the hearts of her children the influence of so lovely a life that we of the third generation have before us the vision of a rare and excellent woman. Five years of loneliness were allotted to the worthy husband, and then he passed away and the hearth stone was without its founders, and desolation reigned at the homestead. "Cahoon Pioneer Celebration," Reunion Notebook, Rose Hill Museum, Newspaper article, 1878.

Mrs. CAHOON was tenderly remembered in one of the family chronicles for her "gentle ways, her dainty personality, her accomplished horsemanship and her ability as a housewife." Many weary travelers were welcomed in the old home. Don Dunham, "History of the Early Settlers in Bay Village," p. 2.

The Memory of ***Mrs. Lydia CAHOON***, the pioneer woman of Dover. This sentiment was responded to by the choir, singing "The bush my mother planted." It is a matter of history that Mrs. Cahoon brought a rose bush from Vermont and planted it on the farm, and that many of the bushes through this part of the country are from that stock. Daily Herald, Northern Ohio News, Dover, Cleveland, August 23d, 1869. Newspaper article in the Cahoon Family Reunion Notebook, Rose Hill Museum, Bay Village, OH.

For Lydia Cahoon

Then calm be the spot where her form now reposeth,
May the friends who so loved her, revisit the grave,
And feel though the cold sod her ashes encloseth,
She lives in the presence of him, who can save.
D. K. Cahoon

Handwritten note, Cahoon Collection, Rose Hill Museum, Bay Village, OH.

OP 4:4 Winsor Monument

WINSOR

Remainder of marker previously read, but currently illegible.

Henry Winsor
born May 16, 1813
died June 1, 1896

Martha Cahoon,
wife of Henry Winsor,
born Sep 5, 1815,
died June 11, 1882
Interment record below states d. 1885.

Henry Winsor
born Sep 3, 1835
died Sep 26, 1855

Nancy M. Winsor
born Mar 25, 1839
died Oct 26, 1849

Cuyahoga County Cemetery Inscriptions, vol. 1, p. 138.

OP 4:4 **Henry Winsor**

Henry is the son of Andrew Winsor and Lydia Winsor as described below. His mother's sister, Elizabeth Winsor (OP 4:1), married Aaron Aldrich (OP 4:1).

Henry, Jr., b. 1813, *(this lot)* is the son of ***Henry WINSOR, Sr.*** who had moved to Dover by way of Cooperstown, NY. Bay Village Historical Society, Bay Village: A Way of Life, p. 27. *This is believed to be incorrect. "Henry Sr.," whose letters are part of the Bay Village Historical Society, would have been the uncle of Henry. The older Henry Winsor was the brother of Lydia Winsor Winsor, Henry's mother. He may have lived in Washington Co., OH dying in 1828. Henry had at least three children: Elizabeth, Henry and Augustus.* Catherine Burke Flament, James Windsor and James Bullock.

Henry WINSOR, Male - 1: 20 under 30 yrs.; Females - 2: under 5, 1: 20 under 30 yrs. Employed in Agriculture. 1840 FC OH CYDO, p. 163, line 4.

Henry WINDSOR, 37, farmer, b. Ohio *(should read Rhode Island according to further documentation)*, real estate value: 1800; ***Martha***, 36, b. Ohio; ***Lydia***, 12, b. Ohio; ***Andrew***, 5, b. Ohio; ***Mary***, 3, b. Ohio; *John WEBER*, 21, laborer, b. Germany. 1850 FC OH CYDO, p. 434, lines 37-42.

2nd Annual Fair of the Dover Agricultural and Mechanical Society, Sept 3, 1858. ***Henry WINSOR***; 1st prize: bull over three years old. 2nd Place: Short Horns, bull, "Sulton". 2nd place: Pumpkins. Domestic Manufacturing: 2nd Place - Carpet. Westlake, Looking Back to Dover, A Collection of Writings.

WINDSOR, Henry, 57, farmer, value of real estate $10,000, personal property $700, b. Rhode Island; ***Marthy C.***, 54, b. Ohio; ***Andrew***, 24, laborer, b. Ohio; ***Maryann***, 21, Miliner *(Milliner)*, b. Ohio; ***Henrietta***, 14, b. Ohio; *KERSTETTER, G___*, 18, Laborer, b. Ohio. 1870 FC OH Cuyahoga Co., Village of Berea, Township of Middleburg, p. 428, dwelling 236, lines 28-33.

WINSOR, Henry, 67, Farmer, b. Rhode Island, fr. and mo. b. RI; ***Martha C.***, 65, Wife, Keeping House, b. Ohio, fr. b. Vermont, mo. b. Conn.; ***Mary M.***, 31, dau., Dress Maker, b. Ohio, fr. b. R.I., mo. b. Ohio. 1880 FC OH CY, Berea, Quarry Street, p. 235A, Family 21, lines 10-12.

Henry WINSOR; res. Berea; interred June 3d, 1896; Original Part. "List of Interments," Lakeside Cemetery, Bay Village, OH.

Ancestors of Henry Winsor:

I. ***Joshua WINSOR*** See *Elizabeth WINSOR ALDRICH (OP 4:1).*

II. ***Samuel WINSOR*** See *Elizabeth WINSOR ALDRICH (OP 4:1).*

III. ***Samuel WINSOR***, b. 18 Nov 1677, Providence, RI; d. 17 Nov 1758, Providence, 80; bur. North Burial Ground, North Main Street, Providence; m. 7 Jan 1703, Providence to ***Mercy*** or ***Mary HARDING*** (dau. of *Abraham HARDING* and *Deborah GARDNER*; b. 1681, Providence; d. 21 Dec 1771, Providence, "in her 89th year."

16 Feb 1713. He testified that he had seen *William TURPIN* and *Edward HAWKINS, Jr.*, play cards at said Turpin's house.

1733. He was ordained pastor of First Baptist Church and preached until his death. *Morgan EDWARDS* says that he was "a man remarkable for preaching against paying ministers, and for refusing invitations to Sunday dinners for fear they should be considerations for Sunday sermons."

20 Dec 1749. Inventory of movable items in his will: money; a linen and woolen wheel, 15 chairs, 2 tables, silver cash £29, 1 shilling, silver cup, 2 large spoons, 3 links of buttons, shoe buckles…cider press, 17 barrels cider…5 barrels cider beer…6 stacks of hay and stacks of oats and thatch, 4 hogs, 10 sheep. 6 cows, &c. John Osborne Austin, The Genealogical Dictionary of Rhode Island; Comprising Three Generations of Settlers Who Came Before 1690, p. 435.

IV. ***Rev. Samuel WINSOR***, b. 1 Nov 1722, Providence, RI; d. 26 Jan 1803, Johnston, RI; m.1 ***Lydia OLNEY*** (dau. of *John OLNEY* and *Patience JENCKS*; b. 25 Aug 1726, Providence; d. 31 Aug 1753, Providence); m.2 3 Mar 1754, ***Anne WINSOR*** (dau. of *Joshua WINSOR* and *Freeborn OLNEY*; b. 3 Oct 1737; d. 13 July 1816, Johnston). Samuel succeeded his father as minister of the First Baptist Church in Providence in 1758. In 1771 he moved to Johnston with a number of other church members, where he continued preaching until his death. Austin, p. 207.

V. ***James WINSOR***, son of James and Anne, b. 28 Mar 1760, probably at Providence, RI; d. 12 Dec 1801, at Johnston, RI, aged 41; m. ***Elizabeth "Betsey" RANDALL*** (of Cranston, RI, the dau. of *Henry RANDALL* and *Dorothy BILLINGS*, b. 30 March 1761, at Providence, and d. 19 May 1829, Johnston, RI, age 68). Dorothy Higson White, Descendants of Roger Williams, "Book I, Waterman Line, Winsor Line," and Representative Men and Old Families of Rhode Island, vol. III, p. 2113.

VI. ***Andrew WINSOR*** (*James* 5, *Samuel* 4, 3, 2, *Joshua* 1), the son of *James WINSOR*. He was b. 5 Feb 1786, at Johnston, RI, and d. 30 Sept 1854, at Smithfield, RI. He married ***Lydia WINSOR***, on 4 Feb 1810, the dau. of *Augustus WINSOR* (*Abraham* 4, *Rev. Joshua* 3, *Samuel* 2, *Joshua* 1) and *Nancy WATERMAN* the dau. of *Captain Andrew WATERMAN* (*Resolved* 4, 3, 2, *Richard* 1), and *Margaret FOSTER*. Lydia was born 22 Feb 1788, and d. 9 Aug 1872. Andrew followed the occupation of farmer, residing at different periods in the towns of Johnston, Scituate and Smithfield. He removed to the latter town a few years before his death. He was a member of the Scituate Congregational Church. Representative Men and Old Families of Rhode Island, vol. III, p. 2113.

Children of Andrew WINSOR and Lydia WINSOR: 1. ***Augustus W. WINSOR***, b. 18 Dec 1810, was a carpenter and farmer; d. 28 Dec 1883 in Providence, RI; m. July 3, 1835, *Almira PETTIS*. 2. ***Henry WINSOR***, b. 16 May 1813, farmer; resided near Berea, Cuyahoga co., Ohio where he died in June 1896. On 26 May 1836, he was married to *Martha CAHOON*, who was born 5 Sept 1814, and who died 30 June 1885. 3. ***Daniel WINSOR***, b. 6 May 1815 (at Johnston, RI; m. *Elizabeth MANTON*). 4. ***Elizabeth WINSOR***, b. 4 May 1817; d. 8 March 1837; m. *George BATTEY*, a farmer, in Dec 1835. Lived in North Scituate where she died. 5. ***Andrew WINSOR***, b. 1 Nov 1818; lumber dealer; d. 11 March 1883, at Providence. He was married Dec 25, 1844 to *Mary J. BROWN*. 6. ***Tillinghast WINSOR***, b. 3 Sept 1820; farmer; d. Nov 1894, in Johnston. He was married March 2, 1843, to *Mary WINSOR*, dau. of *Asa WINSOR*. 7. ***Lydia WINSOR***, b. 3 Aug 1822; m. *Henry IDE*, (d. c1881); lived in Seekonk, Mass where she died 2 May 1843. 8. ***James WINSOR***, 23 August 1824; farmer, resided near Greenville, in the town of Smithfield; d. 31 Jan 1903; m.1 30 Nov 1854 *Mary SWEET*; m.2 28 Jan 1869, *Maria KING*. 9. ***Nancy W. WINSOR***, b. 10 May 1826; d. 26 Aug 1902 at Providence, RI. She resided in San Jose, California, but died while on a visit to Providence. m.1, *Henry IDE*; m.2 *Captain Christian FIELDSTED*, on 22 Feb 1882. 10. ***Huldah WINSOR***, b. 26 May 1828; lived in Oakland, California; m. *Franklin E. PEASLEE* on 14 Aug 1851. 11. ***William W. WINSOR***, b. 6 May 1830, enlisted in Battery C, Rhode Island Volunteers, was taken prisoner Aug 25, 1864, at Ream's Station, Va., and was confined first on Belle Isle and later removed to the Salisbury (N.C.) prison. He died 22 Feb

1865, on the train en route for home, of illness brought on by the prison confinement, and was buried at Danville, Va.; m.1 *Amanda BALLOU*; m.2 *Josephine A. BATTEY*. 12. ***Julia A. WINSOR***, b. 11 May 1832; d. 12 May 1892 in Glocester, R.I.; m. *Henry T. BROWN*, a farmer, 20 May 1857. Representative Men and Old Families of Rhode Island, vol. III, p. 2113. (James Windsor, additional information)

Children of Henry Winsor and Martha Cahoon:

Henry WINSOR *(elsewhere written as Windsor)* m. 14 Sept 1833 to ***Martha CAHOON.*** *Issue:* ***Henry WINSOR***, b. Sept 1835, d. 1855. ***Lydia E. WINSOR***, b. c1837; d. 4 Sept 1864, Dover Twp.; m. *Horace BRAMAN (OP 2: 9-10),* no children. ***Nancy M. WINSOR,*** b. 1839, d. 1849. ***Andrew James*** *(James)* ***WINSOR***, b. c1841; m.1 *Elista HAZELET,* they had at least four children, m.2 *Kate HODGSHORN*; served in the Union Army in the Civil War; res. Berea, O. ***Mary M. WINSOR,*** m. *John McCRODEN,* no children. ***Unnamed child WINSOR,*** b./d. 1849, Cuyahoga Co. ***Henrietta WINSOR,*** b. c1853, Cuyahoga Co.; m. *A. Frank WRIGHT;* they had at least three children. Orval O. Calhoun, Our Calhoun Family, vol. 2, p.148 and Jeff Sigsworth, The Cahoon Family of Scotland (Who Came to Cuyahoga County), p. 10.

Henry WINSOR, b. 3 Sep 1835, Dover Twp., Cuy Co., OH; d. 26 Sept 1855, Dover. *See lot OP 4:5.*

Lydia E. WINSOR, b. 1837, Dover; m. 24 June 1864, Cuy Co. to ***Horace BRAMAN***; d. 24 Sept 1864, bur. Lakeside Cemetery. *See lot OP 2:10.*

Nancy WINSOR, b. 1839, Dover Twp., d. 26 Oct 1849, Dover. *(Buried next lot).*

During the past year, two marriages have taken place-*Miss Electa HEAZLIT* and ***(Andrew) James WINSOR*** of Berea....Two births - a son to James and Electa Winsor... A Pioneer Celebration, Cahoon Reunion Book, Newspaper article, 1875.

The State of Ohio, Cuyahoga County, ss., I Certify that on the 14th day of October, 1875 ***Mr. Andrew J. WNSER*** *(sp.)* and ***Miss Electa M. HEASLIT*** were, by me, legally joined in Marriage. J.S. Broadwell**....**Marriage Record, Cuyahoga County, OH, vol. 18, p. 287

Andrew James 2nd marriage: The State of Ohio, Cuyahoga County, ss., I Certify that on the 20th day of May 1885 ***Mr. Andrew J. Winsor*** and ***Miss Katie J. HODSHON*** were by me legally joined in marriage. Marriage Record, Cuyahoga County, OH, vol. 28, p. 332.

Andrew J. WINSOR, 5 Indpt. Co., Sharp Shooters, Union Private. Pension filed by ***Katie J. WINSOR***. Civil War Pension File.

Andrew James WINSOR, d. May 5, 1915, 1:30 p.m.; Berea, Cuyahoga County, Ohio of Asthma Chronic Gastritis, Chronic Bronchitis; b. Mar 9, 1846, Ohio; 69 yrs. 1 mo. 26 ds.; Retired; fr. ***Henry WINSOR***, b. Rhode Island, mo. ***Martha C. CAHOON***, b. Ohio; informant *Henry WINSOR*, Berea, Ohio; bur. Woodvale Cemetery, Berea, Ohio; undertaker F.W. Eckert, Berea, O. Ohio Certificate of Death, Division of Vital Statistics, 1915, certif. 26768.

Andrew WINSOR: bur. Sect. 6, Lot 20, d. May 8, 1915, 69 yrs. with ***Kate WINSOR***, d. Jan 15, 1916, 58 yrs. Woodvale Cemetery, Middleburg Heights, OH.

The State of Ohio, Cuyahoga County, ss., I Certify that on the first day of November 1870 ***Mr. John McCRODEN*** and ***Miss Mary M. WINSOR*** were by me legally joined in marriage. Aaron Schuyler. Marriage Record, Cuyahoga County, OH, vol. 23, p. 337.

McCRODEN, Mary, wife of the late ***John McCRODEN,*** sister of ***Mrs. Henrietta M. WRIGHT***. Private services at the late residence 3104 Yorkshire Rd., Friday Feb 3 at 2 p.m. Burial at Ridgewood, NJ. Please omit flowers. Cleveland Necrology File, Feb 3, 1928.

Mary Martha McCRODEN, buried Feb 1928; ***John McCRODEN,*** buried Sept 1914, Lot 1142. No other burials in this lot. Valleau Cemetery, Ridgewood, NJ.

Henrietta "Etta" M. WINSOR, b. 1853, Cuy; m. ***Amos Frank WRIGHT*** (b. c1854. Cleveland, OH, son of *James WRIGHT* and *Silicia HEATH*). Keith M. Sheldon, Descendants of Early Bay Village Families, pp. 256, 291, 673 and Sigsworth, p. 22.

Henrietta WINSOR and Amos Frank WRIGHT were both great-grandchildren of Joseph and Lydia CAHOON. Henrietta from their son Amos and Frank from Jacob.

The State of Ohio, Cuyahoga County, ss., I Certify that on the 27th day of January, 1880 ***Mr. Amos F. WRIGHT*** and ***Miss Henrietta M. WINSOR*** were by me legally joined in marriage. Rev. F. Tolhurst. Marriage Record, Cuyahoga County, OH, vol. 23, p. 22.

Henrietta M. WRIGHT, d. December 2, 1943, at her residence 3104 Yorkshire Rd., Cleveland Heights, Cuyahoga Co., Ohio of Pneumonia lobar 6 days; 88 yrs. 2 mos. 29 ds.; widow of ***A. Frank WRIGHT;*** Housewife; b. Sept 3, 1855, Dover Township, Ohio fr. ***Henry J. WINSOR***, b. Providence, Rhode Island, mo. ***Martha CAHOON***, b. Cleveland, Ohio; informant *Silicia M. WRIGHT,* 3104 Yorkshire; funeral director David I. Jones, 9419 Miles Ave.; Harvard Grove Cemetery. Ohio Certificate of Death, Division of Vital Statistics, 1943, certif. 74013.

WRIGHT: Henrietta M., wife of the late ***A. Frank***, mother of ***Silisia M.***, ***Linetta M.***, and ***Winsor***, at her residence, 3104 Yorkshire rd., Cleveland Heights, where services will be held Saturday, Dec 4, at 2 p.m. Cleveland Necrology File, Dec 4 1943.

WRIGHT, Silisia M., daughter of the late ***A. Frank*** and ***Henrietta M. WRIGHT***, sister of ***Linetta M.*** and ***Winsor***. Friends received at the David I. Jones Funeral Home, Miles Ave. at E. 95th St., Monday 2 To 4 And 7 To 9 P.M. Services at Calvary Presbyterian Chapel, E. 79th St. and Euclid Ave., on Tuesday, May 29, at 2 p. m. In lieu of flowers contributions may be made to the Senior Board of Women's Hospital. Cleveland Press, May 28, 1956.

WRIGHT, Linetta M., daughter of the late ***A. Frank*** and ***Henrietta WRIGHT,*** sister of ***Winsor*** and the late ***Silisia M.*** Friends received at the David I. Jones Funeral Home, Miles Ave. at E. 95th St., Monday 2-5 And 7-9 P. M., where services will be held Tuesday, Feb 25, at 2 p. m. In lieu of flowers, contributions may be made to the Senior Board of Woman's Hospital. Cleveland Press, Feb 24, 1958.

OP 4:4 **Martha Cahoon Winsor**

Martha Cahoon Winsor is the grand-daughter of Joseph and Lydia Cahoon, and daughter of Amos and Polly Cahoon.

Martha CAHOON WINSOR married ***Henry WINSOR, Jr.*** *(Jr. incorrect)* in 1835. She was born in 1815 and died at the age of sixty-seven in 1882. She and Henry were not living in Dover at the time. She and Henry are buried at Lakeside Cemetery." Bay Village Historical Society, Bay Village: A Way of Life, pp. 27-8.

Martha CAHOON, daughter of ***Amos CAHOON*** (son of ***Joseph*** and ***Lydia CAHOON*** OP 4:3) and ***Mary "Polly" WILLIAMS*** *(see information below)* b. 3 Sept 1815 at Newburgh, Ohio; d. 3 July 1885; m. 14 Aug 1833 ***Henry WINSER*** *(elsewhere written as Winsor)*. Orval O. Calhoun, Our Calhoon Family, vol. 2, p. 148.

In 1836 ***Martha*** and ***Henry WINSOR*** bought 40 acres of land on Bradley Rd. including a small house built about 1831; by 1852, they had purchased an additional 104 acres, and built a larger house (since moved to 281 Bradley Rd). Jeff Sigsworth, The Cahoon Family of Scotland (Who Came to Cuyahoga County), p. 10.

Martha WINSOR, 69; res. Berea; interred July 2, 1885; Original Part. "List of Interments," Lakeside Cemetery, Bay Village, OH.

Parents of Martha Cahoon Winsor:

Amos CAHOON to ***Polly WILLIAMS*** Married July 3d 1814. I hereby Certify that the Marriage Contract was solemnized between Amos Cahoon and Polly Williams July third 1814. The State of Ohio, Cuyahoga County, Just. Thomas Barr Marriage Record, Cuyahoga County, OH, vol. 1, p. 32.

Amos CAHOON stopped when on the way from Vermont with *Mr. WILLIAMS,* the famous Newburgh miller, soon after married "*Polly*," the miller's pretty daughter, living many years in a log house east of Cahoon Creek. Their daughter, ***Martha***, married ***Henry WINDSOR***, and ***Ruth***, who taught in the log school house, and after it burned in her grandfather's mill, was ***Mrs. Porter SMITH.*** The other three daughters live in Wisconsin. Memorial to the Pioneer Women of the Western Reserve, 1896, p. 60.

Parents of Polly Williams Cahoon:

William Wheeler WILLIAMS, son of *Joseph* and *Eunice*, who both descended from Puritan ancestors who settled in Mass. about 1630. William was b. 1760, m. ***Ruth GRANGER***, (b. 1764; dau. of *Zodac* and *Martha GRANGER* of Suffield, Conn.). He came in the spring of 1799 to Newburgh and built a grist mill. Ruth was a very small, alert and very intelligent woman who went blind before her death. The family settled on what is now Woodhill Rd., called Newburgh street in early days. They brought five children with them to Newburgh, ages 12-2 years old: ***Frederick Granger***; ***William Wheeler*** (Jr.); ***Joseph Williams***; ***Martha***, m. *Elijah PEET* and ***Mary***, m. *Amos CAHOON*, pioneer of Rockport. Mary had three children: ***Martha, Joseph*** and ***Hiram***. The grindstones lying in the Public Square in front of the Old Stone Church *(in Cleveland)* were the first ones used in the grist-mill of William Wheeler Williams erected in 1799. Gertrude Van Rensselaer Wickham, Pioneer Families of Cleveland, 1796-1840, pp. 47-48.

"To the oldest grand-daughter of the Cahoon family" brought ***Mrs. Martha CAHOON WINSOR*** to the stand. She said she was the oldest grand-daughter of the Cahoon family and the oldest grandchild in the Williams family, that came to Newburgh in 1799. Her father and mother met when but sixteen and twelve years of age, and "watched each other four years, when they were married." After a happy married life of forty-eight years, the union was separated by death. Mrs. Winsor was loudly cheered. "The Cahoon Pioneer Celebrations," Reunion Notebook, Newspaper article, 1876.

Amos CAHOON, b. 7 Sept 1789, Salisbury, NY; d. 27 Nov 1861 (or 60), Wisconsin; m. 3 July 1813, Newburgh to ***Mary "Polly" WILLIAMS*** (b. 8 Nov 1797, Suffield, Hartford Co., Conn.; d. 17 Mar 1874; bur. Lyons, Wisc.). *Issue:* ***Martha CAHOON,*** b. 3 Sep. 1815, Newburgh Twp., Cuyahoga Co., Ohio; d. 3 July 1885; m. 14 Aug 1833, *Henry WINSOR,*. (b. 1813, d. 1896); seven children. ***Joseph W. CAHOON,*** b. 16 Mar 1817, Ridgeville Twp., Lorain Co., Ohio; d. 1863, Kansas City, Kans.; m. 19 Sept 1842, *Slatera JOHNSON,* (b. Sept 1815, NY); lived in New York; at least one daughter. ***Hiram F. CAHOON,*** b. 27 May 1819, Dover Twp., Cuyahoga Co., Ohio; d. 15 Mar 1897, Minneapolis, Minn.; m. 14 Nov 1842, *Mary A. LOUGHREN* (b. c1824, Vermont); lived in Minneapolis; at least four children. ***Ruth G. CAHOON,*** b. 30 Dec 1820, Dover Twp.; d. 17 June 1885; m. 2 Oct 1841, *Samuel Porter SMITH* (called "*Porter*"); she taught in Dover Twp.'s early schoolhouse, and after it burned in her grandfather *Joseph CAHOON'S* mill; two children. ***Nancy C. CAHOON,*** b. 7 Jan 1823, Dover Twp.; d. 8 Feb 1896; m. 20 Nov 1844, *Sylvester C. SANFORD* (b. 4 Jan 1820 Camden, NY); lived in Wisc.; at least six children. ***William Overton CAHOON,*** b. 15 Mar 1825, Dover Twp.; d. 12 May 1905, Vesta, Minn.; m. 25 Dec 1848, *Eliza BREWSTER* (b. 28 Jan 1827, Vermont; d. 31 Dec 1910; bur. Marshall, Minn.); lived in Cahoon Hills, Wis., and had four children. ***Mary W. (M.) CAHOON,*** b. 2 Feb 1828, Dover Twp.; d. Lyons, Wis.; m. 2 June 1844, *Zenas B. BURKE;* lived in Lyons; had at least four children. ***Lydia Kenyon CAHOON,*** b. 10 Apr 1830, Dover Twp.; d. Hudson, Wisc.; m. 18 June 1855, *Oliver PALMER*; lived in Hudson, Wisc.; had at least eight children. ***Joel B. CAHOON,*** b. 16 Oct 1832, Dover Twp.; d. 24 May 1839, Dover Twp. ***Amos Franklin CAHOON,*** b. 8 July 1835, Dover Twp.; d. 31 May 1848, Dover Twp. Calhoun, vol. 2, pp. 147-148 and Sigsworth, pp. 10-14.

Amos (CAHOON)...lived on the lot adjoining his father's home on the east. He was one of Dover's most active, energetic citizens until 1842. The "Town Book," a record of those early days in Dover, records his name as township officer in various positions, while his genial disposition won many warm friends. He was very clever at his trade, carpenter and builder...Five sons and five daughters came to them in their log cabin home, before they removed to Wisconsin. Ida M. Cahoon, History of the Cahoon Family, pp. 28-29.

A letter bearing the date Dover, O., Nov 13, 1831, from ***Amos CAHOON***, to his brothers ***Joel*** and ***Daniel*** in Frederick, Md., states: "I have been engaged in building a bridge over Rocky River, which has kept me more confined than I could wish, but I made a finish of it last week to the satisfaction of the Commissioners, and the public in general, who pronounce it a fine piece of workmanship, from which I realized $700." A large sum in those days. He had the contract of constructing the bridge over the Rocky River near the mouth, being the one replaced by the present toll bridge. The bridge was said to be the first concrete bridge in the world which was eight years being developed. "Rose Hill Pioneers," Reunion Notebook, Newspaper article, 1885 and Cahoon, p. 29.

***Amos CAHOON**,* 3rd Regiment (Hayes'), Ohio Militia, Private, purchased 120 acres of land on August 1, 1844, Milwaukee, WI, Twp. 2N, Range 17E, Sect. 11. Wisconsin Land Records.

Amos and Mary Cahoon living with their daughter:

Silvester C. SANFORD**,* 30, b. NY*;* ***Nancy M., 27, b. Ohio*;* ***Elijah**,* 12, b. Ohio; ***Emily C**.*, 3, b. Wis.; ***Harland W**.*, 1, b. Wis.; ***Amos CAHOON**,* 62, occup. none, b. Vermont; ***Mary***, 55, b. Vermont; ***Lydia R.***, 20, b. Ohio. 1850 FC Wisconsin, Walworth Co., Geneva, p. 178, lines 19-26, 12th Sept 1850.

William** (Overton) **CAHOON, 25, farmer, value of real estate $600, b. Ohio; ***El__ C.***, 23, b. Vermont; ***Maria W.***, 6/12 yr., b. Wis. Next door to Silvester, lines 16-18.

***Amos CAHOON**,* 70, Gentleman, value of real estate $2000, personal property $200, b. NY; ***Mary**,* 63, b. NY. 1860 FC Wisconsin, Walworth Co., Hudson, p. 304, house 145, family number 132, lines 17-18.

Mary, wife of ***Amos CAHOON***, and daughter of *W.W. (WILLIAMS),* who came to Newburgh in 1799, died at her home in Wisconsin, in March 1874, aged 77 years. In July 1814, she gave her hand with heart in it to Amos Cahoon. In 1842 she removed to Lyons, Wisconsin, paying two visits after that to her Ohio friends. All who saw her sweet face, retaining so much of its girlish beauty, will find the impression indelible, and think of her now as being with the husband she so much loved and mourned. "The Cahoon Pioneer Celebrations," 1874.

OP 4:4 **Henry Winsor, II**

***Henry WINSOR** was the oldest child of **Henry WINSOR** and **Martha CAHOON, b. 3 Sept. 1835 and d. 26 Sept 1855**.*

OP 4:4/5 **Nancy Maria Winsor**

NANCY MARIA
DAUGHTER OF
H. & M. WINSOR
DIED OCT 26, 1849
AE 10 yr. 7 Mo. 1d.

Sleep on sweet one
not drear and alone,
Is the path of light
where though *(thou)* hast gone.
For we know in the land
where our loved one dwells
There are no more partings
and farewells.
And there when the dreams *(dream)* of life is o'er,
May we meet again
on that far distant shore.

Marker cracked and set in concrete.
Nancy has two markers.

They (***Henry WINSOR**, Jr.* and ***Martha CAHOON WINSOR***) had a daughter ***Nancy*** who died in 1849 at the age of 10 and is buried in Lakeside Cemetery. Bay Village Historical Society, Bay Village: A Way of Life, p. 28.

OP 4:6 **Joel Cahoon**

JOEL
Son of
(crack)
CAHOON
Drowned
May 24, 1838
Aged 6 Years 7 Mo. 8 Dy.

Marker cracked and set in concrete.

Cracked section was previously read as "***Amos*** and ***Mary***." Cuyahoga County Cemetery Inscriptions, p. 138.

***Joel CAHOON** is the brother of **Martha CAHOON WINSOR** (OP 4:6) and grandson of **Joseph CAHOON** and **Lydia KENYON** (OP 4:3), he was probably named after his uncle **Joel Butler CAHOON** (Lots 63/64:10).*

Amos, the second son of ***Joseph*** and ***Lydia K. CAHOON***, married ***Mary** ("**Polly**"),* the daughter of ***William WILLIAMS*** of Newburgh on July 3, 1813. The lived on the lot adjoining his father's home on the east. Five sons and five daughters came to them in their log home, before they removed to Wisconsin. ***Amos*** and ***Joel***, died in childhood. Ida M. Cahoon, History of the Cahoon Family, pp. 25, 28-29. *See additional references with Martha Cahoon Winsor, OP 4:6.*

OP 4:7 **Reuben Osborn**

REUBEN
OSBORN
Died
March 24, 1860
AGED
81 Yrs. 4 Mos. 20
D's.
(Quotation illegible)

Reuben Osborn donated the original land for Lakeside Cemetery.

He (***Reuben OSBORN***) was a descendant of ***Thomas OSBORN***, one of the founders of New Haven, Conn., and was born there in 1778. He was a fruit grower in that area before moving in 1803 to Camden (Oneida County), NY. He lived there for several years before coming to Bay Village (old Dover Twp.) in 1810. Julian Krawcheck, "Let us visit vintage homes," Cleveland Press, undetermined date, p. A8, cols. 4-5.

Reuben OSBORN II and ***Sarah JOHNSON*** were married in Bristol, Connecticut, then moved from Woodbridge to Oneida County, New York, March 2, 1803, and from Camden to Dover Township now Bay Village, May 17, 1811. Julia Osborn Scott, "Osborn Family History," p. 3.

Rebecca JOHNSON married ***Asahel PORTER*** who with their two daughters, ***Catherine*** & ***Emaline***, came to Dover on her natal day. Her brothers, ***Leverett JOHNSON*** & ***Reuben OSBORN***, accompanied them, arriving here "on a fine October day, the tenth of that golden month in 1810," the same day that ***Joseph CAHOON*** came with his family. These two families & Leverett Johnson, therefore, have the distinction of being the first settlers of Dover.

Mr. Osborn soon returned to his home in Camden, NY preferring to wait until spring before settling in a new country. Leverett Johnson afterwards became a member of Ohio's Legislature for several terms. Mr. Osborn and his wife ***Sally***, moved from Conn. in 1803, the year that Ohio was admitted to the Union, to Camden, N.Y. Eight years later they came to Ohio bringing with them their daughter ***Polly***, and a son as blithe and active a little lad as ever rode a stick horse. As the canoe which brought them from Cleveland touched the shinning shores of Dover Bay, Mrs. Osborn's brother, sister, Rebecca, with her family, stepped forth to give them a joyous greeting.

One hundred years have swept by since that meeting on that beautiful May day, when the dainty anemone and moccasin flower nodded in the breeze and all nature flung out her delicate banners of leaf and flower to welcome them to their future home. Oh it was such a gala day to them, for after my devout grandfather had returned heartfelt thanks to God for their safe arrival and happy reunion they had been refreshed and the children tucked away....the sisters sat hand-in-hand and talked of the old home. Mrs. Thomas R. (Julia) Mitchell, Berea Enterprise, June 30, 1911.

Reuben OSBORN and his brother-in-law ***Ashael PORTER*** came on the same day that ***Joseph CAHOON*** and family and ***Leverett JOHNSON***, a young lad of seventeen. They came to look over the land and find a location. The Porters remained, but great-grandfather returned to Camden, New York preferring to remain until Spring before settling in a new country. Julia Osborn Scott, "Osborn Family History."

My father, ***Reuben OSBORN***, moved to Ohio A.D. 1811, May 17, from Camden, Oneida Co., N.Y. He came in a schooner owned by *Major CARTER*, from Buffalo, after waiting ten days for passage. On arrival in Cleveland we found the village consisted of two or three frame houses, one drygoods store, two taverns, and a post office building, with as many as ten Indians to every white man, the rest squaws. After seeing the village, we moved on to Township No. 7-15th range in a large canoe, there being no roads west of the Cuyahoga River.

On arriving at a place called Dover, the township contained four families: viz. *Joseph CAHOON (OP 4:3)*, ***Ashael PORTER*** *(OP 6:3)*, *Philo TAYLOR* and *Moses ELDRED,* besides a few Indians. The Indians were quite friendly and furnished good fat raccoon. Their oil supplied the place of lard, and was quite equal for frying cakes and shortening. Also were supplied with good venison, and our meat was plentiful and when it failed the Indians would furnish it in exchange for other articles they needed.

With an occasional piece of bear meat, they also furnished a tolerable amount of maple sugar. Mother objected a little to using it, on account of cleanliness for they used to boil bacon in the sap without skinning it and the hair would come off, which looked rather unpalatable in tea. Some of the squaws were so nice, however, they would strain the syrup through part of their dress, then the difficulty would be obviated. Unless it was so dirty and full of holes they could not.

The County Commissioners soon laid out a road, called Jacob's Ladder and hired *John S. REED* of Black River to make it which was much on the same order of corduroy causeways of Michigan. Our township was bounded on the west by Sandusky and on the east by the Chagrin River. We obtained the lumber for our barns from a sawmill at Grand River and rafted it up. Our floors were of split logs, our wheat was worth a dollar a bushel. Our mail was brought once a week by *Mr. ALLENBAUGH* on foot. Our Justice of the Peace was at Black River. As for lawyers, we did not need any, for if a man got drunk he had to dig up a stump.

After we began to raise corn, we used to guard it by tying a dog back on the lot, then get up every two or three hours, whistle and this would cause the dog to bark and howl, so the coons would leave forthwith.

Bear and wolves were plentiful and often caught our sheep and hogs, which was the cause of the Great Hunt in 1820. I think I was well acquainted with the boy that was treed by the bear - as related in McGuffy's Second Reader of his being pulled down from the tree and of his escape by flight. At the time those that actually measured his strides stated that they were fifteen feet. His name was *Peter MILLER* of Avon, Lorain Co., and brother of *Mrs. WAGER*, now of Rockport.

Once a bear caught a small pig in the road a few rods from our house. We gave chase with a light, it being in the evening and the pig soon came running back, terribly frightened. We were hearing of the battle of *Commodore PERRY* on Lake Erie, but time forbids my telling you more at present. Account written by Seldon Osborn, son of Reuben, Rose Hill Museum, Bay Village, OH.

What years of toil and years of privation, the first families must have endured and experienced. The land was covered by mighty oaks, black and white. *Reuben HALL*, in an early history of Dover, which he wrote for his grandchildren, said, "Three men and a team of oxen were required to cut down the trees and roll into heaps for burning. Then the pioneer had the hard task of getting the seed in, the land could not be ploughed on account of the stumps and roots. He had to take his oxen and hitch them to a three cornered drag and loosed the earth as best he could to receive the seeds for the first crop."

In building their houses wooden pins were used instead of nails, which were scarce and high and had to come from Pittsburgh. There were fireplaces in every room, foot deep beams and foundation walls two feet thick. Being situated on the banks of Lake Erie, made the home attractive and desirable. Scott, pp. 5-6.

After Hull's surrender, ***Deacon OSBORN*** and myself one evening took a boat and went to Cleveland for necessaries. The British fleet was lying off the mouth of the Cuyahoga. By muffling our oars we passed between the vessels and the shore, and returned safely and the same night - distance 14 miles. *Mr. ELDRED (Moses Eldred was one of the first four men who had settled when the Osborn's arrived in 1811)* spoke of the great anxiety of the settlers when Perry's battle was fought. He with others sat upon the bank of the lake, and listened with hope and fear to the distant cannonade. Clark Eldred, son of Moses, "Dover Pioneer Picnic," Cahoon Family Reunion Notebook, Newspaper article, 1861.

My grandfather ***(Reuben OSBORN)*** owned a section of land bought from the Connecticut Land Company for one dollar an acre, which extended from the west, known as the ***Sherman OSBORN*** property (now owned by *Mr. WELLS*) and extended east to the Ellinwood Allotment and south to the Nickel Plate Railroad.

Later, his grandsons: ***Sherman, Reuben, Samuel*** and ***David*** and his granddaughter, ***Betsey*** were each given a parcel for a farm. ***Minerva*** went to Huntsburg to live and ***Julia*** to Dover, they too, married farmers. Mrs. Thomsas R. (Julia) Mitchell, Berea Enterprise, June 30, 1911.

The Reuben Osborn House

One of the oldest if not the oldest standing frame dwelling west of the Cuyahoga was erected in 1814 by ***Deacon Reuben OSBORN*** who came to the village in May of 1811. Tradition has it that the lumber was sawed east of Cleveland and rafted on the lake to this site. The central chimney of soft wire cut brick was burned in this area. The lime in the mortar was made from shells gathered on the lake shore. After his death the home was occupied by his only son ***Selden OSBORN*** (Capt. Of the Ohio Militia) and in turn by his grandson and namesake ***Reuben OSBORN Jr.***, first mayor of Bay Village in 1903. His widow ***"Aunt" Eunice OSBORN*** effected some alterations in the interior including the removal of the chimney and fireplaces. She lived there to the age of 96 years. The home passed from family ownership upon the death of an unmarried daughter ***Rose*** about ten years ago. Part of the farm south of the address 29202 Lake Road is still the homes of ***Mrs. Warren MEDDICK*** and her brother ***David Leslie OSBORN*** nephew of Reuben Jr. - one hundred and fifty one years of continuous ownership (original deed is from the Conn. Land Co.) Document in the Osborn Family Papers, Rose Hill Museum.

The following includes excerpts of an interview with Eunice Chadwick Osborn, Reuben and Sarah's daughter-in-law. The Osborn House, which has been moved next to the Cahoon home, Rose Hill, is the oldest frame home between Cleveland and Lorain.

Home Weathers Storms of 118 Years

"***Grandfather (Reuben) OSBORN*** was four years building this house," the little white-haired lady related, "every bit of lath and siding was cut by hand from the timber he felled from the clearing...

"Reuben stopped at Cleveland first," Grandma *(Eunice)* Osborn said today, "but found hard clay, not fit for farming, so he moved still farther west along the lake to find good soil.

"Everything they ate had to be grown," she continued, "so grandfather wanted to be sure he was getting good land."

There wasn't very much the pioneers could buy or very many places they could spend money if they had any. Reuben did go to market for a pig one day, however and the story of how he finally brought home that very necessary addition to his livestock, still is related by Osborn...

"Reuben got as far as Rocky River without any mishaps," Grandma related, "by leading the pig with a rope tied to its leg.

"Then he came to Rocky River and his troubles began. There wasn't a bridge at that early time, or even a ferry, so he put the pig in a row boat and started across.

"Either the pig objected to going boat riding or grandfather was a poor sailor, because half-way across, the small craft capsized and father headed for one shore and the pig for the other.

"It took two attempts and a heap of chasing around before both Reuben and his livestock got on the west bank of the river at the same time, and after grandfather had walked the poor pig home with the rope still tied to its leg, I don't know which was the more exhausted." Helen Allyn, "Home Weathers Storms of 118 Years," Cleveland Press, Oct 6, 1932, p. 17, cols. 1-5.

Father's ***(Reuben OSBORN)*** first log house long ago fell into the lake. The present house, the eldest between Lorain and Cleveland was built in 1815(14?). Typed paper quoting Selden Osborn, Rose Hill Museum.

Soon after coming to Dover, Grandfather ***(Reuben OSBORN)*** built a log house near the bank of beautiful Lake Erie, which was several yards further north than it is at the present, but the little log house slipped into the lake long ago, as well as the little vale west of it, where as a child I gathered violets and hepaticas. He built the grand new house in 1815, which remodeled today still stands, one of the oldest houses in Dover, now Bay Village, and probably the oldest house between Cleveland and Lorain, and after a century of service is just as attractive and inviting as in the days of long ago. This house to me in childhood was a wonderful haven with the smoke house in the chimney, the brick oven and the many fireplaces. Mrs. Thomas R. (Julia) Mitchell, "Osborn Family History," Berea Enterprise, 1911 and included in the "Osborn Family History."

Rebecca *(JOHNSON* ***PORTER****, OP 6:3)* and son, drown in Rocky River...in 1814. The bodies were the first to be buried in the first cemetery in Bay, now Lakeside Cemetery, which was given by my grandfather and in it are buried the first Osborn families. Mitchell.

Reuben OSBORN gave land on the shores of Lake Erie for Dover's first school. This was near the west end of the township. It was here that in 1816 *Betsey CROCKER*, daughter of *Jedediah* and *Sarah CROCKER*, started Dover's first school. When she left to become Dover's second bride, her sister *Philena* took over as the teacher. The First 100 Years of Dover Schools, p. 3.

The records of Dover Congregational Church recites that ***Reuben OSBORN*** was one of the incorporators of the First Congregational Society, February 9, 1831, together with *Sylvanus CROCKER, Calvin PHINNEY* and *Josiah HURST*. Reuben and ***Sarah***, his wife, were admitted to membership April 12, 1812. Julia Osborn Scott, "Osborn Family History," p. 3.

Reuben OSBORN, 72, farmer, b. Conn.; ***Sarah***, 71, b. Conn.; ***Polly***, 45, b. NY. 1850 FC OH CYDO, p. 433, dwelling 3741.

I, ***Reuben OSBORN***, of Dover Township, Cuyahoga County and State of Ohio do make and publish this last will and Testament...First I give unto my wife ***Sarah OSBORN*** the use of all the land I now own the North side of the highway during her natural Life, also one half of all the stock and moveable property to be at her disposal.

Secondly I give to my daughter ***Polly*** five hundred dollars to be Paid within one year after the decease of her Father.

Thirdly of my son ***Seldon OSBORN*** shall pay Polly Osborn five hundred dollars within one year of my disease then he shall be entitled to the residue of my property not given to any other in this Will and also to the part given to my wife Sarah Osborn after her decease.

Fourth and lastly I constitute and appoint my son Seldon Osborn the Executor of this my last will and Testament in Testimony whence of I have here unto set my hand and seal this seventh day of June. Reuben Osborn. Signed and sealed in the presents of *Aaron ALDRICH* and *Martha CAHOON*. Will of Reuben Osborn, Cuyahoga County Archives, Will Book C, pp. 62-63, Cleveland, OH.

DOVER LAKE

The one hundredth anniversary of the settling of the grandfather of the Osborn's, at Dover Lake, was celebrated at the home of ***Reuben OSBORN***, Wednesday, May 7th. Of the sixty-one remaining descendants forty-five were present. Evening Telegram, Elyria, OH, Thursday, May 25, 1911, p. 6, col. 2.

Ancestors of Reuben Osborn:

I. ***Thomas OSBORN*** of New Haven, Conn., was born in England, probably Herfordshire, and came to America and joined the New Haven Colony of Reverend Davenport in the year 1639 or 1640. This was about two years after the establishment of the New Haven Colony, the date of his arrival in America is not definite, however, we find that the town records of New Haven show that in 1649 Thomas Osborn was registered as a citizen of New Haven, and in 1641, among the names of the proprietors of New Haven, that Thomas Osborn, with a family of six, had an estate valued at £300. Among his holdings was the following land: 30 acres in the 1st Division, 6 acres in the neck, 18 acres in the meadow and 72 acres in the 2nd Division. He became the town tanner and was assisted in the business by his son ***Jeremiah***. The tannery was located on the south side of George Street between Broad and Factory Streets. In 1643 Thomas was reprimanded by the Town Board for spoiling diverse hides in the tanning. Thomas made the excuse that he had not yet become accustomed to the materials he was required to use in the tanning process. He promised to make good any hides he had spoiled, so he continued as town tanner.

Thomas was one of the leaders in the church and was assigned the sixth seat in the middle row. He later moved to East Hampton, Long Island and was one of its early property owners. C.M. Osborn, "The Osborn Family of Bay Village, Ohio," p. 1-2 and Donald Lines Jacobus, Families of Ancient New Haven, p. 1323.

II. ***Jeremiah OSBORN***, who was born in England, came to America with his father, Thomas. [Jeremiah, d. 26 Apr 1676 (New Haven Vital Statistics); m. ***Mary*** ___, who d. 1695, p. 1323] Jeremiah and Mary had a son. Osborn, p. 2 and [Jocobus, p. 1323].

III. ***Joseph OSBORN***, [b. on 15 Dec 1667 *(New Haven Vital Statistics)*]; d. 19 Nov 1735; [m. ***Mary*** (dau of *James BENNETT* and *Mary JOY*, d. 1737)]. Joseph and Mary had a son Joseph. Osborn, p. 2 and [Jocobus, p. 1323, also lists death].

IV. ***Joseph OSBORN***, bap. 18 Feb 1693, [First Congregational Society; d. Dec 1724, ae. 32 (Old Graveyard, North Haven); m. ***Experience TOLLES***, dau. of *Henry TOLLES* and *Dorothy THOMAS*]. He had a son, *Amos*. Osborn, p. 2 and [Jocobus, pp. 1323-1324].

V. ***Amos OSBORN***, b. 6 June 1722 in New Haven, Conn.; d. 1 Nov 1790 [Naugatuck, New Haven, CT], bur. Pine Hill Cemetery, Waterbury; m.1 15 Nov 1743, [New Haven, CT] to ***Joanna WEED***, the dau. of *John WEED* and *Mary BEAMON* (b. 22 April 1724 [in Derby, New Haven, CT]); m.2 25 Mar 1758 to ***Elizabeth HOTCHKISS BENHAM***, b. on 30 Mar 1735, the dau. of *Joshua HOTCHKISS* and *Mary HOTCHKISS*, a widow of *Ebenezer BENHAM*. Amos and three brothers moved to Waterbury, Conn. in time to pay a good sized tax in 1738, buying 100 acres of farm adjoining the holdings of a fourth brother who appeared not to come until 1750.

Waterbury's Military Officers and Company enlist *Ensign Amos OSBORN*, third company in the first society. The Colonial records of Connecticut, vol. 14, p. 168 state, "This assembly do establish Amos Osborn to be Lieutenant of the company or trainband in the Pine Hill Cemetery, Waterbury, Conn." Amos is buried in Pine Hill Cemetery. Amos and Joanna's sixth child was Reuben. Osborn, pp. 2, 3 and [Jocobus, pp. 1326-1327].

VI. ***Reuben OSBORN***, b. 8 Apr 1755 [Waterbury, New Haven, Conn.]; resided in Harwinton; d. 23 Feb 1830, age 75; m. about 1775 to ***Mariam ATWATER***, dau. of *Jonathan ATWATER* and *Miriam CANFIELD*, b. c1755, died 5 Mar 1813, age 58 yrs. Osborn, pp. 2, 3 and [Jocobus, p. 1327].

Reuben and Miriam had the following children: ***Thomas Canfield OSBORN***, b. Sept 12, 1776; d. Apr 21, 1854; m. *Susannah HOTCHKISS* of Chester; resided in Harrington. ***Reuben OSBORN***, b. Nov 4, 1778, Woodbridge, Conn.; d. Mar 24, 1860; m. Dec 9, 1802 to *Sally JOHNSON* (dau. of *Elephalte* and *Mary JOHNSON*, b. 8 Aug 1779, d. 6 Sept 1856). ***Polly OSBORN***, b. Aug 11, 1780; d. Mar 25, 1781. ***David OSBORN***, b. Jan 13, 1782; d. Mar 29, 1859; m. *Esther POTTER* (dau. of *Eliakin(m) POTTER* of Plymouth, resided in Camden, New York). ***Miles OSBORN***, b. Apr 17, 1785; d. Aug 23, 1788. ***Clarissa OSBORN***, b. Dec 3, 1789; d. Nov 4, 1831; m. *Chauncey POTTER*. ***Amos OSBORN***, b. Mar 20, 1792; d. Apr 25, 1859; m. *Laura MARSH*. ***Miriam OSBORN***, b. Mar 31, 1796; d. June 9, 1859; m. *Isaiah Barber LOOMIS*. Osborn, pp. 3, 4 and Jocobus, pp. 1330-1331.

VII. ***Reuben OSBORN*** was born Nov 4, 1778, in Woodbridge, Conn., the son of *Reuben OSBORN* and *Miriam ATWATER*. He married ***Sarah JOHNSON*** at Bristol, Conn. on Dec 9, 1802, by *Rev. G. COWLES* of Bristol. They moved from Woodbridge, Conn. to Camden, New York on March 2, 1803. They left Camden; traveling in a schooner owned by *Major CARTER*, from Buffalo arriving in Dover Township May 17, 1811. The records of the Dover Congregational Church recite that Reuben Osborn was one of the incorporators of the First Cong. Church Society, Feb 9, 1831. Reuben became the second postmaster for Dover following ***Asahel PORTER***.

Issue: ***Polly OSBORN***, b. 27 Feb 1804, Camden, N.Y.; d. 27 Aug 1870, bur. Lake Side Cem. *(OP 4:9/10)*. ***Selden OSBORN***, b. 9 June 1809, Camden, N.Y.; m. 20 Nov 1833, *Nancy RUPLE* (dau. of *Deacon John RUPLE* and *Elizabeth CRAFT* of Euclid, OH); d. 23 Sept 1867, bur. Lake Side Cem.*(OP 5:7)*. ***Julia OSBORN***, b. 3 Apr 1813, Dover; d. 18 Apr 1833, bur. Lakeside *(OP 4:11)*. Julia Osborn Scott, "Osborn Family History" and Osborn, pp. 3-6.

OP 4:8 Sarah Johnson Osborn

SARAH
wife of
REUBEN
OSBORN
Died
SEPT 6, 1858
AGED
79 Yrs. 28 D's.
OUR MOTHER

Sarah (Sally) JOHNSON OSBORN, daughter of ***Eliphalet*** and ***Mary JOHNSON***, was born 8 Aug 1779 in Woodbridge, Conn. Mrs. Thomas R. Mitchell, Berea Advertiser, Berea, OH, June 30, 1911, p. 4.

OSBORN, Mrs. Reuben; maiden name ***JOHNSON, Sally***; Yr. came to Township 1811, Where From and Born: Camden, NY, Last Res. Dover, O. Women of the Western Reserve Prior to 1840, p. 23.

Of grandmother's family (***Sarah OSBORN***), ***Eliphalet*** *(her brother)* came to Dover where he organized the first Methodist Church. ***Rebecca*** *(her sister)* married ***Asahel PORTER***, who…came to Dover. Her brother, ***Leverett JOHNSON***…accompanied them *(to Dover)*…in 1810. … Grandmother spun and wove and walked in the way of the industrious. Having three children of her own and taking to her loving heart and home the three motherless children of her sister, Rebecca Porter, who with her infant son was drowned off Rocky River. Mrs. Thomas R. Mitchell, Berea Advertiser, Berea, OH, June 30, 1911, p. 4.

Upon the landing of the Osborns on the shores of Lake Erie in Bay, ***Mrs. (Sarah) OSBORN'S*** brother and sister, ***Rebecca (PORTER****, OP 6:3)*, with her family stepped forth to give them a joyous greeting...Oh, it was such a gala time for them, for after grandfather had returned heart-felt thanks for their safe arrival and happy reunion and they had been refreshed, the children tucked away in the little trundle bed for an afternoon nap, the sisters sat hand in hand and talked of the old home in the Eastland and all that had happened there, the births, the marriages and all the good things they could remember, and laughed and cried from sheer joy of being together again. Paper by Mrs. Thomas R. (Julia) Mitchell, referred to in the Osborn Family History by Julia Osborn Scott.

Sarah JOHNSON (OSBORN), wife of ***Deacon Reuben OSBORN***, extended a beneficial influence to all about her. Her only son, ***Selden***, married ***Nancy RUPLE***, a member of one of Euclid's old families. Upon the original farm of Deacon Osborn is a colony of his descendents to the third and fourth generation. The hospitable homestead is still inviting and attractive. Pioneer Women of the Western Reserve, Dover, p. 61.

Ancestors of Sarah Johnson Osborn:

I. ***Robert JOHNSON***, b. Kinston-on-hill, England; d. 1661. Rev. Frederick W. Bailey, Early Connecticut Marriages as Found in Ancient Church Records Prior to 1800, p. 47.

II. ***William JOHNSON***, b. 1635, Deacon in Guilford of Wallingford, England; m. ***Sarah HALL***, dau. of *John HALL* and *Jane WOOLEN*; d. 1716, New Haven, New Haven, CT. Bailey, p. 47.

III. ***John JOHNSON***, b. 20 July 1667, New Haven; m. ***Abigail SHERMAN***, dau. of *Daniel SHERMAN* and *Abiah STREET*; d. 1744. Bailey, p. 47.

IV. ***Abraham JOHNSON***, b. 7 Apr 1694, New Haven; m. ***Sarah GILBERT*** (b. 31 July 1694, New Haven); d. 1775. Bailey, p. 47.

V. ***Eliphalet JOHNSON***, b. 8 Jan 1718, New Haven; christening 24 Apr 1731, New Haven; m. ***Mary LINES*** (dau. of *Joseph LINES* and *Hannah BRADLEY*; christened June 1723, New Haven; d. 1769); d. 1769, New Haven.

Eliphalet JOHNSON and ***Mary LINES*** were married on July 7, 1743. Bailey, p. 47.

VI. ***Eliphalet JOHNSON***, b. 1746 Litchfield, Litchfield, CT; christening 20 Apr 1746, Woodbridge, New Haven, CT; m. ***Mary SPENCER*** (b. 1753; d. 26 Feb 1817, Camden, Oneida, NY; bur. Old Burial Ground, Mexico Street, Town of Camden); d. 2 Mar 1818, Camden, Oneida, NY, bur. Old Burial Ground, Mexico Street, Town of Camden.

Issue: ***Polly JOHNSON***, b. 13 Mar 1775, m. *Dr. Andrew CASTLE*. ***Rebecca JOHNSON***, b. 7 April 1777, m. *Asahel PORTER (OP 6:3)*. ***Sarah (Sally) JOHNSON***, b. 8 Aug 1779, Woodbridge; d. 6 Sep 1856; m. *Reuben OSBORN*. ***Eliphalet JOHNSON***, b. 20 Sep 1781, CT; d. 1856; organized the first Methodist Church in Dover in 1827, where he preached for fifteen years before going to Wisconsin in 1842. [*JOHNSON, Mrs. Eliphalet*, Maiden Name *Margery SANFORD*, Where From or Where Born N.Y., Last Residence Clinton Junc., Wis. *Source* Women of the Western Reserve Prior to 1840, p. 28.]. ***Isaac JOHNSON***, b. 14 Feb 1783, CT. ***Calvin JOHNSON***, b. 17 Nov 1785, CT; d. 29 June 1844, Ripley, Chatauqua, NY. ***Spencer JOHNSON***, b. 17 Feb 1788, Farmington, Hartford, CT; d. 9 July 1865, Lander, Warren, PA; bur. Lander. ***David JOHNSON***, b. 1 July 1790. ***Hezekiah JOHNSON***, b. 31 Oct 1792. ***Leverett JOHNSON***, b. 17 July 1794; d. 1856, m. *Abigail CAHOON* of Dover. ***Leonard JOHNSON***, b. 8 Mar 1798. ***Amelia JOHNSON***, b. 11 Mar 1800, Hartford; d. 23 Mar 1882. Mrs. Thomas R. Mitchell, Berea Advertiser, Berea, OH, June 30, 1911, p. 4; C.M. Osborn, "The Osborns of Bay Village, Ohio," p. 3, and Kathleen Johnson.

OP 4:9 **Polly Osborn**

POLLY OSBORN DIED Aug 27, 1870 AGED 66 YRS. 6 MS.

Polly was the oldest of three children of Reuben Osborn and Sarah (Sally) Johnson. She is listed as living with her father in the 1850 census and her brother, Selden, in the 1860 census.

The daughter of ***Reuben*** and ***Sarah OSBORN, Polly,*** arrived in Dover with her parents in 1811, she never married.

Bay Village Historical Society, Bay Village: A Way of Life, pp. 13, 15.

Polly OSBORN, b. Feb 27, 1804, at Camden, NY, d. Aug 27, 1870, buried at Lakeside Cemetery, Bay Village, Ohio. C. M. Osborn, "The Osborn Family of Bay Village," p. 5.

OP 4:10 Polly Osborn

Assumed marker for Polly Osborn.

P. OSBORN

OP 4:11 **Julia Osborn**

Marker cracked and set in concrete.

JULIA OSBORN
REST ...
(Illegible)

Marker previously read as:

Julia OSBORN,
died April 18, 1833,
age 20 yrs., 15 days.

Cuyahoga County Cemetery Inscriptions, vol. 1, p. 138.

Julia was the youngest daughter of Reuben Osborn and Sarah Johnson.

Julia OSBORN, daughter of ***Reuben*** and ***Sally (Sarah) OSBORN***, grew to be a very handsome girl, and was engaged to be married, but like a flower, drooped and died at the early age of twenty years. Some of her writing is still preserved and is almost as fine and even as script. Julia was born in Dover on April 3, 1813 and died April 18, 1833 in Dover-Aged 20 years, 15 days. Mrs. Thomas R. Mitchell, Berea Advertiser, Berea, OH, 1911, p. 4 and "Receipt and Record Book of Selden Osborn," in C.M. Osborn, "The Osborns of Bay Village".

OP 4:12 **Eliza Campbell**

Marker cracked and set in concrete.

ELIZA CAMPBELL
DIED
JULY 17, 1854
IN THE 41 YR.
OF HER AGE

OSBORN, Selden, 40, b. NY, farmer; *Nancy*, 36, b. Ohio; *Sherman*, 16; *Minerva*, 14; *Betsey*, 10; *Samuel*, 9; *John*, 6; *Ruiben*, 4; *Julia*, 1; all children born in Ohio; ***Eliza CAMPBELL***, 30, b. Penn *(no occupation listed)*. 1850 FC OH CYDO, p. 217A, lines 22-31, house 3742.

The will of ***Eliza CAMPBELL*** was filed on September 28, 1854 with *Selden OSBORN* as the executor and signed by *Aaron ALDRICH* at her request on 15th July 1854. Eliza left her money and two dresses to ***Eliza Jane CHURNS*** of Pennsylvania; $5.00 and two dresses to ***Mary CHURNS***, her sister, in Pennsylvania and $5.00 to her brothers, ***Robert*** and ***Stewart***. $20.00 was given to *Nancy OSBORN* and $10.00 to *Minerva OSBORN*. Eliza Jane was also the recipient of a number of treasured items such as a feather bed, under bed tick, flower coverlet, three quilts, three woolen sheets and three linen sheets. She wrote, "It is also my will that Seldom Osborn, my executor, retain money enough to purchase a suitable pair of tombstones." Estate Case File, Cuyahoga County, A1027 *The style of Eliza's tombstone matches Julia Osborn's.*

Possible brother listed above:
Robt. CAMPBELL, 32, farmer; ***Sarah***, 32; ***Curtis***, 8; ***Sylvester***, 5; ***Margaret*** 3; ***John***, 28, deaf. All born Penn. 1850 FC OH CYDO p. 213B, lines 40-42, p. 214A, lines 1-3.

OP 4:13 Dodd Marker

DODD	
CHARLES	ANNIE
1835-1887	1836-1924

OP 4:13 Charles Dodd

Charles DODD was the great-great grandson of ***Thomas COWLEY*** and ***Ann KILLEYS***, Thomas was the son of ***Patrick*** of KK German *(Parish)* and ***Margaret FARGHER.***

Charles and ***Annie DODD*** migrated in 1868 from their home on the Isle of Man. Three children, ***William, Elizabeth*** and ***Eleanor (Nell)*** traveled with them on this journey. The Dodd's arrived in Little Mountain, OH, near Painesville, in the summer. On October 12th a fourth child, ***Wirt***, was born into the family.

The Dodd's temporarily settled in this area because there were a number of Manx who lived there. Shortly after, a traveling tailor arrived reporting that *Sherman OSBORN* of Dover needed a deckhand on a fishing boat. The opportunity seemed promising to Charles and prompted the decision for the Dodd's to relocate.

Annie left family behind on the Isle including a sister, ***Moriah***, nicknamed ***Reah***. This is not the first time the Cowley sisters had family immigrate to another country. Reah had a son who had moved to Australia along with at least two brothers. Although a strenuous trip, Reah would visit her family "down under." The total trip would take a year and Reah would stop in Dover to visit Annie as part of the excursion.

Tragedy struck the Dodd family when Charles was out on a boat near Eagle Cliff at the western end of Dover. Lake Erie, because of its shallowness, has a tendency to become dangerous quickly. Charles was washed overboard from a fishing vessel he was on in 1887 and died. *This does contradict his death certificate that lists the cause of death as typhoid fever.*

The Dodd family lived on Lake Road opposite the two room school house. Wirt Dodd would recall years later, hearing children in the school yard when he was four years, yelling exuberantly for their Presidential hopeful. *Ulysses S. GRANT* was elected from that particular election. Was he the favored presidential candidate?

Wirt did visit family on the Isle of Man in 1912 which could have ended tragically. A cousin of Wirt's tried to persuade him to exchange his return ticket so that he would be able to travel on the much publicized Titanic, departing on April 10th. Anxious to get home, he declined the offer and arrived safely back in the U. S.

Wirt married ***Elvie POWELL STEVENS***, who had been divorced in the 1890's. He was not only a farmer but would become a builder, designing the plans and supervising the homes he built. He purchased 50 acres on Foote Road, east of Bassett where numerous homes were built. Wirt built both his home and Annie's around 1900. Elvie, along with *Belle WILKSHIRE (husband Lot 19/20)*, worked in a millinery factory on W. 9th Street in Cleveland, taking the Lake Shore Electric to get to work.

One of the buildings that Wirt was involved in building was the Bay Village Methodist Church in approximately 1908. The church would hold an annual Christmas party where boxes of candy would be distributed. This was one of the few chances his children would have to get candy throughout the year, unless he took the Interurban to Cleveland, as the local stores didn't carry it.

Wirt's home was located at 28729 Osborn Road and still stands today. He had a large barn built behind the house. On occasion, when a family he was building a house for was unable to move in on time, their furniture would be stored in the barn if necessary.

A slate roof was installed on the barn so the rain water would run off into cisterns. It would be pumped into the basement into large storage tanks. They then had running water starting around World War I, 1917 or so in addition to gas lights. The farm bordered the Nickel Plate Railroad tracks where a milepost, that still exists today, states: "BU 198 CH 325" *(Buffalo 198 miles - Chicago 325 miles from Bay Village).*

Annie lived just to the east of Wirt. She was short in stature and loved to read in the summer in her yard. Although she had Palsy, tremors, she was always active and kept house for she and her daughter Nell. On her 70th or 75th birthday she walked to French Creek in Avon and back to her home on Osborn. Annie did not have a church affiliation.

Nell (Eleanor), their daughter, was a teacher who loved to ride her bike to school each day. The school was located in what is presently Dover Center Rd. in Westlake. Nellie was also an avid reader who enjoyed making collections of plants and flowers. She organized the first parade to lay flowers at Lakeside Cemetery to honor those who are buried there. This tradition has been continued through the years on Memorial Day.

Ashton DODD, the youngest son who went by the name ***Jack***, worked as a carpenter for Wirt. Jack married ***Clara***, whose family was from the French Creek area in Avon. They had one son, ***James Theodore***, who was born Oct 27, 1908. Jack owned a small amount of acreage connecting Bassett and Bradley Roads where Ashton Lane is presently located. His was the only house on the current Ashton Lane for years, which is why the street was named after him. The woods behind bordered the Nickel Plate Railroad tracks. During the nice weather, on Sunday's, a church would lease a train bringing church members to this area for a picnic. The train would proceed on and return later for the picnickers. Sarah Dodd Wymer

Charles DODD, b. 1835, Isle of Man; d. 29 April 1887, Dover Twp., OH; m. ***Ann "Annie" COWLEY*** on the Isle of Man (b. 1836, Isle of Man; d. 9 Sept 1924, Bay Village, OH). *Issue:* ***William DODD***, b. 1862, Isle of Man; d. 10 Sept 1919 Detroit, Wayne Co., MI, bur. Evergreen Cem, Westlake, OH; m. *Abigail*, adopted son *Paul*. ***Elizabeth DODD***, b. 1864, Isle of Man; d. 1949, bur. Evergreen; m. *Charles HANSEN*, no issue. ***Eleanor DODD***, b. 1866, Isle of Man; d. 1926, bur. Evergreen Cem. ***Wirt Wallace DODD***, b. 12 Oct 1868, Little Mountain, Lake Co., OH; d. 12 Sept 1950 Henrietta, Lorain Co., OH, bur. Evergreen; m. *Elvie Emma POWELL STEVENS* (b. 26 Dec, 1872, Dover, dau. of *Perry POWELL* and *Sarah MILNER*; d. 1954); 2 children. ***Charles DODD***, b. 1870, Dover; d. 1871, Dover *(next lot)*. ***Ashton Cowley DODD***, b. 2 July 1874, Dover; d. 11 Mar 1965, Bay Village, OH, bur. Evergreen; m. *Clara BROOKS* (b. 2 Nov 1880, Avon, Lorain Co., OH, dau. of *James BROOKS* and *Mary WOLFE*; d. 25 Feb 1972, Avon), child: *James Theodore*, b. 27 Oct 1908. Wymer

DODD, Charles, 36, farm laborer, b. Isle of Man; ***Ann***, 34, b. Isle of Man; ***William***, 7, b. Isle of Man; ***Elizabeth***, 6, b. Isle of Man; ***Eleanor***, 4, b. Isle of Man; ***Wallace***, 1, b. Ohio; ***Charles***, 4/12, b. Jan, Ohio. 1870 FC OH LRAV p. 340, dwelling 2, lines 4-10.

DODD, Charles, 46, b. Isle of Man, fr. b. Scotland, mo. b. Isle of Man; ***Annie,*** 47, wife, b. Isle of Man, parents b. Isle of Man; ***William R.,*** 17, son, Laborer, b. Isle of Man; ***Nellie E.,*** 14, dau., b. Isle of Man; ***Wirt W.***, 11, At school, b. Ohio; ***Ashton C.***, son, b. Ohio. 1880 FC OH CYDO, p. 100A, lines 15-20.

DODD, Charles. Owned land; Acres: Improved - 8 tilled, including fallow and grass; 2 permanent meadow. Farm Values: Land - $1,000, Machinery - $25, Live Stock - $100. Estimated value of all farm production: $200. Grass lands: acreage: 2 mown, 2 not mown, 2 tons hay. 2 horses, 1 milch cows, 1 calves dropped, 1 cattle sold living. 100 pounds of butter made on the farm. 30 barnyard poultry on farm, 200 dozen eggs produced in 1879. Indian corn: 3 acres, 120 bushels. "Schedule 2. Production of Agriculture in Dover Township, Cuyahoga County, OH," enumerated June, 1880, p. 35.

DODD, Chas., d. April 29, 1887, Dover, married, 54, b. Isle of Man, ---England, farmer, parents: *Robert DODD* and *Elenor (sp.)*, disease Typhoid Fever. PD 3:218.

Charles DODD, 52; res. Dover; nativity Manx; interred Apr 30, 1887, Original Part. "List of Interments," Lakeside Cemetery, Bay Village, OH.

Children of Charles Dodd and Annie Cowley:

DODD, Wm. A., res. Newark, Ohio; 56 yrs.; d. Newark of phthisis pulmonalis, undertaker Clifford Pease, bur. 10 Sept 1919 at Evergreen Cem, Sect. I, Lot 50, Grave 1. Evergreen Cemetery, Westlake, Ohio.

Charles HANSEN, 38, res. Dover, O., b. Denmark, occup. Farmer, fr. *Carl HANSEN,* mo. *Anna PATRISEN;* married ***Elizabeth DODD***, 38, res. Dover, O., b. Isle of Man, occup. Dressmaker, fr. *Chas. DODD,* mo. *Annie COWLEY,* neither previously married. Marriage to be solemnized by Rev. Robinson, Dover, O. The State of Ohio, Cuyahoga County, s.s. I Certify, That on the 26th day of Mar 1905 Mr. Charles Hansen and Miss Elizabeth Dodd were by me legally joined in marriage. Rev. Wm. W. Robertson. Marriage Record, Cuyahoga County, OH, vol. 60, p. 384.

Elizabeth (Bessie) HANSEN, widow of ***Charles***, res. 30513 Link Rd., Bay Village, O., *Link Road is currently called Ashton Lane;* d. July 16, 1949 3 a.m. at res., cause Hypertensive Heart Disease 5 yrs., Senility, 85 yrs.; b. May 22, 1864, Peel, Isle of Man; rel. Methodist, Rev. Alfred Kreke, Bay Village; Evergreen Cemetery, Lot 50, Section I. Pease Funeral Home Records, Mss. 4809, Western Reserve Historical Society, Cleveland, OH, Record of Funeral, p. 282.

DODD, Elenora, 60, res. Dover Village, OH, bur. 10 Aug 1926; Evergreen Cemetery Section I, Lot 50, Grave 3. Evergreen Cemetery, Westlake, OH.

Wirt W. DODD, 32, res. Dover, b. Concord T., Lake Co., O., occup. Carpenter, fr. *Charles DODD*, mo. *Annie COWLEY*, never married. Married ***Elvie POWELL STEVENS***, 27, res. Dover, O., occup. Dressmaker, fr. *Perry POWELL (his mother is Sophia SADLER, dau. of William SADLER OP 3:13)*, mo. *Sarah MILLINER*, previously married once before. The State of Ohio, Cuyahoga County, s.s. I Certify, That on the 20th day of Nov 1900 Mr. Wirt W. Dodd and Miss Elvie Powell Stevens were by me legally joined in marriage. Rev. Vernon Wade Wager, Dover, Ohio. Marriage Record, Cuyahoga County, OH, vol. 51, p. 223.

Elvie's previous marriage: The State of Ohio, Cuyahoga Co., ss., I Certify that on the 27th day of February 1895, *Mr. Chauncey B. STEVENS* and *Elvie E. POWELL* were by me legally joined in marriage. Levi Gilbert, Pastor 1st ME Ch. Marriage Record, Cuyahoga County, OH, vol. 41, p. 421. *(Possibly Chauncey B. STEVENS, OP 2:3)*

DODD, Elvie E., res. Henrietta, Ohio; 81 yrs.; d. Apple Creek, Ohio of senile myocardiopathy; undertaker Marion E. Pease, bur. 28 April 1954 at Evergreen Cemetery, Sect. I west end, Lot 51. Evergreen Cemetery Records, Westlake, OH.

DODD, Wirt, head, 41, married 9 years, b. Ohio, parents b. Eng., General Fruit Farmer; ***Elva***, wife, 37, number of children 2, b. Ohio, parents b. Ohio; ***Charles***, 8, son, b. Ohio;....*POWELL, Perry*, Father-in-law, 73, widower, b. Ohio, fr. b. Un. *(unknown)*, mo. b. Ohio, laborer, farms, number of weeks unemployed 8; *SMITH, Nicholas*, servant, 51, single, b. Ohio. 1910 FC OH CYBV ED 9, p. 3B, lines 85-6.

DODD, Wirt, head, owned free of mortgage, 51, b. Ohio, parents b. Isle of Man, Fruit Farmer on own farm; ***Elva***, wife, 47, b. Ohio, parents b. Ohio; ***Chas***., son, 17, b. Ohio, parents, b. Ohio, attending school; ***Sara***... ; Dodd Road. 1920 FC OH CYBV ED 509, p. 7B, lines 94-97.

DODD, Wirt W., 60, own home valued at $25,000, no radio, age at first marriage 32, b. Ohio, parents b. Isle of Mann *(Man)*, Builder Homes; ***Elvie E.***, 57, age at first marriage 27, b. Ohio, parents b. Ohio; ***Sarah E***., 11, b. O. (d. 4 Sept 2005, Shreve, OH, 96 yrs.). 1930 FC OH CYBV ED 18-534, p. 21A, 28729 Osborn Rd, lines 15-17, Pat Wymer Gnizak.

DODD, Wert *(sp.)* ***W.***, d. Henrietta, Ohio, 81 yrs., generalized arteriosclerosis, undertaker Marion E. Pease, bur. 12 Sept 1950. Evergreen Cemetery, Westlake, OH.

DODD, Ashton C., 36, married 6 years, b. Ohio, parents English, Carpenter, owned home; ***Clara B.***, wife, 29, b.

Ohio, parents b. Ohio; ***James T.***, son, 1, b. Ohio; Link Road, between Bradley and Bassett. Only family listed both years. 1910 FC OH CYDO, p. 2A, lines 8-10. Similar: 1920 census CYBV, ED 509, p. 6B, lines 57-59.

DODD, Ashton C., 55, owns home valued at $10,000, no radio, age at marriage 27, b. Ohio, parents b. Isle of Mann *(Man)*, Carpenter House Construction; ***Clara L.***, 49, wife, age at marriage 23, b. Ohio, parents b. Ohio; ***James T.***, 21, son, single, b. Ohio, Service man at Gasoline Sta. 1930 FC OH CYBV, ED 18-534, 30513 Link Road, p. 19B, lines 95-97.

Bay Street Honors Vet Employe*(e)*, 83

By John Fisher

A street has been named after 83-year-old ***"Jack" DODD***, a Bay Village service department worker. It is Ashton Lane.

Ashton is Dodd's given name, but his friends and co-workers avoid using that name because of Jack's aversion to it. Jack is a nickname that has stuck with Dodd through his 83 years in Bay Village.

Ashton Lane is the former Link Road, also know to some people as Lincoln Road - that is Ashton Lane - at 30513.

Deliveries Went Astray

Residents of that street decided to seek a change in the street's name because deliveries to their home ended up on Lake Road. The new name was suggested by School Superintendent *Charles M. PATTERSON* at a meeting of residents of the street at the home of Councilman *Lake GILES.*

Council approved the change, Dodd and *Carl MEILANDER* of the service department were ordered to erect a new street sign. Meilander got a kick out of the job. His family lived next door to Dodd on Bassett Road when he was born 53 years ago.

Dodd doesn't think much of the new name. "I liked Link as the name of the street. Before that it was known as Lakeland Road and that was a good name, too, but I don't care much for the new name." he said.

25 years in Department

Dodd has worked in the service department for more than 25 years. Prior to that he was a carpenter.

Asked why he hasn't retired, Jack answered, "Those fellows that retire they soon die. I'm not going to retire until I die."

The only hobby Jack admits to is working. He putters around his small farm when he isn't working for the city.

As a boy in the sparsely settled fishing and farming community then known as Dover Township, Jack said he could always be found on the spacious lake beaches, now almost nonexistent.

He swam and fished there. The fishing was so good that three fisheries were located in the township part of what is now Bay Village. The community also was a grape and peach growing center.

Skated to Downtown.

In 1903, Bay Village seceded from the township and became famous for its summer cottages until the demise of the Lake Shore Interurban in the late 30's. With the postwar building boom the complexion of Bay Village has now completely changed.

Jack can remember when he skated clear to downtown on the ice of Lake Erie. He also remembers his first ride on the Nickel Plate Road. He road a flatcar full of ties while the tracks were under construction in 1882.

Dodd's parents came to Dover in 1868 from the Isle of Man. His father, ***Charles***, was a fisherman and ran a small farm on Bassett Road.

Dodd and his wife, ***Sarah*** *(should read* ***Clara****)*, have one son, ***James***, who lives in Rocky River.

Although it may be Ashton Lane to Jack's neighbors, it still is Link Road to Ashton "Jack" Dodd. Cleveland News, 3 Mar 1958.

DODD, Ashton, age 91, late residence, 30513 Ashton Lane, Bay Village, beloved husband of ***Clara*** (nee ***BROOKS***), father of ***James*** of Avon Lake. Friends may call at the Jenkins Funeral Chapel, 2944 Dover Center Rd., Westlake, where services will be held Thursday, March 11 at 11 a.m. Cleveland Necrology File, Mar 11, 1965, reel 104 Died March 8, 1965 of acute circulatory failure, Bay View Hospital, Bay Village; bur. Evergreen Cemetery Sect. A-2, Lot 181, Grave 4. Ohio Certificate of Death, Division of Vital Statistics, 1965, certif. 18558 and Evergreen Cemetery.

DODD, Clara B., 30513 Ashton Lane, Bay Village, OH, 91; b. Avon, Ohio; d. 25 Feb 1972 to Avon, undertaker: Glen Jenkins, bur. Evergreen Cemetery Sect. A-2, Lot 181, Grave 3. Evergreen Cemetery, Westlake, Ohio.

DODD, James T., res. 699 Center Road, Avon Lake, Ohio; 68 yrs.; b. Bay Village, Ohio; d. 15 Jan 1977, Bay Village of acute cir. collapse, undertaker Glen Jenkins; bur. Evergreen Cemetery Sect. A-2, Lot 232, Grave 8. Evergreen Cemetery, Westlake, Ohio.

OP 4:13 Annie Cowley Dodd

When ***Annie COWLEY*** was five years old, she was listed in the census an extra time as she visited her grandparents. ***Ann SHIMMIN***, 50, Farmers wife; ***John SHIMMIN***, 70, Shoemaker, *Hue QUAY*, 30, Male Servant, *Jane CHRISTIAN*, 25, Female Servant; *Cath COOL*, 20, Female Servant; ***Ann COWLEY***, 5, granddaughter. All individuals born "in the Island." Census of the Population in the Islands in the British Seas, 1841, Isle of Man, Ballahosil German.

DODD, Annie C., head, 74, widow, 6 children born, 5 living, b. Eng., parents b. Eng., immigrated 1868, occup. own income, own free house; ***Eleanor***, daughter, 43, single, b. Eng., teacher, Public School, working, number of weeks out of work during the year 14. 1910 FC OH CYBV ED 9, p. 3B, lines 85-6.

DODD, Annie, head, home owned, 83, widow, house owned free, immigrated 1870, naturalized citizen in 1880, b. Isle of Man, parents b. Isle of Man, occup. none; ***Nell***, daughter, 53, single, immigrated 1870, naturalized citizen

1880, b. Isle of Man, parents b. Isle of Man, teacher, high school, working. 1920 FC OH CYBV ED 509, p. 7B, lines 98-99.

DODD-Annie, widow of the late ***Charles DODD***, at her residence on Osborne road, Bay Village, O., Tuesday, Sept 9, aged 85 years, native of the Isle of Man. Funeral from Bay Village M. E. church, Lake road, Stop 32, Thursday, Sept 11, at 3 p.m. Cleveland Necrology File, Sept 11, 1924.

Annie Cowley DODD, Osborn Rd., Bay, Cuyahoga 9:40 p.m., Cardiac Dilatation with Arterio Sclerosis, Contributory Hemiplegia-Cerebral Thrombosis for 18 mos.; b. April 19, 1836, Ballasalla, Isle of Man, fr. ***Wm. COWLEY***, b. Isle of Man, mo. ***Ann SHIMMIN***, b. Isle of Man; occup. Hwf., 88 yrs. 4 mos. 20 ds.; widowed; informant *Nellie E. DODD*, Bay Village, O.; bur. Bay Village, Sept 11, 1924; undertaker C. Pease, Dover Center, O. Ohio Certificate of Death, Division of Vital Statistics, 1924, certif. 48425.

OP 4:14 Charles Dodd II

CHARLES DODD
1870-1871

Son of Charles Dodd and Annie Cowley above.

Like true wives and women,
they braved the solitude's and dangers
of the wilderness,
toiling with a zeal and purpose
that none but women know,
to hand down a right inheritance
of freedom and intelligence
to their children.
May their great success surround
their declining years
with the joy of "faithful servants."

A Toast made to the Pioneer Women of Dover
Cahoon Fifty-first annual celebration
of the Settlement of Dover, Oct 10, 1861.

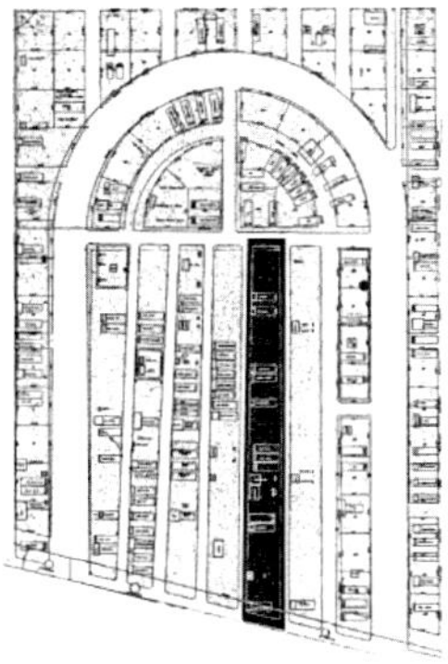

Fifth row east of the west drive starting from the road and proceeding north.

OP 5:1 Sophia Scharnhorst Krumwiede

SOPHIA
SCHARNHARST
Wife of
WM. KRUMWIEDE
BORN
Jan 25, 1822
Died
Aug 8, 1874
Aged 52 Yrs. 6 Mo. 13 D.
Inscription illegible.

Sophia (***KRUMWIEDE)*** arrived in Dover with her husband ***William***, and daughter, ***Mary*** from Hanover, Germany in 1847. Having friends in Cleveland, they traveled directly to that city. William, a carpenter, went to work as a ship's carpenter until they were able to purchase a farm on Walker Rd. in Dover. They built a house on the lot in the early 1860's. Bay Village Historical Society, Bay Village: A Way of Life, p. 52.

Anne Marie Sophia SCHARNHORST, b. 25 Jan 1822 at Baumuhle Su Neustadt on Prunnenberg Konegriede (Kingdom) Hanover, Germany; daughter of ***Velmeirer Fredrick SCHARNHORST*** (b. c1797?, Hanover; m. c1820?, Hanover; d. Germany) and ***Ellnora BRUNS*** (b. c1797?, Hanover, Germany; d. Germany). Carol P. Reed and Rev. Margie Musial Frank.

Anna Marie Sophie SCHARNHORST KRUMWIEDE bore eleven children; only four survived to adulthood. She died when she was 52 years old. Her married daughters no longer lived at home, so ***Minnie***, ten, was expected to stay home and keep house for her father and younger brother, ***Louie***, who was seven. She did the cooking and house keeping from then on, and occasionally helped on the berry farm. Grandma (***Minnie***) told me once how she would put stockings on her arms in the summer when she worked in the fields picking berries, so her arms would not be tan. At that time real ladies did not want to darken and look like field hands. The farm was in an area referred to as Dover, Ohio.

Grandma was expected to make enough pies so her father could have homemade pie with every meal. Of course she also baked bread regularly.

Minnie felt obligated to stay at home and continue to keep house for her father even when ***William Gerrit EPPINK***, was courting her. When she was still not married at 25, apparently late to marry at that time, someone told her that her father had said he didn't know why Grandma didn't get married. It wasn't long after that that Grandma's wedding took place in 1889. Rev. Margie Musial Frank

The name *SCHARNHORST* is famous in Germany, much like Jefferson would be in this country. In one of the famous sea battles of World War II, the German battleship Scharnhorst was sunk. Krumwiede was originally spelled Krummwiede, at some point, one "m" was dropped. Thomas Case

OP 5:1 Heinrich William Krumwiede

(Probable burial site, exact location not identified.)

Heinrich William KRUMWIEDE, son of the English Penshioner Kings Guard, ***Henrich KRUMMWIEDE*** and ***Dorothe*** (nee ***RITTER***) was born at Wendenborstel Amt Wolpe Konigreich Hanover, Germany on December 5, 1816. (There are two small towns north and west of Hanover with these names.)

Wilhelm and ***Sophia*** were married at Stadt Zelle, Germany, on March 25, 1847. In October 1849 they immigrated to America with one child, ***Mary K.*** then 1 1/2 years old. A son, ***William***, was born on the ocean. He lived about two years. Sophia and Wilhelm lived in Cleveland for some time and in 1858 the Krumwiede family moved to Dover, Ohio. There were eleven children, four of which outlived their parents. Stocker Family Reunion papers, early 1950's, in the possession of Carol P. Reed.

The State of Ohio, Cuyahoga County. Be it remembered, That on the 6th day of June A.D. 1853. ***William KRUMWIEDE*** an Alien and Native of Hanover personally appeared before me, *G. GURGHAM* Deputy Clerk of the Court of Common Pleas, in and for said County, and Declared, on his solemn oath, that he first arrived in the United States in the month of October A.D. 1848 and that it is his bona fide intention to become A Citizen of The United States, and to renounce forever all allegiance and fidelity to any Foreign Prince, Potentate, State of Sovereignty whatever, and particularly to *George King of Hanover* and subscribe his name to said Declaration, which remains on file in the office of the Clerk of said Court. Request made to the Cleveland Court on 6 June 1853.

In the matter of the Application of William Krumwiede to become a citizen of the Untied States *David MALLO* of Cleveland being duly sworn, deposes and says, that he is a citizen of the United States; that he has resided within the limits and under the jurisdiction of the United States for five years last past, and for one year last past within the State of Ohio; and that during the same period he has behaved himself as a man of good moral character, attached to the principles of the Constitution of the United States, and well disposed to the good order and happiness of the same. Immigration Records, District Court, National Archives, Chicago #146.

Henry F. KRUMWIDE *(sp.)*, 82 yrs.; res. West Dover; German; interred April 19, 1899; Original Part. "List of Interments," Lakeside Cemetery, Bay Village, OH.

CUMWEDER *(sp.),* ***Wm.***, 54, farmer, value of real estate $1500, personal estate $300, b. Germany; ***Sophia***, 48, keeping house, b. Germany; ***Lizie***, 10, b. Ohio; ***Minnie***, 6, b. Ohio; ***Louie***, 3, b. Ohio. 1870 FC OH CYDO p. 34, lines 32-6.

KRUMWIEDE, John *(assumed to be William),* 63, Farmer, b. Hanover, fr. b. England, mo. b. Hanover; ***Minnie***, 16; ***Louis***, 13. 1880 FC OH CY Rockport, p. 326A. *(Additional mistake with father's place of birth.)*

Children of William Krumwiede and Sophia Scharnhorst:

Heinrich William KRUMWIEDE, a carpenter and farmer, and ***Sophia SCHARNHORST*** arrived from Hanover, Germany in October, 1849. *Issue:* ***Mary KRUMWIEDE***, b. 21 Mar 1848, Hanover, Germ.; d. 6 Jan 1931, Cleveland, OH; m. 10 May 1866 to *Barthlome (Bartholmew) STOCKER* (son of *Andreas STOCKER* and *Magdalena BURRI*, b. 2 Jan 1833, Boltigen, Bern, Switzerland; d. 26 Mar 1923, Cleveland, OH; immig. 22 Apr 1852, NY, NY). ***William KRUMWIEDE***, b. 1849, d. 1852. ***Dora KRUMWIEDE***. ***Sophie KRUMWIEDE.*** ***Henry KRUMWIEDE.*** ***William KRUMWIEDE.*** ***Amelia KRUMWIEDE.*** ***Elizabeth "Lizzie" KRUMWIEDE***, b. 22 May 1860, Cuyahoga Co., OH; m. *Philip HABER*, 6 Dec 1877, Cuyahoga Co., OH. ***Minnie KRUMWIEDE***, b. 27 Mar 1864, Cuy. Co., OH; d. 21 April 1960, OH; m. 27/28 Nov 1889, Cuy. Co., OH to *William EPPINK* (b. July 1858, OH; mo. *Angeline EPPINK*). *Their child is buried in an undetermined lot in the Original Part.* ***Louis***

KRUMWIEDE, b. 24 May 1867, Dover Twp., Cuy Co., OH; d. 1 Oct 1945, Wakeman, OH; bur. Birmingham Cemetery; m.1 16 July 1889 to *Katherine "Katie" QUELL (Lot 9)*, m.2 *Nellie VANDERPLOEG BRUGGERS*, (b. c1880, Holland; d. 25 Dec 1959, Lorain, OH, Wakeman, OH; bur. Birmingham Cemetery). Carol P. Reed, Esther Seitz Matousek and Rev. Margie Musial Frank.

Bartholomew STOCKER, a Swiss immigrant farmer from Bern sometime in the 1840s-50s, joined the Union Cavalry perhaps as a paid substitute for someone who did not want to serve. However, the Union forces quickly needed reinforcements for their Mississippi naval ships, and switched him to the Union Navy.

He served a short while, participating in the Battle of Island No. Ten in the Mississippi between Vicksburg and Memphis. After that he was transferred to a casual ship, the Pittsburg (not 'burgh') and soon mustered out, apparently at the end of his enlistment. He and his wife, ***Mary (KRUMWEIDE)***, also an immigrant, subsequently had 10 children. Thomas Case He was fondly called "*Uncle Bartley*." Frank

STOCKER, Bartholomew, head, 77, married 39 years, b. Switz-German, fr./mo. b. Switz-German, immig. 1852, occup. Own Income, Own house free of mortgage; ***Mary M.***, wife, 62, # children born and living 10, b. Germany, fr./mo. b. Germany; ***Alice B.***, 21, dau., b. Ohio, Stenographer. 1910 FC OH Rockport Village, ED 48, p. 11A, lines 24-6.

STOCKER: Mary, age 82 years, wife of the late ***Bartholomew***, and beloved mother of ***William*** and ***Frank STOCKER, Mrs. C. NYLAND, Mrs. E. PRASSE, Mrs. G. HACKATHORN, Mrs. George C. LANG, Mrs. Edward ZINSER, Mrs. Fred CASE*** and the late ***Lillie*** and ***Sam STOCKER***; grandmother and great-grandmother. Tuesday morning. Funeral Friday, Jan 9, 1931, at 2 p. m., from the home of her daughter, Mrs. C. Nyland, 7001 Lorain Avenue, and 2:30 p. m. from Bethany M. E. Church, corner W. 91st and Willard Avenue. Cleveland Necrology File, Jan 8 1931, reel 078.

STOCKER-Bart, aged 90 years, beloved husband of ***Mary*** (nee ***KRUMWIEDE***), father of ..., Monday p. m. Funeral Thursday, March 29, at 2 p. m., from the late residence and from Bethany M. E. church, corner Willard ave. N. W. and W. 91st street, at 2:30 p. m. Cleveland Necrology File, Mar 26, 1923, reel 078.

Children of Mary Krumwiede and Bartholomew STOCKER:

The State of Ohio, Cuyahoga Co., ss., I Certify that on the 5th day of February 1890, ***Mr. William STOCKER*** and ***Miss Sarah E. FEUCHTER*** were by me legally joined in marriage. O.C. Klocksiem, Pastor. Marriage Record, Cuyahoga County, OH, vol. 34, p. 132.

STOCKER: William, husband of the late ***Sarah***; father of ***Elton, Oliver*** and ***Ray STOCKER*** and ***Mrs. Pearl KNIGHT***; and grandfather; brother of ***Frank*** and ***Mary STOCKER, Mrs. Emma LANG*** and ***Mrs. Alice CASE***; suddenly, Saturday. Friends may call at the Geo. C. Lang Co. Funeral Home, W. 95th St. at Lorain Ave., where services will be held Wednesday, May 15, at 2:30 p. m. Cleveland Necrology File, May 14 1946, reel 078.

STOCKER: Sarah, beloved wife of ***William***, mother of *Elton W., Oliver C., Ray F., Mrs. Pearl KNIGHT*, the late *Wesley, Melvin* and *Hazel*, and grandmother, sister of *William* and *Fred FEUCHTER* and *Mrs. Anna PERKINS*. Sunday evening. At residence, 14131 Lorain ave., until noon Wednesday. Funeral Wednesday, Feb 10, at 2 p. m., from the George C. Lang Co. Funeral Home, W. 95th st. at Lorain ave. Cleveland Necrology File, Feb 10 1937, reel 078.

The State of Ohio, Cuyahoga Co., ss., I Certify that on the 15th day of December 1892, ***Mr. Christopher A. MYLAND*** *(sp.)* and *Miss* ***Lizzie A. STOCKER*** were by me legally joined in marriage. Rev. Chas. Koch *Christopher A. NYLAND* having made application for a Marriage License..signed Christopher A. Nyland. *Note spelling of Nyland.* Marriage Record, Cuyahoga County, OH, vol. 39, p. 56.

NYLAND: Elizabeth A. (nee ***STOCKER***), of 6200 Wakefield ave.; beloved wife of ***Christopher A.***, mother of ***Arthur S., Paul C.*** and the late ***Esther***, also grandmother; sister of ***William, Frank*** and ***Mary STOCKER, Mrs. Sarah PRASSE, Mrs. Emma LANG, Mrs. Rose ZINSER*** and ***Mrs. Alice CASE***; Monday evening. Friends may call at the George C. Lang Co. Funeral Home, W. 95th at Lorain ave. Funeral Thursday, Aug 26 at Christ Methodist Church, W. 138 st. and Lorain, at 2:30 p. m. Cleveland Necrology File, Aug 26 1943, reel 061.

NYLAND, Christopher A., of 15123 Arden Ave., beloved husband of the late ***Elizabeth*** (nee ***STOCKER***); father of ***Arthur S.*** and ***Paul C.***; grandfather of *Paul, jr.*, and *Ted*; brother of *Henry* and *Albert* and the late *Dena TERBEEK, Ellen NYKAMP, Jennie EPPINK* and *Anna DURST*; Wednesday morning. Friends may call at the Geo. C. Lang Co. Funeral Home, W. 95th and Lorain Ave., until Friday Noon. Services at Christ Methodist Church, W. 138th and Lorain, at 2 p. m. (Member of Lakewood Borrowed Time Club.) Cleveland Necrology File, Oct 14 1949, reel 061.

The State of Ohio, Cuyahoga County, ss. I Certify that on the 24th day of June 1896 ***Mr. Emil PRASSE*** and ***Miss Sarah STOCKER*** were by me legally joined in marriage. Rev. J.O. Weidmann Marriage Record, Cuyahoga County, OH, vol. 43, p. 453.

PRASSE: Sarah A., of 1425 Olivewood; wife of the late ***Emil***; beloved mother of ***Harold A.*** and ***Roland E. PRASSE*** and ***Mrs. Erma HART***; sister of ***William, Frank*** and ***Mary STOCKER, Mrs. George C. LANG, Mrs. Alice B. CASE***, the late ***Elizabeth NYLAND, Rose ZINSER, Sam*** and ***Lillie***; also grandmother.

Friday morning. Friends may call at the Geo. C. Lang Co. Funeral Home, W. 95th-Lorain ave., where services will be held Monday, Nov 12, at 3 p. m. Cleveland Necrology File, Nov 12 1945, reel 065.

PRASSE-Emil G., Thursday, July 20. Funeral from his late summer residence, Bonny Bank, Rocky River, Saturday, July 22, 1911, at 2 p. m. 1866 - 1911. Age 45. Riverside Cemetery Cleveland, Ohio. Cleveland Necrology File, July 22, 1911, reel 065.

PRASSE, Sarah A. owner of Lot 29, Section 7, Riverside Cemetery, Cleveland, OH.:

Emil G. PRASSE, 45, d. 21 July 1911 in Cleveland of a gun shot wound, bur. 31 Jul, undertaker Geo. Lang, res. 6109 Wakefield Ave., Cleveland, Grave 1. Stone inscription Emil G. Prasse, Father, 1865-1911.

Samuel E. STOCKER, 31, married, d. 7 May 1917, Cleveland at res. 3227 W. 82nd St., Cleveland of appendicitis, bur. 10 May, Grave 2.

Sarah A. PRASSE, 75, widow; b. Cleveland; d. 9 Nov 1945 in Cleveland of Pulm. Edema, bur. 12 Nov, undertaker Geo. C. Lang at 9437 Lorain Ave.; res. 1425 Olivewood Ave.; grave 3. Stone inscription Sarah, Mother, 1870-1945.

Roland E. PRASSE, 77, married; b. 22 July 1909, Ohio; d. 22 June 1987, Cleveland of Prostate Cancer; services at Mandley Funeral Home, 18871 Lorain Ave., Cleveland. Stone inscription Beloved Husband and Father, Roland E. Prasse, 1909-1987.

Emma HART, 83, widow; b. 3 Oct 1901 in Cleveland; d. 25 Oct 1984 at Elyria Methodist Home of heart failure, bur. 27 Oct, Busch Funeral Home, 4334 Pearl Rd. In loving memory, Emma, 1901-1984.

Riverside Cemetery Records, Cleveland, OH. Inscriptions recorded by Catherine Burke Flament.

Emma STOCKER LANG, the fifth child, was born on the Stocker Farm. She was a partner with her husband, ***George***, in his business as a funeral director and furniture store owner. They had no

children of their own and so dedicated their lives to helping others. Emma Lang Hall, a woman's dormitory, at Baldwin Wallace College and Lang Cottage at the Methodist Children's Home in Berea were just two of their many philanthropies. George died in 1935. In 1952 she was inducted into the Methodist Hall of Fame for Philanthropy "for outstanding contribution to her fellow-man." Her extended family enjoyed many wonderful times at her summer home in Bay, which we called "The Lake House." Alice Case Black *The summer home was next to the cemetery on the east side.*

The State of Ohio, Cuyahoga Co., ss., I Certify that on the 19th day of Jany 1898, ***Mr. George C. LANG*** and ***Miss Emma M. STOCKER*** were by me legally joined in marriage. Rev. F.W. Mueller Marriage Record, Cuyahoga County, OH, vol. 46, p. 34.

LANG. ***Emma M. LANG*** (nee ***STOCKER***), of 2180 West Blvd., beloved wife of the late ***George C. LANG***, sister of ***Mrs. Alice CASE*** and the late ***William, Mary, Frank, Samuel*** and ***Lillian STOCKER, Mrs. Elizabeth NYLAND, Mrs. Sarah PRASSE*** and ***Mrs. Rose ZINSER***, Monday evening. Services Friday, May 19, at Christ Methodist Church, Lorain Ave. at W. 138th St., at 2 p.m. Memorials to Christ Methodist Church, the Methodist Children's Home, Berea, O., or Baldwin Wallace College are suggested. Visiting at The Geo. C. Lang Co. Funeral Home, W. 95th and Lorain Ave. May 19 1967. The Plain Dealer.

LANG: George C., beloved husband of ***Emma M.*** (nee ***STOCKER***), brother of *Mrs. George GRAL* of Dunkirk, N. Y., and *Mrs. John KLINK* of Strongsville, G., Thursday morning. Body will lie in state Saturday, May 11, at the Bethany M. E. Church, Willard and W. 91st St., from 1 p. m. until time of services at 2:30 p. m. 1870-1935. Lakewood Park Cem., Rocky River, Ohio. Cemetery record; Cleveland Necrology File, May 11 1935, reel 049.

Wilber G. HACKATHORN, 45; res. Middlefield, Ohio; b. Chagrin Falls, Ohio; Farmer, fr. *James*, mo. *Mary J. DRAY*; Married Once before (Dec'd). Married ***Mary STOCKER***, 35; res. West Park, Ohio; b. West Park, Ohio; occup. Domestic; fr. *Bart*, mo. *Mary KRUMWIEDE*. The State of Ohio, Cuyahoga Co., ss., I Certify that on the 7th day of September 1910, *Mr. Wilbur G. Hackathorn* and *Miss Mary Stocker* were by me legally joined in marriage. Rev. John W. Kuyper Marriage Record, Cuyahoga County, OH, vol. 76, p. 162.

STOCKER, Mary, sister of ***Frank STOCKER, Mrs. Emma LANG, Mrs. Alice CASE***, and the late ***William*** and ***Samuel STOCKER, Mrs. Elizabeth NYLAND, Mrs. Sarah PRASSE*** and ***Mrs. Rose ZINSER***. Friends may call at the George C. Lang Co. Funeral Home, W. 95 at Lorain Ave., where services will be held Saturday, Sept 13, at 3 p. m. Cleveland Necrology File, Cleveland Press, Sept 12, 1952, reel 159.

The State of Ohio, Cuyahoga Co., ss., I Certify that on the 18th day of November 1896, ***Mr. Frank L. STOCKER*** and ***Miss Jennie TEN HOPPEN*** were by me legally joined in marriage. Rev. F.W. Mueller. Marriage Record, Cuyahoga County, OH, vol. 44, p. 243.

STOCKER. ***Frank STOCKER***, formerly of 1438 Owego Ave., husband of the late ***Jennie***, father of ***Mrs. Janette MAIER*** and ***Barthel***, grandfather and great-grandfather, brother of ***Mrs. Alice CASE, Mrs. Emma LANG*** and the late ***William, Samuel*** and ***Mary STOCKER, Mrs. Elizabeth NYLAND, Mrs. Sarah PRASSE*** and ***Mrs. Rose ZINSER***, Saturday. Friends may call at the Geo. C. Lang Co. Funeral Home,

W. 95th at Lorain Ave. Services Tuesday, Aug 25, at 2 p. m. Member of Lakewood Borrowed Time Club. Aug 25 1964. The Plain Dealer.

STOCKER: Jennie (nee ***TEN HOOPEN***), beloved wife of ***Frank L.***, ... grandmother of *Jean*, sister of *Christina TEN HOOPEN*, *Mrs. Dena BORNEMAN*, the late *Bart, John* and *Ralph TEN HOOPEN* and *Mrs. Johanna SINNEMA*, Wednesday afternoon. Friends may call at the Geo. C. Lang Co. Funeral Home, W. 95 and Lorain ave., where services will be held Saturday, Jan 30, at 3:30 p. m. Cleveland Necrology File, Jan 30, 1943, reel 078.

Edward I. ZINSER, 25, res. 2059 Clark Ave., City, b. El Paso, Ill., occup salesman, fr. *Isaac ZINSER*, mo. *Louisa SCHNEERER*. Married ***Rose M. STOCKER***, 20, res. Rockport, O., b. Rockport, occup. none, fr. *Bartholemew STOCKER*, mo. *Mary KRUMMWIEDE*, neither previously married. The State of Ohio, Cuyahoga Co., ss. I Certify that on the 28th day of June 1899, *Mr. Edward ZINSER* and *Miss Rose M. STOCKER* were by me legally joined in marriage. Rev. F.W. Mueller, Columbus, OH Marriage Record, Cuyahoga County, OH, vol. 49, p. 72.

ZINSER: Rose (nee ***STOCKER***), beloved wife of ***Edward G.***; mother of ***Mrs. Gladys BARBER, Pvt. Earl ZINSER*** and ***Mrs. Fern SEITZ*** and ***Mrs. Ruth DOW*** of California and the late ***Mrs. Myrtle CAMPBELL***, also grandmother, sister of ***William, Frank*** and ***Mary STOCKER, Mrs. Sarah PRASSE, Mrs. Emma LANG, Mrs. Alice CASE***, the late ***Mrs. Elizabeth NYLAND, Sam*** and ***Lilly***; Monday night. Friends may call at the George C. Lang Co. Funeral Home, W. 95 and Lorain ave., where services will be held Thursday, Sept 16, at 2 p. m. Cleveland Necrology File, Sept 16 1943, reel 088.

STOCKER-Lillian K., age 35 years, beloved daughter of ***Mr.*** and ***Mrs. B. STOCKER*** and sister of ***Mrs. George C. LANG, Mrs. C. NYLAND, Mrs. E. E. PRASSE, Mrs. E. ZINSER, Mrs. G. HACKETHORN, Mrs. S. CASE*** and ***Will, Frank*** and ***Sam STOCKER***. Saturday noon. Funeral Tuesday, 1:30 p. m., from her late home, 2200 W. 98th st., and 2 p. m. from the German M. E. church, cor. Willard and W. 91st St. Cleveland Necrology File, Mar 12, 1917, reel 078.

Samuel STOCKER, 23, res. 3109 W. 95th St., b. West Park, O., occup. Manager, fr. *Bartholomew*, mo. *Mary KRUMWIEDE*. Married ***Selma L. GOMMEL***, 22, 2019 W. 48th St., b. Kenndelville, O., occup. Housework, fr. *Jon. C.*, mo. *Caroline BARTH*; neither previously married. The State of Ohio, Cuyahoga Co., ss., I Certify that on the 20th day of October 1909, Mr. Samuel E Stocker and Miss Selma L. Gommel were by me legally joined in marriage. Rev. Elmer Roesner (Gibson Ave.) Marriage Record, Cuyahoga County, OH, vol. 73, p. 398.

STOCKER-Sam E., age 31 years, after a brief illness at Huron Road hospital; beloved husband of ***Selma*** (nee ***GOMMEL***). Funeral Thursday, May 10, 1 p. m. from the home of his father, 2209 W. 98th st., and 2 p. m. from St. Paul's M. E. church, cor. W. 44th and Bridge. 1886-1917. Riverside Cemetery, Cemetery Record and Cleveland Necrology File, May 9, 1917, reel 078.

STOCKER. ***Selma STOCKER*** (nee ***GOMMEL***), wife of the late ***Samuel***, mother of ***John, Raymond*** and ***Carl***, also grandmother, sister of *Mrs. Anita NYLAND, Mrs. Mabel MILLIS* and *Mrs. Hilda REIMERS, Frank, Samuel*, and *Benjamin GOMMEL*, Oct 3, in Phoenix, Ariz. Services in Phoenix, Tuesday, Oct 6. Cleveland Necrology File, Cleveland Press, Oct 5, 1964, reel 159.

Alice STOCKER CASE, the youngest of ten children, was born on the Stocker Farm on Settlement Road, which is now West 130th Street. She was a widow at age 45 and with the help of her sister, ***Emma STOCKER LANG***, was able to raise eight children, six of whom graduated from Parkview High School in Bay. She was a gentle person, gifted and creative in her needlework and poetry that she wrote for her grandchildren. Perhaps the best thing is that she stayed contemporary with each generation which endeared her to her grandchildren. She never complained, she never looked back. Alice Case Black

Alice STOCKER CASE, my mother, widowed with eight children ranging from a year or two up to 18, in the midst of the depression had little time, inclination for laughs. Alice was very quiet, not stern, not given to outbursts of temper or elation. A very sober farmer's daughter who was simply coping during the worst of times. She did attend Baldwin-Wallace college for one year (then called German-Wallace), an accomplishment for the early 1900s. In her later years, kids gone, time on her hands, she began oil painting, a la Grandma Moses' naif style, very creditably. She was quite a reader as are all of her children, grandchildren, and most of her great-grandkids. Thomas Case

Fred B. CASE, 23, res. 667 Parkwood Dr., b. Kingsville, O., occup. Adv. Agt., fr. *Fred C.*, mo. *Jennie VIERS*. Married ***Alice B. STOCKER***, 23, res. 2209 West 98th St., b. West Park, occup. Stenographer, fr. *Bartholomew*, mo. *Mary KRUMWIEDE*; neither previously married. The State of Ohio, Cuyahoga Co., ss., I Certify that on the 25th day of October 1913, Mr. Fred Case and Miss Alice B. Stocker were by me legally joined in marriage. Rev. C.H. Winter. Marriage Record, Cuyahoga County, OH, vol. 86, p. 206.

CASE. Mrs. Alice CASE, 80 years, of 83 North Center St., Seville, passed away at Medina Hospital after a short illness. Born in Cleveland. Resided in Seville past nine years with a daughter *Mrs. Carol CONPARS*, having moved from California. Member of United Methodist Church. Widow of *Fred B. CASE*, survived by children *Mrs. Leila LOFFUS* of Cleveland, *Mrs. Frances PLAGMAN* of Euclid, *Mrs. Emma ZIEGLER* of California, *Thomas CASE* of Bay Village, *Fred CASE* of Minneapolis, *Mrs. Alice BLACK* of Cocoa Beach, Fla., *Mrs. Jean ADAMS* (deceased), 17 grandchildren, nine great-grandchildren. Funeral services Saturday, June 7 at 11 a.m. at The Arrostrong Funeral Home, Seville, where friends may call Friday 2-4 And 7-9 P.M. Burial Lakewood Park Cemetery 1 p.m. Saturday. Contributions may be made to Medina

Community Hospital. June 6 1969, The Plain Dealer.

The State of Ohio, Cuyahoga Co., ss., I Certify that on the Seventh day of December 1877, ***Mr. Philip HABER*** and ***Miss Elizabeth KRUMMWIEDE*** *(sp.)* were by me legally joined in marriage. Philip was twenty years old and needed parental consent to marry. H. Herzer, Minister Marriage Record, Cuyahoga County, OH, vol. 21, p. 261.

HABER, Philip, b. May 1857, 43, married 23 years, b. Ohio, parents b. Germany, Farmer, renting farm; ***Elizabeth***, wife, b. May 1860, 40, 8 children born, 6 living, b. Ohio, parents b. Germany; ***Clara***, dau., b. July 1880, 19, school teacher; ***Louisa***, dau., b. Oct 1882, 17; ***Harvey***, son, b. June 1887, 13; ***Pearl***, dau., b. Dec 1889, 10; ***Emma***, dau., b. June 1892, 8; ***Florence***, dau., 3, b. Mar 1895 *(date and age don't agree)*. 1900 FC OH CY Olmsted Twp., ED 228, p. 167 B, lines 62-69.

HABER, Philip, 53, married 33 yrs., b. Ohio, parents b. Germany, General farmer, own farm free; ***Elizabeth***, wife, 50, 5 children born, 3 living, b. Ohio, parents b. Germany; ***Harvey***, son, 22, Farm laborer at home farm; ***Pearl***, dau., 20; ***Emma***, dau., 18; ***Christine***, mother, 79?, Widow, 4 children born, 3 living?, b. Germany, parents b. Germany. 1910 FC OH CY Olmsted Twp., ED 30, p. 4A, family 78.

HABER, Philip R, 61, b. Ohio, parents b. Germany, farmer, general farm; ***Elizabeth***, 58, b. Ohio, parents b. Germany. 1920 FC OH CY Olmsted Twp., Irish Road, p. 7A, lines 75-6.

HABER: Phillip R., age 84, beloved husband of ***Elizabeth*** (nee ***KRUMWIEDE***), father of ***Mrs. Clara COVILL, Mrs. Louise QUELL, Mrs. Pearl DONVILLE*** and the late ***Harvey***, brother of *Henry HABER*, grandfather and great-grandfather. Friends may call at the residence, Water st., Olmsted Falls. Services at the Community Church, Friday at 2:30 p. m. Cleveland Necrology File, Dec 25 1941, reel 033.

Minnie KRUMWIEDE EPPINK *son buried in an "Undetermined Lot" of the Original Part.*

Louis KRUMWIEDE, *information under wife*, ***Kate QUELL KRUMWIEDE***, *Lot 9:17.*

OP 5:2 James Goodrich

JAMES
SON OF
JAMES & JULIA
GOODRICH
DIED OCT 10, 1848
Aged
19 M. 7 D.

James Goodrich, the oldest of eight children of James Goodrich and Julia Ann Aldrich.

Parents of James Goodrich:

James GOODRICH, b. 18 Nov 1818, Elizabethtown, Essex Co., NY; d. 17 Sep 1895, Colon, St. Joseph Co., MI; m. ***Julia Ann ALDRICH*** (dau. of *Aaron ALDRICH* and *Elizabeth WINSOR, both OP 4:1;* b. 10 Apr 1820, d. 22 Nov 1907).

Issue: ***James GOODRICH***, b. 3 Mar 1847, d. 10 Oct 1848. ***Hiram GOODRICH***, b. 1 Aug 1849, d. 28 Feb 1933, m. *Anna ___*. ***Julia Ann GOODRICH***, b. 8 Mar 1850; d. 18 Oct 1929; m. 3 July 1884, *Wilbur GILLETTE*. ***Eugene GOODRICH***, b. 12 Feb 1852; d. 26 Mar 1918; m. 5 Mar 1885, *Sarah Fern SAGE*. ***Aaron Aldrich GOODRICH***, b. 8 Feb 1853; d. 2 Oct 1931; m. 14 Aug 1883 *Bridget T. KEARNS*. ***Henry W. GOODRICH***, b. 12 May 1856; d. 4 June 1922; m. 23 Jan 1877, *Ella ___*. ***William Waterman GOODRICH***, b. 17 July 1858; d. 4 Sep 1898; m. 28 Feb 1877, *Grace WOODBURY*. ***Philip M GOODRICH***, b. 21 Nov 1861, m. *Mattie CROSS*. George H. Drake, "Aldrich Generation Chart," p. 9.

Rev. James GOODRICH married ***Julie Ann ALDRICH***, daughter of ***Aaron ALDRICH*** and ***Elizabeth WINSOR*** *(OP 4:1)* in North Dover on June 11, 1846 and preached at the Baptist Church there. He left there after three years and in succeeding churches, he met problems of people divided on the subject of slavery.

He died of a malignant carbuncle on Sept 17, 1895. Julie Ann outlived him by several years, as she died Nov 22, 1907. They were always a very religious family and several descendants become missionaries. Gertrude Aldrich Barker Rose, "Genealogy of the Aldrich Family," p. 15.

OBITUARY.

GOODRICH.- September 17, 1895, at the old homestead near Colon, Mich., ***Rev. James GOODRICH***, aged 76 years, 10 months and 6 days.

Deceased was born November 11, 1818, in Elizabethtown, Essex Co., N.Y. His first religious experience was when about ten years old. These continued until at the age of twenty he found peace in believing. Immediately he was drawn to a preparation for the ministry. With this object in view, he entered Madison (now Colgate University), at Hamilton, N.Y., the next year, and in 1845 was ordained and began his life-work at Crown Point, N.Y. The following year he was married to ***Julia Ann ALDRICH***, of North Dover, O., and in 1847 made that place his field of labor. Throughout his entire ministry his choice was to labor with feeble broken-down or divided churches, for such fields his mild and earnest disposition well fitted him. Previous to the late war he settled with a church which seemed hopelessly divided over the slavery question. At the end of three years he closed his labors with them and sought another field because he found another church in the same condition, needing the same kind of help. Both were left after a three years' effort in each, working together in harmony and with any additions as the result.

It was his purpose to make every discourse a direct appeal to the sinner's heart. This followed by his daily pastoral visiting, with religious conversation and prayer made his ministry abundant in spiritual results. During one of his pastorates it is said that "scarcely a monthly meeting but one or more members were taken into the church, who had been baptized since his last monthly meeting. His special or revival efforts were not without results, but were quiet, earnest seasons of seeking God, and often resulted in many conversions."

In 1862 his family consisted of six sons and one daughter, one son having died from being burned in infancy, and he began to cast about him for a plan to get them away from town upon a farm, thinking in this way to have a better opportunity to exert a right influence over them and to make them useful men and women. To accomplish this he moved from Huntington, Ind., to Colon, Mich., and settled on a farm where he lived at the time of his last illness. Here he worked with his boys, teaching them, as he so well knew how, the way of peace. "Every morning," says a son, "after the morning meal, we gathered for family worship. Each one old enough to read, read a portion of scripture; then some appropriate song was sung, and while we all bowed, father commended us to God for the day, earnestly imploring the inspiration of the Holy Spirit, that we might all walk together in the narrow way. Thus he led and taught us."

During a portion of the eight years he lived on the farm he supplied the Baptist Church at Colon; but he could not be satisfied, and after six months' mission labor in the Burr Oak Church, in 1871 he accepted a call to the church at Orland, Ind., where he remained three years. At this time the church at Huntington, O., where he had before labored three years, desired him to return to that field, which he did, remaining with them four years and six months.

During the last few years of his life he was much sought for to solemnize marriages. His presence seemed a benediction on the bridal pair and company present.

During the extreme suffering experienced from a malignant carbuncle which resulted in death, the patient sufferer would often say: "Father, take me, I want to come home."

During his illness he made complete preparation for his funeral, even to the details of selecting the text from which he desired the sermon to be preached, the hymns to be sung, and also a place of burial. At his request his six sons bore him to the tomb. The only daughter was not present, being on an extended tour through England, Ireland, and the Continent. June 3, 1896, would have been his golden wedding, had his life and that of his surviving widow been continued until that date. "Servant of God, well done. Rest from thy loved employ." Baptist Christian Herald (Mich.) Wellington Enterprise, 30 Oct 1895, p. 5, cols. 2-3.

OP 5:3 **Lina (Geuder)**

LINA
daughter of
A&L GEUDRG
DIED
1855
AGED
?
(Inscription worn)

Lina's last name has not been determined, sources vary as described below.

Previously read in 1934 as "***Lena***, dau. of ***A & L Gender***, died Nov 20, 1858, age 2 m. 18 d." Cuyahoga County Cemetery Inscriptions vol. 1, p. 142.

Plot maps for Dover-Bay Village show ownership of the central and eastern section of Lot 94, the lot next to the cemetery, as:

1852	*P. KRAUSS*
1858	***A. GEUIDER**** or ***GUEDER***
1860	***Adolphus GEUDER***, 101 3/4 acres
1874	***A. GENDER***, 101 3/4 acres
1882	Jno. HUNTINGTON

Adolphus GEIDER, 34, farmer, value of real estate $3,200, personal estate $300, b. Bavaria; ***Charlotte***, 30, b. Bavaria; ***Gemett***, female, 7; ***Godlelb?***, 6, male; ***Charlotte***, 5; ***George***, 3, male; *Godery BROIE*?, 64?, b. Bavaria. All children b. Ohio. 1860 FC OH CYDO p. 47, lines 21-27. *Very difficult to read.*

This family is not found in the 1870 census on Lot 94, instead Henry Noek is listed with his family. Numerous mistakes are listed in this census. The family could not be traced after this time period.

OP 5:4

Probably the original marker for Mary E. Osborn, below.

MOTHER

OP 5:5

Probably the original marker for Samuel F. Osborn, below.

FATHER

OP 5:6 Osborn Monument

SAMUEL F.
OSBORN
1842-1897
MARY E.,
HIS WIFE
1851-1922
OSBORN

NETTIE PEARL
1878-1882

OP 5:6 **Samuel Foster Osborn**

Samuel is the fourth child of Selden Osborn and Nancy Ruple (OP 5:8). The inscription above does conflict with the date of birth listed below which is believed to be accurate.

Samuel Foster OSBORN, b. Aug 28, 1841; m. ***Mary CROCKER***; d. April 12, 1897; bur. Lakeside Cemetery. C.M. Osborn, 'The Osborn Family of Bay Village, Ohio" p. 6.

OSBORN, Samuel** F.*, 38, farmer, b. Ohio, fr. b. Conn., mo. Ohio; ***Mary, 28, b. Ohio, fr. b. Mass, mo. b. NY; ***Clayten***, 7, b. Ohio; ***Florence***, 4, b. Ohio; ***Nettie***, 2, b. Ohio; *AHRLING, John*, 20, servant, laborer, b. Ohio, parents b. Hanover. 1880 FC OH CYDO ED 213, p. 94, lines 28-33, house 233. *Mary Crocker, 54, mother of Mary, and her daughter Sarah P., 33, school teacher, were living next door in house 232.*

OSBORN, Samuel; rents for fixed money rental. Acres: Improved: 83 tilled, including fallow and grass, 8 permanent meadows, Unimproved: 25 woodland. Farm Values: Land : $10,000, Machinery: $100, Live Stock: *not legible*. Labor: Paid for wages in 1879: $200; weeks hired 70. Estimated value of all farm production: $600. Grass lands: acreage: 30 mown, 20 not mown, 17 tons hay. 3 horses, 4 milch cows, 4 other. Calves: 5 dropped, 2 cattle sold living, 5 slaughtered, 2 died, stolen or strayed and not recovered. 400 pounds of butter made on the farm. 63 sheep on hand June 1, 1880, 30 lambs dropped in 1879, 36 purchased, 75 sold living, 1 slaughtered, 1 died of disease, 33 fleeces, weight: 165 lbs. 6 swine. 30 barnyard poultry on farm, 125 dozen eggs produced in 1879. Indian corn: 6 acres, 280 bushels; oats: 9 acres, 447 bushels; wheat: 6 acres, 114 bushels; potatoes: 2 acres, 250 bushels. Orchards: apple: 1 acre, 40 bearing trees. Amount of wood cut: 30 cords. Value of forest products: $150. "Schedule 2. Production of Agriculture in Dover Township, Cuyahoga County, OH," enumerated June, 1880, p. 23.

***S. F. OSBORN**,* 56; res. West Dover; interred April 15, 1897; Original Part. "List of Interments," Lakeside Cemetery, Bay Village, OH.

Children of Samuel Osborn and Mary Crocker:

Issue: ***Clayton Seldon OSBORN***, b. 1873, Dover Twp., Cuy. Co., Ohio; d. 22 June 1911, Cleveland, Cuy Co., OH *(Lot 43)*. ***Florence OSBORN***, b. 1876, Dover Twp.; m. *James M. STEWART*. ***Nettie Pearl OSBORN,*** b. 1878, Dover Twp.; d. 1882, Dover Twp. *(this lot)*. ***Nellie A. OSBORN**,* b. Apr 1881, Dover; d. 8 Apr 1936; m. *William M. ALEXANDER*; no issue. ***Ray S. OSBORN**,* b. June 1884, Dover; d. 1948; bur. Evergreen Cem, Westlake, OH. ***Leveret C. OSBORN***, b. Jan 1887, Dover. ***Alice Minerva OSBORN,*** b. July 1889, Dover; d. 1959; bur. Evergreen Cem., m. *Clifford PEASE*. ***Russell F. OSBORN***, b. July 1893, Dover. Keith M. Sheldon, Descendants of Early Bay Village Families, p. 552 and 1900 FC OH CYDO, p. 11A; Certificate of Death, Division of Vital Statistics, 1936, certif 22954.

ALEXANDER: Nellie, 7829 Euclid ave., wife of the late William, sister of …Services at Clifford Pease Funeral Home, 2914 Dover rd., Dover Center, O., Saturday, April 11, at 3 p. m. Cleveland Necrology File, reel 1, Apr 11 1936.

STEWART, Florence M., wife of the late ***J. Mont;*** mother of ***James M.***; grandmother of *John* and *Nancy*; sister of ***Mrs. Alice O. PEASE, Leverett*** and ***Russell OSBORN***, and ***Mrs. Nelle ALEXANDER*** and ***Ray***, deceased. Friends may call at the Clifford Pease Funeral Home, 2914 Dover Center Rd., Westlake, where services will be held Friday, March 17, at 3:30 p. m. Res. and d. Westlake, Ohio; d. breast cancer; bur. Sect. K, Lot 9, Grave 2. Cleveland Necrology File, Mar 16 1950, reel 078; Cleveland Necrology File, roll 143 and Evergreen Cemetery, Westlake, Ohio.

STEWART-James M. (Mont)**,* of 126 River Street, Willoughby, Ohio, husband of ***Florence (nee ***OSBORN***), father of ***James***, son of *Mrs. J. W.(M) STEWART* and brother of *Nina S. WRIGHT*, suddenly Saturday, Dec 15. Remains and services at Clifford Pease Funeral Home, Dover Center, O., Tuesday, Dec 18, at 1:30 p. m. 1874-1928. Evergreen Cemetery, Dover, Ohio; Sect K, Lot 9, Grave 1. Cleveland Necrology File, reel 078 and Evergreen Cemetery.

STEWART, James M., res. 36853 Ridge Road, #514, Willoughby, Ohio; 86 yrs. b. Cleveland; d. 8 Mar 1998, Chardon, Ohio of lymphoma; Jenkins Funeral Home; Evergreen Cem., Sect. K, Lot 9, Grave 4. Evergreen Cemetery, Westlake, Ohio.

Ray S. OSBORN, 51; res. 591 Bradley Rd., Bay Village; b. Dover, O.; occup. Farmer; fr. *Samuel OSBORN*, mo. *Mary CROCKER*. Married ***Sarah E. PALMER***, 45; res. 2907 *(inaccurate house number)* Lake Rd., Bay Village, O.; b. Beaver Falls, Pa.; occup. none; fr. *George PALMER*, mo. *Alice BRAINARD*; neither previously married. On 29th day of June 1934 Ray S. Osborn and Sarah E. Palmer were legally married, Cuyahoga County, OH. Marriage Record, Cuyahoga County, OH, vol. 172, p. 52.

Ray OSBORN dated ***Sallie*** for a long time before they were married and is remembered as an extremely nice individual. He had a cottage or cabin in Hudson, OH. Ronald G. Osborn

OSBORN, RAY S., husband of the late ***Sallie***.... Feb 22, 1948. The Plain Dealer. All rights reserved. Reprinted with permission.

REMODELS HOME, DIES AT WORK

AVON LAKE-***Ray S. OSBORN***, 64, 112 Moorland Dr., Stop 58 1/2, Avon Lake, was found dead in the second story bedroom he was remodeling at his home Saturday afternoon, according to deputy sheriffs.

Dr. S.C. WARD, Lorain, coroner, returned a verdict of death due to natural causes.

Osborn had been suffering from a heart ailment for some time, according to his niece, ***Mrs. Clifford PEASE***, Westlake.

Osborn was the brother of ***Mrs. Alice PEASE***. She and Mrs. Clifford Pease are operators of the Pease funeral home, Westlake.

Osborn had lived alone since the death of his wife, ***Sally***, last Dec 18.

The body was found by Mrs. Alice Pease and another relative, ***James R. PEASE***, Westlake. They came to the home to investigate after neighbors reported not having seen Osborn for some time. Mrs. Alice Pease said she phoned the neighbors because Osborn had failed to come to their house for the week-end as was his custom. Neighbors said they had last heard the sound of Osborn working in the upstairs bedroom last Tuesday.

Osborn had lived in Avon Lake since last summer. In the past several years he had worked as a floor manager at various exhibits at Public Auditorium, Cleveland.

Born in Westlake, Osborn was a member of the Westlake Congregational church and the Bay Village Reading Club.

Surviving are two sisters and two brothers, ***Mrs. Alice PEASE*** and ***Mrs. Florence STEWART***, Westlake; ***Russell OSBORN***, Hudson and ***Leverett OSBORN***, San Francisco, Cal.... Undetermined Newspaper article, Pease Funeral Home Records, Mss. 4809, Western Reserve Historical Society, Cleveland, OH.

Ray Sylvanus OSBORN, b. June 26, 1883, Dover, Cuy. Co., Ohio; widower of ***Sallie*** (nee ***PALMER***); d. 2/17/48, P.M., 64 yrs. 7 mos. 21 days; rel. Cong., Rev. Harold Freer, Westlake. Pease Funeral Home Records, Mss. 4809, Western Reserve Historical Society, Cleveland, OH, Record of Funeral, p. 184.

Leverett OSBORN: His first wife ***Mabel BARNES*** died at child birth. No other children. He married a second time to ***Emily*** from or in Kentucky. No recorded children. Ronald G. Osborn

OSBORN-Mabel L. (nee ***BARNSON***), wife of ***Leverett C. OSBORN***, formerly of Dover and Cleveland, Sunday, Oct 27, at San Francisco, Cal. Funeral services at San Francisco Tues., Oct 29, at 10 a.m. Cleveland Necrology File, Oct 30, 1918.

Leverett Crocker OSBORN, 39 yrs., resident of Oakland, Alameda Co., California. Married ***Emily McCLAIN***, 42, resident of San Francisco; Dec 16, 1924, City of San Francisco. Married by W.J. Fisher. Marriage Certificate with Pease Funeral Home Collection, Mss. 4809, Western Reserve Historical Society, Cleveland, OH.

OSBORN, LEVERETT C., at residence, San Francisco, Cal., Mar 10, husband of ***Emily***, brother of ***Mrs. Alice PEASE*** of Westlake and ***Russell*** of Macedonia. Services in San Francisco. Cleveland Necrology File, Mar 11 1951.

Alice Minerva OSBORN, 21; res. West Dover; Ohio, b. same; occup none. Married ***Clifford PEASE***, 30; res. Dover, Ohio, b. same; occup. Funeral Director; fr. *James A.*, mo. *Asenath ABELL;* neither previously married. Marriage solemnized by A. Aldrich (Dover O). On 28th of September 1909, Alice Minerva Osborn and Clifford Pease of Cuyahoga County, OH. Marriage Record, Cuyahoga County, OH, vol. 73, p. 309.

Clifford PEASE, 30, b. Ohio; ***Alice***, wife, 22, b. Ohio; ***Mary OSBORN***, mother-in-law, 58, b. Ohio. 1910 FC Miracode OH, East Cleveland, Cuyahoga Co., ED 11, visit 178.

PEASE, Clifford, 30, head, b. Ohio, parents b. Ohio, undertaker, married 1 yr., renting house; ***Alice***, wife, 22...; ***OSBORN, Mary***, mother-in-law, 58, widow, 8 children born, 7 living. 1910 FC OH CYDO, p. 8B, lines 89-91.

PEASE, Alice O. (nee ***OSBORN***), beloved wife of the late ***Clifford***; mother of ***Marion E.***, and ***Kenneth*** (deceased); sister of ***Russell***. Friends may call at the late residence, 2940 Dover Center Rd., Westlake, Until 2 P. M. Saturday. Services private. The family suggests that contributions may be made to the Dover Congregational Church Building Fund. Mar 28 1959. The Plain Dealer. All rights reserved. Reprinted with permission. and Cleveland Necrology File, reel 143.

Children of Clifford Pease and Alice Minerva Osborn:

PEASE-Kenneth Osborn, son of ***Clifford*** and ***Alice*** (nee ***OSBORN***), Dover, Ohio, suddenly Saturday, Apr 22, 7 a. m., age 3 years 16 days. Burial Evergreen cemetery, Dover, Saturday, Apr 22, 4 p. m. April 25, 1916. Cleveland Necrology File, reel 063.

Marion E. Pease, 81, was longtime funeral director

AVON

Marion E. PEASE was a graduate of the Cleveland College of Embalmers and received a funeral director's license in December 1933. The following year, she received an embalmer's license and became one of the first women to be licensed as an embalmer in Ohio.

Miss Pease, 81, died Thursday at Avon Oaks nursing home in Avon. She had suffered a stroke two years ago.

Born in Dover, which later became Westlake, Miss Pease was a 1928 graduate of Dover High School, now Westlake High School. She attended Wooster College but graduated from Oberlin College.

Her father, the late ***Clifford PEASE***, was a funeral director in Westlake for 50 years. Mr. Pease's mother was the granddaughter of *Lorenzo CARTER*, who in 1797 became Cleveland's first permanent settler. Miss Pease also was a descendant of the Osborns, who were among the first settlers along Lake Erie in 1810. Her maternal grandparents, *Jedediah* and *Sarah CROCKER*, built the first home site in Westlake, now the location of the Atrium office building on Detroit Rd. The Crockers were among eight families who founded Dover Congregational Church after moving here from Lee, Mass.

After Miss Pease's mother sold the family funeral home, Miss Pease conducted funerals from the *Mark KACIREK* Funeral Home 29060 Lorain Ave., North Olmsted.

Miss Pease was a member of the Ohio and National Association of Funeral Directors and Cleveland and Ohio Embalmers Association. She was past first vice regent of the *Nathan Perry Chapter*, Daughters of the American Revolution; a member of the Cora Griswold Chapter of the Order of the Eastern Star of Westlake; and a member of the Dover Congregational Church of Westlake since 1926.

Services will be at 12:30 p.m. Wednesday at the Kacirek funeral home. December 1, 1991, p. 9B. The Plain Dealer.

PEASE ***Marion E. PEASE***, beloved daughter of the late ***Clifford*** and ***Alice*** (nee ***OSBORN***) ***PEASE***, loving sister of the late ***Kenneth PEASE***, dear "Second Mother" of *Christine Eyon KITCHENS, Mrs. Norman* and *Leonore (Lenny) CRAWFORD*, long-time friend of the *Richard J. REIDY* family of Lorain, Ohio. Also, survived by many cousins. Funeral services Wednesday, December 4, 12:30 p.m. at the Kacirek Funeral Home, 29060 Lorain Rd. North Olmsted where friends may call Tuesday, 3-5 and 7-9 P.M. Interment Evergreen Cemetery. Contributions may be made to the Salvation Army or Cleveland Animal Protective League. December 1, 1991, p. 8B. The Plain Dealer.

Russell Foster OSBORN, b. 18 July 1891, Dover, Ohio; d. 23 Nov 1963, Wadsworth, Ohio; bur. Crown Hill Cem., Twinsburg, Ohio; m. 17 Nov 1917, Akron, Ohio to ***Opal Marie SENTER*** (b. 3 Mar 1895, Macedonia, Ohio; d. 2 Jan 1984, bur. Crown Hill Cemetery). *Issue:* ***Glenn Russell OSBORN***, b. 6 Feb 1920, Macedonia, Ohio; m. 26 April 1941 to *Ruth STAEDTLER* and ***Delbert James OSBORN***, b. 22 Sept 1924, Macedonia; m. May 4, 1957 in Russell Township, Geauga County, Ohio to *Betty Jane BURGENSON* (b. October 25, 1925).

Russell and Opal moved from Dover to Macedonia and bought a farm in 1918. The new Chrysler Stamping Plant in Twinsburg needed rail service and the railroad bought their farm and they moved to Sharon Center, Ohio in 1956.

Russell kept a neat, clean dairy farm with the buildings always painted. He was very respected by his neighbors and had that New England dry sense of humor, as a teen it was always very hard to tell if he was serious or joking. Sunday, other than milking the herd (up at 5:00 every morning and still at it until the evening milking was over at 7:30), was a day of rest. They always had visitors on Sunday, never knowing who it would be. Everyone would sit and talk, then Opal, my grandmother, would serve pie or cake with ice cream. One Sunday, one of the visitors made a comment that it must be nice that I was there helping with the farm work for the summer. My grandfather did not miss a beat and said, "well if we could get him out of bed in the morning and he didn't eat so much, he'd be a much better helper." I guess I really believed him. My grandmother always told that story and how she had to reassure me that that was not how he really felt. (For the record, I worked for free, never ever thought about being paid).

Russ's son, ***Glenn OSBORN*** worked on the farm until his teens and then worked at different local small businesses. He started work at Warner and Swasey in 1938 as a machinist staying until January 1944. He was married to ***Ruth STAEDTLER*** who was a Twinsburg resident in 1941. The couple lived in a apartment on the square in Twinsburg when their first child, ***Carolyn*** was born. Needing more space they purchased a home in Twinsburg. In early 1944 he left his job to go back to the family farm to help his brother because his father, Russell, had a heart attack. He joined the US Navy July 28, 1944 and served through February 13, 1946 as a machinist mate. Glenn sailed from New York City through the Panama Canal in support of different naval operations and ended up in Japan days after the surrender of that country. He served aboard (Patrol Craft) PC1210, PC1413, & PC464. After the war he worked at Bedford Nash, Bedford Ford as a mechanic. His interest in police work started in 1948 as a part time constable for Twinsburg Township until he was appointed as the first Chief of Police of the newly incorporated village of Twinsburg in 1955. He served as Chief of Police until his retirement in 1976. During those years he saw the department grow from 4 to 21 employees. Glenn served as President of the Ohio Chiefs of Police Association and the Cuyahoga County Chiefs of Police for one. One of Glenn's employees once said of him, "I did not always agree with his policies and decisions, but I always respected the man for his decisions, his integrity was impeccable." Issue: ***Carolyn Ann OSBORN***, b. Bedford, OH. ***Ronald Glenn OSBORN***, b. 23 Jan 1947, Bedford; m.1 10 Aug 1968/div. Aug 1979 to *Pearl Jean ZINGARO*; *children Stefanie Denise* and *Amy Therese;* m.2 6 June 1981, Twinsburg to *Linda Joyce BRAUN.* ***Christine Ellen OSBORN***, b. Bedford.

Delbert stayed home and worked the family farm. He learned everything from his father and took control of the operation. During World War II, Del took the exemption farmers had though it was tough because he wanted to serve his country. Though his father worked with him until his death, Del was always ready to keep modernizing and up-grading the farm equipment. He was definitely a jack of all trades. This patient man is an amazingly dedicated person. He never had a vacation because the cows always had to be milked twice a day, morning and night. He married late in life and neighbors helped out with the farm so they could have a honeymoon. In 1956 when the old family homestead was sold to the railroad, Del moved the family farm thirty miles away. Del and ***Betty*** as with his father, had only one child, Russell, stay on to keep on farming, the other Osborn boys opting to have other careers. Delbert is that person that would give you the shirt off his back. As the young teenager working summers, I never saw Delbert show anything but respect to his father. As my uncle he taught me so much about life, machinery, and animals. I loved the respect he gave me and the confidence he had in me, which goes a long way with a teenager. Issue: *Karl James OSBORN, Russell Ray OSBORN and James Delbert OSBORN.* All children b. Wadsworth, OH. Ronald G. Osborn

OSBORN, Russell F. of Wadsworth, O., beloved husband of ***Opal***, father of ***Glenn R.***, and ***Delbert J.*** and grandfather, brother of the late ***Raymond, Leverett, Florence STEWART, Alice PEASE***, and ***Nellie ALEXANDER*** passed away Wednesday…Funeral Home, Hudson, O., Services Saturday, Nov 30, 1963, at 1:30, Interment Crown Hill Cemetery. Nov 29, 1963. The Plain Dealer.

OP 5:6 Mary Crocker Osborn

OSBORN, Mary E., 42, head, b. Nov 1852, Ohio, fr. b. New York, mo. b. Mass., farmer, 8 children born, 7 living; ***Nellie A.***, 19, b. Apr 1881, Ohio; ***Ray S.***, 15, b. June 1884, Ohio; ***Leveret C.***, 13, b. Jan 1887, Ohio; ***Allice M.***, 10, b. July 1889, Ohio; ***Russle F.***, 6, b. July 1893, Ohio; own farm free. 1900 FC OH CYDO p 11, lines 17-22, house 209. *Mary and Sarah CROCKER next-door.*

OSBORN-Mary E., mother of ***Ray, Levrette, Russell, Mrs. J. M. STEWART, Mrs. William ALEXANDER*** and ***Mrs. Clifford PEASE***, Thursday December 28, age 71 years. Funeral from residence of her daughter, Mrs. Clifford Pease, Dover Center, Ohio, Sunday, December 31, at 2:30 p.m. Cleveland Necrology File, Dec 28, 1922.

Mrs. Mary Elizabeth OSBORN, Dover Center Rd., Dover, Cuy. Co.; Dec 28, 1922, 6 a.m. Strangulated umbilical hernia-3ds., Contributory Chronic umbilical hernia-many years; Widow of ***Samuel OSBORN***; occup. Hwf.; b. Nov 22, 1851, Dover, fr. ***Sylvanus CROCKER***, b. Mass., mo. ***Mary O'BRIEN***, b. New York; 71 yrs. 1 mo. 6 ds.; informant *Mrs. Clifford PEASE*, Dover Center, O.; bur. Osborn Cemetery, Dec 31, 1922, undertaker C. Pease. Ohio Certificate of Death, Division of Vital Statistics, 1922, certif. 62613.

Mrs. Mary Elizabeth OSBORN, Dover, 71, Strangulated Umbilical Hernia, undertaker H.S. Weller, Cuyahoga Falls, O., issued Dec 30, 1922, interred Dec 31, 1922. Burial Removal Permit, City of Bay Village, OH.

Sylvanus Crocker, Mary's father, may have been the son of Jedediah and Sarah Crocker:

Jedediah CROCKER of Lee, Massachusetts, bought in Dover and in June, 1811, came west as far as Euclid. He remained there while his son *Noah* with a wife and three children came onto Dover and began clearing on his father's land. After a time he found work in Elyria and worked there from time to time while clearing on his father's farm. This he found more remunerative than farming, and when in 1816 Jedediah came on to Dover with his family, he had sold all the land he bought from *HUBBARD* and *STOWE* of Connecticut except two lots. He sold it for $1.25 per acre, what it cost him. When he came his nearest neighbors were *Barnabas HALL, Thomas FOOT, Sylvanus PHINNEY, Bernard CASE, Jesse LILLY, Jonathan SMITH,* and *Harry* and *Jasper TAYLOR*. William R. Coates, A History of Cuyahoga County and the City of Cleveland, Dover, vol. I, p. 143.

Parents of Mary Crocker Osborn:

Sylvanus CROCKER, 55, farmer, b. Mass.; ***Mary***, 34, b. N.Y.; ***Sarah Polly***, 13, b. Ohio; ***Mary E.***, 8, b. Ohio; ***Jedediah***, 4, b. Ohio; ***Sophrana***, 2, b. Ohio. 1860 FC OH CYDO, p. 50, lines 6-11, dwelling 373.

Sylvanus CROCKER, along with *Reuben OSBORN, Calvin PHINNEY* and *Josiah HURST* were the incorporators of the Dover Congregational Church on February 9, 1831. Bay Village Historical Society, Bay Village: A Way of Life, p. 15.

Sylvanus CROCKER, b. c1797; d. 31 March, 1876; ***Mary*** b. 1826, d. 1904; in the same lot as ***Sophrana*** b. 1857, d. 1864; and ***Sarah P.***, b. 1846, d. 1929. Additional lot ***Sylvanus J.*** 1851-1940 with ***Emeline*** 1859-1945. Evergreen Cemetery, Westlake, OH.

Mary (Mrs. Sylvanus CROCKER), maiden name ***O'BRIEN***; ***Mrs. Thomas O'BRIEN*** (maiden name ***Elizabeth HALL***); ***Ann (Mrs. Aaron Winsor ALDRICH****, (daughter-in-law of Aaron ALDRICH and Elizabeth WINSOR OP 4:1),* maiden name ***O'BRIEN***; are all listed as arriving in Dover in 1835, coming from Clarkson, NY. Women in the Western Reserve, Prior to1840, p. 18. *There is a possibility that Mary may be the sister of Eliza O'Brien Coppin (OP 2:15) and Ann, Mrs. Aaron Winsor Aldrich.*

Sibling of Mary Crocker Osborn:

Sylvanus CROCKER, 23, Farmer, value of real estate $3,200, b. Mass.; ***Mary***, 25, b. NY; ***Sarah***, 4, b. Ohio; ***Sarah,*** 87, b. Mass. 1850 FC OH CYDO p. 218 A, lines 2-23.

OP 5:7 **Nettie Pearl Osborn**

NETTIE

Nettie P. OSBORN, 4; res. Dover; interred April 29, 1880; Original Part. "List of Interments," Lakeside Cemetery, Bay Village, OH.

OSBORN, Ettie, d. Mar 28, 1882; Dover; 4 yrs.; b. Dover, parents ***Saml. OSBORN*** and ***Mary***; disease C___ps. PD 2:131.

OP 5:8 Selden Osborn Monument

SELDEN OSBORN
DIED
APL. 23, 1867
Aged 58 Y. 4 M.

NANCY R.
wife of
SELDEN OSBORN
died
Jan 14, 1890
Aged 76 Yrs. 9 M. 22 D.

MARY R.
died Feb 28, 1844
aged 6 months
JOHN R.
died Aug 28, 1856
aged 11 yrs. 9 months
children of
S. & N. Osborn

Small stone also marked S. Osborn

OP 5:8 **Selden Osborn**

Selden OSBORN, b. 9 June 1809 in Camden, NY, was the son of ***Reuben OSBORN*** and ***Sarah JOHNSON*** *(OP 4:7-8)*. He arrived in Dover Township with his parents on May 17, 1811 and later took ***Nancy RUPLE***, of Euclid, OH as his wife. The Osborns had nine children. Bay Village Historical Society, Bay Village: A Way of Life, pp. 13, 15 and C.M. Osborn, "The Osborns of Bay Village," p. 7.

An account written by Seldon Osborn is included with details regarding his father, Reuben Osborn (OP 4:7).

State of Ohio, Cuyahoga County, ss. Married by me, E. S. Scott, on the twentieth day of November 1833 ***Selden OSBORN*** and ***Nancy RUPLE*** according to law at Euclid. E. S. Scott, Minister of the Gospel. Marriage Record, Cuyahoga County, OH, vol. 3, p. 40.

Selden was an herb doctor, who grew his own herbs and ***Nancy*** brewed them for him. He received his training from a doctor's office. He is described as traveling on horseback with his two saddle bags, one on each side of the saddle. One for his own use and one for his medicine. Many of his recipes are written in long hand...Leeches were used at the time to allay inflammation. Julia Osborn Scott, "Osborn Family History," p. 6.

Herb Recipes from the Original Notes of Selden Osborn

Ague Pills

Take 1 ½ grs. Quinine One lump as a small Pea of Ext Genson & Roll in as much A Capsicum as you can & if to act on the Liver add a little Blue Mass Pill

Directions 1st take a cathartic of Billious Pills & Begin on well day take one Pill at a time once in 2 ½ to 3 hours till you take 8 or 10 & next well day take 2 as before Then wait 10 Days Wait then take 2 or 3 for 2 days. 18 Pills in box

Ague Bitters

Take 2 ozs. Peruvian Bark 40 grains Virginia Snake Root 30 grs of Salts Wormwood to ½ Pint Gin or Whiskey Shake well – Dose One Table Spoonfull Night & Morning + one just as the chill comes on. B. Ruple

Smiths Ague cure

For Cathartic Take Mandrake & Pleurisy Root & Nutgalls Mix. Dose 1 Teaspoonfull one in 20 minutes 4 times
Bitters Take Nanny Bush Bark, Greek Velirean, Prickly Ash Berries, Mandrake Root Pulverized + ¼ part Gum Myruh in one Pint Rum.
Dose 1 Table Spoonfull 3 times per day.
N.B. Take the Cathartic first

Ague & Fever before it comes on remove the cause ie Cleanse & strengthen the stomach or system
1st Take a portion of good Billious Pills then
2d Take one Table Spoonfull each Golden Seal Pulverized & Peruvian Bark (And for Children it is better to add as much white ash Bark) & fill a Pint bottle with this & wild Cherry Bark split fine Then fill the bottle with spirits.

Dose ½ Table Spoonfull 9 Mornings in succession before eating, shaking the bottle before using & no more. Good in the spring.

Dr. Tinny

Ague Cure For...

First Cleanse the system with Emetice or cathartic then Take one Table spoonfull of Peruvian Bark one of Cayenne & one of Blood Root & if needed one of Bitter Root Infused in 2 qts of Cider.

Dose from ½ to a wine Glass three times per Day.

B. Hill

After Cleansing the system in Ague or Chill fever after the fever is broke this invaluable.

Sommers & Miltimores Fever & Ague Pills

Take 20 Grains of Quinine & 60 Grains of capsicum cemented with Ext of Gentin or Dogwood made into 20 pills.
Dose One per hour after the fever is off
First use an emetic or Cathartic or both

Dr. P. Cody

Dr. Thompsons Ague Pills

Take Aloes Casteel Soap & Beefs Gall
Dose 3, 4 or 5 pr Day

Dr. Doyer

Ague Bitters Billious Fever

Take ¼ part White Ash Bark & ¾ W&ahoo *(?)* Bark Boil. Strain the Liquor then simmer to the thickness of molasses. Dose one Table spoonful pr day till it physics off the Ague or 2 or 3 days then decrease & use for a few days till it is cleared out and the stools become as black as your hat.

Sure cure

B. Ruple

Ague Bitters

Take Boxwood or Peruvian B. Cherry Bark & Genson Mix put 2 Table spoons in 1 pint Brandy or other liquor.
Dose 1 Table spoon 3 times per day if the patient can bear.

B. Ruple

Bitters

Take Poplar & White Wood Bark Birdock seed Bitter Root & Wormwood pulverized 1 Table spoonfull each to1 qt. Liquor
Dose 1 Tablespoonful 3 pr day

Bitters in or Syrup

Take ½ Lb each Poplar Bark Blk Cherry Bark White Ash Bark Tag Alder & ¼ Lb Butternut Bark & one handfull Thorough Wort sweeten with Molasses & spirits to preserve it. Good general syrup Dr. Brigam
Dose from ½ to a wine glass 3 times per day.

Jaundice Bitters

Take Iron Wood chips & Black Cherry Bark in Liquor Or Black Alder Bark & Prickly Ash Bark in Do.

Dr. Price

Billius or Jaundice Bitters & Pills

Pills Ext Manroot 1 Pill 3 times per day
Take Greek Velirean Seneca Snake Root & Unicorn On(e) Table Spoonfull each & a small piece June Myrrh to one Pint Rum
Dose 1 Table Spoonfull 3 times per Day

Smith

Aqua Bitters after cleansing the stomach

Take the Juice of Blue Vervain & Extract of Boxwood Bark & Black Cherry & Bark to a Syrup then add Liquor enough to preserve it.
Dose from 1 Teaspoonfull to Table According to Age & consistence. B. Ruple

Dysseptic or Spring Bitters

Take 1 Handfull Each of Black Cohush Root, Boxwood Bark B. Cherry, Spice Bush Torough Root, ½ pint Poplar Do Boil in soft water to 1 quart. Strain & add Molasses 1 quart. Boil till syrup is formed when cool. Bottle. Add 1 pint of Rye Whiskey with small piece Gum Myrrh.
Dose 1 Table spoonfull 3 times per Day before meals. Take perseveringly. A good Tonic Bitter. By a Patent Cured in Pleria. "Journal of Selden Osborn" in the possession of David Osborn Scott, Jr.

The Second Congregational Church of Dover is the outgrowth of a Congregational Church organized in Lee, Massachusetts, June 5, 1811, with eight members. About 1840 the church was divided on the slavery question, and until 1847 one congregation worshiped in the church building and the other in the town house. In that year the two bodies were reunited and reorganized as the Second Congregational Church of Dover, with fifty-one members...The deacons of the reorganized church were *Alfred MILLARD*, *Jonathan OAKES*, ***Selden OSBORN***, and *Josiah HURST*. Since 1847 about two hundred and seventy-five persons have been received into the church. Crisfield Johnson, History of Cuyahoga County, Ohio, p. 440.

Selden OSBORN, son of the pioneer ***Reuben OSBORN*** ***(OP 4:7)***, was commissioned Captain of the 7th Company, 1st Rifle Regiment, 2nd Brigade of the 9th Division of the Ohio Militia on July 20, 1853. Doubtless other men in Dover Township belonged because it was a requirement that they be registered for military service under the newly adopted Ohio state constitution of 1851. Note in Osborn Family Papers regarding a donated flag and copy of original commission, Rose Hill Museum.

A controversy over the boundary line between the Untied States and Canada was going on soon after my grandfather's appointment. "Fifty-four forty or Fight" was a common slogan at the time. It was during this time, while the families were at church, that some men came across the lake and took the guns stored in the house belonging to the militia and escaped. Julia Osborn Scott, "Osborn Family History," p. 7.

Selden OSBORN'S home is now the home of the Meddicks, built in 1832. It is the birth place of three generations. My grandmother, ***Nancy***, lived in it all of her married life. She died at the age of 77. My father lived in it all of his life as well as ***Mrs. MEDDICK***. To it, many of the near great of Cleveland have come for their summer vacations as paying guests. Julia Osborn Scott, "Osborn Family History," p. 7.

The ***Selden OSBORN House*** was said to have the first bathroom in Bay Village. Osborn Family File, Rose Hill Museum, Bay Village, OH.

OSBORN, Selden, 40, b. NY, farmer; ***Nancy***, 36, b. Ohio; ***Sherman***, 16; ***Minerva***, 14; ***Betsey***, 10; ***Samuel***, 9; ***John***, 6; ***Rueben***, 4; ***Julia***, 1; all children born in Ohio; *Eliza CAMPBELL*, 30, b. Penn. 1850 FC OH CYDO, p. 217A, lines 22-31, house 3742.

OSBORN, Selden, 50, farmer, value of real estate $8,000; value of personal estate, $1,000; ***Nancy***, 44; ***Betsy***, 19; ***Samuel***, 19, farmer; ***Ruobin*** *(sp.)*, 13; ***Julia***, 11; ***David***, 6; ***Polly OSBORN***, 56, Value of real estate $1,000. All b. Ohio. 1860 FC OH CYDO p. 47, lines 32-39, house 368.

Children of Selden Osborn and Nancy Ruple.

Sherman OSBORN, b. 3 Oct 1834; d. 5 Nov 1886; m.1 *Angenette "Nettie" PHINNEY (Lot 48)*, m.2 *Myra YODER*. ***Minerva OSBORN***, b. 20 Apr 1836; d. 15 May 1918, bur. Huntsburgh, O; m. *Levi JUDD* of Huntsburgh, Geauga Co., Ohio. ***Betsey OSBORN***, b. 22 Oct 1839; d. 14 Mar 1912, bur. Lakeside Cem. *(Lot 2)*; m. *Barney WILLIAMS*. ***Samuel Foster OSBORN***, b. 28 Aug 1841; d. 12 Apr 1897, bur. Lakeside Cem. *(OP 5:5)*; m. *Mary E. CROCKER*. ***Mary OSBORN***, b. 12 Aug 1843, d. 28 Feb 1844, bur. Lakeside Cemetery *(OP 5:7)*. ***John Ruple OSBORN***, b. 19 Dec 1844; d. 28 Aug 1856, bur. Lakeside Cem.*(OP 5:7)*. ***Reuben OSBORN***, b. 7 Aug 1847; d. 16 June 1919, bur. Lakeside Cem. *(Lot 46)*; m. *Eunice CHADWICK*. ***Julia OSBORN***, b. 22 May 1849; d. 26 July 1912, bur. Dover Cemetery, Dover Center, O. *(Burial is at Evergreen Cemetery, Westlake, OH, Sect J, Lot 30, See info under David DeForrest, Lot 1)*; m. *Thomas MITCHELL*. ***David DeForrest OSBORN***, b. Feb 21, 1853; d. Feb 8, 1902, bur. Lakeside Cem. *(Lot 1, moved to Evergreen Cemetery, Westlake)*; m. *Rose MITCHELL*. C.M. Osborn, "The Osborns of Bay Village, Ohio," p. 6.

The State of Ohio, Cuyahoga Co., ss., I Certify that on the 15th day of September 1858, ***Mr. Levi W. JUDD*** and ***Miss Minerva OSBORN*** were by me legally joined in marriage. Nelson S. Taylor. Marriage Record, Cuyahoga County, OH, vol. 9, p. 130.

Levi West JUDD, b. 27 Sep 1827 in Northampton, Hampshire, Mass.; d. 16 Feb 1907, Huntsburg, Geauga Co., OH; bur. Huntsburg Cemetery, Huntsburg. Marianne Ruple Gardner, The Descendants of Balthazar (Baltus)Ruple Pennsylvania, New Jersey, Ohio, p. 60.

Children of Minerva and Levi Judd: ***Leverett JUDD***, b. May 1861. ***Hubert JUDD***, b. 24 Sept 1870, Huntsburg, Geauga Co., OH; resided Garden City, Kansas in 1934. ***Charles A. JUDD***, b. 19 Aug 1872. ***Luella Minerva JUDD***, b. 8 Oct 1873, Huntsburg; d. 15 Aug 1934, Huntsburg, bur. Huntsburg Cemetery, Huntsburg. ***Howard JUDD***, b. 11 Mar 1875, d. 17 Nov 1918. Violet Warren, Huntsburg's Old Crowd and Related Families, pp. 19, 77-79.

Howard L. JUDD, d. 17 Nov 1917, Geauga Co., OH. Ohio Historical Society Death Index.

Minerva OSBORN JUDD, d. May 15, 1918 in Huntsburg, Geauga Co., Ohio; there was no specific disease but a gradual decline, Old Age; 82 yrs. 25 ds.; Widowed; Housekeeper; b. April 20, 1836, Dover, Ohio to ***Selden OSBORN***, b. Conn. and ***Nancy RUPLE***, b. Ohio; informant ***Chas. A. JUDD***; undertaker W.B. Bincox?, E. Claridon; burial Huntsburg. Ohio Certificate of Death, Division of Vital Statistics, 1918, certif. 31544.

The State of Ohio, Cuyahoga County, ss. I Certify that on the 25th day of April 1882 ***Mr. Thomas R. MITCHELL*** and ***Miss Julia A. OSBORN*** were by me legally joined in marriage. Henry S. Bates. Marriage Record, Cuyahoga County, OH, vol. 25, p. 169.

MITCHELL-Julia A., beloved wife of ***Thomas R. MITCHELL***, Friday morning, July 26th. Funeral from late residence, at North Dover, O., July 29th, 2 p.m. standard. Cleveland Leader, July 27, 1912, p. 13, col. 7. *(See David Deforest Osborn, Lot 1 for more information)*

Mrs. Julia A. MITCHELL, d. July 26, 1912, 8 a.m., Dover, Cuyahoga Co., Ohio of Carcinoma of liver; Married; b. May 22, 1849, Dover, O. to ***Seldom OSBORN***, b. Conn. and ***Nancey RUPLE***, b. Euclid, Ohio; undertaker J.A. Pease and Son, Dover, O.; burial Evergreen. Ohio Certificate of Death, Division of Vital Statistics, 1912, certif. 37386.

Evergreen Cemetery Records for Mitchell surname *(not complete)*:

Section A, Lot 47, owner Y.W. Mitchell: ***Yankee W. MITCHELL***, 79, Dover, inter. 4 Oct 1939 and ***May Minerva MITCHELL***, 66, Dover, 14 Aug 1929.

Section A, Lot 48, owner Y.W. Mitchell: ***John MITCHELL***, 73, Dover, inter. 13 July 1930.

Section G, Lot 26, owner Thomas Mitchell: ***Gladys C. MITCHELL***, 41, Dover, d. Cleveland, Uremia, Undertaker Clifford Pease, inter. 11 Oct 1935; ***Leo. L. MITCHELL***, 44, d. Lakewood, Angina Pectoris, Undertaker Wm. and Roy Daniels-Cleve., inter. 11 May 1941; ***Nina A. MITCHELL***, 1 1/2 yrs., Dover, b. Dover, inter 29 Nov 1894; ***Starr P. MITCHELL***, 62, 2101 Olive Ave., Lakewood, Ohio, d. Lakewood, Coronary Occlusion, inter 14 July 1952, Undertaker William Daniels-Lakewood.

Section G, Lot 27, owner Thomas Mitchell: ***Eliza MITCHELL***, 68, Dover, b. Dover, inter 26 Apr 1888, buried from vault 1886; ***Flora H. MITCHELL***, 87, Westlake, d. Westlake, Chronic Myocarditis, Undertaker Marion Pease, inter 26 Feb 1948; ***Michael MITCHELL***, 72, inter 8 Mar 1927; ***Thomas MITCHELL***, 67, inter 30 Jan 1889.

Section G, Lot 28, owner Thomas Mitchell: ***Alta MITCHELL***, 64, Dover, inter 7 Oct 1929; ***Warren MITCHELL***, 48, Dover, b. Dover, d. Dover, Pneumonia, undertaker James Pease, inter 22 May 1910.

Section J, Lot 30, owner Thomas Mitchell: ***Thomas MITCHELL***, 79, Dover, inter 20 Oct 1927 and ***Julia MITCHELL***, 63, Dover, inter. 29 July 1912, cancer of the liver, undertaker Jas. Pease.

MITCHELL, Thomas, b. 3 May 1821, d. 18 Dec 1883; ***Eliza LETTS***, his wife, born April 26, 1819, d. Mar 8, 1888; ***Nina.*** Evergreen Cemetery, Westlake, OH. Read by Catherine Burke Flament.

OP 5:8 Nancy Ruple Osborn

Nancy RUPLE OSBORN, the daughter of ***Deacon John RUPLE*** and ***Elizabeth CRAFT*** of Euclid, married ***Selden OSBORN***, November 20, 1833. She was born March 14, 1813; d. January 14, 1890. C.M. Osborn, "The Osborns of Bay Village," p. 5.

OSBORN, Mrs. Selden, Maiden Name ***Nancy RUPLE***, Year Came to Township 1833; Where From or Where Born Euclid, O., Last Res. Dover. Women of the Western Reserve Prior to 1840, p. 23.

RUPLES AT MR. REUBEN OSBORN'S DOVER, OHIO - 1915

Several years ago, I'll not tell you just how many, a little girl accompanied her grandfather on his annual visit to his sister in Dover by the lake. 'Twas the fall fishing season and late apple harvest. Everything in and about the place so delighted the child that she wished to stay. ***David*** and ***Julia*** were in Oberlin College, and ***Aunt Nancy*** suggested keeping the little girl. Accordingly, her grandfather, ***Mr. Abram L. RUPLE***, returned to his home in South Euclid alone.

As the pleasant autumn days passed and school in the little brick schoolhouse on ***Betsy's (Betsy OSBORN WILLIAMS)*** place opened, the little girl registered, as one of the pupils, the teacher inscribing her name as Osborn because it seemed easier to remember than her own, that of Ruple. Soon the lake was frozen over, and the fish ponds stood in solid ice. School lunches were hurriedly eaten, often at morning recess, for the children accompanied by the teacher, walked out daily upon the ice, where the sand and snow had blown into hills, in which caves were dug, and play was exercised as well. The recreation, or noon hour, was never long enough for this form of play to become tiresome.

Another memory which stands out bright in this girl's life is the church; the dear old-fashioned, two story church at the Center, painted white, with Sunday School room on the first floor and auditorium with its high-backed white pews closing with doors on the second. This was before the day of the automobile, and our host always drove a good team attached to a nine-passenger, three spring wagon. In which the three seats were well supplied with cushions, blankets and buffalo robes, contributing to every one's comfort for the four-mile ride to service, for the roads were not paved, and were often rough and muddy. But no one thought of staying at home, not even when one of the planks was out in the little bridge which crossed the brook near Oviatt's Mill, for ***Reuben*** simply urged his horses on a little faster and they sprang right over the place without injury to anything. These are little incidents of our first visit to Aunt Nancy's, when only seven years of age.

Aunt Nancy was the second daughter of the eight children of ***Deacon John RUPLE***, who lived and died on that portion of his estate, which is located on the south side of Euclid Avenue east of the East Cleveland "Y" which is now being allotted for an extension to Colonial Heights. She married ***Selden OSBORN***, who brought his bride to Dover and built his home across the street from that of his father, ***Mr. Reuben Osborn***, grandfather of our host, whose namesake he is, and whose house he occupies. In his new home, a long day's journey from his father's house, she and her husband raised their family of nine children in the nurture and admonition of the Lord, for both were from religious families of the Puritan type.

Grandfather Osborn's Sabbath began at six o'clock Saturday night. What a contrast to the present day! Saturday's pleasures often unfit us for Sunday's morning service. Fond of her father and family, she kept in touch with them making the long journey to see him frequently, and taking the children who were always welcome. In the later years, after Uncle Selden's death and her children grown to manhood and womanhood, she had opportunity to visit cousins with whom she had exchanged greetings and for whom she had an affectionate regard: the Coopers of Mt. Vernon, where ***Mrs. COOPER***, her ***Aunt Elizabeth***, lived and a cousin ***Nancy COOPER***.

Looking back I can see the little party, consisting of Grandpa, Abram L. Ruple, Aunt Nancy Osborn, ***Uncle Ben*** and ***Aunt Ann HOUGHLAND***, seated in Aunt Nancy's carriage, the team. Aunt Nancy's cream horse Fannie, and Uncle Ben's bay with white strip on his face, everything trim and in shape when "Aunty Ben" gets her veil adjusted--- Aunt Ann always wore a brown veil, into which an elastic had been drawn, thus making it fit snugly around the brim to her bonnet. It was, and looked more useful than many we see now in machines. At last everyone is ready, and they start on their drive to Washington, Pa., where they visited their uncle ***Colonel James RUPLE***, and their cousins, the Crafts, who returned the visit in fishing season and remarked upon the "right smart sprinkle of fish," after witnessing a haul. The late ***Mr. C. M. RUPLE***, of Washington, told me that the Crafts had expressed a desire to attend a reunion sometime if they were invited. A beautiful friendship existed between Aunt Nancy and her cousin, ***Mrs. Pamela Coleman CUSHMAN***, Euclid, Ohio, whose mother was ***Mimi CRAFT***, sister of ***Elizabeth CRAFT RUPLE***. Twenty-five years ago last January, after a life of usefulness and thrift, Aunt Nancy went home to join the

Reunion above, and we who loved her, cherish her memory, and rejoice in the fellowship of her children. ***Effie RUPLE SMITH***, historian. Marianne Ruple Gardner, The Descendants of Balthazar (Baltus) Ruple Pennsylvania, New Jersey, Ohio, pp. 23-24.

I recall my grandmother, ***Nancy OSBORN***, a woman with a strong will, religiously inclined and somewhat domineering. Sunday began at six on Saturday night. We children must have our baths before that time and all the chores that could be done that were possible, so that the Sabbath could be kept in the Puritan way, which she tried to live up to and her family as well. Our dolls were put away for the day and all kind of play was forbidden. I guess that was one of the reasons we went to church so much. We would come home from church, eat a hasty lunch (which was prepared for the most part the day before) and go to the little Methodist Church at the corner of Bassett and Lake Roads. She always had her parlor heated on Sunday, where after church, she would read us Bible stories. I especially like the stories of her girlhood which were always fascinating to me as a young girl. Julia Osborn Scott, "Osborn Family History," p. 8.

OSBORN, Nancy, 56, b. Ohio; ***Betsy*** *R.*, 28, at home; ***Samuel F.***, value of real estate $4,000, personal property $800, 26, fisherman; ***Julia M.***, 20, Teacher School; ***David***, 17. All b. Ohio. 1870 FC OH CYDO pp. 256, lines 1-5, house 247.

Nancy OSBORN, 76; res. Dover; interred Jan 17, 1890; Org. Part. "List of Interments," Lakeside Cemetery, Bay V., OH.

Ancestors of Nancy Ruple Osborn:

I. ***Balthazar (Baltus) RUPLE***, b. c1740, Rising Sun Area of Philadelphia, PA; d. after June 1794 in Washington, PA where he was buried; m.1 c1767, Philadelphia, PA to ***Rebecca SMITH*** (b. c1740, PA; d. c1786, Somerset, NJ where she was buried). *Children of Baltus and Rebecca*: 1. ***John RUPLE***, b. 1768; d. 1860. 2. ***Catherine RUPLE***, b. 9 July 1769, Philadelphia; d. Ohio. 3. ***Rachel RUPLE***, b. 14 Feb 1771, Germantown, Phil., PA; m. *MILLIBAR*. 4. ***Samuel RUPLE*** b. c1771, Philadelphia, PA; d. 27 Jan 1847, Elkhart, Indiana; m. 1798, Washington, PA to *Rebecca CRAFT*. ***Balthazar*** m.2 before 1786 in Morris Twp., Somerset, NJ to *Annie McCOLLUM* (dau. of *David McCOLLUM* and *Mary HENRY*). *Children of Baltus and Annie:* 5. ***Mary RUPLE***, b. 1787, d. 1840, m. Mar 1805 to *William PARKINSON*. 6. ***James B. RUPLE***, b. 18 Feb 1788, Morris, NJ; d. 8 Jan 1855, Washington, PA. 7. ***David RUPLE***, m. 1815, Greene, PA to___ *DURBIN*. 8. ***Elizabeth RUPLE***, b. Morris, NJ. 9. ***Margaret RUPLE.*** Marianne Ruple Gardner, The Descendants of Balthazar (Baltus)Ruple Pennsylvania, New Jersey, Ohio, pp. 2, 3.

II. ***John RUPLE***, b. 4 Jan 1768, Pennsylvania; d. 22 Nov 1860 in East Cleveland, bur. First Presbyterian Church Cemetery, East Cleveland, Cuyahoga Co., OH; m. c1793, Washington, PA to ***Elizabeth CRAFT*** (dau. of *Lawrence CRAFT* (b. 1737, Maryland; d. 1820, East Cleveland; m. 28 Dec 1769, Baltimore Co., MD) and *Mary LYMES* (d. c1829)). *Issue:* 1. ***Dr. Baltus RUPLE***, b. 21 Mar 1795, Morris Twp., Washington Co., PA; d. 4 Oct 1885, Columbia Twp., Lorain Co., OH; bur. Columbia Cemetery; m. 7 Dec 1819, Euclid, Cuyahoga Co., OH to *Clarissa OSBORN*. 2. ***Lawrence Craft RUPLE***, b. 10 Dec 1797, Morris Twp.; d. 13 Feb 1865, South Euclid, Cuyahoga Co; bur. First Presb. Church; m. *Jemima HICOCK*. 3. ***Sarah RUPLE***, b. 1799, Morris Twp., Washington Co., PA; d. 9 Sept 1808, Euclid Twp.; bur. First Presb. Church. She died when a tree fell on her as she was calling her father to dinner. 4. ***Samuel RUPLE***, b. 1 Sep 1800, Morris Twp.; d. 4 Aug 1876, Euclid; m. 2 Mar 1823, Cuyahoga Co. to *Eunice McVEY*. 5. ***Abram C. RUPLE***, b. 1 July 1803, Morris Twp.; d. 12 Jan 1878, East Cleveland; m. 20 Dec 1828, Cuyahoga Co. to *Hanna STEWART*. 6. ***Cyrus RUPLE***, b. 7 Mar 1806, Collinwood, Cuyahoga Co.; d. 10 Mar 1875, Collinwood; bur. East Cleveland Cemetery; m. 16 Aug 1835, Lorain, OH to *Julia HITCHCOCK (Parents of Finetta Ruple Stevens, see OP 2:1)*. 7. ***Seth Doan RUPLE***, b. 1807, Euclid Twp.; d. 24 Dec 1885, South Euclid; bur. East Cleveland Cemetery; m. 6 July 1829, Cuyahoga Co., *Jane BEERS*. 8. ***James Robinson RUPLE***, b. 12 June 1810, Euclid; d. 18 July 1894, North Olmsted, Cuyahoga Co.; bur. Butternut Cemetery; m. 29 Sept 1833, Lorain to *Alma HITCHCOCK*. 9. ***Nancy RUPLE***, b. 1812, d. 1890, *see below*. 10. ***Anne C. RUPLE***, b. 1814, Cuyahoga; d. 9 Aug 1877, Euclid Twp; bur. Presb. Church Cem.; m. after June 1860, Euclid to *Benjamin HOUGHLAND*. 11. ***Mary Lymes RUPLE***, b. Mar 1816, Euclid, OH; d. 25 July 1842, Euclid Twp.; bur. First Presbyterian Church. Gardner, pp. 4, 8, 13-25.

III. ***Nancy RUPLE***, b. 14 Mar 1812 in Euclid Twp., Cuyahoga Co., OH, and was christened 3 May 1812 in Presbyterian Church, East Cleveland, Cuyahoga Co. Nancy died 14 Jan 1890 in Dover Twp., Cuyahoga Co., at the age of 77, and was buried at Lakeside Cemetery, Bay Village; m. 20 Nov 1833 in Cuyahoga Co. to ***Selden OSBORN*** . Gardner, pp. 23-24.

Parents of Nancy Ruple Osborn:

John RUPLE, b. 4 Jan 1769, Sommerset Co., NJ; d. 27 Nov 1860, East Cleveland; bur. Nela View Cemetery; m. ***Elizabeth CRAFT***, (b. 1 May 1771, Washington Co., PA; d. 1 June 1841, E. Cleveland, OH; bur. Nela View Cemetery) Washington Co., PA. *Issue:* ***Nancy***, b. Euclid Township. William D.H. Heym

Euclid. *Jacob COLEMAN*...moved into Euclid in 1805, as did also ***John RUPLE*** long known as "Deacon" Ruple, who settled on the ground he had selected two years before, a little east of Nine Mile Creek. William R. Coates, A History of Cuyahoga County and the City of Cleveland, Dover, vol. 1, p. 454.

East Cleveland. In August 1803...John Ruple,...from Washington County, Pennsylvania, visited this part of Ohio together. Mr. Ruple located...in what is now Euclid. This location was on the main road which had been laid out from Cleveland to the Pennsylvania line, parallel with the lake shore, but which was then hardly passable even for ox-teams, an axe to clear away fallen timber being the necessary accompaniment of every vehicle. The parties named returned to Pennsylvania and did not begin work on their land til the next spring. Coates, p. 443.

In 1805, John Ruple settled on the line between Euclid and East Cleveland. He too was a noted hunter, and is credited by *William COLEMAN* with killing the first panther slain in the old township of Euclid by a white man, the beast measuring nine feet from tip to tip. He raised a large family and lived to an advanced age, on the place where he first located, amid the respect of all who knew him. Coates, p. 444.

August 27, 1810, John Ruple was appointed a ruling leader of the First Presbyterian Church of Collamer. Coates, p. 448.

Brief Sketch of Deacon Ruple and Brother Samuel's Life

Ninety years ago this month, my great-grandfather, ***John RUPLE***, better known as Deacon Ruple, visited that part of Ohio, now known as Euclid Township. He was one of a party of five men who selected their future homes, and then returned to Washington, Pa., their former home. In August, 1805 he located permanently on his land, which was situated a little east of Nine Mile Creek, on the main road laid out from Cleveland to the Pennsylvania line...The same road is now the far-famed Euclid Avenue. To the privations and hardships of the new county, danger from the Indians and wild beast, came the women as bravely as their lords, among them our grandmother, ***Elizabeth CRAFT***. The following year, ***Samuel RUPLE***, brother of the Deacon, with his wife, ***Rebecca CRAFT***, sister of our grandmother settled at Nine Mile Creek. In the eastern part of what was the village of Collamer, lately called East Cleveland Hamlet. The two brothers began in earnest to build homes, raise their families and help to civilize the country...***Nancy, Mrs. OSBORN***, at whose home we are now celebrating, and whose life we hope to hear a short sketch of from her daughter, ***Mrs. MITCHELL***...The pest of Euclid seems to have been the rattle snake. All the old settlers mention the great number of them. Deacon Ruple at one time, killed thirty-eight, counted and piled them up in a heap, although the poison which the angry reptiles spit forth into the air made him so sick that he had no desire to repeat the work. Article from the Ruple Family Reunion Notes, no author listed, possibly Effie Ruple Smith. Marianne Ruple Gardner, The Descendants of Balthazar (Baltus) Ruple Pennsylvania, New Jersey, Ohio, p. 5.

Death of an Old Soldier

Died - At Collamer (later Euclid) in this county on Thursday, the 22nd instant, ***Deacon John RUPLE***, age 91 years, 11 months and 18 days.

The deceased was a native of Sussex County, N.J., and removed with his parents in early life to Washington County, Pennsylvania, where he married and resided for several years. In 1805 he removed with his family (a wife and eight children) and settled on a farm he occupied until his death....Of a cheerful and happy disposition, he endeavored at all times to infuse a spirit of love and charity among his fellow men, which was followed by the usual happy results, and endeared him to his neighbors and friends. In his dealings with his fellow men he was rigidly just and generous...

During the War of 1812 he performed several tours of camp duty in defense of this city and spent much time in nursing the sick soldiers and otherwise ministering to their wants while stationed here...

In early life, Mr. Ruple united with the Presbyterian Church and on his arrival at Euclid, took a leading part with the small band of professing Christians already there, observing the Sabbath, holding religious meetings as often as circumstances would permit, and on the organization of a church in 1807...Mr. Ruple was unanimously chosen ruling elder, and continued in that relation while his connection with the church lasted, and held the same relation to the one he was connected with at the time of his death.

In the erection of the church, in 1817, at Euclid, he exerted himself greatly in time and means and in the hard times in this region that followed the late war, a large portion of the church debt was assumed by him...

During his last and somewhat painful illness of about four weeks he was calm and resigned in view of death; to him it had no sting, the grave no terror...While free from pain at intervals, he spent much of his time in prayer, and conversing with his friends on the glories that awaited him....Almost the last words he was heard to speak were "Come! May we die the death of the righteous," and soon after fell asleep...His remains were committed on the following Sabbath, to the grave, by the side of his wife who was taken from him by death, June 3, 1841... Obituary found among the papers of Miss Rose Mitchell by C.M. Osborn. Marianne Ruple Gardner, The Descendants of Balthazar (Baltus) Ruple Pennsylvania, New Jersey, Ohio, pp. 5-6.

OP 5:8 Mary R. Osborn

Daughter of Selden Osborn and Nancy Ruple.
Mary R. OSBORN, d. February 28, 1844, aged 6 months. *(b. cAugust 1843).* Lakeside Cemetery, tombstone inscription.

OP 5:8 John Ruple Osborn

Son of Selden Osborn and Nancy Ruple.
John R. OSBORN, d. August 28 1856, 11 years 9 mos. Lakeside Cemetery, tombstone inscription.

OP 5:9-11

Three small tablets set in concrete.
Wording on tops is not legible.

OP 5:12 William Comstock

Marker cracked and set in concrete.

WM. COMSTOCK
DIED
JAN 27, 1855
AGED 28 YEARS

William Comstock

Records and memories handed down to his wife's descendants.

According to records kept in the Bible owned by the second daughter of ***William*** and ***Roxanna COMSTOCK, Martha Washington COMSTOCK,*** William Comstock was born on September 2, 1826 in Albany, New York, the first child of ***Charles COMSTOCK*** and ***Virtue COOPER COMSTOCK***. His nine brothers and sisters listed on the same sheet of paper were ***Isaac, Oliver, Hezekiah, Abigail, Esther, Elizabeth, Matilda, Bulah***, and ***Thomas***. Their mother died June 25, 1841, just twenty days after Thomas's birth.

William may have met Roxanna Britton on a visit to Avon, Ohio where his mother's family lived. A note in the family records links Virtue Cooper Comstock to ***Joanna EDMONDS COOPER***, Roxanna's mother's sister. The marriage license of William Comstock and Roxanna A. Britton dates their wedding on March 18th, 1852 in Lorain County, Ohio. The license, which is among my family documents, is signed by *Schuyler PUTNAM, Justice of the Peace* and by a judge named *P. BLISS*. Her parents were both children of original settlers in the area and farmers of land granted to heirs of soldiers in Washington's army.

The newlyweds went to Cleveland, where, according to family tradition, William was employed as a machinist. Their first child, ***Sylvia Medora***, was born January 10, 1853; the second, Martha Washington, on October 29, 1854. William died just three months later on January 27, 1855. Roxanna, a twenty-two year old mother of two infants, with no means of support, must have been devastated by his death. Possibly because of the intensity of her grief, no account of the cause of his death is included in the family legends.

The young widow went back to her parents in Avon, where they must have already been hard pressed to provide for a family of nine on their fifty-acres of sandy soil at the edge of Lake Erie. Within a few months, they gave up the Britton land grant and moved west to Indiana, where Roxanna's mother's parents and two of her sisters had already settled. All of the Britton family moved into ***Grandmother EDMONDS'*** house, and Roxanna's father took over management of the farm. Under such crowded conditions, Roxanna must have felt pressed to remarry, and in 1857 married a carpenter named ***Amos Ebenezer BOIES*** and moved with her two Comstock daughters to Rome City, a few miles from her grandmother's farm.

My great aunt, ***Emma BOIES WILLIAMS***, the first child of Roxanna's second marriage, whom I knew throughout my childhood, often talked about Rome City, Indiana, where she and her two half-sisters spent their early and apparently happy years from 1857 to 1866. Sylvia and Martha, who could hardly have known their own father, were treated like members of the Boies family for the rest of their lives. During the Civil War, Roxanna gave birth to two more daughters, and the family moved to Cortland, Illinois, probably in search of work for Amos. Either during their stay in Cortland or soon after their subsequent move to Chicago, Sylvia was married to ***John MARCELLUS*** on August 12, 1871 and died little more than a year later on October 17, 1872. Family records have no information about Marcellus, and family legend asserted that Sylvia was murdered by her husband with a knife to the belly, which also killed her eight-month fetus. (In the light of recent research, this legend may be false.)

In about 1876, the Boies family left Chicago to take up a homestead in Chapman, Nebraska. Emma, recently married, remained in Chicago, but Martha Comstock and the two other Boies daughters, *Mary* and *Adele*, accompanied Amos and Roxanna. I believe that William Comstock's sister, ***Elizabeth COMSTOCK***, was now one of the family. A note in the handwriting of Mary Boies, recording Elizabeth's death in Grand Island on March 28, 1892, refers to her as "dear Aunt Lizzie." By then she had been married to a man named ***WALLACE***. It's possible that Roxanna had met Elizabeth during their stay in Cortland, since another of William Comstock's sisters, ***Esther Adeline***, who was married to ***Charlie BAILEY***, lived in nearby DeKalb, where Mary Boies's daughter, *Jean KING*, visited her before her death in 1922. This sister was known to Jean as "Aunt Addie Bailey."

The only other note about William Comstock's siblings in Martha Comstock's Bible is the fact that ***Thomas***, the youngest, died at Gettysburg and is buried on the battle field.

Martha Comstock stayed with her mother on the homestead after Amos's death and the marriage of her sisters. She must have helped her mother improve the land in order to claim the 160 acres for their own. She married ***Thomas Christian GULLIVER*** on January 4, 1880, two years to the day after her stepfather's death. A family photograph, taken in the summer of 1889 (dated by the age of the young children in the picture), shows Martha and Thomas Gulliver (holding a shotgun in one hand) and Roxanna, seated in the center surrounded by visiting members of the Boies and Britton families, all posed outside the house in Chapman, Nebraska.

Family legend says that Gulliver was not kind to his wife. He is reported to have driven the buckboard so wildly that she was thrown out and suffered a broken hip. I can testify to the broken hip, because when I met "Aunt Mattie" on a visit to California with my mother in 1926, I was startled by her walk. She dipped way down on one side with every step. Gulliver is also reported to have shot rounds at Martha's feet while she was in the kitchen "to keep her on her toes." Whether these stories are true or not, Roxanna and Martha suddenly moved to Elsinore, California, shortly after the family photograph was taken. Mary Boies's daughter told me that Roxanna and Martha rode into Elsinore driving a buckboard.

Martha must have obtained an annulment or a divorce from Gulliver, since she married ***Charlie P. CARTER***, a prominent man in the desert frontier community, in Wildomar on April 2, 1894. (The date of Gulliver's death is not entered in the family Bible.) Roxanna gave her new Elsinore house to Martha and went to live with her youngest daughter's family, who had followed them to Elsinore. Charlie Carter died in 1924, and Martha was still living in that house (which has since burned down) when she died on April 17, 1939. Shirley S. Allen, great-granddaughter of his wife, Roxanna Britton and author of Roxanna Britton.

The State of Ohio, Lorain Co., ss., ***William COMSTOCK*** having made application for a Marriage License for himself and ***Roxanna BRITTON***...Subscribed and Sworn to the 18 day of March 1852. Marriage Applications of Lorain County, OH 1852-56, p. 524.

William's parents didn't reside in Ohio, but in New York at the time of his marriage. It is thought that he may have visited his grandparents, ***Isaac*** and ***Elizabeth COOPER,*** and met ***Roxanna***. The Cooper's resided in Avon, Lorain Co. in 1840 and again in 1860. T.J. Aaron

Ancestors of William Comstock:

I. ***William COMSTOCK***, b. England c1595; believed to have d. c1683; m. 2nd ***Elizabeth DANIEL*** (b. 1608, d. after 1665); their youngest and fifth child was Christopher. John Adams Comstock, The Comstocks in America., p. 2.

II. ***Christopher COMSTOCK***, b. c1635; d. Norwalk, Conn., 28 Dec 1702; m. 6 Oct 1663, ***Hannah PLATT*** (dau. of *Richard* and *Mary PLATT* of Milford; b. Milford, Conn., 1 Oct 1643; d. Milford after 1713). Christopher came from England and settled in Fairfield in 1654. 19 Sept 1692 he was a member of a grand jury for witches. All eight of their children were born in Norwalk, the seventh being Samuel. Comstock, p. 4.

III. ***Samuel COMSTOCK***, b. Norwalk, 6 Feb 1679-80; d. 26 Oct 1752; m. 27 Dec 1705 to ***Sarah HANFORD***, dau. of *Rev. Thomas HANFORD* and his wife *Mary*, of Norwalk. He was appointed Captain of South Company of Norwalk and the deputy to the General Assembly. The fourth of their seven children was Nathan. Comstock, p. 8.

IV. ***Nathan COMSTOCK***, b. Wilton, Conn., 1713; d. Wilton, 12 Oct 1794; m. Wilton, 7 Mar 1738-9, ***Bethiah STRONG***, dau. of *Benajah STRONG* of Fairfield. Nathan was Ensign of Third Company in Norwalk in 1757 and in 1759 Lieutenant in Wilton Parish, Norwalk. Six children were born in Wilton and the youngest in Norwalk. The fourth was Aaron. Comstock, p. 19.

V. ***Aaron COMSTOCK***, b. Wilton, 1744; d. Half Moon, NY, 12 Mar 1815; m. Wilton, 9 June 1765 to ***Rebecca** (or **Rebena) DeFORREST*** (b. 1748; d. 7 Nov 1809; bur. Waterford, NY). Aaron settled in Half Moon soon after the Revolution and remained there until his death. He was a farmer and kept a public house near Waterford village. He was Captain, Albany County, 4 Oct 1786; Major, Saratoga County, 9 Mar 1793; Colonel, 8 Apr 1799. They had five children, the fourth being William. Comstock, pp. 43-4.

VI. ***William COMSTOCK***, d. Lockport, NY, 14 Feb 1846; m. Hartford, Conn. to ***Abigail BETTS***. William was a miller and moved to Western, NY. They had eight children, the oldest being Charles. Comstock, p. 92.

VII. ***Charles COMSTOCK***, b. 1804; d. Lowden, Iowa, 23 Apr 1891; m. ***Virtue COOPER*** (d. 25 June 1841). Charles was a piano and melodeon manufacturer of New Albany, Ind. (Charles was living in Garden Plains Twp., Ill., in 1872 and died in Camanche, Iowa at the home of his son, possibly Charles. T.J. Aaron) Family bible of Martha Washington Comstock, now in the possession of Mrs. Terence (Bonnie) Munt and Comstock, p. 185.

Children of Charles Comstock and Virtue Cooper:

1. ***William COMSTOCK,*** b. 2 Sept 1826, Albany N.Y. 2. ***Isaac COMSTOCK***, b. 16 Feb 1828. 3. ***Oliver Levanson COMSTOCK***, b. Poughkeepsie, NY, 9 July 1828; d. Hamilton, Ohio, 7 Apr 1859; m. 4 Dec 1853, New Albany, Ind. to *Sophia Ailade NARDIN* (b. Hamilton, O., 8 July 1828; d. Louisville, KY, 22 May 1907, dau. of *Frederick P. NARDIN* and *Abigail Pearson LOWE*). 4. ***Hezekiah COMSTOCK***, b. 29 Jan 1831, d. 13 Mar 1894. 5. ***Abigail COMSTOCK***, b. 10 Feb 1833, d. 7 May 1889, m. *BRIGGS*. 6. ***Esther Adeline COMSTOCK***, b. 6 Oct 1834, d. 9 Feb 1922 in DeKalb, Illinois. 7. ***Elizabeth COMSTOCK***, b. 9 Apr 1836; m. *WALLACE*; d. 28 Mar 1892, Grand Island, Nebraska. 8. ***Matilda COMSTOCK***, b. 8 Feb 1838, d. 9 Sept 1893, m. *CADY*. 9. ***Bulah COMSTOCK***, b. 3 Dec 1839, d. 30 Mar 1941. 10. ***Thomas C. COMSTOCK***, b. 5 June 1841; Died at Gettysburg, buried on battlefield (too much for mother). Family bible of Martha Washington Comstock, now in the possession of Mrs. Terence (Bonnie) Munt including notes by Muriel S. Campbell stored with it and Comstock, p. 185.

VIII. ***William COMSTOCK,*** b. 2 Sept 1826, Albany N.Y.; d. 27 Jan 1855, Cleveland, Ohio; m. 18 Mar 1852, Lorain County, OH to ***Roxanna Alvira BRITTON*** (b. 8 June 1833, Cleveland; d. 30 Mar 1895, Elsinore, Cal.; dau. of *Edwin Squire* and *Roxanna Elvirie BRITTON*) by

Schuyler Putman, Justice of the Peace. William was a machinist.

Issue: ***Sylvia Medora COMSTOCK****,* b. 10 Jan 1853; d. 17 Oct 1872. She died a violent death at her husband's hands at childbirth or just before; m. 12 Aug 1871. ***Martha Washington COMSTOCK****,* b. 29 Oct 1854.; d. 17 Apr 1939; m.1/div. ***Thos. E. GULLIVER*** (b. 21 Apr 1844, son of *Daniel* and *Mary G. GULLIVER* by 1850 census, Addison Co., Vermont); m.2 ***Charles P. CARTER*** (Mormon, b. maybe Utah, he never wanted to talk about himself but knew a lot about Utah, d. 8 Feb 1924). Family bible and Comstock, p. 185.

Additional notes by Muriel Campbell from Mattie W. Comstock:

Rufus COMSTOCK, b. 1736; d. 17 Apr 1826, 90 yrs.; m. *Mary*?. ***Mary? COMSTOCK***, b. 1743; m. *Rufus*; d. 1 Oct 1827, 84 yrs. ***Isaac COMSTOCK***, b. 1786; d. 29 Aug 1846, 60 yrs.; m. *Clarinda*. ***Clarinda Cooper COMSTOCK***, b. 1787; d. 13 Mar 1874; m. *Isaac*. *Issue: George COMSTOCK*, b. 1811, d. 14 Aug 1835, 24 yrs. and *Emily COMSTOCK*, b. 1818, d. 5 Oct 1835, 20 yrs. Comstock Family Bible Notes.

Father of William Comstock:

Charles COMSTOCK*,* was born in Waterford, Saratoga Co., NY, the son of ***William COMSTOCK*** and ***Abigail BETTS***. He was married four times: m1. ***Virtue COOPER****,* she may have died between 1842-1850; m2. possibly ***Anna*** (married name ***LEWIS***); m3. 6 Sept 1869, Whiteside Co., IL to ***Juliet BEAL***; m4 31 July 1879, Whiteside Cuy., IL, ***Emeline BURLINGAME***. He died at the home of his son (name not determined) in Camanche, south of Clinton, Iowa. T.J. Aaron

COMSTOCK, Charles M. 45, b. NY; ***Anna F****.*, 45, b. NY; ***LEWIS, Mary J. F****.*, 15, b. NY; ***COMSTOCK, Matilda F***., 12, b. NY; ***Thomas M****.*, 9, b. NY; ***Charles M****.*, b. NY. 1850 FC NY Niagara Co, p. 407. Presumed to be the father of William.

Mr. Charles COMSTOCK*,* for many years a citizen of Albany, died at the home of is son in Camanche, Iowa, Thursday, April 23. The body was brought to Albany on Saturday afternoon, and the services were held in the cemetery, conducted by *Rev SHEDFORD*. A number of friends and relatives accompanied the remains to the last resting place where the aged father was laid away after a long life of toil and usefulness. Whiteside Centennial, Morrison, IL, April, 1891.

Chas. COMSTOCK; d. 22 April 1891, 5 p.m. at Camanche, IA; bur. Oak Ridge Cemetery, Albany, IL; married; 87 yrs. 6 mos. 22 ds.; d. Capillary Bronchitis - 15 days/old age, in Iowa four years, Informant L.B. Hitchcock. Death Records Book 2, p.14, certif. 3015, Clinton, Clinton Co., Iowa.

Nephew of William Comstock:

Rev. Oliver Ethan COMSTOCK *(b. 28 Dec 1854, d. 10 Sept 1937)*, son of ***Oliver Levanson COMSTOCK****,* founded the Comstock Hospital in Tucson, AZ. Originally in 1909 it was comprised of tents to care for poor patients with tuberculosis. The first permanent building was erected in 1919 but closed in 1966. Lester N. Inskeep, "Invalid's Suicide Was Hospital's Incentive, Oliver E. Comstock, Who Died Yesterday at Casa Grande, Started Institution Here After Destitute Tubercular Took Own Life, The Arizona Daily Star, Sept 11, 1937, pp. A1 and 3; Comstock Hospital's Closing Ends 50 Years of Service, The Arizona Daily Star, Dec 21, 1965, p. A2 and family information.

Wife of William Comstock, Roxanna Britton:

A biographical novel has been written on the life of Roxanna, beginning with the death of William, Roxanna Britton, by Shirley Allen, Criterion House, 2001. *The book is interesting and very informative, although not always historically accurate, it is well worth reading. Comstock photographs for this book provided by Shirley S. Allen.*

Grandparents of Roxanna Britton Comstock:

Squire and ***Mary HOUGHTON BRITTON****,* Males: 1 10-16 yrs., 1 16-26 yrs., 1 45+ yrs.; Females: 1 45+ yrs. 1820 FC OH Cuyahoga County, Troy.

Parents of Roxanna Britton Comstock:

BRITTIN, Edwin*,* 40, Farmer & Ship Carpenter, value of real estate $1,300, b. Mass.; ***Keziah L***.,36, b. NY; ***Roxana E****.*, 16, b. Ohio; ***Harriett A****.*, 11, b. Ohio; ***Byron J****.*, 9, b. Ohio; ***Mary A****.*, 7, b. Ohio; ***Eleanor A****.*, 4, b. Ohio; ***Marion EDMOND****,* 22, b. NY. 1850 FC OH LOAV, p. 468, lines 19-26. *Living near Otis BRAMAN, John CARTER and George JACOX (JAYCOX). Mary BRITTON,* 79, b. NY, living by herself two farms away, line 31. Edwin Britton and Keziah Edmond are said to have had at least ten children. T.J. Aaron

Edw. BRITTON*,* Farm Laborer, value of real estate $500, b. NY; *Mathew SMITH*, 21, Farm Laborer, b. Germany; *Catherine*, 19, b. Germany. 1860 FC OH LOAV, p. 52, lines 23-25.

Roxana A. BRITTON COMSTOCK Married ***Amos E. BOIES****,* 19 May 1857, Orange Twp., Noble Co., Indiana. The Boies's would have three girls and one boy. Amos passed away in 1878, Grand Island, NB. Aaron

BOICE, Amos*,* 34, b. Vermont, Carpenter, value of real estate $1300, personal property $300; ***Roxana***, 27, b. Ohio; ***Sylvia***, 7, b. Ohio; ***Martha***, 5, b. Ohio; ***Emma***, 2, b. Ind.; ***James***, 3, b. Ind.; *John KNOWEL*, 21, Carpenters Apprentice, b. Ohio. 1860 FC IN Noble Co., Orange Township, p. 130, family # 952, lines 17-22.

Amos's parent's ***Joseph BOICE***, 69, b. Mass., Farmer; ***Melinda***, 69, b. Mass. Family #966, p. 132.

Roxann A. BRITTON, b. 8 June 1833, Avon, Lorain Co, OH; d. 30 March 1895, Lake Elsinore, CA; fr. ***Edwin BRITTON****,* mo. ***Keriah Lampson EDMUNDS***; m.1 ***William COMSTOCK***; m.2 ***Amos E. BOIES*** *(*b. c1833; d. between 1873-1918, Grand Island, Nebraska; fr. *Joseph BOIES,* mo. *Melinda CHILD).* California Death Records.

Mrs. R.A. BOYCE*,* widow, Elsinore, CA; 1893-94 Riverside Directories. The directory was published in 1893. Lake Elsinore Library, Lake Elsinore, CA.

Roxanne Adele BOIES, d. 3/30/1895 *(remarried wife of* ***William COMSTOCK****),* ***Adele BOIES ROGERS*** *(youngest daughter of Roxanna and Amos),* b. 1866, bur. 3/11/1897 Lot H-07-10; #11 empty; ***Mattie W. CARTER*** *(daughter of William and Roxanne)*, b. 10/1854, d. 4/17/1939, Lot H-07-12. ***Charles P. CARTER*** *(husband of Mattie)*, b. 12/1858, d. 2/8/1924, Lot H-07-08.; ***Mattie*** as above #12, #13 empty. Elsinore Valley Cemetery, Lake Elsinore, Riverside, CA. Elsinore Valley Cemetery Records.

The weekly issues of the Elsinore Press are missing for the month of March 1895 (Roxanne Comstock Boies obit.) and for the year 1939 (Mattie Carter obit.). Lake Elsinore Library, Lake Elsinore, CA.

Children of William Comstock and Roxanna Britton:

Sylvia Medora COMSTOCK, b. 10 Jan 1853; d. 17 Oct 1872, in Fulton, Ill.; m. 12 Aug 1871 to ***John MARCELLUS***. John Adams Comstock, The Comstocks in America, p. 297.

John A. MARCELLUS & Sylvia COMSTOCK, Clinton, Iowa, Date of Marriage 12 August 1871; Julius Stevens, Minister. #5067, Marriage Certificate, Clinton, IA *(Clinton, Iowa and Fulton, Ill. are across the river from each other)*

Husband of Sylvia:

John Arthur MARCELLUS, was the seventh of eleven children of *Enoch* and *Rachel R.T. WEEKS (WICKS)*. John was b. 29 Feb 1848 in Fulton, Whiteside Co., IL and died 10 Feb 1933, Stuart, Holt, NB at the home of his son, *P.E. MARCELLUS*. His first wife was ***Sylvia COMSTOCK***. Following her death he married *Elizabeth STANGER* in Fulton, Whiteside, IL, dau. of *William STANGER* and *Anna SCHNETT*. She was born 15 July 1855 in Waukegan, Lake Co., IL and died 11 Nov 1916 in Neligh, Antelope, NB. Nine children were born of this union, eight of whom would survive their father. In 1917, Mr. Marcellus was married for the third time to *Mrs. Helma LUND* of Neligh. She died in Washington in 1923. Bob Mosher

John Arthur MARCELLUS married ***Elizabeth M. STANGER*** 29 Oct 1873. County Records, Whiteside County Clerk, Morrison, IL

Sylvia COMSTOCK MARCELLUS, bur. Protestant Cemetery, Fulton, IL, Lot 384, only burial in lot. Cemetery records.

Mattie Washington COMSTOCK, b. 29 Oct 1854; d. 17 Apr 1939; m. 2 Apr 1894, Elsinore, Cal. to ***Charles P. CARTER***. John Adams Comstock, The Comstocks in America, p. 297.

State of California, County of Riverside, ss. This Certifies, That I, Fred Johnston a clergyman of the County of Riverside, in the state of California, united in marriage at Wildomar, in the County of Riverside on the 2nd day of April A.D., 1894 ***Charles CARTER*** a white person, aged 37 years, and who resided at Wildomar to ***Mattie W. GULLIVER*** a white person, aged 39 years, and who resided at Elsinore as authorized by the above instrument, and in accordance with the laws of the State of California, and that the persons whose names are subscribed were present at the Marriage, Witnesses: *M. CHANEY*, res. Wildomar, Cal. and *M. ROGERS, (Mason Rogers, brother-in-law of Mattie)* res. Elsinor. Groom - married once before, wife died. Charles Carter, native of Utah and Mattie W. Gulliver, native of Ohio. Copy of original marriage certificate, provided by Shirley S. Allen.

CARTER, Charles P., owned, farm, 61, married, b. Utah, fr. and mo. b. Indiana, occup. Justice of the Peace; ***Martha***, wife, 63, b. Ohio, fr. b. New York, mo. b. Ohio. 1920 FC California, Riverside County, Elsinore City, p. 1B, enumerated Jan 2-3, 1920.

ELSINORE PIONEER IS LAID TO REST

LOVING FRIENDS PAID LAST TRIBUTES OF RESPECT TO C.P. CARTER SUNDAY

Charles Phillip CARTER, for over 30 years a resident of Elsinore, passed away at his home at 2 a.m., last Friday, after an illness of several months' duration. He was confident until the last that he would recover, making a valiant fight for life.

Mr. Carter was born in Parowan, Utah, and at the time of his death was 65 years of age. For 25 years he was city clerk of Elsinore, serving as city marshall for 5 years prior to being elected to that office. At all times he was faithful in the performance of his duties.

The latter part of last October he resigned from the city position because of failing health, at the same time tendering his resignation to the board of supervisors as Justice of the Peace of this township. The supervisors refused to accept his resignation and granted him an indefinite leave of absence as a mark of respect and confidence.

He is survived by ***Mattie W. CARTER***, his wife, two sisters, and a brother in St. Louis.

A large number of friends from all over the valley and other nearby sections gathered for the funeral services at the home at 1:30 last Sunday afternoon. The *Reverend Avery G. HUNT* conducted the service. Flowers in great abundance bespoke the love and esteem in which the deceased was held. Interment was in the Elsinore cemetery, in charge of *W.L. EVERETT*.

Pallbearers were *A.G. KECK, Chas. HUDSON, Edy? WILLSEY, A.S. BURNHAM, Mr. GEIGER* and *Mr. LEE*, ***Mr.*** and ***Mrs. A.W. WILLIAMS*** and *Mr.* and *Mrs. C.A. WILLIAMS* and two children of Pasadena were present. ***Mrs. A.W. WILLIAMS*** is the sister of Mrs. Carter. Lake Elsinore Valley Press, Friday, February 15, 1924, p. 5, col. 1.

MRS. MATTIE CARTER SUCCUMBS TUESDAY

Pioneer of Elsinore Had Been a Resident Here For 54 Years

The ranks of Elsinore pioneers were saddened this week by the passing of ***Mrs. Mattie W. CARTER***, 85 years old, who died in her home Tuesday morning. Death was due to a heart attack. Funeral services for the deceased were conducted in the chapel of the Everett and

Peterson mortuary Wednesday afternoon, and interment was in the Elsinore Valley cemetery.

Mrs. Carter was born Mattie Comstock....During her youth in the Midwest, a colorful epoch was passed, and she was in the center of it. The settling of the west, including Indian attacks and all the excitement were part of her life, and at one time she lived in the home of a scout of *Buffalo Bill CODY*, and was acquainted with him. *(The scout referred to is believed to be her husband.)*

She arrived in Elsinore 54 *(50)* years ago, and at that time Elsinore was only planning incorporation. Eight *(five)* years after her arrival, she married ***Charles CARTER***, and moved into the home of her mother on Prospect street. When her mother died, she left Mrs. Carter the home, and lived in it since. Mr. Carter was active in civil affairs, holding positions as city councilman, city clerk, and assessor. He passed away in 1924.

Survivors are a sister in Chicago, ***Mrs. Emma WILLIAMS***, and several nieces, including *Mrs. May Down (Dawn) FOSTER; Mrs. Virginia BIRCH of Illinois, Mrs. S. HAZEL, Miss Grace E. WINN* of Baldwin Park and *Mrs. A. G. LILJEGREN* of San Diego.

Officiating at this service Wednesday was *Rev. J.L. CAMERON* of the Presbyterian church, and *Mrs. HERD* was the soloist. Thursday, April 20, 1939, undetermined newspaper, provided by Shirley S. Allen. Corrections by Shirley S. Allen.

Refer to Cemetery lot for Roxanna, above.

OP 5:13 Jerusha Tillotson Rowell

JERUSHA ROWELL
died
June 11, 1867
aged 86 yrs. 1 month
13 days

William IRISH, 34, *?* Mill Wright, Waggon Maker, b. N.Y.; ***Margarett***, 32, b. O.; could be *Issac THORP*, 5, male; *Margaret*, 3, female; ***Jerusha ROWELL***, 69, female, b. *seems to be C....t, but doesn't look like Conn. Census is extremely light and difficult to read. Jerusha is listed in the 1860 index for Ohio and William is recorded in the Lorain Co. individual index which was used to verify the name of Irish.* 1850 LOAV, p. 936, lines 21-25.

William IRISH, 43, Farmer, b. N.Y.; ***Margaret***, 42, b. N.Y.; *Isaac THORP*, 15, b. O. *Jerusha is not listed as living with the Irish family in 1860.* 1860 FC OH LRAV, p. 27, lines 19-21.

Daughter of Isaac Rowell and Jerusha Tillotson:

William IRISH married ***Margaretta Ann ROWEL***, 22 June 1837. Ohio Historical Society; Marriage Index 1824-1848, Lorain Co. Court No.1, p. 204.

William B. IRISH, d. July 19, 1886, 70 y.; ***Margaret A.***, d. Mar 29, 1907, 90 y; *OWEN, Earl B.*, 1890-1891; *Archie E.* 1890-1891. Lot D, row 34, Monument, Garfield Cemetery, Sheffield Twp., Lorain County, OH. Sheffield City Hall, Sheffield, OH (next to cemetery), read by Catherine Burke Flament and Genealogical Workshops of the Lorain County Historical Society, Cemetery Inscriptions of Lorain County, Ohio 1980, Garfield Cemetery, p. 437.

OP 5:14 Isaac Rowell

ISAAC ROWELL
died
July 7, 1845
AE 69 Y. 8 M. 6 D.

I. ROWELL, Male - 60-70 yrs. old: 1; Females - 15-20 yrs. old: 1; 50-60 yrs. old: 1. 1840 FC OH LOAV, p. 155. Next to *Wm. IRISH, Z. IRISH, D. BATES, J.C. LOOMIS* and *Benj. STEVENS.*

The 164'6" long Rowell Bridge of Hopkinton, NH was built in 1853 in honor of Isaac Rowell. The original bridge using a combination of long trusses and burr arches cost $300.25. Richard G. Marshall, New Hampshire Covered Bridges, <http://www.state.nh.us/nhdhr/bridges/p19.html>, (cited 18 Sept 2005) and David J. Rowell

Ancestors of Isaac Rowell:

I. ***Valentine ROWELL***, b. abt. 1566, Mancetter, Atherstone, Warwick, England; d. 13 Sept 1613; m. ***Elizabeth HAMPTON*** (b. 1570, d. 14 Feb 1647). Howard W. Hildebrand, Thomas Rowell, 400 Years & 8461 Descendants Later; and David J. Rowell.

II. ***Thomas ROWELL***, b. 1590, England; d. 8 May 1662, Andover, MA; m. ***Margaret OSGOOD*** (b. 1594, England, d. 1649, England). Hildebrand and Rowell

III. ***Valentine ROWELL***, b. 1618, England; d. 17 May 1662, Salisbury; m. ***Joanna PINDER***, (b. 1621, S. England, d. Oct 1890, Amesbury, MA; dau. of *Henry PINDER* (b. 1578 England, d. 6 Feb 1661, E. Salisbury, MA) and *Mary ROGERS* (b. 1582, England, d. Salisbury)). Hildebrand and Rowell

IV. ***Phillip ROWELL***, b. 8 Mar 1648, Salisbury; d. 7 July 1690; m. ***Sarah MORRELL*** *(sp.)* (b. 14 Oct 1650, Salisbury; d. 11 Sept 1731, S. Hampton, NH; dau. of *Abraham MORRILL* and *Sarah CLEMENT*). *Issue: Jacob, Sarah, Thomas, John, Hepzibah, Judith, Aaron,* and *Job*. Hildebrand and Rowell

V. ***Job ROWELL***, b. 1685, Amesbury, MA; d. 4 May 1746; m. ***Bethia BROWN*** (b. July 1684, dau. of *Abraham BROWN* and *Elizabeth SHEPHERD*). Hildebrand and Rowell

VI. ***Thomas ROWELL,*** b. 1718?, Salisbury; m. ***Sarah MORRILL*** (b. 22 June 1722, Salisbury, dau. of *Jacob MORRILL* (b. 25 May 1677 at Salisbury, d. 25 Mar 1754 at Salisbury) and *Elizabeth STEVENS* (b. 14 Feb 1677)). Hildebrand and Rowell

VII. ***Abraham ROWELL***, b. 1743, Salisbury, Essex Co., MA; m. ***Elizabeth EASTMAN*** (b. 6 June 1743, Salisbury, dau. of *Jonathan EASTMAN* and *Martha ALLEN*). Hildebrand and Rowell

Children of Mr. Abraham Rowell and *Elizabeth Eastman* his wife: ***Jacob ROWELL***, b. Sept 22, 1768; ***Abraham ROWELL***, in the town, Oct 17, 1770; ***Bette ROWELL***, b. Nov 22, 1772; m. (*possibly same individual) Mr. John TUCKER* of Unity and *Miss Betsy ROWELL* of Hopkinton were put in a marriage covenant at Hopkinton by the Rev. Amos Wood, Nov 17, 1794; ***Isaac ROWELL,*** b. Nov 1, 1774; ***Sarah ROWELL***, b. Sept 6, 1778; ***Molley ROWELL***, b. Sept 10, 1782. Pauline Osterland, Hopkinton, New Hampshire Vital Records, vol. 1, pp. 10-25, 71.

VIII. ***Isaac ROWELL*** was the 6th child of ***Abraham ROWELL*** and ***Elizabeth EASTMAN*** of Hopkinton, NH. Their children were; ***Thomas, Jonathan, Jacob, Abraham, Betsy, Isaac, Moses, Sally, Samuel, Molly, Hannah*** and ***Nancy Ann***. ***Isaac*** m.1 ____***STRONG*** c1800; res. Hopkinton, NH; m.2 ***"Joshua" TILLOTSON***. *This may have been misread since it is not a female name, it is probably Jerusha.* Hildebrand and Rowell

Marriages recorded in Lorain County 1824-1865:
Charles B. ROWELL to *Mary Ann COLE,* April 29, 1845.
Charles B. ROWELL to *Mary E. PARRISH,* Sept 5, 1847.
John L. ROWELL to *Martha TINKER,* July 3, 1845.
John S. ROWELL to *Elizabeth NORTON,* July 10, 1848.
Sullivan ROWELL, to *Harriett CURTIS,* May 28, 1850.
William S. ROWELL to *Emily A. ARNOLD*, Nov 30, 1853.
Marriages of Lorain County, Ohio 1824-1865.

ROWELL: *Sullivan*, d. May 16, 1865, 85y.; *Mabel S.*, wife, d. Dec 4, 1845, 64y.; *Frank*, 1841-1941; *Mary M. GIFFORD*, wife, 1854-1920; *Charles B.*, 1818-19_5; *Margaret A.*, wife, 1827-1845; *Alice E.*, 1854-1908.; *C. Arthur,* 1848-1849; *Clarence*, 1851; *J. L.*, Mar 23, 1818-Jan 8, 1885; *Elizabeth*, wife, Sep 16, 1824-Feb 22, 1906; *George S.*, son *JL&E*, d ?; Hinkley, ?. South Pittsfield or Whitney Cemetery, Wellington, OH, Cemetery Inscriptions of Lorain County, p. 368.

OP 5:15 William Henry Loomis

Marker cracked and set in concrete.

WILLIAM H.
SON OF
J.C. & B.L. LOOMIS
DIED
MAY 24, 1842
Previously read as
May 21, 1812
AGED
7 M. 11 D.

William LOOMIS is thought to be the earliest burial on record in Lake Side Cemetery. Bay Village Historical Society, Bay Village: A Way of Life, p. 142.

After careful examination of the stone, which is difficult to read, the date of death seems to be 1842, not 1812 as recorded earlier. This seems to be in agreement with the following census records which include the parents' middle initials as recorded on the stone of Jonathan Collins and Betsey (Elizabeth) Lovise LOOMIS. If this child were born in 1811, he would have been born one month before Jonathan Collins Loomis, his father. Eber, the father of Jonathan Collins was living in Dover when the 1820 census was taken. 1820 FC OH CYDO, p. 53. *The 1830 census finds him located in La Grange, Ohio.* 1830 FC OH Lorain Co., La Grange, p. 27. *The following lists data about Eber and Jonathan Collins's families. William is listed as a child of Jonathan.*

Paternal Ancestors of William H. Loomis:
Descendants of Joseph Loomis, the first settler in America of the Loomis Family generously donated money for a school to be built on the original family property. Below is a description of the history and some statistics on the boarding school today.

In the early 1870's, four Loomis brothers, *James Chaffee, Hezekiah Bradley, Osbert Burr* and *John Mason*, and their sister, *Abigail Sarah*, wife of *H. Sidney HAYDEN*, united by the loss of all their children, decided to pool their considerable estates to found an institution for secondary education in the hope, as expressed in the will of John Mason, that The Loomis Institute would be "a shrine upon which boys and girls shall take the highest inspirations for better and grander lives." The Founders were closely allied in their vision by a sense of family and obligation to their kin and the fact that the original Loomis family homestead, built by *Joseph LOOMIS* in 1640 at the confluence of the Farmington and Connecticut rivers, provided an ideal site for their dream.

The charter for The Loomis Institute, unusual for private secondary schools at the time, stipulated that the institute should offer a broad curriculum (vocational as well as college preparatory) and that there should be no religious or political criteria for admission. "Free and gratuitous education" was to be provided as far as the endowment would permit.

Upon the death of the widow of John Mason Loomis in 1910, the business of construction began. *Nathaniel Horton BATCHELDER* was chosen as the first headmaster in 1912. The Loomis Institute, a boarding and day school, opened in 1914 with an enrollment of 39 boys and five girls.

The Loomis Chaffee School today is an independent, coeducational college-preparatory, boarding and day school with an enrollment of approximately 725 students and a faculty of 136. The 300-acre campus is located in a rural setting in the historic town of Windsor, six miles north of Hartford, Connecticut. Students are from 29 U.S. states and 21 other countries. Loomis Chaffee, About Loomis Chaffee, "History" and "Key Facts" http://www.loomis.org. (cited 7 July 2004).

I. ***Eber LOOMIS,*** was born 20 Jan 1779, Pittsfield, MA; moved to La Grange, Lorain County, Ohio, in 1815; died 16 Apr 1843, La Grange, Ohio. m.1 ***Rebecca COLLINS,*** 12 May 1808 in La Grange, Ohio. m.2 ***Juliana THOMPSON,*** 5 May 1824. *Children of Eber and Rebecca;* ***Eber Clark LOOMIS,*** b. 16 Feb 1809. ***Norvall Lyman LOOMIS***, b. 11 Aug 1810. ***Jonathan Collins LOOMIS***, b. 16 Nov 1811, Avon, Lorain County; d. 29 Dec 1854, Dover, Cuyahoga County, Ohio. ***Rebecca Lucinda LOOMIS***, b. 13 Apr 1813. ***Otis Henry LOOMIS***, b. 27 Oct 1816. ***Horace Lyman LOOMIS***, b. 30 Mar 1818. ***Woolsey Melancthon LOOMIS***, b. 07 May 1820. ***Mary Rebecca LOOMIS***, b. 11 Dec 1822. Elisha Scott Loomis, Descendants of Joseph Loomis in America and his Antecedents in the Old World, pp. 199-200. *Available at Rhode Island Historical Society.*

LOOMIS, Woolsey m. ***MARTIN, Emeline*** on Dec 16, 1841. Marriages of Lorain County, p. 69.

II. ***Jonathan Collins LOOMIS***, b. Nov 16, 1811; d. Dec 29, 1854, at Avon, O.; m. July 13, 1835, Dover, Cuyahoga Co., O., ***Elizabeth Lovise CROCKER*** (b. July 13, 1816, Dover; d. 1 Dec, 1891, Byron, Mich.; dau. of *Noah L. CROCKER* and *Betsy (FOOTE)*). All 7 children b. Avon.

Issue: ***Leonard Gurley LOOMIS***, b. Aug 4, 1837.* ***Julia Rebecca LOOMIS***, b. June 3, 1839; m. Dec 25, 1865 to *William W. THOMAS*, son of *Aaron* and *Betsy (ROBERTS) THOMAS*. *Issue*: 1. *Letta Eulalia THOMAS*, 2. *Lillian Isabelle THOMAS*. ***William Henry LOOMIS***, b. Aug 10, 1841; d. March 7, 1842. ***Alvin Crocker LOOMIS***, b. June 3, 1843.* ***Jonathan Collins LOOMIS***, b. Aug 4, 1846; m. 1877, *Ella LAWRENCE*. ***Charles Wesley LOOMIS,*** b. June 18, 1849; unm.; d. May 6, 1883, Byron, Mich. ***William Chester LOOMIS***, b. Dec 10, 1852.* Loomis, pp. 279-280, #1937, 4401-4407. * *Indicates additional information available.*

Parents of William Loomis:

J.C. LOOMIS, Males - under 5: 1, 20-30: 1; Females: under 5: 1, 20-30: 1. 1840 FC OH LOAV, p. 155.

Jn-. C. LOOMIS, 38, farmer, b. N.Y.; ***Betsey L.***, 33, b. O.; ***Leonard G.***, 12; ***Julia R.***, 11; ***Alvin C.***, 7; ***Jno. C.***, 3. All children b. O. Living next to *Noah CROCKER*. 1850 FC OH LOAV, house 1239, p. 937.

Betsey LOOMIS, 43, farmer, value of real estate 1500, personal estate 400; ***Alvin***, 17; ***Jonathon***, 13; ***Charles***, 10; ***William***, 7; all b. in Ohio. 1860 FC OH LOAV, p. 26, lines 10-14. *Jonathon Sr. died before this census and they had named a second child William.*

OP 5:16 **Alonson Atwell Grant**

ALONSON A.
GRANT
DIED AT
POTOMAC
.....
MAR 31, 1863
AGED 28 YRS. 6 M.
6D.

Previously read as "***Alanson A. GRANT***, died at Potomac Creek, Va., Mar 31, 1863..." Cuyahoga County Cemetery Inscriptions, 1934.

Alonson died in battle during the Civil War. His second child, Maurice Alonson Grant, was born on Independence Day two months after his death. His wife would remarry and is also buried at Lakeside.

Alonson Atwell GRANT, son of ***Thomas GRANT*** and ***Mary ATWELL***, b. Avon, O., Oct 27, 1835; d. Potomac Station (Columbus), Va., Mch. 30 (20), 1863 (1864); m. A., May 13, 1857, ***Fannie CARTER***, who was b. A., Dec 4, 1839; sailor; Sergt. and 2d Lieut. 6th O. Vol. Cav. 1861-3.* Arthur Hastings Grant, The Grant Family, A Genealogical History of the Descendents of Matthew Grant of Windsor, CT, 1601-1898, p. 193. * Indicates additional information available.

Children of ***Alonson A. GRANT*** *and* ***Fannie CARTER***: ***Sarah E. GRANT*** b. Sep. 9, 1860; d. Burwell, Neb.; m. Pittsfield, ____, a 1876, *Geo. I. GILL.* ***Maurice Alonson GRANT***, b. Avon, O.; July 4, 1863; res. Lorain, O.; form. Omaha, Neb.; grocer; clerk with U.P.R.R. 1883-93; Oberlin Coll. 1882-3. Grant, p. 346.

GRANT, Alanson to ***Fanny CARTER*** on May 13, 1857. Marriages Lorain County, Ohio 1824-1865, p. 46.

I. ***Josiah GRANT,*** m.1 ***Sarah MINER***, m.2 ***Mary HEWITT WILLIAMS***. A son of Josiah and *Sarah* was *Josiah*. Arthur Hastings Grant, The Grant Family, A Genealogical History of the Descendents of Matthew Grant of Windsor, CT, 1601-1898, p. 21

II. ***Josiah GRANT***, b. Stonington, Conn., Aug 18, 1771; d. Warrensville (Willoughby), O., c1843-4; m. in Scotland to ***Sibyl SAFFORD*** (b. near Edinburgh, Scotland; d. Oct 8, 1830, Willoughby, O., c50 yrs. old); res. Stonington, perhaps also for a time near Rockville; removed 1814 by oxteam to N.Y., thence to Willoughby; farmer; went to sea and was shipwrecked, hence his marriage abroad.

Issue: ***Mary GRANT***, b. Stonington, Feb. 10, 1803; d. Geneva, Mich., Sept. 11, 1869; bur. Cleveland, O.; m. Willoughby, O., May 1821, *David LAFLER* (b. Geneva, NY, Aug 10, 1794; d. Rockport, O., May 16, 1854; bur. Cleveland; son of *Jacob LAFLER* and *Mary___*); res. Willoughby; removed 1833 to Warrensville, O., in 1835 to Dover, O., and in 1838 to Rockport; carpenter, farmer and miller. ***Thomas GRANT***, see below. ***Noah Josiah GRANT***, b. Stonington, 1808; d. Des Moines, Iowa, 1853; m. *Julia HOVEY*, of Warrensville, O.; farmer and lay preacher. ***Miner GRANT***, b. Stonington; d. Tomah, Wis., 1870; m. *Abigail PENFIELD*, of Cuyahoga Falls, O., who d. bef. 1870; farmer and lay preacher. ***Joseph GRANT***, b. in N.Y., 1814; m. *Hannah TURNER*; (res. Tomah, Wis.?). Grant, pp. 43, 88.

III. ***Thomas GRANT***, b. in Conn.; killed in battle; m. Dover, O., 1828 to ***Mary ATWELL*** of D. *(Dover)* (b. 14 miles E. of Buffalo, N.Y., July 20, 1807; d. D., Jan 4, 1887; dau. of *Jesse ATWELL* and [*Caroline*] *RICE*). {*Mary GRANT* 1807-1886, with her son, *Alfred A. GRANT* 1837-1904, bur. Evergreen Cemetery, Westlake, put in vault 29 Dec 1886, bur. 29 Jan 1887}; farmer and merchant; private in an Ill. Regt. in Civil War; dea. In M.E. ch. Grant, p. 88.

Issue: ***Alonzo Augur GRANT***, b. Avon (Warrensville), O., Dec 10, 1832 (Nov 1829); d. Erie, Pa. (Cleveland, O), Oct 10, 1870 (1872); 3 yrs. in Union army. ***Alonson Atwell GRANT***, see above. ***Alfred Alfonso GRANT***, b. June 6, 1837; m. July 16, 1870, *Nancy M. GIBSON* [b. Amherst, O., Apr 12, 1848; dau. of *Manhattan GIBSON* and *Maria C. KENDEIGH*]; res. S. Amherst, O.; farmer; sailor 20? Yrs.; served 2 yrs. in Civil War {Alfred A. Grant 1837-1904, b. Avon; bur. 18 Apr 1904, Evergreen Cemetery, Westlake}. ***Lorenzo Wilford GRANT***, b. Rockport, O., Mch. 24, 1841; m. Chicago, Ill., 1871, *Mary A. ROCKWOOD* [b. in Vt.; dau. of *Lyman ROCKWOOD*]; res. Saugatuck, Mich.; house and ship carpenter; dea., mayor. ***Ellen Nancy GRANT***, b. Avon, O., Mch. 31, 1846; m. Dover, O., July 15, 1867, *Thomas Francis DOYLE* [b. Kiltmaugh, Co. Mayo, Ireland, Dec 1849; d. Lakewood, O., Aug 6, 1893; s. of *Owen John DOYLE* and *Catherine DYRE*]; res. Cleveland, O. (40 Walnut St.). Grant, p.193; {Evergreen Cemetery, Westlake}and [Ingrid Abram].

I do hereby certify that on the 31st day of Dec 1831, by virtue of a license from the Clerk of the Court of Common Pleas of Cuyahoga County ***Thomas GRANT*** and ***Mary ATWELL*** were legally joined in marriage by me a Justice of the Peace in and for said County, Given under my hand this 11th day Feby. 1832. Aaron Aldrich, JP Marriage Record, Cuyahoga County, OH, vol. 2, p. 291. *(Aaron married them four days before Thomas B. Powell and Sophia Sadler.)*

Thomas GRANT, 42, farmer, b. Conn.; ***Mary***, 42, b. NY; ***Alonzo***, 17, farmer; ***Alonson***, 16; ***Alfred***, 12; ***Wilford***, 9; ***Safford***, 6; ***Ellen***, 4; all children b. Ohio; illegible name listed as a farmer. 1850 FC OH LRAV pp. 931-932.

Wife of Alonson Grant, Fanny Carter:
Alonson's widow remarried. She and her second husband are buried in OP 1: 1-2. The State of Ohio, Lorain County, ss. I Hereby Certify that on the 24th day of September A.D. 1874, I duly solemnized the Marriage Contract between ***Mr. Alfred WILLIS*** and ***Miss Fanny GRANT***. H.M. Walker, M.G. LCMR: 1872-1888, p. 779 (110).

"Dover -
Her past, present and future.
Proof positive that her pioneers did not 'take hold of the plow and look back.'"

A.P. Johnson, Jamestown, N.Y.
A Pioneer Celebration, 1875

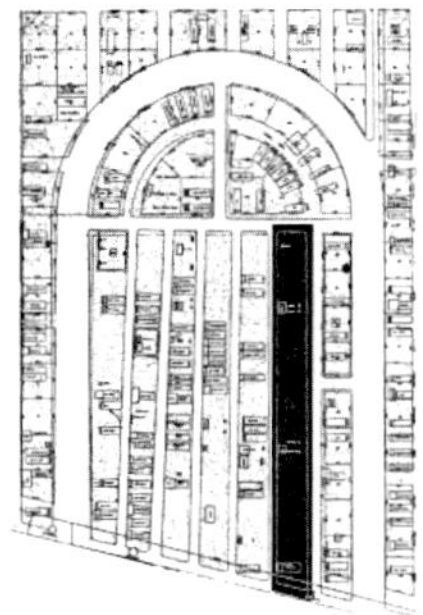

Sixth row east of the west drive starting from the road and proceeding north.

OP 6:1 **Charlotte Burlingame McMahon**

CHARLOTTE
BURLINGAME
WIFE OF
PHILOTAS
MCMAHON
DIED DEC 10, 1862
AGE 26 YEARS
1 M. 18 D.

Charlotte is the daughter of Hiram Burlingame and Rebecca Gant (Lot 44-4).

MCMAHON, Mrs. Flotus, maiden name ***Charlotte BURLINGAME***, last res. Rockport, O. Arrived in Cuy Co. prior to 1840. Women of the Western Reserve Prior to 1840, p. 28.

Hiram BURLINGAME, 51, sailor, b. Vt.; ***Rebecca***, 49, b. Vt.; ***Charlotte***, 23, b. Ohio. 1860 FC OH CY Rockport, p. 9, lines 33-35, house 67.

The State of Ohio, Cuyahoga County, ss, I Certify, That on the 10th day of May 1860 ***Mr. Philotas McMAHON*** and ***Miss Charlotte BURLINGAME*** were by me legally joined in Marriage. J. Barnum, J.P. Marriage Record, Cuyahoga County, OH, vol. 10, p. 17.

Charlotte and Philotas may have had a daughter according to the following census. Charlotte's mother's place of birth is listed as Ohio which would be incorrect if she is, in fact, Charlotte's daughter.

MCMAHON, Philotas, 39, Carpenter, b. Ohio, fr. b. Ireland, mo. b. Conn.; ***Mary***, 40, wife, keeping house, b. Ohio, fr. and mo. b. Conn.; ***Charlotte***, 17, dau., at home, b. Ohio, fr. and mo. b. O.; ***Oza***, 12, son, b. Ohio; ***Grace***, 3, b. Ohio; *Gale WILLIAM*, 33, Servant, Farm Hand, b. NY, mo. and fr. b. Ohio. 1880 FC OH CYRP, p. 314, lines 42-47.

The State of Ohio, Cuyahoga County, SS. I Certify, That on the 14th day of November 1889, ***Mr. Ozra (Oza) J. MCMAHON*** and ***Miss Ida M. BOWER*** were by me legally joined in Marriage. J.W. Utter Marriage Record, Cuyahoga County, OH, vol. 33, p. 447.

The State of Ohio, Cuyahoga County, ss. I certify, That on the 15th day of October 1895, ***Mr. Lucius DEAN Jr.*** and ***Miss Grace Edna MCMAHON*** were by me legally joined in Marriage. Rev. M.W. Reece Marriage Record, Cuyahoga County, OH, vol. 42, p. 474.

Entry showing death of Charlotte's husband. He died just a little over a month after his second wife.

Philotas MCMAHON, *(Detroit Rd.)*, Rocky River, Ohio; d. Jan 31, 1919, Apoplexy; Widower; Carpenter; b. Oct 28, 1840, Dover, Ohio, fr. ***Michael MCMAHON***, b. Ireland, mo. ***Julia BENEDICT***; Informant Irving Dean, Rocky River; bur. West Park Cemetery, Feb 3, 1919, undertaker Clifford Pease. Ohio Certificate of Death, Division of Vital Statistics, 1919, certif. 1135.

West Park Cemetery has no record of ***Philotas MCMAHON*** being buried at the cemetery. There is no one by that name listed under the Feb 3, 1919 burials or in the general list of burials. West Park Cemetery, Cleveland, OH.

Parents of Philotas McMahon:

Michael MCMAHON, 65, farmer, b. Ire.; ***Julia***, 50, b. Vt.?; ***Henry***, 14, b. O. 1860 FC OH CY Rockport, p. 10, lines 37-39.

MCMAHON-M., in West Rockport on the 19th inst., of Consumption, M. McMahon aged 69 years. Mr. M. emigrated from the State of Connecticut in the year 1851, to Rockport Ohio then a wilderness where he resided till his death, an industrious honest citizen. Eastern papers please copy. Cleveland Necrology File, Oct 18, 1861.

Mrs. McMAHON (Julia BENEDICT) probably the oldest pioneer woman in Rockport, was born 1800 in Stanford, Conn. In 1831, she with her husband, came to Ohio. They were considered wealthy in those days, having about $500. She has never had a sick day since, and when eighty-six years old was able to walk ten miles. During the first year of her pioneer life she would take butter and eggs in a basket on her arm and walked to Cleveland, a distance of eleven miles, to exchange them for groceries. Their first crop of potatoes was taken to Cleveland where they were offered but three cents per bushel, the pay in trade. *Mr. McMAHON* in disgust pulled the end board out of the wagon, and let them roll into the river. She remembers seeing Lafayette, she is the mother of nine children, and is at the present living with her son, ***Phiolotas MCMAHON***, at Rocky River. Women of the Western Reserve Prior to 1840, Rockport, p. 271.

HAHN-MCMAHON, cemetery on private property, last house on Lake Rd., in Rocky River. Abandoned. Ohio Cemeteries, p. 75.

Second wife of Philotas McMahon:

MCMAHON-Mary L., wife of ***Philotas MCMAHON***, Thursday, Dec 26, aged 78 yrs. Funeral services from the residence, Detroit Road, Rocky River, Sunday, Dec 29, at 2 p.m. December 29, 1918. Cleveland Necrology File, reel 53.

MCMAHON, Mary E.; d. Dec 26, 1918, 9 a.m., Detroit Road, Rocky River, Cuyahoga Co., O of Broncho Pneumonia; married, Housewife; b. Sept 7, 1840, Dover; fr. *Chas. ALLEN*, b. NY State, mo. *Rachel KIDNEY*, b. Ohio; Informant *Mr. Philotas MCMAHON*, Rocky River; bur. Alger Cem., undertaker Mastick & Daniel, 14622 Detroit. Ohio Certificate of Death, Division of Vital Statistics, 1918, certif. 86579.

OP 6:2 Case Monument

MOSES CASE
DIED
SEPT 19, 1868
CHARLOTTE MILLER
WIFE OF
MOSES CASE
DIED
MAR 2, 1826
"OUR FATHER &
MOTHER"
very difficult to read

OP 6:2 Moses Case

Moses CASE, male 40-50: 1, 10-15: 2, female 30-40: 1, 10-15: 1, 5-10: 1. 1830 FC OH LRAV, p. 6, lines 5-8, dwelling 1175.

Moses CASE, 63, Farmer, value of real estate $450, b. Conn.; ***Chloe***, 18; ***Harvey***, 15, Farmer, attended school during the year; ***Philancy***, 10, attended school; children all b. O. 1850 FC OH LRAV, p. 934, lines 5-8.

Moses LUSE *(sp.)*, 78, b. Conn.; ***Filansy***, 21, b. O. *Listed on the farm next to his, was his son,* ***Isaac***. 1860 FC OH Sheffield, Lorain Co., p. 305, lines 17-18.

CASE.-In Sheffield, on the 19th day of September, of Dropsy of the heart, ***Moses CASE***, in the 88th year of his age. Elyria Independent Democrat, Elyria, Ohio, Wednesday, Sept 30, 1868, p. 2, col. 5.

Ancestors of Moses Case:

James CASE, a genealogist with the Conn. Mayflower Association, related before his death that there are two separate and unrelated Case families, one from Rhode Island and the other, ***John CASE*** from Simsbury, CT. Ruth Cost Duncan, John Case and His Descendants

I. ***John CASE***, Aylesham, Eng.; b. 1616. Aylesham, England; d. 21 Feb 1703/4, Simsbury, Hartford, CT*(VR)*, no tombstone; m.1 1656, Hartford, Hartford Co., MA to ***Sarah SPENCER*** (dau. of *William SPENCER* and *Agnes TUCKER (or HARRIS)* of Hartford, CT.; b. 7 Mar 1635/36, Boston, MA; d. 3 Nov 1691, Simsbury). Sarah's tombstone is the oldest in the Hopmeadow Cemetery, Simsbury); m.2 ***Elizabeth MOORE LOOMIS*** (dau. of *John* and *Abigail MOORE* of Windsor, CT and widow of *Nathaniel LOOMIS*; b. 23 July 1638, Windsor, Hartford Co., CT; d. 23 July 1728, Windsor). Lucius Barnes Barbour, Families of Early Hartford, Conn.; Ruth Cost Duncan; Daphne Gawne and *(Vital Records).*

II. ***Joseph CASE***, b. 6 Apr 1674, Simsbury, Hartford, CT *(VR)*; d. 11 Aug 1748, Simsbury*(VR)*; m. 6 Apr 1699, Simsbury*(VR)* to ***Anna ENO*** (dau. of *James ENO* and *Abigail BISSELL* of Windsor, CT; b. 10 Apr 1682, Windsor, CT; d. 10 June 1760, Simsbury*(VR)*). Barbour, Duncan and Gawne with *(Vital Records).*

III. ***Josiah CASE***, b. 1 Feb 1715/16, Simsbury, CT*(VR)*; m. 22 July 1742*(VR)*, Simsbury to ***Mary HOSKINS*** (dau. of *Robert HOSKINS* and *Mary GILLETT*; she d. 29 Apr 1797 in Simsbury at the age of 74 *(Barkhamsted, Ct Church Record)*). Barbour; Dr. Erastus Ely Case, "Case Family Manuscript," A185, at The Connecticut Historical Society, Hartford, Connecticut; Ruth Cost Duncan, John Case and His Descendants; Daphne Gawne.

IV. ***Josiah CASE***, b. 19 Feb 1753, Simsbury, CT; d. after 1788 in Phelps, Ontario Co., NY; m. ***Ruth PHELPS*** (dau. of *David PHELPS* and *Abigail PETTIBONE* of Simsbury, b. 15 Sept 1743, Simsbury). The marriage was not recorded in the Simsbury VR. Josiah Case settled in Guilford, Conn. Then removed to Vermont. *John HIGLRY?*, of Simsbury deeds land in Norfolk, Conn., to Josiah Case, of Simsbury, Dec 22, 1769. Josiah Case with his family removed from Simsbury to N.Y. about 1800. Some of them went to Albany Co., N.Y. and some to Ohio.

Children of Ruth with her first husband Jonas CASE: ***Bissell CASE***, b. 1764; ***Lucy CASE*** m. *Horatio SEYMOUR*; ***Loyal CASE***, b. 1768, d. 1830, m. *Sally*.

Children of Josiah and Ruth: ***Levi Norman CASE*** *(possibly two individuals with Levi b. 1775)**, b. 1775; ***Ira CASE***, b. 1776, m. *Phebe BODGELEY*; ***Russell CASE***, b. 1777, m. *Jane THOMPSON*; ***Moses CASE***, b. 1 Aug 1781, m. *Charlotte MILLER*, d. Sept 1868, OH; ***Harvey CASE***, b. 1788, m. *Catherine VAN AUKEN*; ***Truman CASE***, b. 1792, m. *Annis*; ***Chloe CASE***, m. ___ *HAWKS*; ***Sally CASE***, m. ____ *CHAPMAN*. Barbour; Case, "Case Family Manuscript," A1856; Duncan; Gawne and *(Vital Records).**

V. ***Moses CASE***, b. Aug 1, 1781, probably Connecticut; d. Sept 1868, in Ohio; m.1 ***Charlotte MILLER*** abt. 1809 in New York (b. abt. 1790 in Phelps, Ontario Co., NY; dau. of *Adam MILLER* and *Anna TREMONT* of Connecticut and Phelps; d. in Avon, Lorain Co., Ohio); m.2 ***Martha LOOMIS***; (b. c1810 [b. 1796], Black River, Jefferson Co., NY; dau. of *Jonathan LOOMIS* and *Mattie BLAKE*; d. 1850, Avon). Moved to Cleveland and later Avon, Ohio. Farmer. Case, [Gawne]

Children of Moses CASE and *Charlotte MILLER*: ***Menzies Raynor CASE***, b. 7 Nov 1810, Wayne Co., NY; d. 23 June 1887, Jersey City, Hudson Co., NJ; m. *Amanda Melvina COON*, 2 Jan 1834, Schenectady Co., NY. ***Archibald Russell CASE***, b. 19 Aug 1813, Phelps, Ontario Co., NY; d. 19 Dec 1881 Baraboo, Sauk Co., Wisconsin. ***Delia Ann CASE***, b. 12 Oct 1816, Phelps; d. 5 July 1880; m. 18 Mar 1833, Lorain Co., OH to *Theron MOORE*. ***Isaac CASE***, b. 25 Jan 1819 Cleveland, Cuyahoga Co., OH; d. 7 May 1886, Sheffield, Lorain Co.; m.1 2 Dec 1840, Avon, Lorain Co. to *Susan A. TITUS*; m.2 22 Aug 1850, Lorain Co. to *Sarah Ann MOORE (should be MOON)*; m.3 26 Jan 1856, Avon, Lorain Co. to *Malinda Caroline GRISWOLD (dau. of Luman GRISWOLD and Margaret SMITH GRISWOLD EDDY OP 1:10-11)*. ***Sarah Catherine CASE***, b. 12 Mar 1821, Lorain Co.; d. 23 Sept 1901; m. 1841, Lorain Co. to *Ichabod BRIGGS*. ***Susan Miller CASE***, b. 15 June 1823, Lorain Co.; d. 22 Mar 1878; m. *David J. FIELD*, 18 June 1847, Lorain Co. Barbour; Case, A18566; Duncan; Gawne.

Parents of Martha Loomis Case, second wife of Moses Case:

Jonathan LOOMIS, Males: 1 10-16 yrs., 1 16-26 yrs., 1 26-45 yrs., 1 45+ yrs.; Females: 1 10-16 yrs., 1 26-45 yrs. 1810 FC NY, Jefferson Co., Champion, p. 49.

Children of Moses Case and Charlotte Miller:

CASE, Menzies R., Broker, 101 Wall, h. N.J. New York City Directory, 1869.

Delia Ann CASE, b. 12 Oct 1816, Phelps, Ontario Co., NY; d. 5 July 1880, m. 18 Mar 1833, Avon, Lorain Co., Ohio to ***Theron MOORE*** (son of *Theron MOORE* (b. 3 Sep. 1786, Granville, Hampshire, MA) and *Keziah ALDRICH* (b. c1790, d. aft 19 Feb 1814, but before Aug 1919), b. 8 Oct 1810, Willsboro, Essex Co., NY; d. 28 Nov 1877, Sheffield Twp., Lorain Co., OH). *Issue:* ***Menzies Raynor MOORE,*** b. 10 Feb 1834, OH; d. 6 Nov 1881, KS, m. *Marion CAHOON*. ***Leonard William MOORE***, b. 9 Feb 1836, Sheffield; d. 5 June 1913, Lorain, OH; m.1 1 Feb

1854 to *Sarah E. ROOT* (d. 8 Sept 1857), m.2 15 Mar 1859, Lorain Co. to *Amanda C. MILLER* (b. 1835, d. aft. 1894), res. Lorain, Ohio. ***Elmina MOORE***, b. 14 June 1838; d. 24 Mar 1915, Lorain; m. *Thomas GAWN*; res. Lorain. ***Melvina MOORE***, b. 10 Sept 1840, OH; d. 24 Nov 1850, OH. ***Amelia Catherine MOORE***, b. 27 Dec 1842, Sheffield; d. 10 Jan 1931, Lorain; m. *John FARAGHER*; res. Lorain. ***Truman Case MOORE***, b. 1 Dec 1844; d. 13 Jan 1919, Lorain; m.1 1863, OH to *Esther CARRON* (b. 15 July 1847, Isle of Man; d. 8 May 1880, Sheffield); m.2 1881, OH to *Rosa RICE* (b. 1848, Medina Co., OH; d. after 1894); res. Lorain. ***Charlotte Parlly MOORE***, b. 3 Oct 1846, d. 1921; m. *Albert BRIGGS*; res. Wayneport, NY. ***Maria MOORE***, b. 3 July 1849, OH; d. aft 1894; m. c1868 *Mair POINTON [Muir POINTOU]* (b. c1849, Yellow Medicine Co., MN; d. aft 1894). ***Rowena Angebella MOORE***, b. 11 Jan 1854, OH; d. 2 May 1918, Cleveland, Cuyahoga Co., OH; m. *Theron T. MERRY*; res. Cleveland. ***George Albert MOORE***, b. 27 Dec 1855, OH; d. 21 Mar 1860, OH. ***Mary Adeline MOORE,*** b. 23 Mar 1858, OH; d. 13 Nov 1933, Cleveland Hts., Cuyahoga Co., OH; m. c1878, *William Arthur JEWITT* (b. Mar 1857, Cleveland; d. 12 Apr 1936, Cleveland Hts.; res. 171 Hough Ave., Cleveland and 2624 Wellington Rd., Cleveland Heights; bur. Knollwood Cemetery). Theron Moore had moved to Ohio with his parents in 1818. He was a cousin of *Kit CARSON*, famed Indian Scout, 1809-1868, whose exploits were closely followed. Daphne Gawne and Dr. Erastus Ely Case, "Case Family Manuscript," A18566, at The Connecticut Historical Society, Hartford, Connecticut. [Case Manuscript conflicting information].

Theram MOORE, 39, Farmer, value of real estate $2000, b. N.Y.; ***Delia***, 33, b. N.Y.; ***Menzies***, 17, Farmer; ***Lenard***, 14; ***Almira***, 12, female; ***Malvina***, 10, female; ***Amelia***, 8, female; ***Truman***, 6, male; (all preceding children attending school during the year); ***Charlotte***, 4; ***Maria***, 2. All children b. Ohio. 1850 FC OH, Lorain Co., Sheffield, p. 765, lines 6-15.

Delia CASE, wife of Theron Moore, d. July 5, 1880, 63y. 8m.; ***Theron MOORE***, d. Nov 28, 1877, 67y.; ***Sarah E.***, wife of L., d. Sept 8, 1857, 24 yrs. ***MOORE, Melvina,*** d. Nov 24, 1850, 10 y. 2 m. 14 d.; ***Birtie,*** d. March 23, 1860, 4 y. 2 m. 26 d. ***MOORE, Lydia Ann,*** *wife of Charles,* d. May 18, 1873, 34 y. 9m. 28 d.; ***Mary***, dau. C & LA d. Sept 9, 1871, 3 m.. ***MOORE, Ira Eugene,*** son C & LA, d. Mar 22, 1865, 5 y. 1 m. 16 d. Lot A, Row 1. Sheffield City Hall, Sheffield, OH (next to cemetery). Read by Catherine Burke Flament; and Genealogical Workshops of the Lorain County Historical Society, Cemetery Inscriptions of Lorain County, Ohio 1980, Garfield Cemetery, p. 432.

Isaac CASE and ***Susan TITUS*** m. Dec 2, 1840. Marriages of Lorain County 1824-1865, p. 21.

Susan A. wife of ***Isaac L. CASE,*** died Jan 15, 1850, Aged 26 years. Lake Shore Cemetery, Avon Lake, OH; read by Catherine Burke Flament.

Isaac L. CASE and ***Sarah MOON***, m. 21 Aug 1850, Lorain County. Marriages of Lorain County 1824-1865, p. 21.

Sarah A. MOON, wife of I. L., d. Apr 15, 1855 In her 31st year. Her ways were ways of pleasantness and her paths were peace. She is buried next to *Oliver MOON*, b. in Tyringham, MA Feb 2, 1787, d. Apr 28, 1867; *Eunice*, wife, b. in Clifton Park, NY Apr 6, 1795, d. June 10, 1877; *Mary,* dau. O & W, d. Mar 14, 1871, 34y. Lot A, Row 3, Garfield Cemetery, Sheffield Twp., Lorain County, OH. Sheffield City Hall, Sheffield, OH (next to cemetery). Read by Catherine Burke Flament; and Genealogical Workshops of the Lorain County Historical Society, Cemetery Inscriptions of Lorain County, Ohio 1980, Garfield Cemetery, p. 432. *Sarah is the daughter of Oliver and Eunice.*

The State of Ohio, Cuyahoga Co., ss., I Certify that on the Twenty fifth day of Jan 1856, ***Mr. Isaac L. CASE*** and ***Miss Malinda GRISWOLD*** were by me legally joined in marriage. Rev. Ira M. Hitchcock, M. E. Church. Marriage Record, Cuyahoga County, OH, vol. 6, p. C7. *Malinda is the daughter of Luman GRISWOLD and Margaret SMITH GRISWOLD EDDY (OP 1:10-11).*

Isaac LUSE *(Case),* 41, Farmer, value of real estate $5000, value of personal property $2000; ***Malinda***, 24; ***Newton***, 12; ***Lilly,*** *1; Hulda PERIGOLD,* 23; *George L?AUD*, 24, occup. *Furin L___,* b. Hess Darmsta. *Living next to Moses Luse (CASE).* 1860 FC OH Lorain Co., Sheffield, p. 305, lines 11-16.

CASE, Isaac V., 51, Farmer, value of real estate $4000, personal property $1800; ***Melinda***, 34, Keeping House; ***Newton S.***, 22, Sailor, value of real estate $1000; ***Lillie D.***, 11; ***Harlow C.***, 9; all b. Ohio; *Stephen SMITH*, 25, Farm Hand, b. Germany. 1870 FC OH Lorain Co., Sheffield, p. 665A-B, lines 36-41.

CASE, Isaac L., Jan 25, 1819-May 7, 1876; ***Malinda C. GRISWOLD,*** wife of Isaac Case 1836-1917; ***Nina Lorett***, dau. IL&MC, d. May 7, 1868, 6y. 18d.; ***Edna***, 1873-1901. Lot owned by *David GRISWOLD.* Lot A, Row 2, Garfield Cemetery, Sheffield Twp., Lorain County, OH. Sheffield City Hall, Sheffield, OH *(next to cemetery)*. Read by Catherine Burke Flament; and Genealogical Workshops of the Lorain County Historical Society, Garfield Cemetery, p. 432.

Melinda CASE, d. Feb 15, 1917, 206 Woodland, Oberlin, Lorain Co., Ohio of Pneumonia; widowed; b. March 10, 1836, Solon, Ohio, fr. ***Luman GRISWOLD***, b. U.S., mo. ***Margaret SMITH***, b. U.S.; 80 yrs. 11 mos. 5 ds.; undertaker Allen & Hayden, Oberlin, bur. Sheffield T.P., Lorain Co.; informant Mrs. L.C. Cuyler, 206 Woodland Ave. Ohio Certificate of Death, Division of Vital Statistics, 1917, certif. 11948.

Sarah Catherine CASE BRIGGS, b. 12 Mar 1821, Phelps, NY; d. 23 Sept 1901, Macedon, NY; m. 1 Jan 1841 ***Ichabod White BRIGGS*** (b. 24 Mar 1809, Duanesburg, NY; son of *Jeremiah BRIGGS* and *Margaret WHITE*; d. 1 Aug 1893, Macedon, NY). Her parents had moved to Lorain County before 1835 and Sarah returned to Phelps, NY shortly thereafter in her 15th year. She made her home in the vicinity until she married Ichabod Briggs, they would have nine children. Sarah and Ichabod are both buried in Wayneport Cemetery (Union Bury Ground), Macedon, NY. Sue Harmon

Ichabod Briggs and his wife, Sarah Catherine, lived at Fairville for a time; removed to West Macedon, NY (Wayneport) with their three small children. The other children were born at West Macedon, NY. Their home still stands and is located on Route 31.

Ichabod Briggs was Postmaster in Wayneport for thirty years, and its chief patron. He was a pioneer in trying to propagate two plants together and it was not until 1940 that it was successfully done. Aside from a farmer he was a contributor to farming periodicals, and conducted a subscription agency. The latter industry grew to proportions, that the West Macedon Post Office did the largest amount of business of any one in the county, and one year, became the presidential class. In his old age he gave up the business, and the post office was abandoned.

Numerous "love letters" exist that were written by the couple. One such letter begins:

-----Catherine_____

doubt not the love and Constancy of me---your Best Friend, the Summit of my ambition is to see you happy and to contribute all within my Power to Render you Perfectly so. This and this alone can make me happy. Your smiles are food to my hopes and your affections though but feebly demonstrated

I cannot seriously doubt, without a Simultaneous Prostration of all those prospectus of Happiness to be enjoyed with you which Fancy has often portrayed to my delighted imagination. Oh! Where! Is happiness to be found if not in the "Union of 2 fond hearts." Certainly not in this world. For sure I am that I have one and perhaps is little cause for being unhappy as most any other mortal in my Situation and Station in Life. Still there is a restlessness, a Kind of Vacuum (Never so sensibly experienced before as Since my acquaintance with you) which nothing can supply but the Love of her Love--No--No--that is not all--I am assured I have that already. It is the Union of Hearts, cemented by kindness and affection. Here is the fountain whence the real pleasures of this Life do flow. May this be our lot. Ichabod Letter in the family papers of Susan Harmon.

David I.M. FIELD, 31, Farmer & o., b. N.Y.; ***Susan M.***, 26, b. O.; ***E__***,1, female, b. Ohio. 1850 FC OH LRAV, p. 931, lines 32-34. Living next to *Thomas GRANT*, son *Alonson (OP 5: 15).*

FIELD David J.M., d. Apr 30, 1857. ***Susan M.***, wife, d. Mar 22, 1878, 54y. Cleveland Street Cemetery, Amherst Twp. Genealogical Workshops of the Lorain County Historical Society, Cemetery Inscriptions of Lorain County, Ohio 1980, Cleveland Street Cemetery, p. 8.

Children of Moses Case and Martha Loomis:

Chloe M. CASE, b. 1 Feb 1832, Lorain Co.; m. 25 Dec 1856, Lorain Co. to *Henry WALLACE*. ***Harvey Henry CASE***, b. 5 Aug 1833, Avon; d. 21 May 1914, Avon; m. 26 July 1857, Jefferson Co., Wisconsin to *Louisa Emily BLISH*. ***Philancy CASE***, b. 9 Jan 1839, Lorain Co.; d. 23 Dec 1923; m. 25 Dec 1870 to *Charles GIBSON*. ***Emeline CASE***, b. Lorain Co., d. in infancy. Glenda Thayer and Dr. Erastus Ely Case, Case Family Manuscript , A18566, at The Connecticut Historical Society, Hartford, Connecticut.

Henry WALLACE, the well-known lake captain and vessel owner, whose residence is in Lorain, was born in County Down, Ireland, in 1828, a son of *Samuel* and *Ann (FINLEY) WALLACE.*

In his native land he was reared on a farm, and educated at the Protestant schools of the vicinity of his place of birth. In 1850 he came to America and to Ohio, making his first home, in the New World, in Cleveland, where he remained till the fall of the same year, when he came to Lorain (then Black River), the flourishing city he has since made his home. Here he worked in shipyards for several years, finally becoming interested in vessel property - small boats chiefly - the firm with which he was connected being known as "Wallace, Gawn & co.," who became very successful in business. For the past several years he has been owner or part owner of some of the A 1 vessels that have sailed the lakes, and among those in which he at present has an interest may be mentioned the propeller "Vulcan" (built of steel), and the steamer *"Robert WALLACE"* and sailing vessel "*David WALLACE*," the "*Thomas GAWN*" and "Lyons;" also the steel propeller "Vega," which was built by the company winter of 1892-93. For about twenty-eight consecutive years he sailed the lakes as captain, and for excellency of seamanship and care in handling his vessels, his reputation stands without blemish.

On Christmas Eve, 1856, Capt. Wallace was united in marriage with ***Miss Chloe CASE***, a native of Avon, Lorain Co., Ohio, and they have three children living, namely; ***Eva***, wife of *J.H. HILLS*, a superintendent of the Brass Works at Lorain (they have three children: *Alma*, *Harry* and *Albert*); ***Elizabeth***, and ***Lillie***, wife of *Welker McEl. FRISH.*

The entire family with the exception of Mrs. Hill, who is Congregationalist, are members of the M.E. Church. Capt. Wallace is a Republican in politics, and is a member of the I.O.O.F. Commemorative Biographical Record of Huron and Lorain Counties, 1894, p. 739.

Henry WALLACE, 30, Sailor, b. Ireland; ***Cloe***, 28, b. *(unclear, possibly Ireland)*; ***Eva E.***, 8/12. Living next to *David WALLACE*, 27, Ship Carpenter, b. Ireland; *Angelina*, 25, b. O.; *Anna D.*, 6/12, b. Ohio. 1860 FC OH Lorain Co., Black River, p. 299, lines 24-29.

WALLACE; Harvey H., d Apr 18, 1890, 19y 8m 25d.; ***Finny D.***, ch. H&C, d Sept 27, 1859, 20m.; ***Bell D.***, ch. H&C d. Aug 13, 1868, 15m.; ***Capt. Henry***, County Down IRE *(Ireland)*, Feb 3, 1828-June 16, 1905; ***Chloe CASE***, wife, Avon OH, Feb 1, 1832-Mar 1, 1904. Cleveland Street Cemetery, Amherst Twp., Ohio, also published in Cemetery Inscriptions of Lorain County, Ohio 1980, p. 9.

Mr. Harvey CASE, d. May 21, 1914, 9 a.m., 350 5th St., Lorain, Lorain Co., Ohio of Chronic Gastritis for 1 yr. and old age; b. Aug 5, 1835, Avon, Ohio, son of ***Moses CASE***, b. Conn. and ***Marth (Martha) LEWIS***, b. Conn.; Retired Farmer; 79 yrs. 9 mos. 16 ds.; undertaker Geo. W. K. Ke?, Lorain, Ohio; bur. Elmwood C., Lorain, Ohio; informant *Cloe WICKENS*, 5th St., Lorain, OH. Ohio Certificate of Death, Division of Vital Statistics, 1914, certif. 29446.

Harvey CASE, b. Avon, d. age 79, buried May 23, 1914, last address 350 5th St. Sect. 74, Lot 2, map page 3. Permit 3119. Elmwood Cemetery Records, Lorain, OH.

Charles GIBSON, painter, with wife ***Philancy***, 202 Franklin Ave., Lorain, Ohio. 1907 City Directory, Lorain, OH.

GIBSON, A. *(Philancy?)*, Head, 71, Widow, children born 0, b. Ohio, fr. b. Conn., mo. b. New York, own farm and house; ***CASE, Harvey***, 76, widower, b. Ohio, fr. b. Conn., mo. b. New York, Farmer, Own farm. 1910 FC OH Black River Twp., Lorain, Ward 1, ED 88, p. 1B, lines 95-6.

Charles GIBSON, b. Isle of Jersey, d. age 71, buried Jan 8, 1907; ***Phalancy H. GIBSON***, b. Avon , d. age 85, bur. Dec 28, 1923, last residence 350 5th St. Section 74, Lot 2, with ***Harvey CASE*** below. Elmwood Cemetery Records, Lorain, OH.

Philancy CASE GIBSON, d. Dec 26, 1923, 7:30 a.m., 350 5th St., Lorain, Lorain Co., Ohio of Broncho Pneumonia for 8 ds., and Carcinoma of the rectum; b. Jan 9, 1839, Avon, Ohio, fr. *Moses CASE*, b. Hartford, Conn., mo. unknown; widowed, husband ***Chas. GIBSON***; 84 yrs. 11 mos. 18 ds.; Housewife; undertaker Sidney B. Royse, Lorain; bur. Elmwood Cem.; informant Mrs. Eliz. Wickins, 222 5th St., Lorain, Ohio. Ohio Certificate of Death, Division of Vital Statistics, 1923, certif. 72528.

OP 6:2 **Charlotte Miller Case**

Charlotte MILLER, the first wife of ***Moses CASE,*** is the dau. of ***Adam*** and ***Anna (TREMONT) MILLER***, of Connecticut, and Phelps, Ontario County, New York. She was born about 1790, in Phelps and d. in Avon, Lorain County, Ohio. Charlotte and Moses had six children: ***Menzies Raynor CASE***, b. Nov 17, 1810; ***Archibald Russell CASE***, b. Aug 19, 1813; ***Delia Ann CASE***, b. Oct 12, 1816; ***Isaac CASE***, b. Jan 25, 1819; ***Sarah Catherine CASE***, b. March 12, 1821 and ***Susan Miller CASE***, b. June 15, 1823. Dr. Erastus Ely Case, Case Family Manuscript, A18566, at The Connecticut Historical Society, Hartford, Connecticut.

OP 6:3 Porter Monument

PORTER

ASAHEL PORTER
JUNE 18, 1782 - MAY 4, 1820
REBECCA PORTER
APR 7, 1777 - APR 6, 1814
DENNIS PORTER
MARCH 1814 - APRIL 1814

OP 6:3 **Asahel Porter**

It is relatively little known that the honor of being the first settler in Bay Village, then known as Dover, was a near thing for *Joseph CAHOON*. Joseph arrived about noon on October 10th and established his camp on the banks of Cahoon Creek, but on the same day, a few hours later the ***Asahel PORTER*** family arrived and settled in the same area. The Porter Wagon had overturned when fording the Rocky River and thereby had lost several hours of traveling time, if it had not been for this mishap it may well have been the Porters who held the title of Dover's First rather than the renowned Cahoons. "Old Houses in Bay Village," Westlife, October 3, 1960, p. 12.

Rebecca (Johnson) married ***Asahel PORTER*** who with their two daughters, ***Catherine*** & ***Emaline*** came to Dover on her natal day. Her brothers, ***Leverett JOHNSON*** & ***Reuben OSBORN*** accompanied them, arriving here "on a fine October day, the tenth of that golden month in 1810," the same day that *Joseph CAHOON* came with his family. These two families & Leverett Johnson, therefore, have the distinction of being the first settlers of Dover. Mrs. Thomas R. Mitchell, Berea Advertiser, Berea, OH, June 30, 1911, p. 4.

By his arrival on the morning of Oct 10, 1810, *Joseph CAHOON* just connected with the honor of being the fist settler in the township, for that evening ***Asahel PORTER***, a 70-year-old *(incorrect age)* pioneer with his family, began living on lot No. 94 of the same tract.

With the help of *George PEAKE,* an earlier colored resident of Rockport, Porter soon built a log home. ***Leverett JOHNSON***, a nephew of Porter, and one of his party, though hardly 17, started almost the next day to clear No. 58 and established a homestead. Undetermined source, Newspaper article, Cahoon Collection, Rose Hill Museum, Bay Village, OH.

George PEAKE, a mulatto, had been a soldier in the British Army, and was in *General WOLF'S* command at the taking of Quebec. Locating in Maryland he had married a black woman reputed to have "a half bushel of dollars." He settled with her in Pennsylvania, had raised a family of children, and then moved to Rockport in 1809... The Peakes introduced an improvement in the form of a hand gristmill, which was exceedingly well liked by the few settlers, as grinding had previously been accomplished by means of the "stump mortar and springpole pestle." George died in September 1827, at the great age of one hundred and five. Crisfield Johnson, History of Cuyahoga County, Ohio, p. 502.

The first township election was held April 6, 1812, at the house of *Philo TAYLOR*, at which eighteen votes were cast. ***Asahel PORTER*** was elected township clerk, one of three "trustees"; Asahel along with *Joseph CAHOON* and *Azariah BEEBE* were overseers of the poor. Asahel was re-elected as the clerk in 1813 and 1814.

The first Postmaster of Dover was Asahel Porter, who kept a store and post office on the Lake Shore near the Avon Township line in 1815. ***Reuben OSBORN*** was his successor. Johnson, Dover, pp. 436, 439.

The property owned by ***Asahel PORTER***, when he was postmaster, was the property known as the C.B. Ellinwood property, located just east of the Lake Side Cemetery, on lot 94. The property was later owned by *Charles HASSLER*. Lake Erie has been constantly encroaching on the land and the land where the Porter house once stood has since disappeared into the lake. C.M. Osborn, "The Osborns of Bay Village, Ohio," p. 6 and William R. Coates, A History of Cuyahoga County and the City of Cleveland, Dover, vol. 1, p. 141.

Asahel sold the property next to the cemetery in 1818 after his wife had died.

"To all People to whom these Presents shall come Greeting" Know that I ***Asahel PORTER*** of Dover in the county of Cuyahoga & State of Ohio for the consideration of three thousand Dollars received to my full satisfaction of *Silas FOOT* and *Moraica COWNOVER* of said Dover & State of Ohio aforesaid Do give grant sell & confirm unto the said Foot & Cownover one certain lot of Land lying in Dover on the Lake shore being Lot No. ninety four in Township No. Seven in the fifteenth Range of Township in the Connecticut Western Reserve So called containing one hundred & forty five acres be the same more or less…In witness where of I have here unto sett my hand & seal Asahel Porter Cleaveland April 14th 1818. Personally appeared Asahel Porter. Received April 14th and Recorded 16th 1818. Horace Perry Recorder. Cuyahoga County Land Deeds, vol. B., p. 630.

PORTER built a log house on lot 94, near the lake, which was later occupied by *Charles HASSLER*. Lake Erie has been constantly encroaching on the land, and the site where stood the log house built by Porter has been washed into the lake…Later he moved to Rockport, but the family was represented in Dover by a daughter, ***Mrs. Catherine FOOT***, who lived past three score and ten there. Of the boy, ***Leverett JOHNSON***, who came with the Porters, a record is preserved of his descendants. While living with the Porter family he began clearing land some distance away, on lot 58. We say living with the Porters but he only came home to spend the weekend, to use the modern phrase. During the week he lived alone in the wilderness…He was carving a home in the forest…for the love of a woman. In 1814 he married ***Abigail CAHOON***. William R. Coates, A History of Cuyahoga County and the City of Cleveland, Dover, vol. 1, pp. 141-142 and Cuyahoga County Land Deeds, vol. B, p. 630.

ORGANIZATION OF ROCKPORT. Rockport was formed as a civil township in February, 1819, and on the first Monday in the following April it held its first election at *Rufus WRIGHT'S* tavern….

The chairman of the meeting was *Charles MILES*; the judges of election were ***Asahel PORTER*** and *Datus KELLEY*. The officers chosen were… The first book of township records has been lost, and the list of those who served the township as trustees, clerks and treasurers, can be given only from 1832 to 1879. Johnson, pp. 504-505.

Children of Asahel Porter and Rebecca Johnson:

Rebecca and *Asahel* had four children*:* ***Catherine PORTER*** m. *Ransom FOOTE (buried OP 2:11-12);* ***Emaline PORTER*** m. *Hiram SMITH*, both of Dover; ***Angeline PORTER*** m. *Mr. HUNTINGTON*; ***Dennis PORTER***, b. March 1814; drowned April 1814 with *Rebeecca.*

After Rebecca's death, Asa moved his family to Rockport…and died six years later, the children were raised by ***Sarah OSBORN***, Rebecca's sister. "Osborn Family History," p. 5 and Bay Village Historical Society, Bay Village: A Way of Life, pp. 11, 35.

I hereby certify that on the twenty first day of May just past, I joined in the state of matrimony ***Hiram SMITH*** and ***Emeline PORTER*** both of Dover and County, who produced a certificate from the clerk of the court of Common pleas for said County. Given under my hand and seal this 3rd day of June A.D. 1826. Noah Crocker, Justice Peace. Marriage Record, Cuyahoga County, OH, vol. 2, p. 101.

Emeline PORTER married ***Hiram SMITH***, son of ***Abner*** and ***Rebecca SMITH***. *Rebecca may have been buried at Lakeside Cemetery and moved to another cemetery, she is listed as such in this publication.*

The first white child born in the township was ***Angelina***, daughter of ***Asahel PORTER***. The date of her birth was April 1, 1812. It is claimed that *Vesta*, daughter of *Nathan BASSETT*, was the first born, but the best available evidence shows the date of her birth to have been June 14, 1812. Crisfield Johnson, History of Cuyahoga County, Ohio, p. 438.

Angeline PORTER married ***George C. HUNTINGTON***, Cleveland Township, Cuyahoga County, Oct. 6, 1833. Marriage Record, Cuyahoga County, OH, vol. 3, p. 31.

George Cabot HUNTINGTON was one of the earliest crockery merchants of the town. He carried on a wholesale and retail business at No. 5 Superior street. In his advertisements he called attention to his sign of a big pitcher, as a guide to customers.

He was the son of ***Erastus HUNTINGTON*** of Norwich, Conn., and about the year 1833 when 26 years of age, came to Cleveland. At the same time he was married to ***Miss Angeline PORTER***, daughter of ***Ashael PORTER*** of Waterbury, Conn. She had two children, and died at the birth of the second one, and was laid away in Erie Street cemetery. Both children died in infancy, some time in the 60's all were removed to a Kelley Island Cemetery.

In 1837 Mr. Huntington married secondly, *Emmeline KELLEY*, daughter of *Datus KELLEY* of Kelleys Island. She lived to be 80 years of age, dying on Christmas day, in 1909, in Denver, Colorado. Two years after his second marriage, and following the disastrous panic of 1837, Mr. Huntington removed to Kelleys Island where he remained until 1870, when he took up his residence in New York City, and died 6 years later in Wallace, Kan., and is buried on Kelleys Island. Gertrude

Van Rensselaer Wickham, The Pioneer Families of Cleveland, 1796-1840, p. 419.

Angelina PORTER (dau. of ***Asahel PORTER***); d. 1836 at Cleveland; m. 6 Oct 1833 to ***George Cabot HUNTINGTON***, oldest of three son's of *Erastus Huntington* (b. 7 Dec 1769, Norwich, CT; m.1 20 Mar 1806; d. 10 Feb 1846, Norwich, CT) and *Nabby HYDE* (b. 12 Nov 1786, d. 1 July 1811); b. 20 July 1807, Norwich, CT; d. 5 July 1876, Wallace KS. *Issue:* ***George HUNTINGTON***, b. 12 Aug 1834, Cleveland; d. 29 Aug 1934. ***Sarah W. HUNTINGTON***, b. 19 June 1836, Cleveland; d. 30 June 1836, Cleveland.

George Cabot Huntington remarried on 9 Nov 1837, Kellys Island, OH to *Emeline KELLY* (dau. of *Datus KELLY* and *Sara DEAN*; b. 10 June 1819, Rockport, OH; d. 25 Dec 1910, Denver, CO) *Issue: Erastus HUNTINGTON*, b. 15 Aug 1838, Cleveland; m. *Elzina HAMILTON*, Kellys Island; d. Cleveland. *Simon HUNTINGTON*, b. 15 Dec 1839, Kellys Island; d. 19 Jan 1863, Nashville, TN. *Daniel Kelley HUNTINGTON*, b. 28 Mar 1845, Cleveland, OH; m. 4 June 1867, Rockport to *Emily FARR*. *Joseph Alfred HUNTINGTON*, b. 10 Feb 1850, Kellys Island, OH; m. 29 May 1877, Kansas City, MO; spouses: m.1 *Theophania HAINES*, m.2 *Eva Caroline PILCHARD*. *(Kelly should be spelled Kelley.)* Huntington Family Association.

OP 6:3 Rebecca Johnson Porter

First Burials at Lakeside.

PORTER, Mrs. Asahel, Maiden Name ***Rebecca JOHNSON***, Year Came to Township 1810, Where From or Where Born Waterbury, Ct. Memorial to the Pioneer Women of the Western Reserve, p. 19.

On the first day of April, 1814, ***Asahel PORTER'S*** wife and infant child, *Noah CROCKER*, and *George*, son of *Jonathan SMITH*, made the journey to Cleveland in an open boat. Upon their return, being overtaken by a storm, they sought to put in at the mouth of Rocky river, when the boat was capsized and Mrs. Porter, her babe, and George Smith were drowned, Crocker alone escaping. Crisfield Johnson, History of Cuyahoga County, Ohio, p. 438.

The sad story of ***Mrs. PORTER'S*** death four years later *(after their arrival in Dover)* cast a shadow over the community that was lasting. While coming from Cleveland the rowboat in which the trip was made over turned at Rocky River. Mrs. Porter and her infant son were drowned, the bodies were recovered, and rest in the Lakeside Cemetery, the first burial place in the town. Memorial to the Pioneer Women of the Western Reserve, p. 58.

Philo TAYLOR had moved from New York to Cleveland in 1806. In 1808, he agreed to settle in Rockport, landing on the 10th of October in an open boat at the mouth of the Rocky river. He selected a place on the east side of the river, put up a cabin and began a clearing. By 1809 he had effected material improvements. At that time, *Mr. CANFIELD*, who had verbally agreed that Mr. Taylor should have the place, informed him that the would have to select another spot, since it had been decided by the proprietors to lay out a town near the mouth of the river, and that the lot originally selected by Mr. Taylor would be wanted for that purpose. At this Mr. Taylor became exceedingly wroth. He sold his improvements to *Daniel MINER*, launched a curse against the mouth of the Rocky River and moved with his family to Dover. Johnson, p. 502.

Information on the siblings of Rebecca Johnson Porter is listed with her sister, Sarah (Sally) Johnson Osborn (OP 4:8) and sister-in-law, Abigail Cahoon Johnson (OP 4:3).

OP 6:3 Dennis Porter

Dennis Porter drowned with his mother and *George SMITH* in an open row boat on April 6, in the Rocky River after returning from Cleveland. Bay Village Historical Society, Bay Village: A Way of Life, p. 9.

OP 6:4-5

Small upright stones located just behind the Porter Memorial. These tablets are assumed to be the original markers for Asahel and Rebecca Porter.

I.P. R.P.

OP 6:6 Unknown Soldier

UNKNOWN SOLDIER
CIVIL WAR

The grave of "Ohio's Unknown Union Soldier" was found in the little Osborn burial lot in Bay Village. The never-identified body was washed ashore by Lake Erie during the Civil War and buried in his uniform by local patriots. "Neglected Legion Honored at Last Forgotten Graves Mapped After WPA Survey," Cleveland Press, May 29, 1940.

Local lore passed on through *George DRAKE* and *Cliff ALDRICH* states that the body of the soldier washed ashore near the Wischmeyer Hotel. It is thought he may have fallen from the cliff near the end of the Civil War. Marty Chomoa

On July 3, 2000, a stone was dedicated to Lakeside's Unknown Soldier. Present were veterans and family members of the American Legion, Sons of Union Veterans, Veterans of Foreign Wars and community members. The ceremony included a prayer by Rev. Timothy W. GAREAU of St. Raphael Church and statements by Dave MAIER, a resident of Bay Village, of the Veterans Affairs Office; Jon SILVIS, Sons of Union Veterans of the Civil War and Cathy BURKE FLAMENT, compiler of this book. Because of the rain, the dedication was held under the shelter at Huntington Park, just east of the cemetery. Near the conclusion, a 21-gun salute honored the Unknown Soldier.

"For whatever the reason he came to be here, it is fitting and proper that we gather here today, on the eve of the 224th anniversary of the founding of our nation..."

Jon Silvis, member, Northeast Chapter, Sons of Union Veterans of the Civil War.

Still 'Unknown' but not forgotten

Veterans of other wars join in ceremony Honoring Anonymous Civil War soldier

By Brian E. Albrecht, Plain Dealer Reporter

BAY VILLAGE - Blue skies battled gray clouds in the meteorological equivalent of a bygone war remembered yesterday at Lakeside Cemetery with the dedication of a tombstone for an unknown Civil War soldier.

Veterans in uniforms of more recent conflicts joined re-enactors in Union blue to salute a fallen comrade who, in his anonymity, could represent both sides in a conflict that pitted brother against brother.

"Unknown, but now never to be forgotten," was read during the dedication's invocation on the eve of Independence Day. "May this Civil War soldier forever be a symbol of that which we hold dear and to which we pledge our allegiance..."

During the Civil War's waning years (1864-65), a dead man wearing a Union uniform washed ashore from Lake Erie, not far from his current gravesite.

Details have been lost to history. Some say he may have been from the USS Michigan, a Union gunboat stationed on Lake Erie. Others speculate he came from the nearby Johnson Island stockade, a prisoner who swapped Confederate gray for Union blue in a doomed escape attempt.

Also lost to time is whatever grave marker the man may have been buried under. An old cemetery plot map noted the location simply for a "soldier."

Cathy FLAMENT, of Bay Village, discovered the marker was missing as part of her research for a genealogical book about Lakeside Cemetery and its estimated 280 burials. The small cemetery has 19 veterans, including soldiers from the Revolutionary War, War of 1812, Civil War, Spanish-American War and World War I.

Flament mentioned the absent marker - and another missing stone for World War I Army veteran *Harry E. REHLING* (buried there in 1989) - to *Richard E. ROSS*, a Vietnam vet and chairman of the Bay Village Memorial Day Parade.

Ross contacted the Cuyahoga County Veterans Service Commission, which provided markers for the two soldiers. (Installation of the stone for the World War I veteran has been delayed until relatives can be located to give their permission.) *Relatives of Mr. Rehling read articles about the soldiers and granted permission immediately for a stone to be procured.*

The commission added a drawing of a vintage cannon to the stone that reads, "Unknown Soldier/Civil War."

About 75 people attended yesterday's dedication, retreating to a nearby Huntington Park picnic shelter in a heavy downpour.

Among them was *Jon SILVIS*, one of several members of the Northeast Ohio chapter of the Sons of Union Veterans of the Civil War.

Silvis cited speculation surrounding the Unknown Soldier, adding he may have been a Union deserter or murdered while home on leave.

"For whatever the reason he came to be here, it is fitting and proper that we gather here today, on the eve of the 224th anniversary of the founding of our nation, the founding of a union...which would be tested from 1861-1865," he added.

The ceremony also may have meant a bit more to Smith than most people attending the event.

Peering from beneath a battered hat to match his Union uniform, Smith assured one spectator that when it comes to honoring the Civil War's fallen-who may have fought with his own ancestors in the blood baths of Gettysburg and Antietam - "This is very, very personal." Brian E. Albrecht, "Still 'Unknown' but not forgotten," Northeast Ohio, Sect. B, Tuesday, July 4, 2000, pp. 1+ cols. 1-3. The Plain Dealer.

UNKNOWN SOLDIER RECOGNIZED

The VSC would like to thank all of those who participated Monday, July 3, 2000, in the 11 AM, memorial ceremony to dedicate a grave marker to an unknown soldier of the U.S.Civil War....*Jim SEARS*,

Director of the Bay Village Service Dept. earlier had the marker set over the grave.

Richard E. ROSS, a local veterans advocate, had contacted *Laurene RUTKOWSKI*, VSC Memorial Affairs Officer, about furnishing the grave marker after he learned from *Cathy BURKE FLAMENT*, a Bay Village author and historian, where the grave was and that it was unmarked. He secured the necessary permission from the City of Bay Village's Cahoon Park Trustees, acted as the master of ceremonies and enlisted *Jon SILVIS*, a Rocky River resident and member of the Sons of Union Veterans of the Civil War, to be the main speaker.

The program began with a musical interlude of civil war era music pre-recorded by *Allan MAIER,* a Bay High senior. As the veterans' organizations presented the colors, *Jean SILVER'S* singing of the national anthem inspired patriotism in our hearts and made her father, *Rocco SCOTTI*, who accompanied her, very proud. The invocation was read, "In the midst of our country's celebration of our independence...We gather and pause to honor...and to bring closure to...the life of the man known only as 'Ohio's unknown soldier'...as we dedicate the stone that now marks his grave." When all the acknowledgements and speeches were over, *Priest Tim GAREAU*, of St. Raphael Catholic Church, led everyone in prayer. A firing squad, led by VVA's *Jeff CAMPBELL*, of combined veterans organizations and civil war reinactors, honored the dead with a 21-gun salute. In the silence that followed, the smoke still hovering from the guns, *Mike HANNA* sounded Taps as perfect as you have ever heard it played. "The Vet's Gazette," Cuyahoga County Service Commission, Volume 5, Issue 5, October 2000, pp. 2-3.

Portion of speech by Catherine Burke Flament at the Memorial Service:

It is unfortunate that this gentleman who was washed ashore in a Union soldier's uniform close to this very spot on the lakeshore, approximately 135 years ago, was never identified. Somewhere I'm sure he had family members who were concerned and never knew his final fate. That uncertainty of sending a loved one off to war, unsure if and when you will see each other again, is difficult. I still remember the day my brother left for Vietnam, it was a very unsettling one for my family.

It is devastating to learn that a loved one has lost his life in battle, but at least the grieving process is allowed to begin. Never knowing what happened to someone must be so much more difficult. Hopefully the soldier we are honoring today and his family are smiling upon us knowing that there has been some recognition for his sacrifice of leaving home and never returning.

Unidentified Graves in the Original Part

Though their forms we miss,
Their memories we will ever cherish.

Toast read by Mr. Ingersoll at the
Cahoon Fifty-Fifth Anniversary Celebration of the Settlement of Dover, Oct 10, 1865

Infant Eppink

Child of William Eppink and Minnie Krumwiede, Grandchild of William Krumwiede and Sophia Scharnhorst (OP 5:1). See Louis Krumwiede obituary below, under "infant" Krumwiede.

Baby EPPINK; res. Cleveland; German; interred Oct 2, 1890; Original Part. "List of Interments," Lakeside Cemetery, Bay Village, OH.

*Name left blank,(**Infant EPPINK**)* b. Oct 2, 1890, Cleveland, Cuyahoga County, female, fr. ***William EPPINK***, 33, nationality Holland, Elevator Man; mo. ***Minnie EPPINK***, 27, nationality German, Housewife; res. 38 Hope St., Cleveland; religion of parents Lutheran. City Birth Records, 1890, 0024, roll: 1852565, Cuy Archives.

Family history states that this first child of ***William*** and ***Minnie,*** died of what would now be considered crib death. ***Engelina*** was their second child, named after her grandmother, who went by the name ***Emmalyn***. Minnie lost an infant after scrubbing floors when she was almost full term expecting her third infant. ***Harold, Florence, Walter*** and ***Gladys*** would follow. Rev. Margie M. Frank

Ancestors of Infant Eppink:

Johann Heinrich EPPINK, m. 11 Jan 1815, Buchwald, Westphalia, Prussia to ***Johanna TE KOTTE***. *Issue:* ***Christine Elizabeth EPPINK***, b. 19 Mar 1815; ***Heinrich EPPINK***, b. 11 Aug 1816; ***Hermannus Lambertus EPPINK***, b. 20 Dec 1818; ***Gerhard EPPINK***, b. 21 Jan 1821; ***Arnold Johann EPPINK***, b. 22 Feb 1823; ***Johanna Gertruda EPPINK***, b. 23 Mar 1825; ***Aldheit EPPINK***, b. 11 Mar 1827.

Arnold Johann EPPINCK was born 22 February 1823 at Bocholt (Buchwald) in Westphalia. This German province was next to the Netherlands and had been given to Prussia eight years before Arnold was born. The name Eppinck is Dutch. Arnold was married 22 June 1854 in the Netherlands, at the age of 31. The following year he immigrated to the US and moved to Olmsted Falls, Ohio, where his wife probably had a brother. Arnold became a farmer and continued in this occupation until his death in 1886 at the age of 63.

His wife, ***Engelina Grada TE GROTENHUIJS*** was born on 20 October 1826 in Grote Breedenbroek, Gelderland, Netherlands. She was 27 when she married Arnold. Although she lived over half a century in Olmsted Falls, she generally only spoke Dutch at home while her husband also spoke English. She was sometimes referred to as Angelina. Three of their nine children died young.

The 1880 census shows that ***William***, age 22 and ***Theodore***, 20 were unmarried and living at home as farm laborers helping Arnold, and listed as farmers. The 1892 Cleveland City Directory shows Angelina was the widow of Arnold who had died six years earlier and that she lived at 38 Hope Street on Cleveland's west side, probably with her unmarried children, ***Hannah*** and ***Herman***. She died in 1906 at age 79.

Children of Arnold EPPINK and Engelina Te Grotenhuijs:

John S. EPPINK, b. 11 Aug 1855, d. 15 Mar 1864. ***Johanna (Hannah) EPPINK,*** b. 13 Apr 1857, d. 11 Jan 1923, never married. ***William Gerrit EPPINK,*** b. 3 July 1858; d. 14 Apr 1929; m. Thanksgiving, 28 November 1889 to *Minnie KRUMWIEDE* (dau. of *William KRUMWIEDE* and *Sophia SCHARNHARST (OP 5:1)*, b. 1864, d. 1960). ***Theodore EPPINK,*** b. 30 Mar 1860, d. 26 Oct 1948, m. *Jennie NYLAND* (b. 6 July 1866, d. 11 May 1949). ***Mary EPPINK,*** b. 20 Feb 1862, d. 7 May 1938, m. *Frank BARGE*. ***John L. EPPINK,*** b. 1 Feb 1864, d. 20 June 1865. ***Caroline (Lena) G. EPPINK,*** b. 7 Jan 1866, d. 1948, m. *John HOFTYZER*. ***Arnold J. EPPINK,*** b. 9 Feb 1868, d. 4 May 1881, 13 yrs. old. ***Herman EPPINK,*** b.16 Mar 1870, d. 1 June 1934, m. *Katherine KOCH*. All of the above are buried at Olmsted Falls Cemetery, Olmsted Falls, Ohio except William, Mary and Herman. Richard Eppink and Mary Milne Jamba.

Parents of Infant EPPINK:

Minnie Krumwiede Eppink, My Grandmother

When ***Minnie KRUMWIEDE*** married, her new husband, ***William EPPINK***, decided to leave the family farm and move to the city, three years after his father had died. William got a job at the Worthington Hardware Company in downtown Cleveland, Ohio, where he continued until the company retired him, not really his choice.

Grandma had five children plus a late term little boy she miscarried and a baby who died of crib death. I was told she lost the little boy, after a day of very hard work, scrubbing floors, as I recall, my Grandpa sat down and cried over the loss. Grandma's multiple pregnancies resulted in bad vericose veins in her legs which resulted in the complication of ulcerated sores on her legs.

Grandma herself told me of the story of having had all her teeth pulled (she wore upper and lower dentures) as a young girl, right in the kitchen. I wonder if there was any anesthesia used?

Louie KRUMWIEDE, Minnie's brother, brought the family fresh food in the summer, from the family farm. He would stop on his trip to sell items at the West Side Market in Cleveland. The trip would have been a ten to fifteen mile trip for him, a long ride in a horse and wagon! Minnie would then can the food he brought, resenting anyone who wanted to eat any as there wouldn't be enough left to can.

In her younger years she knit, and in her declining years she pieced and quilted beautiful quilts by hand. I recall seeing a large homemade quilting frame in her home; it seems to me that it was supported on the tops of chairs at each end.

Later while she was in care homes she often sold some of the beautiful pillow tops she continued to piece and quilt by hand. They were made from silk and rayon, which were elegant fabrics to her. Her sons and others would give Grandma neckties they were no longer wearing, and she would take them apart and use the lovely fabrics for her quilts. Grandma's usual design for her quilts and pillow tops were traditional Log Cabin designs. I believe she sold her pillow tops for $1. She felt very good about the money that she earned herself.

Minnie was remembered by her daughter as being a feisty person with quite a temper while she was growing up. This was certainly not the grandmother that I knew who was soft spoken. I remember her telling me, "Margie, always remember to be kind!" Rev. Margie M. Frank

The State of Ohio, Cuyahoga County, ss. ***William EPPINK*** having made application for a Marriage License for himself and ***Minnie KRUMWIEDE*** of said County and being duly sworn, on his oath that he is of age of not less than twenty-one years, that he has no wife living, that said Minnie Krumwiede is of age of not less than eighteen years, that she has no husband living, and that said person are not nearer kin than second cousins…I certify that one the 27th day of Nov 1889…were legally joined in marriage. Frank D. Stevick Marriage Record, Cuyahoga County, OH, vol. 34, p. 31.

EPPINK, William; Minnie, wife; ***Emaline***, dau, b. Oct 1892, 7; ***Harold*** , son , b. 1897, 3; ***Edna***, dau., b. Mar 1900, 2 1/2 mos.; *Angeline*, mother, b. Oct 1826, 73, b. Germany; *Hannah*, sister, b. Apr 1857, 43; *Lena*, sister, b. Jan 1866, 34; *Herman*, b. Mar 1870, 30. FC 1900 OH CY, census extract by Carol P. Reed.

EPPINK, William G., 51, b. Ohio; ***Minnie E.,*** 46, b. Ohio; ***Emmaline***, dau., 17; ***Harold W.***, son, 12; ***Florence***, dau., 10; ***Walter***, son, 7; ***Gladius***, dau., 3; *HELLER, Frank*, boarder, 18. 7616 Colgate Ave. 1910 FC OH CY Cleveland, ED 63, p. 21.

EPPINK, William, 60, own with mortgage, b. Ohio, fr. b. Westphalia, Germany, mo. b. Holland, Shipping Clerk, Hardware; ***Minnie***, 55, b. Ohio, parents b. Germany; ***Emmalyne***, dau., 27, no occup.; ***Harold***, son, 22, Cashier at bank; ***Florence***, dau. 19, Clerk at bank; ***Walter K.***, son, 17, Accountant Steel?; ***Gladys***, dau. 13. Colgate Ave. 1920 FC OH CY Cleveland, Ward 3, ED 37, sheet 10A, lines 11-17.

Garret William EPPINK, d. 4/14/1929, 2070 Lewis Drive, Lakewood, Cuyahoga Co., Ohio; b. July 3, 1858, Berea, Ohio. Married ***Minnie KRUMWIEDE EPPINK***; occup. Retired, Shipping Dept., Worthington's; fr. *Arnold J.* --, b. Holland, mo. *Engeline TEGROTENHAUS*, b. Holland; Informant *Walter EPPINK*, 2070 Lewis Drive. Cause Myocardial Decomposition, 1 mo., Senile Arteriosclerosis, 2 yrs. Buried at West Park Cem, Apr 17, 1929; Undertaker Geo C. Lang, 9437 Lorain. Ohio Certificate of Death, Division of Vital Statistics, 1929, certif. 27272.

EPPINK-William, age 70 years, beloved husband of ***Minnie*** (nee ***KRUMWIEDE***), father of ***Harold W., Walter K., Emmalyn, Mrs. Florence MUSIL*** and ***Gladys*** (deceased), brother of *Theodore, Herman, Mrs. Mary BARGE, Mrs. Lena HOFTYNER* and *Hanna EPPINK (deceased),* Sunday afternoon at residence, 2070 Lewis Drive, Funeral Wednesday, April 17, at 2:30 p. m., from St. Paul's M. E. Church, Bridge Avenue, corner W. 44th Street. Friends invited. Cleveland Necrology File, Apr 15 1929, reel 023.

Minnie EPPINK, d. 21 Apr 1960, Ferry Nursing Home, Elyria, Lorain Co., OH, res. 1 yr.; Usual residence 1015 Middle Ave., Elyria; b. 27 Mar 1864, Bay Village, fr. ***Wm. KRUMWIEDE***, mo. ***Sophia SCHORNHURST***, age 96; housewife; Cause Medullory failure, Cerebral Thrombosis 1 week, Arteriosclerosis 6 yrs.; Funeral Home The Geo. C. Lang Co., 9437 Lorain Ave., Cleveland, OH, Burial 4-25-60, West Park Cemetery, Cleveland; informant *Florence MUSIL*. Ohio Certificate of Death, Division of Vital Statistics, 1960, certif. 029972.

EPPINK, Minnie, beloved wife of the late ***William G.***, mother of ***Harold*** and ***Walter EPPINK, Mrs. Florence MUSIL*** and the late ***Emmalyn*** and ***Gladys***, grandmother and great-grandmother. Thursday evening. Friends may call at the Geo. C. Lang Co. Funeral Home, W. 95th at Lorain Ave., Saturday 7 To 9. Sunday 2 To 5 And 7 To 9. Services Monday, Apr 25, at 1:30 p. m. Cleveland Necrology File, Cleveland Press, Apr 23 1960, reel 107.

Memoirs of the sister of Infant Eppink:

Selections From the Autobiography of Florence Louise Eppink Musil

(3 March 1900 - 6 June 1992)

A LITTLE GIRLS EARLIEST IMPRESSIONS – 7009 HOPE AVENUE

How well I remember the house where all five of my parents' ***(William EPPINK** and **Minnie KRUMWIEDE)*** children were born. The address was 7009 Hope Avenue on Cleveland, Ohio's west side. The house still stands – as sturdy as ever even though it is well over 100 years old.

My grandmother and two maiden aunts and a bachelor uncle lived with my parents and their children for the first several years of their married life. Actually this statement should be reversed, for it was my parents who lived with my grandparents and their remaining unmarried children. This was to be expected for according to European custom of the day, the eldest son had the responsibility of his parents placed upon his shoulders for as long as they lived. This meant that when my father married he had to bring his bride to his parents' home. The young wife took over her share of the household duties, but unfortunately under this arrangement it was not long before a bride became more like a maid in the household than a mistress in her own home for she was expected to fall into the pattern of homemaking and kind of cooking long ago established by her newly acquired husband's mother. My grandparents liked their new home in America but still the habits and customs taught to them during all their most impressionable years could not be cast aside lightly. Both my father's parents were fine upright Christian church loving people, and all their children turned out to be fine Christian citizens.

In those days of long ago, elderly people were not expected to be active. When they got into their 60's and 70's they were considered very old. It was time for them to rest themselves in their comfortable rocking chairs and enjoy the fruits of their labor in earlier years. Now they could enjoy the luxury of being waited upon by younger hands and feet. Grandparents did make good sitters, however, for the children in the home and as they sat and rocked themselves often they held one of the grandchildren in their lap and rocked them to sleep. Often I was held by my grandmother and rocked.

How well I recall the old coal oil lamps in the house, which not only were used for light but also served as heat to warm up the curling iron, which in those days was very popular and an important tool to keep the hair of all the girls and ladies in becoming style. Permanents and beauty parlors had not yet been born. My older sister ***Emmalyn*** had long hair, just as did all girls at that time for short hair for girls was also still unheard of... There was always a piece of paper handy to test the heat of the iron on before touching the iron to the hair lest the locks become scorched. My mother was very lucky in that she had naturally curly hair. All she had to do was dampen the comb and when she had combed through her hair – there were the beautiful waves.

My parents had a large portrait of my sister Emmalyn framed, and it stood on an easel, which was quite a popular custom in those days. This sister was not well. She had fallen prey to some sort of respiratory infection when very young. Being in the days before antibiotics, doctors seemed not to be able to cure her permanently and the disease became chronic. Due to the fact that my sister was ailing so much, everyone made a fuss over her and seemed to cater to her and bring her extra gifts, etc. This was no doubt understandable, but it did make the other children a little envious, and when we were "lucky" enough to become ill and go to bed we made the most of it.

Sometimes my grandmother helped my mother prepare fruit and vegetables during the canning season. This she was able to do sitting down. My mother canned hundreds of jars of fruit, and put up many crocks of salted vegetables and grape jam. The green beans had to be cut into very thin slivers. These were salted down well and then a plate put over the top of that. The process was similar to making sour kraut, another vegetable they made a lot of. These of course kept all winter. Also, in the fall enough potatoes were bought and put into a bin for that purpose.

OUR KITCHEN

When I was about five some very important improvements came into being in our house. We had water piped into the kitchen. Before that all our water was drawn from the well in the yard. Also, gas lines were installed and now our house was modernized in that we had gaslights instead of coal oil lamps.

Our kitchen there on Hope Avenue was typical of those in other houses of the day. Wainscoting panels lined the walls on the lower part to about four feet high. This was stained a dark color. There was a large coal and wood burning stove with a warming oven at the top, some sash curtains on the lower window – the top window pane was bare, no doubt to let in more light. There was a large round table although we ate all our meals in the dining room. From the kitchen there were the constant aromas of fresh bread, pies, cakes, cookies, jellies, apple butter, and about every kind of tempting pleasant fragrance one could imagine.

My grandmother liked candy. Her favorite kinds were anise drops, horehound candy, licorice, and old-fashioned rock candy, which were strung on a string like huge beads. Usually she carried candy in her pocket, and we children knew where to go when it was something sweet we wanted.

GOING TO THE PARK

About once a year we had an outing at Edgewater Park, which was a little less than a two-mile walk from where we lived. There was no public transportation to this park so the distance had to be walked. Those were not as yet the days of at least one car in every family.

My mother would pack a wonderful picnic supper. The large oblong baby buggy with the parasol fastened on had room not only for my little brother (***Walter***) but also the picnic basket in the middle, and somehow I could also get squeezed into the middle of the buggy if I got too tired to walk all the way.

Edgewater Park was very hilly and we children loved to climb the hills and run down. Also, there was a lovely wide sandy beach and we were allowed to take off our shoes and wade in the lake where the water was very shallow. That soft wet sand felt heavenly and cool to our bare feet. And what fun to build castles in the sand. Then there were swings and teeters and lots of green grass and picnic tables in the grove.

TROUBLE IN OUR HOME

My mother, who was expecting her fifth child in a few months, was washing a lamp chimney, which suddenly broke in the water and cut her finger very badly. The next day she did the family laundry, and as always, had bluing in the last rinse water. Her finger became very badly infected. Home remedies failed. The doctor was called as Mother walked the floor night and day in excruciating pain. Blood poisoning set in. The family doctor recommended a surgeon who had to amputate the finger. Mother almost lost her life. I still remember the hush around the house and trying to be helpful setting dishes on the table.

DEATH OF MY GRANDMOTHER

(Engolina TeGrotenhuis Eppink, 1827-1906)

One morning not long after the above incident, I was awakened with the news that my grandmother had died. It was my first close contact with death. I was now a little past six. It seemed that people were supposed to look sad when someone passed away. I saw my father sitting on the steps of the back porch and he had his head in his hands and he was quietly weeping. It was the first time I had ever seen my father cry.

I still remember how Grandma looked. She was laid out in the parlor of our home – the room that was not used as commonly as our living rooms are today. She was dressed in her very best beautiful black dress. (Old people always wore black clothing for dressed up occasions, and so all her clothes were black.) The casket was black, as was every other thing to do with the funeral. The hearse, the carriages – everything. All of the nearest relatives wore solid black and long black veils on their hats. This complete somber color was worn by all the mourners for at least a year after the funeral. Even in the hot days of summer they could not be seen in public in another color. To do so might invite criticism from some who might say or feel that there had been little sincere grief over the loss if they could be so disrespectful in shedding their mourning clothes too soon.

Now came the day of the funeral. What excitement! How I loved rides in the horse drawn buggies whenever we visited aunts and uncles in the country. Now I was going to have the longest ride in a beautiful carriage that I had ever had in my life. I'd be riding practically the whole day, which time it would take to drive the distance to the cemetery and back. First we would attend the funeral services at the church and then ride in the beautiful black carriage drawn by beautiful horses. Each carriage could seat four people. The two seats faced each other – two people in a seat – and the driver sat outside – similar to a stagecoach.

Something else I remember about that eventful day was my new hat. Of course little children were not expected to dress in mourning clothes. The latest style in hats for little girls, and which I admired very much but probably never would have had if it not been for the funeral, was a white leghorn straw tricorn shaped, with a fluffy white pompom sewed on the front left side of the crown. I thought it the most beautiful hat I had ever seen and felt sure of the admiration I would receive by all who would attend the funeral.

My mother was unable to go to the cemetery. Her hand was still all heavily bandaged, and also it was getting too close to the time of the expected birth of her baby.

A NEW BABY IN OUR HOME

Not many days later I was awakened with another surprise. I was told I had a new baby sister named ***Gladys Alberta*** (b. 7-31-06). Now my mother was really sick it seemed. She was in bed and the doctor had been there.

Where did our new baby come from? That was an easy question for parents to answer in those days. The doctor brought the baby when he came to tend the sick mother. But why didn't any woman ever get the doctor to bring a baby when she wasn't sick? To me that seemed more sensible than having to be sick in bed with all the excitement and fun of having a new baby in the house. Well, so it was—so might as well accept it and not worry about it.

BACK TO SCHOOL

The following September I started back to school in the first grade. I loved school and was very fond of my teacher whose name I still remember – *Miss STREITEL*. We used slates to write our lessons on and after the lesson was over a child would be appointed to take a little oil can, which was filled with water instead of oil, and squirt a little water over each slate and then every child would wipe and dry the slate with a little piece of rag we kept for this purpose. The slate was now put away clean in readiness for the next time it would be used.

FAMILY PLEASURE

My family loved music and hymns. Both my sister, Emmalyn and I were born with a talent in music and somehow both of us learned how to read music -- simple melodies and hymns, before either of us had had formal instruction. Of course my sister learned to play long before I did being 7 years younger. We both played on our lovely organ in the parlor. Making our own music in those days undoubtedly brought more real delight and satisfaction than all the mechanical entertainment people seem to depend on today.

My father's brothers, *Herman* and *Theodore*, and two sisters *Mary BARGE* and *Lena HOFTYZER* all lived within a two-mile radius. They all loved to get together for reunions or birthdays which were usually celebrated in our home, at least while Grandma lived, because that was still home to all of them, and it was easier for Grandma not to have to go out. It would have meant getting someone, perhaps hiring them, to come and get her with a horse and buggy, because she could not have walked that far.

OUR NEW HOME
7616 COLGATE AVENUE

The September after I had my seventh birthday was a very eventful time. We moved. My parents bought a home on Colgate Avenue, which was in the same neighborhood -- perhaps three quarters of a mile away.

This house was more modern. It had a bathroom – something my mother had long coveted. At that time bathrooms were not just taken for granted. To have one was a great privilege. No longer would we have to take a bath in a tub in the kitchen on Saturday night, or visit the privy in the back in freezing weather. When we lived on Hope Avenue there was a public bathhouse about a quarter mile away. For a small fee adults were able to get a better bath there than in a small tub. However, it was more convenient to bathe the children in the kitchen.

We had a very pretty yard with three apple trees in the back and also a very cute little summerhouse for the children to play in. Ours was the only house on the whole street, which had a summerhouse and also three apple trees. Who wouldn't be proud of that?

MY PLAYMATES

There were not many children my age on Colgate Avenue for me to play with. However, there was one girl about two years older and we seemed to enjoy doing the same things. We both liked to play with our dolls. We liked to sew for small dolls and collected all the left over dress material we could get a hold of or trade. To "make" a dress we took a piece of straight material about two or three inches wide and about six inches long. We turned up the bottom about half an inch and ran a basting stitch through it to hold it. Then we turned in about a quarter of an inch at the top of the piece of material and ran another basting stitch through it, but this time gathered it to fit around the little doll's neck. Then we cut two little holes for the doll's arms to go through, and there was the dress! We could make a dozen in a couple of hour's time and so our little dolls had big wardrobes.

This little girl, whose name was *Edna*, had a cute doll with real human hair which could be combed. I thought she was very lucky to be able to comb the doll's hair in many styles. Sometimes she let me do it

Another game we enjoyed was Jacks. We loved to throw the ball up and gather the jacks and both of us became quite expert at it. There were about a dozen different parts to the game – each involved considerable skill. Each time we missed catching the ball or touched a jack we were not supposed to touch, we had to wait for another turn to continue on. Of course the one who finished going through all the different skills first won the game.

Often in the summer time we would sit for hours playing a game of jacks. We'd put them away for a while and do something else and then we were back playing with the jacks and ball again.

CHRISTMAS AT THE EPPINK HOME

Christmas was always a very happy time in our home. We looked forward to the lighted Christmas tree on Christmas Eve (with candles). That was also when gifts were exchanged. The Christmas tree had a very special place in the parlor and no one, except the one who decorated, was allowed to see it until it was completely trimmed and lit up.

For those of us who believed in Santa Claus, we were expectantly waiting until we heard Santa's horn, which he blew from outside the window to let us know he had been there and was now on his way to pay a visit to the neighbor. After we no longer believed in a physical Santa Claus, we pretended we did and still found much pleasure in the traditional custom set up so long ago within the family.

Christmas that year was very different though. Just a couple weeks before Christmas my older brother, ***Harold***, was hurt in his chest and pneumonia developed. It was a peculiar kind of pneumonia and had out family doctor baffled. The doctor had been our physician so long he was almost like one of the family and extremely conscientious. One night my brother's temperature was so high that the doctor stayed nearly all night. He promised my parents that he would not leave them until he got the fever down some. He didn't. I believe he left around 4:00 in the morning. For many days in a row life hung on as by a thread. My mother nearly collapsed from fatigue and anxiety because she had sat up with him next to the bedside day and night during all that time.

A couple of days before Christmas my mother called my younger brother, ***Walter***, and I to her and explained that due to

my older brother's grave illness we could not have a Christmas tree or celebrate Christmas as we usually did. She told us we would each be allowed to buy ourselves one gift which we especially wanted.

I had seen a doll in the window of a store, which I thought very beautiful. It was about 12 or 15 inches long and I'm sure at this writing would sell at three or four dollars. This doll was priced at 25 cents. It seems unbelievable now but there it was. The doll had a kid body and the head was made of bisque, an unglazed porcelain used to make the heads of all the better dolls. It had a very beautiful face – brown eyes and dark brown curls. Of course the doll was not dressed. That would take quite a bit off the price. I was perfectly satisfied and played with the doll a long time. Fortunately, my brother recovered.

TWO WEEKS IN THE COUNTRY

That same year my mother began having trouble with a large varicose ulcer on her leg. It was very painful and would not heal. The physician insisted that the only way it could ever heal would be complete rest – keep off the foot and keep it elevated. This was no easy solution with a family of seven.

All that next year my mother hobbled around and suffered day and night with her sore leg. Finally it seemed a solution had been found so that my mother could get away from home for about three weeks during which time her leg might respond to the rest treatment and become healed. My mother's relatives all lived in the country but in different cities. One of my aunts invited my mother and my little sister to visit her, during which time my mother would do nothing but rest for three weeks. My older bother, Harold, was to stay with my mother's other sister in a different city, and my younger brother and I were invited to stay with my mother's brother, ***Uncle Louie*** *(Louie KRUMWIEDE, see OP-unidentified lots, and Lot 9-17)* and his second wife, ***Aunt Nellie*** – who also lived in the country. My older sister was going to stay home and keep house for my father who would be going to work every day. It seemed like a wonderful arrangement for everyone concerned.

I was now ten and my younger brother was eight. We didn't know this aunt and uncle very well and were not used to being in the country. We had never been away from home without my parents except for the times I went to visit *Aunt Hannah* and that was almost like being with our parents.

Unfortunately, after only a couple of days and nights there in the country we both became dreadfully homesick. People who have never been homesick cannot possibly appreciate the meaning of that word. When one is homesick there is no cure for it except to get home with the ones who can satisfy that lonely feeling. Both my aunt and uncle and their children did everything they could to make us happy, and during the daytime seemed to succeed quite well. But night time came and the crickets began to sing and it was so terribly, terribly dark – no shadows shining into any windows from the street lights, and never the sound of a person's heels on the sidewalk, or a streetcar stopping to let a passenger off. (We could hear streetcars 'though they were a block away.)

Finally we could stand it no longer. When everyone had retired and we were supposed to be asleep we were sobbing our hearts out. We missed our mother most at bedtime because she always tucked us in and listened to our prayers. Now we were completely on our own in a house so far away and we didn't even know if Mama was getting better.

After about two weeks of this, my uncle finally took us back to the city even though my mother would not be home for another week. With my father at home nights, my sister could manage during the day, and I was now old enough to help with some of the household chores. The next week went much faster and never was there a happier reunion than when we were all together again.

My mother was an extremely good neighbor. There never was sickness or trouble anywhere around that my mother didn't know about it or do something to help them. How well I recall when little *Clifford NICHOLS*, one of the neighbor's children became desperately sick with spinal meningitis and had to give up his life at the age of nine. My mother seemed to be able to find time to be over there every day to help them. All of the neighbors loved and were true friends to my mother through all of her long life as long as they all lived.

OUR CHURCH

My father and his two brothers and two sisters were all active in the same church (St. Paul's German Methodist Episcopal Church, on Cleveland's near West Side) living as they did in the same general area. His other sister, *Aunt Lena*, joined the church her husband's family had been active in. But with so many uncles, aunts, and cousins all attending the same church, we had a family reunion every Sunday.

Often when we had visiting ministers, they came to our house for dinner. If they didn't come home with my father, then they went to my uncle's. My parents loved company and it seemed we were always having guests for meals.

SUNDAY SCHOOL PICNIC

No doubt the day that we thought of as the biggest fun day of the year was our Sunday School Picnic.

In the days before automobiles were so popular that every family owned one, it was not possible to go to many picnics, and so the one big picnic everyone looked forward to was the Sunday School Picnic.

Usually the park chosen to have the picnic was about fifty miles away from Cleveland. Several times we went to Linwood Park in Vermilion, which was considered a very ideal place for a church picnic. It was a beautiful shady park located on the picturesque Vermilion River. There was boating on the river and a few people went bathing in the river, not knowing how very dangerous it was.

The most exciting part of the trip was the ride on the train, which in order to get on, everyone had to go down to the old Union Depot downtown. The train left about eight or nine in the morning; I can't remember exactly, but it did give us a long day.

Then there were the days before the picnic when the lunch was planned: baking, picnic basket to be packed. I believe my mother stayed up until midnight the night before the picnic, and got up at dawn to finally get everything together in the basket, and get all the children dressed and ready and be downtown early enough so we did not miss the train. The men folk took off the day from work if it was possible. How exciting and happy everyone on the train was! Of course it was a special train and everyone knew each other.

Linwood Park was not known as an amusement park. About the only thing of that sort was a merry-go-round. But to us children, that was the most important thing anyway and so nothing else was missed. The ride on the merry-go-round cost a nickel and since it was about the only time or chance we ever got to ride the horses, usually we were allowed to have several rides. It seemed like forever would not be long enough for me to get enough rides on the merry-go-round.

Then in the afternoon there were races planned for all ages to participate. One race was for men and women. My father walked off with the men's prize, my mother with the women's. The race for the men was hanging up clothes on a clothesline. The one who could do it the fastest won a prize. The women were given a piece of wood and a saw, which could show who could saw a board the fastest. My mother won this one very easily. All in all, it seemed to prove that my mother and father really worked together as a team.

Later it was time to eat our second meal at the park, and just get the food packed again, if any was left over before it was time to board the train again to return home – tired but very happy with memories to last to next year.

A HAPPY ANNIVERSARY

Fortunately, there was a happy event that same year near Thanksgiving time. It was my parents' twenty-fifth wedding anniversary. My older sister now was twenty-two and she urged them to celebrate in a big way which they certainly did. All my aunts and uncles and a few cousins were invited. The event took place in our home – even to the serving of the big meal to about sixty-seven people.

I'm not sure I can remember all the kinds of food on the tables (for everyone was served at tables which had been borrowed from the church). We even had tables upstairs in a large room up there, which was sort of a hall, since from it all the bedrooms were entered. (Actually, it was a foolish plan in the architecture, for had it not been for all this wasted space the bedrooms might have been larger.) I do recall that we had lots of potato salad, cold cuts, pickles and olives and two kinds of homemade cake. How well I remember that I baked all the cakes – a yellow cake and a spice cake with rich brown sugar icing. The yellow cake had white icing and I believe a filling between the layers.

I can't recall exactly how many cakes I baked, but it seemed it was fourteen – and we did not have an electric mixer. Every stroke was done by hand and my mother was proud of the fact that the cakes turned out so well and that I was able to do it at the age of fourteen. We did have lots of cake left over but with a large family who did enjoy sweets I'm sure none of it was wasted.

My sister planned a program. One of the exciting things I remember was that one of my cousins, who was the manager of a furniture store, sent a record player and quite a few records just to be used that night. We didn't have a record player, and so we had enjoyment from this for a number of days afterwards. We were a family of music lovers. Being a silver anniversary, my parents received many beautiful gifts.

WORLD WAR I

At the age of twenty-one my older brother *(Harold)* was drafted and had to go into the Army. Never shall I forget the concern in the hearts of every member of our family. This Great War was being fought on foreign shores and it was only a matter of a few months before the newest boys were sent overseas.

My brother had to leave for training very early one morning. Everyone in our family, including *Aunt Hannah* went downtown to the Union Depot, from which his train left to see him off. It was one of the saddest times of our whole lives.

After he was in service a few weeks, he was given a short furlough, at which time he was allowed to come home, and we could see how he looked in his Army uniform.

We had a star in the window for him, because most families who had someone in service were proud to display a "service flag," which told how many sons were away defending our country. If there were more than one in the family gone, there would be a star for each one. Also, service pins were worn with the same design and colors, but small, of course. There was a special design for the ones who were serving overseas. These were shaped like a Liberty Bell with a star in the center. Some who had several sons or brothers and perhaps a sweetheart might be wearing as many as three service pins: one an overseas pin with one or more stars and perhaps one for one of more sons or brothers still here in this country and if someone had a sweetheart in the service there would be another pin for him. Of course these pins were not always expensive jewelry; they sold for a quarter or more depending upon the quality desired.

Everyone was singing the marching and popular war songs, which while some of them were sad – they also had a rhythm, which made it difficult to keep from tapping the beat with either the feet or fingers.

It seemed just about every day downtown there would be a parade of solders being moved closer to the coast to be shipped overseas. Our boss never objected to us going to the window to watch our boys marching along to the steps of the popular marches. (Many of them were *SOUSA'S* marches.)

It was very exciting to see all these young men in Uncle Sam's uniform marching perfect step, and yet it made one's heart ache to know how many of them would be killed or badly wounded "over there."

After my brother had been in service about six months my parents received word that he would be shipped to the Eastern Coast. If they wished to see him before he left they would have to make the trip to his training camp, Fort Knox, Kentucky, right away.

Of course they wanted to see him before he left, so immediately they packed and were off. It was a very difficult trip for them to make, because they were eager and looking forward to seeing him. Under the circumstances they were mixed with a great deal of sadness – not knowing what would happen before the next time they saw him.

And so farewell to him was sad and then my mother and father were on their way home. That day the most wonderful thing that possibly could have happened did happen. It was November 11, 1918. Whistles began to blow, paperboys were shouting as loud as they could scream, church bells rang, people were hollering and hugging each other. Everyone was so excited and happy they almost acted wild. The great news of the signing of the armistice, which meant the END OF THE WAR, was really TRUE! Thank God! – The war was over! Even if my brother was sent overseas now, they felt sure he would not be in combat service. As it was he was not sent overseas even though he was kept in the service for sometime after that.

When my parents got home from Kentucky instead of the sad faces we had expected to see, we saw more happiness than we had ever seen since the day my brother left.

Everyone hoped that this "War to End War" would be the last. With this hope and the joy of having the boys come back home a few at a time both from camps and overseas those next months were hilariously happy ones. As one might expect, there was some problem of getting employment again – with so many young men all needing jobs at once. Before the war women did not hold the kind of jobs they were now holding. They had come to like their work in offices, factories and many other fields. They were earning good wages. This was the beginning of competition between men and women in the field of employment. This was the time when woman really began to fight seriously for equal rights and in less than two years had established the right to vote. Up until that time in 1920 only men in the U.S.A. were allowed the privilege of voting.

I must have been lucky because I didn't lose my job at the bank although several boys did return form the service to reclaim their old jobs.

Needless to say wedding bells rang often as the soldier boys returned home. Sweethearts who had been separated for so long did not wait to make plans for a big elaborate wedding. The only thing that mattered to them was the ceremony that would bind them together forever – there would never be another war to tear them apart! How little did they realize that their sons and daughters – the very next generation, would face exactly the same problem! And even now – the third generation lives in fear of this happening again. How we hope and pray that the futility of war has been learned! There must be a better way!

THE FIRST CAR

Those first years of the 1920's were very gay. People were prosperous and spending money madly. They were making up for the unhappy years of the war. Before that, very few people except the very wealthy could afford a family car. Now, one by one, it seemed that someone in more and more families owned a car – if not a new one, a second hand one.

In our family my younger brother, *Walter*, managed to buy a second hand jalopy, and how well I remember that old car! It was no problem to go down hill – but when it came to climbing up the other side – that was something different. How I recall our first ride in that old car. We got to a spot and the car wouldn't climb the little slope. There we sat and got out and stood and everyone was raking his brain trying to figure out how to get out of that place. Just whose idea was the best I can't remember – but finally chug-by-chug – like a little steam engine – we finally managed to get up on level ground again, and luckily arrive back home with no further trouble. There was another problem, however, with this old car, the top of it like all those first cars, folded up like a convertible today – except that it was much, much more difficult to put the top up and down. If the top happened to be down and suddenly it started to sprinkle and my brother got out of the car to put the top up – usually it was such a big job and took so long that by the time it finally gave us protection from the rain – we were already drenched. Also, it seemed the tops of those old cars always leaked anyhow, and the rain poured in from the cracks in the sides. But in spite of all this, we were wonderful sports about it all – for after all being able to go places in one's own car instead of having to use public transportation was well worth a little trouble and discomfort and inconvenience. I'm quite sure my brother did not find it difficult to take his "dates" out riding in it.

By 1923, however, it seems he had had enough of it and so traded it in on a brand new Buick. This was a beautiful car we all thought and certainly enjoyed being able to ride in it. Now my brother really was popular with the fair sex – having the additional good fortune of being very attractive and handsome. It seemed he had so many girlfriends that all of us thought he would marry very young. It did not work out that way, however. His was the last wedding in our family.

1923 – A SAD YEAR

Not long after my *Aunt Hannah* passed away in January, my younger sister ***Gladys***, began ailing. Her illness was very perplexing to the family doctor. He did not consider it serious, yet she did not seem to improve under the medication provided, but rather, kept getting steadily worse. Later after consulting another physician she was taken to the hospital for x-rays and while the x-rays seemed to be able to pinpoint where her trouble lay, the second doctor was unable to diagnose the disease either.

Early in July she began running a very high fever. This was thought by the doctor to be unrelated to her other trouble and diagnosed it as pneumonia. Suddenly she lost consciousness due to the very high temperature.

A third doctor was called in. He took tests and his report from the tests was that she had spinal meningitis. The fluid from the spine, which he had taken, was sent to the hospital to be analyzed. He told us that there might be a slight chance of her recovery provided no tuberculosis germs were found in the fluid. These germs were found, and now, just a few days before her death, they were able to put things together as to what had been wrong with her all those months. She had tuberculosis of the bowel. She did not have pneumonia at all. The high temperature at the end from the tuberculosis was what caused complications – the fever going to her brain and thus causing the meningitis – or so it was explained at the time in July 1923.

On her birthday, on July 31st she was very, very ill. Some of her friends had a birthday card shower on her. I can't exactly recall how many cards there were but it was quite a bundle. She was too sick to notice them at all.

The following morning she went into a coma from which she never regained consciousness – and so on August 1, 1923 we had to part with her. Her death is one I shall never be able to forget, not only due to the change and adjustment the family had to make, but also the significance of it in a spiritual way.

That night we were all assembled around her bedside for the last time, just moments before the end came – even though it seemed she was unconscious, suddenly she looked up at the ceiling and as she gazed around a beautiful smile crossed her lips. My mother noticed it at once and remarked, "she sees something." I'm sure she did – it may have been her first glimpse into the Eternal even before her heart beat for the last time. Her face was almost scarlet in color from the heat of the fever. Her breathing which had been very loud and heavy all day finally was coming to an end. Suddenly as in a flash the breathing stopped and the color of her face changed from the red color to a waxy white. She still had a smile on her face and I can still recall the thought, which came to me at that moment. It was, "she looks so beautiful, just like a beautiful white lily." And then this thought, so significant to me now as it has been through the years: "Heaven can't be very far away; why a moment ago she was here – and now she's there!"

FATHER'S RETIREMENT

The following winter my father became ill. He had a severe case of bronchitis and he was sick for a long time. The company for which he had worked for a long time, nearly his whole life time, decided that since he was of retirement age it would be kind to him to retire him on a pension.

However, this came as a tremendous shock as he had not intended to retire for some time. He always enjoyed his work even though it was hard work. He enjoyed the fellowship with his working companions. This shock, added to by the death of *Gladys* and his sister, *Hannah*, were too much for him. There seemed to be nothing, which could restore his robust health.

A ROMANCE

We always had a church service on Sunday evening and I usually attended – even all summer long. One evening I happened to glance around during the service and was so surprised to see a young man in the congregation, who was none other than the elderly minister's nephew, ***Frank (MUSIL)***. Outside of my brothers, he was the only fellow I knew who drove a car – a very small car with only one seat. He was a carpenter by trade and it was very necessary for him to have a car because the tools were heavy and the carpenter jobs spread all over the big city.

While there were some things about Frank's personality which I did not understand or admire there were other things which did seem to win me to him. He was so strong. I had always been so sensitive about my height. He never objected to that. His parents had died when he was young and he had to make his own way from the time he was fourteen. I felt sorry for him not having had the shelter of a home and the love of parents surrounding him. He liked to attend church and did go regularly. That fact was very important to me. He was very ambitious and saved his money – also good qualities when not carried to the extreme. While I had never met his parents, I did like his aunt and uncle and cousin very much, and had met his brother and sister-in-law.

The next summer he decided to go into the building business – to work for himself instead of other contractors. In August we became engaged and in September I received my engagement ring. The night he put the ring on my finger we were sitting on a bench in Edgewater Park – the park my family had their picnics in when I was a child, about which I wrote in earlier chapters.

A WEDDING

We were not married until the next May. The date was May 2, 1925. We did not have a large wedding but instead a very simple home wedding with only the immediate families being invited, some of my friends urged me to have a big church wedding. This was something I had never planned to do. I liked the way my older brother and sister-in-law had been married in our home and that was the way I wanted to be married. We did start out in a brand new house. Actually it was the first house Frank built and he had intended to sell it and then build another one. But the house was finished at the wrong time of year. It was early Spring (before our marriage). The street was unpaved and terribly muddy. Nearly everyone who came down the street got stuck in the mud, which was lots worse than being stuck in a snowdrift.

Since it was so close to the date of our wedding, Frank thought that we ought to move into the house for a while, while the street was in such bad condition. Then having the house furnished with new furniture might make it more attractive to prospective buyers.

For about a year or so after our marriage there was quite a building program in progress – but the following year – a couple of years before the big depression of 1929, the building trades were beginning to feel a big slump. It became very difficult – almost impossible – to get carpenter work.

Frank knew how hopeless it was to continue seeking carpenter work when there was no building, so he became a salesman. This was not easy for him since he had never done anything like that – and having to meet the public in this way was a tremendous adjustment to make. He began first to sell sewing machines. This did not prove very profitable. So then he tried selling Fuller Brushes. He did some better with this, but still it was all commission and certainly not enough to meet our financial obligations.

That summer I knew that within a year there would be three in our family. During that time Frank continued with his selling and now and then got a little carpenter work to help a little.

Our little daughter, ***Margie***, was born in St. John's Hospital. The first time Frank saw the baby in my arms he spoke of the time she would go to college – for of course she would go to college as neither of us had been able to go. It almost made me smile planning ahead so far in the future – for that time seemed almost an eternity away. Florence Eppink Musil, sister of Infant Eppink, and granddaughter of William Krumwiede and Sophia Scharnhorst, *(OP 5:1)*.

Siblings of Infant Eppink:

Emmalyn EPPINK, [b. Oct 1892], never married, died age 58. ***Harold EPPINK***, b. 17 May 1897, d. July 1965, m./div. *Marion RUGGLES* (b. 28 Jan 1898, d. Apr 1978). ***Florence EPPINK***, b. 3 Mar 1900, d. 6 July 1992, m. *Frank MUSIAL*. ***Walter EPPINK***, b. 20 June 1902, d. Aug 1982(4), m. *Marion DORAN* (b. 17 Oct 1909, d. May 1987). ***Gladys EPPINK***, b. 1906, d. 1 Aug 1923, never married, d. age 17. Richard Eppink, Mary Milne Jamba and [Census records 1870].

EPPINK, Emmalyn, of 14204 Superior Ave., beloved daughter of ***Minnie*** and the late ***William***, sister of ***Harold*** and ***Walter EPPINK***, and ***Mrs. Florence MUSIL***, and the late ***Gladys***, Friday morning. Friends may call Friday evening at the George C. Lang Co. Funeral Home, W. 95 St. at Lorain Ave. Services Saturday evening, at 8 p. m., at the Young- Koebler Funeral Home, 1966 E. 82 St. In lieu of flowers friends may contribute to the Cancer Fund. Cleveland Necrology File, Cleveland Press, Dec 1950, reel 088.

EPPINK-Gladys A. age 17, beloved daughter of ***William G.*** and ***Minnie*** (nee ***KRUMWIEDE***), sister of ***Emmalyn, Harold, Florence*** and ***Walter***, Wednesday, at 8:10 p. m., after a lingering illness. Funeral services to be held at 2 p. m., at late residence, 7616 Colgate avenue and at 2:30 p. m., at St. Paul's Methodist Episcopal church, W. 44th street and Bridge avenue N. W. Cleveland Necrology File, Aug 1, 1923, reel 023.

Henrich (Henry) Wilhelm Krumwiede

Henry F. KRUMWIDE *(sp.)*, 82 yrs.; res. West Dover; German; interred April 19, 1899; Original Part. LI *It is assumed he is buried with his wife, Sophia Krumwiede. See OP 5:1.*

Infant Krumwiede

Child of Louis KRUMWEIDE (first husband of Kate QUELL KRUMWIEDE, see Lot 9) and his second wife, Nellie VANDERPLOEG; grandson of William and Sophia KRUMWIEDE (see OP 5:1).

"***Infant Krumweide***," male; b. March 14, 1909, Bay Village, Cuyahoga Co., Ohio; d. March 14, 1909, duration ½ day, Asphyxia due to compression of the umbilical cord at birth. Transverse presentation with prolapse of cord; fr. ***Louie KRUMWIEDE***, b. Dover, O., mo. ***Nelly BRUGGER***, b. Germany. Ohio Certificate of Death, Division of Vital Statistics, 1909, certif. 11654.

Infant KRUMWIEDE; res. Bay Village; German; interred Mar 15, 1909; Original Part. "List of Interments," Lakeside Cemetery, Bay Village, OH.

Bay, male, Asphyxia due to compression of the Umbilical Chord at birth, undertaker Jas. A. Pease, Dover, Ohio, issued Mar 15, 1909. Burial Removal Permit, City of Bay Village.

Parents of Infant Krumwiede:

Louis KRUMWEIDE, (b. 24 May 1867, Dover, Cuyahoga Co., OH; d. 1 Oct 1945, Wakeman, Huron Co., Ohio) and ***Nellie VANDERPLOEG*** (b. 3 Jan 1880, Provence Grogingen, Munaplity, T Zandt, Holland; d. 25 Dec 1959, Wakeman, OH; bur. Birmingham Cemetery, Birmingham, OH). This was the second marriage for Nellie, she was the widow of *George BRUGGERS* (b. 16 Dec 1874, Deaconess Hosp., Cleveland, OH; m. 4 June 1902, probably, Cuyahoga County; d. 25 May 1906, Deaconess Hosp., bur. Monroe Street Cemetery, Cleveland, OH). Louie and Nell would have another child, ***Kenneth*** (b. 19 Nov 1911; m. *Hazel*; d. 3 Jan 2000, Wakeman, OH; bur. Birmingham Cemetery). *(See section on Kate Quell Krumwiede, Lot 9).* Esther Seitz Matousek

Louis KRUMWIEDE, 40, Bay Village, b. same, farmer, fr. *Wm. KRUMWIEDE*, mo. *Sophie SCHOENHURST*, married prev. Once (dead) married ***Nellie BRUGGES***, 27 yrs., 277 Dare St., b. Holland, occup. none, fr. *John VANDERPLOEG*, mo. *Jennie*, married prev. once, married name *Nellie BRUGGES*. The State of Ohio, Cuyahoga County, ss. I Certify, That on the 31st day of July 1907 Louis Krumwiede and Nellie Brugges were by me legally joined in marriage. Marriage solemnized by Karmen *[listed later A. Karreman]* (Colgate St.) Marriage Record, Cuyahoga County, OH, vol. 68, p. 59.

KRUMWEEDIE, Louie, 52, head, parents B. Hanover, Germany; ***Nell***, 39, wife, b. Holland, parents b. Holland, immig 1898, Al; ***Will***, 26, son, single, RFD Mail Carrier; ***Louise***, dau., 19, single, clerk, steam railroad; ***Dorthy BRUGGERS***, 14, step-dau., b. Ohio, fr. b. Ohio, mo.- b. Holland, ***Kenneth KRUMWEIDIE***, 8 son, b. Ohio, fr. b. Ohio, mo. b. Holland; Own, mortgage, farm, Fauther Road. 1920 FC OH CYBV, p. A1, lines 1-6.

Louie KRUMWIEDE died October 1, 1945 in Wakeman, Huron County, Ohio. He is buried in the family plot at Birmingham Cemetery, Birmingham (Wakeman area), OH along with ***Nellie, Kenneth***, and Kenneth's wife, ***Hazel***. Matousek

KRUMWEIDE: Lewis, beloved husband of ***Nellie*** (nee ***VANDERPLOEG***). Father of ***Sophia SEITZ, Louise BEARD, Dorothy HINKEL, William, Arthur, Kenneth***, grandfather and great-grandfather, brother of ***Mrs. Minnie EPPINK***, the late ***Elizabeth HABER*** and ***Mary STOCKER***. Friends may call at the Geo. C. Lang Co. Funeral Home, W. 95th and Lorain ave. until Thursday a.m. Funeral from Brownhelm Evangelical Church, Brownhelm, O. 2:30 p.m. Cleveland Necrology File, Oct 4, 1945.

KRUMWIEDE, Nellie (nee ***VANDERPLOEGE***), wife of the late ***Louis***, mother of ***Sophia SEITZ, William, Arthur, Louise BEARD, Dorothy HINKEL*** and ***Kenneth***, grandmother and great-grandmother, passed away Dec 25, sister of *Gertrude VANDERPLOEGE, Esther BELGRAVE* and *Elmer*. Friends received at the Garland Funeral Home Amherst, O., where services will be held Monday, Dec 28, at 2 p. m. Cleveland Necrology File, Cleveland Press, Dec 28 1959.

Sibling of Infant Krumwiede:
Kenneth KRUMWIEDE, b. 19 Nov 1911; d. 3 Jan 2000, Wakeman, OH (born on the twenty-first birthday of his half-sister ***Sophie***); m. 2 Dec 1936 to ***Hazel BRILL*** (b. 15 February 1913, d. 20 Oct 1984). Esther Seitz Matousek and Carol P. Reed.

David Miller

MILLER, David F., 29, Farmer, Value of Real Estate 2000, Value of Personal Estate 600; ***Marietta***, 30, Keeping House; ***Louis E.***, 3; ***Willard R.***, 1; all b. Ohio. 1870 FC OH Sheffield, Lorain Co., p. 655. *They were living two farms from William Irish, who is the son-in-law of Jerusha and Isaac Rowell (OP 5:13-14).*

DIED

MILLER.- On the 9th instant, in Avon, of heart disease, ***Mr. David MILLER***. The deceased leaves a wife and four small boys to mourn their loss. The bereaved ones have the heartfelt sympathy of the community. Elyria Weekly Republican, Elyria, OH, Thursday, April 17, 1879, p. 5. col. 5.

David MILLER; Sheffield; interred April 11, 1879; Original Part. "List of Interments," Lakeside Cemetery, Bay Village, OH.

Parents of David Miller:
The following census was found that may be the family of David as a child. This has not been proven but seems very possible. According to David's date of birth in November and the census being taken in June, the age is correct.

Alexis MILLER, 53, Farmer, b. NY; ***Caroline***, 50, b. Mass.; ***Diana***, 20, b. O.; ***David***, 18, Farm Laborer, b. O; ***Lorenzo***, 15, b. O.; *(unable to read the next name)*, female, 11, b. O. 1860 FC OH LRAV, pp. 77-78. *Caroline is the daughter of David Foote and Betsey Hamblin (OP 3:3-4)*

METHODIST EPISCOPAL CHURCH

In 1822 *Rev. William REYNOLDS* organized a class at the Titus school house in Avon township, but a large portion of the members were from Sheffield township. Meetings were held previous to this at the house of ***Alexas MILLER***. The following persons composed this class: *Adam MILLER* and wife *Anna*, Alexas Miller and wife ***Caroline***, *Susanah PARSHALL, Delia Ann CASE*, now widow of *Theron MOORE (dau. of Moses Case, OP 6:2), Norman MOORE, Anson TITUS* and *Susan* his daughter. This church was removed to Sheffield in 1843, and meetings have since that date been held in the school house in district number three. It belongs to the Avon charge. The membership is now only small; *Rev. N.J. CHASE,* present pastor. A Baptist church was formed in Sheffield in 1833, also in the school district three. It was not in operation but a few years, disbanding, and the members, a portion of them uniting with the Methodist Episcopal church, the remainder joining the Baptist church in Avon. History of Lorain Co., Sheffield, p. 254.

Wife of David Miller, Marietta Robinson Foote:
MILLER, Mrs. David; Maiden name ***Maryette FOOTE***, Year Came to Township 1840; Where From or Where Born Dover, O.; Last Residence Dover, O. Women of the Western Reserve Prior to 1840, p. 17.

Marietta Robinson FOOTE, dau. of ***Ransom FOOTE*** *(OP 2:11-12)* and ***Catherine PORTER*** *(OP 2:12)*, b. 17 Mar 1840, Dover; m. 22 Dec 1864 ***David F. MILLER*** (b. 6 Nov 1841, Avon, Lorain Co., OH), res. 537 E. Ocean Ave., Long Beach, Cal. *Issue:* ***Louis Everett MILLER***, b. 10 Dec 1866, Sheffield, Lorain Co., OH; m. 25 July 1894, *Mary KRAMER* (b. E. St. Louis, Ill., 21 Aug 1864); res. Annaheim, Cal; ch.: *Edwin Louis MILLER,* b. 18 Aug 1895, Anneheim. ***Willard Earl MILLER***, b. 24 Aug 1868, Sheffield; m. 10 Jan 1906, *Grace HOUSE* (b. 31 Jan 1880, Columbus, OH); res. Long Beach, Cal. ***George Irving MILLER***, b. 13 June 1874, Dover. ***Arthur Clair MILLER***, b. 29 Mar 1876, Dover. Abram W. Foote, Foote Family Comprising the Genealogy and History of Nathaniel Foote, vol. 1, p. 231.

MILLER, Mary _, 40; ***Lewis E.***, 13; ***Williard E.***, 11, ***George***, *6;* ***Arthur***, 4. 1880 FC OH LRAV, p. 340B, house 371.

A note states (source unknown) that ***Marietta*** died in CA in 1897. Note in the possession of Harry Colbonn.

Children of David Miller and Marietta Foote:
Louis Everett MILLER, b. 12/10/1866, Ohio, maiden name mo. *TOOTE (Foote)*, fr. *MILLER*; d. Orange Co., 12/27/1955, 89 yrs. California Death Index

Edwin Louis MILLER, b. 18 Aug 1895; d. Aug 1978; res. 92028 Fallbrook, San Diego, CA. Soc. Sec. Index

MILLER, Louie E., owns farm, 52, b. Ohio, parents b. Ohio, Salesman, Hardware; ***Mary K.***, wife, 55, b. Illinois, parents b. Germany, no occup.; ***Edwin L.***, son, 24, b. Calif, no occup.; *Earl E. SMITH*, b. Lodger, 31, b. Missouri, Cashier, Bank; *Edward S. ROBERTS,* Lodger, 40, b. England, Salesman, Dry Goods; *Carl E. THOMPKIN*, Lodger, 33, b. S. Dak., Dentist, Own business; *Arthur H. STRIPKEY?*, 25, b. Montana, Salesman, Union Oil. 1920 FC California, Orange Co., Anaheim Twp., Anaheim City, ED 54, p. 7, lines 1-6, South Lemon St.?, recorded Jan. 10.

MILLER, Willard E., 51, b. Ohio, parents b. Ohio, occup. None; ***Grace***, wife, 39, b. Ohio, parents b. Ohio, occup. None. 1920 FC California, Los Angeles Co., Long Beach Twp., ED 82, p. 5B, lines 52-53, East First Street.

George I. MILLER, Lodger, 45, b. Ohio, parents b. Ohio, Laborer, Fruit House; Boarding with *Willard COPPS?*. 1920 FC California, San Bernardino Co., Upland Twp., ED 207, p. 1B, dwelling 16, lines 56-63, 9th Street.

George I. MILLER, head of household, owns home worth $1,800, not a farm, 56, single, b. Ohio, parents b. Ohio, Contractor, painter, not a veteran; ***Arthur C.***, brother, 54,

b. Ohio, Contractor, painter, not a veteran. 1930 FC California, Orange Co., Anaheim Twp., ED 30-17, p. 3A, lines 6-7.

Arthur C. MILLER, b. 3/29/1876, Ohio, mo. *FOOTE*; d. Orange, 5/23/1959, 82 yrs. California Death Index.

Robbie D. Peake

Robbie and his brother, Horace Peake, died within two days of each other of pneumonia, they were the sons of Fred Peake.

PEAK, Rob; d. 1899, Jan 15; 2 yrs. 9 mo., Avon; b. Avon; white; pneumonia. PDL 4:61.

Robbie D. PEAKE, 2 yrs.; res. Avon; interred Jan 15, 1899; Original Part. "List of Interments," Lakeside Cemetery, Bay Village, OH.

Grandparents of Robbie and Horace Peake:

PEAKE, Robert, 49, Farmer, value of real-estate $3500, value of personal estate $800, b. England; ***Margaret,*** 42, Keeping House, b. England; ***Lucy,*** 19, No Occupation, b. England; ***Richard,*** 14, At home, b. Ohio, attended school; ***Mary,*** 14, b. Ohio, attended school; ***Robert,*** 11, b. Ohio, attended school; ***Edward,*** 8, b. Ohio; ***William,*** 6, b. Ohio; ***George,*** 4, b. Ohio. 1870 FC OH Lorain Co., Elyria, p. 347, house 115, lines 23-31.

PEAKE, Robert, 58, Farmer, b. England, parents b. England; ***Margaret***, 52, b. England, parents b. England; ***Perry***, 19, Working on farm, b. Ohio; ***William***, 16, Work on farm, attended school, b. Ohio; ***George***, 14, Work on farm, attended school; ***Frederick***, 7, b. Ohio. 1880 FC OH LRAV, p. 334 B, lines 27-32.

PEAK Robert, Nov 13, 1822-Dec 21, 1899; ***Margaret***, wife, Jan 14, 1828-Aug 23, 1893; ***Perry***, 1860-1896. ***PEAK George E.***, 1866-1945; ***Mattie E***., 1866-1934; ***Margaret***, 1897-1917. Avon Center (Mounds) Cemetery, Avon, OH.

Parents of Robbie and Horace Peake:

Father, Fred, living with his brother: ***PEAK, George***, head, b. Apr 1866, 34, married, 5 yrs., b. Ohio, fr. b. England, mo. b. England, farmer; ***Matie***, wife, b. Dec 1866, 33 yrs., 3 children born, 3 living, b. Ohio, fr. b. England, mo. b. England; ***Grace***, dau., b. Nov 1895, 4 yr.; ***Margaret***, dau., b. Apr 1897, 3 yrs.; ***Edith***, dau., b. Oct 1899, 7/12 yr.; all children b. Ohio; ***Fred,*** brother, b. Aug 1872, 27, married, b. Ohio, parents b. England, Farm Laborer. *No wife or children listed with Fred.* 1900 FC OH LRAV, p. 51. *Census enumerated June 23, 1900*

PEAKE, Fred H. (Ethel B.), Beach Park, farmer; ***Theodore,*** Center Rd. *PEAKE, Geo. E. (Mattie B.),* Beach Park, farmer; *Grace B.; Margaret P, Edith E; Rachael I.; Helen M.,* M&S Center Rd. 1910 Lorain County Rural Directory, Avon.

Mrs. Fred PEAK is on the sick list. Elyria Evening Telegram, Mar 15, 1919, p. 7, col. 4.

PEAK, Frederick, 1872-1938; ***Ethel B***. 1886- ; *Beatrice GREEN*, 1909-1937; *Gladys,* 1909-1962; *Herbert D.,* 1916-1931. Mounds (Center) Cemetery, Avon, OH.

Horace Leroy Peake

Horace, brother of Robbie:

PEAK, Horace Leroy; b 1897, Nov 18, Avon, Lorain Co., Ohio; fr. ***Fred H. PEAK***, mo. ***Harthy S. BRAMMAN***; res. of parents Avon. PBL 4:105.

PEAK, Horace; d. 1899, Jan 18, Avon; 1 year, 2 mos., b. Avon; white; pneumonia. PDL 4:61.

Horace L. PEAKE, 1 yr.; res. Avon; interred Jan 19, 1899; Original Part. "List of Interments," Lakeside Cemetery, Bay Village, OH.

Those Interred in an Unspecified Area

Our ancestors; may we assimilate their virtues,
Cherish fondly their memories and associations,
And practice their teachings,
Especially that one beautiful recompense in life taught us
That in doing good to others we bring happiness to ourselves.

Sentiment by Rev. Mr. Walker
Cahoon Anniversary Celebration, August 28, 1878.

Jenny Mary Vogt Brais

Possible connection to the Bambam family in Lot 23.

Arthur Daniel BRAIS, 20, res. 74 Dartmouth St., b. Canada, carpenter, fr. *Fred BRAIS*, mo. *Virginia BRAIDRAI.* Married ***Jennie Mary VOGT***, 21, res. N. Dover, O., b. Cleveland, O., fr. *Henry VOGT*, mo. *Minnie BAMBAM;* neither previously married. Marriage solemnized by Wm. Brown, J.P. The State of Ohio, Cuyahoga County, ss. I Certify, That on the 2nd day of June 1905 Mr. Arthur Daniel Brais and Miss Jennie Mary Vogt were by me legally joined in marriage. Marriage Record, Cuyahoga County, OH, vol. 73, p. 487.

Jenny Mary BRAIS, d. June 16, 1909, 11:20 p.m., Dover, Cuyahoga Co., Ohio, cause Asthenia Phthisis for 2 days, contributory Phthisis for 1 yr.; married; b. Dec 17, 1883, Cleveland, Ohio, fr. ***Henry VOGT***, b. Germany, mo. ***Minnie BAMBAM***, b. Germany; 25 yrs. 7 mos. old; bur. Bay Village, undertaker Jas. A. Pease & Son, Dover, O.; informant *Arthur D. BRAIS*, North Dover, O. Ohio Certificate of Death, Division of Vital Statistics, 1909, certif. 29454

Mrs. Jenny Mary BRAIS, 24; res. Bay Village; German; Interred June 19, 1909. "List of Interments," Lakeside Cemetery, Bay Village, OH.

Mrs. Jenny Mary BRAIS, Dover, 24, Asthenia-Phthisis, removed to Bay Village via hearse, undertaker Jas. Pease & Co., Dover, O., issued June 19, 1909. Burial Removal Permit, City of Bay Village, OH.

Parents of Jennie Vogt Brais:

VOGT, Henry C., b. Jan 1848, 57 yrs., married 30 yrs., b. Germany, parents b. Germany, day laborer; ***Minnie L.***, wife, b. May 1852, 48 yrs., 10 children born, 7 living, b. Germany, parents b. Germany; ***Jennie M.***, dau., b. Dec 1884, 15 yrs., b. Ohio; ***Bertha M.***, dau., b. Mar 1886, 14 yrs., b. Ohio; ***Lilly C.***, dau., Mar 1888, 12 yrs., b. Ohio, at school. 1900 FC OH CYDO, p. 3B, lines 59-63.

Henry VOGT, d. Sept 28, 1924, 12 p.m., First Street, Dover, Cuyahoga Co., Ohio of myocarditis. Husband of ***Minnie VOGT;*** b. Jan 21, Mechlinburg, Germany; 81 yrs. old, Retired Farmer; fr. ***Henry VOGT***, b. Germany; mo. ***Sophie CLEVE***, b. Mechlinburg, Germany; informant *Mrs. E. GRUGLE* (daughter), North Dover; bur. Monroe Cemetery; undertaker The S.W.Mather Co., 3227 W. 25th St., Cleve., O. Ohio Certificate of Death, Division of Vital Statistics, 1924, certif. 48427.

Minnie VOGT, d. Sept 26, 1927, 5:20 a.m., Myocarditis (senilis); 26527 East Oviatt Rd., Bay *(Village)*, Cuy Co., Ohio; widow of ***Henry VOGT;*** 75 yrs. 4 mo.; housewife, retired; b. May 23, Mechlinburg, Germany; fr. ***John BAMBAM***, b. Germany, mo. ***Freda BRANDT***, b. Germany; informant *Mrs. E. Grugle*, 26527 East Oviatt Rd.; Cemetery Monroe Cem., undertaker The S.W.Mather Co., 3227 W. 25th St. Ohio Certificate of Death, Division of Vital Statistics, 1927, certif. 54914.

Siblings of Jenny Vogt Brais:

Edward J. O'NEILL, 24, res. 1436 E. 61st. Bl., b. Brooklyn, NY, occup. Finisher, fr. *Martin*, mo. *Mary OLDFIELD.* Married ***Bertha M. VOGT***, 23, res. 1436 E. 61st. Bl., b. Cleveland, O., occup. Clerk, fr. *Henry L.*, mo. *Minnie D. BAMBAM;* neither previously married. I Certify that on the 3rd day of Feby 1910…were by me legally married. John J. MacEwen. Marriage Record, Cuyahoga County, OH, vol. 41, p. 293.

David PENFOLD, 33; res. 1404 E. 49th St.; b. Cleveland, O.; occup. Machinist; fr. *W.C.*, mo. *Naomie MARTIN*, previously married Once (Dec'd). Married ***Lillian VOGT***, 20; res. Dover, Ohio; b. Cleveland, O.; occup. Housework; fr. *Jno. VOGT*, mo. *Minnie BONBON*; previously married Once (Div.) *BLAKE*. The State of Ohio, Cuyahoga County, ss. I certify that on the 20th day of Nov 1907 David Penfold and Lillian Vogt were by me legally joined in marriage. Marriage Record, Cuyahoga County, OH, vol. 69, p. 32.

Ernest GRUGLE, 40, res. 1197 E. 74 St., b. Cleveland, occup. Machinist, fr. *John GRUGLE,* mo. *Mary KAUSE,* previously married once. Married ***Lillian PENFOLD***, 35, res. 1197 E. 74th St., b. Cleveland, fr. *Henry VOGT,* mo. *Minnie BAMBARY,* previously married twice, married name *BLAKE--PENFOLD*, 1st Div. 2nd Div June 1-23 C.P.Ct., Marriage solemnized by Rev. E. Wright, Hippodrome 207950. The State of Ohio, Cuyahoga County, ss. I certify that on the 5th day of July 1923 Ernest Grugle and Lillian Penfold were by me legally joined in marriage. Marriage Record, Cuyahoga County, OH, vol. 131, p. 265.

GRUGLE, Ernest C., 46, owned home and radio, age at first marriage 17, b. Ohio, parents b. Germany, Machinist, manufactures machines; ***Lillian***,42, wife, age at first marriage 23, b. Ohio, parents b. Berlin, Germany, occup. Housework at private house; ***Harry***, 21, son, b. Ohio, Wire Drawer at General Electric. 1930 FC OH CYBV, ED 18-534, 26527 East Oviatt, p. 15 A, lines 17-19.

Husband of Jenny Vogt Braise, Arthur D. Braise:

After Jenny's death, Arthur married Josephine, the widow of John Close, Lot 8. Arthur died July 17, 1923, in Bay Village.

The State of Ohio, Cuyahoga County, ss. ***Arthur BRAIS***, 26, res. N. Dover, O., b. Canada, carpenter, fr. *Fred*, mo. *Virginia BROUDEU*, Arthur's wife deceased. Married ***Josephine CLOSE***, 33, res. N. Dover, O., b. N. Dover, O., housewife, fr. *John SUNK*, mo. *Frieda FRANK*, previously married once; Marriage solemnized by Rev. Carl Weiss. I Certify, That on the 10th day of November 1909 Arthur Brais and Josephine Close were by me legally joined in marriage. Marriage Record, Cuyahoga County, OH, vol. 73, p. 487.

BRAIS, Arthur, beloved husband of ***Josephine***, son of *Fred* and *Virginia BRAIS*; brother of *Eugene, Henry, Charles, Mrs. J.L. LANCER, Mrs. W.R. WHITE*. Funeral Friday, July 20th, at 2 p. m., from late residence, Bay Village, Stop 23. Cleveland Necrology File, July 19, 1923, reel 009.

Arthur D. BRAIS, d. 7-17-1923, 12 noon, Lutheran Hospital, Cleveland, Ward 7, Cuyahoga County, Ohio; res. Bay Village; b. June 13, 1884, Canada; 39 yrs. 1 mo. 4 days. Married ***Josephine BRAIS***; occup. Carpenter; fr. *Frederick BRAIS*, b. Canada; mo. *Virginia BROWDO*, b. Canada. Informant *Mrs. C.L. Hopkins*, Bay Village, O. Cause of death Aortic Aneurism, 4 mos., bur. Evergreen - Dover, O.; Undertaker C. Pease, Dover Center, O. Ohio Certificate of Death, Division of Vital Statistics, 1923, certif. 42873.

Parents of Arthur Braise:

BRAIS, Frederick, husband of ***Elizabeth*** and the late ***Virginia***, father of *Dr. E.J., Henry F., Charles W., Mrs. William MORGAN* and *Mrs. William WHITE*, the late *Arthur* and stepfather of *August J., Mrs. MANETTY*?, and *Mrs. George SCHOLL*… Cleveland Necrology File, Feb 9, 1941.

Frederick BRAIS, d. Feb 6, 1941, Lakewood City Hospital, Broncho Pneumonia; res. 1472 West 110th, Cleveland; husband of ***Elizabeth BRAIS***; retired carpenter, 80 yrs. 3 mos. 21 days; b. 16 Oct 1859, Montreal, Canada, fr. ***Paul BRAIS***, b. Canada, mo. ***Agba LYNCH***, b. Canada; informant *Dr. E.J. BRAIS*, 3714 Washington Blvd., St. Louis; funeral home Wm. & Roy Daniels, Cleveland, 15800 Detroit Ave.; bur. Evergreen Sect. A-2, Lot 150, Grave. 2. Ohio Certificate of Death, Division of Vital Statistics, 1941, certif. 9692 and Evergreen Cemetery.

BRAIS, Virginia, 78 yrs., d. Cleveland, OH, cause myocarditis, undertaker Saxton-Daniels, Cleveland; internment 7/5/1933, Section A-2, Lot 150, Grave 1, lot owner *W.R. WHITE.* Evergreen Cemetery, Westlake.

___ Burlingame

___ ***BURLINGAME***; res. Avon; interred Nov 30, 1882. "List of Interments," Lakeside Cemetery, Bay Village, OH.

Two of Hiram Burlingame's (Lot 44-4) brothers lived in the Sheffield area, Henry H. and Ewin Rufus. This individual may have descended from their families. No documentation was found to substantiate who this individual was.

Ludwig Deutsel

L. DEUTSEL; res. Bay Village; German; interred Aug 3, 1910. "List of Interments," Lakeside Cemetery, Bay Village, OH.

Ludwig DEUTSCH, appendectomy, Aug 3, 1910, C.F. Ford, MD. Burial Removal Permit, City of Bay Village, OH, 5312, 132.

Ludurah DEAUTAH *(difficult to read)*, servant, male, 45, single, b. Germany, parents b. Germany, laborer, general farm, able to read, not write. He was living with the *August MEILANDER* family on Bradley Rd. in Bay Village. *This may be the deceased person listed above. Census recorded April 18, 1910.* 1910 OH CYBV p. 1B, line 61.

Infant Fichle

Male, b. Oct 12, 1925, stillborn at 3:10 p.m., Cuyahoga Co., Bay Village, Glenn *(Glen)* Park Dr.; fr. ***Preston FICKLE***, white, 27 yrs. old, b. Tenn., laborer; mo. ***Bira RAPIER***, white, 24 yrs. old, hwf., 2 children born and living, Prophylactic against Ophthalmia Neonatorum used; attending physician Russell A. Pease, Dover Village, O. CB 1925: 3553.

Still Born FICHLE, age x, male, cause of death still born - , burial Lakeside Cemetery, undertaker C. Pease, Dover Center, O., Cuyahoga County, Ohio, issued Oct 13, 1925. Burial Removal Permit, City of Bay Village, OH.

William J. Johnson

William J. JOHNSON, 47, res. 3806 Franklin Ave., b. Saybrook, O., occup. machinist, fr. *Maurice W.*, mo. *Ann J. HARLOW*, No. of times prev. married 1st. dec'd 2nd

Div. 1921 Boston, Mass. Married ***Hilga E. RICHARDS***, 35, res. 3806 Franklin Ave., b. Norway, occup. none, fr. *John*, mo. *Hannah NELSEN*, prev. married none. Marriage to be solemnized by Rev. Anderson, Akron, O. The State of Ohio, Cuyahoga County, ss. I Certify, That on the 10th day of March 1924 William J. Johnson and Hilga E. Richards were by me legally joined in marriage. Rev. P. J. Norris. Marriage Record, Cuyahoga County, OH, vol. 134, p. 135.

William J. JOHNSON, 25943 Lake Rd, Bay Village; d. Dec 11, 1934, 12:15 p.m., Lakewood City Hospital, Lakewood, O., Acute broncho pneumonia (12/10/34) and Cardiac dilatation (12/11/34), contributory Cerebral embolism 1 yr., hypertension 5 yrs.; married to ***Hilga JOHNSON***; b. Mar 18, 1875, Saybrooke, Ohio, fr. ***Horace JOHNSON***, b. unknown, mo. ***Nettie HARLOW***, b. unknown; carpenter, last worked 1932; 59 yrs. 8 mos. 23 ds.; informant *Hilga Johnson*; bur. Bay, Dec 13, 1934, undertaker Clifford Pease, Dover Center, embalmed. Ohio Certificate of Death, Division of Vital Statistics, 1934, certif. 71957.

Hilga JOHNSON was found living alone at 25943 Lake Rd in the 1939-41 Bay Village City Directories, but is not listed as living in Bay Village in the 1944 Directory. The 1942 and 1943 were not available. Bay Village City Directories, Rose Hill Museum.

Martha Jane Pickering

Mrs. Martha Jane PICKERING, 71; res. Bay; cause of death Hypostatic Pneumonia; Bay Village Cemetery, undertaker C. Pease, Dover Center, O.; interment Apr 16, 1930. Burial Removal Permit, City of Bay Village, OH. *It is assumed that Martha is buried with her husband, George, see Lot 21 for more information.*

Elizabeth Bender Scheible

Elizabeth SCHEIBLE, 77; res. Avon Lake; cause of death Acute Cardiac Dilation; removed to Bay Village; undertaker E.C. Haag, Berea; issued Oct 30, 1929. Burial Removal Permit, City of Bay Village, OH.

Elizabeth may be buried with her husband, George, see Lot 29 for more information.

Wilbur Lawrence Seitz

Wilbur Lawrence SITES, 19 mo.; res. Bay Village; German; interred Apr 15, 1915. "List of Interments," Lakeside Cemetery, Bay Village, OH. *It is assumed that he is buried with his parents Jay H.W. Seitz and Lillian "Sophie" Krumwiede. See Lot 9 for further information.*

Jacob Wagner

Jacob WAGNER, 19; res. Cincinnati; nativity unknown; interred June 16, 1880. Drowned, washed ashore at S. Osborn, Dover, Bay. "List of Interments," Lakeside Cemetery, Bay Village, OH.

There were no newspaper accounts or other records found relating to Jacob's death.

Infant Yanko

Not named *(Infant YANKO)*, male, b. Sep. 22, 1927, stillborn at 5 p.m., Cuyahoga Co., Bay; fr. ***Joe YANKO***, Spanish-dark, 42 yrs. old, b. Muskoka, Oklahoma, occup. Gypsy Travelers; mo. ***Mary STEVE***, Spanish-dark, 37 yrs., b. Brazil, hwf. (housewife); 7 children born alive, 7 living, Prophylactic against Ophthalmia Neonatorum not used; attending physician C.W. Stoll, Dover Center, O., physician. CB 1927: 2270, Registration 3412.

Still Born YANKO, bur. Lakeside Cemetery, Dover Center, Ohio, date of death Sept 22, 1927, stillborn, interment September 23, 1927, undertaker C. Pease. Burial Removal Permit, City of Bay Village, OH 71.

Each year two or three colorful gypsy wagons would arrive in Bay Village, settling on the ridge near where the old Gun Club was on Lake Road. Their stay would only be for two weeks or so, but the community never seemed to mind when they came.

When the Yanko family faced the tragedy of a stillborn child, they turned to *Julia OSBORN SCOTT* for help. Julia was the town librarian at the time and she arranged for the infant to be buried in Lakeside Cemetery. M. Patricia Meddick Read, interview at Rose Hill Museum, 12 July 2004.

Gypsies occasionally traveled through town, along the dusty roads on the ridges. The kids were scared of them, because of the old stories about gypsies stealing children, and sometimes ran and hid if they saw them coming. They occasionally stole food or horses if they had a chance, but were otherwise harmless. They made a picturesque sight, with the brightly decorated wagons and horses, their unusual clothing, jewelry and jangling bells, and more than one person succumbed to the wheedling "Cross my palm with silver and I'll tell your fortune..." A History of Westlake, Ohio 1811-1961, Book II, Chapter I.

Mexican Gypsies - from Russia/Serbia moved back and forth between Mexico and the US for awhile. The Mexican vistas/clans are Bokurschti, Chokurschti and Yonkurschi. The surnames common to these vistas are Costello, Flores, John, Spiro, Steve and Yanko. Joseph Mitchell, Up in the Old Hotel, p. 191.

Individuals Who Were Moved to Another Cemetery or Are Included in the Cemetery Records But May Never Have Been Buried Here.

A place is indelibly and forever stamped
By the character and personality of the people
Who first settled and lived in the community.
Mrs. Caroline Dale Snedecker

Lena Bambam

Lena is listed on the cemetery plot map in the same plot as her husband, Frederick, but Lena may be buried at Brooklyn Heights Cemetery with her son. See lot 23 for more information.

Henry Davider

Heinrich DAVIDER was moved from Lakeside to St. Paul Lutheran Church Cemetery, Westlake, OH, in 1910. St. Paul Lutheran Church, Westlake, OH. *See lot 24 for more information.*

Erdine Seitz Dranse

Erdine DRANSE is listed on the cemetery plot map. There may have been preliminary plans for Erdine to be buried at Lakeside. Erdine is buried at Lakeview Cemetery, Cleveland, OH. Plot map, Lakeside Cemetery, Bay Village, OH and Evelyn Albers Badt. *See lot 9 for more information..*

Calvin Riley Edson

Riley EDSON; res. Dover; interred, Sept 5, 1880; Lot 43; Removed to Cld. "List of Interments," Lakeside Cemetery, Bay Village, OH.

The State of Ohio, Cuyahoga County, ss. I Certify that on the 22nd day of May A.D. 1854, I duly solemnized the Marriage Contract between the said ***Calvin Riley EDSON*** and ***Lovisa TILTON***. C.A. Slater, Minister. Marriage Record, Cuyahoga County, OH, vol. 35, p. 226. *Note: Rinda M. Edson married George H. Babcock on the same day by the same minister. Relative?*

EDSON, Riley, 48, farmer, b. NY, parents b. NY; ***Lovisa***, 48, wife, b. Canada, fr. b. NH, mo. b. NJ; ***Alwilda***, 25, dau., at home, b. Ohio; ***Eugene***, 21, son, fisherman, b. Ohio. 1880 FC OH CYDO, p. 99, lines 24-9, house 315. *Living between Theadore Lieberich and William Saddler.*

EDSON, Riley. Owned land. Acres: Improved - 11 tilled, including fallow and grass, 9 permanent meadow. Farm Values: Land and buildings - $3500, Machinery - $150, Live Stock - $225. Estimated value of all farm production: $250. Grass lands: acreage: 5 mown, 5 tons hay. 2 horses, 1 milch cow, 1 calf dropped, 1 cattle sold living. 100 pounds of butter made on the farm. 25 barnyard poultry on farm, 150 dozen eggs produced in 1879. Indian corn: 3 acres, 150 bushels ; oats: 2 acres, 150 bushels; potatoes: 1 acre, 80 bushels. Orchards - apple: 5 acres, 282 bearing trees, 750 bushels; peaches: 1 acre, 100 bearing trees. Total value of orchard products: $300. "Schedule 2. Production of Agriculture in Dover Township, Cuyahoga County, OH," enumerated June, 1880, p. 33.

Riley EDSON, 18 3/100 acres on Lake Rd. 1880 Map of Dover Twp.

EDSON, Calvin d. Sept. 4, 1880, Dover; married; 48 yrs. 6 mos. days; b. New York; Fisherman; fr. ***Calvin EDSON***, mo. ***Margaret EDSON***; disease: Typhoid Pneumonia; last residence: Dover. Record of Death, Cuyahoga County, Ohio, vol. 2, p. 82, recorded June 11, 1881.

EDSON-C. R., September 4, at his residence, North Dover, C.R. Edson, aged 48 years. Funeral Monday, at 2 o'clock.

Friends are invited. Leader, Sept 6, 1880; Cleveland Necrology File.

Riley EDSON; res. Dover; interred Sept 5, 1880; Lot 43, removed to Cld *(Cleveland)*. "List of Interments," Lakeside Cemetery, Bay Village, OH.

EDSON, Calvin Riley, married, 49, b. Cazenovia, *(Madison Co.),* NY, d. Dover, O., Sept 4, 1880, Typhoid Pneumonia, interment Aug 8, 1892, sec. No. 10, Lot 63, Grave 2. Lot owned by E. R. Edson and Allie S. Rice. Removed from Dover, Ohio. Buried in the same lot with ***Lovina E. EDSON, Alfred RICE*** and ***Sarah A. RICE***. Riverside Cemetery, Cleve., OH.

Parents of Calvin Riley Edson:

EDSON, Calvin, Males: 15-20 yr. - 1; 20-30 yrs. 2, 50-60 yrs. 1. Females: under 5 - 1; 5-10 yrs. - 3; 10-15 yrs. - 1; 15-20 yrs. 1, 40-50 yrs. - 1. 1830 FC NY Madison Co., Lenox Twp., p. 328. *This is the same area that Riley was born.*

EDSON, Calvin, 45, Peddler, b. N.Y.; ***Margaret***, 41, b. N.Y.; ***Sarah A***., 22, b. NY; ***John***, 20, Fisherman, b. NY; ***Margaret***, 10, b. NY, attending school; ***Lucy***, 17, b. NY; ***Maria***, 14, b. NY, attending school; ***Martha***, 12, b. Ohio, attending school. 1850 FC OH CY Brooklyn, p. 56, lines 12-19.

EDSON, Calvin, 63, Fish Dealer, value of real estate $2500, personal property $2000, b. New York; ***Margaret***, 61, Keeping House, b. New York; *LAPIERRE, Maggie*, 13, Attending School, b. Ohio; *ORTLI?, Anna*, 15, Domestic Servant, b. Ohio, parents of foreign birth. 1870 FC OH Cuyahoga Co., Cleveland, Ward 12, p. 108, dwelling 76, lines 25-28.

EDSON - Margaret. Thursday, February 20, at 6 o'clock a.m., Margaret Edson, wife of ***Calvin EDSON***, No. 1 Empress st. A kind neighbor, a devoted wife and loving mother, passed on to a higher sphere of usefulness, after thirty-seven years of painful illness here below, of cancer, aged 60 years and 10 months. She was a resident of the West Side for forty-two years. Funeral will take place at 11 o'clock Sunday morning, at Clark Mission Church, Lorain st. Cleveland Necrology File, Leader, Feb. 21, 1879.

EDSON - Calvin. Tuesday, June 2, 1885, at 2:30 a.m., at 913 Empress st., Calvin Edson, of inflammation of the lungs, aged 79 years and 8 months. He was a resident of the West Side for fifty years, well known and respected by all as a kind neighbor, a devoted father. He passed away without a struggle; his end was peace, and with a smile passed away to join his wife in Heaven. Funeral will take place Thursday at 2 o'clock, at Clark Mission Church, Lorain st. Friends invited. Cleveland Necrology File, June 3, 1885.

Wife of Calvin Riley, Lovina Tilton.

EDSON-Lovina E., aged 75 years. Funeral Dec 26, 2 o'clock, 3103 Clinton ave. N.W. Cleveland Necrology File, Dec 26, 1906.

EDSON, Lovina E., widow, 75, b. Canada, d. Cleve., Dec 24, 1906, bur. Feb 26, 1907, undertaker Sharer, late address 3103 Clinton St., Section 10, Lot 63, Grave 4. Riverside Cemetery, Cleveland, OH.

Children of Calvin Riley and Lovina Tilton:

The State of Ohio, Cuyahoga County, ss. I Certify that on the 1st day of Jany. 1888 ***Mr. Alfred RICE*** and ***Miss Alwilda S. EDSON*** were by me legally joined in marriage. Marriage Record, Cuyahoga County, OH, vol. 31, p. 267.

RICE: Sarah Alwilda (Allie) S., age 86, beloved wife of the late ***Alfred***, mother of ***Mrs. Lettie R. VOGT***, sister of ***E. R. EDSON***, grandmother of *Mrs. Catherine SPITLER* and *Mrs. Betty POORMAN* and great-grandmother of *Shirley Jean POORMAN*. Residence, 3138 W. 84. Friends may call at Klanke Funeral Parlor, 12629 Detroit ave., Lakewood. Services Saturday, June 14, at 3 p. m. Cleveland Necrology File, June 14 1941, reel 068.

RICE-Alfred Rice, on Tuesday, February 24, 8:30 p. m., aged 44 years. Funeral February 27, 2 p. m., from his late residence, No. 12 Irvington st. Friends invited. Burial private. Syracuse papers please copy. 1847-1891, age 44, Riverside Cemetery, Cleveland, Ohio. Cleveland Necrology File, Feb 26, 1891, reel 068.

The State of Ohio, Cuyahoga County, ss. I Certify that on the 1st day of December 1880 ***Mr. Eugene R. EDSON*** and ***Miss May Juliette OVIATT*** were by me legally joined in marriage. Lewis Burton, Rector of St. Mark's Church Marriage Record, Cuyahoga County, OH, vol. 23, p. 404.

May Juliet EDSON- On Tuesday evening, February 7, at 7 p.m. at the residence of her father, ***L. M. OVIATT***, 150 Huron st., Mrs. May Juliet Edson, aged 23 years, wife of ***Eugene R. EDSON***, of North Dover, Ohio. Funeral at residence, No. 150 Huron st., on Friday, the 10th inst., at 2:30 p.m. Cleveland Necrology File, Feb 9, 1882, reel 022.

The State of Ohio, Cuyahoga County, ss. I Certify that on the 1st day of December 1886 ***Mr. Eugene R. EDSON*** and ***Miss Anna WEST*** were by me legally joined in marriage. Marriage Record, Cuyahoga County, OH, vol. 30, p. 164.

EDSON: Eugene R., husband of the late ***Anna***; father of ***Clarence E., Carl R.*** and ***Mrs. Ruth BRAMAN***; grandfather and great-grandfather; residence, 17817 Lake Ave. Friends may call at William R. & Roy A. Daniels Funeral Home, 15800 Detroit Ave., where services will be held Friday, April 5, at 3 p. m. Cleveland Necrology File, Apr 3, 1946, reel 022.

EDSON: Anna Elisabeth, beloved wife of ***Eugene R. EDSON***, mother of ***Carl R.*** and ***Clarence E. EDSON***, entered into rest late Friday night. Services at the residence, 17817 Lake ave., Lakewood, Monday, Jan 13, at 2:30 p. m. Interment private. Riverside Cemetery. Please omit flowers. Cleveland Necrology File, Jan 13, 1936, reel 022.

Frederick R. Hahn

Frederick R. HAHN, 3; res. Dover; German; interred July 26, 1882; Lot 38. Body removed to Cleveland Aug 28th, 1884. "List of Interments," Lakeside Cemetery, Bay Village, OH. *(See Lot 38/39 for more information.)*

Frances Willard Jaycox

Francis W. JAYCOX; Avon, 1894, Lot 62. Removed to Lorain, Ohio. "List of Interments," Lakeside Cemetery, Bay Village, OH.

Frances Willard JAYCOX, was the daughter of ***James M. JAYCOX*** and ***Ida Lorinda HILLIARD*** *(See Lot 62 for more information.)*

David Deforest Osborn

David OSBORN, 49; res. Bay Village; interred Feb 10, 1902; Lot 1. "List of Interments," Lakeside Cemetery, Bay Village, OH.

David D. OSBORN was moved and interred at Evergreen Cemetery on Nov 20, 1945. Evergreen Cemetery, Westlake, OH. *(See Lot 1 for more information.)*

Cuvier H. Peters

Spellings varied throughout the records, the correct spelling is believed to be Cuvier Peters.

DOVER LAKE

Culver *(sp.)* ***PETERS***, a gas driller was fatally scalded last Friday morning by the boiler explosion near Cleveland. He was taken to St. Alex's hospital, Cleveland, but died in a few hours. His remains were brought to the home of his parents at West Dover. He was a bachelor, 39 years old, had lived at West Dover all his life. The funeral will occur at the Lake Methodist church Monday at one p.m. conducted by Rev. Endley, of Elyria, Interment at Lakeside cemetery, Bay Village. Elyria Republican and Telegram, Elyria, OH, Thursday, Dec 19, 1912, p. 8, col. 2.

Cuver PETERS, d. Dec 13, 1912, St. Alexis Hosp., 13th Ward, Cleveland, Cuyahoga Co.; Gross Scalds, Explosion of Boiler, accidental; male, b. West Dover, Nov 2, 1883, 39 yrs., occup Engineer; fr. ***Henry PETERS***, b. Hanover, Germany, mo. ***Elizabeth POWELL***, b. West Dover; informant Henry F. Peters, bur. West Dover, Dec 16, 1912, undertaker E.V. Raus & Son, 5040 Broadway. Ohio Certificate of Death, Division of Vital Statistics, 1912, certif. 64494. *Year of birth is incorrect, should be 1873.*

Cuver PETERS; res. Bay Village; interred Dec 14, 1912. Removed to Evergreen Cemetery, Westlake, OH. "List of Interments," Lakeside Cemetery, Bay Village, OH.

Nov 11, 1919, ***Cuvier PETERS*** (Removal from Bay to Dover, OH). Box $10, op & c grave at Bay $4.00, op & c grave at Dover $4.00, auto service $6.00. Pd B.J. Reed $4.00. PFH, Register of Funerals 1919-1922, p. 171.

PETERS, Cuvier *(baby)*, W. Dover, Ohio, d. W. Dover, Ohio, cause scalding, undertaker Clifford Pease, date of interment 11/11/19, Lot No. 35, Section 1, Lot Owner *Mrs. Henry PETERS. "baby" incorrect.* Evergreen Cemetery, Westlake, OH.

Parents of Cuvier Peters:

The State of Ohio, Cuyahoga County, ss. I Certify that on the 18th day of December 1872 ***Mr. Henry F. PETERS*** and ***Miss Elizabeth S. POWELL*** were, by me, legally joined in marriage. John Crocker White Marriage Record, Cuyahoga County, OH, vol. 18, p. 309

Henry F. was the son of Henry William (Wilhelm) Peters, 1859-1885, bur. St. Paul's Cemetery. Cuvier's aunt is Annie Peters, Lot 59. See additional information with Annie.

PETERS, Henry, 36, carpenter and joiner, b. Hanover, parents b. Hanover; ***Elisabeth***, 26, wife, b. Ohio, parents b. NY; ***Cuvier H.*** 6, son, b. Ohio; ***Charlie***, 4, son, b. Ohio; ***Elisabeth S.***, 9/12, b. Sep., Ohio. 1880 FC OH CYDO, p. 95 A.

PETERS, Henry F., head, b. Aug 1845, 55, b. Germany, parents b. Germany, Farmer, ***Elisabeth S.***, wife, b. Mar 1848, 52, married 28 yrs., 4 children born, 4 living, b. Ohio, parents b. New York; ***Cuvier H.***, son, b. Nov 1873, 26 yrs., farm laborer; ***C. Mable A.***, dau., b. Dec 1884, 15 yrs., b. Ohio, at school. 1900 FC OH CYDO p. 7B, lines 69-73.

Henry Frederick PETERS, d. April 6, 1916, 12:15 p.m., Bay, Cuyahoga Co., Ohio, Primary Hypertrophy and dilatation of heart - 5 yrs.; 70 yrs. 8 months 1 day; married; b. Germany; machinist; fr. ***Wm. F. PETERS***, b. Germany, mo. ***Marie PETERS***, b. Germany; bur. Dover, Ohio; undertaker James A. Pease and Son, Dover. Ohio Certificate of Death, Division of Vital Statistics, 1916, certif. 23385.

PETERS, Henry; W. Dover, 70; place of death W. Dover, Ohio; undertaker Jas. Pease, interment 4/29/1916; Lot 35, Section I, Lot owner *Mrs. Henry PETERS*. Evergreen Cemetery, Westlake, OH.

Elizabeth Sophia PETERS, d. Jan 12, 1924, 3421 Poe Ave., Cleveland, Cuy Co., Ohio, cause Chronic Myocarditis - 10 yrs., and Edema of Lungs - 3 days; widow of ***Henry PETERS***; hwf., b. Mch. 22, 1843, Bay Village, Ohio; fr. ***Unknown POWELL***, b. Do not know, mo. ***Elizabeth SADLER***, b. Do not know; 80 yrs. 9 mos. 20 days; Informant *Mrs. Elizabeth WILEY*, 3421 Poe. Ave; bur. Evergreen, Dover, O., undertaker C. Pease, Dover Center. Ohio Certificate of Death, Division of Vital Statistics, 1924, certif. 1175.

PETERS, Elizabeth; Dover, Ohio, 80 yrs., date of interment 1/14/1924, Lot 25, Section J., Lot owner Charles Asplin. Evergreen Cemetery, Westlake, OH.

Sibling of Cuvier Peters:

PETERS, Charles; Denver, Colorado, 37 yrs., b. W. Dover, Ohio; d. Bay Village, Ohio of Dropsy, undertaker Jas. Pease, internment 5/2/1914; Lot 30, Section B, lot owner *Thomas B. POWELL*. Evergreen Cemetery, Westlake, OH.

Rebecca Smith

The first death in Dover township is suppose to have been that of ***Mrs. Abner SMITH***, who was buried upon the Smith farm and afterwards removed to the cemetery on the lake shore, that being the first public burial ground laid out in the township. Crisfield Johnson, History of Cuyahoga County, Ohio, p. 442.

It is unclear if Rebecca Smith was ever buried at Lakeside. It is known that Rebecca Johnson Porter, who died in 1814, was buried at Lakeside when she died. The above source states that Mrs. Abner Smith, was moved to Lakeside, the cemetery on the lake shore, after being buried on their farm. She is presently in Evergreen Cemetery. Could the above be a mistake and instead of her being moved twice, she was moved from her farm to Evergreen Cemetery when it opened, which is near the family farm on Center Ridge Road.

Eunice SMITH, b. 30 Sep 1781; ***Rebecca SMITH***, b. 2 Apr 1784; ***Ozias SMITH***, b. 15 July 1786; ***Anne SMITH***, b. 30 Sep 1788; ***Ozias SMITH***, b. 3 Feb 1791; ***Sally SMITH***, b. 27 Mar 1793; ***Lucy SMITH***, b. 10 Mar 1795; ***Ruth SMITH***, b. 11 Mar 1797; ***Hiram SMITH***, b. 7 Sep 1799. Ashfield, Massachusetts Birth Records.

Abner and ***Rebecca SMITH*** were one of three families who brought the Church Charter of Dover Congregational Church with them from Hawley, Mass. When the church was built it was located in the geographical center of Dover Township. The Smith's had several children. The Smith's built the home on Center Ridge that would become the "1820 Gift Company." The home is thought to have been built before 1820 due to a stone that is located in the basement stating "181-," the last number is illegible. It was decided to go to the next decade in regard to dating the house since records are not available to authenticate the precise date. A son of Abner Smith built a home which still stands today to the west of the family house. The old sandstone home positioned near the street has been named "The Weston House." A more appropriate name may be the Smith-Weston House since the Smiths built it and the Westons lived in the home some fifteen years, moving into it after their home near Center Ridge and Bradley Roads burned. The Westons moved in 1872 to Hall Road, now Columbia Road, and lived there until 1995 when it was sold. Lollie Cooley, former owner of the 1820 Gift Company, and Doris Weston, Westlake.

1820 Gift Company, 27748 Center Ridge. Originally built and used as a home, this home was plaqued as Circa 1820, and was owned for many years by ***Abner SMITH*** and his heirs. It is believed that Abner Smith, like most of the early settlers in Dover Township, was a farmer. At one time, the 1820 was believed to have been the Peacock Tavern, one of several taverns that served as a stopping place on the stagecoach route that ran from Cleveland to Oberlin. A more recent owner of the 1820 even included the Westlake Board of Education. The home is a two-story frame with brick facing and the style is of the Federal Period. "The Home Place," 1986, p. 3. *The current occupant of the home is the orthodontist, Dr. Bruce Harwood.*

SMITH, Mrs. Abner; Maiden Name _____, ***Rebecca***; Yr. Came to Township 1812; Where From Hawley, Mass.; Last Res. Dover. Women of the Western Reserve Prior to 1840, Dover, p. 27.

Jonathan SMITH, Died December 14th, 1824, Age 62 years. *Stone next to Jonathan's of Abner's brother who traveled with them to Dover.* Tombstone inscription at Evergreen Cemetery, Westlake, OH. Read by Catherine Burke Flament.

In Memory of ***Rebecca***, Wife of ***Abner SMITH*** who died September 27, 1811 in her 52nd year. ***Abner SMITH***, 1759-1825, The Revolutionary War of 1776 *(tombstone of her husband)*. Tombstone inscriptions at Evergreen Cemetery, Westlake, OH. Read by Catherine Burke Flament.

Children of Abner and Rebecca Smith:

Ozias SMITH married ***Ruth FOX***, 14 Oct 1821, Cuyahoga County, OH. Marriage Record, Cuyahoga County, OH, vol. 1, p. 175.

There was no wedding in the township *(Rockport)* until January, 1814. ***Chester DEAN***, of Rockport, and ***Lucy***, daughter of ***Abner SMITH*** of Dover, were united by George Wallace, Esq., at the house of *Datus KELLEY*. Visitors to this wedding came from miles around upon ox-sleds, and the occasion, so says tradition, "was one of great merriment." Crisfield Johnson, History of Cuyahoga County, Ohio, Rockport, p. 503.

Lucy SMITH married ***Chester DEAN***, 9 Jan 1814, Cuyahoga County, OH. Marriage Record, Cuyahoga County, OH, vol. 1, p. 22.

Chester DEAN married ***Abigal TAYLOR***, 15 Mar 1818, Cuyahoga County, OH. Marriage Record, Cuyahoga County, OH, vol. 1, p. 91.

Ruth SMITH married ***Amos R. SPERRY***, 23 Aug 1815, Cuyahoga County, OH. Marriage Record, Cuyahoga County, OH, vol. 1, p. 49.

Mrs. Ransom SPERRY, maiden name ***Ruth SMITH***, came to township in 1815 from Ashfield, Mass., last residence: Dover. Women of the Western Reserve Prior to 1840, Dover, p. 27.

Amos SPERRY came with his family from Oneida, New York, in 1815 and bought lot 60 from *Lyman ROOT*, who moved to Ridgeville. Sperry opened a blacksmith shop and tavern in 1818, but he did not put up a tavern sign till 1824. Supposedly the customers at the blacksmith shop sufficiently advertised the tavern before that time. Believing as Washington said that "agriculture is the most healthful, most useful, most noble employment of man," he in a few years dropped the shop and the tavern and farmed until his death in 1848 at the age of eighty-seven. His son, ***Amos R. SPERRY***, who came a year before him, also lived out his life on the farm leaving a descendant, *Junia SPERRY*. Amos R. Sperry married the widow of *Junia BEACH* of Elyria. William R. Coates, A History of Cuyahoga County and the City of Cleveland, Dover, vol. 1, p. 144.

I hereby certify that on the twenty first day of May just past, I joined in the state of matrimony ***Hiram SMITH*** and ***Emeline PORTER*** both of Dover and County, who produced a certificate from the clerk of the court of Common pleas for said County. Given under my hand and seal this 3rd day of June A.D. 1826 Noah Crocker, Justice Peace. Marriage Record, Cuyahoga County, OH, vol. 2, p. 101.

Hiram SMITH married ***Jemima PORTER***, 10 Nov 1836, Cuyahoga County, Ohio. Marriage Record, Cuyahoga County, OH, vol. 3, p. 243.

SMITH, Mrs. Hiram; formerly ***Jemima PORTER*** who came from Ashfield, Mass., last residence Dover, O. Women of the Western Reserve Prior to 1840, Dover, p. 26.

Hiram SMITH, 52, Farmer, value of real estate: 3200, b. Mass.; ***Abner***, 21; ***Lucy***, 19; ***Asel***, 17; ***Hiram***, 9; ***Ozias***, 7; ***Amanda***, 5; all children b. Ohio; *David TAYLOR*, 30, laborer, b. Ohio. 1850 FC OH CYDO, p. 212A, family 3877.

Hiram SMITH**,* 60, farmer, value of real estate $10,000, value of personal estate $2000, b. M.; ***Elizabeth, 46, b. Mass.; ***Hiram***, 17, student; ***Ozias***, 16, farmer; ***Asel***, 25, farmer; ***Amanda***, 13; all children b. Ohio; *William SANDER?,* 20, farm laborer, b. Ohio. 1860 FC OH CYDO, p. 64, lines 11-17.

Hiram SMITH 1799-1868, buried Evergreen Cemetery, Westlake, OH. Cleveland Necrology File.

Dexter Tuttle

Dexter TUTTLE, 71; res. Dover Lake Shore; interred Feb 26, 1879; Lot 40 *(note year)*. "List of Interments," Lakeside Cemetery, Bay Village, OH. *See lot 40 for more information.*

Dexter TUTTLE, Evergreen Cemetery, Lot 31, interment in 1878. Evergreen Cemetery Records, Westlake, OH.

Addendum

We cherich the memory of absent friends ,
who were wont to mingle with us here.
May his many social virtues long be green in memory.

Sentiments offered by Wm. O. Cahoon of Elyria,
The Cahoon Pioneer Celebration, 1876

Addendum only has individuals interred at Lakeside Cemetery listed in the index.

Lot 1 *Owner: D.D. Osborn of Dover purchased March 1877 for $4.24* SL

David Deforest Osborn was originally buried in Lot 1 in 1902. Widening of Lake Road was considered by the city and the family was concerned that if this did come to fruition, what would happen to the remains? When his wife, Rose Mitchell Osborn, passed away, it was decided to have Rose buried at Evergreen Cemetery, Westlake. David was moved to Evergreen and his plot remained empty. Mabel Meddick Read, being a descendant, requested to have she and her husband buried in the vacant lot.

Lot 1 Read Marker

READ
TRUE ELLIS
OCT. 11, 1919 – SEPT. 13, 2003
VET WWII
MABEL PATRICIA MEDDICK
DEC. 12, 1922 – AUG. 22, 2016
DESCENDANT OF SELDEN OSBORN

Lot 1-1 True Ellis Read

True is the son of ***Fenton "Finney" R. READ***, b. 24 May 1878, West Salem, Wayne, Ohio; d. 26 Dec 1949, Mansfield, Richland, Ohio and married 4 Jan 1900, Medina, Ohio to ***Ruby Filora D. FREYMAN***, b. 27 Feb 1880, Homerville, Median, OH; d. 3 May 1964, Woodland Nursing Home, Mansfield, OH. Medina County, Ohio Marriage Records, 1900, p. 93, U.S. Find a Grave Index and News Journal, Mon, May 4, 1964, p. 3.

F.R. READ, head, renting home, male, 41, can read and write, b. Ohio, parents b. Ohio, res. 107 Congress Street, Drayman [driver of a dray, a low flat wagon without sides transporting goods], employed own account. ***Ruby READ***, wife, female, 39, married, can read and write, b. Ohio, parents b. Ohio, no occupation. ***Ralph W. READ***, son, 5, attended school, can read, b. Ohio. ***True E. READ***, daughter, female, 1/12 years, b. Ohio. 1920 FC Ohio, Wayne, Congress Township, West Salem Village, SD 15, ED 198, Sheet 4B.

Finn R. READ, head, owns home, value: $3,000, has radio set, not living on a farm, male, white, 52, married, first married at 21, able to read and write, b. Ohio, parents b. Ohio, Brick Layer of buildings, wage salary, employed, not a veteran. ***Ruby READ***, wife, female, white, 50, age at first marriage 19, b. Ohio, parents both b. Ohio, occup.: none. ***Ralph READ***, son, 15, single, attended school, able to read and write, b, Ohio. ***True READ***, son, 10, single, attended school, able to read and write, b. Ohio. 1930 FC OH, Wayne, Congress Township, West Salem District ED 85-15, SD 14, Sheet 1A.

Finn R. READ, head, male, 61, married, completed 2 years of high school, b. Ohio, residence in 1935: 272 Rowland Ave. Mansfield, same house, hours worked the week prior to census: 20, occup.: Captain of Guard, State Reformatory, weeks worked in 1935: 50, no other income sources. ***Ruby READ***, wife, female, 60, completed 2 years of high school, b. Ohio, housewife. ***Ralph W. READ***, son, 25, single, not attending school, completed 2 years of high school, b. Ohio, worked 40 hrs. week before census, Group Leader, Elect App., worked 52 weeks prior year. ***True Ellis READ***, 21, b. c1919, male, white, b. Ohio, single, son, 2nd year college, residence in 1935 Mansfield. 1940 FC OH, Richland, Mansfield, S.D. No.17, ED. 70-28, 10B.

True Ellis READ, b. Oct. 11, 1919, West Salem, Ohio; Residence: 276 Rowland Ave., Mansfield. Richland, Ohio; Phone Mid 2953, 21, Registration 16 Oct 1940; Employer: The Ohio State University, Height 5'10", Weight 150, Complexion Light, Hair Color Blonde; Eye Color Gray; Next of Kin: ***Mr. Finn R READ***, father, 276 Rowland Ave., Mansfield Registration Date 16 Oct 1940. U.S., World War II Draft Cards Young Men, 1940-1947. Serial Number 3403, Order Number 1473. https://www.fold3.com/image/681534300/read-true-ellis-page-1-us-wwii-draft-registration-cards-1940

True E. READ, Male, b. 11 Oct 1919, Enlistment Branch ARMY, Enlistment Date 25 Feb 1943, Discharge Date 10 Apr 1946. U.S. Department of Veterans Affairs BIRLS Death File, 1850-2010.

DRAFTEES WHO DEPARTED FROM BOARD 1 LISTED

Names Included in Contingent Leaving City Yesterday Announced.

One of the largest groups of selective service inductees to leave from the Board 1 district in Mansfield went to the Fort Benjamin Harrison, Ind., induction station Wednesday.

Included in the group of inductees were two registrants of boards outside the county who were inducted from Mansfield. On the same date, a number of Board 1 registrants who have moved out of the city since the registered were scheduled to go to the army from other cities. All of them are listed here:... ***True Ellis READ***, 276 Rowland avenue... News Journal, Mansfield, Ohio, Thursday, August 20, 1942, p. 5, col. 1.

READ, True E, head, 30, married, Ohio, working 40 hrs. week, assistant salesman wholesale drug, worker class: Private; ***Mabel P.***, wife, female, 27, married, b. Ohio. 1950 FC MI Wayne, Northville, 82-287.

True E (M Patricia) asst sls. mgr McKesson-Robbins h29025 Foote rd. (BV) Lakewood, Ohio, City Directory, 1958, p 612.

True Ellis READ, male, non-Hispanic, Married, 83, b. 11 Oct 1919, Ohio, res.: Other, Carteret, North Carolina, 28570; educ 4 years of college; d. 13 Sep 2003 Newport, Carteret, North Carolina, 28570; father's last name: Read. State Center for Health Statistics North Carolina 2003.

True Ellis READ, d. 13 Sep 2003, Nursing home, Newport, Carteret, North Carolina. North Carolina State Center for Health Statistics

True Ellis READ: Buried on 12.09.2009 Plot #1, (West side). City of Bay Village, OH, Lakeside Cemetery Records.

Ancestors of True Ellis Read

Read is identified in some early records as REED and READE.

I. ***John READ***, b. c1646, was admitted freeman by the General Assembly of Plymouth Colony at Newport, RI, May 2, 1666; d. 3 Jan 1721; m.1 to ***Hannah*** (***PEABODY***?, d. 12 Apr 1727). Issue: ***John READ***, b. c1668/9. ***Hannah READ***, b. c1670; m. *SHEARMAN*. ***Joseph READ***, b. c1687. Some of the descendants of John Read, Senior, of Newport, Rhode Island, and Freetown, Massachusetts: 1646-1924, 1924, p. 6-9. "Wescott History and Genealogy", p. 38.

II. ***John READ***, b. c1668/9, Freetown, Bristol, Massachusetts Colony, UK; d. 5 Jun 1750, Swansey, Bristol, MA; m.1 c1689/90 to ***Mary PEARCE*** of Tiverton, RI, (d. 6 May 1726, dau. of *John PEARCE* and *Mary TALLMAN*). Issue: ***Mary READ***, b. 19 Nov 1690; m. 22 Jan 1728 to *Samuel FOREMAN*. ***John READ***, b. 12 Jun 1694; m. 31 Oct 1719 to *Sarah BORDEN* (widow of Joseph Borden, Sr.). ***Thomas READ***, b. 9 May 1696; m. *Deborah*. ***Hannah READ*** (b. 12 Oct 1697; d. 17 Oct 1718). ***William READ***, b. 9 Sep 1699; m. 1727 to *Sarah SMITH*. ***Oliver READ***, b. 1701, d. 1777. ***Penelope READ***, b. 12 Oct 1703; m.1 3 Feb 1725 to *Stephen BORDEN* (d. 10 Aug 1738), m.2 3 Jul 1739 to *John BOWMAN*. ***Jonathan READ***, 23 Jan 1705; m. 28 Mar 1730 to *Hope DURFEE* of Tiverton. ***Joseph READ***, b. 5 Mar 1708; m. 5 Mar 1732/3 to *Grace PRAY*. ***Sarah READ***, b. 1 Feb 1709/10; d. 3 Jun 1728. ***Nathan READ***, b. 23 Feb 1711. ***Susannah READ***, b. 27 Sep 1715; m. 19 Feb 1736 to *Joseph BORDEN, Jr.* ***John*** m.2 29 Mar 1727, Tiverton, RI to *Susannah BROWNELL* of Portsmouth, RI, (b. 25 Jan 1676; d. 25 Aug 1735; dau. of *George BROWNELL* and *Susannah PEARCE*), No issue. m.3 3 Oct 1737 to *Sarah CHASE* of Swansea (b. c1677, widow of *Joseph CHASE*), No Issue. Pierce, Col. Frederick C. Pearce genealogy, being the record of the posterity of Richard Pearce, an early inhabitant of Portsmouth, in Rhode Island, Rockford, IL. 1888. p. 39. Read, George Henry. Some of the descendants of John Read, Senior, of Newport, Rhode Island, and Freetown, Massachusetts: 1646-1924. 1924, p. 6-13. Rhode Island, U.S., Vital Extracts, 1636-1899, Swansey Friends Record – Marriage, p.25- 28. "Wescott History and Genealogy", p. 38.

III. ***Oliver READ***, b. 14 Oct 1701, Freetown, Bristol, MA; d. 3 Jun 1777, Freetown, Bristol, MA; m. 28 Jan 1730, Portsmouth, RI to ***Martha DURFEE***, (b. 22 Feb 1702, Portsmouth, Newport, RI; d. 3 Jun 1777, Freetown, MA). Issue: ***Oliver READ*** b. 1734, d.1780. ***Jonathan READ***, b. 13 Nov 1737, Freetown; d. Freetown; m.1 24 Apr 1757, Freetown, MA to *Eunice WEAVER*; (dau. of *Benjamin WEAVER* and *Ruth SHEFFIELD*). m.2 *Hannah Cook SLOCUM*. ***Joseph READ***, b. 11 Dec 1732, Freetown, MA; d. 1791, Freetown; m. 10 Jan 1760 to *Mary KNOWLS* of Swansea (d. Oct 1816). ***Mary READ***, b. 31 Mar 1736, Freetown, MA; d. 12 Mar 1806, Pittstown, Rensselaer, NY; bur. Slade Cemetery, Pittstown; m. 9 Oct 1755 to *Philip SLADE* (son of *Edward SLADE* and *Phebe CHASE*; b. 1732; d. 31 Jul 1803). ***Nathan READ***, b. 16 Jun 1742, Freetown; m. 11 May 1775 to *Phebe TERRY* of Freetown. ***Waite READ*** [female], b. 6 Dec 1739; m. 9 Jan 1761, Freetown, MA to *Samuel WEAVER* (son of *Benjamin WEAVER* and *Ruth SHEFFIELD*, b. 1732). ***Benjamin READ***, b. 28 Mar 1744, Freetown; m. 27 Mar 1766 *Elizabeth DODSON*. ***Gideon READ***, b. 5 Feb 1746, Freetown; d. bef Jun 1777; m. *Mercy WINSLOW*. Freetown Records, 1836-1871, Book 5, p. 217. Geneanet Community Tree Index. Rhode Island Vital Extracts, 1636-1899, Portsmouth Marriages, p.19, 35. SAR Membership Applications 1889-1970, #43075. Wescott History and Genealogy, p. 38.

IV. ***Oliver READ,*** b. 21 Aug 1734, Freetown, Bristol, MA Bay; Will signed 29 Sep 1814, Freetown. Served as a lieutenant in Captain Durfee's company, MA militia, Rev. War; m.1 14 Feb 1754 to ***Patience BRAYTON*** (b. 1 May 1740, Swansea, Bristol, MA; d. 1794, Swansea, MA; dau. of *Baulston BRAYTON* and *Margaret LEE*). Issue: ***Isaac READ*** b. 1754; d. 1844. ***Nancy "Anna" READ***, b. 7 Sep 1756, Freetown, Freetown, MA; m.1 *Thomas FREELOVE*; m.2 23 Jun 1824 to *George HATHAWAY*. Oliver m.2 16 Jul 1759 to ***Hannah COLLINS***. Issue: ***Mary READ***, b. 20 Mar 1761, Freetown, MA; m. 8 Dec 1789 to *Thos. COLLINS*. ***Job READ***, b. 24 Oct 1763, Freemont, MA; m. 26 Oct 1797 to *Sylvia CLEAVELAND*. ***Content (Constant) READ***, b. 23 Jul 1765, Freetown, MA; m.1 *Joseph CLEVELAND*, m.2 *David BUTTS*, m.3 *LATHROP* additional record lists 19 Jul 1793 to *Joseph DOTEE (DOTTA)*. ***Patience READ***, b. 9 Aug 1767, Freetown, MA; m. 23 Nov 1789 to *Thomas KNIGHT* of Tiverton. ***Gideon READ***, b. 2 Mar 1770, Freetown, MA; m. 16 Apr 1789 to

Margaret (Peggy) HILTON. ***Martha READ***, b. 21 Jun 1772, Freetown, MA; m. 18 Mar 1799 to *Elisha HATHAWAY.* ***Oliver READ***, b. 20 Apr 1778, Freetown, MA; m. *Sarah.* ***Brayton READ***, b. 19 Dec 1780, Freetown, MA; d. 1849; m. 20 Nov 1799 to *Elisha HATHAWAY.* ***Mahaly REED*** [Listed in Oliver's will as his 6th daughter] Descendants of John Read, Senior, p. 26. DAR Lineage Book of Charter Members, Vol. 083, p. 218, 82569. Massachusetts, U.S., Town and Vital Records, Freetown, 1795-1847, Number 3, p. 123. Massachusetts, U.S., Wills and Probate Records, 1635-1991, Massachusetts County, District and Probate Courts, Bristol Probates, Vol 49-50, 1814-1815, pp. 311-312, film pp.509-510. Oliver Read. Wescott History and Genealogy, p. 38.

V. ***Isaac READ***, b. 26 Dec 1754, Freetown, Bristol, Massachusetts Bay, MA; d. 11 Apr 1844, Sykes Hollow Rd., N. Rupert, Bennington, VT; Rev. War drummer, bricklayer, m. 25 Sep 1781, Baptist Church, Freetown, Bristol, MA *to* ***Diadama Shearman GRAY*** dau. of *Matthew GRAY* and *Sarah BARBER*; b. 21 Jan 1765, Freetown, MA; d. c7 Sep 1844, Rupert, Bennington, VT. Issue: ***David READ***, b. 16 Sep 1782, Freetown. ***Abigail READ***, 30 Nov 1784, Freetown. ***Isaac READ***, b. 7 Jan 1787, Freetown. ***Susannah READ***, b. 14 Feb 1789, Freetown. ***James READ***, b. 12 Apr 1791, Freetown; m. 25 Aug 1796 to *Rebeccah BARTON* of Warren, RI. ***Elijah READ***, b. 5 Oct 1793, Freetown. ***Patience READ***, b. 4 Apr 1795, Freetown. ***Benjamin Durfee (Durfey) READ***, b. 6 Aug 1799, Pawlet, Rutland, VT; d. 24 Oct 1885, Dorset Bennington, VT; m. 1821 to *Submit HOLTON* (1803; d. 3 Nov 1868, Dorset, VT). ***Solomon D. READ***, b. 15 May 1801, Pawlet, Rutland, VT; d. 2 May 1888, Rupert, Bennington, VT. ***Elizabeth READ***, b. 1806, VT. ***Nelson READ***, b. 16 Oct 1808, Pawlet, VT; d. 1878; m. 1832, *Ruth HARRINGTON* (1810-1880). Geneanet Community Tree Index. Massachusetts, U.S., Town and Vital Records, Freetown, 1795-1847, Number 3, p. 123. Massachusetts, U.S. Town and Vital Records, Freetown Birth, Marriages and Deaths Index, 1686-1844, Book 16, p. 55 and 125. Massachusetts, U.S. Town and Vital Records, Freetown Birth, Marriages and Deaths Index, Records 1795-1847, Book 3. Read, George H. Some of the descendants of John Read, Senior, of Newport, Rhode Island, and Freetown, Massachusetts: 1646-1924. unknown: unknown, 1924. U.S., Federal Census Mortality Schedules, 1850-1885, Rutland, VT, No. 1, ED 183, line 21. U.S., Revolutionary War Pensioners, 1801-1815, 1818-1872, National Archives and Records Administration, Vermont, p. 89. Wescott History and Genealogy, p. 38.

VII. ***Nelson READ***, b. 16 Oct 1808, Pawlet, VT; d. 13 Jul 1878; bur. West Salem Cemetery, West Salem, Wayne, OH; m. ***Ruth HARRINGTON***, dau. of *Gideon HARRINGTON* and *Aurilla PHELPS*; b. 1810, VT; d. after 1870. Issue: ***Aurilla READ***, b. 18 Sep 1830, VT; d. 25 Aug 1907, Auburn, DeKalb, IN; bur. Woodlawn Cemetery, Auburn, IN; m. *William Jasper WILCOX* (b. 1825, OH; d. 6 Jun 1903, Auburn, DeKalb, IN). ***Jane READ***, b. 11 Sep 1832, VT; d. 13 Jun 1913, Martinsville, Clark, IL; bur. Baird Cemetery, Martinsville, Clark, IL; m. *Jeremiah HILLS* (b. 29 May 1829, Portage Co.; d. 20 Jan 1915, Neadmore, Clark, IL). ***Nelson G. READ***, b. 1839; d. 1891; bur. West Salem Cemetery; m. *Isabella SPENCER* (b. 1840, d. 1925). ***Washington George READ***, 1842-1932. Find-a-Grave, 1600s-Current. Harrington, Hills, Read and Wilcox. US Federal Census, Ohio 1850-1870.

VIII. ***Washington George (George W.) READ***, b. 14 Feb 1842, Medina Co., OH; private during the Civil War; d. 17 Jul 1932, West Salem, Wayne, OH; bur. Woodlawn Cemetery, Lodi, Median, OH; m.1 26 Oct 1865, Medina, OH to ***Caroline J. ROGERS***. Issue: ***Orlin A./Orliss/Rollin L. READ***, b. 29 Nov 1867, Ohio; m.5 June 1888, Hudson, MI to *Mary PETIT*. Washington m.2 3 Aug 1872, Medina, OH to ***Hannah WINTER***, (dau. of *William WINTER* and *Ann FREEMAN*; b. Aug 1849, OH; d. 29 Apr 1925, West Salem, OH; bur. Woodlawn Cemetery, Lodi, OH). Issue: ***Vernon Sinclair READ***, b. 10 Aug 1873; d. 6 Jul 1926, West Salem, Wayne, OH; bur. Lodi, Medina, OH. ***Fenton READ***, 1878-1949. Ohio County Marriage Records 1774-1993. Ohio, U.S., Rutherford B. Hayes Presidential Center Obituary Index, 1810s-2016. Ohio, U.S., Births and Christenings Index, 1774-1973. U.S. Federal Census Records, Ohio 1860-1930. U.S. Find-a-Grave, Read.

IX. ***Fenton "Finney" R. READ***, b. 24 May 1878, West Salem, Ohio; d. 1949; bur. Homer Reformed Cemetery, Homerville, Medina, Ohio; m. 4 Jan 1900, Medina, OH to ***Ruby Filora FREYMAN*** (dau. of *Elias FREYMAN* b. 2 Mar 1864, Homerville, OH; d. 13 Sep 1929, Lodi, Median, OH; m. 10 Dec 1865, Wayne Co., OH to *Sarah Jane KIME* (Ruby b. 27 Feb 1880, Medina; d. 3 May 1864, Mansfield, OH)). Children: ***Ralph William READ***, b. 12 Jun 1914, West Salem, Wayne, OH; d. 15 Jul 1980, Mansfield, OH; bur. Homer Reformed Cemetery, Homerville, Medina, Ohio; m. 27 Jul 1940, Covington, KY to *Margaret KOHUT* (dau. of *John KOHUT* and *Mary Victoria GASPER*, b. 11 Oct 1915, West Salem, Summit Co., OH; d. 21 Jun 2003, Paducah, KY). ***True Ellis READ***, b.1878, d. 1964. Marriage Index; WWWII draft cards 1940-1947. News Journal, Mansfield, OH, Thursday, July 17, 1980, p. 34, col. 4. U.S. Find-a-Grave Index.

X. ***True Ellis READ***, b.24 May 1878; d. 3 May 1964.

Lot 1-2 Mabel Patricia Meddick Read

MEDDICK, Warren A., head, owns home, value: 10000, radio, not a farm, 40, married, age at first marriage: 23, able to read and write, b. Michigan, parents b. Michigan, occup.: Sales Manager, Manuf. Road Equip., wage, not veteran; ***Mabel J.***, wife, 38, age at first marriage 23, able to read and write, b. Ohio, father b. Ohio, mother b. England, occup. none; ***Jack W.***, son, male, 13, b. Ohio, father b. Ohio, occup. none; ***Mabel P.***, daughter, female, 7, single, attending school, b. Ohio, occup. none; Osborn, Rose, mother-in-law, female, 71, widow, able to read and write, b. Eng., parents b. England, speaks Eng., Immigration year 1859, not a naturalized citizen, occup. none. 1930 FC OH CUY Bay, Sheet 16B.

MEDDICK, Warren A., head, 50, married, white, highest grade completed: high school, 4th year, b. Missouri, residence since 1935 [for entire family]: same home, employed for pay, hours worked week before census: 42, salesman at electric trucks, weeks worked in

1939: 52, income: 4800, income other sources: yes; ***Mabel J.***, wife, 48, married, highest grade completed: high school, 4th year, b. Ohio, not employed for pay; ***John W.***, son, 23, single, attended school or college: college 4 year, b. Ohio, employer for pay, hours worked week prior to census: 30, office clerk dept. store; ***Mabel P.***, daughter, 17 single, highest grade completed: high school, 3rd yr., b. Ohio; ***OSBORN, Rose***, mother in law, 81, widowed, highest grade completed: elementary 8th grade, b. England, naturalized citizen, employment: other. 29059 Lake Rd, Bay Village. 1940 FC OH CUY Bay, Sheet 41A.

Patsy "Pat" MEDDICK, Friendship Club 2-3-4; President, 4; Annual Staff, 4; Glee Club 1-2-3-4; Play, 3-4. 1940 Bay High School, Bay Blue Book, p. 16.

Mabel Patricia MEDDICK, Class of 1944, Westminster Hall, Ohio State University.

Meddick-Read Wedding Details are Revealed

Of interest to social circles here is the announcement of the wedding of ***Miss Patricia MEDDICK,*** and ***True Ellis READ*** March 1. The bride is the daughter of Mr. and ***Mrs. Warren MEDDICK,*** of Bay Village and the bridegroom is the son of Mr. and Mrs. F.R. Read of this city.

The couple were married in the Bay Methodist church by Rev. Thurman F. Alexander, officiating.

The bride was attended by Mrs. Leo W. Usher and ***Ralph W. Read*** was his brother's best man.

Ushers for the ceremony were Major Marcks of Bay Village and Paul R. Cropper of Mansfield.

The former ***Miss Meddick*** is a graduate of Ohio State university where she was affiliated with Kappa Kappa Gamma sorority.

Mr. READ attended Ohio State university prior to serving two and a half years in the South Pacific. The couple will reside in Columbus where he will continue his studies. Mansfield News-Journal, Mansfield, Ohio, Tuesday, May 07, 1946, p. 6, col.3.

Mabel Patricia READ, 93, b. 12 Dec. 1922, Bay Village; d. 22 Aug 2016, New Jersey. New Jersey, U.S. Death Index, State File Number: 20160045470, 2001-2017. https://www.newjerseydeathindex.com/

Mabel Patricia READ d.12 Dec 1922, burial Lakeside Cemetery, Bay Village, Cuyahoga County, Ohio https://www.findagrave.com/memorial/61596221/mabel_patricia-read.

Mabel Patricia Meddick READ: Buried on 11.04.2016. Plot #1 (East side, closer to path). City of Bay Village, OH, Lakeside Cemetery Records.

Ancestors of Mabel Patricia Meddick Read:

I. ***Peter MEDDICK***, b. 1780 Readington, Hunterdon, NJ; d. 1853 Lodi, Seneca, NY; m. ***Sarah BIRD***, b. 1779, d. 1850. *[Information was unable to be documented, but a daughter, Eliza Meddick Covert (1811-1877), wife of Freeman Covert, lived on land three houses from Frederick, possibly her brother. Her parental information has been verified.]* 1850 United States Federal Census, New York, Seneca, Lodi, p. 26. Michigan, U.S., Deaths and Burials Index, 1867-1995.

II. ***Frederick MEDDICK***, b. 12 Feb 1816, NJ; d. Feb 1893; bur. Oakwood Cemetery, Adrian, Lenawee, MI with both wives. m1. ***Jane KELLY***, (dau. of *Joseph C. KELLY* and *Sarah SMITH*; b. 14 Oct 1817, Seneca Cty., NY; d. 10 Jan 1874). Issue: ***Joseph Warren MEDDICK***, b. 1843, Lodi, Seneca, NY; d. 25 Jun 1911, Buffalo, NY; m. 5 Feb 1874, Geneva, NY to *Sophia M. CLAPP* (dau. of *Clark R. CLAPP* and *Eleanor KNOWLES*; b. 1849, NY; d. 1925, NY). ***Alice Mariah MEDDICK***, b. 14 Jun 1846, Ovid, Seneca, NY; d. 5 Aug 1889, Emmett, MI; bur. Brookside Cemetery, Battle Creek, MI; m. 24 Mar 1869, Adrian, Lenawee, MI to *Thomas Jefferson KENNEDY* (b. 1846, MI; d. 1922, Jackson, MI). ***Clarence S. MEDDICK***, b. Jun 1850, Lodi, Senecca, NY; d. btw 1900-1920; m. 1 Mar 1876, Lucas, OH to *Laura Bennett NORTON* (dau. of *Chester W. NORTON* and *Sophia R. BLOOMFIELD*; b. 5 Sep 1851, Perrysburg, OH; d. 5 Sep 1926, Lucas, OH). ***Charles V. MEDDICK***, b. 1852, d. 21 Dec 1890; bur. Lake Cemetery, Lamar Hts, Barton, MO. *Frederick* m2. 10 Sep 1879 to *Mary Jane YOUNG* (dau. of *William YOUNG* and *Jane*; b. 1840, Monroe Co., NY; d. 8 May 1894, Adrian, Lenawee, MI). Democrat and Chronicle, Tue, Jun 27, 1911, p 10. Kelly, Lloyd E. "The Charles Kelly Family, 1769-1963," manuscript, p. 6. Michigan, U.S., Marriage Records, 1867-1952, Cty. of Lenawee. New York, U.S., Episcopal Diocese of Rochester Church Records, 1800-1970. Reformed Dutch Church of Farmerville, Members, Minutes, Marriages, Baptisms, Deaths, 1830-1850. 1850 United States Federal Census, Lodi, Seneca, NY, p. 28. 1850-1880 Ohio US Federal Census. 1860 United States Federal Census, MI, Lenawee, Adrian, p. 13, lines 34-39. U.S., Find a Grave Index.

III. ***Charles V. MEDDICK***, b. 1852, New York; d. 21 Dec 1890; bur. Lake Cemetery, Lamar Heights, Barton, MO; m. 15 Apr 1885, Adrian, Lenawee, MI to *Cora E KNIGHT* (b. Apr 1861, Michigan; d. Jun 1925, Lakewood, OH; m2 1902 *Herbert C. BRAGG*). Issue: *Warren Andrew MEDDICK*, b. 1888, d. 1968. Find-a-Grave, Bragg and Meddick. Michigan, U.S., Marriage Records, 1867-1952. The Plain Dealer, 3 Jun 1925, p. 21. 1860 United States Federal Census, MI, Lenawee, Adrian, p. 13, lines 34-39.

IV. ***Warren Andrew MEDDICK***, b. 27 Jun 1888, Lamar, Missouri; d. 11 Dec 1968, Detroit, MI; m. 15 Apr 1914 to ***Mabel Irene OSBORN*** (dau. of *David Deforest OSBORN* and *Rose MITCHELL*, b. May 1891, Bay Village, OH; d. 11 Mar 1969, Bay Village, OH). Issue: ***John Warren MEDDICK,*** b. 5 Jul 1916, Bay Village; d. 5 May 2002, Newport, NC; m. 16 Aug 1941 to *Mary Jane BRYAN* (dau. of *Earl James BRYAN* and *Blanche Marie HORN*, b. 14 Dec 1917, East Cleveland, OH; d. 5 Dec 2008, New Haven, CT). ***Mabel Patricia MEDDICK***, b. 1922, d. 2016. 1930-1950 United States Federal Census, Ohio, Cuyahoga, Bay Village, District 0534. Connecticut Death Index, 1949-2012, Hartford, CT. Ohio, U.S., County Marriage Records, 1774-1993. The Plain Dealer, Mon, Dec 16, 1968, p. 46, cols 7-8. World War II Draft Registration Cards, 1942.

Lot 14 *Owner: Elizabeth R. Martin of Bay Village purchased May 13, 2011 for $1,000*

MOTION to approve the creation of Sublot 14-C in Lakeside Cemetery for purchase by T. Richard and Betsy Martin. This sublot has been reviewed in connection with the publication Retracing Footsteps of Lakeside Cemetery and upon the physical, on-site review of an available lot to be created at Lakeside Cemetery. The use would be for ashes only due to the available space and location…Mr. Ebert stated that based on the fact of all the years of service that

Mr. T. Richard Martin contributed to the City of Bay Village it would be a good gesture. The fee will be determined at the rate scale, or slightly higher, for burial. Motion carried 7-0. The City of Bay Village, Cahoon Memorial Park Trustees, Minute of Meeting held July 12. 2010, p. 1.

Lot 14 Martin Marker

MARTIN

T. RICHARD	ELIZABETH R.
MAR 5, 1930	JUNE 4, 1930
SEPT. 20, 2011	MAY 30, 2016

Korean War grave marker to the lower left of the stone.

Lot 14C Treagh Richard "Dick" Martin

MARTIN, Tony J., renting, residence: 3411 W. 126th St., Cleveland, monthly rent 40, 29, married, age at first marriage 27, able to read and write, b. Norway, parents b. Norway, language at home: Norwegian, year immigrated: 1923, naturalized, occup.: Machinist, Industry: Machine Shop, not at work yesterday, line number of unemployment schedule: Line 2-18, not a veteran. ***Mabel F. MARTIN***, wife, 29, year at first marriage 27, able to read and write, b. Wisconsin, father and mother b. Sweden, occup: none; ***Treag MARTIN***, son, male, age 1/12, b. Ohio. 1930 FC OH CUY Cleveland City, Ward 33, Block 158, Sheet ED18-283, SD 6, lines 57-59.

MARTIN, Thomas, res: 308 Elsienna Avenue, head, 39, married, highest grade completed: 8th, b. Norway, naturalized citizen, residence in 1935: same place, employed for pay: yes, hours worked in week prior to census: 35, industry: painting contractor own, private work, weeks worked in 1939: 36, income other sources: yes; ***Mabel MARTIN***, wife, 39, completed 1 yr. high school, b. Wisconsin, home housework; ***Richard MARTIN***, son, 10, attended school, elementary school 3rd grade, b. Ohio; ***Jean C.***, daughter, age 7, attended school, grade 1, b. Ohio. 1940 FC OH CUY, Cleveland, Ward 33, Block Nos. 48, SD No. 22, ED No. 92-884, pp. 15AB.

Richard J. MILLER, housefellow of rooming house. ***T. Richard MARTIN*** one of 17 roomers, 106 N. Prospect, 20 yrs. old, b. OH, occup. other, worked last week: 8 hrs., bus boy, cafeteria, industry: State University 1950 FC WI Dane, Madison, Sigma Phi Fraternity, Large Rooming House, ED 72-53, Line 19.

Bay Village

T. Richard MARTIN who has been a member of the Bay Village Council since 1967, was elected president of the council last night, beating *Charles P. AKER* and *William A. CLARK*... Cleveland Plain Dealer, November 3, 1971, p. 11.

T. Richard Martin 2008 Dedication

T. Richard MARTIN was born in Cleveland, Ohio and graduated from John Marshall High School where he excelled in track. He attended the University of Wisconsin, graduated from their School of Commerce, and was inducted into the Iron Cross Society Honorary.

After college, Dick married ***Betsy***, a fellow University of Wisconsin graduate. They honeymooned while Dick served stateside in the Army in the Military Police. They moved to Bay Village in the late 1950's to the house they currently call home. They welcomed daughter, ***Susan*** and son, ***Ross***.

Dick Martin was appointed to Bay Village City Council in April 1967 to replace *Donald GRESHAM*, who passed away in March 1967. Dick was re-elected thereafter for two-year terms beginning January 1, 1968 through January 1, 1990. He was elected to the office of President of Council for the term beginning January 1, 1972 and every four years thereafter.

In the mid 1990's, City officials and citizens alike realized the need for a private foundation in Bay Village. With help from then *Mayor Tom JELEPIS* and Law Director, *Gary EBERT*, the charter for The Village Foundation was written. In 1995, *Dick Martin, Wayne REESE and Tom Jelepis* signed the Articles of Incorporation. The Founding Trustees of The Village Foundation exists to provide support for projects and programs fostering Bay Village's social, historical, cultural and educational heritage.

The mission of The Village Foundation is to preserve the quality of life in Bay Village, Ohio by using the talents and resources of private citizens and non-government funding. The Village Foundation exists to provide support for projects and programs fostering Bay Village's social, historical, cultural and educational heritage.

Dick is the leading contributor to The Village Foundation with many of his donations made in honor and in memory of outstanding citizens who dedicated much of their life in the service of the City of Bay Village.

T. Richard Martin has had an enormous influence on the Bay Village we know today, demonstrating a love of community, willingness to serve and dedication to the future that is rarely seen. We will all reap the benefits of his vision for years to come. Bay Village Foundation Bronze Memorial Plaques, Bay Village Foundation, Cahoon Memorial Bridge, Bay Village, Ohio, 2008 Dedication.

MARTIN T. "Dick" RICHARD MARTIN, age 81, passed away peacefully on Tuesday, Sept. 20th. Devoted husband, of 59 years, to ***Betsy*** (nee ***ROSS***). Loving father of ***Susan MARTIN*** (*Larry FOURNIER*) and ***Ross MARTIN*** (*PJ*). Dear grandfather of ***Andrew, Grace, Ellie and Katherine***. Brother of ***Jean Kniess***. Dick served on Bay Village City Council for 38 years, City Council President for 32 years. Retired financial advisor for several investment firms. Memorial Services Monday, Oct. 10th, at 12 p.m., at Bay Presbyterian Church, 25415 Lake Rd., with a reception to follow. Internment private. The family suggest donations to University of Wisconsin Foundation, 1848 University Ave., Madison, WI 53726-4090, The Bay Village Foundation, P.O. Box 14022, Bay Village, OH 44140 or a charity of your choice. A special note of thanks to the staff at Brighton Gardens. Arrangements by DONLON FUNERAL HOME 216-251-7300. The Plain Dealer, September 22, 2011, p. 5, col.1.

Internment at Lakeside Cemetery, 10/10/11. Deed for Cemetery Lot. Lot No. 14 KNOW ALL MEN BY THESE PRESENTS: That we, the Mayor and Council of the City of Bay Village in the County of Cuyahoga and State of Oho...to them paid by ***ELIZABETH R. MARTIN*** and her heirs, forever, the following named lot of ground in LAKESIDE Cemetery, to wit: Lot No. 14 in Square 84 2/10 as described upon the plat of said Cemetery, on file in the office of the Clerk of said City.

AND TO HOLD the same to the said ELIZABETH R. MARTIN and her heirs, to be used for the purposes of burial for ashes only, subject to the laws of this State regarding Cemeteries...We have set our hands and seals on this the 13th day of May A.D. 2011. Deborah L. Sutherland, Mayor of the City of Bay Village in Cuyahoga County, State of Ohio...Gary A Ebert, Atty. Deed for Cemetery Lot. City of Bay Village.

T. Richard MARTIN: Buried on 10.10.2011, Plot# 14-C. City of Bay Village, OH, Lakeside Cemetery Records.

Parents of Treagh Richard "Dick" Martin:

Trygve MARTIN (Gustavsen): Trygve Gustavsen, Ufift (single), b. 1901, Drammen, Last Known Residence: Fana, Emigration Date 16 Jun at Bergen, Norge, Emigration Destination: Amk, Cleveland Ohio Melvankel. Norway Emigration Records 1867-1960, Bergen Politidistrikt, 1922-1923, line 1458.

Lot 14 Elizabeth Roseberry Ross Martin

ROSS-MARTIN

Also in the social news is the engagement of ***Miss Elizabeth Roseberry ROSS*** to ***Treagh Richard MARTIN***, son of ***Mr.*** and ***Mrs. Thomas MARTIN***, Cleveland, O.

No date has been set for the wedding of the daughter of ***Mr.*** and ***Mrs. Frederick Allan ROSS***, W. Webster avenue, and ***Mr. MARTIN***. Green Bay Press-Gazette, Fri, June 13, 1952, p. 6, cols. 2-3.

ROSS, Fred A., head, 41, married, completed 4 years high school, b. New York, hours worked week prior to census 44 hrs., Vice President Printing Shop, weeks worked in 1939: 52, income $5,000+; ***Helen R.***, wife, 42, completed 4 years high school, b. New Jersey; Allan M., son, 11, b. Ohio; ***Elizabeth R.***, daughter, 9, b. Ohio; Turnley, ***Elizabeth***, maid, negro, 40, widow, b. Tennessee, employed 48 weeks, private home, income $624. Residence in 1935, same house: 13857 Lake Road, Lakewood, Ohio. 1940 FC OH CUY, Lakewood City, S.D.No. 22, E.D.No. 18-19, sheet 8A.

Miss Elizabeth Ross Weds Treagh Martin Saturday

Miss ***Elizabeth R. ROSS*** and ***Treagh Richard MARTIN*** were married at 3 o'clock Saturday afternoon in Union Congregational church. The *Rev. John W. CLAXTON* returned to Green Bay to perform the ceremony for the daughter of ***Mr. and Mrs. Frederick Allan ROSS***, route 6, and the son of the ***Thomas MARTINS***, Cleveland, Ohio.

Miss Ross chose a full-length gown of Chantilly lace, fashioned from princess lines and finished in a Cathedral train. The bodice was accented with a Peter Pan collar. The bride's veil of imported pure silk illusion was fingertip in length, and caught to a Juliet cap of matching lace. As her father gave her in marriage, Miss Ross was carrying white roses and ivy.

As Matron of Honor

The matron of honor, *Mrs. Robert H. MEIER*, and the *Misses Genevieve KILLINS* and *Virginia BUSH*, were identically gowned in Nile green nylon net and satin. Their strapless gowns were worn with Empire waist jackets of matching satin. The yellow and rust colored mums in their hair were repeated in cascade bouquets.

Best man at the ceremony was *Jack Randall GAY*. Ushers were *Michael R. TORPHY, John S. BAUMAN, William R. KUHNS*, ***Allan M. ROSS***, brother of the bride, and *James E. GRANT.*

Evan B. STEVENS, uncle of the bride, was at the organ during the ceremony, which was followed by a reception in Pilgrim hall. As she received guests with her daughter, Mrs. Ross was wearing a slate blue taffeta dress with grey accessories. Mrs. Martin was in navy blue lace. Both wore corsages of yellow roses and mums. Expected were *Mr. and Mrs. E.B. STEVENS*, Plainfield, N.J., *Mr. and Mrs. Judson S. CROSS*, Sycamore, Ill.; and *Mrs. Robert MEIER*, Minneapolis, Minn.

Honeymooning In Chicago

The Martins are now honeymooning in Chicago, and will be at home at 751 Jennifer street, Madison. Mrs. Martin attended Carleton college for two years and is a graduate of the University of Wisconsin, where she was a member of Delta Gamma sorority. Her husband, a law student at the University, is a member of Sigma Phi fraternity.

The rehearsal dinner was held at the Beaumont hotel. Green Bay Press-Gazette, Mon. Sep 08, 1952, p. 14, cols. 1-2.

Elizabeth Ross Martin 2012 Dedication

Elizabeth ROSS MARTIN (Betsy) was born in Cleveland in 1930. Her family moved to Lakewood when she was three years old, and remained there until 1943. At that time, her family moved to Green Bay, Wisconsin, where she graduated from high school. Betsy then attended Carleton College in Minnesota for two years before transferring to the University of Wisconsin-Madison where she received her Bachelor of Business Administration from the School of Commerce. While at the University of

Wisconsin, Betsy met her future husband, ***T. Richard MARTIN (Dick)***. They were married in 1952. They spent two years at Fort Knox, Kentucky while Dick served in the army during the Korean War. After military service, Dick and Betsy moved back to the area. They spent two years in Rocky River before moving to Bay Village in 1957. Betsy worked at National City Bank as a credit analyst for two years before their daughter, Susan was born. Susan was followed by, a son, Ross three years later. Betsy then devoted her time to her family and she became involved in community projects and activities. During her children's school years, she was very active in the P.T.A. She participated in the League of Women Voters, P.E.O. and their church. She currently serves as a volunteer at the Lake Erie Nature and Science Center and has served as a volunteer for the Juvenile Diabetes Research Association for many years. Betsy has lived in Bay Village for over 55 years and she still considers it to be the BEST PLACE TO LIVE. Bay Village Foundation Bronze Memorial Plaques, Bay Village Foundation, Cahoon Memorial Bridge, Bay Village, Ohio, 2012 Dedication.

Elizabeth R. "Betsy MARTIN, age 85, died peacefully on Monday, May 30, 2016 surrounded by family and friends at her home in Bay Village. She was born in Cleveland to ***Frederick*** and ***Helen Ross***, the younger of two children. Her family moved to Green Bay, WI, where her father started a company to produce business forms. She attended the University of Wisconsin-Madison, became a member of the Delta Gamma sorority, and in 1952 was one of a small number of women graduates of its School of Business. That same year she married ***T. Richard "Dick" MARTIN***, also of Cleveland. In 1957 they settled in Bay Village where they raised two children, ***Susan*** and ***Ross***, and she supported Dick in all his endeavors. She was active in various organizations, including P.E.O., Lake Erie Nature & Science Center, and the League of Women Voters, and was a member of Bay Presbyterian Church. Betsy was a wonderful host, beloved friend and always enjoyed telling a good joke. She is survived by her two children, son-in-law *Larry Fournier*, daughter-in-law *PJ Martin (Schinski)*, and four grandchildren, ***Andrew, Grace, Ellie and Katherine***. Her husband, parents and brother preceded her in death. A Memorial Service will be held on Friday, July 22nd at 1:00 pm at Bay Presbyterian Church (Lake and Columbia Roads, Bay Village). Reception to follow. Interment private, Lakeside Cemetery, Bay Village. Special thanks to her friends at Griswold Home Care of Western Cuyahoga, who loved and cared for her in her last months. Memorials may be made in Betsy's name to Lake Erie Nature and Science Center, 28728 Wolf Rd., Bay Village, Ohio 44140. McGorray-Hanna Westlake. https://www.mcgorray.com/obituaries/ELIZABETH-R-BETSY-MARTIN?obId=2236907., accessed 9/5/2025.

Elizabeth (Ross) MARTIN Buried on (sometime after June 1, 2016), Plot #14-C. City of Bay Village, OH, Lakeside Cemetery Records.

Ancestors of Elizabeth R. Ross Martin:

I. ***Frederick William Sandford ROSS***, b. 20 May 1861, Blythswood, Glasgow, Lanark, Scotland; d. 27 Dec. 1907; m. ***Mary [Duncan] ROSS***, she b. Nov 1871, Scotland; d. 1944, United States. Issue: ***William ROSS***, b. Jan 1898, New York; d. 17 Sep 1918. ***Frederick Allan ROSS*** 1899-1978. ***Jessie D. ROSS***, b. c1904, New York; d. Mar 1993, Plainfield, Union, New Jersey; m. 22 Dec 1925, New York, New York to ***Evan Blish STEVENS***, b. 1898, d. 1964. 1871 England Census, London, Hackney St. John, Hackney, 14 b, p. 68j, line 5; Scotland, Select Births and Baptisms, 1564-1950, New York, New York, U.S., Index to Birth Certificates, 1866-1909.

II. ***Frederick Allan ROSS***, b. 21 Oct 1899, Brooklyn, Kings, New York; d. 17 May 1978, Green Bay, Brown, Wisconsin; m. 7 Aug 1926 to ***Helen R. Roseberry***, she b. 29 Apr 1898, Plainfield, New Jersey; d.6 Aug 1994, Green Bay, Brown, Wisconsin. Issue: ***Allan Melville ROSS***, b. 28 May 1928, Cleveland, Cuyahoga, Ohio; d. 25 Oct 2008, Green Bay, Brown, Wisconsin; m. *Betty Ann Koeller*, 6 Oct 1951. ***Elizabeth Roseberry ROSS***, b.1930-2016. Green Bay Press-Gazette, Green Bay, Wisconsin, Fri. Oct 31, 2008, p. 15. New York, New York, U.S., Index to Birth Certificates, 1866-1909. U.S. Federal Census 1920-1950.

III. ***Elizabeth Roseberry ROSS***, b. 4 Jun 1930, Cleveland, Cuyahoga, Ohio; d. 30 May 2016, Bay Village, Cuyahoga, OH; m. ***T. Richard MARTIN*** U.S. Find A Grave Index, Elizabeth R. Martin.

Military Dedication

May time deal gently with the living,
And embalm in all hearts the memory of the departed.

Sentiments offered by Mr. and Mrs. J.A. Harris, of Cleveland,
The Cahoon Pioneer Celebration, 1874

The marker above is located in the central section of the cemetery just south of the two quarter circles, north of the original section. An American flag flies with the marker. Individual service markers were installed at each soldier's grave by the Bay Village Post 135 of the American Legion on Memorial Day of 2004. They allow for individual flags to be place at each of the grave sites.

MEMORIAL DAY SERVICE AT LAKESIDE CEMETERY

Those buried at Lakeside have been remembered in a special observance since 1913. Nellie (Eleanor) Dodd (1866-1926, daughter of Charles and Annie Dodd, OP4:15) began the tradition of honoring those at the cemetery with a walk originating at the Methodist church. Sarah Wymer Dodd recalls service men and children alike walked together with the children placing flowers on graves. They would then return to the church for a picnic.

Sometime in the 1920's the parade developed into one very similar to the observance we participate in today.

Commander introduces a local clergyman who reads the opening prayer.

"This day is sacred with the almost visible presence of those who have gone before us. We honor the memory of those who gave their lives in the service of our country and of those others who have dropped their burdens by the wayside of life and are gone to eternal rest. May the ceremonies of today deepen your reverence for our dead. Let us resolve by work and deed to emphasize the privilege and duty of patriotism."

Sermon provided by clergyman.

Commander: "Color Guard, Present Arms!"

Decoration of Graves

The graves of servicemen who are buried at Lakeside Cemetery are decorated by Bay Village Brownie and Bluebird troops accompanied by soft music from the Bay High Band while the commander reads their names.

Revolutionary War

David Foote (Private, Capt. Ezra Whittelsey's Co., Col J. Brown's det. Of Berkshire Co. Militia)
Christopher Sadler (Dragoon in independent corps under General Count Pulaski)

War of 1812

Joel Cahoon (Private Capt. Delanne Mills' Company, probably Portage Co.)
Caleb Eddy
Asahel Porter
William Saddler (Corporal under Captain Harris, 58th Regiment)
John Wolf (Private, 2nd Co., 3rd Regiment, Strongs Ohio Militia)

Civil War

James Conklin *(Probably served with New York)*
Washington Elmer (Private Co. I, 10th Regiment, N.Y.Heavy Artillery)
Alonson Grant (Sergeant And 2d Leiut. 6th O. Vol. Cav.)
Lumon Griswold (Private, Co. I, 8th Regiment, US OVI)
John Schultz (*possible:* Thirty-Seventh Infantry, Company H.)
Chauncey Stevens (Sergeant, Co. I 21 Ohio Inf.)
Alfred Wolf (Private, Co. I, Regiment: 150 O.N.G., Inf.)
Michael Wolf
Unknown Union Soldier

Spanish American War

Walter S. Wilkshire (L5 Ohio Inf (S), Sgt. Maj+B 46 US Vol. Inf.)

World War I

Harry E. Rehling (National Army, LB 1)
Sterling Rumbaugh (United States Navy)

World War II

True Ellis Read (United States Army)

Korea

T. Richard Martin (United States Army)

Commander: "Firing squad, salute the dead."
FIRING SQUAD SALUTE (3 volleys)
TAPS AND ECHO
STAR SPANGLED BANNER

Benediction

Commander: "We will move out to the Memorial Rose Garden. Please regroup in the same parade order."

The parade, comprised of local dignitaries and organization representatives in convertibles, scouts walking with their leaders, the Bay Village High School Marching Band and various veterans groups will then parade east down Lake Road to the gazebo area at Cahoon Park where local dignitaries will speak. Residents line the street on both sides waving flags as the cars slowly pass and designated organizations walk by.

Family References

My eternal gratitude is extended to the following individuals who assisted with the project through interviews, sharing family files, Bible records, photographs, etc.

Aaron, Thomas J., New Braunfels, TX 78130-8715 *(Comstock Family)*
Allen, Shirley, Walnut Creek, CA 94595-5203 *(Comstock Family)*
Ames, Lucille Bennett, Cedar Hill, TX 75103 *(Eddy and Griswold Families)*
Aslaksen, Arthur, Avon Lake, OH 44012 *(Aslaksen Family)*
Badt, Evelyn, (Mrs. Edward), Westlake, OH 44145 *(Dranse Family)*
Bakker, Cheryl A., Crystal River, FL 34429 *(Burlingame Family)*
Bangert, Martha, previously Bay Village, OH 44140 *Deceased (Hassler Family)*
Beheim, Lois C., Bay Village, OH 44140 *(Sunk Family)*
Bircher, Helen Hassler, formerly of Willoughby, OH 44094 *Deceased (Hassler Family)*
Black, Alice Case, Rockledge, FL 32955-2244 *(Krumwiede, Case Family)*
Black, Terrill Bates, (Mrs. D.), Wharton, NJ 07885 *(Carter and Willis Families)*
Boas, Karen, Venice, FL 34285 *(Aldrich, Eddy, Jaycox, Hilliard and Griswold Families)*
Bonnes, Harry P., Fairfax, VA 22030-2004 *(Foote Family)*
Bradley, Donna, Anza, CA 92539 *(Comstock Family-cemetery inscriptions)*
Braman, Frank, New Braunfels, TX 78132 *(Braman, Foote and Stevens Families)*
Butler, James N., Queensbury, NY 12804 *(Wuestenburg Family Reference)*
Caldwell, W. Wilson, formerly of Bay Village, OH 44140 *Deceased (Hassler Family)*
Calhoun, Owen, Burlington, Ontario, Canada L7R 3TI *(Cahoon Family)*
Case, Thomas S.; Surprise, AZ 85374-3813 *(Krumwiede and Case Family)*
Cavalier, Paul, Massapequa, NY 11758 *(Ottawa County, OH records, Scheible Family)*
Childs, Jeanette M. (Taylor), Mrs. David, Kechi, KS 67067 *(Elmer Family)*
Clifford, Betty, (Mr. Robert C.), Westlake, OH 44145 *(Heckerman Family)*
Cooley, Lollie, (Mrs. Roger M.), Westlake, OH 44145 *(Former owner of the home built by Abner and Rebecca Smith)*
Coppin, Roy, Southend-on-Sea, England *(Coppin Family)*
Crane, Theodore R., Boulder CO, 80302-5717 *(Osborn, Chadwick and Stocking Families)*
d'Acunzo, Leslie Hinz, (Mrs. Aldo), Avon Lake, OH 44012 *(Hinz Family)*
DeChant, Donna, (Mrs. Woodie), Avon Lake, OH 44012 *(Tomanek Family)*
DeMaso, Carlene Burlingame, Springfield, MI 49015 *(Burlingame Family)*
Dougherty, Lois Irvin, Westlake, OH 44145 *(Bay Village Families)*
Dyke, Hon. Ann, Bay Village, OH 44140 *(Hinz Family)*
Eddy, Thomas, Fayetteville, GA 30214 *(Eddy Family)*
Eppink, Richard H., Williamsville, NY 14221 *(Eppink Family)*
Evanson-Myers, Suzanne, Williamsville, NY 14221 *(Knaggs Family)*
Fanta, Wayne, Cincinnati, OH 45247 *(Schmit and PetersFamilies)*
Frank, Rev. Margie M., Washington, PA 15301 *(Eppink Family)*
Freeman, Cameron Stuart, Reseda, CA 91335*(Foote Family)*
Gaddy, Phyllis J., Garrison, IA 52229 *(Willis Family)*
Garber, Norma Wolf, Bay Village, OH 44140 *Deceased (Wolf Family)*
Gardner, Marianne Ruple, Willoughby, OH 44094 *(Osborn and Ruple Family)*
Garoutte, Pat, Springfield, MO *(Loomis Family)*
Gawne, Daphne M., (Mrs. Michael), Saint Albans, VT 05478 *(Case, Foote and Perry Families)*
Griswold, Coralee, Elko, NV 89801 *(Griswold Family Association)*
Haag, Richard L., Wellington, OH 44090 *(Haag and Scheible Families)*
Hardway, Geraldine A. (Mrs. James B.), Milan, OH 44846 *(Saddler and Stevens Families)*
Harmon, Sue A., Millington, TN 38053 *(Case Family)*
Heym, William D.H., Lakewood, OH 44107 *(Osborn and Ruple Family)*
Heys, Sue E., Berlin Heights, OH 44814 *(Darby Family)*
Hillard, Victor Grant, Jr., N. Chelmsford, MA 01824 *(Hilyar, Hilliard, Jaycox Families)* Website: Descendants of William Hilliard http://members.aol.com/vichillard/hillard/hillard.htm
Hoerrle, Thomas K., Sheffield Village 44055-2840 *(Burrell Family and Garfield Cemetery Inscriptions)*
Hoff, Robert W., Lawndale, CA 90266 *(Wuestenberg Family)*
Hutchins, Janice (Mrs. Jack Randolph), New Market, Maryland 21774 *(Griswold Family)*
Jacox, Marilyn E., Montgomery Village, MD *(Burlingame, Jaycox Families)*

Jackson, Sarah Ellis, North Olmsted, OH 44070-4902 *(Westlake References)*
Jamba, Mary Milne, (Mrs. Mark), Fairview Park, OH 44126 *(Eppink Family)*
Johnson, Kathryn O'Connor, (Mrs. Randall B.), Prospect, OH 43342 *(Osborn and Morgan Families)*
Johnson, Kathleen, Hoodsport, WA 98548 *(Johnson Family)*
Jones, Mike *(Stiles-Cahoon Family)*
Krulik, Leah, (Mrs. Frank), North Olmsted, OH 44070 *(Oviatt Family)*
Laird, Linda D., Spokane, WA 99207 *(Braman Family)*
Laughlin, Kay, (Mrs. Gerald L.), Bay Village, OH 44140 *(Bay Village History)*
Lenard, Carol M. Sadler, (Mrs. Frank), Frankenmuth, MI 48734 *(Sadler Family)*
Lewit, Nancy Rowell, (Mrs. Peter G.), Cornwall, NY 12518 *(Rowell Family)*
Loomis, Mark, Portland, Oregon 97219 (*Loomis Family)*
Matousek, Esther Seitz, Brook Park, OH 44142 *(Burko, Dranse, Eppink, Krumwiede and Seitz Families)*
McCutcheon, Hazel Walker; (Mrs. Wm. Douglas), Avon Lake, OH 44012 *(Beard Family)*
Meermans, Carol K., (Mrs. Ralph E.), Bay Village, OH 44140 *(Bay Village United Methodist Church)*
Menning, Gay, (Mrs. Raymond F.), Bay Village, OH 44140 *Deceased (Bay Village History)*
Meyer, Louella Parsons, (Mrs. Charles), Bay Village, OH 44140 *(Bay Village Women's Club)*
Miller, Donald Britton, Saratoga, CA 95070-555- *(Britton Family)*
Mosher, Bob, Surprise, AZ 85374-4528 *Deceased (Comstock Family)*
Munt, Bonnie, (Mrs. Terence), Julian, CA 92036 *(Comstock Family)*
O'Connor, Sally, Marion, OH 43302 *(Osborn and Morgan Families)*
Osborn, J. Marshall, Madison, WI 53705 *(Osborn Family)*
Osborn, Ronald G., Dixmont, ME 04932 *(Osborn Family)*
Offutt, Mildred, Cleveland, OH 44102 *(Heckerman Family)*
Palmer, May Aslaksen, (Mrs. Ernest M.), Avon Lake, OH 44012 *(Aslaksen Family)*
Philiben, Anne, Hopkinton, NH 03229 *(Rowell Family)*
Porter Robert John III and Helen J., Westlake, OH 44145 *(Wolf Family)*
Price, Sally Irvin, Bay Village, OH 44140 *(Bay Village Families)*
Raz, Carolyn Jo Ames, Ovilla, TX 75154 *(Eddy and Griswold Families)*
Read, Patricia Meddick (Mrs. True), Westlake, OH 44145 *(Osborn and Yanko Families)*
Reed, Carol, Fairview Park, OH 44126 *(Krumwiede Family)*
Reehorst, Robert E., Westlake, OH 44145 *(Cahoon Family {Property)*
Rose, Gertrude Aldrich Barker, Houston, TX 77063 (*Aldrich, Bassett and Windsor Families)*
Ross, Marilyn, OH *(Jaycox Family)*
Rowell, David J., Yorktown, NY 10598 *(Rowell Family)*
Sanford, Jean Osborn, former address Ashland, OH 44805 *Deceased (Osborn Family)*
Sarles, Florence (Mrs. Raymond), Princeton, WV 24740 *(Sarles Family)*
Schwartz, Billie Jo (B.J., Mrs. Edward), Bay Village, OH 44140 *(Osborn Family and Lakeside Cemetery History)*
Scott, David Osborn, Jr., Carrizozo, NM 88301 *(Osborn Family)*
Serb, George, Bay Village, OH 44140 *Deceased (Bay Village History)*
Siek, Carl, Escondido, CA 92027 *(Krumwiede, Schulz and Wischmeyer Families)*
Sigsworth, Jeff, Elyria, OH 44035 *(Cahoon Family)*
Slaby, Ima Aldrich, (Mrs. Jerome T.), Traverse City, MI 49686 *(Aldrich Family)*
Sleasman, John, Solon, OH 44139 *(Westlake history)*
Stocking, Theodore L., Lakewood, OH 44107 *(Stocking and Osborn Families)*
Szabo, Karen Sue; Ashtabula, OH 44004 *(Jaycox and Rehling Families)*
Stave, Carrie, Roseville, MN 55113 *(Griswold Family)*
Taylor, Arline, Cedar Hill, TX 75104 *(Conkey Family)*
Thayer, Glenda, Tacoma, WA *Case descenedent and former editor of Case newsletter, "Brief Case."*
Thielen, Susy O'Connor, (Mrs. Bruce E.), Keena, NH 03431 *(Osborn and Morgan Families)*
Thompson, Millard, Ventura, CA 93001 *(Phinny Family)*
Trayte, Herbert J., Fairview Park, OH 44126 *(Wilkshire and Knaggs Families)*
Turner, Mary Jane, Tucson, AZ *(Braman Family)*
Veits, Nancy, Rancho Palos Verdes, CA 90275 *(Aslaksen and Tomanek Families)*
Vulku, James and Linda, Omaha, NE 68135-2398 *(Martin Family)*
Weston, Doris, Westlake, OH 44145 *(Smith Family)*
Williams, John, Euclid Historical Museum, Euclid, OH 44117 *(Cahoon Family)*
Windsor, James, San Francisco, CA 94110 *(Winsor Family)*
Wolf, Edgar H. and Susan, Reno, NV 89511 *(Wolf Family)*
Wymer, Sarah Dodd, Scio, OH 43988 *Deceased (Dodd, Sadler and Powell Families, general Bay Village history and assisted with other family lines)*

Please excuse any ommisions that may have accidently occurred.

Bibliography

Abbott, Susan Woodruff. Families of Early Milford, Connecticut. Baltimore: Genealogical Publishing Co., Inc., 1979.

Adair County Historical Society. History of Adair County, Iowa. Adair County Historical Society, 1976.

Adjutant General of Ohio. Roster of Ohio Soldiers in the War of 1812. OH: Adjutant General of Ohio, 1916.

Albrecht, Brian E. "Still 'Unknown' but Not Forgotten." The Plain Dealer. Northeast Ohio, 4 July 2000: Sect. B., pp. 1+.

Allen, Shirley. Roxanna Britton. Oceanside, CA: Criterion House, 2001.

Allyn, Helen. "Home Weathers Storms of 118 Years." The Cleveland Press 6 October 1932: p. 17.

Annals of Cleveland, 1818-1876. Microfiche. *A digest and index of the newspaper records of events and opinions abstracted principally from the Cleveland Register, Cleveland Herald, Cleveland Daily True Democrat, and Cleveland Leader organized by year.*

Atlas of Cuyahoga County, Ohio, from actual surveys by and under the directions of D. J. Lake, C. E. Titus. Philadelphia: Titus, Simmons & Titus, 1874.

Atlas and Directory of Lorain County, Ohio. Cleveland: The American Atlas Company, 1896.

Atlas of Lorain County, Ohio, from actual surveys by and under the directions of D. Lake and C. E. Titus. Philadelphia: Simmons & Titus, 1874.

Austin, John Osborne. The Genealogical Dictionary of Rhode Island: Comprising Three Generations of Settlers Who Came Before 1690. 1887. Reprinted, Baltimore: Genealogical Publishing Co., 1969.

"Avon Lake." Elyria Democrat [Elyria, OH] 12 June 1913: p. 1.

Bailey, Rev. Frederick W., B. D. Early Connecticut Marriages as found in Ancient Church Records Prior to 1800. Seventh Book. 1906. Reprinted, Baltimore: Genealogical Publishing Co., Inc., 1976.

Bamberger, Werner. "James Osborn, 70, A Literary Scholar Specialist in 17th-and 18th-Century English Literature, Was at Yale." New York Times. 19 October 1976.

Barbour, Lucius Barnes. Families of Early Hartford, Connecticut. Reprinted, Baltimore: Genealogical Publishing Co., 1977.

Bay View Hospital Records. Bay Village, OH. Records in the possession of City of Bay Village, Bay Village, OH.

Bay Village City Council Minutes (Hamlet of Bay) 1903-. Records in the possession of Bay Village City Hall, Bay Village, OH.

Bay Village Historical Society. Bay Village: A Way of Life. Compiled by Mrs. Raymond F. Menning, Jr. and Dale F. Harter. Bay Village, OH: The Society, 1974.

Bay Village Historical Society. "The Joel Butler Cahoon Family." Pamphlet written for a Cahoon exhibit at Rose Hill Museum. Bay Village: The Society, 2003.

"Bay Village Historical Society Family Papers Collection, 1816-1995." Rose Hill Museum, Bay Village, OH. Microfilmed by the Western Reserve Historical Society.

Beebe, Mr. Aldrich Family Papers. Rose Hill Museum, Bay Village, OH

Beers, F. W. History of Herkimer County, N.Y. "The Town of Salisbury and Early Settlers and Settlements." New York: F. W. Beers & Co., 1879.

The Biographical Annals of Ohio: A Handbook of the Government and Institutions of the State of Ohio. Compiled under authority of the Act of 12 May 1902. Revised and enlarged edition of Ohio Statesmen and Hundred Year Book. Col. W. A. Taylor, 1892: pp. 878-879.

Blanton, Monty. "Testimony by Monty Blanton, President." OCSEA Assembly for Mental Health/Mental Retardation/Ohio Veteran's Home. <http://www.ocsea.org/mrdd_testimony.html>. Cited 31 July 2004.

Briggs, Ichabod White. Family Papers of Susan Harmon. Millington, TN.

Burlingame, Nelson B. and Henry Allen Burlingame. "Burlingame Manuscript." Roger Burlingame Descendents, Eleven Generations in North America. 8 vols. Self published. Housed at Rhode Island Historical Society, Providence, RI 02906.

Busch-Burmeister Family Funeral Chapels Records. 163 Avon-Belden Rd., Avon Lake, OH 44012.

Butler, Margaret Manor. The Lakewood Story. New York: Stratford House, 1949.

"Cahoon Annual Celebration Notebook." Accumulated newspaper articles 1860-1907+. Rose Hill Museum, Bay Village, OH.

Cahoon, Ida M. History of the Cahoon Family. Cleveland: published privately by W. A. Robertson, c1910. Copies in the possession of Rose Hill Museum, Bay Village, OH.

"Cahoon, Leverett J." Obituary. Morning Leader [Cleveland, OH] 18 August 1886: p. 5.

Cahoon, Margaret Van Allen. "Autobiography of Margaret Van Allen Cahoon." Handwritten copy. Rose Hill Museum, Bay Village, OH. 1880s.

Calhoun County, Michigan Death Records. Book 2. Sheridan Twp., p. 61.

Calhoun, Orval O. Our Calhoun Family: 800 Years of Colquhoun, Colhoun, Calhoun, and Cahoon Family History in Ireland, Scotland, England, United States of America and Canada. vol. 2. Baltimore, MD: Gateway Press, Inc., 1982.

California Death Index. California Home Page, Vital Search. <http://www.vitalsearch-ca.com/gen/ca/_vitals/cadeathm.htm>. Cited 2000-2003.

Calvary Cemetery. Cemetery records and inscriptions. Cemetery R 555 North Ridge Rd., Lorain, OH.

"Car Victim is Hero of Daring Rescue at Sea." Lorain Times-Herald [Lorain, OH] 3 August 1921: p. 2.

Case, Dr. Erastus Ely. "Case Family Manuscript." Self published. A18566, at The Connecticut Historical Society, Hartford, Connecticut.

Centennial History of Fairview General Hospital. Cleveland: The Health Cleveland, 1992.
Chabek, Dan. "Today's prime land once laid an egg." Lakewood Sun Post. 18 January 1990. Available online: <http://www.lkwdpl.org/lore/lore167.htm>.
Chaney, Charles. "History of the West Park Neighborhood, Cleveland, Cuyahoga County, OH." General History. Early Settlers and Their Legacies: George Peake. <http://www.westparkhistory.com/index.htm> Cited: 26 February 2006.
Christ Church Anglican Church Records. 34 Boucher St. E., Meaford, Ontario, Canada N4L 1B9.
Christiansen, Harry. New Lake Shore Electric, Trolley Trails. vol. 4. Lakewood, OH: Western Reserve Historical Society, 1978.
City Cemeteries. Cleveland, OH, General Office: 21400 Chagrin Blvd., Cleveland, OH.
Erie Cemetery, 2291 E. 9th St., Cleveland, OH.
Highland Park Cemetery, 21400 Chagrin Blvd., Cleveland, OH.
West Park Cemetery, 3942 Ridge Rd., Cleveland, OH.
Woodland Cemetery, 2367 E. 65th St., Cleveland, OH.
Civil War Pension Files. National Archives, Washington, D.C.
Cleveland City Directories. Published 1837-1977. Microfilm. Available at Fairview Park Regional Library
Cleveland Leader. Cleveland: Cowles and Company. 1847-1918. Microfilm.
Cleveland Plain Dealer [Cleveland, OH] Plain Dealer Published 1885-1961.
Cleveland Public Library. Preservation Office. Cleveland Necrology File. 169 Microfilm reels. Cleveland, Ohio: Cleveland Public Library Preservation Office, 1950-1975. [Originally published as "Card Index to Paid Death Notices Published in: Cleveland Plain Dealer, 1850-1975, the Cleveland Herald, 1833, 1847-1848, 1876, 1878-1879 and the Cleveland Press, August 16, 1941 - 1975," Cleveland Public Library Staff, n.d.], <http://www.cpl.org/LinksLibrary.asp?FormMode=SubCategory&ID=151&CatID=17>, Cited 2001-2004.
Cleveland Weekly Leader. Cleveland: Medill Cowles & Co., 1854-1885. Microfilm.
Coates, William R. A History of Cuyahoga County and the City of Cleveland. 1924. Reprint, Salem, MA: Higginson Book Co., 1997. 3 vols. in 2.
Comstock Family Bible, in the possession of Mrs. Terence (Bonnie) Munt, Julian, CA.
Comstock, John Adams. A History and Genealogy of the Comstock Family In America. Privately printed for the author. Los Angeles: The Commonwealth Press Inc., 1949.
"A Compilation of Histories, The Lakewood Public Schools." Lakewood, OH: Lakewood Board of Education, 1984.
Connecticut Western Reserve. Wikipedia. Answers.com <http://www.answers.com/topic/connecticut-western-reserve> Cited 31 January 2006.
"Coppin-Richardson." Lorain Constitutionalist [Elyria, OH] 12 February 1868: p. 2.
"Cuyahoga County Cemetery Inscriptions." vol. 1. Dover Township, Cuyahoga County, Ohio. Bay Village. Cleveland: The Western Reserve Historical Society, 1934. pp. 138-143.
Cuyahoga County Recorders Office. Veterans Services, Graves Site. <http://recorder.cuyahoga.oh.us/GraveResults.cfm>. Cited 21 July 2004.
The Cleveland Press. Cleveland: Scripps Publ., 1878-1982. Currently housed at Cleveland State University Library, Special Collections.
Dailey, Jane Dowd. The Official Roster of the Soldiers of the American Revolution Buried in the State of Ohio. Columbus, OH: F. J. Heer Printing, 1929.
Daughters of the American Revolution. Lineage Books of the Charter Members of the National Society of the Daughters of the American Revolution. 166 vols. Washington, D.C.: The Society, 1895-1939.
Didick, Deborah A. Cahoon, Famous and Infamous Cahoons. Taunton, MA: Coma Graphics, 1999.
"Died." Obituary of Joseph Cahoon. Elyria Advertiser [Elyria, OH] 16 March 1839: p. 3.
"Died." Obituary of David Foote. Lorain Argus [Elyria, OH] 18 February 1851: p. 3.
"Died." Obituary of Elizabeth Foote. Lorain Republican [Elyria, OH] 17 January 1844: p. 3.
Dillman, Alma G. Marriage Application Index to Elyria, Ohio Newspapers 1830-1874. Elyria Public Library: Elyria, OH, 1973.
---. Obituary Index to Elyria, Ohio, Newspapers 1830-1874. Elyria Public Library: Elyria, OH, 1968.
---. Obituary Index to Elyria, Ohio, Newspapers 1875-1883. Elyria Public Library: Elyria, OH, 1982.
"Dover." Reference to Mrs. Fred Peake. Elyria Evening Telegram [Elyria, OH] 15 March 1919: p. 7.
Dover Cook Book. Bay Village, OH.: No publisher, Undetermined publication date.
"Dover Lake." Obituary of Cuvier Peters. Elyria Republican and Telegram [Elyria, OH] 19 December 1912: p. 8.
Drake, George H. "Aldrich Family - Thirteen Generation Chart." Undetermined year. Hand written charts at Rose Hill Museum, Bay Village, OH.
Dunham, Don. "The Early Settlers of Bay Village." Undetermined year. Osborn Family File. Rose Hill Museum, Bay Village, OH.
Duncan, Ruth Cost. John Case and His Descendants. Decorah, Iowa: The Anundsen Publishing Co., 1991.
Dunker, Mary Jean. Undetermined newspaper, Letter to the Editor. October 1991. Pamphlet File. Avon Lake Library, Avon Lake, OH.
Early Records of Lorain County, Ohio, Abstracts of Wills and Estates Years 1824-1847 *(with additions to 1865)* From Lorain County Probate Court films, and the Common Pleas Court Journals Court House, Elyria, Ohio. Compiled by Mary Parker Gray. Elyria Chapter Daughters of the American Revolution, 1962.
Eddy, Ruth Story Devereux. The Eddy Family in America. Boston: The Eddy Family Association, 1930.
Ellis, William D. and Mary Ellen Wobbecke. A History of Westlake, Ohio 1811-1961. No publisher.

Elsinore Valley Cemetery. Cemetery records and inscriptions. 18170 Collier Avenue, Lake Elsinore, CA 92530.
Elyria Constitution [Elyria, OH] Published March 1875-September 1887.
Elyria Independent Democrat [Elyria, OH] Published August 1852-April 1876 and 1900 to 1928 irregular.
Elyria Republican [Elyria, OH] Published 1834-1939 and July 1839-December 1875.
Ennis, Edward. "History of Avon Lake, Ohio." c1941. Seven page manuscript at Avon Lake Public Library, Avon Lake, O.
Euclid Cemetery. Cemetery records and inscriptions. 20239 Concordia Drive, Cleveland, OH 44117.
Elyria Evening Telegram. [Elyria, OH] Published January 1916-June 1919.
Evangelical Lutheran Church at Elizabethtown (Hagerstown). Family Tree Maker. CD 178. Church Records, MD and DE, 1600's-1800's, Washington Co., MD. ©Broderbund Software, Inc. Banner Blue Division 10 November 1998.
Evening Telegram [Elyria, OH] Citations from 1911.
Evergreen Cemetery. Cemetery records and inscriptions. 29535 Center Ridge Road, Westlake, OH.
Fairview Park Cemetery (formerly Rockport Cemetery). Cemetery records and inscriptions. Fairview Park, OH. Original records at Fairview Park City Hall; copies housed at Fairview Park Regional Library, Fairview Park, OH.
Falkland Islands, South America. Division of Health Services – Vital Records. Birth Registry. Louisa Malvina Hardy, 1877.
Falmouth Historical Society. "Falmouths Whaling History. " Falmouths History. Falmouth, Massachusetts. <http://www.falmouthhistoricalsociety.org/history.html>. Cited July 2003.
Foote, Abram W. Foote Family Comprising the Genealogy and History of Nathaniel Foote of Wethersfield, Conn. and His Descendants. vol. I. Rutland, Vermont: Marble City Press -The Tuttle Company, 1907.
---. Foote Family Comprising the Genealogy and History of Nathaniel Foote of Wethersfield, Conn. and His Descendants. vol. II. Burlington, VT: Free Press Printing Company, 1932.
French, Esther Griswold and Robert Lewis French. The Griswold Family: The First Five Generations in America. Weathersfield, Connecticut: The Griswold Family Association, 1990.
French, Robert L. and Esther G. French. The Greswolde Family: 12 Generations in England. Compiled by Coralee Griswold. Weathersfield, Connecticut: The Griswold Family Association, 1999.
"Gallipolis, Ohio." Wikipedia, the On-line Encyclopedia. <http://en.wikipedia.org/wiki/Gallipolis,_Ohio>. Cited 31 July 2004.
Gardner, Marianne Ruple. The Descendants of Balthazar (Baltus) Ruple; Pennsylvania, New Jersey, Ohio. Willoughby, OH: Self published, 2000.
Garfield Cemetery. Cemetery records and inscriptions. Sheffield Village City Hall, Sheffield Village, OH.
Genealogical Workshops of the Lorain County Historical Society. Cemetery Inscriptions of Lorain County, Ohio 1980. Elyria, OH: The Workshop, 1980.
Genealogies of Connecticut Families from The New England Historical and Genealogical Register. 3 vols. Baltimore: Genealogical Publishing Co., Inc. 1983.
Geographical Gazetteer of Jefferson County, NY 1684-1890. Part 1. Ed. Hamilton H. Horton, 1890. Reprinted, Salem, MA: Higginson Book Co., 1993.
"George Scheible Dies in Avon Lake." Lorain Journal [Lorain, OH] 20 August 1947: p. 9.
Gutgesel, Stephen. Guide to Ohio Newspapers 1793-1973. Columbus, Ohio: Ohio Historical Society, 1974.
Goebelt, Margaret Schaefer. Fairview Park in Historical Review. Cleveland: John S. Swift Co., Inc., 1978.
Goodwin, Nathaniel. Genealogical Notes or Contributions to the Family History of Some of the First Settlers of Connecticut and Massachusetts; Hartford, Conn. 1856. Reprinted, Baltimore: Genealogical Publishing, 1978.
Grant, Arthur Hastings. The Grant Family: A Genealogical History of the Descendents of Matthew Grant of Windsor, CT, 1601-1898. Poughkeepsie, NY: A. V. Haight, 1898.
The Griswold Family Association. The Griswold Family Association Home Page. http://www.griswoldfamily.org/. Wethersfield, CT. Cited 12 July 2003.
Hadsell, R.S. and Hazel Rutherford. A History and Civics of Dover Village. Dover Village Board of Education, 1941.
"Maplewood Park" Target Investment Area Hubbard Township. Historical Information for the Target Investment Areas Trumbull County and the Historic Western Reserve. Trumbull County Planning Commission. History <http://planning.co.trumbull.oh.us/History_CAS.htm." Cited 20 January 2006.
Hall, Reuben. "Reminiscences of Dover Pioneer Life, 1810-1910." Unpublished paper. Undetermined date. Available on line: <http://www.westlakelibrary.org/reubenhall.htm>.
Hatcher, Harlan. Western Reserve: The Story of New Connecticut in Ohio. Indianapolis: The Bobbs-Merrill Company, 1949. 2nd edition, Cleveland: World Publishing, 1966. 2nd edition paperback, Kent State University Press, 1991.
Hayden, Amos S. Early History of the Disciples of the Western Reserve, Ohio; with Biographical Sketches of the Principal Agents in Their Religious Movement. Cincinnati: Chase & Hall Publishers, 1875. <http://sidneyrigdon.com/1875Hay1.htm>. Cited 31 January 2006.
"Henry Wallace." Commemorative Biographical Record of the Counties of Huron and Lorain, Ohio Containing Biographical Sketches of Prominent and Representative Citizens and of Many of the Early Settled Families. 1894. Reprinted, Evansville, IN: Unigraphic Inc., 1977: p.739.
Heys, Sue E. "Darby Family Descendant Report." Berlin Heights, OH. 2000.
Hildebrand, Howard W. Thomas Rowell, 400 Years & 8,461 Descendants Later: Also His Parents, His Siblings and His English Family. Kettering, OH: Self published, 1993.
Hillmer, Paul. "John D. Rockefeller and Civic Affairs in Cleveland." Research Report. Sleepy Hollow, NY: Rockefeller Archive Center, Spring 2000: p. 3-6. <www.rockefeller.edu/archives.ctr>. Cited 5 December 2003.

History of La Cross County, Wisconsin, Containing an Account of Its Settlement, Growth, Development & Resources; Biographical Sketches & Portraits of Prominent Men & Early Settlers. 1881. Reprinted, Salem, MA: Higginson Book Co., 1998.
History of Lorain County Ohio, with Illustrations & Biographical Sketches of Some of Its Prominent Men and Pioneers. 1879. Reprinted, Salem, MA: Higginson Book Co., 1997.
"History of the Early Settlers in Bay Village." Osborn Family File. Rose Hill Museum, Bay Village, OH.
History of the Town of Lee, Mass. Lee, Mass: French & Royce, 1854.
"The Holzer Heritage." Holzer Medical Center. Gallipolis, OH. <http://www.holzer.org/heritage2.html>. Cited 31 July 2004.
Hoff, Robert Woodrow. "Wuestenberg Family Group Sheets." Manhattan Beach, CA. February 1998.
Howe, Henry, LL.D. Historical Collections of Ohio in Two Volumes. Cincinnati, OH: Published by the State of Ohio, 1904.
Hubbard House Anti-Slavery Museum. About Us. <http://www.hubbardhouseugrrmuseum.org/about.htm.> Cited 7 April 2006.
Huntington Family Association. HFA Project Version 2. <www.huntington.tierranet.com/>. Cited 4 June 2002.
Hutchins, Jack Randolph. Geneology of Thomas Hutchins of Salem, Massachusettes. Washington, D.C.: Goetz Press, 1972.
"Ichabod White Briggs to Catherine Case." Family Papers of Susan Harmon. Millington, TN.
Index to Marriage License Applications, Cuyahoga County, OH 23 February 1829-August 1851, Volumes 1 through 6. Compiled by Cuyahoga West Chapter of the Ohio Genealogical Society. Fairview Park, OH: Cuyahoga West Genealogical Society, 1985.
"Influenza Hits Camps." Elyria Evening Telegram [Elyria, OH] 12 December 1918: p. 5.
"Influenza of 1918." History of Great Lakes. Naval Station Great Lakes, Great Lakes, MI. United States Navy<www.ntcgl.navy.mil/history.htm>. June 2002.
"The Influenza Epidemic of 1918 and the Music of Life." History of Great Lakes. Great Lakes Naval Training Center. United States Navy. <http://www.nsgreatlakes.navy.mil/history/index8.html>. Cited 14 July 2004.
Inskeep, Lester N. "Comstock Hospital's Closing Ends 50 Years of Service." The Arizona Daily Star [Tucson, AZ] 21 December 1965: p. A2.
"Invalid's Suicide Was Hospital's Incentive, Oliver E. Comstock, Who Died Yesterday at Casa Grande, Started Institution Here After Destitute Tubercular Took Own Life. The Arizona Daily Star [Tucson, AZ] 11 September 1937: pp. A1 and 3.
Izant, Grace Goulder. Hudson's Heritage. Kent, OH: Kent State University Press, 1985.
Jacobus, Donald Lines. Families of Ancient New Haven. Rome, NY: Clarence D. Smith, 1923.
Jacobus, Donald Lines and Edgar Francis Waterman. The Waterman Family: Descendants of Richard Waterman of Providence, Rhode Island. vol. 3. Hartford, CN: Connecticut Historical Society, 1954.
"James M. Osborn Dies; Noted for Yale Collection." New Haven Register 19 October 1976.
"James Osborn, 70, A Literary Scholar." New York Times 19 October 1976.
Jensen, Elizabeth. Pleasant Grove United Church of Christ Records. Compilation of historical records, Pleasant Grove, IA.
"The Joel Butler Cahoon Family." Rose Hill Museum Pamphlet. Rose Hill Museum, Bay Village, OH. 2003.
"John E. Osborn." Obituary. Dayton Journal Herald 15 May 1962: p. 30.
Johnson, Crisfield. History of Cuyahoga County, Ohio, with Portrait & Biographical Sketches of Some of Its Prominent Men & Pioneers. 1879. Reprinted, Salem, MA: Higginson Book Co., 1993.
Johnson, Mary Ann. A Field Guide to Flight: On the Aviation Trail in Dayton, Ohio. Dayton, OH: Landfall Press, 1996.
"Julia Winsor Weld to Elizabeth Aldrich." 1850. Aldrich Papers. Rose Hill Museum, Bay Village, OH.
Kellogg, Dale Cosnett. Marriages, Lorain County, OH 1824-65. Compiled by Elyria Chapter, Daughters of the American Revolution and Genealogical Workshop, Lorain County Historical Society. Elyria, Ohio, 1980.
Kennedy, James Harrison. A History of the City of Cleveland, it's Settlement Rise and Progress, 1796-1896. Cleveland: The Imperial Press, 1896. Also available online: <http://web.ulib.csuohio.edu/ebooks/kennedy/c02.html>
Kirchen Buch I Der Deutschen Ev. Protestantischen St. Johannes Gemeinde Zu Cleveland, Ohio West Seite. Independent Evangelical Church. Abstracted/Compiled by Ingrid Abram.
Knepper, George W. Ohio and Its People. Kent, OH: The Kent State University Press, 1989.
Knepper, George W., Dr. The Official Ohio Land's Book. The Auditor of State, OH. Columbus, OH. 2002 Available online: <http://www.auditor.state.oh.us/StudentResources/OhioLands/ohio_lands.pdf>.
Krawcheck, Julian. "Let us Visit Vintage Homes." Cleveland Press. Press Magazine. First in the series, "Cleveland Historical Houses." 24 August 1976: p. A8.
Lake Shore Cemetery Records, Lake Road, Avon Lake, OH: Busch-Burmeister Family Funeral Chapel, 163 Avon-Belden Road, Avon Lake, OH 44012.
Lakeside Cemetery File, Bay Village City Hall, Bay Village, OH.
Lake Side Cemetery Ledger. Bay Village, OH. List of interments and financial lot transactions. 1879-present. Bay Village City Hall, Bay Village, OH.
Lakeview Cemetery. Cemetery records and inscriptions. 12316 Euclid Avenue, Cleveland, OH 44106-4393. <www.lakeviewcemetery.com>.
Lakewood Park Cemetery Assn. Cemetery records and inscriptions. 22025 Detroit Rd., Rocky River, OH 44116.
Leelanau Enterprise [Northport, Leelanau Co., MI]. Aldrich newspaper citations 1880-1884 as extracted by Ima Aldrich Slaby.
Lenard, Carol M. "Sadler Family Group Sheets and Pedigree Charts." Frankenmuth, MI. October 1981.
Lindsey, Daird. Ohio's Western Reserve: The Story of Its Place Names. Cleveland: The Press of Western Reserve University, 1955, revised 1962.
Lorain Times-Herald [Lorain, OH] Published May 1901-December, 1932.
Lynch, Charles P. "Lakewood Public Schools." Lindstrom, E. George. Story of Lakewood, OH. Lakewood, OH: self published.

Loomis Chaffee School. "History of Loomis Chaffee." <http://www.loomis.org>. Cited 5 July 2003.

Loomis, Elisha Scott, Ph.D. Descendants of Joseph Loomis in America and his Antecedents in the Old World. 1875. Reprinted, Elias Loomis, L.L.D, ed. Berea, OH: 1908.

Lorain County Directory. vol.1. Lorain, OH, 1906.

Lorain County Rural Directory. Lorain, OH, 1910.

Lorain County Library Obituary File. Lorain County Main Branch, Lorain, OH.

"Lorain County Researcher." Ohio: Lorain County Chapter, Ohio Genealogical Society. Winter 1996: pp. 6-7.

Maher, Melbourne Funeral Home. 4274 Mayfield Road, South Euclid, OH.

Maple Ridge Cemetery, Westlake, OH. Limited inscriptions recorded by Catherine Burke Flament. 2001.

Marriage Applications Rec. From 4/1872 to 4/1885. Ohio Historical Society. Probate Court, Lorain, Lorain County, OH. Court #3. Microfilm. *Available at Lorain Public Library, Main Branch.*

Marshall, Richard G. New Hampshire Covered Bridges. "A Link with Our Past." New Hampshire Department of Transportation. Updated 1994. <http://www.state.nh.us/nhdhr/bridges/p19.html>. Cited 14 September 2004.

Massachusetts. Office of the Secretary of State. Massachusetts Soldiers and Sailors of the Revolutionary War. 17 vols. Boston: Wright and Potter Printing Co., State Printers, 1896-1908.

Matteson, Porter. Mattesons in America. No publication date. *A series of papers privately published as information was accumulated.*

"Matthias Mawby." Edmonds Tribune-Review [Edmonds, Washington] 8 May 1974: p. 2.

McGunagle, Fred. "Park Superintendent Traces Family to First Settlement." Newspaper article provided by Sally O'Connor, undetermined source.

Meermans, Carol K. "Bay United Methodist Church, 175th Anniversary Booklet." Bay Village, OH: Bay Village United Methodist Church, 2002.

Memorial Record of the County of Cuyahoga and City of Cleveland, Ohio. 1894. Reprinted, Evansville, IN: Whipporwill Publications, 1988.

Memorial to the Pioneer Women of the Western Reserve. Ed. Mrs. Gertrude Van Rensselaer Wickham. Part 1. 1896.

Memorial to the Pioneer Women of the Western Reserve. Ed. Mrs. Gertrude Van Rensselaer Wickham. Part 4. February 1897. Available online: http://www.rootsweb.com/~usgenweb/oh/cuyahoga/history-index.html.

Meyer, Frieda. "Couple to Observe Golden Anniversary." Lorain Journal [Lorain, OH] Oct 18, 1954.

Military Pension Records. National Archives. Washington D.C.

Miller, Tabitha. Letter in the private collection of Norma Wolf Garber, Bay Village, OH. December 21· 1931.

Minderman, Edith Johnson. Marriages from the Probate Court, Ottawa County, Ohio, 1840-1890. The Ottawa County Chapter of The Ohio Genealogical Society. Ozark, MO: Dogwook Printing, 1982.

"Miss Mae Everard." Obituary. Chronicle Telegram [Elyria, Ohio] 2 October 1936: p. 2.

Mitchell, Joseph. Up in the Old Hotel and Other Stories. Stories previously published in the New Yorker. New York: Pantheon Books, 1992.

"Mrs. Alfred Bates." Obituary. Elyria Telegram [Elyria, OH] 3 October 1913.

"Mrs. Emma Beard." Obituary. Lorain Times-Herald [Lorain, OH] 25 April 1927: p. 2.

Mitchell, Mrs. Thomas R. The Berea Advertiser [Cleveland, OH] 30 June 1911: p. 4.

Morris, John E. The Felt Genealogy. Hartford, CN: The Case, Lockwood and Brainard Company, 1893.

Musil, Florence Louise Eppink. "Autobiography of Florence Louise Eppink Musil." Manuscipt in the private collection of Rev. Margie M. Frank, Washington, PA.

Musselman, Barbara. Fairview Park Cemetery (Rockport Cemetery), Cuyahoga County, OH. Fairview Park, OH: Fairview Park Cemetery Restoration Committee, 1991.

Myers, Margaret E. Marriage Licenses of Frederick County, 1811-1840. 2nd ed. Pawtucket, RI: Quintin Publications, 1997.

"Neighborhood Tour." Welcome to Clark-Fulton. Neighborhood Link. Cleveland: Cleveland State University. <http://www.nhlink.net/neighborhoodtour/clark-fulton/>. Cited 12 July 2004.

Non-Military Death Notices from the Lorain County News 1860-1867. Compiled by Glenn A. Carruthers. Oberlin, OH: 1983.

"Northern Ohio News." "Dover, Cleveland." Article with references to Lydia Cahoon. Daily Herald [Cleveland] 23 August 1869.

"Obituary." Obituary of Rev. James Goodrich. Wellington Enterprise [Wellington, OH] 30 October 1895: p. 5.

The Official Roster of Ohio Soldiers in the War with Spain, 1898-99. Compiled under the direction of Willis, Frank B., Governor, Charles Q. Hildebrant, Secretary of State, and Benson W. Hough, Adjutant General. Published by Authority of the General Assembly. Columbus, OH: E. T. Miller Co., 1916. p. 387.

Official Roster of Ohio Soldiers, Sailors and Marines, World War 1917-18. vol. 14 POK-ROS. Columbus, OH: The F. J. Heer Printing Co., 1928.

Ohio. City of Cleveland. Records of Death, 1840-1908. Microfilm. Cuyahoga County Archives.

Ohio Cemeteries. Ed. Smith, Maxine Hartmann. Ohio Genealogical Society. Mansfield, OH: The Ohio Genealogical Society. 1978.

Ohio Historical Society. Ohio Death Certificate Index, Searchable Database, 1913-1937. [Originally published Ohio Department of Health Division of Vital Statistics, 1970]. Online: Ohio Historical Society, 1998. <http://www.ohiohistory.org/dindex/search.cfm>. Cited 1999-2004.

Ohio Genealogical Society. Ohio Cemeteries. Ed: Maxine Hartmann Smith. Mansfield, OH: The Society, 1978.

Ohio's Western Reserve, A Regional Reader. Ed. Harry F. Lupold and Gladys Haddad. Kent, OH: The Kent State University Press, 1988.

"Old Houses in Bay Village." West Life [Westlake, OH] 3 October 1960: p. 12.
Osborn, C. M. "The Osborn Family of Bay Village." Typed transcript. 1934. *Copy available at Bay Village Historical Society, Bay Village, OH.*
Osterland, Pauline. Hopkinton, New Hampshire Vital Records. vol. I. Bowie Maryland: Heritage Books, Inc., 1998.
Palmer, May Aslaksen. Personal interview by Jeanne Parks. United Methodist Church, Avon Lake, OH. 9 Oct 2002.
Pease Funeral Home Records. Mss. 4809. Western Reserve Historical Society, Cleveland, OH.
Penfield Cemetery. Cemetery records and inscriptions. Penfield, Lorain County, OH.
Physicians' and Dentists' Directory of the State of Ohio, 1905. Cincinnati, OH: Galen Gonsier and Co., 1905.
Pioneer and General History of Geauga County. 1880. Reprinted, Evansville, IN: Unigraphic, Inc., 1973.
Pioneer Women of the Western Reserve Prior to 1840. Microfilm, Cuyahoga County Public Library: Fairview Park Branch, Fairview Park, OH.
Plain Dealer. [Cleveland, OH] Plain Dealer, 1961-current.
Probate Court Estate Case Files, Cuyahoga County, Ohio. Wills from 1813-1913. Indexes, 1813-1941. Cuyahoga County Archives, Cleveland, OH.
Probate Court Death Records, Cuyahoga County, Ohio. vol. I. (3 July 1868-20 April 1879).
Probate Court Death Records, Cuyahoga County, Ohio. vol. II. (4 July 1878-14 March 1884).
Probate Court Death Records, Cuyahoga County, Ohio. vol. III. (11 March 1884-22 March 1889). Probate Court Death Records, Cuyahoga County, Ohio. vol. IV. (1 April 1888-30 April 1890)
Probate Court Death Records, Cuyahoga County, Ohio. vol. V. #1-6174. (1 May 1890-7 August 1891, August 1-May 1892).
Probate Court Death Records, Cuyahoga County, Ohio. vol. VI. #6175-12235. (1 February 1890-19 June 1892; 26 May 1892-13 May 1893).
Probate Court Death Records, Cuyahoga County, Ohio. vol. VII. #12236-18296. (27 April 1893-21 September 1893; 10 June 1893-18 June 1894).
Probate Court Death Records, Cuyahoga County, Ohio. vol. VIII. #18301-24399. (20 September 1893-11 March 1895; 18 June 1894-24 June 1895).
Probate Court Death Records, Cuyahoga County, Ohio. vol. IX. #24410-30584. (March 1895-9 March 1896; and 2 August 1895-3 September 1896).
Probate Court, Marriage Records 1810-1941, Cuyahoga County, Ohio. *Vols. 1-200 originals available at Cuyahoga County Archives.*
Quit Claim Deed from D.D. Osborn to Trustees of Dover, August 6, 1877, Cuyahoga County, Vol. 295, p. 89.
Read, M. Patricia Meddick. 2004. Catherine Burke Flament, interviewer. Oral interview at Rose Hill Museum, Bay Village, OH. 12 July 2004.
"Rehling, George H." Dayton Daily News 5 February 1973: p. 39.
Renfrew, Flora Tuttle. "Tuttle Family Story." Unpublished, undetermined date.
Representative Men and Old Families of Rhode Island. vol. III. Chicago: J.H. Beers & Co., 1908.
Riverside Cemetery and Columbarium. The Riverside Cemetery Association, 3607 Pearl Road (West 25th Street), Cleveland, OH.
"Robert Everard." Obituary. Chronicle Telegram [Elyria, OH] March 1945: p. 2.
Rose, Gertrude Aldrich Barker, "Genealogy of William Bassett and Descendents 1620-1973." *Copy at Rose Hill Museum, Bay Village, OH.*
---. "Genealogy of Descendants of George Aldrich and Roger Williams as it Concerns Descendants of the Families of Aaron Aldrich III and William Waterman Aldrich I of Dover, Ohio." 1977. *Copies at Rose Hill Museum, Bay Village, OH and Western Reserve Historical Society, Cleveland, OH.*
Rose Hill Museum, Bay Village Historical Society, P.O. Box 40187, Bay Village, OH. *The home of Joseph Cahoon and later the Joel B. Cahoon Family.*
Rose Hill Museum, Family Paper Collection and File, Rose Hill Museum, Bay Village, OH.
Rose, Kenneth W. "John D. Rockefeller's Philanthropy and Problems in Fundraising at Cleveland's Floating Bethel Mission and the Home for Aged Colored People." Ohio History. vol. 108. pp. 145-157. Adapted with permission.
Rose, William Ganson. Cleveland: The Making of a City. Cleveland: The World Publishing Co., 1950.
St. James Parish Register, Burials, 1799, Family Tree Maker, CD 178, Church Records, MD and DE, 1600's-1800's, Washington Co., MD, ©Broderbund Software, Inc., Banner Blue Division, November 11, 1998.
Saint Paul Lutheran Church Records, Westlake, OH.
Saxton-Parker-Daniels-Busch Family Funeral Chapels, 15800 Detroit Ave., Lakewood, OH.
"Schedule 2. Production of Agriculture in Dover Township, Cuyahoga County, OH," enumerated June, 1880. Microfilm. National Archives, Washington, D.C.
Scott, Julia Osborn. "Osborn Family History for the One Hundred Fiftieth Anniversary." 1961.
Sheffield, The Lorain County Metropolitan Park District, Elyria, OH, 1971. Reprint of "A History of the First Fifty Years of Sheffield" by Norman Day, 1865.
Sheffield Preservation Project. Sheffield, Lorain County, OH. http://members.tripod.com/~Range17/.
Sheldon, Keith M. Descendants of Early Bay Village Families. No publisher. 1999. *Two copies printed and kept in the collection at Rose Hill Museum, Bay Village and Western Reserve Historical Society, 10825 East Blvd., Cleveland, OH 44106-1777.*
Sigsworth, Jeff. "The Cahoon Family - From Scotland to Lorain Co". Lorain County Researcher, Fall 1995, p. 42-3.
---. "The Cahoon Family - From Scotland to Lorain Co." Lorain County Researcher, Winter 1996, p. 6-8.

---. The Cahoon Family in Scotland, Mass., Rhode Island, Vermont, and New York (Who Came to Cuyahoga Co. and the Future Lorain Co., Ohio 1810-14, Elyria, OH, 7 November 1995. *(Available at Lorain Public Library and Rose Hill Museum)*
Slaby, Ima M. "Family Group Sheets and Pedigree Charts". Documented. Aldrich, Bassett and Winsor Families. 1998.
Smith, Taylor J. Historical Sketch of Avon, Ohio, to 1974. on line <http://www.centuryinter.net/tjs11/hist/hto74.htm>. Cited 5 February 2006.
Special Schedule.-Surviving Soldiers, Sailors, and Marines, and Widow, etc., S.D. 6; E.D. 157; Dover, OH. Microfilm.
A Standard History of Lorain County, Ohio. Ed. G. Frederick Wright. vols. I and II. Chicago: The Lewis Publishing Company, 1916. Reprinted, Salem, MA: Higginson Book Co., 1994.
Stercula, Beverly M. "The Thompson Family Magazine," published 1960-1972.
Stiles, Henry R. History of Ancient Wethersfield, Connecticut. New England History Press, 1904. Reprinted, Somersworth: New Hampshire Pub. Co., 1974-1975.
---, History and Genealogies of Ancient Windsor, Connecticut. Hartford, Conn.: Press of the Case, Lockwood & Brainard Co. vol. I, 1892; vol. II, 1893.
Stocking, George. The Stocking Ancestry, Comprising the Descendants of George Stocking Founder of the American Family. Chicago: The Lakeside Press. 1903.
"Stow, Joshua." Local History. Stowe-Monroe Public Library. <http://www.smfpl.org/joshua.htm>. Cited 7 April 2006.
Suburban News and Herald. Weekly paper of the western suburbs of Cleveland. 1911-
Traverse Region. Chicago: H. R. Page & Co., 1884. p. 242.
"Those Who Came," Brochure on the Cahoon Family, Rose Hill Museum, 2003.
Trumbull County Cemetery Inscriptions, 1800-1930. Trumbull Co.: Ohio Genealogical Society, 1983.
Various U. S. Federal Census, 1810-1930, some of which are the following:
United States. Census Office. Fourth Census of the United States, 1820. Population Schedules: Ohio: Clinton, Cuyahoga, Logan, Hardin, and Median Counties. Roll 90. Dover: pp. 52A-53A, Rockport: pp. 58A-59A, Orange 59A. Washington, D. C.: National Archives and Records Administration, 1949, 1958-1960. Microfilm.
United States. Census Office. Fifth Census of the United States, 1830. Population Schedules: Coshocton Cuyahoga, Crawford, and Clinton Counties. Roll 129. Dover: pp. 119-121, Rockport: pp. 116-118. Microfilm.
United States. Bureau of the Census. Sixth Census of the United States, 1840. Federal Population Schedules. Ohio: Cuyahoga County. Bountiful, Utah: AGLL, 19--??. Roll 389. Dover: pp. 159-164. Microfilm.
United States. Bureau of the Census. Seventh Census of the United States, 1850. Federal Population Schedules. Ohio: Cuyahoga County (part). Roll 673. Dover, pp. 211-224, 10–16 October 1850, enumerated by S. O. Griswold. Bountiful, Utah: AGLL, 19--??. Microfilm.
United States. Bureau of the Census. Seventh Census of the United States, 1850: Federal Population Schedules. Ohio: Lorain County. Roll 705. Avon Lake, pp. 452-473, enumerated from 17-24 September 1850. Bountiful, Utah: AGLL, 19--??. Microfilm.
United States. Bureau of the Census. Eighth Census of the United States, 1860. Federal Population Schedules: Indiana: Noble Co., Orange Township. Roll 286. p. 130, family # 952, lines 17-22. Bountiful, Utah: AGLL, 19--??. Microfilm.
United States. Bureau of the Census. Eighth Census of the United States, 1860. Federal Population Schedules: Ohio: Cuyahoga (part) County, (exc. City of Cleveland). Roll 954. Rockport pp. 1-48; Dover, pp. 49-78, enumerated from 4-9 June 1860 by William Abbey. Bountiful, Utah: AGLL, 19--??. (microfilm).
United States. Bureau of the Census. Ninth Census of the United States, 1870: Federal Population Schedules. Ohio: Cuyahoga County, City of Cleveland, wards 11 thru 15, and Dover and East Cleveland. Roll 1192. Dover, pp. 22-36, enumerated from 29 June–8 July 1870 by Gardner Stearns. Bountiful, Utah: AGLL, n.d. Microfilm.
United States. Bureau of the Census. Ninth Census of the United States, 1870: Federal Population Schedules. Ohio: Lorain County. Roll 1192. Avon Township: pp. 1-47, enumerated from 20 June–2 July 1870 by Theo. L. Faxon. Original data, Washington, D.C.: National Archives and Records Administration. Microfilm.
United States. Bureau of Census. Tenth Census of the United States, 1880: Federal Population Schedules. Ohio: Lorain (part) and Lucas (part) Counties. Roll 1042. Original data, Washington, D.C.: National Archives and Records Administration. Microfilm.
United States. Bureau of Census. Tenth Census of the United States, 1880: Federal Population Schedules. Ohio: City of Cleveland, Ward 18 (cont 53/7 - end), and Cuyahoga County (excluding City of Cleveland; begin - 73-18). Roll 1009. Dover Township, pp. 93-101B, enumerated from 17-30 June 1880, by Wilbur Beutty. Original data, Washington, D.C.: National Archives and Records Administration. Microfilm.
United States. Bureau of Census. Tenth Census of the United States, 1880: Federal Population Schedules. Michigan, Calhoun Co., Sheridan Twp. Roll 574-5. Original data, Washington, D.C.: National Archives and Records Administration. Microfilm.
United States Special Schedule, Surviving Soldiers, Sailors and Marines, and Widows, Etc., Ohio, County of Cuyahoga, 1890. Roll 71. Dover Township, pp. 1-4. Original data, Washington, D.C.: National Archives and Records Administration. Microfilm.
United States. Bureau of the Census. Twelfth Census of the United States, 1900: Federal Population Schedules. Ohio: Cuyahoga County (part: EDs 1-7) and City of Cleveland (part: EDs 8-18, 238, 19-35). Roll 1252. ED 23, Dover Township, pp. 1-14A, enumerated from 7-21 June 1900, by John Mitchell. Bountiful, Utah: Heritage Quest, 19--??. Microfilm.
United States. Bureau of the Census. Twelfth Census of the United States, 1900: Federal Population Schedules. Ohio: Lorain County. Roll 1294. Avon, pp. 1A-p. 21A, enumerated from June 5-July 7, 1900. Bountiful, Utah: Heritage Quest, 19--??. Microfilm.

United States. Bureau of the Census. Thirteenth Census of the United States, 1910. Federal Population Schedules. Ohio: Drake and Cuyahoga Counties. Roll 1164. ED 1, Bay Township, pp. 1A-5A, enumerated from April 15-30, by Earl J. Darby. Bountiful, Utah: AGLL, 19--??. Microfilm.

United States. Bureau of the Census. Fourteenth Census of the United States, 1920. Federal Population Schedules. Ohio: Drake Co. (EDs 89-91 and 108-123) and Cuyahoga Co., Cleveland City (EDs 1-12). Roll 1359. ED 3, Avon. Bountiful, Utah: AGLL, 19--??. Microfilm.

United States. Bureau of the Census. Fourteenth Census of the United States, 1920. Federal Population Schedules. Ohio: Cuyahoga Co., Cleveland City (EDs 47-65, 614, 631, 639, 66-82, 630, 83-86, 626, and 628). Roll 1361. ED 63, Sheffield. Bountiful, Utah: AGLL, 19--??. Microfilm.

United States. Bureau of the Census. Fourteenth Census of the United States, 1920. Federal Population Schedules. Ohio: Cuyahoga (EDs 509-526, 609, 527-534, 624, 535, 536, 623, 537-543, 622, 544, 547) County CY. Roll 1374. Ed 509, Bay Village: pp. 1A-8A, enumerated from January 2-14, 1920 by Chas. H. Drake. Bountiful, Utah: AGLL, 19--??. Microfilm.

United States. Bureau of the Census. Fourteenth Census of the United States, 1920. Federal Population Schedules. Ohio: Cuyahoga (EDs 545, 546, 548-565, 593-596, and 566-585) County CY. Roll 1375. ED 593, Rocky River. Bountiful, Utah: AGLL, 19--??. Microfilm.

United States. Bureau of the Census. Fourteenth Census of the United States, 1920. Federal Population Schedules. Ohio: Cuyahoga Co., Cleveland City (EDs 13-46). Roll 1360. ED 37, Ward 3, sheet 10A, lines 11-17. Bountiful, Utah: AGLL, 19--??. Microfilm.

United States. Bureau of the Census. Fourteenth Census of the United States, 1920. Federal Population Schedules California: Riverside County. Roll 125. ED 101, Elsinore City. p. 1B, enumerated 2-3 January 1920. Bountiful, Utah: AGLL, 19--??. Microfilm.

United States. Bureau of the Census. Fifteenth Census of the United States, 1930. Federal Population Schedules. Ohio: Cuyahoga Co. Roll 1761. ED18-534, Bay Village: pp. 1A-23B enumerated 23-30 April by Bessie M. Hoag. Ann Arbor, MI: Proquest, 2002. Microfilm.

United States. Bureau of the Census. Fifteenth Census of the United States, 1930. Federal Population Schedules. Ohio: Cuyahoga Co. Roll 1784. ED18-584, Dover Village: pp. 1A-27A enumerated 2-25 April by A. J. Pierce. Ann Arbor, MI: Proquest, 2002. Microfilm.

Valleau Cemetery Records, 660 East Glen Avenue, Ridgewood, NJ 07450.

Van Tassel, David D. and John J. Grabowski. The Encyclopedia of Cleveland History. Bloomington, Indiana: Indiana University Press, 1987.

"The Vet's Gazette." Cuyahoga County Service Commission, vol. 5, issue 5, October 2000, pp. 2-3.

Veteran Pension Records. Microfilm. Washington, D.C.: National Archives, Records held with Veterans Administration.

The Village Cookbook. Bay United Methodist Church. Bay Village, OH, c1911-15.

"Yensen, Howard Magruder 'Pete'." Virginia Gazette [Williamsburg, VA] 23 January 1980: vol. 51, no. 4, p. 24.

Walker, Milburn. "The Avon Lake Story." Kiwanis Club of Avon Lake, c1965.

Warranty Deed from D.D. Osborn to Trustees of Dover, August 6, 1877, Cuyahoga County, vol. 295, p. 90.

Warren, Violet. Huntsburg's Old Crowd and Related Families: Huntsburg Township, Geauga County, OH. Gregath Company: Wyandotte, OK. 1990.

West Park Cemetery, Cleveland, OH.

Westlake Arts Council. "The Home Place, A Tour of Selected Century Homes in Westlake in Celebration of Our 175th Anniversary (1811-1986)." Westlake, OH, 1986.

Weston, May E. The First 100 Years of Dover Schools. Westlake Historical Society, Westlake, OH, 1969.

White, Virgil D. Genealogical Abstracts of Revolutionary War Pension Files. Waynesboro, Tenn.: National Historical Pub. Co., 1990-1992.

White, Dorothy Higson, (the Waterman line) and Mr. Kay Kirlin Moore (the Winsor line), Descendants of Roger Williams, "Book 1, Waterman Line, Winsor Line," for the Roger Williams Family Association; published by Gateway Press, Baltimore, Maryland, 1991.

Wickham, Mrs. Gertrude Van Rensselaer. The Pioneer Families of Cleveland 1796-1840. vols. I and II, Evangelical Publishing House, 1914. Reprinted, Salem, MA: Higginson Book Co., 1993.

"William K. Steves." Commemorative Historical Biographical Record of Wood County, Ohio. Chicago: J.H. Beers & Co., 1897. p. 1362.

"William L. Lippert." Obituary. New York Times 10 April 1943.

Wood County, Ohio Atlas 1875-1912.

Woodland Cemetery & Arboretum, Dayton, OH.

Woodvale Cemetery, 7535 Engle Road, Middleburg Heights, OH 44130.

Workman, Jeanne B. and Jayne A. Broestl. Maple Ridge Cemetery, Westlake, Cuyahoga County, Ohio. Cuyahoga West Chapter, O.G.S. p. 72.

Acknowledgements and Related Genealogical Sources

The following organizations graciously assisted with the book:

Family Associations:

The William Cahoone Society. <http://personal.tmlp.com/richard/wilsoc.html>.
Eddy Family Association. Thomas Eddy, 140 Bentley Way, Fayetteville, GA 30214. <http://www.eddyfamily.com/>.
Foote Family Association of America. < http://www.footefamily.org/>.
The Griswold Family Association. 116 Garden St., Wethersfield, CT 06109. The Griswold Family Association Home Page. <http://www.griswoldfamily.org/>.
Huntington Family Association, Charles A. Huntington, Jr., Burbank, IL 60459
Loomis Families of America, P.O. Box 31963, Seattle, WA < http://loomis-family.org/>
Matteson Historical Congress. Betty Matteson Rhodes. <http://www.matteson.us/congress.html>.
Roger Williams Family Association. (Winsor line) <http://www.rogerwilliams.org>.

Historical Societies, Libraries and Local Organizations:

Bay Village City Council and Cahoon Trustees, Bay Village, OH
Bay Village Historical Society, Rose Hill Museum, Bay Village, OH 44140
Buffalo and Erie County Public Library, 1 Lafayette Square, Buffalo, NY 14203 (716) 858-8900.
Busch Funeral and Crematory Services, Harlan F. Saxton, 15800 Detroit Ave., Lakewood, OH 44107
Chicago Public Library, Harold Washington Library Center, 400 South State Street, Chicago, IL 60605
Cleveland Public Library, 325 Superior Ave., N.E., Cleveland, OH 44114. (216) 623-2800 <http://www.cpl.org/>.
Cleveland State University Library, 2121 Euclid Avenue Cleveland, Ohio 44115-2214 Information: (216) 687-2475 Reference: (216) 687-5300. <http://www.ulib.csuohio.edu/>.
Connecticut Historical Society, One Elizabeth Street at Asylum Avenue, Hartford, CN 06105 (860) 236-5621.
Cuyahoga County Archives, 2905 Franklin Blvd NW, Cleveland 44113; (216) 443-7250 <http://www.cuyahogacounty.us/cs/archives/default.htm>.
Cuyahoga County Public Library, Fairview Park Regional Branch, Genealogy Collection, 21255 Lorain Road, Fairview Park, OH 44126-2120, (440) 333-4700.
Dayton Public Library, 215 E. Third St., Dayton, OH 45402 (937) 227-9500. Clinton Lowell, Magazines Division and Nancy Horlacher, Collection Librarian.
Defiance Public Library, 320 Fort Street, Defiance, OH 43512 (419)782-1456.
Elyria Public Library, 320 Washington Ave., Elyria, OH 44035.
Fairview General Hospital, 18101 Lorain Road, Cleveland, OH 44111.
Glen Avon Regional Library, Riverside County Library Systems, Riverside, CA. Diane I. Drake, Manager.
Herrick Memorial Library, 101 Willard Memorial Square, Wellington, OH 44090
Kenilworth Historical Society, 415 Kenilworth Avenue, P.O. Box 181, Kenilworth, IL 60043-1134
Lakewood Public Library, 15425 Detroit Ave., Lakewood, OH 44107 (216) 226-8275 <http://www.lkwdpl.org/lfiles/>. Lakewood, Ohio history
Lake Elsinore Library, Riverside County Library Systems, Lake Elsinore, CA.
Loomis Chaffee School, Batchelder Rd., Windsor, CT 06095
Lorain County Historical Society, 509 Washington Ave., Elyria, OH 44035
Lorain Public Library System, Main Branch, 351 Sixth Street, Lorain, OH 44052 (440)-244-1192
National Archives and Record Service, 8th Street and Pennsylvania Avenue, N.W., Washington, DC 20408
National Archives and Records Administration, 8601 Adelphi Road, College Park, MD 20740-6001, <http://www.archives.gov/genealogy/>.
National Archives of Canada, Ottawa, 395 Wellington St., Ottawa, Ontario, Canada <http://www.genealogy.gc.ca/index_e.html>.
Naval Training Center Great Lakes, John Sheppard, United States Navy, Great Lakes, IL
Ohio Genealogical Society, 713 Main St., Mansfield, OH 44907-1644 <http://www.ogs.org/>.
Ohio Historical Society Archives-Library Division, 1982 Velma Ave., Columbus, OH 43211 <http://www.ohiohistory.org/resource/archlib/>.
Olan Mills Portrait Studio, 4325 Amnicola Highway, Chattanooga, TN 37422-3456
The Plain Dealer, Tom Coscarelli, Asst. Managing Editor, 1801 Superior Ave., Cleveland, OH 44114
San Jose Public Library, California Room, San Jose, California

Sno-Isle Regional Library System, Edmonds Library, 650 Main Street, Edmonds, WA 98020. T. Reynold
Trumball County Chapter of the Ohio Genealogical Society, Warren, OH 44482-0309
Tucson-Pima Public Main Library, Tucson, AZ 85726-7470
Warren-Trumbull County Library, 444 Mahoning Avenue NW, Warren, OH 44483 (330) 399-8807
Westlake Porter Public Library, 27333 Center Ridge Road, Westlake, OH 44126 (440) 871-2600
Western Reserve Historical Society Library and Archives, 10825 East Boulevard, Cleveland, OH 44106 10825 East, Cleveland, Ohio, 44106; 216-721-5722 x 224, FAX 216-721-5702 <http://www.wrhs.org/>.
Williamsburg Regional Library, 7700 Croaker Road, Williamsburg, VA 23188

Religious Organizations:
Baltimore-Washington Conference, Commission on Archives and History, United Methodist Church, Lovely Lane Museum, Baltimore, MD < http://lovelylanemuseum.org/archives.html>
Bay United Methodist Church, 29931 Lake Road, Bay Village, OH 44140 <http://www.bayumc.org/>
Christ Church Anglican, Fr. Gary Parker, Meaford, Ontario, Canada N4L 1B9 <https://christchurchanglican.ca/>
Jesus Christ Church of the Latter Day Saints, Family History Center, Cleveland Branch Library. 25000 Westwood, Westlake, OH 44145 (440) 777-1518 <http://www.familysearch.org/>.
St. Paul Lutheran Church, Rev. L.F. Wesolik, 27981 Detroit Rd., Westlake, OH 44145 <https://www.stpaulwestlake.org/>

Local Cemeteries:
Calvary Cemetery. Cemetery records and inscriptions. Cemetery R 555 North Ridge Rd., Lorain, OH. <https://www.clecem.org/>
Cleveland City Cemeteries, 21400 Chagrin Blvd., Cleveland, OH.
Evergreen Cemetery, 29535 Center Ridge Rd., Westlake, OH 44145 (440) 835-6431 caretaker, Ray Mariner, retired 2002, Gayle Hill, current. <https://www.cityofwestlake.org/380/Cemeteries>
Fairview Park Cemetery, Lorain Road, Fairview Park, OH. *Records located at Fairview Park City Hall and Fairview Park Regional Public Library.* < https://fairviewparkcemetery.org/>
Garfield Cemetery, SR 254, Sheffield Village City Hall, Sheffield Village, OH 44035 < https://range17.tripod.com/garfield.html>
Lake Shore Cemetery, Lake Road, Avon Lake, OH *Records located at Busch-Burmeister Family Funeral Chapel, 163 Avon-Belden Road, Avon Lake, OH 44012.* Resource:< https://www.arcadiapublishing.com/Products/9781467103718>
Lake View Cemetery Assn., 12316 Euclid Avenue, Cleveland, OH 44106. (216) 421-2665 < https://www.lakeviewcemetery.com/>
Lakewood Park Cemetery Assn., 22025 Detroit Road, Rocky River, OH 44116 (440) 333-1922
Maple Ridge Cemetery, Columbia Rd., between Hall Dr. and Westwood Rd., Westlake, OH records kept at: Evergreen Cemetery, 29535 Center Ridge Rd., Westlake, OH 44145 (440) 835-6431 <http://www.rootsweb.com/~ohgcgg/cemeteries/mapleridge/>.
Riverside Cemetery, William R. Holley, Gen Mgr., 3607 Pearl Road, Cleveland, OH 44109 (216) 351-4800. < http://www.riversidecemeterycleveland.org/>

Cuyahoga County web sites of interest:
Bay Village Historical Society. <http://www.bayhistorical.com/BVHSocHome.htm>.
Case Western Reserve University. Encyclopedia of Cleveland History and Dictionary of Cleveland Biography.
<http://ech.cwru.edu/index.html>.
Cuyahoga County Genealogy and History. <http://www.rootsweb.com/~ohcuyah2/index.html>.
<http://www.myohiogenealogy.com/oh_county/cu.html>.
Cuyahoga County Births. <http://www.rootsweb.com/~ohcuyah2/births/index.html>.
Cuyahoga County Probate Death Index 1867-1890: <http://www.rootsweb.com/~ohcuyah2/deaths/coarch/part1/index.html>.
Cuyahoga County Public Library. Genealogy. <http://www.cuyahogalibrary.org/onlineresources/websites/Genealogy.htm>.
Ohio Death Certificate Index. 1913-1937. <http://www.ohiohistory.org/dindex/>.
Historical Marriage License Index 1810 to April 1998. <http://probate.cuyahogacounty.us/ml/>.
Rockport History. <http://www.lkwdpl.org/history/4.htm>.
Memorial To The Pioneer Women Of The Western Reserve, 1896 Local histories. <http://www.rootsweb.com/~ohcuyaho/cities/>.
Cuyahoga County Naturalizations. <http://www.rootsweb.com/~ohcuyah2/nats/index.html>.
Cuyahoga County Necrology File. Obits 1833, 1847-1975. <http://www.cpl.org/>.
Social Security Death Index. <http://ssdi.genealogy.rootsweb.com/cgi-bin/ssdi.cgi>.
Westlake Public Library. <http://www.westlakelibrary.org/reubenhall.htm>, photo collection: <http://history.westlakelibrary.org/cdm4/browse.php>.

Lorain County web sites of interest:
Lorain County Gen-web site. <http://resources.rootsweb.com/~clusters/USA/OH/Lorain>.
USGenWeb Site, Lorain County. <http://home.centurytel.net/lorgen/>.
Lorain County Cemeteries with cemetery inscriptions listed <http://home.centurytel.net/lorgen/cemetery/cemetery.htm>.
Historical Sketches of Avon. <http://www.centuryinter.net/tjs11/hist/hto74.htm>
Avon Genealogy. <http://www.centuryinter.net/tjs11/gen/genindex.htm>
History of Sheffield. <http://members.tripod.com/~Range17/>.

Index

The index has been created to be as complete as reasonably possible. Due to the preponderance of evidence, all misspellings were not included in the index. This is especially true if the variation was close to the correct spelling and/or found infrequently in sources. Individuals have been listed by their formal name. Aaron Aldrich may be found in the text as A. Aldrich, A.A. Aldrich, Aaron Aldrich or Deacon Aldrich, etc. but is included in the index only under Aaron A. Aldrich III, Deacon. When checking a reference, a name may appear on a page more than once.

Those buried in, or those who were included in, the cemetery records (were moved or burial may never have taken place) are listed in bold. Bold was used to identify the page numbers referring to the main reference for each individual buried at the cemetery.

Women who married are listed under their maiden and married names, even when the citation does not include both. For instance, the listing for Lorinda Griswold Hilliard Aldrich includes her first name, maiden name, first marriage and second marriage. Lorinda is referenced under all three last names.

( ) - a variation of a name commonly used in references. i.e. Mary (Marcy) Waterman

/ - both spellings used in references i.e. ATWELL/ATWILL

[ ] - incorrect spelling

The index has been designed to be as complete as possible. Due to the thousands of names entered, please excuse any omissions or mistakes that may have inadvertently occurred. Great care was taken when entering and proofreading

A

C

E

F

H

I

J

L

M

P

Q

R

T

U

V

Y

Z

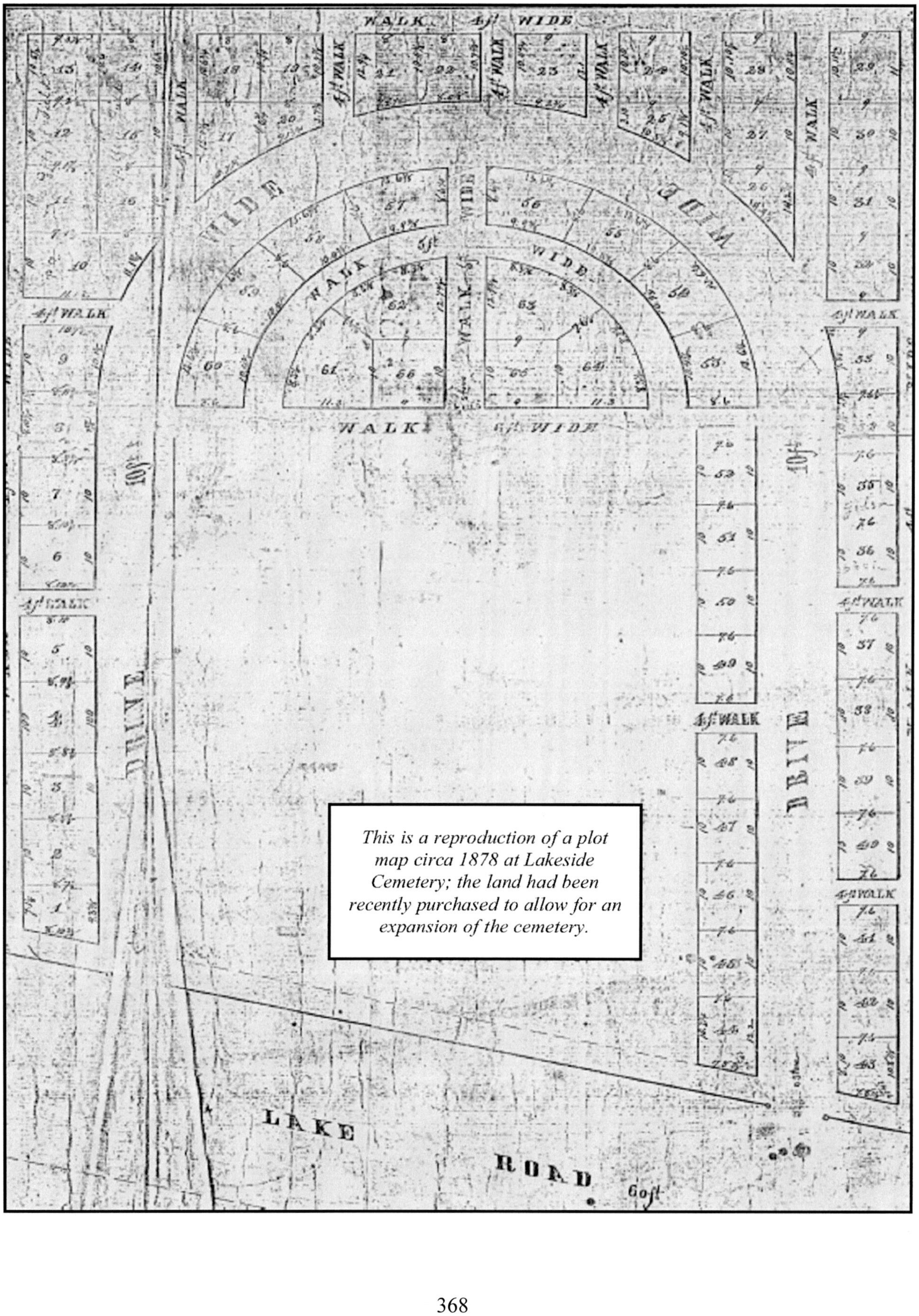

This is a reproduction of a plot map circa 1878 at Lakeside Cemetery; the land had been recently purchased to allow for an expansion of the cemetery.